UNITED STATES PRISON LAW

SENTENCING TO PRISON, PRISON CONDITIONS, AND RELEASE—THE COURT DECISIONS

Selected and with Comments
By

Erwin C. Surrency
Professor of Law and Law Librarian
University of Georgia

With Editorial Assistance By
MICHAEL MOORE
DEBORAH DANCE

VOLUME IX

Supplementing
Volumes I-VIII

1988
OCEANA PUBLICATIONS, INC.
DOBBS FERRY, N.Y.

Library of Congress Cataloging in Publication Data

Rubin, Sol., comp.
    United States prison law.

    CONTENTS: V.1. Sentencing to prison.
    V.2. State Power and its limits.
    V.3. Prisoners' Rights. V.4. Parole
    and other release procedures. V.5. Civil rights;
Index to v. 1–5. V.6. Supplement to v. I–V, Index to
v. VI. V.7. Supplement to v. I–VI; Index to v. VII.
V.8. Supplement to v. I–VII; Index to v. VIII; Index
to v. I–VIII. V.9. Supplement to v. I–VIII; Index to
v. IX; Index to v. I–IX.
        1. Correctional law — United States — Cases.
I. Title
KF9728.A7R8   345'.73'077   74-23142
ISBN 0-379-10050-9 (Series)
ISBN 0-379-10059-2 (Vol. 9)

THIS VOLUME IS DEDICATED TO ONE WHO HAS PATIENTLY
ENDURED DAILY REPORTS ON THE PROGRESS AND PROBLEMS
OF COMPLETING THIS VOLUME — IDA, MY WIFE.

CONTENTS

TABLE OF CASES

VOLUME THREE SUPPLEMENT — PRISONERS' RIGHTS

Chapter 1 PRINCIPLES GOVERNING PRISONERS' RETENTION
OF RIGHTS

Chapter 2 RIGHTS IN LEGAL PROCEEDINGS

Chapter 3 RELIGIOUS RIGHTS, RIGHT TO NONDISCRIMINA-
TION FOR RACE OR SEX

Chapter 4 CONTACTS WITH THE OUTSIDE WORLD

Chapter 5 REHABILITATION AND HEALTH CARE

TABLE OF CASES - Decisions Reported Vol. IX

ACKNOWLEDGMENTS

The author would like to express his appreciation to the West Publishing Company and especially to its President, Dwight D. Opperman, for permission to reproduce all the cases in this volume which originally appeared in units of the National Reporter System. All the cases reproduced in this volume are copyrighted by West Publishing Company, and are copied with permission from the appropriate National Reporter volumes.

INTRODUCTION TO VOLUME IX

During 1986, there were few dramatic court cases in the area of prison law or prisoner's rights. However, the fact that the majority of cases seemed to reiterate principles which have been stated previously does not obliterate a need for a collection of significant cases for the time period. The purpose of this volume is to collect cases decided in 1985 and 1986 that contribute to an understanding of law regulating relationships between prisoners and authorities. Essentially, this is a matter of federal law arising under the Constitution of the United States rather than of local state law, although local forums continue to consider similar questions. After examining several hundred cases, the editors feel the cases presented in this volume are the most significant. They have attempted to reference other cases of lesser importance in the introductions. Together with other volumes of the set, this book is designed to present a fairly complete library of important cases in this area over the past two decades.

Parameters of this area of the law have been set in previous decades, but in litigation, principles continually have been applied to new situations. In applying the law, courts must ever be alert to circumstances that might not accord with established principles. Unfortunately, those in authority may become insensitive to conditions that may develop beyond the expectations of the courts. Law suits can only adjust a few grievous situations, as much depends on the good will of all parties concerned, including an awareness on the part of the public as to the needs and conditions of prisons.

Courts have frequently stated that they will defer judgment in certain areas to prison authorities, but this does not mean that challenges to their actions are not merited. Challenges to disciplinary actions and to the granting or denial of parole continue to demand a modicum of fair hearings, a legal concept that is difficult to define with precision. The result of these challenges has been a change in the perception of the status of a prisoner versus the control of authorities. It is the expectation of the editors that these volumes will contribute to an understanding of changes that are taking place in the law governing prisoners.

The author is indebted to many individuals for their contributions to the compilation of these cases. Michael Moore served as project researcher, initially locating important cases and bringing them to the attention of the editor. His work has been thorough in this regard. Another research assistant, Deborah Dance, has contributed immeasurably to this book - doing the editorial work and proofreading. Her past experience as a newspaper woman proved an asset in this regard. Katrina DeFoor Wingate has patiently typed the editorial material, such as the chapter introductions and the table of cases for this volume with her usual precision. Rarely do authors and editors acknowledge the contributions of publishers and the editorial assistance received from the publishing house. Philip F. Cohen, a friend of long standing, encouraged the editor to undertake this project. Edwin Newman, a vice-president, and a former practicing attorney who was interested in this area, has been most encouraging. James McCue, a super salesman, has made many useful comments, for which I am grateful.

Finally, the editor is indebted to a person who patiently endured daily reports at breakfast and dinner on the progress and problems of completing this volume, my wife, Ida, to whom this volume is affectionately dedicated.

VOLUME I
SUPPLEMENT

SENTENCING TO PRISON

VOLUME I

CHAPTER 1 INTRODUCTION: WHEN COMMITMENTS MAY BE QUESTIONED

As was earlier pointed out in the introduction to Volume I, "Prison law does not begin with life in prison, the incidents of imprisonment, and the prison program. It begins with the defendant's main concern - liberty which need not always await the service of the term of the sentence." The defendant may, in various ways, attack the sentence when it is imposed.

This section does not necessarily deal with illegal sentences, which are those not authorized by statute, but with legally imposed sentences that may be subject to review. Courts have generally declared that they do not have power to reduce a sentence that is within statutory limitations, which is usually described as the "hands-off" policy. Courts do review sentences, however, and may reduce them for a variety of reasons. Increasingly, statutes are rather specific, not only as to the length of sentences, but with regard to steps that should be taken before a sentence is imposed. Gone are the days when the jury pronounced a verdict of guilty and a judge asked the defendant if he had anything to say before the sentence was imposed at that time. In practically all states, the sentencing procedure is postponed for a reasonable period after the verdict.

Cases set out in this section illustrate various attacks on sentences imposed. *United States v. Kamer,* 781 F.2d 1380 (9th Cir. 1986), reproduced in Chapter 2 of this supplementary volume, involved a question of whether the court adhered to the plea bargain. More troubling, was the case of *United States v. Santamaria,* 788 F.2d 824 (1st Cir. 1986), which, among other points, involved the remark of a judge that indicated his bias against the defendant.

Appellate courts continue to challenge the concept that they have the authority to review a sentence.

Introductions in previous volumes:

I:1; VI: 2; VII: 3; VIII: 3

UNITED STATES of America, Appellee,

v.

Juan C. SANTAMARIA,
Defendant, Appellant.

No. 85–1679.

United States Court of Appeals,
First Circuit.

April 23, 1986.

Before COFFIN and BREYER, Circuit Judges, and MALETZ,* Senior Judge.

MALETZ, Senior Judge.

Defendant-appellant Juan Santamaria appeals from denial of his motion to correct or reduce sentence, Fed.R.Crim.P. 35, contending that the manner in which he was sentenced violated due process. Santamaria argues also that the district court erred in failing to attach to the presentence investigation report its findings as to contested information in the report. Additionally, the government has stated for the first time on this appeal that the court erred in imposing a special parole term. We affirm, with modifications, and remand.

I. *Introduction*

Santamaria was indicted for (1) conspiring in violation of 21 U.S.C. § 846 to knowingly and intentionally distribute and possess with intent to distribute in excess of one kilogram of a mixture containing co-

caine, *id.* § 841(a)(1) and (b)(1)(A), and (2) knowingly and intentionally possessing with intent to distribute one kilogram or more of a mixture containing cocaine, *id.* Santamaria pleaded guilty to both counts of the indictment pursuant to a plea agreement providing for a maximum sentence of twenty years, with a fine and a special parole term to be set in the discretion of the court. He was sentenced on Count II to a term of twenty years, a special parole term of ten years, and a fine of $50,000, and on Count I to a concurrent suspended sentence of ten years. Subsequently, his motion to correct or reduce sentence was denied. This appeal followed.

II. *Background*

On November 15, 1984, Santamaria was recruited by an individual in Rhode Island to go to Florida to pick up four kilograms of cocaine. He then paid his wife, from whom he was separated, $2,000 to accompany him to Florida, where he picked up

* Of the United States Court of International   Trade, sitting by designation.

the cocaine, then returning to Rhode Island. On December 5, 1984, Santamaria again went to Florida with his wife, paid $100,000 for the cocaine previously received, obtained five additional kilograms on consignment, and drove back to Rhode Island with the cocaine hidden in secret compartments built into his Porsche. While en route he was apprehended. A search of his house in Rhode Island revealed additional cocaine, scales, and other implements used in the distribution of cocaine.

Shortly after his arrest, Santamaria made two voluntary statements in which he provided the details of the November and December transactions and gave the names of a number of major cocaine dealers. Thereafter, however, he stopped cooperating, with the result that the information he provided was of little use to the government. Santamaria then moved to suppress the statements he had made during the course of his cooperation. At the hearing on that motion, he testified that he had stopped cooperating out of fear, and that he initially had been misled by government agents into believing that any information he provided would not become public. The court found, contrary to this testimony, that there had been no deception by government agents.

Information available to the court at the time of sentencing included the fact that Santamaria was a twenty-two-year-old unemployed high school graduate with some community college education and no criminal record. At the time of his arrest, he owned four cars: the Porsche in which he had transported the cocaine; two cars admittedly purchased with the proceeds of drug sales; and a car purchased for $8300 in cash shortly after the November trip to Florida. Bank records showed that he had deposited an additional $11,300 in cash shortly after that trip. Santamaria's four cars had been forfeited, as had his house, following a magistrate's determination that although the house was held in the name of his mother and stepfather, Santamaria had provided the $30,000 cash down payment.

At sentencing, defense counsel contested two aspects of the presentence report. The first objection was to a characterization of Santamaria's refusal to continue cooperating as reflecting a "change of heart." Counsel argued that because the defendant had initially been under a misapprehension as to the manner in which the information he provided would be used, it was misleading to say that he had had a "change of heart." The court indicated that its understanding of the phrase was that when Santamaria had realized cooperation would require him to testify, he decided that was not his original intention and that he would not do it. Defense counsel agreed with this characterization.

Counsel's second objection concerned an assertion in the presentence report that Santamaria had been involved in a Canadian drug transaction. Rather than granting counsel's request for a hearing on that aspect of the report, the court indicated that it would not take the alleged transaction into account.

III. *Alleged Violations of Due Process*

Santamaria contends that statements of the court indicate that it did in fact consider the Canadian transaction, despite its representation to the contrary, and that the denial of a hearing regarding that transaction was thus a denial of due process. The statements objected to include the court's comments at sentencing that Santamaria was a "kingpin of this industry that is rattling this country and eating alive our young," and that he was a "villain" and "beyond rehabilitation." Santamaria argues that there was nothing in the facts before the court to support these conclusions, and that the court therefore must have taken the Canadian transaction into account. But given the serious nature of the drug transactions that provided the basis for Santamaria's plea, and in light of the additional information properly before the sentencing court, there is no reason to doubt the judge's assertion that he was not considering the Canadian transaction. *Cf. United States v. Gonzales*, 765 F.2d 1393, 1397 (9th Cir.1985) (district court's statement that it will disregard certain matter in presentence report must be taken at face value), *cert. denied,* —— U.S. ——, 106 S.Ct 826, 88 L.Ed.2d 798 (1986). Thus, there was no constitutional violation, since there is no due process right to contest the accuracy of information not relied upon by the court. *See United States v. Brown,* 715 F.2d 387, 389 (8th Cir.1983) (due process affords the defendant no right to rebut evidence not relied upon in the sentencing process).

Santamaria also argues that the comments of the district court indicated that it employed a rigid sentencing policy rather than considering the defendant as an individual. *See United States v. Foss,* 501 F.2d 522, 527 (1st Cir.1974) (sentences dictated by a mechanistic concept of what a particular type of crime deserves may be vacated by appellate court); *accord United States v. Miller,* 589 F.2d 1117, 1138 (1st Cir.1978), *cert. denied,* 440 U.S. 958, 99 S.Ct 1499, 59 L.Ed.2d 771 (1979). We find the contention without merit. For the record shows specific consideration by the court of factors peculiar to this defendant, including the use of his wife as a "front," the secret compartments in his car, the fact that greed was apparently his only motive, and the amount of narcotics involved.

Santamaria further argues that the court penalized him because he had refused to continue to cooperate. This contention is based in part upon the court's statement that "[w]hat has been termed as forthrightness and candor I see as a cautious venturing forward governed only by self-interest, without the slightest sign of genuine remorse or even a true recognition of the enormity of the wrong which you have committed."

We cannot agree that this or any other statement of the district court indicates that the defendant was being penalized for his failure to cooperate. To the contrary, the court's statements indicate merely an assessment that the defendant's limited cooperation had reflected only self-interest, and not a step towards rehabilitation. Accordingly, the court did not abuse its dis-

cretion by its apparent refusal to consider that cooperation as a ground for leniency. *See United States v. Reed,* 674 F.2d 128, 129–30 (1st Cir.1982) (the premium to be placed on cooperation is a policy judgment left to the discretion of the trial court); *United States v. Miller,* 589 F.2d 1117, 1138 (1st Cir.1978) (there is a distinction between punishing a defendant for asserting his innocence and merely considering a failure to recant when evaluating his prospects for rehabilitation), *cert. denied,* 440 U.S. 958, 99 S.Ct. 1499, 59 L.Ed.2d 771 (1979); *cf. Roberts v. United States,* 445 U.S. 552, 556–61, 100 S.Ct. 1358, 1362–65, 63 L.Ed.2d 622 (1980) (cooperation with the authorities is a laudable endeavor that bears a rational connection to a defendant's willingness to change his behavior); *United States v. Tracey,* 675 F.2d 433, 441 (1st Cir.1982) (defendant's lack of cooperation with the government is a legitimate factor in sentencing).

More troubling is Santamaria's contention that he was denied due process by the sentencing court's conclusion that: "I think from what I know of your case that you are beyond rehabilitation, that punishment for punishment's sake is deserving, that punishment for the sake of deterrence is deserved...." Santamaria argues that a conclusion that he—a twenty-two-year-old with no prior criminal record—was beyond rehabilitation lacked any foundation in the record. He therefore argues that his sentence was based in part upon a false premise, and so violates due process.

A sentence within statutory limits is generally not subject to substantive review. *See Dorszynski v. United States,* 418 U.S. 424, 443, 94 S.Ct. 3042, 3052–53, 41 L.Ed.2d 855 (1974) (well-established doctrine bars review of the exercise of sentencing discretion); *United States v. Talavera,* 668 F.2d 625, 632 (1st Cir.), *cert. denied,* 456 U.S. 978, 102 S.Ct. 2245, 72 L.Ed.2d 853 (1982). However, a case will be remanded for resentencing if a sentence was based on erroneous information or erroneous assumptions of constitutional magnitude. *See*

United States v. Tucker, 404 U.S. 443, 447, 92 S.Ct. 589, 591–92, 30 L.Ed.2d 592 (1972) (case would be remanded for reconsideration of sentence where sentence was founded at least in part upon misinformation of constitutional magnitude); *United States v. Kimball,* 741 F.2d 471, 475 (1st Cir.1984) (sentence within statutory limits and not based on misinformation of constitutional magnitude is within the discretion of the sentencing judge); *United States v. Tracey,* 675 F.2d 433, 441 (1st Cir.1982).

The sentencing court's conclusion as to Santamaria's being beyond rehabilitation did not amount to an erroneous assumption of constitutional magnitude. First, in considering Santamaria's prospects for rehabilitation, the court acted within the proper bounds of discretion. *See United States v. Grayson,* 438 U.S. 41, 47–48, 98 S.Ct. 2610, 2614, 57 L.Ed.2d 582 (1978) (to an unspecified degree the sentencing judge is obligated to make his decision on the basis, among others, of predictions regarding the defendant's potential or lack of potential for rehabilitation). Second, although, given Santamaria's youth and lack of a criminal record, this court might not similarly have concluded that Santamaria was "beyond rehabilitation," it does not follow that that conclusion of the sentencing court was without basis in the record.

Santamaria's November and December drug transactions had involved substantial amounts of cocaine of a high degree of purity; the defendant apparently had access to large amounts of cash, and, although unemployed, his lifestyle was apparently luxurious. He had obtained large amounts of cocaine on consignment, arguably suggesting that he was known, trusted, and no beginner in the area of drug dealing. He owned a car with specially constructed compartments in which to hide drugs; he was able to provide the names of major drug dealers; and he had employed his estranged wife to assist him in his drug transactions. Additionally, the district court had concluded that Santamaria's initial cooperation was based solely on self-interest rather than on a desire to reform his behavior, and had rejected his testimony

that he was misled by federal agents. In light of all this information, we cannot say that the court's assessment of Santamaria's prospects for rehabilitation was so unreasonable as to rise to the level of a false premise of constitutional magnitude. *Cf. United States v. Hartford,* 489 F.2d 652, 656 (5th Cir.1974) (sentencing court's statement that there may be no such thing as rehabilitation for people who push drugs, although not approved of by appellate court, did not indicate that the court had imposed sentence mechanistically); *see also United States v. Hendrix,* 752 F.2d 1226, 1234–35 (7th Cir.) (inference drawn by court that bank teller's death by cancer had been speeded by the trauma of bank robbery was not so unsupported by record as to have denied defendant due process), *cert. denied,* — U.S. —, 105 S.Ct. 2032, 85 L.Ed.2d 314 (1985).

Also significant is the district court's articulation of additional factors for the sentence imposed, *e.g.,* the amount of narcotics involved, Santamaria's use of his estranged wife, and the secret compartments built into his car. This lessens any concern we might have that the defendant's sentence was based upon an improper assumption. *See United States v. Miller,* 589 F.2d 1117, 1139 (1st Cir.1978) (articulation by sentencing court of additional reasons for maximum sentence allayed fear that sentencing decision was tainted by impermissible considerations), *cert. denied,* 440 U.S. 958, 99 S.Ct. 1499, 59 L.Ed.2d 771 (1979); *United States v. Stevenson,* 573 F.2d 1105, 1107 (9th Cir.1978) (even assuming that court in sentencing defendant to higher term than that of his co-defendant relied upon a false understanding that the co-defendant had no prior record, that inaccuracy, which was pointed out to the sentencing court, when balanced against other substantially accurate factors that were considered, was not of constitutional magnitude). For the foregoing reasons, we hold that Santamaria was not denied due process.

IV. *Failure to Attach Findings to Presentence Report*

Santamaria correctly argues that the requirements of rule 32 of the Federal

Rules of Criminal Procedure were not fully complied with in this case. Rule 32(c)(3)(D) provides that, where the defendant alleges factual inaccuracies in a presentence report, the court shall make findings as to any controverted matter or make a determination that no such finding is necessary because the matter will not be taken into account in sentencing. The rule further provides that a written record of such findings and determinations shall be appended to and accompany any copy of the presentence report thereafter made available to the Bureau of Prisons or the Parole Commission.

Here, although the sentencing court indicated that it would not take into account information in the presentence report regarding the alleged Canadian drug transaction, it did not attach a record of that determination to the report. Nor did the court attach a record of its finding regarding the interpretation to be given to the assertion in the presentence report, objected to by defense counsel, that Santamaria had had a "change of heart" regarding cooperation. However, the failure to append the required materials does not necessitate resentencing. The function of the provision of rule 32 requiring attachment of a court's findings and determinations to the presentence report is to prevent a defendant from being prejudiced in the future by errors in the report, which may accompany him throughout his dealings with the correctional system. As the Advisory Committee note on rule 32(c)(3)(D) states:

[T]he Bureau of Prisons and the Parole Commission make substantial use of the presentence investigation report. Under current practice, this can result in reliance upon assertions of fact in the report in the making of critical determinations relating to custody or parole.

See United States v. Castillo-Roman, 774 F.2d 1280, 1285 (5th Cir.1985) (transcript reflecting determination of sentencing court would be attached to presentence report on remand so that disputed information would not be relied upon as having been previously established and thereby adversely affect defendant's confinement or

chance of parole). This function is served by a remand for the required attachments to the report. See id. at 1284–85 (failure to attach finding does not call for vacation of sentence as the remedy contemplated will be afforded by remand for attachment); accord United States v. Eschweiler, 782 F.2d 1385, 1390 (7th Cir.1986). We therefore remand for that purpose.

V. Special Parole Term

Santamaria pleaded guilty, under Count II, to knowingly and intentionally possessing with intent to distribute one kilogram or more of a mixture containing cocaine in violation of 21 U.S.C. § 841(a)(1) and (b)(1)(A), and was sentenced on that count to a sentence of twenty years, a special parole term, and a fine. The government now concedes that the special parole term was improperly imposed.

Prior to amendment in October 1984, the penalty provisions set forth in 21 U.S.C. § 841(b)(1)(A) (1982) required imposition of a special parole term upon a person convicted under 21 U.S.C. § 841(a) of an offense involving a narcotic drug. Those penalty provisions were recast by section 502 of the Comprehensive Crime Control Act of 1984, 21 U.S.C.A. § 841(b)(1)(A) (West Supp. 1985). The new provisions prescribe penalties of different magnitudes depending upon the amount of narcotics involved in an offense, and raise the maximum penalties. Under the new provisions, however, a special parole term, while mandatory for offenses involving less than one kilogram of a narcotic drug, is not authorized for an offense that involves one kilogram or more of a narcotic drug—an offense for which Santamaria was convicted. Thus, there is no basis here for the imposition of a special parole term, and that provision of the sentence is vacated.

VI. Conclusion

The judgment of the district court is affirmed except: (1) the special parole term is vacated, and (2) the case is remanded for compliance with Fed.R.Crim.P. 32(c)(3)(D).

Affirmed as modified and remanded.

VOLUME I

CHAPTER 2   IMPROPERLY BASED COMMITMENTS

Bargained Pleas of Guilty

Bargaining a guilty plea is common in American criminal practice, and many defendants, rightly or wrongly, are induced to enter such an agreement. Once reached, a bargain has been compared by the courts to a contract by which both parties must abide. The federal courts, as many state courts, require that the judge question a defendant extensively about the voluntariness of his agreement. The case of *United States v. Kamer,* 781 F.2d 1380 (9th Cir. 1986), reiterates many points raised in plea bargaining. In *Mabry v. Johnson,* 467 U.S. 504, 104 S.Ct. 2543 (1984), the question was raised as to whether the defendant could enforce the first bargain offered by the prosecutor. Significantly, the Supreme Court stated that a plea bargain standing alone is without constitutional significance. The bargain is only raised to the level of constitutional significance after conviction. In essence, the defendant had not relied exclusively on the plea bargain and had been misled in the process.

Many state courts consider similar cases.

Presentence Investigations

The most frequent source of litigation is the presentence investigation. The law in this area has changed significantly over the past decades. Approximately two decades ago, courts considered such reports as confidential to the judge. They were not made available to the defendant or his counsel. Since then, the law has changed, and the federal rules of criminal procedure require that a copy be given to the defendant and his counsel sometime prior to the sentencing hearing. Practices governing presentence investigations are set out in Fed. R. Crim. P. 32.

The new rule, which takes effect in November 1987, provides that the judge proceed to impose a sentence without unnecessary delay. During the sentencing hearing, the judge must determine whether the defendant and counsel have had an opportunity to read and discuss the presentence report, which must contain the history and characteristics of the defendant's criminal record and the classification of the offense under new sentencing guidelines. The report is to set out the range of sentences that may be imposed - in sentence types and in factors that differentiate the sentence. A new requirement is that presentence reports identify non-prison programs and resources available for the defendant's rehabilitation.

The Illinois statute, Section 1005-4-1, is similar to federal requirements, but allows a victim impact statement, as do many states. *See* Connecticut Statutes 54-91(A).

The case of *United States v. Rone,* 743 F.2d 1169 (7th Cir. 1984) provides a good discussion of the rule.

Introductions in previous volumes:

I: 11; VI: 5; VII: 15; VIII: 5

Articles:

Willis, *Statutory Entitlement to a Presentence Investigation,* 41

J. Mo. Bar 181-182 (1985).

UNITED STATES of America,
Plaintiff/Appellee,

v.

Reink KAMER, Defendant/Appellant.

No. 85–5013.

United States Court of Appeals,
Ninth Circuit.

Argued and Submitted Sept. 6, 1985.
Decided Feb. 5, 1986.

Sneed, Circuit Judge, filed specially concurring opinion.

Appeal from the United States District Court for the Central District of California.

Before SNEED, NELSON and NORRIS, Circuit Judges.

NELSON, Circuit Judge:

Defendant Reink Kamer was charged with 57 counts of conspiracy, mail fraud, and wire fraud, in violation of 18 U.S.C. sections 371, 1341, and 1343, respectively. Pursuant to a binding plea agreement with the government, Kamer withdrew his plea of not guilty and pled guilty to three counts. Kamer appeals to this court contending that the judgment must be vacated because (1) his guilty plea violated Rule 11 of the Federal Rules of Criminal Procedure in that the trial court failed to (a) ascertain whether the plea was voluntary, (b) establish the factual basis for the plea, and (c) inform Kamer of the nature of the charges against him; and because (2) his sentence did not comply with the terms of the plea agreement. Alternatively, and yet interrelated, Kamer argues that the indictment should be dismissed for failure to comply with the Speedy Trial Act because there was no basis for excludable time for trial preparation.

We vacate the district court's judgment with respect to each of Kamer's Rule 11 claims; we hold similarly with respect to his contention that his sentence did not conform to the plea agreement. We affirm, however, the district court's judgment that there was not a violation of the Speedy Trial Act.

BACKGROUND

On October 26, 1983, a federal grand jury charged Kamer, a citizen of the Netherlands, and an American co-defendant, Bernard Whitney, with 57 counts of conspiracy, mail fraud, and wire fraud, in violation of sections 371, 1341, and 1343 of Title 18 of the United States Code. The indictment alleged that Kamer and Whitney jointly owned and operated entities which sold American land at greatly inflated prices to European investors. Apparently, it was not disclosed to investors that the land was inappropriate for large-scale development and that Whitney and Kamer lacked the expertise and financing to insure development. In fact, Kamer and Whitney made no effort to develop the properties, and the prices charged for the land were such that it was highly unlikely that any of the investors could ever make a profit. Investors were also misled about potential sources of financing for the projects and about placement of their money in trust accounts. As a result of this scheme, investors lost millions of dollars.

After extradition from Europe, Kamer was arraigned on July 10, 1984. Trial was set for September 18, 1984, but on August 23, 1984, despite Kamer's objections, his appointed Deputy Public Defender made an application for, and was granted, a continuance of trial until January 8, 1985. Kamer thereafter made a motion to represent himself, and the motion was granted on September 25, 1984. The Deputy Public Defender, however, was appointed standby counsel.

On December 11, 1984, Kamer, acting *pro se*, entered into a binding plea agreement whereby Kamer agreed to plead guilty to three counts. In return, Kamer would receive a maximum sentence of three years with full credit for time already served.

The trial court accepted the plea and on January 21, 1985, sentenced Kamer to sixteen months in custody with credit for time served. The trial court also imposed a five-year probationary sentence on the condition that Kamer make restitution and that he re-enter the United States only with the approval of the Attorney General.

ISSUES PRESENTED

I. Did the trial court violate Rule 11 by failing to (A) ascertain whether the plea was voluntary, (B) establish the factual basis for the plea, or (C) inform defendant of the nature of the charges against him?

II. Did the sentence comply with the plea agreement?

III. Should the indictment be dismissed for failure to comply with the Speedy Trial Act?

DISCUSSION

I. THE GUILTY PLEA: RULE 11

A. *Failure to inform as to the nature of the charges and penalties: Rule 11(c)(1)*

Section (c)(1) of Rule 11 provides, in pertinent part:

Before accepting a plea of guilty or nolo contendere, the court must address the defendant personally in open court and inform him of, and determine that he understands...:

(1) the nature of the charge to which the plea is offered....

The government maintains that Kamer's "over-technical" focus on the plea proceeding ignores the overall effort made by the court *throughout the entire criminal proceedings*. The government argues that a thorough examination of the *entire record* reveals compliance with the mandates of Rule 11(c)(1). We disagree; the trial court's inquiry was wholly inadequate and thus does not comply with Rule 11.

One of the purposes of Rule 11 is to develop a complete record at the plea proceeding so as to decrease the number and facilitate the disposition of often frivolous post-conviction attacks. *McCarthy*, 394 U.S. 459 at 465, 89 S.Ct. 1166 at 1170, 22 L.Ed.2d 418 at 424 (1969). As the *McCarthy* Court noted, "[t]here is no adequate substitute for demonstrating *in the record at the time the plea is entered* the defendant's understanding of the nature of the charge against him." *Id.* at 470, 89 S.Ct. at 1172 (emphasis in original). The dictates of Rule 11 and the federal policy of fair and efficient judicial administration require that the reviewing court look solely to the record of the plea proceeding. *United States v. Coronado*, 554 F.2d 166, 170 n. 5 (5th Cir.1977) ("[C]laims of noncompliance with rule 11 must be resolved solely on the basis of the rule 11 transcript. That transcript provides all that is needed and all that is allowed for the resolution of such claims."); Fed.R.Crim.P. 11(h) advisory committee note (1983 Amendment) (same). *See also United States v. Dayton*, 604 F.2d

931, 939 (5th Cir.1979), *cert. denied,* 445 U.S. 904, 100 S.Ct. 1080, 63 L.Ed.2d 320 (1980) ("it will be a rare case and one that we cannot presently envision in which we look beyond the transcript of the arraignment in passing on an appeal after a guilty plea."). The requirement that the trial judge adequately inquire of the defendant, at the plea proceeding, as to the nature of the charge effectuates the purposes of Rule 11 and the policy of efficient judicial administration. The government's contention that this court should review the *entire* record, therefore, is baseless.

In his prepared pre-sentencing statement to the court, Kamer declared in conclusory fashion that he violated several sections of the United States Code. Kamer's statement, however, does not indicate that he, in fact, understood the charges to which he pled. Nevertheless, the trial judge discussed with Kamer the nature of the charges only to the extent of the following colloquy:

THE COURT: You understand the nature of the charges here against you, I think, very thoroughly, because the statement you just made demonstrates that. You don't have any questions about what the nature of the charges are?

DEFENDANT KAMER: After fourteen months, no more.

Clearly, the sufficiency of any particular colloquy between the judge and the defendant as to the nature of the charges will "vary from case to case, depending on the peculiar facts of each situation, looking to both the complexity of the charges and the personal characteristics of the defendant, such as his age, education, intelligence, the alacrity of his responses, and also whether he is represented by counsel." *United States v. Wetterlin,* 583 F.2d 346, 351 (7th Cir.1978), *cert. denied,* 439 U.S. 1127, 99 S.Ct. 1044, 59 L.Ed.2d 88 (1979). In the instant case, the district court judge neither caused the indictment to be read, *see United States v. Punch,* 709 F.2d 889, 892–94 (5th Cir.1983) (in non-complex cases, a reading of the indictment *may* suffice);

Dayton, 604 F.2d at 938 (same); nor did he give *any* explanation as to the nature of the charges to which the plea was offered. *See Wetterlin,* 583 F.2d at 350–52; *Irizarry v. United States,* 508 F.2d 960, 965–66 (2nd Cir.1974) (trial judge should at least set out the bare bones elements of the offense). *See also McCarthy,* 394 U.S. at 467 n. 20, 89 S.Ct. at 1171 n. 20.

In *Wetterlin,* the Seventh Circuit vacated a guilty plea to a complex conspiracy charge for failure to ascertain whether the defendant understood the nature of the charges. Similar to the case *sub judice,* the Court of Appeals observed that "the judge made no effort to explain the law of conspiracy generally or by reference to the specific charge of this case, nor did he personally inquire and determine that the defendant understood the nature of the charges." 583 F.2d at 350 (footnote omitted).

Granted, Kamer exhibited above-average intelligence. As the trial judge noted, however, this was a complex case. And, although there was standby counsel, Kamer essentially represented himself. That Kamer did not fully appreciate the nature of the charge against him is reflected in his conclusory and somewhat contradictory prepared statement to the court. Indeed, the statement tends to evidence a misunderstanding of the alleged offenses and their requisite elements. The charged offenses all require a showing of specific intent. *See United v. Clevenger,* 733 F.2d 1356, 1358 (9th Cir.1984); *United States v. Andreen,* 628 F.2d 1236, 1248 (9th Cir. 1980). Nonetheless, reading from his declaration to the court, Kamer stated that he was advised that United States law was not applicable to his activities and that mail fraud and wire fraud are unknown to the Netherlands. These remarks, coupled with Kamer's conclusory admission to criminal nondisclosure "because of [his] culpable ignorance of the necessity of disclosing information of that sort." should have alerted the judge to the fact that Kamer may not have pled guilty with a full awareness of the nature of the charges. *See McCarthy,*

394 U.S. at 470, 89 S.Ct. at 1172; *Punch*, 709 F.2d at 893–94.

It is incumbent upon a district judge accepting a plea to make the minor investment of time and effort necessary to set forth the meaning of the charges and to demonstrate on the record that the defendant understands. "There is no excuse for failing to undertake procedures of such utility in ensuring voluntary and intelligent pleas that are susceptible to meaningful review." *Coronado,* 554 F.2d at 172. Under the circumstances, the trial judge should not have accepted Kamer's plea until his understanding was manifest. A district court should not rely upon a *pro se* defendant's bald representation that he does not have any questions. Rather, the trial judge is required to engage in a colloquy with the defendant and elicit responses from him which demonstrate, on the record, that the accused does so understand. Accordingly, we agree with the *Wetterlin* court that

> the judge should not have assumed that the defendant already knew and understood what the charges were, but rather the court should have assumed he was ignorant of the charges and thus used the hearing to inform the defendant "of some aspects of legal argot and other legal concepts that are esoteric to an accused."

583 F.2d at 350 (quoting *Coronado,* 554 F.2d at 172. *See also McCarthy,* 394 U.S. at 467, 89 S.Ct. at 1171 (Rule 11 is not followed when, instead of personally inquiring of the defendant, the district judge

1. This case is distinguishable from the situation that was presented in *United States v. Coronado,* 554 F.2d 166 (5th Cir.1977). Although admonishing the trial judge for "fail[ing] sufficiently to make the required explication of the charges," the *Coronado* court found no reversible error because the Rule 11 transcript, "as a whole," made clear that Coronado had the requisite understanding. 554 F.2d at 173. On the present transcript, however, with the exception of Kamer's prepared presentencing statement (which, as we previously stated, demonstrates a lack of understanding), there is nothing which this court can review to discern substantial compliance with Rule 11(c)(1). We conclude, therefore, that the error here is not harmless.

resorts to "assumptions" as to the defendant's understanding).[1]

B. *Failure to inquire as to voluntariness: Rule 11(d)*

Section (d) of Rule 11 provides that "the court shall not accept a plea of guilty or nolo contendere without first, by addressing the defendant personally in open court, determining that the plea is voluntary and not the result of force or threats or of promises apart from a plea agreement."

The government asserts that after weeks of vigorous negotiations with Kamer, all of which were summarized and memorialized on the record, the trial judge had a sufficient basis for finding that Kamer's plea was entered voluntarily and free from any sort of influence. This contention, however, is legally unfounded. Although the trial judge may have satisfied himself that Kamer's plea was indeed voluntary, Rule 11 "expressly requires the court to address the defendant personally in the course of determining that the plea is made voluntarily...." Fed.R.Crim.P. 11, Notes of Advisory Committee on Rules, 1966 Amendment. "[T]he Rule is intended to produce a complete record *at the time the plea is entered* of the factors relevant to this voluntariness determination." *McCarthy,* 394 U.S. at 465, 89 S.Ct. at 1170 (emphasis added).

The transcript of the plea proceeding is absolutely devoid of any inquiry. As discussed in Section I.A, *supra,* by developing a complete and searching record, the trial court can, and should, ensure the thor-

> There would *not* be harmless error under subdivision (h) where, for example, as in *McCarthy,* there had been *absolutely no inquiry* by the judge into defendant's understanding of the nature of the charge and the harmless error claim of the government rests upon nothing more than the assertion that it may be "assumed" defendant possessed such understanding merely because he expressed a desire to plead guilty.
> Fed.R.Crim.P. 11(h) advisory committee note (1983 Amendment) (first emphasis added; second emphasis in original).

ough and effective administration of justice. Evidently, the trial judge found Kamer's plea to have been made voluntarily. On the bare record before us, however, we cannot adequately perform a review of the district judge's determination. When, as here, we are unable to establish, beyond doubt, that the defendant voluntarily entered his plea, we have no choice but to find noncompliance with Rule 11(d).[2]

C. Failure to establish a factual basis for the plea: Rule 11(f)

Kamer's alleged violation of sections 371, 1341, and 1343 all derive from a failure to disclose material facts. See United States v. Mandel, 591 F.2d 1347, 1363 (4th Cir. 1979), cert. denied, 445 U.S. 961, 100 S.Ct. 1647, 64 L.Ed.2d 236 (1980). Kamer argues that the plea must be vacated because the court did not make "such inquiry as shall satisfy it that there is a factual basis for the plea." Fed.Crim.P. 11(f). Specifically, he alleges that there was insufficient evidence of intent to defraud, a requisite element of the offenses to which he pled guilty. See United States v. Clevenger, 733 F.2d 1356, 1358 (9th Cir.1984); United States v. Andreen, 628 F.2d 1236, 1248 (9th Cir.1980).

In McCarthy, the Supreme Court observed, Rule 11(f) requires the court accepting the plea of guilty to make an "examination of the relation between the law and the acts the defendant admits having committed, a task designed to expose the defendant's state of mind on the record through personal interrogation...." McCarthy, 394 U.S. at 467, 89 S.Ct. at 1171).

As noted in I.A., supra, Kamer was apparently under the impression that U.S. law was not applicable to his activities. Moreover, he expressed that the offenses involved herein are unknown to his country, "[a]nd for that reason, [Kamer] was unaware of the possibility of such a viola-

tion." These statements, uncontroverted by the government, tend to negate a showing of the requisite scienter.

Kamer's alleged violation of sections 371, 1341, and 1343 all derive from a failure to disclose material facts. See Mandel, 591 F.2d at 1363. Absent a duty to speak, however, nondisclosure does not rise to criminal proportions. See id. at 1362-63. Kamer's statements indicate that he was advised he owed no such duty. His failure to disclose, therefore, may not have been motivated by an intent to deceive. From the present record, "we cannot infer that [Kamer] had, beyond doubt, the specific intent to defraud." United States v. McDonald, 576 F.2d 1350, 1359 (9th Cir.), cert. denied sub nom. Stewart v. United States, 439 U.S. 830, 99 S.Ct. 105, 58 L.Ed.2d 124 and cert. denied sub nom. Bresbis v. United States, 439 U.S. 927, 99 S.Ct. 312, 58 L.Ed.2d 320 (1978). Accordingly, we hold that the court below failed to comply with Rule 11(f).

II. THE SENTENCE: COMPLIANCE WITH PLEA AGREEMENT

Kamer entered his guilty plea pursuant to a written plea agreement conditioned upon acceptance by the court in conformance with Rule 11(e)(1)(A) and (C). The written plea agreement provided that Kamer would enter a guilty plea to counts 1, 2, and 21 of the indictment, and in return, "[t]he maximum sentence imposed by the Court shall be three (3) years or less, with full credit for time served since October 11, 1983." On December 11, 1984, the court accepted the agreement. When sentenced on January 21, 1985, however, Kamer received 16 months imprisonment with credit for time served and was placed on probation for five years. The court further imposed as conditions of probation that Kamer "make restitution as ordered by the probation office or the court," that he not re-enter the United States "without the

---

2. If it is elsewhere evidenced, a trial judge's failure to demonstrate *on the Rule 11 transcript* that a defendant's plea was voluntary may be harmless error. See Fed.R.Crim.P. 11(h).

Here, however, we cannot discern voluntariness from even the *entire record*. Therefore, we need not decide that issue now.

permission of the Attorney General or an authorized agent thereof," and that he "report to the nearest probation office within forty-eight hours" of re-entry. Kamer complains that the sentence imposed fails to comply with the terms of the agreement.

Plea agreements are subject to contract-law standards of interpretation. *United States v. Arnett*, 628 F.2d 1162, 1164 (9th Cir.1979). As this court previously stated:

In determining whether a plea agreement has been broken, courts look to "what was 'reasonably understood by [the defendant] when he entered his plea of guilty.'" *United States v. Arnett*, 628 F.2d 1162, 1164 (9th Cir.1979) (quoting *United States v. Crusco*, 536 F.2d 21, 27 (3d Cir.1976)). If disputed, the terms of the agreement will be determined by objective standards.

United States v. Travis, 735 F.2d 1129, 1132 (9th Cir.1984). In order to determine whether the sentence imposed comports with the reasonable understanding and expectations of the defendant as to the sentence for which he had bargained, we look to the objective proof on the record.

As previously mentioned, the written plea agreement refers to a "maximum sentence" of three years or less, but is silent as to any probationary term. The government argues that imposition of the probationary term did not breach the plea agreement because Kamer's only desire was to avoid *incarceration* of more than three years. *See Gammarano v. United States*, 732 F.2d 273, 276 (2d Cir.1984). The government further contends that the probationary term should stand even if probation exceeded Kamer's expectations. Essentially, the government asserts that the plea agreement was silent on this issue

because probation is not part of a "sentence." Therefore, it claims that Kamer unreasonably concluded that probation could not be imposed.

The government contends that *Gammarano* supports its claim that Kamer intended only to avoid *incarceration*. *Gammarano*, however, is distinguishable on its facts. Determining the "reasonable understanding and expectations of the parties," the *Gammarano* court looked to counsel's argument at the sentencing hearing and Gammarano's reaction immediately after the sentence had been imposed. 732 F.2d at 276. The court stressed the fact that counsel had "argued eloquently in favor of a noncustodial term," that Gammarano and his counsel thanked the court after sentencing, and that he did not immediately file a direct appeal. *Id.* The Second Circuit interpreted Gammarano's behavior as objective "evidence that his reasonable expectations [that he would not be incarcerated for more than two years] had been fulfilled." *Id.*

By contrast, Kamer filed a notice of appeal immediately after the sentence was imposed. Also unlike *Gammarano*, nowhere in the record is there *any* reference by anyone to a noncustodial term prior to actual sentencing. *See* 732 F.2d at 276. Finally, while the record does not indicate that Kamer objected at the time sentence was imposed, he was acting as his own counsel and may not have believed that oral objection was appropriate at the time. *See id.* Accordingly, Kamer appears reasonably justified in expecting the sentence to comply with the "literal terms of the agreement." *Travis*, 735 F.2d at 1132.

There appears to be a split in the circuits regarding the government's contention that probation is not a "sentence,".[3]

3. *Compare Sims v. United States,* 607 F.2d 757, 759 (6th Cir.1979) (imposition of five-year prison term upon revocation of probation for two years is not double jeopardy because defendant "had not been sentenced"); *United States v. Becker,* 536 F.2d 471, 473 (1st Cir.1976) ("probation and sentence are separate and distinct"); *United States v. Fultz,* 482 F.2d 1, 4 (8th Cir. 1973) ("Probation . . . is in no sense a sentence

as that term is used in the [Probation] Act") *with United States v. Condit,* 621 F.2d 1096, 1098 (10th Cir.1980) ("for purposes of 28 U.S.C. § 2255 and 18 U.S.C. § 3653 . . . probation is merely one form of sentence"); *United States v. Rodgers,* 588 F.2d 651, 654 (8th Cir.1978) ("probation is a sentence within the meaning of 18 U.S.C. § 3653"); *Nicholas v. United States,* 527 F.2d 1160, 1162 (9th Cir.1976) ("probation is a

However, we find Judge Wisdom's analysis in *Smith v. United States*, 505 F.2d 893 (5th Cir.1974), instructive. Writing for the Fifth Circuit, he explained: "In determining whether probation is properly defined as a 'sentence,' we avoid needless terminological distinctions of artificial origin; we focus on the reality of probationary status." 505 F.2d at 895. We similarly urge that antiquated semantic distinctions be laid aside. "Probation and similar dispositions are, and should be viewed as, sentences just like any other disposition following conviction.... Probation is an attempt by society to impose a sanction that will accomplish its goals, just as any other sentence is." III A.B.A., *Standards for Criminal Justice* 18.80 (1980). We are of the opinion that within the plea bargaining context, where the reasonable understanding and expectations of the parties prevail, probation is commonly understood to be a sentence.

Our conclusion that probation is a sentence within the plea bargaining context is further supported by the Second Circuit's holding in *United States v. Burruezo*, 704 F.2d 33 (2d Cir.1983). The defendant in *Burruezo* entered into a plea agreement with the government. The government agreed that "any prison sentences imposed on [the] pleas of guilty shall not exceed ten years." *Id.* at 34. At sentencing the trial court imposed "imprisonment for eight years with a consecutive five-year term of probation, $3,000 in fines, and a requirement that [defendant] make restitution." *Id.* at 35. The Second Circuit vacated the district court's judgment, however, observing that "the court did not follow the sentencing limitations incorporated in the plea arrangement: the sentence imposed was materially different from the terms of the agreement because the possible length

of sentence exceeded ten years (including the period of probation)...." *Id.* at 38.

It is not uncommon for probation to be one of the considered elements of a plea bargain. Thus, failure to expressly provide for a probationary term must be construed as an intentional omission designed to preclude its imposition.

Burruezo additionally suggests that the district court's imposition of restitution likewise amounts to a breach of the plea agreement. There, the appellate court found that "the comparative magnitude of the amount of restitution [$400,500] ... created a material change in the plea bargain." 704 F.2d at 38 (quoting *United States v. Runck*, 601 F.2d 968, 970 (8th Cir.1979), *cert. denied*, 444 U.S. 1015, 100 S.Ct. 665, 62 L.Ed.2d 644 (1980)). In *Runck*, the district court judge imposed as a condition of probation restitution of $87,-400. The *Runck* court reversed because, as in *Burruezo* and the instant case, the plea agreement was silent on the issue of restitution:

While the condition of restitution of a small amount might be acceptable because it would not necessarily materially alter the expectations of the parties to the bargain, restitution of a large amount should have been part of the plea bargain or the possibility of its inclusion as a condition or probation made known and agreed to by the bargainers.

601 F.2d at 970.

Here, the written plea agreement fails to mention restitution. Nonetheless, the government urges that throughout the negotiations Kamer was aware of the possibility of its imposition. The record, however, indicates to the contrary; several times the court seemed to indicate that restitution would *not* be ordered.[4] Further, subsequent to signing the plea agreement Kamer told the judge it was his

'sentence' within the meaning of section 3653"); *Napoles v. United States*, 536 F.2d 722, 725 (7th Cir.1976) ("probation is a sentence within the meaning of the provisions of § 2255 and § 3653"); *Smith v. United States*, 505 F.2d 893, 895 (6th Cir.1974) ("probation is a sentence like any other sentence").

4. At one point the court told Kamer that "it's not likely that there would be material financial conditions attached to whatever happens here, okay?"

understanding that no restitution would be imposed.

Restitution, here, is presumably in the millions. Under the circumstances, we agree that "[i]f restitution of less than $90,000 [in *Runck*] is material enough to demand express inclusion in a plea agreement, it follows ineluctably that restitution of some [one million-plus] must likewise be included." *United States v. Garcia*, 698 F.2d 31, 36 (1st Cir.1983) (restitution in amount of $900,000 is material alteration of plea agreement).

With respect to the court's imposition of re-entry restrictions, the government maintains there is no material variance with the plea agreement since Kamer would already be subject to such restrictions as a general matter of law. The government, however, appears only partially correct. Present law enables the Attorney General to exclude aliens who have been convicted of crimes involving moral turpitude. 8 U.S.C. § 1182(a)(9) (1970 & 1985 Supp.). Moreover, Kamer's offense would be considered a crime of moral turpitude within the meaning of section 1182. *See McNaughton v. Immigration and Naturalization Service*, 612 F.2d 457 (9th Cir.1980) (fraud is a crime involving moral turpitude).

Accordingly, ordering Kamer "not to enter the United States without the permission of the Attorney General or an authorized agent thereof" merely subjects Kamer to conditions he was already required to obey. The imposition of this restriction, therefore, is harmless error.

As to the requirement that Kamer report to a probation office within 48 hours of re-entry, however, the government cites no authority for the proposition that Kamer would have been required to do so absent the court's imposition of sentence. In light of the express language of the agreement and Kamer's expectations that probation

would not be imposed at all, we find this additional requirement to be a material breach of the bargain.

Since we agree with Kamer that the plea agreement was breached, we vacate the judgment. *Santobello v. New York*, 404 U.S. 257, 262–63, 92 S.Ct. 495, 498–99, 30 L.Ed.2d 427 (1971).

III. SPEEDY TRIAL ACT

Kamer complains that the district court erred in entering an "ends of justice" continuance pursuant to 18 U.S.C. § 3161(h)(8)(A).[5] Kamer's trial was originally scheduled for September 18, 1984. On August 23, 1984, however, Kamer's court-appointed attorney moved for a four-to-five month continuance. Counsel indicated to the court on August 29 that Kamer wanted to go to trial as scheduled, but said that if the court did not grant a continuance, counsel would be forced to withdraw because of inadequate trial preparation. The government agreed that in order to insure a fair trial, a continuance should be granted. On September 11, 1984, pursuant to a section 3161(h)(8)(A) hearing, the district court found that (1) the complexity of the case required additional time for trial preparation and (2) even if the case was not complex, Kamer's counsel needed additional time for trial preparation. Kamer does not challenge these findings, and, moreover, they do not appear to be clearly erroneous. *See United States v. Perez-Reveles*, 715 F.2d 1348, 1351 n. 2 (9th Cir. 1983) (findings that ends of justice require continuance reviewed for clear error). Rather, Kamer argues that on September 25, 1984, when his motion for self-representation was granted, his appointed counsel's need of additional time for trial preparation ceased being a factor. Accordingly, he concludes that the period between September 25, 1984, and January 8, 1985, was not properly excludable, and, therefore, a

5. Section 3161(h)(8)(A) of Title 18 provides, in pertinent part:

No such period of delay resulting from a continuance granted by the court in accordance with this paragraph shall be excludable under this subsection unless the court sets

forth, in the record of the case, either orally or in writing, its reasons for finding that the ends of justice served by the granting of such continuance outweigh the best interests of the public and the defendant in a speedy trial.

Speedy Trial Act violation occurred. Kamer fails to note, however, that although the district court granted Kamer's motion for self-representation, the trial judge retained the appointed Deputy Public Defender as standby counsel. Contrary to Kamer's assertion, therefore, preparation of his appointed counsel did *not* cease being a factor on September 25.

As the district judge observed, the case was a complex one. There were numerous overseas documents, most of which are in the Dutch language. And, of the more than 70 witnesses, many reside in Europe. Accordingly, we are of the opinion that the trial court's grant of an "ends of justice" continuance pursuant to 18 U.S.C. § 3161(h)(8)(A) was within its discretion, and, therefore, no Speedy Trial Act violation occurred.

CONCLUSION

We agree with Kamer that the district court did not comply with several of Rule 11's requirements, and, thus, the judgment should be vacated. Similarly, we hold the plea agreement to have been breached and therefore vacate the judgment on this independent ground. Finally, we find no Speedy Trial Act violation and thus decline to dismiss the indictment.

Accordingly, we vacate the judgment and remand the cause to the district court for proceedings consistent with our above holdings.

SNEED, Circuit Judge, concurring separately:

I concur in Judge Nelson's opinion. I do this while harboring the belief that the appellant has represented himself in this prosecution considerably better than he would have been served by most attorneys. That belief provides no basis for affirmance, however.

Rule 11 imposes upon trial courts fairly precise formal requirements designed to reduce the opportunities for misunderstanding on the part of the defendant or the court. The price that must be paid for this benefit is an occasional reversal solely on the basis of failure to conform to the formalities. This is the usual price that must be paid if formalities are to be taken seriously, as in the instance of Rule 11 they should be. Not to pay the price leads to forfeiture of the benefits that the formalities were intended to achieve.

Formalism in the last century or so has had harsher critics than it deserved. It is reassuring to see its beneficent aspects be recognized in a setting in which that recognition is bolstered by our more honored concern for those accused of crime.

James MABRY, Commissioner,
Arkansas Department of
Correction

v.

George JOHNSON.

No. 83–328.

Argued April 16, 1984.

Decided June 11, 1984.

Syllabus *

After respondent was convicted in an Arkansas state court on charges of burglary, assault, and murder, the Arkansas Supreme Court set aside the murder conviction, and plea negotiations ensued. A deputy prosecutor proposed to respondent's attorney that in exchange for a guilty plea to a charge of accessory after a felony murder, the prosecutor would recommend a 21-year sentence to be served concurrently with the concurrent burglary and assault sentences. However, when defense counsel called the prosecutor three days later and communicated respondent's acceptance of the offer, the prosecutor told counsel that a mistake had been made and withdrew the offer. He proposed instead that in exchange for a guilty plea he would recommend a 21-year sentence to be served consecutively to the other sentences. Respondent rejected the new offer, but after a mistrial was declared, he ultimately accepted the prosecutor's second offer, and the trial judge imposed a 21-year sentence to be served consecutively to the previous sentences. After exhausting state remedies, respondent sought habeas corpus re-

* The syllabus constitutes no part of the opinion of the Court but has been prepared by the Reporter of Decisions for the convenience of the reader. See *United States v. Detroit Lumber Co.*, 200 U.S. 321, 337, 26 S.Ct. 282, 287, 50 L.Ed. 499.

lief in Federal District Court with respect to his guilty plea. The court dismissed the petition, holding that respondent had understood the consequences of his guilty plea, that he had received effective assistance of counsel, and that because it was not established that he had detrimentally relied on the prosecutor's first proposed plea agreement, respondent had no right to enforce it. However, the Court of Appeals reversed, holding that "fairness" precluded the prosecution's withdrawal of the plea proposal once accepted by respondent.

Held: Respondent's acceptance of the prosecutor's first proposed plea bargain did not create a constitutional right to have the bargain specifically enforced, and he may not successfully attack his subsequent guilty plea. Plea agreements are consistent with the requirements that guilty pleas be made voluntarily and intelligently. If a defendant was not fairly apprised of its consequences, his guilty plea can be challenged under the Due Process Clause. And when the prosecution breaches its promise with respect to an executed plea agreement, the defendant pleads guilty on a false premise, and hence his conviction cannot stand. However, respondent's plea was in no sense induced by the prosecutor's withdrawn offer, and it rested on no unfulfilled promise; he knew the prosecution would recommend a 21-year consecutive sentence. Thus, because it did not impair the voluntariness or intelligence of his guilty plea, respondent's inability to enforce the prosecutor's first offer is without constitutional significance. Neither is the question whether the prosecutor was negligent or otherwise culpable in first making and then withdrawing his offer relevant. Cf. *Santobello v. New York*, 404 U.S. 257, 92 S.Ct. 495, 30 L.Ed.2d 427. Pp. 2546–2548.

707 F.2d 323 (CA8 1983), reversed.

John Steven Clark, Brinkley, Ark., for petitioner.

Jerrold J. Ganzfried, Washington, D.C., for the United States as amicus curiae, by special leave of Court.

Richard Quiggle, Little Rock, Ark., for respondent.

Justice STEVENS delivered the opinion of the Court.

The question presented is whether a defendant's acceptance of a prosecutor's proposed plea bargain creates a constitutional right to have the bargain specifically enforced.

In the late evening of May 22, 1970, three members of a family returned home to find a burglary in progress. Shots were exchanged resulting in the daughter's death and the wounding of the father and respondent—one of the burglars. Respondent was tried and convicted on three charges: burglary, assault, and murder. The murder conviction was set aside by the Arkansas Supreme Court, *Johnson v. State*, 252 Ark. 1113, 482 S.W.2d 600 (1972). Thereafter, plea negotiations ensued.

At the time of the negotiations respondent was serving his concurrent 21- and 12-year sentences on the burglary and assault convictions. On Friday, October 27, 1972, a deputy prosecutor proposed to respondent's attorney that in exchange for a plea of guilty to the charge of accessory after a felony murder, the prosecutor would recommend a sentence of 21 years to be served concurrently with the burglary and assault sentences. On the following day, counsel communicated the offer to respondent who agreed to accept it. On the next Monday the lawyer called the prosecutor "and communicated [respondent's] acceptance of the offer." App. 10. The prosecutor then told counsel that a mistake had been made and withdrew the offer. He proposed instead that in exchange for a guilty plea he would recommend a sentence of 21 years to be served consecutively to respondent's other sentences.

Respondent rejected the new offer and elected to stand trial. On the second day of trial, the judge declared a mistrial and plea negotiations resumed, ultimately resulting in respondent's acceptance of the prosecutor's second offer. In accordance with the plea bargain, the state trial judge imposed a 21-year sentence to be served consecutively to the previous sentences.

After exhausting his state remedies, respondent filed a petition for a writ of habeas corpus under 28 U.S.C. § 2254.[1] The District Court dismissed the petition, finding that respondent had understood the consequences of his guilty plea, that he had received the effective assistance of counsel, and that because the evidence did not establish that respondent had detrimentally relied on the prosecutor's first proposed plea agreement, respondent had no right to enforce it. The Court of Appeals reversed, 707 F.2d 323 (CA8 1983), over Judge John R. Gibson's dissent. The majority concluded that "fairness" precluded the prosecution's withdrawal of a plea proposal once accepted by respondent. Because of a conflict in the Circuits,[2] coupled with our

concern that an important constitutional question had been wrongly decided, we granted certiorari, 464 U.S. 1017, 104 S.Ct. 547, 78 L.Ed.2d 722 (1983). We now reverse.[3]

Respondent can obtain federal habeas corpus relief only if his custody is in violation of the Federal Constitution.[4] A plea bargain standing alone is without constitutional significance; in itself it is a mere executory agreement which, until embodied in the judgment of a court, does not deprive an accused of liberty or any other constitutionally protected interest.[5] It is the ensuing guilty plea that implicates the Constitution. Only after respondent pleaded guilty was he convicted, and it is that conviction which gave rise to the deprivation of respondent's liberty at issue here.[6]

It is well settled that a voluntary and intelligent plea of guilty made by an accused person, who has been advised by

---

1. The petition was referred to a Magistrate who conducted an evidentiary hearing and made recommended findings of fact and conclusions of law, which the District Court subsequently adopted.

2. Compare *Virgin Islands v. Scotland,* 614 F.2d 360 (CA3 1980), and *United States v. Greenman,* 700 F.2d 1377 (CA11), cert. denied, 464 U.S. 992, 104 S.Ct. 482, 78 L.Ed.2d 680 (1983), with *Cooper v. United States,* 594 F.2d 12 (CA4 1979).

3. This case is not moot despite the fact that respondent has been paroled. Respondent remains in the "custody" of the State, see *Jones v. Cunningham,* 371 U.S. 236, 83 S.Ct. 373, 9 L.Ed.2d 285 (1963); see generally *Justices of Boston Municipal Court v. Lydon,* 466 U.S. 294, 300–302, 104 S.Ct. 1805, 1809–1810, 80 L.Ed.2d 311 (1984); *Hensley v. Municipal Court,* 411 U.S. 345, 93 S.Ct. 1571, 36 L.Ed.2d 294 (1973); and whether respondent must serve the sentence now under attack consecutively to his prior sentences will affect the date at which his parole will expire under state law, see Ark.Stat.Ann. § 43–2807(c) (Supp.1983). Respondent's challenge to the duration of his custody therefore remains live.

4. *E.g., Townsend v. Sain,* 372 U.S. 293, 312, 83 S.Ct. 745, 756, 9 L.Ed.2d 770 (1963). In pertinent part, the habeas statute provides:

"The Supreme Court, a Justice thereof, a circuit judge, or a district court shall entertain an application for a writ of habeas corpus in behalf of a person in custody pursuant to the judgment of a State court only on the ground that he is in custody in violation of the Constitution or laws or treaties of the United States." 28 U.S.C. § 2254(a).

5. Under Arkansas law, there is no entitlement to have the trial court impose a recommended sentence since a negotiated sentence recommendation does not bind the court, see *Varnedare v. State,* 264 Ark. 596, 599, 573 S.W.2d 57, 60 (1978); *Marshall v. State,* 262 Ark. 726, 561 S.W.2d 76 (1978); Ark.Rule Crim.Proc. 25.3(c); there is a critical difference between an entitlement and a mere hope or expectation that the trial court will follow the prosecutor's recommendation, see *Olim v. Wakinekona,* 461 U.S. 238, 248–251, 103 S.Ct. 1741, 1747–1748, 75 L.Ed.2d 813 (1983); *Jago v. Van Curen,* 454 U.S. 14, 19–21, 102 S.Ct. 31, 34–35, 70 L.Ed.2d 13 (1981) (*per curiam*); *Connecticut Board of Pardons v. Dumschat,* 452 U.S. 458, 465–467, 101 S.Ct. 2460, 2464–2465, 69 L.Ed.2d 158 (1981); *Meachum v. Fano,* 427 U.S. 215, 226–227, 96 S.Ct. 2532, 2539, 49 L.Ed.2d 451 (1976).

6. See *Boykin v. Alabama,* 395 U.S. 238, 89 S.Ct. 1709, 23 L.Ed.2d 274 (1969); *Kercheval v. United States,* 274 U.S. 220, 223, 47 S.Ct. 582, 583, 71 L.Ed. 1009 (1927).

competent counsel, may not be collaterally attacked.[7] It is also well settled that plea agreements are consistent with the requirements of voluntariness and intelligence—because each side may obtain advantages when a guilty plea is exchanged for sentencing concessions, the agreement is no less voluntary than any other bargained-for exchange.[8] It is only when the consensual character of the plea is called into question that the validity of a guilty plea may be impaired. In *Brady v. United States*, 397 U.S. 742, 90 S.Ct. 1463, 25 L.Ed.2d 747 (1970), we stated the applicable standard:

> " '[A] plea of guilty entered by one fully aware of the direct consequences, including the actual value of any commitments made to him by the court, prosecutor, or his own counsel, must stand unless induced by threats (or promises to discontinue improper harassment), misrepresentation (including unfulfilled or unfulfillable promises), or perhaps by promises that are by their nature improper as having no proper relationship to the prosecutor's business (e.g. bribes).' " *Id.*, at 755, 90 S.Ct., at 1472 (quoting *Shelton v. United States*, 246 F.2d 571, 572, n. 2

7. See *Tollett v. Henderson*, 411 U.S. 258, 266–267, 93 S.Ct. 1602, 1607–1608, 36 L.Ed.2d 235 (1973); *North Carolina v. Alford*, 400 U.S. 25, 31, 91 S.Ct. 160, 164, 27 L.Ed.2d 162 (1970); *Parker v. North Carolina*, 397 U.S. 790, 797–798, 90 S.Ct. 1458, 1462–1463, 25 L.Ed.2d 785 (1970); *McMann v. Richardson*, 397 U.S. 759, 772, 90 S.Ct. 1441, 1449, 25 L.Ed.2d 763 (1970); *Brady v. United States*, 397 U.S. 742, 747–748, 90 S.Ct. 1463, 1468, 25 L.Ed.2d 747 (1970). See also *Henderson v. Morgan*, 426 U.S. 637, 96 S.Ct. 2253, 49 L.Ed.2d 108 (1976); *Menna v. New York*, 423 U.S. 61, 96 S.Ct. 241, 46 L.Ed.2d 195 (1975) (*per curiam*).

8. See *Corbitt v. New Jersey*, 439 U.S. 212, 219–220, 222–223, 99 S.Ct. 492, 497–498, 499, 58 L.Ed.2d 466 (1978); *Bordenkircher v. Hayes*, 434 U.S. 357, 363, 98 S.Ct. 663, 667, 54 L.Ed.2d 604 (1978); *Blackledge v. Allison*, 431 U.S. 63, 71, 97 S.Ct. 1621, 1627, 52 L.Ed.2d 136 (1977); *Santobello v. New York*, 404 U.S. 257, 260–261, 92 S.Ct. 495, 497–498, 30 L.Ed.2d 427 (1971). For example, in *Brady v. United States*, we wrote: "For a defendant who sees slight possibility of acquittal, the advantages of pleading guilty and

(CA5 1957) (en banc) (in turn quoting 242 F.2d 101, 115 (Tuttle, J., dissenting to panel opinion)), rev'd on other grounds, 356 U.S. 26, 78 S.Ct. 563, 2 L.Ed.2d 579 (1958).

Thus, only when it develops that the defendant was not fairly apprised of its consequences can his plea be challenged under the Due Process Clause. *Santobello v. New York*, 404 U.S. 257, 92 S.Ct. 495, 30 L.Ed.2d 427 (1971), illustrates the point. We began by acknowledging that the conditions for a valid plea "presuppose fairness in securing agreement between an accused and a prosecutor.... The plea must, of course, be voluntary and knowing and if it was induced by promises, the essence of those promises must in some way be made known." *Id.*, at 261–262, 92 S.Ct., at 498. It follows that when the prosecution breaches its promise with respect to an executed plea agreement, the defendant pleads guilty on a false premise, and hence his conviction cannot stand: "[W]hen a plea rests in any significant degree on a promise or agreement of the prosecutor, so that it can be said to be part of the inducement or consideration, such promise must be fulfilled." *Id.*, at 262, 92 S.Ct., at 499.[9]

limiting the probable penalty are obvious—his exposure is reduced, the correctional processes can begin immediately, and the practical burdens of a trial are eliminated. For the State there are also advantages—the more promptly imposed punishment after an admission of guilt may more effectively attain the objectives of punishment; and with the avoidance of trial, scarce judicial and prosecutorial resources are conserved for those cases in which there is a substantial issue of the defendant's guilt or in which there is substantial doubt that the State can sustain its burden of proof. It is this mutuality of advantage that perhaps explains the fact that at present well over three-fourths of the criminal convictions in this country rest on pleas of guilty, a great many of them no doubt motivated at least in part by the hope or assurance of a lesser penalty than might be imposed if there were a guilty verdict after a trial to judge or jury." 397 U.S., at 752, 90 S.Ct., at 1471 (footnotes omitted).

9. See also 404 U.S., at 266, 92 S.Ct., at 501 (Douglas, J., concurring); *id.*, at 269, 92 S.Ct., at 502 (MARSHALL, J., concurring in part and dissenting in part).

Santobello demonstrates why respondent may not successfully attack his plea of guilty. Respondent's plea was in no sense induced by the prosecutor's withdrawn offer; unlike Santobello, who pleaded guilty thinking he had bargained for a specific prosecutorial sentencing recommendation which was not ultimately made, at the time respondent pleaded guilty he knew the prosecution would recommend a 21-year consecutive sentence. Respondent does not challenge the District Court's finding that he pleaded guilty with the advice of competent counsel and with full awareness of the consequences—he knew that the prosecutor would recommend and that the judge could impose the sentence now under attack.[10] Respondent's plea was thus in no sense the product of governmental deception; it rested on no "unfulfilled promise" and fully satisfied the test for voluntariness and intelligence.

Thus, because it did not impair the voluntariness or intelligence of his guilty plea, respondent's inability to enforce the prosecutor's offer is without constitutional significance.[11]   Neither is the question whether the prosecutor was negligent or otherwise culpable in first making and then withdrawing his offer relevant. The Due Process Clause is not a code of ethics for prosecutors; its concern is with the manner in which persons are deprived of their liberty.[12] Here respondent was not deprived of his liberty in any fundamentally unfair way. Respondent was fully aware of the likely consequences when he pleaded guilty; it is not unfair to expect him to live with those consequences now.

The judgment of the Court of Appeals is *Reversed.*

10. Respondent suggests that the prosecutor's withdrawal of the initial offer undermined his confidence in defense counsel, in violation of his Sixth Amendment right to counsel. This argument is simply at odds with reason. Prosecutors often come to view an offense more seriously during the course of pretrial investigation for reasons entirely unrelated to what defense counsel has done or is likely to do. See *United States v. Goodwin,* 457 U.S. 368, 381, 102 S.Ct. 2485, 2493, 73 L.Ed.2d 74 (1982). We fail to see how an accused could reasonably attribute the prosecutor's change of heart to his counsel any more than he could have blamed counsel had the trial judge chosen to reject the agreed-upon recommendation, or, for that matter, had he gone to trial and been convicted. The District Court and the Court of Appeals concluded that counsel effectively advised respondent; that is all the Constitution requires. See *United States v. Cronic,* 466 U.S. 648, 656–657, n. 19, 104 S.Ct. 2039, 2045, n. 19, 80 L.Ed.2d 657 (1984); *Tollett v. Henderson,* 411 U.S., at 266–268, 93 S.Ct., at 1607–1608; *Parker v. North Carolina,* 397 U.S., at 797–798, 90 S.Ct., at 1462–1463; *McMann v. Richardson,* 397 U.S., at 770–771, 90 S.Ct., at 1448–1449.

11. Indeed, even if respondent's plea were invalid, *Santobello* expressly declined to hold that the Constitution compels specific performance of a broken prosecutorial promise as the remedy for such a plea; the Court made it clear that permitting Santobello to replead was within the range of constitutionally appropriate remedies. See 404 U.S., at 262–263, 92 S.Ct., at 498–499; see also *id.,* at 268–269, 92 S.Ct., at 502 (MARSHALL, J., concurring in part and dissenting in part). It follows that respondent's constitutional rights could not have been violated. Because he pleaded after the prosecution had breached its "promise" to him, he was in no worse position than Santobello would have been had he been permitted to replead.

12. *Santobello* itself rejected the relevance of prosecutorial culpability: "It is now conceded that the promise to abstain from a recommendation was made, and at this stage the prosecution is not in a good position to argue that its inadvertent breach of agreement is immaterial. The staff lawyers in a prosecutor's office have the burden of 'letting the left hand know what the right hand is doing' or has done. That the breach of agreement was inadvertent does not lessen its impact." *Id.,* at 262, 92 S.Ct., at 499. Cf. *United States v. Agurs,* 427 U.S. 97, 110, 96 S.Ct. 2392, 2400, 49 L.Ed.2d 342 (1976).

Richard JOHNSON,
Petitioner-Appellant,

v.

UNITED STATES of America,
Respondent-Appellee.

No. 85–1378.

United States Court of Appeals,
Seventh Circuit.

Argued May 29, 1986.

Decided Nov. 4, 1986.

Rehearing and Rehearing En Banc
Denied Jan. 14, 1987.

Before BAUER, Chief Judge, POSNER, Circuit Judge, and SWYGERT, Senior Circuit Judge.

POSNER, Circuit Judge.

This appeal from the denial of Richard Johnson's petition to vacate his sentence requires us to consider in what circumstances a criminal defendant can use 28 U.S.C. § 2255, the federal prisoner's substitute for habeas corpus, to correct violations of Rule 32 of the Federal Rules of Criminal Procedure. As amended in 1983, Rule 32 requires that the report of the presentence investigation be shown to the defendant personally (not just to his lawyer) before sentencing, so that he can point out any factual inaccuracies to the sentencing judge. Violation of Rule 32 is reversible error (requiring that the defendant be re- sentenced) if a claim that the judge relied on inaccurate information in the presentence report in sentencing the defendant is made and not resolved. *United States v. Eschweiler*, 782 F.2d 1385, 1389 (7th Cir. 1986); *United States v. Rone*, 743 F.2d 1169 (7th Cir.1984). And in administering this standard we have been reluctant to characterize violations of the rule as harmless. See *United States v. Sosa*, 789 F.2d 1257, 1264 (7th Cir.1986); *United States v. Eschweiler, supra*, 782 F.2d at 1390–91.

Johnson had been the president of a small-loan company that had gotten into financial trouble, and he had devised a scheme by which his company discounted phoney loan contracts to Walter E. Heller & Co., receiving some $141,000 in advances from Heller on these contracts. Johnson had involved his wife and mother, who were officers of his company, in the scheme. He pleaded guilty, after the effective date of the amended Rule 32, to two counts of mail fraud. At his sentencing hearing, when asked whether he had anything to say on his own behalf, Johnson said, "Only that I'm sincerely sorry, even more sorry that I involved my family in it." The presentence investigation report, which was shown to Johnson's counsel but not to Johnson, indicated that he had previously been arrested eight times, had served one year in a pretrial diversion program for having committed bank fraud and embezzlement, had served 10 days in jail for contempt of court, and had indeed involved his family in the scheme to defraud. It also described Johnson as a "mover" and "shaker" and indicated that Walter E. Heller & Co. claimed to have lost $919,000 as a result of the fraud. During the sentencing hearing the assistant U.S. attorney commented on a fraud that had not been mentioned in the presentence report, but defense counsel objected and the judge said he would not consider this incident in sentencing Johnson.

The judge then explained the basis on which he would sentence Johnson:

The court has always adhered to the view in most cases that everyone is entitled to a second chance. Mr. Johnson had his chance. He had his second chance. And he proved to the court and apparently to the government that he is not a proper candidate for probation. Albeit he did plead guilty, I also agree with the government. Mr. Johnson shows utterly no remorse whatever for his actions. I think to grant probation in Mr. Johnson's case would be a mockery. I don't know how else to characterize it. Not only did he engage in this scheme after he had been treated with compassion by the U.S. Attorney and after the court had treated him compassionately, he involved his family members, and that requires some period of incarceration in the court's humble opinion.

The court then sentenced Johnson to three years in prison to be followed by three years on probation, fined him $2,000, and ordered him to make restitution to Heller of $75,000.

About a year later Johnson, who had not appealed from his conviction or sentence, moved to vacate the sentence on the ground that the judge had violated Rule 32 and relied on false information in sentencing him. Johnson complained that listing his arrests in the presentence report without explaining their circumstances had given a misleading impression of his propensity to commit crimes, that the words "mover" and "shaker" should not have been used, that one of the charges mentioned in the report was not, in fact, on his record, and that Heller hadn't lost $919,000 and indeed had received $135,000 in interest payments from Johnson. The district judge, without resolving the accuracy of these charges, refused to vacate the sentence. He said that in sentencing Johnson he had not relied on any of the alleged misinformation in the presentence report, but had

relied only upon the incident involving the prior pretrial diversion program and not upon the list of prior arrests or the claimed loss of the victim. The Court's reference to a first chance given to the defendant by the court and by the U.S. Attorney can only refer to the pretrial diversion program since none of the other incidents contained in the presentence report involved federal crimes.... The only other factor mentioned was the involvement of defendant's family in the fraudulent loan scheme. Since neither of these two factors were challenged by the defendant as inaccurate, the Court did not rely on any controverted matter in passing sentence on the defendant and therefore no ground exists to grant him a new sentencing hearing.

Johnson moved for reconsideration, arguing that the presentence report had also been inaccurate in saying that he had involved his family in the scheme. The judge denied the motion for reconsideration, and this appeal followed.

Johnson makes three principal arguments: Rule 32 was violated; he was denied due process of law; he did not receive effective assistance of counsel.

1. Rule 32 was indeed violated, and we find the violation both inexplicable and inexcusable. We can understand how a busy district judge might overlook a recent amendment to the Federal Rules of Criminal Procedure but not how an assistant U.S. attorney could fail to draw the oversight to the judge's attention at the sentencing hearing so that the mistake could be corrected on the spot. If Johnson had appealed from the sentence we would have reversed and directed the judge to comply with Rule 32 and resentence Johnson.

But Johnson did not appeal. Instead he waited almost a year and then filed a motion for postconviction relief under section 2255. The grounds for relief under this section are narrower than the grounds for relief on direct appeal. On direct appeal a defendant can complain of any error committed in the district court, other than a harmless error; in a section 2255 proceeding he must show that "the sentence was imposed in violation of the Constitution or laws of the United States, or that the court was without jurisdiction to impose such sentence, or that the sentence was in excess of the maximum authorized by law, or is otherwise subject to collateral attack." The legislative history shows, and the Supreme Court has held, that the purpose of section 2255 was "simply to provide in the sentencing court a remedy exactly commensurate with that which had previously been available by habeas corpus in the court of the district where the prisoner was confined." *Hill v. United States*, 368 U.S. 424, 427, 82 S.Ct. 468, 470, 7 L.Ed.2d 417 (1962) (footnote omitted). And, of course, habeas corpus is not a proper route for complaining about simple trial errors. The policy of finality in criminal cases, attenuated though it is compared to the policy of finality in civil cases, retains some strength—enough to make the direct appeal (which the defendant must file within 60 days of being sentenced—habeas corpus and section 2255 have no time limits) the exclusive route for complaining about errors that demonstrate neither "a fundamental defect which inher-

ently results in a complete miscarriage of justice, nor an omission inconsistent with the rudimentary demands of fair procedure." *Id.* at 428, 82 S.Ct. at 471. The Supreme Court applied this standard in *Hill* to the question whether a violation of Rule 32 could be corrected under section 2255, and held that it could not be. The Court reaffirmed *Hill* in *United States v. Timmreck*, 441 U.S. 780, 99 S.Ct. 2085, 60 L.Ed.2d 634 (1979). See also *United States v. Addonizio*, 442 U.S. 178, 185, 99 S.Ct. 2235, 2240, 60 L.Ed.2d 805 (1979).

That would be the end of Johnson's case, at least insofar as it rests on the violation of Rule 32, but for language in *Timmreck* suggesting that while a "technical" violation of one of the Federal Rules of Criminal Procedure cannot be corrected in a proceeding under section 2255, conceivably a violation that "occurred in the context of other aggravating circumstances" could be. 441 U.S. at 784–85, 99 S.Ct. at 2087–88. The Court did not hold it could be; it merely left the question open. All that we understand by this language is that if the circumstances of violation are such that the defendant's right to due process of law has been denied, he may be able to complain under section 2255—not of the rule violation as such, however, but only of the violation of due process. We find it hard to imagine an error that was either "a fundamental defect which inherently results in a complete miscarriage of justice" or "an omission inconsistent with the rudimentary demands of fair procedure," yet would not violate the due process clause of the Fifth Amendment. And we also think these formulations come to much the same thing, for the most "rudimentary demand" of "fair procedure" is that the trial not be infected by the kind of error likely to lead to a miscarriage of justice, i.e., the conviction of an innocent person. Cf. *Darden v. Wainwright*, —— U.S. ——, 106 S.Ct. 2464, 2473 and n. 15, 91 L.Ed.2d 144 (1986); *Donnelly v. De Christoforo*, 416 U.S. 637, 642–43, 94 S.Ct. 1868, 1871, 40 L.Ed.2d 431 (1974). In any event the due process clause requires compliance with at least "the rudimentary demands of fair procedure," whatever precisely they are. It therefore is not necessary to discuss Johnson's Rule 32 complaint further; we can turn directly to his claim that the district court deprived him of due process of law.

In taking this approach, we have not overlooked *Davis v. United States,* 417 U.S. 333, 345, 94 S.Ct. 2298, 2304, 41 L.Ed.2d 109 (1974), which holds that in applying the standard of *Hill,* the courts are not confined to "claims 'of constitutional dimension.' " Davis had claimed that his "conviction and punishment [were] for an act that the law does not make criminal," and the Court held that such a claim is actionable under section 2255. *Id.* at 346–47, 94 S.Ct. at 2305. To punish a person criminally for an act that is not a crime would seem the quintessence of denying due process of law, and it seems that what the Court had in mind in saying that section 2255 is not limited to claims of constitutional dimension is simply that in some cases a defendant may be able to make a statutory argument the basis for a due process claim. If you argue that Statute X does not make your act a crime, you are making a statutory argument, but in support of a due process claim. This is not because every erroneous statutory interpretation is a denial of due process—a ridiculous proposition. It is because punishing a person for engaging in conduct that the polity has not made criminal is inconsistent with the proposition that state or federal government may not, consistently with the Constitution, deprive persons of life, liberty, or property, except through due process of law.

Another distinction builds on the fact that habeas corpus (for which as we have said section 2255 is designed to be an identical substitute, so far as the issues in this case are concerned) for prisoners requires a showing that the prisoner "is in custody in violation of the Constitution or laws ... of the United States." 28 U.S.C. § 2241(c)(3). The custody could be lawful even though a violation of law had occurred at the trial or sentencing. Indeed, without this distinction the difference between direct and collateral attack on crimi-

nal judgments would be erased. Custody is unlawful if the prisoner is being held for committing a crime that does not exist, but not if there just was some irregularity in the procedure by which his guilt or punishment was determined. If *Davis* goes further than we are supposing and makes all violations of federal statutes or rules actionable under section 2255, it is inconsistent with *Hill, Timmreck,* and many other cases, and indeed with the whole distinction between direct appeal and collateral attack.

Our decision in *Krilich v. United States,* 502 F.2d 680, 682 and n. 3 (7th Cir.1974), suggests in dictum that statutory violations are actionable under section 2255 even if they do not involve a fundamental defect or breach of rudimentary principles of fair procedure—even if they do not violate due process. But this dictum cannot be considered authoritative in light of *Timmreck* and, indeed, *Davis* itself. Granted, our recent decision in *Kramer v. United States,* 788 F.2d 1229, 1231, supplementary opinion, 798 F.2d 192 (7th Cir. 1986), considered the merits of a Rule 32 violation presented in a motion under 28 U.S.C. § 2255. But the only issue we considered was whether Kramer had waived his right to collateral relief by failing to press his Rule 32 claim on direct appeal. The issue whether such a claim can be made in a collateral attack on the sentence was neither raised nor considered, and was treated as open in still another *Kramer* opinion, see *Kramer v. United States,* 803 F.2d 896, 899 (7th Cir.1986).

2. If as Johnson claims the district court relied on false information in sentencing him, without giving him a chance to correct the information, he may have been denied due process of law. *United States v. Tucker,* 404 U.S. 443, 447, 92 S.Ct. 589, 591, 30 L.Ed.2d 592 (1972); *United States ex rel. Welch v. Lane,* 738 F.2d 863, 864–65 (7th Cir.1984). (We say "may" rather than "was" to avoid getting tangled in the question, irrelevant to our disposition of this appeal, what the Supreme Court meant in *Tucker* by "misinformation of constitutional magnitude." 404 U.S. at 447, 92 S.Ct. at

591.) But there is no factual basis for this claim. The district judge was emphatic, in his order denying Johnson's motion to vacate the sentence, that he had not relied on any of the information in the presentence report that Johnson claims is false. Pointing out that this order was rendered more than a year after the sentencing, Johnson argues that the judge surely could not remember what parts of the presentence report he had or had not relied on. This would be a more powerful argument if the judge's recollection were not entirely consistent with his remarks at sentencing. The remarks purport to give the judge's reasons for imposing the sentence he did: that Johnson had breached the trust implied in allowing him to participate in a pretrial diversion program—which is to say, allowing him to escape punishment—for his previous fraud, and that he had involved his family in the fraud. The first fact is uncontested, and the second Johnson admitted at his sentencing hearing. His belated attempt to deny that he involved his family is entirely unconvincing, given what he said at the hearing and his failure to try to substantiate the denial.

Of course it is possible that the judge's memory was playing tricks on him, that in fact when he sentenced Johnson he was under the influence of information in the presentence report that he didn't bother to mention, and that over the course of a busy year he forgot about his unrecorded mental processes. But although this is possible we have no ground for concluding that it is probable. Judge Bua is an experienced and responsible judge, who is sensitive to the rights of criminal defendants. We have no basis for discrediting his unequivocal report of his recollections, which persuade us that he did not in fact rely on inaccurate information in sentencing Johnson. See *Lawary v. United States*, 599 F.2d 218, 226–27 (7th Cir.1979) (per curiam).

We do not suggest that the type of ex post facto determination that Judge Bua made can always cure a Rule 32 violation; *Sosa* and *Eschweiler* suggest not, and for the practical reason that it is easier for the district judge to comply with Rule 32 and resentence the defendant than to rack his brain to recall what parts of the presentence report he relied on in sentencing the defendant the first time. But the issue on this appeal is not whether Rule 32 was violated; it is whether the violation denied Johnson due process of law. It did not.

Johnson also argues that the judge's failure to tell him that he had a right to read the sentencing report, and failure to give him a chance to correct any errors in the report, denied him due process of law. Even before the 1983 amendments to Rule 32 required the sentencing judge to show the defendant the presentence report, it was the better practice to do so; among other things it was a good way of making sure the judge did not inadvertently deny the defendant due process by sentencing him on the basis of inaccurate information. But no one thought that the old Rule 32, let alone those basic concepts of fair procedure that are encompassed by the term "due process of law," *required* that the report be shown to the defendant, especially when (as in this case) it was shown to the defendant's counsel. If we accepted Johnson's contention we would come close to elevating the 1983 amendment, which required that the defendant be given the report personally, to constitutional status, thereby perhaps giving the amendment an indefinite retroactive effect. Prisoners sentenced many years ago but still in prison, on probation (like Johnson), or suffering collateral consequences (such as an enhanced sentence for another crime), might demand to be resentenced.

In any event, the failure to show Johnson the report could not have caused a miscarriage of justice, since Judge Bua did not rely on any contested or contestable portions of the report in sentencing him. As suggested earlier in this opinion, there can be no denial of due process by a procedural irregularity that is not itself a constitutional violation and that is unlikely to have changed the outcome of the criminal proceeding. *United States v. Mazzone*, 782 F.2d 757, 763 (7th Cir.1986). The point is not that a harmless error is not reversible but that a procedural irregularity which does not contravene some specific constitutional right does not achieve constitutional significance through the due process clause unless it is not only an egregious but a highly prejudicial error—one quite likely to have changed the outcome, and thus to have infected the trial with fundamental, and not merely technical, unfairness. See *Darden v. Wainwright, supra,* 106 S.Ct. 2473 and n. 15; *United States ex rel. Bonner v. DeRobertis,* 798 F.2d 1062, 1067–69 (7th Cir.1986). A prosecutor who in closing argument impugns the honesty of the defendant's lawyer, or argues that the government would not prosecute a person who wasn't guilty, or otherwise injects improper considerations into the case infringes the defendant's procedural rights; but there is a denial of due process of law only if the defendant can show that probably he was convicted *because* of the improper conduct, in which event his conviction was a miscarriage of justice. *United States v. Mazzone, supra,* 782 F.2d at 763–64. "Miscarriage of justice" is legalese for convicting an innocent person, more precisely a person who under the rules of the criminal justice process should have been acquitted. The standard announced in *Hill* is similar, see 368 U.S. at 428–29, 82 S.Ct. at 471–72, and is not satisfied here.

We emphasize that prejudicial error and nonharmless error are not the same thing. An error is deemed harmless when the court is confident that it made no difference to the outcome, prejudicial when the court thinks it probably (not certainly) did make a difference; there is a fine, but discernible, difference between the two standards. See *United States v. Silverstein,* 732 F.2d 1338, 1349 (7th Cir.1984).

3. Johnson's argument that his counsel was ineffective is based primarily on counsel's failure to bring the Rule 32 violations to the district judge's attention at or after the sentencing hearing, or failing that to advise Johnson to appeal from the sentence on the basis of those violations. Denial of effective assistance of counsel can of course be raised in a motion under section 2255; and if the denial were proved, a suitable remedy would be to order that Johnson be resentenced in a proceeding that complied with Rule 32.

The issue of ineffective assistance of counsel was not raised before the district judge—it was raised for the first time in this appeal—and ordinarily we would not attempt to decide it without the benefit of the district judge's views. But of course we can decide it if the issue is sufficiently clear-cut. *United States v. Dyer,* 784 F.2d 812, 816 (7th Cir.1986). It is in this case. Even assuming that Johnson's counsel fell below minimum professional standards in representing him, it is apparent that Johnson was not denied his constitutional right to effective assistance of counsel. To be actionable, ineffective assistance must be prejudicial; Johnson must show that if his counsel had rendered effective assistance, it probably would have made a difference in the sentence. *Strickland v. Washington,* 466 U.S. 668, 695, 104 S.Ct. 2052, 2068, 80 L.Ed.2d 674 (1984). This appears to be much the same, perhaps exactly the same, standard used to decide whether a procedural irregularity is sufficiently egregious to rise to the level of a due process violation and whether an error to which no timely objection was made is nevertheless reversible because "plain." *United States v. Wolf,* 787 F.2d 1094, 1098 (7th Cir.1986); *United States v. Silverstein, supra,* 732 F.2d at 1349. At least we doubt the practical ability of courts to multiply the distinctions among kinds and degrees of harm or prejudice more than they have done already (as in *Murray v. Carrier,* — U.S. ——, 106 S.Ct. 2639, 2650, 91 L.Ed.2d 397 (1986)). In any event we are confident that the alleged ineffective assistance of counsel was not prejudicial, since as we have said Judge Bua did not rely on any of the allegedly false information in the presentence report in sentencing Johnson. Nonprejudicial oversights by counsel no more violate the Sixth Amendment's right to counsel than they do the Fifth Amendment's right to due process.

An issue we need not resolve is whether Johnson's failure to take a direct appeal from his sentence operated as a waiver of his right to attack the sentence collaterally. Ordinarily a criminal defendant is not allowed to raise by way of motion under section 2255 a ground that he could have raised in a direct appeal from his conviction (or sentence), *Norris v. United States*, 687 F.2d 899 (7th Cir.1982), but there are various exceptions, including ineffective assistance of counsel. Since we have held that Johnson is not entitled to relief under section 2255 wholly apart from any waiver, we need not decide whether he also waived the right to seek such relief.

Insofar as Johnson wants to correct inaccuracies in his presentence report that might affect the date of his parole, he must use the procedure outlined in *United States v. Mittelsteadt*, 790 F.2d 39 (7th Cir.1986) (per curiam).

The order denying his motion to set aside his sentence is

AFFIRMED.

SWYGERT, Senior Circuit Judge.

I respectfully dissent. In the circumstances of this case, petitioner Richard Johnson had the right to be sentenced after full compliance with Rule 32 of the Federal Rules of Criminal Procedure. That Rule provides that the sentencing court shall afford the defendant and his counsel the opportunity to read and discuss the presentence investigation report before the imposition of sentence and to comment on the report. Section 32(c)(3)(D) provides that if the defendant and his counsel allege any factual inaccuracy in the report, the court shall make a finding whether the report did in fact contain inaccurate information or that no determination on that point is necessary because the controverted matter will not be considered by the court in forming its sentence. The Rule further provides that a written record of such findings and determinations shall be made. In *United States v. Rone*, 743 F.2d 1169 (7th Cir.1984), this court elaborated upon the Rule, stating: "The district court at the sentencing hearing need directly ask the defendant only three questions—whether he or she had an opportunity to read the report, whether the defendant and defense counsel have discussed the report, and whether the defendant wishes to challenge any facts in the report." *Id.* at 1174.

There can be no question that the district court here violated Rule 32 by not inquiring of the defendant and his counsel whether they had discussed the presentence report and whether the defendant wished to challenge any facts in the report. In fact, the record indicates that although his counsel was furnished a copy of the report, the petitioner was not allowed to read it before sentencing so that he might detect the alleged inaccuracies that he now asserts. Today this court acknowledges that the Rule was not complied with: "Rule 32 was indeed violated, and we find the violation both inexplicable and inexcusable.... If Johnson had appealed from the sentence we would have reversed and directed the judge to comply with Rule 32 and resentence Johnson."

Johnson did not appeal because he was unaware of the alleged inaccuracies until he read the presentence report during a parole hearing while incarcerated. Thereafter, he secured the services of a new lawyer who instituted a section 2255 proceeding.

I agree with the majority that when considering a violation of Rule 32, the grounds for relief under 28 U.S.C. § 2255 are more restrictive than those that can be asserted in a direct appeal. Section 2255 may reach only errors occurring during the sentencing procedure that constitute a "fundamental defect which inherently results in a complete miscarriage of justice" or an "omission inconsistent with the rudimentary demands of fair procedure." *Hill v. United States*, 368 U.S. 424, 428, 82 S.Ct. 468, 471, 7 L.Ed.2d 417 (1962).

The purpose of Rule 32(c)(3)(D) is to ensure a fundamental requirement of fair procedure: that a defendant be sentenced on the basis of accurate information. If the district court considers inaccurate information in determining the sentence, an error of constitutional dimension occurs and is cognizable in a section 2255 proceeding. I do not comprehend that the majority takes a contrary view. Indeed, this court in *United States v. Eschweiler*, 782 F.2d 1385 (7th Cir.1986), specifically held that Rule 32(c)(3)(D) "protects a defendant's due process right to be sentenced on the basis of accurate information" and, as I interpret our recent decision in *Kramer v. United States*, 788 F.2d 1229 (7th Cir.1986), a section 2255 proceeding is appropriate in circumstances quite similar to those presented in the case at bar. An earlier decision of this court is to the same effect. *Krilich v. United States*, 502 F.2d 680, 682 (7th Cir.1974) ("Non-compliance with a statute which has as one of its purposes the effectuation of a constitutional right presents an issue of sufficient constitutional dimension to warrant consideration under 28 U.S.C. § 2255.").

The determinative issue in the instant case is not whether section 2255 may be an appropriate vehicle to remedy a Rule 32 violation in egregious situations, but whether the district judge can cure a defect in the sentencing proceeding by a *post hoc* determination that the alleged inaccuracies had no role in the fashioning of the sentence.

Although there is authority in this circuit to the effect that the sentencing judge may rely on his memory and rule that he did not rely on inaccurate information, *Lawary v. United States*, 599 F.2d 218 (7th Cir.1979), that proposition is not without exception. Reversal is required when reliance is "manifest and incontrovertible" from the record even in the face of the court's disclaimer of reliance. *Id.* at 227. The converse should be equally true. If nonreliance is not manifest and incontrovertible from the record, reversal should be required despite a disclaimer of reliance. Here the record is far from clear as to what the district judge relied on in imposing sentence. Indeed, the judge in his memorandum decision denying Johnson's section 2255 petition stated: "[H]ere, it is unclear from the record whether the judge relied on alleged inaccurate information in the sentencing proceeding...." When the question of whether there was reliance on the alleged misinformation contained in the presentence report is admittedly unclear from the record, a determination of nonreliance made by the district court one year after sentencing cannot cure the error. *United States v. Harris*, 558 F.2d 366 (7th Cir.1977); *United States v. Eschweiler*, 782 F.2d at 1390 n. 11 ("[W]here it is unclear whether the sentencing judge relied on the contested information, resentencing would resolve the matter."). Only a clear record can allow a judge to state with the requisite assurance that he did not rely on the disputed information in imposing sentence. Absent such support in the record, a belated determination of nonreliance, if permitted, might well result in complete circumvention of the salutary purpose of the Rule.

I would remand for a fresh sentencing.

UNITED STATES of America,
Plaintiff-Appellee,

v.

Dennis D. RONE, Defendant-Appellant.

No. 83–3132.

United States Court of Appeals,
Seventh Circuit.

Argued June 6, 1984.

Decided Sept. 4, 1984.

Before CUDAHY, EDWARDS* and   ESCHBACH, Circuit Judges.

---

* Honorable George Clifton Edwards, Jr., United   sitting by designation.
States Court of Appeals for the Sixth Circuit, is

CUDAHY, Circuit Judge.

This appeal challenging appellant's sentence, imposed after he pled guilty to a one-count information charging him with possession with intent to distribute marijuana in violation of 21 U.S.C. § 841(a)(1), presents the first opportunity, at least in this circuit, to consider the new rules governing presentence investigations, Fed.R. Crim.P. 32(a)(1)(A) and (c)(3)(A) and (D). Because the district court did not apply these new rules correctly, we vacate the sentence and remand to the district court for new sentencing.

I

Defendant-appellant, Dennis Rone, pled guilty on October 7, 1983, to a count of cultivating two of ten separate patches of marijuana in the Shawnee National Forest. Rone is a veteran with an honorable discharge and no prior criminal history. At the guilty plea proceedings, Rone admitted having cultivated two of the patches but denied responsibility for any others. The government, however, stated that it was prepared to show, in aggravation of sentencing, that Rone was responsible for at least eight patches. The court noted the "substantial dispute," accepted the guilty plea, ordered a presentence report and set the date of November 21, 1983, for sentencing. Plea to Information at 14–17.

The presentence report indicated that 856 Sinsemillia cannabis plants weighing approximately 1090 pounds and with a street value of $1,646,000 were seized. At the sentencing hearing, defense counsel attempted to clarify the point that Rone claimed responsibility for only two of the patches, which contained approximately 450 to 500 plants (Disposition Hearing at 3; Plea to Information at 15). Defense counsel then stated, "[a]nything else in the presentencing report ... we agree with fully and completely ... and have no additions, corrections, deletions or any other points of clarification." Disposition Hearing at 3. The defense counsel thus never raised any issue concerning the *value* of the marijuana seized, other than his objection to the

amount seized, and the court never directly asked the defendant whether he had seen the report or whether he had any objection to the factual accuracy of the report.

Following defense counsel's statement quoted above, Rone made a personal statement attempting to present mitigating factors. The government then recommended to the court a sentence of four years of incarceration and a fine of $10,000 based upon the seriousness of the crime in light of the fact that, even if the defendant had been responsible for only the two patches to which he admitted, the weight of the marijuana would have still been 520 pounds with a street value of over $750,000. The court sentenced Rone to three years imprisonment and an additional special parole term of three years. During the sentencing hearing, the court made the following comments:

There is a substantial amount of marijuana involved in this. I suppose to some extent it's anybody's speculation as to the total amount that would have been realized from it had it gone on the street, but it looks like it was in the neighborhood of maybe a million dollars .... I bring it [the question of the number of patches involved] up because it is my impression in talking with different people involved in this matter that have talked with you, and the overall knowledge I have about the matter is that there was a certain amount of sophistication involved in this; and I think you are a fairly sophisticated individual....

*   *   *   *   *   *

I feel strongly that one of the real bad things that we have going on in this country is the business of drugs. And I have said it—if I have said it once, I have said it several hundred times, that I think one thing that will bring this country to its knees could be this drug situation, if it gets out of hand and if it's not stopped. Now why do I say that? I say that because one of the primary reasons in me doing what I am going to do with you in this case is that it may have some effect on somebody else. And still, the one big purpose that the Court has in sentencing, if not the biggest purpose, is deterrence. In many ways you have probably suffered enough. I am not saying you have; but in many ways you may have. The only way that the Court feels that it can send a message to the community is through, hopefully, others seeing what has happened to you or other people that the court sentences.

Disposition Hearing at 5–8.

Appellant asserts that the presentence report contained a gross exaggeration of the street value of the marijuana.[1] Appellant also alleges that the district court clearly relied on the high value of the marijuana given in the presentence report when he stated that, because of the monetary value involved, the defendant appeared to be sophisticated and that he should be made an example to deter others—presumably other sophisticated drug dealers.

Appellant raises two arguments on appeal: first, that the district court failed to assure him access to his presentence report and an opportunity to dispute material factual inaccuracies contained in the report, and, second, that he was denied effective assistance of counsel during sentencing. Because we vacate the sentence and remand for new sentencing based on the district court's failure to assure the defendant access to his presentence report at a reasonable time before the sentencing hearing, we do not reach appellant's second argument concerning ineffective assistance of counsel.

II

Convicted defendants, including those who plead guilty, have a due process right to a fair sentencing procedure which includes the right to be sentenced on the basis of accurate information. *United States v. Tucker*, 404 U.S. 443, 447, 92 S.Ct. 589, 591, 30 L.Ed.2d 592 (1972); *Townsend v. Burke*, 334 U.S. 736, 741, 68 S.Ct. 1252, 1255, 92 L.Ed. 1690; *United States ex rel. Welch v. Lane*, 738 F.2d 863 at 864–865 (7th Cir.1984). A sentence must be set aside where the defendant can demonstrate that false information formed part of the basis for the sentence. The defendant must show, first, that the information before the sentencing court was false, and, second, that the court relied on the false information in passing sentence. *United States v. Harris*, 558 F.2d 366, 375 (7th Cir.1977).

Several provisions of Rule 32(c) of the Federal Rules of Criminal Procedure are intended to protect that due process right by ensuring that the sentence is fair and based on accurate information. Changes amending this rule with respect to presentence investigations became effective August 1, 1983. Three of the amended subsections clarify considerably the role of the sentencing judge in assuring that the defendant and defense counsel have a meaningful opportunity to review the presentence report and to contest alleged factual inaccuracies. These sections read as follows:

(a) Sentence.

(1) Imposition of Sentence. Sentence shall be imposed without unreasonable delay. Before imposing sentence the court shall

(A) determine that the defendant and his counsel have had the opportunity to read and discuss the presentence investigation report ...;

*   *   *   *   *   *

---

1. Appellant has submitted with his brief the affidavit of Richard Evans Schultes, Jeffrey Professor of Biology at Harvard University. This affidavit states that only approximately 2% of the total weight of the uprooted plants (1090 pounds) constituted "useable" marijuana. Therefore, even if one assumes that the defendant was responsible for all 856 plants seized and that the approximate street value of $1500 per pound (a point also disputed by the defendant)

was correct, then the value of the marijuana seized was, in fact, according to the information in the affidavit, closer to $32,700, than to $1,600,000. The concept that the entire plant as pulled from the ground does not constitute saleable marijuana seems intuitively correct, although there obviously remain several factual disputes which the district court will be in a better position to evaluate than we.

(c) Presentence Investigation.

*　　*　　*　　*　　*　　*

(3) Disclosure.

(A) At a reasonable time before imposing sentence the court shall permit the defendant and his counsel to read the report of the presentence investigation .... The court shall afford the defendant and his counsel an opportunity to comment on the report and, in the discretion of the court, to introduce testimony or other information relating to any alleged factual inaccuracy contained in it.

*　　*　　*　　*　　*　　*

(D) If the comments of the defendant and his counsel or testimony or other information introduced by them allege any factual inaccuracy in the presentence investigation report or the summary of the report or part thereof, the court shall, as to each matter controverted, make (i) a finding as to the allegation, or (ii) a determination that no such finding is necessary because the matter controverted will not be taken into account in sentencing. A written record of such findings and determinations shall be appended to and accompany any copy of the presentence investigation report thereafter made available to the Bureau of Prisons or the Parole Commission.

Before the 1983 amendments, the availability of presentence reports varied markedly among the different districts. The prior rules contained no equivalent to Rule 32(a)(1)(A) or 32(c)(3)(D), while 32(c)(3)(A) only required that the court permit the defendant or defense counsel to read the report upon request. In suggesting the 1983 changes, the Advisory Committee relied extensively on an empirical study by Fennell and Hall, *Due Process at Sentencing: An Empirical and Legal Analysis of the Disclosure of Presentence Reports in Federal Courts*, 93 Harv.L.Rev. 1613 (1980). This study found that the extent and nature of disclosure of these reports were not only inconsistent among the district courts but also too often insufficient

to ensure accuracy of sentencing information.

Amended subsection (a)(1)(A) requires that the sentencing court "determine that the defendant and his counsel have had the opportunity to read and discuss the ... report." The Notes by the Advisory Committee state that this subsection now imposes "upon the sentencing court the additional obligation of determining that the defendant and his counsel have had an opportunity to read the presentence investigation report .... This change is consistent with the amendment of subdivision (c)(3) ... providing for disclosure of the report ... to *both* defendant *and* his counsel *without request*" (emphasis in original). The Fennell and Hall study concluded that the extent of disclosure under the prior rule was often inadequate and "that some form of judicial prodding is necessary to achieve full disclosure." *Id.* at 1651. The specific mention in the amended rule of both the "defendant *and* his counsel" was thus deliberate and the amended subsection, for the first time, imposes the affirmative obligation on the sentencing judge to determine whether the defendant, *in addition to counsel*, has read the report and whether they have reviewed the report together.

Amended Rule 32(c)(3)(A) involves three principal changes from the prior rule: disclosure of the report is not limited to those situations in which a request is made; disclosure is provided to *both* the defendant and defense counsel; and disclosure is required a reasonable time before sentencing. In order to promote accuracy in the presentence report under the amended rules, the *defendant* is to be permitted to review the report and to contest erroneous information. To accomplish this purpose, the report must be disclosed sufficiently before sentencing to permit assertion and resolution of claims of inaccuracy and to permit the defendant to make submissions of additional information and to make informed comments on the report.

The Notes thus emphasize the role of the defendant, in contrast even with that of counsel, in reviewing the report so as to "significantly reduce[ ] the likelihood that false statements will [not] be discovered, as much of the content of the presentence report will ordinarily be outside the knowledge of counsel." Subsection (c)(3)(D), which is an entirely new provision concerning the district court's obligation to make findings regarding contested facts if they are relied on in sentencing, can only be rendered truly meaningful if amended subsection (c)(3)(A) is given full effect.

The record in the present case as to the extent of disclosure of the presentence report is unclear, and one of the primary purposes of the amended rule, particularly subsection (a)(1)(A), is to require the court to establish a clear record on this issue. Defense counsel had access to the report at some time before the sentencing hearing, although it is unclear exactly when before the hearing the report was available. The record does not show, and the defendant now denies, that he had access to the report before the hearing. It is precisely for this reason that the amended rules specifically place upon the sentencing judge the responsibility of ascertaining whether the defendant had the opportunity to read the report and of establishing a record on this issue.[2] The requirements of the rule were thus not satisfied by the procedures followed in this case.

The government asserts that, even if the defendant did not see the report before the hearing, his counsel's oral statements *during* the hearing were sufficient to alert him to the portions of the report which he now claims were inaccurate. Listening to parts of the report recited during the hearing is not enough. The rule specifically requires that the defendant *and* defense counsel *shall* be permitted to *read* the report *at a reasonable time before* the imposition of sentence. This requirement of the rule was simply not satisfied.

The Notes make clear that merely making the presentence report available upon request, as did many district courts before

---

2. The dissent relies upon defense counsel's use of the term "we" during the sentencing hearing to establish that the defense counsel at least discussed the report with the defendant. The defendant, however, was incarcerated up to the day of sentencing, and his attorney apparently never visited him during that time. The use of the first person plural pronoun is not persuasive because attorneys often use the word loosely for various reasons. Further, as the dissent notes, defense counsel's statement, at the most, only suggests that he *discussed* the report with the defendant. Again, this is not all that the rule requires; rather, it requires that the defendant be given a reasonable opportunity to *read* the report and that the sentencing judge determine whether the rule has been complied with.

Our comments concerning the availability of the report are based on the appellant's brief and statements at oral argument as well as the appellee's description at oral argument of the usual procedures followed (at least at that time) for presentence reports. The government has not attempted to refute or deny appellant's assertions about the availability of the report, other than through its reliance on defense counsel's use of the word "we" at the sentencing hearing. Neither has the government refuted or denied appellant's explanation of the manner in which the government calculated the total street value of the marijuana involved. It is precisely because there are so many factual disputes, involving issues which amended Rule 32 requires be clearly established in the record, that a remand is required.

We note that if the defense counsel was given an adequate opportunity to review the report but did not contest the report's apparent inaccuracies, his performance might appear to fall below the minimum standards of professional competence. On the other hand, if counsel used the term "we" misleadingly so as to effect a waiver of his client's rights (as the dissent implies), when he had not in fact discussed the report with his client, such a misrepresentation would also cast doubt on counsel's competence. The Supreme Court, in *Strickland v. Washington,* — U.S. —, 104 S.Ct. 2052, 80 L.Ed.2d 674 (1984), recently articulated the analysis to be applied to determine ineffective assistance of counsel. Judged under that standard, appellant's allegations seem to support a belief that defense counsel's apparent incompetence affected the outcome in the present case. These allegations might thus seem to warrant at least a remand for a hearing on the issue whether appellant's sixth amendment right to effective assistance of counsel has been violated. However, in light of our remand for resentencing solely on the basis of the procedures followed under Rule 32, we do not remand for consideration of the ineffectiveness of counsel issue. Neither do we attempt to decide that issue.

the amendments were enacted, is not adequate. Instead, the amended rule was intended to give the defendant a more clearly defined opportunity to read the report. The recognition that many of the facts included in the report are within the exclusive knowledge of the defendant—and not that of the defense counsel—led to the formulation of amended subsection (a)(1), which imposes on the district court an affirmative duty to ensure that the defendant has had an opportunity to read the report a reasonable time before the hearing is held. As with other rights which are personal to the defendant, the defendant would, of course, be able to waive this right to read the report. Such a waiver, however, must be clear and unequivocal.

The defendant claims on appeal that the total value of the marijuana seized, as presented in the presentence report, was grossly overvalued, see supra n. 1. This error was primarily the result of the fact that the report figures are based not merely on the weight of the useable parts of the marijuana plant but on the weight of the entire plant, including roots, stems and dirt. We cannot, without the benefit of an evidentiary hearing, determine the correct value of the marijuana seized. The defendant, however, has met the burden, which would have been imposed even under the old rules and our precedent in *United States v. Harris*, of raising grave doubt about the reliability and accuracy of the value given in the presentence report.[3] In addition, the sentencing judge's comments make it clear that he was relying on the high value of the marijuana in determining the type of sentence which he was imposing.

In the interest both of establishing a clear record and of carrying out the terms and intent of the amendments, therefore, the rules require a definite yet simple procedure. The district court at the sentencing hearing need directly ask the defendant only three questions—whether he or she has had an opportunity to read the report, whether the defendant and defense counsel have discussed the report and whether the defendant wishes to challenge any facts in the report. This brief questioning of the defendant would be somewhat analogous to the questioning of a defendant by the court upon entry of a guilty plea, although the sentencing situation is much simpler and the extent of questioning would be much more limited. The rules require only that the court make a record during the sentencing hearing, which reflects that the defendant has had a realistic opportunity to read and discuss the report and to raise objections.

By placing the responsibility on the court, the amended rule should clarify the record, particularly in a case like this in which the defendant was unable to make bond and was held in custody throughout the time when the report would usually have been available. Appellant's serious

---

3. The dissent impliedly criticizes the appellant for not having raised his allegations in the sentencing court under Fed.R.Crim.P. 35. In *Harris*, 558 F.2d at 375–76, the appellant also had not challenged the inaccuracies in his presentence report until his appeal and had apparently brought no Rule 35 motion. Nevertheless, as we stated in *Harris*, "several considerations persuade us that, under the circumstances of this case, justice would not be disserved if defendant is simply afforded the opportunity to deny and rebut the allegations ... in the presentence report." *Id.* at 375. The primary consideration which led to this conclusion was appellant's contention, admittedly without factual support in the record, that his trial counsel had apparently neglected to examine the presentence report. *Id.* at 376. A defendant may thus raise on direct appeal the possibility that the sentence was based on information of highly questionable reliability. The appropriate remedy is ordinarily, as here, a remand for further factual inquiry and resentencing, at least in a situation in which the defendant has not knowingly and voluntarily waived his right to challenge the report. There is no requirement of a separate Rule 35 motion. *See id.* at 375–76 (direct appeal); *United States v. Weston*, 448 F.2d 626, 631–34 (9th Cir.1971) (direct appeal; no indication that Rule 35 motion was filed), *cert. denied*, 404 U.S. 1061, 92 S.Ct. 748, 30 L.Ed.2d 749 (1972). However, waiver under the prior rules, as in *Harris*, is not the issue in this case. Rather, the amended rules require the sentencing judge to make a record precisely so as to spare a reviewing court from disputes concerning the record such as the one which now divides this panel.

allegations concerning the effectiveness of his counsel further illustrate the necessity of having the district court question the defendant directly rather than relying on the assertions of defense counsel as to the accuracy of the report. Uncertainty about the practical availability of the report to the defendant, such as is present here, would be eliminated by requiring the district court to question the defendant personally. If the defendant has not been permitted to read the report (whether because of practical difficulties arising from routine procedures followed by the relevant officials or for other reasons) and has not waived the right to do so, the court should ensure that the defendant had an opportunity to review it. To make the report available in a nominal sense but to deny the defendant (who may not even know of the report's existence) a real opportunity to see it is to defeat the purpose of the amended rule as effectively as if disclosure were denied after a request had been made.

Once the court ascertains that the defendant has had an opportunity to read the report a reasonable time before the sentencing hearing, the court must then merely ask the defendant and defense counsel whether there are any contested statements of fact. In this way, the record will be clear as to when there are allegations of factual inaccuracies and when the requirements of Rule 32(c)(3)(D) have been triggered. The fundamental changes brought about by the amended rules and by the procedures adopted here thus relate to the emphasis to be placed on the defendant's opportunity (in addition to that of counsel) to read the report before the hearing. That opportunity is, in turn, closely related to the sentencing court's obligations under Rule 32(c)(3)(D).

During the sentencing hearing here, defense counsel clearly disputed the number of patches for which the defendant was responsible and, on that sole basis, the value of the marijuana at stake. Once that allegation of factual inaccuracy in the report was made, the requirements of Rule 32(c)(3)(D) were triggered, and the sentencing judge was obligated to make a finding

as to the allegation or determine that the finding was not necessary because the controverted matter would not be relied upon in sentencing.

The district judge, in this case, clearly did not state that the number of patches for which the defendant was responsible would not be relied on, and he therefore did not comply with 32(c)(3)(D)(ii). On the other hand, it is unclear whether the judge made a finding as to the truthfulness of the allegedly inaccurate statement. The fact that the judge relied on the amount of marijuana seized as given in the presentence report may imply that he rejected the defense counsel's contention. However, an implication which we must draw by reading between the lines scarcely seems to comport with the rule's requirement that the court squarely address the factual dispute. Our remand is thus also based on the district court's failure to comply with Rule 32(c)(3)(D), as well as on its failure to comply with Rule 32(a)(1)(A).

The defendant's allegations of inaccuracy concerning the weight and value of the marijuana seized, which in all likelihood would have been timely made if the defendant had had a reasonable opportunity to read the report, would have triggered the requirements of Rule 32(c)(3)(D). Clearly, no finding was made as to the weight or street value of the marijuana seized. The report's estimate of more than $1,600,000 compared with the estimate of a little over $30,000, based on an intuitive understanding of the facts of the case and on information in the affidavit, reveals a wide, and apparently significant, discrepancy. It is the sentencing judge's reliance on precisely this sort of important yet disputed information, without there being a finding as to its reliability, which the amended rules were intended to prevent. By following the procedures outlined in the amended rules as interpreted by this opinion, a sentencing judge will be able to eliminate gross errors and thus ensure greater accuracy and fairness in the sentencing process.

The amended rule, as the dissent notes, was admittedly intended to apply to the situation in which the report refers to criminal activity for which the defendant was never convicted. The rule, however, is also intended to apply to the type of information disputed in this case and to other situations in which the government might have been careless with the facts and thus significantly exaggerated the extent and nature of the defendant's culpability. Particularly in this case, where the defendant has absolutely no prior criminal record and admitted during the sentencing hearing that he has no familiarity with the technical aspects of the legal system (Disposition Hearing at 4), the amended rules and the purposes which inspired them should be given full scope, and their specific prescriptions should be followed.

The sentence is therefore vacated and the matter is remanded to the district court with instructions to resentence the defendant.

GEORGE CLIFTON EDWARDS, Jr., Circuit Judge, concurring specially.

I concur in Judge Cudahy's opinion remanding this case for a rehearing on sentence. I believe that the new amendments governing the hearing on sentence should be interpreted as requiring the District Judge to address the Defendant personally and thus learn from him that he has had time to read and understand the report. The rehearing may, of course, shed no new light and may cause no change in the sentence. But it is clear to me that the 1983 changes (See Rule 32(c)(3)(A)) mandate our remand for the reasons ably outlined in Judge Cudahy's opinion.

In my opinion the opportunity for the subject of the sentencing hearing to be addressed personally by the judge and have any relevant dispute of fact resolved through testimony, if within the trial judge's discretion it is found necessary, will strengthen the appearance and the reality

of fairness. It may send the person sentenced to the appointed place of confinement somewhat less resentful and more subject to rehabilitation than he would be otherwise.

ESCHBACH, Circuit Judge, dissenting.

The majority holds that this case must be remanded to the district court for resentencing. In doing so, it concludes that the district court erred in neither assuring the defendant access to his presentence report nor making specific findings about the exact number of marijuana fields for which the defendant was to be held responsible. The majority also concludes that the defendant has met his burden of establishing that the district court relied on materially false information in imposing sentence. *United States v. Harris*, 558 F.2d 366 (7th Cir.1977).

In so holding, the majority relies primarily on the defendant's unsubstantiated allegations, made for the first time in this court. While it is undisputed that the defendant's attorney read the report, the defendant claims that he never saw the report and that his attorney never visited him during the interim period between the entry of his guilty plea and the sentencing hearing. Further, the majority suggests—with no apparent basis in the record [1]—that the report was not available at least a reasonable time before sentencing.

No attempt was made to present any of these allegations to the sentencing court in the first instance under Fed.R.Crim.P. 35. *See United States v. Papajohn*, 701 F.2d 760 (8th Cir.1983); *United States v. Madonna*, 582 F.2d 704, 705 (2d Cir.1978), *cert. denied*, 439 U.S. 1069, 99 S.Ct. 838, 59 L.Ed.2d 34 (1979). Had the defendant done so, we would be able to review his claims on the basis of more than speculation. What can be said on the basis of the record, however, is the following. Defense counsel, who was representing only one defendant, stated:

1. The only possible explanation in the record for the majority's statement is that the report is dated four days before the sentencing hearing

was held. Whether this was reasonable or not under the circumstances is a factual determination that we are not competent to make.

In reference to the pre-sentencing report, *we* have only one point of clarification .... Anything else in the pre-sentencing report ... *we* agree with fully and completely.

(Emphasis added.) The majority interprets counsel's use of the plural as either an indication that he intended misleadingly to effect a waiver of his client's rights or as evidence of counsel's incompetence. I believe that counsel's representations are equally—and more plausibly—susceptible to the interpretation that counsel and the defendant had reviewed the report. Indeed, counsel's statements make no sense unless he had at least discussed the report with his client, since most of the report was concerned with the defendant's family situation and the circumstances of his arrest.[2]

Moreover, as the majority points out, the only dispute the defendant now raises with the facts contained in the presentence report which he did not also raise before the sentencing court is his contention that the government overvalued the market price of the marijuana. In support of its remand, the majority relies on the rationale behind amended Rule 32:

> The [Advisory Committee] Notes thus emphasize the role of the defendant, in contrast even with that of counsel, in reviewing the report so as to "significantly reduce [ ] the likelihood that false statements will [not] be discovered, as much of the content of the presentence report will ordinarily be outside the knowledge of counsel."

Ante at 1173. As the Advisory Committee Notes also make clear, the reason for mandating that the defendant be given an opportunity to view the report is that the report is likely to contain historical facts, the truth of which only the defendant could dispute. For instance, many presentence reports contain allegations that the defendant has been involved in other criminal activity for which he has not been convicted. Defense counsel could not know

whether these allegations are true or not; such information is peculiarly within the knowledge of the defendant.

Rone's challenge to the valuation of the marijuana is not based on any claimed expertise on his part in valuing narcotics. On the contrary, he relies in this court on the affidavit of a Harvard professor of biology to contest that valuation. *See ante* at 1171. This evidence was not presented to the court below, nor did the defendant dispute the value assigned to the marijuana below, although he was present when his attorney, in open court, repeated the valuation given in the report and the government attorney stated his lesser estimation based on the marijuana for which Rone actually claimed responsibility. *See Disposition Hearing*, 3–5.

Perhaps a simple inquiry, such as the one the majority now requires, would assure that a record is developed demonstrating compliance with Rule 32. But on the record before us, where there is no clear indication of noncompliance with the disclosure provisions of the rule, I cannot agree with the majority's holding that the district court erred in this regard.

I also cannot agree with the majority's holding that the defendant has met his burden of establishing that the district court relied on materially false information in making its sentencing decision. *United States v. Harris*, 558 F.2d 366, 375 (7th Cir.1977). Relying on the aforementioned affidavit submitted in this court, the defendant claims that only two percent of the marijuana plant is valuable (a contention which the majority finds "intuitively correct"). The majority accepts the defendant's claim that "the report figures are based not merely on the weight of the useable parts of the marijuana plant but on the weight of the entire plant, including roots, stems, and dirt." *Ante* at 1174. There is simply no evidence that the report figures were derived in the manner suggested by the majority: the report itself

---

2. If this is not the case, then defendant's silence in the face of his attorney's representations is inexplicable, especially in light of the fact that

after his attorney concluded his remarks, defendant himself addressed the court.

merely states that subsequent to defendant's arrest, "856 Sinsemillia cannabis plants weighing approximately 1090 pounds with a street value of $1,646,000 ... were seized." Moreover, I do not believe that the district court's reliance on the figures in the report has been shown. While stating that "it looks like [the value] was in the neighborhood of maybe a million dollars," the judge also noted, "I suppose to some extent it's anybody's speculation as to the total amount that would have been realized had it gone on the street...." *Disposition Hearing*, 5–6.

What is manifestly clear from the district court judge's sentencing comments is that he relied on his concern for deterring other potential drug growers and the "substantial amount" of marijuana seized. The majority holds that the judge erred again in failing to make findings about the number of marijuana fields for which he was holding defendant responsible. A reading of the remarks at sentencing shows that the judge, noting that defendant was arrested in the fields for which he claimed responsibility, and that those fields were in the same area as the other fields, expressly discredited defendant's denial of more extensive involvement:

> I think it would have meant more to the Court if you had made a complete [sic] breast of everything. Now you may say you have and you may have. You just haven't convinced the Court.

Disposition Hearing, 6–7. I do not believe, as does the majority, that we need "read[ ] between the lines" to find that the district court judge rejected defendant's contention.

For the reasons expressed above, I cannot join the majority opinion. I respectfully dissent.

UNITED STATES of America,
Plaintiff-Appellee,

v.

Arria Chyvonne GRAVES a/k/a Karen
Lynn McAfee, Defendant-Appellant.

No. 84–1119.

United States Court of Appeals,
Tenth Circuit.

March 12, 1986.

Before HOLLOWAY, Chief Judge, and
SETH, Circuit Judge, and WINDER, District Judge.*

WINDER, District Judge.

Appellant claims the district court erred in denying her motion to strike certain alleged offenses from the "prior record" section of her presentence report because evidence of those alleged crimes had been obtained in violation of her constitutional rights. We find no violation of appellant's constitutional rights in the inclusion of this information in the presentence report and affirm the ruling of the district court.

Appellant was indicted on May 3, 1983 by a federal grand jury in the Western District of Oklahoma on one count of forging an endorsement of a United States treasury check with the intent to defraud the United States, in violation of 18 U.S.C. § 495, and on one count of conspiracy to take from the United States mails, unlawfully possess and forge an endorsement of a United States treasury check with the intent to defraud the United States, in violation of 18 U.S.C. § 371. Under Rule 20 Fed.R.Crim.P., the case was transferred to the United States District Court for the District of Kansas, and on November 8, 1983 appellant pled guilty to the conspiracy charge.

Prior to appellant's sentencing, the probation department prepared an extensive presentence report. The "prior record" portion of this report listed seventeen prior offenses in which appellant was allegedly involved. One of the alleged offenses was possession of marijuana for which appellant was arrested, but not charged, because it was ruled there was an illegal search and seizure of the vehicle in which the marijuana was found. Another alleged offense was conspiracy and possession with intent to distribute heroin and cocaine; these charges were dismissed after the court determined that the search warrant by which the controlled substance was obtained was illegal. The presentence report also listed other alleged offenses involving arrests only and appellant requested that the district court strike these from the report because of their lack of probative value and potential for inaccuracy. On appeal, however, appellant makes no claim respecting those arrests.

The district court heard appellant's motion to strike on January 12, 1984. The court denied appellant's motion although the district judge indicated that he would not consider the two alleged offenses described above in imposing sentence. He did, however, decline to strike the alleged offenses from the presentence report or to have a new report prepared containing no mention of these matters because he did not believe that he should prevent the Federal Bureau of Prisons, the United States Parole Commission or the United States Probation Department from considering these matters at the post-sentencing stage of appellant's case. After denying appellant's motion to strike, the district court sentenced her to three years imprisonment and recommended confinement in an institution where she would be evaluated and would receive treatment for drug addiction. Thereafter, appellant filed this appeal.

On appeal, appellant seeks no relief from the sentence imposed by the district court. Her sole contention is that the failure of the district court to strike from the report

---

* Honorable David K. Winder, United States District Judge for the District of Utah, sitting by   designation.

the two matters described above will unjustly prejudice the post-sentencing handling of her case by the Bureau of Prisons, the Parole Commission and the Probation Department, in violation of her constitutional rights.

Rule 32(c)(2) Fed.R.Crim.P. specifies the information to be included in the presentence report and, as pertinent here, states:

(A) Any prior criminal record of the defendant;

.   .   .   .   .

(D) any other information that may aid the court in sentencing ...

The contents of the presentence report are intended to be extremely broad in order to provide the court a thorough description of the defendant's background. In fact, 18 U.S.C. § 3577 provides that "[n]o limitation shall be placed on the information concerning the background, character, and conduct of a person convicted of an offense which a court of the United States may receive and consider for the purpose of imposing an appropriate sentence."

Appellant acknowledges the breadth of the permissible scope of the information included in a presentence report, but contends that constitutional limitations require exclusion of the information in question here. The marijuana that appellant allegedly possessed was discovered during the illegal search of a vehicle. The charges of conspiracy and possession with intent to distribute heroin and cocaine were dismissed after the court determined that the search warrant used in that case was illegal. Appellant, therefore, claims that the availability of information concerning these alleged offenses to federal agencies having control over the nature and duration of her incarceration will result in prejudice to her in violation of her constitutional rights.

With few limitations, a court has almost unlimited discretion in determining what information it will hear and rely upon in imposing sentence. *United States v. Tucker*, 404 U.S. 443, 446, 92 S.Ct. 589, 591, 30 L.Ed.2d 592 (1972). However, two exceptions have been generally recognized by the courts, including this circuit: (1) a defendant has a due process right to have his or her sentence based on accurate information, and (2) in limited cases certain information linked to the denial of a constitutional right cannot form the basis for sentencing. *United States v. Jones*, 640 F.2d 284, 286 (10th Cir.1981).

In *Smith v. United States*, 551 F.2d 1193 (10th Cir.1977), *cert. denied*, 434 U.S. 830, 98 S.Ct. 113, 54 L.Ed.2d 90 (1977), this court rejected the defendant's contention that inclusion of his previous arrest history in the presentence report was improper. 551 F.2d at 1195–96. The court cited *Tucker*, 404 U.S. at 446, 92 S.Ct. at 591, wherein it was stated that a presentence investigation inquiry may be "broad in scope, largely unlimited either as to the kind of information ... [considered], or the source from which it may come." 551 F.2d 1196. This court recognized that consideration at sentencing of convictions obtained when the defendant was not afforded the benefit of counsel was limited by the *Tucker* decision, but in affirming the trial court in *Smith*, recognized the clear authorization given the trial judge by 18 U.S.C. § 3577 to rely upon information concerning alleged criminal activity for which the defendant had not been prosecuted. 551 F.2d at 1196. Other circuit courts have also upheld the trial judge's right to consider evidence of crimes allegedly committed by the defendant even if the defendant had not been brought to trial for the alleged offenses, or no final disposition had been made concerning those offenses. *United States v. Ochoa*, 659 F.2d 547, 549 (5th Cir.1981) (appeal of state conviction not yet decided), *cert. denied*, 455 U.S. 959, 102 S.Ct. 1472, 71 L.Ed.2d 678 (1982); *United States v. Metz*, 470 F.2d 1140, 1142 (3rd Cir.1972) (indictments pending), *cert. denied*, 411 U.S. 919, 93 S.Ct. 1558, 36 L.Ed.2d 311 (1973); *United States v. Doyle*, 348 F.2d 715, 721 (2nd Cir.1965) (the defendant pled guilty to one count in the indictment; the other counts were dismissed, but considered at sentencing), *cert. denied*, 382 U.S. 843, 86 S.Ct. 89, 15 L.Ed.2d 84 (1965).

Appellant argues that neither the sentencing judge nor the federal agencies that will later consider her parole should be allowed to consider illegally seized evidence which could not be admitted at a trial. The government, on the other hand, urges that the exclusionary rule is a judicially created remedy designed to safeguard fourth amendment rights by deterring official misconduct and that under *United States v. Calandra*, 414 U.S. 338, 94 S.Ct. 613, 38 L.Ed.2d 561 (1974), this court should balance the incremental deterrent effect of applying the exclusionary rule at sentencing and in post-sentencing administrative proceedings against the costs of impairing effective and suitable punishment of proven offenders and unduly complicating sentencing procedures.

We agree with the government's argument. We have already mentioned the district judge's duty to "conduct [a presentence] inquiry broad in scope, largely unlimited either as to the kind of information he may consider, or the source from which it may come." *Tucker*, 404 U.S. at 446, 92 S.Ct. at 591. It is true that in *Tucker* the Court barred the consideration at sentencing of convictions obtained without affording the defendant the benefit of counsel. *Tucker* recognized that the absence of counsel impugns the integrity of the fact finding process so that a conviction obtained under such circumstances is unreliable. *See* 404 U.S. at 447 n. 5, 92 S.Ct. at 592 n. 5. Most illegally obtained evidence is not inherently unreliable, but "is excluded at trial on the theory that exclusion will deter the making of illegal searches." *United States v. Lee*, 540 F.2d 1205, 1211 (4th Cir.1976), *cert. denied*, 429 U.S. 894, 97 S.Ct. 255, 50 L.Ed.2d 177 (1976). *See also, United States v. Calandra*, 414 U.S. 338, 347–48, 94 S.Ct. 613, 619–20, 38 L.Ed.2d 561 (1974) (the prime purpose of the exclusionary rule is to deter unlawful police conduct). To decide whether illegally obtained evidence should be kept from the court or from federal agencies who may later consider such information in determining the post-sentencing status of appellant, an evaluation must be made of the degree of deterrence which might be promoted by exclusion, and that degree of deterrence must be weighed against the concomitant limitation of the right of the sentencing judge to impose sentence in light of all relevant facts. *Calandra*, 414 U.S. at 349–52, 94 S.Ct. at 620–22.

In the opinion of this court, extension of the exclusionary rule to sentencing or post-sentencing proceedings before federal agencies would, in the ordinary case, have a deterrent effect so minimal as to be insignificant. In the usual case, law enforcement officers conduct searches and seize evidence for the purpose of obtaining convictions, not for the purpose of increasing the sentence in a prosecution already pending or one not yet commenced. It is apparent that the significant deterrent to official lawlessness is the threat that an illegal search and seizure would render the prosecution ineffective. The additional threat that the sentence imposed in a future criminal prosecution might be less severe or that the defendant in a future case might be paroled earlier would appear to have little practical effect.

It also appears that sentencing proceedings could be intolerably delayed and disrupted if it became necessary to determine whether every item of information to be relied on by the sentencing judge had a lawful origin. The same considerations apply to post-sentencing administrative hearings.

This court has been made aware of only one circuit court decision in which evidence obtained in violation of the fourth amendment was excluded from consideration at sentencing. That decision is *Verdugo v. United States*, 402 F.2d 599 (9th Cir.1968), *cert. denied*, 397 U.S. 925, 90 S.Ct. 931, 25 L.Ed.2d 105 (1970). In *Verdugo*, the government, knowing that it already possessed sufficient evidence to convict the defendant of selling heroin, illegally searched his home in the hope of locating a larger supply of heroin because "the length of Verdugo's sentence would be quite different if it could be shown that Verdugo was involved in the narcotics traffic on a large scale rather than merely as the seller in a single small transaction." 402 F.2d at 612. The court concluded that, under these circumstances, exclusion at trial would be of little significance and exclusion at sentencing would be the only meaningful deterrent. 402 F.2d at 612–13.

In two subsequent decisions, the Ninth Circuit appears to have disavowed a broad reading of *Verdugo*. In *United States v. Vandemark*, 522 F.2d 1019 (9th Cir.1975), the court upheld the district judge's right to revoke probation on the basis of illegally seized evidence when, at the time of the illegal search, the law enforcement officers had neither known nor had reason to believe that the suspect was on probation. 522 F.2d at 1020–21. The court additionally held that the district judge could consider the illegally obtained evidence in imposing sentence after revocation of probation. 522 F.2d at 1021. The court noted that *Calandra* provided the analytical framework for determining whether the exclusionary rule should apply to sentencing after revocation of probation. 522 F.2d at 1021. In *Calandra* the Supreme Court, holding that the exclusionary rule did not apply in grand jury proceedings, weighed "the potential injury to the historic role and functions of the grand jury against the potential benefits of the rule as applied in this context." 414 U.S. at 349, 94 S.Ct. at 620. Using the *Calandra* balancing approach, the Ninth Circuit held that "extension of the exclusionary rule to sentencing subsequent to revocation of probation would have a disruptive effect far out of proportion to any incremental deterrence of police misconduct." 552 F.2d at 1021.

The court further explained that "[t]he detrimental effect of the exclusionary rule upon sentencing is apparent. It deprives the district judge of information necessary to effectuate the federal policy of individualized sentencing." 522 F.2d at 1021 (citing *Williams v. New York*, 337 U.S. 241, 248, 69 S.Ct. 1079, 1083, 93 L.Ed. 1337 (1949) (dictum)). The court supported its conclusion that "[a] sentence can be properly tailored to fit an individual defendant only to the extent that the judge is aware

of the major facts relevant to needed correction," 522 F.2d at 1021, by quoting *Williams:*

A sentencing judge ... is not confined to the narrow issue of guilt. His task within fixed statutory or constitutional limits is to determine the type and extent of punishment after the issue of guilt has been determined. Highly relevant—if not essential—to his selection of an appropriate sentence is the possession of the fullest information possible concerning the defendant's life and characteristics. And modern concepts individualizing punishment have made it all the more necessary that a sentencing judge not be denied an opportunity to obtain pertinent information by a requirement of rigid adherence to restrictive rules of evidence properly applicable to the trial.

522 F.2d at 1021 (quoting *Williams v. New York*, 337 U.S. 241, 247, 69 S.Ct. 1079, 1083, 93 L.Ed. 1337 (1949)).

The second case in which the Ninth Circuit rejected a broad reading of *Verdugo* was *United States v. Larios*, 640 F.2d 938 (9th Cir.1981). In *Larios* the court considered "whether it was reversible error for the sentencing judge to consider evidence found through an illegal search and seizure when deciding the appropriate sentence for the appellant." 640 F.2d at 941. The court held that, under the facts of that case, the trial court acted properly in considering such evidence. 640 F.2d at 942. The court noted that the police had obtained a search warrant and that there was no indication that the search was overextensive or inappropriately conducted. 640 F.2d at 942. The court further explained that the illegality was caused by a technical error in the affidavit supporting the warrant and that any police misconduct that may have been involved was not sufficient to justify interfering with individualized sentencing. 640 F.2d at 942. In support of its decision, the Ninth Circuit cited its *Vandemark* opinion, 522 F.2d at 1021–22, and noted that in *Verdugo*, the evidence had been excluded from sentencing because the search was conducted without a warrant, was "blatantly illegal," and the *Verdugo* court had found that deterrence against illegal searches was required under the circumstances there involved. 640 F.2d 942.

Other circuit courts have also applied the *Calandra* balancing approach. In *United States v. Schipani*, 435 F.2d 26 (2nd Cir. 1970), *cert. denied*, 401 U.S. 983, 91 S.Ct. 1198, 28 L.Ed.2d 334 (1971), the Second Circuit concluded that certain evidence obtained in violation of the fourth amendment should not be excluded from the consideration of the sentencing judge. 435 F.2d at 27. In *Schipani*, the illegal wiretap evidence which the defendant sought to have excluded at sentencing had been gathered in the course of an investigation which led to the defendant's conviction. 435 F.2d at 28. The court reasoned that the government's principal objective in gathering the evidence had been to convict the defendant, so the fear of exclusion at trial would have been a significant deterrent, but any further deterrence achieved by exclusion at sentencing would have been minimal. 435 F.2d at 28.

In *United States v. Lee*, 540 F.2d 1205 (4th Cir.1976), *cert. denied*, 429 U.S. 894, 97 S.Ct. 255, 50 L.Ed.2d 177 (1976), the Fourth Circuit concluded that "reliable but illegally obtained evidence may generally be considered by the sentencing judge." 540 F.2d at 1207. The court based its conclusion on the finding that "the disadvantages of applying the exclusionary rule at sentencing are large, the benefits small or non-existent, and that the rule should therefore not be extended." 540 F.2d at 1212. That court noted that the facts in *Lee* were not those presented in *Verdugo* where it appeared that the government had illegally seized additional evidence for the purpose of enhancing the defendant's sentence, and that in such circumstances the rationale of the exclusionary rule can be served only by excluding illegally seized evidence from consideration at sentencing. 540 F.2d at 1212.

Although this court has not previously decided the precise issue presented in this case, the holding in *United States v. Majors*, 490 F.2d 1321 (10th Cir.1974), *cert. denied*, 420 U.S. 932, 95 S.Ct. 1136, 43 L.Ed.2d 405 (1975), foreshadowed our present decision. The *Majors* court affirmed the sentencing judge's right to consider a charge that had been dismissed when the defendant pled guilty to the charge for which he was being sentenced. 490 F.2d 1324. Several principles applicable to this case underly the *Majors* decision. The court there stated that "[i]n the exercise of the difficult discretionary function of imposing sentence upon a convicted ... criminal, the sentencing judge is entitled to all the help he can get." 490 F.2d at 1322. Such help includes knowledge of the history, background, character and criminal activities of the defendant as well as aggravating and mitigating circumstances. 490 F.2d at 1322. Finally, the court relied on the principle that "[p]ertinent information is not generally to be disregarded because of exclusionary rules of evidence." 490 F.2d at 1322 (citations omitted).

The principal function of the presentence report is to give the sentencing judge the assistance described in *Majors*, 490 F.2d at 1322. The report also serves other vital functions. It aids the probation officer in supervision efforts during probation and parole. It assists the Federal Bureau of Prisons in classification, institutional programs and release planning. It furnishes the United States Parole Commission with information pertinent to consideration of parole and, finally, it serves as a source of information for research. *See* Administrative Office of the United States Courts, *Guide to Judiciary Policies and Procedures*, (Probation Manual) Vol. X, p. 2–3, § 2002; *United States v. Charmer Industries*, 711 F.2d 1164, 1170 (2nd Cir.1983). When the sentencing court has authorized its use, as it did here, the information contained in the presentence report unquestionably serves to aid in crucial determinations made by the Parole Commission, the Bureau of Prisons and the Probation Department.

In this case the trial judge ruled that, in imposing sentence, he would not consider the matters requested to be stricken. He did, however, decline to strike those matters from the report that would be provided to the various agencies for post-sentencing adjudication. It is the opinion of this court that, in ruling as he did, the trial judge went beyond what he was required to do in not considering these alleged offenses. He did correctly rule that the matters should not be stricken from the report provided to the agencies.

There is no suggestion in this case that the two alleged offenses which were the subject of the motion to strike resulted from any attempt on the part of the arresting officers to enhance the sentence imposed in this case. The arrest for possession of marijuana occurred in 1974, nine years before this sentence was imposed. The information contained in the presentence report concerning that arrest is straightforward and relatively innocuous. It simply indicates that appellant was arrested but exonerated the same day because of the illegal search and seizure of the vehicle in which the marijuana was found. It is difficult to see how the inclusion of this information in the presentence report could unfairly prejudice the sentencing judge or federal agencies to whom such information might thereafter be transmitted.

The information contained in the presentence report concerning the 1982 arrest for conspiracy and possession with intent to distribute heroin and cocaine is more extensive, but also appears to be accurate and untainted by any relation to the present offense, and would be highly relevant to the sentencing judge and to the federal agencies to which such information might later be transmitted. Appellant has not denied the accuracy of this information or, for that matter, the accuracy of the information concerning the 1974 arrest for possession of marijuana. Appellant simply claims that, because the evidence of both alleged offenses was obtained in violation of the fourth amendment, neither the sentencing court nor federal agencies to which the presentence report is later transmitted, may be allowed to see or consider information concerning those alleged offenses.

This court rejects that argument. The purpose of the exclusionary rule is to protect, by means of deterrence, fourth amendment rights generally, rather than the personal constitutional rights of the aggrieved party. *United States v. Calandra,* 414 U.S. 338, 348, 94 S.Ct. 613, 620, 38 L.Ed.2d 561 (1974). The principal, if not sole, reason for excluding evidence obtained in violation of the fourth amendment at trial is to deter illegal law enforcement conduct. 414 U.S. at 347, 94 S.Ct. at 619. The degree of deterrence achieved by excluding illegally obtained evidence from the presentence report must be weighed against the concomitant limitation of the right of the trial judge and the post-sentencing administrative tribunals to make their decisions in light of all relevant facts. *See* 414 U.S. at 349, 94 S.Ct. at 620.

As the court recognized in *United States v. Lee,* 540 F.2d 1205 (4th Cir.1976), *cert. denied,* 429 U.S. 894, 97 S.Ct. 255, 50 L.Ed.2d 177 (1976), the additional deterrent effect of extending application of the exclusionary rule to sentencing procedures, in the ordinary case, would be so minimal as to be insignificant. 540 F.2d at 1211. This court believes that this is the ordinary case given the length of time between the arrests complained of and the sentencing date of this case. Both the sentencing court and the post-sentencing administrative agencies are entitled to know all of the facts, including prior alleged offenses that did not result in a conviction. They are, of course, limited to a consideration of information that is accurate, but they are not precluded from considering prior charges that were dismissed or alleged offenses for which charges were not filed because of illegally obtained evidence.

The ruling of the district court is, therefore. AFFIRMED.

UNITED STATES of America,
Plaintiff-Appellee,

v.

Andrew ESCHWEILER,
Defendant-Appellant.

Nos. 85–1058, 85–1536.

United States Court of Appeals,
Seventh Circuit.

Argued Sept. 23. 1985.

Decided Jan. 30, 1986.

Before CUMMINGS, Chief Judge, EAST-
ERBROOK, Circuit Judge, and GRANT,   Senior District Judge.*

CUMMINGS, Chief Judge.

Andrew Eschweiler pled guilty to one count of distribution of cocaine, a violation of 21 U.S.C. § 841(a). He received a two-year sentence to run consecutive to a previous five-year sentence. The defendant appeals from the sentencing hearing, claiming a violation of Federal Rule of Criminal Procedure 32(c)(3)(D). He also appeals from the district court's refusal to exonerate his bail bond pursuant to Federal Rule of Criminal Procedure 46(f). This Court has jurisdiction pursuant to 28 U.S.C. § 1291. We affirm.

Statement of the Case and Facts

On April 12, 1984 the defendant Andrew Eschweiler was arrested while on appeal bond from a previous federal narcotics conviction.[1] He was indicted on May 3, 1984 with three counts of sales of cocaine and marijuana in violation of 21 U.S.C. § 841(a)(1). Bail was set at $50,000 cash, which the defendant's brother posted, designating the defendant as recipient. The government requested a *Nebbia*[2] hearing to determine the source of the funds. The hearing was never held, but Eschweiler was released on April 24, 1984 after additional security was posted.

On November 2, 1984 Eschweiler pled guilty to Count I (sale of 13.26 grams of cocaine) under a conditional plea agreement in accordance with Fed.R.Crim.P. 11(e)(1)(C). At the December 28, 1984 sentencing hearing, although not specifically asked, the defendant raised several objections to the presentence report. The judge did not refer to the objections, make findings, or state that he would not rely on the disputed facts in sentencing the defendant. The judge did, however, state the basis on which he was sentencing the defendant. Eschweiler received the maximum sentence under the plea agreement, two years to run consecutive to his previous five-year sentence. Eschweiler appeals from the sentencing hearing, claiming a violation of Fed.R.Crim.P. 32(c)(3)(D).

After the defendant was sentenced and he surrendered, he moved to exonerate the bond pursuant to Fed.R.Crim.P. 46(f). Judge Hart denied that motion on March 29, 1985 because the Internal Revenue Service (IRS) had levied against the $50,000 bail bond for back taxes it had assessed against the defendant.[3] The defendant appeals from the denial of his bond exoneration motion.

There are two issues before this Court on appeal.[4] First, whether the case should be remanded due to a violation of Fed.R. Crim.P. 32(c)(3)(D). Second, whether the bond posted as defendant's bail should be released to its proper owner under the mo-

---

* The Honorable Robert A. Grant, Senior District Judge for the Northern District of Indiana, is sitting by designation.

1. Eschweiler's earlier conviction was upheld in *United States v. Eschweiler*, 745 F.2d 435 (7th Cir.1984), certiorari denied, — U.S. —, 105 S.Ct. 1188, 84 L.Ed.2d 334 (1985).

2. *United States v. Nebbia*, 357 F.2d 303 (2d Cir. 1966). A *Nebbia* hearing is conducted to determine the source of funds deposited as bail bond. The hearing is conducted to ensure that the funds provided are adequate to compel the defendant to return.

3. The judge had issued an earlier order releasing the additional security (real estate deeds) posted by the defendant's family.

4. Eschweiler does raise a further issue. He claims that the mandatory special parole provision of 21 U.S.C. § 841 is unconstitutional. However, we find it unnecessary to address this argument because the exact issue was recently decided in *United States v. Bridges*, 760 F.2d 151 (7th Cir.1985). In the *Bridges* decision this Court stated, "clearly sections 841(b)(1)(A) and (C) are not unconstitutional ...," 760 F.2d at 154, and addressed the very arguments raised here. See *id.* at 154 and n. 5.

tion to exonerate. We affirm both the sentence and the denial of the bail exoneration motion, but remand for full compliance with Rule 32(c)(3)(D).

I. RULE 32(c)(3)(D)

A. Purpose

When a defendant alleges inaccuracies in his or her presentence report, Fed.R. Crim.P. 32(c)(3)(D) [5] requires that the sentencing judge make written findings as to the allegations or a written determination that the disputed matters will not be relied upon for sentencing. The rule also requires that these written findings or determinations be attached to the presentence report. This rule was contained in the 1983 amendments to Rule 32.

Rule 32(c)(3)(D) serves a dual purpose. First, it protects a defendant's due process right to fair sentencing procedures, particularly the right to be sentenced on the basis of accurate information. Fed.R. Crim.P. 32 Advisory Committee notes; see *United States v. Tucker*, 404 U.S. 443, 447, 92 S.Ct. 589, 591, 30 L.Ed.2d 592; *Townsend v. Burke*, 334 U.S. 736, 741, 68 S.Ct.

1252, 1255, 92 L.Ed. 1690; *United States ex rel. Welch v. Lane*, 738 F.2d 863, 864–865 (7th Cir.1984). Thus, in order to show a due process violation, the defendant must raise grave doubt as to the veracity of the information and show that the court relied on that false information in determining the sentence.[6] *United States v. Harris*, 558 F.2d 366, 375 (7th Cir.1977).

The second purpose of Rule 32(c)(3)(D) is to provide a clear record of the disposition and resolution of controverted facts in the presentence report. Advisory Committee notes, *supra; United States v. Rone*, 743 F.2d 1169 (7th Cir.1984). This record aids both appellate courts in their review of sentencing hearings and administrative agencies that use the report in their own decisionmaking procedures.[7] For example, if the court finds that information in the report is unreliable or simply decides not to rely on the disputed facts in sentencing, by following Rule 32(c)(3)(D) that decision will become part of the presentence report. This reduces the likelihood of later decisions being made on the basis of improper information. *United States v. Petitto*, 767 F.2d 607, 609 (9th Cir.1985). Moreover, if

---

5. Federal Rule of Criminal Procedure 32(c)(3)(D) provides:

> If the comments of the defendant and his counsel or testimony or other information introduced by them allege any factual inaccuracy in the presentence investigation report or the summary of the report or part thereof, the court shall, as to each matter controverted, make (i) a finding as to the allegation, or (ii) a determination that no such finding is necessary because the matter controverted will not be taken into account in sentencing. A written record of such findings and determinations shall be appended to and accompany any copy of the presentence investigation report thereafter made available to the Bureau of Prisons or the Parole Commission.

6. However, this standard need not be met to show a violation of Rule 32(c)(3)(D) requiring resentencing. See *infra* at I.B.

7. The 1983 amendments to Rule 32 came as a result of an empirical study that found abuses in the use of the presentence investigation report at sentencing. See Fennell & Hall, *Due Process at Sentencing: An Empirical and Legal Analysis of the Disclosure of Presentence Reports in Federal Courts*, 93 Harv.L.Rev. 1613, 1651

(1980). That study recognized the important role the presentence report plays following sentencing:

> The defendant's interest in an accurate and reliable presentence report does not cease with the imposition of sentence. Rather, these interests are implicated at later stages in the correctional process by the continued use of the presentence report as a basic source of information in the handling of the defendant. If the defendant is incarcerated, the presentence report accompanies him to the correctional institution and provides background information for the Bureau of Prisons' classification summary, which, in turn, determines the defendant's classification within the facility, his ability to obtain furloughs, and the choice of treatment programs. The presentence report also plays a crucial role during parole determination. Section 4207 of the Parole Commission and Reorganization Act directs the parole hearing examiner to consider, if available, the presentence report as well as other records concerning the prisoner. In addition to its general use as background at the parole hearing, the presentence report serves as the primary source of information for calculating the inmate's parole guideline score.

the record does not clearly reflect whether or not the information was relied on, appellate courts or prison officials may make incorrect assumptions about the disposition of alleged inaccuracies. Thus a court that fails to follow Rule 32(c)(3)(D) may not necessarily violate a defendant's right to due process; nonetheless, a violation of the Rule could require a remand for resentencing. See *id.; United States v. O'Neill*, 767 F.2d 780 (11th Cir.1985).

Both of these objectives are met when sentencing judges follow the procedures set forth in *United States v. Rone*, 743 F.2d 1169 (7th Cir.1984). *Rone* requires that the sentencing judge ask the defendant three questions in order to comply with Rule 32.[8] (1) whether the defendant has had an opportunity to read the report; (2) whether the defendant and defense counsel have discussed it; and (3) whether he or she wishes to challenge any facts in the report. *Id.* at 1174. This questioning process establishes a record reflecting that the defendant has had a realistic opportunity to read, discuss, and object to the report.[9]

If the defendant disputes a fact in the report, the requirements of subsection (D) are triggered. *Rone*, 743 F.2d at 1175. The sentencing judge is then obligated either to make written findings concerning the disputed matter or a written determination that the disputed matter will not be relied on for sentencing, and then attach it to the presentence report. *Id.* at 1175. These procedures, when strictly followed, ensure that the defendant's sentence is based on accurate and reliable information and that subsequent recipients of the re-

port are aware of whatever resolutions occurred at sentencing.

B. Standard

The government in its brief has raised the issue of what burden the defendant must meet before resentencing under Rule 32(c)(3)(D) is required. The government argues that there should be no resentencing because the defendant has failed to show that the contested facts in the presentence report are actually false. The government incorrectly cites *Rone* as holding defendants to the *Harris* burden of raising grave doubt about the reliability or accuracy of the presentence report information in order to show a violation of the Rule. See *supra*, discussion at 1387. However, the court in *Rone* simply noted that the defendant had met the *Harris* standard for demonstrating a due process violation. The court stated, "The defendant, however, has met the burden, *which would have been imposed* even under the old rules and our [*Harris*] precedent ..." to show a due process violation. 743 F.2d at 1174 (emphasis added). The showing necessary to demonstrate a constitutional violation should not be confused with that required to make out a Rule 32 violation. Resentencing may be necessary under the Rule even though a defendant's right to due process has not been violated. *Petitto*, 767 F.2d at 610 ("although the due process sentencing standards ... were satisfied, rule 32 still requires a remand"); *United States v. O'Neill*, 767 F.2d 780, 787 (11th Cir.1985)(court found it unnecessary to address defendant's due process claim because the trial court's failure to comply

---

8. Rule 32(a) provides in pertinent part:
  (a). Sentence.
    (1) Imposition of Sentence. Sentence shall be imposed without unreasonable delay. Before imposing sentence, the court shall
    (A) determine that the defendant and his counsel have had the opportunity to read and discuss the presentence investigation report made available pursuant to subdivision (c)(3)(A) or summary thereof made available pursuant to subdivision (c)(3)(B);
    (B) afford counsel an opportunity to speak on behalf of the defendant; and

    (C) address the defendant personally and ask him if he wishes to make a statement in his own behalf and to present any information in mitigation of punishment.

9. From the record it appears that the sentencing judge failed to meet the requirements of *Rone*. None of the questions was asked, except to the extent that the judge asked the defendant if he had anything to say before sentencing. Transcript, Dec. 28, 1984, at 9. However, the defendant does not argue on appeal that this violation requires resentencing.

with Rule 32(c)(3)(D) required resentencing); *United States v. Velasquez*, 748 F.2d 972, 974 (5th Cir.1984) (court ordered resentencing because district court failed to comply with a procedural rule). Thus all a defendant needs to show in order to be resentenced for a violation of Rule 32(c)(3)(D) is that (1) allegations of inaccuracy were before the sentencing court and (2) the court failed to make findings regarding the controverted matters or a determination that the disputed information would not be used in sentencing. See *United States v. Travis*, 735 F.2d 1129, 1132–1133; *Petitto*, 767 F.2d at 611; *O'Neill*, 767 F.2d at 787; *Velasquez*, 748 F.2d at 974.[10] Unless the government can then demonstrate that the disputed facts were not relied upon, the defendant must be resentenced.

C. *Application*

In this case the sentencing judge failed to meet the requirements of Rule 32(c)(3)(D). At the sentencing hearing the defendant objected to certain information contained in the report, alleging it to be false:

> First of all, I wanted to mention that I am very upset about the numerous erroneous information that was given to you in the presentence report. They are false, many of them are false, and I would like to mention a few for the record.
>
> I am not a big drug dealer. I was not making $15,000 a year—a night breaking up large quantities of five ounces in a pack.

Transcript, December 28, 1984, at 9.

According to *Rone*, when the defendant raises inaccuracies in the presentence report, the requirements of Rule 32(c)(3)(D) are triggered, 743 F.2d at 1175. Despite the defendant's allegations, the court here failed to make any findings to resolve the dispute. Nor did the court expressly determine that it would not rely on the allegations. The court did, however, state its reasons for the sentence imposed.

The government stressed during the sentencing hearing that the defendant was arrested on this drug charge while on appeal bond for a previous drug-related conviction. The government noted that to impose less than the maximum sentence (two years consecutive to the earlier five-year imprisonment) would leave the defendant virtually unpunished for this conduct. The court agreed:

---

10. Two recent court of appeals decisions are arguably contrary to this view. In *United States v. Castillo-Roman*, 774 F.2d 1280 (5th Cir.1985), the Fifth Circuit decided a case appealed under Fed.R.Crim.P. 35. The defendant objected to presentence report allegations that he was the leader of a group that smuggled illegal aliens across the Mexico-Texas border. He claimed that the district court made no findings or determination as required by Rule 32(c)(3)(D). The court opened its opinion by stating that to prevail on the Rule 35 motion the defendant was required to demonstrate that the information in the presentence report was materially inaccurate and that the judge relied on the information. *Id.* at 1283. The court held that the defendant failed to show reliance because the district court stated that it would not take into account the disputed information and on that basis denied the Rule 35 motion. *Id.* But then, after holding no abuse of discretion in denying the Rule 35 motion, the court went on to discuss the defendant's Rule 32 argument and found a technical violation that did not require resentencing. *Id.* at 1284–1285. Because the court proceeded to discuss the Rule 32 violation after

determining that the defendant did not demonstrate inaccuracy and reliance, the court implicitly recognized that a lesser standard is sufficient for resentencing under Rule 32.

Similarly, in *United States v. Stewart*, 770 F.2d 825, 832 (9th Cir.1985) (citing *United States v. Ibarra*, 737 F.2d 825, 827 (9th Cir.1984), the Ninth Circuit stated that (1) the defendant must show the contested information was false or unreliable and (2) relied upon by the judge when challenging sentencing procedures under Rule 32(c)(3)(D). *Id.* at 832. However, the court remanded for resentencing because, unlike *Ibarra*, the district court did not substantially comply with Rule 32. The court so held because it was left without knowing whether the disputed information was relied upon by the sentencing court. *Id.* (citing *United States v. Donn*, 661 F.2d 820, 825 n. 4 (9th Cir.1981). The court never discussed the falsity or unreliable requirement except for its initial statement requiring that the defendant so demonstrate. Instead, after simply finding that the sentencing court did not respond to allegations of falsity, the Ninth Circuit remanded.

I believe that there is truth in the Government's statement that if *any less of a sentence* were imposed in this case, it would be a travesty on the law and it would be an indication that your conduct can be condoned, and it cannot be condoned.

Transcript, December 28, 1984, at 12 (emphasis added).

The court obviously imposed the maximum sentence only because the defendant continued to deal in narcotics while on appeal from a previous narcotics conviction. This case is thus distinguishable from cases in which the sentencing judge clearly did rely on contested information·in sentencing, see *Rone, id.* at 1175, and also from cases where it is unclear on what the sentence was based, see *Petitto,* 767 F.2d at 611. In so determining, we are mindful of the *Rone* Court's admonition not to "read between the lines" as to what took place at the sentencing hearing. 743 F.2d at 1175. Because the controverted facts clearly did not form any part of the basis for the sentence, a remand for sentencing is not required. In fact, 28 U.S.C. § 2111 compels this Court to ignore errors that are harmless. See also Fed.R.Crim.P. 52(a) ("Any error ... which does not affect substantial rights shall be disregarded.").

Recent cases from other circuits hold somewhat contrary to this result. In *United States v. Petitto,* 767 F.2d 607, 611 (9th Cir.1985), the Ninth Circuit held that any noncompliance with Rule 32(c)(3)(D) requires a remand for resentencing. See also *United States v. Travis,* 735 F.2d 1129, 1132–1133 (9th Cir.1984). Although the record in *Petitto* left it unclear whether the sentencing judge relied on the disputed information, the court noted that the same result had been reached in *Travis* where the record demonstrated that the court had not considered the relevant facts. *Petitto,* 767 F.2d at 610 (citing *Travis,* 735 F.2d at 1132–1133). Similarly the Eleventh Circuit in *United States v. O'Neill,* 767 F.2d 780,

787 (1985), held that a plain violation of Rule 32(c)(3)(D) without more mandated a remand for resentencing.

But requiring resentencing when the record is clear that the sentencing judge did not rely on a contested matter does not further the purpose of Rule 32(c)(3)(D). Because the sentencing judge here did not rely on the contested information, there is no concern that the defendant was sentenced on the basis of inaccurate or unreliable information.[11] Therefore, to the extent that these circuits hold that every violation of Rule 32(c)(3)(D) requires a resentencing, we decline to follow their strict interpretation of the Rule.

A remand is necessary, however, to fulfill the second purpose of Rule 32(c)(3)(D). Because the sentencing judge did not make a written determination and attach it to the presentence report, there is no record of this disposition of Eschweiler's allegations. Requiring attachment will further the Rule's goal of providing this Court and administrative agencies with a complete record to use in their decision-making processes. See *United States v. Castillo-Roman,* 774 F.2d 1280 (5th Cir. 1985); *United States v. Hill,* 766 F.2d 856, 858 (4th Cir.1985), certiorari denied, — U.S. ——, 106 S.Ct. 257, 88 L.Ed.2d 263.

At oral argument, the government conceded that remand is necessary under *Petitto.* But on brief it argued that the defendant is not harmed by this omission because the contested material is merely a summary of defendant's previous trial and conviction, which is already contained in a previous presentence report and is part of his file. This "harmless error" argument is unpersuasive. The purpose of Rule 32(c)(3)(D) will be hindered by failing to correct and clarify the record for the future use of the presentence report. First, without the attached determination there will be no record that the defendant alleges the information to be false. Furthermore, agencies could infer both that the informa-

---

11. However, where it is unclear whether the sentencing judge relied on the contested infor-

mation, resentencing would resolve the matter.

tion was used in sentencing and that the defendant did not contest it. Thus the absence of the determination could attest to the veracity of the disputed facts when a finding of veracity was never made. For these reasons, the Court remands the case for attachment to the presentence report of a written determination that the contested facts were not relied upon in sentencing. As the Advisory Committee on the Criminal Rules has pointed out, this does not "impose an onerous burden." 8A Moore's Federal Practice 32.20.

II. BAIL BOND LEVY

The second issue raised by the defendant is whether his bail bond should be exonerated and the funds returned to their proper owner. Eschweiler appeals from the denial of his Rule 46(f) motion to exonerate. Because this is not the proper vehicle for challenging the levy, we hold that the district court properly denied the motion.

The defendant attacks the levy on several grounds. First, he claims that the levy is invalid because he did not receive notice of a deficiency assessment as required by 26 U.S.C. § 6212.[12] Additionally, the defendant asserts that the IRS failed to comply with the 10-day waiting period of 26 U.S.C. § 6331,[13] rendering the subsequent levy invalid. See 26 U.S.C. § 6213. Finally, the defendant argues that levying against bail bonds is impermissible under the Eighth Amendment.

Unfortunately, the defendant failed to raise these issues properly below. A motion to exonerate is not the proper forum to present the district court with sufficient evidence upon which to make a decision. The defendant raised his factual contentions as to notice only in memoranda in support of the motion to exonerate. The government, particularly the IRS, did not have adequate opportunity to respond to the factual assertions.[14] Many factual issues need to be resolved before the validity of the levy can be established. For example, these significant facts remain unknown: (1) the date the IRS deficiency assessment was made; (2) the date the notice of deficiency was mailed; (3) the address to which the deficiency notice was mailed; (4) whether the defendant had actual or constructive notice of the deficiency; and (5) to whom the property belongs.

The government argues that the defendant cannot proceed in district court because he is barred by *United States v. Doyal*, 462 F.2d 1357 (5th Cir.1972), and 26 U.S.C. § 7421(a). In *Doyal*, the Fifth Circuit held that a defendant who asserted no interest in the attached bail bond funds could not recover the funds pursuant to a motion to exonerate. *Id.* The court found that the motion was an attempt to enjoin collection of a tax and was thus barred by § 7421(a).[15] *Id.* at 1358. The court went on to say that the proper action was for the owner of the property to bring a wrongful levy action under 26 U.S.C. § 7426(a)[16] to

---

12. 26 U.S.C. § 6212 provides that:

If the Secretary determines that there is a deficiency in respect of any tax imposed * *, he is authorized to send notice of such deficiency to the taxpayer by certified mail or registered mail.

13. 26 U.S.C. § 6331 provides that:

If any person liable to pay any tax neglects or refuses to pay the same within 10 days after notice and demand, it shall be lawful for the Secretary or his delegate to collect such tax * * * by levy upon all property and rights to property * * * belonging to such person or on which there is a lien provided in this chapter for the payment of such tax.

14. Furthermore, the IRS was not a party to the motion, and thus had no opportunity to refute the defendant's notice allegations.

15. 26 U.S.C. § 7421(a) provides:

Except as provided in sections 6212(a) and (c), 6213(a), and 7426(a) and (b)(1), no suit for the purpose of restraining the assessment or collection of any tax shall be maintained in any court by any person, whether or not such person is the person against whom such tax was assessed.

16. 26 U.S.C. § 7426(a) provides:
(a) Actions permitted.—
(1) Wrongful levy.—If a levy has been made on property or property has been sold pursuant to a levy, any person (other than the

contest the validity of the attachment. *Id.;* see also *United States v. Neely,* 357 F.Supp. 713 (S.D.Fla.1973).

Doyal is distinguishable on three grounds. First, the defendant in *Doyal* was not alleging that the IRS had failed to follow proper notice and levy procedures. Second, he was asserting that the money belonged to someone else. Third, that defendant did not raise a constitutional claim.

In this case § 7421(a) does not apply because Eschweiler contends that the IRS failed to provide notice of the deficiency, as is required by § 6212, and attached the levy prior to the ten-day waiting period required by § 6331. Section 6213 states that § 7421(a) does not apply when the government seeks to enforce collection of a tax before the required waiting period.[17] Where the IRS fails to follow procedures for deficiency assessment and collection, § 7421(a) is inapplicable. *Laing v. United States,* 423 U.S. 161, 96 S.Ct. 473, 46 L.Ed.2d 416; *Valley Finance, Inc. v. United States,* 629 F.2d 162 (D.C.Cir.1980) (notice of deficiency is a jurisdictional prerequisite to the imposition of a tax lien and levies), certiorari denied *sub nom. Pacific Development, Inc. v. United States,* 451 U.S. 1018, 101 S.Ct. 3007, 69 L.Ed.2d 389; *Shapiro v. Secretary of State,* 499 F.2d 527 (D.C.Cir.1974) (power of the IRS to levy is inoperative until failure or refusal

of taxpayer to pay the required amount), affirmed, 424 U.S. 614, 96 S.Ct. 1062, 47 L.Ed.2d 278. Accordingly the district court has jurisdiction to determine the validity of the levy and enjoin its enforcement.

Although the defendant contends in his brief that it is unnecessary to determine who owns the funds in question, a party challenging a levy must have sufficient interest in the levied property. See *Rosenblum v. United States,* 549 F.2d 1140, 1145 (8th Cir.1977), certiorari denied, 434 U.S. 818, 98 S.Ct. 58, 54 L.Ed.2d 74; *Flores v. United States,* 551 F.2d 1169, 1171 (9th Cir.1977). If the property belongs to someone other than the taxpayer, that person must bring suit under 26 U.S.C. § 7426. *Doyal,* 462 F.2d at 1358. If the taxpayer owns the property but wants to contest the validity of notice, he or she can file suit to enjoin enforcement of the levy in district court,[18] see § 6213; *Laing v. United States,* 423 U.S. 161, 96 S.Ct. 473, 46 L.Ed.2d 416; *Austin v. Voskuil,* 493 F.Supp. 780, 781 (E.D.Mo.1980); *Needham v. United States,* 564 F.Supp. 419, 421 (W.D.Okla.1983). A tricky question may arise if the defendant does not own the property, yet wants to raise a constitutional question; where is his or her forum? But that question is not before us because the defendant has sufficient property interest to challenge the levy.

---

person against whom is assessed the tax out of which such levy arose) who claims an interest in or lien on such property and that such property was wrongfully levied upon may bring a civil action against the United States in a district court of the United States. Such action may be brought without regard to whether such property has been surrendered to or sold by the Secretary or his delegate.

17. 26 U.S.C. § 6213 provides in pertinent part:

(a) Time for filing petition and restriction on assessment.—Within 90 days, or 150 days if the notice is addressed to a person outside the United States, after the notice of deficiency authorized in section 6212 is mailed * * *, the taxpayer may file a petition with the Tax Court for a redetermination of the deficiency. * * * *[N]o levy or proceeding in court for its collection shall be made, begun, or prosecuted until such notice has been mailed to the taxpayer,* nor until the expiration of such 90-day or 150-day period, as the case may be, nor, if

a petition has been filed with the Tax Court, until the decision of the Tax Court has become final. *Notwithstanding the provisions of section 7421(a), the making of such assessment or the beginning of such proceeding or levy during the time such prohibition is in force may be enjoined by a proceeding in the proper court.* (Emphasis added.)

18. The defendant complains that he will be forced to file a "full blown suit" against the IRS if the bond funds are not released to the designated recipient. This "argument" does not persuade the Court. The defendant fails to explain why he should be treated any differently than any other citizen whose funds have been attached by the IRS for alleged back taxes owing. The proper course of action in such a situation is for the taxpayer or owner of the property to bring a suit against the IRS claiming improper notice or wrongful levy. See *United States v. National Bank of Commerce,* —— U.S. ——, 105 S.Ct. 2919, 2929, 86 L.Ed.2d 565.

When Eschweiler's bond was posted in April 1984, he was designated as the recipient of the $50,000 cash bail bond. The IRS attached the bond in August of 1984. It was not until well after that attachment that the designated recipient was changed.[19] That change in designation cannot defeat the prior interest of the IRS in the funds. Therefore, although the defendant had sufficient property interest to bring suit to enjoin enforcement of the levy, see *United States v. National Bank of Commerce,* — U.S. —, 105 S.Ct. 2919, 2929, 86 L.Ed.2d 565 (tax liens attach to rights to property), the district court's denial of his motion to exonerate was proper.

III. CONCLUSION

For the reasons set out in this opinion, we affirm the district court's sentence of the defendant and denial of the motion to exonerate, but remand for full compliance with the attachment provision of Rule 32(c)(3)(D).

UNITED STATES of America, Appellee,

v.

Giuseppe PUGLIESE and Pietro
Pugliese, Defendants-Appellants.

Nos. 1181, 1182, Dockets
85–1460, 85–1461.

United States Court of Appeals,
Second Circuit.

Argued May 13, 1986.
Decided Nov. 21, 1986.

Before LUMBARD, CARDAMONE and
WINTER, Circuit Judges.

CARDAMONE, Circuit Judge:

These appeals from judgments imposing
in each case 30-year terms of imprisonment
question whether the sentencing court's
consideration of testimony regarding Pietro
Pugliese at a sentencing proceeding before
another judge comports with due process.
Recognizing the long held necessity for a
sentencing court to have vast discretion in
order to individualize punishment, the Supreme Court, in *Williams v. New York*,
337 U.S. 241, 69 S.Ct. 1079, 93 L.Ed. 1337
(1949), cautioned lower courts not to treat
the due process clause as a reason to abandon the widely accepted practice of considering out-of-court material, generally contained in a probation report, in order to
reach a just sentence. *Id.* at 250–51, 69
S.Ct. at 1084–85. Yet, the Supreme Court
has also stated that due process concerns
are implicated at sentencing. *See Townsend v. Burke*, 334 U.S. 736, 741, 68 S.Ct.
1252, 1255, 92 L.Ed. 1690 (1948). Because
these divergent views as to where the em-

phasis should be placed when imposing a
sentence make the footing unsure, one cannot tread too confidently in this area of the
law. Yet, we must decide whether the
district court here heeded the admonishment of *Williams*, without foregoing the
due process rights noted in *Townsend*.

I BACKGROUND

A. *Facts*

Pietro and Giuseppe Pugliese appeal
from the sentences imposed in a judgment
of the United States District Court for the
Eastern District of New York (Bramwell,
J.), following a jury trial at which both
were found guilty of having violated 18
U.S.C. §§ 2, 371, 472, and 473 through their
participation in a large-scale organized conspiracy to counterfeit fifty dollar bills.
Pietro Pugliese was also convicted of aiding and abetting another sale of counterfeit
money in violation of 18 U.S.C. §§ 472, 473.
Based on these convictions, the district
court sentenced each appellant to identical
cumulative 30-year terms of imprisonment.
In addition, both appellants were fined
$20,000 and Pietro Pugliese was given a

concurrent 10–year term on his separate conviction.

Appellants were first indicted in February 1982. When the government was unable to proceed to trial because its principal witness refused to testify, Judge Bramwell denied a motion for a continuance and dismissed the indictment under Fed.R.Crim.P. Rule 48(a), stating:

> I will tell you one thing, I have a great deal of resentment for people like these who are foreigners and come here and are involved in crime. I did this thing because this is what the situation called for. But these people are foreigners who come here and are involved in crime and they think we are supposed to give them special consideration. This type of people [sic] are the worst things we have and I am telling you that for you to tell it to each of the defendants.

On April 2, 1985, after the appellants were reindicted, a motion for the trial judge to recuse himself based on the above statements was denied. The case then proceeded to trial on October 3, 1985 and resulted in guilty verdicts. Judge Bramwell sentenced the Puglieses on December 3, 1985.

During the sentencing proceedings the district court judge said that he would consider allegations that appellants had sanctioned an attempt to murder an adverse federal witness. In considering these allegations the sentencing court further stated that it would review the transcript of a hearing being held before another district court judge pursuant to *United States v. Fatico*, 579 F.2d 707 (2d Cir.1978) (*Fatico I*). Appellants assert that the sentencing proceedings violated their rights to due process and that the sentencing judge should have recused himself based upon his pretrial remarks.

B. *Sentencing Hearings*

We examine first the facts relevant to the due process challenge. Both Puglieses' presentence reports contained identical allegations that appellants were involved in an attempted murder of a government witness who was shot while enroute to the courthouse to testify against them. When defense counsel questioned the propriety of the sentencing judge considering this information, the following colloquy took place on November 14, 1985 at the first of two sentencing hearings held before Judge Bramwell.

THE COURT: You know, I would say this to you as to the shooting of Mr. Quagliata at the time the witness was on his way to Court, he was driving and I can't say that either of these two defendants actually did the shooting or anything of that nature, that, I can't say but in some way, this Court must believe that these defendants are somehow involved in this, the Court must believe that. Of course, it would be—other than that, it would be utterly ridiculous, the Court must believe that.

MR. FISHER [DEFENSE]: Well, your Honor, in that regard, first, as I understand it, the government does not even allege the involvement in anyway at all by Pietro Pugliese in that incident, that's the first thing.

THE COURT: Let me say this to you, the history of what has happened with this case would almost dictate to this Court that these defendants were involved in some way in that shooting and I'm standing on that statement, I'm not going to change it.

MR. FISHER: Your Honor, the defendants, each of them deny [sic] categorically any involvement whatsoever in the shooting.

THE COURT: I will let you say that as long as you want to stand there and as long as you want to say it and I will listen to you but my statement, I stand by it and it's not going to change.

The history mentioned by the sentencing judge refers to the disappearance and intimidation of prior witnesses. Specifically, one government witness who disappeared in violation of his bail conditions stated when he was apprehended that the Puglieses had told him to flee and had financed his flight. Later, this same witness was again asked to cooperate with the prosecution. While awaiting an interview with an Assistant United States Attorney (AUSA), he was detained in the same facility as Giuseppe Pugliese. Ultimately, he declined to testify. A second government witness also refused to testify. Threats—recounted more fully below—were also made against the witness who was actually shot.

The summarized history was relied upon and read into the record at the behest of the trial court. Shortly afterwards, this colloquy ensued.

THE COURT: The history of this case lends itself to any reasonable person to believe that these defendants were part of what happened to Vincenzo Quagliata.

DEFENSE: Your Honor, I appreciate the candor of the Court in telling me as you have where you are at with regard to these considerations.

THE COURT: This is something, this I will say without hesitation is something I rarely do on a sentence but in this situation, I'm almost compelled to accept what has happened here as against these two defendants.

The district judge then learned that Judge Wexler of the Eastern District was conducting a *Fatico* hearing regarding Giuseppe's participation in the attempted assassination. Judge Bramwell expressed an interest in the records of that proceeding,

even offering to look at them, though the court still maintained that "[t]he record will be ample and I will still take the same position, in some way these defendants are involved...." The hearing concluded with the district judge stating that his "position has not changed, it's going to be the same up to the sentence, through the sentence, it's not changing."

Judge Bramwell conducted a second sentencing hearing on December 3, 1985. Initially he read a prepared text representing his findings as to appellants' involvement in the shooting.[1] Testimony adduced at Judge Wexler's *Fatico* hearing, which Judge Bramwell had requested to see on his own motion, corroborated the circumstantial evidence of intimidation of other witnesses. Judge Bramwell summarized his view of these matters as follows:

In short, the overwhelming circumstantial evidence in this matter, coupled with testimony offered during Judge Wexler's hearing, compelled this Court to find that Giuseppe Pugliese and Pietro Pugliese were in some way responsible for the intimidation and attempted murder of the witness Vincenzo Quagliata. For this Court to ignore the evidence connecting the Puglieses with the shooting of Quagliata would be to turn a blind

---

1. THE COURT: Before we proceed, the Court is going to put a statement on the record.

In light of defense counsel's concern about the extent of this Court's belief that the defendants were involved with the shooting of Vincenzo Quagliata the Court will put the following statement on the record.

To begin with, there is ample circumstantial evidence supporting the finding that the Pugliese brothers were in some way connected with the intimidation and shooting of Quagliata.

This case against the Pugliese brothers has had a disturbing history of witnesses mysteriously disappearing, often literally on the eve[ ] of trial, allegedly at the command of the Puglieses.

The mere fact that, after other government witnesses had become unavailable under suspicious circumstances, the witness Quagliata was shot on the way to Court for a meeting with Assistant U.S. Attorney Savitt, would by itself lead this Court to reject the contention that the defendants were not at all responsible.

This circumstantial evidence, moreover, is directly supported by testimonial evidence elicited at a presentence hearing conducted by Judge Wexler in August of this year.

At that hearing, for example, detective Alphonse Ripandelli of the New York City Police Department testified that one Carmello Lovacco, who admitted to being the driver of the vehicle from which the shots were fired at Quagliata, stated that Quagliata was to be shot at the behest of Joe [Giuseppe] Pugliese because Quagliata "was a rat."

Detective Ripandelli further testified to information that Lovacco performed this criminal act to obtain status in the criminal organization run by Joe Pugliese.

Special Agent Jerry Williams of the United States Secret Service also testified at the hearing. Agent Williams testified that approximately one week before Quagliata was shot in the head, another associate of Joe Pugliese accosted Quagliata with a warning that if he, Quagliata, testified against Joe or Pete [Pietro] Pugliese that he would, "lose his head."

eye to reality, and would be in gross dereliction of this Court's duty to see that justice is done in this courtroom. Because the district court's ultimate findings, made after it had examined the *Fatico* material, were substantively identical to its preliminary statement, defense counsel questioned whether Judge Bramwell's findings were fair and objective.

Appellants were sentenced during this second hearing. The district court's conclusion that the Puglieses had participated in the shooting plainly influenced it as to the sentences imposed. For example, in sentencing Giuseppe Pugliese, the court noted that appellant "intimidated, threatened and tried to have murdered a witness against him." The attempt was mentioned again when Pietro Pugliese was sentenced. "The Pugliese brothers tried to hinder and prevent their prosecution again in 1985 by attempting to have murdered another primary witness against them, fortunately he survived and is recovering."

C. *The* Fatico *Hearing*

We turn now to Judge Wexler's *Fatico* hearing upon which Judge Bramwell relied. Judge Wexler conducted four separate hearings. The first three hearings occurred prior to the first sentencing hearing before Judge Bramwell and were considered by him at the second sentencing hearing of December 3, 1985. The fourth and last *Fatico* hearing held by Judge Wexler took place after Judge Bramwell had sentenced appellants.

During the first *Fatico* hearing, the AUSA stated that Quagliata was shot shortly after his status as a witness was made known to the defense. A detective testified that his informant had a conversation with the driver of the vehicle used during the murder attempt. In the conversation, the driver admitted that the shooting had been planned because Quagliata was going to testify against Giuseppe Pugliese and that the driver undertook the mission for the purpose of "obtain[ing] status in the organization run by Giuseppe Pugliese." When Judge Wexler became aware that tapes existed of the conversation between the informer and Lovacco (the

driver) he ordered them produced for his *in camera* inspection. A Secret Service agent also testified to a conversation that he had with Quagliata in which Quagliata told him that approximately a week prior to the shooting, he was approached by an individual named Tony whom he had known for approximately five years and who worked for Giuseppe Pugliese. The agent testified that Quagliata had also said that "Tony came up to him by himself" and threatened " 'if you testify against Joe or Peter you're going to lose your head.' " Defense counsel was given ample opportunity to cross-examine the detective and the Secret Service agent.

Judge Wexler found at the second hearing held the next day that the tapes corroborated the detective's testimony of the previous day and stated: "I will go one step further, I find nothing inconsistent." Up until this point in the hearings all of the allegations of involvement in the shooting referred to both appellants. Significantly, for the first time the government admitted at the third hearing that only Giuseppe Pugliese was implicated in the shooting and that "there is no statement that Pietro Pugliese was involved in it".

At the final *Fatico* hearing, held January 31, 1986, Judge Wexler refused to consider Giuseppe Pugliese's alleged participation in the attack on Quagliata. Neither counsel objected to this ruling as they had agreed among themselves that the murder attempt allegations had already influenced the sentencing decision of Judge Bramwell who had sentenced the Puglieses earlier on December 3, 1985 (without the benefit therefore of the January 31 hearing and decision).

II DISCUSSION

Appellants contend that it violates due process for the sentencing judge to examine the transcript of an ongoing *Fatico* hearing before another judge involving only one appellant, and then use the evidence there revealed in sentencing both appellants. The Puglieses additionally urge that the Court's statements during sentencing demonstrate that it was already firmly convinced of their connection to the murder attempt, and that therefore it refused to conduct a full hearing on this point. The government responds that the Puglieses had an adequate opportunity to challenge the allegations regarding their involvement in the Quagliata shooting at the hearing conducted by Judge Wexler on those identical claims.

A. *Due Process at Sentencing*

Historically, sentences were rigidly imposed. Blackstone relates how those felonies to which the benefit of clergy extended were all punishable by death, 4 W. Blackstone, *Commentaries* 94 (Univ. of Chicago Press ed. (1979)), giving no option to the sentencing court upon conviction except that of imposing the fixed sentence. Discretion crept in gradually. Presently, sentencing is a highly subjective exercise of judgment—seldom successfully challenged—because a sentence imposed by a district court within statutory limits, and not illegal, or based on inaccurate information, or procedures that offend due process will not be interfered with on appeal. *United States v. Slocum*, 695 F.2d 650, 657 (2d Cir.1982), *cert. denied*, 460 U.S. 1015, 103 S.Ct. 1260, 75 L.Ed.2d 487 (1983).

Moreover, a district court judge's discretion in sentencing is "largely unlimited either as to the kind of information he may consider, or the source from which it may come." *See United States v. Tucker*, 404 U.S. 443, 446, 92 S.Ct. 589, 591, 30 L.Ed.2d 592 (1972). We have consistently acknowledged a sentencing court's wide discretion to consider all circumstances that shed light on a convicted person's background, history and behavior. *Billiteri v. United States Bd. of Parole*, 541 F.2d 938, 944 (2d Cir.1976); *see also United States v. Charmer Industries, Inc.*, 711 F.2d 1164, 1170–71 (2d Cir.1983) (hearsay statements bearing no relationship to the crime charged may be included); *United States v. Mennuti*, 679 F.2d 1032, 1037 (2d Cir.1982) (similar though uncharged crimes may be considered); *United States v. Hendrix*, 505 F.2d 1233, 1235 (2d Cir.1974), *cert. denied*, 423 U.S. 897, 96 S.Ct. 199, 46 L.Ed.2d 130 (1975) (claimed perjury, though neither charged nor tried, may be taken into account); *United States v. Needles*, 472 F.2d 652, 654–56 (2d Cir.1973) (a dropped count in an indictment may be considered); *United States v. Sweig*, 454 F.2d 181, 184 (2d Cir.1972) (criminal activity for which a defendant has been acquitted may be included).

Sentencing is nonetheless a critical stage in a criminal case where due process protects a convicted person as it does an accused at trial. A convicted defendant has a right to procedural safeguards, such as the right to counsel, *see Mempa v. Rhay*, 389 U.S. 128, 134, 88 S.Ct. 254, 256, 19 L.Ed.2d 336 (1967). As a consequence, sentencing no longer stands like an island separate from the mainland of criminal law.

Further, the Supreme Court instructs us that a defendant has a due process right to question the procedure leading to the imposition of his sentence. *Gardner v. Florida*, 430 U.S. 349, 358, 97 S.Ct. 1197, 1204, 51 L.Ed.2d 393 (1977). What process is due at sentencing must be evaluated in light of four factors: (1) the nature of the individual interest, (2) the risk of error inherent in present methods of obtaining information, (3) the value of additional procedural safeguards, and (4) the government's interest, including fiscal burdens, of any proposed additional safeguards. *Mathews v. Eldridge*, 424 U.S. 319, 335, 96 S.Ct. 893, 903, 47 L.Ed.2d 18 (1976).

We apply these factors to the facts in the instant case, testing whether Judge Bramwell's use of the *Fatico* hearing before Judge Wexler violated procedural due process. Obviously the interest of an offender at sentencing could not be greater because his sentence in large measure determines that individual's future destiny. Yet, when a sentencing judge reads the transcript of another judicial proceeding where the defendant has had the opportunity to cross-examine witnesses, the risk of prejudice is minimal. Since the borrowed hearing was used simply to corroborate certain statements contained in the Puglieses' presentence reports, additional procedural safeguards are not required. Nor is the government's interest affected by this method of obtaining information.

Beyond the application of the *Mathews v. Eldridge* factors, it is plain that to review the transcript of a judicial hearing is certainly no less trustworthy than the ordinary kinds of information found in a presentence report that a district judge reads and relies upon. *Hendrix,* 505 F.2d at 1235. Analyzing the method Judge Bramwell used against the four factors we conclude that, on balance, it may not be faulted on due process grounds, particularly when heeding the Supreme Court's lesson in *Williams* that sentencing courts should not abandon the practice of considering out-of-court sources of information. 337 U.S. at 246, 69 S.Ct. at 1082. Thus, we are satisfied that the wide discretion vested in a district court at sentencing permitted Judge Bramwell to consider the information developed at the hearing before Judge Wexler.

B. *No Requirement for Evidentiary Hearing*

Appellants nonetheless insist that they were entitled to a full-blown hearing in their challenge to the presentence reports. When hearsay is admitted into evidence through a presentence report and the defendant challenges the veracity of that evidence, the government must introduce corroborating proof. Corroboration is required to ensure "the reliability of evidence that is difficult to challenge . . . through cross-examination or otherwise. . . ." 579 F.2d at 713 (*Fatico I*). The cases suggest that corroboration may be provided simply by a government proffer, but leave silent how that proffer may be challenged.

Due process as well as Rule 32 requires that a defendant be allowed in some manner to challenge the prosecution's proffer to assure the reliability of presentence report information. The defendant may challenge the prosecution's affidavits, letters, and other submissions to the court; he may direct comment to the court, and may

cross-examine witnesses. Both sides should have an effective opportunity to rebut allegations likely to affect the sentence, *see* 3 *Standards for Criminal Justice, Sentencing Alternatives and Procedures,* Standard 18–6.4 at 448 (1986 Supp.), including, for example, the right to examine sentencing material, and the right to challenge allegations in the presentence report. *See* Note, *Procedural Due Process at Judicial Sentencing for Felony,* 81 Harv.L.Rev. 821, 825 (1968).

But a convicted defendant has no absolute right to present his own witnesses, since sentencing proceedings are not designed to be full-blown evidentiary hearings, *Needles,* 472 F.2d at 657–58, or minitrials, because of the costly burden that would impose on the court. Sentencing hearings ultimately are conducted within the discretion of the district court. *Charmer Industries,* 711 F.2d at 1172. Under Fed.R.Crim.P. 32(c)(3)(A) a district court's options include affording a defendant, at the minimum, "an opportunity to comment on the report" and, in the district court's discretion, "to introduce testimony or other information relating to any alleged factual inaccuracy contained in it." The choice followed rests in the sound discretion of the sentencing court. Hence, it is clear that the Puglieses had no right to a mandatory evidentiary sentencing hearing.

C. *Requirement That Information on Which Sentence Based Be Reliable and Accurate*

Nevertheless, as *Townsend v. Burke,* 334 U.S. 736, 68 S.Ct. 1252, 92 L.Ed. 1690 (1948), recognizes, due process requires that a convicted person not be sentenced on "materially untrue" assumptions or "misinformation." *Id.* at 741, 68 S.Ct. at 1255. In addition, Congress' interest in reliable sentencing information can be clearly discerned in the various amendments to Federal Rule of Criminal Procedure 32. In 1975, subdivision (c)(3)(A) was amended to allow a defendant *or* his or her counsel to review a presentence report to comment on it at sentencing to insure "that the presentence report be completely accurate in every material respect." H.R.Rep. No. 247, 94th Cong., 1st Sess. 18, *reprinted in* 1975 U.S.Code Cong. & Ad.News 674, 690. More recently in 1983, subdivision (c)(3) was further amended to provide for disclosure of the report to *both* defendant *and* his counsel *without request.* See Fed. R.Crim.P. 32(c)(3)(A), 18 U.S.C. app. at 124 (Supp. III 1985). Moreover, subdivision (a)(1) was amended to impose on the sentencing court the obligation to determine "that the defendant and his counsel have had the opportunity to read and discuss the presentence investigation report made available pursuant to subdivision (c)(3)(A) or summary thereof made available pursuant to subdivision (c)(3)(B)." Fed.R.Crim.P. 32(a)(1)(A), 18 U.S.C. app. at 123 (Supp. III 1985).[2]

Consequently, a district court has an obligation to assure itself that the information upon which it relies in sentencing defendants is both reliable and accurate. In the instant case, the district court did not satisfy this Rule 32 obligation. Instead, it relied on the allegations of the presentence reports and its belief in the appellants' prior history of witness intimidation, and announced its "unalterable" conclusion that the Puglieses were implicated in the murder attempt. The district court made clear that regardless of what it might later learn, it would remain convinced that appellants participated "in some way" in the shooting. Expressions of a fixed view based on the presentence report made prior to a hearing are inconsistent with the due process obligations imposed on a sentencing court to consider only reliable and accurate information. As such, they call into question a sentencing judge's impartiality, and thus cast doubt on the fair and impartial administration of justice at a critical stage of a criminal proceeding. Even when subsequent evidence is produced in support of the district court's earlier statement, public confidence in the reliability of the sentencing procedure has been weakened.

The gathering of information contained in a presentence report is not an exact science, as this case illustrates. Because the information in a presentence report may be unfounded malicious gossip, inaccurate, or materially false, sentencing courts must tread warily, without acting blindly upon serious allegations, absent guarantees of reliability. The Puglieses' presentence reports before Judge Bramwell each contained the same Parole Guideline Worksheet which, under "Particularly Aggravating Factors," stated: "Witness Vincenzo Quagliata was shot and seriously wounded while on his way to federal court to provide testimony against the defendant on May 23, 1985." Of course, the government later conceded that it had no proof of Pietro Pugliese's involvement in that shooting. In our view, the district court's failure to ascertain the reliability and accuracy of the presentence reports constitutes plain error and is also an abuse of discretion that mandates vacatur of the sentences. Therefore, we remand the matter for resentencing before a different district court judge. *See United States v. Robin,* 545 F.2d 775, 778 (2d Cir.1976).

D. *Resentencing*

Upon resentencing the court should adopt whatever method it believes will best insure the reliability and accuracy of the sentencing information. The resentencing we are now directing should not be regarded as an adjudication of appellants' claim that they were not involved in the shooting. Rather the district court may consider relevant evidence linking Giuseppe Pugliese with the murder attempt. Pietro Pugliese was not a defendant at the hearing before Judge Wexler, and the government admitted that it had no evidence linking him to the shooting. The evidence before Judge Wexler thus does not support the allegation that Pietro Pugliese participated in some manner in the shooting. The government must therefore produce other evidence, if such exists, to substantiate its

---

2. Congress subsequently amended subdivision (a)(1). None of the changes is relevant to our discussion. *See* Continuing Appropriations,

1985—Comprehensive Crime Control Act of 1984, Pub. 98–473, Title II, § 215(a), 98 Stat. 2014 (1984) (effective November 1, 1986).

claim that he was implicated in the murder attempt. Of course, in assuring the reliability of the presentence report the government is not held to a "beyond a reasonable doubt standard", *see United States v. Fatico*, 603 F.2d 1053, 1057 & n. 9 (2d Cir.1979), *cert. denied*, 444 U.S. 1073, 100 S.Ct. 1018, 62 L.Ed.2d 755 (1980) (*Fatico II*). *See also Williams*, 337 U.S. at 246–47, 69 S.Ct. at 1082–83.

III RECUSAL

Finally, appellants made a motion of recusal pursuant to 28 U.S.C. § 455(a) and the Fifth Amendment. This motion was based upon the statements made by the district court in its 1982 dismissal of the preceding indictment against the Puglieses. Section 455(a) requires recusal when the impartiality of the court is "reasonably" suspect. We have noted that 28 U.S.C. §§ 144 and 455 should be construed in *pari materia* and that the test is the same under both sections: "The determination should be made on the basis of conduct extrajudicial in nature as distinguished from conduct within a judicial context." *In re International Business Machines Corp.*, 618 F.2d 923, 928 (2d Cir.1980) (quoting *Davis v. Board of School Commissioners*, 517 F.2d 1044, 1052 (5th Cir. 1975), *cert. denied*, 425 U.S. 944, 96 S.Ct. 1685, 48 L.Ed.2d 188 (1976)). "The rule of law, [for § 144 and therefore § 455(a)], without belaboring the point, is that what a judge learns in his judicial capacity— whether by way of guilty pleas of codefendants or alleged coconspirators, or by way of pretrial proceedings, or both—is a proper basis for judicial observations, and the use of such information is not the kind of matter that results in disqualification." *United States v. Bernstein*, 533 F.2d 775, 785 (2d Cir.1976).

The statement challenged here, though admittedly strong, is a product of the district court's observations and information derived from the pretrial proceedings. As such, it may not serve as a basis for a successful motion to recuse.

IV CONCLUSION

The case is remanded to another district court judge for resentencing consistent with this opinion.

Kenneth Michael JULIAN,
Plaintiff-Appellee,

v.

UNITED STATES DEPARTMENT OF
JUSTICE, Defendant-Appellant.

Margaret J. WALLACE,
Plaintiff-Appellee,

v.

UNITED STATES PAROLE COMMIS-
SION, and Charles Turnbo, Warden,
F.C.I., Pleasanton, CA, Defendants-Ap-
pellants.

Nos. 85–2649, 85–2751.

United States Court of Appeals,
Ninth Circuit.

Argued and Submitted Sept. 11, 1986.

Decided Dec. 30, 1986.

Before WALLACE, ALARCON and BEEZER, Circuit Judges.

BEEZER, Circuit Judge:

Kenneth Michael Julian and Margaret J. Wallace requested copies of their presentence investigation reports under the Freedom of Information Act, 5 U.S.C. § 552. In separate summary judgment motions Julian and Wallace obtained orders requiring release of the reports. The government has appealed both judgments and the cases have been consolidated. We affirm.

I

On November 1, 1984, Wallace, who was at that time incarcerated, made a request under the Freedom Of Information Act (FOIA) for disclosure of all records pertaining to her in possession of the United States Parole Commission. On March 25, 1985, the Commission sent Wallace all of the relevant documents she had requested except for her presentence investigation report. Wallace filed suit seeking a copy of this report and on September 6, 1985, Judge Henderson ordered the presentence report released.

Julian, who is currently incarcerated, requested a copy of his presentence investi-gation report on October 17, 1984. This request was denied, prompting Julian to appeal to the Department of Justice, Office of Information and Privacy, which refused his request. Julian filed suit on January 30, 1985. On August 5, 1985, Judge Bilby granted Julian's motion for summary judgment and held that there was no basis to withhold the presentence investigation report.

II

The probation service of a district court compiles presentence investigation reports after a criminal defendant has been found guilty. The report contains detailed factual information concerning the criminal record and background of the defendant. The report includes inter alia: 1) the defendant's official arrest and conviction record; 2) an official version of the offense in question obtained from the United States Attorney; 3) information concerning harm or loss suffered by the victim of the crime; 4) information on the defendant's contacts with the military, schools, banks, and credit bureaus; 5) summaries of interviews with social service agencies, employers, family and friends; and 6) clinical evaluations of the defendant's physical and mental health. The report concludes with the probation officer's sentencing recommendation. Fennell and Hall, *Due Process at Sentencing: An Empirical and Legal Analysis of the Disclosure of Presentence Reports In Federal Courts*, 93 Harv.L.Rev. 1615, 1623 (1980).

The presentence report serves three purposes. The district court considers the report while formulating a sentencing decision. Second, if the convicted defendant is incarcerated, the report accompanies him to the correctional institution, where the Bureau of Prisons utilizes the contents of the report to classify the prisoner for the facility and to determine an appropriate treatment program. There is no statutory directive that the Probation Service furnish a copy of the report to the Bureau of Prisons, but it does so. Finally, the Parole Commission considers the report when it makes its parole eligibility determination.

The convicted defendant has several opportunities to read his presentence investigation report. Under Federal Rule of Criminal Procedure 32(c)(3), the convicted defendant and his attorney may examine all or certain portions of the report a reasonable time before sentencing. Rule 32(c)(3) states in pertinent part,

(A) At a reasonable time before imposing sentence the court shall permit the defendant and his counsel to read the report of the presentence investigation exclusive of any recommendation as to sentence, but not to the extent that in the opinion of the court the report contains diagnostic opinions which, if disclosed, might seriously disrupt a program of rehabilitation; or sources of information obtained upon a promise of confidentiality; or any other information which, if disclosed, might result in harm, physical or otherwise, to the defendant or other persons.

Judges must provide an oral or written summary of any exempted information which they rely on in sentencing decisions and provide the defendant or his counsel an opportunity to comment on the summary. Fed.R.Crim.P. 32(c)(3)(B). The convicted defendant may not keep a copy of the report. Fed.R.Crim.P. 32(c)(3)(E). However, he may take extensive or verbatim notes from the report if he so chooses. Fennell and Hall, *supra* at 1646–47.

The convicted defendant has a second opportunity to view the report after he has been incarcerated and before his parole hearing. The Parole Commission and Reorganization Act of 1976, 18 U.S.C. § 4201, et seq. (PCRA), dictates the procedures for disclosing the report at this stage. The disclosure procedures applicable during the parole eligibility process mirror the procedures applicable during sentencing. 18 U.S.C. § 4208(b) provides in part:

(b) At least thirty days prior to any parole determination proceeding, the prisoner shall be provided with (1) written notice of the time and place of the proceeding, and (2) reasonable access to a report or other document to be used by the Commission in making its determination.

The statute identifies certain types of information which shall not be revealed to the convicted defendant except in summary form. These exempted items are identical to those listed in Rule 32(c)(3).[1] A prisoner may obtain a copy of his presentence report during the parole hearing process, but only if the sentencing court which prepared the report consents. 28 C.F.R. § 2.56(b) (1985).

The government contends that presentence investigation reports are exempt from disclosure under FOIA provisions 5 U.S.C. § 552(b)(3) (hereinafter "Exemption 3") and 5 U.S.C. § 552(b)(5) (hereinafter "Exemption 5"). Alternatively, the government argues that FOIA is displaced by the special statutory procedures for obtaining presentence investigation reports set forth

---

1. 18 U.S.C. § 4208(c) provides that "subparagraph (2) of subsection (b) shall not apply to— (1) diagnostic opinions which, if made known to the eligible prisoner, could lead to a serious disruption of his institutional program; (2) any document which reveals sources of information obtained upon a promise of confidentiality; or (3) any other information which, if disclosed, might result in harm, physical or otherwise, to any person."

in Fed.R.Crim.P. 32(c)(3) and 18 U.S.C. § 4208. The district courts rejected these claims. Because this case involves questions of law, we review de novo. *United States v. McConney*, 728 F.2d 1195, 1200–01 (9th Cir.), *cert. denied*, 469 U.S. 824, 105 S.Ct. 101, 83 L.Ed.2d 46 (1984).

III

Presentence investigation reports are "agency records" when they are in the possession of the Parole Commission. *Fendler v. United States Parole Commission*, 774 F.2d 975, 977 (9th Cir.1985); *Berry v. Department of Justice*, 733 F.2d 1343, 1349 (9th Cir.1984). The government has not argued to the contrary in this case.[2] Consequently, the Commission must disclose presentence reports to prisoners unless it can demonstrate that they fall within one of FOIA's nine enumerated exemptions. *United States v. Weber Aircraft Corp.*, 465 U.S. 792, 793–94, 104 S.Ct. 1488, 1489, 79 L.Ed.2d 814 (1984). FOIA is to be liberally construed in favor of disclosure and its exemptions narrowly construed. *FBI v. Abramson*, 456 U.S. 615, 630–31, 102 S.Ct. 2054, 2063–64, 72 L.Ed.2d 376 (1982) (citing *Department of Air Force v. Rose*, 425 U.S. 352, 361, 96 S.Ct. 1592, 1599, 48 L.Ed.2d 11 (1976)).

[5, 6] We are required to decide whether FOIA provides a *per se* exemption for withholding an entire presentence report when it is requested by the subject of the report. There is no doubt that portions of the report may be withheld. Both Rule 32(c)(3) and PCRA authorize the withholding of certain classes of information which appear in the presentence report. The probation officer's sentencing recommendation, diagnostic opinions which might dis-

rupt the prisoner's rehabilitation if disclosed, and information obtained upon a promise of confidentiality may all be withheld pursuant to Rule 32(c)(3) and PCRA. FOIA does not override these provisions. In fact, it ensures their vitality.[3] However, FOIA requires that "[a]ny reasonably segregable portion of a record shall be provided to any person requesting such record after deletion of the portions which are exempt under this subsection." 5 U.S.C. § 552(b). Thus, the Parole Commission has a duty under FOIA to release any nonexempt, segregable portions of a presentence investigation report to the requesting party. The burden is on the Commission to justify nondisclosure. *FBI v. Abramson*, 456 U.S. 615, 626, 102 S.Ct. 2054, 2061, 72 L.Ed.2d 376 (1982); *NLRB v. Robbins Tire and Rubber Co.*, 437 U.S. 214, 224, 98 S.Ct. 2311, 2318, 57 L.Ed.2d 159 (1978); *Lykins v. United States Department of Justice*, 725 F.2d 1455, 1462–63 (D.C.Cir.1984).

We conclude that neither Exemption 3 nor Exemption 5 provides a blanket exemption for presentence investigation reports. We recognize that the process of segregating nonexempt information from exempt information, and furnishing the nonexempt data to prisoners may be time consuming and expensive, but we are bound by the express language of 5 U.S.C. § 552(b). We expressly limit our holding to FOIA requests made by the subject of the presentence investigation report. FOIA exemptions which are inapplicable in this context may be applicable to third party requests for presentence reports. *See infra* n. 4.

A. *Exemption 3*

The statutory framework of FOIA requires the disclosure of agency records un-

---

2. Until recently the government asserted that presentence reports are not agency records since they are initially prepared by courts, which are not viewed as agencies under 5 U.S.C. § 551(1)(B). We rejected this argument in *Berry v. Department of Justice*, 733 F.2d 1343, 1349 (9th Cir.1984) (concluding that "court-generated documents are agency records if they are 1) in the possession of an agency and 2) prepared substantially to be relied upon in agency decisionmaking"). The First Circuit reached the opposite conclusion in *Crooker v. United States*

Parole Commission, 730 F.2d 1 (1st Cir.), *vacated and remanded*, 469 U.S. 926, 105 S.Ct. 317, 83 L.Ed.2d 255 (1984). The government abandoned its contention that presentence reports held by the Parole Commission are not agency records in the Solicitor General's certiorari petition in *Crooker*.

3. FOIA Exemption 3 allows the withholding of "matters that are specifically exempted from disclosure by statute." 5 U.S.C. § 552(b)(3).

less they may be withheld pursuant to one of the nine enumerated exemptions listed in 5 U.S.C. § 552(b); *United States v. Weber Aircraft Corp.*, 465 U.S. 792, 793–94, 104 S.Ct. 1488, 1489, 79 L.Ed.2d 814 (1984). Pursuant to Exemption 3, records may be withheld from disclosure that are

[S]pecifically exempted from disclosure by statute (other than section 552b of this title) provided that such statute (A) requires that the matters be withheld from public in such a manner as to leave no discretion on the issue, or (B) establishes particular criteria for withholding or refers to particular types of matters to be withheld.

5 U.S.C. § 552(b)(3). The government argues that Fed.R.Crim.P. 32(c)(3) and PCRA § 4208(c) specifically exempt presentence investigation reports from disclosure.

Neither Rule 32(c)(3) nor section 4208 of the PCRA establish complete exemptions. Each provision requires that presentence reports be disclosed to convicted defendants. In fact, Rule 32 was amended in 1983 to require disclosure to the defendant and his attorney even when they fail to request disclosure. This change in Rule 32 was prompted by findings that the disclosure of presentence reports was insufficient under the pre–1983 version of the rule to ensure accuracy of sentencing information. Fed.R.Crim.P. 32 advisory committee note. Thus, the provisions are exempting statutes only in the sense that they identify subclasses of information within the entire report that may be withheld.

Berry v. Department of Justice, 733 F.2d 1343 (9th Cir.1984)., was primarily concerned with the issue of whether presentence reports were agency records. In *Berry* we also considered the scope of Ex-

emption 3 in response to the government's claim that dissemination of presentence reports would improperly intrude on the prisoner's right to privacy and undermine the government's efforts to rehabilitate prisoners.[4] We found that PCRA was designed to maintain the confidentiality of specific portions of presentence reports and was therefore a withholding statute under Exemption 3. *Id* at 1354. However, we concluded only that *"potentially harmful parts* of the presentence report and Report on Sentenced Offender will not be disclosed under the FOIA." *Id.* (emphasis added). The clear implication of our holding in *Berry* was that Exemption 3 was not a valid basis for a *per se* exemption for presentence reports, but only allowed the withholding of those specific types of information expressly identified in section 4208(c) of PCRA.

Accordingly, we conclude that Exemption 3 permits withholding the probation officer's sentencing recommendation, diagnostic opinions which might disrupt the inmate's rehabilitation if disclosed, and information obtained on a promise of confidentiality and any other information which, if disclosed, might result in harm to any person. If there is data contained in the report which falls within the purview of section 4208(c), it may be withheld pursuant to Exemption 3. However, the Commission has a duty to supply the FOIA applicant "[a]ny reasonably segregable portion of a record ... after deletion of the portions which are exempt." 5 U.S.C. § 552(b). A presentence report containing none of the items specified in section 4208(c) should be disclosed in its entirety. The government bears the burden of justifying nondisclosure of any withheld

---

4. The government hypothesized in *Berry* and in the case at bar that if presentence reports are subject to disclosure under FOIA, there will be an avalanche of requests by third parties seeking prisoners' reports, who under FOIA will have just as much right to copies of the reports as the subjects of the reports themselves. Initially, FOIA Exemption 6, 5 U.S.C. § 552(b)(6), which exempts the disclosure of records "which would constitute a clearly unwarranted invasion of personal privacy" may provide an exemption

for requests by third parties. A presentence report typically contains highly personal data and its disclosure to third parties could constitute an unwarranted invasion of the subject's privacy. The exemption is inapplicable when the FOIA request is made by the subject of the report. Moreover, despite the government's forecast of doom, history has shown that third party requests for presentence reports are uncommon. *Berry*, 733 F.2d at 1352.

records or segments of records. *NLRB v. Robbins Tire and Rubber Co.*, 437 U.S. 214, 224, 98 S.Ct. 2311, 2318, 57 L.Ed.2d 159 (1978); *Lykins v. United States Department of Justice*, 725 F.2d 1455, 1462–63 (D.C.Cir.1984).

B. *Exemption 5*

Title 5, United States Code, section 552(b)(5) exempts from FOIA disclosure "inter-agency or intra-agency memorandums or letters which would not be available by law to a party other than an agency in litigation with the agency." The government contends that presentence investigation reports are exempt under this provision.

On its face, Exemption 5 could encompass virtually everything an agency reduces to writing. Note, *The Freedom of Information Act and The Exemption for Intra-Agency Memoranda*, 86 Harv.L.Rev. 1047, 1048 (1973). The provision has been construed narrowly to "exempt those documents, and only those documents, normally privileged in the civil discovery context." *NLRB v. Sears, Roebuck and Co.*, 421 U.S. 132, 149, 95 S.Ct. 1504, 1515, 44 L.Ed.2d 29 (1975). Thus, to invoke the protection of Exemption 5 the government must identify a privilege which it "enjoys under the relevant statutory and case law in the pretrial discovery context." *Renegotiation Board v. Grumman Aircraft Engineering Corp.*, 421 U.S. 168, 184, 95 S.Ct. 1491, 1500, 44 L.Ed.2d 57 (1975).

The Court of Appeals for the District of Columbia recently concluded that presentence reports fell within the purview of Exemption 5. *Durns v. Bureau of Prisons*, 804 F.2d 701, 702 (D.C.Cir.1986). Our analysis leads us to an opposite conclusion.[5]

The government has failed to identify an existing statutory or common law privilege that exempts presentence reports from discovery. The government apparently claims that section 4208(c) of PCRA and Rule 32(c)(3) create such a privilege or, in the alternative, that such a privilege may be inferred from a line of criminal cases where defendants requested presentence reports of codefendants to be used for impeachment purposes.

Rule 32 and PCRA do not create a civil discovery privilege. Both provisions mandate the disclosure of presentence reports to the subject of the report to ensure the report's accuracy. Each provision exempts a narrow class of information. However, these narrow exemptions do not create a blanket privilege for the entire report.

The government claims that a line of criminal cases creates a common law discovery privilege which justifies withholding presentence reports from the subject of the report. These cases hold that when a defendant requests a copy of a witness's presentence report for the purpose of impeaching the witness, the report will be disclosed only if it is necessary to meet the ends of justice.[6] These cases are inapposite when the party requesting the

---

5. The Court of Appeals for the District of Columbia found two recent Supreme Court cases addressing the scope of Exemption 5 persuasive. In *United States v. Weber Aircraft Corp.*, 465 U.S. 792, 104 S.Ct. 1488, 79 L.Ed.2d 814 (1984) the Court held that confidential statements obtained during an Air Force investigation of an airplane crash were protected from disclosure under Exemption 5. Such statements are privileged from discovery under the well-established rule of *Machin v. Zuckert*, 316 F.2d 336 (D.C. Cir.), *cert. denied*, 375 U.S. 896, 84 S.Ct. 172, 11 L.Ed.2d 124 (1963). Similarly, in *FTC v. Grolier, Inc.*, 462 U.S. 19, 103 S.Ct. 2209, 76 L.Ed.2d 387 (1983), the Supreme Court concluded that Exemption 5 encompasses the attorney work-product rule. In both cases the Supreme Court

applied Exemption 5 only after identifying a well recognized privilege. We do not find an established privilege in this case.

6. *See United States v. Anderson*, 724 F.2d 596 (7th Cir.1984); *United States v. Charmer Indus., Inc.*, 711 F.2d 1164 (2d Cir.1983); *United States v. Martinello*, 556 F.2d 1215 (5th Cir.1977); *United States v. Cyphers*, 553 F.2d 1064 (7th Cir.), *cert. denied*, 434 U.S. 843, 98 S.Ct. 142, 54 L.Ed.2d 107 (1977); *United States v. Dingle*, 546 F.2d 1378 (10th Cir.1976); *United States v. Figurski*, 545 F.2d 389 (4th Cir.1976); *United States v. Walker*, 491 F.2d 236 (9th Cir.), *cert. denied*, 416 U.S. 990, 94 S.Ct. 2399, 40 L.Ed.2d 769 (1974).

presentence report is the *subject* of the report. In the seminal decision on this subject, the Fourth Circuit stated

Rule 32(c)(3), F.R.Cr.P., relates to the disclosure of presentence reports, and it is applicable to reports made by the Bureau of Prisons under 18 U.S.C. § 4208(b). Rule 32(c)(3)(E). *In general, the rule provides for the disclosure of such reports to a defendant who is the subject of the report, or his counsel, except for certain information and recommendations that may be withheld. The rule is silent about disclosure to anyone else.* We are in accord with the construction placed on the rule in *Hancock Brothers, Inc. v. Jones*, 293 F.Supp. 1229, 1233 (N.D.Cal.1968): "information contained in a presentence report should not be disclosed to third parties unless lifting confidentiality is required to meet the ends of justice."

United States v. Figurski, 545 F.2d 389, 391 (4th Cir.1976) (emphasis added). *See also* Fennell and Hall, *supra* at 1683–84. The *Figurski* court recognized that Rule 32 and section 4208 require the disclosure of presentence reports to the subject of the report but that these provisions offer no guidance governing the disclosure of reports to third parties. Accordingly, the Fourth Circuit fashioned a different rule concerning disclosure requests made by third parties. However, the Fourth Circuit refused to tamper with the standards controlling disclosure to the subject of the report. *Figurski* and its progeny do not create a privilege which justifies withholding presentence reports when a FOIA re-

quest is made by the subject of the report. *See also United States v. Charmer Industries, Inc.*, 711 F.2d 1164, 1172–73 (2d Cir. 1983). In fact, *Figurski* expressly disavows this result.[7]

A rule that presentence reports are exempt from disclosure would not further the objectives underlying Exemption 5. Exemption 5 was created to prevent the disruption of a free flow of ideas, opinions, advice and frank discussions within agencies concerning their policies and programs. *See* S.Rep. No. 813, 89th Cong., 1st Sess. 9 (1965); H.R.Rep. No. 1497, 89th Cong., 2d Sess. 10 (1966), U.S.Code Cong. & Admin. News 1966, p. 2418. In furtherance of this objective the courts have allowed the government to withhold memoranda containing advice, opinions, recommendations and subjective analysis. Note, *supra* at 1049. However, communications containing purely factual material are not typically within the purview of Exemption 5. In *EPA v. Mink*, 410 U.S. 73, 93 S.Ct. 827, 35 L.Ed.2d 119, the Supreme Court held that

in the absence of a claim that disclosure would jeopardize state secrets, memoranda consisting only of compiled factual material or purely factual material contained in deliberative memoranda and severable from its context would generally be available for discovery by private parties in litigation with the Government.

EPA v. Mink, 410 U.S. at 87–88, 93 S.Ct. at 836 (citations omitted). *See also Mead Data Central, Inc. v. United States Department of the Air Force*, 566 F.2d 242, 256 (D.C.Cir.1977) ("Under this facet of exemption five, the courts have required

---

7. Even if the government could identify a common law or statutory privilege, it has waived its right to assert that privilege. Rule 32 and section 4208 of PCRA constitute a Congressional mandate which waives the government's privilege to withhold presentence reports from the subject of the report. The mandate is grounded in Congress' belief that convicted defendants must have an opportunity to read their presentence reports in order to ensure the accuracy of the information contained therein. The government asserts that there can be no waiver because convicted defendants, who are permitted to read their reports, are not allowed to copy them. This argument is meritless. In *Berry* we

stated that "FOIA speaks in terms of disclosure and nondisclosure. It does not recognize degrees of disclosure, such as permitting viewing, but not copying, of documents." *Berry*, 733 F.2d at 1355 n. 19. Thus, under FOIA, the government's required disclosure pursuant to Rule 32 and section 4208 of PCRA constitutes a waiver. It is irrelevant that the prisoners have never had the opportunity to copy their reports. *Cf. North Dakota ex rel. Olson v. Andrus*, 581 F.2d 177 (8th Cir.1978) (government waived right to claim privilege pursuant to Exemption 5 after voluntarily disclosing documents requested by North Dakota to the National Audobon Society in separate litigation).

disclosure of essentially factual material but allowed agencies to withhold documents which reveal their deliberative or policy-making processes").

A presentence investigation report is composed primarily of factual data about the prisoner. *See supra* p. 1414. This essentially factual, nonprivileged material may not be withheld under Exemption 5. *United States v. Weber Aircraft Corp.*, 465 U.S. at 800 n. 17, 104 S.Ct. at 1493 n. 17 (1984). Presentence reports exhibit none of the traditional indicia of privileged documents. They are not prepared with an expectation of secrecy.

In *EPA v. Mink*, the Supreme Court further observed that

Exemption 5 ... requires different treatment for materials reflecting deliberative or policy making processes on the one hand, and purely factual, investigative matters on the other.

Mink, 410 U.S. at 89, 93 S.Ct. at 837. The process of compiling presentence reports is primarily factual and investigative. Disclosure of presentence reports will not chill deliberative or policy-making processes. The government contends that disclosing the reports will hamper its efforts in obtaining information from confidential sources. This claim is untenable. Both Rule 32 and section 4208 of PCRA authorize withholding "information obtained upon a promise of confidentiality." Moreover, FOIA Exemption 7 allows withholding records which would "disclose the identity of a confidential source." 5 U.S.C. § 552(b)(7)(D). Thus, the government's resort to Exemption 5 for protection of data acquired from confidential sources is unnecessary.

We do not conclude that factual material can never qualify for protection under Exemption 5. We only hold that Exemption 5 does not create a *per se* exemption for presentence reports.

C. *PCRA and Rule 32 Do Not Supersede FOIA*

The government's final claim is that section 4208 and Rule 32(c)(3)(E) constitute an alternative disclosure scheme and, as such, supersede FOIA.

We addressed a similar argument in *Long v. IRS*, 742 F.2d 1173 (9th Cir.1984). In *Long*, the IRS argued that the Internal Revenue Code sections governing the confidentiality and disclosure of tax returns, 26 U.S.C. § 6103, preempted FOIA and provided the sole standard for disclosure of returns. We examined the text of section 6103 and its legislative history and found nothing to indicate that Congress intended section 6103 to operate independently of FOIA. Accordingly, we rejected the government's claim. *Long*, 742 F.2d at 1177.

Our analysis in *Long* requires us to find that FOIA is not implicitly supplanted by Rule 32 and section 4208 of PCRA. Nothing in the text of either provision or the legislative history of PCRA supports the claim that Congress intended to supersede FOIA.

The government relies on *Ricchio v. Kline*, 773 F.2d 1389 (D.C.Cir.1985), to support its contention that Rule 32 and PCRA supersede FOIA. In *Ricchio* the Court of Appeals for the District of Columbia held that a doctoral candidate's request of transcripts of tape recordings of White House conversations involving former President Nixon was governed by the Presidential Records and Materials Preservation Act, 44 U.S.C. § 2111, rather than FOIA. Without passing on the wisdom of this decision we observe that a more compelling argument for displacing FOIA could be made in *Ricchio* than in the instant case. The Materials Preservation Act, unlike PCRA, is a comprehensive, detailed and carefully tailored provision governing disclosure of Presidential records. In addition, the legislative history of the MPA indicates that Congress intended it to displace FOIA. *Ricchio*, 773 F.2d at 1392 (quoting H.R. Rep. No. 1507, 93 Cong., 2d Sess. 1 (1974)). In contrast, the scheme prescribed by Rule 32 and section 4208 does not approximate the specificity or particularity required to displace FOIA. Thus, we find that *Ricchio* is inapposite.

The judgments of the district courts are AFFIRMED.

VOLUME I

CHAPTER 3 POWER TO SUSPEND SENTENCE, A RIGHT TO PROBATION

There is little doubt that the sentencing judge has a wide range of discretion and can suspend a sentence, giving the defendant credit for a previous offense or for time spent in custody. Commonly, if upon retrial, a defendant is found guilty on one charge and not guilty on another and has spent more time in prison than the sentence of the crime for which he is found guilty, the defendant is entitled to credit for the time spent in custody. Few cases have challenged the power of the courts in such cases.

Another alternative of the court is to grant probation. Generally, a prisoner has no right to probation, but some cases seem to indicate the opposite. See Vol. I: 176. Still, in *People v. Allegri,* 487 N.E.2d 606 (Ill. 1985), set out here under Volume IV, Chapter 4, a defendant excused her violation of probation by insanity and insisted she had a right to probation. The court, calling probation a "privilege," refused to recognize her defense.

There are no cases that appear to challenge these concepts.

Introductions in previous volumes:

I: 141; VI: 45; VII: 29; VIII: 49.

VOLUME I

CHAPTER 4   IMPRISONMENT NOT A SANCTION FOR FINE

Restitution has become a more common requirement of sentencing. It may work as a fine in that it may be imposed as a requirement of probation and serve as a substitute for imprisonment. A problem arises when restitution is not paid, and the person is then sentenced to prison. *Bearden v. Georgia,* 103 S.Ct. 2064 (1983), held that the court could not revoke probation because the defendant failed to pay a fine and make restitution absent a showing that he was responsible for the failure and that any other form of punishment would be inadequate.

No cases decided during the period of this book seem to deal with restitution either as a substitute for imprisonment or as a form of punishment, although restitution has become a standard feature of sentencing. *Commonwealth of Kentucky v. Bailey,* 721 S.W.2d 706 (Ky. 1986), involved a Kentucky statute ordering restitution. Statutes providing restitution will become more prevalent, raising new issues for the courts.

Introductions in previous volumes:

I: 241; VI: 47; VII: 37; VIII: 71.

COMMONWEALTH of
Kentucky, Movant,

v.

Lowell T. BAILEY, Respondent.

Supreme Court of Kentucky.

Nov. 6, 1986.

Rehearing Denied Jan. 22, 1987.

GANT, Justice.

Respondent was indicted on four counts of theft by deception of over $100. He entered a plea of guilty to each count and was sentenced to four terms of three years each, to be served concurrently, and concurrently with an additional sentence respondent was serving from the Fayette Circuit Court. The offenses involved four worthless checks totalling $1,830.80.

Inasmuch as respondent was ineligible for probation, the Commonwealth sought to invoke the provisions of KRS 431.200, which reads as follows:

431.200 **Reparation for property stolen or damaged, from person convicted**

Any person convicted of a misdemeanor or felony for taking, injuring or destroying property shall restore the property or make reparation in damages if not ordered as a condition of probation. The court in which the conviction is had, if applied to by verified petition made within ninety (90) days of the date the sentence was pronounced, may order restitution or give judgment against the defendant for reparation in damages, and enforce collection by execution or other process. In a petition for restitution or reparation, the court shall cause the defendant, if in custody, to be brought into court, and demand of him if he has any defense to make to the petition. If he consents to the restitution or to reparation in damages in an agreed sum, the court shall give judgment accordingly. Otherwise a jury shall be impaneled to try the facts and ascertain the amount and the value of the property or assess the damage, as the case may be. A failure to pursue this remedy shall not deprive the person aggrieved of his civil action for the injury sustained.

Technically, the Commonwealth Attorney failed to precisely conform to the statute, as he proceeded by "Motion To Order Restitution" rather than by verified petition as required by the cited statute. However, no objection to form was made in the trial court, the Court of Appeals, or here. The remainder of the statute was complied with. The motion was filed within 30 days; the respondent was in custody; he was brought to court, along with his attorney; and a judgment and order of restitution was entered. The order itself directed three things. First, it directed the respondent to make designated restitution to each of the four victims. Second, it directed the Correction Cabinet or other custodian of the respondent or his records to notify the court of his date of release. Third, it directed the respondent to report to the Franklin Circuit Court at 9 a.m. on the first Monday following his release from incarceration for the purpose of establishing a payment schedule for restitution.

Conceding the authority of the trial court to grant the first part of the order (the restitution), under KRS 431.200, respondent appealed to the Court of Appeals on the second and third parts of the order (the enforcement portions), on the grounds that they were not explicitly authorized by statute and constituted imprisonment for debt in violation of § 18 of the Kentucky Constitution. The Court of Appeals reversed the Franklin Circuit Court on these two issues.

To dispose of the last argument, we find no imprisonment for debt or even threat thereof in the order of the Franklin Circuit Court, and this contention has no standing in this particular case.

It is the opinion of this court that the remedy provided under KRS 431.200 is an additional statutory remedy. It is exercised only if the defendant is in custody for the period immediately following his determination of guilt, and the last sentence of the statute specifically contrasts this action

with the civil action which may be filed by the person or persons aggrieved. The legislature has taken a commendable action to ascertain that the victim of a misdemeanor or felony involving the taking, injuring or destroying of his property may have a simple method of obtaining restitution of that property. It would be an anomaly to permit restitution to a victim as a part of the probation process of a first offender, which is recognized as available, and then to deny such restitution when the criminal, because of his own conduct, is ineligible for probation.

We also do not feel this is additional punishment exacted by the criminal justice system. It is neither imprisonment as envisioned by KRS Chapter 532, nor fine as set out in KRS Chapter 534. It is merely a system designed to restore property or the value thereof to the victim. It is not punishment to make the criminal give back something which was never his and which was obtained by him only by commission of a crime.

The present thrust of the law, through victims' relief funds, the Federal Victim and Witness Protection Act of 1982 (18 U.S.C. §§ 3579, 3580), etc., has been to assist the victim and to reduce the profit from crime. KRS 431.200 is but another step.

It is also not fatal to the judgment or order herein that the final establishment of the payment schedule for restitution was deferred until such time as respondent is released from custody. It is only then that the court and respondent will have the complete information from which a fair and comprehensive plan may be evolved, taking into consideration such things as employment, dependents, other debts, etc. Although deferment is not specifically mentioned in the statute, it is implicit that the court, once empowered to order restitution, may make such act workable, meaningful and considerate of the rights of all the parties.

Respondent argues that the Court of Appeals was correct in its holding that "... any orders by the trial court which purport to affect the appellant after his release from imprisonment are outside the scope of the statute and therefore invalid."

We feel this is error. A judgment was entered within 30 days from the date of conviction, and assumes the status of any other judgment. It is enforceable just as any other judgment is enforceable, by use of "execution or other process" as set out in the statute.

That portion of the opinion of the Court of Appeals affirming the order of restitution is affirmed. The remainder of the opinion is reversed, and the order of the Franklin Circuit Court is reinstated.

STEPHENS, C.J., and WHITE and WINTERSHEIMER, JJ., concur.

LEIBSON, STEPHENSON and VANCE, JJ., dissent.

STEPHENSON, J., files a dissenting opinion in which LEIBSON and VANCE, JJ., join.

STEPHENSON, Justice, dissenting.

I have an uncomfortable feeling when this court amends an act of the legislature by opinion.

The restitution statute, by its plain terms, entitles a victim to a *civil* judgment if he desires to pursue the right granted in the statute. The legislature was careful to avoid making this procedure an exclusive remedy by providing in the last sentence that failure to pursue the remedy in the statute should not deprive the victim of his civil action for the injury sustained.

The authority of the trial court to order a defendant into court for the purpose of restitution or reparation in damages is strictly statutory. This statute provides that the defendant, *if in custody*, may be ordered into court. The statute does not have any provision, nor is there any authority bestowed upon the trial court, to *order* the defendant into court after he is released from custody in order to establish a payment schedule.

The reasons set out in the majority opinion to justify ordering the defendant into court after release from custody may be desirable, but there is no authority, express or implied, for the trial court's action in this proceeding, and implying such authority effectively amends the statute.

This is a civil judgment and may be enforced according to well-established procedures. Established procedures and the statute do not provide for a coerced attendance in court in order for the court to establish a payment schedule. The trial court simply exceeded its authority in this order.

Accordingly, I dissent.

LEIBSON and VANCE, JJ., join in this dissent.

VOLUME I

CHAPTER 5   VALIDITY OR INVALIDITY OF MANDATORY SENTENCES

Frequently, mandatory sentences are required in certain drug dealing cases, following the third or fourth conviction of a crime of violence, and in similar circumstances. Such mandatory sentences generally have been upheld; however, the question arises as to the standard of proof required in a criminal case for imposing a mandatory sentence. For example, in providing a mandatory sentence for possession of a firearm during the commission of a crime, the question is whether the charge must be proven beyond a reasonable doubt. The Supreme Court of the United States has discussed this issue in the case of *McMillan v. Pennsylvania*, ——— U.S. ———, 106 S.Ct. 2411 (1986), which is included in this text.

Introductions in previous volumes:

I: 265; VI: 49; VII: 51; VIII: 81.

Dynel McMILLAN, Lorna Peterson,
James J. Dennison and Harold L.
Smalls, Petitioners

v.

PENNSYLVANIA.

No. 85–215.

Argued March 4, 1986.

Decided June 19, 1986.

Syllabus *

Pennsylvania's Mandatory Minimum   Sentencing Act (Act) provides that anyone

---

* The syllabus constitutes no part of the opinion of the Court but has been prepared by the Reporter of Decisions for the convenience of the reader. See *United States v. Detroit Lumber Co.,* 200 U.S. 321, 337, 26 S.Ct. 282, 284, 50 L.Ed. 499.

convicted of certain enumerated felonies is subject to a mandatory minimum sentence of five years' imprisonment if the sentencing judge—upon considering the evidence introduced at the trial and any additional evidence offered by either the defendant or the Commonwealth at the sentencing hearing—finds, by a preponderance of the evidence, that the defendant "visibly possessed a firearm" during the commission of the offense. The Act, which also provides that visible possession shall not be an element of the crime, operates to divest the judge of discretion to impose any sentence of less than five years for the underlying felony, but does not authorize a sentence in excess of that otherwise allowed for the offense. Each of the petitioners was convicted of one of the Act's enumerated felonies, and in each case the Commonwealth gave notice that at sentencing it would seek to proceed under the Act. However, each of the sentencing judges found the Act unconstitutional and imposed a lesser sentence than that required by the Act. The Pennsylvania Supreme Court consolidated the Commonwealth's appeals, vacated petitioners' sentences, and remanded for sentencing pursuant to the Act. The court held that the Act was consistent with due process, rejecting petitioners' principal argument that visible possession of a firearm was an element of the crimes for which they were sentenced and thus must be proved beyond a reasonable doubt under *In re Winship*, 397 U.S. 358, 90 S.Ct. 1068, 25 L.Ed.2d 368, and *Mullaney v. Wilbur*, 421 U.S. 684, 95 S.Ct. 1881, 44 L.Ed.2d 508.

Held:

1. A State may properly treat visible possession of a firearm as a sentencing consideration rather than an element of a particular offense that must be proved beyond a reasonable doubt. This case is controlled by *Patterson v. New York*, 432 U.S. 197, 97 S.Ct. 2319, 53 L.Ed.2d 281, which rejected a claim that whenever a State links the "severity of punishment" to the "presence or absence of an identified fact" the State must prove that fact beyond a

reasonable doubt. While there are constitutional limits beyond which the States may not go in this regard, the applicability of the reasonable-doubt standard is usually dependent on how a State defines the offense that is charged in any given case. Here, the Pennsylvania Legislature has made visible possession of a firearm a sentencing factor that comes into play only after the defendant has been found guilty of one of the enumerated crimes beyond a reasonable doubt, and the constitutional limits to a State's power are not exceeded by the Act, which only raises the minimum sentence that may be imposed and neither alters the maximum sentence nor creates a separate offense calling for a separate penalty. *Specht v. Patterson*, 386 U.S. 605, 87 S.Ct. 1209, 18 L.Ed.2d 326, distinguished. Pp. 2415–2419.

2. There is no merit to petitioners' contention that even though States may treat visible possession of a firearm as a sentencing consideration rather than an element of a particular offense, due process nonetheless requires that visible possession be proved by at least clear and convincing evidence. The preponderance standard satisfies due process. Sentencing courts have traditionally heard evidence and found facts without any prescribed burden of proof at all. Nothing in Pennsylvania's scheme warrants constitutionalizing burdens of proof at sentencing. Pp. 2419–2420.

3. Nor is there merit to petitioners' claim that the Act denies them their Sixth Amendment right to a trial by jury. There is no Sixth Amendment right to jury sentencing, even where the sentence turns on specific findings of fact. P. 2420.

508 Pa. 25, 494 A.2d 354, affirmed.

REHNQUIST, J., delivered the opinion of the Court, in which BURGER, C.J., and WHITE, POWELL, and O'CONNOR, JJ., joined. MARSHALL, J., filed a dissenting opinion, in which BRENNAN and BLACK-

MUN, JJ., joined. STEVENS, J., filed a dissenting opinion.

Leonard N. Sosnov, Philadelphia, Pa., for petitioners.

Steven J. Cooperstein, Philadelphia, Pa., for respondent.

Justice REHNQUIST delivered the opinion of the Court.

We granted certiorari to consider the constitutionality, under the Due Process Clause of the Fourteenth Amendment and the jury trial guarantee of the Sixth Amendment, of Pennsylvania's Mandatory Minimum Sentencing Act, 42 Pa.Const.Stat. § 9712 (1982) (the Act).

I

The Act was adopted in 1982. It provides that anyone convicted of certain enumerated felonies is subject to a mandatory minimum sentence of five years' imprisonment if the sentencing judge finds, by a preponderance of the evidence, that the person "visibly possessed a firearm" during the commission of the offense. At the sentencing hearing, the judge is directed to consider the evidence introduced at trial and any additional evidence offered by either the defendant or the Commonwealth. § 9712(b).[1] The Act operates to divest the judge of discretion to impose any sentence of less than five years for the underlying felony; it does not authorize a sentence in excess of that otherwise allowed for that offense.

Each petitioner was convicted of, among other things, one of § 9712's enumerated felonies. Petitioner McMillan, who shot his victim in the right buttock after an argument over a debt, was convicted by a jury of aggravated assault. Petitioner Peterson shot and killed her husband and, following a bench trial, was convicted of voluntary manslaughter. Petitioner Dennison shot and seriously wounded an acquaintance and was convicted of aggravated assault after a bench trial. Petitioner Smalls robbed a seafood store at gunpoint; follow-

---

1. Section 9712 provides in full:

"(a) Mandatory sentence.—Any person who is convicted in any court of this Commonwealth of murder of the third degree, voluntary manslaughter, rape, involuntary deviate sexual intercourse, robbery as defined in 18 Pa.C.S. § 3701(a)(1)(i), (ii) or (iii) (relating to robbery), aggravated assault as defined in 18 Pa.C.S. § 2702(a)(1) (relating to aggravated assault) or kidnapping, or who is convicted of attempt to commit any of these crimes, shall, if the person visibly possessed a firearm during the commission of the offense, be sentenced to a minimum sentence of at least five years of total confinement notwithstanding any other provision of this title or other statute to the contrary.

"(b) Proof at sentencing.—Provisions of this section shall not be an element of the crime and notice thereof to the defendant shall not be required prior to conviction, but reasonable notice of the Commonwealth's intention to proceed under this section shall be provided after conviction and before sentencing. The applicability of this section shall be determined at sentencing. The court shall consider any evidence presented at trial and shall afford the Commonwealth and the defendant an opportunity to present any necessary additional evidence and shall determine, by a preponderance of the evidence, if this section is applicable.

"(c) Authority of court in sentencing.—There shall be no authority in any court to impose on an offender to which this section is applicable any lesser sentence than provided for in subsection (a) or to place such offender on probation or to suspend sentence. Nothing in this section shall prevent the sentencing court from imposing a sentence greater than that provided in this section. Sentencing guidelines promulgated by the Pennsylvania Commission on Sentencing shall not supersede the mandatory sentences provided in this section.

"(d) Appeal by Commonwealth.—If a sentencing court refuses to apply this section where applicable, the Commonwealth shall have the right to appellate review of the action of the sentencing court. The appellate court shall vacate the sentence and remand the case to the sentencing court for imposition of a sentence in accordance with this section if it finds that the sentence was imposed in violation of this section.

"(e) Definition of firearm.—As used in this section 'firearm' means any weapon (including a starter gun) which will or is designed to or may readily be converted to expel a projectile by the action of an explosive or the expansion of gas therein."

ing a bench trial he was convicted of robbery. In each case the Commonwealth gave notice that at sentencing it would seek to proceed under the Act. No § 9712 hearing was held, however, because each of the sentencing judges before whom petitioners appeared found the Act unconstitutional; each imposed a lesser sentence than that required by the Act.[2]

The Commonwealth appealed all four cases to the Supreme Court of Pennsylvania. That Court consolidated the appeals and unanimously concluded that the Act is consistent with due process. 508 Pa. 25, 494 A.2d 354 (1985). Petitioners' principal argument was that visible possession of a firearm is an element of the crimes for which they were being sentenced and thus must be proved beyond a reasonable doubt under *In re Winship*, 397 U.S. 358, 90 S.Ct. 1068, 25 L.Ed.2d 368 (1970) and *Mullaney v. Wilbur*, 421 U.S. 684, 95 S.Ct. 1881, 44 L.Ed.2d 508 (1975). After observing that the legislature had expressly provided that visible possession "shall not be an element of the crime," § 9712(b), and that the reasonable doubt standard " 'has always been dependent on how a state defines the offense' " in question, 508 Pa., at 34, 494 A.2d, at 359, quoting *Patterson v. New York*, 432 U.S. 197, 211, n. 12, 97 S.Ct. 2319, 2327, n. 12, 53 L.Ed.2d 281 (1977), the Court rejected the claim that the Act effectively creates a new set of upgraded felonies of which visible possession is an "element." Section 9712, which comes into play only after the defendant has been convicted of an enumerated felony, neither provides for an increase in the maximum sentence for such felony nor authorizes a separate sentence; it merely requires a minimum sentence of five years, which may be more or less than the minimum sentence that might otherwise have been imposed. And consistent with *Winship*, *Mullaney*, and *Patterson*, the Act "creates no presumption as to any essential fact and places no burden on the defendant"; it "in no way relieve[s] the prosecution of its burden of proving guilt." 508 Pa., at 35, 494 A.2d, at 359.

Petitioners also contended that even if visible possession is not an element of the offense, due process requires more than proof by a preponderance of the evidence. The Supreme Court of Pennsylvania rejected this claim as well, holding that the preponderance standard satisfies due process under the approach set out in *Addington v. Texas*, 441 U.S. 418, 99 S.Ct. 1804, 60 L.Ed.2d 323 (1979). The Commonwealth's interest in deterring the illegal use of firearms and insure punishment for those who commit crimes with guns is as compelling as a convicted defendant's contervailing liberty interest, which has been substantially diminished by a guilty verdict. Moreover, the risk of error in the context of a § 9712 proceeding is comparatively slight—visible possession is a simple, straightforward issue susceptible of objective proof. On balance, the Court concluded, it is reasonable for the defendant and the Commonwealth to share equally in any risk of error. The Court vacated petitioners' sentences and remanded for sentencing pursuant to the Act. One Justice concurred and filed a separate opinion.

We granted certiorari, 474 U.S. ——, 106 S.Ct. 58, 88 L.Ed.2d 47 (1985), and now affirm.

---

2. McMillan was sentenced to a term of 3 to 10 years for aggravated assault; he was also convicted of possession of instruments of crime, 18 Pa.Cons.Stat. § 2503 (1982), for which he received a concurrent term of 2½ to 5 years. Peterson received a sentence of 1 to 6 years on the manslaughter charge, as well as a concurrent term of 6 to 18 months for possession of instruments of crime. Dennison received concurrent sentences of 11½ to 23 months for aggravated assault and possession of instruments of crime. Smalls was sentenced to concurrent 4- to 8-year terms for robbery and criminal conspiracy; he was also convicted of violating of the Uniform Firearms Act, § 6101 *et seq.*, and reckless endangerment, § 2705, for which he was sentenced to concurrent terms of 2½ to 5 years and 1 to 2 years respectively. He received a suspended sentence for possession of instruments of crime.

II

Petitioners argue that under the Due Process Clause as interpreted in *Winship* and *Mullaney*, if a State wants to punish visible possession of a firearm it must undertake the burden of proving that fact beyond a reasonable doubt. We disagree. *Winship* held that "the Due Process Clause protects the accused against conviction except upon proof beyond a reasonable doubt of every fact necessary to constitute the crime with which he is charged." 397 U.S., at 364, 90 S.Ct., at 1073. In *Mullaney v. Wilbur*, we held that the Due Process Clause "requires the prosecution to prove beyond a reasonable doubt the absence of the heat of passion on sudden provocation when the issue is properly presented in a homicide case." 421 U.S., at 704, 95 S.Ct., at 1892. But in *Patterson v. New York*, 432 U.S. 197, 97 S.Ct. 2319, 53 L.Ed.2d 281 (1977), we rejected the claim that whenever a State links the "severity of punishment" to "the presence or absence of an identified fact" the State must prove that fact beyond a reasonable doubt. *Id.*, at 214, 97 S.Ct., at 2329; see also *id.*, at 207, 97 S.Ct., at 2325 (State need not "prove beyond a reasonable doubt every fact, the existence or nonexistence of which it is willing to recognize as an exculpatory or mitigating circumstance affecting the degree of culpability or the severity of the punishment"). In particular, we upheld against a due process challenge New York's law placing on defendants charged with murder the burden of proving the affirmative defense of extreme emotional disturbance.

Patterson stressed that in determining what facts must be proved beyond a reasonable doubt the state legislature's definition of the elements of the offense is usually dispositive: "[T]he Due Process Clause requires the prosecution to prove beyond a reasonable doubt all of the elements *included in the definition of the offense* of which the defendant is charged." *Id.*, at 210, 97 S.Ct., at 2327 (emphasis added).

While "there are obviously constitutional limits beyond which the States may not go in this regard," *ibid.*, "[t]he applicability of the reasonable-doubt standard ... has always been dependent on how a State defines the offense that is charged in any given case," *id.*, at 211, n. 12, 97 S.Ct., at 2327. *Patterson* rests on a premise that bears repeating here:

"It goes without saying that preventing and dealing with crime is much more the business of the States than it is of the Federal Government, *Irvine v. California*, 347 U.S. 128, 134 [74 S.Ct. 381, 384, 98 L.Ed. 561] (1954) (plurality opinion), and that we should not lightly construe the Constitution so as to intrude upon the administration of justice by the individual States. Among other things, it is normally 'within the power of the State to regulate procedures under which its laws are carried out, including the burden of producing evidence and the burden of persuasion,' and its decision in this regard is not subject to proscription under the Due Process Clause unless 'it offends some principle of justice so rooted in the traditions and conscience of our people as to be ranked as fundamental.' *Speiser v. Randall*, 357 U.S. 513, 523 [78 S.Ct. 1332, 1341, 2 L.Ed.2d 1460] (1958)." *Id.* 432 U.S., at 201–202, 97 S.Ct., at 2322 (citations omitted).

We believe that the present case is controlled by *Patterson*, our most recent pronouncement on this subject, rather than by *Mullaney*. As the Supreme Court of Pennsylvania observed, the Pennsylvania legislature has expressly provided that visible possession of a firearm is not an element of the crimes enumerated in the mandatory sentencing statute, § 9712(b), but instead is a sentencing factor that comes into play only after the defendant has been found guilty of one of those crimes beyond a reasonable doubt. Indeed, the elements of the enumerated offenses, like the maximum permissible penalties for those offenses, were established long before the Mandatory Minimum Sentencing Act was passed.[3] While visible possession might well have been included as an element of the enumerated offenses, Pennsylvania chose not to redefine those offenses in order to so include it, and *Patterson* teaches that we should hesitate to conclude that due process bars the State from pursuing its chosen course in the area of defining crimes and prescribing penalties.

As *Patterson* recognized, of course, there are constitutional limits to the State's power in this regard; in certain limited circumstances *Winship*'s reasonable doubt requirement applies to facts not formally identified as elements of the offense charged. Petitioners argue that Pennsylvania has gone beyond those limits and that its formal provision that visible possession is not an element of the crime is therefore of no effect. We do not think so. While we have never attempted to define precisely the constitutional limits noted in *Patterson*, *i.e.*, the extent to which due process forbids the reallocation or reduction of burdens of proof in criminal cases, and do not do so today, we are persuaded by several factors that Pennsylvania's Mandatory Minimum Sentencing Act does not exceed those limits.

We note first that the Act plainly does not transgress the limits expressly set out in *Patterson*. Responding to the concern that its rule would permit States unbridled power to redefine crimes to the detriment of criminal defendants, the *Patterson* Court advanced the unremarkable proposition that the Due Process Clause precludes States from discarding the presumption of innocence:

" '[I]t is not within the province of a legislature to declare an individual guilty or presumptively guilty of a crime.' *McFarland v. American Sugar Rfg. Co.*,

241 U.S. 79, 86 [36 S.Ct. 498, 500, 60 L.Ed. 899] (1916). The legislature cannot 'validly command that the finding of an indictment, or mere proof of the identity of the accused, should create a presumption of the existence of all the facts essential to guilt.' *Tot v. United States*, 319 U.S. 463, 469 [63 S.Ct. 1241, 1246, 87 L.Ed. 1519] (1943)." *Patterson*, 432 U.S., at 210, 97 S.Ct., at 2327.

Here, of course, the Act creates no presumptions of the sort condemned in *McFarland v. American Sugar Rfg. Co.*, 241 U.S. 79, 36 S.Ct. 498, 60 L.Ed. 899 (1916) (presumption from price sugar refiner paid for sugar that refiner was party to a monopoly), or *Tot v. United States*, 319 U.S. 463, 63 S.Ct. 1241, 87 L.Ed. 1519 (1943) (presumption that convicted felon who possessed a weapon obtained it in interstate commerce). Nor does it relieve the prosecution of its burden of proving guilt; § 9712 only becomes applicable after a defendant has been duly convicted of the crime for which he is to be punished.

The Court in *Mullaney* observed, with respect to the main criminal statute invalidated in that case, that once the State proved the elements which Maine required it to prove beyond a reasonable doubt the defendant faced "a differential in sentencing ranging from a nominal fine to a mandatory life sentence." 421 U.S., at 700, 95 S.Ct., at 1890. In the present case the situation is quite different. Of the offenses enumerated in the Act, third-degree murder, robbery as defined in 18 Pa.Cons. Stat. § 3701(a)(1) (1982), kidnapping, rape, and involuntary deviate sexual intercourse are first-degree felonies subjecting the defendant to a maximum of 20 years' imprisonment. § 1103(1). Voluntary manslaughter and aggravated assault as defined in § 2702(a)(1) are felonies of the second degree carrying a maximum sentence of 10 years. § 1103(2). Section 9712 neither alters the maximum penalty for the crime committed nor creates a separate offense

3. The elements of the enumerated offenses were established in essentially their present form in 1972. See 1972 Pa.Laws No. 334, which compiled, amended and codified the Pennsylvania "Crimes Code." The Mandatory Minimum Sentencing Act was passed in 1982.

calling for a separate penalty; it operates solely to limit the sentencing court's discretion in selecting a penalty within the range already available to it without the special finding of visible possession of a firearm. Section 9712 "ups the ante" for the defendant only by raising to five years the minimum sentence which may be imposed within the statutory plan.[4] The statute gives no impression of having been tailored to permit the visible possession finding to be a tail which wags the dog of the substantive offense. Petitioner's claim that visible possession under the Pennsylvania statute is "really" an element of the offenses for which they are being punished—that Pennsylvania has in effect defined a new set of upgraded felonies—would have at least more superficial appeal if a finding of visible possession exposed them to greater or additional punishment, cf. 18 U.S.C. § 2113(d) (providing separate and greater punishment for bank robberies accomplished through "use of a dangerous weapon or device"), but it does not.

Petitioners contend that this Court's decision in *Specht v. Patterson*, 386 U.S. 605, 87 S.Ct. 1209, 18 L.Ed.2d 326 (1967), requires the invalidation of the Pennsylvania statute challenged here. Again, we think petitioners simply read too much into one of our previous decisions. Under the Colorado scheme at issue in *Specht*, conviction of a sexual offense otherwise carrying a maximum penalty of 10 years exposed a defendant to an indefinite term to and including life imprisonment if the sentencing judge made a post-trial finding that the defendant posed "a threat of bodily harm to members of the public, or is an habitual

offender and mentally ill," *id.*, at 607, 87 S.Ct., at 1211. This finding could be made, without notice or any "hearing in the normal sense," based solely on a presentence psychiatric report. *Id.*, at 608, 87 S.Ct., at 1211. This Court held that the Colorado scheme failed to satisfy the requirements of due process, and that the defendant had a right to be present with counsel, to be heard, to be confronted with and to cross-examine the witnesses against him, and to offer evidence of his own.

Petitioners suggest that had *Winship* already been decided at the time of *Specht*, the Court would have also required that the burden of proof as to the post-trial findings be beyond a reasonable doubt. But even if we accept petitioners' hypothesis, we do not think it avails them here. The Court in *Specht* observed that following trial the Colorado defendant was confronted with "a radically different situation" from the usual sentencing proceeding. The same simply is not true under the Pennsylvania statute. The finding of visible possession of a firearm of course "ups the ante" for a defendant, or it would not be challenged here; but it does so only in the way that we have previously mentioned, by raising the minimum sentence that may be imposed by the trial court.

Finally, we note that the specter raised by petitioners of States restructuring existing crimes in order to "evade" the commands of *Winship* just does not appear in this case.[5] As noted above, § 9712's enumerated felonies retain the same elements they had before the Mandatory Minimum Sentencing Act was passed. The

---

4. By prescribing a mandatory minimum sentence, the Act incidentally serves to restrict the sentencing court's discretion in setting a maximum sentence. Pennsylvania law provides that a minimum sentence of confinement "shall not exceed one-half of the maximum sentence imposed." 42 Pa.Cons.Stat. § 9756(b) (1982). Thus, the shortest maximum term permissible under the Act is 10 years.

5. We reject the view that anything in the Due Process Clause bars States from making changes

in their criminal law that have the effect of making it easier for the prosecution to obtain convictions. "From the vantage point of the Constitution, a change in law favorable to defendants is not necessarily good, nor is an innovation favorable to the prosecution necessarily bad." Jeffries & Stephan, Defenses, Presumptions, and Burden of Proof in the Criminal Law, 88 Yale L.J. 1325, 1361 (1979).

Pennsylvania legislature did not change the definition of any existing offense. It simply took one factor that has always been considered by sentencing courts to bear on punishment—the instrumentality used in committing a violent felony—and dictated the precise weight to be given that factor if the instrumentality is a firearm. Pennsylvania's decision to do so has not transformed against its will a sentencing factor into an "element" of some hypothetical "offense."

Petitioners seek support for their due process claim by observing that many legislatures have made possession of a weapon an element of various aggravated offenses.[6] But the fact that the States have formulated different statutory schemes to punish armed felons is merely a reflection of our federal system, which demands "[t]olerance for a spectrum of state procedures dealing with a common problem of law enforcement," *Spencer v. Texas*, 385 U.S. 554, 566, 87 S.Ct. 648, 655, 17 L.Ed.2d 606 (1967). That Pennsylvania's particular approach has been adopted in few other States does not render Pennsylvania's choice unconstitutional.[7] See *Patterson*, 432 U.S., at 211, 97 S.Ct., at 2327; cf. *Spaziano v. Florida*, 468 U.S. 447, ——, 104 S.Ct. 3154, ——, 82 L.Ed.2d 340 (1984). Nor does the historical test advanced by the *Patterson* dissent, on which petitioners apparently also rely, materially advance their cause. While it is surely true that "[f]or hundreds of years some offenses have been considered more serious and the punishment made more severe if the offense was committed with a weapon or while armed," Brief for Petitioners 17, n. 11, petitioners do not contend that the particular factor made relevant here—visible

possession of a firearm—has historically been treated "in the Anglo-American legal tradition" as requiring proof beyond a reasonable doubt, *Patterson*, 432 U.S., at 226, 97 S.Ct., at 2335 (POWELL, J., dissenting). See also *id.*, at 229, n. 14, 97 S.Ct., at 2337, n. 14 (POWELL, J., dissenting) (approving new scheme under which State put burden on armed robbery defendant to prove that gun was unloaded or inoperative in order to receive lower sentence).

We have noted a number of differences between this case and *Winship*, *Mullaney*, and *Specht*, and we find these differences controlling here. Our inability to lay down any "bright line" test may leave the constitutionality of statutes more like those in *Mullaney* and *Specht* than is the Pennsylvania statute to depend on differences of degree, but the law is full of situations in which differences of degree produce different results. We have no doubt that Pennsylvania's Mandatory Minimum Sentencing Act falls on the permissible side of the constitutional line.

III

Having concluded that States may treat "visible possession of a firearm" as a sentencing consideration rather than an element of a particular offense, we now turn to petitioners' subsidiary claim that due process nonetheless requires that visible possession be proved by at least clear and convincing evidence. Like the court below, we have little difficulty concluding that in this case the preponderance standard satisfies due process. Indeed, it would be extraordinary if the Due Process Clause as understood in *Patterson* plainly sanctioned Pennsylvania's scheme, while the same

---

6. The Commonwealth argues that the statutes on which petitioners rely typically differ from that at issue here. In particular, most of the statutes are directed at all deadly weapons rather than just firearms, and most treat the armed crime as a higher grade of offense than the unarmed crime. Brief for Respondent 11.

7. At least two States—New Jersey, see N.J.Stat. Ann. § 2C:43–6c (West 1982); *State v. Gantt*, 186 N.J.Super. 262, 452 A.2d 477 (1982), aff'd, 195 N.J.Super. 144, 478 A.2d 422 (App.Div.1984), and Kansas, see Kan.Stat.Ann. § 21–4618 (1981); *State v. Mullins*, 223 Kan. 798, 577 P.2d 51 (1978)—have statutory schemes similar to Pennsylvania's.

clause explained in some other line of less clearly relevant cases imposed more stringent requirements. There is, after all, only one Due Process Clause in the Fourteenth Amendment. Furthermore, petitioners 'do not and could not claim that a sentencing court may never rely on a particular fact in passing sentence without finding that fact by "clear and convincing evidence." Sentencing courts have traditionally heard evidence and found facts without any prescribed burden of proof at all. See *Williams v. New York*, 337 U.S. 241, 69 S.Ct. 1079, 93 L.Ed. 1337 (1949). Pennsylvania has deemed a particular fact relevant and prescribed a particular burden of proof. We see nothing in Pennsylvania's scheme that would warrant constitutionalizing burdens of proof at sentencing.[8]

Petitioners apparently concede that Pennsylvania's scheme would pass constitutional muster if only it did not remove the sentencing court's discretion, *i.e.*, if the legislature had simply directed the court to *consider* visible possession in passing sentence. Brief for Petitioners 31–32. We have some difficulty fathoming why the due process calculus would change simply because the legislature has seen fit to provide sentencing courts with additional guidance. Nor is there merit to the claim that a heightened burden of proof is required because visible possession is a fact "concerning the crime committed" rather than the background or character of the defendant. *Ibid.* Sentencing courts necessarily consider the circumstances of an offense in selecting the appropriate punishment, and

we have consistently approved sentencing schemes that mandate consideration of facts related to the crime, *e.g.*, *Proffitt v. Florida*, 428 U.S. 242, 96 S.Ct. 2960, 49 L.Ed.2d 913 (1976), without suggesting that those facts must be proved beyond a reasonable doubt. The Courts of Appeals have uniformly rejected due process challenges to the preponderance standard under the federal "dangerous special offender" statute, 18 U.S.C. § 3575, which provides for an enhanced sentence if the court concludes that the defendant is both "dangerous" and a "special offender." See *United States v. Davis*, 710 F.2d 104, 106 (CA3) (collecting cases), cert. denied, 464 U.S. 1001, 104 S.Ct. 505, 78 L.Ed.2d 695 (1983).

IV

In light of the foregoing, petitioners' final claim—that the Act denies them their Sixth Amendment right to a trial by jury—merits little discussion. Petitioners again argue that the jury must determine all ultimate facts concerning the offense committed. Having concluded that Pennsylvania may properly treat visible possession as a sentencing consideration and not an element of any offense, we need only note that there is no Sixth Amendment right to jury sentencing, even where the sentence turns on specific findings of fact. See *Spaziano v. Florida*, 468 U.S., at ——, 104 S.Ct., at ——.

For the foregoing reasons, the judgment of the Supreme Court of Pennsylvania is affirmed.

It is so ordered.

---

8. *Addington v. Texas*, 441 U.S. 418, 99 S.Ct. 1804, 60 L.Ed.2d 323 (1979), and *Santosky v. Kramer*, 455 U.S. 745, 102 S.Ct. 1388, 71 L.Ed.2d 599 (1982), which respectively applied the "clear and convincing evidence" standard where the State sought involuntary commitment to a mental institution and involuntary termination of parental rights, are not to the contrary. Quite unlike the situation in those cases, criminal sentencing takes place only after a defendant has been adjudged guilty beyond a reasonable doubt. Once the reasonable doubt standard has been applied to obtain a valid conviction, "the criminal defendant has been constitutionally de-

prived of his liberty to the extent that the State may confine him." *Meachum v. Fano*, 427 U.S. 215, 224, 96 S.Ct. 2532, 2538, 49 L.Ed.2d 451 (1976). As noted in text, sentencing courts have always operated without constitutionally imposed burdens of proof; embracing petitioners' suggestion that we apply the clear and convincing standard here would significantly alter criminal sentencing, for we see no way to distinguish the visible possession finding at issue here from a host of other express or implied findings sentencing judges typically make on the way to passing sentence.

Justice MARSHALL, with whom Justice BRENNAN and Justice BLACKMUN join, dissenting.

I agree with much in Justice STEVENS' dissent, *post*, at 2421. Whether a particular fact is an element of a criminal offense that, under *In re Winship*, 397 U.S. 358, 90 S.Ct. 1068, 25 L.Ed.2d 368 (1970), must be proved by the prosecution beyond a reasonable doubt is a question that must be decided by this Court and cannot be abdicated to the States. "[I]f *Winship* were limited to those facts that constitute a crime as defined by state law, a State could undermine many of the interests that decision sought to protect without effecting any substantive change in its law." *Mullaney v. Wilbur*, 421 U.S. 684, 698, 95 S.Ct. 1881, 1889, 44 L.Ed.2d 508 (1975). The deference that the majority gives to the Pennsylvania legislature's statement that the visible possession of a firearm should not be considered an element of the crime defined by 42 Pa.Cons.Stat. § 9712 (1982) is thus wholly inappropriate.

I would not, however, rely in this case on the formalistic distinction between aggravating and mitigating facts. The "continued functioning of the democratic process," *post*, at 2424 (Justice STEVENS, dissenting), might provide us with some assurance that States will not circumvent the guarantee of *Winship* by criminalizing seemingly innocuous conduct and then placing the burden on the defendant to establish an affirmative defense, *post*, at ——. But this Court nonetheless must remain ready to enforce that guarantee should the State, by placing upon the defendant the burden of proving certain mitigating facts, effectively lighten the constitutional burden of the prosecution with respect to the elements of the crime. See *Patterson v. New York*, 432 U.S. 197, 206–207, 97 S.Ct. 2319, 2324–2325, 53 L.Ed.2d 281 (1977) (allowing State to require defendant to prove extreme emotional disturbance by preponderance of the evidence but noting that this affirmative defense "does not serve to negative any facts of the crime which the State is to prove in order to convict of murder").

I would put off until next Term any discussion of how mitigating facts should be analyzed under *Winship*. This issue will be aired when the Court considers *Martin v. Ohio*, 21 Ohio St.3d 91, 488 N.E.2d 166, cert. granted, 475 U.S. ——, 106 S.Ct. 1634, 90 L.Ed.2d 180 (1986), in which a defendant challenges Ohio's requirement that the accused bear the burden of proving a claim of self-defense by a preponderance of the evidence. For now, it is enough to agree with Justice STEVENS that "if a state provides that a specific component of a prohibited transaction shall give rise both to a special stigma and to a special punishment, that component must be treated as a 'fact necessary to constitute the crime' within the meaning of our holding in *In re Winship*," *post*, at 2426. Pennsylvania has attached just such consequences to a finding that a defendant "visibly possessed a firearm" during the commission of any aggravated assault, and, under *Winship*, the prosecution should not be relieved of proving that fact beyond a reasonable doubt. I dissent.

Justice STEVENS, dissenting.

Petitioner Dennison, a 73-year-old man, committed an aggravated assault upon a neighborhood youth whom he suspected of stealing money from his house. After a trial at which the Commonwealth proved the elements of the offense of aggravated assault beyond a reasonable doubt, the trial judge imposed a sentence of imprisonment of 11½ to 23 months. Because he had concluded that Pennsylvania's recently enacted Mandatory Minimum Sentencing Act, 42 Pa.Cons.Stat. § 9712 (1982), was unconstitutional, the trial judge refused to impose the 5–year minimum sentence mandated by that Act whenever the Commonwealth proves—by a preponderance of the evidence—that the defendant "visibly possessed a firearm during the commission of the offense," § 9712(b).

The judge presiding over Dennison's trial, as well as the judges in the other three petitioners' trials and the superior court judges hearing the appeals, all concluded that visible possession of a firearm was an element of the offense. " 'Visibly possessed a firearm' is inarguably language which refers to behavior which the legislature intended to prohibit." App. to Pet. for Cert. A35. As a consequence, the prohibited conduct had to be established by proof beyond a reasonable doubt. The Pennsylvania Supreme Court agreed that visible possession of a firearm is conduct that the Pennsylvania General Assembly intended to prohibit, *Commonwealth v. Wright*, 508 Pa. 25, 42, 494 A.2d 354, 363 (1985) (Larsen, J., concurring); *id.*, at 49, 494 A.2d, at 366 (concurring opinion joined by the majority opinion), and it recognized that evidence of such conduct would mandate a *minimum* sentence of imprisonment more than twice as severe as the *maximum* the trial judge would otherwise have imposed on petitioner Dennison, *id.*, at 28, n. 1, 494 A.2d, at 356, n. 1. But it nonetheless held that visible possession of a firearm was not an element of the offense because the Pennsylvania General Assembly had the foresight to declare in § 9712(b) that "Provisions of this section shall not be an element of the crime."

It is common ground that "the Due Process Clause requires the prosecution to prove beyond a reasonable doubt all of the elements included in the definition of the offense of which the defendant is charged." *Patterson v. New York*, 432 U.S. 197, 210, 97 S.Ct. 2319, 2327, 53 L.Ed.2d 281 (1977). Today the Court holds that state legislatures may not only define the offense with which a criminal defendant is charged, but may authoritatively determine that the conduct so described—*i.e.*,

the prohibited activity which subjects the defendant to criminal sanctions—is *not* an element of the crime which the Due Process Clause requires to be proved by the prosecution beyond a reasonable doubt. In my view, a state legislature may not dispense with the requirement of proof beyond a reasonable doubt for conduct that it targets for severe criminal penalties. Because the Pennsylvania statute challenged in this case describes conduct that the Pennsylvania legislature obviously intended to prohibit, and because it mandates lengthy incarceration for the same, I believe that the conduct so described is an element of the criminal offense to which the proof beyond a reasonable doubt requirement applies.

Once a State defines a criminal offense, the Due Process Clause requires it to prove any component of the prohibited transaction that gives rise to both a special stigma and a special punishment beyond a reasonable doubt. This much has been evident at least since *In re Winship*, 397 U.S. 358, 90 S.Ct. 1068, 25 L.Ed.2d 368 (1970). In that case, the Court "explicitly" held that "the Due Process Clause protects the accused against conviction except upon proof beyond a reasonable doubt of every fact necessary to constitute the crime with which he is charged." *Id.*, at 364, 90 S.Ct., at 1073. In reasoning to this conclusion the Court reviewed the heritage of the rule that Justice Frankfurter characterized as "basic in our law and rightly one of the boasts of a free society,"[1] and—of critical importance to the decision before us—explained the reasons that undergird the rule:

"The reasonable-doubt standard plays a vital role in the American scheme of criminal procedure. It is a prime instrument for reducing the risk of convictions resting on factual error. The standard provides concrete substance for the presumption of innocence—that bedrock 'ax-

---

1. *Leland v. Oregon*, 343 U.S. 790, 803, 72 S.Ct. 1002, 1009, 96 L.Ed. 1302 (1952) (Frankfurter, J., dissenting). Later in his opinion he noted that the "duty of the State of establishing every fact of the equation which adds up to a crime,

and of establishing it to the satisfaction of a jury beyond a reasonable doubt is the decisive difference between criminal culpability and civil liability." *Id.*, at 805, 72 S.Ct., at 1011.

iomatic and elementary' principle whose 'enforcement lies at the foundation of the administration of our criminal law.' *Coffin v. United States*, [156 U.S. 432,] 453 [15 S.Ct. 394, 403, 39 L.Ed. 481 (1895)]. As the dissenters in the New York Court of Appeals observed, and we agree, 'a person accused of a crime ... would be at a severe disadvantage, a disadvantage amounting to a lack of fundamental fairness, if he could be adjudged guilty and imprisoned for years on the strength of the same evidence as would suffice in a civil case.' 24 N.Y.2d [196], 205 [299 N.Y.S.2d 414, 420], 247 N.E.2d [253], 259 [1969].

"The requirement of proof beyond a reasonable doubt has this vital role in our criminal procedure for cogent reasons. The accused during a criminal prosecution has at stake interests of immense importance, both because of the possibility that he may lose his liberty upon conviction and because of the certainty that he would be stigmatized by the conviction. Accordingly, a society that values the good name and freedom of every individual should not condemn a man for commission of a crime when there is reasonable doubt about his guilt." *Id.*, at 363–364, 90 S.Ct., at 1072. *In re Winship* thus took a purposive approach to the constitutional standard of proof: when the State threatens to stigmatize or incarcerate an individual for engaging in prohibited conduct, it may do so only if it proves the elements of the prohibited transaction beyond a reasonable doubt.[2]

It is true, as the Court points out, that " '[t]he applicability of the reasonable-doubt standard ... has always been dependent on how a State defines the offense that is charged in any given case.' " See *ante*, at 2416 (quoting *Patterson v. New York*, 432 U.S., at 211, n. 12, 97 S.Ct., at

2327, n. 12). A State's freedom in this regard, however, has always been understood to reflect the uncontroversial proposition that a State has power, subject of course to constitutional limits, to attach criminal penalties to a wide variety of objectionable transactions; when it does so, the prosecution need establish beyond a reasonable doubt only the constituent elements of the specified criminal transaction. Nothing in *Patterson* or any of its predecessors authorizes a State to decide for itself which of the ingredients of the prohibited transaction are "elements" that it must prove beyond a reasonable doubt at trial.

Indeed, contrary to the supposition of the majority, *Patterson v. New York* is entirely in keeping with the limit on state definitional power implied in *Winship*. Patterson was charged with second-degree murder, a crime which in New York included two elements: " 'intent to cause the death of another person' " and " 'caus[ing] the death of such person or of a third person.' " 432 U.S., at 198, 97 S.Ct., at 2321 (quoting N.Y. Penal Law § 125.25 (McKinney 1975)). "Malice aforethought [was] not an element of the crime." 432 U.S., at 198, 97 S.Ct., at 2321. Because "causing the death of another person with intent to do so," *id.*, at 205, 97 S.Ct., at 2324, was "an act which ... the State may constitutionally criminalize and punish," *id.*, at 209, 97 S.Ct., at 2326; accord, *id.*, at 208, 97 S.Ct., at 2326, and because New York in fact proscribed and punished that conduct, *id.*, at 206, 97 S.Ct., at 2324, the Court upheld the State's refusal to "prove beyond a reasonable doubt every fact, the existence or nonexistence of which it [was] willing to recognize as an *exculpatory or mitigating circumstance* affecting the degree of culpability or the severity of the punishment," *id.*, at 207, 97 S.Ct., at 2325 (emphasis added)—in that case, the affirmative

---

2. "The combination of stigma and loss of liberty involved in a conditional or absolute sentence of imprisonment sets that sanction apart from anything else the law imposes." Packer, *Mens Rea* and the Supreme Court, 1962 Sup.Ct.Rev. 107, 150. The requirement that conduct subject-

ing an individual to a special stigma and a special punishment be proved beyond a reasonable doubt therefore casts no doubt on the constitutionality of criminal restitution ordered on a lesser standard of proof.

defense of extreme emotional disturbance. The Court explained that "the Due Process' Clause did not invalidate every instance of burdening the defendant with proving *an exculpatory fact.*" *Id.,* at 203, n. 9, 97 S.Ct., at 2323, n. 9 (emphasis added). "To recognize at all a *mitigating circumstance* does not require the State to prove its nonexistence in each case in which the fact is put in issue." *Id.,* at 209, 97 S.Ct., at 2326 (emphasis added). *Patterson* thus clarified that the Due Process Clause requires proof beyond a reasonable doubt of conduct which exposes a criminal defendant to greater stigma or punishment, but does not likewise constrain state reductions of criminal penalties—even if such reductions are conditioned on a prosecutor's failure to prove a fact by a preponderance of the evidence or on proof supplied by the criminal defendant.[3]

The distinction between aggravating and mitigating facts has been criticized as formalistic. But its ability to identify genuine constitutional threats depends on nothing more than the continued functioning of the democratic process. To appreciate the difference between aggravating and mitigating circumstances, it is important to remember that although states may reach the same destination either by criminalizing conduct and allowing an affirmative defense, or by prohibiting lesser conduct and enhancing the penalty, legislation proceeding along these two paths is very different even if it might theoretically achieve the same result. Consider, for example, a statute making presence "in any private or public place" a "felony punishable by up to five years imprisonment" and yet allowing "an affirmative defense for the defendant to prove, to a preponderance of the evidence, that he was not robbing a bank." Dutile, The Burden of Proof in Criminal Cases: A Comment on the *Mullaney-Patterson* Doctrine, 55 Notre Dame Law. 380, 383 (1980). No democratically-elected legislature would enact such a law, and if it did, a broad-based coalition of bankers and bank customers would soon see the legislation repealed.[4] Nor is there a serious dan-

---

3. The *Patterson* Court also recognized other "constitutional limits beyond which the States may not go in this regard," 432 U.S., at 210, 97 S.Ct., at 2327, citing *Tot v. United States,* 319 U.S. 463, 469, 63 S.Ct. 1241, 1245, 87 L.Ed. 1519 (1943), and other cases invalidating statutory presumptions. It was on the basis of these cases that *Patterson* distinguished the Maine statute struck down in *Mullaney v. Wilbur,* 421 U.S. 684, 95 S.Ct. 1881, 44 L.Ed.2d 508 (1975). The Maine murder statute prescribed life imprisonment for "Whoever unlawfully kills a human being *with malice aforethought,*" Me.Rev. Stat.Ann., Tit. 17, § 2651 (1964) (emphasis added), and the trial judge had charged the jury that "'malice aforethought is an essential and indispensable element of the crime of murder," *Mullaney v. Wilbur,* 421 U.S., at 686, 95 S.Ct., at 1883 (quoting App. in No. 74-13, O.T. 1974, p. 40). Likewise, the Government conceded that the federal enactment in *Tot* proscribed only receipt of firearms in interstate commerce. See *Tot v. United States,* 319 U.S., at 466, 63 S.Ct., at 1244. *Patterson* clarified that *Mullaney,* like *Tot,* stood for the proposition that "shifting of the burden of persuasion with respect to a fact which the State deems so important that it must be either proved or *presumed* is impermissible under the Due Process Clause." 432 U.S., at 215, 97 S.Ct., at 2329 (emphasis added). Cf. *United States v. Romano,* 382 U.S. 136, 138, 144, 86 S.Ct. 279, 280, 283, 15 L.Ed.2d 210 (1965).

Thus, although Maine could have punished all unlawful, intentional killings with life imprisonment, just as Congress in *Tot* could have punished possession of a firearm by one convicted of a crime of violence, in neither case did the legislature do so. This explanation, although not entirely satisfactory, see *State v. Lafferty,* 309 A.2d 647, 664–665 (Me.1973); *id.,* at 672–673 (Wernick, J., concurring), is consistent with the Maine Supreme Court's explanation on direct appeal that State law presumed malice. See *State v. Wilbur,* 278 A.2d 139, 145–146 (Me. 1971). The state court downplayed this presumption because "no burden is imposed upon defendant until the State has first convinced the jury beyond a reasonable doubt that defendant is guilty of a voluntary and intentional homicide," at which point the issue "is no longer guilt or innocence of felonious homicide but rather the degree of the homicide." *Id.,* at 146. As we held in *Mullaney,* "[t]he safeguards of due process are not rendered unavailable simply because a determination may already have been reached that would stigmatize the defendant and that might lead to a significant impairment of personal liberty." 421 U.S., at 698, 95 S.Ct., at 1889. Accord, *Specht v. Patterson,* 386 U.S. 605, 608–611, 87 S.Ct. 1209, 1211–1213, 18 L.Ed.2d 326 (1967).

4. Cf. Ashford & Risinger, Presumptions, Assumptions, and Due Process in Criminal Cases:

ger that a state will soon define murder to be the "mere physical contact between the defendant and the victim leading to the victim's death, but then set up an affirmative defense leaving it to the defendant to prove that he acted without culpable *mens rea." Patterson v. New York*, 432 U.S., at 224, n. 8, 97 S.Ct., at 2334, n. 8 (POWELL, J., dissenting). No legislator would be willing to expose himself to the severe opprobrium and punishment meted out to murderers for an accidental stumble on the subway. For similar reasons, it can safely be assumed that a State will not "define all assaults as a single offense and then require the defendant to disprove the elements of aggravation." *Mullaney v. Wilbur*, 421 U.S. 684, 699, n. 24, 95 S.Ct. 1881, 1890, n. 24, 44 L.Ed.2d 508 (1975). The very inconceivability of the hypothesized legislation—all of which has been sincerely offered to illustrate the dangers of permitting legislative mitigation of punishment in derogation of the requirement of proof beyond a reasonable doubt—is reason enough to feel secure that it will not command a majority of the electorate.[5]

It is not at all inconceivable, however, to fear that a State might subject those individuals convicted of engaging in antisocial conduct to further punishment for aggravating conduct not proved beyond a reasonable doubt. As this case demonstrates, a State may seek to enhance the deterrent effect of its law forbidding the use of firearms in the course of felonies by mandat-

ing a minimum sentence of imprisonment upon proof by a preponderance against those already convicted of specified crimes. But *In re Winship* and *Patterson* teach that a State may not advance the objectives of its criminal laws at the expense of the accurate fact-finding owed to the criminally accused who suffer the risk of nonpersuasion.

It would demean the importance of the reasonable doubt standard—indeed, it would demean the Constitution itself—if the substance of the standard could be avoided by nothing more than a legislative declaration that prohibited conduct is not an "element" of a crime. A legislative definition of an offense named "assault" could be broad enough to encompass every intentional infliction of harm by one person upon another, but surely the legislature could not provide that only that fact must be proved beyond a reasonable doubt and then specify a range of increased punishments if the prosecution could show by a preponderance of the evidence that the defendant robbed, raped, or killed his victim "during the commission of the offense."

Appropriate respect for the rule of *In re Winship* requires that there be some constitutional limits on the power of a State to define the elements of criminal offenses. The high standard of proof is required because of the immense importance of the individual interest in avoiding both the loss of liberty and the stigma that results from

A Theoretical Overview, 79 Yale L.J. 165, 178 (1969) ("In the first statute, a legislature has deemed three factors germane to punishment: (a) presence of the individual; (b) the presence of narcotics in the house; and (c) the defendant's knowledge. In the second statute, only two factors are deemed germane to whether an individual will be punished: (a) presence of the individual; (b) the presence of narcotics in the house. The electorate might approve of the passage of the first statute, but not the passage of the second. The fact that a legislature might pass the second statute does not mean that, given the political temperament of the state, the legislature would in fact have passed it. If the legislature nominally recognizes knowledge as germane (as it did in the first statute) and further, as the type of germane issue to be proved by the state, and then arranges its process so that most of those who lack knowledge are still

sent to jail (as though the second statute had been passed), then those individuals are being punished for a crime which has never undergone the political checks guaranteed by representative government"); Note, The Constitutionality of Affirmative Defenses after *Patterson v. New York*, 78 Colum.L.Rev. 655, 667 (1978) ("[A]lthough a state legislature might have decided to define an offense without the mitigating or exculpatory factor, there is no reason to suppose it would have done so, or given the political climate of the state, could have done so").

5. See J. Ely, Democracy and Distrust 183 (1980) ("constitutional law appropriately exists for those situations where representative government cannot be trusted, not those where we know it can"). See also *id.*, at 182–183.

a criminal conviction. It follows, I submit, that if a state provides that a specific component of a prohibited transaction shall give rise both to a special stigma and to a special punishment, that component must be treated as a "fact necessary to constitute the crime" within the meaning of our holding in *In re Winship*.

Pennsylvania's Mandatory Minimum Sentencing Act reflects a legislative determination that a defendant who "visibly possessed a firearm" during the commission of an aggravated assault is more blameworthy than a defendant who did not. A judicial finding that the defendant used a firearm in an aggravated assault places a greater stigma on the defendant's name than a simple finding that he committed an aggravated assault. And not to be overlooked, such a finding with respect to petitioner Dennison automatically mandates a punishment that is more than twice as severe as the *maximum* punishment that the trial judge considered appropriate for his conduct.

It is true, as the Court points out, that the enhanced punishment is within the range that was authorized for any aggravated assault. That fact does not, however, minimize the significance of a finding of visible possession of a firearm whether attention is focused on the stigmatizing or punitive consequences of that finding. See *Mullaney v. Wilbur*, 421 U.S., at 697–698, 95 S.Ct., at 1888–1889.[6] The finding identifies conduct that the legislature specifically intended to prohibit and to punish by a special sanction. In my opinion the constitutional significance of the special sanction cannot be avoided by the cavalier observation that it merely "ups the ante" for the defendant. See *ante*, at 2418. No matter how culpable petitioner Dennison may be, the difference between $11\frac{1}{2}$ months and five years of incarceration merits a more principled justification than the luck of the draw.

I respectfully dissent.

---

6. It is likewise irrelevant that petitioners had first been convicted of predicate felonies. "Under our system of criminal justice even a thief is entitled to complain that he has been unconstitutionally convicted and imprisoned as a burglar." *Jackson v. Virginia*, 443 U.S. 307, 323–324, 99 S.Ct. 2781, 2791, 61 L.Ed.2d 560 (1979). See n. 3, *supra*.

VOLUME I

CHAPTER 6   CORRECTING UNEQUAL SENTENCES

The most common problem in the area of unequal sentencing occurs when two defendants are tried separately for the same offense and one defendant receives an extraordinarily longer sentence than the other. Courts have usually followed a hands-off policy in this context, except in the most grievous situations. Increasingly, the trend has been for courts to look at sentences and modify them where there is some reason to do so.

There have been no cases during the period of this volume relating to sentences awarded to two defendants in similar circumstances. However, there were cases arising under the Youth Correction Act and cases concerning resentencing after a conviction is reversed.

Women, Youth and Blacks

The Youth Correction Act, 18 U.S.C. 5005, was repealed by Act of October 12, 1984, sec. 218, 98 Stat. 2027. In its place, the Sentencing Guidelines are to take into consideration age where relevant. 28 U.S.C. 994(d). The original theory of the Youth Correction Act was that the sentence of a youth could be longer than that of an adult because the youth would receive greater attention in rehabilitation. This assumption was challenged. Early cases set forth in Volume I, following p. 312, declared that it was unconstitutional for a youth to receive a greater sentence than an adult. In the future, differences in sentencing for youths can only arise when state laws involving juvenile delinquency are considered.

Several cases did arise where, as in *Johnson v. Rodgers,* 756 F.2d 79 (10th Cir. 1985), the defendant who was sentenced under the Youth Corrections Act did not receive as much good time-credit as that of an adult prisoner. A typical case that will not present itself until the Sentencing Guidelines are fully integrated into our legal system is represented by *United States v. Hemby,* 753 F.2d 30 (4th Cir. 1985). In *Hemby,* an individual convicted under the Youth Correction Act and sentenced as an adult for another crime, was required to serve the balance of his term under the Youth Correction Act.

The classical case discussing the purpose of the Youth Correction Act was *Dorszynski v. United States,* 418 U.S. 424, 94 S.Ct. 3042, found in Vol. VI: 51, which stated that the purpose of the act was rehabilitation in exchange for an indeterminate sentence. In *Scott v. United States,* 778 F.2d 1444 (10th Cir. 1985), the court held that the youth was not entitled to credit for having served some time in an adult facility.

In *United States v. McDonald,* 775 F.2d 724 (6th Cir. 1985), the court held that an individual sentenced under the Youth Correction Act could not be given a greater period of time than that of an adult. Further, the youth would earn no credits toward the sentence for time served on probation when the terms of probation were denied. Since the issues will not be important in the future, the case is not included here.

There appear to be no cases decided where longer sentences were imposed upon women based upon their sex or upon blacks based upon their race.

Resentenced after Conviction

The question has continued to plague the courts as to whether a person's sentence can be increased upon conviction after a second trial. The classic case is *North Carolina v. Pearce,* 395 U.S. 711, 89 S.Ct. 2089 (1969), found in Vol.I: 388, which sets out certain principles. The chief requirement is that the second sentence can not be vindictive. A greater sentence, if imposed, must be based on facts discovered since the first trial. Double jeopardy does not come into play in these cases. The Supreme Court had occasion to consider the same question in *Texas v. McCullough,* 106 S.Ct. 976 (1986), included here, which upheld a greater sentence on the ground that new evidence was discovered after the first trial and introduced at the second trial.

Another case, included here, from the same term of the Supreme Court was *Poland v. Arizona* 106 S.Ct. 1749 (1986), which presented an interesting question of double jeopardy in the second sentencing.

In *United States v. Garcia,* 785 F.2d 214 (8th Cir. 1985), a co-defendant who testified against other defendants was given a lesser sentence, which was upheld.

Introductions in previous volumes:

I: 295; VI: 51; VII: 61; VIII: 103

Jerry Wayne WATTS, et al., Petitioners,

v.

John T. HADDEN, Warden, et
al., Respondents.

Civ. A. No. 78–M–495.

United States District Court,
D. Colorado.

Feb. 5, 1986.

MEMORANDUM OPINION AND ORDER

MATSCH, District Judge.

This class action on behalf of persons who have been committed for treatment under the Youth Corrections Act ("YCA"), 18 U.S.C. §§ 5005 *et seq.*, is again before this court pursuant to its continuing jurisdiction to implement the mandate issued in *Watts v. Hadden*, 651 F.2d 1354 (10th Cir. 1981). The present dispute concerns the manner in which the Parole Commission determines the conditional release date of a YCA inmate, and the respective roles of the Parole Commission and the Bureau of Prisons. While the YCA was repealed on October 21, 1984 in 98 Stat. 2027, and while this court did, on November 4, 1985, authorize the Bureau of Prisons to implement an amended plan to use FCI, Englewood, a designated YCA facility, to house some non-YCA offenders, the repeal is of no effect on the present issues because persons committed under the Act must be treated according to the requirements of the statute.

The court of appeals made it clear in *Watts, supra*, that the Parole Commission was failing to follow the requirements of the YCA because the Commission had mistakenly believed that the enactment of the 1976 Parole Commission Act had impliedly repealed certain provisions of the YCA. More particularly, the court concluded that the inmates' response to treatment must be considered with the criteria contained in 18 U.S.C. § 4206(a).

The respondents received further instructions on the law from the Tenth Circuit Court of Appeals in *Benedict v. Rodgers*, 748 F.2d 543 (10th Cir.1984), which concerned two habeas corpus petitions out of this court. In that opinion, as modified by an order entered on January 14, 1985, the appellate court affirmed this court's finding and conclusion that by the use of a presumptive release date, with an alternate date, contingent upon satisfactory program completion, the Parole Commission was failing to give adequate consideration to the individual's response to treatment. The circuit court used the following language:

> We believe that such prospective "consideration" of rehabilitation as a factor in parole determinations does not satisfy the requirements of the YCA as analyzed in *Watts*. A proposed formulaic reduction of sentence for completion of a program plan does not approximate an evaluation of an individual offender's response to treatment as mandated by *Watts*. Nor does it amount to consideration of rehabilitation as a determinative factor in parole decisions as *Watts* explicitly requires.

> We are concerned that without more inherent flexibility, such a rigid, prospectively-applied formula converts an indeterminate sentence into a determinate one, thereby divesting the trial court of its sentencing function, a result expressly proscribed by the Supreme Court in *Dorszynski*, 418 U.S. [424] at 440, 94 S.Ct. at [3042] 3051 [41 L.Ed.2d 855 (1974)]. See *Watts*, 651 F.2d at 1376. In addition, the knowledge that the Parole Commission will re-evaluate the extent of rehabilitation and response to treatment following completion of the program plan will provide a much stronger incentive for the offender to do well.

Id. at 546–47.

The habeas corpus petitions considered in *Benedict* were filed after the Parole Commission had refused to change the alternate release dates in consideration of the Warden's report of program completion and recommendation for an earlier release date. The evidentiary hearings which have since been held in this class action, and the briefs which have been filed, make it clear that the response to the *Benedict* decision by the Bureau of Prisons was an abdication of authority and a shifting of full responsibility to the Parole Commission to determine release dates. While the previous practice had been for the Warden (as the Director's delegate) to certify program completion and recommend a release date,

the new approach is simply to certify program completion and make no recommendation. The stated justification for this position is that the Bureau of Prisons is not in the rehabilitation business, and has no "expertise" to make any such determinations. That is a facile evasion of a difficult decision. The question is not "expertise" but responsibility.

The purposes and structure of the YCA have been examined and articulated repeatedly by the courts. In *Dorszynski v. United States*, 418 U.S. 424, 94 S.Ct. 3042, 41 L.Ed.2d 855 (1974), the Supreme Court considered the overall plan for the YCA in great detail, and emphasized that:

> An important element of the program was that once a person was committed for treatment under the Act, the execution of sentence was to fit the person, not the crime for which he was convicted.

Id. at 434, 94 S.Ct. at 3048.

There is a joint responsibility for both the Bureau of Prisons and the Parole Commission to act together to determine the appropriate treatment required for an individual inmate, and to determine the time when he has responded to that treatment sufficiently to warrant release after consideration of the other two criteria in section 4206(a). Under section 5014, the Bureau of Prisons must make an initial classification study within thirty days of commitment, and report the findings from that study with recommendations for treatment to the Parole Commission. A parole interview must be conducted as soon as practicable after commitment. It seems apparent that the Act contemplates participation by the Parole Commission in the treatment program design for each inmate. There would be no other purpose for the statutory requirements that it receive the classification report with recommendations and that it conduct an early parole interview.

Under section 5016, the Director must cause periodic examinations and re-examinations to be made on all YCA inmates with reports to the Parole Commission as to each offender. Under section 5017(a), the Parole Commission may make the conditional release decision at any time; but, that subsection also contains the following language:

When, in the judgment of the Director, a committed youth offender should be released conditionally under supervision he shall so report and recommend to the Commission.

Since the *Benedict* decision, the Bureau of Prisons has read that language to mean that it need report only on matters "within its knowledge and expertise: the offenders completion of the individualized treatment plan at the institution, along with any comments on particularly good or poor adjustment on his part." Bureau of Prisons' Response at page 2. That view contradicts the explicit language of the statute which requires the Director to report when a *"committed youth offender should be released conditionally under supervision."* The Director does not have the option of refusing to make a judgment as to when an offender should be released conditionally because the Bureau of Prisons has a philosophical disagreement with a policy of rehabilitative treatment, or because it is difficult to predict human behavior, or because the staff does not include persons with adequate knowledge or training. The plain language of the statute compels the Bureau of Prisons to make a recommendation for a release date. While the Director may choose the particular means and manner for making the judgment, he cannot avoid the responsibility for recommending a release date to the Parole Commission.

For its part, the Parole Commission continues to contend that regardless of program participation, the offense severity is a primary factor, and that emphasis on offense severity is necessary to reduce disparity which erodes confidence in the criminal justice system. The YCA expressly contemplates disparity in the length of confinement of inmates convicted of the same or similar offenses. That is precisely why the Act was adopted as an alternative to the sentence which would otherwise be required by law. Again, it is necessary to emphasize that which the Supreme Court said thirteen years ago in *Dorszynski*. *The execution of the sentence must fit the person, not the crime for which he was convicted.* What has been shown here, yet again, is the same resistance to recognize and respond to the requirements of the law that these respondents have demonstrated throughout the years in which this litigation has been in this court. It seems incredible that the respondents still sing the refrain that they cannot determine when "rehabilitation" has been achieved. In this regard, it should again be noted that nowhere in the YCA is the word "rehabilitation" used. The statute speaks to "treatment" which is defined in section 5006(f) as:

(f) "treatment" means corrective and preventive guidance and training designed to protect the public by correcting the anti-social tendencies of youth offenders.

The Congress recognized that no one can foretell future conduct of any individual when it required that the initial release must be a "conditional release," subject to close supervision. Obviously, the best measure of the ability of a person to function in free society is to put him back there under close supervision and adequate control.

While this court has consistently sought to avoid intrusion into the discretionary authority of the respondents in performing their respective duties under the Act and has, accordingly, directed the submission of plans for compliance with the Act as it has been interpreted in this circuit, it now becomes clear that more specific direction is required to avoid prolonging this litigation beyond the time when the last YCA inmate will be in the system. Moreover, the giving of some specific direction seems necessary to avoid the continuing proliferation of habeas corpus petitions by inmates in this district. Those who are serving the YCA commitments should be given more adequate guidance with respect to the goals and objectives of their individual institutionalization and the requirements which they must meet to obtain conditional release. Toward that end, the Bureau of Prisons and Parole Commission should agree upon the treatment program plan for each inmate. Since most of the inmates now in this class are well beyond the initial classification stage, some mechanism should be developed for the Parole Commission to review their program plans and indicate approval or disapproval at the earliest possible time.

A second requirement is that the Director through his delegate, the Warden, or some other staff position, shall develop a system for periodic reporting on the inmate's progress in treatment, with written reports and interim evaluations to go to the Parole Commission no less frequently than at six-month intervals. Additionally, the Director shall, through the Warden or other delegate, cause a section 5017(a) recommendation for conditional release to be made to the Parole Commission, with a report of findings and a sufficient statement of reasons to give the Parole Commission an understanding of the individual inmate's status and the basis for the Director's judgment.

To make these periodic reports and release recommendations meaningful, the Parole Commission will be required to conduct conditional release interviews with each inmate within ninety days of the receipt of the interim reports and within sixty days of receipt of the release recommendation. Those interviews must be attended by the inmate's unit leader, or some other person from the institution having direct knowledge of the inmate's participation in programs and conduct within the institution, who can respond to questions from the hearing examiners and the inmate.

It should be made clear to all inmates that they may not rely on any previous presumptive release date determinations or alternative release date determinations. Counsel for the plaintiff class has asserted that all of the class members should be given new opportunities for hearings without the threat of losing the existing alter-

nate release dates. That would be inconsistent with and violate the provisions of section 5018, giving the Parole Commission the express authority to revoke or modify any of its orders respecting a committed youth offender, excepting an order of unconditional discharge. It also would be inconsistent with this court's criticism of the previous conduct of the Parole Commission in using guidelines to transform indeterminate sentencing to determinate sentences.

While the Parole Commission may continue to use the guidelines for purposes of evaluating the section 4206(a) criteria, it must not continue the policy of refusing to release any inmate earlier than would be dictated by the "very good" category plus the maximum reduction for superior program achievement provided at 28 C.F.R. § 2.60. There can be no strict requirement for any minimum time to be served under a YCA sentence.

These are the directions to be followed. The details for implementing them are matters which must be determined by the respondents. In directing further action, this court is, of course, aware that the YCA inmate population is declining. In that regard, there is the flexibility provided in section 5015(b) giving the Director the authority to transfer committed youth offenders from one agency or institution to another agency or institution, and the additional authority granted in section 5013 to contract with any appropriate public or private agency for the training of committed youth offenders. It may well be that with the declining population the use of contract facilities will become more appropriate for the particular treatment needs of individuals under the YCA, and that for appropriate and articulated reasons, an inmate may be placed with a contract agency even though there would then be no segregation from adults. These are matters which are not now before this court in this case. They are mentioned only to remind the respondents that there are alternatives which can be considered in performing the difficult task of treating YCA inmates under the changed circumstances resulting from repeal of the Act.

Upon the foregoing, it is

ORDERED that on or before March 31, 1986, the respondents Bureau of Prisons and Parole Commission shall file a joint plan for the implementation of the directions given herein.

Peter H. JOHNSON, Petitioner-Appellee,

v.

George RODGERS, Warden,
Respondent-Appellant.

No. 83–2636.

United States Court of Appeals,
Tenth Circuit.

March 5, 1985.

Before McKAY and LOGAN, Circuit Judges and RUSSELL, District Judge.[*]

McKAY, Circuit Judge.

The issue in this case is whether the trial court erred in awarding petitioner good-time credits as equitable relief for failure to provide him with treatment and rehabilitation as required under the Youth Corrections Act.

Petitioner was convicted of assaulting a federal officer in violation of 18 U.S.C. § 111. He was sentenced to a zero-to-six year sentence pursuant to 18 U.S.C. § 5010(b) of the Youth Corrections Act, and was sent to the Federal Correctional Institution in Englewood, Colorado. Petitioner filed a petition for habeas corpus alleging, *inter alia*, that he was entitled to good-time credit because he was being denied the rehabilitation programs to which he was entitled under the YCA. The petition was referred to a magistrate, who held an evidentiary hearing and recommended that all of petitioner's claims be dismissed. Petitioner filed extensive objections to these findings and recommendations. The district court reviewed the file, the magistrate's recommendations, and the objections, and entered an order awarding good-time credits to the petitioner. The government appeals.

We have reviewed the trial court's order and find it to be supported in the record and in accordance with the law. Because the trial court did not publish its order, we here summarize its findings and rationale.

The core purpose of the Youth Corrections Act is rehabilitation. *Dorszyn-*

ski v. United States, 418 U.S. 424, 94 S.Ct. 3042, 41 L.Ed.2d 855 (1974). To accomplish this purpose, a youthful offender may receive an indeterminate sentence, during which he is to undergo a comprehensive program of rehabilitation, followed by a period of conditional release. 18 U.S.C. §§ 5010(b) and 5017(c). The time of release is based upon a determination that the offender has acquired the stability and redirection to overcome the past and begin life anew. As a result, it is possible for a youthful offender to be confined longer than an adult who has been convicted of the same offense. An offender sentenced under the YCA is not eligible for good-time credit since the indicator for early release is not the sentence as reduced by good time, but demonstrated progress toward rehabilitation. *See Staudmier v. United States*, 496 F.2d 1191, 1192 (10th Cir.1974).

The rehabilitation thus "may be regarded as a quid pro quo for a longer confinement." *Carter v. United States*, 306 F.2d 283, 285 (D.C.Cir.1962). Accordingly,

[w]here YCA offenders are not given special treatment in accordance with the law but instead have the same terms and conditions of confinement as other offenders, the imposition of a sentence which tends to be longer on youth offenders raises a potential stumbling block of constitutional dimension.

Watts v. Hadden, 651 F.2d 1354, 1365 (10th Cir.1981). *See Johnson v. Smith*, No. 78–71747, slip op. (E.D.Mich. March 18, 1983) (unfair for YCA offenders to serve longer sentences than adults without either good-time allowances or specialized treatment.)

---

[*] Honorable David L. Russell, United States District Judge for the Districts of Oklahoma, sitting by designation.

For petitioner this "constitutional stumbling block" was not merely potential, but starkly real. He is serving a zero-to-six year sentence. The comparable sentence for an adult who commits the same offense is a three-year maximum. In April of 1982, he unfortunately witnessed a prison assault and thus became a target for possible inmate violence. He was placed in administrative detention for his own safety and remained there until he was transferred to the Federal Correctional Institution in Morgantown, West Virginia, in February 1984. The district court found that while he was in protective custody he could not participate in the minimum required YCA rehabilitative programs, because a number of them are group functions and were not accessible to petitioner while he was housed in administrative isolation.**

As a result, the district court found that petitioner was confined under substantially worse terms and conditions than an adult offender. He lacked the rehabilitative benefits of the YCA, yet he was serving a longer sentence than would an adult, and without the incentive of early release based on good-time credit that an adult would enjoy. In view of the clear congressional intent expressed in the YCA, the conditions of petitioner's incarceration were legally unacceptable.

The respondent has attempted to shift the burden of this dilemma to the petitioner. But it is the prison administration, not petitioner, that Congress instructed to implement the YCA. If the prison administration could not, under the circumstances, provide petitioner with rehabilitative programs, it should have taken effective remedial action. As the district court found, since petitioner was not accorded the rehabilitative opportunities that were the *quid pro quo* for his longer sentence, he is entitled, in equity and conscience, to

the good-time credit he would have earned had he been serving an adult sentence. *See Johnson v. Bell*, 487 F.Supp. 977 (E.D. Mich.1980), and subsequent remedial order, *Johnson v. Smith*, No. 78–71747, slip op. at 6 (E.D.Mich. March 18, 1983) (ordering statutory good-time credit for youths held under conditions violative of the Youth Corrections Act).

The only issue raised on appeal not dealt with in the district court's opinion is the question of whether, after rejecting the magistrate's recommendations, the district court erred in making new fact findings without either remanding the petition to the magistrate for further findings or holding a hearing. The district court is required to make a *de novo* determination of the portions of the magistrate's report to which objections are made. Rule 8(b)(4), Rules Governing Proceedings in the United States District Courts under Section 2255 of Title 28, United States Code (1984). Thus we find no merit in the contention that the court should have remanded the case to the magistrate for fact findings. The requirement of a *de novo* determination does not, however, mean that a *de novo* hearing is required. *United States v. Raddatz*, 447 U.S. 667, 674, 100 S.Ct. 2406, 2411, 65 L.Ed.2d 424 (1980). As the House Report makes explicit, "the use of the words 'de novo determination' *is not intended to require the judge to actually conduct a new hearing* on contested issues." H.R.Rep. No. 94–1609, p. 3 (1976) (quoted in *Raddatz*, 447 U.S. at 675, 100 S.Ct. at 2412). The district court acted within its discretion in finding, based on the record before it, that petitioner was denied rehabilitation, and its conclusion is supported by the record. The award of good-time credits was, therefore, appropriate.

AFFIRMED.

** In November 1983 petitioner received material for a correspondence course in accounting, a form of rehabilitative training. Petitioner only claims entitlement to good-time credit for the period of March 1982 through November 1983.

UNITED STATES of America, Appellee,

v.

John D. HEMBY, Appellant.

No. 84–6112.

United States Court of Appeals,
Fourth Circuit.

Argued Dec. 6, 1984.

Decided Jan. 17, 1985.

Before WINTER, Chief Judge, and HALL and ERVIN, Circuit Judges.

HARRISON L. WINTER, Chief Judge:

The question presented by this appeal is whether the district court after sentencing defendant, John David Hemby, in 1979 to three years' imprisonment as an adult with service to begin after the completion of service of an earlier sentence imposed pursuant to the Federal Youth Corrections Act (YCA), 18 U.S.C. § 5010(c), properly ordered in 1983 that defendant serve the remainder of the earlier sentence as an adult. The district court ruled that it could properly exercise that authority, and it directed that defendant serve the remainder of his earlier sentence as an adult.

We affirm, albeit for reasons different from those assigned by the district court.

I.

On March 2, 1977, defendant pled guilty to a charge of bank robbery in violation of 18 U.S.C. § 2113. The district court for the Eastern District of New York sentenced defendant pursuant to 18 U.S.C. § 5010(c) of the YCA to an indeterminate sentence not to exceed ten years.

On March 30, 1979, Judge Warriner of the Eastern District of Virginia sentenced defendant to three years' imprisonment as an adult following defendant's plea of guilty to a charge of assaulting a correctional officer in violation of 18 U.S.C. § 111. Judge Warriner found that defendant "would not benefit from sentencing under the [YCA]," and imposed the adult sentence to be served consecutively to defendant's unexpired YCA sentence. On June 19, 1980, a U.S. Magistrate for the Western District of Tennessee sentenced defendant to an additional six-month consecutive adult term of imprisonment following another conviction for assault.

On December 2, 1981, the Supreme Court decided *Ralston v. Robinson*, 454 U.S. 201, 102 S.Ct. 233, 70 L.Ed.2d 345 (1981), which held that a "judge who sentences a youth offender to a consecutive adult term may require that the offender also serve the remainder of his youth sentence as an adult." *Id.* at 217, 102 S.Ct. at 243. The only condition on the exercise of this authority is a finding by the second sentencing judge that defendant will not benefit further from YCA treatment during the remainder of his youth term. *Id.* at 219, 102 S.Ct. at 244. *Ralston* also held that such an abolition of the YCA requirements of segregation and treatment could only be performed by the judiciary, and not by the Bureau of Prisons as had been its prior practice.

On May 31, 1983, the United States filed a motion in the Eastern District of Virginia seeking a clarification or modification of Judge Warriner's 1979 sentence as to defendant. It sought to end his YCA treatment and to confine him as an adult. Judge Warriner ruled that while he had not explicitly made the requisite "no benefit" finding when he imposed sentence, he had the authority to make the finding now. He therefore made that finding and ruled that defendant should serve the remainder of his YCA sentence as an adult. *United States v. Hemby*, 583 F.Supp. 58 (E.D.Va. 1983). Defendant appeals from that order.

II.

On appeal defendant advances a number of contentions.* In our view, most of them need not be addressed because we think that Judge Warriner *implicitly* made the requisite finding when he imposed the adult sentence. Although Judge Warriner candidly admitted that he had not made the explicit "no benefit" finding in his 1979 sentencing, that sentencing predated the Supreme Court's statement of its expectation that "[i]n the future, we expect that judges will eliminate interpretive difficulties by making an explicit 'no benefit' finding with respect to the remainder of the YCA sentence." *Id.* 454 U.S. at 219, 102 S.Ct. at 244. Thus, his failure to be explicit is not only understandable but also does not negate the possibility that the finding is implicit.

Judge Warriner in the 1979 sentencing did make the explicit finding that for the crime of assault "defendant would not benefit from sentencing under the Federal Youth Corrections Act." We deem this finding the functional equivalent of a finding that defendant would not benefit further from continued treatment under the YCA in accordance with his original sentence. A finding that an offender will not benefit from treatment under the YCA at a point five years in the future must of necessity be made on the facts available to the judge at the time he makes the finding. Since it is inconceivable to us how the judge could find that events which will occur after sentence is imposed will indicate the need for treatment as an adult some years later, we can only conclude that a "no benefit" finding for a sentence to begin at a future date necessarily includes a parallel finding that the offender also will not benefit from the YCA as of the time of sentencing.

* He contends that the district court (1) lacked jurisdiction to entertain such a motion, (2) violated Fed.R.Crim.P. 35 by entertaining the motion more than 120 days after sentencing, (3) incorrectly applied *Ralston v. Robinson*, 454 U.S. 201, 102 S.Ct. 233, 70 L.Ed.2d 345 (1981), retroactively, (4) lacked statutory authority to modify the sentence in the absence of an additional criminal offense, (5) subjected him to double jeopardy by increasing the severity of his sentence, and (6) granted the modification without due process of law.

Ralston is authority for us to interpret the 1979 specific finding by Judge Warriner. *Ralston* involved the failure of a second sentencing judge to make an explicit change in the defendant's unexpired YCA sentence, although he did find that defendant would not benefit "further" from treatment under the YCA. The lack of an explicit finding did not trouble the Court:

> [W]e conclude that the second sentencing judge made a sufficient finding that respondent would not benefit from YCA treatment during the remainder of his youth term. The judge found that respondent would not benefit "further" under the YCA, and he declined to sentence under that Act, imposing instead a consecutive adult sentence. *In the future*, we expect that judges will eliminate interpretive difficulties by making an explicit "no benefit" finding with respect to the remainder of the YCA sentence.

Id. at 219, 102 S.Ct. at 244 (emphasis added). So, too, for the reasons stated, we think that as a matter of interpretation the action of Judge Warriner necessarily included the requisite "no benefit" finding.

We therefore conclude that Judge Warriner's 1979 sentencing finding was sufficient to transform the remainder of defendant's YCA sentence to an adult sentence.

This disposition precludes any need to consider the jurisdictional arguments raised by defendant.

III.

In the view that we take of the case, the factual basis for the defendant's due process argument disappears, as does his argument concerning the retroactivity of *Ralston*. His double jeopardy argument remains and merits brief discussion. Succinctly stated, it is that he has been subjected to double jeopardy when his YCA sentence was altered to an adult sentence.

The double jeopardy issue was not squarely before the Court in *Ralston*. Since the decision of the court of appeals had been favorable to the prisoner on statutory grounds, there had been no reason to decide the constitutional issues, *see Robinson v. Ralston*, 642 F.2d 1077, 1079 n. 4 (7 Cir.1981). It was raised, however, by Justice Stevens in dissent. 454 U.S. at 224 n. 3, 102 S.Ct. at 247 n. 3. The suggestion that the YCA might be unconstitutional on this ground was rejected by the majority. *Id.* at 220 n. 14, 102 S.Ct. at 245 n. 14.

Absent further expression from the Supreme Court, we deem the issue settled adversely to defendant's argument.

AFFIRMED.

TEXAS, Petitioner

v.

Sanford James McCULLOUGH.

No. 84–1198.

Argued Dec. 10, 1985.

Decided Feb. 26, 1986.

Syllabus

Respondent was tried before a jury in　　a Texas District Court and convicted of

---

* Note: The syllabus constitutes no part of the opinion of the Court but has been prepared by the Reporter of Decisions for the convenience of the reader. See *United States v. Detroit Lumber Co.,* 200 U.S. 321, 337, 26 S.Ct. 282, 287, 50 L.Ed. 499.

murder. He elected to be sentenced by the jury, as was his right under Texas law, and the jury imposed a 20-year sentence. The trial judge then granted respondent's motion for a new trial on the basis of prosecutorial misconduct. Respondent was retried before a jury, with the same trial judge presiding, and again was found guilty. This time he elected to have the judge fix his sentence, and she imposed a 50-year sentence. To justify the longer sentence, the judge entered the following findings of fact: the testimony of two state witnesses who had not testified at the first trial added to the credibility of the State's key witness and detracted from the credibility of respondent and a defense witness; the two new witnesses' testimony directly implicated respondent in the commission of the murder and shed new light upon his life and conduct; and it was learned for the first time on retrial that respondent had been released from prison only four months before the murder. The Texas Court of Appeals reversed and sentenced respondent to 20 years' imprisonment, considering itself bound by *North Carolina v. Pearce*, 395 U.S. 711, 89 S.Ct. 2072, 23 L.Ed.2d 656, wherein it was held that the Due Process Clause of the Fourteenth Amendment prevented increased sentences on retrial when the increase was motivated by the sentencing judge's vindictiveness, and that to show the absence of vindictiveness the reasons for imposing the increased sentence must affirmatively appear. The Texas Court of Criminal Appeals, while holding that, as a matter of procedure, the case should have been remanded to the trial judge for resentencing, also held that under *Pearce* vindictiveness must be presumed even though a jury had fixed punishment at the first trial and a judge had fixed it at the second trial.

Held: The Due Process Clause was not violated by the trial judge's imposition of a greater sentence on retrial. Pp. 978–982.

(a) The facts of this case provide no basis for a *Pearce* presumption of vindictiveness. In contrast to *Pearce*, respondent's second trial came about because the trial judge herself concluded that the prosecutor's misconduct required it. Granting respondent's motion for new trial hardly suggests any vindictiveness on the judge's part toward him. The presumption is also inapplicable because different sentencers assessed the varying sentences, the second sentencer providing an on-the-record, logical, nonvindictive reason for the longer sentence. Pp. 978–980.

(b) Even if the *Pearce* presumption were to apply here the trial judge's findings on imposing the longer sentence overcame that presumption. Those findings clearly constituted "objective information justifying the increased sentence," *United States v. Goodwin*, 457 U.S. 368, 375, 102 S.Ct. 2485, 2489, 73 L.Ed.2d 74. Pp. 980–982.

— S.W.2d —— (Tex.Cr.App.1983), reversed and remanded.

BURGER, C.J., delivered the opinion of the Court, in which WHITE, POWELL, REHNQUIST, and O'CONNOR, JJ., joined. BRENNAN, J., filed an opinion concurring in the judgment. MARSHALL, J., filed a dissenting opinion, in which BLACKMUN and STEVENS, JJ., joined.

———

Randall L. Sherrod, Canyon, Tex., for petitioner.

Jeff Blackburn, Amarillo, Tex., for respondent, pro hac vice, by special leave of Court.

Chief Justice BURGER delivered the opinion of the Court.

We granted certiorari to decide whether the Due Process Clause was violated when the defendant in a state court received a greater sentence on retrial where the earlier sentence was imposed by the jury, the trial judge granted the defendant's motion for a new trial, the defendant requested that in the second trial the judge fix the sentence, and the judge entered findings of fact justifying the longer sentence.

I

In 1980, Sanford James McCullough was tried before a jury in the Randall County, Texas, District Court and convicted of murder. McCullough elected to be sentenced by the jury, as was his right under Texas law. Tex.Code Crim.Proc.Ann., Art. 37.07 (Vernon 1981). The jury imposed a 20-year sentence. Judge Naomi Harney, the trial judge, then granted McCullough's motion for a new trial on the basis of prosecutorial misconduct.

Three months later, McCullough was retried before a jury, with Judge Harney again presiding. At this trial, the State presented testimony from two witnesses who had not testified at the first trial that McCullough rather than his accomplices had slashed the throat of the victim. McCullough was again found guilty by a jury. This time, he elected to have his sentence fixed by the trial judge. Judge Harney sentenced McCullough to 50 years in prison and, upon his motion, made findings of fact as to why the sentence was longer than that fixed by the jury in the first trial. She found that in fixing the sentence she relied on new evidence about the murder that was not presented at the first trial and hence never made known to the sentencing jury. The findings focused specifically on the testimony of two new witnesses, Carolyn Hollison McCullough and Willie Lee Brown, which "had a direct effect upon the strength of the State's case at both the guilt and punishment phases of the trial." App. to Pet. for Cert. A–23. In

addition, Judge Harney explained that she learned for the first time on retrial McCullough had been released from prison only four months before the later crime had been committed. *Ibid.* Finally, the judge candidly stated that, had she fixed the first sentence, she would have imposed more than twenty years. *Id.*, at A–24.[1]

On appeal, the Texas Court of Appeals reversed and resentenced McCullough to 20 years' imprisonment. 680 S.W.2d 493 (1983). That court considered itself bound by this Court's decision in *North Carolina v. Pearce*, 395 U.S. 711, 89 S.Ct. 2072, 23 L.Ed.2d 656 (1969), and held that a longer sentence upon retrial could be imposed only if it was based upon conduct of the defendant occurring after the original trial.[2] Petitioner sought review in the Texas Court of Criminal Appeals, and that court limited its review to whether the Texas Court of Appeals had authority to limit respondent's sentence to 20 years. The court concluded that, as a matter of procedure, the case should have been remanded to the trial judge for resentencing. On petitioner's motion for rehearing, the court concluded that under *Pearce* vindictiveness must be presumed even though a jury had fixed punishment at the first trial and a judge had fixed it at the second trial. We granted certiorari. 472 U.S. ——, 105 S.Ct. 2699, 86 L.Ed.2d 716 (1985). We reverse.

II

In *North Carolina v. Pearce, supra*, the Court placed a limitation on the power of a sentencing authority to increase a sentence after reconviction following a new trial. It held that the Due Process Clause of the Fourteenth Amendment pre-

---

1. Later Judge Harney sentenced two other defendants for their role in the same murder. She gave both defendants 50 year sentences identical to McCullough's.

2. The Texas Court of Appeals in applying *Pearce* observed:

   "This case demonstrates the excessive scope of *Pearce*. The trial judge filed detailed and valid reasons for the heavier punishment and there is nothing in the record to indicate that the in-

creased punishment resulted from vindictiveness. However, the reasons affirmatively supported by evidence are based on events occurring during or after the crime but before the first trial. Although those matters were not brought out at the first trial, they cannot be used [under *Pearce*] to increase punishment because none occurred *after* the first trial." 680 S.W.2d, at 496, n. 2.

vented increased sentences when that increase was motivated by vindictiveness on the part of the sentencing judge. The Court stated:

"Due process of law, then, requires that vindictiveness against a defendant for having successfully attacked his first conviction must play no part in the sentence he receives after a new trial. And since the fear of such vindictiveness may unconstitutionally deter a defendant's exercise of the right to appeal or collaterally attack his first conviction, due process also requires that a defendant be freed of apprehension of such a retaliatory motivation on the part of the sentencing judge.

"In order to assure the absence of such a motivation, we have concluded that whenever a judge imposes a more severe sentence upon a defendant after a new trial, *the reasons for his doing so must affirmatively appear.*" *Id.*, at 725–726, 89 S.Ct., at 2080–2081 (emphasis added).

Beyond doubt, vindictiveness of a sentencing judge is the evil the Court sought to prevent rather than simply enlarged sentences after a new trial. The *Pearce* requirements thus do not apply in every case where a convicted defendant receives a higher sentence on retrial. Like other "judicially created means of effectuating the rights secured by the [Constitution]," *Stone v. Powell*, 428 U.S. 465, 482, 96 S.Ct. 3037, 3046, 49 L.Ed.2d 1067 (1976), we have restricted application of *Pearce* to areas where its "objectives are thought most efficaciously served," 428 U.S., at 487, 96 S.Ct., at 3049. Accordingly, in each case, we look to the need, under the circumstances, to "guard against vindictiveness in the resentencing process." *Chaffin v. Stynchcombe*, 412 U.S. 17, 25, 93 S.Ct. 1977, 1982, 36 L.Ed.2d 714 (1973) (emphasis omitted). For example, in *Moon v. Maryland*, 398 U.S. 319, 90 S.Ct. 1730, 26 L.Ed.2d 262 (1970), we held that *Pearce* did not apply when the defendant conceded and it was clear that vindictiveness had played no part in the enlarged sentence. In *Colten v.*

Kentucky, 407 U.S. 104, 92 S.Ct. 1953, 32 L.Ed.2d 584 (1972), we saw no need for applying the presumption when the second court in a two-tier trial system imposed a longer sentence. In *Chaffin, supra*, we held *Pearce* not applicable where a *jury* imposed the increased sentence on retrial. Where the prophylactic rule of *Pearce* does not apply, the defendant may still obtain relief if he can show actual vindictiveness upon resentencing. *Wasman v. United States*, 468 U.S. ——, ——, 104 S.Ct. 3217, ——, 82 L.Ed.2d 424 (1984).

The facts of this case provide no basis for a presumption of vindictiveness. In contrast to *Pearce*, McCullough's second trial came about because the trial judge herself concluded that the prosecutor's misconduct required it. Granting McCullough's motion for a new trial hardly suggests any vindictiveness on the part of the judge towards him. "[U]nlike the judge who has been reversed," the trial judge here had "no motivation to engage in self-vindication." *Chaffin*, 412 U.S., at 27, 93 S.Ct., at 1983. In such circumstances, there is also no justifiable concern about "institutional interests that might occasion higher sentences by a judge desirous of discouraging what he regards as meritless appeals." *Ibid.* In granting McCullough's new trial motion, Judge Harney went on record as agreeing that his "claims" had merit. Presuming vindictiveness on this basis alone would be tantamount to presuming that a judge will be vindictive towards a defendant merely because he seeks an acquittal. Thus, in support of its position, the dissent conjures up visions of judges who view defendants as temerarious for filing motions for new trials, *post*, at 986, and who are "annoyed" at being forced "to sit through ... trial[s] whose result[s] [are] foregone conclusions," *post*, at 985. We decline to adopt the view that the judicial temperament of our Nation's trial judges will suddenly change upon the filing of a successful post-trial motion. The presumption of *Pearce* does not apply in situations where the possibility of vindictiveness is this speculative, particularly since the presumption may often "operate in the absence of any proof of an improper motive and thus ... block a legitimate response to criminal conduct," *United States v. Goodwin*, 457 U.S. 368, 373, 102 S.Ct. 2485, 2488, 73 L.Ed.2d 74 (1982). Indeed, not even "apprehension of such a retaliatory motivation on the part of the sentencing judge," *Pearce*, 395 U.S., at 725, 89 S.Ct., at 2080, could be present in this case. McCullough was entitled by law to choose to be sentenced by either a judge or a jury. Faced with that choice, on retrial McCullough chose to be sentenced by Judge Harney. There can hardly be more emphatic affirmation of his appraisal of Judge Harney's fairness than this choice. Because there was no realistic motive for vindictive sentencing, the *Pearce* presumption was inappropriate.

The presumption is also inapplicable because different sentencers assessed the varying sentences that McCullough received. In such circumstances, a sentence "increase" cannot truly be said to have taken place. In *Colten v. Kentucky, supra*, which bears directly on this case, we recognized that when different sentencers are involved,

"[i]t may often be that the [second sentencer] will impose a punishment more severe than that received from the [first]. But it no more follows that such a sentence is a vindictive penalty for seeking a [new] trial than that the [first sentencer] imposed a lenient penalty." *Id.*, 407 U.S., at 117, 92 S.Ct., at 1960.

Here, the second sentencer provides an on-the-record, wholly logical, nonvindictive

reason for the sentence. We read *Pearce* to require no more particularly since trial judges must be accorded broad discretion in sentencing, see *Wasman, supra*, 468 U.S., at ——, 104 S.Ct., at ——.

In this case, the trial judge stated candidly her belief that the 20-year sentence respondent received initially was unduly lenient in light of significant evidence not before the sentencing jury in the first trial. On this record, that appraisal cannot be faulted. In any event, nothing in the Constitution prohibits a state from permitting such discretion to play a role in sentencing.[3]

III

Even if the *Pearce* presumption were to apply here, we hold that the findings of the trial judge overcome that presumption. Nothing in *Pearce* is to be read as precluding a rebuttal of intimations of vindictiveness. As we have explained, *Pearce* permits "a sentencing authority [to] justify an increased sentence by affirmatively identifying relevant conduct or events that occurred subsequent to the original sentencing proceedings." *Wasman*, 468 U.S., at ——, 104 S.Ct., at 3225; see also *id.*, at ——, 104 S.Ct., at 3225–3226 (POWELL, J., concurring in part and concurring in judgment). This language, however, was never intended to describe exhaustively all of the possible circumstances in which a sentence increase could be justified. Restricting justifications for a sentence increase to *only* "events that occurred subsequent to the original sentencing proceedings" could in some circum-

---

3. *Pearce* itself apparently involved different judges presiding over the two trials, a fact that has led some courts to conclude by implication that the presumption of vindictiveness applies even where different sentencing judges are involved. See, *e.g., United States v. Hawthorne*, 532 F.2d 318, 323 (CA3), cert. denied, 429 U.S. 894, 97 S.Ct. 254, 50 L.Ed.2d 177 (1976). That fact, however, may not have been drawn to the Court's attention and does not appear anywhere in the Court's opinion in *Pearce*. Clearly the Court did not focus on it as a consideration for its holding. See *Hardwick v. Doolittle*, 558 F.2d 292, 299 (CA5 1977), cert. denied, 434 U.S. 1049, 98 S.Ct. 897, 54 L.Ed.2d 801 (1978). Subsequent opinions have also elucidated the basis for the *Pearce* presumption. We held in *Chaffin v. Stynchcombe*, 412 U.S. 17, 93 S.Ct. 1977, 36 L.Ed.2d 714 (1973), for instance, that the presumption derives from the judge's "personal stake in the prior conviction," *id.*, at 27, 93 S.Ct., at 1983, a statement clearly at odds with reading *Pearce* to answer the two-sentencer issue. We therefore decline to read *Pearce* as governing this issue. See also n. 4, *infra*.

stances lead to absurd results. The Solicitor General provides the following hypothetical example:

"Suppose ... that a defendant is convicted of burglary, a non-violent, and apparently first, offense. He is sentenced to a short prison term or perhaps placed on probation. Following a successful appeal and a conviction on retrial, it is learned that the defendant has been using an alias and in fact has a long criminal record that includes other burglaries, several armed robbery convictions, and a conviction for murder committed in the course of a burglary. None of the reasons underlying *Pearce* in any way justifies the perverse result that the defendant receive no greater sentence in light of this information than he originally received when he was thought to be a first offender." Brief for United States as *Amicus Curiae* 26.

We agree with the Solicitor General and find nothing in *Pearce* that would require such a bizarre conclusion.[4] Perhaps then the reach of *Pearce* is best captured in our statement in *United States v. Goodwin*, 457 U.S., at 374, 102 S.Ct., at 2489:

"In sum, the Court [in *Pearce*] applied a presumption of vindictiveness, which may be overcome only by objective information ... justifying the increased sentence."

Nothing in the Constitution requires a judge to ignore "objective information ... justifying the increased sentence." In refusing to apply *Pearce* retroactively we observed that "the *Pearce* prophylactic rules assist in guaranteeing the propriety of the sentencing phase of the criminal process." *Michigan v. Payne*, 412 U.S. 47, 52–53, 93 S.Ct. 1966, 1969, 36 L.Ed.2d 736 (1973). Realistically, if anything this focus would *require* rather than *forbid* the consideration of the relevant evidence bearing on sentence since " '[h]ighly relevant—if not essential—to [the] selection of an appropriate sentence is the possession of the fullest information possible concerning the defendant's life and characteristics.' " *Wasman, supra,* at —, 104 S.Ct., at 3220–3221 (quoting *Williams v. New York*, 337 U.S. 241, 247, 69 S.Ct. 1079, 1083, 93 L.Ed. 1337 (1949)).

To be sure, a defendant may be more reluctant to appeal if there is a risk that new, probative evidence supporting a longer sentence may be revealed on retrial. But this Court has never recognized this "chilling effect" as sufficient reason to create a constitutional prohibition against considering relevant information in assessing sentences. We explained in *Chaffin v. Stynchcombe*, 412 U.S., at 29, 93 S.Ct., at 1984, "the Court [in *Pearce*] intimated no doubt about the constitutional validity of higher sentences in the absence of vindic-

---

4. The dissent contends that this objection "was considered in *Pearce* and rejected there." *Post,* at 988. In fact, the issue, like the two-sentencer issue just discussed, was not before the Court because in neither *Pearce* nor its companion case did the State offer "any reason or justification" for the increased sentence. 395 U.S., at 726, 89 S.Ct., at 2081. Moreover, *Pearce* was argued on the assumption that the Constitution either absolutely forbade or permitted increased sentences on retrial. None of the briefs advanced the intermediate position ultimately relied upon by the Court that the Constitution permits increased sentences only in certain circumstances. Cf. Brief for American Civil Liberties Union et al. as *Amici Curiae* in *North Carolina v. Pearce*, O.T. 1968, No. 413, pp. 8–10 (quoted *post,* at 987–988) (arguing that "[t]o subject an accused to the risk of harsher punishment ... as a condition of appeal ... is an unconstitutional condition which violates the Due Process Clauses of the Fifth and Fourteenth Amendments"). Thus, as the Solicitor General points out, "in formulating the standard set forth in *Pearce*, the Court was completely without the 'sharpen[ing of]' the presentation of issues' provided by the adversary process, 'upon which the court so largely depends for illumination of difficult constitutional issues.' " Brief for United States as *Amicus Curiae* 22–23 (quoting *Baker v. Carr*, 369 U.S. 186, 204, 82 S.Ct. 691, 703, 7 L.Ed.2d 663 (1962)). But even if *Pearce* could be read to speak definitively to this situation, we are not reluctant to tailor judicially-created rules to implement constitutional guarantees, like the *Pearce* rule, see *Michigan v. Payne*, 412 U.S. 47, 51, 93 S.Ct. 1966, 1968, 36 L.Ed.2d 736 (1973), when the need to do so becomes apparent. Cf. *United States v. Leon*, 468 U.S. —, 104 S.Ct. 3405, 82 L.Ed.2d 677 (1984).

tiveness despite whatever incidental deterrent effect they might have on the right to appeal." We see no reason to depart from this conclusion.

It is clear that the careful explanation by the trial judge for the sentence imposed here fits well within our prior holdings. Judge Harney relied on the testimony of two new witnesses which she concluded "had a direct effect upon the strength of the State's case at both the guilt and punishment phases of the trial." App. to Pet. for Cert. A-23. The judge supported this conclusion with specific findings, noting that "[t]he testimony [of the two new witnesses] added to the credibility of the State's key witness ... and detracted from the credibility of Dennis McCullough and [respondent] who both testified for the defense." *Ibid.* The judge also found that "[t]he testimony of these two witnesses directly implicated the defendant in the commission of the murder in question and showed what part he played in committing the offense." *Id.,* at A-22. Finally, the judge concluded that their testimony "shed new light upon [McCullough's] life, conduct, and his mental and moral propensities." *Id.,* at A-23. These findings clearly constitute "objective information ... justifying the increased sentence."

Judge Harney also found that McCullough had been released from confinement only four months before the murder, *ibid.,* another obviously relevant fact not before the sentencing jury in the first trial. We have recognized the state's legitimate interest "in dealing in a harsher manner with those who by repeated criminal acts have shown that they are simply incapable of conforming to the norms of society as established by its criminal law." *Rummel v. Estelle,* 445 U.S. 263, 276, 100 S.Ct. 1133, 1140, 63 L.Ed.2d 382 (1980). A defendant who commits new crimes within four months of his release from prison clearly poses a greater danger to society than one who commits crimes less often. To foreclose reliance on the kind of pertinent new information developed in the second trial would be wholly incompatible with modern sentencing standards. This new objective information also amply justified McCullough's increased sentence.

In setting aside the second sentence, the Texas Court of Appeals recognized that the new information bore legitimately on the appropriate sentence to impose, but concluded, reluctantly, that *Pearce* precluded reliance on this information. It is appropriate that we clarify the scope and thrust of *Pearce,* and we do so here.

The case is remanded to the Texas Court of Criminal Appeals for further proceedings not inconsistent with this opinion.

Reversed and remanded.

Justice BRENNAN, concurring in the judgment.

After respondent was sentenced to twenty years imprisonment upon his conviction for murder, Judge Harney granted respondent's motion for a new trial based on prosecutorial misconduct. Under these circumstances, I believe that the possibility that an increased sentence upon retrial resulted from judicial vindictiveness is sufficiently remote that the presumption established in *North Carolina v. Pearce,* 395 U.S. 711, 89 S.Ct. 2072, 23 L.Ed.2d 656 (1969), should not apply here. Because respondent has not shown that the fifty-year sentence imposed by Judge Harney after respondent's retrial resulted from actual vindictiveness for having successfully attacked his first conviction, I would reverse the judgment below.

I emphasize, however, that were I able to find that vindictiveness should be presumed here, I would agree with Justice MARSHALL that "the reasons offered by Judge Harney [were] far from adequate to rebut any presumption of vindictiveness." *Post,* at 986. The Court's dictum to the contrary, see *ante,* at 980-982, serves in my view only to distort the holding of *Pearce.*

Justice MARSHALL, with whom Justice BLACKMUN and Justice STEVENS join, dissenting.

With little more than a passing nod to the considerations that prompted this Court, in *North Carolina v. Pearce*, 395 U.S. 711, 89 S.Ct. 2072, 23 L.Ed.2d 656 (1969), to safeguard due process rights by establishing a prophylactic rule of presumptive vindictiveness, the majority first refuses to apply that rule in a case where those considerations are clearly relevant, and then proceeds to rob that rule of any vitality even in cases in which it will be applied. Because I believe that under the rationale of *Pearce* we must presume vindictiveness here and that the findings of the trial judge with respect to respondent's second sentence should not be permitted to defeat that presumption, I must dissent.

I

After the jury in Sanford James McCullough's first trial imposed a sentence of 20 years' imprisonment, the Randall County Criminal District Attorney thought McCullough had been treated much too leniently. A local newspaper quoted the prosecutor as commenting: "A guy's life ought to be worth more than that." Amarillo Globe-Times, Sept. 24, 1980, p. 25, col. 1; Record, Defendant's Exhibit 5. Luckily for the District Attorney, McCullough was not satisfied with the results of his first trial either. McCullough filed a motion with the trial court requesting a new trial and raising two challenges to Judge Harney's conduct of the first trial:

"I.

"The Trial Court erred in not granting Defendant's Motion for Mistrial subsequent to the prosecutor's improper jury argument concerning the fact that the jury, if they only gave the Defendant ten to fifteen years in the penitentiary, would look outside their window at the end of that period of time and wonder if the criminal out there was the Defendant.

"II.

"The Trial Court erred in overruling Defendant's Motion for Mistrial subsequent to the prosecutor's cross-examination of the witness, DENNIS McCULLOUGH, as to a purported 'confession' given by a Co-Defendant, KENNETH McCULLOUGH. Such conduct constituted error in light of *Bruton v. United States* [, 391 U.S. 123, 88 S.Ct. 1620, 20 L.Ed.2d 476 (1968)]." Defendant's Motion for a New Trial, App. 17.

When Judge Harney entertained this motion on October 6, 1980, there was no argument to be heard. The Assistant District Attorney noted the State's full agreement to a retrial. Statement of Facts, vol. II, pp. 432–433. The next day's newspaper made the prosecutor's motives clear.

"In a rare occurrence, the Randall County Criminal District Attorney Randy Sherrod said yesterday he has joined a defense motion calling for a new trial in the case of Sanford James McCullough, who was found guilty Sept. 24 of the murder of George Preston Small and sentenced to 20 years in the penitentiary.

"Sherrod said it was the first time in his experience that he had been in agreement with a defense attorney in granting a new trial.

"He said one of the biggest factors influencing his decision to join the defense motion was the possibility of a [sic] getting a harsher sentence in a new trial." Amarillo Daily News, Oct. 7, 1980, p. C-1, col. 1; Record, Defendant's Exhibit 2. See also Amarillo Globe-Times, Oct. 7, 1980, p. 21, cols. 1–6 ("DA Agrees to New Trial for Man Convicted in Murder Case"). Record, Defendant's Exhibit 1.

In the face of this publicity, the defense moved for a change of venue, but its motion was denied. 2 Tr. 518 (Nov. 7, 1980). Having failed in this attempt to ensure that McCullough's second jury had no knowledge of his conviction and sentence in the first trial, the defense postponed its election of sentencer until it could hear the results of *voir dire*. 3 Tr. 7–8 (Dec. 10–12, 1980). During *voir dire* at least 13 prospective jurors were excused after indicating that their knowledge of the first trial's results would affect their ability to give McCullough a fair trial. *Id.*, at 17–33. Immediately after the close of *voir dire*, the defendant elected to be sentenced by the trial judge if convicted. *Id.*, at 122; App. 25–26. McCullough's election likely was affected by his counsel's belief that while *Chaffin v. Stynchcombe*, 412 U.S. 17, 93 S.Ct. 1977, 36 L.Ed.2d 714 (1973), had made the rule of *North Carolina v. Pearce, supra*, inapplicable to resentencing by a different jury, that rule would still bar Judge Harney from imposing a sentence greater than the 20 years defendant had received in his first trial. But fears that *voir dire* had not been sufficient to purge the jury of all knowledge of McCullough's first trial could well have played as great a part in that decision.

After McCullough was convicted a second time, Judge Harney heard argument on sentencing. Defense counsel urged that "there being no additional evidence on the part of the conduct or action of the Defendant subsequent to the prior conviction," the court was bound by *North Carolina v. Pearce, supra*, to impose a sentence of not more than 20 years. 2 Tr. 273–274 (Dec. 10–12, 1980). The prosecution replied that because defendant had elected to be sentenced by the trial judge, *North Carolina v. Pearce*, would not bar the court "from assessing a range of punishment greater than what was received by a jury." 2 Tr. 277 (Dec. 10–12, 1980). Judge Harney sentenced McCullough to 50 years' imprisonment. In response to defendant's motion, she later filed an order in which, while holding the rule of *North Carolina v. Pearce* inapplicable, she gave her reasons for imposing a heavier sentence in order to make remand unnecessary should the Court of Criminal Appeals hold the rule applicable. App. 33. She found that the testimony of two new witnesses, Carolyn Sue Hollison McCullough and Willie Brown, implicated defendant in the crime, added to the credibility of certain prosecution witnesses, and detracted from that of certain defense witnesses. The testimony also "shed new light upon the defendant's life, conduct, and his mental and moral propensities," especially his "propensity to commit brutal crimes against persons and to constitute a future threat to society." *Id.*, at 34. Judge Harney noted further that had defendant "elected to have the court set his punishment at the first trial, the court would have assessed more than the twenty (20) year sentence imposed by the jury." *Ibid.* Finally, the court found:

"Upon retrial after having been found guilty of murder for a second time by a jury and after having made known to the court that he had been involved in numerous criminal offenses and had served time in the penitentiary, the defendant never produced, or even attempted to produce, any evidence that he intended to change his life style, habits, or conduct, or that he had made any effort whatsoever toward rehabilitating himself. Again upon retrial, the [sic] failed to show this court any sign or indication of refraining from criminal conduct in the future, nor did he give any indication upon retrial that he no longer posed a violent and continuing threat to our society." *Id.*, at 35.

II

A

At the outset, one must reject the majority's suggestion, *ante* at ——, that the fact that McCullough elected to be sentenced by Judge Harney has any relevance to the question whether *Pearce* requires us to presume that the increase in his sentence was the product of the judge's vindictiveness. The message of *Pearce* is not that a defendant should be given a chance to choose the sentencing agency least likely to increase his sentence as a price for his decision to pursue an appeal. Rather,

Pearce held that under the Due Process Clause, "vindictiveness against a defendant for having successfully attacked his first conviction must play no part in the sentence he receives after a new trial." 395 U.S., at 725, 89 S.Ct., at 2080. Thus, in *Chaffin v. Stynchcombe, supra,* where the defendant had been tried and sentenced by a jury at his first trial, the Court assumed that if the defendant had elected to be tried and sentenced by a judge at his retrial, *Pearce* would circumscribe the sentence the judge could impose should defendant be convicted again. See 412 U.S., at 33, n. 21, 93 S.Ct., at 1986, n. 21.

Had McCullough's first conviction been overturned on appeal, rather than nullified by Judge Harney's order for a retrial, it would make no sense to allow McCullough's decision to be sentenced by the court to deprive him of the safeguards against judicial vindictiveness established in *Pearce.* Whether or not that judge had been the sentencing authority in the first proceeding, we would fear that the judge would have had a "personal stake in the prior conviction" and a "motivation to engage in self-vindication," as well as a wish to "discourag[e] what [s]he regards as meritless appeals." *Chaffin, supra,* at 27, 93 S.Ct., at 1983. Moreover, it would not be appropriate to find a waiver of McCullough's due process right in his exercise of his statutory right to elect his sentencer, especially in a case where defendant's choice might have been influenced by a desire to avoid being sentenced by a jury from a community that had been exposed to the considerable publicity surrounding his first trial.

B

In *Pearce,* recognition of the possibility that personal animosity and institutional prejudices might infect a trial judge's resentencing of a defendant after a successful appeal led this Court to establish a rule of presumptive vindictiveness. The question here is whether these same personal and institutional prejudices may infect a judge's sentencing following a retrial that the judge herself ordered.

The majority reasons that "[i]n contrast to *Pearce,* McCullough's second trial came about because the trial judge herself concluded that the prosecutor's misconduct required it. Granting McCullough's motion for a new trial hardly suggests any vindictiveness on the part of the judge towards him." *Ante,* at ——. Such an observation betrays not only an insensitivity to the motives that might underlie any trial judge's decision to grant a motion for a new trial, but also a blindness to the peculiar circumstances surrounding the decision to grant a retrial in this case.

The mere grant of a new trial motion can in no way be considered a guarantee, or even an indication, that the judge will harbor no resentment toward defendant as a result of his decision to exercise his statutory right to make such a motion. Even where a trial judge believes that the assignments of error are valid, she may still resent being given a choice between publicly conceding such errors and waiting for her judgment to be put to the test on appeal. This will be especially true when the errors alleged, however substantial as a matter of constitutional or statutory law, are considered by the judge not to cast doubt on the defendant's guilt. In such a case, the judge might well come to defendant's sentencing annoyed at having been forced to sit through a trial whose result was a foregone conclusion, and quite ready to vent that annoyance by giving the defendant a sentence stiffer than he otherwise would have received. Even if a trial judge is confident that her conduct of a trial was error-free, she may still grant a new trial if she has any doubts as to whether the courts reviewing her ruling will agree. In this situation, the feelings of resentment already alluded to might be augmented by the judge's annoyance with the courts that review her judgments.

Turning to the facts here, I believe the possibility of vindictiveness is even greater in this case than in the general run of cases in which a trial judge has granted a retrial. It is far from clear that Judge Harney's decision to grant a new trial was made out of either solicitude for McCullough or recognition of the merits of his claims. Defendant's motion was uncontested and, if the press coverage is any indication, the judge's decision to grant it was at least as much a boon to the prosecution as it was to defendant. Indeed, the most cynical might even harbor suspicions that the judge shared the District Attorney's hope that a retrial would permit the imposition of a sentence more commensurate with the prosecution's view of the heinousness of the crime for which McCullough had been brought to bar. At any rate, one can imagine that when it fell to Judge Harney to sentence McCullough after his second conviction, his decision to seek a retrial after receiving such a comparatively light sentence from his first jury was counted against him.

Whether any of these considerations actually played any part in Judge Harney's decision to give McCullough a harsher sentence after his retrial is not the issue here, just as it was not the issue in *Pearce*. The point is that the possibility they did play such a part is sufficiently real, and proving actual prejudice, sufficiently difficult, that a presumption of vindictiveness is as appropriate here as it was in *Pearce*. See Van Alstyne, In Gideon's Wake: Harsher Penalties and the "Successful" Criminal Appellant, 74 Yale L.J. 606, 612, and n. 22 (1965) (noting difficulties faced by defendant seeking to show actual vindictiveness).

III

The majority holds that "[e]ven if the *Pearce* presumption were to apply here, we believe that the findings of the trial judge overcome that presumption." *Ante*, at ——. I find the reasons offered by Judge Harney far from adequate to rebut any presumption of vindictiveness. Moreover, I believe that by holding those reasons sufficient, the Court effectively eviscerates the effort made in *Pearce* to ensure both

that vindictiveness against a defendant for having successfully attacked his first conviction "play no part in the sentence he receives after a new trial," 395 U.S., at 725, 89 S.Ct., at 2080, and that the "defendant be freed of apprehension of such a retaliatory motivation on the part of the sentencing judge." *Ibid.*

A

The presumption of vindictiveness established in *Pearce* was made rebuttable. The Court there held that where a judge decides to impose a more severe sentence on a defendant after a new trial,

"the reasons for his doing so must affirmatively appear. Those reasons must be based upon objective information concerning identifiable conduct on the part of the defendant occurring after the time of the original sentencing proceeding. And the factual data upon which the increased sentence is based must be made part of the record, so that the constitutional legitimacy of the increased sentence may be fully reviewed on appeal." *Id.*, at 726, 89 S.Ct., at 2081.

Whether this formulation allowed a sentencing judge to rely on any event occurring after a defendant's first sentencing or only on actual "conduct" by the defendant since that time might have been open to some speculation, at least until *Wasman v. United States*, 468 U.S. ——, 104 S.Ct. 3217, 82 L.Ed.2d 424 (1984) resolved that "matter of semantics," *id.*, at ——, 104 S.Ct., at 3226, (POWELL, J., concurring in part and concurring in judgment). But the Court was quite clear that the conduct or event used to justify an increased sentence must have taken place after the original sentencing proceeding. Indeed, the majority's insistence upon this restriction led to the refusal of Justice WHITE to subscribe to one part of the Court's opinion. He wrote:

"I join the Court's opinion except that in my view Part II–C should authorize an increased sentence on retrial based on any objective, identifiable factual data not known to the trial judge at the time of the original sentencing proceeding." *Pearce*, 395 U.S., at 751, 89 S.Ct., at 2089 (WHITE, J., concurring in part).

The Court's rejection of the standard proposed by Justice WHITE is no doubt explained by the majority's desire to "protect against reasonable apprehension of vindictiveness that could deter a defendant from appealing a first conviction." *Wasman*, 468 U.S., at ——, 104 S.Ct., at 3226 (POWELL, J., concurring in part and concurring in judgment). As a majority of the Court recently recognized, the need to eliminate this apprehension was as much a concern of the Court in *Pearce* as actual vindictiveness. See 468 U.S., at ——, 104 S.Ct., at 3226; *id.*, at ——, 104 S.Ct., at 3226 (BRENNAN, J., concurring in judgment); *id.*, at ——, 104 S.Ct., at 3226 (STEVENS, J., concurring in judgment). Recognizing that in the course of any retrial, or merely by virtue of the passage of time, new information relating to events prior to a defendant's original sentencing would become available to a sentencer after retrial, the Court decided that allowing this information to justify a harsher sentence would make the intended guarantee of fairness sound quite hollow to the defendant deciding whether to pursue his statutory right of appeal.

B

By finding the reasons given by Judge Harney adequate to rebut a presumption of vindictiveness, the majority not only disregards the clear rule in *Pearce*. It announces a new regime in which the "chill" that plagued defendants in the days before *Pearce* will once again be felt by those deciding whether to contest their convictions.

I do not doubt Judge Harney's assertions that the testimony of Carolyn Sue Hollison McCullough and Willie Lee Brown strengthened the prosecution's case against McCullough by corroborating evidence and testimony that had already been produced at his first trial and by adding a

few brush strokes to the portrayal in the first proceeding of McCullough's role in the crime and of his character. However, "[i]n the natural course of events upon the retrial of a case, one might normally expect the Government to have available additional testimony and evidence of a defendant's guilt if for no other reason than that the Government has had additional time to prepare and refine its presentation." *United States v. Tucker*, 581 F.2d 602, 606, n. 8 (CA7 1978). That such new evidence will be available to a trial judge sentencing a defendant after a retrial is thus inevitable. And if that judge wishes to punish defendant for having asserted his right to a fair trial, she will always be able to point to that new information as the basis for any increase in defendant's sentence the second time around. As one authority has noted: "If a court on retrial could justify an increased sentence on the ground that it now had additional knowledge concerning the defendant's participation in the offense, then the *Pearce* limitation could be evaded in almost every case." 3 W. LaFave & J. Israel, Criminal Procedure 176 (1984). This limitation would be even more easily avoided if a trial judge could rebut a presumption of vindictiveness merely by indicating that she would have given defendant a harsher sentence at his first trial had she been given the chance. That leaves, as the only "new" information to support 30 additional years' imprisonment, the fact that between his two trials, McCullough did not evince a desire to rehabilitate himself. Surely something more is required.

There is neither any reason nor any need for us to believe that dishonest and unconstitutionally vindictive judges actually hold sway in American courtrooms, and even less call for us to doubt the integrity of Judge Harney. The message of *Pearce* is that the fear of such vindictiveness is real enough. And a defendant plagued by such an apprehension is likely to take small comfort in any presumption of vindictiveness established for his benefit if the means of rebutting that presumption will always be within the easy reach of the judge who will sentence him should the challenge to his conviction prove unsuccessful. As far as defendants are concerned, today's decision, by permitting references to new, often cumulative, information about the crime charged to satisfy *Pearce*'s demand for "objective information concerning identifiable conduct on the part of the defendant," 395 U.S., at 726, 89 S.Ct., at 2081, nullifies the guarantee held out in *Pearce*.

Persuaded by the Solicitor General's hypothetical involving a defendant whose prior convictions are not apparent to the trial judge until after defendant's appeal and retrial, the majority concludes that "[r]estricting justifications for a sentence increase to *only* "events that occurred subsequent to the original sentencing proceedings" could in some circumstances lead to absurd results." *Ante*, at ——. However, this objection to such a restriction was considered in *Pearce* and rejected there, as it should be here. As one *amicus curiae* brief advised the *Pearce* Court:

"In the unlikely event that some prior offense escaped the notice of the court when the accused was under consideration for sentencing, moreover, the government is free to bring a separate proceeding under its habitual offender (recidivism) acts. To the little extent that states may be concerned that sentences generally tend to be imposed in some instances without due consideration of the nature of the offense or the char-

acter of the accused, moreover, each state is constitutionally free to make ample provision for staffing and presentence reports to guard against unduly lenient sentencing to whatever extent that government feels to be appropriate. Indeed, each state presumably has done this to the precise extent that it has been genuinely concerned with the securing of sentences which are both fair to the accused and adequate for the public safety." Brief for American Civil Liberties Union et al. as *Amici Curiae* in *North Carolina v. Pearce*, O.T.1968, No. 413, pp. 9–10.

IV

A lot has happened since the final day of the October 1968 Term, the day *North Carolina v. Pearce* was handed down. But nothing has happened since then that casts any doubt on the need for the guarantee of fairness that this Court held out to defendants in *Pearce*. The majority today begins by denying respondent the promise of that guarantee even though his case clearly calls for its application. The Court then reaches out to render the guarantee of little value to all defendants, even to those whose plight was the explicit concern of the *Pearce* Court in 1969. To renege on the guarantee of *Pearce* is wrong. To do so while pretending not to is a shame. I dissent.

Patrick Gene POLAND, Petitioner,

v.

ARIZONA.

Michael Kent POLAND

v.

ARIZONA.

Nos. 85–5023, 85–5024.

Decided May 5, 1986.

Syllabus [*]

Petitioners robbed a bank van of $281,-000 in cash and killed the guards by dumping them into a lake in sacks weighted with rocks. Petitioners were convicted of first-degree murder in an Arizona state court. At a separate hearing, while finding that the statutory aggravating circumstance that the offense was committed for "pecuniary gain" was not present because it applied only to contract killings, the trial judge sentenced petitioners to death upon finding that the statutory aggravating circumstance that the offense was committed

[*] The syllabus constitutes no part of the opinion of the Court but has been prepared by the Reporter of Decisions for the convenience of the reader. See *United States v. Detroit Lumber Co.*, 200 U.S. 321, 337, 26 S.Ct. 282, 287, 50 L.Ed.2d 499.

in "an especially heinous, cruel, or depraved manner" was present. The Arizona Supreme Court, while reversing and remanding for a retrial on other grounds, held that the evidence was insufficient to support a finding of the "especially heinous" circumstance, but that the trial judge erred in finding the "pecuniary gain" circumstance limited to contract killings, and that if petitioners were again convicted the judge might find this circumstance present. On remand, petitioners were again convicted of first-degree murder and the trial judge again sentenced them to death, finding that both the "pecuniary gain" and "especially heinous" circumstances were present. The Arizona Supreme Court affirmed, rejecting petitioners' argument that the Double Jeopardy Clause barred reimposition of the death penalty. The court found the evidence still insufficient to support the "especially heinous" circumstance but sufficient to support the "pecuniary gain" circumstance.

Held: Reimposing the death penalty on petitioners did not violate the Double Jeopardy Clause. Pp. 1753–1756.

(a) When a conviction is reversed on appeal, it is nullified and " 'the slate wiped clean,' " so that if the defendant is convicted again, he may constitutionally be subjected to whatever punishment is lawful. *Bullington v. Missouri*, 451 U.S. 430, 442, 101 S.Ct. 1852, 1860, 68 L.Ed.2d 270. This rationale is, however, inapplicable where a jury agrees or an appellate court decides that the prosecution "has not proved its case." *Id.*, at 443, 101 S.Ct., at 1860. Therefore, the relevant inquiry in these cases is whether the sentencing judge or the reviewing court has "decided that the prosecution has not proved its case" for the death penalty and hence has "acquitted" petitioners. *Bullington v. Missouri, supra; Arizona v. Rumsey*, 467 U.S. 203, 104 S.Ct. 2305, 81 L.Ed.2d 164. Pp. 1753–1754.

(b) The trial judge's rejection of the "pecuniary gain" aggravating circumstance was not an "acquittal" of that circumstance for double jeopardy purposes, and did not foreclose its consideration by the reviewing court. Moreover, because the reviewing court did not find the evidence legally insufficient to justify imposition of the death penalty, there was no death penalty "acquittal" by that court. The Double Jeopardy Clause, therefore, did not foreclose a second sentencing hearing at which the "clean slate" rule applied. Pp. 1754–1756.

144 Ariz. 388, 698 P.2d 183, and 144 Ariz. 412, 698 P.2d 207 (1985), affirmed.

WHITE, J., delivered the opinion of the Court, in which BURGER, C.J., and POWELL, REHNQUIST, STEVENS, and O'CONNOR, JJ., joined. MARSHALL, J., filed a dissenting opinion, in which BRENNAN and BLACKMUN, JJ., joined.

W.K. Wilhelmsen, for petitioner in each case.

Gerald R. Grant, Phoenix, Ariz., for respondent in each case.

Justice WHITE delivered the opinion of the Court.

The question presented is whether the Double Jeopardy Clause bars a further capital sentencing proceeding when, on appeal from a sentence of death, the reviewing court finds the evidence insufficient to support the only aggravating factor on which the sentencing judge relied, but does not find the evidence insufficient to support the death penalty.

I

In 1977 petitioners Patrick and Michael Poland, disguised as police officers, stopped a Purolator van that was making cash deliveries to various banks in northern Arizona. After removing some $281,000 in cash from the van, petitioners took the two Purolator guards to a lake and dumped them into the water in sacks weighted with rocks. Autopsies indicated that the most probable cause of the guards' death was drowning, although one may have died of a heart attack. It was not possible to determine if the guards were drugged, but there was no evidence of a struggle.

The jury disbelieved petitioners' alibi defense and convicted them of first-degree murder. Pursuant to former Ariz.Rev. Stat.Ann. § 13–454(A) (Supp.1973), the trial judge then sat as sentencer in a separate proceeding. At the hearing, the prosecution, relying on the evidence presented at trial, argued that two statutory aggravating circumstances were present: (1) that petitioners had "committed the offense as consideration for the receipt, or in expectation of the receipt, of [something] of pecuniary value," former Ariz.Rev.Stat.Ann. § 13–454(E)(5) (Supp.1973); and (2) that petitioners had "committed the offense in an especially heinous, cruel, or depraved manner," former Ariz.Rev.Stat. § 13–454(E)(6) (Supp.1973). The trial judge made the following finding with respect to the "pecuniary gain" aggravating circumstance:

"The court finds the aggravating circumstance in § 13–454E(3) *[sic]* is not present. This presumes the legislative intent was to cover a contract killing. If this presumption is inaccurate, the evidence shows the defendants received something of pecuniary value, cash in the amount of $281,000.00.

"This, then, would be an aggravating circumstance." App. 15–16.

The judge found that the "especially heinous, cruel, [or] depraved" aggravating circumstance was present, stating that the murders were "shockingly evil, insensate, and marked by debasement." *Id.*, at 16. Finding that this aggravating circumstance outweighed the mitigating evidence, the judge sentenced petitioners to death. *Id.*, at 14.

On appeal, petitioners argued that the evidence was insufficient to support the judge's finding of the "especially heinous, cruel, or depraved" aggravating circumstance. They also argued that the jury's verdict was tainted by a jury-room discus-

sion of evidence not admitted at trial. The Arizona Supreme Court agreed that the jury's verdict was tainted, necessitating reversal and retrial. *State v. Poland,* 132 Ariz. 269, 283–285, 645 P.2d 784, 798–800 (1982). The court next held that the evidence on which the State relied at the first sentencing hearing was insufficient to support a finding of the "especially heinous, cruel, or depraved" aggravating circumstance. *Id.,* at 285, 645 P.2d, at 800. Finally, the court stated that the trial court "mistook the law when it did not find that the defendants 'committed the offense as consideration for the receipt, or in expectation of the receipt, of anything of pecuniary value.'" *Ibid.* The court explained that this aggravating circumstance is not limited to situations involving contract killings, see *State v. Clark,* 126 Ariz. 428, 616 P.2d 888 (1980), and added that "[u]pon retrial, if the defendants are again convicted of first degree murder, the court may find the existence of this aggravating circumstance." 132 Ariz., at 286, 645 P.2d, at 801.

On remand, petitioners were again convicted of first-degree murder. At the sentencing hearing, the prosecution, relying on the evidence presented at the second trial and also presenting additional evidence, argued that the "pecuniary gain" and "especially heinous, cruel, or depraved" aggravating factors were present in each petitioner's case. The prosecution alleged a third aggravating circumstance in petitioner Patrick Poland's case: previous conviction of "a felony ... involving the use or threat of violence on another person," Ariz. Rev.Stat.Ann. § 13–454(E)(2) (Supp.1973).[1] The trial judge found all of the aggravating circumstances alleged by the prosecution, and again sentenced both petitioners to death.

Petitioners argued on appeal, as they had at their second sentencing hearing, that the Double Jeopardy Clause barred reimposition of the death penalty. Their theory

1. On October 5, 1981, petitioner Patrick Poland, in an unrelated case, was convicted of bank robbery and use of a dangerous weapon in a bank robbery.

was that the Arizona Supreme Court's decision on their first appeal that the evidence failed to support the "especially heinous, cruel, or depraved" aggravating circumstance amounted to an "acquittal" of the death penalty. Cf. *Bullington v. Missouri*, 451 U.S. 430, 101 S.Ct. 1852, 68 L.Ed.2d 270 (1981); *Arizona v. Rumsey*, 467 U.S. 203, 104 S.Ct. 2305, 81 L.Ed.2d 164 (1984). A majority of the Arizona Supreme Court rejected this argument, stating:

"Our holding in *Poland I* ... was simply that the death penalty could not be based solely upon [the 'especially heinous, cruel, or depraved'] aggravating circumstance because there was insufficient evidence to support it. This holding was not tantamount to a death penalty 'acquittal.'" *State v. Poland (Patrick)*, 144 Ariz. 388, 404, 698 P.2d 183, 199 (1985); accord, *State v. Poland (Michael)*, 144 Ariz. 412, 698 P.2d 207 (1985).

The court found the evidence still insufficient to support the "especially heinous, cruel, or depraved" aggravating circumstance, but sufficient to support the "pecuniary gain" aggravating circumstance with respect to both defendants and the "prior conviction involving violence" circumstance with respect to Patrick Poland. *State v. Poland (Patrick), supra*, at 404–406, 698 P.2d, at 199–201; accord, *State v. Poland (Michael), supra*. After again reviewing and independently weighing the mitigating and aggravating circumstances, the court concluded that the death penalty was appropriate in each petitioner's case. We granted certiorari to consider whether reimposing the death penalties on petition-

ers violated the Double Jeopardy Clause. 474 U.S. ——, 106 S.Ct. 60, 88 L.Ed.2d 49 (1984). We hold that it did not.

II

In *Bullington v. Missouri, supra,* this Court held that a defendant sentenced to life imprisonment by a capital sentencing jury is protected by the Double Jeopardy Clause against imposition of the death penalty in the event that he obtains reversal of his conviction and is retried and reconvicted. The Court recognized the usual rule to be is that when a defendant obtains reversal of his conviction on appeal,

"the original conviction has been nullified and 'the slate wiped clean.' Therefore, if the defendant is convicted again, he constitutionally may be subjected to whatever punishment is lawful, subject only to the limitation that he receive credit for time served." *Id.*, 451 U.S., at 442, 101 S.Ct., at 1860 (quoting *North Carolina v. Pearce*, 395 U.S. 711, 721, 89 S.Ct. 2072, 2078, 23 L.Ed. 656 (1969)).

However, the Court found that its prior decisions had created an exception to this rule: "[T]he 'clean slate' rationale ... is inapplicable whenever a jury agrees or an appellate court decides that the prosecution has not proved its case." *Bullington, supra*, 451 U.S., at 443, 101 S.Ct., at 1860.[2] Although it is usually "impossible to conclude that a sentence less than the statutory maximum 'constitute[s] a decision to the effect that the government has failed to prove its case,' " *ibid.* (quoting *Burks v. United States*, 437 U.S. 1, 15, 98 S.Ct.

---

2. Thus, a defendant charged with first-degree murder but only convicted of the lesser-included offense of second-degree murder has been acquitted of the greater charge for purposes of the Double Jeopardy Clause. In the event his conviction is reversed on appeal, "a retrial on the first-degree murder charge [is] barred by the Double Jeopardy Clause, because the defendant 'was forced to run the gantlet once on that charge and the jury refused to convict him.' " *Bullington, supra*, 451 U.S., at 443, 101 S.Ct., at 1860 (quoting *Green v. United States*, 355 U.S. 184, 190, 78 S.Ct. 221, 225, 2 L.Ed.2d 199 (1957)).

Also, when a defendant's conviction is overturned on appeal on the grounds that the evidence was insufficient to convict, the Double Jeopardy Clause forbids a retrial. " 'Since we necessarily accord absolute finality to a jury's *verdict* of acquittal—no matter how erroneous its decision—it is difficult to conceive how society has any greater interest in retrying a defendant when, on review, it is decided as a matter of law that the jury could not properly have returned a verdict of guilty.' " *Bullington, supra*, 451 U.S., at 442–443, 101 S.Ct., at 1859–1860 (quoting *Burks v. United States*, 437 U.S. 1, 16, 98 S.Ct. 2141, 2150, 57 L.Ed.2d 1 (1978)).

2141, 2149, 57 L.Ed.2d 1 (1978)), the Court found that Missouri, by "enacting a capital sentencing procedure that resembles a trial on the issue of guilt or innocence, ... *explicitly requires* the jury to determine whether the prosecution has 'proved its case,'" *id.*, at 444, 101 S.Ct., at 1861 (emphasis in original).[3] Accordingly, the Court held that the jury's decision to sentence Bullington to life imprisonment after his first conviction should be treated as an "acquittal" of the death penalty under the Double Jeopardy Clause.

Recently, the Court held that the rationale of *Bullington* applies to the Arizona capital sentencing scheme at issue in this case. *Arizona v. Rumsey*, 467 U.S. 203, 104 S.Ct. 2305, 81 L.Ed.2d 164 (1984).[4] In *Rumsey*, the trial judge erred in exactly the same way as the trial judge did at petitioners' first sentencing hearing in this case. by construing the "pecuniary gain" aggravating circumstance as limited to "murder for hire" situations. Unlike the trial judge in this case, however, the trial judge in *Rumsey* found no aggravating circumstances, and entered a sentence of life imprisonment. This Court held that "[t]he double jeopardy principle relevant to [Rumsey's] case is the same as that in-

voked in *Bullington:* an acquittal on the merits by the sole decisionmaker in the proceeding is final and bars retrial on the same charge." *Id.*, at 211, 104 S.Ct., at 2310.

Under *Bullington* and *Rumsey*, therefore, the relevant inquiry in the cases before us is whether the sentencing judge or the reviewing court has "decid[ed] that the prosecution has not proved its case" for the death penalty and hence has "acquitted" petitioners. *Bullington*, 451 U.S., at 443, 101 S.Ct., at 1860.

III

At no point during petitioners' first capital sentencing hearing and appeal did either the sentencer or the reviewing court hold that the prosecution had "failed to prove its case" that petitioners deserved the death penalty. Plainly, the sentencing judge did not acquit, for he imposed the death penalty. While the Arizona Supreme Court held that the sentencing judge erred in relying on the "especially heinous, cruel, or depraved" aggravating circumstance, it did not hold that the prosecution had failed to prove its case for the death penalty.

3. The "case" to which the Court referred in *Bullington* was the prosecution's case that the defendant deserved the death penalty. The analogy drawn was between a death sentence and a verdict of guilty, a life sentence and a verdict of innocent. The Court emphasized that the sentencer was required to make a choice between "two alternative verdicts," 451 U.S., at 438, 101 S.Ct., at 1858, a statement inconsistent with the view that for double jeopardy purposes the capital sentencer should be seen as rendering a series of mini-verdicts on each aggravating circumstance. See also *Arizona v. Rumsey*, 467 U.S. 203, 209–210, 104 S.Ct. 2305, 2309–2310 (1984) ("The sentencer—the trial judge in Arizona—is required to choose between two options: death, and life imprisonment without possibility of parole for 25 years").

4. The Court explained the similarities between the Arizona and Missouri systems as follows: "The capital sentencing proceeding in Arizona shares the characteristics of the Missouri proceeding that make it resemble a trial for purposes of the Double Jeopardy Clause. The sentencer—the trial judge in Arizona—is required to choose between two options: death, and life

imprisonment without possibility of parole for 25 years. The sentencer must make the decision guided by detailed statutory standards defining aggravating and mitigating circumstances; in particular, death may not be imposed unless at least one aggravating circumstance is found, whereas death must be imposed if there is one aggravating circumstance and no mitigating circumstance sufficiently substantial to call for leniency. The sentencer must make findings with respect to each of the statutory aggravating and mitigating circumstances, and the sentencing hearing involves the submission of evidence and the presentation of argument. The usual rules of evidence govern the admission of evidence of aggravating circumstances, and the State must prove the existence of aggravating circumstances beyond a reasonable doubt.... [T]hese characteristics make the Arizona capital sentencing proceeding indistinguishable for double jeopardy purposes from the capital sentencing proceeding in Missouri." 467 U.S., at 209–210, 104 S.Ct., at 2309–2310 (citations omitted).

Indeed, the court clearly indicated that there had been no such failure by remarking that "the trial court mistook the law when it did not find that the defendants 'committed the offense as consideration for the receipt, or in expectation of the receipt, of anything of pecuniary value,'" and that "[u]pon retrial, if the defendants are again convicted of first-degree murder, the court may find the existence of this aggravating circumstance," 132 Ariz., at 285, 286, 645 P.2d, at 800, 801.

Petitioners argue, however, that the Arizona Supreme Court "acquitted" them of the death penalty by finding the "evidence [insufficient] to support the sole aggravating circumstances found by the sentencer." Brief for Petitioners 16. Petitioners' implicit argument is, first, that the sentencing judge "acquitted" them of the "pecuniary gain" aggravating circumstance, and second, that the Double Jeopardy Clause rendered this "acquittal" final, so that the evidence relating to this circumstance was effectively removed from the case at the time of petitioners' first appeal.[5]

We reject the fundamental premise of petitioners' argument, namely, that a capital sentencer's failure to find a particular aggravating circumstance alleged by the prosecution always constitutes an "acquittal" of that circumstance for double jeopardy purposes. *Bullington* indicates that the proper inquiry is whether the sentencer or reviewing court has "decided that the prosecution has not proved its case" *that the death penalty is appropriate.*[6] We are not prepared to extend *Bullington* further and view the capital sentencing hearing as a set of mini-trials on the existence

of each aggravating circumstance. Such an approach would push the analogy on which *Bullington* is based past the breaking point.

Aggravating circumstances are not separate penalties or offenses, but are "standards to guide the making of [the] choice" between the alternative verdicts of death and life imprisonment. *Id.*, at 438, 101 S.Ct., at 1858. Thus, under Arizona's capital sentencing scheme, the judge's finding of any particular aggravating circumstance does not of itself "convict" a defendant (*i.e.*, require the death penalty), and the failure to find any particular aggravating circumstance does not "acquit" a defendant (*i.e.*, preclude the death penalty).

It is true that the sentencer must find *some* aggravating circumstance before the death penalty may be imposed, and that the sentencer's finding, albeit erroneous, that no aggravating circumstance is present is an "acquittal" barring a second death sentence proceeding. *Arizona v. Rumsey.* This is because

"the law attaches particular significance to an acquittal. To permit a second trial after an acquittal, however mistaken the acquittal may have been, would present an unacceptably high risk that the Government, with its vastly superior resources, might wear down the defendant so that 'even though innocent he may be found guilty.'" *United States v. Scott,* 437 U.S. 82, 91, 98 S.Ct. 2187, 2194, 57 L.Ed.2d 65 (1978) (quoting *Green v. United States,* 355 U.S. 184, 188, 78 S.Ct. 221, 2 L.Ed.2d 199 (1957)).

Petitioners seem to attach importance to the fact that the prosecution did not cross-appeal the trial judge's finding regarding the "pecuniary gain" aggravating circumstance. However, the Arizona Supreme Court did not accord any significance to the prosecution's failure to cross-appeal, and we certainly cannot say that as a matter of state law the court was precluded from considering the evidence regarding the "pecuniary gain" aggravating circumstance.

---

5. Petitioners have not made this argument with any clarity, but we can discern no other plausible basis for their contention that the Arizona Supreme Court "acquitted" them of the death penalty at the time of their first appeal. Any suggestion that the court *intended* to acquit them is negated by the language in *Poland I* and is rendered even more untenable by the court's statement at the time of the second appeal that "[o]ur holding in *Poland I, however,* was ... not tantamount to a death penalty 'acquittal.'" *State v. Poland,* 144 Ariz., at 404, 698 P.2d, at 199.

6. See n. 3, *supra.*

This concern with protecting the finality of acquittals is not implicated when, as in this case, a defendant is sentenced to death, *i.e.*, "convicted." There is no cause to shield such a defendant from further litigation; further litigation is the only hope he has. The defendant may argue on appeal that the evidence presented at his sentencing hearing was as a matter of law insufficient to support the aggravating circumstances on which his death sentence was based, but the Double Jeopardy Clause does not require the reviewing court, if it sustains that claim, to ignore evidence in the record supporting another aggravating circumstance which the sentencer has erroneously rejected. Such a rule would have the odd and unacceptable result of requiring a reviewing court to enter a death penalty "acquittal" even though that court is of the view that the State has "proved its case." Our decisions in *Burks* and *Bullington* do not support such a rule, which would certainly give the prosecution cause to "complain of prejudice." *Burks*, 437 U.S., at 16, 98 S.Ct., at 2149. We hold, therefore, that the trial judge's rejection of the "pecuniary gain" aggravating circumstance in this case was not an "acquittal" of that circumstance for double jeopardy purposes, and did not foreclose its consideration by the reviewing court. Furthermore, because the reviewing court did not find the evidence legally insufficient to justify imposition of the death penalty, there was no death penalty "acquittal" by that court. The Double Jeopardy Clause, therefore, did not foreclose a second sentencing hearing at which the "clean slate" rule applied.

The judgment of the Supreme Court of Arizona is

Affirmed.

Justice MARSHALL, with whom Justice BRENNAN and Justice BLACKMUN join, dissenting.

There is one difference between these cases and *Arizona v. Rumsey*, 467 U.S. 203, 104 S.Ct. 2305, 81 L.Ed.2d 164 (1984), in which seven Members of this Court interpreted the Double Jeopardy Clause to bar imposition of a death sentence after a life sentence has been reversed on appeal: the sentencing judge in petitioners' case made two errors of state law, while Rumsey's judge made only one. According to the majority, that makes the difference between life and death.

In *Rumsey*, the defendant was convicted of murder and robbery; the trial judge sentenced him to life imprisonment upon finding that none of the statutory aggravating circumstances provided by Arizona law applied to the defendant's case. One of those aggravating circumstances—murder committed as consideration for pecuniary gain—the court rejected in the belief that it applied only to murders for hire. On appeal, the Supreme Court of Arizona held that murder for pecuniary gain could also include murder in the course of a robbery. Accordingly, it set aside Rumsey's life sentence and remanded for resentencing. This time, Rumsey was given a death sentence, supported by the aggravating circumstance of murder for pecuniary gain. On writ of certiorari, this Court concluded that the Arizona death-sentencing procedure is equivalent to a trial for purposes of the Double Jeopardy Clause, under the doctrine of *Bullington v. Missouri*, 451 U.S. 430, 101 S.Ct. 1852, 68 L.Ed.2d 270 (1981). We then concluded that Rumsey's initial life sentence had constituted an "acquittal" on the merits of the central issue of the proceeding: whether death was the appropriate punishment for the offense. Under traditional double jeopardy principles, retrial of that issue was thereafter precluded, even though the "acquittal" was predicated upon a mistaken interpretation of state law. *Rumsey, supra,* at 211, 104 S.Ct., at 2310.

Petitioners, Patrick and Michael Poland, were convicted of the murders of two guards in the course of a robbery. Like the trial court in *Rumsey*, the sentencing court rejected the aggravating circumstance of murder for pecuniary gain, believing that it applied only to murders for hire. Unlike the *Rumsey* court, however, the trial judge did not then impose a life sentence. Instead, he concluded that another of the statutory aggravating circumstances was present: that the murders were "especially heinous, cruel, or depraved." Based on this sole aggravating circumstance, therefore, the court sentenced petitioners to death. On joint appeal, the Arizona Supreme Court reviewed the death sentences and concluded that the evidence was insufficient as a matter of state law to establish that the murders had been "especially heinous, cruel, or depraved," because the State had not proven that the victims had suffered, as state law requires. App. 61. Before remanding, however, the court took the opportunity, *sua sponte*, to note that murder for pecuniary gain was not limited to murders for hire, and therefore was available as a possible alternative basis for a death sentence. On remand, the trial court once more sentenced petitioners to death, again concluding that the murders were "especially heinous, cruel, or depraved," and also that they were committed for pecuniary gain.* The Arizona Supreme Court again reversed the aggravating circumstance of "especially heinous, cruel, or depraved," but this time upheld the death sentences on the ground of pecuniary gain.

The Court makes much of the fact that, unlike Rumsey, petitioners never received sentences of life imprisonment. Yet the majority fails to recognize the teaching of *Burks v. United States*, 437 U.S. 1, 98 S.Ct. 2141, 57 L.Ed.2d 1 (1978). In *Burks*, we held that an appellate reversal of a conviction, based on the legal conclusion that the evidence was insufficient to support the verdict, has the same effect under the Double Jeopardy Clause as an acquittal at trial. *Id.*, at 16, 98 S.Ct., at 2150. "To hold otherwise," the Court concluded, "would create a purely arbitrary distinction between those in petitioner's position and

others who would enjoy the benefit of a correct decision by the District Court." *Id.*, at 11, 98 S.Ct., at 2147. That arbitrary distinction is precisely the one that the Court creates today. The initial death sentences that petitioners received were "convictions," see *Rumsey, supra,* and their reversal for insufficiency of the evidence to support the sole aggravating circumstance found by the sentencing judge must, under *Burks,* be accorded the same effect as an "acquittal" at trial—the same effect as Rumsey's life sentence. As much as Rumsey's life sentence constituted the all-important "acquittal on the merits," even though predicated on an error of law, so, too, did the reversal of petitioners' death sentences.

The analogy, first drawn in *Bullington v. Missouri, supra,* between an acquittal at trial and an "acquittal" of death at sentencing, is not perfect, and the imperfections perhaps can explain the majority's mischaracterization of the issue in these cases. At trial, a defendant is charged with an offense containing certain specified elements; he is either convicted or acquitted of that offense, the trier of fact having concluded that the prosecution has or has not proved all the elements of the offense. The sentencing proceeding, however, is quite different. In Arizona, for example, a death sentence may be imposed if any one of seven statutory aggravating factors is proven. While it might be possible to treat each aggravating circumstance as a separate "offense," of which a defendant is either convicted or acquitted, this Court has taken a different approach. We have said that "on the merits" of a capital proceeding, the "central issue [is] whether death was the appropriate punishment for [the] offense." *Rumsey,* 467 U.S., at 211, 104 S.Ct., at 2310. Thus, the "offense" for which the defendant receives his "conviction" or "acquittal" is that of the appropriateness of the death penalty, not the elements of any particular aggravating factor. *Ante,* at 1754, n. 3.

---

* With respect to petitioner Patrick Poland, an additional aggravating factor was invoked to support the second death sentence, based on events subsequent to the first penalty proceeding.

In these cases, the trial judge found death to be the appropriate punishment because petitioners' offenses were "especially heinous, cruel, or depraved." On appeal, the Arizona Supreme Court held that the sole basis offered by the trial court to support its "conviction" of petitioners was insufficient as a matter of law.

The majority believes that, since other aggravating circumstances might have been found to support the "convictions," it was permissible to remand the cases for further factfinding on those alternative factors. But this overlooks what our cases have said a conviction *is* in the sentencing context—a determination that death is the appropriate penalty, not separate trials on the existence of all statutory aggravating circumstances, conducted *seriatim*. In these cases, that determination was reversed because there was insufficient evidence to support the ground relied on by the trial judge in reaching it. Any remand for further factfinding on the question whether the death sentence should be imposed was thereafter prohibited. See *Rumsey, supra,* at 211–212, 104 S.Ct., at 2310–2311. In no other circumstance would the Double Jeopardy Clause countenance the offer of a second chance to the State and the trial judge to find a better theory upon which to base a conviction. Nor should it do so here. I dissent.

VOLUME I

CHAPTER 7   CORRECTING EXCESSIVE SENTENCES

Courts continue to wrestle with problems of imposing sentences. Gradually, to insure equal sentences for the same crimes, the federal government has introduced sentencing guidelines. When these guidelines go into effect, the court will assign numerical values to certain factors and from a tabulation of the values will determine the length of sentences. Parole will be abolished. Whether these reforms will attain their stated goals remains to be seen.

One state which has sentencing guidelines is Washington. *State v. Ammons,* 713 P.2d 719 (Wash. 1986), is included as illustrative of a case where the guideline concept was held constitutional. Of course, future volumes of this series will follow closely the application of sentencing guidelines in the federal courts.

The case of *Kohley v. United States,* 784 F.2d 332 (8th Cir. 1986), rejected a statistical analysis of previous sentences in the same court. The case of *United States v. Meyer,* 802 F.2d 348 (9th Cir. 1986), which is not included here, brought to the judge's attention a study showing individuals convicted of "lewd and lascivious acts with a child under age 14" who were sentenced for a short period, whereas in *United States v. Hale,* 784 F.2d 1495 (9th Cir. 1986), the defendant was fined and given probation. In *Hale,* the defendant argued that the trial judge was obliged to harmonize his sentence with the sentences of the cited case and study. The court disagreed.

United States v. Rhodes, 779 F.2d 1019 (4th Cir. 1985), has a general discussion of factors to be considered when an appellate court reviews a sentence.

In *United States v. Barker,* 771 F.2d 1362 (9th Cir. 1985), the sentence was reversed. The case of *United States v. Rosenberg,* 806 F.2d 1169 (3d Cir. 1986), discussed the length of a sentence and bias on the part of the judge. Rosenberg is an important case on the topic.

In *People v. Strait,* 451 N.E.2d 631 (Ill.App.3d Dist. 1983), the court did not lessen an extended sentence, but sanctioned the judge's imposition of an extended sentence based on his findings that the offense was committed in an exceptionally brutal and henious manner. The case is not included.

In *Hutto v. Davis,* 454 U.S. 370, 102 S.Ct. 703 (1982), the Court sanctioned a sentence of forty years for the possession of nine ounces of marijuana. The defendant claimed the sentence was excessive, but the Supreme Court disagreed, for Virginia law authorized a greater punishment.

Introductions in previous volumes:

I: 429; VI: 63; VII: 93; VIII: 137

Articles:

Alperin, *Length of Sentence as Violation of Constitutional Provisions Prohibiting Cruel and Unusual Punishment,* 33 A.L.R.3d 335.

Michalik, *Review for Excessiveness of Sentence in Narcotics Case,* 55 A.L.R.3d 812.

A.B.A. Standards Relating to Appellate Review of Sentences, (§ 1.1, Appendix A).

105 Wash.2d 175

STATE of Washington, Respondent,

v.

Roy Lee AMMONS, Dale R. Barton, and Eugene Garrett, Appellants.

Nos. 51550–6, 51580–8 and 51587–5.

Supreme Court of Washington,
En Banc.

Jan. 30, 1986.

GOODLOE, Justice.

The appellants, Roy Lee Ammons, Dale R. Barton, and Eugene Garrett, challenge the constitutionality of the Sentencing Reform Act of 1981, RCW 9.94A (hereafter referred to as the SRA), pursuant to which they were sentenced. We hold the SRA is constitutional and affirm their sentences.

The SRA became effective on July 1, 1984. The SRA is a comprehensive sentencing system which establishes a standard presumptive sentencing range for most criminal offenses. The presence and nature of prior convictions determine, in part, the presumptive sentence range. RCW 9.94A.360 and .370.

Because the cases were consolidated on appeal, the factual settings of each appellant must be outlined.

Ammons: Roy Lee Ammons was found guilty of second degree burglary by a King County Superior Court jury on September 13, 1984, the Honorable Terrence A. Carroll presiding. The sentencing hearings were held on October 23 and 29, 1984. The standard sentence range for second degree burglary as a first offense is 0–90 days. The State presented to the court certified copies of four prior convictions: all from Skagit County, all for second degree burglary; three of them based on guilty pleas and one based on a jury verdict. Inclusion of the four prior convictions elevated the sentence range to 33 to 43 months.

Ammons asked the court to rule that before any prior conviction can be used to enhance a sentence, the State must prove the prior conviction beyond a reasonable doubt. The sentencing court ruled the State need only establish the prior convictions by a preponderance of the evidence.

Ammons also asked the court to rule that the State must prove the constitutional validity of any prior conviction, whether it is based on a guilty plea or a jury verdict. Ammons offered specific evidence of jury instructions which called into question the constitutional validity of his prior jury verdict conviction. The sentencing court found the State did not have to prove the constitutional validity of the prior convictions.

The sentencing court further found that the defendant did not have the right to remain silent with regard to the existence of prior convictions. Ammons was sentenced to 40 months in prison.

Barton: Dale R. Barton pleaded guilty, pursuant to a plea agreement, to the charge of second degree burglary on September 18, 1984 in King County Superior Court before the Honorable Stephen M. Reilly. The sentencing hearing was held on October 25, 1984. The standard sentence range for second degree burglary as a first offense is 0–90 days. The State presented to the court certified copies of four prior convictions: two for theft, one for forgery and one for burglary. Inclusion of the four prior convictions elevated the sentence range to 12 to 14 months. The court sentenced Barton to 14 months in prison.

Barton on appeal makes several constitutional challenges which will be addressed in the analysis section. He also argues that this court should not consider the certified copies of the four prior convictions which were discussed and reviewed at the sentencing but which were not included in the Superior Court's Clerk's Papers. RCW 9.94A.210(5). On June 4, 1985, the State moved to supplement the record. On June 24, 1985, we ordered that the record be supplemented.

Garrett: Eugene Garrett pleaded guilty to charges of second degree robbery and first degree theft on August 20, 1984 in King County Superior Court before the Honorable Donald D. Haley. At the plea proceeding, Garrett disputed the prosecutor's statement of his criminal history, arguing he knew of no prior convictions which the State could prove the existence, identity, and constitutional validity of beyond a reasonable doubt. The sentencing hearing was held on November 6, 1984. The standard sentence range for second degree robbery as a first offense is 6 to 12 months and for first degree theft as a first offense is 2 to 6 months. The State offered a certified copy of a judgment and sentence for second degree burglary. Inclusion of the prior conviction elevated the sentence range to 12 to 14 months for second degree robbery and 3 to 9 months for first degree theft.

Garrett objected to the use of the prior conviction, but submitted a certified copy of the statement on plea of guilty in order to challenge the constitutional validity of the plea. The court found the State's presentation of the judgment met the burden of preponderance of the evidence. The court imposed a sentence of 14 months for the second degree robbery and 3 months for the first degree theft.

To the extent possible, the overlapping issues raised by the appellants have been grouped together. The issues will be examined in the order deemed most sensible to the court.

I

The first challenge, made by Barton, is that the SRA violates the separation of powers doctrine. Barton presents three different theories. We find all three theories without merit.

The first theory is that the SRA is unconstitutional as a violation of the separation of powers doctrine because the Legislature's enactment of the SRA impinges on the judicial power to sentence. This theory begins with a faulty premise because the Legislature, not the judiciary, has the authority to determine the sentencing process.

This court has consistently held that the fixing of legal punishments for criminal offenses is a legislative function.

As early as 1909, the court stated:

The spirit of the law is in keeping with the acknowledged power of the legislature to provide a minimum and maximum term within which the trial court may exercise its discretion in fixing sentence

. . .

State v. Le Pitre, 54 Wash. 166, 169, 103 P. 27 (1909).

In *State v. Mulcare*, 189 Wash. 625, 628, 66 P.2d 360 (1937), the court stated: "Fixing of penalties or punishments for criminal offenses is a legislative function, and the power of the legislature in that respect is plenary and subject only to constitutional provisions against excessive fines and cruel and inhuman punishment."

The court in 1975 recognized that "it is the function of the legislature and not of the judiciary to alter the sentencing process." *State v. Monday*, 85 Wash.2d 906, 909–10, 540 P.2d 416 (1975). Recently, the court again reiterated that sentencing is within the Legislature's power. *State v. Bryan*, 93 Wash.2d 177, 181, 606 P.2d 1228 (1980).

Barton offers as support for his position our decision in *State ex rel. Schillberg v. Cascade Dist. Court*, 94 Wash.2d 772, 621 P.2d 115 (1980). It does not support his position. *Cascade Dist. Court* determined that the decision to refer an accused for diagnostic evaluation of amenability for a deferred prosecution is essentially a sentencing alternative and, therefore, at least partially a judicial act which does not infringe upon the prosecutor's charging function. The court recognized that the prosecutor could have input if the Legislature provided guidelines but, as written, the statute gave the prosecutor the ability to arbitrarily veto a partial judicial decision and therefore violated the separation of powers doctrine. We stated: "If the legislature wishes to make the initial eligibility decision one for the prosecutor ... then standards for guiding decision making are necessary to prevent an unconstitutional delegation of the *legislative* authority to alter the sentencing process." (italics ours.) *Cascade Dist. Court*, at 781, 621 P.2d 115.

We find no violation of the separation of powers doctrine by the Legislature's enactment of the SRA because it is within the Legislature's power.

The second theory is that the SRA is unconstitutional as a violation of the separation of powers doctrine because the SRA's limitation on the trial court's discretion in sentencing infringes upon a judicial power.

Barton argues that alteration of a judge's discretion, by requiring a sentence within a certain range unless there are substantial and compelling reasons, violates judicial authority. This argument fails to recognize that the trial court does not have absolute discretion to do whatever it pleases. The trial court's discretion in sentencing is that which is given by the Legislature.

The SRA by its language still gives the trial court discretion in sentencing but it changes the parameters in which the discretion can be exercised. RCW

9.94A.010 specifically states that the SRA "structures, but does not eliminate, discretionary decisions affecting sentences ..." The court continues to have discretion. The SRA allows "[t]he court [to] impose any sentence within the [presumptive sentence] range that it deems appropriate." RCW 9.94A.370. The court is allowed to impose a sentence outside the standard range, either higher or lower, as long as it finds "considering the purpose of [the SRA] that there are substantial and compelling reasons justifying an exceptional sentence." RCW 9.94A.120(2). The Legislature's structuring of the trial court's discretion does not infringe upon a judicial power.

The Juvenile Justice Act of 1977, RCW 13.40, in which the Legislature gave trial courts new guidelines for the sentencing of juveniles has been upheld. *State v. Rhodes*, 92 Wash.2d 755, 600 P.2d 1264 (1979); *State v. Adcock*, 36 Wash.App. 699, 676 P.2d 1040 (1984).

The third theory is that the SRA is unconstitutional as a violation of the separation of powers doctrine because the SRA's structuring of the Court of Appeals review of sentences outside the standard range infringes upon a judicial power.

Appellate review of sentences outside the standard range is governed by RCW 9.94A.210, which provides, in pertinent part:

> (2) A sentence outside the sentence range for the offense is subject to appeal by the defendant or the state. The appeal shall be to the court of appeals in accordance with rules adopted by the supreme court.

> .   .   .   .

> (4) To reverse a sentence which is outside the sentence range, the reviewing court must find: (a) Either that the reasons supplied by the sentencing judge are not supported by the record which was before the judge or that those reasons do not justify a sentence outside the standard range for that offense; or (b)

that the sentence imposed was clearly excessive or clearly too lenient.

Similar standards were given to the Court of Appeals in the Juvenile Justice Act of 1977, RCW 13.40.230. This court applied them without question in *State v. Rhodes, supra,* 92 Wash.2d at 760, 600 P.2d 1264. The SRA's structuring of the Court of Appeals review of sentences outside the standard range does not infringe upon judicial power.

II

The second challenge, made by Barton, is that RCW 9.94A.210(1), which provides: "A sentence within the standard range for the offense shall not be appealed" is unconstitutional. Although article 1, section 22 of the Washington State Constitution provides: "In criminal prosecutions the accused shall have ... the right to appeal in all cases", our construction of RCW 9.94A.210(1) makes it constitutional.

We read RCW 9.94A.210(1) as only precluding appellate review of challenges to the amount of time imposed when the time is within the standard range. The Legislature by establishing presumptive sentence ranges has structured the trial court's discretion. When the sentence given is within the presumptive sentence range then as a matter of law there can be no abuse of discretion and there is no right to appeal that aspect. An appellant, of course, is not precluded from challenging on appeal the procedure by which a sentence within the standard range was imposed.

III

The third challenge, made by Barton and Ammons, is that RCW 9.94A.100 and 9.94A.370 violate the constitutional rights of a defendant against self-incrimination and against having to produce evidence which are protected by the fifth amendment to the United States Constitution and article 1, section 9 of the Washington State Constitution.

RCW 9.94A.100 provides, in pertinent part, that:

The prosecuting attorney and the defendant shall each provide the court with their understanding of what the defendant's criminal history is prior to a plea of guilty pursuant to a plea agreement.

RCW 9.94A.370 provides, in pertinent part:

In determining any sentence, the trial court may use no more information than is admitted by the plea agreement, and admitted to or acknowledged at the time of sentencing. Acknowledgement includes not objecting to information stated in the presentence reports. Where the defendant disputes material facts, the court must either not consider the fact or grant an evidentiary hearing on the point.

Criminal history means the list of a defendant's prior convictions, and may include certain juvenile convictions. RCW 9.94A.030(8)(a) and (b).

RCW 9.94A.100 requires the defendant to disclose any prior convictions but applies only when the defendant enters a plea of guilty pursuant to a plea agreement. A defendant has no constitutional right to plead guilty. *State v. Martin,* 94 Wash.2d 1, 4, 614 P.2d 164 (1980). However, the State may confer such a right by statute. *Martin,* at 4, 614 P.2d 164, *citing North Carolina v. Alford,* 400 U.S. 25, 38 n. 11, 91 S.Ct. 160, 168 n. 11, 27 L.Ed.2d 162 (1970). Because a plea agreement has been analogized to a contract, *Santobello v. New York,* 404 U.S. 257, 262, 92 S.Ct. 495, 498, 30 L.Ed.2d 427 (1971), the State can, pursuant to statute, condition the plea agreement on a defendant's giving his criminal history of convictions. Disclosure of a defendant's criminal history prior to the plea of guilty also enables the court to apprise the defendant of the sentencing consequences of his plea. *See In re Baca,* 34 Wash.App. 468, 471, 662 P.2d 64 (1983). We find the requirement of RCW 9.94A.100 does not violate a defendant's constitutional rights.

RCW 9.94A.370 applies at any sentencing proceeding. Under RCW 9.94A.370, the defendant is not required to disclose prior convictions; however, his failure to object to information contained in the presentence reports allows the court to use it in determining the sentence.

The issue of whether the rights against self-incrimination and having to produce evidence apply at a sentencing is one of first impression for this court. The United States Supreme Court has recognized a Fifth Amendment right in the sentencing phase of a capital punishment case, where it stated in dicta: "Any effort by the State to compel [a defendant] to testify against his will at the sentencing hearing clearly would contravene the Fifth Amendment." (Footnote omitted.) *Estelle v. Smith*, 451 U.S. 454, 463, 101 S.Ct. 1866, 1873, 68 L.Ed.2d 359 (1981).

In *Estelle*, the defendant's unwarned statements to a psychiatrist in a pretrial examination were used against him in a post-trial death penalty proceeding. Statements made by a convicted defendant to a probation officer or psychiatrist revealing prior criminal, but unconvicted, behavior, have not been allowed to influence a sentencing decision. *United States v. Jones*, 640 F.2d 284, 287 (10th Cir.1981); *Jones v. Cardwell*, 686 F.2d 754, 756 (9th Cir.1982). The essence of the principle is that the state must " 'produce the evidence against [the defendant] by the independent labor of its officers, not by the simple, cruel expedient of forcing it from his own lips.' " *Estelle*, 451 U.S. at 462, 101 S.Ct. at 1872, quoting *Culombe v. Connecticut*, 367 U.S. 568, 581–82, 81 S.Ct. 1860, 1867–68, 6 L.Ed.2d 1037 (1961). However, all encounters, examinations and interviews do not necessarily present the same Fifth Amendment concerns. *Estelle*, 451 U.S. at 469 n. 13, 101 S.Ct. at 1876 n. 13, *Jones v. Cardwell, supra.*

RCW 9.94A.370 does not compel a defendant to provide any information. The defendant has the right to know of and object to adverse facts in the presentence reports. If he contests any facts, an evi-

dentiary hearing must be held before they are used. We hold RCW 9.94A.370 does not violate the defendant's constitutional rights.

IV

The fourth challenge, made by all three appellants, is that the SRA's requirement that the existence of prior convictions be proved by a preponderance of the evidence denies them due process. They assert that the standard of beyond a reasonable doubt is constitutionally required. We hold the beyond a reasonable doubt standard is not required and affirm the SRA's adoption of a preponderance of the evidence standard.

The sections dealing with proof of prior convictions state, in pertinent part:

If the court is satisfied by a preponderance of the evidence that the defendant has a criminal history, the court shall specify the convictions it has found to exist.

RCW 9.94A.110.

"Criminal history" means the list of a defendant's prior convictions ...

RCW 9.94A.030(8)(a).

We recognize that in some proceedings we have required that the state prove the existence of prior convictions beyond a reasonable doubt when a sentence beyond the statutory maximum or a mandatory additional sentence could be imposed. *See State v. Tongate*, 93 Wash.2d 751, 754, 613 P.2d 121 (1980) (deadly weapon enhancement); *State v. McKim*, 98 Wash.2d 111, 117, 653 P.2d 1040 (1982) (knowledge that codefendant armed with a deadly weapon); *State v. Murdock*, 91 Wash.2d 336, 340, 588 P.2d 1143 (1979) (proof of prior convictions in habitual criminal proceedings); *State v. Nass*, 76 Wash.2d 368, 370, 456 P.2d 347 (1969) (proof of sale of narcotics to a minor to impose a greater sentence).

In other proceedings, we have not required the state to prove the existence of prior convictions, even though the prior conviction was an element of the present crime. *See State v. Gonzales*, 103 Wash.2d

564, 693 P.2d 119 (1985); *State v. Hall*, 104 Wash.2d 486, 706 P.2d 1074 (1985) (escape).

We find the sentencing court's determination of prior convictions under the SRA to be most analogous to the former parole board's determination of criminal activity in a parole revocation proceeding. Pursuant to RCW 9.95.125, the parole board determined criminal activity by a "preponderance of the evidence." We held this standard to be constitutionally sufficient. *Standlee v. Smith*, 83 Wash.2d 405, 409, 518 P.2d 721 (1974); *Standlee v. Rhay*, 557 F.2d 1303, 1307 (9th Cir.1977); *Pierce v. Department of Soc. and Health Servs.*, 97 Wash.2d 552, 559–60, 646 P.2d 1382 (1982). The defendant has similar interests at stake in an SRA sentencing proceeding and a parole revocation proceeding because the individual has been convicted and the sentencing body is determining the terms and conditions of the sentence within a lawful maximum.

We have consistently recognized that a convicted defendant has a liberty interest which minimal due process protects. *State v. Nelson*, 103 Wash.2d 760, 697 P.2d 579 (1985); *In re Sinka*, 92 Wash.2d 555, 599 P.2d 1275 (1979). Use of the evidentiary standard of preponderance of the evidence satisfies minimal due process.

V

The fifth challenge, made by all three appellants, is that due process requires that the state must prove a prior conviction, considered in sentencing a defendant, is constitutionally valid and was imposed upon this defendant.

Prior convictions are used to determine the offender score which in turn is used to determine the applicable presumptive standard sentence range. RCW 9.94A.360; .370. The presumptive standard sentence range, regardless of how many prior convictions, can never exceed the statutory maximum sentence for the current offense. RCW 9.94A.420.

The SRA itself does not explicitly require the state prove the constitutional validity of a prior conviction before it can be con-

sidered in sentencing. *See* RCW 9.94A.110 and .030(8)(a). In only two situations has this court held that the state, before using a prior conviction, had to affirmatively show its constitutional validity: (1) a proceeding to establish a status of habitual criminal or habitual traffic offender, *State v. Chervenell*, 99 Wash.2d 309, 312, 662 P.2d 836 (1983); *State v. Holsworth*, 93 Wash.2d 148, 157, 607 P.2d 845 (1980); *State v. Ponce*, 93 Wash.2d 533, 611 P.2d 407 (1980); and (2) a proceeding to establish the crime of felon in possession of a firearm. *State v. Swindell*, 93 Wash.2d 192, 607 P.2d 852 (1980); *State v. Gore*, 101 Wash.2d 481, 681 P.2d 227, 39 A.L.R.4th 975 (1984), in which the prior conviction was an essential element.

We have refused to apply such a requirement in other situations. *See State v. Gonzales, supra* (use of prior conviction in prosecution for escape); *State v. Williams*, 98 Wash.2d 428, 656 P.2d 477 (1982); *State v. Thompson*, 95 Wash.2d 888, 632 P.2d 50 (1981) (use of prior conviction for impeachment purposes); *In re Bush*, 26 Wash.App. 486, 616 P.2d 666 (1980), aff'd 95 Wash.2d 551, 627 P.2d 953 (1981) (use of prior conviction to establish minimum term).

We hold that the state does not have the affirmative burden of proving the constitutional validity of a prior conviction before it can be used in a sentencing proceeding. However, a prior conviction which has been previously determined to have been unconstitutionally obtained or which is constitutionally invalid on its face may not be considered. *See In re Bush, supra* at 497–98, 616 P.2d 666; *United States v. Tucker*, 404 U.S. 443, 92 S.Ct. 589, 30 L.Ed.2d 592 (1972); *Burgett v. Texas*, 389 U.S. 109, 88 S.Ct. 258, 19 L.Ed.2d 319 (1967). Constitutionally invalid on its face means a conviction which without further elaboration evidences infirmities of a constitutional magnitude.

To require the state to prove the constitutional validity of prior convictions before they could be used would turn the sentencing proceeding into an appellate review of all prior convictions. The defendant has no right to contest a prior conviction at a subsequent sentencing. To allow an attack at that point would unduly and unjustifiably overburden the sentencing court. The defendant has available, more appropriate arenas for the determination of the constitutional validity of a prior conviction. The defendant must use established avenues of challenge provided for post-conviction relief. A defendant who is successful through these avenues can be resentenced without the unconstitutional conviction being considered.

A similar conclusion was explained by Judge Ringold, and affirmed by this court, with respect to the use of prior convictions by the Board of Prison Terms and Paroles to establish the defendant's minimum term.

If an inmate wishes to challenge the use of the prior conviction, the remedy is to seek a judicial determination that the conviction cannot constitutionally be used as a basis for setting a minimum term. The inmate may either collaterally attack the conviction in the state or federal court where it was entered or file a personal restraint petition pursuant to RAP 16.3 *et seq.* in the appropriate division of the Court of Appeals or in the Supreme Court. In the latter situation, the petitioner will be required to demonstrate that he or she is being unlawfully restrained because of the unconstitutional present use by the Parole Board of an involuntary guilty plea in setting the mandatory minimum term of confinement.

In re Bush, 26 Wash.App. at 497, 616 P.2d 666.

A review of the challenges made by the appellants in this case will elaborate on the meaning of constitutionally invalid on its face and will explain why none of their challenges were sufficient to withdraw the existence of the prior convictions from the sentencing courts' consideration. All of the prior convictions used against the appellants were based on guilty pleas, except one used against Ammons was based on a jury verdict.

Garrett raised specific challenges before the sentencing court for why his prior conviction on a guilty plea in King County No. 65061 was not constitutionally valid and therefore should not be used to enhance his sentence. Garrett argued that the guilty plea form failed to show that he was aware of his right to remain silent, failed to set forth the elements of the crime of burglary, and failed to set forth the consequences of pleading guilty. Furthermore, he argued the statement "I broke into the welfare office looking for food stamps" was an insufficient factual basis for the court's accepting the plea. Report of Proceedings (Garrett), at 4. Garrett may have a valid argument that his prior conviction was unconstitutional. However, such a determination cannot be made from the face of the guilty plea form. There is no indication that Garrett was told he did not have the right to remain silent or that he was not informed of the elements of the crime or the consequences of the plea. Absent such an affirmative showing, Garrett must pursue the usual channels for relief.

Barton challenges the use of his prior guilty plea convictions to prove his criminal history because they do not reflect that constitutional safeguards were provided. Similar to Garrett's plea, there is no affirmative showing that the constitutional safeguards were not provided. Barton's recourse is to the appellate courts.

Ammons asks this court to allow collateral attacks on the constitutional validity of prior jury trial convictions. Even in the habitual criminal proceeding this has not been allowed. *See State v. Serr*, 35 Wash.App. 5, 9, 664 P.2d 1301, *review denied*, 100 Wash.2d 1024 (1983); *State v. Heaps*, 36 Wash.App. 718, 724, 677 P.2d 1141, *review denied*, 101 Wash.2d 1013 (1984). Ammons argues that the jury instructions used in his prior trial denied him his constitutional rights. Ammons also appears to raise valid challenges, but the validity cannot be determined facially. The trial court would have to go behind the verdict and sentence and judgment to make such a determination. We hold this should not be done.

Each appellant also argues that the State must prove that he and the defendant named in the prior conviction is the same person. Of course, there must be some showing that the defendant before the court for sentencing and the person named in the prior conviction are the same person. We hold that the identity of names is sufficient proof, which may be rebutted by the defendant's declaration under oath that he is not the same person named in the prior conviction. The defendant's declaration under oath will suspend the use of the prior conviction in assessing the presumptive standard sentence range until the State proves by independent evidence, for example, fingerprints, court personnel present at prior adjudication, or institutional packets, that the defendant before the court for sentencing and named in the prior conviction are the same.

These requirements achieve the proper balance. In these cases, the defendant in the certified copies of judgments and sentences had the same name as the defendant currently being sentenced. The prosecutor offered no other independent corroborating evidence. Not one of the appellants, however, alleged that he was not the same person as the one named in the prior conviction. Ammons and Garrett made no objection at their sentencing hearings. They only argued that the State has the burden of proving identity, without alleging they were not the same person, in their hearing memoranda. Barton, in both his memorandum and at the sentencing hearing, argued that the State had the burden of showing, and had not shown, that he was the same person as the one named in the prior conviction. The sentencing court independently ascertained that Barton was the same person as the defendant in one of his four alleged prior convictions by asking Barton's counsel if this was the same person that he had represented in the earlier proceeding. Defense counsel answered truthfully. Barton, also, was given the opportunity, but refused, to testify under oath that he was not the same person named in the prior convictions. Due process is satisfied when the defendant is informed of the prior convictions being utilized and given the opportunity to deny that he is the same person.

VI

Because we are not remanding any of the appealed sentences for resentencing, we do not reach the sixth challenge, made by Barton, of whether double jeopardy would be violated if on a remand for resentencing additional prior convictions were shown which could result in a higher presumptive standard sentence range.

VII

Finding the challenged SRA sections and the sentencing courts' applications of them pass constitutional scrutiny, we affirm the sentences imposed upon Roy Lee Ammons, Dale R. Barton, and Eugene Garrett.

DOLLIVER, C.J., and UTTER, BRACHTENBACH, DORE, PEARSON, ANDERSEN, CALLOW and DURHAM, JJ., concur.

Robert L. KOHLEY, Appellant,

v.

UNITED STATES of America, Appellee.

No. 85–2149.

United States Court of Appeals,
Eighth Circuit.

Submitted Dec. 20, 1985.
Decided Feb. 20, 1986.

Before ARNOLD, Circuit Judge, HEN-
LEY, Senior Circuit Judge, and JOHN R.
GIBSON, Circuit Judge.

PER CURIAM.

Robert L. Kohley appeals the district
court's [1] denial of his 28 U.S.C. § 2255 petition without a hearing. We affirm.

---

1. The Honorable Elmo B. Hunter, United States
   Senior District Judge, Western District of Mis-   souri.

Kohley, a former president of the Grandview Bank & Trust Company of Grandview, Missouri, pleaded guilty to a one-count information charging a violation of 18 U.S.C. § 656 (embezzlement and misapplication of bank funds of more than $100.00), and was sentenced to a fifty-four month term of imprisonment. He filed a § 2255 petition alleging that (1) in violation of his right to due process, he was sentenced on the basis of a materially false presentence report which he had no meaningful opportunity to rebut; (2) he was coerced by other inmates into taking a "passive role" during the sentencing hearing; and (3) his sentence is so harsh as to violate the eighth amendment.

I. Presentence Report.

Kohley's principal contention is that he was not given a meaningful opportunity to rebut erroneous information included in his presentence report. We reject his contention. It is true that a sentence based on material misinformation may violate due process if the defendant's opportunity for rebuttal was not meaningful. *Barton v. Lockhart*, 762 F.2d 712, 713 (8th Cir.1985) (per curiam); *Ryder v. Morris*, 752 F.2d 327, 332 (8th Cir.1985). However, we are not convinced that the presentence report contained material misinformation. Due process does not require reconsideration of a sentencing decision " 'where the defendant is given a full and fair opportunity to reveal inaccuracies in the information relied upon by the sentencing court and fails to do so.' " *United States v. Manko*, 772 F.2d 481, 482 (8th Cir.1985) (per curiam) (quoting *United States v. Brown*, 715 F.2d 387, 389 (8th Cir.1983)). The district court found that Kohley was given an opportunity to comment on the presentence report prior to imposition of sentence, and the transcript of the sentencing hearing reveals that Kohley did in fact do so. Accordingly, no due process violation occurred.

Kohley contends that he did not personally see the report prior to the sentencing as required by Fed.R.Crim.P. 32(c) and that resentencing is therefore required. However, we are satisfied from our review of the record that Kohley had the opportunity to see the report and probably did see the report prior to sentencing, that his attorney saw the report, and that Kohley made specific objections to matters in the report at the sentencing hearing. Rule 32(c) does not require more.

II. Coercion by Other Inmates.

In his § 2255 motion, Kohley alleges that the United States Attorney coerced him into taking a "passive role" during the sentencing hearing by suggesting that harm would come to Kohley's family if Kohley spoke. In the "Formal Motion of Apology to John Osgood" filed in the district court on June 19, 1985, Kohley appears to have withdrawn this allegation. He alleges for the first time on appeal that the coercion came from other inmates. We do not consider issues of fact raised for the first time on appeal. Even if we were to do so, we would find Kohley's contention without merit, because there is no indication that Kohley concealed anything from the district court as a result of the alleged coercion.

III. Harshness of Sentence.

Finally, Kohley alleges that his fifty-four month sentence is too harsh and violates the eighth amendment, citing *Solem v. Helm*, 463 U.S. 277, 103 S.Ct. 3001, 77 L.Ed.2d 637 (1983). He states:

Kohley's sentence is disparit [sic] to sentences given in this district for the same crime and to the same criminal background. Between 7/1/82 through 6/30/83; 29 people were sentenced for a similar offense; 27 people received probation, with the other 2 persons receiving a split sentence comprised of 90 days in prison and 5 years probation. Under the same test, Kohley's sentence is disparit [sic] when compared to sentences given for the same crime and same offender background nationally. For a 12 month period ending June 30, 1984, convictions of similar offenses totalled 957. Only 23 persons received a longer sentence and the majority of those was greater because of consecutive sentences to serve. The statute under which Kohley was convicted provides for a fine of not more than $5,000.00 or imprisonment for not more than five years, or both. 18 U.S.C. § 656.

The factors to be considered under *Solem* are (1) the gravity of the offense and the harshness of the penalty; (2) how the sentence compares with other sentences imposed for the same crime in the same jurisdiction; and (3) how the sentence compares with sentences imposed for the

same crime in other jurisdictions. 463 U.S. at 290–92, 103 S.Ct. at 3009–10. Given that Kohley was accused of the wrongful application of approximately $950,000.00 and in his capacity as bank president, we cannot say that his sentence, which was less than the maximum sentence, was unfairly harsh. *See United States v. Lewis*, 759 F.2d 1316, 1333–35 (8th Cir.1985); *United States v. Stead*, 740 F.2d 657, 659 (8th Cir.) (per curiam), *cert. denied*, — U.S. —, 105 S.Ct. 600, 83 L.Ed.2d 709 (1984).

No basis for § 2255 relief appearing, the judgment of the district court is affirmed.

UNITED STATES of America,
Plaintiff-Appellee,

v.

Michael James O'DRISCOLL,
Defendant-Appellant.

Colorado Criminal Defense Bar,
Amicus Curiae.

No. 84-1795.

United States Court of Appeals,
Tenth Circuit.

May 7, 1985.

Rehearing Denied June 4, 1985.

Before BARRETT and SETH, Circuit Judges, and SEAY,* District Judge.

BARRETT, Circuit Judge.

The sole issue presented in this appeal is whether the sentence imposed by the trial court upon appellant O'Driscoll, for kidnapping, following conviction by a jury, of three hundred years in prison, with eligibility of parole following service of ninety-nine years, is outside the applicable statutory limits and thus illegal and an abuse of the trial court's discretion. 586 F.Supp. 1486 (1984). O'Driscoll entered a guilty plea to a charge of armed robbery prior to his trial on the kidnapping charge. A review of the facts relative to O'Driscoll's commission of the crimes of armed robbery and kidnapping will aid in placing the issue presented on appeal in focus.

Facts of Case

The evidence in this trial record discloses that on November 12, 1982, O'Driscoll bought a nine millimeter Smith & Wesson gun from the Mile Hi Pawnshop in Denver, Colorado. He used a false driver's license for identification. On December 16, 1982, he bought a Smith & Wesson model 29 .44 magnum at Foothills Shooting Center in Lakewood. He again used a false driver's license for identification. On January 20,

1983, O'Driscoll attempted to pawn the Smith and Wesson .44 magnum at the Lakewood Gem and Trading Post. The owner, Irwin Kass, informed O'Driscoll that he did not have a license to pawn goods; he recommended another shop. Within an hour, O'Driscoll returned to Mr. Kass's store, where Mr. Kass was then alone. O'Driscoll drew the gun, told Mr. Kass that it was a stick-up and ordered Mr. Kass to the floor. Mr. Kass complied. O'Driscoll then beat Mr. Kass on the head with the revolver until he was rendered unconscious. O'Driscoll stole Mr. Kass's wallet and some $400 from the store. Mr. Kass was hospitalized for a week and unable to work for more than three months. His injuries required more than 100 stitches in his scalp. In addition, he suffered two broken fingers, three cracked teeth, and his left ear was half torn off. Mr. Kass positively identified O'Driscoll as the man who had robbed and beaten him.

Karen Tietgens, who was O'Driscoll's girlfriend, testified that just before O'Driscoll assaulted Mr. Kass and robbed his store, she and O'Driscoll had attempted unsuccessfully to sell the yellow van he was driving in an effort to raise money. They then drove to Mr. Kass's store, where O'Driscoll entered carrying his gun and a newspaper. O'Driscoll returned to the van with the gun wrapped in the newspaper, covered with blood.

After the robbery, O'Driscoll and Karen Tietgens drove to the JCRS Shopping Center in Lakewood. O'Driscoll drove to a parking space next to that of Kent Leslie Martin. O'Driscoll ordered Mr. Martin to move over and he ordered Tietgens to get in Mr. Martin's car. O'Driscoll drove Mr. Martin's car to their motel where he paid the bill with the robbery money. O'Driscoll and Tietgens then departed for Kansas with Mr. Martin as a hostage. Throughout the kidnapping, O'Driscoll held Mr. Martin at gunpoint. Near Salina, Kansas, O'Driscoll dropped Karen Tietgens off at the Red

* The Honorable Frank H. Seay, Chief Judge, United States District Court for the Eastern District of Oklahoma, sitting by designation.

Coach Inn truck stop at an interchange off I-135. O'Driscoll then drove Mr. Martin some three miles west and two miles south to a wooded area. Karen Tietgens testified that O'Driscoll told her he shot Mr. Martin and that he did so for her sake so that Mr. Martin could never identify them. Mr. Martin died of ten gunshot wounds. One wound in Mr. Martin's chest was inflicted when O'Driscoll pressed the gun against the flesh and pulled the trigger. Mr. Martin had several grazing gunshot wounds on his left hand, incurred from his attempts to shield his body with his hands while being shot.

Following the killing of Mr. Martin, O'Driscoll drove Karen Tietgens to Ohio, where they parted company temporarily. O'Driscoll went on to Springfield, Massachusetts, where he met Christie Blake, another girlfriend, on January 30, 1983. O'Driscoll picked up Ms. Blake in Mr. Martin's car, and he told her not to leave her fingerprints in the car because it was a dead man's car. The following day, O'Driscoll and Christie Blake robbed the People's Savings Bank in Holyoke, Massachusetts.

O'Driscoll then left Springfield and Ms. Blake, and drove to Groton, Connecticut, where he abandoned Mr. Martin's car in a parking lot. When the Connecticut police subsequently searched the car, they found a box of license plates from different states in the trunk. The police removed the rear view mirror of the car and examined it for fingerprints. The mirror contained the print of O'Driscoll's right ring finger.

O'Driscoll next paid a man to drive him to New York, where, after a brief reconciliation with Karen Tietgens, he continued cross-country, ending up in Puyallup, Washington, where he was arrested in the company of a Patty Case. When arrested, O'Driscoll was carrying a nine millimeter automatic weapon, which had been sold by Mile Hi Pawnshop to O'Driscoll in November of 1982. It matched the shell casings and slugs taken from Mr. Martin's body and the scene of the murder in Kansas. A subsequent search of Ms. Case's trailer residence, where O'Driscoll had been living,

revealed numerous other weapons, including a Smith & Wesson Model 29 .44 magnum, which had been sold by Foothills Shooting Center to O'Driscoll in December of 1982.

O'Driscoll testified that he arranged with a friend named Jay, who he met at a bar but whose last name he could not remember, to borrow some money and to let Jay drive his yellow van from Las Vegas, Nevada, to Ohio. O'Driscoll stated that he had left both the nine millimeter and the .44 magnum in the back of the van because he had to fly from Las Vegas to San Diego and could not take the guns on the plane. He stated that the arrangement was for Jay to drive Tietgens to Ohio, and then proceed on with O'Driscoll to Massachusetts to rob a bank. O'Driscoll said that he flew from San Diego to Cleveland on January 24 or 25, 1983, and met Jay at the Cleveland airport, where Jay told him that "he had some problems and he took this guy's car ... and somewhere in Kansas him and Karen disposed of him." (Vol. V, pp. 545, 546). O'Driscoll also testified that he used Kent Martin's car to drive from Lorain, Ohio, to Springfield, Massachusetts, and that if he had known that either the nine millimeter or the .44 magnum had been used to murder a man, he would not have held onto them.

On cross-examination, O'Driscoll acknowledged that: he had pled guilty and was convicted in Massachusetts federal court of kidnapping a 68-year-old woman after a bank robbery on November 10, 1982; he had no explanation as to why Jay would have used O'Driscoll's favorite gun to kill Mr. Martin; and the reason why he had left Denver on December 21, 1982, was because he had held up the Western Federal Savings and Loan Association bank there the day before.

O'Driscoll was charged with kidnapping and armed bank robbery. He pled guilty to the armed bank robbery charge, and was sentenced to twenty-five years imprisonment. His trial before a jury on the instant kidnapping charge began on March 26, 1984, and on April 2, 1984, he was unanimously found guilty. On May 24, 1984, O'Driscoll was sentenced to serve three hundred years in prison, and to become eligible for parole after serving ninety-nine years.

Other Facts Before The Court at Sentencing

With regard to the guilty plea entered by O'Driscoll to the charge of armed bank robbery of the Western Federal Savings and Loan Association of Denver on December 20, 1982, while accompanied by one Christina Blake who was also carrying a hand gun, the trial court noted, *inter alia:* O'Driscoll was very aggressive; he pushed people around; he brandished his gun in making numerous demands while using loud profanities; he destroyed bank property; he fired a shot inside the bank and while leaving, he fired a shot through the window and threatened to kill all of the bank personnel. He robbed the bank of $3,384. The trial court found that the worst part was the fear that O'Driscoll instilled in all of the bank employees.

O'Driscoll, born August 6, 1953, at Springfield, Massachusetts, was the product of a broken marriage which resulted in his commitment to a training school at an early age; he married at an early age, became a father of two children and was divorced. He has never given any financial support to his children. In the seventh grade, O'Driscoll became a habitual truant. In April, 1978, he received a certificate of accomplishment in welding and was immediately hired by a manufacturing concern; however, between April, 1978, to date of sentencing, O'Driscoll had held down four jobs for a total working period of eighteen months. After his divorce, O'Driscoll became involved with many paramours, many of whom joined him in thefts and robberies. O'Driscoll admitted to commission of seven bank robberies. He further admitted to heavy consumption of alcohol, use of cocaine and many other drugs. During the presentence investigation process, O'Driscoll attempted to strike a "bargain" with the trial court: O'Driscoll would provide

the location of some $98,000 he had "salted away" from his bank robberies if the court would order that he receive conjugal visits from his woman friends. Since age 17 to date of sentencing in this case, O'Driscoll was convicted of at least eight misdemeanor offenses, six serious traffic violations and three or four felonies. Even so, O'Driscoll had served only a total of twenty days in jail under these sentences. The court noted that O'Driscoll was convicted in California state courts for burglary, theft and false impersonation and in each instance he was placed on probation. The court reviewed specific cases involving O'Driscoll's criminal conduct in specific instances which established O'Driscoll's mean, cruel, malicious character. At the time of sentencing, O'Driscoll had 71 charges in seven different courts pending against him involving charges of assault on a federal officer, escape, murder, assault with dangerous weapons, armed robbery, malicious injury, assault with intent to rape, threat to murder and eight charges of kidnapping.

Trial Court Basis for Sentence Imposed

Based upon the evidence in the case at bar and the presentence record aforesaid, the trial court detailed the viciousness of O'Driscoll's conduct, attitude and propensities, *inter alia:*

It is difficult, indeed impossible, to describe accurately the physical and emotional suffering and loss which this defendant has caused to so many, yet he demonstrates not even a scintilla of remorse. Instead, he is preoccupied with the immediate gratification of his own needs. He appears uncommonly successful in manipulating a number of women and exploiting them in ways that not only injure their lives, but also create significant problems with the security measures necessary to control and monitor him.

The evidence is clear, convincing and beyond serious disputation that the defendant has a chronic sociopathic personality ... the defendant fails to demonstrate even the existence of a conscience.

Results of psychometric testing show that he is chronically maladjusted, immature and self-indulgent, manipulative of others, obnoxious, hostile and aggressive. He is incapable of respecting authority, demonstrates difficulty in interpersonal relations and refuses to accept responsibility for problems. He is hedonistic and over-uses alcohol and drugs. He is excessively impulsive and acts out against others without considering the consequences. His capacity for rage has already been more than adequately demonstrated. In his wake he has left nothing but carnage and devastation.

Any leniency in sentencing in this case would depreciate the seriousness of the defendant's crimes and would promote a clearly understandable disrespect for the law and the judicial system. Further, I consider it mandatory to impress upon all who learn of this defendant's sordid criminality what certain and terrible penalties would be imposed upon them for similar conduct. This defendant has demonstrated himself to be such a danger to the public that I believe it is incumbent upon me to do all that I can to see that he is never again let loose to wreak violence and devastation upon the innocent, the weak and the aged.

... It is devastating to say, but this defendant's record establishes that it is simply too late to indulge in quixotic notions of rehabilitation and redemption.

The maximum penalty for armed bank robbery is imprisonment for not more than twenty-five years and a fine of not more than $10,000 or both such fine and imprisonment. The defendant has already been sentenced to twenty-five years imprisonment for a similar offense and I do not perceive any reason to impose a lesser sentence in this case.

The penalty for the crime of kidnapping is any term of years or for life. Upon first impression, it would seem reasonable to impose a sentence of life imprisonment in this case. Upon reflection, however, I have decided to impose a term of years. My decision is based upon the provisions of law set forth by Congress in the United States Code. Title 18 of the United States Code, Section 4205 provides that whenever a prisoner is serving more than one year in prison, he or she becomes eligible for release on parole after serving one-third of the sentence or sentences imposed by the courts. If a life sentence is imposed, or if the total of sentences imposed exceeds thirty years, the the defendant becomes eligible for release on parole after serving ten years.

I do not know what some parole authority in the future might be disposed to do with this defendant, but even the possibility of this defendant obtaining release in ten or so years reduces the seriousness of his crimes to the point of triviality. Accordingly, I have found authorization for an appropriate sentence in subparagraph (b) of Section 4205 which reads as follows:

Upon entering a judgment of conviction, the court having jurisdiction to impose sentence, when in its opinion the ends of justice and *the best interest of the public* require that the defendant be sentenced to imprisonment for a term exceeding one year, may (1) designate in the sentence of imprisonment imposed a minimum term at the expiration of which the prisoner shall become eligible for parole, which term may be less than but shall not be more than one-third of the maximum sentence imposed by the court, or (2) the court may fix the maximum sentence of imprisonment to be served in which event the court may specify that the prisoner may be released on parole at such time as the Commission may determine.

(Emphasis added.) It is my clear intent to sentence this defendant in accordance with this statute. I have reviewed the legislative history, which is scant, and find that the sentence I shall announce is not in conflict with congressional purpose.

I specifically find the ends of justice and the best interest of the public require that this defendant be sentenced to imprisonment for a term exceeding one year and that I should designate in the sentence a minimum term at the expiration of which the defendant shall become eligible for parole which is less than one-third of the maximum. It should be clear to all who review this sentence that my intent is to announce that this defendant will not be released from prison at any time insofar as it is within the power of the judicial branch of the government to prevent such a release. In the unlikely event that this defendant ever becomes deserving of release in full appreciation of the wrong he has done and awareness of the danger to others he presents, the laws of the United States provide for action by the executive branch of government. In other words, his release, if ever, should be a matter of executive clemency and not legal entitlement.

Accordingly, I pronounce the following sentence:

Michael James O'Driscoll, on the charge of armed bank robbery in violation of 18 1U.S.C. [18 U.S.C.] § 2113 (a)(d), 2., I sentence you to the custody of the Attorney General of the United States for a term of twenty-five (25) years. This sentence shall be consecutive to the two concurrent 25 year sentences imposed December 29, 1983 by the United States District Court for the District of Massachusetts in Case No. 82–305–01. It is my specific recommendation that this sentence never run concurrently with any sentence imposed by any state court.

In case number 84–CR–14–1 charging you with the crime of kidnapping, I sentence you to the custody of the Attorney General of the United States of America for a term of three-hundred years. I specifically order that this sentence shall run consecutive to and not concurrent with the sentence of 25 years imposed in case number 83–CR–63–1 charging you with armed bank robbery. Further, in accordance with 18 U.S.C. § 4205 (b)(1), I specifically order that you shall become eligible for release on parole only on

completion of serving ninety-nine years which is one year less than one-third of the maximum sentence of three-hundred years. (Footnotes omitted.)

R., Vol. I, pp. 70–72.

Discussion and Decision

On appeal O'Driscoll contends that the trial court erred in that (1) O'Driscoll's sentence is outside of applicable statutory limits and therefore illegal, and (2) the imposition of O'Driscoll's sentence was an abuse of the trial court's discretion.

We are cognizant that the unbridled power of the sentencing courts to be arbitrary and discriminatory has been the subject of much discussion. *See United States v. DiFrancesno*, 449 U.S. 117, 101 S.Ct. 426, 66 L.Ed.2d 328 (1980). It is our view, based on the record which we have detailed, that the sentence imposed by the trial court upon O'Driscoll is not arbitrary, discriminatory, unlawful or cruel and unusual punishment. We hold that (1) the sentence imposed is within the range of the sentence for the crime of kidnapping, (2) the trial court was fully, adequately and reliably informed by presentence investigations and reports, and (3) the trial court did not infringe upon the power or authority of the Parole Commission.

I.

O'Driscoll contends that the sentence imposed is outside of applicable statutory limits and therefore illegal. Relying on the rule that the fixing of penalties for crimes is a congressional function, *Hayes v. United States*, 238 F.2d 318, 322 (10th Cir. 1956), *cert. denied*, 353 U.S. 983, 77 S.Ct. 1280, 1 L.Ed.2d 1142 (1957), and that proper apportionment of punishment is peculiarly a question of legislative, not judicial, policy, *Gore v. United States*, 357 U.S. 386, 78 S.Ct. 1280, 2 L.Ed.2d 1405 (1958), O'Driscoll argues:

(a) The penalty for kidnapping set forth in 18 U.S.C. § 1201 "imprisonment for any term of years or for life" does not permit, based on general principles of statutory construction and certain "minimal legislative history," (Brief of Appellant, p. 3), a sentence in excess of "life imprisonment." Appellant argues that if the Congress intended to permit a three hundred year sentence, the language allowing the imposition of a sentence of life imprisonment would be superfluous. Such is not the case, argues O'Driscoll, because Congress took steps to add the life imprisonment language to the predecessor statute to § 1201, 18 U.S.C. § 408a, in 1948, and the Reviser's Note states that the amendment was added to remove all doubt as to whether a court could impose a life sentence. Thus, argues O'Driscoll, the most sensible construction of § 1201 is that "life imprisonment" is meant to be the maximum permissible sentence under the statute.

The Government counters with the argument that O'Driscoll ignores the legislative intent behind the predecessor to 18 U.S.C. § 4205(b)(1), which was 18 U.S.C. § 4208. The predecessor statute contained the identical language as § 4205(b)(1) and its legislative history states that the section "would permit the court, at its discretion, *to share with the executive branch the responsibility for determining how long a prisoner should actually serve.*" S.Rep. No. 2013, 85th Cong., 2d Sess. 2, *reprinted in* 1958 U.S.Code Cong. & Ad.News 3891, 3892. (Emphasis added.) (Brief of Appellee, p. 9.) Further, argues the Government, the interpretation urged by O'Driscoll of 18 U.S.C. § 1201 renders superfluous the provision allowing sentences "for *any* term of years" in that had Congress intended life imprisonment to be the maximum sentence, it would have so specified. (Brief of Appellee, p. 10.) We agree.

The trial court recognized the distinction between a sentence of life imprisonment and one for a term of three hundred years. A prisoner serving a life sentence becomes eligible for parole no later than ten years after his incarceration. 18 U.S.C. § 4205(a).[1] A prisoner sentenced to a term of three hundred years with eligibility for parole specifically fixed following service of a minimum term of ninety-nine years based on the trial court's finding, as here, that such sentence is required to satisfy the "ends of justice and best interest of the public" is not eligible for parole under 18 U.S.C. § 4205(b)(1)[2] until he has served ninety-nine years, a period one year less than one third of the full sentence imposed. Such a sentence, the Congress determined, is permissible if the "ends of justice and the best interests of the public" require. The Congress did clearly delineate the distinction between § 4205(b)(1) and § 4205(b)(2). The former permits the court to determine any eligibility date up to one-third of the maximum sentence imposed by the court, while the latter permits the court to impose only the maximum sentence, in which event the Board of Parole (now Parole Commission) would be authorized to release a prisoner at any time. *See* S.Rep. No. 2013, 85th Cong., 2d Sess. 2, *reprinted in* 1958 U.S.Code Cong. & Ad. News, 3891, 3901–02. It is our view that the Congress, in enacting § 4205(b)(1) specially allowed the trial courts to bypass the Parole Commission if the "ends of justice and the best interests of the public" so require. We hold that the evidence before the court at the O'Driscoll sentencing was such that the "ends of justice and the best interests of the public" fully support the

1. Whenever confined and serving a definite term or terms of more than one year, a prisoner shall be eligible for release on parole after serving one-third of such term or terms or after serving ten years of a life sentence or of a sentence of over thirty years, except to the extent otherwise provided by law.

2. Upon entering a judgment of conviction, the court having jurisdiction to impose sentence, when in its opinion the ends of justice and best interest of the public require that the defendant be sentenced to imprisonment for a term ex-

ceeding one year, may (1) designate in the sentence of imprisonment imposed a minimum term at the expiration of which the prisoner shall become eligible for parole, which term may be less than but shall not be more than one-third of the maximum sentence imposed by the court, or (2) the court may fix the maximum sentence of imprisonment to be served in which event the court may specify that the prisoner may be released on parole at such time as the Commission may determine.

district court's imposition of the 300 year sentence.

In assessing the punishment commensurate with the crime for which the defendant was convicted, the trial court may consider a broad range of information even though it was not contained in the presentence report. *Roberts v. United States*, 445 U.S. 552, 100 S.Ct. 1358, 63 L.Ed.2d 622 (1980) (sentencing judge may consider defendant's attitude toward society and the prospects for rehabilitation); *Williams v. New York*, 337 U.S. 241, 69 S.Ct. 1079, 93 L.Ed. 1337 (1949).

The sentencing judge originally determines the extent of a criminal defendant's confinement within the permissible range authorized by the Congress; the Parole Commission may order conditional release any time after the prisoner has served one-third of his fixed term. *United States v. Grayson*, 438 U.S. 41, 98 S.Ct. 2610, 57 L.Ed.2d 582 (1978); *United States v. Schell*, 692 F.2d 672 (10th Cir.1982).

Court review of a sentence generally ends once it is determined that a sentence is within statutory limits. *Rummell v. Estelle*, 445 U.S. 263, 100 S.Ct. 1133, 63 L.Ed.2d 382 (1980); *Dorsznski v. United States*, 418 U.S. 424, 94 S.Ct. 3042, 41 L.Ed.2d 855 (1974); *Schick v. Reed*, 419 U.S. 256, 95 S.Ct. 379, 42 L.Ed.2d 430 (1974); *United States v. Tucker*, 404 U.S. 443, 92 S.Ct. 589, 30 L.Ed.2d 592 (1972); *Gore v. United States*, 357 U.S. 386, 78 S.Ct. 1280, 2 L.Ed.2d 1405 (1958). A federal prisoner sentenced to a definite term exceeding one year is eligible for parole after serving one-third of the sentence. 18 U.S.C. § 4205(a)(1976). Alternatively, the court may set a maximum term which permits parole eligibility at any point up to one-third of the term. 18 U.S.C. § 4205(b)(1). Thus, under this latter section, district courts may enter sentences which set parole eligibility at any point of time during the first one-third of the sentence imposed. *United States v. Addonizio*, 442 U.S. 178, 189 n. 15, 99 S.Ct. 2235, 2242 n. 15, 60 L.Ed.2d 805 (1979); *United States v. Pry*, 625 F.2d 689 (5th Cir.1980); *Wilden v. Fields*, 510 F.Supp. 1295, 1306–1307 (W.D.Wis.1981) (judges may, pursuant to § 4205(b), designate a minimum sentence to be served, up to one-third of the term imposed, before a prisoner is eligible for parole; nothing in the legislative history indicates that prisoners serving § 4205(b)(2) sentences should be treated differently from prisoners sentenced under any other statutory provision); *United States v. Whitley*, 473 F.Supp. 23, 24 (E.D. Mich.1979) (§ 4205(b) allows the district court judge to impose a sentence which by-passes the one-third or ten-year provision of § 4205(a)).

Fundamental rules of statutory construction require that the court presume legislative enactments to be reasonable and logical and that legislative intent be ascertained from the language of the statute whenever possible. The legislature will not be presumed to intend futile results. *Jackson v. Kelly*, 557 F.2d 735, 740 (10th Cir. 1977); *Whiteis v. Yamaha Intern. Corp.*, 531 F.2d 968 (10th Cir.1976), cert. denied, 429 U.S. 858, 97 S.Ct. 157, 50 L.Ed.2d 135 (1976). It is fundamental that legislative acts dealing with related matters must be considered *in pari materia* and the meaning of each such statute be correlated so as to give intelligent meaning to both whenever possible. In attempting to give full force and effect to a statute, the court must read it in the light of its purpose; when Congress uses words in a statute without defining them and those words have a judicially settled meaning, it is presumed that Congress intended that meaning. *Hardy Salt Company v. Southern Pacific Transp. Co.*, 501 F.2d 1156, 1168 (10th Cir.1974), cert. denied, 419 U.S. 1033, 95 S.Ct. 515, 42 L.Ed.2d 308 (1974).

When the term "or" is used, it is presumed to be used in the *disjunctive* sense unless the legislative intent is clearly contrary. *Azure v. Morton*, 514 F.2d 897, 900 (9th Cir.1975); *United States v. Snider*, 502 F.2d 645, 655 (4th Cir.1974); Sutherland, Statutory Construction, 4th Ed., Vol. 1A, § 21.14; 82 C.J.S., Statutes, § 335;

73 Am.Jur.2d, Statutes, § 241; Anno., 118 A.L.R. 1367, 1375. And in penal statutes the word "or" is seldom used other than as a disjunctive and can never be interpreted as meaning the conjunctive "and" if the effect would be to increase the punishment; the word "or" indicates permissible alternative sentences. 21 Am.Jur.2d, Criminal Law, § 540, p. 897; *Smith v. City of Casper*, 419 P.2d 704 (Wyo.1966); *State v. Evans*, 245 P.2d 788 (Idaho 1952); *State v. Dickens*, 66 Ariz. 86, 183 P.2d 148 (1947); *Rasmussen v. Zundel*, 67 Utah 456, 248 P. 135 (1926); *Re McNeal*, 74 P. 1110 (Kan. 1904). Applying this standard, we hold that the trial court's imposition of the three hundred year sentence was permissible under 18 U.S.C. § 1201 which permitted the penalty range for the conviction of the crime of kidnapping of "imprisonment for *any* term of years *or* for life." (Emphasis added.)

It is argued that the above interpretation ignores 18 U.S.C. § 4206(d) which authorizes the Parole Commission to release a prisoner sentenced to more than 45 years, including a life term, when he has served 30 years, unless "there is reasonable probability that he will commit any Federal, State or local crime." (Brief of *Amicus Curiae*, p. 4.) The difficulty with this contention is that the trial court's sentence under 18 U.S.C. § 1201 and 18 U.S.C. § 4205(b)(1) does not interfere with the application of the Parole Commission's guidelines. It simply fixes the date that the parole mechanism shall become operative.

It is fundamental that a judgment must conform to the statutory provision and that a variation in the extent of the punishment imposed renders the judgment void. *Weems v. United States*, 217 U.S. 349, 30 S.Ct. 544, 54 L.Ed. 793 (1910). When there are two statutes addressing the same general subject matter (here sentencing under 18 U.S.C. § 1201 and 18 U.S.C. § 4205), one being special and one being general, the special act controls as effective, and all matters coming within the scope of the special act are governed by its provisions. *Preiser v. Rodriguez*, 411 U.S.

475, 93 S.Ct. 1827, 36 L.Ed.2d 439 (1973); *Glover Const. Co. v. Andrus*, 591 F.2d 554, 561 (10th Cir.1979), *affd* 446 U.S. 608, 100 S.Ct. 1905, 64 L.Ed.2d 548 (1980); *Missouri K. & T. Ry. Co. v. Jackson*, 174 F.2d 297 (10th Cir.1949); Sutherland, Statutory Construction, 4th Ed., Vol. 2A, § 51.05. Here the special act is 18 U.S.C. § 1201 which delineates the range of penalty the trial court may impose on one convicted of kidnapping. We have heretofore held that the 300 year sentence imposed by the trial court in the case at bar is within the legislative range, i.e., "imprisonment for any term of years." Reading this special act in *pari materia* with the general act relating to parole eligibility, i.e., 18 U.S.C. § 4205, we hold that the three hundred year sentence is not void in light of the trial court's specific finding that "the ends of justice and the best interest of the public" require said sentence which, in accord with § 4205(b)(1), permits O'Driscoll to become eligible for release on parole on completion of service of a term of imprisonment of ninety-nine years, which is one year less than the one-third maximum sentence of three-hundred years. Statutes are to be construed in a manner as to effectuate the intent and interest of the enacting body. In *Glover, supra*, we quoted Sutherland, Statutory Construction, 4th Ed., Vol. 2A, § 51.05 as follows:

General and special acts may be in pari materia. If so, they should be construed together. When one statute deals with a subject in general terms, and another deals with a part of the same subject in a more detailed way, the two should be harmonized if possible; but if there is any conflict, the latter will prevail, regardless of whether it was passed prior to the general statute, unless it appears that the legislature intended to make the general act controlling....

591 F.2d at 561.

II.

O'Driscoll contends that the trial court's imposition of a three hundred year sentence, with no possibility of parole for ninety-nine of those years, was an abuse of discretion and must be stricken as excessive under the prohibition against cruel and unusual punishment in the Eighth Amendment to the United States Constitution. We disagree.

O'Driscoll relies upon the practice "during the past seventy years" of releasing prisoners on parole before the end of their sentence as an integral part of the penological system recognized in *Morrissey v. Brewer*, 408 U.S. 471, 92 S.Ct. 2593, 33 L.Ed.2d 484 (1972). (Brief of Appellant, p. 6.) Predicated thereon, O'Driscoll argues that the trial court, contrary to the purpose of 18 U.S.C. § 4205(b) used it, in conjunction with 18 U.S.C. § 1201, "to increase, rather than decrease, the amount of time that O'Driscoll would be imprisoned." (Brief of Appellant, p. 7.) This action, he contends, effectively defeated the purpose of the statutory scheme and constitutes cruel and unusual punishment. We have already held that the sentence imposed was within statutory limits and therefore legal.

With respect to the charge that the O'Driscoll sentence, as a practical matter, amounts to life imprisonment without the possibility of parole and therefore constitutes cruel and unusual punishment, we observe that *Schick v. Reed*, 419 U.S. 256, 267, 95 S.Ct. 379, 385, 42 L.Ed.2d 430 (1974) rejected this contention. *See also, Government of Virgin Islands v. Gereau*, 592 F.2d 192 (3rd Cir.1979). *See also*, Anno., 33 ALR 3d 335. It is fundamental that punishment should be tailored to the particular criminal and not necessarily to the severity of the crime. *Williams v. New York*, 337 U.S. 241, 69 S.Ct. 1079, 93 L.Ed. 1337 (1949). Certainly, the sentence imposed in the case at bar was fine-tuned to the particular criminal, O'Driscoll. Rehabilitation is not the only constitutionally permissible goal of incarceration; retribution is equally permissible. *Atiyeh v. Capps*, 449 U.S. 1312, 101 S.Ct. 829, 66 L.Ed.2d 785 (1981) (Per Justice Rehnquist as Circuit Justice).

[13, 14] The Eighth Amendment's prohibition against imposition of cruel and unusual punishment requires that the sentence cannot be disproportionate to the severity of the crime or involve unnecessary infliction of pain. *Solem v. Helm*, 463 U.S. 277, 103 S.Ct. 3001, 77 L.Ed.2d 637 (1983); *Coker v. Georgia*, 433 U.S. 584, 97 S.Ct. 2861, 53 L.Ed.2d 982 (1977); *Gregg v. Georgia*, 428 U.S. 153, 96 S.Ct. 2909, 49 L.Ed.2d 859 (1976). Again, the guiding rule is that the fixing of penalties for crimes is a legislative function, and the determination of what constitutes adequate punishment is left to the trial court's discretion; and if the sentence is within statutory limits, the appellate court will not regard it as cruel and unusual or excessive. *United States v. Le Mon*, 622 F.2d 1022 (10th Cir.1980); *United States v. Baer*, 575 F.2d 1295 (10th Cir.1978); *Adam v. United States*, 266 F.2d 819 (10th Cir.1959). The imposition of a severe sentence, within legal limits, is not error. Insofar as standard sentencing is concerned, not every offense in a like category calls for identical punishment. *Williams v. State of Okl.*, 358 U.S. 576, 79 S.Ct. 421, 3 L.Ed.2d 516 (1959), rehearing denied, 359 U.S. 956, 79 S.Ct. 737, 3 L.Ed.2d 763 (1959).

A sentence of imprisonment for a very long term of years, the effect of which is to deny a prisoner eligibility for parole until a time beyond his life expectancy, does not violate the Eighth Amendment prohibition of imposition of cruel and unusual punishment. Anno., 33 A.L.R.3d 335, 310, pp. 369–371. In *Bailey v. United States*, 74 F.2d 451, 452 (10th Cir.1934), Bailey was convicted of conspiracy to transport a kidnapped person in violation of 18 U.S.C. § 408 (predecessor to 18 U.S.C. § 1201), which provided that, upon conviction, the defendant shall be imprisoned for a term of years as the court, in its discretion, shall determine. This court held that the imposition of the sentence "during the term of his natural life" was permissible and definite and tantamount "... [t]o a sentence for a definite possible life span of the person sentenced." 74 F.2d at 452. And in *United States v. Ragen*, 146 F.2d 349 (7th Cir. 1945), *cert. denied*, 325 U.S. 865, 65 S.Ct.

1194, 89 L.Ed. 1985 (1945), the court, in a habeas corpus challenge to a 199-year sentence fixed by the jury as sentence for murder, held that the sentence was authorized by the Illinois statute which provided, "punishment of death or imprisonment in the penitentiary for his natural life or for a term of not less than fourteen years," and that the sentence did not constitute cruel and unusual punishment.

In this case, given the basis in fact for the trial court's sentence, we hold that the three hundred year term of imprisonment was completely justified. The appellant O'Driscoll is one of the worst type of offenders. We recognize that the law has long recognized that retribution is not the dominant, primary objective of the criminal justice system. Rather, reformation and rehabilitation are primary, hopeful goals.

However, a severe penalty is required where vindication of the law and the common good of society are at stake because of the callous, vicious propensities of the defendant and his lack of any semblance of good character and respect for human life. We fully agree with the trial court's conclusion that a criminal defendant such as O'Driscoll must be prevented from ever again inflicting on the public his heineous, cruel conduct. The punishment imposed by the trial court is proportioned to the offense committed and the vile criminal record of O'Driscoll. This appellant is a threat and danger to the peace and safety of the community. The punishment imposed by the trial court in this case was properly tailored to the criminal.

WE AFFIRM.

UNITED STATES of America, Appellee,

v.

James Alvin RHODES, a/k/a Mickey
Rhodes, Appellant.

UNITED STATES of America, Appellee,

v.

Garvey Martin CHEEK, Jr., Appellant.

Nos. 84–5241, 84–5242.

United States Court of Appeals,
Fourth Circuit.

Argued March 6, 1985.

Decided Dec. 26, 1985.

Before WIDENER, PHILLIPS and SNEEDEN, Circuit Judges.

WIDENER, Circuit Judge:

Garvey Martin Cheek and James Alvin "Mickey" Rhodes were convicted under 21 U.S.C. § 848 and other statutes for engaging in a continuing criminal enterprise (CCE) and other offenses on the basis of their dealings in controlled substances. Cheek received a 75–year sentence without parole under § 848, while Rhodes received a 50–year sentence without parole under that statute. Both received various other sentences. Cheek and Rhodes appeal their convictions on several grounds, but we find no reversible error and affirm.

Cheek and Rhodes were convicted after a jury found them guilty of several charges in a multicount indictment. Count 1 of the indictment charged that from August 1978 through April 1980 Cheek and Rhodes and others conspired together and with yet others to possess and distribute cocaine and marijuana in violation of 21 U.S.C. §§ 841(a)(1), 846. Counts 4 and 5 charged that on or about November 22, 1979 Cheek, Rhodes and others unlawfully possessed with intent to distribute more than 1000 pounds of marijuana, and that they did distribute same in violation of 21 U.S.C. § 841(a)(1) and 18 U.S.C. § 2. Counts 6 and 7 of the indictment charged Cheek, Rhodes and others with an April 1980 unlawful possession with intent to distribute and with the distribution of greater than 1000 pounds of marijuana in violation of 21 U.S.C. § 841(a)(1), 18 U.S.C. § 2. In Counts 2 and 3, Cheek and others were charged with the unlawful possession with intent to distribute and the distribution of approximately four kilograms of cocaine in or about October 1979. Counts 8, 10, and 11 charged Cheek with separate Travel Act violations under 18 U.S.C. § 1952, and Count 12 charged that Cheek engaged in a continuing criminal enterprise from October 1979 to April 1980 in violation of 21 U.S.C. § 848. Count 16 of the indictment charged Rhodes with engaging in a continuing criminal enterprise from October 1978 to April 1980 in violation of 21 U.S.C. § 848. Cheek was convicted on the charges in all eleven counts and received total sentences of 75 years on the felony violations other than for a continuing criminal enterprise, to run concurrently with a 75-year no parole sentence on the continuing criminal enterprise conviction. Rhodes was convicted of the charges in all six counts and received total sentences of forty-five years on the felony convictions other than for a continuing criminal enterprise, to run concurrently with a 50-year no parole sentence on the continuing criminal enterprise conviction.

No question is raised as to the sufficiency of the evidence to support any of the convictions except those of the continuing criminal enterprise under 21 U.S.C. § 848.

Cheek's and Rhodes' convictions arose out of various illegal drug operations through which large quantities of cocaine and marijuana were transported from either Florida or South Carolina into the Western District of North Carolina. The evidence showed that both Cheek and Rhodes were involved in bringing controlled substances into North Carolina on several occasions. While the evidence regarding Cheek's and Rhodes' involvement in the smuggling operations overlaps to a certain extent, we will discuss separately the evidence as it relates to each.

CHEEK

Viewing the evidence in the light most favorable to the government, *Glasser v. United States*, 315 U.S. 60, 80, 62 S.Ct. 457, 469, 86 L.Ed. 680 (1942), the record shows that Cheek was involved in several drug transactions during the relevant time period charged in the continuing criminal enterprise count. The evidence shows that during late October and early November 1979, Cheek at his residence in Perrine, Florida arranged for the purchase of four kilograms of cocaine from one Maynard Gonzalez, Jr. for a price of $208,000. Gonzalez let Cheek take possession of all four kilograms of the cocaine in exchange for payment of one-half of the purchase price. After paying $104,000 to Gonzalez, Cheek took possession of the cocaine in Florida. Cheek and Rocky Townsend, a witness for the government, loaded the cocaine into a car and drove to Wilkes County, North

Carolina, where the cocaine was distributed to Shelton Wiles. Several weeks after Cheek and Townsend had delivered the cocaine to Wiles in North Carolina, Cheek called upon Townsend to deliver the balance of the cocaine purchase price to Gonzalez at a motel in Charlotte, North Carolina. Townsend complied and delivered the money to Gonzalez for Cheek.

The evidence shows that Cheek undertook this large cocaine transaction to make enough money to cover expenses on an upcoming marijuana transaction that was scheduled to occur around Thanksgiving of 1979. Government witness Jorge Felix Aragon testified that he and his brother, Fred Aragon, arranged to import 5000 pounds of marijuana from Columbia, South America into Florida and that they intended to sell the marijuana to Cheek, Rhodes, and an unnamed individual. Like the Aragons had done on previous marijuana importations, on the Thanksgiving deal they were responsible for obtaining the marijuana in Columbia and for the transportation and offloading of such in southern Florida. The record fairly shows that Cheek was responsible for making the arrangements to receive the marijuana from the offloaders and to transport it to a "stash house" for later distribution into North Carolina. Cheek directed two women, Dorothy Hodges and Peggy Jordan, to rent rooms at two motels in Homestead, Florida, where the marijuana would be received from the offloaders. Townsend, at Cheek's direction, accompanied Hodges and Jordan to two motels, and two rooms were rented. From the two motel rooms, the marijuana would be transported to the stash house which had been secured by Jorge Aragon. As planned, the offloaders drove the marijuana from the coast to the motel rooms, and several individuals who knew where the stash house was located, but who had no relationship with the offloaders, drove the marijuana to the stash house for unloading and weighing. Cheek, Aragon, and Duke Shew waited at the stash house and were responsible for weighing and numbering the bales of marijuana. Within a few days, the transfer process was completed and all but 1200 pounds of wet marijuana was taken from the stash house for distribution. Cheek, Aragon, and Dorothy Hodges soon thereafter flew into Charlotte, North Carolina, and went to Rhodes' house in North Wilkesboro, where they met Rocky Townsend who had driven a load of the wet marijuana out of Florida. Cheek and Aragon spread out the wet marijuana in Rhodes' garage and worked for a few days to dry it out. Thereafter, Aragon stayed in Wilkesboro waiting for Cheek and Rhodes to sell the marijuana from the Thanksgiving deal so that they would be able to pay Aragon with the proceeds. Shortly thereafter, however, Cheek arranged for Rocky Townsend to leave North Carolina and to drive down to Cheek's house in Florida to pay Aragon $500,000 for the marijuana. At Cheek's direction, Townsend drove to Cheek's house in Florida and paid Aragon $500,000 for the marijuana.

The evidence shows that Cheek was involved in another marijuana transaction with Jorge Aragon in the spring of 1980. Cheek accompanied Aragon to Barranquilla, Columbia in preparation for an upcoming deal. Through the Aragon brothers' Columbian connection, 10,000 pounds of marijuana would be airdropped to a yacht off the Florida Keys, unloaded at a house in Islamorada in the Keys, and distributed to Cheek, Rhodes, and unnamed "people up north." Fred Aragon arranged for the Islamorada house and instructed his brother Jorge to stay in the Florida Keys and monitor Coast Guard movement. Before the airdrop, Jorge Aragon contacted Cheek and told him that he needed more money for expenses on the Islamorada operation. Cheek contacted Shelton Wiles and told him to get someone to bring down more money to Florida for expenses. The next day, Cheek's wife flew down to Florida and gave Cheek $10,000. Cheek gave Aragon the money and directed Rocky Townsend to assist Aragon in monitoring Coast Guard activity. The airdrop was successful and the marijuana was unloaded at the Islamorada house. Cheek, Aragon, Townsend, and an unnamed Cuban weighed the marijuana, separated out the bales that were wet, and loaded the dry bales into cars. Townsend testified that he remembered loading the cars for Tony Sidden and his wife, Gloria Sidden, and Wayne Shepherd; and such testimony is consistent with Jorge Aragon's testimony to the effect that he recalled these three individuals were working for Cheek. When the marijuana had been weighed and loaded into cars, Townsend drove a carload of marijuana to Statesville, North Carolina, and Aragon went up to North Carolina to collect from Cheek and Rhodes for their respective purchases of 6500 and 1100 pounds of the Islamorada marijuana.

RHODES

The record shows that Rhodes was involved in several marijuana transactions during the relevant time period charged in the CCE count, October 1978 through April 1980. Government witness Jeffrey VanMeter testified that he and Rhodes had been involved in several marijuana deals in 1978 and 1979. The evidence shows that in late 1978 Cheek unloaded 17,000 pounds of marijuana (that Cheek had been involved in importing through Myrtle Beach, South Carolina) at a farm in Alexander County, North Carolina which Rhodes had used previously for distribution of marijuana. In the words of VanMeter, part of the 17,000-pound load did not go to Rhodes but, rather, went to someone else. The record shows that Rhodes, VanMeter, and Russell Gambill worked together to' sell their portion of the 17,000-pound load and that when Cheek went to Rhodes' house to collect the money on the marijuana that he had fronted, they returned 2000 pounds of the marijuana they could not sell.

The evidence shows that Rhodes became involved with the Aragon brothers in the fall of 1978 when the Aragons smuggled a load of marijuana into Miami, Florida from Columbia, South America and through VanMeter sold a quantity of marijuana to Rhodes. In early 1979, Rhodes met with the Aragons in Wilkesboro and they discussed whether Rhodes would help finance an airplane so that the Aragons could continue their smuggling ventures by air rather than sea. Although the record does not show clearly whether Rhodes agreed to finance the venture, it does show that the Aragons were able to purchase an airplane and that they planned to airdrop a load of marijuana in the spring of 1979, promising to give at least 2000 pounds to Rhodes in exchange for some money that he had paid to them. Jorge Aragon testified that from this airdrop operation they did not have 2000 pounds of marijuana to give to Rhodes and that he was not sure how much Rhodes actually received.

Aside from Rhodes' involvement with the Aragons, the evidence shows that Rhodes obtained marijuana from another source in Florida. The record shows that in May or June of 1979 Rhodes sent several cars from North Wilkesboro to Fort Lauderdale to pick up marijuana from two friends named Patty and Rob. VanMeter testified that he went to Fort Lauderdale and loaded the marijuana in the cars that Rhodes had sent from North Carolina. VanMeter testified that after he loaded the cars he went to North Wilkesboro, where Rhodes gave him $600,000 to take back to Patty and Rob in Fort Lauderdale. VanMeter, accompanied by Clay Green, went to Florida and paid Patty and Rob for Rhodes.

The evidence shows that after the Fort Lauderdale transaction Rhodes became involved with the Aragons and Cheek in the Thanksgiving marijuana deal of 1979. Before the importation, Rhodes sent VanMeter down to Florida, and Jorge Aragon filled VanMeter in on the details of the operation to transport the marijuana from the two motel rooms, which Cheek had arranged to be rented, to the stash house for distribution. VanMeter drove two carloads of marijuana to the stash house but quit and went to Fort Lauderdale because he was disgusted that the marijuana was wet. While the record shows that Wayne McNeil took VanMeter's place in the Thanksgiving operation, VanMeter testified that he later helped McNeil load up a motor home with marijuana at Cheek's house in Florida. When the distribution had been accomplished, Cheek and Aragon arrived at

Rhodes' house in Wilkesboro and attempted to dry out a load of the wet marijuana which had been brought out of Florida. After Cheek and Aragon had finally dried the marijuana, Rhodes refused to let them stay at his house. VanMeter further testified that shortly after the Thanksgiving deal with Cheek and Aragon, he drove a load of 600 to 700 pounds of marijuana supplied by Patty and Rob from Florida to North Carolina and that for his efforts Rhodes paid him $1,000.

The record shows that Rhodes was again involved with Jorge Aragon and Cheek in the 1980 marijuana importation off Islamorada, although it does not indicate that Rhodes was involved in any planning of the operation with Aragon and Cheek. However, the evidence does show that Aragon called Rhodes and told him that the Islamorada marijuana load was in and to send some people down to pick up what Aragon could give him from the load. Aragon testified that four drivers came to Florida and picked up approximately 1100 pounds of the marijuana for Rhodes. Aragon could identify two of the drivers as Wayne McNeil and Kim Edmiston but was unable to identify the other two drivers.

In addition to the detailed evidence which was presented by the government with respect to the aforementioned marijuana deals, Peggy Jordan and Dorothy Hodges testified that they went to Florida to pick up carloads of marijuana for Rhodes in the summer of 1979. Dorothy Hodges further testified that during this time period Wayne McNeil, Kim Edmiston, and a man named "Clay" drove her car to Florida to pick up marijuana for Rhodes.

Cheek and Rhodes appeal their CCE convictions on several grounds. Cheek and Rhodes assert: that they were improperly convicted of engaging in a continuing criminal enterprise under 21 U.S.C. § 848; that their respective sentences of 75 years without parole and 50 years without parole violate the Eighth Amendment's prohibition against cruel and unusual punishment since the sentences are disproportionate to the crimes for which they were convicted; that the district court committed reversible error by admitting evidence of other wrongs or acts committed by both defendants which were not charged in the indictment; and that the district court improperly admitted the contents of a spiral notebook, allegedly containing drug business records between Rhodes and Cheek, because the notebook was seized in violation of the defendants' Fourth Amendment rights. Rhodes separately argues that the court improperly admitted a statement he made to police officers that allegedly was the product of custodial interrogation. We will address these contentions in order.

CCE CONVICTIONS

To obtain a CCE conviction under § 848, the government must prove that the accused violated a specified federal drug law, the violation of which is punishable as a felony, *see* 21 U.S.C. § 801 *et seq.*,[1] and that such violation was part of a "continuing series of violations" of the specified federal drug laws. Section 848(b)(2) sets forth the essential elements for what constitutes a continuing series of violations by providing in relevant part that:

[S]uch violation is a part of a continuing series of violations [of the specified drug laws]—

(A) which are undertaken by such person in concert with five or more other persons with respect to whom such person occupies a position of organizer, a supervisory position, or any other position of management, and

(B) from which such person obtains substantial income or resources.

21 U.S.C. § 848(b)(2). Cheek and Rhodes argue that their CCE convictions were improper because the government failed to prove that either defendant occupied a managerial, organizational, or supervisory position over the requisite number of people within the proscription of § 848(b)(2)(A). They contend that § 848 requires the

government to prove that an accused occupied a managerial position with respect to at least five persons on each of the underlying felony drug violations constituting the continuing series of violations. The government, on the other hand, takes the position that § 848 merely requires proof that an accused occupied a managerial, organizational, or supervisory position with respect to at least five people during the course of the overall series of violations.

To support the contention that the CCE convictions were improper because the government failed to prove that either defendant occupied a managerial position with respect to at least five people on each underlying violation, defendants contend that the language of the statute itself indicates that the numerosity requirement relates to each individual violation as opposed to the series of violations as a whole. In this regard, they point to the relevant part of § 848 which provides that the government must prove that a specific felony drug violation "is a part of a continuing series of violations ... which *are* undertaken by such person in concert with five or more other persons with respect to whom such person occupies a position of organizer, a supervisory position, or any other position of management." *Id.* § 848(b)(2)(A) (emphasis added). The argument goes that if Congress had intended for the numerosity requirement to relate to the entire series of violations as a whole, Congress would have used the word "is" instead of "are" as the proper verb form to indicate that the numerosity inquiry focuses on whether the *series* of violations *is* undertaken in concert with five or more other persons. The use of the word "are" indicates, the defendants say, that Congress intended for the five-person requirement to relate to the term "violations" rather than to the term "series" and that, consistent with this legislative intent, the five-person minimum must be proven with respect to each underlying felony drug vio-

---

1. Controlled Substances Act, Pub.L. No. 91–513, 84 Stat. 1242 (codified as amended at 21 U.S.C. §§ 801–904); Controlled Substances Import and

Export Act, Pub.L. No. 91–513, 84 Stat. 1285 (codified as amended at 21 U.S.C. §§ 951–970).

lation. Cheek and Rhodes assert that since the government did not prove that either of them occupied a managerial position with respect to five people during any of the underlying drug violations, their CCE convictions were improper and should be reversed.

We have found no cases to support the sought for construction of § 848. Defendants have candidly admitted that courts considering the five-person requirement uniformly have found that the five people under a defendant's management need not have worked in the drug business at the same moment. *See United States v. Smith,* 690 F.2d 748, 750 (9th Cir.1982), *cert. denied sub nom. Fisherman v. United States,* 460 U.S. 1011, 103 S.Ct. 1435, 75 L.Ed.2d 793 (1983); *United States v. Losada,* 674 F.2d 167, 173–74 (2d Cir.), *cert. denied,* 457 U.S. 1125, 102 S.Ct. 2945, 73 L.Ed.2d 1341 (1982); *United States v. Phillips,* 664 F.2d 971, 1013 (5th Cir.1981), *cert. denied sub nom. Meinster v. United States,* 457 U.S. 1136, 102 S.Ct. 2965, 73 L.Ed.2d 1354 (1982); *United States v. Barnes,* 604 F.2d 121, 157 (2d Cir.1979), *cert. denied,* 446 U.S. 907, 100 S.Ct. 1833, 64 L.Ed.2d 260 (1980); *United States v. Bolts,* 558 F.2d 316, 320–21 (5th Cir.), *cert. denied sub nom. Hicks v. United States,* 434 U.S. 930, 98 S.Ct. 417, 54 L.Ed.2d 290 (1970); *United States v. Sperling,* 506 F.2d 1323, 1344 (2d Cir.1974), *cert. denied,* 420 U.S. 962, 95 S.Ct. 1351, 43 L.Ed.2d 439 (1975). They contend, however, that these cases do not stand for the proposition that the required five people need only act sometime during the course of the related drug violations. Instead, the claim is that these cases simply find that the five people need not have been acting at the same moment during each specific violation, and, accordingly, defendants concede that for each underlying violation it would be sufficient for the five people to have been involved in such at different times.

We, however, are unpersuaded by either of defendants' constructions of § 848. The Second Circuit in *United States v. Sperling,* 506 F.2d 1323 (2d Cir.1974), *cert. denied,* 420 U.S. 962, 95 S.Ct. 1351, 43

L.Ed.2d 439 (1975), rejected a defendant's contention that his CCE conviction was improper because the evidence failed to show that five people were working in his narcotics business at the same moment. The court noted that the defendant Sperling was an operational kingpin of a highly organized, structured and on-going narcotics network and that the evidence clearly showed that during the relevant time period charged in the indictment, greater than five people were engaged in Sperling's narcotics operation and were directly under his supervision. *Id.* at 1344. In deciding that § 848 did not require proof that at least five people worked under the defendant at the same moment, the court found the statute merely required proof that the person charged acted " 'in concert with five or more other persons' and as to them that he occupied 'a position of organizer, a supervisory position, or any other position of management.' " *Id.*

As stated, defendants argue that *Sperling* and the cases which later followed are distinguishable on the ground that these cases did not hold specifically that five people need only work for a defendant some time during the course of the violations comprising the series, regardless of the number of people who participated in the underlying violations. Accordingly, they argue that we would not be in conflict with other circuits if we were to hold that § 848 requires proof that at least five people worked under a defendant's supervision on each violation comprising the series of violations, whether or not the minimum five people worked simultaneously on each violation.

We disagree. In *United States v. Smith,* 690 F.2d 748 (9th Cir.1982), *cert. denied sub nom. Fisherman v. United States,* 460 U.S. 1011, 103 S.Ct. 1435, 75 L.Ed.2d 793 (1983), the defendant challenged his CCE conviction by arguing that the government failed to prove that he directly supervised five people for each of the acts embodying the continuing series of violations. *Id.* at 749. The jury convicted the defendant on six counts in the fifteen-count indictment. To support his claim of improper CCE conviction, the defendant emphasized that four of the substantive counts of the indictment involved fewer than five people. Notwithstanding, the Ninth Circuit, in *Smith*, relied on *Sperling* and rejected the defendant's construction of § 848 by reasoning that it was not necessary for the government to show that "the organizer worked with five or more persons at the same moment." *Id.* at 750. Needless to say, we consider the holding of the case to be more important than the use of the *Sperling* language.

We agree with the Ninth Circuit's construction of § 848 and hold that the five other persons mentioned in the statute need not be under a defendant's supervision at the same moment nor in the conduct of the same underlying felony. It is enough that they are found to be under the defendant's supervision in the conduct of the same continuing criminal enterprise, as here.

We think the record fairly shows that both Cheek and Rhodes acted in concert with five or more other persons and that each occupied a position of organizer, supervisor, or manager with respect to those individuals. There is credible evidence to show that from the period of October 1979 through April 1980 Cheek occupied a position of organizer, supervisor, or manager with respect to Rocky Townsend, Dorothy Hodges, Peggy Jordan, Judy Cheek, Shelton Wiles, Tony Sidden, Gloria Sidden, and Wayne Shepherd, to name a few. Thus, as to Cheek, the evidence clearly was sufficient to support his CCE conviction. Likewise, we think the evidence is sufficient to support Rhodes' conviction since it fairly shows that from October 1978 through October 1980 Rhodes occupied a managerial, supervisory or organizational position with respect to at least six individuals, including Jeffrey VanMe-

ter, Clay Green, Wayne McNeil, Kim Edmiston, Peggy Jordan, and Dorothy Hodges.

EIGHTH AMENDMENT

Cheek and Rhodes assert that imposition of their respective sentences is cruel and unusual punishment in violation of the Eighth Amendment because the sentences are disproportionate to the crimes for which they were convicted. At the time Cheek received his sentence of 75 years without parole, we are told he was 38 years old. Assuming the maximum amount of good time credit as provided in 18 U.S.C. § 4161, Cheek would have to serve approximately 50 years, thereby becoming eligible for release at the age of 88. At the time Rhodes received his 50-year sentence without the possibility of parole, he was 42 years old. Accounting for maximum good time credit, Rhodes would have to serve approximately 33⅓ years of this sentence and would become eligible for release at the age of 76.[2] Cheek and Rhodes argue that their respective sentences are effectively life sentences without parole, given their advanced years, upon their prospective release dates under present law. Because, they argue, the sentences are *de facto* life sentences without possibility of parole, they maintain that the Supreme Court's recent decision in *Solem v. Helm*, 463 U.S. 277, 103 S.Ct. 3001, 77 L.Ed.2d 637 (1983), requires us to undertake an extensive proportionality review of defendants' sentences in accordance with a three-part test announced by the Court.

In *Solem*, the Supreme Court declared unconstitutional a sentence of life imprisonment without possibility of parole and, in so doing, set forth a three-part test involving "objective factors" to use in reviewing the proportionality of sentences under the Eighth Amendment. 463 U.S. at 290–303, 103 S.Ct. at 3010–16. Significantly, the Court in *Solem* held for the first time that a noncapital sentence was disproportionate

2. These prospective dates for release are only illustrative, however. Cheek currently is serving another sentence, and the sentencing judge found that the CCE sentence would run consecutively with that sentence. Rhodes, on the other hand, has been free on bond since his CCE conviction.

to the crime committed and stated, "we hold as a matter of principle that a criminal sentence must be proportionate to the crime for which the defendant has been convicted." *Id.* at 290, 103 S.Ct. 3010. In declaring the life sentence imposed under South Dakota's recidivist statute disproportionate, *Solem* distinguished the earlier decision of *Rummel v. Estelle*, 445 U.S. 263, 100 S.Ct. 1133, 63 L.Ed.2d 382 (1980), which had upheld imposition of a life sentence under Texas' recidivist statute, on the ground that the defendant Rummel was eligible for parole, while, under South Dakota law, no prospect of parole attached to Helm's life sentence.[3] 463 U.S. at 297 & n. 24, 300–03, 103 S.Ct. at 3013 & n. 24, 3015–16. The question left open after *Solem* is whether, because a life sentence without possibility of parole will cause a proportionality review, a severe sentence of a term of years, as here, similarly requires review. We note this issue to emphasize the fact that notwithstanding the Court's review of such a life sentence in *Solem* the Court has never set aside as cruel and unusual punishment a sentence for a term of years that is within the limits set by statute. *See Hutto v. Davis*, 454 U.S. 370, 372, 102 S.Ct.

703, 704, 70 L.Ed.2d 556 (1982) (per curiam).

In *Hutto v. Davis*, 454 U.S. 370, 102 S.Ct. 703, 70 L.Ed.2d 556 (1982) (per curiam), the Supreme Court reversed an *en banc* decision of this court in which we had affirmed the district court's invalidation of consecutive sentences for a total term of 40 years upon finding such sentences disproportionate to the crime committed. *See Davis v. Zahradnick*, 432 F.Supp. 444 (W.D.Va.1977), *aff'd sub nom. Davis v. Davis*, 646 F.2d 123 (4th Cir.1981) (en banc) (per curiam), *rev'd. sub nom. Hutto v. Davis*, 454 U.S. 370, 102 S.Ct. 703, 70 L.Ed.2d 556 (1982). Relying on its earlier pronouncement in *Rummel*, the Court in *Davis* emphasized that courts "should be 'reluctant to review legislatively mandated terms of imprisonment'" and, moreover, that "'successful challenges to the proportionality of particular sentences' should be 'exceedingly rare.'" 454 U.S. at 374, 102 S.Ct. at 706, *quoting Rummel*, 445 U.S. at 272, 274, 100 S.Ct. at 1138, 1139. Therefore, to the extent that *Solem* does not overrule the reasoning of *Rummel* and *Davis* but, rather, explicitly accepts the posi-

3. The defendant Rummel was convicted in a Texas state court for two separate felonies: fraudulent use of a credit card to obtain $80 worth of goods or services and passing a forged check in the amount of $28.36. *Rummel v. Estelle*, 445 U.S. 263, 100 S.Ct. 1133, 63 L.Ed.2d 382 (1980). Rummel pleaded guilty to the 1964 credit card offense and was sentenced to three years' imprisonment. He also pleaded guilty to the 1969 forgery offense and was sentenced to four years' imprisonment. In 1973, Rummel was charged with obtaining $120.75 by false pretenses. Since the latter offense was classified as a felony under Texas law, the prosecution proceeded against Rummel under Texas' recidivist statute and, pursuant to such, Rummel received a mandatory life sentence with the possibility of parole. 445 U.S. at 265–66, 278, 100 S.Ct. 1134–35, 1141.

In *Solem v. Helm*, 463 U.S. 277, 103 S.Ct. 3001, 77 L.Ed.2d 637 (1983), the defendant Helm was convicted of what the Court classified as six nonviolent felonies under South Dakota law during the period between 1964 and 1975. 463 U.S. at 279, 103 S.Ct. at 3004. These convictions included third-degree burglary in 1964, 1966, and 1969; obtaining money under false pretenses in 1972; grand larceny in 1973; and,

in 1975, a third offense of driving while intoxicated, punishable as a felony. In 1979, Helm was charged with uttering a "no account" check for $100 and pleaded guilty to the uttering offense, which, ordinarily, would have carried with it a sentence of five years' imprisonment and a $5,000 fine. However, because of his prior record, Helm was subject to the South Dakota recidivist statute. Under the statute, Helm received a life sentence without possibility of parole. *Id.* at 281–82, 103 S.Ct. at 3065.

In distinguishing *Rummel*, the *Solem* Court noted that Helm's sentence was far more severe than Rummel's because, at the time the Court considered Rummel's sentence, it was likely that Rummel would have been eligible for parole within 12 years of his initial confinement. *Id.* at 297, 103 S.Ct. at 3013. On the other hand, given the fact that Helm was sentenced for life with no possibility of parole, the Court commented that capital punishment was the only punishment exceeding Helm's in severity. *Id.* Furthermore, the Court specifically refused to decide *Solem* under the reasoning of *Rummel* by equating the possibility of parole that existed in Texas with the possibility of executive clemency that existed in South Dakota. *Id.* 463 U.S. at 300, 103 S.Ct. at 3013.

tion asserted in those cases, that in noncapital cases successful proportionality challenges will be extremely rare, 463 U.S. at 289–90, 103 S.Ct. at 3009, it seems to us that *Solem* requires an extensive proportionality analysis only in those cases involving life sentences without parole. We are inclined to interpret *Solem* in this light, especially given the *Solem* Court's refusal to overrule *Rummel* and *Davis*, and accordingly uphold the terms of years' sentences herein as appropriate sentences within the limits set by Congress.

Such a disposition is complicated, however, by the fact that defendants equate their sentences for terms of years without parole with life sentences without parole because of their ages. Thus, as an alternate ground for our decision, we uphold the sentences because they withstand an analysis under *Solem*. Defendants rely on *United States v. Darby*, 744 F.2d 1508 (11th Cir.1984), *cert. denied*, — U.S. —, 105 S.Ct. 2322, 85 L.Ed.2d 841 (1985), as authority for this court to undertake an extensive proportionality review. In *Darby*, the court determined that *Solem* required an extended analysis of the proportionality of two 60-year sentences imposed under § 848 because it found the scheme prescribing enhanced penalties for federal drug violations to be similar to the recidivist statutes involved in *Rummel* and *Solem*, 744 F.2d at 1526. The court then undertook a thorough review by applying the three-part *Solem* test to consider "(i) the gravity of the offense and the harshness of the penalty; (ii) the sentences imposed on other criminals in the same jurisdiction; and (iii) the sentences imposed for commission of the same crime in other jurisdictions." *Id.*, *quoting Solem*, 463 U.S. at 292, 103 S.Ct. at 3011. After the court conducted its extensive review, it determined that although the sentences were severe, they were "not so grossly disproportionate to their crime to constitute cruel and unusual punishment." *Id.* at 1526–29.

With respect to the appropriate steps we should now take, we note that the Supreme Court in *Solem* warned:

Reviewing courts, of course, should grant substantial deference to the broad authority that legislatures necessarily possess in determining the types and limits of punishments for crimes, as well as to the discretion that trial courts possess in sentencing convicted criminals.

463 U.S. at 290, 103 S.Ct. at 3010. By way of footnote, the majority further added:

... we do not adopt or imply approval of a general rule of appellate review of sentences. Absent specific authority, it is not the role of an appellate court to substitute its judgment for that of the sentencing court as to the appropriateness of a particular sentence; rather, in applying the Eighth Amendment the appellate court decides only whether the sentence under review is within constitutional limits. In view of the substantial deference that must be accorded legislatures and sentencing courts, *a reviewing court rarely will be required to engage in extended analysis to determine that a sentence is not constitutionally disproportionate.*

Id. at 290 n. 16, 103 S.Ct. at 3010 n. 16 (emphasis added).

Unlike the court in *Darby*, we do not think that the sentences imposed in this case require an extended proportionality analysis. Given the substantial deference that should be accorded Congress and the sentencing court, our duty is to decide whether the sentences under review are within the constitutional limits. *See* 463 U.S. at 290 n. 16, 103 S.Ct. at 3010 n. 16. Such a review, as one court has noted, often requires at least a perfunctory *Solem* analysis. *See Moreno v. Estelle*, 717 F.2d 171, 180 & n. 10 (5th Cir.1983). While we would not use the same adjective to describe the analysis because of its overtones, we think that court meant less than extended and are of opinion that in cases where an Eighth Amendment claim is made concerning the length of a sentence which may not be disposed of as so obviously within the prerogative of Congress and the district court to require no comment, that a simple matching of the facts of a particular case against the *Solem* principles will suffice without extended discussion. That is what we do here.

After reviewing Cheek's and Rhodes' sentences under the principles set forth in *Solem*, we are of opinion that they are not disproportionate within the meaning of the Eighth Amendment. There is no doubt that their crimes were indeed serious. They were involved in many importations and distributions of cocaine and marijuana. There was evidence that Rhodes and Cheek opened up the Wilkes County market for illegal drugs for Jorge Aragon. Time after time during 1978 through April 1980, both defendants actively participated in bringing large quantities of controlled substances into North Carolina. The marijuana involved was measured by the ton and the cocaine by the kilogram; millions of dollars were involved; so this was not the operation of small scale dope peddlers selling on street corners. Continuous large-scale drug trafficking is a grave offense and Congress chose to impose severe penalties for it. *See* H.R.Rep. No. 1444, 91st Cong., 2d Sess., *reprinted in* 1970 U.S.Code Cong. & Ad.News 4566, 4576. Furthermore, many defendants convicted under § 848 have received sentences comparable to those Cheek and Rhodes received. *See United States v. Love*, 767 F.2d 1052 (4th Cir.1985); *Darby*, 744 F.2d at 1528–29 (citing cases). In many of these cases, moreover, the validity of the severe sentences was not attacked. We note that while cases under § 848 involve many different fact situations which may appear to be either more or less serious than the offenses involved here, insofar as sentencing is concerned Congress drafted the penalty provisions of the Controlled Substances Act, *see* 21 U.S.C. §§ 801 *et. seq.*, to "give maximum flexibility to judges, permitting them to tailor the period of imprisonment...to the circumstances involved in the individual case." H.R.Rep. No. 1444, *supra*, at 4576. We also note that the House Report above referred to, 1970 U.S. Code Cong. & Ad.News, p. 4575, quotes with approval the Prettyman Report (Report of the President's Advisory Committee

on Narcotics and Drug Abuse, November 1963), which we think fairly states the intent of Congress as follows:

The illegal traffic in drugs should be attacked with the full power of the Federal Government. The price for participation in this traffic should be prohibitive. It should be made too dangerous to be attractive.

Considering the large amount of illegal drugs involved, the huge amounts of money, the extent of the operation, and the number of people involved, we do not think that the sentencing court abused its discretion in imposing severe sentences on the defendants, particularly in light of the fact that Congress intended for judges to tailor specific sentences according to the circumstances involved in each case to make participation in the drug traffic too dangerous to be attractive.

We conclude that the sentences, although they are indeed severe, are not disproportionate to the crimes committed so as to constitute cruel and unusual punishment.

BAD ACTS EVIDENCE

Cheek and Rhodes individually raise several assignments of error concerning the admission of evidence of other crimes and wrongs which were not charged in the indictment. We will address their contentions separately.

Cheek objects to the admissibility of evidence surrounding his purchase of two Ferrari automobiles for $33,000 each, which he paid for in cash, for which payment he declined to accept receipts. He had the cars titled in the name of his mistress. The argument is that this was proof of inadmissible bad acts under FRE 404(b). We think, however, that proof of such large cash purchases in the circumstances present here was relevant evidence under 21 U.S.C. § 848(b)(2)(B) which requires proof that a defendant obtain substantial income or resources on account of one or more of the series of violations mentioned in the statute.

The evidence introduced by the government as to Cheek's personal drug use, as well as the general pattern of his personal life, we do not think was plain error.

Finally, with respect to this aspect of Cheek's argument, as his brief may be read to object to the closing argument of the United States Attorney, even if the argument went too far, which is doubtful and which we do not decide, it was not reversible error because there was no motion for a mistrial.

We next consider Rhodes' claim of reversible error based on the admission of three state court convictions: misdemeanor possession of less than one ounce of marijuana on February 12, 1981; misdemeanor possession of cocaine on April 9, 1980; and simple felonious possession of cocaine on November 1, 1983. Rhodes argues that admitting evidence of the three convictions was improper because it was irrelevant and, even if it was relevant on a disputed issue, it nevertheless was highly prejudicial because it depicted him as a bad person, drug user, and convicted drug offender. Specifically, Rhodes claims that the convictions were inadmissible under Rule 404(b) because there was no disputed issue concerning his motive, opportunity, intent, preparation, plan, knowledge, identity, or absence of mistake. The trial judge, however, specifically stated that he was admitting the convictions because of the line of defense Rhodes had raised and that in his opinion the probative value of the convictions outweighed the prejudicial effect.

Rhodes was charged in Count 1 with conspiring with others to possess and distribute cocaine and marijuana from August 1978 through April 1980. The government charged as a manner and means of the conspiracy that three individuals, not including Rhodes, were involved in a four kilogram cocaine transaction in November 1979. While the indictment charged Rhodes specifically with conspiracy to possess and distribute cocaine and marijuana, it did not otherwise charge or connect Rhodes to any specific cocaine transaction.

Notwithstanding Rhodes' apparent lack of involvement in the specific cocaine transaction charged as a manner and means of the conspiracy, it was the government's theory that the cocaine transaction was undertaken to generate money to cover the expenses for an upcoming marijuana transaction. The indictment charged Rhodes with participation in the subsequent marijuana transaction. Rhodes maintains that since the government was able to tie the cocaine and marijuana operations into one conspiracy and since there was no proof that Rhodes was involved in the four kilogram cocaine sale, the government introduced the two cocaine convictions so that the jury would think that Rhodes nevertheless was involved in the November 1979 cocaine transaction. Such admission, Rhodes asserts, was improper under Rule 404(b) since his defense was not lack of knowledge or intent, but, rather, that he was not involved in the specific four kilogram transaction. Moreover, he claims that he was prejudiced by the introduction of the cocaine convictions, which were subsequent in time to the 1979 cocaine transaction and involved only possession of cocaine. He argues that, even though the government could not prove his involvement in the large cocaine distribution transaction, the jury could infer on the basis of his past cocaine possessions that he was involved in it. Similarly, Rhodes contends that it was improper to admit the misdemeanor marijuana conviction because his defense was not lack of motive, intent, or knowledge regarding the charges against him for marijuana possession and distribution. As with the cocaine charge, Rhodes argues that his defense on the marijuana charges was that he did not participate in the specific acts.

During opening statements, counsel for Rhodes depicted Rhodes as a professional gambler who sought to ingratiate himself with people who had money so that he could win their money by gambling. Counsel painted Rhodes as never an organizer or importer of drugs and proposed that he merely stayed around to collect from those

who owed him gambling debts.[4] Throughout presentation of the government's case-
in-chief, Rhodes' counsel on cross examination raised the issue of Rhodes' involvement with cocaine. For example, on cross
examination of Rocky Townsend, counsel
asked, "You've never known Mr. Rhodes to
be involved in any cocaine transaction
whatsoever, have you?," and the witness
responded "No." Similarly, on cross examination of Dorothy Hodges, counsel asked
"You've never known Mr. Rhodes to be
involved in any cocaine distribution at all,
have you?," to which the witness responded, "Not a large amount, no." Upon further questioning concerning Hodges'
knowledge of Rhodes' involvement with cocaine, Hodges responded that she had obtained a gram or two of cocaine from
Rhodes.   Counsel also cross examined
Jorge Aragon and Jeffrey VanMeter on the
matter of Rhodes' involvement with cocaine. Aragon stated that he had never
been involved in a cocaine transaction with
Rhodes, and VanMeter testified that he had
never known Rhodes to sell and distribute
cocaine.

    We think that the cocaine convic-
tions were properly admitted under FRE
404(b) and that the district court did not
abuse its discretion in determining that the
probative value outweighed the prejudicial
effect.   Rhodes defended himself on the
ground that as a professional gambler he
merely associated with the real drug con-
spirators so they could gamble away their
drug money. He consistently questioned
the government's witnesses concerning
their knowledge of his involvement with
cocaine in an attempt to divorce himself
from connection with the drug. To the
extent then that Rhodes defended on the
ground that he was present but innocent,
he placed his intent in issue. By asking
government witnesses whether they had
ever known him to be involved with co-

caine, the cocaine convictions became admissible to contradict the attempt to disas-
sociate Rhodes from connection therewith.
We think that under the liberal construction lately given by this circuit to Rule
404(b) and like theories, it was not reversible error to admit the cocaine convictions
on the issue of Rhodes' intent. *See United
States v. Hadaway*, 681 F.2d 214 (4th Cir.
1982); *United States v. Masters*, 622 F.2d
83 (4th Cir.1980); *United States v. DiZen-
zo*, 500 F.2d 263 (4th Cir.1974); *United
States v. Woods*, 484 F.2d 127 (4th Cir.
1973), *cert. denied*, 415 U.S. 979, 94 S.Ct.
1566, 39 L.Ed.2d 875 (1974).

    Additionally, we find that the marijuana
conviction was properly admitted.   The
conviction was based on the discovery of
marijuana that police officers found in a
drain in Rhodes' garage during the course
of lawful search on March 22, 1980. This
search, as we will describe more fully below in relation to the Fourth Amendment
claim, uncovered a spiral notebook with
names and figures which the government
at trial introduced to show that Rhodes
was in fact in the drug business and was
involved with Cheek in such. The officer
who conducted the search of Rhodes' house
and garage testified as to what he found on
the premises. We agree that admitting
proof of the conviction was admissible under Rule 404(b) since Rhodes' defense that
he was present but innocent placed his
intent with respect to marijuana in issue.
Moreover, we do not think that the trial
court abused its discretion in ruling that
the probative value outweighed the prejudicial effect.

REMAINING ISSUES

    During a search of Rhodes' house
on March 22, 1980, police officers seized a
spiral notebook that allegedly contained
drug business records which related to the

---

4. Just as an opening statement does not make
admissible evidence to contradict it, *see United
States v. Basic Construction Co.*, 711 F.2d 570,
574 (4th Cir.), *cert. denied*, 464 U.S. 956, 104
S.Ct. 371, 527, 78 L.Ed.2d 330 (1983), neither
does it call for admitting bad acts of the defend-

ant into evidence. *United States v. Hadaway*,
681 F.2d 214, 218 (4th Cir.1982). But an opening statement as here certainly may be taken
into account by the trial court in ascertaining a
theory of defense.

dealings between Cheek and Rhodes on the November 1979 marijuana importation. The search was conducted pursuant to a search warrant which authorized seizure of certain containers of brown vegetable material and rolling papers. At the suppression hearing, Officer Hamilton testified that the closed notebook was next to some marijuana on a kitchen counter and that he picked it up and flipped through the pages. The notebook contained names, numbers, and figures. Hamilton testified that he looked at the notebook because, based on his experience as a law enforcement officer, he was aware that drug dealers customarily kept records of their drug dealings. The government maintains that the seizure was justified under the plain view exception to the warrant requirement since the search warrant did not extend to authorize seizure of the notebook. The government further contends that admission of photocopies of the notebook's contents was proper under FRE 1003 and 1001(4). We agree that under the authority of *United States v. Crouch*, 648 F.2d 932 (4th Cir.), *cert. denied*, 454 U.S. 952, 102 S.Ct. 491, 70 L.Ed.2d 259 (1981), the seizure of the notebook was justified by the plain view exception and that photocopies of the contents of such were admissible. Upon such a finding, we need not decide whether Cheek had a protectable privacy interest in the notebook seized from Rhodes' house.

Rhodes separately alleges that it was error for the court to admit a statement Rhodes made allegedly during the course of custodial interrogation. When Officer Hamilton picked up the spiral notebook during the search of Rhodes' house, Rhodes said, "You can't take that." Hamilton then asked, "Why," to which Rhodes responded, "I can't run my business without that." Rhodes moved to suppress the second statement on the ground that his response to Hamilton's question "Why" amounted to custodial interrogation. Since

he had not been given his warnings under *Miranda v. Arizona*, 384 U.S. 436, 86 S.Ct. 1602, 16 L.Ed.2d 694 (1966), Rhodes claims that the statement should have been suppressed. The government claims that the statement was admissible because Rhodes was not in custody at the time and because no interrogation occurred.

We do not need to decide the issue whether Rhodes' statement was made while he was "in custody," *see Minnesota v. Murphy*, 465 U.S. 420, 104 S.Ct. 1136, 79 L.Ed.2d 409 (U.S.1984), because we think the district court correctly determined that Rhodes made a spontaneous statement which was not the product of interrogation. Before Rhodes told Officer Hamilton that he could not have the spiral notebook, Hamilton had had no communication with Rhodes beyond reading the search warrant to him. It is apparent that the police officer did not initiate the conversation that ensued. Viewing the context within which Rhodes made the statement he now seeks to suppress, we agree that Rhodes' response was spontaneous and not the product of interrogation. Thus, we find that the statement was admissible and follow the reasoning of *United States v. Grant*, 549 F.2d 942, 946 (4th Cir.), *cert. denied*, 432 U.S. 908, 97 S.Ct. 2955, 53 L.Ed.2d 1081 (1977), where we stated that *Miranda* does not protect an accused "from a spontaneous admission made under circumstances not induced by the investigating officers or during a conversation not initiated by the officers."

We have considered the other assignments of error and find them to be without merit.

Accordingly, the judgment of the district court is

AFFIRMED.

UNITED STATES of America,
Plaintiff/Appellee,

v.

Robert Wayne BARKER,
Defendant/Appellant.

UNITED STATES of America,
Plaintiff/Appellee,

v.

William Bernard McKINNEY,
Defendant/Appellant.

UNITED STATES of America,
Plaintiff/Appellee,

v.

Jeffrey Martin ENGLE,
Defendant/Appellant.

UNITED STATES of America,
Plaintiff/Appellee,

v.

George Leland TIMMONS, III,
Defendant/Appellant.

UNITED STATES of America,
Plaintiff/Appellee,

v.

Jason ENGLE, Defendant/Appellant.

Nos. 84–1240 to 84–1242, 84–1244
and 84–1280.

United States Court of Appeals,
Ninth Circuit.

Argued and Submitted April 8, 1985.

Decided Sept. 20, 1985.

Appeal from the United States District Court for the Northern District of California.

Before MERRILL, CANBY and NORRIS, Circuit Judges.

CANBY, Circuit Judge:

Each appellant pleaded guilty to one count arising from participation in a single shipment of marijuana that was part of a large and protracted marijuana smuggling operation. Each was sentenced to the maximum term permitted by statute. On appeal, each contends that the district court abused its ordinarily wide discretion in sentencing by failing adequately to consider individualized factors. We agree, vacate appellants' sentences, and remand for individualized resentencing in accord with this opinion.

BACKGROUND

From 1977 to 1981, a large-scale drug smuggling organization known as the "Coronado Company" imported and distributed approximately twenty-four tons of marijuana from Thailand. More than twenty-five persons participated. The five appellants here, Robert Barker, William McKinley, Jeffrey Engle, Jason Engle, and George Timmons, were each charged with multiple substantive and conspiracy counts stemming from their involvement in the Company's importation of five tons of marijuana in 1981.

Count One charged each with conspiring to import five tons of marijuana in violation of 21 U.S.C. § 963. Count Two charged defendants with conspiracy to possess and distribute. Counts Three and Four charged that Jeffrey and Jason Engle had actually imported the marijuana in violation of 21 U.S.C. § 952, and had possessed it

with intent to distribute in violation of 21 U.S.C. §§ 841(a)(1) and 841(b)(6).

Separate superceding informations were filed against Barker, McKinney, and Timmons. Barker and McKinney were charged with unlawful possession, respectively, of 140 and 45 pounds of marijuana with intent to distribute, in violation of 21 U.S.C. § 841(a)(1). Timmons was charged with conspiracy to possess 180 pounds of marijuana with intent to distribute, in violation of 21 U.S.C. §§ 841(a)(1) and 846.

Each defendant ultimately pleaded guilty to a single count, and remaining counts were dismissed upon government motion. Barker, McKinney, and Timmons each entered guilty pleas to the superceding informations. Jeffrey and Jason Engle each pleaded guilty to Count One of the indictment.

Each defendant's involvement in the smuggling operation was described by his respective counsel at the sentencing hearing. Jeffrey and Jason Engle were crew members on a boat that delivered the marijuana from Thailand. Timmons invested $100,000 in the operation and was repaid with 180 pounds of marijuana. Barker invested $50,000 and received 45 pounds of marijuana in return. McKinney "lent" $75,000 to the principals of the smuggling ring, and was also repaid with 45 pounds. Although the entire conspiracy extended for over five years, the record does not reflect any other involvement in the smuggling operation by any of these defendants.

By the time appellants entered their guilty pleas, most of the other members of the "Coronado Company" had been sentenced in separate proceedings. After comparing relative levels of culpability and considering the sentences imposed in other districts on more prominent members of the Company,[1] the government recommended prison sentences for each defendant ranging from one year for crew members Jeffrey and Jason Engle, to 18 months for the "investors" Barker, McKinney, and Timmons. The court, however, rejected these recommendations. Describing marijuana smuggling as "a plague on society," and expressing its dismay at what it viewed as the government's leniency, the court sentenced each defendant to the maximum five-year term permitted by statute.[2] This appeal follows.

DISCUSSION

A. Reviewability

It is generally accepted that trial courts are accorded virtually unfettered discretion in imposing sentence. *See Dorszynski v. United States*, 418 U.S. 424, 94 S.Ct. 3042, 41 L.Ed.2d 855 (1974); *but see* 3 C. Wright, *Federal Practice and Procedure* § 533 at 168–69 (1982) (rule arguably based on misconstruction of 1891 statute creating courts of appeals); *Woosley v. United States*, 478 F.2d 139, 141–42 (8th Cir.1973) (en banc) (discussing 1891 statute and noting that Supreme Court support for this proposition "is pure dicta"). While there are exceptions, *see United States v. Garrett*, 680 F.2d 650, 652 & n. 3 (9th Cir.1982), a sentence is generally not subject to appellate review if it is within

statutory limits. *See United States v. Tucker*, 404 U.S. 443, 447, 92 S.Ct. 589, 591, 30 L.Ed.2d 592 (1972); *United States v. Lopez-Gonzales*, 688 F.2d 1275, 1276 (9th Cir.1982).[3]

The exceptions to this rule, while limited, are well supported. Courts have remanded for resentencing "where the sentencing court in effect refuses to exercise its discretion," *United States v. Wardlaw*, 576 F.2d 932, 938 (1st Cir.1978), and where the district court "exceeded the bounds of its sentencing discretion" by failing to individualize sentences. *Id.* In *Lopez-Gonzales*, we held that because trial courts are obligated actually to exercise their discretion, we may conduct a limited review of the sentencing process to insure that discretion has, in fact, been exercised by the district court. 688 F.2d at 1276 (citing *Dorszynski*, 418 U.S. at 443, 94 S.Ct. at 3052). In *Garrett*, we noted that sentences imposed on a mechanical basis have been vacated as an *abuse* of the sentencing judge's discretion. 680 F.2d at 652 n. 3 (citing *Woosley*, 478 F.2d at 141–43); *see also United States v. Hartford*, 489 F.2d 652, 655 (5th Cir. 1974) (rigid policy of imposing maximum sentence for narcotics violations both "an abuse of judicial discretion" and "under no reasonable conception an exercise of judicial discretion").

---

1. Louis Villar, the Company's kingpin, had received a 14-month prison term. *See* note 7 *infra*.

2. Section 21 U.S.C. § 841(b)(1)(B) provides for a maximum prison sentence of five years for a marijuana offense involving less than 1,000 pounds. The court also imposed five year special parole terms on Timmons, Barker and McKinney, fined McKinney and Timmons $5,000 each, and fined Barker the maximum $15,000. Our disposition makes it unnecessary to reach the propriety of the special parole term given Timmons. We note, however, that a special parole term is inappropriate where defendant is convicted under the conspiracy statute. *See Bifulco v. United States*, 447 U.S. 381, 100 S.Ct. 2247, 65 L.Ed.2d 205 (1980).

3. Wide criticism of this rule has led to congressional action. "That appellate courts should have the power to review sentences is a proposition strongly urged by the American Bar Associ-

ation, and has been endorsed by the President's Crime Commission, the National Advisory Commission, and numerous commentators." A.W. Campbell, *Law of Sentencing* § 126 at 387 (1978) (footnotes omitted). *See* ABA Standards Relating to Appellate Review of Sentences 26 (App. Draft 1968) ("It is shocking, to say the least, that the United States is the only country in the free world where not only can a single man sentence without explaining why, but where there is no regular channel for review of his work."). *See also* C. Wright, *supra*, at § 533. The Sentencing Reform Act of 1984, Pub.L. No. 98–473, 98 Stat. 1837, establishes a commission to set sentencing ranges for each federal criminal offense, and authorizes defendants to appeal sentences harsher, and the government to appeal sentences more lenient, than commission guidelines. *Id.* at § 213, 98 Stat. at 2011 [codified at 18 U.S.C. § 3742] (effective Nov. 1, 1986).

Whether the failure to individualize sentences is described as an abuse or an abdication of discretion, however, it is the failure itself which warrants defendants' resentencing. It is that failure to which we turn.

B. Individualized Sentencing

Few legal principles are either as ancient[4] or deeply etched[5] in the public mind as the notion that punishment should fit the crime. This familiar maxim, however, is only half-true. "[I]n the present century the pendulum has been swinging away from ... the philosophy that the punishment should fit the crime and toward one that the punishment should [also] fit the criminal." W. LaFave & A. Scott, *Handbook on Criminal Law* § 5 at 25 (1972).

While we do not suggest that this trend has been without reverses, past or present, the concept of individualized sentencing is firmly entrenched in our present jurisprudence. As the Supreme Court has observed,

> [p]unishment should fit the offender and not merely the crime. The belief no longer prevails that every offense in a like legal category calls for an identical punishment without regard to the past life and habits of a particular offender.

Williams v. New York, 337 U.S. 241, 247, 69 S.Ct. 1079, 1083, 93 L.Ed. 1337 (1949) (citation omitted); *United States v. Foss*, 501 F.2d 522, 527 (1st Cir.1974); *Wardlaw*, 576 F.2d at 938. In each case, a criminal sentence must reflect an individualized assessment of a particular defendant's culpability rather than a mechanistic application of a given sentence to a given category of crime. As we said in *Lopez-Gonzales*, 688 F.2d at 1276–77,

> [t]he exercise of sound discretion requires consideration of all the circumstances of the crime.... The sentencing judge is required to consider all mitigating and aggravating circumstances involved. There is a strong public interest in the imposition of a sentence based upon an accurate evaluation of the particular offender and designed to aid in his personal rehabilitation. Thus, appellate courts have vacated sentences reflecting a preconceived policy always to impose the maximum penalty for a certain crime.

Accord Foss, 501 F.2d at 527; *United States v. Thompson*, 483 F.2d 527, 529 (3d Cir.1973).

In *Lopez-Gonzales*, the district court had stated that it automatically imposed the maximum sentence whenever an illegal alien is apprehended after flight and pursuit. 688 F.2d at 1275; *see Thompson*, 483 F.2d at 529. Although the court here did not announce a fixed or predetermined policy to sentence drug offenders to the maximum statutory term, a full reading of the record does reveal that the court sentenced defendants as essentially undifferentiated units, ignoring both their differences from one another, and from others who might be charged under the same statute. This failure adequately to individualize sentences ignores the goal that punishment fit the criminal.

This is not to suggest that any, or even all, of the defendants here could not legitimately have been sentenced to the maximum statutory term. Our concern is less the appropriateness of a given criminal sentence than the propriety of the process through which sentence was imposed. Specifically, do the four corners of the record indicate that the district court actually and adequately considered the factors neces-

---

4. *Cf. Solem v. Helm*, 463 U.S. 277, 103 S.Ct. 3001, 3006, 77 L.Ed.2d 637 (1983) ("principle that a punishment should be proportionate to the crime is deeply rooted and frequently repeated in common-law jurisprudence"); *see also* Hammurabi's Code § 196 (c. 2100 B.C.) ("If a man destroy the eye of another man, they shall destroy his eye."); Deuteronomy 19:21 ("eye for eye, tooth for tooth, hand for hand, foot for

foot"); Matthew 7:2 (King James) ("And with what measure ye mete, it shall be measured to you again.").

5. *See e.g.*, W.S. Gilbert, *The Mikado*, Act ii (1885) ("My object all sublime/I shall achieve in time/To let the punishment fit the crime/The punishment fit the crime").

sary to insure that each individual defendant was assessed and sentenced *as* an individual?

While the duty of the sentencing courts to individualize is clear, it may well be impossible to propound for purposes of review a single test or standard sufficient to insure individualized sentencing. *Cf. Solem*, 103 S.Ct. at 3010 n. 17 (no single criterion can identify when a sentence is constitutionally disproportionate). The danger in specifying sentencing standards is the potential for any such test to become as mechanistic in application as the mechanized sentencing which we seek to avoid. To require the exercise of sound discretion is not to fall into that trap, however. *See Lopez-Gonzales*, 688 F.2d at 1277 (requiring exercise of discretion need not lead to "hollow ritual"). Whether sound discretion has been exercised must be answered in each case through a thorough review of the record. Here, we cannot answer in the affirmative.

To begin with, the record is replete with comments suggesting that it was the category of crime, rather than the culpability of each individual criminal, that led the court to impose the maximum statutory term. Typical, for example, was the court's statement upon sentencing Jason Engle. Although Engle had demonstrated remorse and rehabilitation, the court observed

> Well, if I could ever chastise the government [for its sentencing recommendation] it would be in this case here. I never saw anything so ridiculous ... with a crime of this magnitude. I have been a judge for 17 years and I never saw a crime with such an amount of marijuana in my life and with such a lenient sentence for this massive of a conspiracy is incomprehensible, how a person could be involved in such a plague on society that involves so much marijua-

na, and the defendant has contributed to the spread of that plague.

At the sentencing hearing, counsel stressed (and the presentence report confirmed) that Jason's brother Jeffrey did not realize the boat was involved in smuggling marijuana until after they were at sea. He had apparently boarded the boat because his older brother had indicated they would be going fishing. Although he did eventually help load and unload the marijuana, when he learned of the indictment he immediately turned himself in and was consistently contrite. Nevertheless, the court observed, after the government's recommendation of one year in prison,

> Well, there again, if I could chastise the government more fully, I would certainly do so. This is a terrible crime, tons and tons of marijuana coming into the country and people being sorry and your life and what-have-you. What about the lives of the other people that have been affected by the young people taking the stuff; just because you want to have a good time and make some money out of it.

The court made similar statements in sentencing the three defendants who contributed money to the scheme, first criticizing the government's recommendations and then commenting on the severity of the crime. There is no indication that the court seriously considered arguments made in mitigation.[6] Instead, the record suggests that in imposing sentence, the court was overwhelmingly motivated by its assessment of the crime rather than its individual evaluation of each defendant.

In addition, several factors support the inference that, in this case, the district court's imposition of sentence was more "mechanistic," *Foss*, 501 F.2d at 522, than measured. First, the court chastised the government for its recommendations and

---

6. Timmons' only involvement, for example, was to lend money at the request of Louis Villar, *see* note 1 *supra*, to help finance what he was told were necessary ship repairs. Timmons was to be repaid in money, but when the ship returned, he was told that if he didn't accept marijuana instead, he might not be paid at all. Although he accepted the marijuana, the record suggests that Timmons promptly realized that he did not wish to be involved in drug trafficking and that Timmons had rehabilitated himself prior to arrest.

imposed sentences more than three times as long. Although this fact alone would not justify appellate intervention, *Wardlaw*, 576 F.2d at 938, it does reinforce the impression created by the court's comments before sentencing, that usual individual considerations played little if any part in its thinking.

Second, the district court imposed the same maximum statutory prison term upon each defendant, despite the differences in their levels of involvement. Although imposition of a maximum term does not alone justify appellate intervention, the district court's failure to differentiate among defendants ignores that defendants "were entitled to have their sentences set primarily in terms of the seriousness of their own crimes and associated individual factors." *Wardlaw*, 576 F.2d at 939. *Cf. Solem*, 103 S.Ct. at 3011 (relative culpability relevant in assessing sentence challenged under eighth amendment).

Similarly, although the district court correctly noted that it is not required to harmonize its view of appropriate sentencing with that of other district courts,[7] the court's statements at sentencing suggest that it was motivated by the desire to deter this "profitable business ... involving millions and millions of dollars" to the exclusion of determining what these particular defendants deserved. *See* note 9 *infra*; *Wardlaw*, 576 F.2d at 936.

Finally, we point out that 21 U.S.C. § 841(b)(1)(B), which provides for a maximum sentence of five years for a marijuana offense involving less than one thousand pounds, "'is an express legislative sanction ... of meting out sentences substantially less than five years in prison ... where there are appropriate mitigating circumstances.'" *Hartford*, 489 F.2d at 655

(citing *United States v. Daniels*, 446 F.2d 967, 971–72 (6th Cir.1971)). Although the establishment of a maximum sentence for offenses involving *up to* one thousand pounds does not require that defendants involved in smuggling lesser amounts receive sentences proportionally reduced, "from this express legislative authorization there is clearly evidenced an 'implied legislative will to impose a lesser sentence where appropriate.'" *Id.* at 655. By routinely entering the maximum sentence without differentiating among defendants, the district court "failed to abide by the implied congressional mandate to frame the punishment to address the particular circumstances of the individual defendant." *Id.*

We emphasize that neither the court's comments nor these additional factors, taken alone, would necessarily justify appellate intervention. Taken together, however, they leave us with the clear impression that the sentences imposed by the district court reflect more its personal view of the opprobrium of the crime charged— its view that "this is a terrible crime, tons and tons of marijuana coming into the country.... a plague on society...." —than a careful weighing of mitigating factors and the relative levels of culpability and involvement of each defendant.[8]

C. General Deterrence

In sentencing appellants to the maximum statutory term, the district court repeatedly alluded to the enormous societal harm it attributed to marijuana smuggling. As the government notes, implicit in the court's comments was the desire to stem the tide of marijuana smuggling through the deterrent effect maximum sentences would pre-

---

7. Counsel for McKinney noted that kingpins in the smuggling operation received sentences far less harsh than those imposed here. In response, the court noted "counsel, just because somebody else does something that I consider highly inappropriate, doesn't mean that I have to follow those footsteps, that's one of the things that concerned me about this case more than anything else."

8. As we have said, our remand should not be construed as suggesting that the imposition of the maximum statutory term would be necessarily impermissible for any defendant in this case. Similarly, our remand should not be construed as rejection of the sentiments expressed by the district court.

sumably have on others.[9]   In this sense, both the court's comments at sentencing and the sentences themselves were aimed at a wider audience than simply these defendants.

We do not find this desire to "send a message" through sentencing inappropriate *per se*.   Indeed, perhaps paramount among the purposes of punishment is the desire to deter similar misconduct by others.[10]   This doctrine, commonly called "general deterrence,"[11] boasts an impressive lineage,[12] was long-recognized at common law,[13] and continues to command "near unanimity . . . among state and federal jurists. . . ."   *United States v. Bergman*, 416 F.Supp. 496, 499 (S.D.N.Y.1976) (Frankel, J.); *see also United States v. Moore*, 599 F.2d 310, 315 (9th Cir.1979), *cert. denied*, 444 U.S. 1024, 100 S.Ct. 687, 62 L.Ed.2d 658 (1980); *United States v. Elliott*, 674 F.2d 754, 756 (8th Cir.1982); *United States v. Hedman*, 630 F.2d 1184, 1201 (7th Cir.1980), *cert. denied*, 450 U.S.

965, 101 S.Ct. 1481, 67 L.Ed.2d 614 (1981); *Foss*, 501 F.2d at 528; (general deterrence appropriate objective in imposing sentence). Notwithstanding our admonishment that punishment fit the offender, we too recognize the legitimacy of considering general deterrence in passing sentence.[14]

Nevertheless, deterrence as a sentencing rationale is subject to limitation.   Tailoring punishment to the individual criminal may reduce the efficacy of deterrence, but that reduction is an inevitable cost of a system that eschews mechanistic punishment.[15] General deterrence is a legitimate aim, but it has never been the *sole* aim in imposing sentence.

Central to our system of values and implicit in the requirement of individualized sentencing is the categorical imperative that no person may be used merely as an instrument of social policy, that human beings are to be treated not simply as means to a social end like deterrence, but also—

---

9.   The following colloquy is illustrative:

COUNSEL: On the other hand, we have two defendants that were all arrested in 1977, all of whom were much more involved than Mr. McKinney, and every one of them got probation.

THE COURT: That's one of the reasons why we have a high crime rate in this country, why it's successful to peddle tons of marijuana, because people know they can get away with it. That's the reason. It's a profitable business. This is involving millions and millions of dollars. . . . If you were going to get probation, why not do it? So you have children dying on the streets, . . . involved in burglaries and robberies to get the money to pay for it. Sure, fine and dandy.

10.   *See generally* M.P. Golding, *Philosophy of Law* 69–86 (1975); LaFave & Scott, *supra* § 5; Campbell, *supra* note 3, at § 5; J. Andenaes, *Punishment and Deterrence* (1974); F. Zimring & G. Hawkins, *Deterrence* (1973).

11.   While the sentencing factors that compete in this case are those of general deterrence and individualization of sentencing, we do not mean to suggest that there are no other factors to be considered. *See United States v. Bergman*, 416 F.Supp. 496, 500 (S.D.N.Y.1976).

12.   *See, e.g.*, Deuteronomy 21:21; Plato's *Laws:* "The purpose of [punishment] is not to cancel the crime—what is once done can never be made undone—but to bring the criminal *and all*

who witness his punishment in the future to complete renunciation of such criminality. . . ." Bk. xi, 934a-b, reprinted in *The Collected Dialogues of Plato* 1484 (Taylor trans. 1961) (emphasis added).

13.   As Lord Halifax, Lord Privy Seal and Chief Minister of the Crown, observed, "[m]en are not hang'd for stealing Horses, but that Horses may not be stolen." George Savile, Marquess of Halifax, *Political, Moral, and Miscellaneous Reflections* (1750), reprinted in *The Complete Works of George Savile* 229 (1912). *See also Hopt v. Utah*, 110 U.S. 574, 579, 4 S.Ct. 202, 204, 28 L.Ed. 262 (1884) (citing 4 W. Blackstone, *Commentaries* 11).

14.   As the First Circuit has observed, "[T]he view that punishment should fit the offender has never yet been held to eliminate general deterrence as a factor to be considered along with others. This is so even though general deterrence concerns itself not with the individual offender but with the sentence's impact on others." *Foss*, 501 F.2d at 527 (citation omitted); *see also Pell v. Procunier*, 417 U.S. 817, 822, 94 S.Ct. 2800, 2804, 41 L.Ed.2d 495 (1974).

15.   Indeed, even a policy of making the punishment fit the crime precludes the unfettered pursuit of deterrence. Deterrence might be well served by a death penalty for double parking, but no one suggests that such a punishment would be appropriate.

and always—as ends in themselves. *See, e.g.,* I. Kant, *Groundwork of the Metaphysic of Morals* 66–67 (H.J. Paton trans. 2d ed. 1964) ("Act in such a way that you always treat humanity, whether in your own person or in the person of any other, never simply as a means, but always at the same time as an end" [16]); *see also* I. Kant, *Philosophy of Law* 196 (W. Hastie trans. 1887) ("one man ought never to be dealt with merely as a means subservient to the purposes of another"); *accord United States v. Barker,* 514 F.2d 208, 231 (D.C. Cir.1975) (en banc) (Bazelon, J., concurring); L. Tribe, *American Constitutional Law,* 463 (1978); R. Dworkin, *Taking Rights Seriously* 198 (1977). Deterrence is not inconsistent with this principle,[17] but the principle does demand that a balance be struck between the goal of general deterrence and the enlightened imperative of individualized sentencing. *Cf.* Golding, note 10, *supra,* at 79 (distinguishing between deterrence as a legitimate *purpose* of punishment and the "moral fit" nevertheless necessary between a given offense/offender and the *amount* of punishment).

How that balance is to be struck is committed to the sound discretion of the trial court; that it *be* struck is what we require today. *See Lopez-Gonzales,* 688 F.2d at 1277.[18] A court's "conclusions as to deterrence," however, "may never be so unbending as to forbid relaxation in an appropriate case...." *Foss,* 501 F.2d at 528; *accord Wardlaw,* 576 F.2d at 938–39.[19]

Because we find, after a careful review of the record, that the district court's imposition of sentence was motivated by the desire for general deterrence to the exclusion of adequate consideration of individual factors, we vacate and remand for resentencing.[20]

Sentences VACATED and REMANDED for resentencing.

---

16. In Kant's imperative that we treat others "never as a means only but always as an end also," the modifiers "only" and "also" are central to the meaning. *See* W. Kaufman, *The Faith of a Heretic* 291 (1959).

17. *See. e.g., Foss,* 501 F.2d at 528 (when individualizing a sentence, district court may consider general deterrence); *United States v. Elliott,* 674 F.2d at 756; *Bergman,* 416 F.Supp. at 499 (citing H.L.A. Hart, *Punishment and Responsibility* 243–44 (1968); Andenaes, "The Morality of Deterrence," 37 U.Chi.L.Rev. 649 (1970); O. Holmes, *The Common Law* 43–44, 46–47 (1881)).

18. "The court's duty to 'individualize' the sentence simply means that, whatever the judge's thoughts as to the deterrent value of a jail sentence, he must in every case reexamine and measure that view against the relevant facts and other important goals such as the offender's rehabilitation. Having done so, the district judge must finally decide what factors, or mix of factors, carry the day...." *Foss,* 501 F.2d at 528.

19. While the Sentencing Reform Act of 1984 requires district courts to consider the need, in imposing sentence, "to afford adequate deterrence to criminal conduct," *supra* note 2 at § 212, 98 Stat. at 1989 [codified at 18 U.S.C. § 3553(a)(2)(B)], deterrence is simply one of several mandatory factors, first of which is "the nature and circumstances of the offense and the history and characteristics of the defendant." *Id.* [codified at 18 U.S.C. § 3553(a)(1)].

20. Although we are confident that the original judge would fully comply with the spirit and intent of this opinion, we nevertheless think it appropriate that defendants be resentenced by a different district court judge. *See, e.g., U.S. v. Alverson,* 666 F.2d 341, 349 (9th Cir.1982); *Wardlaw,* 576 F.2d at 939. We so direct.

UNITED STATES of America

v.

ROSENBERG, Susan Lisa.

Appeal of Susan Lisa ROSENBERG,
Appellant in 85–5360.

UNITED STATES of America

v.

BLUNK, Timothy.

Appeal of Timothy BLUNK,
Appellant in 85–5361.

Nos. 85–5360, 85–5361.

United States Court of Appeals,
Third Circuit.

Argued Sept. 11, 1986.
Decided Nov. 28, 1986.

Before ALDISERT, Chief Judge,
HIGGINBOTHAM and HUNTER, Circuit
Judges.

OPINION OF THE COURT

JAMES HUNTER, III, Circuit Judge:

Susan Lisa Rosenberg and Timothy
Blunk appeal their convictions and sen-

tences before the United States District Court for the District of New Jersey on nine counts of possession of firearms, explosives and false identification documents. This case requires us to determine, *inter alia*, whether the district court abused its discretion in sentencing these defendants to the maximum prison terms provided by the applicable statutes, whether these sentences resulted from impermissible bias on the part of the district judge, and whether consecutive sentences properly may be imposed for possession of explosives in violation of 26 U.S.C. § 5861(d) (1982) and for the carrying of explosives during the commission of a felony under 18 U.S.C. § 844(h)(2) (1982). The American Civil Liberties Union of New Jersey, the National Lawyers Guild—New Jersey Chapter, the Center for Constitutional Rights and the National Emergency Civil Liberties Committee, concerned that the defendants' sentences may be related to their political beliefs, have submitted a brief to this court on the issue as amici curiae.

The district court's jurisdiction stemmed from 18 U.S.C. § 3231 (1982); we have appellate jurisdiction pursuant to 28 U.S.C. § 1291 (1982). For the following reasons, we will affirm the judgments and sentences in all respects.

I.

Defendants do not challenge the government's evidence. This evidence showed that on November 3, 1984, Susan Rosenberg rented a storage bin at a public storage facility in Cherry Hill, New Jersey. Identifying herself to the facility's manager with a New York driver's license issued in the name of "Barbara Grodin," Rosenberg provided several telephone numbers at which she could be reached, paid for the storage bin in cash, and received an entrance code number which would provide access to the facility. Rosenberg did not unload anything into the bin at that time.

Several days later, when the manager was not in the office, an employee rented out the bin that had been assigned to "Barbara Grodin" to another party. When the

manager returned to the office, he requested the new party to remove his belongings from the bin. The new renter refused, however, and the manager reassigned "Barbara Grodin" to another storage bin and attempted to contact her to inform her that both her bin and her entrance code had been changed to reflect the reassignment. When the manager was unable to contact her using the phone numbers she had supplied, he wrote a letter to "Barbara Grodin" and sent it to the address listed on the driver's license Rosenberg had given him. Soon thereafter he received a phone call from the real Barbara Grodin who informed the manager that she had not rented a storage bin. Moreover, Ms. Grodin wrote the manager that her wallet, containing her driver's license, had been stolen. The manager suggested that Grodin contact the Cherry Hill police concerning the matter, which she did. After a number of phone conversations between Grodin, the manager, and the Cherry Hill police, the parties agreed that if Rosenberg returned to the storage facility the manager would contact the police.

On November 29, 1984, Rosenberg and Timothy Blunk drove up to the facility in a car towing a rented trailer. Unable to enter with the old access code, Rosenberg knocked on the office's window to request admission. The manager recognized Rosenberg as the woman who had identified herself as Barbara Grodin. The manager directed Rosenberg to a new storage bin, provided her with a new access code, and returned to the office to phone the police.

Officer Di Francisco responded to the call. After speaking with the manager, Di Francisco proceeded to the storage area where he observed the defendants covering certain items on the floor of the bin with opaque plastic. Di Francisco noted that one of the items appeared to be an ammunition box and that another item, a large tubular object, bore the clearly visible label "blasting agent." Di Francisco also observed that both Rosenberg and Blunk were wearing glasses and wigs. Di Francisco asked the defendants for identification, and both produced New York driver's licenses. Rosenberg's identified her as Barbara Grodin, and Blunk's was issued in the name of William Hammond. When Rosenberg was unable to provide Di Francisco with the correct birthdate on her license, she volunteered to retrieve additional identification from her car.

Di Francisco did not permit her to return to the car, but instead led the two outside the bin where they met with Officer Martin who had just arrived. Di Francisco told Martin to stay with Blunk while he and Rosenberg returned to the manager's office. At the office, Di Francisco called headquarters, confirmed that the license was stolen, and again asked Rosenberg for her birthdate. She gave him a date that was different from the one she had earlier given him, as well as different from the one on the license. At this point, the officer arrested Rosenberg and placed her in the rear seat of his car, drove back to the storage area, arrested Blunk, and placed him in Officer Martin's car.

Di Francisco then proceeded to defendants' car in an effort to locate the additional identification that Rosenberg mentioned. On the front seat of the defendants' car, Di Francisco found two purses each containing a fully loaded semi-automatic pistol with additional ammunition clips.

After obtaining a search warrant, the police searched the bin, discovering a stockpile of ammunition, weapons, explosives, and false identification documents. In particular, the bin contained twelve assorted guns, two of which—an Uzi 9mm. semi-automatic rifle and an Ithaca twelve-gauge shotgun with its barrel "sawed-off"—were required to be registered to defendants in the National Firearms Registration and Transfer Record under 26 U.S.C. §§ 5861(d); nearly two hundred sticks of dynamite, more than one hundred sticks of DuPont Trovex, a high explosive, a wide array of blasting agents, blasting caps, batteries and switches; and hundreds of false identification documents, including various drivers' licenses, social security cards, and FBI and DEA identification badges.

On December 6, 1984, a federal grand jury returned an indictment charging Blunk and Rosenberg with conspiracy, firearms offenses, and possession of false identification documents. Trial commenced on March 7, 1985. From the beginning of the proceedings, it was evident that Blunk and Rosenberg styled themselves as "political prisoners" rather than criminal defendants. They insisted on being absent from most of the trial proceedings and directed their retained counsel to remain inactive during the trial. To accommodate them, the trial judge provided Blunk and Rosenberg with closed circuit television through which they could monitor the proceedings, and appointed a public defender to remain in the courtroom for the trial to protect the defendants' interests. Both defendants made opening statements to the jury in which they asserted that their conduct was justified by reference to "a higher body of laws." On March 17, 1985, the jury returned a verdict of guilty on all submitted counts. The court imposed the maximum prison sentence on each count and ordered that each sentence run consecutively.[1] The

---

1. On Count 1, which charged both defendants with conspiracy to possess unregistered firearms and false documents in violation of 18 U.S.C. § 371 (1982), the court imposed a five year sentence. On Count 2, which charged defendants with possession of unregistered firearms (the explosives) in violation of 26 U.S.C. § 5861(d), defendants received ten years. On Count 3, which charged defendants with the possession of unregistered firearms (the sawed-off shotgun), defendants received ten years. For Count 4, which charged defendants with the possession of unregistered firearms (the Uzi semi-automatic rifle), defendants received ten years. For Count 5, which charged defendants with the carrying of explosives during the commission of a felony in violation of 18 U.S.C. § 844(h)(2), defendants received ten years. On Count 6, which charged defendants with the possession with intent to use false identification documents in violation of 18 U.S.C. § 1028 (Supp. II 1984), they received three years. On Count 7, which charged Rosenberg with falsely representing a social security account number with the intent to deceive in violation of 42 U.S.C. § 408(g)(2) (1982), she received five years. On Count 8, which charged Blunk with falsely representing a social security account

defendants' statements at sentencing indicated that their only regret was that they had not been successful.

Blunk and Rosenberg timely filed this appeal.

II. SENTENCING ISSUES

A. *Length of Sentence*

Appellants argue that the district court abused its discretion in imposing the maximum term of imprisonment provided by statute. Our standard of review over this claim is limited. It is well settled that absent procedural defects, an appellate court will not disturb the district court's sentence if it falls within the statutory limits. *See Gardner v. Florida,* 430 U.S. 349, 357, 97 S.Ct. 1197, 1204, 51 L.Ed.2d 393 (1977); *United States v. Tucker,* 404 U.S. 443, 447, 92 S.Ct. 589, 591, 30 L.Ed.2d 592 (1972); *United States v. Matthews,* 773 F.2d 48, 52 (3d Cir.1985); *United States v. Felder,* 744 F.2d 18, 20 (3d Cir.1984); *United States v. Del Piano,* 593 F.2d 539, 540 (3d Cir.) (per curiam), *cert. denied,* 442 U.S. 944, 99 S.Ct. 2889, 61 L.Ed.2d 315 (1979). Blunk and Rosenberg invite us to find the required procedural defects in the trial court's alleged anticommunist statements and remarks concerning defendants' parole eligibility. For the reasons set out in our

discussion of the defendants' bias claims, we conclude that the record does not support their contention.

B. *Bias*

Appellants also argue that their sentences resulted from the district judge's bias or prejudice against them, and therefore that we should vacate their sentences and remand the matter for resentencing before a different judge. The proper procedure for disqualification for bias or prejudice is governed by 28 U.S.C. § 144 (1982).[2] For the purpose of this statute, the alleged bias or prejudice must stem from an extra-judicial source rather than from facts which the judge has learned from his participation in the case. *See United States v. Grinnell Corp.,* 384 U.S. 563, 583, 86 S.Ct. 1698, 1710, 16 L.Ed.2d 778 (1966); *Beverly Hills Bancorp,* 752 F.2d 1334, 1341 (9th Cir.1984). Recusal motions pursuant to this statute must be timely filed, contain a good faith certificate of counsel, and include an affidavit stating material facts with particularity which, if true, would lead a reasonable person to the conclusion that the district judge harbored a special bias or prejudice towards defendants. *See generally United States v. Thompson,* 483 F.2d 527 (3d Cir.1973). No such motion was here made.[3]

---

number with the intent to deceive, he received 5 years. For Count 9, which charged both defendants with the possession of counterfit social security cards in violation of 42 U.S.C. § 408(g)(3) (1982), defendants received five years.

The court imposed the sentences to run consecutively for a total prison term of fifty-eight years for each defendant. Although many of the offenses also provided for monetary penalties, the court declined to include fines in the defendants' sentences.

2. This section provides:

Whenever a party to any proceeding in a district court makes and files a timely and sufficient affidavit that the judge before whom the matter is pending has a personal bias or prejudice either against him or in favor of any adverse party, such judge shall proceed no further therein, but another judge shall be assigned to hear such proceeding. The affidavit shall state the facts and the reasons for the belief that bias or prejudice ex-

ists, and shall be filed not less than ten days before the beginning of the term at which the proceeding is to be heard, or good cause shall be shown for the failure to file it within such time. A party may file only one such affidavit in any case. It shall be accompanied by a certificate of counsel of record stating that it is made in good faith.

3. A disqualification motion filed after trial and judgment is usually considered untimely unless good cause can be shown for the delay, for otherwise a party alleging bias would always await judgment in the hopes of a favorable decision. *See Crowder v. Conlan,* 740 F.2d 447, 453–54 (6th Cir.1984); *Waggoner v. Dallaire,* 649 F.2d 1362, 1370 (9th Cir.1981). Even assuming appellant's brief to this court could constitute a motion for the purposes of 28 U.S.C. § 144, it must be denied as untimely, and as lacking the substantive requirements of legal sufficiency. *See Thompson,* 483 F.2d at 528.

There is also a rarely invoked exception to § 144's statutory procedure that requires disqualification when a judge displays "pervasive bias" towards defendants regardless of the source of the bias. *See Three Mile Island Alert, Inc.*, 771 F.2d 720, 739 (3d Cir.1985), *cert. denied,* — U.S. ——, 106 S.Ct. 1460, 89 L.Ed.2d 717 (1986); *United States v. Meester,* 762 F.2d 867, 885 (11th Cir.), *cert. denied,* — U.S. ——, 106 S.Ct. 579, 88 L.Ed.2d 562 (1985); *Davis v. Board of School Commissioners,* 517 F.2d 1044, 1051 (5th Cir.1975), *cert. denied,* 425 U.S. 944, 96 S.Ct. 1685, 48 L.Ed.2d 188 (1976). Appellants argue that the district court's adverse decisions concerning bail and security, the court's antagonistic attitude toward defense counsel, its remarks concerning communism, and its letter to the Bureau of Prisons recommending against parole for defendants evidence such bias.

We do not believe that these allegations prove any bias against Blunk and Rosenberg, much less the pervasive bias necessary to disqualify the judge at this juncture. Adverse decisions alone do not support a finding of bias. *See Meester,* 762 F.2d at 885; *International Business Machines Corp.,* 618 F.2d 923, 929-30 (2d Cir. 1980); *Botts v. United States,* 413 F.2d 41, 44 (9th Cir.1969). The court's trial orders seem to us reasonable, and lacking in any indicia of bias. We are unable to discern in the record evidence of the alleged antagonism on the part of the court toward either

of the defense attorneys.[4] As for the alleged bias against communism, the defendants cite the judge's comments during sentencing that "[t]he only advice I give you is that you read what an earlier generation of revolutionaries who have embraced Communism have written. 'The God that Failed.' Read what Arthur Koestler and other disillusioned ex-Communists have written. It may help you." This statement, by itself does not suggest a bias against Blunk and Rosenberg. In the context of the sentencing minutes, the remark is addressed to the defendants' lack of remorse for their conduct and declared intention to continue these activities once released. As such, the remark is directed toward the defendants' chances for a successful rehabilitation, a proper concern of the trial court. *See United States v. Grayson,* 438 U.S. 41, 47-48, 98 S.Ct. 2610, 2614, 57 L.Ed.2d 582 (1978).

Finally, appellants urge that the district judge's letter to the Bureau of Prisons recommending against parole for these defendants after ten years of imprisonment, a possibility provided by 18 U.S.C. § 4205(a) (1982),[5] demonstrates bias towards them. We disagree. In this letter, the district judge reiterated his statement during sentencing that "it will be a terrible mistake if these defendants were to be released from prison after serving only 10 years if their attitude then is as it is now." As the letter itself indicates, the court drew this conclu-

---

4. We are unpersuaded by appellants' suggestion that the court's comment concerning the connection between Rosenberg and her attorney, Susan Tipograph, in the court's post-sentence letter to the Bureau of Prisons demonstrates the alleged antagonism. In the letter, the court stressed the importance of ensuring a secure confinement for the defendants:

As to the place of incarceration, it will be remembered that Rosenberg's "comrade", Marilyn Buck, was permitted to walk out of Alderson on a legal furlough to visit her attorney, Tipograph. Tipograph and Rosenberg are more than just attorney and client. They have been associates, companions, and roommates. I am sure the Bureau of Prisons will make certain that Rosenberg does not profit from the same mistake that was made as to Buck. Careful consideration must be given to the security of any prison to which Rosenberg

is sent. She is under indictment in the Southern District of New York, charged with aiding in the prison escape of Joanne Chesimard. I cannot emphasize too much the fact that a minimum-security prison will not hold Rosenberg.

In context, the remark shows only the court's concern that the Bureau of Prisons be aware of the possibility that Rosenberg might attempt to escape.

5. This section provides:

Whenever confined and serving a definite term or terms of more than one year, a prisoner shall be eligible for release on parole after serving one-third of such term or terms or after serving ten years of a life sentence or of a sentence of over thirty years, except to the extent otherwise provided by law.

sion from the facts presented at trial together with his observation of the defendants' lack of remorse at sentencing. No charge of bias can be assigned to the court's recommendation.

In sum, in the context of this case, the district court's actions do not provide a basis for the operation of the pervasive bias exception.

C. Proportionality

Blunk and Rosenberg maintain that the district court's sentence of fifty-eight years for each defendant violates the eighth amendment's guarantee against cruel and unusual punishment.[6] Appellants rely on the Supreme Court's decision in *Solem v. Helm*, 463 U.S. 277, 103 S.Ct. 3001, 77 L.Ed.2d 637 (1983) which held that a life sentence without the possibility of parole for the crime of uttering a "no account" check imposed under South Dakota's recidivist statute violated the eighth amendment.[7]

Appellants have not directed us to, nor have our own efforts uncovered, a federal case which has reversed a lower court's imposition of consecutive sentences under the eighth amendment. *See, e.g., United States v. Golomb*, 754 F.2d 86, 90 (2d Cir. 1985) (collecting cases). Although the *Solem* Court admonished that "no penalty is *per se* constitutional," 463 U.S. at 290, 103 S.Ct. at 3009, the Court also cautioned that our scope of review for this claim is extremely limited, for "[o]utside the context of capital punishment, *successful* challenges to the proportionality of particular sentences [will be] exceedingly rare." *Id.* at 289–90, 103 S.Ct. at 3009, *quoting Rummel v. Estelle*, 445 U.S. 263, 272, 100 S.Ct. 1133, 1138, 63 L.Ed.2d 382 (1980) (emphasis

added by the *Solem* Court); *see Hutto v. Davis*, 454 U.S. 370, 374, 102 S.Ct. 703, 705, 70 L.Ed.2d 556 (1982); *Government of the Virgin Islands v. Ramos*, 730 F.2d 96, 98 (3d Cir.1984); *cf. United States v. Darby*, 744 F.2d 1508, 1525 (11th Cir.1984), *cert. denied*, 471 U.S. 1100, 105 S.Ct. 2322, 85 L.Ed.2d 841 (1985) (scope of review "greatly restricted"). The *Solem* Court explained that appellate courts "should grant substantial deference to the broad authority that legislatures necessarily possess in determining the types and limits of punishments for crimes, as well as to the discretion that trial courts possess in sentencing convicted criminals." 463 U.S. at 290, 103 S.Ct. at 3009. This principle of substantial deference in turn restrains us from an extended analysis of proportionality save in rare cases. *Id.* at 290 n. 16, 103 S.Ct. at 3009 n. 16.

We agree with the Fourth and Fifth Circuits that apart from *Solem's* particular factual context—a life sentence without the possibility of parole—an abbreviated proportionality review following the *Solem* guidelines satisfies eighth amendment demands. *See United States v. Rhodes*, 779 F.2d 1019, 1028 (4th Cir.1985), *cert. denied*, — U.S. —, 106 S.Ct. 2916, 91 L.Ed.2d 545 (1986); *Moreno v. Estelle*, 717 F.2d 171, 180 n. 10 (5th Cir.1983), *cert. denied*, 466 U.S. 975, 104 S.Ct. 2353, 80 L.Ed.2d 826 (1984). These factors include: (i) a consideration of the gravity of the offense and the harshness of the penalty; (ii) the sentences imposed on criminals in the same jurisdiction; and (iii) the sentences imposed for the same crime in other jurisdictions. *Solem*, 463 U.S. at 292, 103 S.Ct. at 3010. Because defendants' crimes are federal and lack clear state analogues,

---

6. The Eighth Amendment to the United States Constitution states that "[e]xcessive bail shall not be required, nor excessive fines imposed, nor cruel and unusual punishments inflicted."

7. *Solem* was the first, and so far the only, Supreme Court case to hold a noncapital punishment violative of the eighth amendment. Three years prior to *Solem*, the Court held that a life sentence imposed on a defendant under Texas's recidivist statute for a conviction of obtaining

$120.75 by false pretenses did not offend the eighth amendment's cruel and unusual punishment clause. *Rummel v. Estelle*, 445 U.S. 263, 100 S.Ct. 1133, 63 L.Ed.2d 382 (1980). In distinguishing *Rummel*, the *Solem* Court observed that Helm had received a life sentence without the possibility of parole, whereas Rummel would have been eligible for parole within twelve years of his initial confinement. *Solem*, 463 U.S. at 297, 103 S.Ct. at 3013.

our determination rests on the first two factors.

In analyzing the first factor, we look to "the harm caused or threatened to the victim or society, and the culpability of the offender." *Id.* at 292, 103 S.Ct. at 3010. Blunk and Rosenberg contend that because they were convicted of "possessory" offenses, the consecutive imposition of the maximum sentences for these offenses must necessarily be grossly disproportionate to their crimes. This, however, is not the test.[8] We agree with the district court that the harm threatened by defendants' possession of a cache of arms and explosives combined with defendants' in court statements expressing their continued willingness to use violent methods to achieve their goals justifies the sentence. There is no doubt that this is a severe sentence; but the deference due Congress in providing for such sentences and that due the district court's finding of the magnitude of harm threatened by defendants' conduct supports our conclusion that the sentence is appropriate. *Cf. United States v. Kimberlin,* 781 F.2d 1247, 1258 (7th Cir.1985). Moreover, there can be no doubt as to the culpability of Blunk and Rosenberg. Neither denied the conspiracy and possession charges during trial. Defendants instead chose to pin their defense on the revolutionary "justification" for their conduct.

With regard to the second factor, appellants have provided us with statistics designed to show that their sentences are greater than the average sentences imposed for other federal crimes and for weapons and explosives possession, and invite us to compare dissimilar crimes and sentences with theirs. Because we do not believe that this case warrants an extended eighth amendment analysis, we need not attempt to match defendants' sentences with the statistics. We hold that the sentences imposed are appropriate to the spe-

cific facts of this case and within the constitutional limits.

III. POSSESSION OF EXPLOSIVES

A. *Cumulative Sentences*

Blunk and Rosenberg also suggest that the court improperly pyramided their sentences by imposing consecutive sentences for Counts 2 and 5. Count 2 charged both defendants with the possession of an unregistered firearm in violation of 26 U.S.C. § 5861(d) (1982), specifically the possession of blasting caps, switches, wire, and one hundred and ninety-nine sticks of dynamite.[9] Count 5 charged defendants with carrying explosives during the commission of a felony in violation of 18 U.S.C. § 844(h)(2) (1982). The underlying felonies for this count were the possession of the sawed-off shotgun and the Uzi semi-automatic rifle which were the subject of Counts 3 and 4 of the indictment.

Courts are reluctant to impose two penalties for the same criminal conduct absent clear congressional intent otherwise, reasoning that doubts in the interpretation of criminal statutes "will be resolved against turning a single transaction into multiple offenses." *Bell v. United States,* 349 U.S. 81, 84, 75 S.Ct. 620, 622, 99 L.Ed. 905 (1955). Thus, in *United States v. Gomez,* 593 F.2d 210 (3d Cir.) (in banc), *cert. denied,* 441 U.S. 948, 99 S.Ct. 2172, 60 L.Ed.2d 1052 (1979), we held that consecutive sentences could not be imposed under the Comprehensive Drug Abuse Prevention and Control Act for possession of a controlled substance with the intent to distribute and for the actual distribution when the convictions stemmed from the same transaction. In so doing, we observed that consecutive sentences in that case would undermine the Act's detailed penalty scheme and violate "the established rule of construction that 'ambiguity concerning the

---

8. In this regard, we note that the Supreme Court upheld a sentence of forty years in prison for the possession with the intent to distribute less than nine ounces of marijuana. *See Hutto v. Davis,* 454 U.S. 370, 102 S.Ct. 703, 70 L.Ed.2d 556 (1982).

9. Firearms are defined in 26 U.S.C. § 5845(a)(8) as including "a destructive device." Section 5845(f)(1)(A) further defines destructive devices as "any explosive ... bomb."

ambit of criminal statutes should be resolved in favor of lenity.'" *Gomez*, 593 F.2d at 214, quoting *Simpson v. United States*, 435 U.S. 6, 98 S.Ct. 909, 55 L.Ed.2d 70 (1978). Similarly, in *United States v. Gomberg*, 715 F.2d 843 (3d Cir.1983), *cert. denied* 465 U.S. 1078, 104 S.Ct. 1440, 79 L.Ed.2d 760 (1984), we determined that cumulative sentences for a continuing criminal enterprise pursuant to 21 U.S.C. § 848 (1982) and the substantive offenses comprising the enterprise could not be imposed under the Comprehensive Drug Abuse Prevention and Control Act because the structure of the penalties in the Act showed that Congress intended section 848 to operate exclusively for sentencing purposes. *Gomberg*, 715 F.2d at 851.

We find neither an ambiguity nor evidence of congressional intent prohibiting cumulative sentences in the instant case. Instead, we find that the language and legislative history of 18 U.S.C. § 844(h)(2) clearly authorize the sentences here. The legislative history for this provision indicates that Congress intended to extend the "stringent provisions" of 18 U.S.C. § 924(c) (1982), a nearly identical statute that provides for increased punishment for felons who carry or use a gun during the commission of a felony, to the area of explosives. *See* H.Rep. No. 1549, 91st Cong., 2d Sess., *reprinted in* 1970 U.S.Cong. & Ad.News 4007, 4046. Section 924(c) provides for enhanced sentences unless the underlying substantive offense was one that already provided for enhanced punishment where the felony was committed with a dangerous weapon. *See Busic v. United States*, 446 U.S. 398, 403, 100 S.Ct. 1747, 1751, 64 L.Ed.2d 381 (1980) (assault with a firearm); *Simpson*, 435 U.S. at 13 (bank robbery with a dangerous weapon). The Supreme Court's interpretation in these two cases rests in part on statements by the Act's sponsor that § 924(c) would not extend to

the particular offense in question. See *Busic*, 446 U.S. at 406, 100 S.Ct. at 1752; *Simpson*, 435 U.S. at 13, 98 S.Ct. at 913. Congress neither provided for enhanced penalties in the underlying offense for carrying an explosive device while possessing an unregistered firearm, nor expressed an intention in the legislative history that § 844(h)(2)'s scope would not extend to such felonies. We therefore hold the consecutive sentences to be proper.[10]

B. *Lack of Relational Element*

Appellants maintain that their conviction on Count 5, for carrying explosives during the commission of a felony (possession of firearms), must be reversed. Appellants contend reversal is justified because no specific connection was shown between the carrying of the explosives and the felony. Because this issue implicates the interpretation and application of a statute, our review is plenary. *Universal Minerals*, 699 F.2d at 101–02.

The basis for Count 5, 18 U.S.C. § 844(h)(2), prohibits the "carr[ying of] an explosive unlawfully during the commission of any felony which may be prosecuted in a court of the United States...." No court has explicitly decided whether the statute requires the government to prove a connection between the explosive and the underlying felony. Cases involving § 844(h)(2) indicate varying results. *See United States v. Lopez*, 586 F.2d 978, 979 (2d Cir.1978) (per curiam) (felony was assault and no indication explosives were connected to assault), *cert. denied*, 440 U.S. 923, 99 S.Ct. 1251, 59 L.Ed.2d 476 (1979); *United States v. Tiche*, 424 F.Supp. 996, 1000 (W.D.Pa.) (in general discussion of statute, court stated "All that is required is that the explosives were used in the commission of a felony...."), *aff'd mem.*, 564 F.2d 90 (3d Cir.1977); *United States v. Pliskow*, 354 F.Supp. 369, 370 (E.D.Mich.)

---

10. Appellants argue that because the underlying felony for the purposes of § 844(h)(2) could have been the possession of explosives—which are also "firearms" for the purposes of the explosives chapter of title 26, *see supra* note 8—the sentence could have been improperly cumula-

tive. Because the indictment clearly identified the underlying felonies as the possession of the sawed-off shotgun and the Uzi semi-automatic rifle, however, we need not entertain this argument.

(defendant apparently used explosives in an attempted aircraft hijacking), *aff'd mem.*, 480 F.2d 927 (6th Cir.1973).

The legislative history of § 844(h) is similarly unilluminating. The section was part of Title XI of the Organized Crime Control Act of 1970. The impetus for Title XI was the recurring bombs and bomb threats during that period. Congress stated that: "The absence of any effective State or local controls clearly attest to the urgent need to enact strengthened Federal regulation of explosives." H.R. No. 1549, 91st Cong., 2d Sess., *reprinted in* 1970 U.S.Code Cong. & Ad.News 4007, 4013. Title XI also was intended to strengthen federal criminal law with respect to the illegal use, transportation, or possession of explosives. *Id.* at 4011. Section 844(h) itself "carries over to the explosives area the stringent provisions of the Gun Control Act of 1968 relating to the use of firearms and the unlawful carrying of firearms to commit, or during the commission of a Federal felony." *Id.* at 4046.

Both sides rely on cases interpreting the Gun Control Act provision. Prior to its amendment, 18 U.S.C. § 924(c) prohibited carrying a firearm during the commission of a felony. As amended (now § 924(c)),[11] the statute now prohibits carrying a firearm *during and in relation to* the commission of a felony.

In *United States v. Stewart*, 779 F.2d 538 (9th Cir.1985), relied on by appellants, the court required a specific connection between the firearm and the underlying felony. The basis for the court's decision was that the legislative history to the 1984 amendment "strongly implie[d]" that the "in relation to" phrase did not affect the

scope of the statute as originally written. *Id.* at 539–40. The court decided that the amending Congress recognized that the earlier Congress had intended to require such a relation. *Id.* at 540. The second case advanced by appellants, *United States v. Robertson*, 706 F.2d 253 (8th Cir.1983), is inapposite. The court reversed the conviction, not because the government failed to prove a connection between the firearm and the felony, but because the proof did not establish that the defendant was even carrying a gun on his person.

We find that the *Stewart* court's analysis of § 924(c) is not helpful to our analysis of § 844(h)(2). First, we do not find that the legislative history to the 1984 amendment "strongly implied" that the "in relation to" language did not affect the scope of the statute as originally drafted. At most, we find that the legislative history fails to explain why the "in relation to" phrase was added to the statute. *See* S.Rep. No. 225, 98th Cong., 2d Sess. 312–14, *reprinted in* 1984 U.S.Cong. & Ad.News 3182, 3490–92. Second, even if the *Stewart* court was correct in its analysis of why Congress amended § 924(c), Congress has not seen fit to modify § 844(h) in the same manner. Thus, even if Congress's subsequent pronouncements clarify previously enacted statutes, Congress's decision to amend § 924(c), but not § 844(h), is, at best, open to a multiplicity of interpretations.

Finding the legislative history to the 1984 amendment in this state, we return to the plain language of § 844(h). Section 844(h)(2) by its terms only requires that the government show that the defendant unlawfully carried an explosive "during the commission of any felony." The plain

---

11. Until 1984, 18 U.S.C. § 924(c) provided, in part:

Whoever—
(1) uses a firearm to commit any felony for which he may prosecuted in a court of the United States, or
(2) carries a firearm unlawfully during the commission of any felony for which he may be prosecuted in a court of the United States, shall be sentenced to a term of imprisonment for not less than one year nor more than ten years.

Section 924(c) now reads, in part:
Whoever, during and in relation to any crime of violence, including a crime of violence which provides for an enhanced punishment if committed by the use of a deadly or dangerous weapon or device, for which he may be prosecuted in a court of the United States, uses or carries a firearm, shall, in addition to the punishment provided for such crime of violence, be sentenced to imprisonment for ten years.
18 U.S.C. § 924(c) (Supp. II 1984).

everyday meaning of "during" is "at the same time" or "at a point in the course of." *See*, Webster's Third New International Dictionary 703 (1961). It does not normally mean "at the same time and in connection with...." It is not fitting for this court to declare that the crime defined by § 844(h)(2) has more elements than those enumerated on the face of the statute. If Congress sees fit to add a relational element to § 844(h)(2), it is certainly free to do so, in the same manner that it added a relational element to § 924(c). Until such time, we will hold that § 844(h)(2) has no relational element, and accordingly, we now hold that the district court correctly denied the defendants' motion to dismiss Count 5.

IV. FIRST AMENDMENT ISSUE

Amici urge that we vacate defendants' sentences and remand for resentencing on the grounds that the sentences resulted from the trial court's adverse reaction to the defendants' statements advocating revolutionary social change. According to amici, the trial court imposed its sentences "at least partly" in retaliation for the defendants' political philosophy.

We agree with the courts that have considered the issue that the imposition of a sentence on the basis of a defendant's beliefs would violate the first amendment's guarantees. *See United States v. Lemon*, 723 F.2d 922, 937 (D.C.Cir.1983); *United States v. Bangert*, 645 F.2d 1297, 1308 (8th Cir.), *cert. denied*, 454 U.S. 860, 102 S.Ct. 314, 70 L.Ed.2d 158 (1981); *cf. Bordenkircher v. Hayes*, 434 U.S. 357, 363, 98 S.Ct. 663, 667, 54 L.Ed.2d 604 (1978). A trial judge may consider a wide range of factors in fashioning a sentence to fit the crime and the individual defendant, however. *See United States v. Tucker*, 404 U.S. 443, 446, 92 S.Ct. 589, 591, 30 L.Ed.2d

592 (1972); *United States v. Baylin*, 696 F.2d 1030, 1038–39 (3d Cir.1982); 18 U.S.C. § 3577 (1982).[12] Specifically, the sentencing judge properly may consider the defendant's amenability to rehabilitation and expressions of remorse for the crime committed when the judge selects an appropriate sentence. *See United States v. Grayson*, 438 U.S. 41, 47–48, 98 S.Ct. 2610, 2614, 57 L.Ed.2d 582 (1978); *Bangert*, 645 F.2d at 1308–09.

Although trial courts are not required to articulate their reasons for a particular sentence in this circuit, *see United States v. Montoya*, 612 F.2d 792, 793 (3d Cir.1980); *United States v. Del Piano*, 593 F.2d at 540, the district court, recognizing the value of the practice for appellate review, placed its reasons on the record.[13] The court specifically admonished the defendants that it was not imposing its sentence on the basis of their political views or remarks, stating,

[l]et me make this clear. You are not on trial here because of your beliefs and your statements. Unlike the Soviet Union, whose political faith you embrace as Communists, here you can believe and say what you want to. Your distorted rhetoric about this being a political trial is best described as "hogwash."

The court then proceeded to give its reasons for the sentences:

You purportedly think because you adhere to certain beliefs and political views you can, when the time comes, as you see it, unleash guns, ammunition, and explosives to kill and destroy. You can't. If all you did was denounce this country you'd be free. Under your philosophy here you could murder anyone you selected and do it with impunity, because you decided it was necessary to advance your Communist cause. You had two guns on the front seat of that car, to kill.

---

12. This statute provides:

Use of information for sentencing

No limitation shall be placed on the information concerning the background, character, and conduct of a person convicted of an offense which a court of the United States may receive and consider for the purpose of imposing an appropriate sentence.

13. Effective November 1, 1987, district courts are required to state their reasons for the imposition of particular sentences by statute. *See* 18 U.S.C. § 3553(c) (Supp. III 1985).

In the trailer you had 600 plus pounds of explosives and dynamite, to kill and destroy. You carried a silhouette target of a man to practice your killing. You had books to aid you in using your arms.... In short, you are a present danger to the community, you show no remorse, all you promise with your conduct at this trial is that if and when released you'll kill the first time you perceive it to be justified.

The court's comments clearly show that the sentences it selected are based on its assessment of defendants' lack of remorse and potential for rehabilitation. We find that the record, and in particular, the sentencing minutes, do not justify amici's concern that the court imposed the sentences as a punishment for the defendants' exercise of their first amendment rights. *Cf. Bangert*, 645 F.2d at 1308 (trial court stated that its sentence was unrelated to defendants' political beliefs and placed proper reasons on the record).

V.

Having considered defendants' contentions, and finding each without merit, we will affirm the judgment of the district court.

A. LEON HIGGINBOTHAM, Jr., Circuit Judge, dissenting in part.

Although I join the majority in rejecting the aggregate sentencing, eighth amendment and first amendment claims raised by appellants Rosenberg and Blunk, I respectfully dissent from its treatment of appellants' convictions and sentences on Counts 2 and 5 for illegally possessing explosives. Because the majority has disregarded central principles of statutory construction in upholding appellants' convictions and sentences for violating 18 U.S.C. § 844(h)(2) (1982), I write separately to express my views.

I.

In Count 5 of the indictment, appellants Blunk and Rosenberg were charged with violating § 844(h)(2), which makes it a felony to "carr[y] an explosive unlawfully during the commission of any [federal] felony...." At the close of the trial, the district court denied appellants' motion to dismiss Count 5 on the ground that the government had failed to offer any proof of a relationship between the explosives illegally possessed by the appellants and any accompanying federal felony they may have committed. The district court also refused appellants' subsequent request that the jury be charged that it had to find that "some connection" existed between appellants' carrying explosives and their possession of unregistered firearms—i.e., that carrying explosives "played some role" in the latter crimes—to convict them under § 844(h)(2).[1] After the jury convicted appellants on Count 5, the district court sentenced each of them to a ten year sentence, the maximum term prescribed by § 844(h), such sentences to run consecutively to each appellant's other sentences. Because the trial court refused to instruct the jury as to what I find to be an essential element of this crime, appellants' convictions on Count 5 should be vacated. Accordingly, I dissent from the majority's holding. All criminal defendants, regardless of their ideology or the destructive potential of their crimes, deserve a fair reading of the applicable law.

My analysis begins with the plain language of § 844(h)(2). Unlike the majority, I construe the statute's phrasing—its prohibition against carrying explosives unlawfully "during the commission of" a federal felony—as explicitly and rather clearly connecting the possession of illegal explosives to the *perpetration* of some other feloni-

---

1. Appellants proposed the following jury charge: in order to find appellants guilty on Count 5, the jury must "first determine that they are guilty of one or more" of the other federal felonies charged and, "further," "that there is some connection between the carrying of explosives" and those other felonies. Jt.App. at A63. "That is, you must determine that the carrying of explosives played some role in the alleged possession of unregistered firearms ... If you do not find that the carrying of explosives played such a role, you may not find the defendants guilty ..." *Id.* The district court denied this request.

ous act.[2] Appellants have not asked "this court to declare that the crime defined by § 844(h)(2) has more elements than those enumerated on the face of the statute." Maj. typescript at 24. They have, rather, simply asked this court to give meaning to *each* of the words that Congress chose to use to define the elements of this crime. In my view, the majority amends a clear statute so as to eliminate an essential element of the crime that the statute expressly describes.

Even though the legislative history of § 844(h)(2) is, as the majority notes, otherwise "unilluminating," *id.* at 21, the sparse history available to us supports my reading of the statute. The House Report for what became § 844(h)(2) refers us to 18 U.S.C. § 924(c)(2) (1982), the gun control statute that served as a model for § 844(h),[3] and the legislative history of § 924(c)(2), as viewed by the Ninth Circuit in *United States v. Stewart*, 779 F.2d 538 (9th Cir. 1985), corroborates appellants' position. I respectfully submit that the Ninth Circuit's construction is correct.

Stewart determined that "the evident purpose" of the original § 924(c)(2), which is identical in structure to the current

§ 844(h)(2),[4] "was to impose more severe sanctions where firearms facilitated, or had the potential of facilitating, the commission of a felony." *Id.* at 540. Mr. Stewart was convicted of violating § 924(c)(2) at a time when its prohibition still mirrored the language of § 844(h)(2).[5] Between the time of Stewart's crime and his appeal to the Ninth Circuit, however, Congress amended § 924(c)(2), replacing the word "during" with the phrase "during and in relation to."[6] In *Stewart*, the court thus ascertained the meaning of § 924(c)(2) in light of the 1984 amendments thereto. The Ninth Circuit read the legislative history of the amendments to § 924(c) as indicating that "the 'in relation to' language was not intended to create an element of the crime that did not previously exist, but rather was intended to make clear a condition already implicit in the statute." *Id.* at 539. Here, the majority rejects that conclusion, "find[ing] that the legislative history fails to explain why the 'in relation to' phrase was added to the statute." Maj. at 1178. This position ignores the logical explanation offered in *Stewart:* "because the amendment [also] eliminated the requirement that the firearm be carried unlawfully, the 'in relation to' language was added

---

2. By offering dictionary definitions of the word "during," *see* maj. at 1178, the majority by implication offers an alternative construction of the statute—one that reads the phrase "during the commission of" to mean only "during." The only way to give some independent meaning to the words "the commission of"—i.e., to *all* the words employed by Congress—is to construe § 844(h)(2) as containing the relational element the majority has read out of the statute. I choose such a construction because, " '[i]n construing a statute[,] we are obliged to give effect, if possible, to every word Congress used.' " *United States v. DiSantillo*, 615 F.2d 128, 135 (3d Cir.1980) (Aldisert, J., joined by Hunter and Van Dusen, JJ.) (quoting *Reiter v. Sonotone Corp.*, 442 U.S. 330, 339, 99 S.Ct. 2326, 2331, 60 L.Ed.2d 931 (1979)). *Accord Mountain States Telephone & Telegraph Co. v. Pueblo of Santa Ana*, 472 U.S. 237, 105 S.Ct. 2587, 2595, 86 L.Ed.2d 168 (1985); *Colautti v. Franklin*, 439 U.S. 379, 392, 99 S.Ct. 675, 684, 58 L.Ed.2d 596 (1979); *Bell v. United States*, 754 F.2d 490, 498–99 (3d Cir.1985).

3. *See* H.Rep. No. 1549, 91st Cong., 2d Sess., *reprinted in* 1970 U.S.Code Cong. & Admin.

News 4007, 4046 ("Section 844(h) carries over to the explosives area the stringent provisions of the Gun Control Act of 1968 relating to the use of firearms and the unlawful carrying of firearms to commit, or during the commission of a Federal felony.").

4. Section § 924(c)(2) originally provided that whoever "carries a firearm unlawfully during the commission of any felony for which he may be prosecuted in a court of the United States, shall, in addition to the punishment provided for the commission of such felony, be sentenced to a term of imprisonment for not less than one year nor more than ten years." 18 U.S.C. § 924(c)(2) (1982). Section 844(h)(2) provides that whoever "carries an explosive unlawfully during the commission of any felony which may be prosecuted in a court of the United States, shall be sentenced to a term of imprisonment for not less than one year nor more than ten years." 18 U.S.C. § 844(h)(2) (1982).

5. *See supra* note 4.

6. For the original and amended text of § 924(c), see *supra* maj. at 1178 n. 11.

to allay explicitly the concern that a person could be prosecuted under section 924(c) for committing an entirely unrelated crime while in possession of a firearm." 779 F.2d at 539. The majority has, in other words, failed to note that § 924(c) was amended in *two* interrelated ways; by disregarding one of the two amendments, the majority misconstrues what the amendment process as a whole tells us about the original intention underlying § 924(c)(2).[7] *Stewart*'s reading of the legislative intent behind § 924(c)(2), and its conclusion that Congress meant to require some proof that the firearm facilitated the underlying felony, convinces me that Congress included a similar relational element in the crime defined by § 844(h)(2).

United States v. Robertson, 706 F.2d 253 (8th Cir.1983) (per curiam), which my colleagues dismiss as "inapposite," maj. at 1178, is indeed additional authority for appellants' position. While the *Robertson* decision did, as the majority observes, focus upon the meaning of the word "carries" in § 924(c)(2),[8] its analysis and holding also had much to say about the statute's use of the words "during the commission of":

> The Government produced no evidence that Robertson ever carried the weapon *or that the weapon played any role in Robertson's seeking collection of the unlawful debt.* Without some evidence showing that Robertson carried the weapon at some time *in connection with the commission of the offenses charged,* the Government's case on this count must fall.

706 F.2d at 256 (emphases added). As I read *Robertson*, there is simply no basis to conclude, as the majority does, that the court *did not* reverse the § 924(c)(2) conviction "because the government failed to prove a connection between the firearm

and the felony," maj. at 1178; even if the government had established that Mr. Robertson *was* carrying a gun on his person, it seems that a failure *also* to prove some connection between the firearm and felony would have moved that court to invalidate the conviction.

The very most one could claim, after reading the statutory language and reviewing the legislative history, is that the relational element of § 844(h)(2) is ambiguous. While I obviously dispute such a claim, even it should not defeat appellants' attacks on their Count 5 convictions. A "time-honored tenet of statutory construction [declares] that ambiguous laws are to be strictly construed against the Government." *United States v. Margiotta*, 688 F.2d 108, 120 (2d Cir.1982), *cert. denied,* 461 U.S. 913, 103 S.Ct. 1891, 77 L.Ed.2d 282 (1983). *Accord Dowling v. United States,* — U.S. —, 105 S.Ct. 3127, 3132, 87 L.Ed.2d 152 (1985) ("Due respect for the prerogatives of Congress in defining federal crimes prompts restraint in this area, where we typically find a 'narrow interpretation' appropriate.") (*quoting Williams v. United States,* 458 U.S. 279, 290, 102 S.Ct. 3088, 3094, 73 L.Ed.2d 767 (1982)); *Busic v. United States,* 446 U.S. 398, 406, 100 S.Ct. 1747, 64 L.Ed.2d 381 (1980) (interpreting 18 U.S.C. § 924(c)); *Bell v. United States,* 349 U.S. 81, 83, 75 S.Ct. 620, 622, 99 L.Ed. 905 (1955) ("when Congress leaves to the Judiciary the task of imputing to Congress an undeclared will, the ambiguity should be resolved in favor of lenity"); *United States v. Cotoia,* 785 F.2d 497, 502 (4th Cir.1986) (same); *Castaldi v. United States,* 783 F.2d 119, 121 (8th Cir.1986) (applying the "'rule of lenity[ ]' established in the *Bell* case"); *United States v. Diaz,* 778 F.2d 86, 88 & n. 2 (2d Cir.1985) (per curiam) (apply-

---

7. The majority offers this fallback justification for its interpretation: "even if the *Stewart* court was correct in its analysis of why Congress [added the phrase "in relation to" to] § 924(c), Congress has not seen fit to modify § 844(h) in the same manner." Maj. at 1178. To my mind, it is inappropriate to delete an element of a statutory crime simply because "Congress has not seen fit" to restate emphatically that statute's meaning.

8. In *Robertson,* there was "no evidence" that the defendant displayed a gun while committing his federal extortion crimes, or, indeed, that the defendant had *ever* carried the gun in question. 706 F.2d at 256. The Eighth Circuit accordingly vacated Mr. Robertson's § 924(c)(2) conviction. *See id.*

ing *Margiotta* to the interpretation of § 924(c)); *United States v. Waechter*, 771 F.2d 974, 978 (6th Cir.1985) ("we are mindful of the thoroughly established principal [sic] that the conduct prohibited by a criminal statute is to be narrowly construed"); *United States v. Anzalone*, 766 F.2d 676, 680–81 (1st Cir.1985) (applying "the proposition ... that criminal laws are to be strictly construed"); *United States v. Bushey*, 617 F.Supp. 292, 298–99 (D.Vt. 1985) (rejecting the government's broad reading of § 924(c)). *Cf. Sedima, S.P.R.L. v. Imrex Co., Inc.,* — U.S. —, 105 S.Ct. 3275, 3283 n. 10, 87 L.Ed.2d 346 (1985) (rejecting the lower court's "rather convoluted" application of this "strict construction principle"). This "well-known" tenet is, as Chief Justice Marshall noted long ago, "perhaps not much less old than construction itself. It is founded on the tenderness of the law for the rights of individuals; and on the plain principle, that the power of punishment is vested in the legislative, not the judicial department." [9] *United States v. Wiltberger*, 18 U.S. (5 Wheat.) 76, 95, 5 L.Ed. 37 (1820). Though the majority notes the precept of lenity, *see* maj. at 1177–1178, it fails to apply the teaching of this tenet. The majority appears to reason as follows: Since § 844(h)(2) makes it a crime to carry explosives illegally in furtherance of a federal felony, it might as well make it a crime to carry explosives unlawfully even when they have nothing to do with any other

federal felony one may be committing. As the majority sees things, in other words, a court must ignore any ambiguity in § 844(h)(2) and read the felony it defines as broadly as possible until Congress sees fit to declare explicitly otherwise. Because this approach usurps the legislative function at the same time it abandons the judicial duty to interpret ambiguous criminal statutes with lenity, I dissent from this portion of the panel's holding.

II.

I also dissent from the majority's treatment of appellants' cumulative sentencing claims. On their convictions under Count 2, appellants each received ten year sentences for possession of explosives in violation of 26 U.S.C. § 5861(d) (1982).[10] On their convictions under Count 5, appellants each received sentences of ten additional years for carrying explosives in the course of possessing firearms, a violation[11] of § 844(h)(2).[12] Appellants thus argue that, pursuant to their convictions under an indictment that was "designed to maximize the number of offenses which could be charged from [a] single event," Brief for Appellants at 52, they have been impermissibly sentenced to consecutive terms for the same act: illegally possessing explosives. With his customary thoughtfulness, Judge Lacey recognized that the imposition of consecutive sentences as to Counts 2 and 5 was not without difficulty.[13] I find the

9. For a further, contemporary discussion of the rationales underlying this principle of construction, *see United States v. Bass*, 404 U.S. 336, 347–49, 92 S.Ct. 515, 522–23, 30 L.Ed.2d 488 (1971) (identifying the policies of fair warning and separated powers).

10. Section 5861(d) makes it "unlawful for any person—

   to receive or possess a firearm which is not registered to him [or her] in the National Firearms Registration and Transfer Record[.]"

26 U.S.C. § 5861(d) (1982). A "firearm," for purposes of both this provision and "the extensive dealer registration and gun control provisions of the same title (for which it was obviously primarily designed)," *Parker v. United States*, 801 F.2d 1382, 1383 (D.C.Cir.1986) (Scalia, J.), includes any "destructive device." 26 U.S.C.

§ 5845(a) (1982). A subsection of this provision defines the term "destructive device" as including "any explosive [or] incendiary ... (A) bomb, (B) grenade, ... or (F) similar device," as well as "any combination of parts either designed or intended for use in converting any device into a destructive device ... and from which a destructive device may be readily assembled." 26 U.S.C. § 5845(f) (1982).

11. I, of course, dispute the statutory validity of appellants' convictions on Count 5. *See supra* p. 1–9.

12. For the language of § 844(h)(2), see *supra* note 4.

13. At sentencing, Judge Lacey made these remarks:

   "I indicated in connection with Count 5 that I would have more to say about it. It's argua-

resolution of this issue more difficult than has the majority.

Analysis of this argument is guided by the well-established rule of *Blockburger v. United States*, 284 U.S. 299, 52 S.Ct. 180, 76 L.Ed. 306 (1932). *See, e.g., Ball v. United States*, 470 U.S. 856, 105 S.Ct. 1668, 1672, 84 L.Ed.2d 740 (1985) (The Supreme "Court has consistently relied on the [*Blockburger*] test of statutory construction"). As the Second Circuit recently noted,

> [t]he *Blockburger* rule is a principle of statutory construction used to determine whether Congress has provided that two statutory offenses may be punished separately. *Whalen v. United States*, 445 U.S. 684, 691, 100 S.Ct. 1432, 1437, 63 L.Ed.2d 715 (1980), cited in *Albernaz v. United States*, 450 U.S. 333, 337, 101 S.Ct. 1137, 1141, 67 L.Ed.2d 275 (1981).[14] The rule provides that
>
> > 'where the same act or transaction constitutes a violation of two distinct statutory provisions, the test to be applied to determine whether there are two offenses or only one, is whether *each* provision requires proof of a fact which the other does not.'
>
> *Blockburger*, 284 U.S. at 304, 52 S.Ct. at 182 [emphasis added].

United States v. Langella, 776 F.2d 1078, 1081–82 (2d Cir.1985). "If so, it is appropriate to conclude that the possibility of cumulative punishment was intended. If not and if no other evidence of an intention to create separate offenses is found, it will be presumed that cumulative punishment was not intended." *Lovgren v. Byrne*, 787 F.2d 857, 863 (3d Cir.1986).

Under *Blockburger*, appellants have clearly received separate sentences for the same criminal offense, for, in establishing a violation of § 844(h)(2), the government has also, by definition, proven every fact necessary to show a violation of 26 U.S.C. § 5861(d).[15] The facts of this case—appellants' convictions under both statutes for one act of possessing a cache of explosives in their warehouse bay—demonstrate a textbook example of a *Blockburger* violation, *cf. Brown v. Ohio*, 432 U.S. 161, 168, 97 S.Ct. 2221, 2226, 53 L.Ed.2d 187 (1977) ("the prosecutor who has established auto theft necessarily has established joyriding as well"); at the very least, it is not, to quote (now Chief) Justice Rehnquist's articulation, for a unanimous Court, of the showing required to pass the *Blockburger* test, "beyond peradventure" that conviction under each of these statutes requires proof of a fact that conviction under the other does not. *Albernaz*, 450 U.S. at 339, 101 S.Ct. at 1142.

In addition, there is no "clearly expressed legislative intent" favoring cumu-

---

ble that a separate sentence should not be imposed on each of Counts 2 and 5. This is based on the argument that establishing every element of an offense under 18 U.S.C. Section 844(h)(2), carrying explosives while committing a felony, which is the subject of Count 5, will also establish a violation of 18 [sic] U.S.C. Section 5861(d), the subject of Count 2. If on appeal the Court of Appeals decides that this argument is valid, I state now that my sentence covering those two counts, 2 and 5, would be a term of imprisonment for 10 years, consecutive to the sentences imposed on all other counts."
Transcript of Proceedings (Sentence) (May 20, 1985) at 52.

14. In *Albernaz*, the Supreme Court employed the *Blockburger* test to evaluate the propriety of consecutive sentences for the crimes of conspiracy to import marijuana and conspiracy to distribute marijuana. Because the two statutes at issue "specif[ied] different ends as the pro-

scribed object of the conspiracy—distribution as opposed to importation— ... it [wa]s beyond peradventure that 'each provision require[d] proof of a fact [that] the other [di]d not.'" 450 U.S. at 339, 101 S.Ct. at 1142 (quoting *Blockburger*). The unanimous Court thus made "the unequivocal determination" that the statutes prescribed separate offenses, "violations of which c[ould] result in the imposition of consecutive sentences." *Id.*

15. A violation of § 844(h)(2) is proven by showing the following facts: (1) carrying (2) an explosive (3) unlawfully (4) during the commission of a felony. A violation of § 5861(d) is proven by showing these facts: (1) receiving or possessing (2) an explosive (3) that is not registered. As these appeals demonstrate, the former list of facts includes each element of the latter.

lative sentences for this single criminal act.[16] Section 844(h)(2) is designed to add a punishment for possessing explosives to the punishment prescribed for the federal crime that those explosives were used to further. But there is no indication that Congress, by passing § 844(h)(2), meant to impose an additional punishment on those who had already violated federal *explosives* laws. "Nothing ... in the legislative history [that] has been brought to our attention discloses an intent contrary to the pre-

sumption [that] should be accorded to these statutes after application of the *Blockburger* test. In fact, the legislative history is silent...." *Albernaz*, 450 U.S. at 340, 101 S.Ct. at 1143. Since "[t]he assumption underlying the *Blockburger* rule is that Congress ordinarily does not intend to punish the same offense under two different statutes," *Ball*, 105 S.Ct. at 1672, I am convinced by this absence of legislative intent to the contrary that the double sentences of each appellant may not stand.[17]

---

16. The Supreme Court has consistently decreed that, under *Blockburger*, cumulative sentences for the same criminal offense are invalid unless Congress has "specially authorized" such sentences. *Whalen*, 445 U.S. at 693, 100 S.Ct. at 1438. *See, e.g., Ohio v. Johnson*, 467 U.S. 493, 499, 104 S.Ct. 2536, 2541, 81 L.Ed.2d 425 (1984) ("the question under the Double Jeopardy Clause whether punishments are 'multiple' is essentially one of legislative intent"); *Missouri v. Hunter*, 459 U.S. 359, 367, 103 S.Ct. 673, 678, 74 L.Ed.2d 535 (1983) ("the result in *Whalen* [invalidating cumulative sentences for the crimes of rape and killing the same victim in the perpetration of the rape] turned on the fact that the Court saw no 'clear indication of contrary legislative intent'") (quoting *Whalen*, 445 U.S. at 692, 100 S.Ct. at 1438). Perhaps the majority's conclusion is explained by the fact that it applies this rule backwards. *See* maj. at 1177 ("Congress ... [did not] express[ ] an intention in the legislative history that § 844(h)(2)'s scope would *not* extend to such felonies.") (emphasis added).

17. If this court were vacating appellants' convictions on Count 5, this cumulative sentencing problem would, at least temporarily, leave the

case. Were the government then to decide to reprosecute on that count and, after proving a relationship between the possession of explosives and an underlying federal felony, obtain a proper conviction under § 844(h)(2), however, the sentencing judge would again confront the problem now before us. To prevent the relitigation of this question at some later date, I would hold now as a matter of law that an accused already sentenced under § 5861(d) may not also be sentenced under § 844(h)(2)—and vice versa—for the same incident of illegally possessing the same explosives.

Because this court has affirmed appellants' convictions on both Counts 2 and 5, however, the *Blockburger* violation I find is actual, not hypothetical. In this Circuit, the remedy for such an injury is to vacate the cumulative sentences and to remand the case to the district court with instructions to impose a general sentence that does not exceed the maximum possible under the statute prescribing the greater punishment. *See Gov't of the Virgin Islands v. Brathwaite*, 782 F.2d 399, 408 & n. 9 (3d Cir. 1986) (Hunter, J., for the court).

VOLUME I

CHAPTER 8   EXTENDED COMMITMENTS FOR TREATMENT OR DANGEROUSNESS

This chapter focuses on sentencing under the Habitual Criminal Acts statute, which is increasingly applied.   *McLester v. Smith,* 802 F.2d 1330 (11th Cir. 1986), argued that the Habitual Criminal Act should not be applied when several crimes arise from a single episode. The defendant further argued that before the Habitual Criminal Act could be applied, he must have been incarcerated for previous crimes. The contentions were rejected by the court.

In the case of *People v. Morissette,* 501 N.E.2d 781 (Ill. App. 1st Dist. 1986), the Illinois Habitual Criminal Act was challenged as unconstitutional. Although the case contained many procedural arguments which are not pertinent to this book, the discussion of the constitutionality of the Habitual Criminal Act has some application.

Other cases not included in which the habitual offender statutes were applied include *Foots v. State of Louisiana,* 793 F.2d 610 (5th Cir. 1986), in which a purse snatcher was sentenced to ten years, and *United States v. Louis,* 759 F.2d 1316 (1985), in which the defendant was sentenced under the Habitual Criminal Act for continuing his criminal empire. See *Holley v. Smith,* 792 F.2d 1046 (11th Cir. 1986) and *United States v. Amand,* 791 F.2d 1120 (4th Cir. 1986).

Introductions in previous volumes:

I: 511; VI: 79; VII: 125; VIII: 163

Terry Wayne McLESTER,
Petitioner-Appellant,

v.

Freddie V. SMITH, Commissioner of the
State of Alabama, Department of Cor-
rections; Charles Graddick, Attorney
General for the State of Alabama, Wil-
lie Johnson, Warden, Holman Station,
Respondents-Appellees.

No. 86–7038.

United States Court of Appeals,
Eleventh Circuit.

Oct. 20, 1986.

Appeal from the United States District
Court for the Middle District of Alabama.

Before HILL and HATCHETT, Circuit
Judges, and THOMAS *, Senior District
Judge.

HATCHETT, Circuit Judge:

Relying on *Seritt v. State of Alabama,*
731 F.2d 728 (11th Cir.1984), we uphold the
application of the Alabama Habitual Offender Act (Alabama Code 13A–5–9) to the
peculiar facts presented in this case.

The appellant, Terry Wayne McLester,
robbed a grocery store. In the robbery
incident, committed while McLester was intoxicated, he displayed a half-opened knife,
requested money from the cash register,
and suggested that the store clerk leave
the store with him. McLester claims that

although the store clerk took his demands
and actions seriously, he committed all of
the acts in jest. Because McLester had
seven prior convictions for burglary in the
second degree, the court sentenced him to
life imprisonment without parole for the
robbery, pursuant to Alabama's Habitual
Offender Act. On appeal, the Alabama
Court of Criminal Appeals upheld the conviction and sentence.

The life sentence without parole for the
robbery resulted from the fact that in January of 1979, McLester had pleaded guilty
to seven burglaries, all committed on the
same night, in one shopping mall, in one
episode. While intoxicated, McLester had
broken into a shopping mall and burglar-
ized seven different stores.

On December 6, 1984, McLester filed a
petition for habeas corpus in the United

---

* Honorable Daniel H. Thomas, Senior U.S. Dis-
trict Judge for the Southern District of Alabama,   sitting by designation.

States District Court for the Middle District of Alabama. During the proceedings, McLester sought discovery through interrogatories. The district court referred McLester's petition to a United States Magistrate who recommended that the writ of habeas corpus be denied and that the petition be dismissed. The district court adopted the magistrate's recommendations.

CONTENTIONS

McLester contends that his life sentence without parole, based on the seven convictions arising from events occurring during a single episode, violates the eighth amendment prohibition against cruel and unusual punishment because the sentence is disproportionate to the offense for which he was convicted. He also contends that the district court erred in refusing his discovery requests.

DISCUSSION

Title 13A-5-9 provides that a criminal defendant who has been convicted of a felony and is convicted of another felony must be punished by an additional penalty.[1] The term of the additional penalty is determined by the number and class of prior felonies as well as the class of the felony which invokes the imposition of the statute. Application of the statute is mandatory. *Watson v. State*, 392 So.2d 1274 (Ala.Crim. App.1980). "The word 'must' as it is used in this section leaves no discretion with the court as to whether a repeat offender is to be punished under the statute." 392 So.2d at 1276.

McLester argues that the purpose of the recidivist statute is to punish after several attempts to rehabilitate have failed. Therefore, the multiple convictions he received arising from the single burglary episode at the shopping mall, must be considered as one conviction which afforded

the state its sole opportunity at rehabilitation. By treating these convictions as separate and distinct, the state has misconstrued the purpose of the statute. McLester argues that applying the statute in this manner raises an impermissible presumption that numerous unsuccessful attempts have been made to rehabilitate him, when in fact, no rehabilitative effort has been expended. Since this misapplication of the statute has resulted in a life sentence for what amounts to one prior felony, his sentence is disproportionate and constitutes cruel and unusual punishment.

On quick review, McLester's argument sounds plausible; on further consideration of existing law and societal aims, however, his argument proves meritless. *Watson* expressly states that the term "convicted" does not require incarceration as a prerequisite to the application of the recidivist statute. In *Watson*, the court held that the statute must be strictly construed and that the origin of the felonies is irrelevant. "Alabama's Habitual Offender's Act contains no requirement that a repeat offender must have served, partially, or completely, his sentence for a prior felony before he can be sentenced under the Act." *Watson*, 392 So.2d at 1278. Since Alabama law does not require incarceration following the commission of a felony before that felony may be utilized under its recidivist statute, McLester's contention is meritless. It would be strange indeed for a federal court to seek to define the length of time that must pass between the commission of felonies and the type of punishment required following conviction of a felony before a state could utilize the conviction under its recidivist statute. Only when a state's statutory scheme clearly punishes in a disproportionate manner, may a federal court impose its theories of how a

---

1. Title 13A-5-9, Ala.Code, in pertinent part, provides:

    (c) In all cases when it is shown that a criminal defendant has been previously convicted of *any three felonies* and after such convictions has committed another felony, he must be punished as follows:

    . . . .

    (3) On conviction of a Class A felony, he *must* be punished by imprisonment for life without parole.
(Emphasis added.)

state should operate its criminal justice system.

McLester also contends that his sentence was disproportionate under the three-prong test announced in *Solem v. Helm*, 463 U.S. 277, 103 S.Ct. 3001, 77 L.Ed.2d 637 (1983). In *Solem*, the Court found that the following objective factors are relevant in determining whether a person's criminal sentence is disproportionate: (a) the gravity of the offense and the harshness of the penalty; (b) the sentence imposed on other criminals in the same jurisdiction; and (c) the sentence imposed for commission of the same crime in other jurisdictions.

A.   Harshness of the penalty.

McLester submits that an evaluation of the offense he committed when compared to his life sentence without parole, unquestionably establishes an unacceptable harshness that violates his constitutional rights against cruel and unusual punishment. McLester particularly declares this to be true in this instance where the facts of the crime show mitigating factors such as intoxication, absence of physical harm, and a lack of intent. McLester concedes that his offense appears at first blush to be grave; however, he emphasizes that he acted in jest although the alleged victim apparently perceived his acts as being serious.

On this issue, *Seritt v. State of Alabama*, 731 F.2d 728 (11th Cir.1984), controls. The court in *Seritt*, at 732, stated that robbery "is not viewed by society as one of the less serious offenses." It is a serious offense! Whether McLester acted in jest has been determined against him— the jury convicted. *Seritt* forecloses relief for McLester under the first *Solem* factor.

B.   Other sentences in the same jurisdiction.

As to prong two of the *Solem* test, the record contains computer data showing that seventy-eight persons in Alabama are presently serving sentences of less than

life without parole following convictions for first degree robbery with prior convictions for felonies sufficient to invoke the mandatory sentence provisions of Title 13A–5–9. Based on this data, McLester argues that his sentence is disproportionate when compared with these seventy-eight persons who should also be serving life sentences without parole.

Solem affords McLester no relief on this issue. Surely the *Solem* test does not apply to or take into account sentences which are unauthorized or illegal. Consequently, McLester's burden is to show that his sentence is disproportionate when compared with lawful and authorized sentences in the state of Alabama.[2] For these reasons, McLester fails to establish that his sentence is disproportionate to other sentences for like conduct in the state of Alabama.

C.   Sentences in other jurisdictions.

As to the third *Solem* prong, McLester asserts that his sentence is disproportionate to sentences in other jurisdictions. We disagree. Florida law prescribes life imprisonment for a felony of the first degree under its Habitual Felony Offenders Statute. Section 775.084(1)(a) and (4)(a) Fla. Stat.Ann. (1976). Moreover, death or imprisonment are possible sentences provided for by Georgia statutory law for a similar crime in the first degree. Section 16–8–41(b), Ga.Code.Ann. (1984); (*Coker v. Georgia*, 433 U.S. 584, 97 S.Ct. 2861, 53 L.Ed.2d 982 (1977), prohibits the imposition of the death sentence in such instances). McLester's sentence clearly does not support a finding of disproportionality when compared with possible sentences in other jurisdictions.

McLester also contends that the district court abused its discretion in denying his amended discovery request. The discovery requested the names, prior criminal records, and the sentences of all persons convicted of the highest degree of murder, sodomy, kidnapping, and rape since July

---

2.   Since the statute is mandatory, the state of Alabama has a serious problem regarding its recidivist statute that we will be requested to

address in some other case or in further proceedings in this case when the issue is squarely presented.

30, 1979, who were sentenced to less than life without parole. McLester claims that the requested data would show that a large number of murderers, sodomists, rapists, and kidnappers had received lesser sentences than he in spite of the fact that they are second, third, and fourth time habitual offenders. The record supports the district court's finding that records in the possession of the state of Alabama Department of Corrections were made available to McLester, and that more extensive discovery requiring manual examination of thousands of prisoner files would be too burdensome.

No contention was made attacking the constitutionality of the sentence as applied to McLester based on the state's stipulation and evidence in the record showing that Alabama has lacked uniformity in application of this supposedly mandatory recidivist statute. Other theories may afford McLester relief, but those interesting theories are not before us. Accordingly, the judgment of the district court is affirmed.

AFFIRMED.

The PEOPLE of the State of Illinois,
Plaintiff-Appellee,

v.

Sherman MORISSETTE,
Defendant-Appellant.

No. 84–2901.

Appellate Court of Illinois,
First District, Fourth Division.

Nov. 20, 1986.

Rehearing Denied Dec. 29, 1986.

Presiding Justice LINN delivered the opinion of the court:

Following a bench trial, defendant, Sherman Morissette, was convicted of armed robbery (Ill.Rev.Stat.1981, ch. 38, par. 18–2) and armed violence (Ill.Rev.Stat.1981, ch. 38, par. 33A–2). Morissette represented himself *pro se* at trial. At sentencing, Morissette was adjudged an habitual criminal and, pursuant to the Habitual Criminal Act (Ill.Rev.Stat.1981, ch. 38, par. 33B–1 et seq.), was sentenced to the Illinois Department of Corrections for a term of life imprisonment without parole.

On appeal, Morissette contends that the cause should be reversed and remanded for a new trial, or alternatively, that the cause be remanded for resentencing. Morissette bases his contentions on his belief that the trial court prejudicially erred by: (1) failing to suppress evidence concerning a line-up, at which he was identified by the victim as the victim's assailant; Morissette contends the line-up was suggestive; (2) denying his motion to appoint a bar association attorney and subsequently allowing him to represent himself at trial; (3) denying him his Sixth Amendment rights of compulsory process and production of documentary evidence helpful to him; and (4) sentencing him pursuant to the Habitual Criminal Act where the habitual criminal statute (Ill. Rev.Stat.1983, ch. 38, par. 33B–1) is unconstitutional.

We affirm the decision of the trial court.

BACKGROUND:

Sherman Morissette was found guilty of stealing a taxicab in the course of committing an armed robbery against the taxicab driver. The facts adduced at trial indicate that during the evening hours of December 24, 1983, Charlie Adams, the complaining witness, was working as a taxicab driver for Yellow Cab Company. Sometime that evening, Adams picked up a passenger, later identified by Adams as Morissette, at or near the intersection of 87th Street and Stony Island, in Chicago. Morissette was wearing a cap and scarf, but removed the scarf once inside the cab. After driving Morissette to his destination of 91st Street and East End, Adams stopped his cab and turned on the inside light in order to collect Morissette's fare. When Adams turned around to collect the fare, Morissette pointed a black pistol at Adams' head, demanding all of Adams' money. Adams replied that he had no money, and Morrissette ordered Adams out of the cab. Morissette allowed Adams to retrieve his coat from the cab before Morissette drove the cab away, leaving Adams in the street.

After Morissette drove away, Adams hailed a different cab and rode to a drug store where he telephoned the police informing them of the armed robbery. The police directed Adams to come to the station to file a report of the incident. Adams left the drug store and hailed another cab to take him to the police station at 71st and Cottage Grove. On the way to the station,

Adams noticed a police paddy wagon parked in front of Jackson Park Hospital and he asked his cab driver to stop there.

Upon entering the hospital, Adams spotted and approached two police officers to whom he reported the incident. Adams testified that one of the police officers called in over the police radio and related both Adams' description of Morissette and the number (726) of the stolen taxicab. Adams then returned home where he contacted Yellow Cab Company, reporting to the dispatcher that his cab was stolen. The dispatcher later testified that he had received such a call and that he made a notation of it for the cab company manager, although the Yellow Cab Company records did not evidence such a report of the armed robbery.

Chicago police officers James Vellehas, Steve Kubiak and Louis Velez testified for the prosecution as to the events leading up to Morissette's arrest and subsequent line-up identification. Vellehas and Kubiak were working together on the night of the armed robbery and monitored a message over their police radio regarding an incident in which Yellow Cab number 726 was stolen at gunpoint. The "flash" message also described the suspect as a male black in his early thirties. Vellehas and Velez were working together on December 27, 1983, and they arrested Morissette that night after an automobile and foot chase.

According to Vellehas and Velez, they noticed Yellow Cab number 726 proceeding eastbound on 92nd Street on December 27, 1983. The driver was a male black in his thirties. Vellehas noted that he recalled the flash message that he and Kubiak heard three nights earlier so he positioned his squad roll behind the taxicab and began to follow Morissette as he drove. Although a radio check on the status of the cab came up clear, Vellehas attempted to curb the cab by activating the siren and flashing lights on his vehicle. Morissette responded by immediately accelerating the taxicab giving way to the car chase. When Morissette stalled the cab in an alley, a foot chase ensued. Morissette was ap-

prehended after an altercation in which he resisted the police. Morissette identified himself as Charles Adams and asserted that the cab belonged to him. The officers transported Morissette to the Fourth District police station.

On the following evening, Morissette was placed in a line-up where the real Charles Adams identified Morissette as the armed robber who stole his cab from him on the evening of December 24, 1983. Because Morissette had been injured while trying to resist police prior to his arrest, Morissette appeared in the line-up with bandages on his head. He also wore a trench coat and was asked to speak while being viewed by Adams.

Morissette was represented by the public defender on his motion to suppress the above identification. After hearing, the trial court denied the motion. During the hearing on the motion to suppress, Morissette moved the trial court to allow him to proceed *pro se*. The record indicates that the trial court proffered to Morissette, as proscribed by Illinois Supreme Court Rule 401(a) (87 Ill.2d R. 401(a)), the proper admonishments concerning self-representation. Subsequently, Morissette was allowed to proceed *pro se* on the balance of the hearing on the motion and later at trial, where the witnesses named above testified as indicated.

The trial court, after reviewing all of the evidence presented by the State and by defendant, found Morissette guilty of armed robbery and armed violence. Pursuant to the Habitual Criminal Act (Ill.Rev.Stat. 1981, ch. 38, par. 33B-1), the State then petitioned for imposition of a natural life sentence on the basis that Morissette had prior armed robbery convictions, and was therefore subject to sentencing as an habitual criminal.

At the sentencing hearing, the State offered evidence of Morissette's prior armed robbery convictions. The record discloses that in 1979, Morissette was convicted on two counts of armed robbery after pleading guilty to stealing a cab after robbing the driver at gunpoint, and for later robbing at gunpoint a passenger he picked up while driving the stolen cab. He was sentenced to two concurrent terms of eight years. In 1976, Morissette also pleaded guilty to two armed robbery counts, and was convicted and sentenced to two concurrent terms of four years to four years and a day. In mitigation, Morissette stated that he had served in the military, and was a licensed cosmetologist. He also argued that the Habitual Criminal Act was unconstitutional.

The trial court, after reviewing the evidence presented at trial and at sentencing, noted Morissette's extensive criminal record which included eight felony convictions in all. The trial court concluded that Morissette was an appropriate candidate for a natural life sentence, and thereupon sentenced Morissette to the Illinois Department of Corrections for a term of natural life. From his conviction and this sentence, Morissette now appeals.

OPINION:

I.

We first address Morissette's contention that he was prejudiced by the trial court's refusal to suppress evidence concerning the line-up at which he was identified as the offender in this case. Specifically, Morissette contends that the line-up was impermissibly suggestive because in a 2-way mirror arrangement, he was the only participant in the line-up wearing head bandages, and because he was singled out to wear a trench coat, pull the lapel of the coat over his face, and say the words, "This is a stick-up."

It is well settled that where a defendant moves to suppress identification testimony, he has the burden of establishing that the pre-trial identification procedure was unnecessarily suggestive. Once defendant has done so, the evidence will then be suppressed unless the State is able to show, by clear and convincing evidence, an independent basis of reliability. *People v. Garcia* (1983), 97 Ill.2d 58, 73, 73 Ill.Dec. 414, 419, 454 N.E.2d 274, 279; *People v. McTush*

(1980), 81 Ill.2d 513, 520, 43 Ill.Dec. 728, 732, 410 N.E.2d 861, 865.

In the instant case, Morissette cites *U.S. v. Wade* (1967), 388 U.S. 218, 233, 87 S.Ct. 1926, 1935, 18 L.Ed.2d 1149, where the supreme court gave the following examples of suggestive pre-trial identification procedures:

"That the other participants in a line-up were grossly dissimilar in appearance to the suspect, that only the suspect was required to wear distinctive clothing which the culprit allegedly wore, that the witness is told by the police that they have caught the culprit after which the defendant is brought before the witness alone or is viewed in jail, that the suspect is pointed out before or during a line-up, and that the participants in the line-up are asked to try on an article of clothing which fits only the suspect."

These examples, however, are inapposite to this case where there is no evidence of similar improprieties.

In addition, the line-up in this case consisted of five black men. There was no significant difference in their height and weight, and they all wore coats and had mustaches. Morissette and two other participants wore blue jeans. Although Morissette was the only person wearing bandages on his head, we agree with the trial court's reasoning that this was not suggestive, since there were no bandages, cuts, bruises, or marks on Morissette's person when he was first viewed by Adams during the armed robbery. Furthermore, there is no evidence to suggest that Morissette was dressed as he was at the time of the robbery, which, even if true, in and of itself would not necessarily render the line-up unduly suggestive. *See, People v. Lark* (1984), 127 Ill.App.3d 927, 83 Ill.Dec. 121, 469 N.E.2d 728 (requiring defendant to wear clothing identified by witness was permissible); *People v. Guyon* (1981), 101 Ill.App.3d 799, 57 Ill.Dec. 318, 428 N.E.2d 998 (requiring only defendant to wear hairnet and jacket allegedly worn by victim's assailants was permissible).

Morissette also contends that he was prejudiced because he was the only participant in the line-up required to repeat the phrase, "This is a stick-up". Despite conflicting evidence as to whether he was the only participant required to do this, this contention, like all others raised by defendant, must fail since the record evinces clear and convincing evidence of an independent basis of reliability for Adams' identification of Morissette as the offender in this case.

Reliability has been held to be the linchpin in determining the admission of identification testimony. (*Manson v. Brathwaite* (1977), 432 U.S. 98, 114, 97 S.Ct. 2243, 2253, 53 L.Ed.2d 140.) As a guideline for evaluating the likelihood of misidentification we consider: (1) the opportunity of the witness to view the criminal at the time of the crime; (2) the witness' degree of attention; (3) the accuracy of the witness' prior description of the criminal; (4) the level of certainty demonstrated at the time of the confrontation; (5) the length of time between the crime and the confrontation; and (6) any acquaintance with the criminal prior to the crime. (*Neil v. Biggers* (1972), 409 U.S. 188, 199–200, 93 S.Ct. 375, 382, 34 L.Ed.2d 401; *accord., People v. McTush* (1980), 81 Ill.2d 513, 521, 43 Ill.Dec. 728, 732, 410 N.E.2d 861, 865.) These elements of reliability are to be weighed against the corrupting effects of the alleged suggestive identification. (*People v. Nolden* (1980), 91 Ill. App.3d 532, 47 Ill.Dec. 8, 414 N.E.2d 1124), and each case must be considered on its own facts. *People v. Son* (1982), 111 Ill. App.3d 273, 66 Ill.Dec. 952, 443 N.E.2d 1115.

Applying the above analysis to this case, it is clear that there are sufficient indicia of reliability of Adams' line-up identification of Morissette to permit its admission into evidence. Most notably, Adams had ample opportunity to view Morissette during the encounter in Adams' taxicab prior to and after Morissette announced the armed robbery. Adams asked Morissette his destination and then explained that he would not drive to that area prior to driving Morissette to an alternate destination. During the drive, Adams said he viewed Morissette through the rear view mirror, and stated that he saw him face-to-face with the taxicab's inside light on as he turned around to collect the fare from Morissette.

Adams also testified that he further viewed Morissette when he bent down to retrieve his coat after Morissette ordered him from the cab. In addition, due to his attentiveness, Adams gave an accurate description of Morissette to the police prior to Morissette's arrest. So accurate was this description that Officers Vellehas and Velez curbed Morissette in the cab on December 27, 1983, even after a radio license check came back clear. Adams identified Morissette only three days after the incident, and again identified him in open court. Based on the totality of the circumstances in this case, we are convinced that Adams identified Morissette based on his memory of the events at the time of the armed robbery. Accordingly, there is a sufficient independent basis for the identification to remove any risk of misidentification. Thus, we hold that the trial court acted properly in ruling not to suppress evidence of Morissette's line-up identification.

II.

As his next assignment of error, Morissette contends that his case was prejudiced when the trial court denied his motion to appoint a bar association attorney, and subsequently allowed him to represent himself at trial. We disagree.

First, although Morissette has an unqualified right to assistance of counsel, he does not have an unqualified right to choose his court-appointed attorney. (*People v. Johnson* (1982), 109 Ill.App.3d 511, 65 Ill.Dec. 137, 440 N.E.2d 992.) Rather, absent a showing of good cause, it is within the court's discretion to deny such a request. (*People v. Dorsey* (1982), 109 Ill. App.3d 218, 64 Ill.Dec. 842, 440 N.E.2d 394, *cert. denied* 460 U.S. 1053, 103 S.Ct. 1503, 75 L.Ed.2d 933.) A review of the record before us fails to show good cause for appointing a bar association attorney in place of the public defender as Morissette requested.

Morissette argues that the public defender failed to follow Morissette's instructions in defending the case. Specifically, Morissette complained that the public defender failed to subpoena and assess the testimony of key defense witnesses and in his reply brief Morissette argues that the defender's case load was so heavy that he could not properly attend to Morissette's case. Given the public defender's pre-trial preparation of motions, witnesses, and investigations which occurred in this case, we find the record to clearly contradict Morissette's unsubstantiated allegations that the public defender failed to effectively represent him below.

Second, Morissette contends that the trial court erred in granting his motion to defend this case *pro se* because the trial court failed to conduct a hearing to determine his competence to do so. In Illinois, waiver of the right to counsel by the accused is governed by Supreme Court Rule 401(a) (87 Ill.2d R. 401(a)). This rule provides for a procedure to ensure that a defendant understands the nature and consequences of proceeding as his own lawyer. (*See, People v. Baker* (1983), 94 Ill.2d 129, 68 Ill.Dec. 125, 445 N.E.2d 769; *People v. Graves* (1985), 134 Ill.App.3d 473, 89 Ill. Dec. 399, 480 N.E.2d 1142.) In the case at bar, the record clearly demonstrates that Morissette made his waiver of right to counsel only after the trial court followed this procedure by admonishing him in open court (pursuant to Supreme Court Rule 401(a)) of the nature of the charges brought against him, the minimum and maximum sentences prescribed under the law, as well as his right to counsel and the consequences of self-representation. 87 Ill.2d R. 401(a).

Further, although Rule 401(a) does not require a separate hearing to determine whether Morissette had the minimal competence to proceed *pro se*, his competence can be inferred from the objective criteria commonly used to make such determinations, *to-wit:* his age, level of education, capacity, and involvement in prior legal proceedings. (*See, People v. Kessler* (1983), 113 Ill. App.3d 354, 360–63, 69 Ill.Dec. 278, 282, 447 N.E.2d 495, 499.) Here, Morissette was 27 years old, had previously been employed as a licensed cosmetologist, and his criminal record shows familiarity with the criminal justice system. (*See, People v. Black* (1979), 68 Ill.App.3d 309, 24 Ill.Dec. 758, 385 N.E.2d 899.) In fact, throughout the trial, Morissette demonstrated his legal sophistication and his ability to conduct a defense through motion practice, calling and examining witnesses, and arguing to the court. (*See, People v. Jackson* (1978), 59 Ill.App.3d 1004, 17 Ill.Dec. 539, 376 N.E.2d 685; *People v. Smith* (1975), 33 Ill.App.3d 725, 338 N.E.2d 207.) As such, we find that he made an intelligent waiver of his right to counsel such that his contention that he was denied effective assistance of counsel is doomed.

III.

Morissette also contends that he was denied his Sixth Amendment rights of compulsory process and production of documentary evidence in this case when the State only listed one of two Officer Kubiaks on their answers to discovery, and when the State failed to proffer to Morissette copies of the police report, notations of the flash message, and the cab company report concerning the robbery in this case.

First, we do not see the State's failure to list the second Officer Kubiak as prejudicial under the circumstances of this case. Supreme Court Rule 412(a)(i), provides that, "[T]he State shall, upon written motion of defense counsel, disclose * * * the names and last known addresses of persons whom the State intends to call as witnesses, together with their relevant written or recorded statements * * *." (87 Ill.2d R. 412(a)(i).) This rule is in keeping with the overall purpose of the discovery rules to prevent surprise or unfair advantage which prejudices another party at trial. Further, as the state correctly asserts, it is incumbent upon Morissette to show that the State's noncompliance with this rule resulted in prejudice to his case. *People v. Anderson* (1977), 46 Ill.App.3d 607, 4 Ill.Dec. 938, 360 N.E.2d 1371.

In the instant case, even if the State should have included the names of both Officer Kubiaks, Morissette has failed to show any resulting surprise or prejudice to his case due to the fact that the existence of the second Kubiak was undisclosed. Indeed, the State contends that it only intended to call Steve Kubiak, star number 5801, to establish that the armed robbery had actually occurred. Steve Kubiak allegedly heard the December 24, 1983 radio call pertaining to the incident. The second Kubiak, whom the State neither called to testify nor intended to call to testify, was allegedly present only when Morissette was transferred to the station. Nowhere in the record is it evidenced that omission of this information from the discovery sheets, or the second Kubiak's failure to testify, caused Morissette either surprise or prejudice in this case.

Second, we find that Morissette was not denied his Sixth Amendment right to production of documents where, as here, the documents sought from the State were never in the State's possession. It is axiomatic that, as a practical matter, the failure of the prosecutor to disclose allegedly exculpatory evidence not in his possession does not violate due process, since under such circumstances, nothing has been suppressed. (*See, Brady v. Maryland* (1963), 373 U.S. 83, 83 S.Ct. 1194, 10 L.Ed.2d 215; *People v. Parker* (1983), 113 Ill.App.3d 321, 69 Ill.Dec. 240, 447 N.E.2d 457; *People v. Palmer* (1982), 111 Ill.App.3d 800, 67 Ill. Dec. 442, 444 N.E.2d 678.) Here, Morissette argues that he was prejudiced by the State's failure to proffer to him documentation of the arrest (police report), flash message, and cab company report concerning the instant charge. However, the record evinces that in this case this evidence could not be produced by any of the respective custodians, nor was it in the possession of the State or any of its agents. As such,

this evidence was not available to either the prosecution or the defense. Accordingly, we cannot hold the State accountable for failing to provide this evidence to Morissette.

It is also our opinion that production of these documents would not serve to exculpate Morissette given the facts of this case. Here the complaining witness testified as to the details of the robbery and he clearly viewed Morissette during the crime, later identifying him both in a line-up and at trial. In addition, two police officers testified that they monitored an armed robbery call during the evening hours of December 24, 1983, and that one of the officers recognized the stolen cab and defendant three days later as a result of that radio call. The officers also testified that Morissette was arrested by them after an attempt to curb him as he drove Yellow Cab number 726, giving way to an automobile and foot chase. At no time did the police lose sight of Morissette after he abandoned the cab and attempted to elude and later physically resist the police.

The record also evinces that the dispatcher on duty at Yellow Cab Company on the night in question stated that Adams called in to report that cab number 726 was stolen. Further, only three days after the incident, Adams identified Morissette as the man who stole his cab at gunpoint and subsequently identified him at trial. Consequently, evaluated in the context of the entire record, the fact that the reports referred to by Morissette were themselves missing have no bearing on this case and similarly their absence does not create a reasonable doubt as to his guilt, given the instant record.

IV.

Finally, we address Morissette's contention that the habitual criminal statute (Ill.Rev.Stat.1983, ch. 38, par. 33B-1), under which he was sentenced to a mandatory term of life imprisonment without parole, is unconstitutional. The State contends that Morissette has waived our review of this issue by failing to raise this objection at sentencing and in his post-trial motion. (*See, People v. Caballero* (1984), 102 Ill.2d 23, 31, 79 Ill.Dec. 625, 464 N.E.2d 223.) Even constitutional errors not raised before the trial court are generally waived on appeal. (*People v. Visnack* (1985), 135 Ill.App.3d 113, 118, 89 Ill.Dec. 901, 904, 481 N.E.2d 744, 747.) However, since this alleged error affects Morissette's substantial rights, we will address this issue under the plain error doctrine.   87 Ill.2d R. 615(a).

The habitual criminal statute provides that every offender who is three times convicted of a Class X felony or murder within a 20–year period shall be sentenced to life imprisonment. (Ill.Rev. Stat.1983, ch. 38, par. 33B–1.) Defendant offers several arguments that this statutory penalty is unconstitutional. The first of these is his claim that it penalizes him for his prior wrongs in 1976 and 1979, thereby violating constitutional provisions regarding *ex parte* laws and double jeopardy. We find this argument to be unpersuasive.

In *People v. Washington* (1984), 125 Ill. App.3d 109, 80 Ill.Dec. 554, 465 N.E.2d 666, this court held that the habitual criminal statute does not violate either the United States or Illinois constitutional provisions regarding *ex post facto* laws and double jeopardy. In that case we cited *People v. Mason* (1983), 119 Ill.App.3d 516, 524, 75 Ill.Dec. 43, 48, 456 N.E.2d 864, 869, for the proposition that recidivist statutes have been consistently upheld as not violative of *ex post facto* provisions. Further, in *Washington* we determined that the statute does not punish defendant a second time for his previous convictions; rather, these prior adjudications are used only to establish matters in aggravation to support the disposition authorized for a third serious offense. (125 Ill.App.3d 109, 117, 80 Ill.Dec. 554, 559, 465 N.E.2d 666, 671; *cf. People ex rel. Carey v. Chrastka* (1980), 83 Ill.2d 67, 77–78, 46 Ill.Dec. 156, 161–62, 413 N.E.2d 1269, 1274–75 (construing the Juvenile Court Act (Ill.Rev.Stat.1979, ch. 37, par. 701–1 *et seq.*).) Having been presented with no reason to change our opinion in

this case, we continue to hold that the habitual criminal statute does not violate constitutional *ex post facto* and double jeopardy provisions.

Morissette next contends that the statute gives unbridled discretion to the prosecutor to determine whom to seek to sentence to life imprisonment, thereby violating the due process and equal protection clauses of the Fourteenth Amendment and the cruel and unusual punishment clause of the Eighth Amendment. We would discuss the Eighth Amendment argument as part of Morissette's third constitutional challenge.

The argument that the habitual criminal statute is unconstitutional because it gives the prosecution unbridled discretion in deciding whether to seek imposition of a life sentence was refused by us in the *Washington* case. There we recognized that the habitual criminal statute does not explicitly delegate to the prosecutor the power to choose which defendants shall be sentenced under its terms; rather, its provisions apply to all defendants who meet the statute's criteria of two previous Class X felony or murder convictions. (125 Ill.App.3d 109, 80 Ill.Dec. 554, 465 N.E.2d 666; *cf. People v. Withers* (1983), 115 Ill.App.3d 1077, 71 Ill.Dec. 444, 450 N.E.2d 1323 *cert. denied* (1984), 465 U.S. 1052, 104 S.Ct. 1332, 79 L.Ed.2d 726.) Accordingly, the statute places no discretion in the hands of the State to determine which defendants qualify for a term of life imprisonment, rather, precise guidelines are set forth to enable the trial judge to determine the applicability of the recidivist statute. (*See also, People v. McNeil* (1984), 125 Ill. App.3d 876, 881, 81 Ill.Dec. 256, 259, 466 N.E.2d 1058, 1061; *People v. Tobias* (1984), 125 Ill.App.3d 234, 240, 80 Ill.Dec. 496, 501–02, 465 N.E.2d 608, 613–14.) Therefore, we conclude that the habitual criminal statute does not grant to the prosecutor unbridled discretion in deciding whom to seek to sentence to life imprisonment and does not violate due process or equal protection.

Morissette's third argument is that the habitual criminal statute is unconstitutional because it requires the imposition of life imprisonment while foreclosing consideration of any mitigating factors making the sentence proportionate to the offender or the offense, violating due process and the Eighth Amendment protection against cruel and unusual punishment. This same argument was recently rejected by this court in *People v. Hartfield* (1985), 137 Ill.App.3d 679, 92 Ill.Dec. 281, 484 N.E.2d 1136. The *Hartfield* court relied on *People v. Withers* (1983), 115 Ill.App.3d 1077, 1090, 71 Ill.Dec. 444, 453, 450 N.E.2d 1323, 1332 *cert. denied* (1984), 465 U.S. 1052, 104 S.Ct. 1332, 79 L.Ed.2d 726, where the court declared that the act did not violate the Eighth and Fourteenth Amendments because two previous adjudications (here 1976 and 1979) have afforded the defendant the opportunity to present mitigating factors to a court.

Finally, it suffices to note that the habitual criminal statute has been upheld repeatedly against constitutional attacks similar to those offered by Morissette in cases other than those discussed above. *See, People v. Taylor* (1984), 102 Ill.2d 201, 80 Ill.Dec. 76, 464 N.E.2d 1059; *People v. Coleman* (1984), 128 Ill.App.3d 538, 83 Ill.Dec. 857, 470 N.E.2d 1277; *People v. Pettigrew* (1984), 123 Ill.App.3d 649, 78 Ill.Dec. 919, 462 N.E.2d 1273.[1]

In sum, based on the facts and circumstances of this case, we find that Morissette's identification was properly admitted into evidence; that he was not denied effective assistance of counsel; that he knowingly and intelligently waived his right to be represented by an attorney; that he was not prejudiced in discovery; and that the Habitual Criminal Act (Ill.Rev.Stat.1983, ch. 38, par. 33B-1) is constitutional.

Therefore, we affirm defendant's armed robbery conviction and his sentence of natural life imprisonment, without parole.

AFFIRMED.

JIGANTI and McMORROW, JJ., concur.

---

1. Morissette raises an additional question regarding the constitutionality of the Habitual Criminal Act in his second pro se supplemental brief filed August 14, 1986. According to Morissette, the statute (Ill.Rev.Stat.1980, ch. 38, par. 33B-1) violates Article IV of the Illinois Constitution (Ill. Const. 1970, Art. IV, sec. 8) because, upon passage, the statute's purpose was not germane to the bill to which it was attached.

We have reviewed Morissette's second supplemental brief and find that it fails to show that the alleged violation prejudiced his substantial rights. Considering this, and in keeping with the plethora of case law finding the subject statute to be constitutionally sufficient, we hold that Morissette has waived this argument on appeal by failing to raise it at sentencing and in his post-trial motion. (*See, People v. Visnack* (1985), 135 Ill.App.3d 113, 118, 89 Ill.Dec. 901, 904, 481 N.E.2d 744, 747.) Therefore, further consideration of this argument is unwarranted.

VOLUME II
SUPPLEMENT

STATE POWER AND ITS LIMITS

VOLUME II

CHAPTER 1 LIMITS ON STATE POWERS IN PRISONS

Introductions to these sections have frequently commented on the conflict between the mythical and realistic views of prisons. Increasingly, courts have begun to declare that some practices in the administration of a prison are prohibited by the constitutional protection against cruel and unusual punishment. Where relief is necessary, courts can step in to remedy violations. In furtherance of this purpose, courts have appointed monitors to oversee reforms in the prisons. The reality of prison life, however, demands that in many situations the courts defer to those in authority with regard to the reasonableness of prison rules and conditions. An increasing number of such cases are reported, but the decision in *French v. Owens*, 777 F.2d 1250 (7th Cir. 1985), is a soundly reasoned opinion reviewing various conditions and standards required. The decision merits considerable study.

Another case included is *Cody v. Hillard*, 799 F.2d 447 (8th Cir. 1986), which discusses the problem of overcrowding in prisons, as does *Jackson v. Gardner*, 639 F.Supp. 1005 (E.D. Tenn. 1986).

The reader is also referred to *Williams v. Lane*, 646 F.Supp. 1379 (N.D. Ill. 1986), which is a finding by the district court of conditions in a prison under supervision of the court. The case is not included here.

Introductions in previous volumes:

II: 1; VI: 105; VII: 133; VIII: 217

Richard A. FRENCH, et al.,
Plaintiffs-Appellees,

v.

Norman G. OWENS, et al.,
Defendants-Appellants.

Richard A. FRENCH, et al.,
Plaintiffs-Appellees,

v.

Norman G. OWENS, et al.,
Defendants-Appellants,

United States of America,
Amicus Curiae.

Nos. 83-2280, 85-1065.

United States Court of Appeals,
Seventh Circuit.

Argued April 5, 1985.

Decided Nov. 26, 1985.

Rehearing and Rehearing En Banc
Denied Feb. 12, 1986.

Before CUDAHY and ESCHBACH, Circuit Judges, and MORTON, Senior District Judge.*

* The Honorable L. Clure Morton, Senior District Judge of the Middle District of Tennessee, sitting by designation.

CUDAHY, Circuit Judge.

This is an appeal from an order of the United States District Court for the Southern District of Indiana requiring extensive reforms at the Indiana Reformatory at Pendleton, Indiana. Defendants, officials of the Reformatory, allege on appeal that the court erred in finding constitutional violations and exceeded its authority in issuing a detailed injunction. We have reviewed the order and affirm most of its provisions. We vacate with respect to several provisions and remand to the district court for further consideration.

I.

Four prisoners at the Indiana Reformatory at Pendleton ("the Reformatory" or "Pendleton") filed a class action suit under 42 U.S.C. § 1983 on behalf of all persons who are or will be in the facility. The suit complained of overcrowding and of the prison's use of mechanical restraints. It protested poor medical care and food, inadequate recreation, discrimination against those in protective custody, insufficient safety personnel and noncompliance with fire and occupational safety standards. After a 16-day trial, the district judge, exercising his pendent jurisdiction, found that many of these conditions violated various provisions of Indiana law. He also found that the practice of double-celling, in concert with other overcrowded and unsanitary conditions, violated the eighth and fourteenth amendments of the United States Constitution. *French v. Owens*, 538 F.Supp. 910 (S.D.Ind.1982). Therefore, he issued a permanent injunction ordering detailed changes.

Defendants appealed. While the appeal was before this court, the Supreme Court decided *Pennhurst State School and Hospital v. Halderman*, 465 U.S. 89, 104 S.Ct.

900, 79 L.Ed.2d 67 (1984), which held that under the eleventh amendment, federal courts lacked jurisdiction over claims for injunctive relief against state officials based upon state law. In light of *Pennhurst*, we remanded this case to the district court so it could consider whether the conditions that it had found violated state law also violated federal law.

On remand, the court found that most of the conditions which violated state law, offended the eighth amendment as well. It therefore issued an amended order. That order also accounted for improvements that had been made at the facility over the two-year period since conditions had originally been considered.

Defendants again appeal. The United States has filed an amicus brief stating its position in detail on the various alleged violations and on the remedies prescribed.

II.

"In analyzing a challenge to prison conditions based on the Eighth Amendment, a court should examine each challenged condition of confinement ... to determine whether that condition is compatible with the 'evolving standards of decency that mark the progress of a maturing society.'" *Wright v. Rushen*, 642 F.2d 1129, 1133 (9th Cir.1981) (*quoting Trop v. Dulles*, 356 U.S. 86, 101, 78 S.Ct. 590, 598, 2 L.Ed.2d 630 (1958) (plurality opinion)). We therefore examine the specifics of Judge Dillin's order to determine if there have been violations of the eighth amendment and, if so, whether the remedy is appropriate.[1]

A. Double-Celling

Built in 1923, by 1982 the Pendleton reformatory housed almost 2,000 prisoners, over twice its intended capacity. To accommodate the rise in population, prison offi-

---

1. Judge Dillin offered an excellent and thorough description of conditions at Pendleton. *See French v. Owens*, 538 F.Supp. 910 (S.D.Ind. 1982). We, therefore, need not rehash the facts of the case at length but instead touch on them only as they are important in explaining our result.

cials placed two prisoners in cells that were intended for one. More than one-third of all cells were converted to double cells. After reviewing the record and personally visiting the prison site, Judge Dillin concluded that "rampant" double celling, in conjunction with general conditions of overcrowding, violated the eighth and fourteenth amendments.[2]

By 1982, the gross available space per man in the double cells was 24 square feet, the net amount approximately half that. In the Administrative Segregation Unit—where prisoners are kept who need to be separated from the general inmate population—the ceilings are lower and inmates on the top bunks of double cells are unable to sit up. There is no space for a chair on the floor. As a result, some have developed back problems.

The district court found that the forty per cent of prisoners in double cells spend large amounts of time together, up to 20 to 23 hours per day for the several hundred prisoners in protective custody or without work assignments.

Deplorable conditions exist beyond the double-celling problem. All cells and dormitories are inadequately ventilated. There is no means of distributing heat to the cells and, in summertime, no system for circulating air to the cells. Rooms are dirty and odorous. Toilets and lavatories are "virtually uncleanable." Lighting is poor. Cells have no hot water.

Especially in light of the poor supervision, safety, medical care and food preparation at the facility, Judge Dillin found the conditions intolerable. He ordered that the population be reduced to 1,615 and enjoined double celling.

As the district court acknowledged, the mere practice of double celling is not per se unconstitutional. In Rhodes v. Chapman, 452 U.S. 337, 101 S.Ct. 2392, 69 L.Ed.2d 59 (1981), the Supreme Court upheld its use in some instances. The institution at issue in Rhodes, however, was de-

scribed as a "top-flight, first class facility." Id. at 341, 101 S.Ct. at 2396. It had been built in the 1970s. Prisoners there shared double cells of 63 square feet, one-third larger than the cells at Pendleton. Each cell contained a night stand and shelf and radio unit. All cells had hot water. Similarly, this court upheld the use of double celling at the State Prison at Pontiac, Illinois in Smith v. Fairman, 690 F.2d 122 (1982), cert. denied, 461 U.S. 946, 103 S.Ct. 2125, 77 L.Ed.2d 1304 (1983). Pontiac's double cells ranged in size from 55 to 65 square feet, giving prisoners there 20 to 35 per cent more space than their Pendleton counterparts. Most of the cells at the Pontiac facility were "neat and clean" and much of the crowding in prisoners' cells was due to the inmates' books, records, stereos and electronic equipment. Food at Pontiac was found to be nutritious and wholesome. Violence had dramatically declined and medical care was found adequate.

While these institutions passed constitutional muster, the Rhodes court noted that prison conditions could be cruel and unusual when they "deprive inmates of the minimal civilized measure of life's necessities," 452 U.S. at 347, 101 S.Ct. at 2399, or when they result in punishments that " 'involve the unnecessary and wanton infliction of pain' or are grossly disproportionate to the severity of the crime." Id. at 346, 101 S.Ct. at 2399 (citations omitted).

In this circuit, we determine whether there have been "serious deprivations of basic human needs," id. at 347, 101 S.Ct. at 2399, by examining the "totality of conditions of confinement." Madyun v. Thompson, 657 F.2d 868, 874 (7th Cir. 1981). In this light, the picture painted of Pendleton is very different from that seen in Smith or Rhodes, from the lack of space and furnishings, to the unwholesome food, medical neglect and continuous threats to prisoners' safety. We agree that such conditions constitute cruel and unusual punishment. See Toussaint v. Yockey, 722 F.2d

---

2. The eighth amendment is applicable to the state through the fourteenth amendment. Rob-

inson v. California, 370 U.S. 660, 82 S.Ct. 1417, 8 L.Ed.2d 758 (1962).

1490, 1492 (9th Cir.1984) (injunction upheld against double celling where it "engender[s] violence, tension and psychological problems"); *Wellman v. Faulkner,* 715 F.2d 269 (7th Cir.1983), *cert. denied,* — U.S. ——, 104 S.Ct. 3587, 82 L.Ed.2d 885 (1984) (overcrowding can violate eighth amendment).

On appeal, defendants contend that even if the conditions were cruel and unusual, the district court's remedy was too broad. They assert that if the population is reduced, there should be no need to ban double celling.

At this time we disagree. The district court has broad powers to forge an adequate remedy to permanently correct any constitutional violation. As the Supreme Court has stated, "once a constitutional violation is demonstrated, the scope of the district court's equitable powers to remedy past wrongs is broad, for breadth is inherent in equitable remedies." *Swann v. Charlotte-Mecklenburg Board of Education,* 402 U.S. 1, 15, 91 S.Ct. 1267, 1275, 28 L.Ed.2d 554 (1971). Here, where there was narrowly cramped double celling as a feature of severely overcrowded, unsafe and unsanitary conditions, we cannot conclude that the district court exceeded its broad remedial power. Under present conditions, a complete ban on double celling is fully justified. However, since double celling is not *per se* unconstitutional, if the Indiana prison system eliminates the severe overcrowding at Pendleton and the pernicious evils that accompany it, the state can at a later date seek some modification of the ban on double celling. If adequate reasons were shown and overall conditions warrant, such a request would, of course, be entitled to consideration.

B. Mechanical Restraints

Plaintiffs also complained that the use of mechanical restraints at Pendleton was unconstitutional. Mechanical restraint was employed against those who threatened suicide or were physically disruptive. Between January 1980 and January 1982, mechanical restraint was used 84 times. Prisoners were often chained for between 12 and 24 hours, with instances recorded of up to 2½ days. Those restrained were usually chained spread-eagled to their bed, their limbs secured by hard shackles. Often they were stripped. Sometimes the mattress was removed from the bed frame. These prisoners were frequently denied the right to use the toilet and had to lie in their own filth. At least one prisoner suffered permanent nerve damage to his wrists from lying in shackles.

Appalled by this catalogue of inhumanities, the district court issued broad and detailed restrictions on the further use of hard shackles and ordered that mechanical restraint not be used as a form of punishment. It confined the use of restraint to the infirmary and allowed its use only when the superintendent of the prison or his substitute approved. The court required psychiatric approval for the use of restraint. The institution can restrain prisoners only for two hours before receiving the approval of a psychiatrist. During the period of restraint, trained medical personnel must constantly supervise the prisoner. Every 12 hours a psychiatrist must review the need for further restraint. Those in need of restraint beyond 24 hours must be sent to a psychiatric hospital. Inmates must be released at least every four hours to use the toilet and must be kept in proper clothing.

Defendants object that the district court based its conclusion on insufficient findings of fact and determinations of law and that the court's lengthy order was without authority because it restrained "the effective management of dangerous and violent offenders." (Defendant's brief at 33). We disagree.

The court was clearly within its right to enjoin such "outmoded and inhuman" practices. *Landman v. Royster,* 333 F.Supp. 621, 648 (E.D.Va.1971). The image of individuals shackled naked for days to a metal bed frame is a sad reminder of the "soul chilling inhumanity of conditions in America's prisons." *Rhodes v. Chapman,* 452 U.S. 337, 354, 101 S.Ct. 2392, 2403, 69 L.Ed.2d 59 (1981). While some form of temporary restraint may be necessary against those who pose a threat to themselves and others, Pendleton's methods are "too close to the rack and the screw to permit of constitutional differentiation." *Rochin v. California*, 342 U.S. 165, 172, 72 S.Ct. 205, 209, 96 L.Ed. 183 (1952). Other courts have found such practices to be cruel and unusual punishment. *See Stewart v. Rhodes*, 473 F.Supp. 1185, 1790–93 (S.D. Ohio 1979), *appeal dismissed* 661 F.2d 934 (6th Cir.1981); *Owens-el v. Robinson*, 442 F.Supp. 1368 (*modified* 457 F.Supp. 984 (W.D.Pa.1978)).

In dealing with detailed instances of brutality, we cannot say the district court exceeded its broad remedial authority in issuing a detailed injunction, especially where Indiana's efforts to explore alternatives seem lacking. *See Landman v. Royster, supra*, 333 F.Supp. at 648. *Cf. Wells v. Franzen*, 777 F.2d 1258 (7th Cir.1985) (violation of due process to restrain prisoner without the approval of a health professional and the taking of adequate health precautions). With respect to some of its specifics, however, we encourage the court at a proper time and in response to specific requests to allow for more flexibility. For example, if a psychiatrist is not immediately available, such as during the middle of the night, perhaps another qualified physician might approve the initial restraint. On the whole, however, Judge Dillin's order prescribes the necessary initial steps for curbing an obnoxious practice. As experience is gained under a properly regulated regime, the district court may permit modifications which seem fully justified by the circumstances.

For example, the United States has urged that bed restraints be allowed elsewhere than in the infirmary. We think that the urgent need for proper control fully justifies the district court in restricting them to the infirmary at this time. But this restriction might prove unnecessary under some future conditions.

C. Medical Care

As the population at Pendleton skyrocketed, the quality of medical care declined. The district court found the institution severely understaffed. Between 1978 and 1982, the population increased by 62 per cent but the number of physicians affiliated with the facility dropped, as did the number of mental health personnel. While there are over 190 requests for medical care per day, there is only one full-time physician, who speaks little English. Inmates in need of medical help get between one and ten minutes each for evaluation and treatment. As would be expected, there are numerous instances of neglect, misdiagnosis and maltreatment. One patient had tuberculosis that went undiagnosed, another had a broken back that went untreated, a third had an abscessed rectum that went unattended for six months.

"When a state imposes imprisonment as a punishment for a crime, it accepts the obligation to provide persons in its custody with a medical care system that meets minimal standards of adequacy." *Wellman v. Faulkner*, 715 F.2d 269, 271 (7th Cir.1983), *cert. denied*, —— U.S. ——, 104 S.Ct. 3587, 82 L.Ed.2d 885 (1984). The Supreme Court had ruled that the eighth amendment is violated by "deliberate indifference to serious medical needs of prisoners." *Estelle v. Gamble*, 429 U.S. 97, 104, 97 S.Ct. 285, 291, 50 L.Ed.2d 251 (1976). Such indifference may be evinced by "repeated examples of negligent acts which disclose a pattern of conduct by the prison medical staff" or by showing "systematic or gross deficiencies in staffing, facilities, equipment or procedures." *Ramos v. Lamm*, 639 F.2d 559, 575 (10th Cir.1980) (citation omitted), *cert. denied*, 450 U.S. 1041, 101 S.Ct. 1759, 68 L.Ed.2d 239 (1981); *Wellman, supra*, 715 F.2d, at 272. Under either criterion, Pendleton's medical services fall short of accepted standards.

After finding an eighth amendment violation, Judge Dillin ordered a comprehensive overhaul of Pendleton's medical staff. He ordered the appointment of an additional full-time physician, required that there be 5 physician's assistants, a hospital administrator, and a full-time pharmacist. To improve mental health services, Judge Dillin mandated that there be one psychiatrist, two psychiatric social workers, a clinical psychologist and two behavioral clinicians. He also required the appointment of 9 medical technicians and two typists and specified that all medical personnel must be able to speak English.

The United States as amicus objects that detailed medical reforms and other modifications ordered at the facility may not be necessary if population is reduced and argues that the state should have been allowed to submit a plan for reform. While we hesitate to tell the state of Indiana in painstaking detail how to staff the health departments of its prisons, Judge Dillin was within his power in drafting a detailed remedy to curb egregious neglect and mismanagement. Here, too, however, every element of the injunction need not be writ in stone. As the population declines and food, ventilation, sanitation and safety improve, the medical needs of the prisoners may change. To account for such changes, prison officials should be encouraged to report periodically to the district court to determine if modifications of the order are necessary. These reports should provide, *inter alia*, suitable indicia of the demand for services, the rate of utilization of services and the quality of services. Based on such reports, the district court may lower the manning requirements or even abrogate those requirements entirely if those steps would be consistent with a continuing guarantee of constitutional rights.

D. Kitchen Facilities

As the Tenth Circuit noted in *Ramos v. Lamm, supra*, 639 F.2d at 570–71, "the state must provide an inmate with a 'healthy, habitable environment.' This includes providing nutritionally adequate food that is prepared and served under conditions which do not present an immediate danger to the health and well being of the inmates who consume it." The district court found the state in violation of these

standards. The kitchen, commissary and food storage areas were unsanitary and infested with mice and roaches. The floor was found uncleanable due to holes, cracks, crevices, missing tile and gross porosity. Some of the ceiling was missing. Pots and pans were covered with uncleanable grime. Little attention was paid to special diets.

While conditions at the time of filing suit were grossly inadequate, the district court noted that the state allocated $2 million to rehabilitate the kitchen facility. The court therefore issued a general directive requiring that the kitchen be maintained to provide inmates with safe, sanitary and nutritious food. We approve fully of the district court's action.

E. Exercise and Recreation

The district court ordered that prisoners be permitted to engage in at least 90 minutes per day of "meaningful recreation." In so ruling, we believe the court overstepped its bounds. The general population gets 90 minutes of outdoor exercise during good weather. The Pendleton facility has 2 baseball diamonds, handball, volleyball and basketball courts, a football field, a jogging area and a horseshoe pit. In inclement weather, the prisoners exercise indoors in the fieldhouse, which is equipped with sporting goods and a small gym and has a television set. Judge Dillin objected to the time spent in the indoor gym because it was cramped and noisy. He also objected to the treatment of those in Administrative Segregation. These individuals get 2½ hours of exercise twice a week and spend approximately one hour each week in commissary. The judge found that these prisoners receive insufficient daily exercise.

Lack of exercise may certainly rise to a constitutional violation. Where movement is denied and muscles are allowed to atrophy, the health of the individual is threatened and the state's constitutional obligation is compromised. In *Preston v. Thompson*, 589 F.2d 300 (7th Cir.1978), for example, this court found a violation where prisoners were never allowed out of their cells to exercise. Similarly, in *Spain v.*

Procunier, 600 F.2d 189, 199 (9th Cir.1979), the court found it an eighth amendment violation to completely deny some prisoners exercise and to limit the remaining population to less than five hours indoor exercise per week.

However, we cannot say that the prisoners here are denied "the minimal civilized measure of life's necessities" merely because during some periods they cannot hear the television. Nor can we call it a "wanton and unnecessary infliction of pain" to have to exercise in cramped quarters. Even those within the Administrative Segregation Unit are allowed exercise periods within the constitutional minimum. *See Bono v. Saxbe,* 620 F.2d 609, 613 (7th Cir.1980).

F. Protective Custody

Plaintiffs complained that those prisoners who were confined in protective custody did not have equal access to the same vocational, academic and rehabilitation programs as those in the general prison population. In its second opinion, the district court agreed with defendants that the failure to provide such programs did not constitute cruel and unusual punishment, *see French v. Owens,* Mem. No. IP–75–677–C (S.D.Ind. Dec. 14, 1984); *see also Rhodes v. Chapman,* 452 U.S. 337, 348, 101 S.Ct. 2392, 2400, 69 L.Ed.2d 59 (1982) (deprivations of jobs and educational programs "simply are not punishment"), *Madyun v. Thompson,* 657 F.2d 868, 874 (7th Cir. 1981); *French v. Heyne,* 547 F.2d 994, 1002 (7th Cir.1976), but nonetheless ordered that the same programs must be provided to protective custody inmates as to others. It stated that "providing access to rehabilitative programs to general population inmates while denying access to such programs to inmates segregated for nondisciplinary reasons may constitute a violation of the Equal Protection Clause of the Fourteenth Amendment." *French v. Owens,* Mem. op. at 14. The court concluded that treating protective custody inmates differently did not serve any rational interest when the state created conditions necessi-

tating the widespread use of protective custody.

[5] We cannot accept the district court's rationale. This circuit has previously held that security reasons justify limiting the access of prisoners in protective custody to rehabilitative programs. *See Bono v. Saxbe, supra,* 620 F.2d at 615; *Cf. Lock v. Jenkins,* 641 F.2d 488, 494 (7th Cir.1981) ("Prisoners selecting placement in the [protective custody] unit, generally to avoid perceived dangers to themselves, also logically must be subject to significant restrictions."). Neither *Bono* nor *Lock* suggests that limitations on protective custody inmates do not apply when the state creates conditions that increase reliance on protective custody. In urging such an exception to this court's prior rulings, Judge Dillin has, we believe, undermined the state's ability to operate an effective protective custody program. Some argument can always be made that prison conditions have contributed to the violent tendencies that require one prisoner to be locked up to protect him from others and another to be locked up to protect others from him. As the court concluded in *Allgood v. Morris,* 724 F.2d 1098, 1100–01 (4th Cir.1984):

> The rationality of a distinction between privileges for prisoners in the general population and those in protective custody goes to the fundamental purpose of such segregation. Protective segregation is offered to inmates for their safety, the safety of others in confinement, and to insure institutional security and order. To allow prisoners in protective custody to enjoy all of the same privileges to the same degree as those in the general population would eviscerate the nature of protective segregation. Because the differences in treatment among prisoners in protective segregation and the general population has a substantial, rational basis in the legitimate state interest of prison security, we hold that Allgood's rights to equal protection have not been abridged.

Accordingly, we disapprove the court's order regarding protective custody. Of course, this should not discourage the state from providing such rehabilitative programs as are feasible within the limitations of the protective custody program.

G. Correction Officers

While some instances of violence unfortunately may be expected in America's prisons, the record in this case details countless examples of abhorrent beatings and wicked acts. As the district court found, "security of inmates from physical attacks by other inmates is a problem at the Reformatory. Severe forms of violence, including stabbings, bludgeonings, and homosexual rapes, occur with distressing frequency. A number of these instances have resulted in fatalities. Lesser forms of violence, such as harassment, threats, intimidation, striking and beating may be said to be routine." One prisoner was doused with lighter fluid by an inmate attempting to set him aflame. Another was bludgeoned with a 10 pound can opener. A 15 year old youth was raped at knifepoint by a group of inmates.

The constitution cannot countenance such widespread abuses. "The right to personal security constitutes an 'historic liberty interest' protected by the due process clause. *Ingraham v. Wright*, 430 U.S. 651, 673, 97 S.Ct. 1401, 1413, 51 L.Ed.2d 711 (1977). And that right is not extinguished by lawful confinement, even for penal purposes." *Youngberg v. Romeo*, 457 U.S. 307, 315, 102 S.Ct. 2452, 2458, 73 L.Ed.2d 28 (1982). As this circuit has noted, the eighth amendment is violated when attacks occur so frequently as to be "pervasive," *Walsh v. Brewer*, 733 F.2d 473, 475 (7th Cir.1984). The district court so found and its order requiring the state to submit a plan to employ and train sufficient security personnel to ensure the inmates safety is without question reasonable and legitimate.

H. Fire and Safety Violations

Plaintiffs, finally, complain that the Pendleton Reformatory does not meet the constitution's required standards for fire safety or for safety in work areas. The plain-

tiffs alleged that electrical wiring was not properly maintained, that there were inadequate fire exists, and that the facility had no established procedures to respond to fires. (Plaintiffs' Supplemental Brief at 33–37). They noted that paper articles were stored in boiler rooms and that solvents were stored near flames. The district court found numerous violations of the Indiana State Fire Regulations. It found these violations constitutionally unacceptable and ordered that "to secure compliance with the personal safety requirements of the eighth and fourteenth amendments, the defendants shall bring all buildings into compliance with the standards of the Indiana State Fire Marshal." *French v. Owens*, Amended Order No. IP 75–677–C, at 5 (S.D.Ind. Dec. 14, 1984).

Plaintiffs also charged that the work areas had improper ventilation, that prisoners were exposed to lethal fumes and fluids, that power tools lacked safety guards and that there was inadequate eye protection. The district court, using Federal OSHA standards as a guide, agreed that these conditions were constitutionally defective. It therefore ordered full compliance with OSHA regulations.

There is no question that fire and occupational safety are legitimate concerns under the eighth amendment. *Santana v. Collazo*, 714 F.2d 1172, 1183 (1st Cir.1983), *cert. denied*, — U.S. —, 104 S.Ct. 2352, 80 L.Ed.2d 825 (1984); *Leeds v. Watson*, 630 F.2d 674, 675 (9th Cir.1980). However, "not every deviation from ideally safe conditions constitutes a violation of the constitution." *Ruiz v. Estelle*, 679 F.2d 1115, 1152–53. *See Santana, supra*, 714 F.2d at 1183. The eighth amendment does not constitutionalize the Indiana Fire Code. Nor does it require complete compliance with the numerous OSHA regulations. "The district judge may consider these standards, but must order the correction of specific violations and may require only that these corrections bring the conditions above constitutional minima." *Hoptowit v. Ray*, 682 F.2d 1237 (9th Cir.1982). While fire and occupational safety no doubt need improvement at Pendleton, the district court erred in requiring compliance with specific administrative requirements to remedy those defects. On remand, the district court should reconsider these matters and require specific corrections of conditions to meet constitutional standards.

ble celling, mechanical restraints, medical care, kitchen services and correction officers is therefore affirmed. The judgment to the extent it pertains to exercise and recreation, protective custody and fire and occupational safety is vacated and remanded to the district court for further proceedings not inconsistent with this opinion.

III.

The judgment of the district court insofar as it pertains to overcrowding and dou-

AFFIRMED IN PART; VACATED AND REMANDED IN PART.

William R. CODY, individually and on behalf of all other persons similarly situated, Appellees,

v.

Carole HILLARD, President of the Board of Charities and Corrections; Frank Brost, Vice President; Ted Spaulding, Member; D.A. Gehlhoff, Member; Lyle Swenson, Member; James Smith, Executive Secretary; Herman Solem, Warden of the South Dakota State Penitentiary; sued individually and in their official capacities, Appellants.

William R. CODY, Individually and on behalf of all other persons similarly situated, LaVerne Koenig, member, Protective Custody Plaintiffs, Appellant,

v.

Carole HILLARD, President of the Board of Charities and Corrections; Frank Brost, Vice President; Ted Spaulding; D.A. Gehloff, Member; Lyle Swenson, Member; James Smith, Executive Secretary; Herman Solem, Warden of the South Dakota State Penitentiary; sued individually and in their official capacities, Appellees.

Nos. 85–5270, 85–5302.

United States Court of Appeals, Eighth Circuit.

Submitted Feb. 13, 1986.

Decided Sept. 2, 1986.

Rehearing Granted Oct. 28, 1986.*

Before HEANEY and BOWMAN, Circuit Judges, and HANSON,* Senior District Judge.

HEANEY, Circuit Judge.

This is an appeal from an order of the district court requiring officials at the South Dakota State Penitentiary (SDSP) to cease double celling inmates at SDSP, both in the general population and in protective custody. On appeal, the officials contend that the trial court erred in finding that double-celling inmates at SDSP violates the Eighth and Fourteenth Amendments to the United States Constitution. They also claim the court erred in using the "rated capacities" of the American Corrections Association as a referent for measuring constitutional violations. Protective custody inmates cross-appeal claiming that they are treated differently from inmates in the general population in violation of equal protection guarantees. We affirm.

BACKGROUND

William R. Cody filed this class action suit under 42 U.S.C. § 1983 on behalf of all persons who are now or will be incarcerated in the South Dakota State Penitentiary at Sioux Falls, South Dakota or in the Women's Correctional Facility at Yankton, South Dakota. Cody complained of overcrowding and living conditions hazardous

---

* See 8th Cir., 804 F.2d 440.

* The Honorable William C. Hanson, Senior United States District Judge for the Northern and Southern Districts of Iowa, sitting by designation.

to the health of the inmates. He protested, among other things, poor medical care, inadequate recreation, contaminated food, and noncompliance with fire safety standards. After an eleven day trial, the district court found that many of these conditions violated the eighth and fourteenth amendments to the United States Constitution. The trial court ordered the prison officials to prepare plans to cure the constitutional violations, which prison officials submitted by the summer of 1985. After extensive negotiation, the parties entered into a consent decree covering certain improvements to be made at the SDSP.

Following a hearing on July 8, 1985, the trial court entered the partial consent decree, and a second judgment on the remaining contested issues, which is the subject of this appeal. It ordered: 1) That except in the case of certain emergencies, the daily population of the SDSP be reduced in compliance with a schedule aimed at reducing the population to 95% of that specified by the American Corrections Association (ACA) as the capacity of SDSP; 2) that SDSP will stop double-celling inmates in protective custody; and 3) further improvements in health services. The state appeals orders one and two which concern double-celling.

On appeal, the officials claim that they have already ended the practice of double-celling general population inmates and have greatly reduced the double-celling of protective custody inmates, but they do not believe this is required by the Constitution, and they want to retain the flexibility to double-cell, if necessary, in the future. They also claim that the district court erred in requiring them to comply with American Correctional Association guidelines for setting prison population maximums.

1. The physical plant, built in the early 1970s, was "unquestionably a top-flight, first-class facility." *Rhodes,* 452 U.S. at 341, 101 S.Ct. at 2396. The cells there averaged sixty-three square feet and contained a cabinet-type night stand, a shelf and radio built into the wall, a wall-mounted sink with hot and cold running water and a

DISCUSSION

The Eighth Amendment to the United States Constitution prohibits cruel and unusual punishment. In *Rhodes v. Chapman,* 452 U.S. 337, 101 S.Ct. 2392, 69 L.Ed.2d 59 (1981), the Supreme Court considered for the first time the limitation that the eighth amendment imposes upon the conditions in which a state may confine those convicted of crimes. The Court stated that conditions of confinement "must not involve the wanton and unnecessary infliction of pain, nor may they be grossly disproportionate to the severity of the crime warranting imprisonment." *Rhodes,* 452 U.S. at 347, 101 S.Ct. at 2399.

The *Rhodes* Court specifically considered whether double-celling at an Ohio prison constituted cruel and unusual punishment. The Court held that in light of the otherwise exceptionally good conditions of confinement at the institution,[1] double-celling was not unconstitutional because it "did not lead to deprivations of essential food, medical care, or sanitation. Nor did it increase violence among inmates or create other conditions intolerable for prison confinement." *Rhodes,* 452 U.S. at 348, 101 S.Ct. at 2400. Thus, in determining whether prison conditions such as double-celling violate the eighth amendment, courts must consider all of the circumstances surrounding the conditions of confinement.

Applying this test, we affirm the district court's holding that SDSP's practice of double-celling, in light of the numerous deficient conditions of confinement at the prison, constitutes a violation of the eighth amendment under *Rhodes.* We point out that the prison officials did not appeal from the district court's detailed findings of deficient conditions at SDSP. Accordingly, in assessing SDSP's appeal of the double-celling orders, we accept as true

flush toilet. All cells had a heating and air circulation vent near the ceiling and more than half of them had a window that the inmates could open and close. All cells used to house two inmates were equipped with two-tiered bunk beds. Medical, food and other services were good.

the district court's findings as to the conditions at SDSP.

At the time of trial, the SDSP housed 538 general population inmates in 440 single occupancy cells. One hundred and ninety-six inmates were doubled up. The cells ranged in size from fifty-five square feet to sixty-three square feet. Some of the cells lacked adequate ventilation, and other cells lacked running hot water. The electrical wiring in the cells is substandard.

The court found that fire safety measures are inadequate: exit doors insufficient, night staff insufficient to respond in an emergency, ventilation inadequate, no fire alarm system, sprinkling system, or automatic unlocking device for the cells doors, and that there were plastic pipes throughout the prison with the potential to emit toxic vapors during a fire. The court further found that kitchen conditions are unsanitary and unsafe, including an inadequate milk pastuerization procedure, improper storage of canned goods and uncleanable dishes and pots. Additionally, medical and dental care available to prisoners is grossly inadequate. The medical and dental units are understaffed, and SDSP resorts to the use of untrained inmates to examine and x-ray patients.

The district court also made findings as to the impact of double-celling on the inmates, which SDSP officials again have not appealed from. The court found that:

Double-celling at the SDSP has resulted in crisis management with respect to the maintenance of ancillary support facilities such as food services, laundry services, medical services, plumbing and electrical wiring.

Double-celling at the SDSP has resulted in an overloading of services such as the work, recreation and school programs.

Since the advent of double-celling in the first part of 1981, there has been one recorded instance of a riot involving approximately twenty persons in November, 1981, and approximately sixty incidents * * * of fighting or assaults between inmates and/or inmates and staff.

The SDSP is grossly under-staffed. The level of prison staff has not increased in proportion to the level of the general inmate population.

Cody v. Hillard, 599 F.Supp. 1025, 1033 (D.S.D.1984).

Moreover, the court found that double-celling creates a serious potential for the spread of communicable diseases due to cramped living spaces and an increased potential for inmates to contact upper respiratory diseases.

We now turn to the district court's findings with respect to protective custody inmates. Out of forty-five inmates housed in protective custody at the SDSP, twenty-two were double-celled. The district court found that "[t]he negative impact attributed to double-celling in other areas of the institution is exacerbated in the protective custody area due to the inordinately limited out-of-cell time available to these inmates." *Cody,* 599 F.Supp. at 1034.

In light of the uncontested findings of fact that we have summarized, we conclude that the district court did not err in banning double-celling both in the general population and in protective custody cells. The facts found serve as an adequate basis to constitutionally require more space for inmates, not only to improve the health and safety conditions for the inmates, but to enhance security and to reduce violence. Our finding is supported by numerous decisions holding double-celling unconstitutional where there are other serious deficiencies in the conditions of confinement. *See e.g., French v. Owens,* 777 F.2d 1250, 1252 (7th Cir.1985), (Seventh Circuit upheld a ban on double-celling "in light of the poor supervision, safety, medical care and food preparation at the facility[.]"); *Toussaint v. Yockey,* 722 F.2d 1490, 1492 (9th Cir. 1984) (injunction upheld against double-celling where it "engenders violence, tension and psychological problems"); *Wellman v. Faulkner,* 715 F.2d 269 (7th Cir.1983), *cert. denied,* 468 U.S. 1217, 104 S.Ct. 3587, 82 L.Ed.2d 885 (1984) (overcrowding can violate eighth amendment).

The SDSP, like the institutions at issue in *French, Toussaint,* and *Wellman,* is very different from the prison under scrutiny in *Rhodes.* It is anything but "a top flight institution," and the horrible conditions are greatly exacerbated by double-celling of inmates.

In so holding, we do not intimate that the order banning double-celling cannot be modified in the future. Prison officials apparently have submitted progress reports—which are not part of the record on this appeal—alleging that improvements have been made at the SDSP. Prison officials should apply to the district court for an evidentiary hearing to determine the extent of the improvements. Upon a proper showing, the district court may determine that the ban on double-celling is no longer justified.

Finally, the state attacks the district court's use of the ACA standards for prison capacity as the guidelines for constitutional requirements. It is true that *Rhodes v. Chapman,* suggested that district courts refrain from overreliance on expert opinions on prison capacity. However, the Court did not prohibit such consideration and several post-*Rhodes* decisions have approved the use of such guidelines as the ACA guidelines where the conclusions therein are supported by other independent evidence. *See e.g., Touissaint,* 722 F.2d 1490 (9th Cir.1984). The district court's use of these guidelines is appropriate in light of its detailed factual findings, based on a wide-range of evidence.

The final issue on appeal is the cross-appeal by the protective custody inmates. They claim that the ban on double-celling is not enough and that they are entitled to additional relief such as more exercise time. Their argument essentially is that conditions in the protective custody unit are not as good as conditions in the general population units and that this violates their rights to equal protection. We have previously stated that "[t]o succeed on an equal protection claim the [protective custody inmates are] required to show that they received treatment which was invid-

iously dissimilar to that received by other inmates." *Lyon v. Farrier,* 730 F.2d 525, 527 (8th Cir.1984). We conclude that the cross-appellants have made no such showing.

BOWMAN, Circuit Judge, concurring in part and dissenting in part.

I concur only in the Court's holding concerning the cross-appeal by the protective custody inmates. The remainder of the Court's decision, in my view, both "wrench[es] the Eighth Amendment from its language and history," *Rhodes v. Chapman,* 452 U.S. 337, 348, 101 S.Ct. 2392, 2400, 69 L.Ed.2d 59 (1981), and engages in analysis directly foreclosed by Supreme Court precedent. I respectfully dissent.

Initially, I believe a more complete exposition of Eighth Amendment standards is necessary than the Court's opinion provides. In *Rhodes,* the Supreme Court stated that "when the conditions of confinement compose the punishment at issue," those conditions "must not involve the wanton and unnecessary infliction of pain, nor may they be grossly disproportionate to the severity of the crime warranting imprisonment." *Id.* at 347, 101 S.Ct. at 2399. The Court referred to conditions that are "totally without penological justification," *Gregg v. Georgia,* 428 U.S. 153, 183, 96 S.Ct. 2909, 2930, 49 L.Ed.2d 859 (1976), as the kind of conditions that violate the Eighth Amendment. 452 U.S. at 346, 101 S.Ct. at 2399. Recently, the Court elaborated further on this standard in *Whitley v. Albers,* — U.S. —, 106 S.Ct. 1078, 89 L.Ed.2d 251 (1986). Justice O'Connor, writing for the Court, observed that "[i]t is obduracy and wantonness, not inadvertence or error in good faith, that characterize the conduct prohibited by the Cruel and Unusual Punishments Clause, whether that conduct occurs in connection with establishing conditions of confinement, supplying medical needs, or restoring official control over a tumultuous cellblock." *Id.* at 1084.

The Eighth Amendment leaves very broad latitude to the states in the administration of their prisons. "[C]onditions that cannot be said to be cruel and unusual under contemporary standards are not unconstitutional. To the extent that such conditions are restrictive and even harsh, they are part of the penalty that criminal offenders pay for their offenses against society." *Rhodes*, 452 U.S. at 347, 101 S.Ct. at 2399. Moreover, the federal courts traditionally

> have adopted a broad hands-off attitude toward problems of prison administration. In part this policy is the product of various limitations on the scope of federal review of conditions in state penal institutions. More fundamentally, this attitude springs from complementary perceptions about the nature of the problems and the efficacy of judicial intervention. Prison administrators are responsible for maintaining internal order and discipline, for securing their institutions against unauthorized access or escape, and for rehabilitating, to the extent that human nature and inadequate resources allow, the inmates placed in their custody. The Herculean obstacles to effective discharge of these duties are too apparent to warrant explication. Suffice it to say that the problems of prisons in America are complex and intractable, and, more to the point, they are not readily susceptible of resolution by decree. Most require expertise, comprehensive planning, and the commitment of resources, all of which are peculiarly within the province of the legislative and executive branches of government. For all of those reasons, courts are ill equipped to deal with the increasingly urgent problems of prison administration and reform. Judicial recognition of that fact reflects no more than a healthy sense of realism. Moreover, where state penal institutions are involved, federal courts have a further reason for deference to the appropriate prison authorities.

Procunier v. Martinez, 416 U.S. 396, 404–05, 94 S.Ct. 1800, 1807, 40 L.Ed.2d 224 (1974). All of these observations aptly fit this case.

Even granting that the District Court's factual findings are correct, I do not agree that double-celling at SDSP evidences the "obduracy and wantonness" necessary to constitute a violation of the Eighth Amendment. Double-celling at SDSP is not "totally without penological justification." *Rhodes*, 452 U.S. at 346, 101 S.Ct. at 2399 (quoting *Gregg*, 428 U.S. at 183, 96 S.Ct. at 2929). While double-celling may not be desirable, it allows the continued detention of persons convicted of serious crimes when they might otherwise have to be released at the peril of law-abiding members of our society. As the Court's opinion notes, double-celling would be cruel and unusual punishment under *Rhodes* only if the double-celling "[led] to deprivations of essential food, medical care, or sanitation" or if it "increase[d] violence among inmates or create[d] other conditions intolerable for prison confinement." 452 U.S. at 348, 101 S.Ct. at 2400. In my judgment, the record in this case falls far short of supporting the Court's conclusion that the line drawn by *Rhodes* has been crossed by double-celling at SDSP. Accordingly, I believe there is no constitutional basis for the remedial order that the Court today affirms.

The District Court's final order provides that

> in the event that the daily population of the SDSP, other than Protective Custody inmates, shall exceed 95% of total American Corrections Association (ACA) rated capacities for 60 consecutive days, the defendants shall commence to develop programs to reduce that population; if such population shall exceed 110% of such ACA capacities for 60 consecutive days, the State within 180 days shall reduce said population to 95% of the total ACA capacities of these facilities; provided, however, that days during which populations may exceed these percentages as a consequence of riot, fire, acts of God, labor unrest, war, civil disturbance, or any other emergencies shall be excluded in applying the foregoing.

Cody v. Hillard, Civ. No. 80–4039, at 1–2 (D.S.D. July 8, 1985) (Final Order). This order could not conceivably be proper unless the ACA standards relied upon by the District Court represented the constitutional norm. But the Supreme Court explicitly has rejected this approach. In *Bell v. Wolfish*, the Court stated that "while the recommendations of these various groups [such as ACA] may be instructive in certain cases, they simply do not establish the constitutional minima; rather, they establish goals recommended by the organization in question." 441 U.S. 520, 543–44 n. 27, 99 S.Ct. 1861, 1876 n. 27, 60 L.Ed.2d 447 (1979). In *Rhodes*, the Court quoted the foregoing statement from *Wolfish* and further observed in regard to Eighth Amendment claims that

> generalized opinions of experts cannot weigh as heavily in determining contemporary standards of decency as "the public attitude toward a given sanction." We could agree that double celling is not desirable, especially in view of the size of these cells. But there is no evidence in this case that double celling is viewed generally as violating decency.

452 U.S. at 348–49 n. 13, 101 S.Ct. at 2400 n. 13. Contrary to this clear instruction from the Supreme Court, the order of the District Court effectively transforms the ACA standards into Constitutional requisites under the Eighth Amendment, and it does so without a shred of evidence for the counter-intuitive proposition that double-celling is viewed generally as violating decency. Thus, it is apparent that neither the District Court nor our Court has properly applied the Constitutional standards to the facts of this case.

The District Court found that "[d]ouble-celling over time has a negative impact on all programs and services" and "has resulted in crisis management with respect to the maintenance of ancillary support facilities such as food services, laundry services, medical services, plumbing and electrical wiring." *Cody v. Hillard*, 599 F.Supp. 1025, 1033 (D.S.D. 1984). The District Court detailed such problems in these areas as unsanitary practices in storing and preparing food, the use of untrained inmates to provide medical services to other inmates, inadequate ventilation and plumbing, and substandard electrical wiring and other fire hazards. Whatever the merit of these findings, there has been no showing, and the District Court has made no finding, that the elimination of double-celling will alleviate these problems to any perceptible degree. An appropriate remedy would relate to correction of the constitutionally deficient conditions that have been found to exist, if any there be, rather than to the elimination of double-celling.

The Court's opinion quotes with approval the District Court's finding that double-celling "has resulted in an overloading of services such as the work, recreation and school programs," *id.*, but never tells us why this matters for purposes of Eighth Amendment scrutiny. In fact, the Supreme Court dismissed precisely this sort of contention as a basis for finding cruel and unusual punishment in *Rhodes*, stating that "limited work hours and delay before receiving education do not inflict pain, much less unnecessary and wanton pain; deprivations of this kind simply are not punishments." 452 U.S. at 348, 101 S.Ct. at 2400.

The District Court found, as the Court's opinion notes, that "[s]ince the advent of double-celling in approximately the first part of 1981, there has been one recorded instance of a riot involving approximately twenty persons ... and approximately sixty incidents ... of fighting or assaults between inmates and/or inmates and staff." 599 F.Supp. at 1033. Prison violence is, of course, not a recent development and occurs with similar frequency in institutions that do not double-cell. There is nothing in the record to show the comparable number of incidents of violence at SDSP before and after double-celling. Accordingly, there is no evidentiary basis for a conclusion that double-celling has caused an increase in such incidents, and we note that the District Court did not make a finding on this question of fact.

The Court's opinion also is notable for those portions of the District Court opinion that it does not mention. No mention is made of the District Court's finding that "[t]here is a relatively low level of tension between inmates and staff at the SDSP." *Id.* at 1033. Nor does the Court discuss the District Court's findings that the level of sanitation at SDSP is adequate or that the prison administrators and staff have made sincere efforts to maintain a healthful environment. *Id.* at 1052. Similarly, the Court does not acknowledge the District Court's finding that the prison

administration has attempted to reduce the negative impact of double-celling by expanding the amount of out-of-cell time afforded inmates, by making a reasonable effort to double-cell only those inmates who volunteer to live with another inmate in the same cell, and by increasing the placement of inmates: (1) into trustee status in a detached unit of SDSP ...; (2) into trustee status in a unit located at the Human Services Center in Yankton; (3) into a detached dormitory, outside the walls of the prison, known as the "West Farm"; (4) into public service restitution programs in various communities in South Dakota.... The SDSP has also attempted to place inmates in work release or school release programs throughout the state.

Id. at 1033. As the District Court recognized, the prison administration is striving within the limits of available resources to limit the amount of double-celling that must be done to accommodate the rising tide of convicted felons. This hardly reflects "obduracy and wantonness" on the part of those whose job it is to manage SDSP. *See Whitley*, 106 S.Ct. at 1084.

I fail to comprehend how the conditions described in this record can be said to inflict pain or amount to punishment and how prison administrators making "sincere efforts" can be said not to be acting in "good faith." *Id.* at 1084. The present case is light years removed from the type of torture, deprivation, and sadistic punishment with which the Cruel and Unusual Punishments Clause is concerned. *See Hutto v. Finney*, 437 U.S. 678, 681–84 & nn. 3–6, 98 S.Ct. 2565, 2568–70 & nn. 3–6, 57 L.Ed.2d 522 (1978) (conditions included use of a

five-foot long leather strap to whip inmates for minor offenses, use of a device to administer "electrical shocks to various sensitive parts of an inmate's body," and use of inmate guards authorized to use deadly force against "escapees" and who therefore could "murder another inmate with practical impunity"). The lack of anything in this record even remotely approaching these conditions, or even remotely showing any conditions of confinement that fall below the Constitutional standards elucidated in cases such as *Rhodes* and *Whitley*, reveals the impropriety of the Court's action today.

Further, it seems to me that the incongruity of the order prohibiting double-celling of inmates who voluntarily have chosen to live together in the same cell should cause the Court to pause. The necessary implication from this feature of the order— that voluntary "double-bunking" constitutes "wanton and unnecessary infliction of pain" amounting to cruel and unusual punishment—is insupportable. What is worse, it trivializes the Constitution and mocks the purposes of the Eighth Amendment.

Finally, the District Court also enjoined the State from double-celling in the protective custody area of the prison. The court found that 22 out of 45 protective custody inmates were double-celled and concluded that this was "inappropriate and without correctional justification." 599 F.Supp. at 1034. The court further noted that "[t]hese inmates need protection not only from other inmates in the general population but also from other protective custody inmates" and concluded that the negative impact of double-celling was exacerbated for these inmates "due to the inordinately limited out-of-cell time available to these inmates." *Id.* I believe that the District Court here merely has substituted its "judgment for that of officials who have made a considered choice." *Whitley*, 106 S.Ct. at 1085. Whether an inmate in protective custody needs protection from someone with whom he is assigned to share a cell is a matter more appropriately left to the prison officials who are charged with making decisions of this nature. Courts should be mindful that our authority in such questions "spring[s] from constitutional requirements and that judicial answers to them must reflect that fact rather than a court's idea of how best to operate a detention facility." *Wolfish*, 441 U.S. at 539, 99 S.Ct. at 1874 (citations omitted). I have found nothing in the record or the District Court's findings of fact to persuade me that my views concerning double-celling generally should be different in regard to the protective custody area of the prison.

The record before us at most demonstrates that SDSP is not always comforta-

ble. As the Supreme Court noted in *Rhodes*, however, "the Constitution does not mandate comfortable prisons, and prisons of [SDSP's] type, which house persons convicted of serious crimes, cannot be free of discomfort. Thus, these considerations properly are weighed by the legislature and prison administration rather than a court." 452 U.S. at 349, 101 S.Ct. at 2400. Because I do not believe that double-celling in the circumstances presented by this record is violative of the Eighth Amendment, I would reverse the District Court's order with respect to double-celling.

Larry Warren JACKSON, et al.

v.

Sheriff Mike GARDNER and Lon
Boyd, County Executive.

No. CIV-2-84-263.

United States District Court,
E.D. Tennessee,
Northeastern Division.

July 2, 1986.

MEMORANDUM AND ORDERS

HULL, Chief Judge.

This is a 42 U.S.C. § 1983 case in which inmates of the Sullivan County Jail have challenged the constitutionality of the conditions of their confinement. By Order of April 4, 1986, this action was certified as a class action to be maintained on behalf of all inmates confined in the Sullivan County Jail and "workhouse". Through a series of pretrial and status conferences, discovery, and negotiation between the parties, the issues upon which proof needed to be taken were limited. Resolution of some of the conditions complained of occurred by way of settlement.[1] Other conditions have been admitted or stipulated as existing, leaving only the issues of overcrowding and fire safety for trial. Plaintiffs seek only injunctive relief in this action which came on for trial without intervention of a jury on June 25, 1986. After carefully considering the evidence in the record, the proof adduced at trial and the arguments and briefs of counsel, the Court makes the following findings of fact and conclusions of law:

The Sullivan County Jail houses both convicted inmates and pretrial detainees. As to pretrial detainees, "the proper inquiry is whether [the] conditions [of confinement] amount to punishment of the detainee." *Bell v. Wolfish*, 441 U.S. 520, 535, 99 S.Ct. 1861, 1872, 60 L.Ed.2d 447 (1979). One may not be "punished" in accordance with due process unless one has been adjudicated guilty of some offense. As to the convicted inmates, the appropriate standard is whether the conditions of confinement amount to cruel and unusual punishment.

The present Sullivan County Jail consists of a main facility adjacent to the Sullivan County Courthouse, and a smaller structure known as the "workhouse". The main facility is an antiquated[2] two-story structure which not only houses inmates, but provides office space for the Sullivan County Sheriff's Department. The "workhouse" is the old Sheriff's house. It is a two-story, mostly wood structure of some historical significance and a cause of great concern for seemingly everyone associated with Sullivan County principally because of fire safety concerns. The main facility con-

---

1. The defendants are to be credited for the many affirmative steps taken at the jail since the inception of this lawsuit.

2. This facility was built in 1955, but in terms of the demands placed upon it and the current standards in the field of corrections, it is sorely in need of renovation or replacement.

tains 122 bunks. The workhouse has 30 bunks. Total population at the jail as of the day of trial was 167. Obviously, there is a problem providing beds for all the inmates. According to the testimony of representative plaintiffs, inmates are often forced to sleep on the floors of the cells. Even when enough beds are available, the jail is still overcrowded.

Pictures of bunk areas in both the workhouse and the main facility reveal the fact that the Sullivan County Jail is unable to accommodate the number of prisoners for which they are responsible. There simply does not appear to be enough room for inmates to move about freely. Michael Jenkins, the state jail inspector from the Tennessee Corrections Institute [3] who has been responsible for inspection of the Sullivan County facility since 1981 testified that Sullivan County does not meet the State's minimum space requirement per inmate. The State requires the provision of at least 25 square feet per inmate. This requirement must be met, along with several others, for a county jail to receive state certification. The American Correctional Association's (A.C.A.) minimum standard is 60 square feet per inmate assuming that the inmate spends no more than ten hours per day locked into this area.[4] This was the minimum standard preferred by plaintiff's expert witness, Gordon Kamka, who possesses impressive credentials in the field of corrections management. The majority of those confined in Sullivan County live in cells which average little more than 20 square feet per inmate (this includes space in bunk areas and the adjoining day area) according to jail inspector Jenkins. This figure would decrease when the fact that the prisoners are locked into their bunk areas from approximately 9:00 p.m. to 7:00 a.m. is taken into consideration.

The cells in the main facility consist of three or four bunk areas side by side,

which open into a common "day area". The day area contains a shower, toilet, sink, table mounted on the wall (actually a counter), and a bench. Each bunk area also contains a toilet and sink; however, the bunk areas are so cramped that the toilet is only a few inches from one of the bottom bunks. Pictures of these areas introduced by the plaintiffs reveal living conditions which could fairly be described as deplorable. Jail Administrator Lynn Hawkins testified that cleaning supplies were available to the inmates, and that it was basically just up to them whether they lived in clean, sanitary cells or not. Although sanitation is one of the issues excluded from trial because of improvements developed during preliminary proceedings, the Court notes that inmate testimony contradicts that of Hawkins on the issue of availability of cleaning supplies. Hawkins testified that the availability of supplies was a policy, but that he did not personally oversee the distribution of such supplies. Whether cleaning supplies are available or not, the photographs introduced reveal conditions so decrepit that it would be nothing short of a major project to make the jail palatable from a sanitary and cleanliness standpoint. Moreover, the crowded conditions which force overuse of the facilities must inevitably diminish the appearance, cleanliness and functionability of the entire jail.

The Court recognizes the fact that many of the prisoners themselves are responsible for creating or exacerbating the unsightly conditions, but to a certain extent, when you confine that many people into that small a space, deterioration is inevitable over a period of time whether those so confined are deputy sheriffs or convicted felons. The squalid conditions of the Sullivan County Jail are even more offensive to notions of decency when one considers the

3. The Tennessee Corrections Institute (T.C.I.) is statutorily empowered to establish minimum standards for jails, inspect same, and establish and enforce procedures to insure compliance with the standards. T.C.A. § 41-4-140.

4. The T.C.I. standards are to "approximate, insofar as possible, those standards established by the inspector of jails, federal bureau of prisons, and by the American Correctional Association's Manual of Correctional Standards ..." T.C.A. § 41-4-140(a)(1).

fact that some prisoners are forced to sleep on the floor, and that most of the prisoners are kept in their cells twenty-four hours a day.

The Sullivan County Grand Jury which, as part of its duties to the County Court, inspects county facilities and makes recommendations, has found the present jail facilities to be substandard and mandated that conditions be improved "before a law suit and/or a federal judge forces construction of a new facility resulting in excessive cost." (Exhibit 18, Minutes of the Sullivan County Grand Jury filed December 4, 1984). Both the Grand Jury and the Sullivan County Jail inspection committee have recommended that the workhouse be closed because of its disrepair and the fire hazard it posed.

Those in the workhouse are misdemeanants or work release inmates, and are allowed some exposure to the outside and have some chance for recreation.[5] The majority however, are never exposed to fresh air and sunlight, have no chance for exercise or recreation, (save the push-ups and sit-ups that might be done in the cell), have no television and are allowed only one non-contact visit per week for fifteen minutes. The single weekly visit is limited to blood relatives. Inmates may have radios, but only with headphones. Lighting in the cells is substandard. Inadequate lighting has long been a complaint of prisoners in Sullivan County. Since the inception of this lawsuit, additional lighting has been added, however, there is no direct in-cell lighting. Mr. Kamka testified that the bunk areas of the cells were so dark that one could not even see the toilet until one's eyes adjusted to the darkness. Mr. Jenkins testified that the jail's lighting did not meet the minimum state requirements, but that he had not checked it since the additional lighting was installed.[6]

Until recently, very little had been done to provide for the safety of the inmates in the event of fire. The Sheriff had testified at previous proceedings that communicating fire escape routes to the inmates presented too great a security risk. There is no sprinkler system. There are no smoke detectors or heat detectors in the jail. A television surveillance system in the corridors serves to alert jail personnel to the presence of smoke. A December 10, 1985 fire safety inspection by the State Division of Fire Prevention found the jail to have ten deficiencies or hazardous conditions at that time. (Exhibit No. 24).

Improvements in fire safety have been made. Jail Administrator Hawkins testified at trial that they had posted fire escape routes, (although they may not have remained posted), that the jailers wore notched keys to facilitate release from the cells in the event of fire, that the escape routes were drawn on the floor of the jail from the cells to the outside, and that the jail personnel conducted fire drills once a month. These improvements have apparently been made since Mr. Jenkins' latest inspection of the jail September 4, 1985 which cited the jail for lack of fire drills, lack of a written evacuation plan, and lack of notched keys for emergency identification. The inspection reports also reveal other offensive conditions.

Inspection reports from as far back as 1977 were admitted into evidence and they reveal that the jail has had problems for several years with inoperable sinks, toilets, and showers, ventilation, lighting, sanitation, and lack of hot water for sinks and showers. Although ten years ago these problems may not have been of Constitutional significance, their significance has increased as the number of inmates has increased over the years. In the September 4, 1985 report it was noted that insects were clearly visible; that cell areas were

---

5. The workhouse contains only 4 square feet per inmate at a population of 30 inmates. Workhouse population often exceeds 30. Obviously, access to the outside is imperative under such circumstances.

6. The Court understands that the defendants could do little more, if any, to correct the lighting deficiency in the present facility without complete renovation and rewiring.

not adequately cleaned, thus posing a possible health problem; that sinks and toilets
were in need of cleaning and repair; that
no library service was provided; and, that
no record was kept of when mattresses
were disinfected. The March 1, 1984 inspection found sixteen sinks, five toilets
and one shower inoperable. The report
cited the jail for failure to disinfect mattresses quarterly and failure to launder
prisoner clothing twice a week. Of course,
these reports contain many other citations,
but not that relate as directly to the living
conditions imposed upon those imprisoned.
There is no storage available for personal
belongings, which results in their being
placed under the bottom bunks and/or generally strewn throughout the cells. The
inmates receive two meals a day and there
was some evidence that portions sometimes
ran short. If they have money, they can
buy vending machine items through the
trusties.

The inmates are basically idle and crowded together in their cells day and night.
This inevitably escalates the normal problem of inmate assaults upon one another as
well as upon jail personnel. Of course,
greater security problems, which arise with
increased numbers of inmates, necessitate
the imposition of more restrictive conditions. James Cody, who spent over 300
days in the jail, testified that being exposed
to the overcrowded, unsanitary, unsafe,
conditions 24 hours a day, day after day,
presented a "strain on your brain," and
engendered hostility and despair. Mr.
Kamka, whose experience in corrections is
complemented by a masters degree in psy-
chology, testified that the conditions he
observed at the jail would be stressful,

unsafe, hazardous, and debilitating on an
individual depending upon the length of
confinement.[7]

County jails are generally thought of as
short-term facilities with a population constantly under transition, but in Tennessee,
some convicted felons can be sentenced to
terms of up to six years in the county jail.
The representative plaintiffs in this action
spent anywhere from a few days to over a
year in the Sullivan County Jail. Thus,
exposure to the offensive conditions cannot
be considered minimal. The greater the
length of confinement, the more debilitating such conditions would be. Although
the jail population will constantly be in
transition, many of those incarcerated in
Sullivan County remain for several months.

The Court finds, from the facts outlined
above that the conditions of confinement at
the Sullivan County Jail violate the rights
of those confined to be free from cruel and
unusual punishment under the Eighth
Amendment.[8]

The primary cause of Sullivan County's
Constitutional violation is the overcrowding. However, it is not simply the
number of square feet per inmate which is
determinative,[9] the Court must look to the
totality of the circumstances in determining
whether a particular confinement violates
the Constitutional rights of an inmate.
Rhodes v. Chapman, 452 U.S. 337, 101
S.Ct. 2392, 69 L.Ed.2d 59 (1981); *Jones v.
Diamond*, 636 F.2d 1364 (5th Cir.1981);
Bradford v. Gardner, 578 F.Supp. 382
(E.D.Tenn.1984). This Court previously
considered the constitutionality of the living conditions of the Sullivan County Jail in
the *Bradford* case. *Id.* However, in that
case, the decision was limited to the condi-

---

7. *See, Campbell v. Cauthron*, 623 F.2d 503, 506
(8th Cir.1980) ("detrimental physical consequences of enforced idleness in a small living
space, and the negative effect of overcrowding
on prisoner's mental states is well documented....").

8. The Court's finding that the conditions of confinement amount to cruel and unusual punishment presupposes that those same conditions of
confinement violate the rights of pretrial detainees to be free from punishment without due

process of law. *See, Campbell v. Cauthron*, 623
F.2d 503 (8th Cir.1980).

9. "No static 'test' can exist by which courts determine whether conditions of confinement are
cruel and unusual...." *Rhodes v. Chapman*,
452 U.S. 337, 346, 101 S.Ct. 2392, 2399, 69
L.Ed.2d 59 (1981), *but see, Gates v. Collier*, 423
F.Supp. 732 (N.D.Miss.1976), *aff'd*, 578 F.2d
1241 (5th Cir.1977) ("50 sq. ft. of living space
per inmate is the minimal acceptable requirement to comport with the Constitution.")

tions of a single inmate and "the only serious constitutional question ... [was] whether the crowded sleeping quarters were *per se* unconstitutional." *Id.* at 383–384. In *Bradford*, this Court refused to impose a minimal square foot requirement in light of the Supreme Court's decision in *Rhodes v. Chapman.*

In the present case, the inquiry is into the totality of circumstances surrounding an inmate's confinement in the Sullivan County Jail, and involves not a single individual, but an entire class. Thus, the *Bradford* decision is of no precedential value in this case in regard to the determination of whether the conditions of confinement at the Sullivan County Jail are constitutional. Moreover, since conditions change over time, "the use of precedents as to prison conditions is suspect." *Kirby v. Blackledge*, 530 F.2d 583 (4th Cir.1976).

Whether prison conditions amount to cruel and unusual punishment must be determined " 'from the evolving standards of decency that mark the progress of a maturing society.' " *Rhodes v. Chapman, supra*, 452 U.S. at 346, 101 S.Ct. at 2399, *quoting, Trop v. Dulles*, 356 U.S. 86, 101, 78 S.Ct. 590, 598, 2 L.Ed.2d 630 (1958) (plurality opinion). It is by applying these "standards of decency" that the Court reached its opinion that the prison conditions at issue do violate the Eighth Amendment. In making this determination the Court relies upon the reports and suggestions of the Sullivan County Grand Jury, the reports and suggestions of the Sullivan County Grand Jury, the reports and suggestions of the Sullivan County Jail Com-

mittee, the reports and suggestions of Jail Inspector Jenkins, the expert testimony of Gordon Kamka, who characterized the jail as one of the three worst he has ever seen in his over twenty years in the field, the testimony of the representative plaintiffs, the T.C.I. and A.C.A. recommended standards, other exhibits admitted into evidence, the Court's own perception of decency and humane treatment, and similar decisions from other jurisdictions.[10]

It is neither the province, nor the desire of this Court to impose its views of how best to run a jail upon the officials of Sullivan County.[11] Such considerations are the responsibility of the legislative and executive branches of state and county governments, and must be accorded deference so long as they comport with constitutional requirements. However, when jail conditions run afoul of the Constitution, it is not only the province, but the duty of this Court to intervene.

In the present case, we are not dealing with policies and considerations which are properly left to the wisdom and discretion of jail administrators. We are not talking about peripheral issues such as whether inmates can receive the book-of-the-month in hardback, or must wait until it comes in paperback. We are dealing here with the bottom-line conditions of basic human existence. "Nothing less than the dignity of man" has been implicated by the offensive conditions of the Sullivan County Jail. *Trop v. Dulles*, 356 U.S. 86, 100, 78 S.Ct. 590, 597, 2 L.Ed.2d 630 (1958).

---

10. *E.g., Campbell v. Cauthron*, 623 F.2d 503 (8th Cir.1980) (17–26 square feet per inmate found unconstitutional); *Jordan v. Wolke*, 460 F.Supp. 1080 (E.D.Wisc.1978) (22½ square feet per inmate of cell space, plus 17 square feet per inmate of day room space found unconstitutional); *Rutherford v. Pitchess*, 457 F.Supp. 104 (C.D.CA 1978) (approximately 25 square feet per inmate approved given the frequent and substantial periods of time out of the cell); *Ahrens v. Thomas*, 434 F.Supp. 873 (W.D.Mo.1977) (10–12 square feet per inmate found unconstitutional, ordered new jail to provide 70 square feet per inmate); *Anderson v. Redman*, 429 F.Supp. 1105 (D.Del.1977) (Constitutional compliance re-

quired provision of 75 square feet per inmate); *Ambrose v. Malcolm*, 414 F.Supp. 485 (Constitutional compliance required provision of 75 square feet per inmate). *Compare, Delgado v. Cady*, 576 F.Supp. 1446 (E.D.Wisc.1983) (10–17 square feet not constitutionally inadequate where inmates allowed daily outdoor exercise, daily visitation and were out of cell anywhere from 2–12 hours per day).

11. *See, Bell v. Wolfish*, 441 U.S. 520 (1979) at 539, 540, 547, 548, 562, fn. 23, 29, 99 S.Ct. 1861, 1874, 1875, 1878, 1879, 1886, fn. 23, 29, 60 L.Ed.2d 447.

Simply crowding more than one inmate in a limited living area has been described as "among the most debasing and most dehumanizing aspects of present prison life. It rips away the sense of privacy—of dignity—which can make bearable many things which otherwise could not be endured." *Delgado v. Cady*, 576 F.Supp. 1446, 1448 (E.D.Wis.1983). The court in *Rutherford v. Pitchess*, 457 F.Supp. 104 (C.D.Cal.1978) found the practice of requiring some inmates to sleep on mattresses on the floor because of a shortage of beds to be "intolerable" and unconstitutional. *Id* at 109.

Lack of opportunity for regular outdoor recreation alone has been held to violate the Eighth Amendment. *Ahrens v. Thomas*, 434 F.Supp. 873 (W.D.Mo.1977); *Sinclair v. Henderson*, 331 F.Supp. 1123 (E.D.La.1971). In the case at bar, the offensiveness of this restriction is exacerbated, as are most other debilitating conditions, by the overcrowding and constant confinement to the cell areas. The result is that the average inmate is confined 24 hours a day in a physically delapidated, insect infested, dimly lit, poorly ventilated area averaging under 20 square feet per inmate, without any available recreation or diversion other than some reading or letter writing, sharing a shower, which may or may not have hot water, with twelve to fourteen others, sharing a sink and toilet, which may or may not be operable, with three or four others, possibly sleeping on the unsanitary floor, or within inches of the toilet, in clothing that may not have been recently washed. The totality of these conditions offend notions of decency and are offensive to the Eighth Amendment prohibition against cruel and unusual punishment.

Much has been made by the defendants of constraints placed upon them which are beyond their control—most notably, the refusal of the state corrections system to accept sentenced inmates from the jail at times because of the state's own problems with overcrowding. However, as the proof revealed, the Sullivan County Jail has been overcrowded since before the state began refusing newly sentenced inmates. Moreover, the various causes of the jail's present situation are of little consequence to this inquiry. The defendants have not acted in bad faith. They have simply been faced with the ever-increasing challenge of fiscal management, recent passage of more severe criminal laws and society's demand for the imposition of punishment upon those convicted. The result has been further deterioration of the conditions in an already marginal facility. That there may be some justifications for these conditions is irrelevant. The Constitution mandates that those incarcerated not be subjected to cruel and unusual punishment. Upon a finding of such a violation it is the duty of this Court to intervene and order it corrected, regardless of the fact that it may result in additional expenditures.

Sullivan County has broken ground in the last month or so for the construction of a new jail facility, a project originally initiated several years ago. Completion of the new facility is projected to be fifteen months away. Thus, this Court is faced with the issue of what must be done in the interim at the present facility to assure the constitutional rights of those incarcerated therein.

Jail Inspector Jenkins' recommendations at trial included reducing the population in the main facility to 69, allowing at least one hour of visitation per week per inmate and the initiation of a program of exercise or recreation. These recommendations are based upon the minimum state requirements.

Mr. Kamka had several recommendations including reducing the population in the main facility to 64 assuming visitation will be increased and regular out of cell recreation opportunities will be provided.[12]

---

12. Kamka actually recommended reduction of population to 32, but stated that during the pendency of the new construction, housing 64 inmates in the main facility would be acceptable given the assumptions mentioned.

Defendants themselves offered, prior to trial, to reduce the population in the main facility to 100 within 90 days, close the workhouse, and construct a prefabricated 3500 square foot metal building on the grounds of the new jail site for the housing of misdemeanants and work-release inmates.

After evaluation of the circumstances and careful consideration of the evidence and recommendations set forth above, the Court holds, that to provide constitutionally acceptable confinement, the population at the main facility must be reduced to 70, regular out-of-cell recreation must be provided, visitation must be increased, and fire escape plans must be communicated to the inmates and prominently displayed in the corridors at all times.[13] Obviously, compliance with Constitutional requirements, as set forth more specifically in the Orders that follow will take the cooperation and creativity of both state and county officials working in conjunction with the Sheriff, and the Court would expect nothing less.

Accordingly, it is hereby ORDERED that the population of the main facility at the Sullivan County Jail be reduced to one hundred (100) inmates within ninety (90) days, and seventy (70) inmates within one hundred eighty (180) days. The maximum number of inmates so confined thereafter may fluctuate between 65 and 75, but shall not exceed 75. It is further ORDERED that within ninety (90) days total visitation for the entire population in the main facility be increased from four (4) hours per week to eight (8) hours per week, one (1) hour of out-of-cell exercise/recreation be provided for every inmate at least five (5) time per week, blown-up fire escape plans be conspicuously placed on the walls of the jail under sheets of plexiglass as described by Captain Hawkins at trial; that the workhouse, as it is presently constituted, be closed within ninety (90) days; and that the county proceed with the construction of a prefabricated metal building which will comply with State T.C.I. requirements, as a replacement for the workhouse.

---

13. Defendants have assured the Court that the workhouse will be closed as a part of the jail, and no longer used to house inmates.

VOLUME II

CHAPTER 2   THE RESPONSIBILITY TO HOLD SECURELY

Prisons officials are charged with the responsibility of preventing injury to inmates by other inmates or by prison officials. Should a prisoner be held in a manner that violates his constitutional protection, prison officials are subject to a Section 1983 civil rights action. Obviously, protection within the prison can not be assured.

Several cases included here are illustrative. In *Whitley v. Albers,* 106 S.Ct. 1078 (1986), the court considered whether too much force was used in an effort to rescue hostages. The plaintiff was shot during the rescue. The court held that "it is obduracy and wantoness, not advertence or error in good faith, that characterize the conduct prohibited by the Cruel and Unusual Punishments Clause."(p.1084). In the opinion by Justice O'Connor, the Court considered and discussed in detail the inmate's claim for injuries suffered during the course of the attempt to quell a prison riot.

Baker v. State Department of Rehabilition, 502 N.E.2d 261 (Ohio App. 1986), discussed the responsibility of the state for injuries to an inmate by another inmate. The officers were held not to be negligent.

Introductions in previous volumes:

II: 9; VI: 107; VII: 135; VIII: 219

Articles:

Blackburn, *Prisoners' Rights: Will They Remain Protected after Whitley?* 16 Stetson L. Rev. 385 (1987).

West, *Constitutional Law: Quelling a Prison Riot: Cruel and Unusual Punishment or a Necessary Infliction of Pain?* 26 Washburn L. Rev. 208 (1986).

Supreme Court Affirms Prison Officials' Use of Deadly Force, 17 Crim. Just. Newsletter 7 (1986).

Harol WHITLEY, Individually and as
Assistant Superintendent, Oregon
State Penitentiary, et al., Petitioners

v.

Gerald ALBERS.

No. 84-1077.

Argued Dec. 10, 1985.
Decided March 4, 1986.

Syllabus *

During the course of a riot at the Oregon State Penitentiary, a prison officer was taken hostage and placed in a cell on the upper tier of a two-tier cellblock. In an attempt to free the hostage, prison officials worked out a plan that called for the prisoner security manager to enter the cellblock unarmed, followed by prison officers armed with shotguns. The security manager ordered one of the officers to fire a warning shot and to shoot low at any inmates climbing the stairs to the upper tier since he would be climbing the stairs to free the hostage. One of the officers, after firing a warning shot, shot respondent in the left knee when he started up the stairs. Respondent subsequently brought an action in Federal District Court against petitioner prison officials pursuant to 42 U.S.C. § 1983, alleging, *inter alia*, that they had deprived him of his rights under the Eighth and Fourteenth Amendments. At the conclusion of the trial, the District Court directed a verdict for petitioners. The Court of Appeals reversed and remanded for a new trial on respondent's Eighth Amendment claim.

Held:

1. The shooting of respondent did not violate his Eighth Amendment right to be free from cruel and unusual punishments. Pp. 1084-1088.

(a) It is obduracy and wantonness, not inadvertence or error in good faith, that characterize the conduct prohibited by the Cruel and Unusual Punishments Clause, whether that conduct occurs in connection with establishing conditions of confinement, supplying medical needs, or restoring control over a tumultuous cellblock. The infliction of pain in the course of a prison security measure, therefore, does not amount to cruel and unusual punishment simply because it may appear in retrospect that the degree of force authorized or applied for security purposes was unreason-

---

* The syllabus constitutes no part of the opinion of the Court but has been prepared by the Reporter of Decisions for the convenience of the reader. See *United States v. Detroit Lumber Co.,* 200 U.S. 321, 337, 26 S.Ct. 282, 287, 50 L.Ed.2d 499.

able, and hence unnecessary in the strict sense. The general requirement that an Eighth Amendment claimant establish the unnecessary and wanton infliction of pain should also be applied with due regard for differences in the kind of conduct involved. Thus, where a prison security measure is undertaken to resolve a disturbance, such as occurred in this case, that poses significant risks to the safety of inmates and prison staff, the question whether the measure taken inflicted unnecessary and wanton pain and suffering ultimately turns on whether force was applied in a good-faith effort to maintain or restore discipline or maliciously and sadistically for the purpose of causing harm. Pp. 1084-1086.

(b) Viewing the evidence in the light most favorable to respondent, as must be done in reviewing the decision reversing the trial court's directed verdict for petitioners, it does not appear that the evidence supports a reliable inference of wantonness in the infliction of pain under the above standard. Evidence arguably showing that the prison officials erred in judgment when they decided on a plan that employed potentially deadly force, falls far short of a showing that there was no plausible basis for their belief that this degree of force was necessary. In particular, the order to shoot, qualified by an instruction to shoot low, falls short of commanding the infliction of pain in a wanton and unnecessary fashion. Nor was the failure to provide for a verbal warning, in addition to a warning shot, so insupportable as to be wanton, since any inmate running up the stairs after the prison security manager could reasonably be thought to pose a threat to the rescue attempt. And the failure to take into account the possibility that respondent might climb the stairs in an effort to return to his cell does not rise to the level of an Eighth Amendment violation. Assuming that the prison officer shot at respondent rather than at the inmates as a group does not establish that the officer

shot respondent knowing that it was unnecessary to do so. Under all these circumstances, the shooting was part and parcel of a good-faith effort to restore prison security. Pp. 1086-1088.

2. In this case, the Due Process Clause of the Fourteenth Amendment cannot serve as an alternative basis for affirmance, independently of the Eighth Amendment. In the prison security context, the Due Process Clause affords respondent no greater protection than does the Cruel and Unusual Punishments Clause. P. 1088.

743 F.2d 1372 (CA9, 1984), reversed.

O'CONNOR, J., delivered the opinion of the Court, in which BURGER, C.J., and WHITE, POWELL, and REHNQUIST, JJ., joined. MARSHALL, J., filed a dissenting opinion, in which BRENNAN, BLACKMUN, and STEVENS, JJ., joined.

Justice O'CONNOR delivered the opinion of the Court.

This case requires us to decide what standard governs a prison inmate's claim that prison officials subjected him to cruel and unusual punishment by shooting him during the course of their attempt to quell a prison riot.

I

At the time he was injured, respondent Gerald Albers was confined in cellblock "A" of the Oregon State Penitentiary. Cellblock "A" consists of two tiers of barred cells housing some 200 inmates. The two tiers are connected by a stairway that offers the only practical way to move from one tier to another.

At about 8:30 on the evening of June 27, 1980, several inmates were found intoxicated at the prison annex. Prison guards attempted to move the intoxicated prisoners, some of whom resisted, to the penitentiary's isolation and segregation facility.

This incident could be seen from the cell windows in cellblock "A", and some of the onlookers became agitated because they thought that the guards were using unnecessary force. Acting on instructions from their superiors, Officers Kemper and Fitts, who were on duty in cellblock "A", ordered the prisoners to return to their cells. The order was not obeyed. Several inmates confronted the two officers, who were standing in the open area of the lower tier. One inmate, Richard Klenk, jumped from the second tier and assaulted Officer Kemper. Kemper escaped but Officer Fitts was taken hostage. Klenk and other inmates then began breaking furniture and milling about.

Upon being informed of the disturbance, petitioner Harol Whitley, the prison security manager, entered cellblock "A" and spoke with Klenk. Captain Whitley agreed to permit four residents of cellblock "A" to view the inmates who had been taken to segregation earlier. These emissaries reported back that the prisoners in segregation were intoxicated but unharmed. Nonetheless, the disturbance in cellblock "A" continued.

Whitley returned to the cellblock and confirmed that Fitts was not harmed. Shortly thereafter, Fitts was moved from an office on the lower tier to cell 201 on the upper tier, and Klenk demanded that media representatives be brought into the cellblock. In the course of the negotiations, Klenk, who was armed with a homemade knife, informed Whitley that one inmate had already been killed and other deaths would follow. In fact, an inmate had been beaten but not killed by other prisoners.

Captain Whitley left the cellblock to organize an assault squad. When Whitley returned to cellblock "A", he was taken to see Fitts in cell 201. Several inmates assured Whitley that they would protect Fitts from harm, but Klenk threatened to kill the hostage if an attempt was made to lead an assault. Klenk and at least some other inmates were aware that guards had assembled outside the cellblock and that shot-

guns had been issued. Meanwhile, respondent had left his cell on the upper tier to see if elderly prisoners housed on the lower tier could be moved out of harm's way in the event that tear gas was used. Respondent testified that he asked Whitley for the key to the row of cells housing the elderly prisoners, and Whitley indicated that he would return with the key. Whitley denied that he spoke to respondent at any time during the disturbance. Tr. 380.

Whitley next consulted with his superiors, petitioners Cupp, the prison superintendant, and Kenney, the assistant superintendant. They agreed that forceful intervention was necessary to protect the life of the hostage and the safety of the inmates who were not rioting, and ruled out tear gas as an unworkable alternative. Cupp ordered Whitley to take a squad armed with shotguns into cellblock "A".

Whitley gave the final orders to the assault team, which was assembled in the area outside cellblock "A". Petitioner Kennicott and two other officers armed with shotguns were to follow Whitley, who was unarmed, over the barricade the inmates had constructed at the cellblock entrance. A second group of officers, without firearms, would be behind them. Whitley ordered Kennicott to fire a warning shot as he crossed the barricade. He also ordered Kennicott to shoot low at any prisoners climbing the stairs toward cell 201, since they could pose a threat to the safety of the hostage or to Whitley himself, who would be climbing the stairs in an attempt to free the hostage in cell 201.

At about 10:30 p.m., Whitley reappeared just outside the barricade. By this time, about a half hour had elapsed since the earlier breaking of furniture, and the noise level in the cellblock had noticeably diminished. Respondent, who was standing at the bottom of the stairway, asked about the key. Whitley replied "No," clambered over the barricade, yelled "shoot the bastards," and ran toward the stairs after Klenk, who had been standing in the open areaway along with a number of other inmates. Kennicott fired a warning shot into the wall opposite the cellblock entrance as he followed Whitley over the barricade. He then fired a second shot that struck a post near the stairway. Meanwhile, Whitley chased Klenk up the stairs, and shortly thereafter respondent started up the stairs. Kennicott fired a third shot that struck respondent in the left knee. Another inmate was shot on the stairs and several others on the lower tier were wounded by gunshot. The inmates in cell 201 prevented Klenk from entering, and Whitley subdued Klenk at the cell door, freeing the hostage.

As a result of the incident, respondent sustained severe damage to his left leg and mental and emotional distress. He subsequently commenced this action pursuant to 42 U.S.C. § 1983, alleging that petitioners deprived him of his rights under the Eighth and Fourteenth Amendments and raising pendent state law claims for assault and battery and negligence. Many of the facts were stipulated, see Tr. 53–60, but both sides also presented testimony from witnesses to the disturbance and the rescue attempt, as well as from expert witnesses with backgrounds in prison discipline and security. At the conclusion of trial, the District Judge directed a verdict for petitioners. He understood respondent's claim to be based solely on the Eighth Amendment as made applicable to the States by the Fourteenth Amendment. See *Robinson v. California*, 370 U.S. 660, 82 S.Ct. 1417, 8 L.Ed.2d 758 (1962). The District Judge held:

> "[D]efendants' use of deadly force was justified under the unique circumstances of this case. Possible alternatives were considered and reasonably rejected by prison officers. The use of shotguns and specifically the order to shoot low anyone following the unarmed Whitley up the stairs were necessary to protect Whitley, secure the safe release of the hostage and to restore order and discipline. Even in hindsight, it cannot be said that defendants' actions were not reasonably

necessary." 546 F.Supp. 726, 735 (Ore. 1982).

In the alternative, he held that petitioners were immune from damages liability because the constitutional constraints on the use of force in a prison riot were not clearly established. Finally, the District Judge held that respondent was barred from recovery on his pendent state law claims by virtue of an immunity conferred on public officers by the Oregon Tort Claims Act as to claims arising out of riots or mob actions.

A panel of the Court of Appeals for the Ninth Circuit reversed, with one judge dissenting. 743 F.2d 1372 (1984). The court held that an Eighth Amendment violation would be established "if a prison official deliberately shot Albers under circumstances where the official, with due allowance for the exigency, knew or should have known that it was unnecessary," *id.*, at 1375, or "if the emergency plan was adopted or carried out with 'deliberate indifference' to the right of Albers to be free of cruel unusual punishment." *Ibid.* The Court of Appeals pointed to evidence that the general disturbance in cellblock "A" was subsiding and to respondent's experts' testimony that the use of deadly force was excessive under the circumstances and should have been preceded by a verbal warning, and concluded that the jury could have found an Eighth Amendment violation. *Id.*, at 1376.

The Court of Appeals also ruled that petitioners could not prevail on their qualified immunity defense, because "[a] finding of deliberate indifference is inconsistent with a finding of good faith or qualified immunity." *Ibid.* Accordingly, the court remanded for a new trial on respondent's Eighth Amendment claim, while agreeing with the District Judge that respondent could not prevail on his state law claims, *id.*, at 1377, and that he had not asserted an independent violation of the Fourteenth Amendment. *Id.*, at 1374, n. 1. We granted certiorari, 472 U.S. ——, 105 S.Ct. 2700, 86 L.Ed.2d 716 (1985), and now reverse.

II

The language of the Eighth Amendment, "[e]xcessive bail shall not be required, nor excessive fines imposed, nor cruel and unusual punishments inflicted," manifests "an intention to limit the power of those entrusted with the criminal-law function of government." *Ingraham v. Wright*, 430 U.S. 651, 664, 97 S.Ct. 1401, 1408, 51 L.Ed.2d 711 (1977). The Cruel and Unusual Punishments Clause "was designed to protect those convicted of crimes," *ibid.*, and consequently the Clause applies "only after the State has complied with the constitutional guarantees traditionally associated with criminal prosecutions." *Id.*, at 671 n. 40, 97 S.Ct., at 1412 n. 40. See also *Revere v. Massachusetts General Hospital*, 463 U.S. 239, 244, 103 S.Ct. 2979, 2983, 77 L.Ed.2d 605 (1983); *Bell v. Wolfish*, 441 U.S. 520, 535, n. 16, 99 S.Ct. 1861, 1872, n. 16, 60 L.Ed.2d 447 (1979). An express intent to inflict unnecessary pain is not required, *Estelle v. Gamble*, 429 U.S. 97, 104, 97 S.Ct. 285, 291, 50 L.Ed.2d 251 (1976) ("deliberate indifference" to a prisoner's serious medical needs is cruel and unusual punishment), and "conditions of confinement" may constitute cruel and unusual punishment because such conditions "are part of the penalty that criminal offenders pay for their offenses against society." *Rhodes v. Chapman*, 452 U.S. 337, 347, 101 S.Ct. 2392, 2399, 69 L.Ed.2d 59 (1981).

Not every governmental action affecting the interests or well-being of a prisoner is subject to Eighth Amendment scrutiny, however. "After incarceration, only the 'unnecessary and wanton infliction of pain' ... constitutes cruel and unusual punishment forbidden by the Eighth Amendment." *Ingraham v. Wright, supra*, 430 U.S., at 670, 97 S.Ct., at 1412 (quoting *Estelle v. Gamble, supra*, 429 U.S., at 103, 97 S.Ct., at 290) (citations omitted). To be cruel and unusual punishment, conduct that does not purport to be punishment at all must involve more than ordinary lack of due care for the prisoner's

interests or safety. This reading of the Clause underlies our decision in *Estelle v. Gamble, supra*, at 105–106, 97 S.Ct., at 291–292, which held that a prison physician's "negligen[ce] in diagnosing or treating a medical condition" did not suffice to make out a claim of cruel and unusual punishment. It is obduracy and wantonness, not inadvertence or error in good faith, that characterize the conduct prohibited by the Cruel and Unusual Punishments Clause, whether that conduct occurs in connection with establishing conditions of confinement, supplying medical needs, or restoring official control over a tumultuous cellblock. The infliction of pain in the course of a prison security measure, therefore, does not amount to cruel and unusual punishment simply because it may appear in retrospect that the degree of force authorized or applied for security purposes was unreasonable, and hence unnecessary in the strict sense.

The general requirement that an Eighth Amendment claimant allege and prove the unnecessary and wanton infliction of pain should also be applied with due regard for differences in the kind of conduct against which an Eighth Amendment objection is lodged. The deliberate indifference standard articulated in *Estelle* was appropriate in the context presented in that case because the State's responsibility to attend to the medical needs of prisoners does not ordinarily clash with other equally important governmental responsibilities. Consequently, "deliberate indifference to a prisoner's serious illness or injury," *Estelle, supra*, at 105, 97 S.Ct., at 291, can typically be established or disproved without the necessity of balancing competing institutional concerns for the safety of prison staff or other inmates. But, in making and carrying out decisions involving the use of force to restore order in the face of a prison disturbance, prison officials undoubtedly must take into account the very real threats the unrest presents to inmates and prison officials alike, in addition to the possible harms to inmates against whom force might be used. As we said in *Hudson v. Palmer*, 468 U.S. —, —, 104 S.Ct. 3194, 3200, 82 L.Ed.2d 393 (1984), prison administrators are charged with the responsibility of ensuring the safety of the prison staff, administrative personnel, and visitors, as well as the "obligation to take reasonable measures to guarantee the safety of the inmates themselves." In this setting, a deliberate indifference standard does not adequately capture the importance of such competing obligations, or convey the appropriate hesitancy to critique in hindsight decisions necessarily made in haste, under pressure, and frequently without the luxury of a second chance.

Where a prison security measure is undertaken to resolve a disturbance, such as occurred in this case, that indisputably poses significant risks to the safety of inmates and prison staff, we think the question whether the measure taken inflicted unnecessary and wanton pain and suffering ultimately turns on "whether force was applied in a good faith effort to maintain or restore discipline or maliciously and sadistically for the very purpose of causing harm." *Johnson v. Glick*, 481 F.2d 1028, 1033 (CA2) (Friendly, J.), cert. denied *sub nom. John v. Johnson*, 414 U.S. 1033, 94 S.Ct. 462, 38 L.Ed.2d 324 (1973). As the District Judge correctly perceived, "such factors as the need for the application of force, the relationship between the need and the amount of force that was used, [and] the extent of injury inflicted," *ibid.*, are relevant to that ultimate determination. From such considerations inferences may be drawn as to whether the use of force could plausibly have been thought necessary, or instead evinced such wantonness with respect to the unjustified infliction of harm as is tantamount to a knowing willingness that it occur. See *Duckworth v. Franzen*, 780 F.2d 645, 654 (CA7 1985) (equating "deliberate indifference", in an Eighth Amendment case involving security risks, with "recklessness in criminal law," which "implies an act so dangerous that the defendant's knowledge of the risk can

be inferred"); cf. *Block v. Rutherford*, 468 U.S. —, —, 104 S.Ct. 3227, 3231, 82 L.Ed.2d 438 (1984) (requiring pretrial detainees claiming that they were subjected to "punishment" without due process to prove intent to punish or show that the challenged conduct is not "reasonably related to a legitimate goal," from which an intent to punish may be inferred); *Bell v. Wolfish, supra*, 441 U.S., at 539, 99 S.Ct., at 1874. But equally relevant are such factors as the extent of the threat to the safety of staff and inmates, as reasonably perceived by the responsible officials on the basis of the facts known to them, and any efforts made to temper the severity of a forceful response.

When the "ever-present potential for violent confrontation and conflagration," *Jones v. North Carolina Prisoners' Labor Union, Inc.*, 433 U.S. 119, 132, 97 S.Ct. 2532, 2541, 53 L.Ed.2d 629 (1977), ripens into *actual* unrest and conflict, the admonition that "a prison's internal security is peculiarly a matter normally left to the discretion of prison administrators," *Rhodes v. Chapman*, 452 U.S., at 349, n. 14, 101 S.Ct., at 2400, n. 14, carries special weight. "Prison administrators ... should be accorded wide-ranging deference in the adoption and execution of policies and practices that in their judgment are needed to preserve internal order and discipline and to maintain institutional security." *Bell v. Wolfish*, 441 U.S., at 547, 99 S.Ct., at 1878. That deference extends to a prison security measure taken in response to an actual confrontation with riotous inmates, just as it does to prophylactic or preventive measures intended to reduce the incidence of these or any other breaches of prison discipline. It does not insulate from review actions taken in bad faith and for no legitimate purpose, but it requires that neither judge nor jury freely substitute their judgment for that of officials who have made a considered choice. Accordingly, in ruling on a motion for a directed verdict in a case such as this, courts must determine whether the evidence goes beyond a mere dispute over the reasonableness of a particular use of force or the existence of arguably superior alternatives. Unless it appears that the evidence, viewed in the light most favorable to the plaintiff, will support a reliable inference of wantonness in the infliction of pain under the standard we have described, the case should not go to the jury.

III

Since this case comes to us from a decision of the Court of Appeals reversing the District Court's directed verdict for petitioners, we evaluate the facts in the light most favorable to respondent. The Court of Appeals believed that testimony that the disturbance was subsiding at the time the assault was made, and the conflicting expert testimony as to whether the force used was excessive, were enough to allow a jury to find that respondent's Eighth Amendment rights were violated. We think the Court of Appeals effectively collapsed the distinction between mere negligence and wanton conduct that we find implicit in the Eighth Amendment. Only if ordinary errors of judgment could make out an Eighth Amendment claim would this evidence create a jury question.

To begin with, although the evidence could be taken to show that the general disturbance had quieted down, a guard was still held hostage, Klenk was armed and threatening, several other inmates were armed with homemade clubs, numerous inmates remained outside their cells, and the cellblock remained in the control of the inmates. The situation remained dangerous and volatile. As respondent concedes, at the time he was shot "an officer's safety was in question and ... an inmate was armed and dangerous." Brief for Respondent 25. Prison officials had no way of knowing what direction matters would take if they continued to negotiate or did nothing, but they had ample reason to believe that these options presented unacceptable risks.

Respondent's expert testimony is likewise unavailing. One of respondent's experts opined that petitioners gave inadequate consideration to less forceful means of intervention, and that the use of deadly force under the circumstances was not necessary to "prevent imminent danger" to the hostage guard or other inmates. Tr. 266. Respondent's second expert testified that prison officials were "possibly a little hasty in using the firepower" on the inmates. Tr. 314. At most, this evidence, which was controverted by petitioners' experts, establishes that prison officials arguably erred in judgment when they decided on a plan that employed potentially deadly force. It falls far short of a showing that there was no plausible basis for the officials' belief that this degree of force was necessary. Indeed, any such conclusion would run counter to common sense, in light of the risks to the life of the hostage and the safety of inmates that demonstrably persisted notwithstanding repeated attempts to defuse the situation. An expert's after-the-fact opinion that danger was not "imminent" in no way establishes that there was no danger, or that a conclusion by the officers that it *was* imminent would have been wholly unreasonable.

Once the basic design of the plan was in place, moreover, it is apparent why any inmate running up the stairs after Captain Whitley, or interfering with his progress towards the hostage, could reasonably be thought to present a threat to the success of the rescue attempt and to Whitley—particularly after a warning shot was fired. A sizable group of inmates, in defiance of the cell-in order and in apparent support of Klenk, continued to stand in the open area on the lower tier. Respondent testified that this was not "an organized group," Tr. 113, and that he saw no inmates armed with clubs in that area. Tr. 114. But the fact remains that the officials had no way of knowing which members of that group of inmates had joined with Klenk in destroying furniture, breaking glass, seizing the hostage, and setting up the barricade, and they certainly had reason to believe that some members of this group might intervene in support of Klenk. It was perhaps also foreseeable that one or more of these inmates would run up the stairs after the shooting started in order to return to their cells. But there would be neither means nor time to inquire into the reasons why each inmate acted as he did. Consequently, the order to shoot, qualified as it was by an instruction to shoot low, falls short of commanding the infliction of pain in a wanton and unnecessary fashion.

As petitioners' own experts conceded, a verbal warning would have been desirable, in addition to a warning shot, if circumstances permitted it to be given without undue risk. See Tr. 446, 556. While a jury might conclude that this omission was unreasonable, we think that an inference of wantonness could not properly be drawn. First, some warning was given in the form of the first shot fired by Officer Kennicott. Second, the prison officials could have believed in good faith that such a warning might endanger the success of the security measure because of the risk that it would have allowed one or more inmates to climb the stairs before they could be stopped. The failure to provide for verbal warnings is thus not so insupportable as to be wanton. Accordingly, a jury could not properly find that this omission, coupled with the order to shoot, offended the Eighth Amendment.

To be sure, the plan was not adapted to take into account the appearance of respondent on the scene, and, on the facts as we must take them, Whitley was aware that respondent was present on the first tier for benign reasons. Conceivably, Whitley could have added a proviso exempting respondent from his order to shoot any prisoner climbing the stairs. But such an oversight simply does not rise to the level of an Eighth Amendment violation. Officials cannot realistically be expected to consider every contingency or minimize every risk, and it was far from inevitable that respondent would react as he did. Whitley was about to risk his life in an effort to rescue

the hostage, and he was understandably focusing on the orders essential to the success of the plan. His failure to make special provision for respondent may have been unfortunate, but is hardly behavior from which a wanton willingness to inflict unjustified suffering on respondent can be inferred.

Once it is established that the order to shoot low at anyone climbing the stairs after a warning shot was not wanton, respondent's burden in showing that the actual shooting constituted the wanton and unnecessary infliction of pain is an extremely heavy one. Accepting that respondent could not have sought safety in a cell on the lower tier, the fact remains that had respondent thrown himself to the floor he would not have been shot at. Instead, after the warning shot was fired, he attempted to return to his cell by running up the stairs behind Whitley. That is equivocal conduct. While respondent had not been actively involved in the riot and indeed had attempted to help matters, there is no indication that Officer Kennicott knew this, nor any claim that he acted vindictively or in retaliation. Respondent testified that as he started to run up the stairs he "froze" when he looked to his left and saw Kennicott, and that "we locked eyes." Tr. 119. Kennicott testified that he saw several inmates running up the stairs, that he thought they were pursuing Whitley, and that he fired at their legs. Tr. 459. To the extent that this testimony is conflicting, we resolve the conflict in respondent's favor by assuming that Kennicott shot at respondent rather than at the inmates as a group. But this does not establish that Kennicott shot respondent knowing it was unnecessary to do so. Kennicott had some basis for believing that respondent constituted a threat to the hostage and to Whitley, and had at most a few seconds in which to react. He was also under orders to respond to such a perceived threat in precisely the manner he did. Under these circumstances, the actual shooting was part and parcel of a good faith effort to restore prison security. As such, it did not violate respondent's Eighth Amendment right to be free from cruel and unusual punishments.

IV

As an alternative ground for affirmance, respondent contends that, independently of the Eighth Amendment, the shooting deprived him of a protected liberty interest without due process of law, in violation of the Fourteenth Amendment. Respondent correctly observes that any ground properly raised below may be urged as a basis for affirmance of the Court of Appeals' decision, see *United States v. New York Telephone Co.*, 434 U.S. 159, 166, n. 8, 98 S.Ct. 364, 369, n. 8, 54 L.Ed.2d 376 (1977), and argues that he has maintained throughout this litigation that his "constitutional protection against the use of excessive and unnecessary force, as well as the use of deadly force without meaningful warning," derives from the Due Process Clause as well as the Eighth Amendment. Brief for Respondent 25, n. 13.

The District Court was correct in ruling that respondent did not assert a *procedural* due process claim that the State was obliged to afford him some kind of hearing either before or after he was shot. See 546 F.Supp. at 732, n. 1. But we believe respondent did raise a claim that his "substantive rights under the Due Process Clause of the Fourteenth Amendment," *Youngberg v. Romeo*, 457 U.S. 307, 309 (1982), were infringed by prison officials when he was shot. His complaint alleged violations of the Eighth and Fourteenth Amendments, App. 2, 7 (First Amended Complaint), and at argument on petitioners' motion for a directed verdict, counsel for both petitioners and respondents treated the Fourteenth Amendment as a distinct though overlapping source of substantive protection from state action involving excessive force. See App. 21, 27. Accordingly, we consider whether the Due Process Clause could serve as an alternative basis for affirmance.

We need say little on this score. We think the Eighth Amendment, which is specifically concerned with the unnecessary and wanton infliction of pain in penal institutions, serves as the primary source of substantive protection to convicted prisoners in cases such as this one, where the deliberate use of force is challenged as excessive and unjustified. It would indeed be surprising if, in the context of forceful prison security measures, "conduct that shocks the conscience" or "afford[s] brutality the cloak of law," and so violates the Fourteenth Amendment, *Rochin v. California*, 342 U.S. 165, 172, 173, 72 S.Ct. 205, 210, 96 L.Ed. 183 (1952), were not also punishment "inconsistent with contemporary standards of decency" and " 'repugnant to the conscience of mankind,' " *Estelle v. Gamble*, 429 U.S., at 103, 106, 97 S.Ct., at 290, 292, in violation of the Eighth. We only recently reserved the general question "whether something less than intentional conduct, such as recklessness or 'gross negligence,' is enough to trigger the protections of the Due Process Clause." *Daniels v. Williams*, — U.S. —, — n. 3, 106 S.Ct. 662, 667 n.3, 88 L.Ed.2d 662 (1986). Because this case involves prison inmates rather than pretrial detainees or persons enjoying unrestricted liberty we imply nothing as to the proper answer to that question outside the prison security context by holding, as we do, that in these circumstances the Due Process Clause affords respondent no greater protection than does the Cruel and Unusual Punishments Clause.

Petitioners also ask us to hold that the Court of Appeals erred in ruling that they did not enjoy qualified immunity. We decline to review that holding, because our decision that petitioners were entitled to a directed verdict on the merits makes it unnecessary to do so.

The judgment of the Court of Appeals is *Reversed.*

Justice MARSHALL, with whom Justice BRENNAN, Justice BLACKMUN, and Justice STEVENS join, dissenting.

I share the majority's concern that prison officials be permitted to respond reasonably to inmate disturbances without unwarranted fear of liability. I agree that the threshold for establishing a constitutional violation under these circumstances is high. I do not agree, however, that the contested existence of a "riot" in the prison lessens the constraints imposed on prison authorities by the Eighth Amendment.

The majority has erred, I believe, both in developing its legal analysis and in employing it. First, the especially onerous standard the Court has devised for determining whether a prisoner injured during a prison disturbance has been subjected to cruel and unusual punishment is incorrect and not justified by precedent. That standard is particularly inappropriate because courts deciding whether to apply it must resolve a preliminary issue of fact that will often be disputed and properly left to the jury. Finally, the Court has applied its test improperly to the facts of this case. For these reasons, I must respectfully dissent.

I

The Court properly begins by acknowledging that, for a prisoner attempting to prove a violation of the Eighth Amendment, "[a]n express intent to inflict unnecessary pain is not required, *Estelle v. Gamble*, 429 U.S. 97, 104, 97 S.Ct. 285, 291, 50 L.Ed.2d 251 (1976)." *Ante*, at 1084. Rather, our cases have established that the "unnecessary and wanton" infliction of pain on prisoners constitutes cruel and unusual punishment prohibited by the Eighth Amendment, even in the absence of intent to harm. *Ibid.*; see also *Ingraham v. Wright*, 430 U.S. 651, 670, 97 S.Ct. 1401, 1412, 51 L.Ed.2d 711 (1977); *Gregg v. Georgia*, 428 U.S. 153, 173, 96 S.Ct. 2909, 2925, 49 L.Ed.2d 859 (1976) (joint opinion of Stewart, POWELL, and STEVENS, JJ.). Having correctly articulated the teaching of our cases on this issue, however, the

majority inexplicably arrives at the conclusion that a constitutional violation in the context of a prison uprising can be established only if force was used "maliciously and sadistically for the very purpose of causing harm," *ante*, at 1085 thus requiring the very "express intent to inflict unnecessary pain" that it had properly disavowed.[1]

The Court imposes its heightened version of the "unnecessary and wanton" standard only when the injury occurred in the course of a "disturbance" that "poses significant risks," *ante*, at 1085. But those very questions—whether a disturbance existed and whether it posed a risk—are likely to be hotly contested. It is inappropriate, to say the least, to condition the choice of a legal standard, the purpose of which is to determine whether to send a constitutional claim to the jury, upon the court's resolution of factual disputes that in many cases should themselves be resolved by the jury.

The correct standard for identifying a violation of the Eighth Amendment under our cases is clearly the "unnecessary and wanton" standard, which establishes a high hurdle to be overcome by a prisoner seeking relief for a constitutional violation. The full circumstances of the plaintiff's injury, including whether it was inflicted during an attempt to quell a riot and whether there was a reasonable apprehension of danger, should be considered by the factfinder in determining whether that standard is satisfied in a particular case. There is simply no justification for creating a distinct and more onerous burden for the plaintiff to meet merely because the judge believes that the injury at issue was caused during a disturbance that "pose[d] significant risks to the safety of inmates and prison staff," *ante*, at 1085. Determination of whether there was such a disturbance or

---

1. This intent standard ostensibly derives from an opinion of Judge Friendly in *Johnson v. Glick*, 481 F.2d 1028, 1033 (CA2), cert. denied sub nom. *John v. Johnson*, 414 U.S. 1033, 94 S.Ct. 462, 38 L.Ed.2d 324 (1973). That opinion, however, considered maliciousness not as a pre-

requisite to a constitutional violation, but rather as a factor that, if present, could enable a plaintiff to survive a motion to dismiss when otherwise the facts might be insufficient to make out a claim. 481 F.2d, at 1033.

risk, when disputed, should be made by the jury when it resolves disputed facts, not by the court in its role as arbiter of law. See *Byrd v. Blue Ridge Cooperative*, 356 U.S. 525, 537, 78 S.Ct. 893, 900, 2 L.Ed.2d 953 (1958).

II

The Court properly begins its application of the law by reciting the principle that the facts must be viewed in the light most favorable to respondent, who won a reversal of a directed verdict below. See *Galloway v. United States*, 319 U.S. 372, 395, 63 S.Ct. 1077, 1089, 87 L.Ed. 1458 (1943). If, under any reasonable interpretation of the facts, a jury could have found the "unnecessary and wanton" standard to be met, then the directed verdict was improper. The majority opinion, however, resolves factual disputes in the record in petitioners' favor and discounts much of respondent's theory of the case. This it is not entitled to do.

The majority pays short shrift to respondent's significant contention that the disturbance had quieted down by the time the lethal force was employed. *Ante*, at 1086. Respondent presented substantial testimony to show that the disturbance had subsided, Tr. 112, 165, 188, 193; that only one prisoner, Klenk, remained in any way disruptive, *id.*, at 212; and that even Klenk had calmed down enough at that point to admit that he had " 'gone too far.' " *Id.*, at 117. The majority asserts that "a guard was still held hostage, Klenk was armed and threatening, several other inmates were armed with homemade clubs, numerous inmates remained outside their cells, and ... [t]he situation remained dangerous and volatile." *Ante*, at 1086. Respondent's evidence, however, indicated that the guard was not, in fact, in danger. He had been put into a cell by several inmates to prevent Klenk from harming him. Tr. 161. Captain Whitley had been to see the guard, and had observed that the inmates protecting him from Klenk were not armed and had promised to keep Klenk out. *Id.*, at 58

(stipulation), 163. According to respondent's evidence, moreover, no other inmates were assisting Klenk in any way when the riot squad was called in; they were simply "milling around," waiting for Klenk to be taken into custody, or for orders to return to their cells. *Id.*, at 188. Respondent's evidence tended to show not that the "situation remained dangerous and volatile," *ante*, at 1086, but, on the contrary, that it was calm. Although the Court sees fit to emphasize repeatedly "the risks to the life of the hostage and the safety of inmates that demonstrably persisted notwithstanding repeated attempts to defuse the situation," *ibid.*, I can only point out that respondent bitterly disputed that any such risk to guards or inmates had persisted. The Court just does not believe his story.

The Court's treatment of the expert testimony is equally insensitive to its obligation to resolve all disputes in favor of respondent. Respondent's experts testified that the use of deadly force under these circumstances was not justified by any necessity to prevent imminent danger to the officers or the inmates, Tr. 266; that the force used was excessive, *ibid.*; and that even if deadly force had been justified, it would have been unreasonable to unleash such force without a clear warning to allow non-participating inmates to return to their cells. *Id.*, at 269. Insofar as expert testimony can ever be useful to show that prison authorities engaged in the "unnecessary and wanton" infliction of pain, even though it will always amount to "after-the-fact opinion" regarding the circumstances of the injury, see *ante*, at 1086, respondent's expert evidence contributed to the creation of a factual issue.

The majority characterizes the petitioners' error in using deadly force where it was not justified as an "oversight." *Ante*, at 1087. This is an endorsement of petitioners' rendition of the facts. As portrayed by respondent's evidence, the "error" was made in cold blood. Respondent's involvement started when, at the request of one of the inmates, he approached petitioner Whitley, who was talking to Klenk, to ask if Whitley would supply a key to a gate so that the elderly and sick patients in so-called "medical cells" near the area of disturbance could be removed before any tear gas was used. Tr. 115–116. Captain Whitley said that he would go and get the key, and left the cellblock. *Ibid.* In two or three minutes, Whitley returned. *Id.,* at 118. Respondent went to the door of the cellblock, and asked Whitley if he had brought the key. Whitley responded " 'No,' " turned his head back and yelled, " 'Let's go, let's go. Shoot the bastards!' " *Ibid.*

Respondent, afraid, ran from his position by the door and headed for the stairs, the only route back to his cell. *Id.,* at 118–119. He caught some movement out of the corner of his eye, looked in its direction, and saw petitioner Kennicott. According to respondent, " 'I froze. I looked at him; we locked eyes, then I looked down and seen the shotgun in his hand, then I seen the flash, and the next thing I know I was sitting down, grabbing my leg.' " *Id.,* at 119. Losing a great deal of blood, respondent crawled up the stairs and fell on his face, trying to get out of range of the shotguns. *Ibid.* After about 10 minutes, an officer grabbed respondent by the hair and dragged him downstairs. *Id.,* at 194. As he lay there, another officer came and stood over respondent and shoved the barrel of a gun or gas pistol into respondent's face. *Id.,* at 122. Respondent was left lying and bleeding profusely for approximately 10 or 15 more minutes, and was then taken to the prison hospital. *Id.,* at 194. He suffered very severe injury. Meanwhile, Klenk had been subdued with no resistance by Whitley, *id.,* at 164, 234, who was unarmed, *id.,* at 233.

Other testimony showed that, although most of the inmates assembled in the area were clearly not participating in the misconduct, they received no warning, instructions, or opportunity to leave the area and return to their cells before the officers

started shooting. *Id.,* at 163. Neither respondent nor any other inmate attempted to impede the officers as they entered the cellblock. *Id.,* at 234. The officers were described as "wild," "agitated, excited," not in full control of their emotions. *Id.,* at 192. One officer, prior to entering Cellblock A, told the others to " 'shoot their asses off, and if Klenk gets in the way, kill him.' " *Ibid.* At the time of this assault, the cellblock was described as "quiet." *Id.,* at 193.

If a jury credited respondent's testimony and that of his witnesses, it would have believed that there was only one inmate who was temporarily out of control, Klenk —"scared," *id.,* at 165, and "high," *id.,* at 117—and ready to give up. The disturbance in the block had lasted only 15 or 20 minutes when it subsided, and there appeared to be no lasting danger to anyone. Respondent was shot while he stood motionless on the stairs, and was left to bleed for a perilously long time before receiving any assistance.

III

Part III of the Court's opinion falls far short of a rendition of the events in the light most favorable to respondent. In that light, the facts present a very close question as to whether the prison officials' infliction of pain on respondent could be said to display the level of wantonness necessary to make out a constitutional violation. At the very least, it is clear that fair-minded people could differ on the response to that question, and that is all it takes to preclude a directed verdict.

The majority suggests that the existence of more appropriate alternative measures for controlling prison disturbances is irrelevant to the constitutional inquiry, but surely it cannot mean what it appears to say. For if prison officials were to drop a bomb on a cellblock in order to halt a fistfight between two inmates, for example, I feel confident that the Court would have difficulty concluding, as a matter of law, that such an action was not sufficiently wanton to present a jury question, even though concededly taken in an effort to restore order in the prison. Thus, the question of wantonness in the context of prison disorder, as with other claims of mistreatment under the Eighth Amendment, is a matter of degree. And it is precisely in cases like this one, when shading the facts one way or the other can result in different legal conclusions, that a jury should be permitted to do its job. Properly instructed, a jury would take into account the petition-ers' legitimate need to protect security, the extent of the danger presented, and the reasonableness of force used, in assessing liability. Moreover, the jury would know that a prisoner's burden is a heavy one, if he is to establish an Eighth Amendment violation under these circumstances.[2] Whether respondent was able to meet that burden here is a question for the jury. From the Court's usurpation of the jury's function, I dissent. I would affirm the judgment of the Court of Appeals.

---

2. The majority also rejects the pure Fourteenth Amendment due process claim asserted by respondent before the District Court. For the reasons stated in Justice BLACKMUN's dissent in *Davidson v. Cannon,* 474 U.S. —, —, 106 S.Ct. 668, ___, 88 L.Ed.2d 677 (1986), which I joined, I believe that the evidence precluding a directed verdict under the "unnecessary and wanton" standard also precludes directed verdict on respondent's due process claim. Justice STEVENS does not join this footnote.

28 Ohio App.3d 99

BAKER, Appellant,

v.

The STATE of Ohio, DEPARTMENT OF REHABILITATION AND CORRECTIONS, et al., Appellees.

No. 85AP–873.

Court of Appeals of Ohio,
Franklin County.

May 6, 1986.

MOYER, Presiding Judge.

This matter is before us upon an appeal from a judgment of the Court of Claims in favor of appellees.

On April 1, 1981, appellant, Robert Baker, was an inmate at the Columbus Correctional Facility. He was assaulted by three other inmates, was badly beaten, and required hospitalization. Appellant filed a complaint in the Court of Claims and alleged that his injuries were sustained as a result of the negligence of correctional officers.

Appellant was confined to the A–B block of the facility. This area was divided into two sections, A block and B block. On each block, there were six floors, or ranges, and on each range there were seventeen cells. The usual procedure for taking the inmates to dinner was to unlock all the cells and allow the inmates to remain on their respective ranges until they were all taken to the dining hall. It was during this time that appellant was assaulted by inmates known to him.

Appellant contended in his complaint that the guards failed to follow procedure by remaining on the ranges while the inmates were out of their cells. Appellant also alleged that the guards negligently failed to follow procedure when he reported his fear of being assaulted. Normally, an inmate who makes such a report is placed in protective custody.

The trial court ruled in favor of appellees and dismissed appellant's claims. The court found that the guards discharged their duties with reasonable care and were not negligent. Further, the court held that the guards did not have notice of appellant's fear of being assaulted.

Appellant asserts the following assignment of error:

"The trial court erred as a matter of law in failing to find that guards employed by the Appellee, State of Ohio, Department of Rehabilitation and Corrections, were negligent in failing to prevent an assault upon Appellant by fellow inmates at the Columbus Correctional Facility."

Appellant contends, as he did below, that R.C. 2921.44(C) establishes appellees' duty of care and that the decision of *Reynolds v. State* (1984), 14 Ohio St.3d 68, 471 N.E.2d 776, requires a finding of negligence on the part of appellees. We do not agree with appellant's contention.

R.C. 2921.44(C) provides in part that:

"(C) No officer, having charge of a detention facility, shall negligently do any of the following:

" * * *

"(3) Fail to control an unruly prisoner, or to prevent intimidation of or physical harm to a prisoner by another;

" * * *

"(5) Fail to observe any lawful and reasonable regulation for the management of the detention facility."

Appellant urges that the guards violated R.C. 2921.44(C)(3) by failing to place appellant in protective custody after he expressed his fear of being assaulted. However, a review of the testimony at trial indicates that appellant did not specifically request protective custody or directly express his fear of an impending assault. Rather, appellant made vague statements that he needed to get off the range or be moved off the range. In spite of the fact that appellant was slapped in the face by another inmate earlier that day, he did not specifically request protective custody. Accordingly, the trial court did not err in holding that the guards did not have adequate notice of an impending assault and that, therefore, appellees were not negligent in failing to place appellant in protective custody.

Appellant also urges that appellees violated R.C. 2921.44(C)(5) by negligently failing to observe management regulations when a guard failed to stay on appellant's range after all the cells were open and the inmates could move freely among themselves.

Appellant does not assert that there was an insufficient number of guards. There was expert testimony that the procedures followed were adequate and that it was not required that a guard stay on each range after the cells were opened. Indeed, it would be impossible for this to occur, since four guards were responsible for twelve ranges.

Contrary to appellant's view, *Reynolds, supra,* is inapplicable to the case at bar. There, the Supreme Court held that, when a statute mandates a particular procedure and creates a duty, the failure to conform to the statute is negligence *per se.*

In the instant case, there was no formal, written rule. The procedure followed by the guards was considered adequate by an expert witness. There was testimony that the guards followed their normal procedure on the day appellant was assaulted. Therefore, appellees did not violate R.C. 2921.44(C)(5) by negligently failing to follow procedure and there was no negligence *per se.*

Appellant's assignment of error is overruled, and the judgment of the Court of Claims is affirmed.

Judgment affirmed.

McCORMAC and VICTOR, JJ., concur.

VICTOR, J., retired, of the Ninth Appellate District, was assigned to active duty pursuant to Section 6(C), Article IV, Ohio Constitution.

VOLUME II

CHAPTER 3 THE RESPONSIBILITY TO HOLD SAFELY

It is now an accepted principle that the state must prevent any deliberate injury to the prisoner during incarceration. In *Alberti v. Klevenhagen,* 790 F.2d 1220, 1223 (5th Cir. 1986), the court stated that "[j]ail conditions must not fall below a minimum standard of decency required by the Eighth Amendment. Conditions which 'alone or in combination may deprive inmates of the minimal civilized measure of life's necessities . . . could be cruel and unusual under the contemporary standard of decency.'" The decision examined evidence of jail conditions and remedies to correct them. The case is not reproduced here.

The classical case in the area is that of *Bell v. Wolfish,* 441 U.S. 520, 99 S.Ct. 1861 (1979), reproduced in Vol. VI: 139 of this series. The decision merits close study and attention.

Obviously, for a prison to meet Eighth Amendment standards, it must maintain a reasonable sanitary condition. Courts have said that "persons involuntarily confined by the states have a constitutional right to safe conditions of confinement." *Hoptowit v. Spellman,* 753 F.2d 779, 784 (9th Cir. 1985). The *Hoptowit* court reviewed many standards, including adequate lighting, plumbing, fire safety, ventilation and the correction of safety hazards.

The two cases reproduced in this section focus on constitutional requirements that attention be directed toward conditions of prisoners. In *Miga v. City of Holyoke,* 497 N.E.2d 1 (Mass. 1986), the prisoner was drunk and demonstrated suicidal tendencies when arrested. Later, while in custody, she hung herself. The court held that her civil rights were violated.

In *Randall v. Thompson,* 635 F.Supp. 145 (N.D. Ill. 1986), the court considered whether prison authorities had accorded the injured inmate sufficient protection from fellow inmates.

Introductions in previous volumes:

II: 105; VI: 135; VII: 191; VIII: 249

Dolores MIGA, individually and as
administratrix,[1]

v.

CITY OF HOLYOKE et al.[2]

Supreme Judicial Court of Massachusetts,
Hampden.

Argued May 5, 1986.

Decided Sept. 2, 1986.

Before HENNESSEY, C.J., and WIL-
KINS, LIACOS, ABRAMS and LYNCH,
JJ.

HENNESSEY, Chief Justice.

The city of Holyoke and two of its police
officers, Joseph Dudek and John J. McMullan, appeal from Superior Court jury verdicts awarding compensatory and punitive
damages for the suicide-by-hanging of the
plaintiff's decedent while in the defendants'
protective custody.

The plaintiff, the mother of the decedent,
brought suit against the city of Holyoke,
its chief of police, and various police officers, seeking recovery for wrongful death,
G.L. c. 229, § 2 (1984 ed.), and for the
deprivation of the decedent's civil rights, 42
U.S.C. § 1983 (1982).[3] Motions by the defendants for   directed verdicts and judgments notwithstanding the verdicts were
made and denied. On special questions,
the jury found that the city was responsible
for the death of the plaintiff's decedent and
awarded $20,000 damages for wrongful
death and $2,100 for funeral and burial
expenses. In addition, the jury found that
the city was sixty per cent negligent and,
therefore, the damage awards were reduced to $12,000 and $1,260, respectively.
The jury also found defendants Dudek and
McMullan liable under 42 U.S.C. § 1983
(1982), and assessed compensatory damages of $20,000 and punitive damages of
$50,000 against each of these defendants.[4]

On appeal, the defendants challenge the
denial of their motions for directed verdicts
and judgments notwithstanding the ver-

1. Of the estate of Sandra J. Smigiel.

2. Joseph Dudek and John J. McMullan. The
record indicates in a few places that McMullan's
first name is "Gerald," but we leave that nicety
to the discretion of the trial judge, if the matter
now requires amendment. The plaintiff's
amended complaint named several other individual defendants who, like defendants Dudek
and McMullan, were employed by the Holyoke

3. The plaintiff's complaint also stated claims for
violations of the Massachusetts Civil Rights Act,
G.L. c. 12, § 11 (1984 ed.), and for intentional
infliction of emotional distress. Directed verdicts were allowed in favor of all defendants on
each of these State law claims.

4. In the defendants' brief, only three pages are
devoted to argument on the issues presented for
appeal. We found the brief woefully inadequate in all respects and at several points in this
opinion are compelled to make mention of specific problems caused by this inadequacy.
The defendants state in their brief that the
judge awarded attorney's fees and that they ap-

police department. The plaintiff does not appeal from the allowance of motions for directed
verdicts on all counts for Harold F. Skelton,
Alan G. Fletcher, and Russell Paquette. In addition, the plaintiff does not appeal from directed
verdicts and jury verdicts which disposed of all
claims in favor of defendants James Sullivan,
Russell Labbe, Jean King, and Dennis Egan.

peal from that award. The briefs and record do
not reflect the amount of the award and the
record does not include the defendants' notice
of appeal, although the filing of the notice is
reflected on the Superior Court docket entries.
In view of these omissions and the one-sentence
mention of the issue in the defendants' brief, we
conclude that the defendants' treatment of this
issue does not rise to the level of appellate
argument as required by Mass.R.A.P. 16(a)(4),
as amended, 367 Mass. 921 (1975). See *Langlitz
v. Board of Registration of Chiropractors*, 396
Mass. 374, 376 n. 2, 486 N.E.2d 48 (1985).

dicts, and the damage awards. Specifically, the defendants contend that the evidence was not legally sufficient to establish a constitutional violation under § 1983, that the existence of an adequate State remedy foreclosed the right to sue for violation of civil rights under § 1983, and that the issue of punitive damages should not have been submitted to the jury.[5] We transferred the case here on our own motion and affirm the judgments.

We summarize the facts. The decedent, Sandra Smigiel (Sandra), had poor mental health and was under care for mental illness continuously from 1974 until her death in September, 1979. She was a certified nurse's aide. Sandra married Daniel Smigiel (Daniel) in February, 1978.

On September 10, 1979, Sandra went to the Holyoke police station and informed a police detective that her husband was threatening to kill himself with a gun. As the detective accompanied Sandra to her home, she informed him that she had a drinking problem and that earlier on the same evening she had been a patient at a local detoxification center. When they arrived at Sandra's residence, the police disarmed Daniel. Daniel then advised the detective to be careful with Sandra, told the detective that Sandra had suicidal tendencies and that she had been hospitalized for that reason. The detective wrote a report regarding Sandra, which was read and signed by Lieutenant James Sullivan of the Holyoke police department.

Eleven days later, on September 21, 1979, Sandra tried unsuccessfully to obtain a drink from a drinking establishment as it was closing. The proprietor followed as Sandra drove away from the bar and observed that Sandra's car was weaving as it proceeded along the road. When Sandra pulled over to the side of the road, the proprietor stopped behind her. He then hailed a passing cruiser, occupied by Lieutenant Sullivan and another officer.

The police officers asked Sandra to get out of her car. Sandra did not respond. The officers turned off the ignition and removed Sandra from the car. She was unable to stand or walk by herself, her breath smelled of alcohol and her speech was slurred. Sandra was able to tell the officers her name and the street where she lived. The officers then drove her there, but went to the wrong house and were told that she did not live at that address. The officers made no attempt to search her pocketbook or otherwise determine her correct address, but instead radioed for another cruiser to take Sandra to the police station. On the way to the police station in the second cruiser, Sandra lapsed into unconsciousness. An officer carried her into the police station, but made no attempt to obtain medical attention for her.

The commanding officer at the police station was defendant John J. McMullan, who had been a police officer for twenty-eight years. He had been off-duty, but had been called to the station to administer a breathalyzer test. McMullan remained while Lieutenant Sullivan, who otherwise would have been commanding officer, was out of the station. The defendant Joseph Dudek was the house officer at the police station on the midnight to 8 *A.M.* shift. He was responsible for checking on prisoners, including female prisoners, although in practice a female dispatcher usually checked on female prisoners.

There was testimony that, at the time Sandra was taken into protective custody, rules and regulations promulgated by the chief of police required: that an attempt be made to bring such a person home prior to calling the treatment center; that at no

---

5. In their statement of the issues presented and throughout their brief, the defendants appear to address only matters relating to the judgments against the individual defendants on the § 1983 claims. The defendants in their conclusion, however, also purport to challenge the entry of judgment against the city in the amount of $12,-000 for compensatory damages on the plaintiff's wrongful death claim under G.L. c. 229, § 2. This one-sentence challenge to the judgment against the city fails to meet the standards for appellate argument set forth in Mass.R.A.P. 16(a)(4). We decline, therefore, to consider the defendants' perfunctory claim of error regarding the wrongful death judgment against the city.

time should an unconscious person be placed in a cell except on orders of a physician; and that prisoners with known suicidal tendencies be checked at least every half hour.

Sandra arrived at the police station at 3 A.M. McMullan observed her to be in a "very drunken condition," and filled out a protective custody form with her name and address and her husband's name. McMullan made no attempt to communicate with Sandra's husband. There was evidence that McMullan did not notify the nearest detoxification center. McMullan took no action to obtain proper care and treatment for Sandra even though she was obviously intoxicated and had lapsed into unconsciousness periodically since being taken into custody by the police. There was evidence that McMullan knew that his failure to take these actions was contrary to department regulations. Shortly thereafter, Lieutenant Sullivan returned to the station and McMullan departed.

After Sandra was booked, she again lapsed into unconsciousness. Two other officers carried her, unconscious, downstairs to a cell. Because she thrashed about when they attempted to place her on a bench, they placed her on the concrete floor. An officer removed her belt, eyeglasses, and necklace, and checked her pockets.

Subsequently, Sandra began banging on the cell wall, asking for belts or shoelaces from other prisoners, and stating that she would commit suicide with her shirt. A woman in another cell began calling for the police to come down to the cell area to help with the situation. There was evidence that a police officer responded from the

stairs with an obscene, racial epithet and that Dudek was the police officer who uttered the response. The woman yelled that Sandra was trying to kill herself; other prisoners also yelled for help. No one came. Defendant Dudek heard the yelling, but made no attempt to find out what was happening. At one point Dudek testified that he told the prisoners to quiet down. At 6 *A.M.* Sandra's body was discovered hanging from the bars of her cell.

1. *Sufficiency of the Evidence Under 42 U.S.C. § 1983.*

In evaluating the judge's denial of the defendants' motions for directed verdicts, and for judgments notwithstanding the verdicts on the § 1983 claims, we view the evidence in the light most favorable to the plaintiff.[6] *Michnik-Zilberman v. Gordon's Liquor, Inc.*, 390 Mass. 6, 7 n. 1, 453 N.E.2d 430 (1983). *Uloth v. City Tank Corp.*, 376 Mass. 874, 876, 384 N.E.2d 1188 (1978). We must determine whether "anywhere in the evidence, from whatever source derived, any combination of circumstances could be found from which a reasonable inference could be drawn in favor of the plaintiff." *Poirier v. Plymouth*, 374 Mass. 206, 212, 372 N.E.2d 212 (1978), quoting *Raunela v. Hertz Corp.*, 361 Mass. 341, 343, 280 N.E.2d 179 (1972). "That the inferences be reasonable requires that they be based on 'probabilities rather than possibilities' and not the result of 'mere speculation and conjecture.'" *Poirier v. Plymouth, supra*, quoting *Alholm v. Wareham*, 371 Mass. 621, 627, 358 N.E.2d 788 (1976).

To establish a claim based on 42 U.S.C. § 1983,[7] a plaintiff must show that the conduct complained of was committed

---

6. In reviewing the denial of the defendants' motions for directed verdict and judgment notwithstanding the verdict, we employ the same standard. *Curtiss-Wright Corp. v. Edel-Brown Tool & Die Co.*, 381 Mass. 1, 3, 407 N.E.2d 319 (1980); *D'Annolfo v. Stoneham Hous. Auth.*, 375 Mass. 650, 657–658, 378 N.E.2d 971 (1978).

7. Section 1983 provides: "Every person who, under color of any statute, ordinance, regulation, custom, or usage, of any State or Territory or the District of Columbia, subjects, or causes

to be subjected, any citizen of the United States or other person within the jurisdiction thereof to the deprivation of any rights, privileges, or immunities secured by the Constitution and laws, shall be liable to the party injured in an action at law, suit in equity, or other proper proceeding for redress. For the purposes of this section, any Act of Congress applicable exclusively to the District of Columbia shall be considered to be a statute of the District of Columbia."

by a person acting under color of State law and that the conduct deprived a person of rights, privileges, or immunities secured by the Constitution or laws of the United States. *Parratt v. Taylor,* 451 U.S. 527, 535, 101 S.Ct. 1908, 1912, 68 L.Ed.2d 420 (1981). *Temple v. Marlborough Div. of the Dist. Court Dep't,* 395 Mass. 117, 122, 479 N.E.2d 137 (1985). There is no question that defendants Dudek and McMullan were acting under color of State law when Sandra was in the custody of the Holyoke police. Thus, the focus of our inquiry is on whether the defendants violated a right secured by the Constitution or laws of the United States.

The plaintiff claims that the conduct of Officers Dudek and McMullan in placing Sandra in a cell unattended when she was obviously intoxicated and unconscious, in failing to attempt to transfer her to a detoxification facility, and in failing to check her every half hour, in violation of the department rules, resulted in a violation of Sandra's constitutional rights. Further, she alleges that those acts, along with the failure of Dudek to respond to the cries of other prisoners for help, constituted deliberate indifference to serious medical needs of a person in police custody. We conclude that there was sufficient evidence to permit a jury to find a violation of § 1983.

In *Estelle v. Gamble,* 429 U.S. 97, 97 S.Ct. 285, 50 L.Ed.2d 251 (1976), the Supreme Court of the United States held that deliberate indifference to the serious illness or injury of prisoners constitutes a violation of the Eighth Amendment to the United States Constitution and states a cause of action under § 1983.[8] *Id.* at 104–105, 97 S.Ct. at 291–292. Mere negligent or inadvertent failure to provide medical care to prisoners does not, however, rise to the level of a constitutional violation. *Id.* at 105, 97 S.Ct. at 291. Moreover, Eighth Amendment scrutiny of the

treatment of persons in State custody is appropriate only after a State has complied with the constitutional requirements associated with criminal prosecutions. *Ingraham v. Wright,* 430 U.S. 651, 671–672 n. 40, 97 S.Ct. 1401, 1412–1413 n. 40, 51 L.Ed.2d 711 (1977). A pretrial detainee, like Sandra, is not protected by the prohibitions against cruel and unusual punishment found in the Eighth Amendment. *Revere v. Massachusetts Gen. Hosp.,* 463 U.S. 239, 244, 103 S.Ct. 2979, 2983, 77 L.Ed.2d 605 (1983). *Bell v. Wolfish,* 441 U.S. 520, 536–537, 99 S.Ct. 1861, 1872–1873, 60 L.Ed.2d 447 (1979). Rather, "[w]here the State seeks to impose punishment without [a constitutional] adjudication [of guilt], the pertinent constitutional guarantee is the Due Process Clause of the Fourteenth Amendment." *Ingraham v. Wright, supra. Revere v. Massachusetts Gen. Hosp., supra.*

The substantive protections of the due process clause limit what a State may do regardless of what procedures are followed. *Rochin v. California,* 342 U.S. 165, 173, 72 S.Ct. 205, 210, 96 L.Ed. 183 (1952). Substantive due process is a source of rights where the conduct complained of shocks the conscience or offends the community's sense of fair play and decency. *Id. White v. Rochford,* 592 F.2d 381, 383 (7th Cir.1979). *Johnson v. Glick,* 481 F.2d 1028, 1032–1033 (2d Cir.1973). *Madden v. Meriden,* 602 F.Supp. 1160, 1166–1167 (D.Conn.1985). While the Eighth Amendment does not serve as a direct source of rights for a person in protective custody, the Federal courts have applied Eighth Amendment analysis by analogy to determine what protections detainees are afforded pursuant to the principles of substantive due process. See, e.g., *Madden v. Meriden, supra* at 1163; *Meshkov v. Abington Township,* 517 F.Supp. 1280, 1284 (E.D.Pa. 1981). See also *Brewer v. Perrin,* 132 Mich.App. 520, 529 n. 3, 349 N.W.2d 198

---

8. The strictures of the Eighth Amendment were made applicable to the States by the Fourteenth Amendment. *Robinson v. California,* 370 U.S. 660, 666, 82 S.Ct. 1417, 1420, 8 L.Ed.2d 758 (1962). See *Estelle v. Gamble,* 429 U.S. 97, 101, 97 S.Ct. 285, 289, 50 L.Ed.2d 251 (1976). A

prisoner has a right to medical care in circumstances when a reasonable person would seek medical care for physical as well as psychological needs. See *Brewer v. Perrin,* 132 Mich.App. 520, 529–530, 349 N.W.2d 198 (1984), and cases cited.

(1984). Persons in police custody who have not been convicted of any crimes, therefore, "retain at least those constitutional rights that [the Supreme Court has] held are enjoyed by convicted prisoners." *Bell v. Wolfish, supra,* 441 U.S. at 535 n. 16, 545, 99 S.Ct. at 1872 n. 16, 1877. *Revere v. Massachusetts Gen. Hosp., supra,* 463 U.S. at 244, 103 S.Ct. at 2983. See *Johnson v. Glick, supra* at 1032 (it would be absurd to hold that a pretrial detainee has less constitutional protection against acts of prison guards than one convicted of a crime); *Brewer v. Perrin, supra* (same).

Applying the substantive due process standard informed by Eighth Amendment principles [9] to the facts of this case, we conclude that there was sufficient evidence here to permit a jury to find that the defendants acted with deliberate indifference to Sandra's medical needs. From the circumstances surrounding McMullan's failure to obtain proper care for Sandra when she was brought to the station, even though she was obviously intoxicated and had difficulty remaining conscious, the jury could have concluded that McMullan was deliberately indifferent to her serious medical needs. The failure of both defendants to follow department rules relating to the care and monitoring of unconscious, intoxicated, and suicidal persons in their custody when faced with an obviously intoxicated and unconscious person, defendant Dudek's

profane and racially insulting verbal response to the efforts of other prisoners to summon help when Sandra was making preparations to hang herself, and Dudek's blatant disregard of the warnings of other prisoners, certainly rise to the level of constitutional violation. The Holyoke police department rules specifying the care and monitoring intoxicated, unconscious, and suicidal persons in custody should receive dictate the minimum level of care to which standards of basic human decency entitle such persons. A jury could find that the defendants' failure to meet these standards and to respond to cries for help was more than mere negligence, that it was shocking to the conscience, and that it constituted deliberate indifference to the serious needs of a detainee in violation of Sandra's rights to substantive due process. The judgments based on the jury verdicts must stand.

2. *Availability of State Remedy.*

The defendants argue that the availability of a State remedy under G.L. c. 229, § 2, for the wrongful death of the decedent precludes an action against the police officers under 42 U.S.C. § 1983. Even assuming that the wrongful death recovery against the city provides an adequate State remedy for the police officers' actions in this case,[10] we conclude that the plaintiff's

---

9. In instructing the jury that, in order for the defendants to be held liable for a violation of § 1983, the plaintiff must demonstrate that the defendants acted with deliberate indifference to Sandra's serious physical and mental medical needs, the judge employed the Eighth Amendment standard without direct reference to the standards under substantive due process analysis. This instruction was essentially correct because, as we have mentioned earlier in this opinion, the substantive protections afforded detainees under the due process clause are equivalent to the protections enjoyed by convicted prisoners pursuant to the Eighth Amendment. *Bell v. Wolfish, supra,* 441 U.S. at 545, 99 S.Ct. at 1877. *Revere v. Massachusetts Gen. Hosp., supra,* 463 U.S. at 244, 103 S.Ct. at 2983. Even if the instruction were error, the defendants failed to object to this aspect of the instruction and have thus waived any right to appeal based on such error. See Mass.R.Civ.P. 51(b), 365 Mass. 816 (1974). See *Webster v. Kowal,* 394 Mass.

443, 446 n. 6, 476 N.E.2d 205 (1985); *Cassamasse v. J.G. Lamotte & Son,* 391 Mass. 315, 320, 461 N.E.2d 785 (1984).

10. We note that direct recovery against the police officers under G.L. c. 229, § 2, is barred by the Massachusetts Torts Claims Act, G.L. c. 258, § 2 (1984 ed.), and that the plaintiff's action for wrongful death lies only against the city of Holyoke.

In addition, we express some doubt as to whether the plaintiff's recovery for wrongful death may seriously be considered an adequate remedy for the police officers' unconstitutional treatment of the decedent. Recovery for wrongful death represents damages to the *survivor* for the loss of value of the decedent's life, including but not limited to compensation for loss of the decedent's expected net income, services and companionship. G.L. c. 229, § 2. The plaintiff's claim under 42 U.S.C. § 1983 seeks recovery on behalf of the *decedent* for the police

claims under § 1983 are not barred as a matter of law.

In *Monroe v. Pape*, 365 U.S. 167, 81 S.Ct. 473, 5 L.Ed.2d 492 (1961), the Supreme Court upheld a civil rights action under the predecessor statute to 42 U.S.C. § 1983 against Chicago police officers for an unreasonable search and seizure in violation of the Fourth and Fourteenth Amendments. The Court explicitly rejected the defendants' argument that, because State law provided a remedy for the defendant's unlawful conduct, the plaintiff could not recover under the Federal law. "It is no answer that the State has a law which if enforced would give relief. The federal remedy is supplementary to the state remedy, and the latter need not be first sought and refused before the federal one is invoked." *Id.* at 183, 81 S.Ct. at 482.

The defendants' argument that the plaintiff's § 1983 claim is barred by the availability of a State remedy under G.L. c. 229, § 2, is based upon an incorrect reading of *Parratt v. Taylor*, 451 U.S. 527, 101 S.Ct. 1908, 68 L.Ed.2d 420 (1981). In *Parratt*, a Nebraska prison inmate brought an action under 42 U.S.C. § 1983, alleging that State officials who had lost his hobby kit had deprived him of property without due process of law in violation of the Fourteenth Amendment. The Supreme Court agreed that the plaintiff had been deprived of property, *id.* at 536–537, 101 S.Ct. at 1913–1914, but concluded that this deprivation was not without "due process of law." *Id.* at 540–544, 101 S.Ct. at 1915–1917. The Court reasoned that because a predeprivation hearing is not feasible when deprivations of property are affected through random and unauthorized acts of State employees, the availability of a postdeprivation remedy under Nebraska's Tort Claims Act satisfied the due process requirements of the Fourteenth Amendment. *Id.* The Supreme Court's ruling in *Parratt* indicates that an adequate State remedy may

satisfy the requirements of procedural due process when the plaintiff alleges a deprivation of liberty or property. Subsequent courts have applied the *Parratt* rule to deprivations of liberty and property. See *Temple v. Marlborough Div. of the Dist. Court Dep't*, 395 Mass. 117, 126, 479 N.E.2d 137 (1985) (postdeprivation safeguards afforded involuntarily committed plaintiff satisfy procedural due process requirements of Fourteenth Amendment). See also *Hudson v. Palmer*, 468 U.S. 517, 533, 104 S.Ct. 3194, 3203–3204, 82 L.Ed.2d 393 (1984); *Ingraham v. Wright*, 430 U.S. 651, 672, 97 S.Ct. 1401, 1413, 51 L.Ed.2d 711 (1977). In reaching its conclusion in *Parratt*, however, the Court clearly indicated that the availability of a postdeprivation remedy, although relevant to the issue of procedural due process, would not be relevant to the alleged violation of substantive constitutional rights. "[R]espondent's claims differ from the claims which were before us in *Monroe v. Pape, supra*, which involved violations of the Fourth Amendment, and the claims presented in *Estelle v. Gamble*, 429 U.S. 97, 97 S.Ct. 285, 50 L.Ed.2d 251 (1976), which involved alleged violations of the Eighth Amendment. Both of these Amendments have been held applicable to the States by virtue of the Fourteenth Amendment. ... Respondent here refers to no other right, privilege, or immunity secured by the Constitution or federal laws other than the Due Process Clause of the Fourteenth Amendment *simpliciter*." (Citations omitted.) *Parratt, supra*, 451 U.S. at 536, 101 S.Ct. at 1913. The Supreme Court limited its holding and discussion in *Parratt* to procedural due process claims under 42 U.S.C. § 1983.

Numerous courts which have confronted the issue since *Parratt* have held that the availability of a State remedy does not bar a § 1983 claim where the plaintiff alleges a violation of a substantive constitutional right. See, e.g., *Williams v. St. Louis*, 783

---

officers' deprivation of her right to substantive due process under the Fourteenth Amendment. These remedies, though they may be parallel, are sufficiently distinct to counter any argument of double recovery. See *Hall v. Tawney*,

621 F.2d 607, 613 (4th Cir.1980) (public school student's substantive due process claim as to corporal punishment is quite distinct from claim of assault and battery under State tort law).

F.2d 114, 118 (8th Cir.1986) (equal protection); *Gilmere v. Atlanta*, 774 F.2d 1495, 1501 (11th Cir.1985), cert. denied, — U.S. ——, 106 S.Ct. 1970, 90 L.Ed.2d 654 (1986) (police brutality "shocks the conscience"); *Augustine v. Doe*, 740 F.2d 322, 326 (5th Cir.1984) (unreasonable search and seizure); *Wolf-Lillie v. Sonquist*, 699 F.2d 864, 872 (7th Cir.1983) (unreasonable seizure). See also *Hall v. Tawney*, 621 F.2d 607, 613 (4th Cir.1980) (corporal punishment); *Temple, supra*, 395 Mass. at 130–131, 479 N.E.2d 137 (specifically noting that court not confronted with substantive due process claim). Unlike procedural due process, which permits the deprivation of life, liberty, or property when such deprivation comports with due process of law, substantive due process imposes absolute limits on State action, irrespective of what procedures are provided. See *Gilmere, supra* at 1500; *Augustine, supra* at 326–327. See also *Parratt, supra*, 451 U.S. at 545, 101 S.Ct. at 1918 (Blackmun, J., concurring) ("there are certain governmental actions that even if undertaken with a full panoply of procedural protection, are, in and of themselves, antithetical to fundamental notions of due process"). Where the right asserted stems from a substantive constitutional guarantee, the availability of a post-deprivation remedy under *Parratt* is of no consequence, because the constitutional violation exists independent of any procedures available to redress the deprivation.[11] See generally Wells & Eaton, Substantive Due Process and the Scope of Constitutional Torts, 18 Ga.L.Rev. 201, 222–223 (1984).

Because the plaintiff alleges a violation of the decedent's right to substantive due process under the Fourteenth Amendment, her claim under 42 U.S.C. § 1983 is not barred by the availability of a remedy for wrongful death under G.L. c. 229, § 2.

3. *Punitive Damages.*

The defendants argue that there was insufficient evidence to submit the issue of punitive damages to the jury. We disagree. Punitive damages are recoverable in a § 1983 suit where the defendant's conduct is motivated by an evil motive or intent, or where it involves reckless or callous indifference to the plaintiff's federally protected rights. *Smith v. Wade*, 461 U.S. 30, 50–51, 103 S.Ct. 1625, 1637–1638, 75 L.Ed.2d 632 (1983).[12] *Clark v. Taylor*, 710 F.2d 4, 14 (1st Cir.1983). There was evidence that defendant McMullan, the officer who placed Sandra Smigiel in protective custody, violated department regulations clearly promulgated for safety and protection of detainees: first, by failing to attempt to transfer an intoxicated person to a treatment facility; and then, by placing an unconscious person in a cell. There was also evidence that defendant Dudek, the house officer on duty the night of Sandra Smigiel's detention, ignored the other prisoners' cries for help, and replied with profanity and a racial epithet. The police officers in their testimony denied these contentions, but the jury were, of course, free to disbelieve the police. Thus, there was evidence of reprehensible conduct, shocking to the conscience and offensive to all standards of common decency, which clearly rises to the threshold level of "callous disregard" for the decedent's substantive due process rights, and the judge did not err in submitting the issue of punitive damages to the jury.

Judgments affirmed.

---

11. The application of *Parratt* outside of the procedural due process context would emasculate 42 U.S.C. § 1983, as a meaningful Federal remedy. See *Augustine, supra* at 326–327; *Frost v. City & County of Honolulu*, 584 F.Supp. 356, 363 (D. Hawaii 1984). Since it is hard to imagine a violation of substantive due process which would not provide a concomitant remedy under State law, most if not all Federal civil rights claims under 42 U.S.C. § 1983, would in effect be precluded by a novel and unintended form of State law preemption.

12. In *Smith v. Wade, supra*, 461 U.S. at 56, 103 S.Ct. at 1640; the Supreme Court upheld an award of punitive damages in factual circumstances analogous to this case, where a correctional officer failed to protect an inmate from beatings and sexual assault by his cellmates.

Alan RANDALL, Plaintiff,

v.

James R. THOMPSON, Michael D. Lane,
Gayle Franzen, Richard DeRobertis,
and Michael P. O'Leary, Defendants.

No. 83 C 233.

United States District Court,
N.D. Illinois, E.D.

April 18, 1986.

MEMORANDUM OPINION AND ORDER

ROVNER, District Judge.

Alan Randall brings this pro se civil rights action pursuant to 42 U.S.C. § 1983 seeking damages against Governor James Thompson, the current and former Director of the Illinois Department of Corrections, and the present and former warden at the Stateville Correctional Center. On October 2, 1984, Judge Charles P. Kocoras dismissed the complaint as to defendant Thompson. The remaining four defendants are now before the Court on a motion for summary judgment.

On January 26, 1983, unknown assailants attacked Randall in the E–House tunnel at Stateville. They beat him with iron pipes and stabbed him with sharpened screwdrivers, causing serious eye damage and permanent physical injury. Randall's complaint alleges an Eighth Amendment violation and seeks to hold defendants accountable for his assault due to their authorization of a 1979 prison renovation that closed off all escape exits from the tunnel. Randall contends the design modifications in the tunnel where the attack took place and lack of sufficient personnel to secure the area created an inherent risk of harm to inmates who passed through the tunnel. He alleges several inmates have been victims of attack in the tunnel.

Relying on portions of Randall's deposition and the investigatory facts set out in reports prepared shortly after the assault, defendants maintain the assault on Randall was isolated and not attributable to any inherently dangerous condition of the E–House tunnel. They contend that to hold them liable as supervisory officials, Randall must establish their personal involvement in the attack. They assert that the single attack alleged in the complaint is insufficient to state a claim against them for supervisory malfeasance.

In response to the summary judgment motion, Randall has submitted his own affidavit and the affidavits of two fellow prisoners, Thomas Jefferson and James Terry. Jefferson's affidavit avers that since 1948 he has served thirty years at Stateville on four separate convictions. He states that from 1943 until 1978 the tunnels running from the cellhouses to the main tunnel contained escape exits. He asserts in that all but one of the forty inmate assaults he observed between 1943 and 1974, the inmate being pursued in the tunnels was able to escape through the exits. According to Jefferson, the escape exits led to areas that were under the surveillance of guards in gun towers who could protect an inmate under attack by other prisoners. Jefferson states that when he returned to Stateville in 1979, he discovered that all the emergency escape exits in the tunnels were closed and replaced with remote control gates. In March 1981, Jefferson witnessed the murder of another inmate in the C–Cellhouse tunnel. Jefferson states that the guard stationed at the door between the Cellhouse and the tunnel refused to open the door to allow the inmate access to safety.

Terry's affidavit states that a gang fight broke out in the E–Cellhouse tunnel in July 1984. He states he ran to the cellhouse door and knocked, but the officer at the door would not let him enter. He then had to fight his way back to the other end of the tunnel to escape. He does not indicate if he suffered any injuries in the incident.

In his affidavit, Randall reiterates that between 1971 and 1979 the escape exits and the two guard towers that protected inmates who used the tunnel were closed. He asserts he has witnessed "many prisoners stabbed and bludgeoned who would easily have escaped their attackers" had the safety exits in the E–Cellhouse tunnel still been available for use.

To prevail on a motion for summary judgment, the moving party has the burden of establishing that there is no genuine issue of material fact. *Korf v. Ball State University*, 726 F.2d 1222, 1226 (7th Cir. 1984). Any inferences to be drawn from the underlying facts must be viewed in the light most favorable to the non-moving party. *Hermes v. Hein*, 742 F.2d 350, 353 (7th Cir.1984). The existence of a factual dispute, however, only precludes summary judgment if the disputed fact is outcome-determinative. *Big O Tire Dealers, Inc. v. Big O Warehouse*, 741 F.2d 160, 163 (7th Cir.1984). " 'A material issue of fact is one that affects the outcome of the litigation and requires a trial to resolve the parties'

differing versions of the truth.' " *Korf*, 726 F.2d at 1226, *quoting Admiralty Fund v. Hugh Johnson & Co.*, 677 F.2d 1301, 1306 (9th Cir.1982). With these precepts in mind, the Court turns to the arguments defendants advance in support of their motion.

Defendants maintain Randall's complaint, read in the light of his deposition testimony, is a classic isolated assault case where, despite the best efforts of Stateville's administration, Randall and another inmate were injured at the hands of other inmates. Defendants point to deposition testimony wherein Randall contradicts his assertion that no correctional officers secured the area where the attack took place. Citing the presence of security staff in the vicinity of the attack and the lack of reason to anticipate any assault on Randall, defendants contend the undisputed facts fail to show that they knowingly created a condition inherently hazardous to the safety of the inmates at Stateville.

Supervisory prison officials may be held liable under the Eighth Amendment where they deliberately maintain prison conditions in such a manner as to create an inherent risk of harm to an inmate committed to their custody. *Walsh v. Brewer*, 733 F.2d 473, 476 (7th Cir.1984). Nonetheless, as the Supreme Court recently recognized in *Whitley v. Albers*, —— U.S. ——, 106 S.Ct. 1078, 1085, 89 L.Ed.2d 251, 54 U.S. L.W. 4236, 4238 (1986), "[t]o be cruel and unusual punishment, conduct that does not purport to be punishment at all must involve more than ordinary lack of due care for the prisoner's interests or safety." Thus, as the Seventh Circuit noted in *Benson v. Cady*, 761 F.2d 335, 339 (7th Cir. 1985), mere negligence or inadvertence is not sufficient to sustain a claim for relief under the Eighth Amendment. To gain relief for an alleged Eighth Amendment claim, plaintiff must prove that officials knew or had reason to know there was a strong likelihood that violence would occur. *Id.* at 340.

Randall cites two conditions as factors in his attack—the absence of any prison officials in the tunnel where the attack took place and the closing of safety exits in the tunnel. Randall's allegation that defendants' failure to ensure the presence of guards created an unconstitutional risk of harm to inmates passing through the tunnel is not, however, supported by the record. From Randall's deposition it appears that the tunnel was at least partially monitored by a camera. Moreover, Randall further stated that correctional officers routinely patrolled the tunnel. Furthermore, although Randall asserts no officer was in the tunnel at the time of the attack, documentary evidence submitted by defendants shows that a guard just outside the tunnel responded immediately to Randall's shouts and intervened to disperse his assailants. Thus, even when read in the light most favorable to Randall, the record does not reveal such a complete absence of security as to evidence more than ordinary lack of due care on the part of defendants.

But the fact that correctional officers routinely monitored the tunnel does not defeat Randall's claim that modification of the design of the tunnel to eliminate escape exits created an inherently dangerous condition. Defendants do not directly address Randall's design modification theory of liability. Randall maintains that in altering the tunnel, defendants changed a relatively safe area of the prison into a "death trap ... leaving both prisoners and prison officials 100% vulnerable for physical assaults." He alleges "[i]n the past, a hot-pursued, unarmed victim had merely to reach one of the many escape exits, and either escape to safety or scream desperately for assistance from one of the numerous 24 hour manned gun towers." To re-

but defendants' characterization of Randall's claim as a single, isolated assault, Randall submits affidavits attesting to other assaults in Stateville tunnels following the 1979 closing of the exits leading out of the tunnels. These affidavits detail only two concrete incidents involving attacks upon inmates in Stateville tunnels. One attack, which took place two years before Randall's stabbing, did not occur in the same tunnel. The other attack took place nearly eighteen months after the assault on Randall. While it may be questionable whether the two widely spaced attacks Randall specifically relies on to support his claim are enough to create an inference that defendants deliberately ignored a known risk of harm, the onus is on defendants to sufficiently respond to the theory of liability underlying Randall's complaint and to demonstrate the absence of any genuine issue of material fact. Randall, whose pro se status may have limited his ability to engage in the discovery necessary to prove his claims, also makes general allegations of other attacks. In the absence of any evidence to the contrary, the Court must conclude that a factual dispute exists as to whether attacks in the Stateville tunnels were so frequent as to put defendants on notice of the dangers caused by changes in the design of the tunnel system. Deliberate indifference to a pervasive risk of violence violates the Eighth Amendment. *See Benson*, 761 F.2d at 340.

Accordingly, for the reasons stated, the Court denies defendants' motion for summary judgment. The Court shall appoint counsel from the trial bar to represent Randall.

VOLUME II

CHAPTER 4   DISCIPLINARY PUNISHMENTS

Courts are now creating a body of law relating to due process in hearings regarding disciplinary punishments. The principles do not apply to the situation in which a prisoner is transferred to protective custody. *Wolff v. McDonnell*, 418 U.S. 539, 94 S.Ct. 2963 (1974), a controlling case, is reproduced in Vol. II: 276. In *Wolff*, the Court stated that "[p]rison officials must have the necessary discretion to keep the hearing within a reasonable limit and to refuse to call witnesses that may create a risk of reprisal or undermine authority."

There have been a number of significant cases in this area. In *Berg v. Kincheloe*, 794 F.2d 457 (9th Cir. 1986), the court found a civil rights action against prison authorities because they were deliberately indifferent or recklessly disregarded prisoner safety. *Sanchez v. Miller*, 792 F.2d 694 (7th Cir. 1986), involved the matter of whether the reliability of confidential informants was a question in a disciplinary proceeding. In *Ponte v. Real*, 105 S.Ct. 2192 (1985), a prisoner requested certain witnesses at a disciplinary hearing. Prison officials are required to give in writing their reasons for refusing to summon certain witnesses requested by the prisoner, but not necessarily at the time of the hearing. In *Freeman v. Rideout*, 808 F.2d 949 (2d Cir. 1986), the court discussed the decision of prison authorities to protect allegedly assaulted inmates "from potential retaliation against inmate witnesses." The test to be applied by the courts was whether the decision was "logically related to prevent undue hazards to institutional safety" (p. 954).

Other cases, not included here, include *Franklin v. Aycock*, 795 F.2d 1253 (6th Cir. 1986), which involved an alleged beating by prison authorities in placing a prisoner in disciplinary segregation. In *Graham v. Baughman*, 772 F.2d 441 (1985), reproduced here in the supplement to Vol. III, Chapter 5, the court held that prison authorities should have summoned witnesses requested to corroborate the prisoner's testimony that he was trying to keep burning materials from his cell. *Green v. Ferrell*, 801 F.2d 765 (5th Cir. 1986), raised the issue of due process in "tight celling." The case of *Stokes v. Fair*, 795 F.2d 235 (1st Cir. 1986), involved a challenge to the concept of "awaiting action status." Essentially, the case turned on a determination of whether state statutes created a liberty interest in the proceeding, entitling the inmate to due process in the initiation and continuance of the status. The use of confidential information was discussed in *Wagner v. Williford*, 804 F.2d 1012 (7th Cir. 1986).

Introductions in previous volumes:

II: 179; VI: 217; VII: 251; VIII: 271

Keith A. BERG, Plaintiff-Appellant,

v.

**Larry KINCHELOE, et al.,
Defendants-Appellees.**

Nos. 84–4310, 85–3963.

United States Court of Appeals,
Ninth Circuit.

Submitted April 7, 1986 *.

Decided July 14, 1986.

Before GOODWIN, HALL and THOMP-
SON, Circuit Judges.

THOMPSON, Circuit Judge:

Keith A. Berg, appearing pro se, appeals
from the district court's grant of summary
judgment in favor of the defendants in this
action under 42 U.S.C. § 1983. Berg contends that summary judgment was improper because triable issues of material fact
exist. We affirm in part, reverse in part
and remand.

I

FACTS

In August 1983 Berg, a prisoner at the
Washington State Penitentiary (the "prison"), filed a pro se civil rights complaint
under 42 U.S.C. § 1983. He named as defendants five employees of the prison: Kincheloe, Marsh, Steinbeck, Fleming and Iverson. Berg alleged that prison officials
placed him in the prison's protective custody unit because his life was in danger; that
while in that unit, Sergeant Marsh, an officer at the prison, ordered him to report to a
"tier porter job" in the protective custody
unit; that he told Marsh his life would be
in danger if he reported to the job, but
Marsh threatened him with disciplinary action if he refused to report to the site; that
he complied, and about one hour later he

was beaten and raped at the site by his cell
partner; that he was then taken to the
prison hospital but Iverson destroyed the
physical evidence (stool sample) to "cover-
up" the incident. Berg requested monetary damages for the defendants' "[callous]
disregard" of his "right to be free from
cruel and unusual punishment," and for
their "criminal negligence" in the operation
of the protective custody unit.

The defendants answered and moved for
dismissal or summary judgment. In support of their motion, the defendants
presented internal memoranda from officials at the prison and investigators of the
Walla Walla Police Department, and a
sworn affidavit from Fleming, a custodial
unit supervisor in the prison admissions
unit. The memoranda revealed that prison
officials reported the incident to police after the assault, and that both prison and
police officials conducted investigations.
Berg refused to identify his assailant to the
police, and the police disposed of the physical evidence of the rape because it could be
preserved only for a short period of time.

Fleming stated he had personally investigated the incident and had forwarded his
findings to a prison hearing committee.
According to Fleming, Berg initially had
maintained that he did not know who committed the rape, because he had been hit
from behind and had blacked out. Fleming
also stated that "the local police department closed the case because Berg refused
to prosecute and the evidence was destroyed."

Berg filed two responses to the defendants' motions. In these he stated, under
oath, that he rested on the "averments to
his pleadings ...;" that prison officer
Marsh's order to report to the tier porter
job "assisted the rape and assault ...;"
and that "other prisoners ... can enlarge
to prison discipline, assault and rapes, [and]
are relevant to determine the peril ... to
the plaintiff ... [of] said rapes and as-

---

* The panel unanimously finds this case suitable
for disposition without oral argument. Fed.R.
App.P. 34(a); Ninth Circuit Rule 3(f).

saults—and such witnesses will be called by the plaintiff." In subsequent papers, Berg stated he was twenty-six years old, weighed one hundred thirty pounds and was five feet seven. He also sought to introduce affidavits from other prisoners who had allegedly suffered rapes and beatings.

The district court granted the defendants' summary judgment motion, ruling that Berg had failed to present any genuine issue of material fact or demonstrate that the defendants' actions proximately caused the rape and beating. Berg appeals.

II

STANDARD OF REVIEW AND APPLICABLE LEGAL STANDARD

We review de novo the district court's grant of summary judgment, and apply the same standard as applied by the district court under Fed.R.Civ.P. 56(c). *Hope v. International Brotherhood of Electrical Workers*, 785 F.2d 826, 828–29 (9th Cir. 1986). Summary judgment is appropriate if, viewing the evidence in the light most favorable to the party opposing the motion, there is no genuine issue of material fact and the moving party is entitled to judgment as a matter of law. *Swayze v. United States*, 785 F.2d 715, 717 (9th Cir.1986). The party opposing summary judgment may not rest on conclusory allegations, but must set forth specific facts showing that there is a genuine issue for trial. *Mosher v. Saalfeld*, 589 F.2d 438, 442 (9th Cir.1978) (involving a pro se litigant), *cert. denied*, 442 U.S. 941, 99 S.Ct. 2883, 61 L.Ed.2d 311 (1979).

A prisoner may state a section 1983 claim under the eighth and fourteenth amendments against prison officials where the officials acted with "deliberate indifference" to the threat of serious harm or injury by another prisoner. *See e.g., Hoptowit v. Ray*, 682 F.2d 1237, 1250 (9th Cir.1982); *Franklin v. Oregon*, 662 F.2d 1337, 1347 (9th Cir.1981) (and cases cited

infra). The "deliberate indifference" standard requires a finding of some degree of "individual culpability," but does not require an express intent to punish. *Haygood v. Younger*, 769 F.2d 1350, 1354–55 (9th Cir.1985) (en banc), *petition for cert. filed sub nom, Crake v. Haygood*, 54 U.S. L.W. 3489 (U.S. Jan. 21, 1986) (No. 85–908). The standard does not require that the guard or official " 'believe to a moral certainty that one inmate intends to attack another at a given place at a time certain before that officer is obligated to take steps to prevent such an assault. But, on the other hand, he must have more than a mere suspicion that an attack will occur.' " *State Bank of St. Charles v. Camic*, 712 F.2d 1140, 1146 (7th Cir.) (*quoting Vun Cannon v. Breed*, 391 F.Supp. 1371, 1374–75 (N.D. Cal.1975)), *cert. denied*, 464 U.S. 995, 104 S.Ct. 491, 78 L.Ed.2d 686 (1983).

III

ANALYSIS

The eighth and fourteenth amendments of the United States Constitution prohibit the infliction of "cruel and unusual" punishment. *See, e.g., Ingraham v. Wright*, 430 U.S. 651, 664–68, 97 S.Ct. 1401, 1408–11, 51 L.Ed.2d 711 (1977); *Haygood*, 769 F.2d at 1354. We have recognized that a prisoner may assert a valid cause of action under section 1983 against state prison officials where the prisoner has suffered "cruel and unusual" punishment. *See, e.g., id.* at 1354–55. *See also Whitley v. Albers*, — U.S. —, 106 S.Ct. 1078, 1084, 89 L.Ed.2d 251 (1986). To violate this constitutional proscription, the "punishment must be incompatible with 'the evolving standards of decency that mark the progress of a maturing society,' " *Haygood*, 769 F.2d at 1354 (*quoting Trop v. Dulles*, 356 U.S. 86, 101, 78 S.Ct. 590, 598, 2 L.Ed.2d 630 (1958)), "or must involve unnecessary or wanton pain disproportionate to the severity of the crime." *Id.* (*citing Solem v. Helm*, 463 U.S. 277, 288, 103 S.Ct. 3001, 3008, 77 L.Ed.2d 637 (1983)).

A prison authority need not brandish a gun or employ a billy club to transgress the evolving standards of decency. History and precedent teach that the cruel and unusual punishments clause reaches other contexts, as well. *Ingraham*, 430 U.S. at 664–68, 97 S.Ct. at 1408–11. A prisoner may state a valid section 1983 claim (under the eighth and fourteenth amendments) against a prison official who was aware that the prisoner was seriously ill but ignored his request for assistance. *See, e.g., Estelle v. Gamble*, 429 U.S. 97, 102, 97 S.Ct. 285, 290, 50 L.Ed.2d 251 (1976); *Broughton v. Cutter Laboratories*, 622 F.2d 458, 460 (9th Cir.1980). In these circumstances, the court will impose liability where the official acted with "deliberate indifference" to the prisoner's plight. *Estelle*, 429 U.S. at 104–06, 97 S.Ct. at 291–92; *May v. Enomoto*, 633 F.2d 164, 167 (9th Cir.1980). Although prison officials are ordinarily accorded "wide-ranging deference" in the administration of prisons, *Bell v. Wolfish*, 441 U.S. 520, 547, 99 S.Ct. 1861, 1878, 60 L.Ed.2d 447 (1979), " 'deliberate indifference to a prisoner's serious illness or injury,' ... can typically be established or disproved without the necessity of balancing competing institutional concerns for the safety of prison staff or other inmates." *Whitley*, 106 S.Ct. at 1084 (citation omitted).

But a prisoner will not always obtain recovery solely upon a showing of "deliberate indifference." Protecting the safety of prisoners and staff involves difficult choices and evades easy solutions. *Bell*, 441 U.S. at 547, 99 S.Ct. at 1878. Courts often lack competence to evaluate fully prison administrative decisions. *Id.* at 547–48, 99 S.Ct. at 1878–79. *See generally Hudson v. Palmer*, 468 U.S. 517, ——, 104 S.Ct. 3194, 3200, 82 L.Ed.2d 393 (1984). In certain situations—as when prison officials respond to an outbreak of violence—the "deliberate indifference standard does not adequately capture the importance of such competing obligations, or convey the appropriate hesitancy to critique in hindsight decisions necessarily made in haste, under pressure, and frequently without the luxu-

ry of a second chance." *Whitley*, 106 S.Ct. at 1085. In these cases, liability involves a balancing of a number of factors, and turns upon " 'whether force was applied in a good faith effort to maintain or restore discipline or maliciously and sadistically for the very purpose of causing harm.' " *Id.* (*quoting Johnson v. Glick*, 481 F.2d 1028, 1033 (2d Cir.), *cert. denied* 414 U.S. 1033, 94 S.Ct. 462, 38 L.Ed.2d 324 (1973)). The Supreme Court has stated that deference to the decisions of prison officials also extends to "prophylactic or preventive measures intended to reduce the incidence of these or any other breaches of prison discipline." *Id.*

Turning to Berg's allegations, we consider separately his claims against defendants Kincheloe, Steinbeck, Fleming and Iverson from those asserted against Marsh. As to the former defendants, Berg failed to demonstrate the existence of any evidence which would substantiate his allegations. He failed to come forward with facts showing that these defendants had any reason to believe he would be attacked by the assailant. *See, e.g., Porm v. White*, 762 F.2d 635, 638 (8th Cir.1985); *Walsh v. Brewer*, 733 F.2d 473, 477 (7th Cir.1984). *See generally Mosher*, 589 F.2d at 442 (involving a pro se litigant). Further, the evidence indicates that Berg's allegations of a "cover-up" are unfounded. Prison officials investigated the incident and delivered all physical evidence to the police (who are not defendants in this case). We find no evidence of "individual culpability," and summary judgment was appropriate as to defendants Kincheloe, Steinbeck, Fleming and Iverson.

However, viewing the evidence in the light most favorable to Berg, we cannot say he has failed to present a genuine issue of material fact as to the liability of defendant Sergeant Marsh. Berg alleged he had been placed in the protective custody unit because his "life was in danger." He further alleged that he specifically told Marsh his life would be in danger if he reported to the tier porter job, but that Marsh ignored that plea and ordered him to report to that job anyway; and that shortly thereafter, he was beaten and raped. Marsh did not present any supporting affidavit to refute Berg's allegations. Berg's pro se complaint, read liberally, states a prima facie cause of action against Marsh under the eighth and fourteenth amendments, and his complaint may not be dismissed "unless it appears certain that [he] can prove no set of facts which would entitle him ... to relief." *Haddock v. Board of Dental Examiners*, 777 F.2d 462, 464 (9th Cir.1985). Berg has provided sufficient detail in his complaint and other pleadings to withstand Marsh's unsupported request for summary judgment. *See Watts v. Laurent*, 774 F.2d 168, 172-74 (7th Cir.1985), *cert. denied*, — U.S. —, 106 S.Ct. 1466, 89 L.Ed.2d 722 (1986).

Berg's allegations with respect to defendant Marsh are analogous to a case in which a prisoner-patient seeks but is denied relief from an infirmity. *See, e.g., Estelle*, 429 U.S. 97, 97 S.Ct. 285. Here the danger comes not from the untreated disease, but the unprevented attack. The similarities between the two situations, as measured by the existence of warning and availability of redress, are obvious. As noted, in both cases, liability is measured by the "deliberate indifference" standard. *See, e.g., Hoptowit*, 682 F.2d at 1250; *Franklin*, 662 F.2d at 1347. *See also Riley v. Jeffes*, 777 F.2d 143, 147 (3d Cir.1985); *Porm*, 762 F.2d at 636-37.

We recognize, however, that, unlike the "medical emergency" case, a case involving an individual prisoner's safety from attacks by other prisoners may implicate "competing institutional concerns for the safety of prison staff or other inmates." *Whitley*, 106 S.Ct. at 1084. Removing a prisoner from a hostile or vengeful inmate may protect the prisoner, but the move may endanger others—particularly if the prisoner is himself dangerous. *See generally Marchesani v. McCune*, 531 F.2d 459, 462 (10th

Cir.), *cert. denied*, 429 U.S. 846, 97 S.Ct. 127, 50 L.Ed.2d 117 (1976); *Lee v. Carlson*, 564 F.Supp. 1048, 1053 (M.D.Pa.1983). Further, "[p]risons, by definition, are places of involuntary confinement of persons who have a demonstrated proclivity for antisocial, criminal, and often violent, conduct." *Hudson*, 468 U.S. at —, 104 S.Ct. at 3200. As the Tenth Circuit observed, "[m]any prisoners are unpredictable. [The] [p]rison setting is, at best, tense. It is sometimes explosive, and always potentially dangerous." *Marchesani*, 531 F.2d at 462. *See also Riley*, 777 F.2d at 145-46; *McLaughlin v. Royster*, 346 F.Supp. 297, 312 (E.D.Va.1972).[1] Public "deliberate indifference" or manpower limitations may place constraints on the choices available to prison officials. *See Wright v. Rushen*, 642 F.2d 1129, 1134 (9th Cir.1981) (costs often constrain ability to act). In deciding how to protect a prisoner, officials may face a number of choices, each posing potential dangers to the prisoner and others. Choosing the optimal "prophylactic or preventive measures" to prevent violence and maintain safety is difficult and not readily susceptible to judicial evaluation. *Whitley*, 106 S.Ct. at 1085; *Bell*, 441 U.S. at 547-48, 99 S.Ct. at 1878-79; *Pell v. Procunier*, 417 U.S. 817, 827, 94 S.Ct. 2800, 2806, 41 L.Ed.2d 495 (1974) (recognizing the difficulties in "maintaining internal order").

The allegations in Berg's complaint illustrate some of these concerns. Berg stated he was placed in the protective custody unit because his "life was in danger," and he was sent to a job assignment in the protective custody unit. This suggests that in deciding how best to protect Berg, prison officials (Marsh included) may have been guided by considerations of safety to other inmates, or they may have made a practical judgment as to the best means of protecting Berg, given the inherent dangers of the prison environment. *See generally Martin v. White*, 742 F.2d 469, 475 (8th Cir.1984) (requiring not only a showing

---

1. In *McLaughlin*, the court stated: "In a penal institution there is always the danger of riots, or lesser disturbances, which may result in injuries to nonparticipants. This exists, probably, so long as each inmate is not confined behind bars at all hours." *Id.* at 312.

of "deliberate indifference" or reckless disregard of prisoner's safety, but also an unreasonable response by officials to the risk); *Lee*, 564 F.Supp. at 1053 (considerations of safety for others may affect decisions).

We believe that in applying the "deliberate indifference" standard in this particular context, the trier of fact (judge or jury) must take into account the foregoing considerations. Specifically, the trier must consider whether, in allegedly exposing the prisoner to danger, the defendant prison official(s) were guided by considerations of safety to other inmates, whether the official(s) took "prophylactic or preventive measures" to protect the prisoner, *Whitley*, 106 S.Ct. at 1085, and whether less dangerous alternatives were in fact available. More generally, the legal standard must not be applied to an idealized vision of prison life, but to the prison as it exists, and as prison official(s) are realistically capable of influencing. In short, the trier must consider context, as well as consequences. If the evidence only involves a "dispute over the ... existence of arguably superior alternatives," *id.*, at 1085–86, then the Supreme Court has indicated that the plaintiff has not met his burden and the case should not be presented to a jury. *Id.*

We recognize that a further airing of the evidence may indicate that at most Berg may only be able to prove an isolated incident of negligence for which he is not entitled to recovery from Marsh. *See Williams v. Field*, 416 F.2d 483, 485 (9th Cir. 1969) (also involving claim under equal protection), *cert. denied*, 397 U.S. 1016, 90 S.Ct. 1252, 25 L.Ed.2d 431 (1970).[2] Alternatively, the evidence may establish that Marsh acted with "deliberate indifference" under the totality of the circumstances in this case when he compelled Berg to report to the tier porter job in the protective custody unit where he was beaten and raped.[3]

In deciding that the district court erred in granting Marsh's motion for summary judgment, we express no opinion as to whether Berg is entitled to a recovery under the "deliberate indifference" standard we have discussed. We hold only that summary judgment dismissing Berg's claim against Marsh at this stage of the proceedings was inappropriate.

AFFIRMED as to defendants Kincheloe, Steinberg, Fleming and Iverson. REVERSED as to defendant Marsh, and REMANDED.

---

2. *See also* 51 A.L.R. 3d § 8[a], at 157 (1973 & Supp. 1985).

3. *Williams* is consistent with our resolution of this case. There, we held that the plaintiff had failed to state a cause of action under the eighth amendment applying "three tests [that] have been used to determine whether the conduct complained of constitutes cruel and unusual punishment." *Id.* at 486. Specifically, we held that the plaintiff's complaint failed to indicate that the defendants' actions "shock[ed] the conscience," or involved "punishment greatly disproportionate to the offense," or "beyond legitimate penal aims." *Id.* While Berg has also failed to state a cause of action under these three tests, we hold that he has stated a cause of action under the "deliberate indifference" standard enunciated by the Court in *Estelle*, 429 U.S. 97, 97 S.Ct. 285, which was decided after *Williams*.

Ruben Ramirez SANCHEZ,
Petitioner-Appellant,

v.

H.G. MILLER, Warden, United States
Penitentiary, Marion, Illinois,
Respondent-Appellee.

No. 84–2872.

United States Court of Appeals,
Seventh Circuit.

Argued May 21, 1985.

Decided June 9, 1986.

Rehearing Denied Aug. 5, 1986.

Before BAUER and ESCHBACH, Circuit
Judges, and SWYGERT, Senior Circuit
Judge.

ESCHBACH, Circuit Judge.

The petitioner, an inmate in a federal
penitentiary, filed this action for habeas-
corpus relief in federal district court challenging the constitutionality of an institution disciplinary hearing conducted in 1980
that resulted in the loss of his good-time
credits. The district court concluded that
the petitioner's due-process rights had not
been violated and granted summary judgment for the respondent.[1] For the reasons
stated below, we will affirm.

I

On November 20, 1979, Charles Hughes,
an inmate at the United States Penitentiary
in Lompoc, California, was stabbed to
death in the prison. On November 21,
1979, the petitioner, Ruben Ramirez Sanchez, was placed in administrative segregation pending an investigation into Hughes's
death. On December 13, 1979, Sanchez
received an incident report charging him
with (1) "Killing" and (2) "Aiding Another

and Making Plans to Commit" the killing.[2]
The incident report stated that "[c]onfiden-
tial information has named you as being
one of the assailants in the stabbing death
of inmate HUGHES, Charles[,] Reg[.] No.
68858–012(C)" that occurred in "C–Unit,
Cell A–12" at "10:30 a.m." on "November
20, 1979."

On December 19, 1979, the Unit Disciplinary Committee ("UDC") at Lompoc found
Sanchez guilty of both offenses, and stated
in its written decision that its findings were
based on "[c]onfidential information obtained by institution staff, confidential
memos and statement by reporting officers." The UDC referred the matter to the
Institution Disciplinary Committee ("IDC")
at Lompoc for a hearing. Sanchez was
provided with notice that the IDC hearing
was scheduled for December 27, 1979, and
signed a form acknowledging that he had
been informed of his rights.

On December 27, 1979, Sanchez's request
for a two-week postponement was granted,
and the IDC hearing was held on January
10, 1980. At the hearing, Sanchez denied
that the incident report was "true as written" and maintained that he was in the
C-Unit at the time of the murder, but on a
different tier. Three inmates testified on
behalf of Sanchez, and his remaining three
witnesses were excused because Sanchez
had indicated that their testimony would
have been essentially the same as that of
the first three. The IDC report includes a
summary of the statements of the three
inmates who testified. The IDC considered
the testimony of the witnesses, as well as
the "[c]onfidential memo from [Investiga-
tor Tom Lynch] identifying two inmate witnesses and their confidential information"
in reaching its decision, and concluded that
Sanchez's "plans resulted in the death of
inmate Charles HUGHES." After finding

1. Sanchez brought this suit against H.G. Miller
in the latter's official capacity as warden at
Marion. Jerry Williford is now the warden of
that institution. Pursuant to Fed.R.App.P. 43(c),
"[w]hen a public official is a party to an appeal
or other proceeding in the court of appeals in
his official capacity and during its pendency ...

ceases to hold office, the action does not abate
and his successor is automatically substituted as
a party."

2. The delivery of the charge had been delayed
pending an FBI investigation into the incident.

Sanchez guilty, the IDC ordered (1) a forfeiture of his statutory good time, (2) continued custody in administrative segregation, and (3) a disciplinary transfer.

Sanchez then filed an initial administrative appeal with the warden at Lompoc seeking restoration of his good-time credits and expungement of the incident report; relief was denied on January 25, 1980.[3] He then appealed to the Regional Director of the Bureau of Prisons, who on March 12, 1980, found that the evidence before the IDC only supported the charge of aiding another and making plans to commit the murder, but not the murder charge. The Regional Director instructed the warden to correct any reports that indicated Sanchez had been found guilty of the actual killing. Further relief was denied. Sanchez attempted to file an appeal with the General Counsel, but it was untimely.

Sanchez was indicted by a grand jury and tried in 1982 in federal district court for the Central District of California for the murder of Hughes, conspiracy to commit murder, and aiding and abetting. The jury returned a verdict of not guilty. Sanchez then filed another series of administrative appeals relating to the 1980 IDC action. These appeals were rejected as untimely.[4]

Sanchez was later incarcerated at the United States Penitentiary at Marion, Illinois, and filed this action in the federal district court for the Southern District of Illinois on January 9, 1984. He sought federal habeas-corpus relief on the ground that he was denied due process at the 1980

IDC hearing at Lompoc.[5] By consent of the parties, the case was submitted to a magistrate pursuant to 28 U.S.C. § 636(c). The warden transmitted to the court under seal the documents relied upon by the IDC (including the investigator's memoranda). Each party moved for summary judgment. The magistrate granted the warden's motion and denied that of Sanchez, and the petition for a writ of habeas corpus was accordingly denied. This appeal followed.

II

A. *Failure to Exhaust Administrative Remedies*

It is beyond dispute that Sanchez failed to exhaust his administrative remedies. The respondent brought this issue to the attention of the district court in its first motion for summary judgment, and filed two affidavits that documented the administrative appeals Sanchez had filed. Sanchez did not deny that he failed to meet the exhaustion requirement. After counsel was appointed to represent Sanchez, the original habeas petition was amended to include additional due-process claims. The respondent supplemented his motion for summary judgment to address these new allegations. The magistrate decided the case on the merits and did not discuss the exhaustion issue. The respondent now urges that the judgment below may be affirmed on the ground that Sanchez did not exhaust his administrative remedies. It is, of course, proper for the party in whose favor the judgment was entered to

---

3. There are three levels of appeals within the federal prison system. The inmate appeals the IDC decision first to his warden, then to the Regional Director, and finally to the General Counsel. *See* 28 C.F.R. §§ 541.19, 542 (1985). Appeal to the Office of General Counsel is the final administrative appeal in the Bureau of Prisons. *Id.* § 542.15. The current regulations governing administrative appeals went into effect on November 1, 1979. *See* 44 Fed.Reg. 62,248 (1979). For a general discussion of the administrative process, see *Anderson v. Miller*, 772 F.2d 375, 377 (7th Cir.1985), *cert. denied*, — U.S. —, 106 S.Ct. 1210, 89 L.Ed.2d 322 (1986).

4. The notice from the General Counsel informing Sanchez that his second round of appeals was untimely did state, however: "Judicial and administrative standards differ considerably. Accordingly, your acquittal in court would not automatically result in expungement of the IDC action."

5. Sanchez initially proceeded *pro se.* Howard B. Eisenberg, Associate Professor of Law at Southern Illinois University School of Law, was subsequently appointed to represent Sanchez before the district court and on appeal. We are grateful to Professor Eisenberg for his able and distinguished representation of Sanchez.

assert any ground appearing in the record in support of the judgment, whether or not that ground was relied upon by the trial court. *Whitley v. Albers,* — U.S. —, —, 106 S.Ct. 1078, 1088, 89 L.Ed.2d 251 (1986); *Farmer v. Prast,* 721 F.2d 602, 606 n. 7 (7th Cir.1983).[6]

Federal prisoners are ordinarily required to exhaust administrative remedies before petitioning for a writ of habeas corpus. *Jackson v. Carlson,* 707 F.2d 943, 949 (7th Cir.), *cert. denied,* 464 U.S. 861, 104 S.Ct. 189, 78 L.Ed.2d 167 (1983); *see also Anderson v. Miller,* 772 F.2d 375, 377 (7th Cir.1985), *cert. denied,* — U.S. —, 106 S.Ct. 1210, 89 L.Ed.2d 322 (1986); *Brice v. Day,* 604 F.2d 664 (10th Cir.1979), *cert. denied,* 444 U.S. 1086, 100 S.Ct. 1045, 62 L.Ed.2d 772 (1980); *Guida v. Nelson,* 603 F.2d 261 (2d Cir.1979); *United States ex rel. Sanders v. Arnold,* 535 F.2d 848 (3d Cir.1976); *Hardwick v. Ault,* 517 F.2d 295 (5th Cir.1975); *Willis v. Ciccone,* 506 F.2d 1011 (8th Cir.1974). Because the time limits for the administrative appeals have long since elapsed and because the Bureau of Prisons has in no way indicated that it will waive the applicable time limits for those appeals, *cf. Anderson,* 772 F.2d at 378, Sanchez cannot now complete the process. His failure to pursue his administrative remedies to their conclusion constitutes a procedural default. *Cf. Engle v. Isaac,* 456 U.S. 107, 124–25 & n. 28, 102 S.Ct. 1558, 1570 & n. 28, 71 L.Ed.2d 783 (1982); *Nutall v. Greer,* 764 F.2d 462, 464 (7th Cir.1985).

The question presented under these facts is what should be the effect of such a default. The respondent urges that the appeal should be dismissed. We disagree, and find instead that Sanchez should be required to make a showing of "cause and prejudice." This court adumbrated such a requirement in *Anderson,* 772 F.2d at 378. However, the issue was apparently not properly presented in that appeal, and we ruled that the prisoners had deliberately failed to comply with the established proce-

dures for prosecuting appeals before the Bureau of Prisons, even though they had twice been warned of the inadequacies of their submissions. *Id.*

The cause-and-prejudice rule was originally articulated in *Davis v. United States,* 411 U.S. 233, 93 S.Ct. 1577, 36 L.Ed.2d 216 (1973). *Davis* involved a federal prisoner who, petitioning under 28 U.S.C. § 2255, sought to challenge for the first time the composition of the grand jury that had indicted him. The government argued that such a challenge was barred because the prisoner failed to comply with Fed.R. Crim.P. 12, which provides that objections to grand-jury composition be presented at trial, and that failure to do so constitutes a waiver of the objection, but that the court "for cause shown may grant relief from the waiver." The Supreme Court concluded that review of the claim on a petition for habeas should be barred in the absence of a showing by the prisoner of cause for the failure to comply with procedural requirements and of actual prejudice resulting from the alleged constitutional violation. 411 U.S. at 243–45, 93 S.Ct. at 1583–84.

In *Francis v. Henderson,* 425 U.S. 536, 96 S.Ct. 1708, 48 L.Ed.2d 149 (1976), the Court applied the rule of *Davis* to a case involving a state procedural requirement that a challenge to the composition of the grand jury be raised before trial. The Court noted that the federal judiciary had the power to entertain such a challenge, but rested its holding on "considerations of comity and concerns for the orderly administration of criminal justice." *Id.* at 538–39, 96 S.Ct. at 1710. Although the state rule at issue in *Francis* did not allow for an exception upon a showing of cause, the Court concluded that the cause-and-prejudice standard of *Davis* should nonetheless apply, because there was no reason to give greater preclusive effect to procedural defaults by federal prisoners than to similar defaults by state prisoners. *Id.* at 542, 96 S.Ct. at 1711. The rule of *Francis* was

---

6. Sanchez maintains on appeal that the respondent waived the exhaustion issue by failing to press the claim below. As the discussion in the text indicates, Sanchez's description of the respondent's presentation below is inaccurate.

extended in *Wainwright v. Sykes*, 433 U.S. 72, 97 S.Ct. 2497, 53 L.Ed.2d 594 (1977), in which the Court held that federal habeas review was barred, absent a showing of cause and prejudice, when the prisoner waived, under state law, his objection to the admission of his confession at trial. *See also Engle v. Isaac*, 456 U.S. 107, 129, 102 S.Ct. 1558, 1572–73, 71 L.Ed.2d 783 (1982). In *United States v. Frady*, 456 U.S. 152, 167–68, 102 S.Ct. 1584, 1594, 71 L.Ed.2d 816 (1982), the Court applied a requirement of cause and prejudice in a § 2255 action involving Fed.R.Crim.P. 30, which, unlike Rule 12, contained no explicit exception to the requirement of a timely challenge to jury instructions. *See also Nutall v. Greer*, 764 F.2d 462 (7th Cir.1985) (state prisoner who fails to seek leave to present to highest state court constitutional objections forming basis of his habeas petition waives those objections unless he can show cause and prejudice); *Norris v. United States*, 687 F.2d 899 (7th Cir.1982) (cause-and-prejudice standard applicable in determining whether constitutional issue not raised on direct appeal from conviction could be considered in § 2255 proceeding).

As the discussion above indicates, the cause-and-prejudice requirement is generally applied to resurrect a federal habeas petition otherwise precluded by a procedural default, whether the default occurs in federal or state court, at trial or on appeal, and whether or not the procedural rule expressly incorporates a cause-and-prejudice standard.[7] Although courts in cases involving state prisoners usually cite comity as the reason for the cause-and-prejudice requirement, *see Wainwright*, 433 U.S. at 84, 97 S.Ct. at 2505, that rationale does not, of course, support its application to those convicted in federal courts. *See Frady*, 456 U.S. at 162–66, 102 S.Ct. at 1591–93. Rather, the underlying policy seems to be that, before either a state or federal prisoner may seek federal habeas relief, he must first present his claim to the forum initially available, primarily because of the costs

associated with granting a writ of habeas corpus. *See Engle*, 456 U.S. at 126–29, 102 S.Ct. at 1571–72 (discussion of costs). The forum with the primary jurisdiction does not simply provide a preliminary determination, but a final one, and the grant of a habeas writ is intended to be the exception, not the rule. For state prisoners challenging their convictions, that initial forum is the state court system. For federal prisoners challenging their convictions, it is the federal courts in the direct appeal process. For federal prisoners challenging disciplinary proceedings, it is the administrative process. It would be anomalous to allow prisoners challenging their convictions to overcome the bar of a procedural default in the court system through a showing of cause and prejudice, but to dismiss outright the claims of the same prisoners challenging prison disciplinary actions because of a procedural default in the administrative process. *Cf. Francis*, 425 U.S. at 542, 96 S.Ct. at 1711.

In addition, the reasons for requiring that prisoners challenging disciplinary actions exhaust their administrative remedies are analogous to the reasons for requiring that they exhaust their judicial remedies before challenging their convictions; thus, the effect of a failure to exhaust in either context should be similar. As the Supreme Court noted in *Schlesinger v. Councilman*, 420 U.S. 738, 756–57, 95 S.Ct. 1300, 1312, 43 L.Ed.2d 591 (1975):

The [exhaustion] rule, looking to the special competence of agencies in which Congress has reposed the duty to perform particular tasks, is based on the need to allow agencies to develop the facts, to apply the law in which they are peculiarly expert, and to correct their own errors. The rule ensures that whatever judicial review is available will be informed and narrowed by the agencies' own decisions. It also avoids duplicative proceedings, and often the agency's ulti-

---

7. For the reasons stated in *United States ex rel. Spurlark v. Wolff*, 699 F.2d 354, 357–61 (7th Cir.1983) (en banc), and *Norris v. United States*, 687 F.2d 899 (7th Cir.1982), we conclude that the "deliberate bypass" rule does not apply in this case.

mate decisions will obviate the need for judicial intervention.

We also observe that circumvention of the administrative process diminishes the effectiveness of the agency by encouraging prisoners to ignore its procedures. *See McKart v. United States*, 395 U.S. 185, 195, 89 S.Ct. 1657, 1663, 23 L.Ed.2d 194 (1969); *see also Brice*, 604 F.2d at 666–68; *Smith v. Fenton*, 424 F.Supp. 792, 795–99 (E.D.Ill.1976).

Thus, we reaffirm that a federal prisoner challenging a disciplinary decision within the federal institution must exhaust his administrative remedies before seeking federal habeas relief. In addition, we hold that, if the prisoner has failed to exhaust and the administrative process is now unavailable, his habeas claim is barred unless he can demonstrate cause and prejudice. As noted above, the district court did not rule on the exhaustion question. We could remand for further proceedings, but, as the discussion in the following section will indicate, a remand is unnecessary, because Sanchez cannot demonstrate prejudice. *See Nutall*, 764 F.2d at 465.

B. *Prejudice*

1. *Use of Confidential Information*

Sanchez's primary claim on appeal is that he was denied due process of law at the 1980 IDC hearing that led to his adjudication of guilt and the loss of his good-time credits. He specifically alleges that the hearing was constitutionally infirm because the IDC did not determine that the confidential informants were reliable and because a showing was not made that the informants were in fact reliable. Sanchez rests his claim on the decision of the Supreme Court in *Wolff v. McDonnell*, 418 U.S. 539, 94 S.Ct. 2963, 41 L.Ed.2d 935 (1974) and this court's decision in *McCollum v. Miller*, 695 F.2d 1044 (7th Cir.1982).

In *Wolff*, the Supreme Court set forth the due-process requirements for prison disciplinary proceedings. The Court noted that, although a prisoner is not wholly stripped of constitutional protections when he is imprisoned, lawful imprisonment necessarily makes unavailable many rights and privileges of the ordinary citizen.[8] In addition, the Court noted that disciplinary proceedings are not part of a criminal prosecution and, therefore, that the full panoply of rights due a defendant in criminal cases does not apply. Although prisoners may have a liberty interest in good-time credits, there must be a mutual accommodation between (1) the needs and objectives of the correctional institution and (2) the provisions of the Constitution that are of general application. *Id.*, 418 U.S. at 555–57, 94 S.Ct. at 2974–75.

The Court in *Wolff* looked to the procedures developed in the context of revocation of parole and probation,[9] and concluded that some, but not all, of these procedures should apply to disciplinary proceedings implicating a constitutionally protected interest. After noting that parole and probation revocation and prison discipline implicate different interests and that the respective proceedings are conducted in different settings, *id.* at 558–63, 94 S.Ct. at 2976–78, the Court held that, in the context of disciplinary proceedings, prisoners were entitled to 24 hours' advance written notice of the charges against them; the right to call witnesses and present documentary evidence in their defense, unless doing so would jeopardize institutional safety or correctional goals; the aid of a staff member or inmate in presenting a defense, provided the accused inmate is illiterate or the issues complex; and an impartial tribunal. *Id.* at 563–72, 94 S.Ct. at 2978–82. The Court also concluded that there must be a "written statement by the factfinders as to the evidence relied on and reasons for the disciplinary action." *Id.* at 563–72, 94 S.Ct. at 2978–82. The Court stated that "[w]ithin the limits set forth in this opinion we are content for now to leave the continuing

---

8. *See also Hudson v. Palmer*, 468 U.S. 517, 104 S.Ct. 3194, 82 L.Ed.2d 393 (1984).

9. *See, e.g., Gagnon v. Scarpelli*, 411 U.S. 778, 93 S.Ct. 1756, 36 L.Ed.2d 656 (1973); *Morrissey v. Brewer*, 408 U.S. 471, 92 S.Ct. 2593, 33 L.Ed.2d 484 (1972).

development of measures to review adverse actions affecting inmates to the sound discretion of corrections officials administering the scope of such inquiries." *Id.* at 568, 94 S.Ct. at 2981.

At issue in *McCollum v. Miller*, 695 F.2d 1044 (7th Cir.1982), were the due-process requirements for disciplinary proceedings where the evidence in support of a finding of guilt was provided by confidential informants. *Wolff* requires written notice of the disciplinary charge sufficient to mount a defense. The general notice the prisoner in *McCollum* received of the charges against him precluded the preparation of an effective defense. More detailed notice could not be given, however, without revealing the identities of the informants. In addition, the investigator did not give his report under oath, and he did not testify at the hearing. The IDC would not vouch for the credibility of the informants, but did indicate that the use of informants had proved reliable in the past, although it was apparently not referring to the specific informants involved. This court found that, because there was a significant risk of error under these facts, these procedures did not comport with due process, but concluded that the record was not sufficiently developed to permit a determination of what "additional safeguards" were appropriate in light of *Wolff.* We noted that it should be "feasible to insist that the [IDC] require that its investigative reports be under oath and that the investigator appear in person and be available for cross-examination; but we are not sure whether it is feasible to go further and require the [IDC] to interview—*in camera,* of course—some or all of the informants." [10] This court did not explicitly hold that the IDC must make a reliability finding in all disciplinary proceedings.

Confidential informants were again at issue in *Jackson v. Carlson*, 707 F.2d 943 (7th Cir.), *cert. denied*, 464 U.S. 861, 104 S.Ct. 189, 78 L.Ed.2d 167 (1983), a consolidated appeal of the habeas claims of five federal prisoners. The IDC found one of the prisoners guilty on the basis of an unsworn investigator's report, and the charge was supported by evidence from informants and a prison employee. The investigator did not testify, and the prisoner was not given the report or the names of the informants. He was, however, given detailed notice of the charges against him. His hearing was held to comport with due process. *Id.* at 948. Another prisoner was found guilty on the basis of confidential information, but had adequate notice of the incident, which should have allowed him to identify the informants. In addition, the chairman of the IDC stated on the record that he had firsthand knowledge of the informants and considered them reliable because of "their past record of reliability." These proceedings were also considered constitutional. *Id.* This court in *Jackson* did not read *McCollum* to require an express reliability finding from the IDC in every case. *Id.* at 947, 948.

In *Dawson v. Smith*, 719 F.2d 896, 899 (7th Cir.1983), *cert. denied*, 466 U.S. 929, 104 S.Ct. 1714, 80 L.Ed.2d 186 (1984), however, *McCollum* was apparently interpreted to require a reliability finding whenever information relied upon by the IDC was obtained from confidential informants. In that case, the investigator's report stated that the confidential source was considered reliable, and it appeared that the IDC adopted the credibility determination of the investigator. Thus, due process had been observed. 719 F.2d at 899. In *Mendoza v. Miller*, 779 F.2d 1287, 1293 (7th Cir.1985), it was stated that "[t]o protect the inmate's interest in a fair hearing, our court requires some indication of the reliability of confidential informants when confidential information is the basis for a prison disciplinary decision." *McCollum* was read to require that information "supplied by prison informants must be supported by some indication of reliability." 779 F.2d at 1295.

---

10. The district court issued its decision following the remand on May 8, 1985. That decision has been appealed to this court. *McCollum v.* *Miller*, No. 85–1985 (7th Cir. Argued February 10, 1986).

As the discussion above indicates, *McCollum* addressed the risk of error in (thus, in a general sense, the reliability of) the IDC's use of confidential informants in a specific prison disciplinary proceeding. The aggravating factor, however, was the generality of the notice given the prisoner, which precluded the preparation of an adequate defense. This court concluded that under those facts, when the notice requirements of *Wolff* could not be met (a situation never addressed in *Wolff* itself), "additional safeguards" were necessary. In *Dawson* and *Mendoza*, however, we read *McCollum* more broadly and departed from a case-by-case analysis to set forth a general rule that no longer focused primarily of the type of notice that the prisoner received, but rather on the quality of the evidence upon which the IDC relied. It should be noted that, although in Anglo-American jurisprudence a tribunal is not ordinarily required to provide an assessment of the reliability of witnesses,[11] the setting of disciplinary proceedings departs from the Anglo-American model of a judicial tribunal. *See generally Cleavinger v. Saxner,* —— U.S. ——, 106 S.Ct. 496, 502, 88 L.Ed.2d 507 (1985); *Hewitt v. Helms,* 459 U.S. 460, 472–75, 103 S.Ct. 864, 871–73, 74 L.Ed.2d 675 (1983); *Wolff,* 418 U.S. at 561–63, 568, 94 S.Ct. at 2977–78, 2980–81. Indicia of reliability provide additional protection when other rights of the accused have been circumscribed in the relatively informal setting of prison disciplinary proceedings.

2. *Retroactivity*

Even if we assume *arguendo* that Sanchez's characterization of *McCollum* is correct, the rule would not necessarily apply in the instant case. As the Supreme Court stated in *Wolff,* 418 U.S. at 573–74, 94 S.Ct. at 2982–83:

The Court of Appeals held that due process requirements in prison disciplinary proceedings were to apply retroactively so as to require that prison records containing determinations of misconduct, not in accord with required procedures, be expunged. We disagree and reverse on this point.

The question of retroactivity of new procedural rules affecting inquiries into infractions of prison discipline is effectively foreclosed by this Court's ruling in *Morrissey* that due process requirements there announced were to be "applicable to *future* revocations of parole," 408 U.S., at 490, 92 S.Ct., at 2604 (emphasis supplied). Despite the fact that procedures are related to the integrity of the factfinding process, the context of disciplinary proceedings, where less is generally at stake for an individual than at a criminal trial, great weight should be given to the significant impact a retroactive ruling would have on the administration of all prisons in the country, and the reliance prison officials placed, in good faith, on prior law not requiring such procedures. During 1973, the Federal Government alone conducted 19,000 misconduct hearings, as compared with 1,173 parole revocation hearings, and 2,023 probation revocation hearings. If *Morrissey-Scarpelli* rules [dealing with parole and probation] are not retroactive out of consideration for the burden on federal and state officials, this case [involving the application of new procedural requirements in prison disciplinary hearings] is *a fortiori*. We also note that a contrary holding would be very troublesome for the parole system since performance in prison is often a relevant criterion for parole. On the whole, we do

11. As this court observed in *Hameetman v. City of Chicago,* 776 F.2d 636, 644 (7th Cir.1985): Juries, when they render general verdicts, do not explain the basis of the verdict. While the federal district judges are required by Fed.R. Civ.P. 52(a) to issue reasonably detailed findings of fact and conclusions of law in bench trials, we have not heard it suggested that this is required by the Constitution. And when

federal district judges dispose of a case without a trial, as in granting a motion to dismiss or summary judgment, Rule 52(a) expressly excuses them from having to issue findings and conclusions. *See also Scott v. Village of Kewaskum,* 786 F.2d 338, 341 (7th Cir.1986); *United States ex rel. Jones v. DeRobertis,* 766 F.2d 270, 272–73 (7th Cir.1985).

not think that error was so pervasive in the system under the old procedures as to warrant this cost or result.

It is clear then that, as a general matter, new procedural rules for disciplinary proceedings will not be applied retroactively. Thus, the constitutionality of the IDC hearing must be considered under the law in existence at the date of the hearing. *See Cox v. Cook,* 420 U.S. 734, 95 S.Ct. 1237, 43 L.Ed.2d 587 (1975); *Johnson v. Holley,* 528 F.2d 116 (7th Cir.1975) (overruled in part on other grounds, *see Bryant v. Grinner,* 563 F.2d 871, 871–72 (7th Cir. 1977)); *Thomas v. Pate,* 516 F.2d 889 (7th Cir.), *cert. denied,* 423 U.S. 877, 96 S.Ct. 149, 46 L.Ed.2d 110 (1975); *Edwards v. Illinois Department of Corrections,* 514 F.2d 477 (7th Cir.1975); *Chapman v. Kleindienst,* 507 F.2d 1246 (7th Cir.1974). The IDC hearing for Sanchez was held on January 10, 1980. *McCollum* was decided on December 20, 1982. Assuming for the moment that *McCollum* prescribed a new procedural rule, it would appear that Sanchez could not rely on it, as his hearing antedated the decision. It is true that in subsequent cases *McCollum* was discussed in connection with IDC hearings conducted prior to December 20, 1982. *See Mendoza,* 779 F.2d at 1290 (IDC hearing held on April 3, 1981); *Dawson,* 719 F.2d at 897 (IDC hearing held on October 25, 1977); *Jackson,* 707 F.2d at 946 (docket numbers indicate federal appeals filed in 1981 and 1982). However, the propriety of the retroactive application of *McCollum* was not discussed in *Mendoza, Dawson,* and *Jackson,* and is therefore an open question in this circuit. Thus, we must determine whether *McCol-*

lum set forth a new rule, which under *Wolff* can only have prospective application.

Sanchez argues that *McCollum's* requirement of indicia of reliability was inherent in the holding in *Wolff* that there must be a "written statement by the factfinders as to the evidence relied on and reasons for the disciplinary action." [12] We disagree. The *McCollum* rule is not inconsistent with *Wolff,* but neither is it compelled by the earlier decision.[13] *Wolff* has not been read as holding that prisoners are generally entitled to due process in disciplinary proceedings. To the contrary, it sets forth specific minimum procedures and expressly leaves the development of additional safeguards to the discretion of the prison authorities. *See, e.g., Edwards,* 514 F.2d at 479. The Court was unwilling to go further, and has continued to read *Wolff* as calling for no more than the procedures specifically enumerated therein. *See Superintendent v. Hill,* — U.S. —, 105 S.Ct. 2768, 86 L.Ed.2d 356 (1985); *Ponte v. Real,* — U.S. —, 105 S.Ct. 2192, 85 L.Ed.2d 553 (1985). *See also Mendoza,* 779 F.2d at 1301 (Swygert, J., dissenting) (*Wolff* "simply did not address what other procedures were constitutionally necessary as a check on the use by prison officials of confidential, and perhaps unreliable, prison information"); *Dawson,* 719 F.2d at 889; *Kyle v. Hanberry,* 677 F.2d 1386, 1389 (11th Cir.1982) (*Wolff* does not consider use of confidential informants).

The case law of this circuit makes clear that a decision calling for a specific procedural rule for disciplinary proceedings that goes beyond the constitutional mini-

---

12. Sanchez's citation to *Gomes v. Travisono,* 510 F.2d 537, 540 (1st Cir.1974), for the proposition that a requirement of a reliability determination was inherent in *Wolff* is unavailing. First, the First Circuit was construing, in light of *Wolff,* a consent decree that was entered in the case of *Morris v. Travisono,* 310 F.Supp. 857, 871–74 (D.R.I.1970), and adopted as law by the state. The First Circuit concluded that the rules set forth in *Morris* did not impermissibly burden prison authorities and were not inconsistent with *Wolff.* In any event, the state had acquiesced in and adopted the *Morris* procedures. Second, even if the First Circuit had concluded

that a reliability finding was required by *Wolff,* that was not the established law of this circuit in 1980. Finally, *Cox v. Cook,* 420 U.S. 734, 95 S.Ct. 1237, 43 L.Ed.2d 587 (1975), suggests that *Gomes* would only apply in the First Circuit.

13. Sanchez acknowledges in his opening appellate brief that "[t]he Court in *Wolff* did not address what specific procedures were required to guarantee the reliability and credibility of confidential informants relied upon by prison disciplinary committees."

mums of *Wolff* will be given prospective effect only. *See, e.g., Thomas,* 516 F.2d at 890. The passage from *Wolff* quoted above illustrates that the primary question is whether the rule imposes greater burdens on the prison authorities, not whether it increases the accuracy of the proceedings. It is true that the Court in *Wolff* did not say that procedural changes could never be applied retroactively, but indicated that the procedural defects at issue did not so undermine the legitimacy of prior disciplinary hearings as to warrant imposing the burden of retroactivity on prison officials. If the sweeping changes mandated in *Wolff* to reduce the risk of inaccurate results are not to be applied retroactively, then the comparatively small change made in *McCollum* cannot, if it burdens prison officials. If *McCollum* is applied retroactively, then all disciplinary proceedings conducted since *Wolff, i.e.,* June 1974, involving evidence from confidential sources are open to challenge. Tens of thousands of findings of guilt could be subject to invalidation. Such a result, with its highly disruptive effect on the disciplinary, parole, probation, and judicial processes, would be manifestly inconsistent with the ruling in *Wolff.* We, therefore, hold that the rule of *McCollum* cannot be applied to prison disciplinary proceedings held prior to the date of its decision, *i.e.,* December 20, 1982.

As noted above, Sanchez's due-process claim must be determined by the state of the law as it existed in January 1980, the date his IDC hearing was held. As we have concluded, *Wolff* did not mandate a reliability finding. Thus, Sanchez cannot

rest on his citation to that decision. Because *McCollum* cannot be applied retroactively, his reliance on that decision is also unavailing. We cannot be unmindful that Sanchez was represented by counsel. The respondent raised the retroactivity issue below and on appeal. Sanchez did assert that *McCollum* or *Wolff* could be applied to his hearing, but elected not to argue in the alternative and, thus, did not discuss the state of the law in 1980.[14] Rule 28 of the Fed.R.App.P. requires that the appellant present argument with citations to the relevant authorities. It is not the obligation of this court to research and construct the legal arguments open to parties, especially when they are represented by counsel. *See May v. Evansville-Vanderburgh School Corp.,* 787 F.2d 1105, 1118 (7th Cir.1986); *Libertyville Datsun Sales v. Nissan Motor Corp.,* 776 F.2d 735, 737 (7th Cir.1985). Sanchez, therefore, has waived the claim that his disciplinary hearing did not comport with the due process requirements existing in January 1980.[15] *Cf. Walton v. United Consumers Club, Inc.,* 786 F.2d 303, 315 (7th Cir.1986); *Graczyk v. United Steelworkers of America,* 763 F.2d 256, 261 n. 6 (7th Cir.), *cert. denied,* — U.S. —, 106 S.Ct. 335, 88 L.Ed.2d 319 (1985).

III

As developed in Section II, *supra,* the law did not require that there be indications in the administrative record of the reliability of confidential informants when Sanchez's disciplinary hearing was held in January 1980. He cannot, therefore, show

---

14. There is a further wrinkle. The retroactivity rule of *Wolff* means that a court must look to the state of the law on the date of the disciplinary hearing. *Cox v. Cook,* 420 U.S. 734, 95 S.Ct. 1237, 43 L.Ed.2d 587 (1975), suggests that one must also look to the law of the place where the hearing was conducted, which in this case was Lompoc, California, not Marion, Illinois.

15. Sanchez also claims that the written notice of the charge was insufficient. Even applying *McCollum* and its progeny, it is obvious that the notice was adequate. Sanchez also claims that the finding of guilt was not supported by the record. We have reviewed the administrative

record *in camera* and cannot say that "no reasonable adjudicator could have found the prisoner guilty of the offense on the basis of the evidence presented." *Jackson v. Carlson,* 707 F.2d 943, 949 (7th Cir.), *cert. denied,* 464 U.S. 861, 104 S.Ct. 189, 78 L.Ed.2d 167 (1983).

Sanchez also maintains that the incident report should have provided the name of his co-conspirator. This claim was not presented below and is, therefore, waived. *See City of Chicago v. United States Department of Labor,* 753 F.2d 606, 607 n. 1 (7th Cir.1985); *Trotter v. Klincar,* 748 F.2d 1177, 1184 (7th Cir.1984). We express no opinion as to its resolution.

that he was prejudiced by the failure to exhaust his administrative remedies. The judgment of the district court is AFFIRMED.

SWYGERT, Senior Circuit Judge, dissenting.

I agree with the majority's view that the "cause and prejudice" requirement must determine whether an inmate's failure to exhaust administrative remedies should be excused. But I cannot agree that Sanchez failed to demonstrate "prejudice." In my view, the requirement that there be some indicia in the record of the reliability or credibility of confidential informants is implicit in *Wolff v. McDonnell,* 418 U.S. 539, 94 S.Ct. 2963, 41 L.Ed.2d 935 (1974).[1] I would therefore remand this case to take evidence on the question of whether the petitioner had "cause" for failing to exhaust his administrative remedies.[2]

My fundamental difficulty with the majority's approach is its ruling that *Wolff* requires nothing more than the procedures specifically enumerated therein. This ruling means that if prison officials observe, *pro forma, Wolff's* express procedures, prison inmates have no cause to complain. This cannot be correct. In granting specific procedures and discussing in detail the objectives to be promoted thereby, the Court in *Wolff* clearly did not intend to grant inmates a hollow shell of procedural protections, devoid of any meaningful content. *See Kyle v. Hanberry,* 677 F.2d 1386, 1390 (11th Cir.1982); *Helms v. Hew-*

itt, 655 F.2d 487, 495 (3th Cir.1981), *rev'd on other grounds,* 459 U.S. 460, 103 S.Ct. 864, 74 L.Ed.2d 675 (1983). Rather, it intended to compel not only those expressly enumerated procedures, but any other due process requirements necessary to give meaning to those procedures.

Two recent decisions of the Supreme Court support this conclusion: *Superintendent Massachusetts Correctional Institution v. Hill,* —— U.S. ——, 105 S.Ct. 2768, 86 L.Ed.2d 356 (1985); and *Ponte v. Real,* —— U.S. ——, 105 S.Ct. 2192, 85 L.Ed.2d 553 (1985). In each case, the Court considered whether a particular safeguard was required under *Wolff's* assurances of "the minimum requirements of procedural due process." *Wolff,* 418 U.S. at 558, 94 S.Ct. at 2976. In *Superintendent Massachusetts Correctional Institution,* the Court considered whether due process was denied if the prison disciplinary decision was not supported by any evidence in the record. In *Ponte,* the Court considered whether due process required prison disciplinary officials to state their reasons for refusing to hear one of the inmate's proposed witnesses. In both cases, the Court acknowledged that nowhere in *Wolff* did it consider either of the safeguards at issue. Nonetheless, the Court held that each of them was compelled by due process, and it suggested that each of them was, in fact, implicit in one of *Wolff's* expressly articulated procedures. *Superintendent Massachusetts Correctional Institution,* ——

---

1. It is important to focus on the precise question presented for review in this case. The petitioner is not complaining about the prison board's failure to employ any particular method for ascertaining the reliability or credibility of the confidential informants. The petitioner's complaint is that he was found guilty solely on the basis of information provided by confidential informants which the UDC did not find to be either credible or reliable and whose credibility or reliability is not readily verifiable from any facts in the record. Thus, the question is not whether the specific procedures set forth in *McCollum v. Miller,* 695 F.2d 1044, 1048–49 (7th Cir.1982) (and as developed in other cases such as *Mendoza v. Miller,* 779 F.2d 1287 (7th Cir. 1985)) are mandated by *Wolff v. McDonnell,* 418 U.S. 539, 94 S.Ct. 2963, 41 L.Ed.2d 935 (1974). And it is irrelevant for purposes of this appeal

that " '[t]he Court in *Wolff* did not address what *specific* procedures were required to guarantee the reliability and credibility of confidential informants relied upon by the prison disciplinary committees.' " *Ante* at note 13 quoting petitioner's opening brief. Rather, the question is whether *Wolff* implicitly requires that there be some indicia in the record, arrived at by whatever means, that the confidential informants were reliable or credible when this information forms the basis for the disciplinary decision.

2. Because I would find this requirement to be inherent in *Wolff,* I do not address either the question of retroactivity or the question raised by *Cox v. Cook,* 420 U.S. 734, 95 S.Ct. 1237, 43 L.Ed.2d 587 (1975).

U.S. ——, 105 S.Ct. at 2762; *Ponte,* —— U.S. ——, 105 S.Ct. at 2196. As the Court in *Ponte* explained:

> To hold [in *Wolff*] that the Due Process Clause confers a circumscribed right on the inmate to call witnesses at a disciplinary hearing, and then conclude that no explanation need ever be vouched for the denial of that right ... would change an admittedly circumscribed right into a privilege conferred in the unreviewable discretion board. We think our holding in *Wolff* ... meant something more than that.

Id. at ——, 105 S.Ct. at 2197.

In effect, the Court in *Superintendent Massachusetts Correctional Institution* and *Ponte* held that in *Wolff* it had implicitly recognized rights in addition to those that were specifically enumerated therein— those rights that are necessary to fulfill those purposes, although the Court had not gone further and prescribed the specific procedures that must be observed to fulfill those requirements.

Significantly, the Court in each of these cases applied its holding to the facts of the case before it, whereas in *Wolff* it refused to do so on the ground of non-retroactivity. To be sure, the issue of retroactivity was not directly raised in either of those cases. Nevertheless, as the majority in this case recognizes, *Wolff* clearly signalled that retroactivity was an important consideration in any case in which new procedural rules are promulgated. It is not unreasonable to assume, therefore, that had the Court conceived of its holdings in *Superintendent Massachusetts Correctional Institution* and *Ponte* to be something more than articulations of principles already inherent in *Wolff* it would have considered the question of retroactivity.

The right claimed in this case is inherent in *Wolff* for two reasons. First, this court has previously concluded that *Wolff's* requirement of a written statement of evidence relied on and the reasons for the decision presumes the inherent right not to be found guilty except by an "appropriate quantum of evidence." *Aikens v. Lash,*

514 F.2d 55, 60 (7th Cir.1975), *vacated on other grounds,* 425 U.S. 947, 96 S.Ct. 1721, 48 L.Ed.2d 191 *reinstated as modified on other grounds,* 547 F.2d 372 (7th Cir.1976). The Supreme Court has recently approved of this conclusion, holding in *Superintendent Massachusetts Correctional Institution,* —— U.S. at ——, 105 S.Ct. at 2774, that fundamental due process requires that the prison disciplinary decision be justified by "some evidence" in the record. In reaching this result, the Court expressly referred to *Wolff's* requirement of a written statement of evidence relied on and the reasons for the decision and its purpose of protecting the inmate against arbitrary decisionmaking. Lawyers and judges may disagree on how much evidence is "some evidence," but it cannot seriously be doubted that uncorroborated hearsay obtained from confidential informants whose good motives are highly questionable, *see Kyle,* 677 F.2d at 1390; *McCollum v. Miller,* 695 F.2d 1044, 1049 (7th Cir.1982), is tantamount to *no* evidence whatsoever.

Second, other circuits have recognized that the right claimed by the petitioner in this case is inherent in *Wolff's* requirement of a written statement of evidence relied on and the reasons for the decision. For example, in *Gomes v. Travisono,* 490 F.2d 1209 (1st Cir.1973), the First Circuit decided that prison inmates were entitled to due process before being transferred for disciplinary reasons from a prison in one state to one in another. It further decided that the pre-transfer process due was the procedures set forth in the consent decree adopted in *Morris v. Travisono,* 310 F.Supp. 857, 871–74 (D.R.I.1970), and later adopted as law by the State of Rhode Island. *Gomes* was subsequently vacated by the Supreme Court, *Travisono v. Gomes,* 418 U.S. 909, 94 S.Ct. 3200, 41 L.Ed.2d 1155 (1974), and remanded for reconsideration in light of *Wolff.*

On remand the First Circuit specifically addressed the issue of whether any requirements of the *Morris* rules not expressly identified in *Wolff* should apply to interstate transfers which are alleged to have been punitive in nature. *Gomes v. Travisono*, 510 F.2d 537 (1st Cir.1974). One of those requirements was that the prison disciplinary board's findings be supported by substantial evidence. Substantial evidence as defined by the decree included the requirement that "if any of the facts establishing a Board determination are derived from an unidentified informant," "the record must contain some underlying factual information from which the Board . . . [could] reasonably conclude that the informant was credible or his information was reliable." *Id.* at 540.

In affirming this term, upon reconsideration in light of *Wolff*, the First Circuit noted that, "if the written statement is intended to withstand scrutiny and guard against misunderstanding, it cannot indicate reliance on speculation or on facts not in the record." It further implied that this requirement was a "necessity in meeting the requirements of *Wolff*," and that it did not demand anything more than *Wolff*. Other courts have reached the same conclusion. *See Langton v. Berman*, 667 F.2d 231, 235 (1st Cir.1981) ("We continue to advise . . . [prison officials] to follow *Wolff's* mandate to devise regulations to assure that the disciplinary board's procedure is adequate to enable it to reasonably conclude that any confidential information upon which it relied was reliable."); *Rinehart v. Brewer*, 483 F.Supp. 165, 170 (S.D. Iowa 1980) (written statement must indicate why prison officials believe the confidential information relied upon to be credible); *Bartholomew v. Reed*, 477 F.Supp. 223, 228 (D.Oregon 1979), *rev'd in part on other grounds sub nom. Bartholomew v. Watson*, 665 F.2d 915 (9th Cir.1982) (same). *Cf. Chavis v. Rowe*, 643 F.2d 1281, 1287 (7th Cir.), *cert. denied sub nom. Boles v. Chavis*, 454 U.S. 907, 102 S.Ct. 415, 70 L.Ed.2d 225 (1981) (*pro forma* statement of evidence relied on and reasons for guilt with no statement regarding credibility determinations does not fulfill *Wolff's* requirement of written statement of reasons and evidence); *Hayes v. Walker*, 555 F.2d 625, 633 (7th Cir.), *cert. denied*, 434 U.S. 959, 98 S.Ct. 491, 54 L.Ed.2d 320 (1977)

(*pro forma* written statement does not fulfill purposes behind *Wolff's* requirement of written statement of evidence relied on, and therefore does not satisfy due process); *Finney v. Mabry*, 455 F.Supp. 756, 775 (E.D.Ark.1978) ("This Court . . . does not view . . . *Wolff* as a direction to the federal courts to consider no constitutional claims involving prison disciplinary procedures except those explicitly addressed in that case.").

Moreover, this court in *McCollum* also implicitly recognized that it was not promulgating a "new" rule. We held that where the prison disciplinary action is based solely on information provided by confidential informants and where most traditional procedures cannot be afforded because of valid concerns with institutional safety, other procedures were required to guarantee the accuracy of the prison disciplinary decision. The court simply assumed, correctly in my view, that a decision based solely on untested, possibly vindictive hearsay was a denial of due process under *Wolff*. It then went on to discuss particular procedures short of confrontation that prison officials might employ to demonstrate that the confidential informants were either credible or reliable. Thus, the court in *McCollum* did not promulgate a heretofore unheard of due process requirement. In fact, we recognized that that requirement was compelled *a fortiori* by the holding in *Wolff*. In conformity with *Wolff*, however, the court in *McCollum* left to prison officials the task of devising procedures to implement the requirement.

This reading of *McCollum* is supported by our subsequent decision, *Dawson v. Smith*, 719 F.2d 896, 899 (7th Cir.1983), *cert. denied*, 466 U.S. 929, 104 S.Ct. 1714, 80 L.Ed.2d 186 (1984), in which we held that *McCollum* "*recognized . . . that when confidential information is the basis of a prison disciplinary decision, there must be some indication of reliability*" (emphasis added), but that it was up to the Supreme Court to mandate which specific procedures were constitutionally necessary to implement this particular requirement. *See also Kyle*, 677 F.2d at 1390.

Finally, the right claimed by the petitioner in this case is inherent in *Wolff* because it is a *sine qua non* of procedural due process; it is implicitly compelled by any decision that compels due process. The Supreme Court long ago recognized that the essence of due process is the protection against arbitrary deprivations, in particular deprivations resulting from information provided by nameless, biased accusers shielded by anonymity from accountability for lying. *See Greene v. McElroy*, 360 U.S. 474, 496, 79 S.Ct. 1400, 1413, 3 L.Ed.2d 1377 (1959). Other courts have recognized that it is a contradiction in terms to say that although one is entitled to due process he may still be deprived of a protected interest on the basis of uncorroborated, untested hearsay. Such reasoning results in a denial of reasonably accurate decision-making, and hence amounts to a denial of fundamental fairness. *See, e.g., Kyle*, 677 F.2d at 1390–91.

The facts of this case demonstrate why *Wolff* implicitly requires that there must be indicia of reliability or credibility of the confidential informants. Sanchez was found guilty by the prison board solely on the basis of the confidential information contained in the prison investigator's report. The confidential information was uncorroborated, and there was no corroborating physical evidence. As the Government concedes, there was absolutely no attempt to ascertain the reliability or credibility of any of the informants, any one of whom could have had a personal vendetta against Sanchez. None of the confidential information was set forth in detail in any public record and hence none of it was available to Sanchez. Sanchez received notice of the charges, and attended the hearing. He denied participating in the stabbing, and he presented three alibi witnesses. The UDC found him guilty of planning the murder and of the murder itself. According to Sanchez, the UDC official who made this finding had a personal score to settle with Sanchez because the Regional Director had earlier reversed a finding by the UDC that

Sanchez had assaulted a staff member. On appeal the Regional Director overturned the finding of guilty of murder, noting that there was absolutely no evidence to support it; yet, he sustained the disciplinary sanction in its entirety. Sanchez was ultimately acquitted of all three charges by a jury, presumably because the Government's sole evidence was the inadmissible uncorroborated hearsay of the confidential informants.

As these facts demonstrate, although nominally accorded some procedural safeguards, Sanchez in fact was denied any kind of meaningful due process. We have no way of knowing whether the prison disciplinary action had *any* basis in fact or was simply the result of fabricated information provided by a vengeful co-inmate or the aftermath of a vendetta by prison officials who were unhappy with Sanchez' acquittal on an unrelated assault charge. Sanchez was in fact no better off than he would have been if the prison disciplinary board had simply informed him that he was being deprived of good time credits because of his participation in a murder. Indeed, he may be worse off given today's holding because any suspicion that he may have harbored that prison disciplinary proceedings are arbitrary and, in fact, a meaningless set of *pro forma* steps designed to pay lip service to the real holding of *Wolff* was confirmed.

In sum, the reason why the Supreme Court in *Wolff* did not expressly articulate a requirement that there be indicia of the reliability or credibility of confidential informants in the record is that it did not have to. The right to be adjudged guilty on the basis of competent (including reliable) evidence is a prerequisite to the right to a statement of evidence relied on and reasons for the decision. Indeed, it is implicit in any guarantee of meaningful due process. By recognizing a prison inmate's right to due process, the Court in *Wolff* assumed the fundamental right claimed in this case. *McCollum* did nothing more than articulate what was already self-evident in *Wolff* by mandating that prison officials afford some procedures to ensure the credibility or reliability of the confidential informants. The *ratio decidendi* of the majority's holding, non-retroactivity, is therefore irrelevant.

The judgment in the instant case should be reversed and the cause remanded.

Joseph PONTE, Superintendent, Massachusetts Correctional Institution,
Walpole, Petitioner

v.

John REAL.

No. 83–1329.

Argued Jan. 9, 1985.

Decided May 20, 1985.

Syllabus *

Respondent, a Massachusetts prison inmate, as a result of a fight that occurred in a prison office, was charged with violation of prison regulations. At the hearing on these charges, the disciplinary board refused to allow respondent to call witnesses whom he had requested, but the record of the hearing does not indicate the board's reason for such refusal. The board found respondent guilty, and 150 days of his "good time" credits were forfeited. Respondent then sought a writ of habeas corpus in a Massachusetts trial court, which sustained his claim that petitioner prison Superintendent had deprived him of the due process guaranteed by the Fourteenth Amendment, because petitioner advanced no reasons in court as to why respondent was not allowed to call the requested witnesses. The Massachusetts Supreme Judicial Court affirmed, holding that there must be some support in the administrative record to justify a decision not to call witnesses, and that since the administrative record in this case contained no such support, the state regulations governing presentation of proof in disciplinary hearings were unconstitutional to the extent that they did not require the administrative record to contain reasons supporting the board's denial of an inmate's witness request.

Held: The Due Process Clause of the Fourteenth Amendment does not require that prison officials' reasons for denying an inmate's witness request appear in the administrative record of the disciplinary hearing. While the Due Process Clause does require that the officials at some point state their reasons for refusing to call witnesses, they may do so either by making the explanation part of the administrative record or by later presenting testimony in court if the deprivation of a "liberty" interest such as that afforded by "good time" credits, is challenged because of the refusal to call the requested witnesses. Pp. 2195–2198.

390 Mass. 399, 456 N.E.2d 1111, vacated and remanded.

Martin E. Levin, Framingham, Mass., for petitioner, pro hac vice, by special leave of Court.

Jonathan Shapiro, Alexandria, Va., for respondent.

Justice REHNQUIST delivered the opinion of the Court.

The Supreme Judicial Court of Massachusetts held that a prison disciplinary hearing which forfeited "good time" credits of respondent John Real was conducted in violation of the Due Process Clause of the Fourteenth Amendment to the United States Constitution because there did not appear in the administrative record of that hearing a statement of reasons as to why the disciplinary board refused to allow respondent to call witnesses which he had requested. *Real v. Superintendent, Massachusetts Correctional Institution, Walpole*, 390 Mass. 399, 456 N.E.2d 1111 (1983). We granted certiorari, 469 U.S. ——, 105 S.Ct. 77, 83 L.Ed.2d 26 (1984), to review this judgment because it seemed to us to go further than our pronouncement on this subject in *Wolff v. McDonnell*, 418 U.S. 539, 94 S.Ct. 2963, 41 L.Ed.2d 935 (1974). While we agree with the Supreme Judicial Court of Massachusetts that the Due Process Clause of the Fourteenth Amendment requires that prison officials at some point state their reason for refusing to call witnesses requested by an inmate at a disciplinary hearing, we disagree with that court that such reasons or support for reasons must be placed in writing or otherwise exist as a part of the administrative record at the disciplinary hearing. We vacate the judgment of the Supreme Judicial Court, and remand the case to that court.

In 1981 Respondent John Real was an inmate at the Massachusetts Correctional Institution at Walpole. In December of that year he was working in the prison metal shop and heard a commotion in an adjacent office. He entered the office and observed another prisoner fighting with a corrections officer. A second corrections officer attempted to break up the fight, and ordered respondent and other inmates who were watching to disperse immediately. Respondent did not depart, and another corrections officer escorted him to his cell.

One week later respondent was charged with three violations of prison regulations as a result of this imbroglio. He notified prison officials, on a form provided for that purpose, that he wished to call four witnesses at the hearing which would be held upon these charges: two fellow inmates, the charging officer, and the officer who was involved in the fight. A hearing was held on the charges in February 1982. At this hearing the charging officer appeared and testified against respondent, but the board declined to call the other witnesses requested by respondent. Respondent was advised of no reason for the denial of his request to call the other witnesses, and apparently whatever record there may be of this disciplinary proceeding does not indicate the board's reason for declining to call the witnesses. The board found respondent guilty as charged, and after an administrative appeal in which penalties were reduced, respondent received the sanction of 25 days in isolation and the loss of 150 days good time credits.

Respondent challenged these sanctions by seeking a writ of habeas corpus in the Massachusetts trial court. That court sustained respondent's claim that petitioner Joseph Ponte, a superintendent of the M.C.I. at Walpole, had deprived him of that due process guaranteed by the Fourteenth Amendment to the United States Constitution because no reasons whatsoever were advanced by petitioner in court as to why respondent was not allowed to call the requested witnesses at the hearing.

On appeal to the Supreme Judicial Court of Massachusetts, this judgment was affirmed but for different reasons. That court discussed our decision in *Wolff v. McDonnell, supra*, and noted that it "[l]eft unresolved ... the question whether the Federal due process requirements impose a duty on the board to explain, in any fashion, at the hearing or later, why witnesses were not allowed to testify." 390 Mass., at 405, 456 N.E.2d, at 1115. The court concluded that there must be some support in the "administrative record" to justify a decision not to call witnesses, and that the administrative record in this case was barren of any such support. Because of its conclusion, the court declared that the Massachusetts regulations governing the presentation of proof in disciplinary hearings, Mass.Admin.Code, Tit. 103, § 430.14 [1] were

1. Mass.Admin.Code, Tit. 103, § 430.14 (1978) provides in part:

"(4) If the inmate requests the presence of the reporting officer ... the reporting officer shall attend the hearing except when the chairman determines in writing that the reporting officer is unavailable for prolonged period of time [sic] as a result of illness or other good cause...."

unconstitutional as to this point, because those regulations did not require that the administrative record contain facts or reasons supporting the board's denial of an inmate's witness request. 390 Mass., at 405–407, 456 N.E.2d, at 1116, citing *Hayes v. Thompson*, 637 F.2d 483, 487–489 (CA7 1980).

Petitioner does not dispute that respondent possessed a "liberty" interest, by reason of the provisions of Massachusetts state law, affording him "good time" credits, an interest which could not be taken from him in a prison disciplinary hearing without the minimal safeguards afforded by the Due Process Clause of the Fourteenth Amendment. The touchstone of Due Process is freedom from arbitrary governmental action, *Wolff*, 418 U.S., at 558, 94 S.Ct., at 2975, but "[p]rison disciplinary proceedings are not part of a criminal prosecution, and the full panoply of rights due a defendant in such proceedings does not apply." *Id.*, at 556, 94 S.Ct., at 2974. Chief among the Due Process minima outlined in *Wolff* was the right of an inmate to call and present witnesses and documentary evidence in his defense before the disciplinary board. We noted in *Wolff* and repeated in *Baxter v. Palmigiano*, 425 U.S. 308, 96 S.Ct. 1551, 47 L.Ed.2d 810 (1976), that ordinarily the right to present evidence is basic to a fair hearing, but the inmate's right to present witnesses is necessarily circumscribed by the penological need to provide swift discipline in individual cases. This right is additionally circumscribed by the very real dangers in prison life which may result from violence or intimidation directed at either other inmates or staff. We described the right to call witnesses as subject to the "mutual accommodation between institutional needs and objectives and the provisions of the Constitution...." *Baxter, supra*, at 321, 96 S.Ct., at 1559, citing *Wolff, supra*, 418 U.S., at 556, 94 S.Ct., at 2974.

Thus the prisoner's right to call witnesses and present evidence in disciplinary hearings could be denied if granting the request would be "unduly hazardous to institutional safety or correctional goals." *Wolff, supra*, at 566, 94 S.Ct., at 2974; *Baxter, supra*, 425 U.S., at 321, 96 S.Ct., at 1559. See also *Hughes v. Rowe*, 449 U.S. 5, 9, and n. 6, 101 S.Ct. 173, 175, and n. 6, 66 L.Ed.2d 163 (1980). As we stated in *Wolff*:

"Prison officials must have the necessary discretion to keep the hearing within reasonable limits and to refuse to call witnesses that may create a risk of reprisal or undermine authority, as well as to limit access to other inmates to collect statements or to compile other documentary evidence. Although we do not prescribe it, it would be useful for the [disciplinary board] to state its reasons for refusing to call a witness, whether it be for irrelevance, lack of necessity, or the hazards presented in individual cases." 418 U.S., at 566, 94 S.Ct., at 2980.

See *Baxter, supra*, 425 U.S., at 321, 96 S.Ct., at 1559. Notwithstanding our suggestion that the board give reasons for denying an inmate's witness request, nowhere in *Wolff* or *Baxter* did we require the disciplinary board to explain why it denied the prisoner's request, nor did we require that those reasons otherwise appear in the administrative record.

"(5) The inmate shall be allowed but shall not be compelled to make an oral statement or to present a written statement in his own defense or in mitigation of punishment.

"(6) The inmate shall be allowed to question the reporting officer, to question other witnesses, to call witnesses in his defense, or to present other evidence, when permitting him to do so will not be unduly hazardous to institutional safety or correctional goals. The factors that the chairman may consider when ruling on an inmate's questioning of witnesses, offer of other evidence, or request to call witnesses shall include, but shall not be limited to, the following:
  "(a) Relevance
  "(b) Cumulative testimony
  "(c) Necessity
  "(d) Hazards presented by an individual case.

   .   .   .   .   .

"(7) the inmate shall be allowed to present relevant, non-cumulative documentary evidence in his defense."

Eleven years of experience since our decision in *Wolff* does not indicate to us any need to now "prescribe" as constitutional doctrine that the disciplinary board must state in writing at the time of the hearing its reasons for refusing to call a witness. Nor can we conclude that the Due Process Clause of the Fourteenth Amendment may only be satisfied if the administrative record contains support or reasons for the board's refusal. We therefore disagree with the reasoning of the Supreme Judicial Court of Massachusetts in this case. But we also disagree with petitioner's intimation, Brief for Petitioner 53, that courts may only inquire into the reasons for denying witnesses when an inmate points to "substantial evidence" in the record that shows prison officials had ignored our requirements set forth in *Wolff*. We further disagree with petitioner's contention that an inmate may not successfully challenge the board unless he can show a pattern or practice of refusing all witness requests. Nor do we agree with petitioner that "across the board" policies denying witness requests are invariably proper. *Id.*, at 53–55, n. 9.

The question is exactly that posed by the Supreme Judicial Court in its opinion: "whether the Federal due process requirements impose a duty on the board to explain, in any fashion, at the hearing or later, why witnesses were not allowed to testify." 390 Mass., at 405, 456 N.E.2d, at 1115. We think the answer to that question is that prison officials may be required to explain, in a limited manner, the reason

why witnesses were not allowed to testify, but that they may do so either by making the explanation a part of the "administrative record" in the disciplinary proceeding, or by presenting testimony in court if the deprivation of a "liberty" interest is challenged because of that claimed defect in the hearing. In other words, the prison officials may choose to explain their decision at the hearing, or they may choose to explain it "later." Explaining the decision at the hearing will of course not immunize prison officials from a subsequent court challenge to their decision, but so long as the reasons are logically related to preventing undue hazards to "institutional safety or correctional goals," the explanation should meet the Due Process requirements as outlined in *Wolff*.

We have noted in *Wolff, supra,* and in *Baxter, supra,* that prison disciplinary hearings take place in tightly controlled environments peopled by those who have been unable to conduct themselves properly in a free society. Many of these persons have scant regard for property, life, or rules of order, *Wolff,* 418 U.S., at 561–562, 94 S.Ct., at 2977, and some might attempt to exploit the disciplinary process for their own ends. *Id.,* at 563, 94 S.Ct., at 2978. The requirement that contemporaneous reasons for denying witnesses and evidence be given admittedly has some appeal, and it may commend itself to prison officials as a matter of choice: recollections of the event will be fresher at the moment, and it seems a more lawyer-like way to do things.[2] But

---

2. Justice MARSHALL's dissent maintains that a rule requiring contemporaneous reasons which are not made available to the prisoner is the only one permitted by the United States Constitution. If indeed this rule is as beneficial to all concerned as the dissent claims, we may eventually see it universally adopted without the necessity of constitutionally commanding it. But we think that, as we indicate in this opinion, there are significant arguments in favor of allowing a state to follow *either* the approach advocated by the dissent or the approach described in this opinion. While the dissent criticizes our alternative as one which "forces inmates to go to court to learn the basis for witness denials," *post,* page 2207, it is difficult if

not impossible to see how inmates under the dissent's approach which requires contemporaneous reasons kept under seal would be able to get these reasons without the same sort of court proceeding.

We think the dissent's approach would very likely lead to an increasing need for lawyers attached to each prison in order to advise the correctional officials; words such as "irrelevant" or "cumulative," offered by the dissent as possible bases for contemporary denials, *post,* page 2206, are essentially lawyer's words. We think that the process of preparing contemporary written reasons for exclusion of testimony is very likely to require more formality and

the primary business of prisons is the supervision of inmates, and it may well be that those charged with this responsibility feel that the additional administrative burdens which would be occasioned by such a requirement detract from the ability to perform the principal mission of the institution. While some might see an advantage in building up a sort of "common law of the prison" on this subject, others might prefer to deal with later court challenges on a case-by-case basis. We hold that the Constitution permits either approach.

But to hold that the Due Process Clause confers a circumscribed right on the inmate to call witnesses at a disciplinary hearing, and then conclude that no explanation need ever be vouched for the denial of that right, either in the disciplinary proceeding itself or if that proceeding be later challenged in court, would change an admittedly circumscribed right into a privilege conferred in the unreviewable discretion of the disciplinary board. We think our holding in *Wolff, supra,* meant something more than that.. We recognized there that the right to call witnesses was a limited one, available to the inmate "when permitting him to do so will not be unduly hazardous to institutional safety or correctional goals." 418 U.S., at 566, 94 S.Ct., at 2979. We further observed that "[p]rison officials must have the necessary discretion to keep the hearing within reasonable limits and to refuse to call witnesses that may create a risk of reprisal or undermine authority, as well as to limit access to other inmates to collect statements or to compile other documentary evidence." *Ibid.*

Given these significant limitations on an inmate's right to call witnesses, and given our further observation in *Wolff* that "[w]e should not be too ready to exercise oversight and put aside the judgment of prison administrators," *ibid.*, it may be that a constitutional challenge to a disciplinary hearing such as respondent's in this case

will rarely, if ever be successful. But the fact that success may be rare in such actions does not warrant adoption of the petitioner's position, which would in effect place the burden of proof on the inmate to show why the action of the prison officials in refusing to call witnesses was arbitrary or capricious. These reasons are almost by definition not available to the inmate; given the sort of prison conditions that may exist, there may be a sound basis for refusing to tell the inmate what the reasons for denying his witness request are.

Indeed, if prison security or similar paramount interests appear to require it, a court should allow at least in the first instance a prison official's justification for refusal to call witnesses to be presented to the court *in camera.* But there is no reason for going further, and adding another weight to an already heavily weighted scale by requiring an inmate to produce evidence of which he will rarely be in possession, and of which the superintendent will almost always be in possession. See *United States v. New York, N.H. & H.R. Co.,* 355 U.S. 253, 256, n. 5, 78 S.Ct. 212, 214, n. 5, 2 L.Ed.2d 247 (1957); *Campbell v. United States,* 365 U.S. 85, 96, 81 S.Ct. 421, 427, 5 L.Ed.2d 428 (1961); *South Carolina v. Katzenbach,* 383 U.S. 301, 332, 86 S.Ct. 803, 820, 15 L.Ed.2d 769 (1966)

Respondent contends that he is entitled to an affirmance even though we reject the Massachusetts Supreme Judicial Court's holding that § 340.14(6) is unconstitutional. Respondent argues that the Supreme Judicial Court affirmed the trial court on two independent grounds: (1) the trial court's simple finding that petitioner's failure to rebut the allegations in respondent's complaint entitled respondent to relief; and (2) the unconstitutionality of § 340.14(6) because Due Process requires administrative record support for denial of witnesses. We think that the Supreme Judicial Court af-

structure than a practice which requires bringing in an attorney only when a lawsuit is filed. The former may be ideally suited to a heavily populated state of relatively small area such as Massachusetts, but the latter may be more desirable in a sparsely populated state of large area such as Nevada. We think the Constitution permits either alternative.

firmed only on the second ground, and that is the issue for which we granted certiorari. Supreme Court Rule 21.1(a); see also Rule 15.1(a). Respondent is of course entitled to urge affirmance of the judgment of the Supreme Judicial Court on a ground not adopted by that court, but whether the Supreme Judicial Court would have affirmed the judgment of the trial court on the reasoning we set forth today is, we think, too problematical for us to decide.[3] It is a question best left to that court.

The judgment of the Supreme Judicial Court of Massachusetts is vacated, and the case remanded to that court for further proceedings not inconsistent with this opinion.

It is so ordered.

Justice POWELL took no part in the consideration or decision of this case.

Justice STEVENS, with whom Justice BLACKMUN joins as to Part II, concurring.

On March 10, 1983, this case was submitted to the Supreme Judicial Court of Massachusetts along with four others.[1] In each case, prisoners in state correctional institutions challenged the procedural fairness of recurring practices in the prison disciplinary process. The five opinions were all assigned to the same Justice, who eight months later delivered five unanimous opinions for the court interpreting the minimum procedural requirements of state regulations and the Federal Constitution in the prison context. The evident deliberation of the Massachusetts court in these cases suggests a careful effort to establish workable rules for prison disciplinary proceedings in that State.

I

The Court candidly states that it granted certiorari to review the judgment of the Supreme Judicial Court of Massachusetts because that judgment "seems to us to go further than our pronouncement on this subject in *Wolff v. McDonald,* 418 U.S. 539 [94 S.Ct. 2963, 41 L.Ed.2d 935] (1974)." *Ante,* at 2193. As Justice MARSHALL points out, that is a manifestly insufficient reason for adding this case to our argument docket. See *Post,* at 2204–2205, n. 21. The merits of an isolated case have only an oblique relevance to the question whether a grant of certiorari is consistent with the sound administration of this Court's discretionary docket.[2]

When the State petitioned for certiorari, it had a heavy burden of explaining why this Court should intervene in what amounts to a controversy between the Supreme Judicial Court of Massachusetts and that State's prison officials.[3] In determin-

---

3. The record in this case is exceedingly thin, and shows that some confusion existed at trial concerning petitioner's habeas petition seeking review of the February 1982 disciplinary hearing and another unrelated petition arising out of a 1980 disciplinary hearing. The trial court also apparently granted incomplete relief, which was only corrected 10 months later by another judge who then stayed the relief. Moreover, the Supreme Judicial Court did not just affirm the trial court, but remanded to permit petitioner, at his option, to conduct another disciplinary hearing. Given the state of this record, we think it wise to remand for further proceedings.

1. *Nelson v. Commissioner,* 390 Mass. 379, 456 N.E.2d 1100 (1983); *Real v. Superintendent,* 390 Mass. 399, 456 N.E.2d 1111 (1983) (case below); *Lamoureux v. Superintendent,* 390 Mass. 409, 456 N.E.2d 1117 (1983); *Cassesso v. Commissioner,* 390 Mass. 419, 456 N.E.2d 1123 (1983);

Royce v. Commissioner, 390 Mass. 425, 456 N.E.2d 1127 (1983). The court did not reach the constitutional questions presented in *Royce* since it resolved the controversy in favor of the prisoner on the basis of state regulations.

2. Cf. *Watt v. Alaska,* 451 U.S. 259, 276, 101 S.Ct. 1673, 1683, 68 L.Ed.2d 80 (1981) (STEVENS, J., concurring) ("My disagreement in these cases with the Court's management of its docket does not, of course, prevent me from joining [the Court's opinion] on the merits"); *Revere v. Massachusetts General Hospital,* 463 U.S. 239, 246–247, 103 S.Ct. 2979, —— ——, 77 L.Ed.2d 605 (1983) (STEVENS, J., concurring in the judgment).

3. "Because the Supreme Judicial Court of Massachusetts—rather than another branch of state government—invoked the Federal Constitution in imposing an expense on the City of Revere,

ing what process is due in the prison context under the Federal Constitution, the Court emphasizes that we must be cautious to ensure that those requirements will be fair to all parties in the varying conditions found in each of the fifty states and the District of Columbia. *Ante*, at 2196, n. 2. The Court's display of caution would have been more relevant in deciding whether to exercise discretionary jurisdiction in the first place. The denial of certiorari would have left the decision below in effect for the State of Massachusetts, but would have left other jurisdictions to explore the contours of *Wolff*, in the light of local conditions.

The imprudence of the Court's decision to grant certiorari in this case is aggravated by the substantial probability that the Massachusetts court will, on remand, reinstate its original judgment on the basis of the state constitution.[4] In that event, the Court's decision—as applied to the State of Massachusetts—will prove to be little more than a futile attempt to convince a state supreme court that a decision it has carefully made is somehow lacking in wisdom as applied to conditions in that State. "As long as the Court creates unnecessary

work for itself in this manner, its expressions of concern about the overburdened federal judiciary will ring with a hollow echo." *Watt v. Alaska*, 451 U.S. 259, 274, 101 S.Ct. 1673, 1682, 68 L.Ed.2d 80 (1981) (STEVENS, J., concurring).

II

Having granted the petition for certiorari, however, each of us has a duty to address the merits. All of us agree that prison officials may not arbitrarily refuse to call witnesses requested by an inmate at a disciplinary hearing. It is therefore obvious that even if the reason for the refusal is not recorded contemporaneously, it must exist at the time the decision is made.

Moreover, as the Court expressly holds, *ante*, at 2197, the burden of proving that there was a valid reason for the refusal is placed on prison officials rather than the inmate. In many cases, that burden will be difficult to discharge if corrections officers elect to rely solely upon testimonial recollection that is uncorroborated by any contemporaneous documentation. For that reason, the allocation of the burden of proof, together with the policy considerations summarized by Justice MARSHALL,

---

this Court has the authority to review the decision. But is it a sensible exercise of discretion to wield that authority? I think not. There is 'nothing in the Federal Constitution that prohibits a State from giving lawmaking power to its courts.' *Minnesota v. Clover Leaf Creamery Co.*, 449 U.S. 456, 479 [101 S.Ct. 715, 732, 66 L.Ed.2d 659] (1981) (STEVENS, J., dissenting). No individual right was violated in this case. The underlying issue of federal law has never before been deemed an issue of national significance. Since, however, the Court did (unwisely in my opinion) grant certiorari, I join its judgment." *Revere v. Massachusetts General Hospital*, 463 U.S. 239, 247, 103 S.Ct. 2979, ——, 77 L.Ed.2d 605 (1983) (STEVENS, J., concurring in the judgment) (footnote omitted). See also *Michigan v. Long*, 463 U.S. 1032, 103 S.Ct. 3469, 77 L.Ed.2d 1201 (1983) (STEVENS, J., dissenting); *post*, at 2209, n. 21 (MARSHALL, J., dissenting).

4. In a series of recent cases, this Court has reversed a state court decision grounded on a provision in the Federal Bill of Rights only to have the state court reinstate its judgment, on remand, under a comparable guarantee contained in the state constitution. See, *e.g.*, *Massachusetts v. Upton*, —— U.S. ——, 104 S.Ct. 2085, 80 L.Ed.2d 721 (1984), on remand, *Commonwealth v. Upton*, 394 Mass. 363, 370–373, 476 N.E.2d 548, 553–555 (1985); *California v. Ramos*, 463 U.S. 992, 103 S.Ct. 3446, 77 L.Ed.2d 1171 (1983), on remand, *People v. Ramos*, 37 Cal.3d 136, 150–159, 207 Cal.Rptr. 800, 807–814, 689 P.2d 430, 437–444 (1984), cert. pending, No. 84–1227; *South Dakota v. Neville*, 459 U.S. 553, 103 S.Ct. 916, 74 L.Ed.2d 748 (1983), on remand, *State v. Neville*, 346 N.W.2d 425, 427–429 (SD 1984); *Washington v. Chrisman*, 455 U.S. 1, 102 S.Ct. 812, 70 L.Ed.2d 778 (1982), on remand, *State v. Chrisman*, 100 Wash.2d 814, 817–822, 676 P.2d 419, 422–424 (1984) (en banc). This development supports Justice Jackson's observation that "reversal by a higher court is not proof that justice is thereby better done. There is no doubt that if there were a super-Supreme Court, a substantial proportion of our reversals of state courts would also be reversed. We are not final because we are infallible, but we are infallible only because we are final." *Brown v. Allen*, 344 U.S. 443, 540, 73 S.Ct. 397, 427, 97 L.Ed. 469 (1953) (concurring in the result).

will surely motivate most, if not all, prison administrators to adopt "the prevailing practice in federal prisons and in state prisons throughout the country." *Post*, at 2207 (MARSHALL, J., dissenting). Because I am not persuaded that the Federal Constitution prescribes a contemporaneous written explanation as the only permissible method of discharging the prison officials' burden of proving that they had a legitimate reason for refusing to call witnesses requested by an inmate, I join the Court's opinion.[5]

Justice MARSHALL, with whom Justice BRENNAN joins, dissenting.

The court below held there must be "some support in the record" for the denial of an inmate's right to call witnesses at a prison disciplinary hearing. Rejecting this position, the Court today concludes that the Constitution requires only that prison officials explain in court, many months or years after a disciplinary hearing, why they refused to hear particular witnesses. I cannot accept that alleged denials of the vital constitutional right to present witnesses are to be reviewed, not on the basis of an administrative record, but rather on the basis of *post hoc* courtroom rationalizations. I believe the Constitution requires that a contemporaneous record explanation for such a denial be prepared at the time of the hearing. The record need not be disclosed to the inmate but would be available to a court should judicial review later be sought. Upon a proper showing that security or other needs of prison officials so require, the court could review the contemporaneous-record explanation *in camera.* That this process is compatible with the prison setting is demonstrated by the fact that the recording of contemporaneous reasons for denying requests to call witnesses is the current practice in federal prisons and in most state prisons in this country.

5. I do not, however, agree with the second paragraph in n. 2, *ante,* at 2196.

I

The facts of this case, which the Court declines to relate in full, highlight the importance of the right to call witnesses at disciplinary hearings. As the Court describes, respondent John Real was among a group of inmates who left the prison metal shop to observe a fight between an inmate and guard that had broken out in an adjacent office. A supervising officer, John Baleyko, ordered Real and the others to leave the area. The Court blandly observes that Real "did not depart." *Ante,* at 2194. Real's version of the events, however, is considerably more detailed. According to Real, as he began to leave, a dozen or so correctional officers entered the office, one of whom, Officer Doolin, stopped Real for a brief shakedown search and questioning. Officer Baleyko then looked up and noticed that Real was still in the office despite the order to leave. When Real tried to explain that he had been unable to leave because he had been stopped by the other officer, Officer Baleyko cut short Real's explanation and ordered him locked up. On its face, Real's explanation for his failure to obey the order to leave is perfectly plausible, internally consistent, and does not contradict any of the undisputed facts.

Real's disciplinary hearing, then, involved a classic swearing match: Officer Baleyko offered one version of the facts, and Real countered with another version. Under these circumstances, testimony from observers of the incident would seem highly relevant to, and perhaps even dispositive of, the question of Real's responsibility for his failure to obey the order to leave. Real therefore requested that three witnesses be produced for the disciplinary hearing: two inmates who had allegedly been present in the metal shop at the time of the incident and a correctional officer.[1] The disciplinary board, composed of three correctional officials, refused to hear any of these wit-

1. Real appears not to have pursued in the lower courts the failure to produce the correctional officer.

nesses. No reason for excluding this seemingly highly relevant testimony was given at the time. No reason can be deciphered from the record, and indeed no explanation has ever been offered for the refusal to hear these witnesses. Real was found guilty and eventually was deprived of 150 days of good-time credit—a near 5-month prison term on a charged offense against which his only opportunity to defend was to offer his word against that of a prison guard.

II

The Court acknowledges that Real had a constitutional right to present his defense witnesses unless his disciplinary board had a legitimate basis for excluding them. This much is clear from *Wolff v. McDonnell*, 418 U.S. 539, 94 S.Ct. 2963, 41 L.Ed.2d 935 (1974). Drawing on long-standing principles of due process embodied in the Fifth, Sixth, and Fourteenth Amendments,[2] the Court in *Wolff* recognized what might be called a "qualified" constitutional right to call witnesses:

> "[T]he inmate facing disciplinary proceedings should be allowed to call witnesses and present documentary evidence in his defense when permitting him to do so will not be unduly hazardous to institutional safety or correctional goals." *Id.*, at 566, 94 S.Ct., at 2979.

See also *Baxter v. Palmigiano*, 425 U.S. 308, 321, 96 S.Ct. 1551, 1559, 47 L.Ed.2d 810 (1976). This qualified right was one element in what the Court described as an overall effort to create a "reasonable" and "mutual accommodation" between the "provisions of the Constitution" and "the needs of the institution" in the context of disciplinary hearings. 418 U.S., at 556, 572, 94 S.Ct., at 2975, 2982.

Wolff did not consider how best to strike that reasonable accommodation with respect to implementing the right to call witnesses.[3] Two options are presented today. The first would require disciplinary boards to enter on the record contemporaneous written reasons for their exclusion of witnesses; these explanations, while not necessarily available to the inmate, would be subject to judicial review to assure that exclusion of witnesses was not arbitrary but rather was based on permissible factors. The second option would only require disciplinary boards to offer *post hoc*, courtroom rationalizations for a board's refusal to hear requested witnesses; these rationalizations would constitute attempts to justify the board's actions, many months, or years, after a witness had been excluded.

Inexplicably, the Court, with only passing consideration of the first option, chooses the second. But no basis for this choice can be found in the principle of "mutual accommodation" announced in *Wolff*. If *Wolff's* principle of mutual accommodation means, as the State contends, that an inmate "is entitled only to those facets of procedural due process which are consistent with the demands of prison security,"[4] it surely also means that the inmate is entitled to *all* the facets of due process that are consistent with the demands of prison security. Contemporaneous explanations for excluding witnesses are an important element of due process at disciplinary hearings and, as long as prison officials have the option of keeping these explanations from the inmate, a requirement that such explanations be recorded would not intrude on the "institutional needs and objectives" of prisons that *Wolff* identified. In the face of this readily-available means of enforcing the inmate's right, the Court's decision instead to choose the second option, that of after-the-fact courtroom explanations, gratuitously dilutes the constitu-

2. See n. 7, *infra*.

3. *Wolff* did eliminate one possibility: that the Constitution might require disclosure to the inmate, at the time of the hearing, of a board's reasons for refusing to allow requested witness-es to be called. 418 U.S., at 566, 94 S.Ct., at 2979.

4. Brief for Petitioner 13–14.

tional rights of prison inmates and fulfills my previously expressed fear that the "noble holdings" of *Wolff* would become "little more than empty promises." *Wolff, supra,* at 581, 94 S.Ct., at 2987 (opinion of MARSHALL, J.). I therefore dissent.

III

A contemporaneous-explanation requirement would strike the proper balance between the inmate's right to present defense witnesses and the institutional needs recognized in *Wolff.* As a general matter, it is now well understood that contemporaneous-explanation requirements serve two important functions. First, they promote a decision-making process in which the decisionmaker must consciously focus on the relevant statutory criteria of decision.[5] Knowledge that a decision will be tested against the justifications contemporaneously given for it increases the prospect that fair and non-arbitrary decisions will be made initially.

Second, judicial review is most meaningful when based on a record compiled before litigation began. *Post hoc* rationalizations of counsel for administrative action "have traditionally been found to be an inadequate basis for review." *Citizens to Preserve Overton Park v. Volpe,* 401 U.S. 402, 419, 91 S.Ct. 814, 825, 28 L.Ed.2d 136 (1971):

"[A]n advocate's hypothesis that an administrative decision-maker did in fact

conclude thus-and-such because the record shows that he could reasonably have concluded thus-and-such, is not likely to be highly impressive. The courts prefer to appraise the validity of an order by examining the grounds *shown by the record* to have been the basis of decision." W. Gellhorn, C. Byse, & P. Strauss, Administrative Law 361 (7th ed., 1979).

Indeed, even when decisionmakers themselves have been willing to submit affidavits to explain with hindsight the basis of their previous decisions, we have refused to consider such offers of proof for fear that they serve as merely "*post hoc* rationalizations." *Burlington Truck Lines v. United States,* 371 U.S. 156, 168–69, 83 S.Ct. 239, 245–46, 9 L.Ed.2d 207 (1962). The best evidence of why a decision was made as it was is usually an explanation, however brief, rendered *at the time of the decision.*

The considerations that call for contemporaneous-explanation requirements in some contexts apply with particular force in the setting of prison disciplinary hearings. A contemporaneous-explanation requirement would force boards to take the inmate's constitutional right to present witnesses seriously. And when inmates are allowed to call witnesses, the fairness and accuracy of disciplinary board findings are significantly affected, not only because witnesses are often crucial to the presentation of a defense,[6] but particularly because an inmate "obviously faces a severe credibility

---

5. See, e.g., *Goldberg v. Kelly,* 397 U.S. 254, 271, 90 S.Ct. 1011, 1022, 25 L.Ed.2d 287 (1970); see also *Dorszynski v. United States,* 418 U.S. 424, 455, 94 S.Ct. 3042, 3058, 41 L.Ed.2d 855 (1974) (MARSHALL, J., concurring in judgment); *Greenholtz v. Nebraska Penal Inmates,* 442 U.S. 1, 40, 99 S.Ct. 2100, 2120, 60 L.Ed.2d 668 (1979) (MARSHALL, J., dissenting); *Hewitt v. Helms,* 459 U.S. 460, 103 S.Ct. 864, 74 L.Ed.2d 675 (STEVENS, J., dissenting) (1983); *Connecticut Bd. of Pardons v. Dumschat,* 452 U.S. 458, 468, 469, 101 S.Ct. 2460, 2466, 69 L.Ed.2d 158 (1981) (STEVENS, J.,dissenting).

6. "Few rights are more fundamental than that of an accused to present witnesses in his own defense." *Chambers v. Mississippi,* 410 U.S. 284, 302, 93 S.Ct. 1038, 1049, 35 L.Ed.2d 297 (1973).

As the Court said in *Washington v. Texas,* 388 U.S. 14, 19, 87 S.Ct. 1920, 1923, 18 L.Ed.2d 1019 (1967):

The right to offer the testimony of witnesses, and to compel their attendance, if necessary, is in plain terms the right to present a defense, the right to present the defendant's version of the facts as well as the prosecution's to the [factfinder] so it may decide where the truth lies....
This right is a fundamental element of due process of law.

See also *United States v. Valenzuela-Bernal,* 458 U.S. 858, 875, 102 S.Ct. 3440, 3450, 73 L.Ed.2d 1193 (1982) (O'CONNOR, J., concurring) ("[T]he right to compulsory process is essential to a fair trial"); *In re Oliver,* 333 U.S. 257, 273, 68 S.Ct. 499, 507, 92 L.Ed. 682 (1948).

problem when trying to disprove the charges of a prison guard." 418 U.S., at 583, 94 S.Ct., at 2988 (opinion of MARSHALL, J.). Many of the other procedural due process rights recognized in *Wolff* —for example, the right to advance notice of the charges, to a hearing, and to a statement of evidence and reasoning relied on—make sense only if the inmate is allowed to present his or her version of the facts through witnesses and evidence. Apart from such witnesses and evidence, inmates have little else with which to attempt to prove their case or disprove that of the charging officer; they have no constitutional right to confront and cross-examine adverse witnesses, and counsel is typically not present at these hearings to marshal the inmate's case. *Wolff*, 418 U.S., at 568, 94 S.Ct., at 2980; see also *Baxter*, 425 U.S., at 321–322, 96 S.Ct., at 1559. That so much hinges on the right to present witnesses is a particularly compelling reason for assuring, through a requirement of written reasons when witnesses are excluded, that the right is being scrupulously honored. See *Connecticut Bd. of Pardons v. Dumschat*, 452 U.S. 458, 472, 101 S.Ct. 2460, 2468, 69 L.Ed.2d 158 (1981) (STEVENS, J., dissenting);[7] cf. *Harris v. Rivera*, 454 U.S. 339, 344–345, n. 11, 102 S.Ct. 460, 463–464, n. 11, 70 L.Ed.2d 530 (1981) (*per curiam*) ("when other procedural safeguards have minimized the risk of unfairness, there is a diminished justifi-

cation for requiring a judge to explain his rulings").

Moreover, *post hoc* rationalizations are unlikely to be of any practical use in this context. Board officials may well not remember, long after the fact, the actual reasons they refused to hear a particular witness in any given case.[8] As one Court of Appeals has concluded, "[t]he requirement of support in the administrative record is central to the effectiveness of judicial review in insuring that a prisoner has not been subjected to arbitrary action by prison officials." *Hayes v. Thompson*, 637 F.2d 483, 488 (CA7 1980).

These very reasons have led the Court to impose a contemporaneous-explanation requirement when virtually identical procedural rights, guaranteed by the Constitution, were at stake.[9] *Vitek v. Jones*, 445 U.S. 480, 100 S.Ct. 1254, 63 L.Ed.2d 552 (1980), is an example directly on point. There the Court held that an inmate being considered for transfer to a mental institution has a constitutional right to a pretransfer hearing and to present witnesses at that hearing. To this point, *Vitek* is on all fours with this case; inmates in both proceedings have a right to a hearing and to witnesses. Yet in *Vitek* the Court further recognized that witnesses could not be excluded except upon a legitimate record finding of good cause—the very requirement the Court today chooses not to extend to disciplinary hearings.[10] Similarly, *Gag-*

---

7. "Whether the refusal to provide the inmates with a statement of reasons is a procedural shortcoming of constitutional magnitude is, admittedly, fairly debatable. Judges often decide difficult and important cases without explaining their reasons, and I would not suggest that they thereby commit constitutional error. But the ordinary litigant has other substantial procedural safeguards against arbitrary decisionmaking in the courtroom. The prison inmate has few such protections.... Many of us believe that ... statements of reasons provid[e] a better guarantee of justice than could possibly have been described in a code written in sufficient detail to be fit for Napoleon." 452 U.S., at 472, 101 S.Ct., at 2468.

8. In 1980, Massachusetts correctional institutions conducted 6,914 disciplinary hearings. Brief for Petitioner 63, n. 12.

9. Even the Court acknowledges that a requirement of contemporaneous reasons "admittedly has some appeal ... recollections of the event will be fresher at the moment, and it seems a more lawyer-like way to do things." *Ante*, at 2196. Of course, the essence of procedural due process is that institutions adopt "lawyer-like" procedures to assure that decisions are fair, rational, and carefully made.

10. The Court in *Vitek* stated that the right to call witnesses could not be denied "*except upon a finding, not arbitrarily made, of good cause* for not permitting such presentation ..." 445 U.S., at 494–495, 100 S.Ct., at 1264 (emphasis added).

non v. Scarpelli, 411 U.S. 778, 93 S.Ct. 1756, 36 L.Ed.2d 279 (1973), recognized a due-process right to counsel under some circumstances at parole and probation revocation hearings. To assure that this important right was faithfully honored, we further held that "[i]n every case in which a request for counsel at a preliminary or final hearing is refused, the grounds for refusal should be stated succinctly in the record." *Id.*, at 791, 93 S.Ct., at 1764. See also *North Carolina v. Pearce*, 395 U.S. 711, 726, 89 S.Ct. 2072, 2081, 23 L.Ed.2d 656 (1969) (written reasons required when more severe sentence imposed on defendant after second trial); *Gagnon, supra* (written reasons required for probation revocation); *Morissey v. Brewer*, 408 U.S. 471, 489, 92 S.Ct. 2593, 2604, 33 L.Ed.2d 484 (1972) (same for parole revocation decisions); *Goldberg v. Kelly*, 397 U.S. 254, 271, 90 S.Ct. 1011, 1022, 25 L.Ed.2d 287 (1970) (written reasons for termination of public assistance payments); *Kent v. United States*, 383 U.S. 541, 561, 86 S.Ct. 1045, 1057, 16 L.Ed.2d 84 (1966) (written reason required when juvenile court waives jurisdiction, subjecting defendant to trial as adult).

Ignoring these precedents, the Court seems to view the question simply as one of policy; the Court is content that "significant arguments" can be made in favor either of its "approach" or of the result I believe is required. The question, however, is not whether sound penological practice favors one result or the other, but rather what minimal elements of fair process are required in this setting to satisfy the Constitution. Due process requires written reasons for decisions, or for steps in the decisionmaking process, when the individual interest at stake makes the contribution of such reasons to the fairness and reliability of the hearing sufficient to

outweigh whatever burdens such a requirement would impose on the government. See *Black v. Romano*, — U.S. —, 105 S.Ct. —, 84 L.Ed.2d — (1985) (MARSHALL, J., concurring) (collecting cases); see generally *Mathews v. Eldridge*, 424 U.S. 319, 335, 343, 96 S.Ct. 893, 903, 907, 47 L.Ed.2d 18 (1976).

Applying this principle here, there can be little doubt that due process requires disciplinary boards to provide written reasons for refusing to hear witnesses. The liberty interests at stake in these hearings are, of course, of serious magnitude, and the right to call witnesses is integral to assuring the fairness and accuracy of these hearings. Moreover, the reality that disciplinary boards, composed of correctional officials, may be overly inclined to accept the word of prison guards and refuse without reason to hear witnesses cannot be ignored. These hearings include only skeletal due process protections to begin with, which makes judicial review essential to assuring the fairness and reliability of the process as a whole. Yet because extra-record judicial review is likely to be so meaningless a protection of the constitutional right to call witnesses, the process due an inmate requires witness exclusions to be justified with contemporaneous explanations. The Court simply fails to come to grips with the issue of constitutional right posed by this case.

Established principles of procedural due process compel the conclusion that contemporaneous explanations are required for refusals of disciplinary boards to hear requested witnesses. At least in the absence of convincing considerations otherwise, that much should be clear. I turn, then, to consider whether such convincing considerations can be found.

The importance of record explanations for excluding witnesses from disciplinary hearings is probably even greater than in *Vitek*, for there the key witness against an inmate was a neutral physician or psychologist, 445 U.S., at 483, 100 S.Ct., at 1258. A prison guard, who both charges an inmate and is the main witness against him, is significantly more likely to have his own personal reasons, including vindictive or retaliatory ones, for wanting to see the inmate convicted. If contemporaneous explanations for excluding witnesses were required in *Vitek*, surely due process requires similar explanations here.

IV

The Court in *Wolff* identified two considerations that limit the due process rights inmates otherwise have: "institutional safety and correctional goals." 418 U.S., at 566, 94 S.Ct., at 2979. The proposal offered by respondent—sealed contemporaneous explanations followed by *in camera* review—would satisfy these concerns fully. At the same time, this proposal maximizes the ability of the inmate to enjoy his or her constitutional right to present defense witnesses. The proposal therefore constitutes a perfectly sensible, "reasonable accommodation" to the concerns identified in *Wolff*.

A. Institutional Hazards and the Threat of Reprisal

The primary factor that caused the Court in *Wolff* to qualify and restrict the right to call witnesses was said to be "institutional safety." Fearing that inmates might be "subject to the unwritten code that exhorts inmates not to inform on a fellow prisoner," *id.*, at 562, 94 S.Ct., at 2977, and concerned that honoring a witness request might subject the witness to "a risk of reprisal or [might] undermine authority," the Court concluded that the "hazards presented in individual cases" of "reprisal" against testifying inmates made dangerous the disclosure to a charged inmate of a board's reasons for refusing to hear his witnesses. *Id.*, at 566, 94 S.Ct., at 2980. Again today, the Court relies on "the very real dangers in prison life which may result from violence or intimidation directed at

either other inmates or staff." *Ante*, at 2195. Presumably, the Court's concern is that an inmate will intimidate or coerce defense witnesses into testifying falsely, and that a witness who goes to officials to disclose such threats will be the target of retaliation if a disciplinary board announces that "institutional safety" precludes it from hearing the witness.[11]

The option of sealed files, subject to later judicial review *in camera*,[12] would fully protect against the threat of reprisal and intimidation by allowing prison officials to refuse to disclose to the inmate those record statements they feared would compromise institutional safety. The *in camera* solution has been widely recognized as the appropriate response to a variety of analogous disclosure clashes involving individual rights and government secrecy needs. For example, after this Court in *McCray v. Illinois*, 386 U.S. 300, 87 S.Ct. 1056, 18 L.Ed.2d 62 (1967), held that the identity of informants relied on by the police need not always be disclosed to the defense at suppression hearings, lower courts turned to *in camera* hearings to "protect the interests of both the government and the defendant." W. LaFave, Search and Seizure § 3.3, p. 583 (1978). Through such hearings into informant identity, "the government can be protected from any significant, unnecessary impairment of secrecy, yet the defendant can be saved from what could be serious police misconduct." *United States v. Moore*, 522 F.2d 1068, 1073 (CA9 1975).[13] Similarly,

---

11. I have stated previously my view that the Court's fears are exaggerated in this context. The prospect of intimidation and later retaliation is much more real when it comes to confrontation of adverse witnesses than "in the context of an inmate's right to call *defense* witnesses." *Wolff*, 418 U.S., at 584, 94 S.Ct., at 2988 (opinion of MARSHALL, J.). Indeed, the Court recognized as much in *Baxter, supra*, observing that, "in comparison to the right to call witnesses, '[c]onfrontation and cross-examination present greater hazards to institutional interests.'" 425 U.S., at 321, 96 S.Ct., at 1559. "Confrontation and cross-examination ... stand on a different footing [than the right to call witnesses] because of their inherent danger and

the availability of adequate bases of decision without them." *Id.*, at 322, 96 S.Ct., at 1560.

12. As the Court's *in camera* discussion acknowledges, *ante*, at 2197, following inspection *in camera* of the relevant statements a court might, under some circumstances, conclude that no basis existed for failing to disclose the statements to the inmate.

13. See also *United States v. Alexander*, 559 F.2d 1339, 1340 (CA5 1977) ("in camera hearing may be helpful in balancing those interests"); *United States v. Anderson*, 509 F.2d 724 (CA9 1974); *United States v. Hurse*, 453 F.2d 128 (CA8 1971); *United States v. Jackson*, 384 F.2d 825 (CA3

Congress specifically invoked *in camera* review to balance the policies of disclosure and confidentiality contained in the exemptions to the Freedom of Information Act. 5 U.S.C. § 552(a)(4)(B). Congress stated that *in camera* review would "plainly be [the] necessary and appropriate" means in many circumstances to assure that the proper balance between secrecy and disclosure is struck. S.Rep. No. 93–1200, p. 9 (1974). Other examples in which Congress has turned to similar procedures abound, such as the federal wiretapping statute [14] and the Foreign Intelligence Surveillance Act of 1978,[15] both of which rely on closed judicial process to balance individual rights and Government secrecy needs in determining whether wiretapping is justified.

If the compelling Government secrecy needs in all these settings can be safeguarded fully through closed judicial process, it can hardly be gainsaid that the interest of prison officials in keeping confidential the basis for refusing to hear witnesses will be fully protected by the same process. Indeed, the *in camera* solution protects the institutional concerns with which the Court purports to be concerned just as well as does the Court's solution. Under the Court's approach, "prison officials at some point [must] state their reason for refusing to call witnesses ..." *Ante*, at 2194. But if institutional safety or reprisal threats formed the basis for the refusal, stating that reason [16] in open court would create hazards similar to those the Court relies on to eschew a requirement that these reasons be disclosed at the disciplinary hearing. Recognizing this fact, the Court holds that, "if prison security or similar paramount interests appear to require it," *ante*, at 2197 the courtroom justifications for refusing to hear a witness can

"in the first instance" *ibid.*, be presented *in camera.*[17] Yet once the Court acknowledges that *in camera* review adequately protects the "institutional safety" concerns discussed in *Wolff,* such concerns simply evaporate in the consideration of whether due process demands a contemporaneous record explanation for the refusal to hear witnesses. As even the Court acknowledges, then, the combination of sealed files and *in camera* review more than adequately protects "institutional safety," the primary factor that justified *Wolff's* qualification of the inmate's right to present defense witnesses.

B.   Other Correctional Goals

To restrict the right to call witnesses, the Court in *Wolff* also relied, although less centrally, on vaguely defined "correctional goals" that seemed to amount to the need for "swift punishment." 418 U.S., at 566, 94 S.Ct., at 2979. Again today, the Court invokes the "need to provide swift discipline in individual cases," *ante,* at 2195, as a basis for refusing to require that prison officials provide a record statement of reasons for declining to hear requested witnesses.

These statements provide unconvincing support for refusing to require a written explanation when witness requests are denied. If swift discipline is a legitimate overriding concern, then why hold hearings at all? And if the imperatives of swift discipline preclude the calling of witnesses in any particular case, stating that reason would suffice.

More generally, the twinkling of an eye that it would take for a board to offer brief, contemporaneous reasons for refusing to hear witnesses would hardly in-

---

1967); *People v. Darden,* 34 N.Y.2d 177, 313 N.E.2d 49, 356 N.Y.S.2d 582 (1974).

14.   See 18 U.S.C. § 2518.

15.   50 U.S.C. § 1801 *et seq.*

16.   The Court does not state whether the bare recitation of "institutional safety" is sufficient to withstand review, or whether some explanation

supporting this assertion must be provided. I too see no need to decide that question today.

17.   I would not decide today whether defense counsel has a right to be present at the *in camera* proceedings. Cf. *United States v. Anderson,* 509 F.2d 724 (CA9 1974).

terfere with any valid correctional goals. Indeed, the requirement of stated reasons for witness denials would be particularly easy to comply with at disciplinary hearings, for *Wolff* already requires provision of a " 'written statement by the factfinders as to the evidence relied on and reasons' for the disciplinary action." 418 U.S., at 564, 94 S.Ct., at 2979 (citation omitted). To include in this statement a brief explanation of the reason for refusing to hear a witness, such as why proffered testimony is "irrelevant" or "cumulative," could not credibly be said to burden disciplinary boards in any meaningful way in their task of completing disciplinary report forms.

I have expressed previously my view that:

> "[I]t is not burdensome to give reasons when reasons exist ... As long as the government has a good reason for its actions it need not fear disclosure. It is only where the government acts improperly that procedural due process is truly burdensome. And that is precisely when it is most necessary." *Board of Regents v. Roth*, 408 U.S. 564, 591, 92 S.Ct. 2701, 2716, 33 L.Ed.2d 548 (1972) (MARSHALL, J., dissenting).

If ever that view is true, it is surely true here. See also *Hewitt v. Helms*, 459 U.S. 460, 495, 103 S.Ct. 864, 884, 74 L.Ed.2d 675 (1983) (STEVENS, J., dissenting) ("[A] requirement of written reasons [for keeping inmates in segregation] would [not] impose an undue burden on prison officials").

Ironically, the Court's shortsighted approach will likely do more to undermine other "correctional goals" with which the Court purports to be concerned than would respondent's approach. According to the Court, prison officials must come to court, many months or years after a disciplinary hearing, to "state their reason for refusing to call witnesses ..." *Ante*, at 2194. The burdens of discovery and cross-examination could well be part of that litigation process.[18] In contrast, under respondent's approach, once a contemporaneous record was prepared, judicial review would normally be limited to review of that record. Cf. *SEC v. Chenery Corp.*, 332 U.S. 194, 196, 67 S.Ct. 1575, 1577, 91 L.Ed. 1995 (1947). Thus, whatever the proper bearing of other "correctional goals" on the inmate's constitutional right to call witnesses, reliance on those goals to hold that prison officials must explain their refusal to hear witnesses in court, rather in the record, is simply misplaced.

V

In the end, the Court's decision rests more on abstract generalities about the demands of "institutional safety and other correctional goals" rather than on any attempt to come to grips with the specific mechanics of the way in which the principle established below would operate. Yet even these abstract generalities founder on the concrete practical experience of those charged with the continuing implementation of *Wolff.* The requirement the Court declines to adopt today is the prevailing practice in federal prisons and in state prisons throughout the country. Regulations promulgated by the Federal Bureau of Prisons provide that an inmate in federal prison has:

> "the right to submit names of requested witnesses and have them called to testify ... provided the calling of witnesses ... does not jeopardize or threaten institutional or an individual's security.... *The chairman shall document reasons for declining to call requested witnesses in the [Institutional Disciplinary Committee] report.* 28 CFR § 541.17(c) (1984) (emphasis added).

Similarly, at least 29 states and the District of Columbia require their disciplinary boards to provide a record statement of

---

18. See, *e.g., Woods v. Marks*, 742 F.2d 770 (CA3 1984) (summary judgment against inmate inappropriate when based on affidavit offering reason for excluding witness).

reasons for the refusal to hear requested witnesses.[19]

In addition, the practice of preparing contemporaneous explanations for the refusal to hear witnesses is favored by experts who have devoted substantial time and resources to studying the problem and who know quite well what the needs of institutional safety are in this context. For example, the American Correctional Association (ACA), after a study funded by the Department of Justice, has adopted the following standard as an "essential" element of disciplinary-hearing procedures:

> Written policy and procedure provide that the inmate is given an opportunity to make a statement and present documentary evidence, and may request witnesses on his/her behalf; *reasons for the denial of such a request are stated in writing.* (emphasis added). ACA, Standards for Adult Correctional Institutions, Standard 2–4363 (2d ed. 1981).

Similarly, the National Conference of Commissioners on Uniform State Laws (NCUSL) has determined that whenever an inmate's request for a witness is denied, the hearing officer must make "a written factual finding that to [call the witness] would subject a person to a substantial risk of physical harm." NCUSL, Model Sentencing and Correction Act, § 4–507 (1979). A third study of this problem reached the same conclusion: "Reasons for disallowing prisoner's requests for appearance of witnesses should be recorded for purposes of future review." ABA, Standards for Criminal Justice, 23–3.2, p. 23–41, n. 14 (2d ed. 1980) (as added 1983).

These authorities testify to the fact that, as penological experts have implemented *Wolff* over the last 11 years, significantly more has been learned about the sorts of due process protections at disciplinary hearings that are compatible with institutional needs. Recognizing that it was taking a tentative first step in this area, the Court in *Wolff* acknowledged that events in future years might "require further consideration and reflection of this Court." 418

---

19. Alaska Dept. of Corrections, 22 AAC05.430.(c) Completion Instructions § 20 (1984); Alabama Dept. of Corrections, Admin. Regulation No. 403, Part IV 10(g) (1983); Ark. Dept. of Correction, Disciplinary Policy and Procedures ¶ V(C)(2) (1983); Cal.Penal Code Ann. West § 2932(a)(3) (1985); Colorado Dept. of Corrections, Code of Penal Discipline ¶ 7e(3), p. 27 (1981); District of Columbia Dept. of Corrections, Lorton Regulations Approval Act of 1982, § 110.2, p. 16 (1982); Fla. Dept. of Corrections, Rules ¶ 33–22.07(5) (1984); Ga. Dept. of Offender Rehabilitation, State-Wide Disciplinary Plan ¶ 6(c) (1985) and Ga. State Prison, Discipline Procedure ¶¶ 8(c), 14 (1983); Haw. Dept. of Social Services & Housing, Corrections Div., Inmate Handbook § 17–201–17(e)(3) (Board "encouraged" to give written reasons); Illinois Dept. of Corrections, Rules, § 504.80(i)(3) (1984); Indiana Dept. of Corrections, Policies and Procedures, State Form 39586R, Completion Form § 20; Iowa Dept. of Corrections, Inmate Activity, Disciplinary Policy and Procedure §§ II (Procedure) (D)(3), II (Procedure) (E)(5) (1984); Kan.Admin.Reg. § 44–13–405a(g) (Supp.1984); Ky. Corrections Cabinet, Policy No. 15.6, ¶ VI(E)(1)(e) (1985); Maryland Dept. of Public Safety and Correctional Services, Division of Correction, Regulation No. 105–2, § IV-B(2)(b) (1982); Michigan Dept. of Corrections, Hearings Handbook § II–B(3), p. 4 (1981); Mississippi Dept. of Corrections, Rules and Regula-

tions § XII(D)(1), p. 11 (1975); Montana Dept. of Institutions, Inmate Disciplinary Procedures, Conduct of Hearing § 2–PD 85–216, pp. 10–11 (1985); Nebraska Dept. of Correctional Services, Rule 6(6)(e), p. 6–3 (1984); N.H. State Prison, Major Disciplinary Hearing Procedures ¶ 6 (1978), and Added Instructions for Handling Inmate Witness Requests ¶ 2(C); N.J. Dept. of Corrections, Disciplinary Standard 254.18 (1984); N.M. Penitentiary, Policy No. PNM 090301, ¶ II(C)(8) (1983); N.Y. Dept. of Correctional Services, Rules and Regulations § 253.-5(a) (1983); N.C. Dept. of Correction, Policies and Procedures § .0201(c)(4) (1984); Okla. Bd. of Corrections, Policy Statement No. OP-060401, ¶ 2(C)(1)(c) (1985); Oregon Dept. of Human Resources Corrections Division, Rule Governing Inmate Prohibited Conduct, and Procedures for Processing Disciplinary Actions §§ VI(G)(4)(a) and VI(G)(6)(d) (1982); Tenn. Dept. of Correction, Administrative Policies and Procedures, Index No. 502.01, ¶ VI(D)(2)(d) (Dec. 1981); Tex. Dept. of Corrections, Disciplinary Rules and Procedures § V(B)(4) (1984); Utah State Prison, Disciplinary Procedures ¶ III(D)(2)(g) (1984); Wis.Admin.Code, note following § HHS 303.81 (1985).

Some of these States explicitly require that the record be disclosed to the inmate; in other States, it is unclear whether the inmate is entitled to view the statements or how judicial review of these explanations is carried out.

U.S., at 572, 94 S.Ct., at 2982. At the time of *Wolff*, the only option considered by both the majority and dissenting opinions was whether disciplinary boards ought to be required to "state" their reasons for refusing to hear requested witnesses, see *id.*, at 584, 94 S.Ct., at 2988 (opinion of MARSHALL, J.); *id.*, at 597–598, 94 S.Ct., at 2994–2995 (opinion of DOUGLAS, J.); this option seemingly implied disclosure to the inmate. But neither the Court nor the dissenting opinions considered the middle-ground alternative respondent proposes today: that a contemporaneous record be prepared and preserved in case of later legal challenge but not be available to the inmate. The failure to consider this alternative is not surprising, for at the time of *Wolff* the relevant question was simply whether inmates had any right at all to present witnesses; no federal court had yet considered whether reasons had to be given for denying this right, let alone whether such reasons could be recorded but pre-

served in a file to which the inmate would not have access. *Id.*, at 572, n. 20, 94 S.Ct., at 2982, n. 20.[20] Nor was the process of *in camera* review, upon which respondent's alternative depends, as common a solution to clashes between individual rights and government secrecy needs as it is today. Yet despite these developments, and despite *Wolff's* expectation that future developments would make clearer the proper balance between due process and institutional concerns, the Court today inexplicably ignores the evolution of legal approaches and penological policy in this area.[21]

VI

The Court's decision leaves the inmate's constitutional right to present defense witnesses dangling in the wind. Perhaps that is the virtue to the Court of its decision, for I certainly can discern no other basis,

20. Neither the parties nor any of the many *amicus curiae* offered such a suggestion in the voluminous ... :ers filed in the case. Briefs in *Wolff v. McDonnell*, O.T.1973, No. 73–679.

21. No doubt the Court's sparse reasoning in this case and the utter lack of empirical foundation for its bald assertions is in part a product of the fact that *not a single lower court, state or federal*, appears to have considered the alternative of sealed records and *in camera* review that the Court today forecloses. This Court is often called on to strike difficult balances between individual rights and institutional needs, but by precipitously rushing into voids left by lower courts, the Court decreases the likelihood that the balance at which it arrives will properly account for all the relevant interests and available options. In this case, the State simply cried *Wolff* and, despite the absence of any clear conflict, the Court responded. But hastily granting certiorari every time an inmate or criminal defendant prevails below, as the current Court seems wont to do, deprives us of the insight lower court judges could offer on the issues and of the experiential basis that implementation of lower court decisions provides. The result, often as not, is the sort of decision rendered today. Once again, "[p]remature resolution of the novel question presented has stunted the natural growth and refinement of alternative principles." *California v. Carney,* — U.S. —, —, 105 S.Ct. —, —, 84 L.Ed.2d — (STEVENS, J., dissenting).

In light of current discussion over the Court's workload, it is worth noting further that, in the absence of any conflict in the lower courts, the decision to grant certiorari in this case is virtually unfathomable. At most, a State court had imposed more stringent due process requirements on its own institutions than this Court had previously recognized. I continue to believe the justifications for review in this Court are at their weakest in such cases, where no individual rights are alleged to be violated and where a State court speaks to its own institutions. See, *e.g.*, *Oregon v. Hass,* 420 U.S. 714, 726, 95 S.Ct. 1215, 1222, 43 L.Ed.2d 570 (1975) (MARSHALL, J., dissenting); see also *Michigan v. Long,* 463 U.S. 1032, 1065, 103 S.Ct. 3469, —, 77 L.Ed.2d 1201 (1983) (STEVENS, J., dissenting); see generally Developments in the Law, 95 Harv.L.Rev., 1342–1347 (1982). This case should therefore be added to the mounting list of examples that disprove claims that the Court is overburdened; "[m]uch of the Court's 'burdensome' workload is a product of its own aggressiveness" in rushing headlong to grant, often prematurely, the overstated petitions of State Attorneys General distraught with the performance of their own State institutions. *Carney, supra,* — U.S., at —, 105 S.Ct., at — (STEVENS, J., dissenting). Reserving the argument docket for cases of truly national import would go far toward alleviating any workload problems allegedly facing the Court.

grounded in principle or sound reasoning, for it. *Wolff* may give prison officials a privilege to dispense with certain due process rights, but, as always, "[t]he scope of a privilege is limited by its underlying purpose." *Roviaro v. United States*, 353 U.S. 53, 60, 77 S.Ct. 623, 627, 1 L.Ed.2d 639 (1957). The underlying purposes of the privilege recognized in *Wolff*—the promotion of "institutional safety and correction-

al goals"—can be realized fully by contemporaneous explanations not disclosed to the inmate. For that reason, the privilege recognized in *Wolff* ought to evaporate in the face of this means of accommodating the inmate's due process rights. That is the conclusion of penological officials and experts throughout the country and my conclusion as well. The Court, however, concludes otherwise. I therefore dissent.

Gary Wayne FREEMAN,
Plaintiff-Appellee,

v.

Richard RIDEOUT,
Defendant-Appellant.

No. 1513, Docket 86–2153.

United States Court of Appeals,
Second Circuit.

Argued Aug. 15, 1986.

Decided Dec. 30, 1986.

Before PRATT and MINER, Circuit Judges, and RE, Chief Judge, United States Court of International Trade, sitting by designation pursuant to 28 U.S.C. § 293(a).

RE, Chief Judge:

The defendant, Richard Rideout, a prison correctional officer, appeals from a judgment entered against him by the District Court for the District of Vermont, which held him liable for damages under 42 U.S.C. § 1983 (1982). The district court found that Rideout filed unfounded or false charges against plaintiff, Gary Wayne Freeman, a state prison inmate. The charges, which accused Freeman of having assaulted another inmate, were the basis for a prison disciplinary hearing, after which Freeman was found guilty, and sentenced to 30 days of "segregation."

Rideout contends that "the district court erred by improperly holding that Freeman's liberty interest was deprived without due process of law at the time the assault charges were filed."

Two questions are presented on this appeal: first, whether the filing of unfounded or false charges by a prison correctional officer against a prison inmate constitutes a deprivation of a constitutional right which permits recovery under 42 U.S.C. § 1983; and; second, whether the prison disciplinary hearing provided the plaintiff prison inmate with due process of law.

Since the Court holds that the filing of unfounded charges is not *per se* a constitutional violation under section 1983, and that the prison disciplinary hearing provided plaintiff with all the due process rights to which he was entitled, the judgment of the district court is reversed.

Facts

On October 5, 1981, institutional disciplinary charges were presented against plaintiff-appellee, Gary Wayne Freeman, a prisoner at the Woodstock Correctional Facility. Freeman was accused of assaulting another prison inmate, Jeffrey Price. The charges were filed by defendant-appellant, Richard Rideout, a prison correctional officer at the Facility. As a result of the charges filed by Rideout, a prison disciplinary hearing was conducted on the institutional charges the following day. Freeman was not informed of the identity of his accuser, nor was the alleged assault victim allowed to testify at the hearing. In part, because of the perceived need to protect Price from retaliation, Price was not permitted to testify at the disciplinary hearing.

After the prison disciplinary hearing, Freeman was found guilty, and was sentenced to 30 days of "segregation" from the general prison population. The evidence upon which the finding of guilty was based consisted of three documents: an incident report written by defendant-appellant, Richard Rideout; a report written by Correctional Officer John Honymar; and the unsworn statement of Douglas Pratt, another prison inmate.

Thereafter, on July 12, 1982, Freeman sued Rideout in the District Court for the District of Vermont for compensatory damages pursuant to 42 U.S.C. § 1983. Freeman contended that the charges filed against him by Rideout were unfounded and false, and that the filing of false charges constituted a *per se* violation of the due process clause of the fourteenth amendment.

At the trial, Freeman introduced into evidence a deposition of the alleged assault victim, Jeffrey Price, which stated that he had not been assaulted by Freeman, and that he had not told Rideout that he had been assaulted by Freeman.

After trial, the district court found that the charges filed by Rideout against Freeman were unfounded, and concluded that "[t]he filing of unfounded charges against an inmate offends clearly established constitutional rights...." In addition, the district court found that "the reasons given by the chairman of the committee for refusing to allow [Freeman] to confront Price [were] not acceptable." Based on these findings and conclusions, the court awarded Freeman damages of $1500, plus costs. *See Freeman v. Rideout,* No. 82-234 Civ. (D. Vt. Jan. 2, 1986). Rideout has appealed the judgment of the district court.

Discussion

In 1871, in response to continued acts of vigilante terrorism committed by the Ku Klux Klan, Congress passed "An Act to enforce the Provisions of the Fourteenth Amendment to the Constitution of the United States, and for other Purposes." Civil Rights Act of 1871, 17 Stat. 13; *see Allen v. McCurry,* 449 U.S. 90, 98–99, 101 S.Ct. 411, 416–417, 66 L.Ed.2d 308 (1980). This Act, presently codified at 42 U.S.C. § 1983, provides for a broad and comprehensive civil rights jurisdiction, and was intended "to ensure that individuals whose federal constitutional or statutory rights are abridged may recover damages or secure injunctive relief." *Burnett v. Grattan,* 468 U.S. 42, 55, 104 S.Ct. 2924, 2932, 82 L.Ed.2d 36 (1984). For many years, however, the Act was narrowly construed and rarely applied. In 1961, in the seminal case of *Monroe v. Pape,* 365 U.S. 167, 81 S.Ct. 473, 5 L.Ed.2d 492 (1961), the Supreme

Court gave new life to the long dormant statute. Since then, section 1983 has been one of the nation's most frequently litigated statutes, and has been established as a primary source for relief to persons who believe that they have been deprived of a constitutional right under color of state law.

The historical origins of section 1983, and the role it has played in the federal protection of individual rights, were recently discussed by Justice Blackmun. *See* Blackmun, *Section 1983 and Federal Protection of Individual Rights—Will the Statute Remain Alive or Fade Away?*, 60 N.Y.U. L.Rev. 1 (1985). The cases and materials cited by Justice Blackmun reveal that a statute that enshrines constitutional values and protections should not be made to suffer by an unwarranted application or expansion.

Section 1983 provides:

Every person who, under color of any statute, ordinance, regulation, custom, or usage, of any State or Territory or the District of Columbia, subjects, or causes to be subjected, any citizen of the United States or other person within the jurisdiction thereof to the deprivation of any rights, privileges, or immunities secured by the Constitution and laws, shall be liable to the party injured in an action at law, suit in equity, or other proper proceeding for redress....

42 U.S.C. § 1983.

In this case, Freeman alleges that the filing of unfounded charges against him by Rideout, which resulted in his being placed in punitive segregation for 30 days, deprived him of a constitutionally protected liberty interest. Rideout concedes that Freeman had a constitutionally protected right not to be placed in punitive segregation without due process. *See, e.g., Hewitt v. Helms,* 459 U.S. 460, 470–72, 103 S.Ct. 864, 870–72, 74 L.Ed.2d 675 (1983); *Wolff v. McDonnell,* 418 U.S. 539, 555–57, 94 S.Ct. 2963, 2974–75, 41 L.Ed.2d 935 (1974). Rideout, however, also contends that the disciplinary hearing provided Freeman with

all the procedural due process to which he was entitled.

Freeman maintains that, even if procedural due process was provided by the disciplinary hearing, the filing of unfounded charges is *per se* a violation of a constitutionally protected right. The district court agreed, and, having found that the disciplinary charges against plaintiff were false or unfounded, held that the defendant "deprived [plaintiff] of [a] liberty interest without due process when he filed unfounded charges." *Freeman v. Rideout,* No. 82–234 Civ., slip op. at 5 (D. Vt. Jan. 2, 1986).

There appears to be a confusion between the existence of a constitutionally protected right, and the deprivation of that right without procedural safeguards or due process. The constitutionally protected interest in this case is the right of liberty. The fourteenth amendment does not prohibit every deprivation of liberty. It does, however, prohibit the deprivation of liberty without due process of law. *See Patterson v. Coughlin,* 761 F.2d 886, 892 (2d Cir. 1985), *cert. denied,* — U.S. —, 106 S.Ct. 879, 88 L.Ed.2d 916 (1986).

The prison inmate has no constitutionally guaranteed immunity from being falsely or wrongly accused of conduct which may result in the deprivation of a protected liberty interest. The plaintiff, as all other prison inmates, has the right not to be deprived of a protected liberty interest without due process of law. As is shown by the facts of this case, before Freeman could be placed in segregation, due process required that he be granted a hearing on whatever charges had been made against him. *See, e.g., Baxter v. Palmigiano,* 425 U.S. 308, 323, 96 S.Ct. 1551, 1560, 47 L.Ed.2d 810 (1976); *Wolff v. McDonnell,* 418 U.S. 539, 571 n. 19, 94 S.Ct. 2963, 2982 n. 19, 41 L.Ed.2d 935 (1974); *Sher v. Coughlin,* 739 F.2d 77, 81 (2d Cir.1984).

In his brief on this appeal, as before the district court, Rideout relies on the case of *Hanrahan v. Lane,* 747 F.2d 1137 (7th Cir.1984), as support for his contention that the mere filing of false charges does *not* constitute a *per se* constitutional violation. In the *Hanrahan* case, the plaintiff, a prison inmate, brought suit, pursuant to section 1983, against three prison guards, the members of a prison disciplinary committee, and various other prison officials. The three prison guards had "planted" contraband in the prisoner's cell after he had refused to pay to the guards "shake down" or extortion money. On the basis of this planted or false evidence, the plaintiff, after a prison disciplinary hearing, lost 15 days of good conduct credit.

Plaintiff-Hanrahan's section 1983 claim was predicated upon the contention or assertion that "his due process rights were violated when the defendant prison guards planted false evidence and issued a disciplinary ticket in retaliation for failure to pay an extortion demand." 747 F.2d at 1139–40. Alleging that the complaint failed to. state a claim upon which relief could be granted, the defendants moved to dismiss under Fed. R. Civ. P. 12(b)(6). The district court granted the motion and dismissed the complaint, and the Court of Appeals for the Seventh Circuit affirmed the dismissal. 747 F.2d at 1142 (per curiam).

In *Hanrahan*, the court of appeals stated that, although prisoners are entitled to be free from arbitrary action and conduct of prison officials, the protections against arbitrary action "are the procedural due process requirements as set forth in *Wolff v. McDonnell.*" *Id.* at 1140. Accordingly, the court held that "an allegation that a prison guard planted false evidence which implicates an inmate in a disciplinary infraction fails to state a claim for which relief can be granted where the procedural due process protections as required in *Wolff v. McDonnell* are provided." *Id.* at 1141. Since it was not clear whether the plaintiff had been afforded the procedural due process to which he was entitled under the *Wolff* case, the action was remanded to the district court.

The trial court in this case made no reference to the *Hanrahan* case. To support its conclusion that "[h]owever minimal due process rights afforded inmates may be,

they certainly include the right to be free from unfounded charges," the district court cited *Morrison v. Lefevre*, 592 F.Supp. 1052 (S.D.N.Y.1984). The *Morrison* case, however, does not support this conclusion.

In *Morrison v. Lefevre*, the plaintiff, a prison inmate, brought suit against prison officials who had planted contraband in a package which was to be given or delivered to the plaintiff. As a result, the plaintiff, without being informed of the charges against him, was transferred to another prison and placed in a "punitive isolation section." Plaintiff contended that "he suffered two deprivations of liberty without due process as a result of the planting and 'discovery'" of the contraband: first, that he was placed in the punitive isolation section, and, second, that he was transferred from one prison to another. The trial court agreed, and held that plaintiff was "denied the procedural protections to which he was entitled." *Id.* at 1072. The court identified the procedural deficiencies as the failure of the prison officials to give plaintiff notice of the charge, and their failure to afford plaintiff an opportunity to present his views to a prison official. *Id.* at 1073. Hence, it is clear that, in *Morrison*, the district court based its holding on the failure of the prison officials "to provide the proper hearing." *Id.* at 1074.

The district court, in *Morrison v. Lefevre*, also stated that "[h]owever minimal may be *the process due to prisoners* before segregation, that process *is insufficient when it has been contaminated by the introduction through state action of false inculpatory evidence. The introduction of false evidence in itself violates the due process clause.*" *Id.* at 1073 (emphasis added). This broad dictum, however, must be read in the factual context of the *Morrison* case. In *Morrison*, there was no hearing, and it was the mere filing of the charge itself that caused the plaintiff to be segregated. In the present case, Freeman was granted a hearing, and had the opportunity to rebut the unfounded or false charges. The holding in the *Morri-*

son case, therefore, does not support Freeman's claim under section 1983.

Since Freeman was granted a hearing, and was afforded the opportunity to rebut the charges against him, the defendant's filing of unfounded charges did not give rise to a *per se* constitutional violation actionable under section 1983. Plaintiff suffered as a result of the finding of guilty by the prison disciplinary committee hearing, and not merely because of the filing of unfounded charges by the defendant.

Since the validity of the hearing is also in issue, the court must now determine whether the disciplinary hearing provided Freeman with due process. In this case, Freeman asserts that he was deprived of due process because he was not permitted to cross-examine Jeffrey Price. On this question, the Supreme Court has held that, although prison inmates are entitled to due process, "the prisoner's right to call witnesses and present evidence in disciplinary hearings could be denied if granting the request would be 'unduly hazardous to institutional safety or correctional goals.'" *Ponte v. Real*, 471 U.S. 491, 105 S.Ct. 2192, 2195, 85 L.Ed.2d 553 (1985) (quoting *Wolff v. McDonnell*, 418 U.S. 539, 566, 94 S.Ct. 2963, 2979, 41 L.Ed.2d 935 (1974)).

In the *Wolff v. McDonnell* case, a prison inmate filed a complaint, pursuant to 42 U.S.C. § 1983, against the administrators of the Nebraska Penal and Correctional Complex. The prisoner, on behalf of himself and other inmates of the Complex, contended that the prison's disciplinary proceedings did not comply with the due process clause of the fourteenth amendment. The defendant maintained that "the interest of prisoners in disciplinary proceedings is not included in that 'liberty' protected by the Fourteenth Amendment." 418 U.S. at 556–57, 94 S.Ct. at 2974–75. The court of appeals, *inter alia*, held that the prisoners were entitled to certain procedural protections, and that the specific requirements were to be determined on remand by the district court.

The Supreme Court granted *certiorari*, because the case raised "important ques-

tions concerning the administration of a state prison." *Id.* at 542, 94 S.Ct. at 2968. The *Wolff* case is particularly pertinent because the Supreme Court identified certain minimum protections or procedures that a prison inmate may expect at a disciplinary hearing. An inmate charged with a violation must be given (1) advance written notice of the charges at least 24 hours before the hearing; (2) the opportunity to appear at the hearing, to call witnesses, and to present rebuttal evidence; and (3) a written statement by the factfinders as to the evidence relied on for their decision, and the reasons for the prison committee's action. *Id.* at 564–66, 94 S.Ct. at 2987–80. The Court, however, also stated that "[p]rison officials must have the necessary discretion ... to refuse to call witnesses that may create a risk of reprisal or undermine authority, as well as to limit access to other inmates to collect statements or to compile other documentary evidence." *Id.* at 566, 94 S.Ct. at 2980. Because the operation of a prison is an "extraordinarily difficult undertaking," the court added that the prison administrators should be free to exercise their discretion "without being subject to unduly crippling constitutional impediments." *Id.* at 566–67, 94 S.Ct. at 2979–80. The *Wolff* case is instructive because it identifies and sets forth the minimum procedures to which prison inmates are entitled under the fourteenth amendment.

In the more recent case of *Ponte v. Real*, 471 U.S. 491, 105 S.Ct. 2192, 85 L.Ed.2d 553 (1985), the Supreme Court held that the due process clause does not require prison officials to state on the record their reasons for denying an inmate's request to confront a particular witness. In *Ponte*, Chief Justice Rehnquist, writing for the Court, emphasized that "nowhere in *Wolff* or *Baxter* did we require the disciplinary board to explain why it denied the prisoner's request, nor did we require that those reasons otherwise appear in the administrative record." 105 S.Ct. at 2195. Hence, "so long as the reasons are logically related to preventing undue hazards to 'institutional safety or correctional goals,' the explanation should meet the Due Process requirements as outlined in *Wolff.*" *Id.* at 2196.

In determining whether a prison disciplinary committee properly excluded a witness from a hearing, because of the exigencies of the prison environment and the need of prison officials to maintain safety and discipline, a reviewing court must accord due deference to the decision of the administrator. On review, it is the responsibility of the court to balance the concern to safeguard the rights of individual inmates with the legitimate needs and aims of the penal institution. *See Superintendent, Mass. Correctional Inst. v. Hill,* 472 U.S. 445, 105 S.Ct. 2768, 2774, 86 L.Ed.2d 356 (1985); *Ponte v. Real,* 105 S.Ct. at 2195; *Baxter v. Palmigiano,* 425 U.S. at 321, 96 S.Ct. at 1559; *Wolff v. McDonnell,* 418 U.S. at 562–63, 94 S.Ct. at 2977–78. Indeed, the Supreme Court has stressed that the extent to which prisoners may confront and cross-examine witnesses should be left to the sound discretion of prison officials and administrators. *See, e.g., Baxter v. Palmigiano,* 425 U.S. at 321–22, 96 S.Ct. at 1559–60; *Wolff v. McDonnell,* 418 U.S. at 568–69, 94 S.Ct. at 2980–81.

The responsibility of prison administrators for the safety and security of the institution requires that they be granted the discretion to evaluate the potential hazards of allowing inmates to testify. Prison administrators may refuse prisoners the right to call witnesses, when the calling of certain witnesses may create a risk of reprisal or undermine authority. *Ponte v. Real,* 105 S.Ct. at 2197; *Baxter v. Palmigiano,* 425 U.S. at 321, 96 S.Ct. at 1559; *Wolfe v. Carlson,* 583 F.Supp. 977, 980 (S.D.N.Y.1984). In the language of the Supreme Court: "The better course ... is to leave these matters to the sound discretion of the officials of state prisons." *Wolff v. McDonnell,* 418 U.S. at 569, 94 S.Ct. at 2981. Therefore, given the limitations on the inmate's right to call and cross-examine witnesses, courts "should not be too ready to exercise oversight and put aside the judgment of prison administrators." *Wolff v. McDonnell,* 418 U.S. at 566, 94 S.Ct. at 2979.

At the trial before the district court, Assistant Superintendent Lawrence McLiverty, chairman of the prison disciplinary committee, testified that the committee was attempting to protect Jeffrey Price from potential retaliation by not allowing him to testify in the presence of Freeman. The district court found this explanation to be without merit, since "there was no suggestion of institutional disruption or danger to the security of the facility."

The concern of prison officials as to potential retaliation against inmate witnesses has been established as a sufficient reason for the exclusion of a witness from a disciplinary hearing. *Wolff v. McDonnell,* 418 U.S. at 566, 94 S.Ct. at 2979; *Wolfe v. Carlson,* 583 F.Supp. at 980. Indeed, in light of the broad discretion possessed by prison officials, the Supreme Court has indicated that "it may be that a constitutional challenge to a disciplinary hearing ... will rarely, if ever be successful." *Ponte v. Real,* 105 S.Ct. at 2197.

In this case, the concern of the prison official was rejected by the district court as "unsatisfactory," because there was "no suggestion, much less proof, that the security of the Woodstock facility or the safety of its residents would have been impaired by allowing Price to testify." The Supreme Court, however, has not required the prison officials to submit "proof." What has been deemed necessary is that the reasons stated be "logically related to preventing undue hazards to 'institutional safety or correctional goals.'" *Ponte v. Real,* 105 S.Ct. at 2196. In the present case, the district court improperly rejected the explanation provided by the administrator. Therefore, Jeffrey Price was properly excluded from the disciplinary hearing on October 6, 1981, and the procedural safeguards enunciated in *Wolff v. McDonnell* were satisfied.

Once a court has decided that the procedural due process requirements have been met, its function is to determine whether there is some evidence which supports the decision of the prison disciplinary board.

See Superintendent, Mass. Correctional Inst. v. Hill, 105 S.Ct. at 2774; *Hanrahan v. Lane*, 747 F.2d at 1141; *see also Willis v. Ciccone*, 506 F.2d 1011, 1018 (8th Cir. 1974). The Supreme Court has indicated the process to be used in making this determination:

> Ascertaining whether this standard is satisfied does not require examination of the entire record, independent assessment of the credibility of witnesses, or weighing of the evidence. Instead, the relevant question is *whether there is any evidence in the record that could support the conclusion reached by the disciplinary board.*

Superintendent, Mass. Correctional Inst. v. Hill, 105 S.Ct. at 2774 (emphasis added).

In this case, the prison disciplinary committee relied on three documents. In addition to the report submitted by the defendant, Rideout, it also relied upon the report submitted by Officer Honymar, and the statement of inmate Douglas Pratt. The committee also heard the rebuttal testimony of plaintiff, Freeman, and inmate Jeffrey Maynard. On this record, the court holds that there existed sufficient evidence to support the disciplinary committee's finding of guilty, and the imposition of punitive sanctions deemed appropriate by the committee.

Conclusion

In view of the foregoing, it is the holding of this Court that Rideout's filing of unfounded charges did not constitute a violation of plaintiff's rights under 42 U.S.C. § 1983 (1982). The Court also holds that the prison disciplinary hearing provided Freeman with the due process to which he was entitled. The judgment of the district court is, therefore, reversed.

VOLUME II

CHAPTER 5   IMPOSED THERAPY

In considering imposed therapy, the typical situation arises when prison officials forcefully undertake medical treatment to save the inmate's life. The cases presented in this section, however, deal with the constitutional right to health care beyond normal medical attention. In *Young v. Armontrout*, 795 F.2d 55 (8th Cir. 1986), the prisoner tried to force a transfer to another institution so that he could receive psychiatric treatment. The court held the inmate had raised a "potentially viable Eighth Amendment claim."

Baugh v. Woodard, 808 F.2d 333 (4th Cir. 1987), was a class action suit involving the transfer of certain inmates for involuntary treatment at a mental health facility. Among other aspects of the case, the court discussed the hearing requirements for such a transfer.

The chief case in this area is *Estelle v. Gamble*, 429 U.S. 97, 97 S.Ct. 285 (1976), which is reproduced in this series in Vol. VI: 433. The decision merits extensive study.

Introductions in previous volumes:

Keith Stanley YOUNG, Appellant,

v.

Bill ARMONTROUT, Warden, Appellee.

No. 85–1689.

United States Court of Appeals,
Eighth Circuit.

ROSS, Circuit Judge.

Keith Young appeals from the dismissal of his petition for a writ of habeas corpus. We vacate the dismissal and remand for further proceedings.

FACTS

Young is presently incarcerated in the Missouri State Penitentiary. He is serving prison sentences totaling forty-four years for convictions rendered in two separate jury trials on counts of rape, sodomy, felonious restraint, and stealing. His convictions were affirmed on direct appeal. *State v. Young,* 643 S.W.2d 28 (Mo.App. 1982); *State v. Young,* 661 S.W.2d 637 (Mo.App.1983).

Without the aid of counsel, Young submitted a habeas corpus petition to the federal district court for in forma pauperis filing. His asserted ground for relief was:

"Failure to treat, psychiatric services * * * [are] not being provided to the petitioner as to violate his Eighth Amendment rights against cruel and unusual punishment." His supporting facts were stated as follows: "That * * * [he was] sentenced to [a] prison term of 44 years under Section 589.-040 R.S.Mo.1984[1] which clearly contemplated that rehabilitative treatment be concomitant with the sentence, that respondents should be directed to afford the relater [sic] treatment consistent with his sentence, or if such treatment not be readily available at Missouri State prison to transfer the relater [sic] to a correctional prison where treatment is available or to release him." An addendum to the petition stated facts establishing that he had exhausted this claim in state court.

The district court permitted Young to file his petition on an in forma pauperis basis. The court then dismissed Young's petition without an evidentiary hearing, stating: "The petition alleges that Petitioner is not receiving psychiatric services which he believes he should be receiving as part of his original sentence. State sentencing schemes do not raise constitutional issues cognizable in federal habeas corpus proceedings except in exceptional circumstances. * * *; Niemann v. Parrott, 596 F.2d 316, 317 (8th Cir.1979). Such extraordinary circumstances are not present in this case." Order, January 31, 1985. When the court later denied Young's petition for a certificate of probable cause, it further explained: "Petitioner is not attacking the actual imposition of sentence or its length, but rather through self-diagnosis feels that the sentence should have included psychiatric care. The imposition of sentence is a discretionary act, limited only in length of time to be served and/or amount of fine by specific statutes. Petitioner may believe he deserves a different type of sentence, but variations of sentence are left to the trial judge's discretion." Order, June 4, 1985. This court subsequently issued a certificate of probable cause.

On appeal, Young contends that the facts alleged in his petition were sufficient to entitle him to an evidentiary hearing on whether his eighth amendment right to adequate psychiatric care has been violated. He also argues that he was legally incompetent to stand trial and that his court-appointed defense attorney failed to provide him with effective assistance of counsel. These latter two grounds for relief were first raised in a letter brief to this court in February of 1985; the grounds had not been raised in Young's petition. Young's petition did mention, however, that he had filed a motion for post-conviction relief pursuant to Missouri Supreme Court Rule 27.-26, that the motion raised an ineffective assistance of counsel claim, that the motion had been dismissed, and that an appeal of that dismissal was pending in state court. The ineffective assistance of counsel claim and the incompetency to stand trial issue are therefore not ripe for decision at this time.

DISCUSSION

Viewing Young's petition as an attack on the state sentence, the district court was correct in dismissing Young's petition. But reading Young's petition liberally, as is required in this case, it is apparent that Young has also raised a potentially viable eighth amendment claim based on a "deliberate indifference to serious medical needs [(here, psychiatric treatment)] of [a] prisoner[ ]." Estelle v. Gamble, 429 U.S. 97, 104, 97 S.Ct. 285, 291, 50 L.Ed.2d 251 (1976). We therefore instruct the district court on remand to treat Young's petition as a complaint filed under 42 U.S.C. § 1983. Leave to amend the complaint shall be granted liberally as justice requires.

In accordance with the above, the district court's dismissal of Young's petition is vacated and the case is remanded for proceedings not inconsistent with this opinion.

1. This citation was crossed out in the petition.

Paul Mack BAUGH, individually and on behalf of all others similarly situated, Appellee,

v.

James WOODARD, Secretary of North Carolina Department of Corrections; Amos Reed, Former Secretary of North Carolina Department of Corrections; Ralph Edwards, Director of North Carolina Department of Corrections; Richard Kiel, Chief of Medical Services DOC; Charles Smith, M.D.; Sam Garrison, Warden; Frank L. Mahan, Superintendent of Wayne County Unit, individually and in their official capacities, Appellants,

and

Billy Royal, M.D.; Richard Jeffries, Nurse; James Dupree, Nurses' Aide; Sarah T. Morrow, Secretary of North Carolina Department of Human Resources; R.J. Blackley, Acting Director of N.C. Div. of Mental Health, Retardation, etc.; Bruce E. Whitaker, Chairman North Carolina Committee for Mental Health and Retardation, individually and in their official capacities, Defendants.

No. 85–6388.

United States Court of Appeals,
Fourth Circuit.

Reargued July 16, 1986.

Decided Jan. 8, 1987.

Before RUSSELL, WIDENER and CHAPMAN, Circuit Judges.

WIDENER, Circuit Judge:

This appeal arises from a class action brought in the United States District Court for the Eastern District of North Carolina by all persons who have been or will be incarcerated by the North Carolina Department of Correction (DOC) and who have been or will be involuntarily subjected to inpatient treatment at a DOC inpatient mental health facility. Plaintiffs claimed that the procedures followed by the DOC in transferring inmates to inpatient mental health facilities were inadequate to satisfy due process requirements.[1] On cross-motions for summary judgment, the district court held that North Carolina inmates have a constitutional liberty interest in not being transferred to a prison facility exclusively for the mentally ill. 604 F.Supp. 1529. To protect this interest, the district court required the DOC to provide the following procedural protections to inmates before transferring them to correctional inpatient mental health facilities:

1. Written notice to the prisoner that referral to an inpatient mental facility is being considered, including a statement of the reasons for the referral;

2. a hearing sufficiently after notice is given to allow the prisoner to prepare his objections;

3. an opportunity at the hearing for the prisoner to testify in person, present documentary evidence, present witnesses and confront and cross-examine witnesses called by the state, except upon a finding, not arbitrarily made, of good cause for not permitting such presentation, confrontation or cross-examination;

4. a neutral and independent decision maker, who may be from within the prison system, but who has the authority to refuse admission;

5. a written statement by the decision maker as to reasons for his decision to transfer, which decision must be concurred in by two psychiatrists or psychologists;

---

1. The plaintiffs also alleged that they had been and were being forcibly treated with psychotropic medications in violation of their constitutional rights. The parties settled this issue by means of the formal adoption of a policy with respect to involuntary administration of psychotrophic medications and a consent judgment.

We emphasize that this opinion does not concern itself with transfers of a prisoner to an inpatient mental hospital other than for treatment. See *Vitek*, infra, 445 U.S. p. 482, 100 S.Ct. p. 1258. Thus, the frequent referrals and transfers of prisoners by courts to mental hospitals for observation, evaluation, and the like are not affected by our decision.

6. qualified and independent assistance from an adviser, not necessarily an attorney, to help the prisoner prepare his objections;

7. periodic review of the continuing need for treatment; and,

8. effective and timely notice of all the above rights.

The State appeals. We affirm in part and remand for further proceedings consistent with this opinion.

As a result of the compliance by the State with the district court's order and the issuance of new regulations in compliance therewith, there remains but one issue in this appeal, namely the place of and timing of the due process hearing required by *Vitek v. Jones*, 445 U.S. 480, 100 S.Ct. 1254, 63 L.Ed.2d 552 (1980). The State contends that it need not hold a hearing prior to an inmate's physical transfer to an inpatient mental health facility. Rather, the State contends that any hearing required under *Vitek* could be held after the inmate's transfer to the inpatient mental health facility, but prior to the inmate's admission therein and still be constitutionally proper. It is this limited issue that we address in this opinion.[2]

Mental health care of North Carolina inmates is administered by the Department of Prisons (DOP), a division of the DOC. Prior to the judgment in this case, DOP regulations provided that consideration of an inmate's involuntary transfer to an inpatient mental health facility began when referred by medical personnel or when custodial personnel observed the inmate engaging in behavioral abnormalities. See DOP Health Care Procedures Manual § 403.1 (May 1, 1980). The custodial personnel would refer the inmate in question to an outpatient clinic which would either provide treatment or refer the inmate to an inpatient mental treatment facility. Id. at

§ 404.1. At this point in the mental health transfer process, the inmate was informed of his impending transfer and given an explanation of the reasons therefor.

Upon his arrival at the inpatient mental health facility, mental health personnel would evaluate the inmate and decide whether to admit him to the facility for treatment. If the mental health personnel at the receiving facility determined that the inmate should not be admitted to that facility, despite the referral, then the case would be referred to the Directors Mental Health Review Committee for resolution of any disagreement between the mental health personnel at the receiving facility and those at the referring facility. Id. at § 404.2. Upon his admission to an inpatient mental health facility, the inmate would remain in the facility until his treatment team determined that he was capable of returning to the general prison population. Id at § 404.3.

The district court held that these procedures for an inmate's involuntary transfer to an inpatient prison mental health facility did not comport with the procedural requirements for such transfers that the U.S. Supreme Court had set forth in *Vitek v. Jones*, 445 U.S. 480, 100 S.Ct. 1254, 63 L.Ed.2d 552 (1980). The district court then ordered the DOC to submit proposed regulations implementing the procedures outlined above.

Pursuant to the district court's directive, the DOC submitted proposed regulations, which the district court subsequently approved and which were implemented throughout the North Carolina prison system in January 1986. See DOP Health Care Procedures Manual § 416 (December 1985). Under these new regulations, an inmate who refuses a voluntary transfer to an inpatient mental health facility is provid-

---

2. We note that the question of emergency referrals to an inpatient prison mental health facility is not at issue in this case and our holding today is solely concerned with nonemergency referrals to such facilities.

If there be any doubt as to our understanding of the gist of the briefs and argument, we add

that we do not distinguish, for the purpose of compliance with *Vitek*, inpatient mental treatment hospital facilities whether operated by the prison system, as in the case here, or by another state agency as in *Vitek*.

ed with a hearing prior to his physical transfer to said facility, at which the State must present sufficient evidence to show (a) that the inmate is mentally ill; (b) that the inmate requires services that are not currently available to him on an outpatient basis; and (c) that the unit to which the inmate is to be transferred is better able to provide the needed treatment services than the housing unit to which the inmate is currently assigned. See id. at § 416.-4(D)(2). During the hearing, the inmate may present evidence and question any witnesses for the State. Id. at § 416.4(D)(4). The inmate, moreover, has an adviser, not necessarily an attorney, to assist him in the preparation and presentation of his case. Id. at § 416.2(6). The hearing officer must document the results of the hearing, clearly summarizing the evidence presented and the rationale for his decision. Id. at § 416.4(D)(5). Furthermore, for the hearing officer's decision to become final, two psychiatrists or psychologists, one of whom must be located at the receiving unit, must concur in the decision. Id. at § 416.4(D)(7). Finally, upon the inmate's request, a hearing officer must review the case within ninety days after the initial hearing to determine whether the assignment to the inpatient mental health facility should be extended or terminated. Id. at § 416.4(D)(8). Subsequent reviews will take place thereafter every 180 days, upon the inmate's request. Id.

The State acknowledges that these new mental health transfer procedures do not create as much burden on the delivery of mental health care to North Carolina inmates as had been anticipated, and the sole objection that the State continues to press in this appeal regarding these new procedures concerns the place and timing of the hearing which is now required prior to the inmate's physical transfer to the inpatient mental health facility, rather than promptly after his arrival at the receiving facility and before his actual admission therein. It is the propriety of this requirement that we now address.

The United States Supreme Court has consistently stated that due process is a flexible concept that a court must adapt to the particular circumstances of the case at hand. See, e.g., *Hewitt v. Helms*, 459 U.S. 460, 472, 103 S.Ct. 864, 871, 74 L.Ed.2d 675 (1983). To determine what procedures are required in any given case to protect a constitutionally cognizable liberty or property interest, courts must balance those factors that the Supreme Court set forth in its opinion in *Mathews v. Eldridge*, 424 U.S. 319, 96 S.Ct. 893, 47 L.Ed.2d 18 (1976):

> First, the private interest that will be affected by the official action; second, the risk of an erroneous deprivation of such interest through the procedures used, and the probable value, if any, of additional or substitute procedural safeguards; and, finally, the Government's interest, including the function involved and the fiscal and administrative burdens that the additional or substitute procedural requirement would entail.

Id. at 335, 96 S.Ct. at 903.

The district court considered these factors when it determined that additional procedural safeguards were required to protect inmates from erroneous or improper transfers to inpatient mental health facilities. For the most part, we concur in the district court's assessment and balancing of these factors. We conclude, however, that the district court erred in its assessment of the potential for erroneous transfer should the required hearing take place after the inmate's physical transfer, but prior to his admission at the receiving facility. Consequently, we conclude that due process does not require the DOC to conduct a hearing concerning the propriety of an inmate's involuntary mental health transfer prior to the inmate's physical transfer from the unit at which he is currently housed.

In its opinion, the district court stated that should the hearing take place after the inmate's physical transfer from the unit at which he is currently housed, the prisoner would, at that point, have already been deprived of his due process rights and subjected to stigmatization and compelled behavioral treatment. In reaching this conclusion, however, the district court overlooked the fact that, after his physical transfer, an inmate must first be admitted to the receiving inpatient prison mental health facility before his psychiatric treatment will begin. Thus, immediately following the inmate's physical transfer to the receiving facility, but prior to his admission therein, the inmate has yet to suffer few, if any, of the adverse consequences resulting from such a transfer for which the Court in *Vitek* considered due process protections to be required. We accordingly vacate the district court's order to the extent that it can be read to require a hearing prior to an inmate's physical transfer from the unit at which he is currently housed. We hold instead that due process is satisfied if the inmate's hearing is held promptly after the inmate's physical transfer to the receiving facility, but before the inmate's admission therein, so long as the inmate's psychiatric treatment does not begin prior to the inmate's admission to the inpatient facility.[3] Our conclusion in this regard is reinforced by the fact that allowing the DOC to conduct due process hearings at the receiving rather than the referring facility will allow the DOC to centralize its hearing process, thereby decreasing the burden that such hearings may impose on the delivery of

mental health care to inmates in the North Carolina prison system.

In sum, we affirm the district court's judgment below in each respect except that concerning the timing of the hearing required to protect inmates' interest in avoiding involuntary transfers for treatment to inpatient prison mental health facilities. We vacate that portion of the district court's judgment that requires the DOC to conduct these hearings prior to the inmate's physical transfer to the inpatient facility. We hold that a hearing conducted promptly after an inmate's physical transfer to the inpatient facility, but before the inmate's actual admission therein, so long as the inmate's psychiatric treatment does not begin prior to his admission at the inpatient facility, will serve adequately to protect the inmate's interest in avoiding erroneous mental health transfers without imposing undue burdens on the delivery of mental health care to inmates.

Accordingly, the judgment of the district court is

AFFIRMED IN PART, VACATED IN PART, AND REMANDED FOR ACTION NOT INCONSISTENT WITH THIS OPINION.

---

3. The State suggested at oral argument that the hearing should be held within 10 days after the physical transfer, and that the Director's Mental Health Resources Committee would be an appropriate hearing body. While both of these suggestions are apparently reasonable, we think they are matters better left to the district court in the first instance and we express no opinion on them at this time.

VOLUME II

CHAPTER 6   LABOR BY PRISONERS

Jobs for prisoners are few, but inmates have neither liberty interests nor property rights in their jobs. An inmate can be removed from a prison job without prior notice or a hearing. The principle was reinforced in the case of *Williams v. Sumner*, 648 F.Supp. 510 (D.Nev. 1986), in which a Section 1985 civil rights action was brought. In *Glick v. Lockhart*, 759 F.2d 675 (8th Cir. 1985), the court held that the inmate's constitutional right was not violated when he was confined for refusing to work outside the prison.

Introductions in previous volumes:

Harry J. WILLIAMS, Plaintiff

v.

George SUMNER; Robin Bates; John
Slansky; John Ignacio; Gayle Sherman, Individually and in their respective official capacities, Defendants.

No. CV–R–86–72–ECR.

United States District Court,
D. Nevada.

June 24, 1986.

AMENDED ORDER

EDWARD C. REED, Jr., Chief Judge.

The plaintiff, Harry J. Williams, filed a
motion to proceed in forma pauperis, under
28 U.S.C. § 1915(d), accompanied by a complaint alleging violation of his civil rights
under 42 U.S.C. §§ 1983, 1985, 1986 and
1988. Plaintiff's complaint also alleges
possible pendent state claims. Plaintiff appears pro se seeking injunctive relief, declaratory relief, compensatory and punitive
damages, costs of suit and attorney's fees.

Plaintiff, an inmate at the Northern Nevada Correctional Center, was removed

from his employment at the Carson City Conservation Camp on November 18, 1985, after testing positive for Acquired Immune Deficiency Syndrome (AIDS) on three separate occasions (in May of 1985, in September or October of 1985 and again on November 16, 1985). On November 20, 1985, an independent medical firm made the diagnosis that the plaintiff was not infected with the AIDS virus. Plaintiff alleges that the defendants deprived him of his rights to procedural due process by refusing to allow him to return to work at the Carson City Conservation Camp, causing plaintiff to lose "work time" credits and to incur financial loss.

This Court assigned this case to the United States Magistrate, Phyllis Halsey Atkins, in accordance with 28 U.S.C. § 636(b)(1)(A). The Magistrate granted plaintiff's motion to proceed in forma pauperis. The Magistrate filed her Report and Recommendation recommending to this Court that it dismiss the plaintiff's complaint without prejudice and without service on defendants because it is frivolous within the meaning of 28 U.S.C. § 1915(d) in that it fails to allege an arguable claim of constitutional dimension which would give the court subject matter jurisdiction. Plaintiff timely filed objections to the Magistrate's recommendations in accord with 28 U.S.C. § 636(b)(1).

A court may authorize a person who is unable to pay the costs of suit to proceed in forma pauperis, allowing commencement of an action without prepayment of fees and costs or security. 28 U.S.C. § 1915(a). The court may dismiss an in forma pauperis action that is frivolous or malicious. 28 U.S.C. § 1915(d). Because the freedom from economic constraints afforded by 28 U.S.C. § 1915 increases the probability of abuse of the legal process through the filing of frivolous suits, most of the circuits have followed the procedure recommended by the Federal Judicial Center and permit dismissal of in forma pauperis actions before service of process. See, e.g., Franklin v. Murphy, 745 F.2d 1221 (9th Cir. 1984). The court in Franklin adopted as

the standard for frivolity, "an assessment of the substance of the claim presented, i.e., is there a factual and legal basis, of constitutional dimension, for the asserted wrong, however inartfully pleaded." Id. at 1227, quoting Watson v. Ault, 525 F.2d 886 (5th Cir.1976).

Plaintiff's claims under 42 U.S.C. §§ 1985 and 1986 may be disposed of summarily. Claims under § 1985 must be motivated by racial or other class based animus. Mollow v. Carlton, 716 F.2d 627, 628 (9th Cir.1983); Blevins v. Ford, 572 F.2d 1336, 1338 (9th Cir.1978). Plaintiff has failed to allege that the defendants had the requisite motivation, nor has he offered any evidence to that effect. Existence of a conspiracy actionable under § 1985 is an indispensible prerequisite for a § 1986 claim. Wagar v. Hasenkrug, 486 F.Supp. 47, 51 (D.Mont. 1980); Kedra v. City of Philadelphia, 454 F.Supp. 652, 663 (E.D.Pa.1978). Since a claim for relief under § 1985 had not been stated, plaintiff cannot prevail under § 1986.

To prevail under 42 U.S.C. § 1983, plaintiff must show that defendants acted under color of state law to deprive him of "rights, privileges or immunities secured by the Constitution and laws [of the United States]." 42 U.S.C. § 1983. Plaintiff asserts that his procedural due process rights were violated by the defendant's refusal to allow him to return to a community trusty work program.

Incarceration does not isolate the plaintiff from the protection of the constitution. Meachum v. Fano, 427 U.S. 215, 225, 96 S.Ct. 2532, 2538, 49 L.Ed. 451 (1976); Wolff v. McDonnell, 418 U.S. 539, 555, 94 S.Ct. 2963, 2974, 41 L.Ed.2d 935 (1974). However, "[n]ot every 'grievous loss' suffered at the hands of the state will require the procedural protection of constitutional due process." Baumann v. Arizona Dept. of Corrections, 754 F.2d 841, 843 (1985), citing Meachum v. Fano, 427 U.S. at 224, 96 S.Ct. at 2538. "The threshold question in due process analysis is whether a constitutionally protected interest is implicated." Id. at 843, citing Meachum v. Fano, 427

U.S. at 223–24, 96 S.Ct. at 2538. Such a constitutionally protected interest, sufficient to trigger procedural due process rights, may originate in the Constitution or in state laws and regulations. *Hewitt v. Helms*, 459 U.S. 460, 469–72, 103 S.Ct. 864, 870–71, 74 L.Ed.2d 675 (1983); *Meachum v. Fano*, 427 U.S. at 223–27, 96 S.Ct. at 2537–39.

A state prisoner has no independent constitutional right to employment. The plaintiff may avail himself of due process protection here only if the state has created a protected interest in his employment in the community trusty work program. A state may create a protected interest by imposing substantive regulatory limitations on the discretion of prison officials. *Olim v. Wakinekona*, 461 U.S. 238, 249, 103 S.Ct. 1741, 1747, 75 L.Ed.2d 813 (1983). However, the state must additionally express these limitations in language of "an unmistakably mandatory character." *Hewitt v. Helms*, 459 U.S. at 471, 103 S.Ct. at 871. In *Greenholtz v. Inmates of the Nebraska Penal and Correctional Complex*, 442 U.S. 1, 99 S.Ct. 2100, 60 L.Ed.2d 668 (1979), the Supreme Court focused closely on the language of a Nebraska penal statute in finding that it created a protected interest in parole by mandating that parole "shall" be granted "unless" one of four specifically designated exceptions applied. The Ninth Circuit has adopted a restrictive interpretation of *Greenholtz*, finding that the "shall/unless" formula of the Nebraska statute was decisive in that case. *Baumann v. Arizona Department of Corrections*, 754 F.2d at 844.

Nevada law provides that the director of the prison is to establish a program for the employment of offenders. NRS § 209.459. Nevada law, NRS § 209.-461(1) further provides that:

1. The director shall:

(a) To the greatest extent possible, establish facilities which approximate the normal conditions of training and employment in the community.

(b) To the extent practicable, require each offender, except those whose behav-

ior is found by the director to preclude participation, to spend 40 hours each week in vocational training or employment, unless excused for medical reasons.

Read together, NRS §§ 209.459 and 209.-461, while mandating the establishment of an employment program, stop far short of requiring that the director provide a job for each offender. The director is required to employ each offender only to "the extent practicable," and the statute expressly vests in the director the discretion to exclude those offenders whose behavior he finds unsatisfactory. The "shall/unless" formula adopted in *Baumann* is present in NRS § 209.461; however, it is relevant only to the employment of offenders in general. The "shall/unless" formula is not here a mandate for the creation of jobs for each and every offender.

Further, plaintiff was employed as a community trusty. Nevada law provides even greater discretion for the director in the employment of offenders in the community. Nevada law provides that the director, "with the approval of the board, may: [g]rant to reliable offenders the privilege of leaving institutions or facilities of the department at certain times for the purpose of vocational training or employment." NRS § 209.461(2)(b). The "shall/unless" construction is here conspicuously absent.

Lacking language of an "unmistakably mandatory character" with respect to employment for individual offenders, required by the Supreme Court in *Hewitt* and interpreted by the Ninth Circuit in *Baumann*, Nevada's statutory scheme fails to create a constitutionally protected liberty interest in the plaintiff in his employment at the Carson City Conservation Camp. Lacking a liberty interest sufficient to trigger due process protections, plaintiff fails to demonstrate a legal basis of constitutional dimension to sustain his claim under 42 U.S.C. § 1983.

Plaintiff alleges that the defendants entered into a conspiracy to deprive him of his civil rights, presumably to come within the language of §§ 1985 and 1986. Plaintiff may also state a cause of action for conspiracy to deprive him of his civil rights without due process under § 1983. *Wright v. City of Reno*, 533 F.Supp. 58, 62–63 (D.Nv.1981). However, conspiracy allegations must be more than mere conclusory statements. *Mosher v. Saalfeld*, 589 F.2d 438, 441 (9th Cir.1979); *Lockary v. Kayfetz*, 587 F.Supp. 631, 639 (N.D.Cal.1984). Plaintiff's complaint states no facts in support of his allegations that the defendants conspired to deprive him of his civil rights. Plaintiff's conspiracy allegations are thus conclusory and must fall along with his other claims under 42 U.S.C. § 1983.

Plaintiff's claim for attorney's fees under 42 U.S.C. § 1988 must be dismissed because plaintiff did not prevail. Also, 42 U.S.C. § 1988 does not by itself set forth a cause of action. Further, attorney's fees may not be awarded to a non-lawyer pro se litigant under 42 U.S.C. § 1988. *Pitts v. Vaughn*, 679 F.2d 311 (3rd Cir.1982).

When federal claims are dismissed before trial, as plaintiff's here must be, pendent state claims should also be dismissed. *Jones v. Community Redevelopment Agency of Los Angeles*, 733 F.2d 646, 647 (9th Cir.1984).

This Court has reviewed *de novo* the report and recommendations objected to, and for the above stated reasons accepts the recommendations of the Magistrate. *See* 28 U.S.C. § 636(b((1).

IT IS, THEREFORE, HEREBY ORDERED that plaintiff's complaint is dismissed without prejudice and without service on defendants.

Dennis P. GLICK, Appellant,

v.

A.L. LOCKHART, Director, Larry Norris, Warden, Maximum Security Unit, Arkansas Department of Correction, Appellees.

No. 84–2622.

United States Court of Appeals, Eighth Circuit.

Submitted March 11, 1985.

Decided April 17, 1985.

Before HEANEY, Circuit Judge, HENLEY, Senior Circuit Judge, and McMILLIAN, Circuit Judge.

PER CURIAM.

Appellant Dennis P. Glick appeals from a final order entered in the District Court [1] for the Eastern District of Arkansas dismissing his 42 U.S.C. § 1983 complaint. For reversal Glick argues the district court erred in finding that his complaint failed to state a claim under 42 U.S.C. § 1983. For the reasons outlined below, we affirm.

Glick, an inmate of the Arkansas Department of Correction, filed this section 1983 action seeking declaratory and injunctive relief and damages. Glick, who is serving a life sentence plus two hundred and eleven years, alleges that he is being incarcerated in the Maximum Security Unit of the Arkansas Department as punishment for refusing to work outside the prison compound. Glick contends that his history, which includes two escapes and two assaults on other prisoners, and his treatment with "psychotrophy" drugs, makes him a threat to himself and those around him if he is compelled to work outside the prison compound. Thus, Glick contends that being punished for refusing to work is unconstitutional under the eighth and fourteenth amendments to the United States Constitution.

Glick's contentions are without merit. This circuit has followed the general rule that "compelling prison inmates to work does not contravene the thirteenth amendment." Mosby v. Mabry, 697 F.2d 213, 215 (8th Cir.1982).

Glick cites the eighth and fourteenth amendments; however, he has not stated any facts showing that his being compelled to work amounts to cruel and unusual punishment in these circumstances or indeed any lack of due process. In short, Glick's action has raised no colorable constitutional issue.

Accordingly, on the basis of the findings of the district court, the judgment of that court is affirmed. See 8th Cir.R. 14.

---

1. The Honorable Elsijane T. Roy, United States District Judge, Eastern and Western Districts of Arkansas.

VOLUME II

CHAPTER 7   TRANSFER OF PRISONERS

In matters of transfer of prisoners, the right to treatment of those being transferred and the right of inmates to due process in transfer procedures come into play. *Beard v. Livesay*, 798 F.2d 874 (6th Cir. 1986), teaches that although the prisoner has no inherent right to be housed at a particular institution, the state may create a liberty interest which is protected by due process.

Murphy v. Missouri Dep't. of Corrections, 769 F.2d 502 (8th Cir. 1985), reversed a decision to dismiss an action as frivolous to give the petitioner an opportunity to prove he was transferred for a constitutionally impermissible reason.

The important case in this area is *Olim v. Wakinekona*, 461 U.S. 238, 103 S.Ct. 1741 (1983) which is in Vol. VIII: 304.

Introductions in previous volumes:

II: 407; VI: 269; VII: 287; VIII: 303

Articles:

Lilly & Wright, *Interstate Inmate Transfer after Olim v. Wakinekoma*, 12 New Eng. J. Crim. & Civ. Confinement 71 (1986).

William R. BEARD, Jr.,
Plaintiff-Appellee,

v.

Gary J. LIVESAY, Warden; Robert Davies, Acting Warden; and Evans Fine, Director of Offender Classification, Defendants-Appellants.

No. 85–5730.

United States Court of Appeals,
Sixth Circuit.

Argued June 9, 1986.

Decided July 18, 1986.

Before MARTIN and GUY, Circuit Judges, and BROWN, Senior Circuit Judge.

BOYCE F. MARTIN, Jr., Circuit Judge.

The defendants, prison officials of the state of Tennessee, appeal the district court's grant of summary judgment to the plaintiff prisoner, William Beard. The district court held that under Tennessee statutes and regulations the reclassification of a prison inmate from minimum to medium security without a hearing implicated a protectible liberty interest under the fourteenth amendment. The court ordered the prison officials to expunge from Beard's record all references to his transfer and reclassification, but denied his requests for restoration of his Prison Performance Sentence Credits and an injunction covering all inmates within the Tennessee prison system. Beard was also awarded attorney's fees and costs. The prison officials appeal from this order; Beard did not file a cross-appeal.

In March of 1980 Beard began serving a ten-year sentence at Bledsoe County, Tennessee Regional Correctional Facility, where he was initially classified as a medium security prisoner. Beard was reclassified as a "minimum-direct" security prisoner in March 1981. He was still not allowed to work outside the prison, but he received fifteen days of Prison Performance Sentence Credit per month as a result of this reclassification, instead of the ten days of credit per month he received as a medium security prisoner. Prison Performance Sentence Credit may reduce the prison time that must be served before a prisoner's parole and eventual release.

In August, 1981, Beard and another inmate became involved in an altercation, and the prison authorities feared further internal security problems. Both Beard and his assailant were transferred to other prisons within the Tennessee system.

Beard was moved to Tennessee's Brushy Mountain Prison pursuant to an administrative transfer. Brushy is a medium security prison. Upon his transfer, Beard was immediately reclassified from minimum to medium security in order to fit the security designation of the institution. No hearing was held before or after this reclassification. As a medium security prisoner, Beard could earn a maximum of ten PPSC days per month. Beard does not challenge the validity of the administrative transfer, but argues that his reclassification without a hearing violated his liberty interest in his security status.

The issues presented on appeal are whether the Tennessee reclassification system creates a protectible interest in an inmate's security status and whether expungement of the plaintiff's reclassification records was an appropriate remedy.[1]

A liberty interest protectible under the fourteenth amendment may arise only when implicated by the Constitution, or a state law or regulation. *Hewitt v. Helms*, 459 U.S. 460, 469, 103 S.Ct. 864, 870, 74 L.Ed.2d 675 (1983); *Meachum v. Fano*, 427 U.S. 215, 226, 96 S.Ct. 2532, 2539, 49 L.Ed.2d 451 (1976). A prisoner has no inherent constitutional right to be housed in a particular institution, *Meachum*, 427 U.S. at 224, 96 S.Ct. at 2538 or to enjoy a particular security classification. *Moody v. Daggett*, 429 U.S. 78, 97 S.Ct. 274, 50 L.Ed.2d 236 (1976); *Montanye v. Haynes*, 427 U.S. 236, 242, 96 S.Ct. 2543, 2547, 49 L.Ed.2d 466 (1976). Therefore, any liberty interest which exists in Tennessee's reclassification process must be created by the state.

A state, by its own actions, may create liberty interests protected by the due process clause. *Hewitt*, 459 U.S. at 469, 103 S.Ct. at 870; *Bills v. Henderson*, 631 F.2d 1287, 1291 (6th Cir.1980). The Supreme Court described when the action of a state will create such an interest in *Olim v. Wakinekona*, 461 U.S. 238, 249, 103 S.Ct. 1741, 1747, 75 L.Ed.2d 813 (1983):

> These cases demonstrate that a State creates a protected liberty interest by placing substantive limitations on official discretion. An inmate must show 'that particularized standards or criteria guide the State's decisionmakers.' *Connecticut Board of Pardons v. Dumschat*, 452 U.S. 458, 467 [101 S.Ct. 2460, 2465, 69 L.Ed.2d 138] (1981) (BRENNAN, J., concurring). If the decisionmaker is not 'required to base its decisions on objective and defined criteria,' but instead 'can deny the requested relief for any constitutionally permissible reason or for no reason at all,' *ibid.*, the State has not created a constitutionally protected liberty interest. See *id.*, at 466–467 [101 S.Ct. at 2465] (opinion of the Court); see also *Vitek v. Jones*, 445 U.S. [480], at 488–491 [100 S.Ct. 1254, at 1261–1262, 63 L.Ed.2d 552 (1980)] (summarizing cases).

---

1. Beard concedes on appeal that that portion of the district court's judgment ordering expungement of his transfer records was in error, as he does not challenge the transfer itself but only the reclassification.

Prison officials may also create liberty interests by policy statements, regulations, or other official promulgations. *Walker v. Hughes*, 558 F.2d 1247, 1255 (6th Cir.1977). The plaintiffs, however, must have "a legitimate claim of entitlement to the interest, not merely a unilateral expectation of it." *Bills*, 631 F.2d at 1292. The criteria for making this determination are explained in *Bills*, 631 F.2d at 1292-93.

Where statutes or prison policy statements have limited prison officials' discretion by imposing a specific prerequisite to the forfeiture of benefits or favorable living conditions enjoyed by a prisoner, an expectation or entitlement has been created which cannot be taken away without affording the prisoner certain due process rights. On the other hand, when prison officials have complete discretion in making a decision that will affect the inmate, no expectation or protected liberty interest has been created.

Similar analysis was employed in the Supreme Court's *Hewitt* decision, which held that under applicable Pennsylvania statutes and regulations, a prisoner's transfer from a general prison population to administrative segregation implicated a protected liberty interest.[2] The *Hewitt* court first made clear that procedural requirements alone cannot establish a liberty interest:

The creation of procedural guidelines to channel the decisionmaking of prison officials is, in the view of many experts in the field, a salutary development. It would be ironic to hold that when a State embarks on such desirable experimentation it thereby opens the door to scrutiny by the federal courts, while States that choose not to adopt such procedural provisions entirely avoid the strictures of the Due Process Clause. The adoption of such procedural guidelines, without more, suggests that is these restrictions alone, and not those federal courts might also impose under the Fourteenth Amendment, that the State chose to require.

Hewitt, 459 U.S. at 471, 103 S.Ct. at 871. *See also Naegele Outdoor Advertising v. Moulton*, 773 F.2d 692, 703 (6th Cir.1985), *cert. denied*, — U.S. —, 106 S.Ct. 1639, 90 L.Ed.2d 184 (1986); *Bills*, 631 F.2d at 1298-99.

Clearly, therefore, Tennessee's requirement that a hearing be held prior to any reclassification cannot in itself create a protectible liberty interest. However, if Tennessee has gone beyond procedural guidelines by using "mandatory language" in connection with "specific substantive predicates," a liberty interest may be found. *Hewitt*, 459 U.S. at 472, 103 S.Ct. at 871. *Compare Pugliese v. Nelson*, 617

---

2. The Court found a liberty interest implicated by the following Pennsylvania statutes and regulation:

Title 37 Pa.Code § 95.104(b)(1) (1978) provides:
An inmate who has allegedly committed a Class I Misconduct may be placed in close or Maximum Administrative Custody upon approval of the officer in charge of the institution, not routinely but based upon his assessment of the situation and the need for control pending application of procedures under § 95.103 of this title.

Section 95.104(b)(3) of the same Title provides:
An inmate may be temporarily confined to Close or Maximum Administrative Custody in an investigation status upon approval of the officer in charge of the institution where it has been determined that there is a threat of a serious disturbance, or a serious threat to the individual or others. The inmate shall be notified in writing as soon as possible that he is under investigation and that he will receive a hearing if any disciplinary action is being

considered after the investigation is completed. An investigation shall begin immediately to determine whether or not a behavior violation has occurred. If no behavior violation has occurred, the inmate must be released as soon as the reason for the security concern has abated but in all cases within ten days. Finally, a State Bureau of Correction Administrative Directive states that when the State Police have been summoned to an institution:
Pending arrival of the State Police, the institutional representative shall:
1. Place all suspects and resident witnesses or complainants in such custody, protective or otherwise, as may be necessary to maintain security. A hearing complying with [37 Pa. Code § 95.103 (1972)] will be carried out after the investigation period. Such hearing shall be held within four (4) days unless the investigation warrants delay and in that case as soon as possible.
Pa.Admin.Div. BC-ADM 004, § IV(B) (1975).

F.2d 916 (2d Cir.1980) (administrative policy statement held not to create liberty interest because it merely established procedures rather than limiting discretion).

An examination of the statutes and regulation at issue in *Hewitt* is instructive. These pronouncements are arguably quite precatory, yet the Supreme Court held that the use of mandatory language and the requirement of substantive predicates in the procedural regulations themselves ("the need for control," or "the threat of serious disturbance") supported a conclusion that the state had established a protected liberty interest. *See also Olim v. Wakinekona,* 461 U.S. at 249, 103 S.Ct. at 1747 ("A State creates a protected liberty interest by placing substantive limitations on official discretion.")

The Tennessee statutes and regulations governing reclassification are more mandatory in nature than the corresponding promulgations in *Hewitt.* The Tennessee statute provides: "The prisoners shall be graded and classified in such manner as shall be most conducive to prison discipline and the moral status of the prisoner." Tenn.Code Ann. § 41–21–202. Further, Tennessee regulations regarding reclassification provide:

Residents assigned to a particular security cannot be classified/reclassified to a facility outside of the receiving institution's security range, e.g. residents assigned close security cannot be reclassified to Turney Center. In order for this [sic] resident to be sent to Turney Center, his security status must not be greater than medium, obviously a resident must merit a reduction in security before being reclassified to a facility with a lesser security range.

Policies of the Department of Correction, Index 404.00.

Tennessee has also adopted elaborate procedures for the reclassification process which further limit prison official's discretion.[3] These regulations require a hearing

prior to any reclassification, which must be held by a specifically composed committee. This committee "in joint consideration with the subject inmate and on the basis of information received from all available sources, assesses and assigns the inmate, or recommends such assignments." Policies of the Department of Corrections, Index 401.02(IV)(C). The Program Review Board is specifically charged with reviewing transfer reclassifications. Index 401.-02(VI)(A)(4)(b). Further, and equally important, "[a] reclassification hearing shall be scheduled before an appropriate panel of the classification committee, whenever any one of the following circumstances applies: ... The inmate's current security designation is not appropriate to his/her current institution assignment." 401.-04(VI)(C) & (11). Beard's situation was therefore specifically addressed in the Department's own policies.

While procedural safeguards alone cannot create a protectible liberty interest, these very detailed procedures, together with the substantive limitation that an inmate merit a reduction or enhancement of security designation, defined as that which is "most conducive to prison discipline and the moral status of the prisoner" are sufficient to create a protectible liberty interest.

A similar argument has been raised before the Seventh Circuit. In *Matthews v. Fairman,* 779 F.2d 409 (7th Cir.1985), the court held that the Illinois administrative regulation governing prison reassignments established only procedural guidelines governing those reassignments and therefore did not create a protectible liberty interest for purposes of the fourteenth amendment. Matthews was transferred from a medium to a maximum security unit without meriting or receiving a corresponding increase in security classification. Under Illinois administrative regulation 802(11)(C), "a change in assignment may be made for three reasons only: (1) the inmate's inability or incompetence in completing a work,

3. The detail evident in these reclassification procedures is not surprising, given that the original classification of a prisoner is a serious under-

taking which takes about six weeks. *See Grubbs v. Bradley,* 552 F.Supp. 1052, 1060–65 (M.D. Tenn.1982).

training, or study assignment; (2) an in-mate's violation of a rule after the inmate has been adjudged guilty in accordance with the provisions of A.R. 804 (governing the administration of discipline); or (3) placement in segregation under the provi-sions of A.R. 804." *Matthews*, 779 F.2d at 412. Matthews argued that A.R. 802(11)(C) limited prison officials' discretion in assign-ment, creating a protected liberty interest under the precepts of *Hewitt v. Helms.*

The *Matthews* court rejected the prison-er's argument, relying heavily on the fact that Matthews could point to no Illinois *statute* restricting officials' discretion in reassigning an inmate. *Matthews*, 779 F.2d at 414. According to the *Matthews* court, an administrative regulation stand-ing alone cannot create a protected liberty interest. *Id.*

The Sixth Circuit has specifically rejected this reasoning. In *Mayes v. Trammell*, 751 F.2d 175 (6th Cir.1984), the Court found a liberty interest to exist in the Ten-nessee parole scheme, although the Tennes-see parole statute contained none of the required mandatory language. The Court held "although the parole statute itself cer-tainly does not create a liberty interest, we hold that the overall Tennessee parole scheme, particularly Rule 1100–1–1–.06 of the Rules of Tennessee Board of Parole, does create an entitlement protected by the due process clause. *The presence of the decisive language in the Board's rules, rather than in the statute, does not di-minish its significance. See Bills v. Hen-derson*, 631 F.2d at 1291; *Walker v. Hughes*, 558 F.2d at 1255." [emphasis add-ed]. In addition, the mandatory language in *Hewitt* is contained in the *procedural* provisions of the Pennsylvania statute and the relevant Bureau of Correction Adminis-trative Directive. For these reasons, we do not find the *Matthews* analysis to be per-suasive in the present context.[4]

In sum, where substantive limita-tions have in fact been placed on the discre-tion of prison officials in classifying in-mate's security status, a protectible liberty interest has been created. *Meachum*, 427 U.S. at 228, 96 S.Ct. at 2540. Tennessee has combined the explicitly mandatory lan-guage required by *Hewitt* with detailed procedures governing reclassification. We believe that this combination sufficiently restrains officials' actions to give rise to an expectation on the part of Tennessee pris-oners that they will not be arbitrarily re-classified.

Mindful of the discretion to be afforded prison officials in matters of discipline, it bears repeating that Beard does not chal-lenge the warden's right to transfer him to another institution for any reason, or no reason at all. His contention is limited to Tennessee's reclassification procedures, and it is these provisions alone which we hold implicate a liberty interest under the fourteenth amendment.

Once a liberty interest has been found to exist, the next step is to determine what process is due the holder of this inter-est. Beard concedes that in this instance, the panoply of procedural rights afforded prisoners subject to reclassification in the Tennessee system satisfies the require-ments of due process under the fourteenth amendment. We agree. While the process due and the process afforded will not al-ways be identical, *see Bills*, 631 F.2d at 1296–99, we believe that Tennessee has ad-equately safeguarded prisoners' rights upon their reclassification. Thus, if Beard had in fact received the procedural protec-tions described in the Tennessee regula-tions, he would have no constitutional com-plaint.

The district court ordered that in-formation regarding both Beard's transfer and his reclassification be expunged from his prison records. Beard concedes that

4. The Eighth Circuit denied a similar claim be-cause "[a]ppellant has pointed to no statute, regulation or practice which places any substan-tive limitation on Missouri's discretion to trans-fer inmates. Nor does appellant show that any

particularized standards or criteria were estab-lished by the state to govern transfer decisions." *Williams v. Walls*, 744 F.2d 1345, 1346 (8th Cir.1984).

because the district court found no liberty interest was implicated by the transfer regulations, a holding not challenged on appeal, the expungement of his transfer was inappropriate. We therefore vacate that portion of the district court's judgment ordering expungement of Beard's transfer records.

We agree with the district court, however, that Beard's reclassification from minimum to medium should be expunged from his prison record. Because Beard has a protected liberty interest in his reclassification, and was not afforded the requisite due process before he was reclassified, this reclassification should not remain in Beard's file.

The State cites *Wolf v. McDonnell*, 418 U.S. 539, 94 S.Ct. 2963, 41 L.Ed.2d 935 (1974), in arguing against expungement as a permissible remedy. The *Wolff* court denied retroactive application of its holding specifying due process requirements for prison disciplinary proceedings. Prison officials were therefore not required to expunge prison records containing determinations of misconduct made without complying with the required procedures. The denial of expungement was based on the "significant impact a retroactivity ruling would have on the administration of all prisons in the country, and the reliance prison officials placed, in good faith, on prior law not

requiring such procedures." *Id.* at 574, 94 S.Ct. at 2983. The *Wolff* court goes on to compare the number of misconduct hearings held by the federal government in 1973 with the much lower number of parole revocation hearings, which had earlier been denied retroactive application.

[12] Nothing in the record indicates the number of reclassifications that occur in the Tennessee system every year, and we decline to speculate on this issue. As for the other basis of *Wolff's* retroactivity holding, however, we believe that there is little basis for a good faith reliance argument in this case. Given the decisions *Hewitt v. Helms, Olim v. Wakinekona,* and other cases regarding prisoner's liberty interests, and more specifically Tennessee's adoption of its own extensive procedural rules, the prison officials in this case cannot argue reliance on the absence of such procedural requirements.[5]

For these reasons, we believe that *Wolff* is distinguishable from the present case, and the Beard's prison records should be expunged of all references to his reclassification from minimum to medium security. However, all information regarding Beard's administrative transfer should be replaced in his file. The judgment of the district court is therefore affirmed in part and reversed in part.

---

5. This determination whether this rule was "clearly established" for purposes of qualified immunity under *Mitchell v. Forsyth*, ——— U.S. ———, 105 S.Ct. 2806, 2817–18 (1985), and *Harlow v. Fitzgerald*, 457 U.S. 800, 102 S.Ct. 2727 73 L.Ed.2d 396 (1982), is, of course, a separate inquiry.

Michael MURPHY, Appellant,

v.

**MISSOURI DEPARTMENT OF
CORRECTION, Appellee.**

No. 85–1184.

United States Court of Appeals,
Eighth Circuit.

Before HEANEY, Circuit Judge, HENLEY, Senior Circuit Judge, and McMILLIAN, Circuit Judge.

PER CURIAM.

Michael Murphy, an inmate at the Missouri State Penitentiary, filed suit under 42 U.S.C. § 1983 alleging, *inter alia*, that he was transferred from the Missouri Training Center for Men in retaliation for his religious beliefs. The district court dismissed his complaint as frivolous. *See* 28 U.S.C. § 1915(d). We reverse and remand for further proceedings.

Murphy is a member of Aryan Nations Church of Jesus Christ Christian. His pro se complaint alleges that he was transferred from a medium security institution to a maximum security prison solely to punish him for his religious views. The district court, relying on *Meachum v. Fano*, 427 U.S. 215, 96 S.Ct. 2532, 49 L.Ed.2d 451 (1976), summarily dismissed the complaint stating that a prisoner may be transferred to another institution for any reason whatsoever.

We believe the district court abused its discretion in dismissing Murphy's complaint as legally frivolous. While a prisoner enjoys no constitutional right to remain in a particular institution and generally is not entitled to due process protections prior to such a transfer. *Olim v. Wakinekona*, 461 U.S. 238, 103 S.Ct. 1741, 1745, 75 L.Ed.2d 813 (1983); *Meachum v. Fano*, 427 U.S. at 228–29, 96 S.Ct. at 2540; *Williams v. Walls*, 744 F.2d 1345, 1346 (8th Cir.1984) (per curiam), prison officials do not have the discretion to punish an inmate for exercising his first amendment rights by transferring him to a different institution. *Garland v. Polley*, 594 F.2d 1220, 1222–23 (8th Cir.1979); *see also Olim*, 103 S.Ct. at 1747 n. 9 (state may place inmate in any penal institution unless "the reason for confining the inmate in a particular institution is itself constitutionally impermissible"); *Montayne v. Haymes*, 427 U.S. 236, 244, 96 S.Ct. 2543, 2548, 49 L.Ed.2d 466 (1976) (Stevens, J., dissenting); *Matzker v. Herr*, 748 F.2d 1142, 1150 (7th Cir. 1984); *Milhouse v. Carlson*, 652 F.2d 371, 373–74 (3d Cir.1981); *McDonald v. Hall*, 610 F.2d 16, 18 (1st Cir.1979); *Buise v. Hudkins*, 584 F.2d 223, 229–30 (7th Cir. 1978), *cert. denied*, 440 U.S. 916, 99 S.Ct. 1234, 59 L.Ed.2d 466 (1979); *Majid v. Henderson*, 533 F.Supp. 1257, 1270 (N.D.N.Y.), *aff'd*, 714 F.2d 115 (2d Cir.1982). Construed liberally, Murphy's complaint alleges just such a retaliatory transfer.

An action may not be dismissed as frivolous unless it is beyond doubt that the petitioner can prove no facts in support of his claim which would entitle him to relief. *E.g.*, *Horsey v. Asher*, 741 F.2d 209, 211 (8th Cir.1984). Here, Murphy may be able to prove that his transfer was motivated by the prison officials' desire to punish him for protected activity. It follows that the district court erred in dismissing the complaint as frivolous.[1]

Reversed and remanded.

---

1. We express no opinion on the merits of Murphy's claim but hold only that his complaint states a valid cause of action under section 1983. We note that on remand Murphy "will face a substantial burden in attempting to prove that the actual motivating factor for his transfer was as he alleges." *McDonald v. Hall*, 610 F.2d 16, 18 (1st Cir.1979). We also note that Murphy raises other allegations which were not addressed by the district court, including a claim of denial of equal protection and that he was transferred in retaliation for filing a lawsuit

VOLUME II

CHAPTER 8   COURT REMEDIES

This section discusses remedies devised by courts to address violations of prisoner rights. The extent to which a prison authority may examine incoming mail or may restrict the receipt of incoming mail was considered in *Parrish v. Johnson,* 800 F.2d 600 (6th Cir. 1986). *Morrow v. Harwell,* 768 F.2d 619 (5th Cir. 1985), considered remedies for the lack of law books available to inmates. *Craine v. Alexander,* 756 F.2d 1070 (5th Cir. 1985), considered liabilities of prison authorities under a Section 1983 action.

Introductions in previous volumes:

II: 439; VI: 291; VII: 323

George PARRISH and Charles Giles,
Plaintiffs-Appellants,

v.

Perry JOHNSON, Charles Anderson,
K.L. Cole, and Clarence Turner,
Defendants-Appellees.

No. 84–1642.

United States Court of Appeals,
Sixth Circuit.

Argued June 2, 1986.

Decided Sept. 5, 1986.

Before KEITH and BOGGS, Circuit Judges, and CELEBREZZE, Senior Circuit Judge.

CELEBREZZE, Senior Circuit Judge.

Plaintiffs-appellants George Parrish and Charles Giles appeal from a district court's decision finding that Parrish's and Giles' conditions of confinement were unconstitutional and that defendant-appellee Clarence Turner subjected Parrish to cruel and unusual punishment and violated Parrish's First Amendment rights.[1] On appeal, Parrish contends that the district court erred in awarding only nominal damages for the punishment he endured and Giles argues that Turner violated his First, Eighth, and Fourteenth Amendment rights. We reverse.

Since the facts of this case are critical to the resolution of the issues raised before this Court, we set out the district court's factual findings in detail.[2] Both Parrish and Giles were paraplegics incarcerated at the State Prison for Southern Michigan. As a result of their condition, both men exhibited a diminished control over their bladder and bowel functions and, consequently, would frequently soil themselves. While Giles was able to clean himself, Parrish, who suffered from a fused hip joint, needed assistance to change. Assistance, however, due to both staff shortages and intentional neglect on the part of prison personnel, was often slow in arriving forcing Parrish, on a regular basis, to sit in his own feces for several hours. Besides being extremely unpleasant, this situation was medically dangerous because Parrish risked infecting his decubitis ulcers. Although Giles could clean himself, mismanagement and neglect rendered this ability nugatory; Giles was either not supplied with anything with which to clean himself or was given one small rag which quickly became soiled and unusable. Thus, like Parrish, Giles would routinely sit in his

---

1. These holdings have not been challenged on appeal.

2. In considering Turner's conduct toward Giles, the district court judge detailed Giles' testimony and assumed that it was true for purposes of his decision. In resolving the issues presented on appeal, we likewise take Giles' testimony as true.

own waste for significant periods of time. These deplorable hygenic conditions were exacerbated by verbal degradations, sporadic assaults, and acts of malfeasance and nonfeasance committed by Turner, a prison guard, against Parrish and Giles.

Turner aggravated the unsanitary conditions of Parrish's confinement by habitually refusing to relay or procrastinating in transmitting Parrish's requests for aid to the nurses. Turner also committed several assaults upon Parrish. On one occasion, Turner brandished a knife in order to extort cigarettes from Parrish and, on another, in what at best could be described as a bizarre episode, Turner while standing on top of a table shouting obscenities waved a knife at Parrish. Turner further enhanced Parrish's suffering by placing Parrish's food tray in positions in which Parrish was unable to retreive it and by serving the food accompanied with taunts that he had contaminated the food with venereal disease (a disease which Turner, in fact, had). Finally, Turner also interfered with Parrish's private phone conversations and personal mail: he would interrupt Parrish's phone calls by loudly speaking obscenities into the receiver and capriciously refuse to distribute and open and read Parrish's legal and personal mail. Giles received similar treatment.

Turner was equally remiss in relaying Giles' requests for care and twice accosted Giles with a knife. The first assault occurred on an elevator when Turner, for no apparent reason, pulled a knife and waved it in front of Giles' face. Turner repeated this action approximately one month later in order to extort potato chips and cookies from Giles. "Quite frequently" Turner ridiculed and tormented Giles by calling him, among other things, a "crippled bastard" who should be dead and telling Giles that he had defiled his food with venereal disease. Finally, Turner randomly opened and read Giles' personal mail.

Based upon the foregoing factual findings, the district court concluded that Parrish's and Giles' conditions of confinement were unconstitutional and that Turner's conduct had violated Parrish's First, Eighth, and Fourteenth Amendment rights. However, the district court judge refused to find that Turner had violated Giles' constitutional rights because Giles had not been subjected to the full panoply of Turner's misbehavior and had failed to demonstrate a special animus. Turning to the appropriate remedy for the constitutional violations, the district court judge reasoned that since injunctive relief was more appropriate than damages and since Parrish's injuries were not "lasting or severe," Parrish was only entitled to an award of nominal damages. This appeal ensued. Before proceeding to the damage questions presented by this case, we first consider whether the district court erred in holding that Turner's conduct did not violate Giles' First and Eighth Amendment rights.

I. Giles' First and Eighth Amendment Claims

A. First Amendment

Giles testified that Turner would randomly open and read his personal mail and that Turner would also taunt him by waving the open mail in front of him. Giles contends that this conduct violated his First Amendment rights.

While prisoners have some First Amendment rights in receiving mail, *see Pell v. Procunier*, 417 U.S. 817, 822, 94 S.Ct. 2800, 2804, 41 L.Ed.2d 495 (1974); *Meadows v. Hopkins*, 713 F.2d 206, 209–10 (6th Cir.1983), it is clear that prison officials may place reasonable restrictions upon these rights, *Bell v. Wolfish*, 441 U.S. 520, 544–52, 99 S.Ct. 1861, 1876–81, 60 L.Ed.2d 447 (1979). In order to maintain prison security and to check for contraband, prison officials may, pursuant to a uniform and evenly-applied policy, open an inmate's incoming mail. *See Wolff v. McDonnell*, 418 U.S. 539, 574–77, 94 S.Ct. 2963, 2983–85, 41 L.Ed.2d 935 (1974); *Bumgarner v. Bloodworth*, 768 F.2d 297, 301 (8th Cir.1985) (per curiam). Prison security may also require that limitations be placed upon the type and amount of mail a prisoner may receive. *See Jones v. North Carolina Prisoners' Labor Union, Inc.,* 433 U.S. 119, 129–31, 97 S.Ct. 2532, 2539–41, 53 L.Ed.2d 629 (1977). Yet, a prison official's discretion is not unlimited in this regard and several courts have held that mail relating to a prisoner's legal matters may not be read and may only be opened in the prisoner's presence, *Taylor v. Sterrett,* 532 F.2d 462, 477 (5th Cir.1976), *Bach v. Illinois,* 504 F.2d 1100, 1102 (7th Cir.) (per curiam), *cert. denied,* 418 U.S. 910, 94 S.Ct. 3202, 41 L.Ed.2d 1156 (1974); *Smith v. Robbins,* 454 F.2d 696 (1st Cir.1972); *see Harrod v. Halford,* 773 F.2d 234, 236 n. 1 (8th Cir.1985) (per curiam), *cert. denied* — U.S. ——, 106 S.Ct. 2254, 90 L.Ed.2d 699 (1986); *but see Sostre v. McGinnis,* 442 F.2d 178, 201 (2d Cir.1971) (en banc), *cert. denied,* 404 U.S. 1049, 92 S.Ct. 719, 30 L.Ed.2d 740 (1972),[3] and at least one court has extended these protections to media mail, *Guajardo v. Estelle,* 580 F.2d 748, 759 (5th Cir.1978); *see also Nolan v. Fitzpatrick,* 451 F.2d 545, 547 (1st Cir.1971). Further, the burden remains upon the prison officials to put forth legitimate reasons for interfering with a prisoner's incoming mail. *See Procunier v. Martinez,* 416 U.S. 396, 413, 94 S.Ct. 1800, 1811, 40 L.Ed.2d 224 (1974); *Brooks v. Seiter,* 779 F.2d 1177, 1180–81 (6th Cir.1985).

In this case, we are not confronted with a regularly applied regulation requiring the opening of all prisoners' incoming mail, *see Meadows,* 713 F.2d at 208–09, or a random interference with a prisoner's mail based upon a reasonable suspicion that the prison's security was being jeopardized. Rather, this case concerns Turner's arbitrary opening and reading of Giles' personal mail. No justification—other than

harassment—has been forwarded for Turner's conduct. A capricious interference with a prisoner's incoming mail based upon a guard's personal prejudices violates the First Amendment. *Cf. Brooks,* 779 F.2d at 1180. Accordingly, we hold that the district court erred in denying Giles' First Amendment claim and remand this claim for further proceedings.[4]

B. Eighth Amendment[5]

The Eighth Amendment protects prisoners against the imposition of "cruel and unusual punishment." U.S. Const. amend. VIII. By definition, therefore, not every intrusion upon a prisoner's bodily integrity will rise to the level of an Eighth Amendment violation. *See Johnson v. Glick,* 481 F.2d 1028, 1033 (2d Cir.) ("Not every push or shove ... violates a prisoner's constitutional rights."), *cert. denied,* 414 U.S. 1033, 94 S.Ct. 462, 38 L.Ed.2d 324 (1973). The maintenance of prison security and discipline may often require that prisoners be subjected to physical contact which at common law would be actionable as an assault or battery and which, in retrospect, may have been excessive. But, the good faith use of physical force in pursuit of valid penological or institutional goals will rarely, if ever, violate the Eighth Amendment. *See Whitley v. Albers,* — U.S. ——, 106 S.Ct. 1078, 1084, 89 L.Ed.2d 251 (1986); *Rhodes v. Chapman,* 452 U.S. 337, 346, 101 S.Ct. 2392, 2398, 69 L.Ed.2d 59 (1981). A violation of the Eighth Amendment nevertheless will occur if the infliction of pain upon a prisoner is both unnecessary and wanton. *Estelle v. Gamble,* 429 U.S. 97, 103, 97 S.Ct. 285, 290, 50 L.Ed.2d 251 (1976). In determining whether a prisoner's

---

3. The Second Circuit has recently indicated that in light of intervening Supreme Court decisions this aspect of *Sostre* may no longer be good law. *Heimerle v. Attorney General,* 753 F.2d 10, 12–13 (2d Cir.1985).

4. On remand, the district court should make formal factual findings on this claim in accordance with Fed.R.Civ.P. 52(a), *see supra* note 2, and consider whether Turner would be entitled to good faith immunity for his actions.

5. Giles also asserts that Turner's conduct contravened substantive due process under the Fourteenth Amendment. *See Lewis v. Downs,* 774 F.2d 711 (6th Cir.1985) (per curiam). Since the Fourteenth Amendment provides a prisoner with no greater protection than the Eighth Amendment, *Whitley v. Albers,* — U.S. ——, 106 S.Ct. 1078, 1088, 89 L.Ed.2d 251 (1986), we consider Giles' claim only under the Eighth Amendment.

claim rises to this level, the reason or motivation for the conduct, the type and excessiveness of the force used, and the extent of injury inflicted should be considered. *Cf. Lewis v. Downs*, 774 F.2d 711, 713 (6th Cir.1985) (per curiam). This analysis, however, must be carefully circumscribed to take into account the nature of the prison setting in which the conduct occurs and to prevent a prison official's conduct from being subjected to unreasonable *post hoc* judicial second-guessing. *See Whitley*, 106 S.Ct. at 1084–85. We consider the district court's holding in light of these considerations.

The district court held that Giles had failed to establish an Eighth Amendment claim because he was not subjected to the full panoply of Turner's misbehavior and because he failed to demonstrate that Turner's actions were the result of a special animus. While we do not take issue with these factual findings, we do not believe that in order to establish an Eighth Amendment violation Giles had to show that he was subjected to all of Turner's aberrant conduct. The question before the district court was not whether Giles suffered as much as Parrish, but rather was whether Turner inflicted unnecessary and wanton pain upon Giles. Similarly, although demonstrating a particularly malicious intent may be important in determining whether a constitutional violation has occurred, we do not believe that this degree of intent is an indispensable element of an Eighth Amendment claim. *See Whitley*, 106 S.Ct. at 1084 ("An express intent to inflict unnecessary pain is not required...."). As with any other case, Giles' case must be scrutinized based upon its own particular facts.

Initially, the actions of Turner towards Giles are devoid of logic or reason. No legitimate penological or institutional objective was furthered by Turner's unexplained

waving of a knife in Giles' face, knife-point extortion of potato chips and cookies, incessant taunting, or failure to relay Giles' requests for medical care to the nurses. Next, Turner's conduct was extreme. Assaults with a knife, theft, and the deliberate failure to provide needed medical care are serious occurrences in any setting. Another important factor is that Turner's behavior, specifically, the paraplegic slurs, acted to strip Giles of his dignity and reinforce the fact that Giles was dependent upon Turner for his continued well-being. Any reasonable person would suffer significant mental anguish knowing that his health was in the hands of a person performing the type of deviant acts which Turner did. Finally, all of the foregoing is to an extent exacerbated by Giles' paraplegic condition; Giles' condition placed him at the mercy of Turner and prevented him from attempting to avoid or mitigate his contact with or reliance upon Turner.

Considering Turner's behavior towards Giles in its totality, we conclude that Turner's actions inflicted unnecessary and wanton pain upon Giles. Causing a prisoner to sit in his own feces, assaulting a prisoner with a knife, extorting food from a prisoner, and verbally abusing a prisoner are all unnecessary acts which result in pain being inflicted. Further, simply the type, number, and seriousness of the acts committed demonstrate that they were performed wantonly. The assaults, verbal abuse, and failure to relay Giles' requests for care were all done intentionally. We hold, therefore, that the district court erred in determining that Turner had not violated Giles' Eighth Amendment rights and remand this issue for further consideration.[6] We now consider the damages issues presented by this appeal.

II. Damages[7]

The district court held that Parrish was only entitled to nominal damages because

---

6. *See supra* note 4.

7. The district court, although finding that Parrish's and Giles' conditions of confinement were

unconstitutional, held that the defendants committed these violations while acting in their official capacities. Although not considered by the district court or either party on appeal, we note

injunctive relief was more efficacious than damages and because his injuries were not "lasting and severe." We first consider whether the presence of injunctive relief may vitiate a claim for damages.

The starting point for analyzing damages for violations of constitutional rights is the common law. *Memphis Community School District v. Stachura*, — U.S. —, 106 S.Ct. 2537, 2543, 91 L.Ed.2d 249 (1986); *Carey v. Piphus*, 435 U.S. 247, 253–56, 98 S.Ct. 1042, 1046–48, 55 L.Ed.2d 252 (1978). At common law, once an injunction had been granted, damages were commonly given for the torts committed prior to and pending the suit. Restatement (Second) of Torts § 951(a) (1979); Restatement (Second) of Torts § 944 comment g (1979) ("When the injunction is granted against the continuance or repetition of torts, it has long been the practice to give, in the same suit, damages for the tortious

conduct anterior to trial...."); *see Dairy Queen, Inc. v. Wood*, 369 U.S. 469, 82 S.Ct. 894, 8 L.Ed.2d 44 (1962). The district court did not cite nor have we found any precedent expressly holding to the contrary.[8] Furthermore, no reason exists to deviate from the common law rule in this respect. A plaintiff injured by a series of constitutional torts, like any other tort plaintiff, should be able to recover "for all harm past, present and prospective." Restatement (Second) of Torts § 910 (1979). We hold, therefore, that the availability of injunctive relief fails to affect an attendant claim for damages. Hence, we consider the damage standards applicable to this case.

A. First Amendment.[9]

This Court has recently held that general damages[10] are presumed to occur when First Amendment rights are

---

that absent waiver the Eleventh Amendment bars the imposition of damages in an official capacity suit against state officials. *Kentucky v. Graham*, — U.S. —, 105 S.Ct. 3099, 3107, 87 L.Ed.2d 114 (1985); *Spruytte v. Walters*, 753 F.2d 498, 512 (6th Cir.1985), *cert. denied*, — U.S. —, 106 S.Ct. 788, 88 L.Ed.2d 767 (1986). On remand, the district court should consider whether the Eleventh Amendment bars damages for these constitutional violations and, since the district court's holding in this regard may moot the issue, we decline to consider the damages, if any, which Parrish and Giles would be entitled to for these unconstitutional conditions of confinement.

8. Two cases have made statements indicating that the availability of injunctive relief may obviate the need to grant damages for a constitutional violation. *Hunter v. Auger*, 672 F.2d 668 (8th Cir.1982); *Jacobson v. Tahoe Regional Planning Agency*, 474 F.Supp. 901 (D.Nev.1979). In *Hunter*, the court, after holding that insufficient evidence existed to support an award of compensatory damages, noted that "[m]oreover" plaintiff's rights had been "fully vindicated" by declaratory and injunctive relief. *Hunter*, 672 F.2d at 677. We do not read this single statement, without citation of authority, as adopting a rule that injunctive relief may be granted in lieu of damages. Rather, in light of the court's holding that insufficient facts existed to support an award of compensatory damages, we view the court's reference to the adequacy of injunctive relief as gratuitous and unnecessary to the opinion.

In *Jacobson*, the district court judge indicated that damages might not be an appropriate remedy when injunctive and declaratory relief would be adequate. *Jacobson*, 474 F.Supp. at 903. However, the district court's statements, in this regard, were compelled by its holding that, as a matter of law, the plaintiffs were precluded from recovering damages from the defendants. *Id.* Thus, we do not find the language in *Jacobson* inconsistent with the result we reach in this opinion.

9. The district court also held that Turner's interference with Parrish's mail violated substantive due process under the Fourteenth Amendment. We do not believe that, in a suit concerning a prison official's interference with a prisoner's mail, substantive due process provides the prisoner with any greater protection or right to damages than the specific guarantees of the First Amendment. *Cf. Whitley*, 106 S.Ct. at 1088. In any event, we would be hesitant to hold that Turner's conduct in handling Parrish's mail considered by itself and in the prison context was "so offensive to human dignity" as to shock our conscience. *Rochin v. California*, 342 U.S. 165, 172, 174, 72 S.Ct. 205, 209, 210, 96 L.Ed. 183 (1952).

10. Throughout this opinion we use the term "general damages" in accordance with the common-law definition, i.e., " '[g]eneral damages' are compensatory damages for a harm so frequently resulting from the tort that is the basis of the action that the existence of the damages is normally to be anticipated...." Restatement (Second) of Torts § 904(1) (1979).

violated. *Walje v. City of Winchester, Kentucky*, 773 F.2d 729, 731–32 (6th Cir. 1985); *accord Stachura*, 106 S.Ct. at 2545 (noting that it may be appropriate to presume general damages from some constitutional violations). The district court, thus, erred in requiring Parrish to establish a "lasting or severe" injury in this context and, accordingly, we remand Parrish's First Amendment violations for a determination of general damages. We caution the district court, however, that Parrish may not recover any damages for the inherent value of his First Amendment rights violated. *See Stachura*, 106 S.Ct. at 2544 ("no room" for jury's perception of importance of constitutional right). Instead, on remand, the district court judge should determine whether Turner's actions in interfering with Parrish's mail and phone calls caused Parrish any pain, suffering, emotional distress, or impairment of employment prospects. *Hobson v. Wilson*, 737 F.2d 1, 61 & n. 173 (D.C.Cir.1984), *cert. denied*, — U.S. —, 105 S.Ct. 1843, 85 L.Ed.2d 142 (1985). Next, we turn to the violations of Parrish's Eighth Amendment rights.

B.   Eighth Amendment.[11]

We begin our analysis of damages for Eighth Amendment violations recognizing that language exists in some of this Court's prior decisions which indicates that general damages may be presumed for the violation of any substantive constitutional right. *See Walje*, 773 F.2d at 731 ("[I]n Section 1983 actions establishing violations of substantive constitutional rights, general damages may be awarded even if there is no showing of actual injury."); *Brandon v. Allen*, 719 F.2d 151, 154–55 (6th Cir. 1983) (indicating general damages available for violations of substantive constitutional rights), *rev'd on other grounds sub nom. Brandon v. Holt*, 469 U.S. 464, 105 S.Ct. 873, 83 L.Ed.2d 878 (1985); *see generally Owen v. Lash*, 682 F.2d 648, 657–59 (7th

Cir.1982) (Stewart, J., discussing procedural/substantive controversy); *Ganey v. Edwards*, 759 F.2d 337, 340–41 (4th Cir.1985) (citing *Brandon* as adopting procedural/substantive dichotomy). Since the prohibition against the imposition of cruel and unusual punishment is a substantive constitutional right, that is, derived from the Eighth Amendment, the application of a substantive/procedural dichotomy to this case would lead to the result that Parrish would be entitled to general damages for the constitutional violation. We believe, however, that such a dichotomy is contrary to the Supreme Court's teaching in *Carey* and to the analysis developed by this Court in *Walje* and *Brandon*.

First, the Supreme Court recently re-affirmed its holding in *Carey v. Piphus*, 435 U.S. 247, 258, 98 S.Ct. 1042, 1049, 55 L.Ed.2d 252 (1978), that the starting point for analyzing damages under Section 1983 is the common law and indicated that substantive constitutional rights are subject to the same damage principles as procedural rights. *Stachura*, 106 S.Ct. at 2542–43. In *Stachura*, the Court explicitly rejected the argument that damages could be given for the value of *substantive* constitutional rights as misperceiving *Carey*'s analysis; the Court held that *Carey* did "not establish a two-tier system of constitutional rights." *Id.* at 2544. The application of a substantive/procedural dichotomy, therefore, would be contrary to *Carey*'s and *Stachura*'s admonitions for courts to first consider the common law, not whether the constitutional provision violated was substantive or procedural. *See Doe v. District of Columbia*, 697 F.2d 1115, 1122–23 (D.C. Cir.1983); *Lancaster v. Rodriguez*, 701 F.2d 864, 866 (10th Cir.) (per curiam), *cert. denied*, 462 U.S. 1136, 103 S.Ct. 3121, 77 L.Ed.2d 1373 (1983); *see generally* Note, *Damage Awards for Constitutional Torts: A Reconsideration After* Carey v. Piphus, 93 Harv.L.Rev. 966, 972–74 (1979–

---

11. Although the district court also found that Parrish's Fourteenth Amendment rights were violated by Turner's actions, we do not believe that in a suit by a prisoner alleging the imposi-

tion of cruel and unusual punishment that the Fourteenth Amendment provides any greater rights to damages than the Eighth Amendment. *See Whitley*, 106 S.Ct. at 1088.

80). Second, this Court's opinions in *Brandon* and *Walje*, despite some possible language to the contrary, did not apply a substantive/procedural dichotomy. Rather, in both cases, this Court looked to the common law and applied the most analogous common-law rule of damages. *Walje*, 773 F.2d at 731–32 (discussing damages at common law for violations of a person's free speech and voting rights); *Brandon*, 719 F.2d at 154–55 (analogizing Fourth Amendment violations to common-law assault and battery). Third, a substantive/procedural dichotomy focuses upon the wrong issue. The purpose of damages under Section 1983 is to compensate for the injury caused by the constitutional deprivation. *Smith v. Heath*, 691 F.2d 220, 226 (6th Cir.1982); *Morrow v. Igleburger*, 584 F.2d 767, 769 (6th Cir.1978), *cert. denied*, 439 U.S. 1118, 99 S.Ct. 1027, 59 L.Ed.2d 78 (1979). Thus, the focal point of the inquiry must be the injury sustained and the appropriate means of redressing it.

Last, although a cursory glance at the case law would indicate that the circuits are split on whether *Carey*'s actual injury requirement applies to violations of substantive constitutional rights, *see Ganey*, 759 F.2d at 340–41; *Owen*, 682 F.2d at 657–59, this "split" is more illusory than real. Although those courts which have refused to apply *Carey*'s actual injury requirement to substantive constitutional violations have often distinguished *Carey* on the ground that it only concerned the deprivation of procedural rights, the majority of

these cases have, like our decisions in *Brandon* and *Walje*, proceeded to analogize the constitutional interests at issue to the law of torts. *See Bell v. Little Axe Independent School District No. 70 of Cleveland County*, 766 F.2d 1391, 1408–12 (10th Cir.1985) (analogizing First Amendment claims to common-law denial of voting rights actions); *Hobson*, 737 F.2d at 61–63 & n. 173 (analyzing possible damages which might occur from a First Amendment violation); *Doe*, 697 F.2d at 1122–1124 (analogizing cruel and unusual punishment to common-law tort rules); *Herrera v. Valentine*, 653 F.2d 1220, 1229–31 (8th Cir.1981) (analyzing relationship between Fourth Amendment violations and common-law dignitary torts); *Halperin v. Kissinger*, 606 F.2d 1192, 1207 & n. 100 (D.C.Cir. 1979) (Fourth Amendment rights of a much different character than procedural due process rights), *aff'd by an equally divided court*, 452 U.S. 713, 101 S.Ct. 3132, 69 L.Ed.2d 367 (1981) (per curiam). The confusion in this area apparently stems from two decisions in which the courts, with very little analysis, applied *Carey*'s actual injury requirement to the denial of First Amendment rights. *Kincaid v. Rusk*, 670 F.2d 737, 745–46 (7th Cir.1982);[12] *Familias Unidas v. Briscoe*, 619 F.2d 391, 402 (5th Cir.1980);[13] *see also Smith v. Coughlin*, 748 F.2d 783, 789 (2nd Cir.1984) (applying an actual injury requirement to a Sixth Amendment violation without any analysis). Other than these two "literalist" interpretations of *Carey*, however, this Court and other Courts of Appeals have been

---

12. The current vitality of *Kincaid's* literal application of *Carey* in the Seventh Circuit is in question. While *Kincaid* has been followed on its facts, *see Crawford v. Garnier*, 719 F.2d 1317, 1324–25 (7th Cir.1983) (per curiam), two decisions evidence a willingness to follow an analytical approach to damages, *see Lenard v. Argento*, 699 F.2d 874, 888–89 (7th Cir.), *cert. denied* 464 U.S. 815, 104 S.Ct. 69, 78 L.Ed.2d 84 (1983); *Owen*, 682 F.2d at 657–59; *see also Freeman v. Franzen*, 695 F.2d 485, 494 (7th Cir.1982) (since actual injuries shown no need to consider if damages may be presumed for a violation of substantive due process), *cert. denied*, 463 U.S. 1214, 103 S.Ct. 3553, 77 L.Ed.2d 1400 (1983). The latest decision of the Seventh Circuit, *Madison County Jail Inmates v. Thompson*, 773 F.2d

834 (7th Cir.1985), in dictum stated, "It is true that *Owen* and *Lenard* recognize that under certain circumstances it is proper to presume damages." *Id.* at 841 (footnote omitted). Thus, the court's mechanical application of *Carey* in *Kincaid* may be an anomaly.

13. The Fifth Circuit is apparently following its decision in *Familias Unidas* and applying *Carey*'s actual injury requirement mechanically to the violation of all constitutional rights without analysis. *See Farrar v. Cain*, 756 F.2d 1148, 1152 (5th Cir.1985); *Ryland v. Shapiro*, 708 F.2d 967, 976 (5th Cir.1983); *Basiardanes v. City of Galveston*, 682 F.2d 1203, 1220 (5th Cir.1982); *Keyes v. Lauga*, 635 F.2d 330, 336 (5th Cir.1981).

attempting to follow *Carey*'s mandate of "adapting common-law rules of damages to provide fair compensation for injuries caused by the deprivation of a constitutional right." *Carey*, 435 U.S. at 258, 98 S.Ct. at 1049. The Supreme Court in *Stachura* indicated its approval of this analytical approach to damages by acknowledging that in some cases damages may be presumed merely from the act constituting the constitutional violation. *Stachura*, 106 S.Ct. at 2545; *see also id.* at 2546 (Marshall, J., concurring) (emphasizing "that the violation of a constitutional right, in proper cases, may itself constitute a compensable injury"). Accordingly, we decline to adopt a substantive/procedural framework for analyzing damages for violations of constitutional rights and proceed to consider the appropriate measure for damages under the Eighth Amendment.

Our analysis must start with the nature and type of interests protected by the Eighth Amendment. *See Carey*, 435 U.S. at 259, 98 S.Ct. at 1050. In generalities, the Eighth Amendment proscribes disproportionate punishments, *Weems v. United States*, 217 U.S. 349, 366–67, 30 S.Ct. 544, 548–49, 54 L.Ed. 793 (1910), "unnecessary and wanton infliction of pain," *Gregg v. Georgia*, 428 U.S. 153, 173, 96 S.Ct. 2909, 2925, 49 L.Ed.2d 859 (1976) (plurality opinion), and conduct repugnant to "evolving standards of decency," *Trop v. Dulles*, 356 U.S. 86, 101, 78 S.Ct. 590, 598, 2 L.Ed.2d 630 (1958) (plurality opinion). In concrete terms, the Eighth Amendment protects prisoners from being severely beaten, *e.g.*, *Collins v. Hladky*, 603 F.2d 824 (10th Cir.1979) (per curiam), intentionally denied medical care for serious medical needs, *e.g.* *Westlake v. Lucas*, 537 F.2d 857 (6th Cir.1976), recklessly subjected to violent attacks or sexual assaults, *e.g.*, *Martin v. White*, 742 F.2d 469, 474 (8th Cir.1984), and denied "the basic elements of hygiene," *Wright v. McMann*, 387 F.2d 519, 526 (2d Cir.1967). As this short list demonstrates, the Eighth Amendment has been interpreted "in a flexible and dynamic manner," *Gregg*, 428 U.S. at 171, 96 S.Ct. at 2924, to address numerous acts and omis-

sions. With this in mind, we consider what showing is necessary to recover damages for an infringement of Eighth Amendment rights.

Initially, we decline to hold that general damages may be presumed from an Eighth Amendment violation. General damages are presumed to flow from some tortious conduct because "the existence of the harm may be assumed and its extent is inferred as a matter of common knowledge." Restatement (Second) of Torts § 904(1) comment a (1979); C. McCormick, Handbook on the Law of Damages §§ 8, 14, at 33–35, 53 (1935). Due to the numerous interests protected and types of conduct prohibited by the Eighth Amendment, rarely will the existence and extent of harm be apparent from the simple allegation that an Eighth Amendment violation has occurred. Next, unlike suits under the First and Fourth Amendments, Eighth Amendment claims cannot be classified under a single traditional tort doctrine; no one tort doctrine is sufficiently expansive to cover the array of conduct prohibited by the Eighth Amendment. Further, unlike injuries emanating from a First Amendment violation, injuries occurring in an Eighth Amendment context are not likely to be of an evanescent nature. The establishing of cruel and unusual punishment will often require the showing of physical abuse from which injuries and concomitant damages will normally be easy to prove. *See Lancaster*, 701 F.2d at 866 ("would appear much easier to demonstrate damages in a cruel and unusual [punishment] case"); *Doe*, 697 F.2d at 1124 n. 24 (mental suffering easier to prove in cruel and unusual punishment cases). We hold, therefore, that general damages may not be presumed whenever the Eighth Amendment is violated and turn to what type of injury is needed to recover damages.

At first blush, it would seem appropriate to simply follow *Carey* and hold that an "actual injury" is needed to obtain damages under the Eighth Amendment. *See Lancaster*, 701 F.2d at 866; *see also Mad-*

ison County Jail Inmates v. Thompson, 773 F.2d 834, 844 (7th Cir.1985). Upon further examination of the practicalities and the ramifications of requiring a prisoner to *always* establish an actual injury as a prerequisite to obtaining damages, we decline to adopt such a rule. As we have previously discussed, the Eighth Amendment protects prisoners from a wide variety of conduct. The numerous types of tortious conduct and resultant injuries which the Eighth Amendment redresses militate heavily against our adopting an actual injury standard, because we simply cannot be certain that an actual injury requirement would be reflective of the common law or an appropriate prerequisite to obtaining damages in every situation.[14] *Cf. Doe,* 697 F.2d at 1124 n. 24 (noting that in some cases emotional distress might be inferred from an Eighth Amendment violation). In fact, having held that Eighth Amendment violations are not capable of being analogized to any single type of tortious conduct, it would be anomalous for us to assert that one single damage theory will sufficiently redress every act or condition constituting cruel and unusual punishment. Also, a single Eighth Amendment violation may subsume several separate and distinct acts. The requiring of actual injury in such cases provides little guidance: must the prisoner show actual injury flowing from one, the majority, or all of the tortious acts? Besides problems of application, an actual injury requirement in these "totality of the circumstances" cases may be inconsistent with the common law, contrary to the purpose the actual injury requirement is supposed to serve. For example, if the constitutional violation is composed of assaults, batteries, or other dignitary torts, an actual injury requirement would be contrary to the common-law rule which presumes general damages from this type of tortious conduct. *See Walje,* 773 F.2d at 731–32; D. Dobbs, Handbook on

the Law of Remedies §§ 7.1, 7.3 (1973). Finally, a wooden application of an actual injury requirement is contrary to the Supreme Court's decision in *Carey.* The Court, in *Carey,* warned that "the elements and prerequisites for recovery of damages appropriate to compensate injuries caused by the deprivation of one constitutional right are not necessarily appropriate to compensate injuries caused by the deprivation of another." *Carey,* 435 U.S. at 264–65, 98 S.Ct. at 1052–53. Thus, an actual injury should only be required when it appropriately remedies the constitutional violation. Since an across-the-board actual injury requirement in the context of the Eighth Amendment presents serious problems of application and fails to consider that in some instances damages may be inferable merely from the conduct constituting the constitutional violation, we decline to hold that establishing an actual injury is a necessary predicate to receive damages for an Eighth Amendment violation.

Instead, we believe that each tortious act comprising or composing the Eighth Amendment violation should be considered on its own merits. *Accord Doe,* 697 F.2d at 1124 n. 21 (noting that analogies may be drawn to various common-law torts). Although we recognize that this is an *ad hoc* approach, our holding is necessitated by the broad range of conduct which may fall within the ambit of cruel and unusual punishment. In addition, this approach will best serve to implement the common law of damages. By considering the damage consequences of each tortious act, a prisoner will be forced to carry the same burdens and be benefitted by the same presumptions as any other tort plaintiff. More importantly, by tailoring the damages to the specific interests invaded, our approach will greatly reduce the

---

14. For example, in a case in which a person has been unconstitutionally incarcerated for a "status offense," *see Robinson v. California,* 370 U.S. 660, 82 S.Ct. 1417, 8 L.Ed.2d 758 (1962), or in which a prisoner's punitive confinement is grossly disproportionate, *see Wright v. McMann,*

460 F.2d 126, 132–33 (2d Cir.), *cert. denied,* 409 U.S. 885, 93 S.Ct. 115, 34 L.Ed.2d 141 (1972), the closest commonlaw analogy apparently would be false imprisonment for which general damages were presumed at common law. *See McCormick, supra,* § 107, at 375–76.

chances that a prisoner will either be under or over compensated for his injuries. *See Stachura*, 106 S.Ct. at 2543; *Carey*, 435 U.S. at 258–59, 98 S.Ct. at 1049–50. We, therefore, turn to the conduct presented in this case.[15]

Turner's waving of a knife in front of Parrish obviously constituted a common-law assault. *See* Restatement (Second) of Torts § 21 (1979). As previously discussed, at common law general damages were presumed to flow from an assault. *See Brandon*, 719 F.2d at 154–55; D. Dobbs, Handbook on the Law of Remedies § 7.1, at 528–29 (1973). Consequently, we hold that Parrish is entitled to general damages for Turner's assaults upon him.

Turner's deprecation of Parrish presents a less clear case. At common law, verbal abuse alone generally did not rise to the level of tortious conduct in the absence of physical injury resulting from the abuse. 2 F. Harper, F. James & O. Gray, The Law of Torts §§ 9.1, 9.2 (1985). The law, however, has been changing in this area to allow recovery in the absence of a physical injury if the conduct by the tortfeasor is both extreme and outrageous and causes severe emotional distress. Restatement (Second) of Torts § 46 (1979); *see, e.g., Ross v. Burns*, 612 F.2d 271, 273 (6th Cir.1980) (applying Michigan law). In this case, we find it unnecessary to decide which standard applies because even if physical injury is not a prerequisite to recovery, insufficient factual findings exist for us to conclude, for the first time on appeal, that

Turner's taunting was extreme and outrageous or that Parrish suffered severe emotional distress from this abuse. Hence, on remand, the district court should make the necessary factual determinations to resolve these questions.

Finally, we consider the appropriate measure of damages for Turner's deliberate failure to provide Parrish with medical care.[16] This Court previously has dealt with the appropriate standard for damages for a denial of medical care, albeit in the context of pre-trial detainees. *Shannon v. Lester*, 519 F.2d 76 (6th Cir.1975). In *Shannon*, we held that a plaintiff may recover for any injury caused by the delay in care and any concomitant pain, suffering, or mental anguish. *Shannon*, 519 F.2d at 79–80; *accord Fielder v. Bosshard*, 590 F.2d 105, 110–11 (5th Cir.1979); *Walnorch v. McMonagle*, 412 F.Supp. 270, 277 (E.D.Pa.1976). Although *Shannon* was based on the Fourteenth Amendment, we believe that its principles are equally applicable to Eighth Amendment claims since the tortious conduct and resultant injuries are the same and since no principled reason exists why a different standard of damages should apply in an Eighth Amendment context. Thus, on remand, the district court should consider whether and to what extent Parrish was injured by the delay in receiving medical care.

For the foregoing reasons, the judgment of the district court is reversed and remanded for further proceedings not inconsistent with this opinion.[17]

---

15. The district court cited no authority for its holding that a "lasting and severe" injury is needed to establish a claim for damages. Besides lacking any support either in the case law or in the common law, requiring a lasting and severe injury as a prerequisite to the obtaining of damages for an Eighth Amendment violation is inconsistent with the principle of providing "fair compensation for injuries caused by the deprivation of a constitutional right." *Carey*, 435 U.S. at 258, 98 S.Ct. at 1049. We, therefore, reject imposing such a significant burden on Eighth Amendment plaintiffs.

16. We include in this category Turner's placing of Parrish's food tray out of his reach.

17. The district court made no findings concerning the appropriateness of assessing the punitive damages against Turner requested by the plaintiffs. *See Smith v. Wade*, 461 U.S. 30, 103 S.Ct. 1625, 75 L.Ed.2d 632 (1983). On remand, the district court should do so.

Thomas MORROW, Individually and in
Behalf of all others similarly situated,
Plaintiff-Appellee,

v.

Jack HARWELL, Individually and in his
official capacity as Sheriff of McLennan County, Texas, et al., Defendants-
Appellants.

No. 84–1610.

United States Court of Appeals,
Fifth Circuit.

Aug. 2, 1985.

Appeal from the United States District
Court for the Western District of Texas.

Before REAVLEY, JOHNSON and
HIGGINBOTHAM, Circuit Judges.

PATRICK E. HIGGINBOTHAM, Circuit
Judge:

The Sheriff of McLennan County, Texas
and other county officials appeal a magistrate's ordered changes in the County's jail
facilities and rules. The orders followed
trial of a class action suit filed by a prison
inmate who alleged denial of access to the
courts, as well as constitutional deprivations relating to the jail's policies on visitation, mail, and disciplinary procedures. We
affirm the magistrate's declaration that the
County's plan for inmate access to the
courts is inadequate. We reverse the declaration that certain physical facilities for
visitation are inadequate but affirm, for
the most part, the other declarations of
invalidity. We set aside all companion injunctive decrees as having been issued
without sufficient necessitating circumstances.

I

This suit was filed in March 1976, when
McLennan County housed its prisoners in
the "old jail," a facility built in the 1950's.
Thomas Morrow, an inmate representing a
class that included "all past, present and
future inmates of McLennan County Jail,"
complained that inmates' rights under the
First, Sixth, Eighth and Fourteenth
Amendments were being violated by a host
of conditions at the jail, including disciplinary procedures, inmate conduct rules,
grievance procedures, visitation and mail
privileges, supervision, clothing, hygiene,
food, exercise, medical treatment, dental
treatment, mental health services, jail design, jail capacity, jail sanitation, and cell
space, as well as lack of access to legal
materials, attorneys, telephones, newspapers, periodicals, radios and televisions.

At about the time suit was filed, the
County began construction of a new jail
and made plans to upgrade the old jail. It
was the County's objective that when the
two facilities were combined the County
would be in compliance with the Texas Jail
Standards Act, Tex.Rev.Civ.Stat.Ann. art.
5115 et seq. (Vernon 1975). The suit lay
dormant until the new jail was completed in
January 1981. At that time, many of the
complaints fell away.

By consent of the parties, the remaining issues were tried to a magistrate in the fall of 1982. After conducting a post-trial hearing on the principal dispute, whether the County had afforded its prisoners adequate access to the courts as required by *Bounds v. Smith*, 430 U.S. 817, 97 S.Ct. 1491, 52 L.Ed.2d 72 (1977), the magistrate filed a final decree in March 1984. The decree found the County to be in compliance with constitutional standards on the issues of supervision, diet, medical care, education, recreation, overcrowding, and detention conditions for pre-trial detainees, but not on the remaining points. The magistrate ordered the County to provide the following relief: (1) access to the courts through either an adequate law library or legal assistance or a combination of both; (2) modification of visitation policies (a) to permit minors to visit inmates, (b) to permit weekend visitation, (c) to equalize visitation rights of male and female inmates, and (d) to upgrade communication facilities in the visitation areas at the old jail; (3) establishment of disciplinary procedures consistent with *Wolff v. McDonnell*, 418 U.S. 539, 94 S.Ct. 2963, 41 L.Ed.2d 935 (1974); and (4) establishment of written guidelines for mail practices consistent with *Guajardo v. Estelle*, 580 F.2d 748 (5th Cir.1978). After a hearing, the magistrate awarded plaintiffs $47,950.00 in attorney fees. The County challenges the relief granted as well as the award of attorney's fees.

II

1

We turn first to the issue of access to the courts. The relevant facts are not disputed. There is no law library at the jail, but legal sources are available to the inmates through a weekly bookmobile, drawing upon the Waco-McLennan County Public Library. This library contains a number of statutory codes, digests, and form books, as well as the advance sheets of certain reporters from the McLennan County Law Library. Although the County contends that notices explaining availability of this service were posted in the jail library,

the magistrate found that "inmates have not been made aware of this program or of the law books available to check out...." There are no digests or other research materials available at the jail itself; therefore, the inmates cannot determine in advance which books they might wish to request.

McLennan County is located in the central part of Texas. Its seat is the City of Waco, the home of Baylor University. The county jail's library program is supplemented by paralegal assistance from two Baylor University law students who work under the supervision of a practicing attorney. The students, paid an hourly wage by the County, visit inmates who request legal assistance, but are prohibited by state law from giving legal advice. *See* Tex.Rev.Civ. Stat.Ann. art. 320a–1 §§ 10(a), 19 (Vernon Supp.1985). The students can assist prisoners only by providing copies of forms, cases, and other written legal materials. The copies are made for inmates at their request at a rate of ten cents per page, with free copies for indigents. Assertedly to deter abuse, jail officials did not inform indigent inmates that they could obtain copies without charge.

There was testimony that, although the law students employed by the County are not supposed to give legal advice, they interpreted some legal authorities and occasionally helped the inmates to complete legal forms. The County does not rely on these enthusiasms to the extent they may occasionally have gone further than the state law permits.

2

The source of the prisoners' asserted right to a law library is the Supreme Court's decision in *Bounds v. Smith*, 430 U.S. 817, 97 S.Ct. 1491, 52 L.Ed.2d 72 (1977). In *Bounds* the Court held that prisoners have a constitutional right of adequate, effective and meaningful access to the courts, a right which "requires prison authorities to assist inmates in the preparation and filing of meaningful legal papers by providing ... adequate law libraries or adequate assistance from persons trained in the law." *Id.* at 828, 97 S.Ct. at 1498.

Apparently, the right is not extended to all legal filings, but applies only to presentation of constitutional claims, such as civil rights complaints and state and federal habeas petitions. *Id.* at 825, 827–28 & n. 17, 97 S.Ct. at 1496, 1497–98 & n. 17. The inmates' ability to file is not dispositive of the access question, because the Court in *Bounds* explained that for access to be meaningful, post-filing needs, such as the research tools necessary to effectively rebut authorities cited by an adversary in responsive pleadings, should be met. *Id.* at 825–26, 97 S.Ct. at 1496–97. In short, this found right of access includes the ability to file a legally sufficient claim. *Bonner v. City of Prichard,* 661 F.2d 1206, 1212 (11th Cir.1981) (en banc).

Perhaps because their textual footing in the Constitution is not clear, these principles suffer for lack of internal definition and prove far easier to state than to apply. For example, there has been confusion in the cases regarding *Bounds*'s requirement that *all* prisoners be given meaningful access to the courts. Dicta in *Cruz v. Hauck,* 627 F.2d 710, 720–21 (5th Cir.1980) (*Cruz III*) suggests that, given that the right recognized in *Bounds* was one of meaningful access to the courts, a library alone may not satisfy the Constitution, at least for those inmates who cannot read English or who are otherwise illiterate. Other courts have rejected the notion that if a *Bounds* library is provided, something more may nevertheless be required. *See Cepulonis v. Fair,* 732 F.2d 1, 6 (1st Cir. 1984). The issue is not before us because the magistrate concluded that the evidence presented on the literacy and educational backgrounds of the inmates at the jail was "inconclusive."

While *Bounds* did not read its found right of access in a wholly mechanical fashion, the Court was firm in its command that the right be met with books or legal assistance or both; it foreclosed the question of the practical utility of a library, concluding that access to a library is access to the courts. Access to courts can be secured, though, by means other than the furnishing of a law library containing the suggested volumes. A complete library, as described in *Bounds,* or assistance by paralegals or some lesser amount of each in combination might be used. Indeed, access to paralegals and writ writers may bear a rough inverse relationship to the library materials required. 430 U.S. at 831–32, 97 S.Ct. at 1499–1500.

Given the tension inherent in requiring that lawyers' tools be made available despite the absence of any constitutional right to lawyers, the *Bounds* requirement is inevitably inexact. For those who question the utility or cost of a *Bounds* library, access can be met by furnishing legal assistance even though the legal assistance is not independently required by the Constitution. To the extent that the operative reality of *Bounds* is that it leverages legal assistance that cannot be justified in direct terms, it is a leverage built into *Bounds* and, whatever its dissembling dimensions, we must obey it.

3

The magistrate concluded that McLennan County's program is insufficient under *Bounds.* We are constrained to agree. We hold that the bookmobile checkout system, accompanied by circumscribed assistance from law students, does not meet the *Bounds* requirement. In the absence of some sort of direct legal assistance, which need not be by trained lawyers, the inmates must be given access to a library as required in *Bounds.* That access is not met by a system allowing a prisoner to check out books through a weekly bookmobile. The Federal Supplement, the Federal Reporter and the Supreme Court Reporter today consist of a total of approximately fifteen hundred volumes. Even a quick research project by a trained lawyer may require reference and cross reference to numerous volumes. Such a task would be impossible to complete with no legal assistance and only the limited library program presently in place. We affirm the magistrate's declaration that the present jail program is not adequate.

We add separate comment on only one of the County's arguments, one not expressly addressed by the magistrate. The County contends that because most of the 160 inmates who occupy the jail at any one time are confined for only brief periods, the bookmobile/paralegal program is sufficient to meet the needs of those few non-transient inmates who are entitled to *Bounds* access. As we observed in *Cruz v. Hauck*, 515 F.2d 322, 333 (5th Cir.1975) (*Cruz II*), cert. denied, 424 U.S. 917, 96 S.Ct. 1118, 47 L.Ed.2d 322 (1976), there is no right of access to the courts for those prisoners whose "brevity of confinement does not permit sufficient time ... to petition the courts." No easily-stated test has emerged for defining how lengthy a stay must be before the right is triggered. Compare the opinions of Judges Haynsworth and Hall in *Williams v. Leeke*, 584 F.2d 1336 (4th Cir.1978), cert. denied, 442 U.S. 911, 99 S.Ct. 2825, 61 L.Ed.2d 276 (1979).

The principal evidence presented concerning the number of inmates held at the county jail for significant lengths of time was a report, prepared in early October 1982, listing the length of stay for each inmate who entered the jail in July 1982, a "representative" month according to prison official Dan Weyenberg. Of these 482 entering inmates, 33 were still confined at the time of the report; three had been held for over 90 days. In addition, two prisoners testified at the October 1982 trial that they had been held at the jail since June 1982. This record, while sparse, permits an inference that some McLennan County jail inmates were incarcerated long enough to have had a right of access to the courts while there. Although the number of inmates entitled to that right may have been small, the right of access is of an individual rather than a group nature. The magistrate was entitled on these facts to enter a declaration that the bookmobile/paralegal system did not satisfy inmates' rights of access to the courts under *Bounds*.

Of course, the number of inmates at a given facility who are there long enough to have *Bounds* rights is important to what the defendant must do to *remedy* the violation. With only a few nontransient inmates for example, judicial access can be met with much less than otherwise.

The magistrate, though, did not require the County to construct a library or to adopt any specific program for legal assistance, nor do we. Counsel for the inmates indicated at oral argument, and amicus curiae LULAC agrees, that most complaints regarding access to the courts would be alleviated if the Baylor students now performing paralegal work were authorized to practice law subject to supervision by a licensed attorney. *See* State Bar of Texas, *Rules and Regulations Governing Participation of Qualified Law Students and Qualified Unlicensed Law School Graduates in the Trial of Cases in Texas* (unpublished, approved by the Supreme Court of Texas, December 1978). It is not clear that the assistance provided by the Baylor students constituted the unauthorized practice of law. While a program approved by the state bar might end such speculation it is not a prerequisite to a valid system under *Bounds*. We say only that greater access to a library than afforded by the checkout system is required *unless* greater assistance by students, paralegals or writ writers is furnished.

III

The County next attacks the magistrate's orders requiring jail officials to "immediately and permanently operate the McLennan County Jail" in accordance with specified policies on jail visitation. The magistrate sustained the four complaints about visitation: (1) visitation facilities at the old jail afforded inmates less privacy and fewer opportunities for communication than those at the new jail; (2) visitation hours for female inmates were fewer than those for male inmates; (3) persons age seventeen or younger were not allowed to visit inmates; and (4) the jail was open for visits on Tuesdays and Thursdays only—no weekend visitation was permitted. The magistrate enjoined the County to upgrade the visitation facilities at the old jail, to equalize visitation privileges for men and women, and to permit both minor and weekend visitation. We address each in turn.

1

First, the magistrate held that the facilities in the old jail were inadequate for visitation. The record testimony cited by the magistrate in support of his finding refers to the fact that at the old jail, visitors had to speak to inmates through openings below a window. There was some testimony that this arrangement made it awkward for some visitors to look at inmates while speaking to them, and that their conversations were not fully private. At the new jail, by contrast, inmates talked by telephone to their visitors at the visitation windows.

The inmates claim that the visitation facilities of the old jail deny their constitutional rights. They argue that their claimed rights are taken if penological purposes can be achieved in a manner less restrictive of their rights as free citizens. As we will explain, this abstract statement removes a familiar inquiry from its context and significantly skews its focus. It suffers from the not uncommon vice of analogical reasoning untethered to constitutional text, a flaw we have identified and condemned. *See Chrysler Corp. v. Texas Motor Vehicle Commission*, 755 F.2d 1192, 1202 (5th Cir.1985). The beginning point for claims of lost constitutional rights is their textual source. While the magistrate did not identify the source of the found right, there are three possibilities, the First, Fourteenth and Eighth Amendments. We turn to each in turn.

McMurry v. Phelps, 533 F.Supp. 742, 764 (W.D.La.1982), derived a right to jail visitation from a perceived First Amendment guarantee of freedom of association, and found a constitutional deprivation on facts similar to these. In *Thorne v. Jones*, 765 F.2d 1270, 1272–1274 & n. 6 (5th Cir.1985) though, we rejected the notion that the First Amendment necessarily embraces a visit with a prison inmate, and expressly disapproved *McMurry*'s First Amendment analysis. While in *Thorne* we were addressing the asserted rights of convicted felons, we need not pause here to elaborate on the asserted visitation rights under the First Amendment of pretrial detainees. Finding protected speech in ordinary visits with detainees is problematic at best. Any such right, and we see none, is vindicated in the due process inquiry that follows.

Because a significant number of inmates using the old jail's visiting facilities are pretrial detainees, we must weigh the conditions there under the Fourteenth Amendment as outlined in *Block v. Rutherford*, — U.S. ——, 104 S.Ct. 3227, 3231, 82 L.Ed.2d 438 (1984), and *Bell v. Wolfish*, 441 U.S. 520, 535, 99 S.Ct. 1861, 1871, 60 L.Ed.2d 447 (1979). We "must decide whether the disability is imposed for the purpose of punishment or whether it is but an incident of some other legitimate governmental purpose.... [I]f a restriction or condition is not reasonably related to a legitimate goal—if it is arbitrary or purposeless—a court permissibly may infer that the purpose of the governmental action is punishment...." *Rutherford*, 104 S.Ct. at 3231, *quoting Wolfish*, 441 U.S. at 538, 539, 99 S.Ct. at 1874.

The magistrate found that the "inadequacy of the facility [was] not justified by any legitimate security concern," and ordered it upgraded. This approach misconceives the *Rutherford/Wolfish* analysis. The unexplained deficiency must be one from which a purpose of punishment can be inferred. It does not necessarily follow from the fact that more hospitable or convenient facilities can be constructed, as the County did in its new jail, that not doing so is punitive. *Wolfish*, 441 U.S. at 537, 99 S.Ct. at 1873. Rather, the question, directly put, is whether pretrial detainees are being "punished." Restrictions unsupported by state interests may well lead to a conclusion that liberty interests of pretrial detainees are being taken without warrant, in view of those inmates' status as detained but unconvicted citizens. But such restrictions support an inference that they are calculated to punish pretrial detainees because of the lack of any legitimate state purpose behind them; they are properly termed arbitrary. In determining whether the physical facility for visitation was arbitrary, we must consider that the cost of reconstructing it was a factor that the County could weigh against the inmates' asserted needs. Otherwise stated, while the expense of achieving constitutional compliance may not justify the status quo, expense is relevant to whether the Constitution was violated. In *Rutherford*, for example, the Supreme Court viewed the cost of constructing additional facilities to accommodate contact visits as a legitimate ground for denying those visits altogether. 104 S.Ct. at 3233–34 n. 9.

Here, because the expense of building new visitation facilities in the old jail was plainly a legitimate state concern and the old facilities could hardly be termed egregious, the inmates did not make the case for interfering with the discretion of the jail administrators. County officials were entitled to strike a balance between a penological ideal distinctly secured by no constitutional text and the financial cost of change.

Finally, the Eighth Amendment approach is easily dispatched; "for convicted prisoners, visitation privileges are a matter subject to the discretion of prison officials." *Jones v. Diamond*, 636 F.2d 1364, 1376–77 (5th Cir.) (en banc), *cert. dism'd*, 453 U.S. 950, 102 S.Ct. 27, 69 L.Ed.2d 1033 (1981), *quoting McCray v. Sullivan*, 509 F.2d 1232, 1334 (5th Cir.), *cert. denied*, 423 U.S. 859, 96 S.Ct. 114, 46 L.Ed.2d 86 (1975). The jail officials' decision to continue use of the old jail's visiting room was within their discretion. Nor does the confinement in the old jail of some pretrial detainees alter these results. We say without elaboration that the inconvenience of the visitation facility is not cruel and unusual.

It developed at oral argument that the magistrate's order was also, in large part, an indirect effort to correct what the magistrate perceived to be a problem of discriminatory assignment of prisoners. That is, the problem addressed was that the opportunity to assign prisoners to the older, adequate but relatively uncomfortable, jail rather than to the new jail might be a punitive weapon in the hands of the jailer. The magistrate, however, did not find that discriminatory assignment existed as an independent constitutional violation. The remedy for any discriminatory assignment is its prohibition. The magistrate erred in directing changes in the facilities available for visitation in the old jail, and we reverse that aspect of his injunction on the merits.

2

Nor do we agree with the magistrate's conclusion that the County has violated the Equal Protection Clause because the visitation time allotted for male prisoners is one hour greater than that allotted for female prisoners. Over ninety percent of the inmates at the jail were male and no inmate, male or female, may be visited for more than fifteen minutes. Allotting greater time for the public to visit a greater percentage of the jail population justifies this assertedly differential treatment. *See Craig v. Boren*, 429 U.S. 190, 97 S.Ct. 451, 50 L.Ed.2d 397 (1976).

3

The County does not seriously defend its policy of forbidding weekend visitation or of preventing visits by minors, but argues that the matters are moot because jail officials have voluntarily adopted rules that meet these demands of the inmates. We do not agree with the County that these matters are now moot, and are constrained to affirm the magistrate's declaration. When the magistrate ruled, the County had not yet modified its practices on weekend and minor visitation, and the changes that followed the ruling, while commendable, do not moot this case. *City of Mesquite v. Aladdin's Castle, Inc.*, 455 U.S. 283, 289, 102 S.Ct. 1070, 1074, 71 L.Ed.2d 152 (1982). Even had those policies been changed before the magistrate entered his orders, he would nevertheless have had the *power* to grant the inmates injunctive relief. It does not follow, however, that he should have granted more than declaratory relief. Our point is, as we will elaborate, that such a hair-trigger on federal injunctive power aimed at state government can be an abuse of discretion. It was here.

IV

Use of federal injunctive relief as an, if not the, ultimate remedy for unconstitutional practices by state and local governments is now familiar. *See generally* O. Fiss, *The Civil Rights Injunction* (1978). While its familiarity to federal courts, gained particularly in desegregation cases over the past thirty years, gives an appearance of the ordinary to this extraordinary remedy, this familiarity in no way erodes the historic conceptual limits of injunctive relief. The malleable quality of the extraordinary injunction, with its ability to conform to complex facts, greatly enhanced its potency and fueled its popularity in civil rights cases. But the flexibility of the remedy only makes the more conspicuous its non-tailored use. That injunctive relief can be form fitted requires that it be exercised with full appreciation of the sensitive issues of federalism presented in cases of this ilk. As the Court explained in *Rizzo v. Goode*, 423 U.S. 362, 379, 96 S.Ct. 598, 608, 46 L.Ed.2d 561 (1976), "appropriate consideration must be given to principles of federalism in determining the availability and scope of equitable relief."

[T]he principles of federalism which play such an important part in governing the relationship between federal courts and state governments, though initially expounded and perhaps entitled to their greatest weight in cases where it was sought to enjoin a criminal prosecution in progress, have not been limited either to that situation or indeed to a criminal proceeding itself. We think these principles likewise have applicability where injunctive relief is sought, not against the judicial branch of the state government, but against those in charge of an execu-

tive branch of an agency of state or local government....

Id. at 380, 96 S.Ct. at 608.

At the threshold, superintending federal injunctive decrees directing state officials are appropriate only when constitutional violations have been shown *and* when the state officials are demonstrably unlikely to implement the required changes without its spur. Where, as here, constitutional violations are found, but state officials have shown their readiness to meet constitutional requirements, the court should limit its initial response to a grant of declaratory relief.

There is no question but that the passive remedy of a declaratory judgment is far less intrusive into state functions than injunctive relief that affirmatively commands specific future behavior under the threat of the court's contempt powers. This reality underlay the passage of the Federal Declaratory Judgment Act, 28 U.S.C. § 2201, expressly designed "to provide a milder alternative to the injunction remedy." *Perez v. Ledesma*, 401 U.S. 82, 111, 91 S.Ct. 674, 690, 27 L.Ed.2d 701 (1971) (Brennan, J., concurring and dissenting); *id.* at 112–13, 91 S.Ct. at 690–91 (discussing Act's legislative history). *See Doran v. Salem Inn, Inc.*, 422 U.S. 922, 931, 95 S.Ct. 2561, 2567, 45 L.Ed.2d 648 (1975) (after successful suit against state defendant, "a district court can generally protect the interests of a federal plaintiff by entering a declaratory judgment, and therefore the stronger injunctive medicine will be unnecessary."); *Grandco Corp. v. Rochford*, 536 F.2d 197, 208 (7th Cir.1976) (vacating injunction against enforcement of statute, but affirming declaratory judgment of statute's unconstitutionality); *see also Steffel v. Thompson*, 415 U.S. 452, 94 S.Ct. 1209, 39 L.Ed.2d 505 (1974) (declaratory relief is not precluded in suits attacking threatened enforcement of state criminal laws, regardless of propriety of injunctive relief).

Our tolerance of declaratory relief and rejection of injunctive relief in this context is not at odds with the Supreme Court's holding that declaratory and injunctive relief are ordinarily equally inappropriate in cases where a state criminal prosecution is pending. *Samuels v. Mackell*, 401 U.S. 66, 91 S.Ct. 764, 27 L.Ed.2d 688 (1971). In such circumstances declaratory relief, even if not as intrusive as an injunction, is intrusive enough. In *Samuels*, the Court observed that although a declaratory judgment would usually frustrate state criminal proceedings as much as an injunction, there might be "unusual circumstances" in which a declaratory judgment of a statute's unconstitutionality would be proper even if injunctive relief were not. *Id.* at 73, 91 S.Ct. at 768; *see also Steffel*, 415 U.S. at 472–73, 94 S.Ct. at 1222. *Steffel* and *Samuels* support the principle of *Rizzo* that primarily guides us here: that in all cases implicating state/federal relations, federal courts ought to intrude into state affairs no more than is absolutely necessary.

The county officials have demonstrated that superintending injunctive relief was not necessary. As we earlier explained, this suit was dormant for the first five years that it was pending. During that time this largely rural county constructed an entirely new facility designed to meet new state standards on jail conditions. Perhaps it is true, as the inmates suggest, that this suit was the brooding background which gave rise to the reform efforts of county officials, but it is also true that the new jail's construction was completed without the whip of a federal decree. Indeed, to the extent that the record is clear on the efforts of the jail's administrators to remedy the asserted violations, it indicates ready compliance rather than recalcitrance. Where, as here, the defendant makes dutiful progress to remedy the asserted problems, whether or not it is encouraged to do so by a suit, a federal court should exercise restraint. Any other course contradicts our system's principles of shared power.

In so holding, we do not tread on precedents that have upheld continued injunctive relief despite state defendants' protests of compliance. The Supreme Court and this court, when affirming such injunctions,

have uniformly pointed to evidence of noncompliance or foot-dragging in the record below. *See Allee v. Medrano*, 416 U.S. 802, 815, 94 S.Ct. 2191, 2200, 40 L.Ed.2d 566 (1974) (injunction proper upon showing of "persistent pattern of police misconduct"); *Jones v. Diamond*, 636 F.2d 1364, 1375 (5th Cir.) (en banc), *cert. dism'd*, 453 U.S. 920, 102 S.Ct. 27, 69 L.Ed.2d 1033 (1981) (defendants' compliance came only after five years of "hotly contested" litigation, and only after oral argument of Fifth Circuit appeal; at time of trial, jail "still violated some constitutional requirements"); *Gates v. Collier*, 501 F.2d 1291, 1321 (5th Cir.1974) (continuing injunction proper where "protracted inhumane conditions and practices" had existed at penitentiary, "much [was] left to be done" to remedy those conditions, and federal monitor had been appointed based on inmates' complaints that state was not complying with court's orders). Such evidence of recalcitrance is absent from this record.

That principles of federalism compel the conclusion that superintending injunctions such as those issued here should be matters of the last order, not the first, is nothing new. We plow no new ground. The Supreme Court has recently told the Congress that it must state its intention in the statute itself if it is to exercise its power to abrogate Eleventh Amendment immunity; an intent to do so will not be inferred. *Atascadero State Hospital v. Scanlon*, — U.S. —, 105 S.Ct. 3142, 87 L.Ed.2d 171 (1985). In other words, the judiciary has required that the Congress act in such a disciplined manner that intrusion into state affairs be its considered judgment and presumably a product of its felt necessity. It would be incongruous for the judiciary to not impose such discipline upon itself.

V

We turn next to the jail's handling of the inmates' mail. Our task is hampered by the absence of specific findings on the asserted deficiencies in the County's program and by the opaque directive of the magistrate that:

> Within sixty days defendant shall devise written guidelines applicable to mail practices which are consistent with *Guajardo v. Estelle*, 580 F.2d 748 (5th Cir. 1978).

The magistrate concluded that "McLennan County's current policies regarding mail and censorship violate inmates' First Amendment rights," but made no specific findings that explained what he found deficient about those policies. As best we can tell, the problem was the absence of a provision for notifying inmates when their correspondence was confiscated and the absence of a right to appeal those decisions. But that is a speculation. We are forced to conclude that the findings are insufficient for review, especially given that the relief granted was no more than a directive that the County comply with the law. Accordingly, we vacate the magistrate's orders on the jail's mail policies and remand for factual findings.

VI

In fashion parallel to his treatment of prisoner mail, the magistrate ordered jail officials to "institute disciplinary procedures consistent with *Wolff v. McDonnell*, 418 U.S. 539, 94 S.Ct. 2963, 41 L.Ed.2d 935 (1974)." The County does not seriously challenge the merits of the magistrate's findings that jail officials had violated *Wolff* in the past, but, as with its policies on visitation, asks us to vacate the injunction because it has been complied with.

As explained above in part IV, while compliance does not moot this issue, declaratory rather than injunctive relief was appropriate given that there was no recalcitrance on the part of County officials. The necessity for an injunction was never present and, in any event, the injunction issued has little operative effect beyond a grant of declaratory relief, save its own threat of the contempt power. For the reasons we set out in part IV, *supra*, we set it aside, while affirming the declaration as to past practices.

VII

To summarize, we affirm the magistrate's declarations regarding access to the courts. We reverse his orders requiring changes in the visitation facilities at the old jail and those directing that visitation hours for male and female inmates be identical, but otherwise affirm the declarations concerning visitation policy. We vacate the orders regarding mail for lack of sufficient factual findings, and affirm those regarding disciplinary proceedings. We set aside all injunctive orders that accompanied the found deficiencies. Finally, we affirm the magistrate's decision that an award of attorney's fees is appropriate, but we vacate the award and remand for reassessment of its amount in light of our rulings. We express no opinion regarding the amount awarded. *See Hensley v. Eckerhart*, 461 U.S. 424, 103 S.Ct. 1933, 76 L.Ed.2d 40 (1983) (extent of plaintiff's success is a crucial factor in determining the proper amount of attorney's fees).

AFFIRMED IN PART, REVERSED IN PART, VACATED IN PART, AND REMANDED.

Ralph CRAINE, Plaintiff-Appellant,

v.

**Lamar ALEXANDER, et al.,
Defendants-Appellees.**

No. 84–4320.

United States Court of Appeals,
Fifth Circuit.

March 25, 1985.

Appeal from the United States District Court for the Northern District of Mississippi.

Before JOHNSON and HILL, Circuit Judges, and BOYLE,* District Judge.

ROBERT MADDEN HILL, Circuit Judge: **

Pursuant to 42 U.S.C. § 1983, Ralph Craine sought damages for battery from Marshall County, Mississippi, the Sheriff and certain deputies of Marshall County, as well as the Board of Supervisors of the Marshall County Jail. Craine also sought damages under the Antipeonage Act for subjection to "peonage." See 42 U.S.C. § 1994. After being awarded damages on the § 1983 claim only, Craine appealed. Before us are issues of § 1983 responsibility of supervisory personnel, the adequacy of the damages awarded Craine, and the scope of the Antipeonage Act. We affirm the district court's rulings on all three issues.

I.

In August 1981, Craine, a 21-year old black male, was convicted of burglary and sentenced to incarceration for three years in the Mississippi Department of Corrections. However, at the time of the events pertinent to this appeal, Craine was confined at the Marshall County Jail in Holly

Springs, Mississippi, instead of at the Parchman facility. During his confinement at the jail, Craine often worked outside the jail at various tasks including cutting and hauling wood for a state investigator, hauling cattle under the supervision of a state game warden, washing cars and other odd jobs. Craine was occasionally paid for his work although the sums were insignificant. Craine was permitted outside the confines of the jail only in his status as a trustee.

On January 23, 1982, Craine worked outside the jail most of the day on sundry chores. He returned to the jail, but left again. Later that evening Craine was being escorted back to the jail from a pool hall by Chief Deputy Lanny Cummings, Deputy Bobby Barksdale and three city police officers. Cummings was armed with a sawed-off shotgun. Experiencing some difficulty in getting Craine to return to the jail, Cummings struck Craine several times with the shotgun. Craine shouted back at Cummings. The other officers forced Craine to the ground to handcuff him, one of the police officers complaining to Cummings that some of the blows were missing their mark and landing on the officers. Cummings apologized to the officer but swung the shotgun at Craine again. When it struck Craine in the stomach, the shotgun went off, inflicting a serious wound in the area of the abdomen and side.

Craine underwent surgery on the wound. He sustained nerve loss in his left thigh resulting in permanent, untreatable muscle atrophy. His immediate medical expenses amounted to $10,714.28.

Craine filed this action against Cummings, Osborne Bell, the Sheriff of Marshall County, the members of the Marshall County Jail Board of Supervisors in their individual and official capacities (the

---

* District Judge of the Eastern District of Louisiana, sitting by Designation.

** Some of the numerous issues raised on appeal do not have precedential value. Local Rule 47.5 provides: "The publication of opinions that have no precedential value and merely decide particular cases on the basis of well-settled principles of law imposes needless expense on the

public and burdens on the legal profession." Pursuant to that Rule, the Court has determined that non-precedential portions of this opinion should not be published. The place at which the published opinion omits part of the unpublished opinion is indicated by footnote references.

Board), the county itself, and others. In this appeal we are concerned only with the claims against Cummings, Sheriff Bell and the Board.

Craine received a jury trial. At the close of his evidence, the district court directed verdicts in favor of the Board on the § 1983 claim and in favor of all defendants on the peonage claim. At the close of all the evidence, the court directed a verdict against Cummings on liability for the § 1983 claim. The jury awarded Craine $10,714.28 as actual damages and $70,000 as punitive damages against Cummings but found in favor of Sheriff Bell.

II.

The district court directed a verdict in favor of the Marshall County Board of Supervisors. We must reverse if, viewing all the evidence in the light most favorable to Craine, reasonable jurors might reach different conclusions. *Reeves v. City of Jackson*, 608 F.2d 644, 648 (5th Cir.1979) (citing *Boeing Co. v. Shipman*, 411 F.2d 355, 374 (5th Cir.1969) (en banc)).

Before the Board can be held liable under § 1983, Craine must show that it breached some duty owed to him that is imposed by state law. *Howard v. Fortenberry*, 723 F.2d 1206, 1209 (5th Cir.) (citing *Sims v. Adams*, 537 F.2d 829, 831 (5th Cir.1976)), *vacated in part*, 728 F.2d 712

(1984). This inquiry precedes—and a negative answer to it compels us to pretermit discussion of—the question whether there was a breach that had some causal connection with the constitutional deprivation, that is, whether, under *Monell v. Department of Social Services*, 436 U.S. 658, 694, 98 S.Ct. 2018, 2037, 56 L.Ed.2d 611 (1978), "execution of a government's policy or custom [has] inflict[ed] the injury." *See Howard v. Fortenberry*, 723 F.2d at 1210. Thus, Craine argues that the Board's duty to him had two alternative sources: the statutory scheme of Mississippi and the established custom of the Board itself.

Craine argues, first, that certain Mississippi statutes give the Board authority and responsibility over the sheriff's department and the jail. At most, however, those statutes, which are set forth in the note,[1] merely impose upon the Board a duty to inspect the jail itself and give it power to rectify abuses discovered in the inspections. Craine does not argue that the Board breached its duty to inspect the jail itself. In any event, the duty to inspect the jail for unsafe conditions did not impose a duty to protect prisoners from abuse by prison personnel. *Cf. Howard v. Fortenberry*, 723 F.2d at 1211. Moreover, it avails Craine nothing to rely on *Penick v. Columbus Board of Education*, 519 F.Supp. 925 (D.C.Ohio), *aff'd*, 663 F.2d 24

---

1. Craine bases his argument on Miss.Code Ann. §§ 19–5–1, 19–3–51 and 19–25–13. They provide, in part, as follows:

   At least once in every three months, and as often as it may think proper, the board of supervisors shall examine into the state and condition of the jail, in regard to its safety, sufficiency, and accommodation of the prisoners, and from time to time take such legal measures as may best tend to secure the prisoners against escape, sickness, and infection, and have the jail cleansed. If it shall appear from such examination that the sheriff has neglected his duty in the manner of keeping the jail, or keeping and furnishing the prisoners, the board shall fine him, as for a contempt, in any sum not exceeding one hundred dollars.

   Miss.Code Ann. § 19–5–1 (1972).

   The board of supervisors shall have power to subpoena witnesses in all matters coming under its jurisdiction and to fine and imprison

any person for a contempt committed while they are in session, the fine not to exceed fifty dollars, and the imprisonment not to exceed beyond the continuance of the term. The person so fined or imprisoned may appeal to the circuit court, as in other cases, from the order or judgment of the board, and such appeal shall operate as a supersedeas.

Id. § 19–3–51.

The sheriff shall, at the July meeting of the board of supervisors, submit a budget of estimated expenses of his office for the ensuing fiscal year beginning October 1 in such form as shall be prescribed by the director of the state department of audit. The board shall examine this proposed budget and determine the amount to be expended by the sheriff in the performance of his duties for the fiscal year and may increase or reduce said amount as it deems necessary and proper.

Miss.Code Ann. § 19–25–13 (1984 Supp.).

(6th Cir.1981), *cert. denied sub nom., Ohio State Board of Education v. Reed,* 455 U.S. 1018, 102 S.Ct. 1713, 72 L.Ed.2d 135 (1982), in which it was clear that the defendant Ohio Board of Education had neglected its "primary statutory duty, *in first the instance,* to investigate the existence of segregation in the public schools, to ascertain its causes and to use its powers to eradicate it." *Id.* at 27 (emphasis in original). No such breach of duty was either alleged or proved by Craine. Craine has completely failed to articulate any other specific duty arising from these Mississippi statutes that might have even remotely caused him injury.

Craine relies more heavily on his allegation that the Board was responsible for his injury because it had adopted a "custom or usage" of preventing the abuse of prisoners by maintaining direct control over the acts of individual members of the sheriff's department. He apparently suggests that breach of this custom-derived duty caused his injury. Craine attempts to demonstrate the existence of this duty on the strength of three isolated instances of Board action: a hearing, during the tenure of Sheriff Bell's predecessor, on jail abuses; the withholding of funds from the sheriff's budget as a disciplinary measure connected with the hearing; and the withholding of the salary of a former chief deputy until he completed the eight-week law enforcement curriculum of the Mississippi Law Enforcement Officer's Academy pursuant to Miss.Code Ann. § 19-25-21 (1972).

Before Craine's theory can proceed, however, he must show that this custom carried the force of state law; that is, the duty he wishes to enforce must be "imposed by" state law. *Howard v. Fortenberry,* 723 F.2d at 1209; *see also, Sims v. Adams,* 537 F.2d at 832 (duty of supervisory personnel may arise from city charter). Assuming the viability of his legal theory, Craine adduced insufficient evidence to entitle him to have it submitted to the jury. In effect, there was evidence of only one instance of Board action regarding jail abuses and only one instance of Board action regarding deputy training. Under any definition of custom or usage, this evidence would be insufficient to raise a jury issue as to the existence of a custom having the force of a duty imposed by state law.

Craine could not seriously argue that two isolated instances of Board action constituted a "settled State [or County] practice" or "[d]eeply embedded traditional ways of carrying out state policy." *Nashville C. & St. L.R. Co. v. Browning,* 310 U.S. 362, 369, 60 S.Ct. 968, 972, 84 S.Ct. 1254 (1940) (Frankfurter, J.) (equal protection analysis). Nor could he reasonably assert that they embodied "[a] persistent, widespread practice ... [that] is so common and well settled as to constitute a custom." *Bennett v. City of Slidell,* 735 F.2d 861, 862 (5th Cir.1984) (en banc) (definition of "official policy" as used in *Monell*). While these definitions of custom were articulated in different contexts, we think they are sufficient to reveal the want of merit in Craine's theory.

Further, Craine's argument betrays a misunderstanding of the principles of § 1983 liability as applied to "local governmental units." *See Monell,* 436 U.S. at 690, nn. 54, 55, 98 S.Ct. at 2034, nn. 54, 55. The custom-derived duty Craine attempts to establish could not form the premise for imposing liability on the Board. Indeed, proof of the benevolent custom Craine claims existed would have effectively undermined liability under *Monell* which requires that "the action that is alleged to be unconstitutional implements or executes a policy statement" or "custom." *Id.* at 690–91, 98 S.Ct. at 2035–36. Here Craine himself argues, not that Cummings was *executing* the Board's malevolent policy but, rather, that he was *violating* the Board's policy of protecting prisoners from abuse. His own argument contradicts the essential causal link he is required to establish.

The district court directed a verdict in favor of the Board on the ground that Mississippi law imposed upon the sheriff, not the Board, the duty of protecting prisoners from abuse. *See, e.g.,* Miss.Code Ann. § 19-25-69. Whether or not this is a completely accurate understanding of Mississippi law, the sources to which Craine has directed our attention fail to establish the imposition of any such duty on the Board. Accordingly, the district court's dismissal of the claims against the Board is affirmed.

III.[2, 3]

IV.[4–6]

V.

In 1867 Congress passed the Antipeonage Act, which prohibits the holding of individuals to forced servitude. Act of March 2, 1867, c. 187, 14 Stat. 546. The first part of the statute provides:

> The holding of any person to service or labor under the system known as peonage is abolished and forever prohibited in any Territory or State of the United States; and all acts, laws, resolutions, orders, regulations, or usages of any Territory or State, which have heretofore established, maintained, or enforced, or by virtue of which any attempt shall hereafter be made to establish, maintain, or enforce, directly or indirectly, the voluntary or involuntary service or labor of any persons as peons, in liquidation of any debt or obligation, or otherwise, are declared null and void.

42 U.S.C. § 1994.[7] Craine contends that the evidence presented issues for the jury concerning whether his § 1994 rights were violated thus entitling him to damages under § 1983. Assuming that § 1994 provides a federal right that may be vindicated in a damages action pursuant to § 1983,[8] we hold that no reasonable jury could have found that any "acts, laws, resolutions, orders, regulations, or usages of [Mississippi]", or even of Marshall County, caused Craine to be subjected to labor as a peon. Consequently, the district court properly directed a verdict on Craine's peonage claim.

Section 1994 renders invalid only the "acts, laws, resolutions, orders, regulations or usages" of the states that establish or enforce labor as a peon. Craine cites no act, law, resolution, order or regulation of the state of Mississippi as being the source of the alleged peonage. Neither did Craine adduce sufficient evidence that there exists a usage or custom of the state of Mississippi or of Marshall County of subjecting prisoners to labor as peons. While there is some evidence in the record of isolated instances of Craine's having worked outside the confines of the jail at the behest and under the control of various individuals without official positions in the county jail system, it was clearly not a widespread practice engaged in with the knowledge or acquiescence of Marshall County officials; much less, with the knowledge and acquiescence of Mississippi state officials. No abuses at the Marshall County Jail of which Craine complains were the result of any "usage" of Marshall County or of the state of Mississippi. Thus, the evidence did not require submission of Craine's peonage claim to the jury. We therefore express no opinion whether the abuses complained of constituted subjection to "peonage" for purposes of § 1994.

Our conclusion that plaintiffs proceeding under § 1994 must show some state responsibility for the abuse complained of, is buttressed by the Supreme Court's language in *Pollock v. Williams*, 322 U.S. 4, 5, 64 S.Ct. 792, 793, 88 L.Ed. 1095 (1944). There the Court, in overturning a Florida statute that made it a misdemeanor to induce salary advances by a promise to perform labor, wrote:

> Forced labor in some special circumstances may be consistent with the general basic system of free labor. For example, forced labor has been sustained as a means of punishing crime.... But in

---

2, 3. See footnote **, ante.

4–6. See footnote **, ante.

7. The second part of the statute, which makes it an offense for any person to hold, arrest or

return another to the condition of peonage, is now codified in 18 U.S.C. § 1581.

8. *See Whitner v. Davis*, 410 F.2d 24, 30 (9th Cir.1969) (assumed that district court had jurisdiction to grant relief under § 1994).

general the defense against oppressive hours, pay, working conditions or treatment is the right to change employers. When the master can compel and the laborer cannot escape the obligation to go on, there is no power below to redress and no incentive above to relieve a harsh overlordship or unwholesome conditions of work.... Whatever of social value there may be, and of course it is great, in enforcing contracts and collections of debts, Congress has put it beyond debate that no indebtedness warrants a suspension of the right to be free from compulsory service. This congressional policy means that no state can make the quitting of work any component of a crime, or make criminal sanctions available for holding unwilling persons in labor.

Id. at 17–18, 64 S.Ct. at 799. This Congressional policy, even outside the context of a state criminal statute, would have little application unless it is the *state* that is enforcing peonage, whether directly or indirectly, as opposed to an individual. Craine has produced no evidence of governmental enforcement of the abuses of which he complains.

Craine asks us to construe § 1994 broadly so as to give him a right of action for damages under § 1983 "without consideration of the perpetrator." He presents us with no convincing plea why we should ignore what Congress chose to make essential. In defining this right as it did, Congress did not choose to abolish usages or customs of individuals that might be likened to conditions of peonage. The remedy for such individual acts lies in the criminal sanction of 18 U.S.C. § 1581 against holding another to a condition of peonage.[9] Additionally, § 1983 is not a source of substantive federal rights but a remedy provided for their vindication. *See, e.g., Chapman v. Houston Welfare Rights Organization*, 441 U.S. 600, 617, 99 S.Ct. 1905, 1915, 60 L.Ed.2d 508 (1979). We decline to

expand the scope of the § 1994 right in direct contravention of legislative expression. The evidence adduced by Craine did not establish a deprivation of any right created by the language of § 1994.

Craine does not complain of the labor imposed upon him as an aspect of the corrective regimen to which he was subject; nor could he do so with any hope of success. *See Draper v. Rhay*, 315 F.2d 193, 197 (9th Cir.), *cert. denied*, 375 U.S. 915, 84 S.Ct. 214, 11 L.Ed.2d 153 (1963) (prisoner sought damages under the 13th amendment on ground that he could not "be forced to perform *any* labor in the penitentiary." Held, no such federally protected right); *United States v. Dowd*, 271 F.2d 292, 294–95 (7th Cir.1959) (13th amendment does not prohibit involuntary servitude "as a punishment for crime."). Therefore we express no opinion on the more difficult question whether a prisoner can establish a § 1994 deprivation by virtue of labor forced upon him by a custom or usage of the state that is, at the same time, outside the scope of a corrective penal regimen. *Compare Draper v. Rhay*, 315 F.2d at 197; *with Jobson v. Henne*, 355 F.2d 129, 132 (2d Cir.1966) (inmate of state school for mentally retarded stated § 1983 cause of action under 13th amendment by alleging unconstitutional amount and conditions of mandatory work program inside state school) *and Santiago v. City of Philadelphia*, 435 F.Supp. 136, 156–57 (E.D.Pa. 1977) (juveniles confined in detention center stated claim under § 1983 for deprivation of § 1994 and 13th amendment rights based on compulsory work program). Moreover, we do not reach the issue of whether Craine established a violation of his rights under the Thirteenth Amendment since this issue was not raised in his complaint. The district court was correct in directing a verdict on Craine's peonage claim.

---

9. Section 1581(a) provides:

   Whoever holds or returns any person to a condition of peonage, or arrests any person with the intent of placing him in or returning

him to a condition of peonage, shall be fined not more than $5,000 or imprisoned not more than five years, or both.

VI.[10]

For the foregoing reasons the judgment of the district court is AFFIRMED.

See also 5th Cir., 720 F.2d 819 and D.C., 573 F.Supp. 788.

---

10. See footnote **, ante.

Otis **HILLIARD**, Plaintiff,

v.

**Charles SCULLY, Harold J. Smith,
John B. Wong, Defendants.**

No. 81 Civ. 5457 (JES).

United States District Court,
S.D. New York.

Dec. 4, 1986.

OPINION AND ORDER

SPRIZZO, District Judge: ·

Plaintiff *pro se*[1] brings this action pursuant to 42 U.S.C. § 1983 seeking declaratory and injunctive relief as well as money damages against the following defendants: Charles Scully, Superintendent of Green Haven Correctional Facility ("Green Haven"); Harold J. Smith, Superintendent of Attica Correctional Facility ("Attica"); Officer R. Dore, a corrections officer at Green Haven;[2] and John B. Wong, the former Correctional Rehabilitation Program Coordinator at Green Haven.

The Court has previously issued an Opinion and Order in this action denying plaintiff's motions for summary judgment, leave to file a supplemental complaint, and jury trial, and denying defendants' cross-motion for summary judgment. *See Hilliard v. Scully*, 537 F.Supp. 1084 (S.D.N.Y.1982); *see also Hilliard v. Scully*, slip op. (S.D.N.Y. Oct. 29, 1982) (denying plaintiff's subsequent motion for leave to file a supplemental complaint.)[3] The Court has held a

---

1. At the start of the trial, the plaintiff requested an adjournment, claiming that he believed he was brought to Court from prison only for a Pre-Trial Conference. *See* Tr. at 1–13. The plaintiff requested the adjournment because he stated that he needed an attorney. *See id.* at 1. No prior motion for appointment of counsel was ever filed by the plaintiff with the Court. After the Court indicated its unwillingness to grant this belated request, plaintiff then requested an adjournment on the grounds that he already had counsel who had not appeared. *See id.*

At the outset, the Court finds plaintiff's assertion that he thought the Court was only holding a Pre-Trial Conference to be incredible. Two months prior to trial, the Court issued an Order placing the above-captioned action on the Court's ready trial calendar. At trial, plaintiff implicitly acknowledged receiving this scheduling order. Thus, the plaintiff corrected a misstatement by the defense counsel with respect to the ready trial date, a date which plaintiff would not have been aware of unless he received the scheduling order. *See id.* at 10. Moreover, defense counsel stated at trial that, at their last meeting, she handed to plaintiff a copy of the order and she specifically informed plaintiff that the next time he came to Court, it would be for trial. *See id.* at 11.

Given the clear notice to plaintiff that the trial would be held, the preparations by the Court and the defense counsel in anticipation of that trial, and taking into account the expense incurred in bringing the plaintiff to Court from prison, the Court denied plaintiff's last minute request for an adjournment. The Court did, however, inform plaintiff that if he had other evidence which he desired to offer at a later date, the Court would afford him the opportunity to do so. *See id.* at 11–12. Plaintiff has never sought leave to present further evidence to the Court.

Clearly, plaintiff's belated request for appointment of counsel was not a sufficient justification to adjourn the trial. Plaintiff had ample opportunity to move for the appointment of counsel prior to trial. More importantly, in light of the complete lack of even colorable merit to plaintiff's claim, this was not a case where the appointment of counsel would have

been warranted in any event. Although prior to trial, it was not entirely clear, as it is now, that plaintiff's claims were frivolous, at best it appeared that plaintiff's chances for success were slim. This did not justify the appointment of counsel. *See Hodge v. Police Officers*, 802 F.2d 58, 60 (2d Cir.1986).

Moreover, this was not a case where assistance of counsel was necessary either to conduct a factual investigation or effectively cross-examine the defendants' witnesses at trial. *Compare id.* at 61. Thus, the basic facts in this case, *i.e.*, that plaintiff was placed in a Special Housing Unit without a finding that he was guilty of any violation of prison rules, that he was denied the right to cross-examine witnesses at the Superintendent's hearing, and that he was transferred to another prison prior to the hearing on his Article 78 proceeding, were undisputed. *See* Tr. at 156. In addition, as the Court noted at the conclusion of trial, plaintiff ably presented his case to the Court. *See id.* at 153.

The Court also notes that plaintiff's incredible and obviously inconsistent request for an adjournment on the ground that he already had counsel was frivolous. No notice of appearance by an attorney for the plaintiff has ever been filed in this action.

2. The record is unclear as to whether Officer Dore was ever served in this action. *See Hilliard v. Scully*, 537 F.Supp. 1084, 1085 n. 2.

3. In seeking leave to supplement his complaint, plaintiff sought to add allegations against prison officials at Great Meadow. The Court denied leave to supplement the complaint in part because venue was improper for those claims. *See Hilliard, supra*, 537 F.Supp. at 1090 & n. 22. At trial, plaintiff once again sought to raise these allegations, as well as allegations of misconduct by prison officials at Attica not contained in plaintiff's complaint. While the Court informed the plaintiff that the Court would not rule on the merits of those claims due to improper venue, *see* Tr. at 17–19, the Court allowed the plaintiff to fully present any evidence he had with respect to those allegations because that evidence may have been relevant to the claims properly before the Court. *See id.*

bench trial in this action and has received post-trial memoranda from the parties. The following constitutes the Court's findings of facts and conclusions of law pursuant to Fed.R.Civ.P. 52.

BACKGROUND

On February 1, 1981 there was a fire in the cell of an inmate named Flowers, who was then incarcerated at Green Haven. On the same day, corrections officer Dore filled out an "Inmate Misbehavior Report" against the plaintiff. See Def.Ex. A-3. According to the report, the plaintiff and another inmate, Thompson, were suspected of arson in connection with the fire in Flower's cell. The plaintiff was given the report on February 1, and placed in a special housing unit ("SHU")[4] pending an investigation of the charges. See id.; Trial Transcript ("Tr.") at 13-14.

On February 2, 1981, plaintiff appeared before the adjustment committee.[5] See Tr. at 15. Although plaintiff denied the charges at the adjustment committee interview, the adjustment committee, after reviewing the available evidence, recommended that a superintendent's hearing be held. See Def.Ex. A-4. Plaintiff was informed of the adjustment committee's disposition and plaintiff remained in the SHU.

A formal charge[6] was then prepared by corrections officer Egger on February 4, 1981 and Sergeant Holt served the plaintiff with the charge on the next day. See Def.Ex. A-6; Tr. 44, 110. The charge read as follows:

INVOLUNTARY PROTECTION STATUS

On February 1, 1981 at approximately 7:50 a.m. a fire was deliberately set in cell B-1-112 which belongs to inmate Flowers 76A-2565. From information received through investigation and from a confidential source you have been identified as one of the inmates responsible for this fire. Further information indicates that you have also been involved in an extortion ring within the facility.

Based on the above the administration has recommended that you be placed in involuntary protection status for the safety and security of the facility.

See Def.Ex. A-6.

When Sergeant Holt served the formal charge, he asked plaintiff if he needed investigatory assistance in his defense of the charge.[7] See Tr. at 111. Plaintiff indicated that he wanted corrections counselor Stanulwich to assist him. See id. The next day, on February 6, Stanulwich went to the SHU and interviewed the plaintiff. During the interview, however, the plaintiff claimed that he did not need any assistance and that he did not want Stanulwich to interview any witnesses. See Tr. at 116.

The defendant Wong conducted plaintiff's first superintendent's hearing on February 11, 1981. See Tr. 15, 125. At that hearing, the plaintiff again denied that he was involved in the fire and requested that

---

4. A special housing unit is defined by regulation as a group of cells "for confinement of inmates who are not in a program that permits them to commingle with the general inmate population." See 7 NYCRR § 300.2(b). Inmates may be placed in an SHU for a variety of reasons. The relevant classifications are: (a) protective admission, which applies when inmates are potential victims or must, for good cause, be restricted from the general inmate population, see 7 NYCRR § 304.1(b); (b) adjustment admission, which applies when an inmate is confined pending the disposition of an adjustment committee or superintendent's proceeding, see 7 NYCRR § 304.1(d); or (c) disciplinary confinement, see 7 NYCRR § 253.5(4).

All regulations set forth in this Opinion and Order correspond to the New York regulations

in existence during the relevant time periods in this action.

5. The function of the adjustment committee is inter alia "to ascertain the full and complete facts and circumstances of the incidents of inmate misbehavior alleged in reports to the superintendent" and "to ascertain the underlying causes of such incident." See 7 NYCRR § 252.-2(a)(b).

6. See 7 NYCRR § 253.2.

7. 7 NYCRR § 253.3 provides in relevant part that the "person appointed to conduct the [superintendent's] hearing shall designate an employee to furnish assistance to the inmate. This assistance shall be solely of an investigatory nature."

Wong interview an inmate named Carlos Dade. *See* Tr. at 125. Wong then adjourned the hearing so that he could conduct the requested interview. In addition to interviewing Dade, Wong also interviewed the following people: Officer Dore, who was in the prison area when the fire started; Sergeant Cheers, the sergeant in charge of evacuating the prisoners during the fire; Flowers, whose cell was set on fire; and an inmate named Thomas, who was implicated along with the plaintiff as being involved in the alleged arson and the extortion ring. *See* Tr. at 124–26; Def.Ex. A–8.

Wong testified at trial that, as a result of his investigation, he believed the fire in Flower's cell was caused by arson. *See* Tr. at 125, 150–51. Wong testified that, while neither Sergeant Cheers nor Officer Dore claimed to have any personal knowledge with respect to who set the fire, both officers told Wong that other inmates had accused Thomas and the plaintiff of the arson. *See id.* at 128, 139. Moreover, Wong testified that his investigation revealed that the three inmates, the plaintiff, Thomas, and Flowers, were involved in a physical altercation a couple of days prior to the fire. *See id.* at 126.

Following his investigation of the fire, Wong held a second superintendent's proceeding on February 13, 1981. *See id.* at 125. At the hearing, Wong refused to divulge to the plaintiff the name of the inmates who accused him of arson, *see id.* at 134–35, nor would he allow the plaintiff to hear the testimony of Carlos Dade. *See id.* at 137–38. According to Wong, when dealing with inmates within the same prison population, the danger of later violent repercusions between the inmates is too great to allow an accused inmate the opportunity of hearing or cross-examining the testimony of an accusing inmate. *See id.* at 138.

It is significant to note that Wong testified that he never considered these proceedings to be formal disciplinary proceedings against the plaintiff. Instead, Wong testified that the investigations and the hearings were simply designed to ensure that security and peace would be maintained throughout the prison. *See id.* at 139–40. Thus, the only issue Wong claims he set out to resolve at that time, was whether the plaintiff should be segregated from the general prison population and transferred to another institution for security purposes. *See id.* Wong's testimony is corroborated by the formal charge issued against the plaintiff as well as the Superintendent's worksheet, which both indicate that the charge in this case was not disciplinary but merely a charge seeking to place the plaintiff in involuntary protection status. *See* Def.Ex. A–6, A–8. According to Wong, if the evidence had warranted disciplinary sanctions, a formal disciplinary charge would have issued at a later date. *See* Tr. at 140.

At the conclusion of the second superintendent's hearing, on February 13, Wong concluded that the plaintiff, as well as Thomas and Flowers, who had separate hearings, should remain in involuntary protection status in the SHU pending a transfer of all three inmates to three different corrections facilities. *See* Tr. at 128–29; Def.Ex. A–8–11.[8] In addition to the evidence of a prior physical altercation between the three inmates, and the evidence that Thomas and the plaintiff may have set the fire in Flower's cell, Wong testified that at least two of these three inmates informed him that once they were released from the SHU, they would "settle the matter" by themselves. *See id.* at 139, 141–42. Faced with what Wong perceived to be a very real prospect for future violence between the three inmates, Wong concluded that the interests of security required that these inmates be separated from each other. *See* Tr. at 127, 139.

Although Wong found that the plaintiff should remain in the SHU for security pur-

---

8. Wong's disposition was subsequently affirmed by the defendant Superintendent of Green Ha- ven Scully. *See* Def.Ex. A–11.

poses, the Court notes that Wong also concluded that the evidence against the plaintiff with respect to the accusations of arson and extortion was inconclusive. *See* Tr. at 141. This conclusion was duly indicated on the Superintendent's Proceeding Worksheet. *See* Def.Ex. A–8. Moreover, the Superintendent's Proceeding Report, which set forth in writing the reasons for plaintiff's continued segregation, contained no findings with respect to the issue of plaintiff's guilt or innocence, but instead concluded that the plaintiff should remain in the SHU pending transfer "[f]or the safety and protection of each of the inmates." *See* Def.Ex. A–10.

Following Wong's disposition, but before the plaintiff could be transferred to another correctional facility, on March 2, 1981 plaintiff instituted an Article 78 proceeding before the New York Supreme Court, Dutchess County, challenging his confinement in the SHU. The Article 78 proceeding was initially scheduled for April 24. However, when plaintiff was transferred to Attica on April 22, the Article 78 proceeding was temporarily postponed. *See* Tr. at 16.

Consistent with defendant's contention that plaintiff was placed in the SHU at Green Haven for security purposes, the plaintiff was released into the general prison population at Attica. *See* Tr. at 26. The plaintiff remained in the general population for a little over a month, until, on May 24, 1981, prison officials again had to place the plaintiff in involuntary protective custody. The former Deputy Superintendent for Security at Attica, Charles James, testified that while the plaintiff was in the general population at Attica, the prison was having problems with extortion amongst the inmates. *See id.* at 79. James had received written and oral reports from inmates and prison guards claiming that the plaintiff was one of the ringleaders in an extortion ring. *See id.* at 79. James also received anonymous letters from inmates threatening to kill the plaintiff for his involvement in the extortion. *See id.* at 79; Pl.Ex. C.

Based on the allegations and threats made against the plaintiff, James believed that the plaintiff was involved in the extortion and that the plaintiff should be placed in "administrative protective custody" pending a transfer to another correctional facility. *See* Tr. at 90, 105. According to James' testimony, administrative protective custody is simply Attica's term for involuntary protective custody in the SHU. *See id.* On June 5, 1981, pursuant to James' order, the plaintiff was transferred from Attica to Great Meadow Correctional Facility ("Great Meadow"). *See* Tr. at 79. The inmate transfer order indicated that plaintiff's transfer was necessary to keep him "separate from unknown enemies." *See* Pl.Ex. B.

Plaintiff's Article 78 proceeding was transferred to the New York Supreme Court in Washington County along with plaintiff's transfer to Great Meadow. *See* Transcript of Article 78 Proceeding ("Art. 78 Tr.") at 2. In that Article 78 proceeding, which was held on August 20, 1981, the plaintiff was represented by counsel. Plaintiff complained that he was "deprive[d] ... of considerable rights and liberties in the prison" when he was "wrongfully incarcerated for eighty-nine days in the special protection unit" at Green Haven. *See id.* at 2, 4. Plaintiff also argued that his confinement constituted cruel and unusual punishment. *See id.* at 3. After reviewing all of the records in the case, the court held that "all required procedural steps were scrupulously taken," that the hearing officer was "within [his] authority and discretion" in ordering the petitioner confined to the SHU and that there was no "violation or deprivation of any rights of the petitioner." *See id.* at 10. The court also noted that, in any event, the proceeding was moot because the plaintiff was no longer in involuntary protective custody. *See id.* at 11.

DISCUSSION

Plaintiff's primary claim is that the prison officials at Green Haven denied him due process because they used a purported involuntary protective custody proceeding as a pretext to continue his confinement in the SHU for disciplinary reasons, without ever finding him guilty of any infraction. *See* Tr. at 157; Plaintiff's Proposed Findings of Fact at ¶ 9. The plaintiff also complains that he was denied his due process rights at the superintendent's hearing in that he was denied the assistance of a prison staff member, he was not allowed to cross-examine or hear the testimony of the witnesses against him, and he was not provided with a statement setting forth the reasons why his confinement in the SHU was to be continued. *See* Complaint at 4. Finally, the plaintiff argues that the defendants violated his constitutional right of access to the courts by transferring him from Green Haven to Attica and then to Great Meadow in an attempt to thwart his right to the Article 78 proceeding.[9] *See id.;* Plaintiff's Proposed Findings of Fact at ¶ 7. Each of these claims are wholly without merit.

Plaintiff's claim that he was placed in involuntary protective custody at Green Haven merely as a pretext for a disciplinary confinement[10] is without any factual support and therefore must be rejected. The plaintiff has presented the Court with nothing more than bald and conclusory allegations that his continued confinement in the SHU was for disciplinary reasons. On the other hand, the evidence presented by

---

9. Defendants argue in their post-trial brief that plaintiff's Article 78 proceeding is *res judicata* and bars plaintiff's present action for damages pursuant to § 1983. Whatever the merits of this argument at the time when the defendant initially briefed this issue, the Second Circuit has since made it clear that a prior Article 78 proceeding does not bar a subsequent § 1983 action for damages. *See Davidson v. Capuano,* 792 F.2d 275 (2d Cir.1986).

Defendants also argue in their post-trial brief that the plaintiff is collaterally estopped from relitigating the same issues raised before the state court in the Article 78 proceeding and that the Court should dismiss plaintiff's entire cause of action on this ground. In actions pursuant to § 1983, the Court must give the same collateral estoppel effect to the prior state court judgment as would the state courts from which the judgment emerged. *See Migra v. Warren City School District,* 465 U.S. 75, 81, 104 S.Ct. 892, 896, 79 L.Ed.2d 56 (1984); *Allen v. McCurry,* 449 U.S. 90, 96, 101 S.Ct. 411, 415, 66 L.Ed.2d 308 (1980); *cf. University of Tennessee v. Elliott,* ── U.S. ──, 106 S.Ct. 3220, 92 L.Ed.2d 635 (1986). Thus, in accordance with New York law, the plaintiff is collaterally estopped from relitigating issues which he had a full and fair opportunity to litigate in a prior proceeding, which were actually litigated, and which were determined finally on the merits. *See Schwartz v. Public Administrator,* 24 N.Y.2d 65, 71, 246 N.E.2d 725, 729, 298 N.Y.S.2d 955, 960 (1969). Clearly, the Article 78 proceeding, in which the plaintiff was represented by counsel, afforded plaintiff a full and fair opportunity to litigate the issues raised in that proceeding. *See See Powell v. Ward,* 643 F.2d 924, 943 (2d Cir.), *cert. denied,* 454 U.S. 832, 102 S.Ct. 131, 70 L.Ed.2d 111 (1981); *Wilson v. Pfeiffer,* 565 F.Supp. 115, 117–118 (S.D.N.Y.1983); *cf. Winters v. Lavine,* 574 F.2d 46, 58 n. 14 (2d Cir.1978). Moreover, although the state court in the Article 78 proceeding ruled in the alternative that plaintiff's claims were moot, *see* Art. 78, Tr. at 10, because the court also dismissed plaintiff's claims on the merits, collateral estoppel would still apply. This is especially so in light of the state court's rather cursory discussion of the mootness point. *See Winters,* 574 F.2d *supra* at 67; *Wilson,* 565 F.Supp. *supra* at 117; *GTF Marketing, Inc. v. Colonial Aluminum Sales, Inc.,* 108 A.D.2d 86, 488 N.Y.S.2d 219 (2d Dept.1985); 1B J. Moore, W. Taggart & J. Wicker, Federal Practice ¶ 0.443 at 3901–02 (2d ed. 1982).

However, the Court is not persuaded that defendant has demonstrated that the issues litigated in the Article 78 proceeding were identical to the issues presented in the instant action. In the Article 78 proceeding, the plaintiff simply argued that he was "wrongfully" confined in the SHU. The only constitutional deprivation alleged in that proceeding was that the confinement constituted cruel and unusual punishment. *See* Art. 78, Tr. at 2–4. Moreover, the state court simply concluded that the prison officials were justified in confining the plaintiff and that "all required procedural steps were scrupulously taken." *See id.* at 10.

Certainly, the propriety of the plaintiff's transfer to Attica and then to Great Meadow was never raised or litigated in the state court. Moreover, the plaintiff never argued in the state court that his due process rights were violated or, more specifically, that the involuntary custody proceeding was a pretext to issue disciplinary sanctions. Under these circumstances, the Court declines to reject plaintiff's claims on the grounds of collateral estoppel.

10. In *Hewitt v. Helms,* 459 U.S. 460, 476 n. 9, 103 S.Ct. 864, 873 n. 9, 74 L.Ed.2d 675 (1983), the Supreme Court noted "[o]f course, administrative segregation [for security reasons] may not be used as a pretext for indefinite confinement of an inmate."

the defendants, which largely remains undisputed, overwhelmingly supports the conclusion that the plaintiff was never confined in the SHU for disciplinary reasons.

The Inmate Misbehavior Report and the subsequent adjustment committee hearing indicate that the prison officials initially contemplated disciplinary action. However, it does not follow from that circumstance that plaintiff was ever placed in disciplinary confinement. The plaintiff's initial confinement, from February 2 until the conclusion of the superintendent's hearing on February 13, was clearly on an adjustment admission basis. *See* n. 3 *infra;* 7 NYCRR § 304.1(d). Thus, the evidence establishes that plaintiff was initially properly held in the SHU, not as a disciplinary sanction, but merely so that he would be segregated from the general prison population for a short period of time pending the disposition of the superintendent's proceeding.

Moreover, by the time plaintiff received the formal charge on February 5, it was clear that the prison officials were no longer contemplating any disciplinary action but only whether the plaintiff should be placed in involuntary protective custody. Indeed, the formal charge received by the plaintiff plainly indicates that the superintendent's proceeding would only determine if the plaintiff should be placed in involuntary protection status. This is consistent with Wong's testimony, which the Court finds credible, that he only set out to determine if the plaintiff should be segregated and transferred for security reasons.

The superintendent's worksheet, which set forth the reasons for Mr. Wong's decision to continue plaintiff's confinement in the SHU, also indicated that the plaintiff should be segregated "for the safety and protection of each of the inmates." *See* Def.Ex. A–8. Moreover, when plaintiff's transfer to another institution was consummated and, therefore, the risk of future violence between the plaintiff, Flowers, and Thomas had disappeared, the plaintiff was immediately placed in the general population. Plaintiff did not receive any loss of good time credits as a result of his confinement. Clearly, plaintiff's confinement for security reasons was not used by the defendants, as plaintiff alleges, as a pretext to administer disciplinary sanctions.

The Court also notes that Mr. Wong was clearly acting within his discretion when he concluded that the plaintiff should be segregated from the general population for security reasons. Both Sergeant Cheers and Officer Dore reported to Mr. Wong that other inmates were accusing the plaintiff and Thomas of the arson in Flowers' cell. In addition, there was evidence that the plaintiff, Flowers, and Thomas had been involved in a prior physical altercation and the inmates had told Wong that once they were released from the SHU they would settle their differences by themselves. The accusations of the plaintiff's involvement in the arson, whether right or wrong, and the threat of future violence between the inmates, clearly posed a substantial threat to plaintiff's safety as well as the general security of the prison necessitating plaintiff's continued confinement in the SHU. *See Sher v. Coughlin,* 739 F.2d 77, 82 (2d Cir.1984). *Cf. Hewitt v. Helms,* 459 U.S. 460, 474, 103 S.Ct. 864, 872, 74 L.Ed.2d 675 (1983) ("rumor, reputation and even more imponderable factors may suffice to spark potentially disastrous incidents" in "the violatile atmosphere of a prison.").

Plaintiff's claim that he was denied constitutionally mandated procedural rights at the Green Haven superintendent's hearings must also be rejected. First plaintiff's assertions in his complaint that he was denied the assistance of a prison staff member and that he was not given a statement of the reasons for his continued confinement in the SHU, *see* Complaint at p. 3, are factually unsupported. Indeed, at trial, plaintiff never claimed that he was deprived of these rights created by state law. Nor was plaintiff's due process violated by the fact that plaintiff was not allowed to cross-examine or hear the testimony of the witnesses against him.

At the outset, it should be noted that the state law regulatory structure in existence in New York in 1981 sufficiently circumscribed the discretion of prison officials to place an inmate in involuntary protective custody so as to create a liberty interest cognizable under the Fourteenth Amendment. *Cf. Hewitt*, 459 U.S. *supra* at 472, 103 S.Ct. *supra* at 871 (1983); *compare Deane v. Dunbar*, 777 F.2d 871, 876 (2d Cir.1985) (close question as to whether New York regulations in 1973 created a liberty interest; unlike the 1981 regulations, the 1973 regulations did not provide for hearing or review procedures which might limit the prison official's discretion). Nonetheless, in the context of involuntary protective custody the Due Process Clause only requires that the inmate "receive some notice of the charges against him and an opportunity to present his views [ordinarily only in writing] to the prison official charged with deciding whether to transfer him to administrative segregation." *See Hewitt*, 459 U.S. *supra* at 476, 103 S.Ct. *supra* at 873.[11] In short, the only process due an inmate who is to be placed in administrative segregation is an "informal, nonadversary evidentiary review." *See id.* Measured against these requirements, the plaintiff was clearly afforded all of the constitutionally required procedural requirements to which he was entitled.

Thus, the plaintiff did receive prompt notice of the reasons for the segregation in the SHU, the plaintiff was afforded an ample opportunity to present his views to Mr. Wong, and the prison officials reviewed the evidence against the plaintiff one day after he was placed in the SHU and again ten days later. Indeed, the prison officials in this case, in accordance with New York's regulations, afforded the plaintiff procedural protections which went well beyond the requirements of the Due Process Clause. For example, the plaintiff was offered investigatory assistance, the superintendent's hearing was postponed so that Mr. Wong could conduct an interview requested by the plaintiff of another witness, and the plaintiff was allowed to present his position orally to Mr. Wong. Therefore, plaintiff's claim that he was denied process is without merit.

Plaintiff's final claim, that the defendants violated his constitutional right of access to the courts by transferring him from Green Haven to Attica and then to Great Meadow, is equally meritless. While it is well-settled that an inmate in New York has no due process liberty interest in not being transferred from one correctional facility to another, *see Montanye v. Haymes*, 427 U.S. 236, 243, 96 S.Ct. 2543, 2547, 49 L.Ed.2d 466 (1976); *Meachum v. Fano*, 427 U.S. 215, 216, 224–25, 96 S.Ct. 2532, 2534, 2538, 49 L.Ed.2d 451; *Sher, supra*, 739 F.2d at 80, it is also well-settled that a prisoner may not be transferred solely in retaliation for the exercise of his constitutional rights. *See Haymes v. Montanye*, 547 F.2d 188, 191 (2d Cir.1976), *cert. denied*, 431 U.S. 967, 97 S.Ct. 2925, 53 L.Ed.2d 1063 (1977); *McDonald v. Hall*, 610 F.2d 16, 18 (1st Cir.1979); *Respress v. Coughlin*, 585 F.Supp. 854, 857 (S.D.N.Y. 1984); *Hasan Jamal Abdul Majid v. Henderson*, 533 F.Supp. 1257, 1270 (N.D.N. Y.), *aff'd*, 714 F.2d 115 (2d Cir.1982). To establish a claim of retaliatory transfer, however, the plaintiff must prove that he would not have been transferred but for the filing of his Article 78 proceeding. *See McDonald*, 610 F.2d *supra* at 18, *Respress, supra*, 585 F.Supp. at 858. Plaintiff has clearly not satisfied this burden.

As noted above, Wong's decision to transfer the plaintiff was based solely on his concern for security. Indeed, the evidence establishes that Wong was not even aware that plaintiff had filed his Article 78 proceeding when the transfer order was issued. *See Tr.* at 129. Moreover, the

11. The Court notes that the Supreme Court has held that the same minimal due process requirements which apply to involuntary protective custody proceedings also apply to confinements pending the disposition of superintendent's proceedings, regardless of whether the contemplated proceedings are disciplinary or administrative. *See Hewitt*, 459 U.S. *supra* at 476, 103 S.Ct. *supra* at 873.

Court finds credible Mr. James testimony that the plaintiff was transferred from Attica due to James' belief that the plaintiff was extorting other inmates and that plaintiff's life was threatened. Therefore, plaintiff's claim of retaliatory transfer must be denied.

CONCLUSION

As the foregoing discussion makes evident, plaintiff's claims pursuant to § 1983 are without merit and must be dismissed. The Clerk of the Court is therefore directed to enter judgment for the defendants accordingly.

It is SO ORDERED.

VOLUME III
SUPPLEMENT

PRISONERS' RIGHTS

VOLUME III

CHAPTER 1   PRINCIPLES GOVERNING PRISONERS' RETENTION OF RIGHTS

Courts acknowledge that prisoners do not entirely forfeit their constitutional rights, but the extent to which prisoners retain their rights has been examined on a case to case basis. In *Patterson v. Coughlin,* 761 F.2d 886 (2d Cir. 1985), the court stated that "an inmate who is facing prison disciplinary charges that could result in punitive segregation is entitled, at a minimum to advance written notice of the charges against him and of the evidence available to the fact finder." The case somewhat extends the rights of prisoners. In *Procup v. Strickland,* 760 F.2d 1107 (11th Cir. 1985), the court spelled out the constitutional rights of prisoners to the courts. Finally, *Burris v. Kirkpatrick,* 649 F.Supp. 740 (N.D. Ind. 1986), discussed action which amounted to indifference to an inmate's rights.

Azeez v. Fairman, 795 F.2d 1296 (7th Cir. 1986), reproduced here in the supplement to Vol. III, Chapter 3, questioned the prisoner's right to change his name and liabilities of prison officials for not recognizing the change.

Arteaga v. State of New York, 510 N.Y.Supp.2d 280 (1986), teaches that some states have not waived their sovereign immunity to suits for damages resulting from discipline of inmates. The case is not reported here. *Shabazz v. Barnauskas,* 790 F.2d 1536 (11th Cir. 1986) discussed beards and the rights of inmates to their personal appearances. The case is not reproduced here. *Levoy v. Mills,* 788 F.2d 1437 (10th Cir. 1986), discussed the rights of prisoners to refuse an anal body search. *Levoy* is not reproduced here.

Introductions in previous volumes:

III: 1; VI: 315; VII: 397; VIII: 365

Emmanuel D. **PATTERSON,**
Plaintiff-Appellant,

v.

Thomas A. **COUGHLIN,** III, Charles P.
Hernandez (sic Charles P. Herman-
derz), Harold J. Smith, N. DeSantos,
Defendants-Appellees.

No. 904, Docket 84–2266.

United States Court of Appeals,
Second Circuit.

Argued March 12, 1985.

Decided May 9, 1985.

Before TIMBERS, CARDAMONE and
PIERCE, Circuit Judges.

TIMBERS, Circuit Judge:

This appeal is from a judgment entered
December 5, 1983 in the Western District
of New York, Michael A. Telesca, *District
Judge*, dismissing a pro se complaint pursuant to Fed.R.Civ.P. 12(b)(6) for failure to
state a claim upon which relief can be
granted. The appeal presents the question
of whether a claim is stated under 42
U.S.C. § 1983 (1982) when the complaint
alleges that a state prisoner was placed in
isolation by state officials in violation of
state law and without being afforded a
prior hearing that conforms to the due
process requirements enunciated in *Wolff
v. McDonald*, 418 U.S. 539 (1974). The
district court held that *Parratt v. Taylor*,
451 U.S. 527 (1981), required dismissal of
the complaint because the state provides an
adequate postdeprivation remedy. We disagree. We reverse and remand.

I.

For purposes of this appeal we accept as
true the allegations set forth in the complaint. We summarize only those facts and
prior proceedings believed necessary to an
understanding of our rulings on the legal
issues raised on appeal.

Appellant Emmanuel D. Patterson is,
and at all times relevant to this action was,
an inmate of the Attica Correctional Facility at Attica, New York. Appellees are
Thomas A. Coughlin III, the Commissioner
of the New York State Department of Correctional Services; Harold J. Smith, the
Commissioner of the Attica Correctional
Facility; Charles P. Hernandez, Director of
the Special Housing Review Board; and N.
DeSantos, a Captain at Attica.

On April 9, 1982, a fight broke out between two other inmates at Attica. Appellant, who asserts that he was not involved
in the altercation, was placed in the facility's Special Housing Unit (SHU). On April
12, appellant appeared before the Prison
Adjustment Committee and was charged
with "Assault 1.5 and Interference with an
employee 1.75". A Superintendent's Hearing was convened on April 16 to consider
the charges but was adjourned until April
20.

Appellee DeSantos was the hearing officer at the April 20 hearing. The only wit-

ness who testified was the guard who claimed to be the subject of appellant's alleged assault. Appellant was not permitted to call any witnesses in his defense nor did DeSantos interview any such witnesses. Appellant was found guilty of both charges. He was sentenced to confinement in the SHU for sixty days and loss of sixty days "good time". Appellant appealed the decision at the Superintendent's Hearing to appellees Smith and Coughlin. On July 21, 1982, that decision was affirmed by the Housing Review Board.

In the meanwhile, appellant filed an Article 78 proceeding in the Supreme Court of the State of New York, County of Wyoming, in which he sought immediate release from the SHU and restoration of the sixty days good time. Just prior to his scheduled appearance in the Supreme Court, and shortly before his sixty-day sentence had been served,[1] he was released from the SHU. A hearing was held in the Supreme Court on June 10, 1982. Appellees at that hearing were ordered to produce the record of the Superintendent's Hearing. That record was never produced. A second hearing was held in the Supreme Court on February 25, 1983.

On March 4, 1983, the Supreme Court entered an Order of Stipulation dismissing appellant's petition with prejudice but ordering that appellees "through their agents or employees not hold the [appellant] in confinement in Attica'[s] Special Housing Unit because of the disposition issued at [appellant's] Superintendent's Proceeding

of April 20, 1982 at the Attica Correctional Facility." The order specifically provided that appellees had stipulated to restore appellant's good time and to expunge any reference to the disciplinary proceeding from appellant's file.

On or about April 6, 1983, appellant filed his pro se complaint, on a form used by prisoners who are not represented by counsel, in the District Court for the Western District of New York. At the same time, he moved for leave to proceed in forma pauperis and for appointment of counsel; on May 10, 1983, Judge Telesca granted the former, but denied the latter.[2]

On August 15, 1983, appellees moved, pursuant to Fed.R.Civ.P. 12(b)(6), to dismiss the complaint for failure to state a claim upon which relief could be granted, or, in the alternative, for summary judgment pursuant to Fed.R.Civ.P. 56. Apparently no documentary evidence ever was produced, despite the district court's order of August 1, 1983 requiring production of the record of the Superintendent's Hearing.[3] The district court, treating the motion as one under Rule 12(b)(6), dismissed the complaint in a Memorandum Decision and Order dated December 5, 1983 which in relevant part states:

"In the present case, plaintiff alleges that defendants failed to strictly comply with the procedures established in New York's Code of Rules and Regulations for Confinement in a Special Housing Unit. Because the procedures existed, but were allegedly not followed, no

---

1. Appellant alleges that he was detained in the SHU for a total of 65 days—12 days while the Superintendent's Hearing was pending and 53 days of disciplinary detention. Since the Superintendent's Hearing was constitutionally deficient, as appellees concede, it is as if appellant never received a hearing at all. It therefore is unnecessary for us to determine whether the 12 days spent in the SHU before the hearing was unconstitutionally lengthy. See Powell v. Ward, 542 F.2d 101, 103 (2 Cir.1976) (requiring disciplinary hearing within seven days of confinement in the SHU).

2. On this appeal, appellant has been represented by able counsel appointed by this Court.

3. In a letter dated June 28, 1983 addressed to Judge Telesca, appellees' counsel, an Assistant Attorney General for the State of New York, stated that the Attica Facility no longer maintained the records that the district court ordered to be produced because the state had expunged appellant's file pursuant to the Order of Stipulation entered in the state court in the Article 78 proceeding. We note that no explanation for the failure to produce the record in the state court in the Article 78 proceeding is found in the record on this appeal. The Assistant Attorney General stated in his letter to Judge Telesca, however, that copies might be available from other sources. We assume that, upon the remand which we are ordering, those copies will be produced.

meaningful predeprivation hearing was possible.... Plaintiff did seek redress pursuant to New York Civil Practice Law and Rules Article 78 to force defendants to comply with the established procedures and thus, was given an opportunity to be heard at a meaningful time and in a meaningful manner."

As indicated above, we reverse and remand, for the reasons stated below.

II.

Recovery under 42 U.S.C. § 1983 (1982) is premised upon a showing, first, that the defendant has denied the plaintiff a constitutional or federal statutory right and, second, that such denial was effected under color of state law. *Adickes v. S.H. Kress & Co.*, 398 U.S. 144, 150 (1970). Appellant here alleges a deprivation of his liberty interest and a denial of the procedural safeguards guaranteed by the due process clause of the Fourteenth Amendment. That the liberty interest at issue here is of constitutional dimension is not contested. *E.g., Hewitt v. Helms*, 459 U.S. 460, 472 (1983); *Sher v. Coughlin*, 739 F.2d 77, 81 (2 Cir.1984). Moreover, it is not claimed that the officials' conduct did not amount to "state action", which is a prerequisite to finding a constitutional violation, or that it did not occur under color of state law. The only issue presented for our decision, therefore, is whether, upon the facts alleged in the complaint, there has been a denial of constitutionally-mandated procedures.

In its simplest formulation, due process requires an opportunity to be heard "at a meaningful time and in a meaningful manner." *Armstrong v. Manzo*, 380 U.S. 545, 552 (1965); *Giglio v. Dunn*, 732 F.2d 1133, 1135 (2 Cir.), *cert. denied*, — U.S. —, 105 S.Ct. 328 (1984). Determining precisely the process that is due, however, is more complicated than this simple statement might suggest. The level of procedural safeguards that must be afforded before the government may deprive an individual of a protected interest is determined by reference to (1) the private interest at

stake, (2) the risk of error inherent in the use of one form of procedure over another, and (3) the interest of the government. *Mathews v. Eldridge*, 424 U.S. 319, 335 (1976). *See also Cleveland Board of Education v. Loudermill*, — U.S. —, —, 105 S.Ct. 1487, 1494 (1985); *Hewitt v. Helms, supra*, 459 U.S. at 473. Thus, a tenured public employee is guaranteed notice of the charges against him, an explanation of the evidence in the employer's favor and an opportunity to present "his side of the story" *before* his employment is terminated. *Loudermill, supra*, — U.S. at —, 105 S.Ct. at 1495. Moreover, a formal postdeprivation evidentiary hearing must be provided before the employee's loss may become final. *Id.*, — U.S. at —, 105 S.Ct. at 1496.

The procedural safeguards that are required when an individual's liberty is at stake must at least equal those required before he may be deprived of his property, even when the individual's liberty already is curtailed by the fact of being incarcerated in a correctional facility. *Wolff v. McDonnell*, 418 U.S. 539, 558 (1974). Thus, an inmate who is facing prison disciplinary charges that could result in punitive segregation is entitled, at a minimum, to advance written notice of the charges against him and of the evidence available to the factfinder. He must be permitted to marshal the facts and prepare his defense. A written record of the proceedings must be kept. The inmate must be allowed to call witnesses and present documentary evidence in his defense. *Id.* at 564–66; *McCann v. Coughlin*, 698 F.2d 112, 120–21 (2 Cir.1983).

In *Hewitt v. Helms, supra*, the Supreme Court held that administrative segregation of a prison inmate—where the inmate posed a threat to the safety of other inmates and prison employees and where an investigation into the charges against the inmate was continuing—required only "an informal, non-adversary review of the information supporting respondent's administrative confinement, including whatever statement respondent wished to submit, within a reasonable time after confining him to administrative segregation." *Id.* at 472. Where, as here, the state can show no such compelling interest, and the sole purpose of the confinement is punishment, the *Mathews* balancing test tips in favor of the inmate's liberty interest. The state, therefore, is required to provide the procedures required by *Wolff.*

In the instant case, appellees "concede[ ] that the [appellant] was placed in SHU and deprived of his liberty after a Superintendent's Proceeding which failed in certain particulars to conform to the requirements of procedural due process established in *Wolff v. McDonnell,* 418 U.S. 539 (1974)." Appellees argue, despite the conceded infirmities in the predeprivation hearing, that no due process violation resulted from the hearing officer's failure to follow the state's own rules, which conform to the requirements set forth in *Wolff.* The district court held that "[b]ecause the procedures existed, but were allegedly not followed, no meaningful predeprivation hearing was possible." Appellees urge this proposition on appeal. They further urge that the Article 78 postdeprivation remedy, the mere threat of which resulted in appellees stipulating to appellant's release after 65 days confinement, was sufficient to satisfy due process. Appellees place heavy reliance on *Parratt v. Taylor,* 451 U.S. 527 (1981). We fail to see either the logic of appellees' argument or the connection between the instant case and *Parratt* or the Supreme Court's subsequent decision in *Hudson v. Palmer,* 468 U.S. ——, 104 S.Ct. 3194 (1984).

Although a state employee's failure to conform to state law does not in itself violate the Constitution and is not alone actionable under § 1983, *Davis v. Scherer,* 468 U.S. ——, ——, 104 S.Ct. 3012, 3019 (1984); *Pollnow v. Glennon,* 757 F.2d 496, 501 (2 Cir.1985), the state regulation that

was violated in the instant case merely reiterated what already was *required* by the Constitution. It has long been settled that unconstitutional conduct that *also* violates state law is still actionable under § 1983, *e.g., Monroe v. Pape,* 365 U.S. 167, 187 (1961); *Screws v. United States,* 325 U.S. 91, 109–11 (1945) (plurality opinion); *United States v. Classic,* 313 U.S. 299, 326 (1941); *Home Tel. & Tel. Co. v. Los Angeles,* 227 U.S. 278, 282–85 (1913), and that exhaustion of state tort and administrative remedies is not required. *Monroe, supra,* 365 U.S. at 183; *Patsy v. Board of Regents,* 457 U.S. 496, 516 (1982).

Allegations of procedural due process violations by certain individual government employees, as opposed to direct challenges to state procedures or the lack thereof, have long been accepted as constituting state action and forming the basis for a claim under the civil rights statutes. *See, e.g., Monroe, supra,* 365 U.S. at 172; *Home Tel. & Tel. Co., supra,* 227 U.S. at 278, 282–85; *Mansell v. Saunders,* 372 F.2d 573, 576 (5 Cir.1967).[4] The requirements of the due process clauses are directed specifically to the federal and state governments. They require the promulgation of laws and regulations providing for regular procedures which the government must follow before it may deprive an individual of life, liberty or property. The execution of those laws and regulations also must conform to due process; otherwise the due process clause, with its guarantees of regular and predictable procedures, becomes a cipher. It is beyond cavil that due process requires more than the mere *promulgation* of laws and regulations which, if followed, would preserve the most fundamental of rights.

In *Parratt,* the Supreme Court based its decision, in part, on the fact that

---

4. As Justice Harlan stated in his concurrence in *Monroe:*

"No one suggests that there is a difference in the showing the plaintiff must make to assert a claim under § 1983 depending upon whether he is asserting a denial of rights secured by

the Equal Protection Clause or a denial of rights secured by the Due Process Clause of the Fourteenth Amendment."

Monroe, supra, 365 U.S. at 199 (Harlan, J., concurring).

"the deprivation occurred as a result of the unauthorized failure of agents of the State to follow established state procedure." *Parratt, supra*, 451 U.S. at 543. Appellees here argue, based on this statement, that no predeprivation hearing was possible in the instant case because the procedures provided for by the state were not followed.

First, appellees, and the district court, apparently confuse the deprivation of a liberty interest with the denial of the constitutional right to procedural safeguards which is implicated by that interest. It must be remembered that the Constitution does not prohibit deprivations of liberty per se. The Constitution prohibits deprivations of liberty *without due process*. The denial of a constitutionally-sound predeprivation hearing is a separate and distinct injury from the loss of liberty.

Second, although the denial of due process may have been "unauthorized", the deprivation of liberty at issue here does *not* appear to have been "unauthorized" as that term is meant by *Parratt*. *Hudson v. Palmer, supra*, makes clear that the question of whether the deprivation of a protected interest was negligent or intentional is not of constitutional dimension. What does matter, however, is whether the conduct of the state's agent that resulted in the deprivation was such as to make the injury unforeseeable when viewed from the position of one who possesses the state-delegated authority to grant a hearing when circumstances and the Constitution so require. It is at least a question of fact whether the decision to place appellant in the SHU was made by "officials with final authority" over that decision. *Burtnieks v. City of New York*, 716 F.2d 982, 986 (2 Cir.1983). Unlike the deprivation of property that occurred in *Parratt*, here the responsible state officials who had the power to grant appellant a hearing obviously knew that appellant was in peril of being deprived of his liberty interest. In fact, he was *given* a hearing, albeit a deficient one. Thus, the deprivation of liberty was neither "random" nor "unauthorized". *See Loud-*

ermill v. Cleveland Board of Education, 721 F.2d 550, 562 (6 Cir.1983), *aff'd*, — U.S. —, 105 S.Ct. 1487 (1985); *Burtnieks, supra*, 716 F.2d at 988–89.

Finally, *Parratt* did not alter the fundamental tenets of due process. *Parratt, supra*, 451 U.S. at 544. Absent some exigency that requires summary action by the state, *e.g., Ewing v. Mytinger & Casselberry, Inc.*, 339 U.S. 594 (1950); *North American Cold Storage Co. v. Chicago*, 211 U.S. 306 (1908), or circumstances that render a predeprivation hearing impossible as a practical matter as in *Parratt*, the opportunity to be heard *before* the state deprives an individual of life, liberty or property is still the " 'root requirement' " of the due process clause. *Loudermill, supra*, — U.S. at —, 105 S.Ct. at 1493, *quoting Boddie v. Connecticut*, 401 U.S. 371, 379 (1972). It is abundantly clear that disciplinary segregation implicates a sufficiently strong liberty interest as to require notice of the charges and, as the word "hearing" suggests, *some* opportunity to present a defense. *Wolff, supra*, 418 U.S. at 563–72; *McCann v. Coughlin, supra*, 698 F.2d at 121; *Powell v. Ward, supra*, 542 F.2d at 104. The opportunity to be heard at a meaningful time and in a meaningful manner has not been satisfied when the first such real opportunity is afforded after an inmate has already been in the SHU for 65 days. "The point is straightforward: the Due Process Clause provides that certain substantive rights—life, liberty, and property—cannot be deprived except pursuant to constitutionally adequate procedures." *Loudermill, supra*, — U.S. at —, 105 S.Ct. at 1493. Since appellant was denied such adequate procedures before punitively being deprived of his liberty, and since it was not impossible or impracticable to provide such procedures, the conclusion is inescapable that appellant was denied due process. *Parratt* and the other cases upon which appellees rely are not to the contrary. In those cases to which the reasoning of *Parratt* was applied to deprivations of liberty, the deprivation itself was "random and unauthorized" and a predeprivation hearing was impossible. *E.g., Thibodeaux v. Bordelon,* 740 F.2d 329, 338 (5 Cir.1984); *Daniels v. Williams,* 720 F.2d 792, 795 (4 Cir.1983), *cert. granted,* — U.S. —, 105 S.Ct. 1168, 84 L.Ed.2d 320 (1985). *Parratt* and its progeny are inapposite here.

III.

In view of our holding that an adequate prior hearing was required, a post-deprivation hearing, by way of an Article 78 proceeding or an action for damages in the Court of Claims, is inadequate, by definition, to meet the requirements of due process. This may be tautological, but it is a point that appears to have been missed by appellees and by the district court. Once a cause of action for a constitutional violation accrues, nothing that the state does subsequently can cut off the § 1983 claim.

To summarize: We hold that, on the facts alleged in the complaint, the deprivation of appellant's liberty was neither random nor unauthorized and, as such, the state, through its agents, was obligated to provide an adequate hearing *before* the decision to discipline appellant was made final. We therefore reverse the judgment of the district court dismissing the complaint for failure to state a claim and remand for further proceedings consistent with this opinion.

Reversed and remanded.

Robert PROCUP, Plaintiff-Appellant,

v.

C. STRICKLAND, et al.,
Defendants-Appellees.

No. 83-3430.

United States Court of Appeals,
Eleventh Circuit.

May 20, 1985.

Opinion on Granting of Rehearing
En Banc July 10, 1985.

JOHNSON, Circuit Judge:

Appellant, state prisoner Robert Procup, brought this action pro se in the Middle District of Florida against prison officials who had allegedly stolen his mail. After reviewing Procup's complaint and his affidavit seeking permission to prosecute the claim in forma pauperis, the district court *sua sponte* entered an order which (1) noted the volume and nature of Procup's previous lawsuits, (2) expressed concern that Procup was engaging in abuse of the judicial process, and (3) gave Procup thirty days to show cause why he should not be enjoined from filing any further pleadings in the Middle District of Florida. The order also allowed the State of Florida thirty days in which to present its position as to the propriety of such an injunction. After considering responses from Procup and the State of Florida, the district court invoked its powers under the All Writs Act, 28 U.S.C.A. § 1651(a),[1] and permanently enjoined Procup from filing in the Middle District of Florida "any additional cases or pleadings therein ... unless ... submitted on behalf of Procup by an attorney admitted to practice before this Court." *Procup*

v. Strickland, 567 F.Supp. 146, 162 (M.D. Fla.1983). Because the injunction unduly burdens Procup's constitutional right of access to the courts and seeks to absolve the district court of its responsibility to examine prisoner complaints for frivolity or maliciousness on a case-by-case basis, we reverse.

INTRODUCTION

Since 1979, Procup has been increasingly active as a pro se litigant, bringing the majority of his lawsuits under 42 U.S.C.A. § 1983 as challenges to various conditions of his confinement in Florida prisons. Based on Procup's lack of success in any action prosecuted thus far, the patently frivolous nature of several of his claims, the repetitive assertion of various claims, a persistent refusal to abide by local rules, and an apparently malicious motive for initiating certain actions, the district court below found that Procup "has engaged and continues to engage in a gross abuse of the judicial process." *Id.* at 156.

We do not question this finding,[2] as the district court provides ample docu-

---

1. Section 1651(a) states:

   The Supreme Court and all courts established by Act of Congress may issue all writs necessary or appropriate in aid of their respective jurisdictions and agreeable to the usages and principles of law.

   28 U.S.C.A. § 1651(a).

2. Nor do we accept Procup's claim on appeal that he was denied adequate notice and opportunity to be heard before issuance of the injunction. Due process does require notice and an opportunity to be heard, and the standard for measuring the adequacy of these procedural protections increases in proportion to the signif-

mentation for the conclusion that Procup is excessively litigious. *Id.* at 148–56. Our concern, instead, is with the overbroad remedy employed by the district court. No analogous precedent from this or any other circuit has affirmed such a restrictive injunction. Its unlimited scope denies Procup adequate, effective, and meaningful access to the courts. Moreover, inherent in a judicial ruling which completely[3] forecloses an individual's pro se access to federal court is an ominous abandonment of judicial responsibility, the import of which far exceeds the actual abuse attributable even to the exceptional prisoner litigant. The efficient operation of our judicial system does not require the issuance of an unlimited restriction on this pro se litigant's access to the courts. Existing federal rules governing pro se and in forma pauperis appearances and local rules when properly designed to streamline pleadings and ferret out abuse should suffice. The magnitude of Procup's abuse does not justify creating a rule that permits the judicial officer charged with the responsibility of reviewing prisoner complaints on a case-by-case basis to refuse to consider these claims altogether. To the contrary, the magnitude of Procup's abuse serves to emphasize the degree to which the pro se litigant's right of access to our courts retains its constitutional significance.

icance of the interest at stake. See *Morrissey v. Brewer*, 408 U.S. 471, 481, 92 S.Ct. 2593, 2600, 33 L.Ed.2d 484 (1972). Here, the interest at stake, access to the courts, is of constitutional significance. *Bounds v. Smith*, 430 U.S. 817, 821, 97 S.Ct. 1491, 1494, 52 L.Ed.2d 72 (1977). Nevertheless, we hold that the district court gave Procup sufficient notice of its concern that his pattern of litigation constituted an abuse of the judicial process. The show cause order focused specifically on Procup's suspected abuse and the court's intent to examine the volume and nature of his past case filings. The thirty-day period for response was also adequate. It enabled Procup to draft and file a twenty-six page reply. Procup was not entitled to a live hearing as to the validity of every case he had filed. See *United States v. Smith*, 257 F.2d 432, 434 (2d Cir.1958), *cert. denied*, 359 U.S. 926, 79 S.Ct. 609, 3 L.Ed.2d 629 (1959).

3. The district court enjoined Procup from filing "any additional cases or pleadings therein." *Procup v. Strickland, supra*, 567 F.Supp. at 162.

DISCUSSION

A. The Injunction Is Overbroad.

Prisoners have a constitutional right of access to the courts. *Bounds v. Smith*, 430 U.S. 817, 821, 97 S.Ct. 1491, 1494, 52 L.Ed.2d 72 (1977).[4] Though this right is not absolute or unconditional, restrictions which deprive inmates of "adequate, effective, and meaningful" access will be declared invalid. *Id.* at 822, 97 S.Ct. at 1495; *See also Wolff v. McDonnell*, 418 U.S. 539, 579–80, 94 S.Ct. 2963, 2986–87, 41 L.Ed.2d 935 (1974). In our Circuit, for example, a trial court's summary dismissal of an inmate's complaint in order to control court dockets and discourage prisoner litigation has been expressly prohibited. *Mitchum v. Purvis*, 650 F.2d 647, 648 (5th Cir.1981) (Unit B).

The district court below correctly acknowledged that litigiousness alone would not support an injunction depriving Procup of his right of access to the courts. *Procup, supra*, 567 F.Supp. at 151. However, the court went on to justify imposing the injunction by finding that Procup had abused the judicial process. *Id.* at 156. Apart from whether an injunction of any kind is warranted under these circumstances, which is a question we shall address in the latter part of this opinion, we hold that the injunction issued by the district court is

On appeal, the parties disagree as to whether this language prohibits Procup from prosecuting cases previously filed pro se and now pending before the district court. Because the right of access to the courts is of constitutional importance, *Bounds v. Smith*, 430 U.S. 817, 821, 97 S.Ct. 1491, 1494, 52 L.Ed.2d 72 (1977), we would construe the injunction narrowly—as the State proposes—in order to ensure at a minimum Procup's continued access as a pro se litigant in these pending actions. Yet we need not resolve this question of construction, since it is subsumed in our overall holding that the injunction itself is invalid.

4. Citing earlier Supreme Court decisions, the Seventh Circuit has catalogued several constitutional sources for this right. These sources include the Due Process Clause of the Fourteenth Amendment (as well as the Fifth Amendment), the First Amendment, and the "Privileges and Immunities Clause" of Article IV, Section 2, of the Constitution. See *Green v. Warden*, 699 F.2d 364, 369 (7th Cir.), *cert. denied*, 461 U.S. 960, 103 S.Ct. 2436, 77 L.Ed.2d 1321 (1983).

overbroad. The unlimited scope of the in-junction is without precedent, and it denies Procup adequate, effective, and meaningful access to our judicial system.

1. The Injunction Is Without Precedent.

Appellate decisions in this and other cir-cuit courts have affirmed the issuance of injunctions against abusive litigants, but none of the injunctions challenged in these cases have swept so broadly as to deny pro se appearances entirely. Where principles of res judicata and collateral estoppel have proven inadequate to deter abuse, litigants have been enjoined from relitigating specif-ic claims or filing repetitive appeals from a particular adverse ruling. E.g., Harrelson v. United States, 613 F.2d 114, 116 (5th Cir.1980); In re Green, 598 F.2d 1126, 1128 (8th Cir.1979); Hill v. Estelle, 543 F.2d 754 (5th Cir.1976), aff'g Hill v. Estelle, 423 F.Supp. 690 (S.D.Tex.1976). Similarly moti-vated injunctions have required litigants who have abused the judicial process to accompany all future pleadings with affida-vits certifying that the claims being raised are novel. E.g., Green v. Warden, 699 F.2d 364, 370 (7th Cir.), cert. denied, 461 U.S. 960, 103 S.Ct. 2436, 77 L.Ed.2d 1321 (1983); In re Green, 669 F.2d 779, 787 (D.C.Cir.1981). Litigants have also been directed to attach to future complaints a list of all cases previously filed involving the same, similar, or related cause of ac-tion [5] and to send an extra copy of every pleading filed to the law clerk for the chief judge of the district. E.g., Green v. White, 616 F.2d 1054, 1056 (8th Cir.1980).

Injunctions of a different sort have pro-hibited the clerk of the court from filing an abusive litigant's pleadings without leave of court. E.g., Green v. Warden, supra, 699 F.2d at 370; In re Oliver, 682 F.2d 443, 446 (3d Cir.1982); In re Green, supra, 669 F.2d at 787; Pavilonis v. King, 626 F.2d

1075, 1079 (1st Cir.), cert. denied, 449 U.S. 829, 101 S.Ct. 96, 66 L.Ed.2d 34 (1980); Gordon v. United States Department of Justice, 558 F.2d 618 (1st Cir.1977). The clerk has also been instructed not to file pleadings that do not comply strictly with the applicable rules of civil and appellate procedure. E.g., Carter v. Pettigrew, No. 84–8411, slip op. at 5 (11th Cir. Aug. 24, 1984) (unpublished) (order authorizing clerk of appellate court to inspect documents re-ceived from certain litigants for compliance with Fed.R.App.P. 3 and to refuse to file the documents if the judgment or order appealed from is not specified).

All of these injunctions, by exposing the litigants to the possibility of being held in contempt for non-compliance, have created an added incentive for not abusing the judi-cial process. Yet, none of these decisions have completely curtailed a prisoner's pro se access to the courts. At most, the in-junctions have created rebuttable presump-tions of repetition, frivolity, or malicious-ness. In none of the decisions have future non-frivolous and non-malicious claims been preemptively and conclusively fore-closed, as they have been in this case.

Two other appellate decisions have af-firmed injunctions that permit an abusive prisoner litigant to file in forma pauperis only claims alleging actual or threatened physical harm. E.g., In re Green, No. 81–1186 (5th Cir. Apr. 27, 1981) (Unit A) (pub-lished as appendix to the opinion in Green v. Carlson, 649 F.2d 285, 286 (5th Cir.) (Unit A), cert. denied, 454 U.S. 1087, 102 S.Ct. 646, 70 L.Ed.2d 623 (1981)); Green v. White, supra, 616 F.2d at 1055. Imposing this type of injunction creates, in effect, a conclusive presumption that future in for-ma pauperis claims not involving actual or threatened physical harm are ipso facto duplicative, frivolous, or malicious. Apart from whether such an injunction should

---

5. We note that a similar listing requirement already appears in the standard civil rights com-plaint form used by prisoners in the Middle District of Florida. In fact, the form mandates that Procup describe not only each lawsuit pre-viously filed "dealing with the same facts," but also each previous lawsuit "otherwise relating to" his imprisonment. The information sought

is needed to determine whether the claim being filed presents a new, non-frivolous issue and whether it is being brought maliciously. In this case, Procup did not respond in meaningful detail to the questions on the form, and yet the district court did not refuse the complaint as incomplete.

ever be employed,[6] even its scope does not extend as far as the injunction issued in the instant case. Here, the question is not solely a matter of precluding access to a non-repetitive, non-frivolous, and non-malicious claim which does not allege actual or threatened physical harm. Rather, the question is whether access can be denied to *any* non-repetitive, non-frivolous, and non-malicious claim when filed pro se.

2. The Injunction Denies Procup Adequate, Effective, And Meaningful Access To The Courts.

The district court below examined and rejected for instrumental reasons each type

of injunction thus far affirmed by the circuit courts. Because Procup is currently serving a sentence of life imprisonment,[7] the court concluded that additional confinement for contempt, based on violations of an injunction which merely prohibited the relitigation of specific claims or required a certification of novelty, would probably have little effect in deterring Procup's abuse of the judicial process. *Procup v. Strickland*, 567 F.Supp. at 159. Similarly, the district court concluded that requiring leave of court before filing further pleadings would not deter Procup's abuse. Instead, this sort of injunction would continue to demand the expenditure of judicial

6. Opposing any modification to the injunction issued against Procup, the State of Florida contends that the injunctions issued in *In re Green* and *Green v. White* are too limiting because future non-frivolous and non-malicious claims which do not allege actual or threatened physical harm will not be heard. Thus, the State implicitly argues that the injunctions should not have been affirmed in these two cases. Without addressing this argument, the district court below concluded that such an injunction was not limiting enough: Procup's persistent creativity in fabricating claims would simply continue to operate within the subject-matter boundaries encompassing actual and threatened physical harm. *Procup v. Strickland, supra,* 567 F.Supp. at 159–60. The court reached this conclusion even though it had no information concerning the effectiveness of injunctions issued in *In re Green* and *Green v. White. Id.* at 159.

If the merits of an injunction that only recognized allegations of physical harm were at issue in this appeal, we could not vacate the order. *In re Green* is binding precedent in this Circuit until overruled or modified by the Court en banc. *See Bonner v. City of Prichard,* 661 F.2d 1206, 1209 (11th Cir.1981) (en banc). We nevertheless note a disturbing aspect of that decision and a growing tension between it and more recent decisions from the Tenth and District of Columbia Circuits. The injunction affirmed in *In re Green* totally precludes any access to non-repetitive, non-frivolous, and non-malicious claims filed in forma pauperis that do not allege actual or threatened physical harm. The only way these claims can be brought, then, is for the filing fee requirements to be satisfied. And yet the decision in *In re Green* also voided that part of the district court's injunction which made the payment of filing fees mandatory. The Tenth and District of Columbia Circuit Courts have similarly held that requiring the payment of fees unduly burdens an indigent prisoner's constitutional right of access to the courts. *In re*

Green, supra, 669 F.2d at 786; *Carter v. United States,* 733 F.2d 735, 737 (10th Cir.1984).

Moreover, we question the expediency of the subject-matter distinction employed in *In re Green* and *Green v. White.* As did the district court below, we doubt that allegations of actual or threatened physical harm will invariably denote non-frivolous and non-malicious claims. We question further whether a court should rule prospectively and without qualification that complaints involving physical harm are necessarily more worthy of consideration than other complaints. The physical harm requirement does provide a bright-line test, but its application is not a reliable means for distinguishing between important and unimportant claims. The physical harm alleged in some cases may well be insubstantial when compared to non-physical deprivations of civil rights alleged in other cases. For example, the test would apparently not preclude the claim raised in *Procup v. Cooper,* Case No. 82–1064–Civ-J-M (M.D.Fla.) (mistreatment at prison allegedly caused Procup to contract athletes foot), *noted in Procup v. Strickland, supra,* 567 F.Supp. at 152.

Finally, we distinguish *In re Green* and related cases by noting that the abusive litigant there faced a significantly shorter sentence than Procup, who is thus less likely to be deterred by the possibility of contempt proceedings. In fact, the district court below concluded that the threat of receiving additional periods of confinement did not appear at all likely to discourage Procup's abuse. *Procup v. Strickland, supra,* 567 F.Supp. at 159 nn. 11–12. Surely an injunction having a deterrent effect, if it has any merit at all, is more defensible than one issued despite a conclusion that it will not be effective as a deterrent. The purpose of issuing the latter injunction becomes immediately suspect.

7. Procup is serving a life-sentence for first degree murder. Under Florida law, he must serve twenty-five years before becoming eligible for

resources in order to review the mass of petitions for leave to file that Procup would be expected to produce, a process of review similar in form to that already required when Procup requests permission to prosecute a claim in forma pauperis. Finally, the district court concluded that Procup would circumvent an injunction against filing any claim not alleging actual or threatened physical harm. He would simply formulate future claims so as to include the requisite allegations.[8] Yet the inefficacy of the injunctions imposed in all of these cases does not justify the court's issuance of a more restrictive injunction here. The unqualified injunction against pro se access must pass constitutional muster on its own terms. It must not deprive Procup of adequate, effective, and meaningful access to the courts.

The district court concluded that an injunction against pro se appearances would not unduly burden Procup's right to obtain judicial redress in appropriate cases. Two avenues were ostensibly available to ensure adequate representation for Procup's future complaints: (1) attorneys in private practice and (2) the non-profit legal assistance organization located at the prison. The first avenue assumes that ample financial incentives exist under 42 U.S.C.A. § 1988 for private attorneys to invest voluntarily the time and effort needed to represent Procup in cases brought pursuant to Section 1983 of the Civil Rights Act, 42 U.S.C.A. § 1983. Section 1988 does provide for the award of attorney's fees to prevailing litigants in civil rights actions, but this provision may not be operative in every case. Procup may desire to bring claims pursuant to statutes other than Section 1983. Moreover, the award of attorney's fees under Section 1988 is discretionary. The possibility that no award will be made can only serve to blunt whatever incentive the statute provides for members of the private bar to represent Procup in pursuing legitimate claims.

The second avenue relies on the non-profit legal assistance organization that is available at the prison to represent Procup when private counsel is not forthcoming. The assistance of the legal aid organization, however, does not guarantee Procup adequate, effective, and meaningful access to the courts. The resources of this organization are limited and may not be sufficient, both at present and in the future, to ensure that Procup's legitimate claims are represented. Moreover, Procup avers that actions he previously filed pro se are now pending against certain attorneys who work for the legal assistance organization. Thus, conflicts of interest might arise which would prevent the organization from representing Procup in cases not handled by a private attorney.

In short, the competitive market for legal services and the available non-profit legal assistance will not invariably provide adequate, effective, and meaningful representation for Procup's non-frivolous and non-malicious claims. Should these avenues of representation prove fruitless, Procup's only remaining option would require the purchase of legal aid with personal funds that he apparently does not have. Ultimately, then, the injunction may impose financial restrictions that operate to preclude Procup from filing a new and legitimate complaint. It is true that costs are a factor in every litigant's decision to pursue a claim, but here the costs of access to our judicial system have been increased for a specific indigent litigant to levels that may completely foreclose his future access to the courts.

The use of an injunction against a pro se litigant "should be approached with particular caution." *Pavilonis v. King, supra,* 626 F.2d at 1079; *In re Oliver, supra,* 682 F.2d at 445; *Hill v. Estelle, supra,* 423 F.Supp. at 695. Here, the operation of economic incentives and the limited extent of available legal assistance resources indicate that, even if injunctive relief were

---

parole. Fla.Stat. § 775.082(1). That date is approximately fifteen years away. *Procup v. Strickland, supra,* 567 F.Supp. at 147.

8. *See supra,* note 6.

appropriate, it should be structured to ensure the fullest possible scope to Procup's constitutional right of access to the courts. The district court's unlimited injunction against pro se appearances produces the opposite effect. By prohibiting *any* pro se appearances, the injunction impermissibly burdens Procup's constitutional right to adequate, effective, and meaningful access to the courts.

B. The Injunction Is Unwarranted.

The right to appear pro se and, where granted by the district court, to proceed in forma pauperis ensures that indigent litigants will have access to our judicial system that is adequate, effective, and meaningful. Pro se litigants who proceed in forma pauperis, however, are not subject to the usual incentives against filing repetitive, frivolous, or malicious lawsuits. They "are immune from imposition of costs if they are unsuccessful; and because of their poverty, they are practically immune from later tort actions for 'malicious prosecution' or abuse of process." *Jones v. Bales*, 58 F.R.D. 453, 463 (N.D.Ga.1972), *aff'd*, 480 F.2d 805 (5th Cir.1973). The problem can be particularly acute when the litigant is a prisoner who has substantial amounts of idle time and a free supply of writing materials and postage stamps.[9]

Our procedural rules are premised on the assumption that litigants are subject to limitations of time and expense and have a basic respect for accuracy. Thus, we interpret the rules liberally so that only the truly untenable claims are dismissed or decided summarily. Since these assumptions may not always be operative in actions proceeding in forma pauperis, especially where a prisoner has initiated the lawsuit pro se, Congress has authorized special procedures for handling in forma pauperis complaints. *Green v. City of Montezuma*, 650 F.2d 648, 651 (5th Cir.1981) (Unit B); *Jones v. Bales, supra*, 58 F.R.D. at 464. These procedures are codified at 28 U.S.C.A. § 1915. Significantly, the procedures do not provide for the use of injunctions.

Section 1915 mandates a two-stage procedure for processing a prisoner's pro se civil rights complaint filed in forma pauperis. *See Green v. City of Montezuma, supra*, 650 F.2d at 650 n. 3; *Woodall v. Foti*, 648 F.2d 268, 271 (5th Cir.1981) (Unit A); *Watson v. Ault*, 525 F.2d 886, 891 (5th Cir.1976). Initially, the district court must determine whether the plaintiff is unable to prepay costs and fees and is therefore a pauper under the statute. 28 U.S.C.A. § 1915(a). If the complainant's affidavit was falsely sworn or his financial condition makes him ineligible, in forma pauperis status can be denied without considering either the merits of the complaint or whether it was filed maliciously. Only after making a finding of poverty and docketing the case can the court proceed to the next question: whether the claim asserted is frivolous or malicious. 28 U.S.C.A. § 1915(d). If it appears that the claim is without arguable merit in both law and fact or that the claim is repetitive or was filed maliciously, then the complaint may be dismissed with prejudice even before the defendants have been served. *Woodall v. Foti, supra*, 648 F.2d at 271; *Taylor v. Gibson*, 529 F.2d 709, 714 (5th Cir.1976); *Watson v. Ault, supra*, 525 F.2d at 892. If the complaint fails to state a claim—i.e., it appears beyond doubt that the plaintiff can prove no set of facts in support of his claim which would entitle him to relief—the court should enter a dismissal without prejudice so that an amended complaint may be filed. *Mitchell v. Beaubouef*, 581 F.2d 412, 416 (5th Cir.1978), *cert. denied*, 441 U.S. 966, 99 S.Ct. 2416, 60 L.Ed.2d 1072 (1979).

The centerpiece of the Section 1915 procedures is the district court's exercise of its discretion on a case-by-case basis, however tedious this exercise of discretion may become. The statute places the responsibility of reviewing prisoner complaints in the district court alone, and "any order that does not allow a district court the appropriate exercise of discretion under § 1915 is invalid." *In re Green, supra*, 669 F.2d at 786; *see also Carter v. United States*, 733 F.2d

---

9. The supply of writing materials and postage for mailing pleadings to the courts is not unlimited. *See, e.g., Hoppins v. Wallace*, 751 F.2d 1161, 1162 (11th Cir.1985).

735, 737 (10th Cir.1984) (vacating an injunction against the filing of a prisoner's future complaints without payment of fees).[10]

Here, the district court's express purpose in issuing the injunction was to have someone other than the court review Procup's claims and cull out the non-frivolous and non-malicious complaints. *Procup v. Strickland, supra,* 567 F.Supp. at 161 n. 17. Although the order as phrased prohibits pro se filings and is silent regarding requests for in forma pauperis status, it nonetheless was designed to shift the responsibility of the case-by-case review process away from the district court. We hold that the court may not by way of an injunction avoid the responsibility Congress has placed upon it to consider each prisoner complaint when filed. Whether a pro se complaint brought in federal court is properly drawn and whether it states a legitimate claim are questions for the district court alone to determine. *Cf. Ex parte Hull,* 312 U.S. 546, 549, 61 S.Ct. 640, 641, 85 L.Ed. 1034 (1941) (holding invalid a state prison regulation that required all pro se legal pleadings to be approved by a prison official and then a special investigator for the parole board before being sent to the designated court).

Our holding does not confer on Procup a right to receive special advantages not bestowed on other litigants. He must, for example, abide by local rules governing the proper form of pleadings. Complaints "scrawled on toilet paper" or written "on both sides of the paper" need not be filed. *See Procup v. Strickland, supra,* 567 F.Supp. at 154. Nor must exhibits be accepted prematurely. *See id.* On the other hand, the frustrations that may attend such violations of local rules cannot justify a proscriptive denial of constitutional rights. As federal courts, we must not surrender to a state-of-siege men-

tality and abandon our duty to provide a forum for even the abusive pro se litigant's occasional legitimate claim. The judicial time spent in dismissing such complaints and returning the exhibits is minimal at most and comprises a cost which our judicial system should absorb when the alternative ruling so portentously restricts the constitutional right of access to the courts.

Our holding similarly does not proscribe the development of additional local rules to expedite the district court's case-by-case determinations. *See* Federal Judicial Center, *Recommended Procedures for Handling Prisoner Civil Rights Cases in the Federal Courts* (1980). Complaint forms may be refined to elicit information designed to reveal repetition, frivolity, or maliciousness. One particular person or group of persons in the office of the clerk of court may be assigned the task of reviewing all prisoner complaints for compliance with local rules of form. This person or group of persons could maintain a separate file on especially prodigious litigants to aid in discovering and documenting repetitious or malicious case filings. An initial screening of prisoner complaints can be performed by law clerks or a magistrate, with recommendations being forwarded along with the complaints to the district judge. All pleadings filed by one inmate may be directed to the same law clerk or magistrate and district judge.

Review of the recommendations of the law clerk or magistrate and consideration of the complaints individually does not require inordinate amounts of time and effort from the district court. If a pro se complaint is on its face without arguable merit,[11] only a one-line order dismissing it with prejudice need be entered. If the claim is not facially frivolous and was not brought maliciously, the court need simply

---

10. This Circuit has previously reached analogous holdings requiring district courts to exercise their discretion with respect to every prisoner's petition for habeas corpus ad testificandum brought under 28 U.S.C.A. § 2241(c)(5). In *Spears v. Chandler,* 672 F.2d 834, 835 (11th Cir.1982), we held that, by refusing altogether to consider whether a prisoner should be allowed

to appear and testify in a case he is prosecuting pro se, the district court effectively precludes prosecution of the action and thus denies the prisoner adequate access to the courts. *See also Mitchum v. Purvis, supra,* 650 F.2d at 648; *Ball v. Woods,* 402 F.Supp. 803, 811–12 (N.D.Ala. 1975).

enter a one-line order instructing the defendants to show why the complaint is not entitled to the relief sought. If the claim is without merit, the defendants can easily answer, and then move for dismissal or summary judgment, attaching to their pleadings copies of medical records or other documents to establish their defense. The magistrate can and should handle most, if not all, of these proceedings and make recommendations to the district court. If the defendants' reply does not suffice to establish grounds for dismissal or summary judgment, the proceedings should continue as in an ordinary case. The claim would be precisely the sort that should be further developed and not be enjoined altogether.

Within the confines of acceptable procedures such as these, the district court has ample discretion to summarily dismiss frivolous or malicious claims; yet the case-by-case consideration envisioned by Congress is left intact. The speed and accuracy with which the claims are ultimately processed will be, in part, a function of the competency and administrative ability of the particular district court. Accordingly, future judicial efforts to deal with the increasing load of prisoner litigation should be directed toward developing effective procedures and improving our own efficiency, not enjoining the access of litigants to the courts.

REVERSED.

ON REHEARING

Before GODBOLD, Chief Judge, RONEY, TJOFLAT, HILL, FAY, VANCE, KRAVITCH, JOHNSON, HENDERSON, HATCHETT, ANDERSON and CLARK, Circuit Judges.

BY THE COURT:

A majority of the Judges in active service, on the Court's own motion, having determined to have this case reheard en banc,

IT IS ORDERED that the cause shall be reheard by this Court en banc *without* oral argument on a date hereafter to be fixed. The previous panel's opinion is hereby vacated.

The Clerk will specify a briefing schedule for the filing of en banc briefs.

---

11. The complaint must be read liberally under our rules of civil procedure. Moreover, pro se complaints are held to less rigorous standards than formal pleadings drafted by lawyers. *Woodall v. Foti, supra*, 648 F.2d at 271.

Gary BURRIS, Plaintiff,

v.

Officer Jay KIRKPATRICK, Defendant.

No. S 83–190.

United States District Court,
N.D. Indiana,
South Bend Division.

Dec. 11, 1986.

MEMORANDUM AND ORDER

ALLEN SHARP, Chief Judge.

I.

On November 24, 1982 at approximately 8:30 o'clock P.M. the plaintiff, Gary Burris, was an inmate at the Indiana State Prison, housed in a two-man cell on death row there. His cellmate was Michael Daniels. Both are awaiting execution. The defendant, Jay Kirkpatrick, was correctional officer on duty in that death row unit on that particular evening. At the time in question, Burris had on his earphones and was writing. An argument erupted between Officer Kirkpatrick and Daniels over the delivery of some milk by the former to the latter. Burris was in no way involved in the argument. There is no competent evidence to suggest or infer any misconduct at this time and place by Burris.

The cell in question is eleven (11) feet wide and nine (9) feet long or deep. It contains two sleeping bunks, a cabinet, a table, a toilet, and a sink. Two inmates and their personal belongings create a very crowded area with very limited locomotion for the occupants. At no time during this entire incident were the doors to this particular cell unlocked. In other words, at all times, both Daniels and Burris were securely locked in their cells.

As the Daniels-Kirkpatrick argument ensued it became heated in a very literal sense. There is some indication that Daniels may have gone beyond verbal abuse of Kirkpatrick. In any event, Kirkpatrick threw two containers of hot water into this particular cell striking both of its occupants and causing burns to Burris. The hot water was taken from a nearby faucet and was placed in two containers, a five gallon bucket and a one gallon mustard container. Kirkpatrick threw both containers into the cell, striking both Burris and Daniels. Burris sustained burns to his body but there is no permanent residual effect.

After the incident, Kirkpatrick took the unit key home with him until he returned to work there the next day. Sometime later, after a hearing, he was placed on three days suspension but that penalty was suspended and he was placed on six months probation. Kirkpatrick remained in the employment of the Indiana Department of Correction as a correctional officer at the Indiana State Prison until he resigned on August 25, 1984, and now lives outside the State of Indiana.

The complaint in this case was filed *pro se* by the plaintiff on May 9, 1983 alleging a claim under 42 U.S.C. § 1983 and invoking this court's subject matter jurisdiction under 28 U.S.C. §§ 1331 and 1343(3), (4). A bench trial was held at the Indiana State Prison on November 12, 1986 and under the order of the Judicial Council of the Seventh Federal Circuit dated October 4, 1984, supplemental briefs have been filed and this case is now ripe for decision. This memorandum and order will constitute the findings and conclusions as required under Rule 52 of the Federal Rules of Civil Procedure.

In addition to filing a complaint against Officer Jay Kirkpatrick, the plaintiff also sued Jack Duckworth, Edward Cohn and Robert Bronnenberg. The defendants, Duckworth, Cohn and Bronnenberg, have been previously dismissed in this case on the basis that no claim under § 1983 can be based on the concept of respondeat superior as defined in *Monell v. Dept. of Social Services*, 436 U.S. 658, 694, 98 S.Ct. 2018, 56 L.Ed.2d 611 (1978), as most recently summarized in *Rascon v. Hardiman*, 803 F.2d 269 (7th Cir.1986). Those rulings are here and now reconfirmed.

II.

Amendment VIII of the Constitution of the United States states:

Excessive bail shall not be required, nor excessive fines imposed, nor cruel and unusual punishments inflicted.

This amendment has long since been "incorporated" into Amendment XIV and therefore is binding upon the States through the due process clause thereof. *See State of Louisiana, v. Resweber*, 329 U.S. 459, 67 S.Ct. 374, 91 L.Ed. 422 (1947).

Judge Friendly breathed relevant life into Amendment VIII thirteen (13) years ago in *Johnson v. Glick*, 481 F.2d 1028, 1033 (2d Cir.1973), *cert. denied*, 414 U.S. 1033, 94 S.Ct. 462, 38 L.Ed.2d 324 (1973), when he said:

> The management by a few guards of a large number of prisoners, not usually the most gentle or tractable of men and women, may require and justify the occasional use of a degree of intentional force. Not every push or shove, even if it may later seem unnecessary in the peace of the judge's chambers, violates a prisoner's constitutional right. In determining whether the constitutional line has been crossed, a court must look to such factors as the need for the application of force, the relationship between the need and the amount of force that was used, the extent of injury inflicted, and whether force was applied in a good faith effort to maintain or restore discipline or maliciously and sadistically for the very purpose of causing harm.

Johnson v. Glick has since been cited with approval by the Supreme Court of the United States. The first such citation that this court has been able to locate is *Ingraham v. Wright*, 430 U.S. 651, 669, 97 S.Ct. 1401, 1411, 51 L.Ed.2d 711 (1977) and the most recent citation was January 21, 1986 in *Davidson v. Cannon*, — U.S. —, 106 S.Ct. 668, 88 L.Ed.2d 677 (1986).

Johnson v. Glick was also cited with approval the first time by the Court of Appeals for the Seventh Circuit in *Potter v. Clark*, 497 F.2d 1206 (7th Cir.1974) and was first cited with approval by this court in *Lock v. Jenkins*, 464 F.Supp. 541 (N.D. Ind.1978).

Thus, on November 24, 1982, the *Johnson v. Glick* reading of Amendment VIII was clearly established here and elsewhere.

On January 21, 1986, the Supreme Court of the United States decided *Davidson v. Cannon*, — U.S. —, 106 S.Ct. 668 and *Daniels v. Williams*, — U.S. —, 106 S.Ct. 662, 88 L.Ed.2d 662.

The Supreme Court has recently espoused a measure of conduct in two cases which must be shown before a constitutional infringement protected by 42 U.S.C. § 1983 is implicated. Second, and more importantly, the Court emphasized that only those rights directly derived from the Constitution, its Bill of Rights, and Amendment will be protected by 42 U.S.C. § 1983.

In *Daniels v. Williams*, — U.S. —, 106 S.Ct. 662, 88 L.Ed.2d 662 (1986), the Court reviewed the § 1983 complaint of an inmate who argued that his liberty interest of freedom from bodily injury "without due process of law" within the meaning of the Fourteenth Amendment had been abridged when the jail staff left a pillow case on the jail floor which the plaintiff slipped on resulting in physical injury. At 106 S.Ct. 664, the Court cited its prior holding in *Parratt v. Taylor*, 451 U.S. 527, 101 S.Ct. 1908, 68 L.Ed.2d 420 (1981), wherein it held that all that need be shown in a § 1983 suit is that a constitutional deprivation occurred and that there is no requirement of a showing of the defendant's "state of mind". The Court concluded that the unintentional loss of a liberty, a right, property, or personal injury resulting from negligent action does not rise to a level which is protected by the Fourteenth Amendment:

> To hold that injury caused by such conduct is a deprivation within the meaning of the Fourteenth Amendment would trivialize the centuries old principle of due process of law.

106 S.Ct. at 665.

The Court, at 106 S.Ct. 666, made it clear that only those rights which are traditionally derived from an uncluttered and pristine reading of the Constitution, its Bill of Rights and Amendments will trigger Fourteenth Amendment protection:

> Our Constitution deals with the large concerns of the governors and the gov-

erned, but it does not purport to supplant traditional tort law in laying down rules of conduct to regulate liability for injuries that attend living together in society. We have previously rejected reasoning that "would make of the Fourteenth Amendment a font of tort law to be superimposed upon whatever systems may already be administered by the States," *Paul v. Davis*, 424 U.S. 693, 701, 96 S.Ct. 1155, 1160, 47 L.Ed.2d 405 (1976), quoted in *Parratt v. Taylor*, 451 U.S., at 544, 101 S.Ct., at 1917.

The Court in *Daniels* concluded that the actions of the defendants of leaving a towel on a floor did not rise to the level of conduct which implicates the Due Process Clause of the Fourteenth Amendment.

Where a government official's act causing injury to life, liberty or property is merely negligent "no procedure for compensation is constitutionally required." *Parratt*, 451 U.S. at 548 [101 S.Ct. at 1919] (POWELL, J., concurring in result (footnote omitted).

106 S.Ct. at 666.

The Court emphasized its narrow interpretation of those subject matters which legitimately can claim ancestry in the Constitution:

That injuries inflicted by governmental negligence are not addressed by the United States Constitution is not to say that they may not raise significant legal concerns and lead to the creation of protectable legal interests. The enactment of tort claim statutes, for example, reflect the view that injuries caused by such negligence should generally be redressed. It is no reflection on either the breadth of the United States Constitution or the importance of traditional tort law to say that they do not address the same concerns. (footnotes omitted).

106 S.Ct. at 666.

In *Davidson v. Cannon*, — U.S. —, 106 S.Ct. 668, 88 L.Ed.2d 677 (1986), another prison case, the plaintiff, an inmate, filed a § 1983 action against prison administrators alleging that they had abridged his right not to be subjected to cruel and unusual punishment as proscribed by the Eighth Amendment, and his right not to be deprived of personal security without due process of law as protected by the Fourteenth Amendment. Factually, the plaintiff asserted that he had sent a written message to a prison administrator informing the administrator that he had been physically threatened by a fellow inmate and that he feared assault from the inmate whose name was specified. Prison administrators basically ignored the message. The plaintiff was soon thereafter assaulted by the specified inmate by use of a fork, resulting in wounds to plaintiff's face, neck, head and body, and a broken nose. While citing its decision in *Daniels, supra*, the Court again held that the defendants' inattention to the written message did not rise beyond a level of conduct which could be described as negligent. The Court held that even though serious injury resulted from defendants' conduct, the plaintiff was not protected by the Due Process Clause of the Fourteenth Amendment. *Davidson*, 106 S.Ct. at 670.

The plaintiff in *Davidson* attempted to distinguish and isolate the substantive claim (not to be deprived of personal security) from the procedural claim by arguing that his claim was "purely procedural," thus circumventing the requirement that plaintiff must show conduct beyond negligence. The Court reaffirmed that such an argument must fail because the procedural aspect of the Fourteenth Amendment is only triggered if any underlying substantive right is at issue:

In an effort to limit the potentially broad sweep of his claim, petitioner emphasizes that he "does not ask this Court to read the Constitution of an absolute guarantor of his liberty from assault by a fellow prisoner, even if that assault is caused by the negligence of his jailers." Brief for Petitioner 17. Describing his claim as one of "procedural due process, pure and simple," *Id.*, at 14, all he asks is that New Jersey provide him a remedy. But the Fourteenth Amendment does not require a remedy when there has been no "deprivation" of a protected interest. *Davidson*, 106 S.Ct. at 670. The Court in *Davidson* concluded that the complaint failed because "the protections of the Due Process Clause, whether procedural or substantive, are just not triggered by lack of due care by prison officials." *Davidson*, 106 S.Ct. at 671.

Most recently, at least one judge of our Court of Appeals has summarized: "Negligence is not itself actionable. *Daniels v. Williams*, [— U.S. —] 106 S.Ct. 662 [88 L.Ed.2d 662] (1986)." *Kirchoff v. Flynn*, 786 F.2d 320 (7th Cir.1986). *See also Bodine v. Elkhart County Election Board*, 788 F.2d 1270, 1272 (7th Cir.1986).

Given the careful and restrained analysis of Judge Friendly in *Johnson v. Glick* and considering the same in the context of *Davidson* and *Daniels*, it is this court's conclusion that the conduct of Officer Kirkpatrick in this case goes well beyond the concepts of negligence as described in the *Davidson-Daniels* cases.

This court is well aware of the constitutional inhibitions that exist when inmates are locked in a cell. In *Lock v. Jenkins*, an appeal from this judge and court, see 464 F.Supp. 541, Judge Fairchild, speaking for the Court of Appeals in 641 F.2d 488, 496 stated:

The October 11, 1975 tear gassing of Carpenter and Lock was found to be needed under the circumstances then existing "to maintain and restore discipline and order," 464 F.Supp. at 555, and to be in a not unreasonable amount. Although the record demonstrates conflicting testimony about the amount of gas used, the appellant did not challenge that finding as clearly erroneous and we accept it as true. Testimony indicated that the safekeepers were engaged in inciting to riot at a time of tremendous tension in the prison following an attempted escape and the taking hostage of the prison warden and several others. We believe that the facts shown regarding this incident constitute one of the rare occasions when

use of tear gas against persons locked in cells was not justified.

On the contrary, we find that the use of gas on June 25 to retrieve a metal food tray from safekeeper Carpenter was constitutionally impermissible. Although defense witnesses testified, and the court agreed, that the tray constituted a potential weapon, nothing in the record demonstrates how the tray could be used as a weapon as long as Carpenter was locked in his cell. Although we recognize that significant destruction of prison property by a person locked in a cell might justify the use of tear gas, we do not believe that the possible damage to the tray rises to that level.

Similarly impermissible was the use of gas on April 21 to stop safekeepers Hunt and Brown from shouting and uttering threats.

Recognizing as Judge Fairchild did in footnote 8 at page 491 thereof that some differences exist conceptually between pretrial detainees and convicted prisoners, in the case of pretrial detainees the rationalization must be under the Due Process Clause of the Fourteenth Amendment whereas with convicted prisoners that rationalization may be under the Eighth Amendment. In either event, basically the same values are considered and the same kinds of factual situations are presented to the courts for decision.

The above quotation from *Lock v. Jenkins* very clearly indicates the constitutional inhibitions that the Eighth Amendment places on correctional officers in dealing with prisoners who are locked in their cells. It is not accidental that both Judge Fairchild and this court have set out virtually the same quotation from Judge Friendly.

It is not here necessary to determine whether or not the interchange between Daniels and Kirkpatrick justified the latter throwing hot water on the former. This court leans very heavily in the direction that it did not, especially considering the above quoted statement from *Lock v. Jenkins*. What this court must decide, given all of the circumstances whether or not the conduct of throwing approximately six gallons of hot water into a small 9×11 cell occupied by two death row inmates was a manifestation of deliberate indifference as that standard was established by Justice Marshall in *Estelle v. Gamble*, 429 U.S. 97, 97 S.Ct. 285, 50 L.Ed.2d 251 (1976). In this context this court also assumes that claim for a violation of the Eighth Amendment based solely on negligence would fall under the weight of the *Davidson* and *Daniels* decisions and would also be outside of the scope of any claim under § 1983.

In *Shelby County Jail Inmates v. Westlake*, 798 F.2d 1085, 1093 n 10, District Judge Sarah Evans Barker gave the following instruction:

> Mere negligence or inadvertence on the part of the county officials is not sufficient to sustain a violation of the Eighth Amendment. County officials must act in callous indifference to the dangers faced by a prisoner or intentionally inflict cruel and unusual punishment before they will incur liability for an Eighth Amendment violation.
>
> In order to show callous indifference, plaintiffs must prove the existence of a "pervasive risk of harm" from other inmates, and that jail officials failed to reasonably respond, knowing of that risk. A pervasive risk of harm may be established by proving that violence or sexual assaults occur with sufficient frequency that inmates are put in reasonable fear for their safety and to reasonably apprise prison officials of the existence of the problem and the need for protective measures. Once a pervasive risk has been established, it must be determined whether the jail officials reasonably responded to that risk.

That instruction was explicitly approved by Judge Wood, speaking for the Court of Appeals in that case and after considering the array of authority concluded:

> The cases have required the plaintiffs to prove deliberate or callous indifference, evidenced by an actual intent to violate

the inmate's rights or reckless disregard for the inmate's rights, in order to prevail on an Eighth Amendment claim. Citing *Duckworth v. Franzen*, 780 F.2d 645, 652–53 (7th Cir.1985); *Watts v. Laurent*, 774 F.2d 168, 172 (7th Cir.1985), cert. denied, —— U.S. ——, 106 S.Ct. 1466, 89 L.Ed.2d 722 (1986); and *Benson v. Cady*, 761 F.2d 335, 339 (7th Cir.1985).

To decide the question of deliberate indifference of Kirkpatrick, the focus is on his total relevant conduct. Given these circumstances and especially given the fact that the plaintiff in this case was not a direct participant in the interchange between Kirkpatrick and Daniels, his conduct was certainly recklessly indifferent to the rights of Burris as were defined at least 13 years ago by Judge Friendly in *Johnson v. Glick*. It is possible to hold that the mere act of throwing hot water into a small cell occupied by two inmates violates the Eighth Amendment values and that the Court of Appeals' decision in *Lock v. Jenkins* supports that result. Certainly the act of throwing hot water into this cell that might cause burns and the attendant pain and injury to another occupant goes well beyond simple negligence and establishes a deliberate indifference as defined in *Estelle v. Gamble*.

This court had a chance to see and hear the plaintiff testify under oath and finds his version of the events here involved basically credible. A considerable amount of the documentary evidence submitted by the defendant is consistent with the plaintiff's versions of these events. It should also be here emphasized that the court is not following any inference against this defendant for his failure to be present at the trial and testify. This court accepts the defendant's proffered explanation for his absence.

The violation of rights under the Eighth Amendment involved here are substantial rather than just procedural and certainly this court was made aware of that distinction by Justice Stewart in *Owen v. Lash*, 682 F.2d 648 (7th Cir.1982). *See also Red-*

ding v. Fairman, 717 F.2d 1105 (7th Cir. 1983).

Where substantive constitutional rights are violated, damages can be presumed even in the absence of discernible consequential damages. See *Lenard v. Argento*, 699 F.2d 874, 889 (7th Cir.), *cert. denied*, 464 U.S. 815, 104 S.Ct. 69, 78 L.Ed.2d 84 (1983); *Owen v. Lash*, 682 F.2d 648, 658–59 (7th Cir.1982).

In *Carey v. Piphus*, 435 U.S. 247, 98 S.Ct. 1042, 55 L.Ed.2d 252 (1978), the Supreme Court of the United States reversed a decision of the Court of Appeals for the Seventh Circuit, which had held that students were entitled to recover substantial non-punitive damages without a showing of consequential injury when they were denied procedural due process. Since the rights involved here are substantive rather than procedural, this court is not constrained by that holding in *Carey v. Piphus*. This court is also familiar with *Kincaid v. Rusk*, 670 F.2d 737, 745–46 (7th Cir.1982), in which the plaintiff sought damages against the Sheriff of Tippecanoe County, Indiana, for violation of both due process and First Amendment rights in denying him reading material. The Court of Appeals for the Seventh Circuit held that the plaintiff has failed to prove compensible damages, but was entitled to nominal damages.

An examination of the foregoing authorities convinces this court that even in the absence of permanent injuries, this plaintiff is entitled to damages for the mere act of violating substantial constitutional rights which did cause him specific personal pain and suffering. This court has determined that the reasonable amount of such damages should be in the sum of $100.00.

Therefore, judgment shall enter for the plaintiff, Gary Burris, in the sum of $100.00 against the defendant, Officer Jay Kirkpatrick, and costs are assessed in favor of the plaintiff against the defendant.

IT IS SO ORDERED.

VOLUME III

CHAPTER 2   RIGHTS IN LEGAL PROCEEDINGS

Courts have repeatedly stated that an inmate has a constitutional right to redress before the courts. The right embraces a wide range of support to which the inmate is entitled, including a library, a right to prepare a trial and the means to prepare it. In *Milton v. Morris*, 767 F.2d 1443 (9th Cir. 1985), the court found that the prisoner was inhibited in preparing his suit. In *Nordgren v. Milliken*, 762 F.2d 851 (10th Cir. 1985), the court spelled out limitations on the rights of indigent inmates to access the courts and to have assistance in preparing their complaints.

Introductions in previous volumes:

III: 21; VI: 317; VII: 399; VIII: 367

Johnny B. MILTON,
Petitioner-Appellant,

v.

P.J. MORRIS, Warden,
Respondent-Appellee.

No. 83-2499.

United States Court of Appeals,
Ninth Circuit.

Argued and Submitted Dec. 12, 1984.

Decided Aug. 12, 1985.

Before HUG, SCHROEDER, and BEEZER, Circuit Judges.

SCHROEDER, Circuit Judge.

Johnny B. Milton was convicted in California state court of robbery and attempted murder. After exhausting state collateral remedies, he sought relief in federal court and now appeals the district court's denial of his petition for a writ of habeas corpus under 28 U.S.C. § 2253.

Milton chose to represent himself rather than be represented by the public defender who, Milton thought, had a conflict of interest. Despite Milton's and the trial court's efforts to see that he had resources to assist him in the preparation of his defense, he went to trial without having had access to research materials, advisory counsel, means to serve subpoenas, or effective use of a telephone. He claims a denial of due process, relying upon the right of self-representation established in *Faretta v. California*, 422 U.S. 806, 95 S.Ct. 2525, 45 L.Ed.2d 562 (1975), and the right of meaningful access to the courts recognized in *Bounds v. Smith*, 430 U.S. 817, 97 S.Ct. 1491, 52 L.Ed.2d 72 (1977). We hold that the petition should be granted.

FACTS

The facts are not materially disputed. Shortly after his arrest, Milton sought private representation because of an alleged conflict of interest in the public defender's office. The trial court held a hearing on his contentions and denied Milton's motion to appoint private counsel. Milton then chose to represent himself rather than accept the services of the public defender. At the time of the denial of his motion, Milton informed the court that the facilities of the county jail were inadequate for him to prepare a defense and requested five phone calls a day, which the court granted.

A few weeks later Milton moved for access to more current law books. He pointed out that the most recent lawbooks in the county jail were twenty-seven years old. He also complained of a lack of access to the telephone. The court granted him a total of six long distance and seven local telephone calls but denied his request for access to legal materials.

Jail authorities apparently misinterpreted the orders regarding phone calls, and his phone use was in fact severely limited. When this was called to the attention of the trial judge, the trial judge continued the date for trial and granted the request for an investigator. However, because Milton lacked a telephone book, and was still limited by jail authorities in his use of the telephone, he could not find an investigator.

The week before his trial, which was scheduled for a Monday, the trial court appointed a runner to assist in the service of subpoenas. However, jail authorities prevented Milton from contacting the runner on at least one occasion prior to trial. The trial court eventually granted Milton's motion for an expert witness, but not until the Friday immediately preceding the trial.

On the day of trial, Milton had not been able to contact any expert witness or to procure an investigator. Having had no access to current lawbooks, witnesses, or an investigator, Milton, on the day of trial, refused to participate. Not surprisingly, he was found guilty.

DISCUSSION

Milton's difficulties began when he challenged the ability of the assistant public defender to represent him because of a claimed conflict of interest. His threshold position here is that the state trial court failed to conduct an adequate inquiry to determine whether his allegation was correct. See Holloway v. Arkansas, 435 U.S. 475, 482, 98 S.Ct. 1173, 1177, 55 L.Ed.2d 426 (1978). We conclude that the trial court's inquiry was sufficient to determine that no conflict existed that would impede representation. See United States v. Lee, 589 F.2d 980, 991 (9th Cir.) (brief discussion showing the absence of any real conflict is sufficient inquiry), cert. denied, 444 U.S. 969, 100 S.Ct. 460, 62 L.Ed.2d 382 (1979).

We agree with the state that it offered services of an attorney and the state trial court did not violate Milton's due process rights by refusing to order the state to provide private counsel. As a practical matter, when Milton declined the services of the public defender, he put himself in the same position as the defendant who chooses to represent himself, as has been declared his right under Faretta, 422 U.S. 806, 95 S.Ct. 2525, 45 L.Ed.2d 562.

The question thus becomes whether Milton's due process rights were violated when he was tried without having had any meaningful opportunity to prepare his defense. We hold, in the circumstances of this case, that they were. Despite timely and reasonable requests, Milton was isolated from any means to prepare. The trial court's own orders, which recognized the legitimacy of his need and which would have provided possible avenues of preparation through telephone usage and a runner, were not heeded. After Milton elected to represent himself, the state not only affirmatively failed to provide defense resources, but also materially impeded use of the minimal tools for defense preparation which the trial court tried to ensure.

The state offers no justification, such as cost or security exigencies, for what occurred. We do not believe that a defendant who exercises his right, under Faretta, to conduct his own defense must subject himself to the possibility that he will have, through circumstances wholly beyond his control, no opportunity to prepare that defense.[1] The right guaranteed by the fourteenth and sixth amendments to reject a lawyer and represent oneself is premised upon the right of the defendant to make a defense:

The Sixth Amendment does not provide merely that a defense shall be made for the accused; it grants to the accused personally the right to make his defense. It is the accused, not counsel, who must be "informed of the nature and cause of the accusation," who must be "confronted with the witnesses against him," and who must be accorded "compulsory process for obtaining witnesses in his favor." Although not stated in the Amendment in so many words, the right to self-representation—to make one's own defense personally—is thus necessarily implied by the structure of the Amendment. The right to defend is given directly to the accused; for it is he who

---

1. In this case, the defendant rejected the assistance of counsel with the understanding that he would at least have minimal telephone access. Since even that means of access to the defendant was effectively denied, it is doubtful whether the defendant's decision to reject the public defender and represent himself was knowing and voluntary as required by Faretta.

suffers the consequences if the defense fails.

Faretta, 422 U.S. at 819–20, 95 S.Ct. at 2533–34 (footnote omitted). The accused in this case, who made every effort to prepare a defense and was thwarted in those efforts, was denied his "right to make his defense." *Id.* at 819, 95 S.Ct. at 2533.

We need not determine in this case whether *Bounds*, 430 U.S. 817, 97 S.Ct. 1491, 52 L.Ed.2d 72, which involved an unrepresented prisoner seeking collateral review of his conviction, should be interpreted as placing an affirmative duty upon the state to provide a library for the defendant who has rejected the assistance of counsel for trial.[2] *Faretta* controls this case.

Faretta holds that the rights guaranteed by the sixth amendment are personal to the accused. "The rights to notice, confrontation, and compulsory process" mean, at a minimum, that time to prepare and some access to materials and witnesses are fundamental to a meaningful right of representation. *Faretta*, 422 U.S. at 818, 95 S.Ct. at 2532; *see also United States v. Portillo*, 633 F.2d 1313, 1324–25 (9th Cir. 1980) (when defendant has sufficient time and ability to conduct research, his right to self-representation is not denied), *cert. denied*, 450 U.S. 1043, 101 S.Ct. 1763, 68 L.Ed.2d 241 (1981)). An incarcerated defendant may not meaningfully exercise his right to represent himself without access to law books, witnesses, or other tools to prepare a defense. We are mindful that this right is not unlimited. Security considerations and avoidance of abuse by opportunistic or vacillating defendants may require special adjustments. *See United States v. Chatman*, 584 F.2d 1358, 1360 (4th Cir.

1978) (security risk); *United States v. Lane*, 718 F.2d 226, 232–34 (7th Cir.1983) (abuse of judicial process). Yet, as the Supreme Court recently stated, "A defendant's right to self-representation plainly encompasses certain specific rights to have his voice heard." *McKaskle v. Wiggins*, 465 U.S. 168, 104 S.Ct. 944, 949, 79 L.Ed.2d 122 (1984); *cf. Mayberry v. Pennsylvania*, 400 U.S. 455, 468, 91 S.Ct. 499, 506, 27 L.Ed.2d 532 (1971) (Burger, J. concurring) (trial "integrity" mandates that the judge take measures to ensure that due process is met).

The state relies on *United States v. Wilson*, 690 F.2d 1267 (9th Cir.1982), *cert. denied*, —— U.S. ——, 104 S.Ct. 205, 78 L.Ed.2d 178 (1983), in which a defendant who wished to represent himself had counsel appointed to represent him. At trial the defendant complained that he lacked access to a library, but he agreed to have appointed counsel question the witnesses. We held that his conviction should not be reversed simply because he had been denied access to a law library to prepare his defense. We held that since he had an appointed lawyer able to do research had he requested it, and since he received legal assistance in presenting his defense at trial, he was not entitled to "insist on an avenue of [defendant's] own choosing." *Id.* at 1271 (citing *Storseth v. Spellman*, 654 F.2d 1349, 1353 (9th Cir.1981)).

This case is different. Here, the defendant lacked all means of preparing and presenting a defense, and was unjustifiably prevented from contacting a lawyer or others who could have assisted him. We therefore hold that the state may not un-

---

2. In *Bounds*, the Court declared, in a post-conviction context, that prisoners have a right of "adequate, effective, and meaningful" access to the courts. 430 U.S. at 822, 97 S.Ct. at 1495. This right does not mandate use of an up-to-date legal library by the prisoners for post-conviction motions when other adequate outside legal assistance is available. *See, e.g., Spates v. Manson*, 644 F.2d 80 (2d Cir.1981); *Kelsey v. State*, 622 F.2d 956 (8th Cir.1980). The extent to which *Bounds* creates rights for pre-trial detainees who decline counsel remains unsettled.

Compare United States v. Lane, 718 F.2d 226, 230 (7th Cir.1983) (court access as defined in *Bounds* is applicable to pre-trial detainees) (citing *Johnson by Johnson v. Brelje*, 701 F.2d 1201 (7th Cir.1983)) *with United States v. Chatman*, 584 F.2d 1358 (4th Cir.1978) (state satisfied *Bounds* with the offering of counsel for representation). *United States v. Wilson*, 690 F.2d 1267, 1271–72 (9th Cir.1982), *cert. denied*, —— U.S. ——, 104 S.Ct. 205, 78 L.Ed.2d 178 (1983), does not decide the question since the defendant there had accepted representation by counsel.

reasonably hinder the defendant's efforts to prepare his own defense.

Our holding in this case is not inconsistent with *United States v. Chatman*, 584 F.2d 1358 (4th Cir.1978), upon which we relied in *Wilson*, 690 F.2d at 1271–72. At the time that Chatman waived his right to counsel, he was being held in segregated confinement for threatening the judge and repeatedly assaulting prison guards. On the day of his trial he demanded a continuance and access to the law library. The court held that *Bounds*, 430 U.S. 817, 97 S.Ct. 1491, 52 L.Ed.2d 72, did not require that Chatman have access to the law library after he had validly waived his right to counsel. "[W]e do not read *Bounds* to give an option to the prisoner as to the form in which he elects to obtain legal assistance." *Chatman*, 584 F.2d at 1360. The petitioner in this case is not arguing that *Bounds* entitles him to any particular form of legal assistance. He was deprived of the alternative assistance which the trial court tried to provide.

Other circuits, consistent with our decisions here and in *Wilson*, have held that a defendant who chooses to represent himself does not have a due process right of access to a court maintained library, so long as he is afforded some alternative means for assistance in the preparation of his defense. *See United States v. Lane*, 718 F.2d 226 (7th Cir.1983); *United States v. Garza*, 664 F.2d 135, 142 (7th Cir.1981), *cert. denied*, 455 U.S. 993, 102 S.Ct. 1620, 71 L.Ed.2d 854 (1982).

The defendant in this case had no means to prepare a defense. When he was denied communication with the outside world, he was denied due process.

The judgment of the district court is reversed and the matter remanded with instructions to grant the petition.

HUG, Circuit Judge, concurring:

I concur in the majority opinion but add these additional thoughts.

There is a distinction between offering a defendant the services of counsel to conduct his defense and offering the counsel's assistance to a defendant who wishes to conduct his own defense. A defendant has the sixth amendment right under *Faretta v. California*, 422 U.S. 806, 95 S.Ct. 2525, 45 L.Ed.2d 562 (1975) to refuse the former and to elect to conduct his own defense. In doing so, he may be offered the assistance of counsel in a variety of ways—for pretrial preparation and during trial. This assistance of counsel to a confined defendant would provide an adequate access to the resources necessary for him to conduct his defense.

The Supreme Court in *Bounds v. Smith*, 430 U.S. 817, 97 S.Ct. 1491, 52 L.Ed.2d 72 (1977) addressed the question of what constituted meaningful access to the courts by a prisoner seeking collateral relief. Surely no less than those minimum requirements must be afforded to a defendant who is initially defending himself against criminal charges. In conducting his own defense, counsel's assistance would meet these requirements because it would provide access to the outside world and a law library through counsel. However, if a defendant is only offered the services of an attorney to conduct his defense and if he refuses that assistance and is offered no other assistance from counsel, then the defendant must be assured of alternate, adequate access to the resources necessary to conduct his defense through other means.

In this case, other means were authorized by the district court, but not allowed to the defendant. As the majority opinion points out, this deprived the defendant of a reasonable opportunity to conduct his defense. He was not offered counsel's assistance to help him prepare and conduct his own defense.

The case of *United States v. Wilson*, 690 F.2d 1267 (9th Cir.1982) is consistent with this analysis because the defendant in that case was afforded adequate legal assistance from counsel. In *United States v. Chatman*, 584 F.2d 1358 (4th Cir.1978), it appears that the defendant rejected the assistance of counsel in conducting his own defense. *Id.* at 1360. Thus, *Chatman*, as construed, is also consistent with this analysis.

In summary, a defendant in jail is constitutionally entitled to conduct his own defense. If he elects to do so by rejecting the services of an attorney to *conduct* his defense, he cannot be confined to his jail simply to look at the four walls and appear on the day of trial to defend himself. He must be afforded reasonable access to resources, and providing a counsel's assistance in conducting his own defense is one way of accomplishing this. Other reasonable alternatives consistent with jail or prison management can be utilized. The defendant does not have the right to dictate the alternative chosen so long as a reasonable one is afforded. However, the rejection of an attorney to conduct his defense cannot be considered as a waiver of the reasonable access to the resources necessary to defend himself. To do so would render *Faretta* meaningless to a confined defendant.

BEEZER, Circuit Judge, concurring:

I concur in the result but on a much narrower ground. The state court judge in this case reasonably concluded that in order to adequately prepare his defense, appellant needed to make a certain number of local and long distance phone calls, and to have access to a runner, investigator, and expert witness. The court ordered various custodial officials to permit appellant access to these resources, but later expressly found that its order was violated. Under these circumstances, we can conclude that appellant's due process rights were violated without having to address the difficult issue of the exact scope of the right to prepare a defense. *See Bounds v. Smith*, 430 U.S. 817, 97 S.Ct. 1491, 52 L.Ed.2d 72 (1977); *Faretta v. California*, 422 U.S. 806, 95 S.Ct. 2525, 45 L.Ed.2d 562 (1975); *United States v. Wilson*, 690 F.2d 1267 (9th Cir.1982), *cert. denied*, — U.S. —, 104 S.Ct. 205, 78 L.Ed.2d 178 (1983). I therefore concur without expressing any opinion on the application of these three cases to the case at bar.

Steven Richards NORDGREN, Douglas
Yoakam, Ray Dodge and John C.
Bolsinger, Plaintiffs-Appellants,

v.

William MILLIKEN, et al.,
Defendants-Appellees.

No. 82–1668.

United States Court of Appeals,
Tenth Circuit.

May 20, 1985.

Before HOLLOWAY, Chief Judge, BAR-
RETT, Circuit Judge, and BOHANON, District Judge.*

HOLLOWAY, Chief Judge.

In this civil rights action plaintiffs, indigent Utah prison inmates, allege that during their incarceration they were denied
their right to meaningful access to the
courts in violation of the Due Process and
Equal Protection Clauses of the Fourteenth
Amendment. Summary judgment was entered in favor of defendants and plaintiffs
appeal. We affirm.

I

Plaintiffs are involved in legal actions
which they are attempting to prosecute or
defend pro se. Specifically plaintiff Nordgren claims that he is the defendant in a
paternity suit and that he is the plaintiff in
a federal civil rights action brought against
the Salt Lake County Jail and the County
Sheriff which was dismissed, appealed, remanded and is pending in the United States
District Court for the District of Utah.

Plaintiff Yoakam alleges that he is seeking to modify his divorce decree and that
he has filed an action against Salt Lake
County and various officers thereof for
conversion of his guns. Plaintiff Dodge
claims that he has several cases pending in
the United States District Court in the nature of civil rights actions against the staff

---

* The Honorable Luther L. Bohanon, United
States District Judge of the Eastern, Northern
and Western Districts of Oklahoma, sitting by
designation.

of the Utah State Prison as a result of due process and/or cruel and unusual punishment violations. Plaintiff Bolsinger claims that he has several actions pending in the United States District Court in the nature of civil rights actions against the staff of the Salt Lake County jail and other county officials as a result of the treatment he received while incarcerated in the County Jail. I.R. 156–64.

Plaintiffs say that they petitioned the trial courts on various occasions to appoint legal counsel to represent them beyond the initial stages and these courts refused to do so. *Id.* at 157.[1] Plaintiffs also say that two legal aid organizations in Salt Lake County will not assist them, *id.* at 173, and that defendants have refused to provide a law library or provide legal assistance be-

yond assisting plaintiffs in filing the initial pro se pleadings. *Id.* at 157.

The United States magistrate in his report and recommendation on the parties' motions for summary judgment found that "[t]he State of Utah has elected to provide at the prison minimal law library facilities and services of contract attorneys to assist inmates in preparing pleadings to initiate court actions and proceedings."[2] *Id.* at 233. The magistrate also found that "[t]here is no constitutional requirement that the assistance of lawyers be provided to the plaintiffs by the defendants in the defense or prosecution of civil actions beyond the pleading stage." *Id.* at 239. This report of the magistrate was accepted and defendants' motion for summary judgment

---

1. In *Nordgren v. Mitchell,* 716 F.2d 1335, 1339–40 (10th Cir.1983), we held that neither due process nor equal protection requires Utah to appoint counsel for all indigent prisoners who are defendants in paternity cases.

2. The magistrate cited the following provisions of the contract between the State Division of Corrections and the contracting firm as being pertinent:

> "Whereas, the DIVISION ... recognizes the need to provide additional legal assistance to prisoners of the Utah State Prison in the preparation and filing of initial legal documents in any civil matters (state or federal) other than those handled by the Salt Lake Legal Defender Association, including but not limited to civil rights actions, divorce, child custody, guardianship, and tort liability actions ...

>   . . .

> "(4) LAW FIRM agrees to provide attorneys who shall provide legal advice, consultation, and assistance to inmates regarding the preparation and filing of initial pleadings in those civil actions referred to above. In cases determined to be meritorious and founded in law, attorneys provided by LAW FIRM shall have discretion in determining which cases are appropriate for court-appointed counsel, and in those cases shall prepare and file motions to the court for court appointed counsel and motions to proceed in forma pauperis. In cases not appropriate for court appointed counsel or where the inmate is not indigent, or where the court declines to appoint counsel, he/she shall be referred to private counsel. Attorneys provided by LAW FIRM shall make good faith efforts to attempt to secure counsel, through court appointment, private counsel, or legal aid agencies, to pursue legal matters after the initial pleadings. In the

performance of all obligations under this contract, attorneys provided by LAW FIRM shall conform to the requirements imposed on them by the applicable laws of the State of Utah and the Code of Professional Responsibility.

>   . . .

> "Nothing herein shall preclude attorneys provided by LAW FIRM in their discretion from representing inmates at later stages of the proceedings in those civil actions filed; however, monies appropriated by the DIVISION under this contract are strictly for purposes of initial consultation, preparation and filing of initial pleadings and are not to be expended by LAW FIRM for providing attorneys to furnish legal assistance to inmates at later stages of any legal proceedings. Attorneys provided by LAW FIRM shall not be obligated to represent inmates at later stages of the process in those civil actions filed." I R. 234.

The Utah State Department of Social Services, Division of Corrections, and the Salt Lake Legal Defender Association entered into a contract whereby the Salt Lake Legal Defender Association agreed to provide "legal assistance to prisoners (1) in preparation, filing and representing persons on writs of habeas corpus in the Third Judicial District Court and appeals in the Utah Supreme Court, and (2) in the preparation and filing of petitions for writs of habeas corpus in the United States District Court, District of Utah, Central Division, and (3) in advising them of any rights and appropriate procedures to perfect any appeals of their criminal convictions in the Utah Supreme Court." *Id.* at 226–27. These contracts were in force for the years 1981 and 1982 and similar contracts were in force for the year 1980. *Id.* at 217.

was granted by the district judge. *Id.* at 245–48.

II

Plaintiffs argue on appeal that defendants have refused to maintain an adequate and complete law library at the Utah State Prison so that they can properly represent themselves and that there is no adequate alternative to a law library to provide Utah prison inmates with meaningful access to the courts. Plaintiffs say that meaningful access to the courts entails legal assistance at all stages of judicial proceedings at the trial level, not just the initial pleading stage; that legal assistance must be available to prison inmates for all types of civil cases; and that legal assistance must be provided to inmates regardless of whether their claims are deemed meritorious by prison officials.

Defendants say that they do not claim to have an adequate law library at the prison. Brief of Appellees 3. They contend, however, that there is an adequate alternative to a law library which provides inmates at the Utah State Prison with meaningful access to the courts. They say that the obligation of the State to provide meaningful access to the courts is satisfied through the services of contract attorneys; that there is no constitutional requirement that the assistance of attorneys be provided to inmates in the defense or prosecution of civil actions beyond the initial pleading stage; and that what is "meaningful" access to the courts must be considered in light of "reasonableness" in the prison setting, giving deference to prison administrators' discretion.

"The right of access to the courts is basic to our system of government, and it is well established today that it is one of the fundamental rights protected by the Constitution." *Ryland v. Shapiro*, 708 F.2d 967, 971 (5th Cir.1983). Referring to *Chambers v. Baltimore & Ohio Railroad Co.*, 207 U.S. 142, 28 S.Ct. 34, 52 L.Ed. 143 (1907),

the *Ryland* court stated that the Supreme Court "viewed the right of access to the courts as one of the privileges and immunities accorded citizens under article 4 of the Constitution and the fourteenth amendment." *Ryland*, 708 F.2d at 971. The Court found "in the first amendment a second constitutional basis for this right of access: 'Certainly the right to petition extends to all departments of Government. The right of access to the courts is indeed but one aspect of the right of petition.'" *Id.* (citing *California Motor Transport Co. v. Trucking Unlimited*, 404 U.S. 508, 510, 92 S.Ct. 609, 611, 30 L.Ed.2d 642 (1972)). "A third constitutional basis for the right of access to the courts is found in the due process clause." *Id.* at 972. In *Wolff v. McDonnell*, 418 U.S. 539, 579, 94 S.Ct. 2963, 2986, 41 L.Ed.2d 935 (1974), the Supreme Court stated that "[t]he right of access to the courts, upon which *Avery* [*Johnson v. Avery*, 393 U.S. 483, 89 S.Ct. 747, 21 L.Ed.2d 718 (1969)] was premised, is founded in the Due Process Clause and assures that no person will be denied the opportunity to present to the judiciary allegations concerning violations of fundamental constitutional rights." [3]

Access to the courts "encompasses all the means a defendant or petitioner might require to get a fair hearing from the judiciary on all charges brought against him or grievances alleged by him." *Gilmore v. Lynch*, 319 F.Supp. 105, 110 (N.D.Cal. 1970), *aff'd sub nom, Younger v. Gilmore*, 404 U.S. 15, 92 S.Ct. 250, 30 L.Ed.2d 142 (1971) (per curiam). That a state prison inmate has a right of access to the courts was first enunciated in *Ex parte Hull*, 312 U.S. 546, 61 S.Ct. 640, 85 L.Ed. 1034 (1941). Annot., 23 A.L.R. Fed. 1, 14 (1975). There the Supreme Court stated that "the state and its officers may not abridge or impair petitioner's right to apply to a federal court for a writ of habeas corpus." *Ex parte Hull*, 312 U.S. 546, 549, 61 S.Ct. 640, 641, 85 L.Ed. 1034 (1941). In *Johnson v. Avery,*

---

3. We note that plaintiffs also allege a denial of their right to meaningful access to the courts in violation of the Equal Protection Clause of the Fourteenth Amendment. We find no reasoning or authority presented by plaintiffs to support this theory.

393 U.S. 483, 490, 89 S.Ct. 747, 751, 21 L.Ed.2d 718 (1969), the Court held that "unless and until the State provides some reasonable alternative to assist inmates in the preparation of petitions for post-conviction relief, it may not validly enforce a regulation ... barring inmates from furnishing such assistance to other prisoners." (footnote omitted). And in *Wolff*, 418 U.S. at 579, 94 S.Ct. at 2986, the Court stated that "the demarcation line between civil rights actions and habeas petitions is not always clear. The Court has already recognized instances where the same constitutional rights might be redressed under either form of relief."

In *Bounds v. Smith*, 430 U.S. 817, 828, 97 S.Ct. 1491, 1498, 52 L.Ed.2d 72 (1977), the Supreme Court defined the duty of the States to protect the right of prisoners to access to the courts by holding that "the fundamental constitutional right of access to the courts requires prison authorities to assist inmates in the preparation and filing of meaningful legal papers by providing prisoners with adequate law libraries or adequate assistance from persons trained in the law." (footnote omitted). *See Ward v. Kort*, 762 F.2d 856 (10th Cir.1985), filed today. Because defendants do not claim that they have an adequate law library at the prison, Brief of Appellees 3, we must determine whether the State of Utah provides prison inmates with adequate assistance from persons trained in the law. *Ward v. Kort, supra.*

Plaintiffs contend that meaningful access to the courts entails legal assistance at all stages of judicial proceedings at the trial level, not just the initial pleading stage. Defendants deny that there is any constitutional requirement of such extensive assistance by attorneys. In *Wolff*, 418 U.S. at 576, 94 S.Ct. at 2984, the Supreme Court stated that "the Fourteenth Amendment due process claim based on access to the courts, *Ex parte Hull*, 312 U.S. 546, 61 S.Ct. 640, 85 L.Ed. 1034 (1941); *Johnson v. Avery*, 393 U.S. 483, 89 S.Ct. 747, 21 L.Ed.2d 718 (1969); *Younger v. Gilmore*, 404 U.S. 15, 92 S.Ct. 250, 30 L.Ed.2d 142 (1971), has not been extended by this Court

to apply further than protecting the ability of an inmate to prepare a petition or complaint." In *Bounds*, 430 U.S. at 828, 97 S.Ct. at 1498, the Court held that the "right of access to the courts requires prison authorities to assist inmates in the *preparation and filing of meaningful legal papers ....*" (emphasis added). And the Court stated that "... our main concern here is 'protecting the ability of an inmate to prepare a petition or complaint,' *Wolff v. McDonnell*, 418 U.S., at 576 [94 S.Ct., at 2984]...." *Id.* at 828 n. 17, 97 S.Ct. at 1498 n. 17; *Ward v. Kort, supra,* at 859.

Most courts have not interpreted *Bounds* as extending the right of access to the courts so as to require special assistance to inmates further than the initial pleading stage. *See Connecticut Bd. of Pardons v. Dumschat*, 452 U.S. 458, 471 n. 4, 101 S.Ct. 2460, 2467 n. 4, 69 L.Ed.2d 158 (1981) (Stevens, J., dissenting, and citing *Bounds*, stated that the Constitution has been applied to issues affecting prisoners including "right to assistance in the filing of legal papers."); *Branch v. Cole*, 686 F.2d 264, 266 n. 1 (5th Cir.1982) (per curiam) (the explicit concern of *Bounds* "was getting inmates through the courtroom door."); *Ramos v. Lamm*, 639 F.2d 559, 584 n. 29 (10th Cir.1980) (in considering whether alternative to law library was adequate, court found evidence failed to show that inmate law library clerks were capable of helping any inmate draft a legal document), *cert. denied*, 450 U.S. 1041, 101 S.Ct. 1759, 68 L.Ed.2d 239 (1981); *Cruz v. Hauck*, 627 F.2d 710, 721 n. 22 (5th Cir.1980) ("[I]nmates are entitled to either access to legal materials or access to counsel for assistance in *filing* habeas corpus and civil rights actions. 430 U.S. at 825–29 [97 S.Ct. at 1496–98]."); *Cf. Carter v. Kamka*, 515 F.Supp. 825, 831 (D.Md.1980) (Legal Assistance Program met "the 'adequacy' requirement, not only in 'the preparation and filing of meaningful legal papers', as required by *Bounds*, but in the entire gamut of representing D O C inmates in civil rights cases, and habeas corpus cases as well."). *But see Bonner v. City of Prichard, Ala.*, 661

F.2d 1206, 1212 (11th Cir.1981) (en banc) (Inmate access to the courts is not "adequate, effective and meaningful" if "it embraces no more than being permitted to file a paper that, without determination of whether it states a claim legally sufficient and within the court's jurisdiction, is subject to dismissal on grounds of convenience to court and litigants.").

We are mindful of the significant claim involved here and its central importance in the protection of all rights of prisoners. Nevertheless in light of the substantial effort already made by the State and the extent of the burden in requiring more, we are persuaded that we should not hold that the right of access to the courts requires more than the assistance of counsel through completion of the complaint for a federal habeas or civil rights action. *Ward v. Kort, supra,* at 860.

III

Plaintiffs also argue that legal assistance must be provided inmates without regard to a determination by prison officials that their claims are meritorious. Plaintiffs say that under defendants' plan no assistance need be given to an inmate on motions to proceed *in forma pauperis* or motions to appoint counsel where the contracting law firm determines the inmate's case to be unmeritorious. Brief of Appellant 23. Defendants argue that the law firm only has discretion in determining which cases are appropriate for court-appointed counsel and that they will apply for appointment of counsel for inmates when appropriate. They maintain that there is no discretion involved in the preparation of initial pleadings; if the inmate wants to file a complaint, the law firm is bound to help draft the complaint. Brief of Appellees 11.

In *Ex parte Hull,* 312 U.S. at 549, 61 S.Ct. at 641, the Supreme Court held that a regulation is invalid that imposes a screening process between an inmate and the court. The Court stated that "the state and its officers may not abridge or impair petitioner's right to apply to a federal court for a writ of habeas corpus. Whether a petition for writ of habeas corpus addressed to a federal court is properly drawn and what allegations it must contain are questions for that court alone to determine." *Id.* We find that procedures followed by the law firm determine only which cases are appropriate for court-appointed counsel and which should be referred to private counsel. *See* note 2, *supra.* These procedures do not violate the principles laid down by the Supreme Court and do not infringe the right of access to the courts.[4]

IV

Accordingly, we conclude that plaintiffs have not shown any constitutional infirmity in the procedures used by the State of Utah amounting to a denial of access to the courts. The agreements with the law firm and the legal defender association, *see* note 2, *supra,* protect the inmates' basic right of access to the courts in connection with both federal habeas and civil rights cases, which is of primary concern. *See Ward v. Kort, supra,* at 860.

AFFIRMED.

---

4. Plaintiffs also contend that a law library or legal assistance must be available to prison inmates for all types of civil cases. Brief of Appellants 21. The argument seems to have no factual basis because in the contract with the Utah State Department of Social Services, Division of Corrections, the law firm agreed to provide "legal advice, consultation and assistance to inmates regarding the preparation and filing of initial pleadings" "in any civil matters (state or federal) other than those handled by the Salt Lake Legal Defender Association, including but not limited to civil rights actions, divorce, child custody, guardianship, and tort liability actions." I R. 220–21.

In *Ward v. Kort, supra,* at 860, we hold that where the State elects to have contract attorneys as an alternative to an adequate law library, plaintiff is entitled to assistance of counsel through the completion of a federal habeas or civil rights complaint, including necessary research and consideration of the facts and the law.

Paul SIMMONS, Plaintiff, Appellant,

v.

Paul G. DICKHAUT and Tony
Somensini, Defendants,
Appellees.

No. 86–1591.

United States Court of Appeals,
First Circuit.

Submitted Oct. 10, 1986.

Decided Nov. 6, 1986.

Before COFFIN, BOWNES, and BREY-   PER CURIAM.
ER, Circuit Judges.

Paul Simmons appeals from the district court's dismissal of his § 1983 complaint. Simmons alleged that the defendants violated his right of access to the courts when they refused to return to him various legal materials. Named as defendants are the superintendent and property officer of MCI Lancaster.

On motion by the state, the district court dismissed under the authority of *Parratt v. Taylor*, 451 U.S. 527, 101 S.Ct. 1908, 68 L.Ed.2d 420 (1981). Simmons argues on appeal that the *Parratt* analysis does not apply to a right of access deprivation. The State argues that *Parratt* applies and precludes relief; that Simmons' complaint is conclusory; and that the retention of legal materials does not state a cause of action.

We address first the nature of the right of access and whether its violation can be redressed under § 1983. The right of access is a discrete, constitutional right, derived from various constitutional sources. It springs in part from the due process clause, *Wolff v. McDonnell*, 418 U.S. 539, 579, 94 S.Ct. 2963, 2986, 41 L.Ed.2d 935 (1974); the privileges and immunities clause, *Chambers v. Baltimore & Ohio Railroad*, 207 U.S. 142, 148, 28 S.Ct. 34, 35, 52 L.Ed. 143 (1907); and the First Amendment, *California Motor Transport Co. v. Trucking Unlimited*, 404 U.S. 508, 513, 92 S.Ct. 609, 613, 30 L.Ed.2d 642 (1972). *See generally Ryland v. Shapiro*, 708 F.2d 967, 971–72 (5th Cir.1983). The right of access is fundamental. *Bounds v. Smith*, 430 U.S. 817, 828, 97 S.Ct. 1491, 1498, 52 L.Ed.2d 72 (1977).

It follows logically that the allegation of intentional violation of the right of access to the courts states a cause of action under § 1983. *Wright v. Newsome*, 795 F.2d 964, 968 (11th Cir.1986); *Jackson v. Procunier*, 789 F.2d 307, 310–11 (5th Cir. 1986); *Sigafus v. Brown*, 416 F.2d 105, 107 (7th Cir.1969); *Morello v. James*, 627 F.Supp. 1571, 1574 (W.D.N.Y.1986).

Many courts have found a cause of action for violation of the right of access stated where it was alleged that prison officials confiscated and/or destroyed legal materials or papers.[1] *E.g., Wright v. Newsome*, 795 F.2d at 968 (allegation that prison officials seized pleadings and law books and destroyed other legal papers states cause of action); *Carter v. Hutto*, 781 F.2d 1028, 1031–32 (4th Cir.1986) (allegation that prison officials confiscated and/or destroyed legal materials, some of which were irreplaceable, states cause of action); *Tyler v. "Ron" Deputy Sheriff or Jailer/Custodian of Prisoners*, 574 F.2d 427, 429 (8th Cir.1978) (taking of prisoner's legal papers states a § 1983 claim if the taking results in interference with or infringement of right of access); *Hiney v. Wilson*, 520 F.2d 589, 591 (2d Cir.1975) (complaint should not have been dismissed because confiscation of legal papers may constitute a denial of access to the courts); *Sigafus v. Brown*, 416 F.2d at 107 (allegation that jail guards confiscated and destroyed legal papers essential for postconviction hearing states claim); *Morello v. James*, 627 F.Supp. at 1574 (claim stated where plaintiff alleged that legal folders were taken from him, briefs were stolen and records of phone call to attorney taken). *See Nolan v. Scafati*, 430 F.2d 548, 550 (1st Cir.1970) (allegation that plaintiff was denied access to courts when prison

---

1. The State argues that under *Crooker v. Mulligan*, 788 F.2d 809 (1st Cir.1986), "the mere deprivation [of] legal materials does not state a cause of action under 42 U.S.C. Section 1983." Appellees' Brief, 5. This argument misconstrues our discussion in *Crooker*. *Crooker* involved a summary judgment in favor of various local and state police officers against a claim of, among other things, illegal search and seizure of a home and violation of the right to access. We discussed the right of access only as it related to what the state and local police officers knew or should have known to avoid liability under principles of qualified immunity. *Crooker* is, of course, not controlling on the question here at hand: whether a prisoner's allegations that prison officials confiscated materials necessary to prosecute a claim states a cause of action under § 1983.

officials refused to mail his letters to Massachusetts Civil Liberties Union states claim).

We turn, therefore, to Simmons' complaint to see whether it states a cause of action for deprivation of the right of access to the courts. Since Simmons is proceeding *pro se*, we have a special obligation to read his complaint indulgently. *Haines v. Kerner*, 404 U.S. 519, 520, 92 S.Ct. 594, 595, 30 L.Ed.2d 652 (1972). We will not approve the district court's dismissal for failure to state a claim unless it appears to us beyond doubt that plaintiff can prove no set of facts that would entitle him to relief. *Conley v. Gibson*, 355 U.S. 41, 45–46, 78 S.Ct. 99, 101–02, 2 L.Ed.2d 80 (1957).

The complaint alleges that plaintiff escaped from state custody (MCI Lancaster) in early July, 1985, and was reincarcerated (MCI Concord) within three weeks. Apparently a hearing was scheduled at Lancaster, during which plaintiff requested his personal and legal property and was told that all but his legal material would be forwarded to him. *See* Exhibit B. About mid-August, plaintiff filed a complaint/request form with MCI Concord, requesting the return of his legal property (Exhibit A). He mentioned that he had a case pending for which the material was required. *Id.* He was told to petition MCI Lancaster.

Plaintiff filed another complaint/request form on August 19, 1985, with MCI Concord. He asked the grievance coordinator to call or write Lancaster on his behalf. He apprised the prison authorities of their regulatory obligation to return to escapees their personal property "as soon as practicable." He received a letter shortly thereafter saying that three large boxes were being held at Lancaster on his behalf and that no one had come to pick them up (Exhibit A–2).

After plaintiff still did not receive his property, he filed a grievance form. He got a notice back saying that he could, at any time, send a friend or relative to MCI Lancaster to pick up the material. Simmons alleges in his complaint that he sent someone to pick up his property, but that the legal material was not included.

The Code of Massachusetts Regulations (CMR) provides, at 103 C.M.R. § 403.17: *Property of Escapees or Deceased Inmates ...*

(2) Where an escapee is returned to the care and custody of the department within one year from the date of the escape, the property shall be transferred as soon as practicable to the institution where the inmate is presently being housed....

We conclude that Simmons has alleged facts adequate to show an intentional deprivation of his right of access. He requested his material three times before he was told he could pick it up. He pointed out twice that the property he sought included legal materials necessary for a pending case. After he had the property picked up, it was determined that all the legal material was missing. Most importantly, the rules that bind the Department of Corrections state clearly and explicitly that all property of a returned escapee is to be transferred to the site of reincarceration. The rule does not place any burden on the prisoner to request, repeatedly, the return of his own property.

The state's final argument is that Simmons has alleged a simple property deprivation and so *Parratt* applies and precludes relief. *Parratt* involved an alleged procedural due process violation. The Supreme Court held that the Due Process Clause was not violated by a state officer's negligent conduct which deprived plaintiff of property, because the State provided the opportunity for post-deprivation process. *Parratt* was later extended, in *Hudson v. Palmer*, 468 U.S. 517, 104 S.Ct. 3194, 82 L.Ed.2d 393 (1984), to insulate intentional deprivations of property from constitutional reach as long as post-deprivation procedures are available. The Court has recently refined *Parratt*, concluding in *Daniels v. Williams*, — U.S. —, 106 S.Ct. 662, 88 L.Ed.2d 662 (1986) and *Davidson v. Cannon*, — U.S. —, 106 S.Ct. 668, 88 L.Ed.2d 677 (1986) that "the protections of the Due Process Clause, whether procedural or substantive, are just not triggered by lack of due care by prison officials." *Davidson*, 106 S.Ct. at 671.

That Simmons' legal *property* was *taken* does not convert this case to a procedural due process/deprivation of property claim. It is decisive that the harm complained of is not simply the taking of property, protected by the due process clause, but the taking of legal property resulting in denial of access to the courts, protected as a substantive, constitutional right. *See* discussion *supra*, p. 2. And the *Parratt* analysis does not apply where the alleged violation concerns a substantive, fundamental right. *See Daniels v. Williams*, — U.S. —, 106 S.Ct. 677, 678–79, 88 L.Ed.2d 677 (1986) (Stevens, J., concurring); *Creative Environments, Inc. v. Estabrook*, 680 F.2d 822, 832, n. 9 (1st Cir.), *cert. denied*, 459 U.S. 989, 103 S.Ct. 345, 74 L.Ed.2d 385 (1982).

See generally Morello v. James, 627 F.Supp. at 1575 (collecting cases).

We have decided that an allegation of intentional deprivation of the right of access states a cause of action under § 1983. As we read Simmons' complaint, he has made such an allegation. Since *Parratt v. Taylor* does not apply to the alleged deprivation of a substantive and fundamental right, the district court erred in dismissing Simmons' claim.

While Simmons' complaint should, therefore, have survived a motion to dismiss, we caution Simmons that he still faces the task of filling in the particulars of his claim to withstand a motion for summary judgment. We intimate no opinion about the success on the merits of Simmons' allegations.

Reversed and remanded for reinstatement of the complaint.

VOLUME III

CHAPTER 3 RELIGIOUS RIGHTS, RIGHT TO NONDISCRIMINATION FOR RACE OR SEX

There appear to be no cases during the period of this volume involving discrimination based on sex or religion. However, several interesting cases have arisen on the right to religious worship. *Tisdale v. Dobbs,* 807 F.2d 734 (8th Cir. 1986), discussed the right of prison authorities to prohibit religious services except under the leadership of approved sponsors and their failure to provide proper lunches as required by certain religious practices.

Chapman v. Pickett, 801 F.2d 912 (7th Cir. 1986), involved a disciplinary action against an inmate who refused to clean pork off of food trays. The petitioner claimed the task violated his religious principles. The court determined prison officials had violated the inmate's constitutional rights and awarded monetary damages.

Udey v. Kastner, 805 F.2d 1218 (5th Cir. 1986), questioned the responsibility of prison authorities to furnish the prisoner with a special diet because of his religious beliefs.

Introductions in previous volumes:

III: 105; VI: 377; VII: 417; VIII: 387

Qaid Rafeeq AZEEZ and Abdullah
Muhammad, Plaintiffs-Appellees,

v.

James W. FAIRMAN, warden, John E.
Wright, asst. warden, and A. Dodge,
#120 (C.O.), Defendants-Appellants.

No. 85-1330.

United States Court of Appeals,
Seventh Circuit.

Before POSNER and EASTERBROOK,
Circuit Judges, and CAMPBELL, Senior
District Judge.*

POSNER, Circuit Judge.

The plaintiffs, Qaid Rafeeq Azeez and
Abdullah Muhammad, brought suit under
42 U.S.C. § 1983 against the warden and

---

* Honorable William J. Campbell, of the Northern   District of Illinois, sitting by designation.

other officials of the Pontiac Correctional Center, which is Illinois' maximum-security prison, charging that the defendants had deprived the plaintiffs of their religious freedom by refusing to recognize their Islamic names. After a bench trial the district judge ruled in favor of the plaintiffs and entered judgments of $150 for each plaintiff, from which the defendants appeal.

Azeez and Muhammad were committed to Pontiac under the names Stanley Russell and Jessie Fields. They later converted to Islam and adopted their present names. Russell changed his name by means of the statutory procedure provided for this purpose. Ill.Rev.Stat. ch. 96. Fields just started calling himself Abdullah Muhammad. The defendants gave the plaintiffs "a/k/a" cards listing both their "committed" and their new names, but at times refused to let either plaintiff sign for various rights or privileges (such as library access, access to religious and notarial services, and commissary—i.e., snacks, cigarettes) in their Islamic names. The defendants also deprived the plaintiffs of these rights from time to time as punishment for the plaintiffs' refusing to sign their "committed" names. At other times, however, punishment was for their refusing to use the cards merely because their "committed" names were listed before their Islamic names.

The defendants do not contest the district court's finding that $150 is a reasonable amount of money to compensate each of the plaintiffs for not being allowed to sign his Islamic instead of his "committed" name, assuming such refusal was unlawful. Nor do the defendants deny, at least for purposes of this appeal, that they should have recognized Azeez's name change because he followed the prescribed statutory procedure. Rather, they argue that they are immune from having to pay damages to Azeez because they acted in good faith in refusing to recognize his name change, and that they did not violate Muhammad's constitutional rights at all.

A curiosity of the appeal is the defendants' asking us to set aside the declaratory relief that the district judge granted Muhammad, and Muhammad's vigorous opposition to that request. The judge did state in his opinion that he would enter a declaratory judgment, but the actual judgment entered reads in its entirety: "judgment entered in favor of the pltfs & against the dfts in the sum of $300 for deprivation of their religious liberties." There is not a word about declaratory relief. A litigant cannot appeal from a statement of intention to enter a judgment, as distinct from the judgment itself. Rule 58 of the Federal Rules of Civil Procedure says that the judgment must appear on a separate piece of paper—separate, that is, from the court's opinion. We take this requirement seriously. See, e.g., *Stelpflug v. Federal Land Bank*, 790 F.2d 47 (7th Cir.1986) (per curiam). As there was no declaratory *judgment*, there is no issue before us concerning the propriety of declaratory relief. Furthermore, a footnote in the defendants' brief states without contradiction, and the parties confirmed at oral argument, that Muhammad has been released from prison. He has no interest— no interest recognized by federal law, in any event—in obtaining a declaratory judgment concerning the religious liberties that he would be entitled to if he were in prison.

The parties' desire to have us resolve an issue that is not within our power to decide troubles us deeply. The federal courts must confine themselves to the jurisdiction, which is ample, that the Constitution gives them. Counsel must help us to carry out this duty. The determination of the propriety of a declaratory judgment, in a case in which such a judgment was never entered and would be moot if it had been, is not within that jurisdiction.

The award of damages, however, prevents the entire case from being moot, and requires us to consider two substantive issues: whether state prison officials can insist that a prisoner (Muhammad) use a statutory procedure for changing his name before they will recognize the name change, even if the change of name has a religious motivation; and whether they are immune from being held liable in damages for having refused to recognize a name change (Azeez's) made by means of the statutory procedure.

The district judge found, and the defendants do not challenge the finding, that the plaintiffs changed their names for sincere religious reasons and that it is offensive to their religious beliefs to be forced to sign their old names for any purpose. This is as true for Muhammad as for Azeez, even though Muhammad never attempted to change his name by the statutory means. It is also uncontested that a citizen of Illinois, which Muhammad (like Azeez) is, has a common law right to change his name. *Reinken v. Reinken*, 351 Ill. 409, 184 N.E. 639 (1933). The defendants' position, therefore, so far as Muhammad's case is concerned, is that considerations of prison discipline and security justify curtailing a prisoner's common law right to change his name, even when his motivation for exercising that right is religious.

There was a time when federal courts did not intervene in the internal affairs of prisons at all. (cf. *Ruffin v. Commonwealth*, 62 Va. (21 Gratt.) 790, 796 (1871)), and though that time is past, even today these courts regulate prisons with a considerably lighter touch than they regulate other public institutions alleged to deprive their charges or wards or employees of federal constitutional rights; see our extensive recent discussion of cases in *Caldwell v. Miller*, 790 F.2d 589, 595–600 (7th Cir.1986), another case involving prisoners' religious liberties. The security problems of present-day maximum-security prisons are acute. See, e.g., *United States v. Silverstein*, 732 F.2d 1338 (7th Cir.1984); *United States v. Fountain*, 768 F.2d 790 (7th Cir. 1985). Recently we noted that "Pontiac is a den of murderers, rapists, and others with no respect for the law—and all too often nothing to lose from further mayhem." *Walker v. Rowe*, 791 F.2d 507, 512 (7th Cir.1986). We have therefore insisted that district judges in this circuit give great

though not complete deference to the decisions of the prison authorities on matters affecting the maintenance of order. "We accord, as we must, prison officials wideranging deference in adopting policies that are needed to preserve internal order and security." *Caldwell v. Miller, supra*, 790 F.2d at 596.

Although the district court's opinion recognizes that Muhammad was not entitled to mutilate his identification card, threaten prison staff, and require that his name be changed on prison records, it does not recognize the practical difficulties that enforcing the common law right to change one's name would create for the prison authorities. Prisoners in maximum-security prisons do not dedicate themselves to making life easier for the guards and wardens. One way in which they can make life more difficult is by changing their names frequently. Every time a prisoner changes his name the prison staff must unlearn the old name and learn the new. If many prisoners happen to change their old names to the same new name (how many "Abdullah Muhammads" are there in the Illinois prison system today, we wonder?), they can cause chaos. Of course prisoners have numbers as well as names, but the plaintiffs' counsel suggested at argument that if a prisoner had religious scruples against being identified by number, these scruples must be honored too. Compare *Bowen v. Roy*, — U.S. —, 106 S.Ct. 2147, 90 L.Ed.2d 735 (1986). People on the outside rarely change their names (except women upon getting married—and that is changing), because of the confusion that may result. But prisoners may want to cause confusion, and in any event do not pay the same price as a free person who, having changed his name, must inform his friends and business acquaintances and get a new driver's license, credit cards, and so on. The plaintiff in *Salahuddin v. Coughlin*, 591 F.Supp. 353, 358–59 (S.D.N.Y.1984), had two Moslem names (as well as three Christian ones), and "professed contemplation of name changes in the future, which he wants to be able to accomplish at will." *Id.* at 359. So we can imagine a situation where when roll is called one morning Fields refuses to answer his name because last night he changed it to Muhammad; the next day he changes it to Azeez, and the next back to Fields. How are the authorities to keep track of prisoners in these circumstances?

No doubt our hypothetical case would represent an abuse of the common law right to change one's name. Cf. *Chaney v. Civil Service Comm'n*, 82 Ill.2d 289, 45 Ill.Dec. 146, 412 N.E.2d 497 (1980). But the boundaries of the concept of abusing the common law right to change one's name are obscure, and we do not think it can be said as a matter of federal constitutional law that the common law fixes the boundaries for prison officials alleged to have curtailed the federal rights of inmates. If perchance the prison authorities are violating Muhammad's common law rights, the remedy is a proceeding in Illinois court under Illinois law; an error of state law is not a denial of federal due process. *Lynk v. LaPorte Superior Court No. 2*, 789 F.2d 554, 564 (7th Cir.1986).

To our suggestion that chaos might result if prison inmates could change their names at will and require the prison's staff to recognize the change, the plaintiffs' counsel replied at argument that the record of this case contains no evidence that changes of name by prisoners at Pontiac have caused serious confusion, even though it appears that some years ago a number of black prisoners converted to Islam all at once and adopted Islamic names. But prison authorities are not required to wait for catastrophe before acting. They ought to prepare in advance for confusing or harassing or just too frequent name changes. They ought to have a rule, a policy. The rule that the Pontiac authorities have adopted is that they will recognize only name changes effected by the statutory procedure that Illinois provides for changing one's name. True, they didn't always follow their own rule in Azeez's case, which is why they confine their appeal in his case to the issue of immunity; but their lack of consistent observance does not bar them from invoking the rule as a

basis for overturning the judgment in favor of Muhammad. The failure to enforce a rule consistently does not make the rule unconstitutional. See, e.g., *Oyler v. Boles*, 368 U.S. 448, 456, 82 S.Ct. 501, 505, 7 L.Ed.2d 446 (1962); *Hameetman v. City of Chicago*, 776 F.2d 636, 641 (7th Cir.1985).

The rule that requires prisoners at Pontiac to follow the statutory procedure for changing one's name is reasonable, see *Salahuddin v. Coughlin, supra*, 591 F.Supp. at 358–59; *Rahman v. Stephenson*, 626 F.Supp. 886, 888 (W.D.Tenn.1986), at least if the procedure is usable by a prisoner, and it was by Muhammad. All the statute requires is that the prisoner have been a resident of Illinois for six months, which Muhammad had been at the time he adopted his Islamic name, that he petition an Illinois court to change his name, and that he publish the name change in a newspaper for a few weeks. The cost of publication might pose an obstacle to some prisoners but it did not to Azeez and there is no suggestion it would have to Muhammad. We need not consider the case of a prisoner who cannot afford to publish, or who cannot use the statutory procedure because he hasn't lived in Illinois for six months.

By requiring inmates to undergo the formalities of the statutory procedure the prison authorities prevent capricious, incessant, casual, sudden, harassing, on-the-spot name changes. Judging by Azeez's experience the formalities are not burdensome, and there is as we just said no suggestion that they would have been a burden for Muhammad. The prison allows prisoners to change their names and only compels them to do so by a procedure designed (imperfectly—but all human institutions, indeed all human undertakings, are imperfect) to weed out the pranksters, the wise guys, the troublemakers, the insincere.

But are these considerations powerful enough to justify impeding the free exercise of religion, a right which the Supreme Court has held state prisoners enjoy by virtue of the First Amendment as read into the Fourteenth Amendment? It is true that, read literally, the First Amendment (so far as pertinent to this case) seems to prohibit only governmental discrimination against religion or particular religious sects; so understood the amendment would not forbid the application of a general regulation that had been adopted for valid secular reasons to a religious group, whatever the consequences for the group. Recognizing, however, how such an interpretation of the First Amendment would elevate the interests of dominant religious groups over those of minority religious groups—since the normal operation of the political process will assure that governmental regulations do not interfere with the religious practices of the majority—the Supreme Court has held that the government must bend its regulations to accommodate sincere religious practices. See, e.g., *Sherbert v. Verner*, 374 U.S. 398, 83 S.Ct. 1790, 10 L.Ed.2d 965 (1963); *Thomas v. Review Bd. of Indiana Employment Security Division*, 450 U.S. 707, 101 S.Ct. 1425, 67 L.Ed.2d 624 (1981); McConnell, *Accommodation of Religion*, 1985 S.Ct. Rev. 1, 34–40. But how far? No definitive standard has emerged. Compare *Sherbert v. Verner, supra*, 374 U.S. at 403, 406, with *Wisconsin v. Yoder*, 406 U.S. 205, 220, 92 S.Ct. 1526, 1535, 32 L.Ed.2d 15 (1972), and notice the greater receptivity to arguments based on the needs of prison security in our recent *Caldwell* decision, *supra*, than in our earlier decision in *Madyun v. Franzen*, 704 F.2d 954, 960–61 (7th Cir.1983)—though even in *Madyun* we rejected the prisoner's claim and made clear that an inmate "simply cannot expect the same freedom from incidental infringement on the exercise of his religious practices that is enjoyed by those not incarcerated." *Id.* at 958. Maybe in the prison setting the answer to the question how far government must go to accommodate religious beliefs, is, not very far, because of the danger to the other prisoners if the prison authorities lose control and because persons who want to exercise their religious rights without interference can do so just by not committing crimes punishable by imprisonment.

But there is no need to fix on a precise standard in this case, for under any standard Muhammad must lose. The record does not show a significant abridgment of his religious freedom; there may, indeed, have been no abridgment at all. For there is no evidence that requiring an Islamic prisoner to undergo a *nonburdensome* statutory procedure for changing his name imposes a religious hardship on him. Supposing, as we do—because the district judge so found and the defendants do not on this appeal contend otherwise—that Jesse Fields upon converting to Islam was required to adopt an Islamic name, still we find no suggestion that he was required to do so at the moment of conversion. So far as appears, he was required to do so at the first opportune moment—within a reasonable time—and there is no evidence that the time it would have taken him to get a statutory name change would have been thought unreasonable by any of his religious mentors.

We grant that duty and right need not be coextensive in this area; the right to religious freedom may be violated by a public regulation that prevents a practice merely recommended, and not mandatory, for members of a particular faith. See McConnell, *supra*, at 27, 34. But there is no evidence that if told he must use his "committed" name in his dealings with the prison authorities for a brief interval until his statutory name change went through, Muhammad would have thought he was being asked to do something contrary to his religious beliefs.

So this seems to be a case where, as in *Menora v. Illinois High School Ass'n*, 683 F.2d 1030 (7th Cir.1982), the alleged conflict between religious liberty and public safety is a false—nonexistent—imagined conflict, arising from a failure to attend carefully to the specific content of the religious obligation. Just as in *Menora* there was no religious obligation to wear a yarmulke that might fall off because it hadn't been securely fastened and might trip up other basketball players, so in this case there appears to be no religious obligation to adopt an Islamic name at the moment of conversion to Islam.

If no deprivation of Muhammad's religious liberty has been shown, he must of course lose. But if there was a deprivation, still it was very slight and was outweighed by the benefits in security and good order from insisting that prisoners who want their new names recognized by the prison authorities follow (at least where it is feasible to do so) the simple statutory procedure which Illinois provides for changing one's name.

The other question we must decide is whether the defendants are immune from liability to Azeez for having at times refused to let him sign for privileges in his Islamic name even though he had used the statutory procedure to adopt it. This depends on whether the defendants were violating "clearly established ... constitutional rights ... of which a reasonable person would have known." *Harlow v. Fitzgerald*, 457 U.S. 800, 818, 102 S.Ct. 2727, 2738, 73 L.Ed.2d 396 (1982). Azeez does not seek damages for any violation of his rights under state law, so we need not consider whether by insisting on an "a/k/a" designation or otherwise by continuing to use Azeez's "committed" name the defendants violated rights clearly established by Illinois statute. The only question is whether they violated any clearly established federal constitutional right.

At the relevant time, 1981, the only case that had held that a prisoner had a federal constitutional right both to change his name for religious reasons and to insist that the prison authorities recognize the new name was a district court decision outside of this circuit, *Masjid Muhammad-D.D.C. v. Keve*, 479 F.Supp. 1311, 1321–26 (D.Del.1979); and there was contrary authority, in cases holding that prison authorities do not have to recognize a religiously motivated name change on the prison's internal records, see *Akbar v. Canney*, 634 F.2d 339 (6th Cir.1980) (per curiam); *Smalley v. Bell*, 484 F.Supp. 16, 18 (W.D.Okla. 1979). Such cases may be distinguishable from *Masjid* and the present case; indeed

the plaintiffs in the present case no longer insist that the prison change their names on its books. But it was not clear back in 1981 that such cases would be distinguished and that the line would be drawn between the use of "committed" names for record-keeping and for other purposes.

Although it was well recognized in 1981 that prisoners retain their constitutional rights to the extent compatible with the needs of prison discipline and safety, the application of this generality to religiously motivated changes of name in circumstances like those of the present case had yet to be authoritatively determined. The words "clearly established ... constitutional rights" may not be used to read the defense of immunity out of federal tort law by the facile expedient of stating constitutional rights in the most general possible terms, so that anyone who prevails on the merits of a claim based on (for example) the First Amendment's free exercise of religion clause, however novel that claim is, can defeat the defense of immunity simply by pointing out that the right to the free exercise of one's religion has long been a clearly established constitutional right. The right must be sufficiently particularized to put potential defendants on notice that their conduct probably is unlawful.

So the question is whether in 1981, in the absence of any authoritative judicial precedent (for the State of Illinois is not bound to comply with every constitutional ruling by every district judge in the United States, see *Shirley v. Chagrin Falls Exempted Village Schools Bd. of Educ.*, 521 F.2d 1329, 1333–34 (6th Cir.1975); *Benjamin v. Board of Election Comm'rs*, 122 Ill.App.3d 693, 697, 78 Ill.Dec. 507, 462 N.E.2d 626, 628 (1984), especially when as in this case there arguably was contrary authority— some of it at the court of appeals level) dealing with the right of a prisoner to compel recognition of a religiously motivated change of name, that right was clearly established. To ask the question is to answer it. Prison authorities had only slight reason to believe then that the Constitution would be interpreted to forbid them to curtail a prisoner's common law or statutory right to change his name, even if the name change was sincerely motivated by religious belief. The plaintiffs' counsel in this case conceded at argument that some such incursions are constitutional—that the defendants could for example have required Muhammad to put his request for a change of name in writing. So it is all a matter of degree, with Azeez and Muhammad conceding that the common law right can be encroached upon to the extent of requiring a written request to recognize their new names and the defendants insisting (at least in 1981, at least intermittently) that the plaintiffs would have to go by their "committed" names while in prison, at least in dealing with the authorities; the plaintiffs were of course free to use their adopted names as soon as they were released (Muhammad has been released, as we have said), as well as in dealing with other prisoners, family, etc.

Even today it is not obvious that it would violate the Constitution for the defendants to hold to this position. We have not said that the religious claims in this case trump the state's legitimate interest in maintaining prison discipline and safety. Requiring adherence to the statutory procedure does not violate Muhammad's rights, and of course it does not follow that forbidding all changes of names by prisoners violates any prisoner's rights. The test in this circuit for a prison regulation challenged on religious grounds is reasonableness; prison officials are not required to use the least restrictive alternative to attain valid regulatory objectives such as safety. *Caldwell v. Miller, supra,* 790 F.2d at 596 n. 11. Even in 1986 the right to make prison staff recognize a religiously motivated name change in prison is not clearly established, and it certainly was not five years ago; a good illustration of the judicial attitude in that period toward curtailment of religious liberties by prison authorities is *Rogers v. Scurr,* 676 F.2d 1211, 1215 (8th Cir.1982). Granted, *Barrett v. Virginia,* 689 F.2d 498, 503 (4th Cir.1982), invalidated a ban on allowing prisoners to use the statutory procedure for changing one's name; but if

only because *Barrett* postdates the alleged deprivation of Azeez's rights, it is not good evidence that the defendants violated some "clearly established" right of Azeez's. Even today, we doubt that his right could be so described; for we are not sure we agree with *Barrett,* though that is not an issue we need resolve in this case.

The defendants are immune from being ordered to pay damages to Azeez, and they never violated Muhammad's constitutional rights. The judgment for the plaintiffs is reversed with instructions to enter judgment for the defendants.

REVERSED.

CAMPBELL, Senior District Judge, dissenting in part.

I believe we should affirm the damage award given to Azeez and affirm Judge Baker's ruling in this area in doing so. In analyzing this issue, we must follow the principles set forth in *Harlow v. Fitzgerald,* 457 U.S. 800, 102 S.Ct. 2727, 2738, 73 L.Ed.2d 396 (1982) where it was held:

[G]overnment officials performing discretionary functions generally are shielded from liability for civil damages insofar as there conduct does not violate clearly established statutory or constitutional rights of which a reasonable person should have known.

On May 20, 1981 the Illinois Circuit Court issued a Writ of Mandamus, requested by Azeez, requiring prison officials to "hereinafter conduct all official business with [Azeez] using his new name." To paraphrase *Harlow,* supra, I consider the writ to have clearly established Azeez's constitutional right (at least in Illinois) to be referred to by his new Muslim name. Indeed, on June 1, 1981 Azeez was properly issued an identification card bearing only his Muslim name. Yet later that same day his card was inexplicably confiscated and he was given a card reading "Stanley Russell a/k/a Qaid Rafeez Azeez," clearly indicating officials would still primarily "conduct official business" with him using his old name. Azeez stood up for his rights after they were clearly established by the Illinois courts. As a result he was denied all privileges for two weeks.

I believe prison officials had due notice from the Illinois courts about the rights of Azeez and callously (if not deliberately) violated them. This kind of callousness should not be condoned and I would affirm Judge Baker's damage award as to Azeez.

Ed UDEY, Petitioner-Appellant,

v.

**B.C. KASTNER, Warden, et al.,
Respondents-Appellees.**

No. 85–2791.

United States Court of Appeals,
Fifth Circuit.

Dec. 15, 1986.

Before GOLDBERG, WILLIAMS and DAVIS, Circuit Judges.

PER CURIAM:

Petitioner Edwin Udey filed suit in the United States District Court for the Eastern District of Texas under the First Amendment: "Congress shall make no law respecting an establishment of religion, or prohibiting the free exercise thereof." Udey, a prisoner in the Federal Correctional Institution in Texarkana, asked to be provided with a diet consistent with his sincerely held religious beliefs; he primarily requested organically grown produce washed in distilled water. The federal prison officials declined, Udey refused to eat the nutritionally adequate food provided, and Udey has since been force-fed through nasal tubes. The district court found that Udey's religious beliefs were not sincerely held. We reversed and remanded for an evidentiary hearing to determine whether meeting Udey's religious and dietary requirements would place an undue burden on the prison system and whether there was any good reason not to provide him with food that complies with his religious diet (order of July 9, 1986).[1] Judge Hall held the appropriate hearings and found that the prison system was not required to cater to Udey's requests, 644 F.Supp. 1441 (1986). We affirm.

Judge Hall found on four independent grounds that an undue burden would be imposed on the prison system and that good reason existed not to provide Udey with his requests. In particular, Judge Hall found: that it would cost approximately $5.00 per day to meet Udey's requirements, with total accommodation costs in excess of $15,000.00 per year; that hostility from other inmates, theft or "pilferage" of specialty foods, and the potential creation of a black market in such items might result, causing security problems; that administrative costs of providing Udey's requirements would include problems of determination, procurement, preparation, health standards, and storage, requiring three or more hours of additional staff time; and that "the potentially disruptive effect on prison order and discipline [from the probable proliferation of claims for specific individual religious dietary require-

---

1. We note that there is an intercircuit conflict on the appropriate standard for free exercise claims in a prison context. *See, e.g., Barnett v. Rodgers*, 410 F.2d 995, 1000 (D.C.Cir.1969) (compelling state interest and no alternatives that would not infringe upon First Amendment rights); *Shabazz v. O'Lone*, 782 F.2d 416, 420 (3d Cir.1986) (en banc), *petition for cert. filed*, 54 U.S.L.W. 3730 (U.S. Apr. 16, 1986) (No. 85–1722) (important penalogical goals served and no reasonable method by which religious rights can be accommodated). We pray the Supreme Court in *Shabazz v. O'Lone* will bring order to this unholy mess.

ments] is perhaps the most compelling governmental interest articulated...." Second Supplemental Record, Corrected Opinion, at 15.

We are somewhat concerned over the government's argument that the provision to one person of simple dietary requirements poses security concerns, which thereby require a "mutual accommodation" standard with "wide-ranging deference" to prison authorities. *See Bell v. Wolfish*, 441 U.S. 520, 546–47, 99 S.Ct. 1861, 1878, 60 L.Ed.2d 447 (1979); *see also Thorne v. Jones*, 765 F.2d 1270, 1275 (5th Cir.1985) (security decisions of prison officials are to be reviewed only for reasonableness). We are reluctant to believe that the failure to provide adequate security from pilferage can be used by the Government to avoid what otherwise might be constitutionally required under the First Amendment. Similarly, although we recognize that costs are a valid consideration for First Amendment purposes, *see Walker v. Blackwell*, 411 F.2d 23, 26 (5th Cir.1969), we have stated in other prison suits that " 'inadequate resources can never be an adequate justification for depriving any person of his constitutional rights.' " *Smith v. Sullivan*, 553 F.2d 373, 378 (1977) (quoting *Hamilton v. Love*, 328 F.Supp. 1182, 1194 (E.D.Ark. 1971)). We therefore are hesitant to adopt the district court's conclusions of law that the alleged cost, security, and administrative difficulties that might result from providing *one* person with his dietary needs constitute a good reason or an undue burden.[2] Thus, we choose not to review the trial judge's determinations except as regards the potential for proliferation of false claims and the burdens potentially

imposed by *many* individuals on the prison system.

As stated in *Brown v. Dade Christian Schools, Inc.*, 556 F.2d 310, 323 (5th Cir. 1977) (en banc) (Goldberg, J., specially concurring):

[A]mong the most important factors in this respect are the institutional consequences of the alternative decision. When a court can recognize a free exercise claim without inviting numerous additional claims, focusing on the particular consequences of the ruling in the case at bar is appropriate. But when recognizing the claim will predictably give rise to further claims, many of which will undoubtedly be fraudulent or exaggerated, the situation is different. In that event, the court must either recognize many such claims (so that the relevant governmental interest extends beyond the individual claimants in the original action) or draw fine and searching distinctions among various free exercise claimants. The latter course would raise serious constitutional questions with respect to the proper functioning of courts in sensitive religion clause adjudication.... When numerous claims are likely, recognizing some while rejecting others unavoidably forces courts to pick and choose among religions and to draw subtle distinctions on the basis of criteria with which no governmental unit should ever be entangled.

The trial judge cited testimony stating that the potential for proliferation was a "very strong likelihood" and that the number of religious dietary requests has "grown by leaps and bounds." Supplemental Record,

---

2. This is particularly true in the present context, where prison officials have already seen fit to provide an experimental "common fare" *religious* dietary alternative to the standard food provided. Judge Hall found that the per person cost per day of the common fare program was $5.00, *identical* to the cost of providing Petitioner Udey's requirements. Second Supplemental Record, Corrected Opinion, at 5.

The Government maintains that this alternative is not *required* by the First Amendment. Government's Proposed Findings of Fact and Conclusions of Law, Supplemental Record, Vol.

1, at 52 n. 1. Further, the Government recognized that the common fare program "did not satisfy the individual dietary demands of every inmate...." *Id.* at 37. Although we have every desire to encourage the Government to provide religious dietary alternatives, providing alternatives acceptable to practitioners of "majority" religions while failing to provide alternatives acceptable to practitioners of less common, even unique, religions poses serious Equal Protection/First Amendment Establishment concerns. *See Cruz v. Beto*, 405 U.S. 319, 92 S.Ct. 1079, 31 L.Ed.2d 263 (1972).

Vol. 1, at 73–74. The trial judge specifically found that the proliferation effect would place an undue burden on the prison system. *Id.* at 74.

We believe that the probable proliferation of claims, and the concomitant entanglement with religion that processing *multiple* claims would require, does constitute a problem that the state has a good reason to avoid. Such proliferation, and the concomitant need to meet *multiple* distinct dietary requirements, might create undue cost and administrative burdens. We thus AFFIRM the trial court's decision on this ground only.

Adrian Bruce TISDALE, Appellant,

v.

Ronald   DOBBS,   Warden;   Dewie
Williams,   Administrator   Chaplaincy
Services;   Lieutenant   Davis,   Tucker
Unit; and A.L. Lockhart, Director, Ar-
kansas Department of Correction, Ap-
pellees.

No. 85–2352.

United States Court of Appeals,
Eighth Circuit.

Submitted May 14, 1986.

Decided Dec. 19, 1986.

Before HEANEY, JOHN R. GIBSON   and MAGILL, Circuit Judges.

JOHN R. GIBSON, Circuit Judge.

Adrian Bruce Tisdale appeals from the district court's [1] entry of summary judgment against him on his claim that officials of the Arkansas Department of Correction denied him and other Muslim inmates the right to free exercise of their religion by refusing to allow them to conduct religious services except under the leadership of an approved free-world sponsor and by providing Muslim inmates an inadequate sack lunch following the daily Ramadan fast. The district court found that these regulations were applied equally to all inmates, and held that they were not discriminatory and were a reasonable response to legitimate security considerations. It concluded that the regulations did not violate Tisdale's constitutional rights. On appeal, Tisdale argues that the district court erred in failing to determine whether the group worship regulation was more restrictive than necessary, in relying on conclusory affidavits submitted by the prison officials, and in failing to determine whether the challenged regulations had an impermissible discriminatory impact on Muslims and interfered with their observance of Ramadan. We affirm.

Tisdale, an inmate at the diagnostic unit of the Arkansas Department of Correction, filed this action pro se to enjoin certain prison officials from violating his constitutional right to free exercise of religion. Tisdale is a Muslim. He challenged the establishment and application of a regulation that prohibits groups of inmates from holding religious services unless a free-world sponsor is present and in charge. The officials were unable to obtain a Muslim to act as free-world sponsor and enforcement of the regulation foreclosed the Muslims from holding group prayer meetings, including their weekly Jumah prayer meetings. He also alleged harassment, retaliation, and discrimination arising from the prison's policy of providing Muslims who were forced to miss regularly sched-

uled meals during the fast of Ramadan with sack lunches consisting of two bologna sandwiches after fourteen hours of fasting.

The officials of the Department of Correction moved for summary judgment and submitted supporting affidavits. A.L. Lockhart, Director of the Arkansas Department of Correction, stated in his affidavit that the requirement of the presence of a free-world sponsor at all worship services applied to all religious groups and was not intended to discriminate against Muslims. He further stated that "[t]he importance of the enforcement of this rule was underscored in July of 1984 when Muslim services at Cummins were used as a forum for advocating institutional mutiny." Designated Record at 11. On that occasion, the Arkansas state police had to assist in maintaining security. Dewie Williams, Administrator of Chaplaincy Services, stated that Muslims would be allowed to assemble for group services if they did so at proper times and with an approved free-world person present and in charge of the meeting. He stated the Department had made efforts to get an American Muslim mission to have someone present for the Jumah meetings, but had been unsuccessful. Warden Ronald Dobbs stated that worship services were permitted on scheduled dates and times and with an approved free-world person· present and in charge. This requirement, he stated, is not intended to discriminate against any religious group and is based on security considerations. He also stated that those inmates participating in Ramadan, which entails fasting during daylight hours, are given the same sack lunches as any other inmate who is unable to go to the cafeteria at the regularly scheduled times.

In answer to the motion and affidavits, Tisdale filed a sworn response stating that the officials were trying to justify oppression, harassment, and denial of Islamic religious worship in alleging that the Muslim

1. The Honorable William Ray Overton, United States District Judge for the Eastern District of Arkansas.

meetings were a security risk. He stated that the Department and the Chaplaincy Service were "sorting out" the Muslim inmates, and were biased against Muslims because of the "conflict" between Christianity and the Muslim faith. Tisdale also stated that Muslim inmates observing Ramadan were given two bologna sandwiches nightly to break their fast and that this was a departure from the Department's former policy of providing food "from a food cart." He alleged that this diet was nutritionally insufficient and that some Muslims were vegetarians and could not eat the sandwiches.

The district court granted the motion for summary judgment. *Tisdale v. Dobbs*, PB–C–85–343 (E.D.Ark. Oct. 25, 1985). It found that the requirement that a free-world person be present at all religious group services applied to all groups and was not discriminatory. It further found that it was "a reasonable response to a legitimate security consideration in light of prior abuses of the assembly privilege." *Id.* at 2. It observed that the Department of Correction had made efforts to provide a sponsor for the Jumah meetings, and it noted that the regulation did not affect any aspects of the Muslim faith other than the Jumah meetings. It concluded that the regulation did not violate Tisdale's constitutional rights. With regard to Tisdale's allegation that the sack lunches provided Muslims during Ramadan were inadequate, it found that this policy was also applied evenhandedly to all inmates who missed meals. It concluded that this complaint "[did] not rise to the level of constitutional significance." *Id.* at 3.

Tisdale filed a separate motion for appointment of counsel. It was denied. This court appointed counsel to assist Tisdale with his appeal.

We turn our attention first to Tisdale's claim that the district court abused its discretion in denying his motion for appointment of counsel. He argues, citing *Sours v. Norris*, 782 F.2d 106 (8th Cir. 1986), that when a colorable claim of constitutional violation is presented, the trial court is under a mandatory duty to appoint counsel. We have recently clarified and re-stated the considerations which should inform the exercise of a trial court's discretion in granting or denying a motion to appoint counsel in a civil suit such as this one. *See In re Lane*, 801 F.2d 1040, 1042–44 (8th Cir.1986) (factual complexity, ability of prisoner to investigate facts, existence of conflicting testimony, ability to present claims, and complexity of legal issues are all factors to be weighed by trial court); *see also Johnson v. Williams*, 788 F.2d 1319, 1322–23 (8th Cir.1986); *Nelson v. Redfield Lithograph Printing*, 728 F.2d 1003, 1005 (8th Cir.1984). Our cases hold that there is no mandatory duty to appoint counsel in a civil suit. *E.g.*, *Lane*, at 1043. Tisdale, therefore, had no "right" to appointed counsel before the district court, and we conclude that the district court did not abuse its discretion in denying his request for one. The factual allegations in this case are not complex, and were well set forth by Tisdale in his complaint. He also concedes that the legal issues are neither particularly novel nor complex. Opening Brief for Appellant at 12. Moreover, his contentions have been vigorously and ably presented to us by appointed counsel on appeal.

With respect to the requirement that a free-world sponsor be present at group religious services, we draw guidance from a number of our recent decisions. In *Hill v. Blackwell*, 774 F.2d 338 (8th Cir.1985), we set out in detail the legal analysis and considerations applicable to Tisdale's claim. In *Hill*, we considered a regulation preventing inmates at the Missouri State Penitentiary from growing beards. The wearing of facial hair, including beards and mustaches, is a practice of the Muslim religion. *Id.* at 339. We stated that the burden is on the prisoner to show that his belief is religious in nature and sincerely held. *Id.* at 342. He must also show that the challenged regulation infringes upon that belief. *Id.* at 342–43. On the other hand, the responsible prison officials need only show that the exercise of the religious practice "could create a potential threat to a legitimate penological objective." *Id.* at 343. If this showing is made, the trial court must defer to the prison officials' expertise in matters of prison administration, and "the prisoner's right must yield to the prison regulation." *Id.* If, however, the record contains substantial evidence that the officials' belief that the regulation is necessary is unreasonable, or that their response to the penological objective is exaggerated, the district court need no longer defer but rather must determine on the record whether the officials have shown that the regulation is justified. *Id.; see also Gregory v. Auger*, 768 F.2d 287, 290–91 (8th Cir.), *cert. denied*, — U.S. —, 106 S.Ct. 601, 88 L.Ed.2d 580 (1985).

We also employed this two-part standard in *Otey v. Best*, 680 F.2d 1231 (8th Cir. 1982), in which we considered the constitutionality of a regulation that prohibited prisoners in administrative segregation and prisoners subject to the death penalty from attending Jumah prayer meetings. We quoted approvingly a portion of the Third Circuit's opinion in *St. Claire v. Cuyler*, 634 F.2d 109 (3d Cir.1980), which explicitly placed on the prisoner the burden of proving by substantial evidence that the prison officials exaggerated their response to security considerations or that their belief is unreasonable. *Otey*, 680 F.2d at 1233 (quoting *St. Claire*, 634 F.2d at 114–15). This passage from *St. Claire* was also repeated and re-emphasized in *Hill*, 774 F.2d at 342.

We recently considered, in *Little v. Norris*, 787 F.2d 1241 (8th Cir.1986), another regulation impinging on group prayer meetings. The plaintiff was not permitted to participate in group religious meetings after he was involved in a potentially violent group demonstration. We affirmed the district court's entry of summary judgment in favor of the prison officials. The officials had identified a legitimate security

concern as the basis of the regulation—the prevention of any further demonstrations during a period of inmate unrest. The prisoner failed to meet his burden under the standard articulated in *Hill* because "[he] never alleged in his complaint, or in his response to defendant's motion to dismiss, that the prison officials exaggerated their response to the security consideration." *Id.* at 1244. Moreover, the prisoner did not allege that the prison official's concern for safety was unwarranted. We held that the prohibition of attendance at group religious services was a reasonable limitation on the prisoner's right to freedom of religion and there was no violation of his constitutional right. *Id.*

We do not believe the district court erred in its application of the principles developed in these cases to Tisdale's claim. The court concluded that the requirement of a free-world sponsor was a reasonable response to legitimate security considerations—the threat of unsupervised group prayer meetings becoming forums for dissension and unrest as had previously occurred at the Cummins Unit in 1984. Phrased in terms of the two-part standard articulated in *Hill*, the prison officials produced evidence that the unfettered exercise of Tisdale's first amendment right would create a potential danger to institutional safety, and the district court found that the prison officials' opinion as to this potential threat and the necessity of the regulation was "sincerely held and arguably correct."[2] *Hill*, 774 F.2d at 344. Tisdale then had the burden of showing by substantial evidence that the officials' belief was unreasonable or that their response to legitimate security considerations was exaggerated. Absent such a showing, "the district court was obligated to defer to the expert judgment of the prison officials." *Id.* The district court implicitly concluded that Tisdale had not met this heavy burden,

---

2. The prison officials do not dispute, and we accept, that the Jumah prayer meeting is a Muslim religious practice, and that Tisdale is sincere in his adherence to the Muslim faith and its observances. Moreover, the prison officials do not seriously dispute that the challenged regulation infringes on that practice to the extent that no free-world sponsors for the Jumah meetings have yet been found and thus the meetings cannot take place.

and appropriately deferred to the expert opinion of the prison officials. As Tisdale failed to meet his burden under the first part of the *Hill* standard, it was not necessary for the court to reach the second part of the analysis and "determine on the record whether the prison officials have indeed shown that the restrictive regulation is justified." *Id.* at 343.

Our opinion in *Little v. Norris, supra*, demonstrates that this analysis does not change if the parties' contentions and the facts are presented to the district court in the form of a motion for summary judgment with supporting and opposing affidavits rather than through a trial. As in *Little*, 787 F.2d at 1243, the prison officials have admitted the existence of the challenged regulation and have articulated a legitimate penological objective on which it is based. And, again as in *Little*, "[Tisdale] never alleged in his complaint, or in response to the defendants' motion [for summary judgment], that the prison officials exaggerated their response to the security consideration * * * [or] that defendants' concern for security was unwarranted." *Id.* at 1244. The closest Tisdale comes to such an allegation is the statement contained in his response to the motion for summary judgment that the officials' articulated penological objective is "to justify the religion being oppressed." This general, conclusory allegation neither begins to satisfy the heavy burden required of Tisdale under *Hill* nor does it meet our requirements for a response to a motion for summary judgment supported by affi-

davits under Rule 56 of the Federal Rules of Civil Procedure. *See Johnson v. Nix*, 754 F.2d 273, 274 (8th Cir.1985) (prisoner's pro se response to summary judgment motion inadequate because conclusory and disputed only immaterial facts); *Miller v. Solem*, 728 F.2d 1020, 1025–26 (8th Cir.), *cert. denied*, 469 U.S. 841, 105 S.Ct. 145, 83 L.Ed.2d 84 (1984) (same); *Cummings v. Roberts*, 628 F.2d 1065, 1069 (8th Cir.1980) (same). Tisdale's response simply was inadequate to establish an issue of fact or law requiring further balancing by the district court.

What we have said thus far answers Tisdale's first allegation of error by the district court. He contends that the court should have determined whether the group worship regulation was more restrictive than necessary to meet the security consideration. He cites no authority for this proposition. However, such a determination should be made, if at all,[3] during the second part of the two-part *Hill* analysis in deciding whether the prison officials have shown the regulation to be justified. The district court did not reach this stage of the analysis because Tisdale did not meet his burden at the first stage.

Tisdale next complains that the district court erred in granting summary judgment based on what he contends are fatally deficient affidavits. He argues that the affidavits submitted by Lockhart, Williams, and Dobbs were conclusory, and could not support the entry of summary judgment. He cites and relies on the Sixth Circuit's opin-

---

3. We explicitly rejected a "less restrictive alternative" analysis when considering a regulation that prohibited Muslim inmates from wearing robes and prayer caps in *Rogers v. Scurr*, 676 F.2d 1211, 1215–16 (8th Cir.1982). In *Hill*, however, we cited our opinion in *Teterud v. Burns*, 522 F.2d 357 (8th Cir.1975), for the proposition that "a regulation which is more restrictive than necessary to meet institutional objectives * * * will be struck down." *Hill*, 774 F.2d at 341 (quoting *Teterud*, 522 F.2d at 359). We then distinguished *Teterud* from *Hill* by noting that no legitimate security consideration was advanced for the challenged regulation in *Teterud*, so there was no need to proceed with the full *Hill* analysis. If there is confusion on this issue among our prior decisions, *see also Safley v.*

Turner, 777 F.2d 1307, 1313 (8th Cir.1985) (approving a "strict scrutiny"-"narrowly tailored" analysis of prison regulation impinging on right to free speech); *Gregory*, 768 F.2d 287 at 289 (the district court must "determine whether the limitation of first amendment freedoms is no greater than necessary or essential to the governmental interest involved"), we decline to resolve it until we are presented with a case more squarely raising this question. We are satisfied that Tisdale was not entitled to a determination of whether the breadth of this regulation was appropriate because he did not present substantial evidence that the prison officials' belief was unreasonable or that their response to the security consideration was exaggerated.

ion in *Weaver v. Jago*, 675 F.2d 116 (6th Cir.1982). The *Weaver* court observed that the allegations contained in the defendants' affidavits were conclusory in reciting that a hair length regulation was necessary for purposes of identification, security, and hygiene. *Id.* at 118. However, the thrust of the court's opinion was not that the affidavits were inadequate, but that they did not meet squarely the allegations in the prisoner's complaint, and further factual development was necessary to properly assess his claims.

The affidavits submitted by Lockhart, Williams, and Dobbs meet each of the complaints raised by Tisdale. Moreover, the officials did not simply assert that the challenged regulation is justified by a concern for security. Lockhart identified a specific incident that prompted the adoption of the group religious service regulation, the use of Muslim services at the Cummins Unit in 1984 as "a forum for advocating institutional mutiny." Designated Record at 11. All three affidavits note that this regulation applies to all religious groups and not merely to Muslims. Williams stated that efforts were being made to find a Muslim free-world sponsor for the meetings. We think that these affidavits, while not models, are adequate to show that unsupervised group religious meetings posed a potential threat to a legitimate penological objective. In this regard we are mindful of the Supreme Court's admonition that prison officials are not to be required to show that the activity controlled by the challenged regulation is a "present danger to security and order," *Jones v. North Carolina Prisoners' Labor Union*, 433 U.S. 119, 128, 97 S.Ct. 2532, 2539, 53 L.Ed.2d 629 (1977) (quoting *North Carolina Prisoners' Labor Union v. Jones*, 409 F.Supp. 937, 945 (E.D.N.C.1976), *rev'd*, 433 U.S. 119, 97 S.Ct. 2532, 53 L.Ed.2d 629 (1977)), but rather that there is a *potential* threat to institutional security. This standard, we conclude, has been met.

Tisdale next argues, again without citation of authority, that the group religious service regulation had an imper-missible discriminatory impact on Muslims, and that the district court erred in failing to so find. He also argues that the enforcement of this regulation against Muslims, coupled with the provision of Christian chaplains for Christian religious services, constitutes an establishment clause violation. Tisdale did not raise an equal protection or establishment clause claim in his complaint or in his response to the motion for summary judgment, however, and we decline to consider these claims for the first time on appeal. *Little*, 787 F.2d at 1243 n. 4. We have reviewed the record, in any event, and we find no factual support for the contentions Tisdale makes in his brief. Although the Arkansas Department of Correction is obligated to afford Tisdale a reasonable opportunity to practice his faith, *Cruz v. Beto*, 405 U.S. 319, 322, 92 S.Ct. 1079, 1081, 31 L.Ed.2d 263 (1972); *Rogers*, 676 F.2d at 1215, "[a] special chapel or place of worship need not be provided for every faith regardless of size; nor must a chaplain, priest, or minister be provided without regard to the extent of the demand." *Cruz*, 405 U.S. at 322 n. 2, 92 S.Ct. at 1081 n. 2.

Tisdale's final claim is that the district court erred in summarily concluding that his complaint regarding the provision of bologna sandwiches to Muslim inmates during Ramadan "[did] not rise to the level of constitutional significance." *Tisdale*, slip op. at 3. We conclude that the district court did not err in so finding. The affidavits submitted by the prison officials stated that Muslim inmates were given the same meal as was given any other inmate who missed a meal during the day. Tisdale's response did not contest the accuracy of this statement. We think that the Arkansas Department of Correction has provided Muslim inmates a "reasonable opportunity," *Otey*, 680 F.2d at 1233 (quoting *Rogers*, 676 F.2d at 1215), to observe Ramadan by furnishing them a sack lunch equal to that given other inmates who miss scheduled meals. Tisdale has not alleged that he cannot eat the meals provided him because he is a vegetarian, or that as a Muslim, he cannot eat bologna because it is made of pork. Under these circumstances, the district court properly found that Tisdale's allegations did not amount to a constitutional violation.

We affirm the judgment of the district court.

Edward Joseph X. CHAPMAN,
Plaintiff-Appellee,

v.

George W. PICKETT, Warden, U.S.
Penitentiary, Marion, et al.,
Defendants-Appellants.

Nos. 84–2842, 84–2913.

United States Court of Appeals,
Seventh Circuit.

Before CUMMINGS, Chief Judge, CUDAHY and EASTERBROOK, Circuit Judges.

CUDAHY, Circuit Judge.

After refusing on religious grounds to clean pork off food trays, plaintiff, a prisoner at the federal penitentiary in Marion, Illinois, was held in segregated confinement for nine months. He filed suit contending that the punishment was excessive.

After numerous trials and appeals, this court determined that defendants—officials at the prison—had violated plaintiff's eighth amendment rights. On remand, the district court for the Central District of Illinois found defendants individually liable to plaintiff for $7,000. Defendants appeal the size of the award and the finding of individual liability. Plaintiff cross-appeals the award—arguing that it is too small—as well as the district court's failure to grant punitive damages. We affirm.

Edward Joseph X. Chapman was convicted in 1969 of armed robbery and sentenced to 20 years in prison. He was originally detained at the federal penitentiary in Lewisburg, Pennsylvania, then at Leavenworth, Kansas, before being transferred to the Marion Penitentiary on October 4, 1972. On October 9, 1972, Chapman was assigned to kitchen detail. This included removing trays from food carts and cleaning off the carts. Because the food trays had pork on them, plaintiff, a devout Black Muslim whose faith forbids any handling of pork, refused to perform the task. James E. Brown, the supervising officer, warned Chapman that if he did not complete his assignment he would receive a disciplinary citation. Chapman still refused and told Brown that the last person who had written a disciplinary report on him had been "blown out of an oven" at Leavenworth two months earlier.[1]

Brown filed a report with the prison's Adjustment Committee under Prison Code section 303, charging Chapman with "failing to perform work as instructed by supervisor." This report noted Chapman's religious grounds for refusing to work. The report also mentioned Chapman's remark about the Leavenworth incident, although Chapman was not charged with threatening an officer. That same day, an investigation by a member of the Adjustment Committee concluded that Chapman generally had a good attitude and noted that Chapman had found another prisoner to remove the pork and had afterwards completed the task. Chapman also performed his kitchen tasks the following two days without incident.

On October 11, 1972, the Adjustment Committee met on Brown's report and concluded that Chapman should be placed in segregated confinement for an indeterminate period. Thereafter, Chapman's status in segregated confinement was reviewed regularly. At one point, he wrote Warden George W. Pickett and requested immediate release and an explanation of why he was in segregation. This inquiry was not answered. On March 15, 1973, Warden Pickett received a copy of a letter dated March 9, 1973 from the Director of the Federal Bureau of Prisons, Norman A. Carlson, in which the director told Congressman Charles Rangel that prisoners should not be assigned to details involving the handling of pork if their religious beliefs forbade it. Despite this letter, Chapman remained segregated. He was returned to the general population on July 25, 1973, after spending 289 days in segregation.

While in segregation, Chapman had no social contact with other inmates. Many of his religious materials were confiscated and he had no opportunity to attend religious services. While prisoners in the general population were allowed out of their cells up to 12 hours a day, Chapman was only allowed out for exercise a few times each week and then only for 15 to 30 minute intervals. He was unable to bathe as frequently as those in the general population, was unable to request food that complied with his religious dietary restrictions, and received no vocational training.

He initially filed suit in April 1973. After much litigation,[2] this court found Chap-

---

1. In fact, an employee was involved in an oven accident at Leavenworth, but Marion officials were aware that Chapman was not suspected of involvement in the incident.

2. Chapman originally sought declaratory and injunctive relief and damages, alleging violations of his rights under the first amendment's free exercise clause, the fifth amendment's due process clause and the eighth amendment's prohibition against cruel and unusual punishment. After hearing from only two witnesses, the district court entered judgment for defendants on grounds that Chapman failed to prove any of

the allegations in his complaint and that his claim for a mandatory injunction was moot because he had already been released from segregation. On appeal, this circuit affirmed the denial of a mandatory injunction ordering release but reversed the dismissal of claims for damages and for certain declaratory and prohibitory relief. *Chapman v. Kleindienst*, 507 F.2d 1246 (7th Cir.1974). The court held that Chapman had made a prima facie case for a first amendment violation, that he had received procedural due process and that the district court had erred in terminating testimony. The court made no determination on Chapman's man's eighth amendment rights to have been violated by his extended confinement in segregation. *Chapman v. Pickett*, 586 F.2d 22 (7th Cir.1978). The case was then remanded to the district court for determination of who was responsible for the eighth amendment violation, when the violation began and what damages Chapman should receive.[3]

The district court determined that segregating Chapman for more than one week for failure to work was impermissible. Based on prior awards for wrongful segregation, the district court determined that Chapman should receive $7,000. The court determined that the three members of the Adjustment Committee, Jack Culley, E.M. Cage and Earl Buzzard were individually liable because they made the determination that Chapman should be segregated for an indefinite period. The court found Deputy Warden Fred Frey liable for approving this indeterminate sentence. The court also found Warden Pickett liable, based on the specific facts to which he had stipulated. Pickett admitted having the authority to override the Adjustment Committee's determination. He admitted knowing of plaintiff's confinement after October 11, 1972. He also knew of Norman Carlson's letter stating that individuals should not be forced to handle meat in violation of their religious beliefs.

The district court did not award plaintiff punitive damages, finding that the officers had not acted with malice and that they legitimately believed that Chapman had threatened Officer Brown. Defendants now appeal the award of more than nominal damages to Chapman, contending that

evidence of Chapman's threat should be considered in assessing the reasonableness of his confinement. Defendants also contend that they should not be held individually liable. Chapman cross-appeals contending that the award of actual damages was too small in light of the length of his confinement and claiming that his treatment warranted punitive damages.

I.

Defendants first argue that Chapman is not entitled to more than nominal damages because, even if he was wrongfully confined for refusing to work on religious grounds, his comment that the last man who had written a disciplinary report on him had been blown out of an oven provided a reasonable basis for his long-term segregation. Defendants note that this comment was in Officer Brown's report and was admitted by Chapman before the Adjustment Committee. As Chapman was an armed robber confined in a maximum security prison, defendants contend, it was reasonable to take his comment seriously and keep him under stricter supervision for 289 days. Thus, under *Carey v. Piphus*, 435 U.S. 247, 98 S.Ct. 1042, 55 L.Ed.2d 252 (1978)—which holds that damages are only recoverable when a deprivation of a right would not have occurred absent a constitutional violation—they conclude that Chapman is entitled to no more than nominal damages.

[1, 2] In raising this argument, defendants attempt to circumvent the settled law of this case. In 1978, this circuit stated:

---

eighth amendment claim due to the inadequacy of the record. It remanded the case for a new trial.

On retrial, the district court ruled that qualified immunity shielded defendants from Chapman's first amendment claim. It found that plaintiff's eighth amendment rights were violated but refused to award money damages because no actual damages were shown. On appeal this court affirmed the finding of an eighth amendment violation and the determination that the first amendment claim was barred by qualified immunity. The court reversed the finding that no actual damages had been shown.

3. On remand the district court determined that no eighth amendment violation existed in light of *Rummel v. Estelle*, 442 U.S. 939, 99 S.Ct. 2879, 61 L.Ed.2d 309 (1979). *Chapman v. Pickett*, 491 F.Supp. 967 (C.D.Ill.1980). This circuit reversed, ruling that *Rummel* did not apply to this case. *Chapman v. Pickett*, 645 F.2d 73 (7th Cir.1980) (unpublished order). The court found that the district judge had departed from the law of the case and again remanded for a determination of when plaintiff's eighth amendment violation began and a calculation of what damages were appropriate. *Chapman v. Pickett*, 676 F.2d 697 (7th Cir.1982) (unpublished order).

Defendants assert that Chapman's remarks concerning the supervisor at Leavenworth properly may have been considered in determining the length of Chapman's confinement, even though defendants admit the Leavenworth investigation of the oven incident did not raise Chapman as a suspect. If the prison authorities had wished to charge Chapman with threatening another with bodily harm, they could have done so; it was, in fact, a separately listed "Prohibited Act" under Prison Code § 004. No such charge was ever made, nor was any hearing regarding it ever held. Defendant Pickett did not even reply to Chapman's request for a formal explanation of his confinement. The mere fact that the remark was listed in the violation report and the investigator's report is not sufficient. Not having been communicated to Chapman as a ground for the decision, it may not properly be relied on as justifying the punishment of indeterminate segregation. *Chapman v. Pickett*, 586 F.2d 22, 28 n. 4 (7th Cir.1978). Never in the nine months of his segregation did any of the defendants profess that the remark was the reason for Chapman's being penalized. Moreover, the officials knew that Chapman was not suspected of causing any harm to the employee at Leavenworth. We can only conclude that Chapman was punished solely for the offense he was charged with—failing to perform work as instructed by his supervisor. As the Adjustment Committee explained in its Committee Action Report of October 11, 1972:

> The inmate stated that he has a Muslim order and that he always follows them to the letter. It forbids one from being around pork much less touch or eat. It is Allah's way. Now that he is in our house he will do as he is told.

Appendix for Plaintiff-Appellee, Cross-Appellant at A–28. As a result of this determination, Chapman was kept in virtual isolation for nine months with severe restrictions on his mobility and daily routine. We cannot say that Chapman did not suffer actual damage.

II.

Granting that Chapman has suffered actual damage, it is appropriate to consider his argument that he should have received more than $7,000 in compensation for his injuries. He notes that in certain instances courts have overturned damage awards that were substantially out of line with awards in similar cases. *See Levka v. City of Chicago*, 748 F.2d 421 (7th Cir. 1984) ($50,000 award for victim of unwarranted strip search reduced as excessive); *Phillips v. Hunter Trail Community Association*, 685 F.2d 184 (7th Cir.1982) ($25,000 award for victim of Fair Housing Act violation reduced as excessive). Plaintiff points out that he received approximately $25 per day for his injuries while other victims of wrongful segregation have sometimes received more. *See Mary & Crystal v. Ramsden*, 635 F.2d 590 (7th Cir.1980) ($80 per day damages to juveniles who were wrongfully confined); *United States ex rel. Larkins v. Oswald*, 510 F.2d 583, 584 (2d Cir.1975) ($80 per day damages to segregated prisoner who was subjected to strip search and probing of his anal cavity); *Maxwell v. Mason*, 668 F.2d 361 (8th Cir.1981) ($100 per day for wrongful detention in solitary confinement).

The district judge sitting as factfinder has broad discretion in assessing damages. *See Saxner v. Benson*, 727 F.2d 669, 672–73 (7th Cir.1984) ("In view of the general restrictions on appellate review of a jury's award of monetary damages we will not substitute our judgment in these circumstances for that of the judge and jury who heard the testimony."), *aff'd sub nom. Cleavinger v. Saxner*, —— U.S. ——, 106 S.Ct. 496, 88 L.Ed.2d 507 (1985); *Phillips v. Hunter Trail Community Association*, 685 F.2d at 191. His findings will not be overturned unless found to be clearly erroneous. Plaintiff contends that the decision here was clearly erroneous because some prisoners received damages more than four times per day greater than what he received.

An individual can always point to cases in which others received more and say that he received too little. To accept that argument is to say that a court must match the most generous offer made elsewhere, even though the circumstances of the case before it may be different and even though it may be the higher awards that less accurately reflect actual damages. In cases of wrongful segregation, at least one other court has awarded sums to victims of wrongful segregation similar to what Chapman received. *See Riley v. Johnson*, 528 F.Supp. 333, 343 (E.D.Mich.1981) ($25 per day). While some courts have awarded larger amounts, this may have been due to factors not present in Chapman's case. For example, the plaintiffs in *Mary & Crystal v. Ramsden* were juveniles. The plaintiff in *United States ex rel. Larkins v. Oswald* was marched naked to his cell and subjected to a strip search and the probing of his anal cavity. The district judge was aware of these cases when he calculated his award. We cannot say he abused his discretion.

III.

Chapman also seeks punitive damages. A court may award punitive damages "when the defendant's conduct is shown to be motivated by evil motive and intent, or when it involves reckless or callous indifference to the federally protected rights of others." *Smith v. Wade*, 461 U.S. 30, 56, 103 S.Ct. 1625, 1640, 75 L.Ed.2d 632 (1983). Here, the district court found that even though defendants' good faith belief that plaintiff had threatened an officer was not a basis for segregating Chapman, it did provide grounds for denying punitive damages. The award of punitive damages is also within the sound discretion of the district judge and his finding will not be disturbed.

IV.

The final issue raised on appeal is whether defendants may be held personally liable for plaintiffs damage.[4] A plaintiff may establish personal responsibility "if the official acts or fails to act with a deliberate or reckless disregard of plaintiff's constitutional rights, or if the conduct causing the constitutional deprivation occurs at her direction or with her knowledge or consent." *Crowder v. Lash*, 687 F.2d 996, 1005 (7th Cir.1982); *Wellman v. Faulkner*, 715 F.2d 269, 275 (7th Cir.1983). This test was clearly satisfied as to the three members of the Adjustment Committee and Associate Warden Frey. The members of the Adjustment Committee made the initial determination that plaintiff should be confined to segregation. They met repeatedly during his time in segregation to review his case. While in a position to return plaintiff

---

4. Defendants claim they should be immune from liability. They initially argued that they were absolutely immune from liability but this argument was foreclosed by the Supreme Court's decision in *Cleavinger v. Saxner*, — U.S. ——, 106 S.Ct. 496, 88 L.Ed.2d 507 (1985), that members of prison disciplinary committees receive only qualified and not absolute immunity. The defendants now claim they should receive qualified immunity from liability for violations of plaintiff's eighth amendment rights. They did not advance a qualified immunity argument before the district court in this case. In 1978, this circuit rejected defendants' qualified immunity argument and concluded:

There can be no serious contention with the fact that the right to be free from disproportionate punishment has long been 'clearly established.' At least as early as 1910, the Supreme Court declared it to be 'a precept of justice' that punishment for crime must be proportioned to the offenses, lest it be found

to be cruel and unusual. *Weems v. United States*, 217 U.S. 349, 367 [30 S.Ct. 544, 549, 54 L.Ed. 793].

American Intern. Ins. Co. v. Vessel SS Fortaleza, 585 F.2d 22, 28 (7th Cir.1978). Since that time the Supreme Court has decided *Harlow v. Fitzgerald*, 457 U.S. 800, 102 S.Ct. 2727, 73 L.Ed.2d 396 (1982). That case articulated an objective standard for determining qualified immunity. Under that test "government officials performing discretionary functions generally are shielded from liability for civil damages insofar as their conduct does not violate clearly established statutory or constitutional rights of which a reasonable person would have known." *Id.* at 818, 102 S.Ct. at 2738. We do not believe that *Harlow* changes the 1978 result. In 1972 it was established that excessive punishment in segregated confinement for the exercise of a religious right could subject prison officials to liability. *See Bryant v. Harris*, 465 F.2d 365, 367 (7th Cir.1972).

to the general prison population, they kept him in segregation for nine months. Associate Warden Frey participated in many of the meetings concerning Chapman's confinement. In his position as supervisor, he too had the power to correct plaintiff's wrongful confinement. Under similar circumstances in *Crowder* we found the personal responsibility requirement had been met:

> The evidence presented by Crowder indicated that both Moore and Devero sat as members of the disciplinary committee and, thus, participated directly in the "disciplinary hearings" by which Crowder was repeatedly sentenced to confinement in the D.O. seclusion unit. In addition, Crowder testified that Moore and Devero were directly responsible for denying his requests for legal assistance and legal materials.... Moreover, because Moore and Devero were personally accountable for reviewing the status of inmates held in D.O. seclusion, they could properly be held liable for an eighth amendment violation if, at any time, Crowder's continued confinement in D.O. seclusion became unlawfully disproportionate to the seriousness of his prison infractions.

687 F.2d at 1006.

Warden Pickett's personal liability presents a more difficult question. Courts have exacting standards for establishing supervisory officials' personal liability and hesitate to saddle supervisors with responsibility for decisions they did not make. The dissent points to cases that have not met these exacting standards and apparently concludes that "supervisory officials are not liable for failing to intervene to ameliorate things." However, the law does not accord supervisors such sweeping freedom from liability. Rather, established law holds that under certain circumstances supervisors may be personally liable for failing to act when they have knowledge of a constitutional deprivation. *See Crowder v. Lash*, 687 F.2d at 1005; *Cf. McKinnon v. City of Berwyn*, 750 F.2d 1383, 1391 (7th Cir.1984) (failing to supervise subordinates may be actionable). The knowledge that is required is not only that a constitutional deprivation exists but also that the supervisor's personal action is necessary to set it right.

The requisite knowledge is present in this case. Warden Pickett stipulated to knowing of Chapman's confinement and doing nothing about it, even after he received a letter from the Director of Prisons—Pickett's own supervisor. He stipulated before the district court

> that among his duties was to see that discipline was maintained at the prison; that as chief officer of the prison Mr. Picket[t] had the authority to override the decisions of officers at the prison; that Mr. Picket[t] was aware of Plaintiff's placement in segregation on October 11, 1972 and that he was continued and confined there until July 25, 1973; that on March 15, 1973 Mr. Picket[t] received a copy of a letter from Norman A. Carlson, Director, Federal Bureau of Prisons to Representative Charles Rangel. The letter indicated, ... "We have your letter of January 11, 1973 concerning Mr. Edward Chapman. In your letter we take exception to your statement of January 17, 1973, that men of the Black Muslim Faith at our facility were assigned the task of handling pork. We reviewed the situation and have communicated to the heads of the department of instructions not to assign individuals to details where they must work with pork as it is against their religious beliefs."

Transcripts of Proceeding Before District Court, Nov. 3, 1976 at 95.

Pickett was the official at Marion to receive Director Carlson's communication, which should have put him on notice that Chapman was wrongfully segregated. While that placed him in the best position to know that a constitutional deprivation had occurred and while he had the authority to remedy the situation, he did nothing. Chapman remained in segregated confinement for more than four more months. Under these circumstances, the district court was entitled to find Warden Pickett personally liable and we cannot say this disposition was clearly erroneous.[5]

For the foregoing reasons the judgment of the court below is AFFIRMED.

EASTERBROOK, Circuit Judge, dissenting.

This first amendment case has turned into an eighth amendment one because of the court's holding in 1978 that the defendants have qualified immunity from damages for punishing Chapman on account of his religious beliefs. 586 F.2d 22, 25–26. The extent to which public officials may or must accommodate sincere religious beliefs has produced a series of cases that are hard to reconcile and apply. These cases divide the Justices deeply. E.g., *Bowen v. Roy*, — U.S. —, 106 S.Ct. 2147, 90 L.Ed.2d 735 (1986); *Goldman v. Weinberger*, — U.S. —, 106 S.Ct. 1310, 89 L.Ed.2d 478 (1986). See also *Caldwell v. Miller*, 790 F.2d 589, 597–600 (7th Cir. 1986); Michael W. McConnell, *Accommodation of Religion*, 1985 Sup.Ct.Rev. 1. A humane prison administration accommodates religious beliefs when assigning jobs, as the Bureau of Prisons now does, but it was not clear in 1972 that it had to. I do not think it is clear today, given cases such as *Goldman* and the fact that a prisoner is more like a member of the military than of free society. See also *Madyun v. Franzen*, 704 F.2d 954, 958–60 (7th Cir.1983). This establishes the immunity of the defendants from damages under the first amendment.

This left for decision in 1978 the claim that nine months in segregation is "exces-

sive" for the offense of refusing to handle pork in the kitchen. The panel both found a violation of the eighth amendment and rejected the defendants' claim of immunity, stating: "At least as early as 1910, the Supreme Court declared it to be 'a precept of justice' that punishment for crime must be proportioned to the offense, lest it be found to be cruel and unusual. *Weems v. United States*, 217 U.S. 349, 367, 30 S.Ct. 544, 549, 54 L.Ed. 793 (1910). This being so, the question becomes whether defendants 'knew or should have known' that their confinement of Chapman to segregation was or became grossly disproportionate to the offense with which he had been charged. But this question almost answers itself, for if a point in time can be determined when the punishment became so seriously disproportionate as to violate the Eighth Amendment, at that same point defendants 'should have known' that the punishment was grossly excessive. Thus, ... the defense of qualified official immunity is not available for damages arising out of Chapman's Eighth Amendment claim." 586 F.2d at 28–29.

Several components of this decision are untenable. One is that "excessively long" separation from the general population of a prison violates the eighth amendment. A second is that the general enunciation of a right—such as "let the punishment fit the crime"—is the sort of clear articulation that dissipates immunity. A third is that by 1973 this general right had been applied to prison discipline. A fourth is that official immunity does not apply to violations of the eighth amendment.

5. The dissent is in all other particulars an attack on *Chapman v. Pickett*, 586 F.2d 22 (7th Cir. 1978). None of the points raised by the dissent (apart from the immunity arguments) has been argued by the government here for the very good reason that, except under rare circumstances, one panel of this court may not overrule a result reached by another panel. *See Devines v. Maier*, 728 F.2d 876, 880 (7th Cir.), cert. denied, 469 U.S. 836, 105 S.Ct. 130, 83 L.Ed.2d 71 (1984); *Appleton Electric Co. v. Graves Truck Line, Inc.*, 635 F.2d 603, 607 (7th Cir.1980) ("we have long held that 'matters decided on appeal become the law of the case to be followed ... on second appeal, in the appel-

late court, unless there is plain error of law in the original decision.'") (quoting *Kaku Nagano v. Brownell*, 212 F.2d 262, 263 (7th Cir.1954)). The law of the case doctrine has an extremely persuasive rationale in this case as in others, and one can hardly imagine a matter more fraught with Pandora's Box potential than reopening the judgments reached by prior panels in the same case. The "change of law" rationale offered by the dissent for its extraordinary exploration of closed matters seems to us, under the circumstances of this case, a license to second-guess, or apply hindsight, to any number of otherwise settled decisions of this court.

The majority does not discuss these holdings, on which its judgment depends, even though the defendants maintain that the immunity holding in 1978 is incorrect and should be reviewed in light of more recent cases. My brethren rely on the law of the case.[1] It is unwise for one panel to undo the work of another in the same case. Litigants should be able to assume that panels of this court are alike. Otherwise they will spend their time (and ours) trying to convince each panel to follow or upset the last decision. The law of the case is a salutary doctrine even when a judge believes that an earlier decision is wrong. Yet the doctrine has exceptions, the most important being for intervening changes in the law. See *Arizona v. California*, 460 U.S. 605, 618–19 & n. 8, 103 S.Ct. 1382, 1391 & n. 8, 75 L.Ed.2d 318 (1983); *Cameo Convalescent Center, Inc. v. Percy*, 800 F.2d 108, 109–10 (7th Cir.1986); *Chicago & North Western Transportation Co. v. United States*, 574 F.2d 926, 930 (7th Cir.1978). See also, e.g., *Devines v. Maier*, 728 F.2d 876, 880 (7th Cir. 1984) (discussing an exception for clear error in the earlier decision, error that usually becomes "clear" because of intervening decisions); *Christianson v. Colt Industries Operating Corp.*, 798 F.2d 1051, 1056 (7th Cir.1986) (a decision that is "manifestly incorrect" may be reexamined even when there has not been an intervening change of law). Although the majority's opinion applies the principles that have been established in the earlier opinions in this case, it is appropriate to reexamine these principles in light of decisions after 1978 and a few earlier decisions that the panel overlooked in 1978. The portion of that decision based on the eighth amendment is wrong in just about every particular. It ought not stand. Moreover, the majority introduces a new error, which I discuss at the end of this opinion.

1. *Weems*, which the panel cited in 1978 for the proposition that "excessive" punishments are forbidden, was a case about prison conditions, life at hard labor in chains, rather than about the duration of confinement alone. The other applications of the eighth amendment to prisoners also are about conditions—about the amount of space a prisoner has, about the quality of the food, about medical care, about freedom from injury. E.g., *Whitley v. Albers*, — U.S. —, 106 S.Ct. 1078, 89 L.Ed.2d 251 (1986); *Rhodes v. Chapman*, 452 U.S. 337, 101 S.Ct. 2392, 69 L.Ed.2d 59 (1981); *Caldwell*, 790 F.2d at 600–01; *Duckworth v. Franzen*, 780 F.2d 645 (7th Cir.1986); *French v. Owens*, 777 F.2d 1250 (7th Cir. 1985). If Chapman had been sent to a hellhole, he would have a claim under the eighth amendment. But segregation at Marion is not infernal. Many prisoners stay a lot longer than nine months in Marion's Control Unit, which is worse. Chapman does not contend that the conditions of segregation independently violated the Constitution.

If the conditions of segregation at Marion are within the tolerable range, and if damages are not the appropriate response to the *reason* Chapman was put in segregation—as we must assume given the holding that Chapman is not entitled to relief under the first amendment—then the duration of the segregation was not unconstitutional. Chapman did not tell the prison officials that he would start clearing the dishes. He held to his beliefs. Every day Chapman was in segregation was a day on which he would have refused to handle pork. So if the eighth amendment establishes a principle of proportional length of differential treatment within a prison, the defendants did not transgress against it. This was no more a violation of the eighth amendment than nine months' confinement

---

1. Chapman also contends that the defendants have not preserved these issues, because they did not raise them in the district court after the decision of 1978. They have done what they must, however. A litigant need not pester the district court with requests to violate the court of appeals' mandate in order to preserve the right to ask the appellate court to reexamine its earlier holdings.

of a recalcitrant witness before a grand jury would be.

The most substantial problem with our 1978 decision, however, is its assumption that a prisoner has *any* legally protected interest in enjoying the same conditions of confinement as other prisoners. Chapman did not serve an extra day because of his refusal to handle pork. He simply had less pleasant conditions. Suppose he had been transferred from a minimum security prison to Marion because of his refusal to do assigned work. His loss would have been greater than the difference between the general population and segregation at Marion. It is established, however, that a conviction for crime allows executive officials to place prisoners where they will, to subject them to the range of conditions in the Nation's many prisons. *Meachum v. Fano*, 427 U.S. 215, 224–25, 96 S.Ct. 2532, 2538–39, 49 L.Ed.2d 451 (1976); *Moody v. Daggett*, 429 U.S. 78, 88 n. 9, 97 S.Ct. 274, 279 n. 9, 50 L.Ed.2d 236 (1976); *Olim v. Wakinekona*, 461 U.S. 238, 103 S.Ct. 1741, 75 L.Ed.2d 813 (1983).

The question about "disproportionate sentences" under the eighth amendment is whether a state has deprived a person of his liberty for too long, given the nature of the offense. There is a big difference between being in and being out of prison. Chapman's natural liberty, though, was not hanging in the balance. His liberty to select where and how he would live had been extinguished by the judgment of conviction. See *Hudson v. Palmer*, 468 U.S. 517, 524–28, 104 S.Ct. 3194, 3199–3201, 82 L.Ed. 2d 393 (1984). That is why the Court held in *Meachum* that a conviction authorizes the state to confine a prisoner in any of its institutions, even though one may be much less pleasant than another. For the same reason a state may confine its prisoners in any cell within a prison or change the prisoner's regimen—individual meals in segregation instead of group meals in the general population, fewer showers, less exercise, and so on. *Hewitt v. Helms*, 459 U.S. 460, 468, 103 S.Ct. 864, 869, 74 L.Ed.2d 675 (1983) (segregation within a prison "is the sort of confinement that inmates should reasonably anticipate receiving at some point in their incarceration"). There is no constitutional difference between segregation and the general population; prisoners have no entitlement that prisons have "general populations", as our recent decision sustaining the "lockdown" of the entire population at Marion for more than nine months shows. *Caldwell*, 790 F.2d at 600–05.

The panel did not discuss these principles in 1978. It did not cite *Meachum* and similar cases. *Hewitt*, which held that a prisoner does not have a constitutional interest in remaining in the general population, was not decided until 1983. True, *Meachum* and *Hewitt* interpreted the fourteenth rather than the eighth amendment. Yet these cases are not accidents of pleading. The Court would not have rendered a different decision if the prisoners had argued their cases under the eighth amendment instead of the due process clause of the fourteenth. After all, the eighth amendment applies to the states only to the extent it has been "incorporated" in the due process clause of the fourteenth. *Meachum, Hewitt, Hudson* (holding that prisoners have no legitimate expectation of privacy), and similar cases establish that the Constitution does not entitle prisoners to live in the best conditions a prison has to offer.

The state may *create* protected interests. It may, for example, adopt rules providing that people will be sent to Marion (or closer confinement within Marion) only on account of misconduct. Rules restricting the discretion of officials may establish legitimate claims of entitlement of which prisoners may be deprived only with due process of law. The Court ultimately held in *Hewitt* that Pennsylvania's regulations created a legitimate claim of entitlement to remain in the general population even though the Constitution of its own force does not. See also *Wolff v. McDonnell*, 418 U.S. 539, 94 S.Ct. 2963, 41 L.Ed.2d 935 (1974), and the treatment of *Wolff* in *Meachum*, 427 U.S. at 225–27, 96 S.Ct. at 2538–40. The question from this perspective is whether rules restricted the discretion of the defendants to put Chapman in segrega-

CHAPMAN v. PICKETT (922)   431

tion for refusing to work. In 1980 we
remarked on the difference between process and substance in prison discipline, implicitly repudiating the premises of our
1978 decision. *Bono v. Saxbe*, 620 F.2d
609, 611–12 (7th Cir.1980), holds that the
due process clause rather than the eighth
amendment governs the duration of segregated confinement at Marion, unless the
conditions of confinement are unconstitutionally harsh.[2] Ours is not a due process
case. Chapman had a hearing. He does
not contend that the hearing was procedurally defective or that the defendants lacked
authority under the regulations then in
force to put him in segregation. He therefore cannot recover under the due process
clause, and he does not seek to do so.

There is one more way in which this case
may be argued under the eighth amendment. If the prison officials *knew* that
they had no basis to punish Chapman, but
they put him or kept him in segregation
vindictively, this might state a claim. Prison officials must have some reason to impose punishment, if they set up rules confining their discretion. *Superintendent of
Walpole v. Hill*, 472 U.S. 445, 105 S.Ct.
2768, 86 L.Ed.2d 356 (1985). The prison
officials had reason to punish Chapman.
He defied a direct order and said he would
defy it again. He gave a reason for disobedience, but under our 1978 decision the
defendants have immunity from damages
on account of their refusal to accept his
reason. It is as if Chapman had been put
in segregation for refusing to press green
shirts in the laundry, proclaiming that
green shirts look better crinkled. Involuntary servitude is the portion of convicts,
the thirteenth amendment says. A prisoner who decides he will work only on terms
satisfactory to himself must expect his confinement to become even more onerous
than it was. Chapman's disobedience is

justification for discipline under Marion's
rules. More, the district court found that
the prison officials did not act maliciously
or vindictively; this is the basis on which
the court denied punitive damages. This
potential source of liability is foreclosed.

Marion is an explosive place. It is the
Nation's maximum security prison, populated by violent and intractable offenders who
could not adjust to life in other prisons.
Administrators of prisons have hard tasks.
They cannot control the population without
authority over it, yet every exercise of authority may expose them to liability. The
Supreme Court has said over and again
that courts should respect prison officials'
exercise of judgment. We have said over
and again that the officials at Marion,
whose task is especially difficult, deserve
especial deference. E.g., *McCollum v.
Williford*, 793 F.2d 903 (7th Cir.1986) (Marion may discipline prisoners on the basis of
reports withheld even from the disciplinary
committee, although that might be impermissible at other prisons). Officials may
respond to judicial orders reducing their
discretion by exerting control in other
ways. They can change the way the prison
is organized. There will be no more disobedience at Marion during work details.
Work has been cancelled. Guards or con-
tractors clean the dishes and press the
shirts. The prisoners stay locked in their
cells. I doubt that they count the trade a
gain.

It is hard to imagine a rule more enervat-
ing than one that allows a prisoner to collect damages from his keepers on the
ground that they should have returned him
to the general population, after an admitted offense, in six months rather than nine,
or perhaps in three weeks rather than four.
This transfers effective authority from the
warden to a jury; it increases the risk of
taking firm measures. The prison's offi-

---

2. *Bono* replaces the eighth amendment analysis
with one styled "substantive due process", see
620 F.2d at 615–18, and this replacement is as
inconsistent with *Meachum, Moody, Hewitt*, and
Olim as is our 1978 case. *Hewitt* knocked the
struts out from under *Bono* by holding that the
Constitution does not independently regulate
transfers to segregation; an analysis based on

"substantive due process" assumes the contrary.
See also *Gumz v. Morrissette*, 772 F.2d 1395,
1405–09 (7th Cir.1985) (concurring opinion),
cert. denied, —— U.S. ——, 106 S.Ct. 1644, 90
L.Ed.2d 189 (1986). But this is not the time to
deal with substantive due process, which Chapman has not invoked. See also note 3 below.

cials will not know what they may do until the case is over and the decision has been rendered on appeal. Yet if administrators react to this threat to their wallets by going easy on misconduct, the result may be the deaths of prisoners and guards alike. There have been too many deaths at Marion to be sanguine about lax discipline. The Framers did not decide in 1789 (when Congress sent the Bill of Rights to the States) or 1791 (when Virginia provided the ratification necessary to put the first ten amendments into effect) to commit to juries the question whether a prisoner's separation from the general population lasted too long in light of the seriousness of his offense. We have no authority to decide so today.

2. Assume now that this is wrong, that Chapman spent an unconstitutionally long time in segregation. The defendants are entitled to immunity from liability in damages unless their acts violated "clearly established ... constitutional rights of which a reasonable person would have known." *Harlow v. Fitzgerald,* 457 U.S. 800, 818, 102 S.Ct. 2727, 2738, 73 L.Ed.2d 396 (1982). See also *Cleavinger v. Saxner,* — U.S. ——, 106 S.Ct. 496, 504, 88 L.Ed.2d 507 (1985). The panel thought in 1978 that *Weems* had "clearly established" that "excessive" punishments are unconstitutional.

This is sleight of hand. It is always possible to state the constitutional right at a level so general that it "clearly establishes" the right in question. If a question arises, such as whether an Attorney General may authorize a national security wiretap without a warrant, a court could reply that the Supreme Court established a presumption in favor of warrants, and in 1967 the Court applied this to the interception of telephone conversations. So by the time Attorney General Mitchell came to office, it was "clearly established" that there had to be a warrant for an interception. This was not, however, the method the Supreme Court used to decide the case. It asked instead when the general rule had been made specific—that is, when the Court first held that national security wiretaps require a warrant. See *Mitchell v. Forsyth,* 472 U.S. 511, 105 S.Ct. 2806, 2818–20 & n. 12,

86 L.Ed.2d 411 (1985). Similarly, if a question arises whether an affidavit establishes probable cause to obtain a warrant, a court could say: "It has long been established that you need probable cause to get a warrant, so if you got a warrant without probable cause you are liable." But "probable cause" is too general. In *Malley v. Briggs,* — U.S. ——, 106 S.Ct. 1092, 89 L.Ed.2d 271 (1986), the Court concluded that the right question is whether a well trained and careful official should have known that his conduct would be viewed as unconstitutional in light of the available precedents. It wrote: "[d]efendants will not be immune if, on an objective basis, it is obvious that no reasonably competent officer would have concluded that a warrant should issue; but if officers of reasonable competence could disagree on this issue, immunity should be recognized." 106 S.Ct. at 1096; see also *id.* at 1098–99.

Until the constitutional right has been stated so that reasonably competent officers would agree on its application to a given set of facts, it has not been "clearly established" for purposes of *Harlow*. In several cases since 1978 we recognized this. E.g., *Zook v. Brown,* 748 F.2d 1161, 1165 (7th Cir.1984); *Coleman v. Frantz,* 754 F.2d 719, 730 n. 15 (7th Cir.1985); *Lojuk v. Johnson,* 770 F.2d 619, 628 (7th Cir.1985); *Benson v. Allphin,* 786 F.2d 268, 275–76 (7th Cir.1986). *Azeez v. Fairman,* 795 F.2d 1296 (7th Cir.1986), is the most recent, and its discussion is dispositive (*id.* at 1301): "The words 'clearly established ... constitutional rights' may not be used to read the defense of immunity out of federal tort law by the facile expedient of stating constitutional rights in the most general possible terms, so that anyone who prevails on the merits of a claim based on (for example) the First Amendment's free exercise of religion clause, however novel that claim is, can defeat the defense of immunity simply by pointing out that the right to the free exercise of one's religion has long been a clearly established constitutional right. The right must be sufficiently particularized to put potential defendants on notice that their conduct probably is unlawful." See also *Hobson v. Wilson,* 737 F.2d 1, 26

(D.C.Cir.1984), *cert. denied,* — U.S. —, 105 S.Ct. 1843, 85 L.Ed.2d 142 (1985). Our decision of 1978 is a derelict—in this circuit anyway. I recognize that it has company in other circuits, e.g., *Creighton v. City of St. Paul,* 766 F.2d 1269 (8th Cir.1985), *cert. granted* under the name *Anderson v. Creighton,* — U.S. —, 106 S.Ct. 3292, 92 L.Ed.2d 708 (1986), but these decisions predate *Malley* and do not explain why it is appropriate to take a broadly phrased right as "clearly establishing" a particular application. Our court should attorn to the standard of *Azeez,* under which the law in 1972–73 had not "clearly established" that the eighth amendment forbids "excessive" terms of segregated confinement within a prison.[3]

Officers of "reasonable competence could disagree" (*Malley,* 106 S.Ct. at 1096) about the propriety of their conduct in 1973. As this opinion shows, judges still disagree about the constitutional standards. The defendants will take cold comfort in knowing that they have been found liable—on the ground that no reasonably well trained person could have believed they were entitled to act as they did—for doing something that the district court thought they were entitled to do (our decision in 1978 reversed the district court) and that at least one judge of this panel thinks the Constitution allows them to do. Cf. *Nix v. Williams,* 467 U.S. 431, 350–51, 104 S.Ct. 2501, 2512–13, 81 L.Ed.2d 377 (1983) (White, J., concurring).

3. The answer to the question "was it clearly established in 1973 that the eighth amendment forbids 'excessive' administra-

tive punishments" is No. It is not so established today. It certainly was not so established in 1973. Not until June 1983, when it decided *Solem v. Helm,* 463 U.S. 277, 103 S.Ct. 3001, 77 L.Ed.2d 637, did the Supreme Court hold a criminal sentence invalid because too long. Earlier cases had held that the length of a punishment, as opposed to its character (torture, death, and so on), is a matter for the judgment of the legislature and the sentencing court. E.g., *Hutto v. Davis,* 454 U.S. 370, 102 S.Ct. 703, 70 L.Ed.2d 556 (1982); *Rummel v. Estelle,* 445 U.S. 263, 100 S.Ct. 1133, 63 L.Ed.2d 382 (1980); *Badders v. United States,* 240 U.S. 391, 395, 36 S.Ct. 367, 368, 60 L.Ed. 706 (1916); *Howard v. Fleming,* 191 U.S. 126, 136, 24 S.Ct. 49, 50, 48 L.Ed. 121 (1903). *Hutto* and *Rummel,* decided after 1978, show that the eighth amendment does not authorize federal courts to insist that punishments be finely proportioned to the crime. The Supreme Court has not extended the principle of *Solem* to intra-prison sanctions, and *Solem* itself suggests that only outrageous punishments (life in prison for shoplifting) violate the eighth amendment. No court to this day has held that nine months in prison is cruel and unusual punishment for anything, even jaywalking.[4] Statutes often authorize misdemeanors, a rag-tag collection of small offenses, to be punished by a year's imprisonment. And because Chapman was not sent *to* prison for refusing to handle pork, but was just moved to a new cell *in* prison, the analogy to other cases under the eighth amendment is even weaker.

The only case that arguably makes the right in question sufficiently particular is

---

3. The panel intimated in 1978 that the prison officials should have released Chapman to the general population soon after the Bureau of Prisons adopted its policy against assigning people to handle foods forbidden them by their religions. This amounts to saying that the administrative rules of the prison system "established" the constitutional right. *Davis v. Scherer,* 468 U.S. 183, 194 & n. 12, 104 S.Ct. 3012, 2019 & n. 12, 82 L.Ed.2d 139 (1984), holds otherwise. *Davis* establishes that only when the rule establishes the claim for relief sued upon does a violation of a "clear" rule abrogate an immunity. See also *Gramenos v. Jewel Companies, Inc.,* 797 F.2d 432, 434 (7th Cir.1986). Chapman is not entitled to recover damages on account of a violation of the Bureau of Prisons' internal rules,

especially a rule that was adopted after he had been put in segregation and that does not mention the appropriate treatment of prisoners in Chapman's position. It is the eighth amendment or nothing.

4. I put to one side the remark in *Robinson v. California,* 370 U.S. 660, 667, 82 S.Ct. 1417, 1420, 8 L.Ed.2d 758 (1962), that one day is cruel and unusual for the crime of having a common cold. Colds imprison the best of us, and at all events the case dealt with the minimum requirements for criminal punishment, not with the duration of imprisonment in relation to the gravity of the offense.

Adams v. Carlson, 488 F.2d 619, 635–36 (7th Cir. Aug. 23, 1973), which the panel in 1978 said (586 F.2d at 27) establishes that any "disproportionate" punishment in prison is unconstitutional. *Adams*, based on principles of procedural due process, preceded *Meachum, Moody*, and *Hewitt*. It is no longer authoritative. *Adams* did not hold that the eighth amendment directly limits the duration of segregation from the general population. Its discussion of the eighth amendment melds principles of due process with those of proportionality, and it ultimately holds that the claims before it under the eighth amendment were not ripe for adjudication. A decision concluding that it could not resolve the dispute at hand—that Article III forbade a disposition on the merits of the eighth amendment claim—cannot "clearly establish" any legal principles, not unless advisory opinions have become the law of the land.

More to the point, *Adams* was decided after Chapman had been released from segregation! The case arose out of a prison disturbance at Marion, whose officials summarily confined a number of prisoners in indefinite segregation. The prisoners sought an injunction to compel their release. The district court held that this confinement did not violate the constitutional rights of the prisoners. *Adams v. Carlson*, 352 F.Supp. 882, 891–94 (E.D.I!!. Jan. 15, 1973). At the time the defendants decided to keep Chapman in segregation, then, they had recently been told by a district court that prisoners at Marion had no constitutional rights that impeded lengthy segregation. It is beyond me how the defendants were supposed to know the opposite—let alone how the opposite could be said to have been "clearly established" in the spring of 1973. See also *Benson*, 786 F.2d at 278.

4. Our decision of 1978 suggested that there can be no immunity when the right in question is the eighth amendment. The Ninth Circuit apparently takes this view. Compare *Haygood v. Younger*, 718 F.2d 1472, 1483–84 (1983), modified en banc, 769 F.2d 1350, 1358–59 (1985), with *Albers v. Whitley*, 743 F.2d 1372, 1376 (1984), rev'd

on other grounds, — U.S. —, 106 S.Ct. 1078, 89 L.Ed.2d 251 (1986). Another panel of this court has applied the *Harlow* standard of immunity to a violation of the eighth amendment, however, see *Joseph v. Brierton*, 739 F.2d 1244, 1249–50 (7th Cir. 1984), although it rejected the defense on the facts presented, and at least two other circuits hold that officials who violate the eighth amendment may be immune from liability in damages. *Sampson v. King*, 693 F.2d 566 (5th Cir.1982); *McCray v. Burrell*, 516 F.2d 357, 370–72 (4th Cir.1975) (en banc).

The *Harlow* standard logically applies to cases under the eighth amendment. The definition of the violation sometimes includes a mental element (such as "deliberate indifference", see *Whitley* and *Duckworth*), but the test under *Harlow* is objective, so that the mental element does not dispose of the immunity question. It is quite consistent to say that the defendants *wanted* Chapman to suffer, or were indifferent to whether he did, and that a reasonable person would have believed in 1973 that the infliction of punishment was lawful. The police officer who shoots a fleeing subject wants to injure that person, but it does not follow that the officer never can claim immunity for wrongful use of force. If a reasonably well trained officer (*Malley*, 106 S.Ct. at 1098) would have concluded that it was permissible to use force, the defendant's subjective intent to inflict pain does not abrogate the immunity. So here. If a reasonably well trained warden or disciplinary committee would have thought in 1973 that it was permissible to keep someone in segregation for nine months for a nonviolent (but deliberate) infraction of the prison's rules, an infraction the prisoner had pledged to repeat, then there should be qualified immunity. Only when the presence of the mental element that defines the violation also shows that no reasonably well trained official could have thought his behavior proper, as in *Joseph v. Brierton*, is the existence of a violation incompatible with immunity.

5. The discussion so far explores my disagreements with the decision in 1978. I have one disagreement with the decision of

today. The district court held former Warden Pickett liable along with his subordinates. No evidence in the record shows that Pickett authorized Chapman's segregation or approved its duration. The stipulation to which the majority refers shows only that the Warden knew that Chapman was in confinement and did nothing, even after receiving a letter stating that the Bureau of Prisons had adopted a policy relieving people of handling food to which they objected on religious grounds. The record does not show that the Warden read this letter (the stipulation says that he "received" it) or that wardens in federal prisons customarily review disciplinary cases in light of changing directives. For all the record shows, wardens leave these things, along with most of the other tasks of management, to their subordinates. Wardens establish policy and assign tasks; detail work and daily administration are among the tasks parcelled out.

The eighth amendment does not establish superiors' liability. A warden is liable only for what he does, not for what he fails to prevent his subordinates from doing. The division of labor and the delegation of functions within a prison are not unconstitutional. A warden asleep on the job will have to answer to his superiors, but dozing off on company time is not a violation of the Constitution. The proper defendants are those who put Chapman in segregation and, despite regularly reviewing his status, refused to let him out. We have held that supervisory officials are not liable for failing to intervene to ameliorate things. E.g., *Kunzelman v. Thompson*, 799 F.2d 1172–

75 (7th Cir.1986); *Walker v. Rowe*, 791 F.2d 507, 508–09 (7th Cir.1986); *Ustrak v. Fairman*, 781 F.2d 573, 575–77 (7th Cir. 1986); *Duckworth v. Franzen*, 780 F.2d at 650; *McKinnon v. City of Berwyn*, 750 F.2d 1383, 1390 (7th Cir.1984); *Wellman v. Faulkner*, 715 F.2d 269, 275–76 (7th Cir. 1983), cert. denied, 468 U.S. 1217, 104 S.Ct. 3587, 82 L.Ed.2d 885 (1984); *Crowder v. Lash*, 687 F.2d 996, 1005–06 (7th Cir.1982); *Duncan v. Duckworth*, 644 F.2d 653, 655 (7th Cir.1981); *Adams v. Pate*, 445 F.2d 105, 107 (7th Cir.1971). Some of these cases are very similar to this. In *Adams v. Pate*, for example, the court held that notice to a warden that a prisoner was being beaten did not justify damages when the warden did not take steps to prevent future beatings.

A prison may apportion responsibilities among officials without exposing supervisors to liability on the ground that they failed to prevent what the subordinates were doing. The majority does not reconcile its holding with the cases I have cited. The "clearly erroneous" doctrine, to which the majority refers, applies to facts and inferences; I do not think, however, that facts and inferences are disputed. The question is whether on stipulated facts the warden of a prison is liable for failing to prevent a violation of the eighth amendment by his subordinates. The stipulation of facts does not suggest, and the district court did not find, that Warden Pickett had either the personal role or the mental state required for a violation of the eighth amendment.

VOLUME III

CHAPTER 4   CONTACTS WITH THE OUTSIDE WORLD

Inmate contacts by mail with family, friends and other individuals are protected by the First Amendment to the extent that such contacts do not interfere with the security and safety of the prisons. Some types of correspondence are privileged, such as an inmate's correspondence with his lawyer, and are not governed by principles of security and safety. Courts tend to defer to the judgment of prison officials as to whether certain mail interferes with the security and safety of the prisoner. A court's assessment of facts generally relies upon the evaluation by prison officials.

The Supreme Court of the United States, in the case of *Procunier v. Martinez,* 416 U.S. 396, 94 S.Ct. 1800 (1974), set forth in Vol. II: 14, provided some guidelines for the troublesome field. However, new issues continue to arise. *Gaines v. Lane,* 790 F.2d 1299 (7th Cir. 1986) considered rules governing the Illinois Penal System that the plaintiff alleged authorities failed to follow. More specifically, the complainant argued that mail from the news media should be privileged.

In *Martin v. Kelley,* 803 F.2d 326 (1986), an inmate claimed an Ohio regulation governing censorship of prison mail was unconstitutional because it did not require that prison officials notify inmates when letters were censored and did not provide them with the opportunity to protest decisions against mail delivery. The court supported his claim.

A similar case, not set out here, was *Travis v. Norris,* 805 F.2d 806 (8th Cir. 1985), a suit for the violation of an inmate's constitutional rights by prison officials. The officials confiscated as contraband publications received in the prison, including the book, *Gorilla Law.* The court relied upon the finding by prison officials that the publication had a detrimental effect on the rehabilitation of inmates.

In *Vester v. Rogers,* 795 F.2d 1179 (4th Cir. 1986), which involved correspondence between prisoners in different penal institutions, the court held that the prisoner's First Amendment rights were not violated by the prohibition of such correspondence.

Introductions in previous volumes:

III: 175; VI: 391; VII: 419; VIII: 397

Dickey GAINES, Plaintiff-Appellant,

v.

Michael P. LANE and James Thieret,
Defendants-Appellees.

Joe WOODS, et al.,
Plaintiffs-Appellants,

v.

Michael P. LANE, Individually, and as
Director, Illinois Department of Corrections, Michael O'Leary, Individually,
and as Chief Administrative Officer,
Stateville Correctional Center, and Wil-
la Jean Aldworth, Individually, and as
Mail Room Supervisor, Stateville Correctional Center, Defendants-Appellees.

Nos. 85–1449, 85–1745.

United States Court of Appeals,
Seventh Circuit.

Argued Dec. 12, 1985.
Decided May 6, 1986.*

---

* This opinion has been circulated among all judges of this court in regular active service under Circuit Rule 16. No judge voted to rehear this case *en banc* regarding the conflict with *Guajardo v. Estelle*, 580 F.2d 748 (5th Cir. 1978).

Before COFFEY, FLAUM and RIPPLE, Circuit Judges.

RIPPLE, Circuit Judge.

This consolidated appeal presents two similar constitutional challenges to the new Illinois Department of Corrections' regulations governing the treatment of prisoner mail. In both instances, the district courts dismissed the complaints pursuant to Fed. R.Civ.P. 12(b)(6) for failure to state a claim on which relief could be granted.[1] The appellants contend that dismissal at this stage of the litigation was error. We disagree. Accordingly, we affirm the judgments in both actions.

I THE COMPLAINT

The appellants are individuals who have been committed to the custody of the Illinois Department of Corrections (Department). As inmates, they are subject to the Department's regulations covering the handling of incoming and outgoing mail. Prior to August 1, 1984, these rules were codified as Regulation 823. However, on that date, the Department enacted new regulations, Rule 525.100 et seq. The appellants have alleged that these new mail regulations are harsher than the previous rules and constitutionally deficient in a number of ways.

The mail regulations apply to both privileged and non-privileged mail. In general, privileged mail is defined as mail which is either sent to or received from attorneys or specified governmental and judicial officers. Non-privileged mail is, accordingly, comprised of all mail which does not fall within that definition. The appellants have alleged that the regulations are unconstitutional as they affect both types of mail.

Non-Privileged Mail. The appellants allege that the regulations pertaining to non-privileged mail infringe on their first amendment right to substantially unrestricted speech. They first object to Rule 525.130 which, unlike its predecessor, requires all non-privileged *outgoing* mail to be unsealed when delivered to the mail room. That rule also permits prison employees to read all outgoing non-privileged mail and to inspect it for contraband. The regulations are objectionable, contend the appellants, because they do not specify 1) which prison employees may read the mail, or 2) what showing is necessary (i.e.: security, prisoner safety, etc.) to support such an intrusion. The appellants reiterate these same objections with respect to Rule 525.140 which subjects *incoming* non-privileged mail to the same inspection.

In addition, Rule 525.130(h) permits Department employees to censor, reproduce, or withhold from delivery non-privileged mail which they believe presents a threat to

---

1. In case No. 85–1745, Count II of the complaint alleged that the prison mail regulations were unconstitutional *as applied* to the appellants. As such, Count II differed from Count I which only presented a facial challenge to the regula-tions. Count II survived the appellees' motion to dismiss; however, the appellants voluntarily dismissed it without prejudice presumably so that this appeal could be brought. Count II constitutes no part of this appeal.

prison security or safety. (Rule 525.140(g) provides a similar regulation for incoming mail.) The rule continues by enumerating nine instances when such a threat exists. The appellants argue that this regulation is deficient in two respects. First, the regulation includes—as one of the nine potentially dangerous instances—letters which "solicit[ ] gifts, goods or money from other than family members." Rule 525.130(h)(6). The appellants allege that this provision cannot possibly promote prison security. Second, the appellants contend that the nine instances are merely illustrative of the types of situations in which mail restrictions are warranted. Since the list is not exhaustive, the appellants claim that the rules impermissibly give prison employees unfettered discretion to decide which items of mail present a threat to the prison.

Privileged Mail. The regulations do not specifically provide that incoming privileged mail may be read. However, Rule 525.140(b) does allow the mail to be inspected "to determine that nothing other than legal or official matter is enclosed." Further, Rule 525.110 does not include letters to and from the news media within the definition of privileged mail. The appellants contend that both of these provisions unnecessarily intrude upon their first amendment rights and, therefore, should be stricken unless the Department can demonstrate some justification for their necessity.

Other Alleged Violations. In addition to these substantive first amendment claims, the appellants also argue that the regulations are impermissibly vague. Specifically, the appellants point to the restrictions found in Rules 525.130(a) and (b). Those sections allow an inmate to mail—at state expense—the equivalent of three one-ounce, first-class letters each week. Prisoners may also send additional letters provided they have sufficient funds in their prison accounts. If a prisoner does not have sufficient funds, he may nonetheless "send reasonable amounts of legal mail at State expense." The appellants contend that, because the regulations define neither

"reasonable" nor "legal," they are impermissibly vague.

Finally, the appellants claim that the Department's rules violate due process inasmuch as they do not afford expeditious review of decisions to withhold prisoner mail.

In sum, the appellants have alleged that the mail regulations infringe on first amendment interests, are impermissibly vague, and fail to provide adequate procedures for contesting adverse decisions. Faced with these challenges, the district courts in both cases dismissed the complaints for failure to state a claim. They believed that the regulations were consistent with the general guidelines set forth by the Supreme Court in *Procunier v. Martinez,* 416 U.S. 396, 94 S.Ct. 1800, 40 L.Ed.2d 224 (1974), and by the courts of appeals in subsequent cases. We now examine the correctness of these decisions.

II.   DISCUSSION

It is well settled that a "complaint should not be dismissed for failure to state a claim unless it appears beyond doubt that the plaintiff can prove no set of facts in support of his claim which would entitle him to relief." *Benson v. Cady,* 761 F.2d 335, 338 (7th Cir.1985) (quoting *Conley v. Gibson,* 355 U.S. 41, 45–46, 78 S.Ct. 99, 101–02, 2 L.Ed.2d 80 (1957)). While this standard is often difficult for the movant to meet—given the complexities of constitutional litigation—it is not insuperable. A litigant will not be able to bypass the strictures of Rule 12(b)(6) simply by alleging a constitutional challenge. If a complaint alleges that a state regulation, on its face, is inconsistent with a specific provision of the United States Constitution, that complaint will be dismissed where a thoughtful reading of the regulation convinces the district court that the regulation is plainly within the bounds of the Constitution. With this in mind, we now proceed to the appellants' claims.

We begin our analysis with the Supreme Court's opinion in *Procunier v. Martinez,* 416 U.S. 396, 94 S.Ct. 1800, 40

L.Ed.2d 224 (1974). In *Procunier*, the Court held that censorship of prisoner mail would be justified if the following criteria were met: "First, the regulation or practice in question must further an important or substantial governmental interest unrelated to the suppression of expression.... Second, the limitation of First Amendment freedoms must be no greater than is necessary or essential to the protection of the particular governmental interest involved." *Id.* at 413. However, the *Procunier* Court did not simply recite this two-part test. Rather, the Court continued by explaining the degree to which prison administrators must justify their regulations:

> This does not mean, of course, that prison administrators may be required to show with certainty that adverse consequences would flow from the failure to censor a particular letter. Some latitude in anticipating the probable consequences of allowing certain speech in a prison environment is essential to the proper discharge of an administrator's duty. But any regulation or practice that restricts inmate correspondence must be generally necessary to protect one or more of the legitimate governmental interests identified above.

Id. at 414, 94 S.Ct. at 1811 (footnote omitted). In short, a regulation which generally advances a legitimate governmental interest of sufficient importance is not invalid simply because the government does not demonstrate that each and every application of that regulation necessarily furthers that interest.

Non-Privileged Mail

A

With respect to non-privileged mail, the regulations in this case provide that all incoming or outgoing mail may be inspected for contraband (Rules 525.130(g); 525.-140(d)) and "spot check[ed] and read." Rules 525.130(h); 525.140(g). These regulations cannot be the basis of a valid constitutional challenge; this court has already determined that provisions of this type do not impermissibly intrude on first amendment rights. In *Smith v. Shimp*, 562 F.2d 423 (7th Cir.1977), we held that prison officials could read non-privileged mail, on a spot-check basis, in order to detect possible escape plans or other threats to jail security. At that time, we also held that it was entirely proper for prison officials to inspect mail for contraband. Since the same governmental justifications—jail security and the possibility of escape—are obviously present at the institutions managed by the Illinois Department of Corrections, we see no reason to part with our holding in *Shimp*.

B

Rules 525.130(h) and Rule 525.-140(g) are also challenged because they allow incoming and outgoing non-privileged mail to be censored, reproduced, or withheld from delivery if it presents a threat to prison security or safety.[2] Notably, these regulations have a built-in justification; the rules specifically say that prison officials may only take the enumerated actions when the mail "presents a threat to security or safety." The rules then detail the prohibited topics which will trigger their application, including: threats of physical harm, blackmail, extortion; plans to escape; coded letters.

After *Procunier* and *Shimp*, it is clear that prison security is a sufficiently important governmental interest to justify limitations on a prisoner's first amendment rights. *See also Bell v. Wolfish*, 441 U.S.

---

2. Rule 525.140(g), the provision dealing with incoming mail, does not specifically limit its application to non-privileged mail. In fact, by its terms, the rule applies to all "[i]ncoming mail." Yet, it is clear from the regulation's context, and as a matter of statutory interpretation, that Rule 525.140(g) is only to be applied to non-privileged mail. This reading makes subsection (g) consistent with the restrictions found in subsection (b).

Rule 525.140(g) also allows mail to be censored, inspected, reproduced, or withheld if it is *obscene*. However, no serious challenge has been brought concerning this portion of the rule; therefore, we do not consider it to be material to our discussion.

520, 546, 99 S.Ct. 1861, 1877, 60 L.Ed.2d 447 (1979). In this instance, the district court was correct in concluding that nothing would be gained by proceeding past the pleadings stage. The regulations already contain a legislative determination that safety and security are important interests in the proper administration of prison life. Government affidavits could not, and constitutionally need not, show more. Simply put, then, at the pleadings stage of this litigation, we already know 1) the regulation's justification and 2) that the justification is both valid and substantial. Rules 525.130(h) and 525.140(g) therefore meet the first part of the *Procunier* test.

As for the second part of the test, it is equally clear that the regulations are well-tailored to minimize their intrusiveness. First, as we have already noted, the rules only allow prison officials to censor mail which presents a threat to prison security. Second, the rules contain nine examples which explain with greater specificity what actually constitutes a threat to security. As Judge McGarr aptly noted, "these regulations give prison officials and other employees ... sufficient guidance in determining what mail can be censored and they are not overly broad." *Woods v.*

Lane, No. 84 C 7745, Opinion and Order at 6 (N.D.Ill. Mar. 19, 1985).[3] Censorship is hardly left to the prison officials' "unfettered discretion."[4] Finally, the regulations also provide that all prisoners will be given written notice when they have been prohibited from either sending or receiving a letter. Thus, the prisoner may "grieve any action taken by officials; if this is not satisfactory, he still has the state remedy of mandamus to compel prison officials to act in accordance with the prescribed rules, and he may also resort to action in federal court under 42 U.S.C. § 1983 for a specific infringement." *Gaines v. Lane*, No. 84–3269, Order at 5 (S.D.Ill. Feb. 25, 1985).[5] In light of these safeguards, we hold that, as a matter of law, these regulations strike "a proper balance between the constitutional rights of the appellants and the legitimate concerns of prison officials." *Meadows v. Hopkins*, 713 F.2d 206, 211 (6th Cir.1983).

Privileged Mail

A

Rule 525.140(b) is equally justifiable. That rule allows incoming *privileged* mail to "be opened in the presence of the committed person to whom it is addressed to inspect for contraband, to verify the

---

3. The appellants' claim that this list is illustrative only and, therefore, improperly gives the Department unfettered discretion to determine which items will be censored. This regulation must, however, be read as a totality. All censorship must be justified in terms of whether the correspondence "presents a threat to security or safety...." Certainly, this regulation gives as much guidance to prison officials as the one cited with approval in *Procunier v. Martinez,* 416 U.S. 396, 414 n. 14, 94 S.Ct. 1800 n. 14, 1812 n. 14, 40 L.Ed.2d 224 (1974).

4. Appellant Gaines charges that of the nine examples, the sixth is unconstitutional since it prohibits an inmate's letters which "solicit[ ] gifts, goods or money from other than family members." This provision is constitutionally unobjectionable. If, under the rule established in *Bell v. Wolfish*, 441 U.S. 520, 553–55, 99 S.Ct. 1861, 1881–82, 60 L.Ed.2d 447 (1979), a prison can totally exclude all packages in the interest of security, the prison must also have the ability to solve the problem before it starts by preventing the solicitation of packages. The same concerns are present with respect to the solicitation of money. *See Sell v. Parratt*, 548 F.2d 753, 756

(8th Cir.), *cert. denied*, 434 U.S. 873, 98 S.Ct. 220, 54 L.Ed.2d 152 (1977).

The appellants also claim that the regulations are deficient because they do not specifically identify which prison employees may read the mail. This feature does not amount to "vagueness" in the constitutional sense. The regulations are, on their face, permissible. Failure to designate a particular employee does not unnecessarily infringe on the first amendment rights of prisoners.

5. The appellants do not seriously contend that these remedies are unavailable. Accordingly, we hold that the district court properly dismissed the due process claims for failure to state a claim.

These remedies could be invoked, for instance, if a prison employee abused his authority and censored a letter not because it posed a threat to security but because its contents were at odds with his "own personal prejudices and opinions." *Procunier*, 416 U.S. at 415, 94 S.Ct. at 1812.

identity of the sender, and to determine that nothing other than legal or official matter is enclosed." This practice has already been condoned by the Supreme Court. In *Wolff v. McDonnell,* 418 U.S. 539, 94 S.Ct. 2963, 41 L.Ed.2d 935 (1974), the Court stated, with respect to privileged mail:

> As to the ability to open the mail in the presence of inmates, this could in no way constitute censorship, since the mail would not be read. Neither could it chill such communications, since the inmate's presence insures that prison officials will not read the mail. The possibility that contraband will be enclosed in letters, even those from apparent attorneys, surely warrants prison officials' opening the letters.

Id. at 577, 94 S.Ct. at 2985. We therefore decline the appellants' invitation to require the Department to justify anew a clearly permissible regulation. Quite obviously, a different situation would be present if the prison officials actually read the privileged mail. However, that "as applied" argument is not before us today. *See supra* note 1. Rather, the appellants have simply challenged a Department regulation which, on its face, allows prison officials to search privileged mail for contraband while the prisoners look on. That is precisely what

Wolff permits. *See Jensen v. Klecker,* 648 F.2d 1179, 1182 (8th Cir.1981).

B

The appellants also assert that the failure to include mail to and from the news media as privileged mail constitutes a violation of their first amendment rights.[6] Department Rule 525.110 defines fourteen categories of mail which will be treated as privileged.[7] Communication with the news media is not among the listed categories. The only question for our review is whether the first amendment *requires* media correspondence to be treated as *privileged.*

In deciding this issue, we must adhere to the principles established by the Supreme Court in *Pell v. Procunier,* 417 U.S. 817, 94 S.Ct. 2800, 41 L.Ed.2d 495 (1974) (upholding a prison regulation which banned face-to-face interviews between media representatives and inmates of their choosing). Access to the media gives the incarcerated person an opportunity to communicate with the general public and a means of petitioning the government for redress of grievances. However, an inmate retains only "those First Amendment rights that are not inconsistent with his status as a prisoner...." *Id.* at 822, 94 S.Ct. at 2804. Furthermore, in determining whether an inmate's first amendment rights are being unduly impeded, prison

---

6. The prisoners here assert, as they must, their own rights to communicate with the media. We are not confronted with any specific complaint by the media with respect to its own right of access to the prisoners. In any event, the Supreme Court has held that the "First Amendment does not guarantee the press a constitutional right of special access to information not available to the public generally." *Branzburg v. Hayes,* 408 U.S. 665, 684, 92 S.Ct. 2646, 33 L.Ed.2d 626 (1972); *see Houchins v. KQED, Inc.,* 438 U.S. 1, 9, 98 S.Ct. 2588, 2593, 57 L.Ed.2d 553 (1978); *Pell v. Procunier,* 417 U.S. 817, 94 S.Ct. 2800, 41 L.Ed.2d 495 (1974).

To the extent that the right to speak necessarily includes the listener's right to receive the message, *cf. Bigelow v. Virginia,* 421 U.S. 809, 95 S.Ct. 2222, 44 L.Ed.2d 600 (1975), this concern is satisfied by the opportunity of the prisoner to communicate with the general public through alternate channels of communication.

7. The fourteen categories of privileged mail include letters to:
   a) The Director;
   b) The Deputy Director of the appropriate division;
   c) Members of the Office of Advocacy Services;
   d) Members of the Administrative Review Board;
   e) Members of the Prisoner Review Board;
   f) The Governor;
   g) The Attorney General;
   h) Federal, Illinois or local Illinois legislators;
   i) Chief Executive Officers of federal, state or local law enforcement agencies;
   j) The Federal Bureau of Prisons;
   k) The U.S. Department of Justice;
   l) Registered Attorneys;
   m) Judges, magistrates or clerks of any court; and
   n) Legal aid organizations.
   Rule 525.110.

regulations "cannot be considered in isolation but must be viewed in the light of the alternative means of communication permitted under the regulations...." *Id.* at 823, 94 S.Ct. at 2804.

In addressing an inmate's interest in communicating with the general public, *Pell* upheld the interview regulation because the prisoners had sufficient alternative means by which they could communicate with the general public. 417 U.S. at 823–24, 94 S.Ct. at 2804, 2805. One such alternative means was a prisoner's ability to communicate with the general public through the mail. Yet, the Court did not prescribe a totally unfettered, privileged mail. *Id.* at 824, 94 S.Ct. at 2805. Rather, it was talking about mail which could be censored in accordance with its earlier opinion in *Procunier. Id.*

Here, we are faced with a situation similar to that in *Pell.* Since we earlier held that the Department's regulations were constitutional insofar as they dealt with nonprivileged mail to the general public (allowing censorship only when a letter's content poses a threat to prison security), there is no reason why mail communication to the media must be given a special status. The inmates have alternative avenues for reaching the general public. As the Court stated, "[s]o long as reasonable and effective means of communication remain open and no discrimination in terms of content is involved, we believe that, in drawing such lines, 'prison officials must be accorded latitude.' " *Id.* at 826, 94 S.Ct. at 2806 (quot-

ing *Cruz v. Beto*, 405 U.S. 319, 321, 92 S.Ct. 1079, 1081, 31 L.Ed.2d 263 (1972)).

We also hold that prisoners have no interest in having the media serve as an alternate means for petitioning the government. We first note that Illinois prison inmates have "substantial opportunities to petition the executive, legislative, and judicial branches of government directly." *Pell*, 417 U.S. at 828 n. 6, 94 S.Ct. at 2807 n. 6. Indeed, these direct communications are treated as privileged and, therefore, constitute an unimpeded means by which prison inmates may petition the government. Moreover, even if inmates were to choose an alternate avenue via the media, the Department's regulations treat media mail exactly as they treat all other non-privileged mail. Thus, prison officials may not censor it unless it contains information which threatens jail security.[8]

Accordingly, the district court did not err by upholding that portion of the Department's regulations which denied privileged status to media communications. In view of the alternate avenues of communication which are available to an inmate, the media is not essential for communicating with the general public or petitioning the government for redress of grievances. Therefore, the first amendment requires only that media mail be treated like all other non-privileged mail.[9]

Mailings at State Expense

Finally, the appellants claim that Rules 525.130(a) and (b), which govern state-paid

---

8. We have already noted that we do not have before us an "as applied" situation where there is a specific allegation that the censored communication does not reasonably come within one of the areas where prison officials may legitimately censor communications. *See supra* note 1; *see also Procunier,* 416 U.S. at 415, 94 S.Ct. at 1812.

9. We realize that the Fifth Circuit has adopted a different position on this issue. In *Guajardo v. Estelle,* 580 F.2d 748, 759 (5th Cir.1978), a panel of that court held that the prisoner plaintiffs in that case had "a right to send media mail unopened and to receive media mail that had been opened only for the inspection of contraband in the inmate's presence."

We respectfully suggest that *Guajardo* is based on an erroneous reading of *Pell.* The Fifth

Circuit grounded its decision on the belief that the Supreme Court's denial of face-to-face interviews between the media and prisoners was based on the existence of an unrestricted right of correspondence *with the media.* In short, the Fifth Circuit assumed that *Pell* requires some unrestricted communication between the media and the prisoner.

In our view, *Pell* contains no such requirement. Rather, the Court assessed the prohibition of media interviews against the entire panoply of methods by which the prisoner could communicate *with the general public. Id.* at 823–25, 94 S.Ct. at 2804–05. Neither *Pell* nor the cases following it established a special right of the prisoner to communicate with the media.

mail, are unconstitutionally vague and deny them access to the courts. These regulations establish a scheme whereby all inmates are entitled to send three first class letters per week at state expense, and may send an unlimited number of additional letters with postage costs deducted from the inmates' trust accounts. Additionally, inmates without sufficient funds in their trust accounts are allowed to send "reasonable" additional amounts of "legal" mail at state expense.

"It is indisputable that indigent inmates must be provided at state expense" with the basic material necessary to draft legal documents and with stamps to mail them. *Bounds v. Smith*, 430 U.S. 817, 824, 97 S.Ct. 1491, 1496, 52 L.Ed.2d 72 (1977). However, although prisoners have a right of access to the courts, they do not have a right to unlimited free postage. *See Bach v. Coughlin*, 508 F.2d 303, 307 (7th Cir. 1974).[10] Prison authorities are able to make "a reasonable attempt to balance the right of prisoners to use the mails with prison budgetary considerations." *Id.* at 307–08.

Here, the district courts properly determined that, as a matter of law, the Department's regulations were constitutional. The regulations set forth a minimum number of privileged or non-privileged letters which may be sent at state expense. This provision is supplemented by a "safety valve" provision which permits the additional expenditure of state funds for legal mail when such an expenditure is reasonable. We cannot say that, on its face, this regulation amounts to an unconstitutional impediment on an inmate's access to courts. Nor do we believe that the terms "reasonable" and "legal" are, as used in the context of this regulation, necessarily vague in the constitutional sense. These terms are certainly susceptible to constitutional—indeed salutary—application. Should prison officials abuse these regulations by interpreting them in such a way as to block a prisoner's legitimate access to the courts, the prisoner is not without remedy.

III. CONCLUSION

In both actions the district courts were correct in dismissing the complaints for failure to state a claim. The Department's mail regulations are comfortably within the parameters established by the Supreme Court and lower federal courts for the processing of privileged and non-privileged mail. No matter what set of facts the appellants could proffer, these regulations—*taken on their face*—are not constitutionally infirm.

Accordingly, the judgments of the district courts [11] are affirmed.

AFFIRMED.

---

10. In *Bach v. Coughlin*, 508 F.2d 303 (7th Cir. 1974), this court approved Regulation 823, the precursor of the current Department rule. *Id.* at 308. Other courts have authorized more stringent provisions. *See, e.g., Hoppins v. Wallace*, 751 F.2d 1161 (11th Cir.1985) (furnishing two free stamps a week to indigent prisoners is adequate to allow exercise of the right to access to the courts).

11. The magistrate erred in not ruling on appellant Dickey Gaines' request for appointment of counsel. It is clear in this circuit that a "trial court must rule on a request for appointed counsel before ruling on a summary judgment motion or a motion to dismiss." *Brown-Bey v. United States*, 720 F.2d 467, 471 (7th Cir.1983). However, contrary to the appellant's request, we see no reason to remand this case. The magistrate's error was clearly harmless. Although appellant Gaines had no counsel, similar arguments were presented—with the assistance of counsel—in the companion case which was consolidated for appeal in this court. Since we have rejected the merits of the appeals in both actions, we are persuaded that appellant Gaines' claim would have been entirely without merit even if he had been given the assistance of counsel.

William E. MARTIN,
Plaintiff-Appellant,

v.

Sgt. Earl KELLEY, Defendant-Appellee.

No. 84–3907.

United States Court of Appeals,
Sixth Circuit.

Submitted Aug. 4, 1986.

Decided Oct. 8, 1986.

Before KEITH and MERRITT, Circuit Judges, and CONTIE, Senior Circuit Judge.

CONTIE, Senior Circuit Judge.

Plaintiff-Appellant William E. Martin appeals from a decision of the district court dismissing his pro se civil rights complaint.

Appellant's complaint raises First Amendment free speech and Fourteenth Amendment due process challenges concerning the censorship of incoming prisoner mail. Appellant argues that the applicable mail censorship regulation for incoming mail,

Ohio Admin.Code § 5120–9–17, is unconstitutional on its face. For the reasons which follow, we agree with the appellant, reverse the order of the district court, and remand this case for further proceedings.

I.

Appellant is a prisoner at the Southern Ohio Correctional Facility in Lucasville, Ohio (SOCF). He alleges that on October 23, 1981, the assistant mail supervisor, defendant Sgt. Kelley, "intercepted" a letter written to appellant on Ku Klux Klan letterhead signed by one John Kahne. Appellant states that he was denied an opportunity to read the letter, and was forced by Sgt. Kelley to return the letter to the sender. Defendant Kelley had concluded that the letterhead was "inflammatory," as was the text of the letter, and should therefore be withheld from the inmate and returned to the author. Kelley believed the text to be inflammatory because the letter mentioned the possibility of having a Ku Klux Klan meeting at the prison. Appellant asserts that his request to forward the letterhead to the Publication Screening Committee for review before it was returned to the sender was denied by Kelley. The letter was photocopied and placed in appellant's mail file. The appellant further alleges that he returned the letter to the wrong person, having not read the letter and believing another Ku Klux Klan member had authored the letter. Appellant asserts that it is the general practice at SOCF to seize letters without notifying the inmate or author, and without returning the letters to the author.

On December 30, 1981, appellant filed a pro se complaint in the United States District Court for the Southern District of Ohio, naming Sgt. Kelley as the sole defendant. He was granted leave to proceed in forma pauperis. The complaint alleged that the act of interference, and the refusal to submit the letterhead to the Publication Screening Committee, violated the mail censorship regulations and the First, Eighth and Fourteenth Amendments.[1] The complaint requested declaratory and injunctive relief as well as compensatory and punitive damages.

The defendant filed a motion to dismiss on January 18, 1982 which was then referred to a magistrate. The magistrate recommended, on April 19, 1982, that appellant's claims be dismissed for failure to state a claim under the doctrine of *Parratt v. Taylor*, 451 U.S. 527, 101 S.Ct. 1908, 68 L.Ed.2d 420 (1981). On May 13, 1982, District Judge Spiegel rejected the magistrate's reliance on *Parratt*, concluding that appellant had adequately stated a claim under the First Amendment. However, the court held that appellant had failed to state a claim under the Eighth Amendment.

After a series of other motions were filed, appellant was permitted to file an amended complaint on March 29, 1983. The amended complaint and a motion to substitute parties named two other defendants: Ronald Marshall, the Superintendent of SOCF, and Richard Seiter, the Director of the Ohio Department of Rehabilitation and Correction. This complaint realleged appellant's claim that interference with his letter, and the refusal to submit the letterhead to the Publication Screening Committee, violated his First Amendment rights and the mail censorship regulations. The complaint also alleged that photocopying the letter, without cause, violated the First Amendment and section 5120–9–17 of the Ohio Admin.Code. He also alleged that he was denied due process when his letter was censored and photocopied, and that section 5120–9–17 was unconstitutional in that it did not provide adequate procedural safeguards for censoring mail. Appellant again requested declaratory and injunctive relief as well as compensatory and punitive damages.

On June 21, 1983, the defendants filed a motion for partial summary judgment as to the issues raised in appellant's first com-

---

1. The appellant's Eighth Amendment claim was premised on the assertion that he suffered "severe mental anguish" when defendant Kelley, a prison official, violated a rule without consequence.

plaint. On November 3, 1983, the magistrate recommended that summary judgment for defendant Kelley be granted, reasoning that a single act of censorship cannot constitute a First Amendment violation in the absence of proof of damages, principally relying on the case *Morgan v. Montanye*, 516 F.2d 1367 (2d Cir.1975), *cert. denied*, 424 U.S. 973, 96 S.Ct. 1476, 47 L.Ed.2d 743 (1976). The magistrate also ruled that the appellant lacked standing to challenge the prison's routine practice of seizing mail. On February 1, 1984, the district court adopted the magistrate's recommendations, and granted summary judgment on all issues for all of the defendants. However, the district court subsequently vacated this order on March 15, 1984 after recognizing that the new issues raised in the amended complaint had not been addressed by the magistrate. The case, in its entirety, was again referred to the magistrate.

In a final report issued September 13, 1984, the magistrate recommended that summary judgment be granted as to all the defendants on each of the claims. The

magistrate adhered to his original reasoning regarding the issues raised in the initial complaint. He further reasoned that the single instance of photocopying mail, in violation of section 5120–9–17(G)(6),[2] did not amount to a constitutional violation. Further, the magistrate ruled that section 5120–9–17 was not procedurally inadequate under the standards set forth in *Procunier v. Martinez*, 416 U.S. 396, 94 S.Ct. 1800, 40 L.Ed.2d 224 (1974), because the appellant had been notified of the rejection and another provision of the Ohio Admin.Code, section 5120–9–31, provided inmates with adequate process. Finding no constitutional violations, the magistrate did not recommend any form of relief.

The district court adopted the magistrate's recommendations, on October 16, 1984, stating that the appellant's claims should be dismissed pursuant to Fed.R. Civ.P. 12(b)(6). This appeal was filed on November 2, 1984.

On appeal, the appellant does not challenge the district court's disposition of his claims relating to the "interception" of the letter on Ku Klux Klan letterhead,[3] or the

---

2. Section 5120–9–17(G)(6) provides:
Mail which is held as evidence may be photocopied for use by persons involved with any criminal prosecution or disciplinary proceeding.
This section does not authorize photocopying simply because mail is returned, withheld or censored.

3. As previously noted, the district court adopted the magistrate's report holding that, in the absence of a showing of damages, an isolated instance of interference with mail does not state a constitutional claim. The magistrate relied on *Morgan v. Montanye*, 516 F.2d 1367 (2d Cir.1975), *cert. denied*, 424 U.S. 973, 96 S.Ct. 1476, 47 L.Ed.2d 743 (1976). The plaintiff in *Morgan* alleged that prison officials had interfered with one piece of mail from his attorney in violation of the prison mail regulations and the Constitution. The court analyzed the plaintiff's claims as a Sixth Amendment right to effective assistance of counsel claim, and a Fourteenth Amendment right of access to the courts claim. *See, e.g., Martinez*, 416 U.S. at 419, 94 S.Ct. at 1814 (right of access to the courts grounded in Due Process Clause). The Second Circuit did not cite to *Martinez*, nor did it treat the case as a First Amendment free speech case. In disposing of plaintiff's claims, the court focused on the fact that the plaintiff only alleged a single interference with his mail, as well as the fact that he had failed to show that he had been damaged in any way by this interference.

Although the issue of whether the appellant's rights were abridged by the withholding of this letter is not before this court, we note that after *Carey v. Piphus*, 435 U.S. 247, 266, 98 S.Ct. 1042, 1053, 55 L.Ed.2d 252 (1978), where the Court held that a plaintiff was entitled to at least nominal damages for violation of his constitutional rights, the question of whether there has been a constitutional violation should not be considered dependent on whether actual damages have occurred. *See Marohnic v. Walker*, 800 F.2d 613, (6th Cir.1986) (do not need to show actual injury to establish First Amendment violation); *Walje v. City of Winchester, Kentucky*, 773 F.2d 729, 732 (6th Cir.1985) (same). *Cf. Owen v. Lash*, 682 F.2d 648 (7th Cir.1982) (at least nominal damages awarded for interference with inmate's correspondence); *Wolfel v. Bates*, 707 F.2d 932, 934 (6th Cir.1983) (per curiam) (nominal damages awarded for violation of inmate's First Amendment right to "seek redress of grievances"); *McNamara v. Moody*, 606 F.2d 621, 625 (5th Cir. 1979) (nominal damages awarded for interfer-

photocopying of that letter; therefore, we will not review them. Rather, the appellant only argues on appeal that Ohio Admin.Code § 5120–9–17 is unconstitutional on its face under the standards set forth in *Procunier v. Martinez*, 416 U.S. 396, 94 S.Ct. 1800, 40 L.Ed.2d 224 (1974).

II.

The district court's October 16, 1984 order specifies that the appellant's complaint was dismissed pursuant to Fed.R.Civ.P. 12(b)(6) for failure to state a claim upon which relief can be granted; the defendants had requested, and the magistrate had recommended, however, that summary judgment be granted pursuant to Rule 56(c), Fed.R.Civ.P.[4] Since the district court adopted the magistrate's report concluding that the recommendations were correct, the district court in effect held that Ohio Admin.Code § 5120–9–17 was not unconstitutional because another provision supplied

adequate procedural safeguards. This conclusion is the equivalent of a grant of summary judgment rather than a Rule 12(b)(6) dismissal in that it clearly reached the merits of appellant's claim and looked beyond appellant's complaint. Therefore, we will review the district court's order under summary judgment standards; and, since there are no issues of material fact in dispute regarding the contents of the regulation being challenged, we will reach the merits of appellant's claim.

A.

This case, like the controlling prisoner mail censorship case *Procunier v. Martinez*, concerns the constitutionality of a regulation which was promulgated by the director of the State Department of Rehabilitation and Corrections. The regulation being challenged, Ohio Admin.Code § 5120–9–17, provides in relevant part:

---

ence with prisoner mail because there was no showing of actual damages), *cert. denied*, 447 U.S. 929, 100 S.Ct. 3028, 65 L.Ed.2d 1124 (1980). *See also Memphis Community School District v. Stachura*, — U.S. —, 106 S.Ct. 2537, 2543–44, 91 L.Ed.2d 249 (1986) (explaining *Carey v. Piphus*). Since *Morgan* was not analyzed as a First Amendment case, we further note that there are a number of cases which have found that one instance of mail censorship can amount to a constitutional violation under the First Amendment. *See, e.g., Trudeau v. Wyrick*, 713 F.2d 1360 (8th Cir.1983) (interference with one letter was a constitutional violation under *Procunier v. Martinez*); *McNamara*, 606 F.2d 621 (it is a violation of the First Amendment to suppress individual letters without showing that a substantial governmental interest would be met by suppressing such letters); *Nichols v. Knowles*, No. 80–496–7 (D.Mass. May 29, 1985) (absolute censorship of two letters was unconstitutional denial of First Amendment rights). *Cf. Abdul Wali v. Coughlin*, 754 F.2d 1015, 1028 (2d Cir.1985) (First Amendment violated by prison's refusal to permit inmates access to specific report); *Campbell v. Sumner*, 587 F.Supp. 376, 378 (D.Nev.1984) (the decision to withhold a specific letter "must be accompanied by procedural safeguards" to be constitutional). *But see Woods v. Yeager*, 463 F.2d 223, 224–25 (3d Cir.1972) (the single act of interference with prisoner's mail failed to state a claim for injunctive relief or damages). We do not express an opinion on

these issues, but simply question the applicability of *Morgan* to the fact pattern in this case.

4. The two rules have different standards and different results. A Rule 12(b)(6) dismissal should be granted only when the court, upon review of the complaint, is convinced that the complainant can prove "no set of facts in support of his claim which would entitle him to relief." *Conley v. Gibson*, 355 U.S. 41, 45–46, 78 S.Ct. 99, 101–02, 2 L.Ed.2d 80 (1957). *See also Scheuer v. Rhodes*, 416 U.S. 232, 236, 94 S.Ct. 1683, 1686, 40 L.Ed.2d 90 (1974). A summary judgment motion may be granted only when "the pleadings, depositions, answers to interrogatories, and admissions on file, together with the affidavits, if any, show that there is no genuine issue as to any material fact and that the moving party is entitled to a judgment as a matter of law." Fed.R.Civ.P. 56(c). The moving party bears the burden of satisfying Rule 56(c) standards, *Davis v. Robbs*, 794 F.2d 1129, 1130 (6th Cir.1986), and the evidence, and the reasonable inferences therefrom, must be viewed in the light most favorable to the nonmoving party. *Adickes v. S.H. Kress & Co.*, 398 U.S. 144, 153–57, 90 S.Ct. 1598, 1606–08, 26 L.Ed.2d 142 (1970); *Smith v. Hudson*, 600 F.2d 60, 63 (6th Cir.), *cert. dismissed*, 444 U.S. 986, 100 S.Ct. 495, 62 L.Ed.2d 415 (1979). Granting summary judgment, therefore, is a decision on the merits of a party's claim or defense.

(A) There shall be no censorship, copying or reading of first class mail in the form of letters addressed to an inmate, except as provided in paragraph (G) of this rule, nor shall there be any limitation upon the number of first class letters that an inmate may receive nor the number of persons with whom an inmate may correspond.

.   .   .   .   .

(G) Mail to or from an inmate may be opened and read, provided that the managing officer or his designee has a reasonable belief that the written contents of mail other than legal mail, present a clear and present danger to institutional security, and such action has been approved by the director or his designee, pursuant to a request by the managing officer.

.   .   .   .   .

(4) Approval of the director or his designee to open and read and copy such mail shall extend only to the managing officer or his designees.

(5) If, after reading such mail, the managing officer or his designee determines that it does not constitute a clear and present danger to institutional security, it shall be promptly forwarded to the inmate addressee. Otherwise, the mail shall be returned to the sender or held as evidence for a criminal prosecution or disciplinary proceeding.

.   .   .   .   .

Therefore, once it has been decided that a prisoner's mail may be opened and read,[5] the managing officer or his designee has the authority to decide if an item of mail

5. The appellant acknowledges that his mail was properly subject to this review procedure.

6. The freedom of speech is secured against abridgement by the states through the Fourteenth Amendment. *Edwards v. South Carolina*, 372 U.S. 229, 235, 83 S.Ct. 680, 683, 9 L.Ed.2d 697 (1963); *Schneider v. State*, 308 U.S. 147, 160, 60 S.Ct. 146, 84 L.Ed. 155 (1939).

7. In *Pell v. Procunier*, 417 U.S. 817, 822, 94 S.Ct. 2800, 2804, 41 L.Ed.2d 495 (1974), the Court stated that a prisoner did retain

constitutes a "clear and present danger to institutional security;" if the letter does constitute such a danger, it is to be returned to the sender or held for evidence in future proceedings. Section 5120–9–17 does not define "clear and present danger," nor does it require that notice be given to the inmate-addressee or the author-sender when a letter is to be rejected, censored or withheld. It also does not provide for a procedure whereby the managing officer's decision may be appealed to and reviewed by a third party prior to the letter being returned to the sender.

B.

The First Amendment freedoms, including the freedom of speech,[6] have always occupied a preferred status in constitutional jurisprudence for it is these freedoms which ensure a free and democratic society. After the Supreme Court decision in *Procunier v. Martinez*, 416 U.S. 396, 94 S.Ct. 1800, 40 L.Ed.2d 224 (1974), there was no doubt that "first amendment concerns are implicated when restrictions are imposed upon an inmate's correspondence." *United States v. Holloway*, 740 F.2d 1373, 1382 (6th Cir.), *cert. denied*, 469 U.S. 1021, 105 S.Ct. 440, 83 L.Ed.2d 366 (1984). The Court in *Martinez* reasoned that it was unnecessary to determine to what extent prisoners retained First Amendment freedoms, however, since free citizens have a protected First Amendment right to communicate with prisoners through uncensored correspondence, whether as an author or as an intended mail recipient. *Martinez*, 416 U.S. at 408–09, 94 S.Ct. at 1808–09.[7]

First Amendment freedoms which were "not inconsistent with his status as a prisoner or with the legitimate penological objectives of the corrections systems." *See also Jones v. North Carolina Prisoners' Labor Union, Inc.*, 433 U.S. 119, 129, 97 S.Ct. 2532, 2539, 53 L.Ed.2d 629 (1977). Despite the language in the Supreme Court case *Wolff v. McDonnell*, 418 U.S. 539, 575–76, 94 S.Ct. 2963, 2984, 41 L.Ed.2d 935 (1974), stating that the Supreme Court had yet to explicitly decide to what extent prisoners retained First Amendment free speech rights, several cir-

The Court reasoned that in order for a mail censorship regulation to pass constitutional muster, it must satisfy both parts of a two-pronged test:

First, the regulation or practice in question must further an important or substantial governmental interest unrelated to the suppression of expression.... [Prison officials] must show that a regulation authorizing mail censorship furthers one or more of the substantial governmental interests of security, order, and rehabilitation. Second, the limitation of First Amendment freedoms must be no greater than is necessary or essential to the protection of the particular governmental interest involved. Thus a restriction on inmate correspondence that furthers an important or substantial interest of penal administration will nevertheless be invalid if its sweep is unnecessarily broad.

Id. at 413–14, 94 S.Ct. at 1811.[8] Under this test, the Court struck down a mail censorship regulation which disallowed correspondence that "magnif[ied] grievances," "express[ed] inflammatory political, racial, religious or other views or beliefs," pertained to criminal activity, was "lewd, obscene, or

defamatory; contain[ed] foreign matter, or [was] otherwise inappropriate." 416 U.S. at 399–400, 94 S.Ct. at 1804–05. The Court held that no substantial justification was offered for this regulation unrelated to suppressing free speech and that the regulation swept too broadly, providing officials with too much discretion to suppress protected speech. *Id.* at 415–16, 94 S.Ct. at 1812.

The Court also concluded that mail censorship regulations could suffer from another deficiency. Concluding that an individual's interest in uncensored mail is a liberty interest which must be "protected from arbitrary governmental invasion," *id.* at 418, 94 S.Ct. at 1814, the Court further held that due process requires a "decision to censor or withhold delivery of a particular letter ... be accompanied by *minimal procedural safeguards*" to be constitutional. *Id.* at 417, 94 S.Ct. at 1814 (emphasis supplied). The Court thereafter approved the district court's order requiring that: (1) notice be given to the inmate of the rejected letter; (2) a reasonable opportunity be given to the author of the letter to protest the rejection decisions; and (3) complaints concerning the rejection be reviewed by someone other than the individu-

---

cuits, relying on *Pell,* have reasoned that prisoners do have First Amendment free speech rights "not inconsistent with" their prisoner status. *See, e.g., Finney v. Arkansas Board of Corrections,* 505 F.2d 194, 211 (8th Cir.1974); *Guajardo v. Estelle,* 580 F.2d 748, 760 (5th Cir. 1978); *Pittman v. Hutto,* 594 F.2d 407, 410 (4th Cir.1979); *Aikens v. Jenkins,* 534 F.2d 751, 755 (7th Cir.1976). *Cf. Safley v. Turner,* 777 F.2d 1307, 1311–13 (8th Cir.1985) (abolishing rule restricting correspondence between inmates), *cert. granted,* — U.S. —, 106 S.Ct. 2244, 90 L.Ed.2d 691 (1986). *See also Martinez,* 416 U.S. at 422–28, 94 S.Ct. at 1815–18 (Marshall, J., concurring), 428–29, 94 S.Ct. at 1818–19 (Douglas, J., concurring). Since the challenged regulation in the instant case deals with censoring incoming mail, we need not decide whether, or to what extent, prisoners retain the right of free speech since our analysis is controlled by *Martinez* and the First Amendment rights of free, non-incarcerated citizens.

8. This test does not differ significantly from the test previously enunciated by the Court in a different context:

[A] government regulation is sufficiently justified if it is within the constitutional power of the Government; if it furthers an important or substantial governmental interest; if the governmental interest is unrelated to the suppression of free expression; and if the incidental restriction on alleged First Amendment freedoms is no greater than is essential to the furtherance of that interest.

United States v. O'Brien, 391 U.S. 367, 377, 88 S.Ct. 1673, 1679, 20 L.Ed.2d 672 (1968) (upholding statute which made it a criminal offense to burn Selective Service registration certificates). The Court in *Martinez* noted that *O'Brien,* as well as *Tinker v. Des Moines Independent Community School District,* 393 U.S. 503, 89 S.Ct. 733, 21 L.Ed.2d 731 (1969) and *Healy v. James,* 408 U.S. 169, 92 S.Ct. 2338, 33 L.Ed.2d 266 (1972), although not controlling, was analogous in that it involved "incidental restrictions on First Amendment liberties by governmental action in furtherance of legitimate and substantial state interest other than suppression of expression." *Martinez,* 416 U.S. at 411–12, 94 S.Ct. at 1810.

al who originally rejected the letter. *Id.* at 418–19, 94 S.Ct. at 1814.

There are two potential problems with the regulation challenged in the instant case. The first is a concern that the regulation's sweep is too broad, and the second relates to the adequacy of procedural safeguards.

1.

Section 5120–9–17 provides that mail must be withheld from the inmate and returned to the sender if the managing officer determines that it constitutes "a clear and present danger to institutional security." Section 5120–9–17, however, does not define this phrase, nor does it otherwise provide specific guidelines for when mail can be censored. Without guidance, prison officials would be provided with complete discretion to censor mail. If a prisoner mail censorship regulation is not narrowly tailored to meet the articulated governmental interest involved, then it violates the First Amendment. *Martinez,* 416 U.S. at 415–16, 94 S.Ct. at 1812. *Cf. Plain Dealer Publishing Co. v. City of Lakewood,* 794 F.2d 1139, 1143–46 (6th Cir.1986) (vesting unbridled discretion in municipal official for granting newsrack license is not narrowly tailored and is therefore unconstitutional under First Amendment).

However, we do not believe that section 5120–9–17 should be held invalid on the theory that it is overbroad and allows for the censorship of protected speech. If it is possible to interpret a regulation so as to protect it from an overbreadth attack, such an interpretation should be adopted. *See Broadrick v. Oklahoma,* 413 U.S. 601, 613, 93 S.Ct. 2908, 2916, 37 L.Ed.2d 830 (1973) ("Facial overbreadth has not been invoked when a limiting construction has been or could be placed on the challenged statute."). In this instance, Ohio Admin. Code § 5120–9–19, a regulation governing

the censorship of printed material,[9] provides a definition of "clear and present danger to the security or safety of the institution." Pursuant to section 5120–9–19, printed material does not constitute a clear and present danger to institutional safety "solely on the basis of its appeal to a particular ethnic, racial or religious audience." Ohio Admin.Code § 5120–9–19(D)(2). Rather,

[i]n order to constitute a clear and present danger to the security or safety of the institution, the printed material must meet at least one of the following criteria:

(a) Printed material which incites, aids, or abets criminal activity, such as rioting or illegal drug use.

(b) Printed material which incites, aids, or abets physical violence against others, including instruction in making, using, or converting weapons.

(c) Printed material which incites, aids, or abets escape, such as instruction in picking locks or digging tunnels.

Id.

We find, as a matter of statutory interpretation, that section 5120–9–19(D)(2) also defines the phrase "clear and present danger to institutional security" in section 5120–9–17. This is a logical conclusion because words or phrases should be given consistent meaning when used in related regulations unless the regulation specifically provides otherwise. Further, by adopting this interpretation and allowing personal letters to be censored only when one of the listed criteria is met, the requirements in *Martinez* will be satisfied. First, the regulation furthers the important governmental objectives of prison security and order and is unrelated to the suppression of speech; second, the regulation is narrowly tailored to meet that governmental objective. *See, e.g., Martinez,* 416 U.S. at 413, 414 n. 14, 94 S.Ct. at 1811, 1812 n. 14

---

9. "Printed material" is defined as "newspapers; magazines; pamphlets; books; photographs ...; drawings; and prerecorded magnetic tapes." Ohio Admin.Code § 5120–9–19(B)(1). Printed material specifically

"does not include personal letters." *Id.* This regulation's origins can be traced to a court order. *See Taylor v. Perini,* 455 F.Supp. 1241, 1244–45 (N.D. Ohio 1978).

(discussing examples of justifiable censorship and quoting from Policy Statement 7300.1A of the Federal Bureau of Prisons); *Gaines v. Lane*, 790 F.2d 1299, 1304–05 (7th Cir.1986) (upholding regulations which were "well-tailored to minimize their intrusiveness" and which provided prison officials with adequate guidance); *Meadows v. Hopkins*, 713 F.2d 206, 211 (6th Cir.1983) (upholding regulations under *Martinez*). *See also Hopkins v. Collins*, 411 F.Supp. 831 (D.Md.1975) (regulations which lacked specificity and were not narrowly tailored found unconstitutional), *aff'd in part and rev'd in part on other grounds*, 548 F.2d 503 (4th Cir.1977); *Taylor v. Perini*, 455 F.Supp. 1241, 1244–45 (N.D.Ohio 1978) (court order for adopting the specific criteria involved here). With such guidelines, prison officials are not given unfettered discretion to censor personal mail, *see Meadows*, 713 F.2d at 211, and the inherent problems of censoring and chilling protected speech are minimized.

2.

The second possible defect of section 5120–9–17 is a due process defect. As previously noted, the Court in *Martinez* upheld the district court's order which required that three procedural safeguards be followed. Specifically, these requirements were that "an inmate be notified of the rejection of a letter written by or addressed to him, that the author of that letter be given a reasonable opportunity to protest that decision, and that complaints be referred to a prison official other than the person who originally disapproved the correspondence." *Martinez*, 416 U.S. at 418–19, 94 S.Ct. at 1814. None of these safeguards are included in section 5120–9–17.[10]

The *Martinez* Court did not express an opinion, however, as to whether any, or all, of these procedures were required for a regulation to be constitutional. For the reasons below, we believe each of these procedural safeguards are required under *Martinez*.

As an initial matter, we note that the "minimum procedural safeguards" referred to in *Martinez* are not mandated solely because of the Due Process Clause of the Fourteenth Amendment, but are primarily required because of the First Amendment free speech rights that are being protected. It is because of the concerns over protecting the freedom of speech and preventing the chilling of speech that procedural safeguards must be in place before letters are withheld or censored. *See Martinez*, 416 U.S. at 406 n. 10, 418–19, 94 S.Ct. at 1808 n. 10, 1814. *Campbell v. Sumner*, 587 F.Supp. 376, 378 (D.Nev.1984). Therefore, we must determine which procedures are required under the Due Process Clause to adequately protect the important First Amendment interests at stake.

We first hold that an incoming mail censorship regulation must provide that notice of rejection be given to the inmate-recipient. The need for such a requirement is evident: without notice of rejection, censorship of protected speech can escape detection by inmates and therefore go unchallenged. Although prison officials may have occasionally, or even consistently, given notice to inmates, the regulation does not require that notice be given.

Second, we hold that the mail censorship regulation is insufficient because it fails to require that notice and an opportunity to protest the decision be given to the

---

10. We note that § 5120–9–19 provides that notice be given to an inmate when printed material is to be censored, and also provides for detailed appeal and review process culminating in review by a Publication Screening Committee. Ohio Admin.Code § 5120–9–19(E) and (F). Although we have borrowed a definition from § 5120–9–19 to uphold § 5120–9–17 on overbreadth grounds, we believe there is no support for borrowing the procedural safeguards. First, this regulation specifically distinguishes between personal letters and print-

ed materials and provides that personal letters are not "within the scope of this provision...." *Id.* at § 5120–9–19(B)(1). Second, the screening committee is specifically labeled a "publication" screening committee; this is another indication of the distinction which was drawn between personal letters and printed material. Therefore, the constitutionality of § 5120–9–17 must be judged apart from these unrelated procedural provisions.

author of the rejected letter. We reach this conclusion for two reasons. First, the decision in *Martinez*, as previously discussed, was premised on the fact that the First Amendment rights of free citizens were implicated by the censorship of prisoners' mail. Without notifying the free citizen of the impending rejection, he would not be able to challenge the decision which may infringe his right to free speech. *Cf. Trudeau v. Wyrick*, 713 F.2d 1360, 1366 (8th Cir.1983) (author of letter brought a First Amendment challenge);[11] *Abdul Wali v. Coughlin*, 754 F.2d 1015, 1027–28 (2d Cir.1985) (the author would have standing to challenge interference with prisoners' mail). Second, since the inmate-recipient would not have seen the contents of the withheld letter, he may require the aid of the author to meaningfully challenge the rejection decision. *See Cofone v. Manson*, 409 F.Supp. 1033, 1042 (D.Conn.1976) (holding that a publisher must receive notice when a prison official decides to withhold a particular publication since a prisoner "cannot be expected to marshal arguments in favor of its admission without the assistance of someone familiar with the material").

We conclude, finally, that a mail censorship regulation must provide for an appeal of the rejection decision to an impartial third party prior to the letter being returned. This is necessary to ensure that future rejection decisions are fair, and based on appropriate factors.

[8] In the instant case, the district court approved the magistrate's report which reasoned that the grievance procedure of Ohio Admin.Code § 5120–9–31 satisfied the procedural requirements in *Martinez*. Although we agree with the district court's initial premise that *Martinez* did not mandate that one regulation provide all the

requisite safeguards, we nonetheless reject its ultimate conclusion.

Section 5120–9–31 is a general grievance procedure, unrelated to the mail censorship regulations. The purpose of the grievance procedure is to provide inmates with a method of presenting complaints which "relate to any aspect of institutional life. It may concern departmental or local institutional policies, procedures, rules and regulations, or the application of any of these to the grievant." As an initial observation, it is clear that if an inmate is never notified that a letter has been rejected, he would not be able to challenge the decision through a grievance procedure. Since section 5120–9–31 does not address the need for notifying the inmate of rejection, it is deficient under *Martinez*. As noted above, the fact that notification of rejection was given on this particular occasion simply does not address the question of whether the regulation is unconstitutional on its face. Also, the grievance procedures are designed for inmate complaints; an author of a letter who wishes to challenge a rejection decision would not be able to utilize this mechanism. Therefore, section 5120–9–31 fails to provide for the second *Martinez* procedural safeguard. Finally, were this the only procedural safeguard required, mail censorship would occur and the letter would be returned to the sender before the grievance would be resolved, or even filed. Under section 5120–9–17, there is no requirement that the letter be saved pending grievance procedures; rather, the managing officer can make a unilateral decision to return a letter to the sender, apparently on-the-spot. As a result, the grievance procedure is inadequate under *Martinez* in that procedural safeguards should be designed to prevent unjustified censorship, not merely to provide a remedy for an aggrieved inmate. It must also be remembered that the prison officials carry

---

11. In *Trudeau*, the author of the letter filed suit in federal court challenging the prison's interference with one letter. The Eighth Circuit held that the author had a constitutionally protected right "to have [a] letter delivered to the inmate free of unjustified interference by state officials," 713 F.2d at 1364,

and that *Martinez* required that "some form of notice [be given] to the author and to the intended recipient that delivery of the letter was being upheld...." *Id.* at 1366. The plaintiff won the case and was awarded substantial damages.

the burden of justifying a mail censorship decision; it is our belief that a post-rejection grievance procedure would not adequately address the threat of the arbitrary suppression of speech and would place a burden on the inmate, or free citizen, which is not theirs to carry.

For the above stated reasons, we find that section 5120-9-17 is unconstitutional, and this case is REMANDED to the district court for further proceedings consistent with this opinion.

MERRITT, Circuit Judge, concurring in part and dissenting in part.

I agree with our Court and the court below that prison officials do not abridge an inmate's substantive first amendment rights when they refuse to permit the letter in question here to circulate in the prison. The letter, written on stationery headed, "UNITED STATES OF AMERICA, INVISIBLE EMPIRE, KNIGHTS OF THE KU KLUX KLAN, INTERNATIONAL OFFICES," says:

Dear William:

I received your letter today. The one letter i got told me to see the chapl in was in Dayton. Nother one said he was in Columbus. I got one of my officers checking it out now. I have got some good news for you. Get about three people to fill out the application for the Klansman newspaper and send it down to the nat. office along with a check or money order, If they refuse you to have the paper you will have the national office backing you up. We will stand behind you too! I want to come and see you and any one else that is interested in the Klan. Can you set up a meeting for us?

I dont want to come under f alse name. Please let me know what you can do.

Very Truly Yours
For God, Race, Nation
JOHN K. _____
KLEAGLES REALM OF OHIO

A sizeable percentage of the prison population is black, and the circulation of this letter and the Ku Klux literature described

in it, as well as the possibility of the Ku Klux Klan organizational meeting mentioned in the letter, may well lead to fights in the prison. The eighth amendment permits punishment that severely limits the personal liberties of convicted felons, including limits on the right to disseminate Ku Klux Klan literature in a prison that may well lead to strife and violent conduct. The prison officials here believed, and I agree, that introducing Ku Klux Klan materials into the prison population would likely lead to violent conduct. On these facts, the prison officials properly rejected the letter.

I part company with the Court on the due process issue. Due process requires that the prisoner be notified of the rejected letter. *Procunier v. Martinez*, 416 U.S. 396, 94 S.Ct. 1800, 40 L.Ed.2d 224 (1973). He was notified here. Due process does not require that the constitutional notice requirement be reduced to an administrative regulation so long as adequate notice in fact occurs. Notice is notice, and it need not be packaged in some particular way that appeals to the appellate judge's penchant for order and neatness. Of course, if an institution does not give some type of notice in every case, such a set of inconsistent practices under the due process clause must be changed.

Martinez does not suggest that procedures required by due process be separately written out in a regulation. Our court and the parties cite no authority and refer to no legal tradition that requires that the constitutional notice requirement be put in an administrative regulation, and I know of no such authority or tradition.

In addition, due process as articulated in *Martinez* is satisfied so long as some reasonable system exists (1) for sending the rejected letter back to the writer so that the writer receives notice of the rejection and (2) for allowing the writer to initiate a procedure to protest the rejection. Although the due process issue concerning the author of the letter was raised in the complaint below and on appeal, the District

Court did not address this question. We do not know what procedures exist in the prison to provide notice of rejection to the author of a personal letter or to permit the author to protest. The case should therefore be remanded to the District Court for findings of fact and conclusions of law under Rule 52, Fed.R.Civ.P. on this issue.

VOLUME III

CHAPTER 5 REHABILITATION AND HEALTH CARE

The Supreme Court of the United States in *Estelle v. Gamble,* 429 U.S. 97, 97 S.Ct. 285 (1976), which is set forth in Vol. VI: 433, established that an incarcerated individual lawfully is entitled to medical attention. The course is generally held that to sustain an Eighth Amendment claim of cruel and unusual punishment, the inmate must show prison authorities denied him access to adequate medical care because of deliberate indifference. When there is a dispute as to whether the attention is optional or not life-threatening there is no cause of action.

Goff v. Bechtold, 632 F.Supp. 697 (S.D. W.Va. 1986), set forth here, involved the question of whether a failure to provide access to a local chiropractor presented a cause of action. The court held that the correctness of the treatment was a matter of dispute between the prisoner and the authorities.

Because some states are contracting out services such as health care, the question arises as to the extent of the state's responsibility. The issue was raised in *Ancata v. Prison Health Services,* 769 F.2d 700 (11th Cir. 1985), which is included here.

Among other cases decided during this time period, but which are not included here, is *Toombs v. Bell,* 798 F.2d 297 (8th Cir. 1986), which involved the dismissal of a civil rights action against the prison doctor and prison nurse. The defendant alleged he had been to sick call several times and that his complaints had been treated with indifference. Later, the inmate's gall bladder was removed. The case was sent back for consideration by the lower courts. Interestingly enough, the opinion cited *Mullins v. Smith,* 738 F.2d 318 (8th Cir. 1984), in which a suit involving a head injury which was untreated for four hours was dismissed.

Exercise is essential to good health, and some prison system regulations prescribe that an inmate have certain amounts of exercise outside of his cell.

Roberts v. Spalding, 783 F.2d 867 (9th Cir. 1986) discussed the principle that an inmate does not have an independent constitutional right to outside medical care. The anticipation of such a benefit does not create a protective interest. The case is not reproduced here.

Introductions in previous volumes:

III: 221; VI: 431; VII: 425; VIII: 411

Eric M. GOFF, Plaintiff,

v.

Lee W. BECHTOLD, Defendant.

Civ. A. No. A:85–0070.

United States District Court,
S.D. of West Virginia,
Parkersburg Division.

April 18, 1986.

MEMORANDUM OPINION
AND ORDER

HADEN, Chief Judge.

Eric Goff brings this *pro se* action pursuant to 42 U.S.C. § 1983. He alleges that Defendant Bechtold, a former Sheriff of Wood County, denied him medical care and attention while he was incarcerated in the Wood County Correctional Center.[1] The Defendant contends that there is no genu-

---

1. The Plaintiff, in essence, is charging the Defendant with violating the Eighth Amendment's guarantee against cruel and unusual punishment. Implicit in his action is the contention that the Defendant was acting under color of state law.

ine issue as to any material fact and that he is entitled to judgment as a matter of law. Accordingly, he moves for summary judgment pursuant to *Rule* 56. The Plaintiff has been notified of his right to submit responsive materials and the consequences of failing to do so. *See* Order entered March 18, 1986. The Plaintiff has not responded. The Court deems the matter mature for decision.[2]

It is now well settled that a governmental unit, such as Wood County, "has an obligation to provide medical care for those whom it is punishing by incarceration." *Estelle v. Gamble*, 429 U.S. 97, 103, 97 S.Ct. 285, 290, 50 L.Ed.2d 251 (1976). Such care, however, need not be the best possible care; it only has to be "reasonable" care. *Vinnedge v. Gibbs*, 550 F.2d 926 (4th Cir.1977); *see also Blanks v. Cunningham*, 409 F.2d 220 (4th Cir.1969); *Edwards v. Duncan*, 355 F.2d 993 (4th Cir.1966).

In *Estelle* the United States Supreme Court solidly gave its approval to the principle developing in the lower courts that deliberate indifference on the part of prison officials to a prisoner's serious illness or injury stated a cause of action under Section 1983. The Supreme Court cautioned, however, that it was only such indifference as would "offend 'evolving standards of decency' in violation of the Eighth Amendment." *Estelle*, 429 U.S. at 106, 97 S.Ct. at 292. The act or omission complained of must be such as to constitute the intentional infliction of unnecessary suffering. *Id.* at 103, 97 S.Ct. at 290. *See also Russell v. Enser*, 496 F.Supp. 320 (D.S.C.1979), affirmed, 624 F.2d 1095 (4th Cir.1980).

It is self-apparent that the *Estelle* test is two-pronged. First, it requires deliberate indifference on the part of prison officials. Second, the injury or illness of the prisoner must be serious.[3] *Inmates of the Allegheny County Jail v. Pierce*, 612 F.2d 754, 762 (3d Cir.1979); *West v. Keve*, 571 F.2d 158, 161 (3d Cir.1978). Hence, a prisoner cannot state a constitutional claim if he has only minor medical needs. Neither can he state a claim if his needs are inadvertently neglected.

In regard to the last point, the courts are in agreement that mere negligence or inadvertence in treating a prisoner will not supply grounds for a Section 1983 suit. *Estelle*, 429 U.S. 97, 97 S.Ct. 285; *Withers v. Levine*, 615 F.2d 158 (4th Cir.1980), *cert. denied*, 449 U.S. 849, 101 S.Ct. 136, 66 L.Ed.2d 59 (1980); *Peterson v. Davis*, 551 F.Supp. 137 (D.Md.1982), affirmed, 729 F.2d 1453 (4th Cir.1984); *Russell*, 496 F.Supp. 320. Negligence may, of course, give rise to a medical malpractice suit, but malpractice in and of itself does not assume constitutional dimensions.

In further refinement of the law applicable to this type of case, it is noted that "claims of inadequate medical treatment which reflect a mere disagreement with prison authorities over proper medical treatment do not state a claim of constitutional magnitude." *Massey v. Hutto*, 545 F.2d 45, 46 (8th Cir.1976); *see also Ferranti v. Moran*, 618 F.2d 888 (1st Cir.1980). Neither can a prisoner sustain an action where he merely harbors a different opinion than his custodians as to the correctness of his course of treatment. *Randall v. Wyrick*, 642 F.2d 304 (8th Cir.1981);

---

2. In considering this motion, the Court is mindful that the pleadings of *pro se* prisoners are to be liberally construed. *Haines v. Kerner*, 404 U.S. 519, 92 S.Ct. 594, 30 L.Ed.2d 652 (1972). Such liberality, however, can only be extended so far. If the Plaintiff had chosen to respond to this motion, the Court would have evaluated his efforts with appropriate leniency. The Plaintiff, however, has chosen to remain silent and rests upon his pleadings—albeit pleadings which are liberally construed. As a result, the Court now addresses a record replete with uncontroverted facts.

3. With regard to the seriousness of the Plaintiff's medical needs, the Court notes that when the Plaintiff's dorsal spine, lumbar spine and pelvis—areas in which the Plaintiff complained of pain—were x-rayed, the results were negative. This outcome does not, of course, disprove the legitimacy of the Plaintiff's complaints, but it does provide one objective aspect of the Plaintiff's health.

McCracken v. Jones, 562 F.2d 22 (10th Cir.1977), *cert. denied*, 435 U.S. 917, 98 S.Ct. 1474, 55 L.Ed.2d 509 (1978).

Upon reflection, the Court believes that this Plaintiff's complaints fall into the last mentioned category—that is, that he had at the time of his incarceration merely a disagreement with the Wood County officials over his treatment. The Plaintiff complains (1) that he was not allowed to be treated by a doctor of his own choice, and (2) that he was denied medication for pain resulting from a back injury.

It is evident from the record that the Plaintiff wished to be treated by Dr. Bunting, a local chiropractor. He asserts that he had to get a court order to see that particular doctor. The record reflects that the Circuit Court of Wood County issued three orders directing the Sheriff's Department to transport the Plaintiff to the Bunting Clinic. The Court is not convinced, however, that the actions of the state court are evidence of deliberate indifference by the Defendant. First, the orders were prepared by counsel for the Plaintiff. Second, there is no indication that the trips to the chiropractor were of an emergency nature. Third, the orders explictly require the Plaintiff to pay for the treatment. At most, the orders manifest a compromise by which the Plaintiff was able to obtain treatment of his choice. Denial of a preferred course of treatment—if in fact such occurred here—does not infringe a constitutional right. *Layne v. Vinzant*, 657 F.2d 468, 473 (1st Cir.1981); *Gahagen v. Pennsylvania Board of Probation and Parole*, 444 F.Supp. 1326 (E.D.Pa.1978).

The case of *Randall v. Wyrick*, 642 F.2d 304 (8th Cir.1981), possesses facts strikingly similar to the case at bar. The plaintiff in *Randall*, a prisoner, complained of back pain as a result of an automobile accident.[4] He complained that the prison staff refused to allow his access to a chiropractor. Chiropractic services, he contended, were necessary to relieve him of the pain which he suffered. The *Randall* court found that the plaintiff's grievance did not meet the *Estelle* standard of "deliberate indiffernce." The claim, said the court, "involve[d] merely a difference of opinion over desirable treatment." *Id.* at 308, n. 8.

The Plaintiff's allegation that he was not given medication to relieve his back pain is pierced by the record which the Defendant has compiled in support of his motion for summary judgment.[5] For instance, the inmate medication log kept for the Plaintiff contains a total of 36 pages. It details literally hundreds of entries whereby the Plaintiff was supplied with medication ranging from Tylenol and Ben-Gay to prescription drugs. The Plaintiff may yet contend that the medication was insufficient to reduce his pain. Such a contention, however, states a claim for malpractice rather than the constitutional tort of "deliberate indifference."[6]

In conclusion, the Court notes that the Plaintiff in all likelihood has suffered some pain as a result of his automobile accident. And it may be true that the medical attention which he received in the Wood County correctional facility did not meet his standards. These facts alone, however, do not state a case for deprivation of a constitutional right. The *uncontroverted* medical documents establish that the Plaintiff frequently received medication and that he was treated by the jail physician and nurse.[7] It must be remembered that the

---

4. The Plaintiff in this case also contends that his back pain can be traced to a recent automobile accident.

5. The Defendant relies upon the exhibits which were appended to his answer. Those exhibits include "speed letters" from the Plaintiff, notes from treating physicians, releases from custody for medical appointments and medication logs. These documents may properly be considered by the Court. *Rule* 56(c) allows the Court to scrutinize the pleadings, *inter alia*, in reviewing

a summary judgment motion and *Rule* 10(c) makes an exhibit to a pleading "a part thereof for all purposes."

6. Naturally, the Court does not express an opinion as to whether medical malpractice in fact occurred.

7. Insofar as the Plaintiff attacks the professional judgment of Dr. Avery, the jail physician, this Court cannot grant the Plaintiff relief under the

"Constitution does not require that sentenced prisoners be provided with every amenity which one might find desirable." *Wolfish v. Levi*, 573 F.2d 118, 125 (2d Cir. 1978), *reversed on other grounds, sub nom Bell v. Wolfish*, 441 U.S. 520, 99 S.Ct. 1861, 60 L.Ed.2d 447 (1979).

Therefore, the Court finding that the Defendant has established that there is no genuine issue of material fact and that he is entitled to judgment as a matter of law, it is ORDERED that judgment shall be entered in favor of the Defendant and against the Plaintiff on the Plaintiff's complaint.

The Clerk is directed to send a certified copy of this Memorandum Opinion and Order to counsel of record and to the *pro se* Plaintiff, Eric M. Goff.

guise of a Section 1983 suit. It is generally accepted that a Court will not second-guess the judgment of a physician. *Zaczek v. Hutto*, 642 F.2d 74 (4th Cir.1981); *Bowring v. Godwin*, 551 F.2d 44 (4th Cir.1977).

Carol ANCATA, individually, as natural
guardian of Tara Ancata, and as personal representative of Anthony Ancata, deceased, Plaintiff-Appellant,

v.

PRISON HEALTH SERVICES, INC., a
Delaware Corp., Susan Colligan, Karen
Sutton, R. Hargrove, Henry Blady, Rob-
ert Butterworth, and George Brescher,
in his capacity as Sheriff of Broward
County, Defendants-Appellees.

No. 84–5923.

United States Court of Appeals,
Eleventh Circuit.

Aug. 26, 1985.

Appeal from the United States District Court for the Southern District of Florida.

Before HENDERSON and CLARK, Circuit Judges and TUTTLE, Senior Circuit Judge.

CLARK, Circuit Judge:

I. FACTS

A. *Procedural History*

This is an appeal from an order of the district court dismissing all counts of plaintiff's first amended complaint based upon 42 U.S.C. § 1983.

Plaintiff is the personal representative of the deceased's, Anthony Ancata's, estate and the guardian of his minor child Tara Ancata. Defendant Prison Health Services is and was the entity responsible for providing medical care to those housed at the Broward County Jail. Defendants Colligan, Sutton, Hargrove and Blady were all medical personnel employed by Prison Health Services, Inc. Robert Butterworth was sued in his official capacity as the sheriff of Broward County at the time of the incidents forming the basis of this lawsuit. Sheriff Brescher was sued in his official capacity as the current sheriff of Broward County. Broward County was sued for its alleged failure to provide adequate funding to address the medical needs of individuals incarcerated there.

Plaintiff's original complaint was filed in August of 1984. Each defendant, other than Prison Health Services, filed a motion to dismiss.[1] Before the court ruled on the motions to dismiss, the defendants consented to the filing of an amended complaint. This took place in October of 1984. Counts 1 and 2 of the complaint alleged that all the defendants violated plaintiff's decedent's right to be free from cruel and unusual punishment by the deliberate indifference to his serious medical needs. The remaining counts raised pendent state law claims. After the amended complaint was filed, defendant Broward County and defendant Blady filed motions to dismiss. The district court entered an order on November 19, 1984 dismissing all counts of the complaint against all defendants.[2] The district

---

1. Prison Health Services failed to answer and a default was entered on October 3, 1984. Its motion to set aside the default was later granted as part of the district court's order dismissing the first amended complaint as to all defend-ants. Appellant does not contest the vacation of the default order.

2. Motions to dismiss by the other defendants, except Prison Health Services, were filed subsequent to the order of dismissal. However, prior

court determined that counts 1 and 2 of the complaint as amended, alleging the constitutional violations, alleged at most, only medical malpractice. Thus, the court determined that dismissal as to all medical defendants was proper. With respect to the non-medical defendants, the district court found that the allegations against them were grounded on notions of respondeat superior and therefore were subject to dismissal. The district court dismissed the pendent state law claims as it had found no valid federal claim.

B. *The Facts as Alleged in Plaintiff's Complaint*

The facts, as alleged in the plaintiff's complaint, indicate the following. Anthony Ancata was arrested and placed in pre-trial detention at the Broward County Jail on August 20, 1982. On August 29, 1982, he began to suffer from a variety of medical symptoms including swelling of the ankle, inability to sleep, chills, lower back pain, tingling and numbness of his hands, hyperventilation, severe pain in his back and right leg, double vision, and other serious problems. Despite his complaints, Prison Health Services and its employees, defendants Blady, Colligan, Sutton and Hargrove did little or nothing to evaluate the medical needs of Mr. Ancata.[3]

The defendants did administer such non-prescription drugs as Ben Gay and Tylenol II and suggested an orthopedic or psychiatric evaluation. However, they took no steps to have Ancata examined by either an orthopedic specialist or a psychiatrist. Rather, they informed Ancata and his family that he would not be referred to a non-staff specialist without a court order. Furthermore, they refused to acquiesce in the entry of a court order unless plaintiff

agreed to bear the costs of the recommended diagnostic evaluation. Mr. Ancata, however, had already been declared indigent.

Ancata's appointed public defender successfully obtained a court order compelling an evaluation by an orthopedic specialist. The orthopedist recommended a neurological evaluation. However, Prison Health Services would again not agree to a medical evaluation by a neurologist without a court order. The second court order was again obtained by the public defender representing Mr. Ancata. After the neurological examination was conducted, Anthony Ancata was hospitalized. He was soon diagnosed as having leukemia. He died in the hospital on December 30, 1982 from respiratory failure.[4]

The appellant raises the following issues on appeal: (1) whether the complaint sufficiently alleged a case of deliberate indifference to serious medical needs thus rendering dismissal improper; (2) whether the federal claims asserted against the sheriff of Broward County and Broward County itself were premised solely on notions of respondeat superior; and (3) whether the dismissal of the pendent state law claims, if the federal claims are found to state a cause of action, was premature.

II. THE LEGAL ISSUES IN CONTEXT

When reviewing an order granting a motion to dismiss for failure to state a claim, this court must accept the facts as pleaded to be true and resolve them in the light most favorable to the plaintiff. The motion to dismiss should not be granted unless it appears to a certainty, "that the plaintiff can prove no set of facts in support of his claim which would entitle him to relief."

to the filing of the first amended complaint, plaintiff had responded to the motions to dismiss of defendants Brescher, Butterworth and Broward County. However, plaintiff's time to respond to the motions to dismiss of the other defendants had not expired as of the time that the district court dismissed the complaint.

3. Defendant Blady was the jail doctor. Colligan was a registered nurse in charge of medical care

at the jail. Sutton and Hargrove were registered nurses employed by Prison Health Services at the jail.

4. Plaintiff alleged that the respiratory failure was "possibly related to herpes pneumonitis and persistent bone marrow hypoplasia, possibly due to chemotherapy as well as marrow suppression by infection, possibly viral."

Milburn v. United States, 734 F.2d 762, 765 (11th Cir.1984). The threshold of sufficiency that a complaint must meet to survive a motion to dismiss for failure to state a claim is, as we have stated previously, "exceedingly low." *Quality Foods de Centro America, S.A. v. Latin American Agribusiness Devel.,* 711 F.2d 989, 995 (11th Cir.1983).

It should also be noted at the outset in this case that the defendants fall into several different groups. Prison Health Services, as was noted previously, is the entity responsible, pursuant to an agreement between it and the county, for providing medical care to those housed at the Broward County Jail. Defendants Colligan, Sutton, Hargrove and Blady were all medical personnel employed by Prison Health Services. The issue to be resolved as to Prison Health Services and its employees, i.e. the medical defendants, is whether plaintiff's allegations sufficiently stated a constitutional tort of deliberate indifference to serious medical needs.

The county and the current sheriff are sued as public bodies ultimately responsible for providing medical care to those incarcerated in Broward County. Mr. Butterworth was the sheriff at the time of Ancata's death. The issue to be resolved as to these defendants, i.e., the non-medical defendants, is whether the district court properly dismissed the claims against them when it determined that any liability they may be exposed to was based solely upon notions of respondeat superior.

A. *The Medical Defendants and the Deliberate Indifference to Serious Medical Needs Claim*

The question before us is whether the allegations of plaintiff's complaint are sufficient to permit a jury to find that the medical defendants' conduct amounted to a deliberate indifference to serious medical needs. *See Estelle v. Gamble,* 429 U.S. 97, 97 S.Ct. 285, 50 L.Ed.2d 251 (1976).[5]

The medical defendants do not contest, and there can be no serious dispute, that if their actions resulted in a deprivation of Ancata's constitutional rights, they would be subject to liability pursuant to 42 U.S.C. § 1983. Although Prison Health Services and its employees are not strictly speaking public employees, state action is clearly present. Where a function which is traditionally the exclusive prerogative of the state (or here, county) is performed by a private entity, state action is present. *Jackson v. Metropolitan Edison Co.,* 419 U.S. 345, 95 S.Ct. 449, 42 L.Ed.2d 477 (1974); *see also Lawyer v. Kernodle,* 721 F.2d 632 (8th Cir.1983) (private physician hired by county to perform autopsies was acting under color of state law); *Morrison v. Washington County, Alabama,* 700 F.2d 678 (11th Cir.1983) (refusing to dismiss physician employed by county from § 1983 action); *Perez v. Sugarman,* 499 F.2d 761 (2d Cir.1974) (holding that state action was present for private institution's acts where the City of New York removed a child from the mother's custody and placed the child in a private child care institution).

If the complaint is sufficient, then dismissal for failure to state a claim is improper. Accepting plaintiff's allegations as true, and giving the plaintiff the benefit of all legitimate inferences from the complaint as we must, we conclude that the complaint sufficiently alleges a claim of deliberate indifference to serious medical needs.

There are at least three separate although somewhat overlapping aspects to plaintiff's claim of deliberate indifference. The first is plaintiff's allegation that the

---

5. Anthony Ancata was a pretrial detainee. *Estelle v. Gamble, supra,* dealt with individuals already convicted of a crime and incarcerated for those crimes, and thus was based upon the Eighth Amendment. Since Ancata was a pretrial detainee the due process clause and not the Eighth Amendment is the applicable constitu-

tional provision. *See City of Revere v. Massachusetts General Hospital,* 463 U.S. 239, 103 S.Ct. 2979, 77 L.Ed.2d 605 (1983). However, as the Court made clear in *City of Revere,* the due process rights of a pretrial detainee are at least as great as the Eighth Amendment protections available to a convicted prisoner.

defendants failed to provide even that level of diagnostic care that they themselves believed necessary. The knowledge of the need for medical care and intentional refusal to provide that care has consistently been held to surpass negligence and constitute deliberate indifference. *See Robinson v. Moreland,* 655 F.2d 887 (8th Cir.1981). In *Ramos v. Lam,* 639 F.2d 559, 575 (10th Cir.1980), *cert. denied,* 450 U.S. 1041, 101 S.Ct. 1759, 68 L.Ed.2d 239 (1981) the court said:

> Deliberate indifference to serious medical needs is shown when prison officials have prevented an inmate from receiving recommended treatment or when an inmate is denied access to medical personnel capable of evaluating the need for treatment.

In this case the plaintiff alleged that the defendants knew that medical care was necessary but simply refused to provide it. The complaint maintains that the defendants concluded that Ancata required a psychiatric or orthopedic evaluation and refused to take the steps to see that he was properly evaluated. Instead, they placed the burden on decedent to obtain a court order for the very examination they believed necessary. Intentional failure to provide service acknowledged to be necessary is the deliberate indifference proscribed by the Constitution. *See Woodall v. Foti,* 648 F.2d 268, 272–73 (5th Cir.1981).

Second, plaintiff alleges that the defendants failed to secure medical care for Ancata because he would not pay. Delay in medical treatment cannot be justified as a means to coerce payment. *See City of Revere v. Massachusetts General Hospital, supra.* Furthermore, if necessary medical treatment has been delayed for non-medical reasons, a case of deliberate indifference has been made out. *See Archer v. Dutcher,* 733 F.2d 14, 17 (2d Cir.1984). Plaintiff alleged that Ancata was indigent

and that the defendants put the financial interest of Prison Health Services ahead of the serious medical needs of Ancata.

Third, plaintiff alleges that the defendants failed to provide proper medical care. Plaintiff's allegations go far beyond that of simple mistake or negligence. Rather, they maintain that the medical care provided was so cursory as to amount to no treatment at all. Such actions, in the case of serious medical problems, may violate the Fourteenth Amendment. *See Tolbert v. Eyman,* 434 F.2d 625, 626 (9th Cir.1970). As the Third Circuit has noted under similar facts:

> Although the plaintiff has been provided with aspirin, this may not constitute adequate medical care. If, "deliberate indifference caused an easier and less efficacious treatment" to be provided, the defendants have violated the plaintiff's Eighth Amendment rights by failing to provide adequate medical care.

West v. Keve, 571 F.2d 158, 162 (3d Cir. 1978) (citations omitted).

Looking at the above-mentioned allegations in the plaintiff's complaint, as well as the other allegations contained therein, it is clear that the allegations contained in the plaintiff's complaint sufficiently state a constitutional claim that the medical defendants were deliberately indifferent to Ancata's serious medical needs. When the allegations indicate this type of indifference, dismissal prior to discovery is premature. Therefore, the decision of the district court is REVERSED as to this issue.

B. *The Non-Medical Defendants and Respondeat Superior*

As to the non-medical defendants, i.e., the two sheriffs and Broward County, the district court dismissed the claims against them as being solely based upon respondeat superior.[6] We disagree. First,

---

6. The district court relied upon *Estelle v. Gamble,* 554 F.2d 653 (5th Cir.1977) (on remand from the Supreme Court decision *supra*) in its determination that the claims against the non-medical defendants were based upon respondeat superior. In *Estelle* the court stated:

> [W]hile the Director and the warden are parties, not for having failed to provide treatment, but more on respondeat superior principles in line with their official capacities. We can find no evidence in the record that either exhibited "deliberate indifference" to

as to Broward County. The county is responsible for insuring that adequate funds are provided to meet the medical needs of inmates. The complaint alleges that "Defendant Broward County is responsible for providing funds to insure that the medical needs of the inmates of the Broward County Jail are properly met.... The limited funds provided by the County may have contributed to deliberate indifference shown for the serious medical needs of Anthony Ancata." [7] The federal courts have consistently ruled that governments, state and local, have an obligation to provide medical care to incarcerated individuals. *See Estelle, supra.* This duty is not absolved by contracting with an entity such as Prison Health Services. Although Prison Health Services has contracted to perform an obligation owed by the county, the

> Gamble's medical needs by means of interference with the prison doctor's performance or in any other manner which would satisfy the Supreme Court standard.
> 554 F.2d at 654.
> The allegations in this case are different in that the plaintiff alleges that the actions and policies of the county and the sheriff's office did affect in various ways the health care received by Mr. Ancata. The actions are not solely based upon their status as a public body.

7. Fla.Stat.Ann. § 951.032 states in pertinent part:

> (1) A county detention facility or municipal detention facility incurring expenses for providing medical care, treatment, hospitalization, or transportation may seek reimbursement for the expenses incurred in the following order:
>   (a) From the prisoner or person receiving medical care, treatment, hospitalization, or transportation.
>   (b) From an insurance company, health care corporation, or other source if the prisoner or person is covered by an insurance policy or subscribes to a health care corporation or other source for those expenses.

Although the statute makes clear that the county can seek reimbursement from a person incarcerated, the plain wording of the statute indicates that the county has the responsibility for securing adequate medical treatment. A prisoner does not have to bargain for medical care. The county admits as much in its brief; "state law mandates that Broward County pay the medical expenses of prisoners incarcerated in the county jail." Brief of Appellee Broward County at 7.

8. However, if a constitutional tort committed by an employee of Prison Health Services was not

county itself remains liable for any constitutional deprivations caused by the policies or customs of the Health Service. In that sense, the county's duty is non-delegable.[8] *See generally Wilson v. Taylor,* 733 F.2d 1539, 1545 (11th Cir.1984).[9] Lack of funds for facilities cannot justify an unconstitutional lack of competent medical care and treatment for inmates. *See Gates v. Collier,* 501 F.2d 1291 (5th Cir.1974); *see also Miller v. Carson,* 401 F.Supp. 835, 889–91 (M.D.Fla.1975), *aff'd* 563 F.2d 741 (5th Cir. 1977).[10]

Additionally, if Broward County established or utilized a policy or custom requiring that inmates needing medical assistance obtain court orders and the result of that policy or custom played a role in the delay in treatment and deliberate indiffer-

a result of the policy or custom of the entity, then the county would not be liable. Liability for the independent actions of a health service employee would be based upon respondeat superior and thus not actionable against the county under § 1983.

9. *See also Hearn v. City of Gainesville,* 688 F.2d 1328 (11th Cir.1982). In *Hearn,* the court made clear that where a governmental entity delegates the final authority to make decisions then those decisions necessarily represent official policy. 688 F.2d at 1334. The county has a duty to provide adequate medical care both under the United States Constitution and under Florida law. Thus, if Prison Health Services and/or its employees have the responsibility to make final decisions regarding a requirement that a prisoner pay for medical attention before receiving it or obtain a court order, then their acts, policies and customs become official policy. *See also supra* note 5 (explaining that Prison Health Services and its employees act under color of state law).

10. Plaintiff also maintains that if she prevails, she will be entitled to recover attorney's fees and costs pursuant 42 U.S.C. § 1988. She maintains the county is ultimately responsible for any attorney's fees or costs assessed against the sheriff. For this reason alone, she maintains that dismissal of the county is inappropriate, relying upon *Glover v. Alabama Board of Corrections,* 734 F.2d 691, 694 (11th Cir.1984). However, in light of Supreme Court's recent pronouncement in *Kentucky v. Graham,* —— U.S. ——, 105 S.Ct. 3099, 87 L.Ed.2d 114 (1985) this contention appears to be without merit.

ence shown towards Anthony Ancata, then the county may be liable. *See Berdin v. Duggan,* 701 F.2d 909 (11th Cir.1983). Furthermore, if the county permitted the sheriff and/or prison health officials that it contracted with to establish such a policy or custom, it may also be liable. *See Trezevant v. City of Tampa,* 741 F.2d 336 (11th Cir.1984).[11] Such liability would not be based upon notions of respondeat superior. The liability would be a result of the county's own policy. *Monell v. New York City Dept. of Social Services,* 436 U.S. 658, 98 S.Ct. 2018, 56 L.Ed.2d 611 (1978).

As to the defendant Robert Butterworth, he was sheriff at the time medical care was refused to Anthony Ancata. His liability, if any, would not necessarily be solely based upon respondeat superior. If plaintiff can establish, as she alleged, that the sheriff was personally involved in the acts depriving Anthony Ancata of his constitutional rights, or that he breached a duty imposed by state law and that that breach caused the plaintiff's injury, then he would be fully responsible for his own actions and/or policies. *See Baskin v. Parker,* 602 F.2d 1205 (5th Cir.1979); *Douthit v. Jones,* 641 F.2d 345 (5th Cir.1981). Furthermore, if Butterworth himself established or utilized a policy or custom requiring that inmates seek court orders to obtain medical services, then he would be liable if the result of that policy or custom played a role in any deliberate indifference to Ancata's medical needs. *Berdin v. Duggan,* 701 F.2d 909 (11th Cir.1983).

At the stage in the litigation at which Sheriff Butterworth was dismissed, i.e., prior to discovery, it is impossible to say whether Butterworth played a role in demanding the court orders as a condition of obtaining medical care. Nor is it known which, if any, of the defendants chose to place the financial interest of the county ahead of Ancata's medical needs. Thus,

dismissal prior to discovery was unwarranted.

Finally, defendant George Brescher, the sheriff at the time the case was filed, was sued in his official capacity as sheriff of Broward County. The issue of which entity is fiscally responsible, i.e., the sheriff's office or the county should be resolved before either one is properly dismissed. Until that issue is resolved, Brescher should remain a party to this litigation. *See Glover v. Alabama Department of Corrections,* 734 F.2d 691, 694 (11th Cir. 1984).

C. *The Pendent State Law Claims*

As we have determined that plaintiff adequately alleged a federal claim, then we must determine that the district court's dismissal of the pendent state law claims was premature. Obviously, they derive from a common nucleus of operative fact and thus because the court, at present, has jurisdiction over the parties and because the federal claims asserted by the plaintiff are substantial, the pendent law claims are properly before the court. *United Mine Workers v. Gibbs,* 383 U.S. 715, 86 S.Ct. 1136, 16 L.Ed.2d 218 (1966).

Therefore, the decision of the district court is reversed and the case is remanded to the district court for proceedings consistent with this opinion.

REVERSED and REMANDED.

HENDERSON, Circuit Judge, concurring in part and dissenting in part:

I concur in the majority's disposition of this case except that portion of the opinion which reverses the district court's dismissal of George Brescher, the sheriff of Broward County at the time of the filing of this suit. The majority opinion accepts the appellant's argument that Brescher should not be dismissed as a party defendant until there is a resolution of which entity, the county or the sheriff, bears the fiscal re-

---

11. As we noted above, if, either expressly or by default, Broward County permitted others to decide or determine policy, it is liable for their actions if these policies prove unconstitutional.

Wilson v. Taylor, supra (holding that when a municipality gives a police chief the final authority to make a decision *Monell* standards for official policy are satisfied).

sponsibility for funding the jail's medical needs. I respectfully disagree with this conclusion.

The majority opinion states, "The county is responsible for insuring that adequate funds are provided to meet the medical needs of inmates." At 705. It notes that Broward County concedes in its brief that state law mandates that it pay the medical expenses of county prisoners. *Id.* at 705–06 n. 7. Given this admission, there is no need to inquire further into whether Brescher or Broward County would be liable for failure to provide the required funds. Since there are no other charges of liability against Brescher, he should not be required to further defend the action.

VOLUME III

CHAPTER 6   SEXUAL AND MARRIAGE RIGHTS

There was little litigation in the area of prisoner rights to marriage and sexual visitation. However, in the case reprinted here, *Safley v. Turner,* 777 F.2d 1307 (8th Cir. 1985), the court reviewed rules of the state of Mississippi that prevented inmates from corresponding or marrying if the prison administration denied them permission to do so. In *Safley,* the rules were found to have abridged the prisoners' constitutional rights.

Introductions in previous volumes:

Leonard SAFLEY, et al., Appellees,

v.

William R. TURNER; Kathy Crocker; Earl Engelbrecht; Betty Bowen; Bernice E. Trickey; Howard Wilkins; James Purkett; William F. Yeager; Larry Trickey, Appellants.

Leonard SAFLEY, et al., Appellees,

v.

David W. BLACKWELL; Lee Roy Black; Donald Wyrick; Betty Bowen; Earl Engelbrecht, Appellants.

Nos. 84–1827, 84–2337.

United States Court of Appeals, Eighth Circuit.

Submitted June 13, 1985.

Decided Nov. 19, 1985.

Before ROSS, Circuit Judge, BRIGHT, Senior Circuit Judge, and NICHOL,* Senior District Judge.

---

* The HONORABLE FRED J. NICHOL, Senior United States District Judge for the District of South Dakota, sitting by designation.

NICHOL, Senior District Judge.

This is an appeal from a class action in which the district court [1] declared unconstitutional certain regulations of the Missouri prison system. For reversal, appellants argue that the district court applied the incorrect legal standard in determining the constitutionality of the prison rules, and that the district court's findings of fact were clearly erroneous. For the reasons set forth below, we affirm.

BACKGROUND

The challenged regulations were in effect at all institutions within the Missouri Division of Corrections. However, the focus of inquiry at trial was the Renz Correctional Institution (Renz). Renz was originally designed as a minimum security prison farm employing male inmate labor. As such, it has a minimum security perimeter without the usual maximum security elements such as guard towers and walls. Since the late 1970s, Renz has become what is known as a "complex prison"—that is, its population consists of both male and female inmates and inmates of varying security levels. Most of the female inmates at Renz are medium and maximum security level offenders, while most of the male inmates are classified as minimum security.

Two regulations are at issue in this appeal. The first dealt with mail between inmates in different institutions within the state, and was set out in Division of Corrections regulation 20–118.010(1)(e):

Correspondence with immediate family members who are inmates in other correctional institutions will be permitted. Such correspondence may be permitted between non-family members if the classification/treatment team of each inmate deems it in the best interest of the parties involved. Correspondence between inmates in all division institutions will be permitted concerning legal matters.

The challenged portion of the rule was that part permitting mail between non-family members only at the discretion of the classification/treatment team of each inmate involved.[2] The team used psychological reports, conduct violations, and progress reports contained in each inmate's file to decide whether to permit correspondence. The testimony indicated that these materials were not actually consulted on each occasion since the team was familiar with the classification files of most of the inmates. Thus, inmate-to-inmate correspondence was controlled by prior approval or disapproval of particular inmates rather than individual review of each piece of mail.

The district court found in Finding of Fact number 5 that

[t]here have been instances where the divisional correspondence regulation has been violated. For example:

a. Letters have been stopped without notice or explanation to either the correspondent or the recipient; [3]

b. Mail to and from persons not incarcerated has been stopped or refused on factually incorrect grounds or without legitimate justification; [4]

c. Mail to incarcerated family members has been refused or returned without notification or explanation; [5]

---

1. The Honorable Howard F. Sachs, United States District Judge for the Western District of Missouri.

2. At Renz, this team consisted of three persons—a caseworker, Betty Bowen; a classification assistant, Warren Karander; and the particular inmate in question. Each member of the team had an equal vote. Tr., Vol. I at 87–89.

3. Division of Corrections regulations 20–118.010(1)(C) and (2)(C) provide for notification to the sender and addressee when mail containing contraband is confiscated.

4. The regulation places no restrictions on mail to and from non-inmates except for the prohibition against contraband, escape plots, and the like.

5. Regulation 20–118.010(1)(E) provides that inmate correspondence with incarcerated family members "will be permitted." Presumably, the prohibition against contraband and the provisions for notice of confiscation apply to family as well as non-family mail.

d. Mail with former inmates has been refused or returned without notification or explanation.[6]

Safley v. Turner, 586 F.Supp. 589, 591 (W.D.Mo.1984). Moreover, "the rule as practiced [at Renz] is that inmates may not write non-family inmates." *Id.* This practice was set forth in the Renz Inmate Orientation Booklet presented to each inmate upon arrival at Renz. The district court found that correspondence had been denied between married inmates, and between inmates who desired to maintain a friendship. An unwritten rule at Renz required prior approval of inmate-to-inmate legal mail; absent such approval, this mail was routinely opened, stopped and refused despite the divisional regulation stating that such mail "will be permitted." The reasons given for these practices include interception of plans for escape, heading off riots and other disturbances, and controlling the formation and activities of inmate gangs. These matters are of special concern at Renz because of the minimum security perimeter.

The second rule at issue in this appeal involved inmate marriages. Prior to December of 1983, the Missouri prison system operated under divisional regulation 20–117.050, which set out the procedure to be followed when an inmate wished to marry. As the district court noted, this regulation "(a) did not obligate the Missouri Division of Correction to assist an inmate who wanted to get married, but (b) did not authorize the superintendents of the various institutions to prohibit inmates from getting married. Inmates at Renz were, however, frequently denied permission to be married." *Safley*, 586 F.Supp. at 592. On December 1, 1983, after this lawsuit was filed, a new inmate marriage regulation was promulgated providing that "[t]he superintendent may approve the marriage of an inmate when requested when there are compelling reasons to do so." Appellants' Brief, App. E. The burden was on the inmate to provide a compelling reason for the marriage. The term "compelling" was not defined in the regulation. At trial, however, testimo-

ny of prison officials indicated that only a pregnancy or the birth of an illegitimate child would be considered compelling reasons.

The district court found that the marriage restrictions were imposed largely on female inmates at Renz and at the Chillicothe Correctional Center for Women, and that the restrictions were motivated primarily by protective attitudes. Apparently many of the female inmates who were denied permission to marry had come from situations involving domestic abuse. Renz's Superintendent Turner believed "that women prisoners whose crimes were connected to abuse that they had suffered ... needed to concentrate on developing skills of self-reliance." Appellants' Brief at 30. Turner believed it to be in the best rehabilitative interests of the inmates to avoid any personal relationship with another inmate. Security interests were also cited. Appellants contend that "the friction that is caused as a result of a 'love triangle' and the maintenance of 'wholesome' inmate friendships is the basis for a large amount of violence within the prison system." *Id.* at 47–48.

The district court, relying on *Procunier v. Martinez*, 416 U.S. 396, 94 S.Ct. 1800, 40 L.Ed.2d 224 (1974), applied a traditional strict scrutiny standard. The court held the marriage rule to be an unconstitutional infringement upon the fundamental right to marry because it was far more restrictive than was either reasonable or essential for the protection of the state's interests in security and rehabilitation. *Safley*, 586 F.Supp. at 594. Likewise, the mail rule was unnecessarily broad, thus constituting a violation of the inmates' First Amendment rights. *Id.* at 596. The district court also held that the correspondence regulations had been applied in an arbitrary and capricious manner.

THE CORRESPONDENCE RULE

Appellants argue that, because of the plaintiffs' status as prisoners, the district court should have applied a rational basis

---

6. *See* note 3, *supra.*

or reasonableness test rather than strict scrutiny in determining the constitutionality of the restriction on inmate-to-inmate correspondence. The issue is one of first impression in this circuit; in fact, we have found only one other decision addressing the precise question of mail between inmates of different institutions. *See Schlobohm v. U.S. Attorney General,* 479 F.Supp. 401 (M.D.Pa.1979) (applying strict scrutiny and finding the regulation constitutional). A series of Supreme Court cases, however, as well as a number of our own past decisions concerning First Amendment rights of prisoners may provide guidance.

We begin with the observation that, traditionally, a direct governmental prohibition of the right to free speech is permissible only if the restriction furthers a compelling governmental interest and is the least restrictive alternative for achieving that purpose. *United States v. Grace,* 461 U.S. 171, 103 S.Ct. 1702, 1707, 75 L.Ed.2d 736 (1983); *Perry Education Association v. Perry Local Educators' Association,* 460 U.S. 37, 103 S.Ct. 948, 955, 74 L.Ed.2d 794 (1983). Restrictions on the First Amendment rights of prisoners, however, have presented special problems. "[C]ourts are ill equipped to deal with the increasingly urgent problems of prison administration and reform." *Martinez,* 416 U.S. at 405, 94 S.Ct. at 1807. Yet the duty of the federal courts to protect fundamental constitutional guarantees, even in state penal institutions, remains intact. *Id.* Hence, courts have struggled to discern the faint line between appropriate deference to prison administrators, on the one hand, and discharge of the judicial duty, on the other.

In *Martinez,* the Supreme Court considered a prisoner mail censorship regulation which proscribed certain forms of expression in inmate correspondence.[7] The Court determined that, because the regulation applied to mail to and from non-inmates as well as inmates, the case did not require an assessment of the extent to which prisoners may claim First Amendment freedoms but instead could be decided on the basis of incidental restrictions on the rights of members of the general public. *Martinez,* 416 U.S. at 408–09, 94 S.Ct. at 1808–09. In this light, the Court held that censorship of prisoner mail is justified only if it furthers an important or substantial governmental interest unrelated to the suppression of expression, and the limitation is no greater than necessary or essential to protect that interest. *Id.* at 412, 94 S.Ct. at 1810. Under this standard, the regulation in *Martinez* was unconstitutional.

Later in the same Term the Court decided *Pell v. Procunier,* 417 U.S. 817, 94 S.Ct. 2800, 41 L.Ed.2d 495 (1974), which involved, *inter alia,* a challenge to a prohibition against face-to-face visits between prisoners and news reporters. Because the rule restricted only one manner of communication between inmates and the general public, *id.* at 823, 94 S.Ct. at 2804, it was regarded as a "time, place or manner" regulation. *Id.* at 826, 94 S.Ct. at 2806; *see, e.g., Grayned v. City of Rockford,* 408 U.S. 104, 92 S.Ct. 2294, 33 L.Ed.2d 222 (1972). The regulation was upheld because it met the traditional "time, place or manner" test. It furthered the important governmental interests in deterrence, security and rehabilitation; it was content-neutral in that it was applied equally to all reporters and prisoners; and, most significantly, several alternative means of communicating with the public, including with reporters, were available to the prisoners. *Pell,* 417 U.S. at 824–25, 94 S.Ct. at 2805.

In the case at bar, we do not deal with a "time, place or manner" regulation. The challenged mail rule, both on its face and as applied, purports to eliminate all manner of correspondence between inmates not "approved" by the classifi-

---

7. Inmates could not write letters in which they "unduly complain," "magnify grievances," or express "inflammatory political, racial, religious or other views or beliefs," nor could they send or receive letters that "pertain to criminal activi-

ty; are lewd, obscene, or defamatory; contain foreign matter, or are otherwise inappropriate." *Martinez,* 416 U.S. at 399–400, 94 S.Ct. at 1804–1805.

cation/treatment team. Nevertheless, *Martinez* and *Pell* are useful illustrations of the proposition that, although lawful incarceration " 'brings about the necessary withdrawal or limitation of many privileges and rights, a retraction justified by the considerations underlying our penal system,' ... a prison inmate retains those First Amendment rights that are not inconsistent with his status as a prisoner or with the legitimate penalogical objectives of the corrections system." *Pell*, 417 U.S. at 822, 94 S.Ct. at 2804 (citations omitted); *see also Martinez*, 416 U.S. at 422, 94 S.Ct. at 1815 (Marshall, J., concurring). Implicitly, then, those rights which are not inconsistent with the fact of incarceration or with legitimate penalogical objectives retain the highest level of protection afforded by the First Amendment, and their deprivation requires strict scrutiny by the courts. Thus, we must decide whether the right to exchange letters between inmates of different institutions is inconsistent with either of those considerations.

Appellants rely most heavily on two of the Court's more recent decisions. In *Jones v. North Carolina Prisoners' Labor Union, Inc.*, 433 U.S. 119, 97 S.Ct. 2532, 53 L.Ed.2d 629 (1977), prison regulations prohibited inmates from soliciting other inmates to join the Union, barred all meetings of the Union, and prevented the delivery of packets of Union publications that had been mailed in bulk to several inmates for redistribution among other prisoners. The Court upheld the regulations because they were "reasonable, and [were] consistent with the inmates' status as prisoners and with the legitimate operational considerations of the institution." *Id.* at 130, 97 S.Ct. at 2540. However, the Court made clear that First Amendment free speech rights were "barely implicated." *Id.* The only real loss was that of the cost advantages of bulk mailings; individual mailings of Union material were not banned. *Id.* at 130 n. 8, 97 S.Ct. at 2540 n. 8.

First Amendment associational rights, the *Jones* court acknowledged, were more directly implicated but were still subject to a reasonableness standard. *Id.* at 132, 97 S.Ct. at 2541. This was a reflection of the Court's concern with the special dangers inherent in concerted group activity by prisoners.[8] The Court noted the "ever-present potential for violent confrontation and conflagration" among inmates, and the fact that "a prisoners' union, where the focus is on the presentation of grievances to, and encouragement of adversary relations with, institution officials surely would rank high on anyone's list of potential trouble spots." *Id.* at 132–33, 97 S.Ct. at 2541.

Unlike in *Jones*, First Amendment speech rights are directly implicated in the instant case. The right to exchange letters with another is clearly a fundamental free speech value. And the presumption of dangerousness applied by the *Jones* Court to prisoner unions loses its force in the context of mail between two inmates in two different institutions physically separated by many miles.

The other case relied upon by appellants is *Bell v. Wolfish*, 441 U.S. 520, 99 S.Ct. 1861, 60 L.Ed.2d 447 (1979). There, a group of pretrial detainees contended, *inter alia*, that a regulation prohibiting the receipt of hardback books not mailed directly from publishers, book clubs, or bookstores violated the First Amendment. The receipt of paperback books, magazines, and other soft-covered materials from any source was permitted. The Court upheld the regulation, concluding it was a rational response to an obvious security problem. *Id.* at 550, 99 S.Ct. at 1880. "It hardly needs to be emphasized that hardback books are especially serviceable for smuggling contraband into an institution; money, drugs, and weapons easily may be secreted in the bindings." *Id.* at 551, 99 S.Ct. at 1880. There was no evidence that prison officials had exaggerated their response to this security problem. *Id.*

8. For a thorough discussion of *Jones* and other decisions pertinent to this issue, *see Abdul Wali*

v. Coughlin, 754 F.2d 1015, 1029–33 (2d Cir. 1985).

In addition to finding the rule reasonable, the Court in *Wolfish* took an approach similar to the one in *Pell, supra,* regarding the rule as a "time, place, or manner" regulation. *Id.* at 553, 99 S.Ct. at 1881. Thus, the rule served the important governmental interest in security; it was content-neutral; and it left available alternative means of obtaining reading material which were not shown to be burdensome or insufficient. *Id.* at 552, 99 S.Ct. at 1881.

In contrast, no alternative means of communicating with inmates in other institutions were available in the instant case. While phone calls to outsiders were permitted under certain conditions, *see* Tr., Vol. V at 60–64, phone calls to other inmates within the system were prohibited. *Id.* at 62. Moreover, we do not think a letter presents the same sort of "obvious security problem" as does a hardback book. Appellants concede that the primary concern with respect to mail between institutions was the possibility of making plans for escapes, riots, and the like. Appellants' Brief at 15. Yet in the daily operation of the correspondence policy now being challenged, Earl Engelbrecht, a Renz supervisor, examined, opened and scanned the contents of all mail between inmates not on his "approved" list. *Id.* at 4–5; Tr., Vol. V at 80–81, 96–97. This task, Engelbrecht testified, took approximately one hour a day. Tr., Vol. V at 70, 96–97. Under these circumstances, and considering the core First Amendment right involved, we believe that neither *Jones* nor *Wolfish* requires application of a rational basis standard to the issue of inmate-to-inmate mail.

Our own previous decisions do not change this conclusion. In *Rogers v. Scurr,* 676 F.2d 1211 (8th Cir.1982), we held that a prison regulation prohibiting the wearing of prayer caps and robes outside of religious services was reasonable. *Id.* at 1215. We noted that, although restrictions on First Amendment rights generally should be no greater than necessary to protect the governmental interest involved, prison officials must be given wide latitude when maintenance of institutional security is at issue. The plaintiff inmates,

members of the Islamic faith, were permitted to congregate five times daily for prayer, were provided the pork-free diet required by their religion, and were served the special meals of the holy month of Ramadan. *Id.* at 1213. " 'So long as the prison authorities provide the inmate with a reasonable opportunity for the exercise of his religious tenets in a form that is substantially warranted by the requirements of prison safety and order, there is no violation of the inmate's constitutional rights.' " *Id.* at 1215–16 (quoting *Sweet v. South Carolina Department of Corrections,* 529 F.2d 854, 863 (4th Cir.1975)). *See also Otey v. Best,* 680 F.2d 1231 (8th Cir.1982) (upholding prison regulation prohibiting inmates subject to death penalty from attending worship services with general prison population; Muslim plaintiff was allowed visits by Muslim religious leader, was provided with special diet, and had access to religious literature and broadcasts).

In both *Rogers* and *Otey, supra,* the prison rules in question were essentially regulations of the time, place, or manner in which an acknowledged First Amendment right could be exercised. In both cases, the right of free exercise of religion was not completely deprived but was merely limited to the extent necessary to conform to security needs. Alternative means were provided by which the inmates could adhere to their religious tenets.

Closer in point is our recent decision in *Gregory v. Auger,* 768 F.2d 287 (8th Cir. 1985). There, an inmate challenged a prison regulation prohibiting the receipt of all but first class mail while an inmate was on disciplinary detention status (DD1). Inmates were placed on DD1 status for no longer than sixty days. *Id.* at 290. The rule was designed to make DD1 status less pleasant than being out in the general prison population, so as to deter future misconduct. *Id.* We upheld the regulation because of its temporary nature and because of the need of prison officials to " 'have available sanctions that impose incremental disadvantages on those already imprisoned.'" *Id.* (quoting *Daigre v. Maggio*, 719 F.2d 1310, 1313 (5th Cir.1983)). We observed that "the Reformatory could properly have established mail policies far more restrictive than this, so long as the disciplinary withholding of mail was only to be temporary." *Id.*

In the case at bar, however, the mail restrictions were neither temporary nor disciplinary. Although past misconduct was considered by the classification/treatment team in deciding whether an inmate should be "approved" for inter-institutional correspondence, it was but one of several factors. Moreover, the chairman of the team testified that decisions on inmate-to-inmate mail were usually made before they reached the classification team; inmates would stop the superintendent or a supervisor in the hallway and receive a decision on the spot. Tr., Vol. II at 148. The *Gregory* decision teaches that a prisoner mail prohibition is a serious infringement of First Amendment liberties, permissible only in narrowly circumscribed settings such as existed there.

We conclude that the exchange of inmate-to-inmate mail is not presumptively dangerous nor inherently inconsistent with legitimate penalogical objectives. We therefore affirm the district court's application of the *Martinez* strict scrutiny standard and its decision finding the Renz correspondence rule unconstitutional.

THE MARRIAGE RULE

Two regulations concerning marriage are at issue. Prior to December 1, 1983, the rule ("the old rule") set out the procedure to be followed when an inmate desired to marry. The thrust of the old rule was to place responsibility for any and all preparations upon the inmate, and to make clear that any assistance from prison officials would be secondary to the normal functions of the institution. While the rule was silent as to the giving or withholding of permission to marry, Superintendent Turner testified that he believed he had the inherent power to deny permission by virtue of Missouri statutes "which allow me to control my institution." Tr., Vol. I at 70.

On December 1, 1983, a new marriage regulation ("the 1983 rule") was promulgated. Under the 1983 rule, an inmate desiring to marry had to file a written request stating reasons for the marriage. The superintendent was given authority to approve the request "when there are compelling reasons to do so," and to disapprove the request if "the wedding would pose a threat to the security and operation of the institution." While both rules appear applicable to marriages between inmates and outsiders, the record refers only to proposed marriages between two inmates.

The district court apparently assumed that the marriage rules were intended to serve the legitimate state interests in security and rehabilitation. *Safley*, 586 F.Supp. at 594. The court held the rules unconstitutional because they were "far more restrictive than is either reasonable or essential for the protection" of those interests. *Id.* (citations omitted). The court thus effectively applied the *Martinez* standard, *see Martinez*, 416 U.S. at 413, 94 S.Ct. at 1811, albeit without reference to that decision. As with the correspondence regulation, appellants argue the court should have applied a reasonableness standard.

It is well settled that the decision to enter into a marital relationship is a fundamental human right. *Zablocki v. Redhail*, 434 U.S. 374, 98 S.Ct. 673, 54 L.Ed.2d 618 (1978); *Loving v. Virginia*, 388 U.S. 1, 87 S.Ct. 1817, 18 L.Ed.2d 1010 (1967); *Skinner v. Oklahoma ex rel. Williamson*, 316 U.S. 535, 62 S.Ct. 1110, 86 L.Ed. 1655 (1942); *Meyer v. Nebraska*, 262 U.S. 390, 43 S.Ct. 625, 67 L.Ed. 1042 (1923). Appellants initially contend, however, that a prisoner has no right to have a marriage ceremony performed in prison. In support of this proposition, appellants cite us to *Johnson v. Rockefeller*, 365 F.Supp. 377 (S.D.N.Y.), *aff'd without opinion sub. nom., Butler v. Wilson*, 415 U.S. 958, 94 S.Ct. 1479, 39 L.Ed.2d 569 (1973); *Polmaskitch v. United States*, 436 F.Supp. 527 (W.D.Okla.

1977); and *Wool v. Hogan*, 505 F.Supp. 928 (D.Vt.1981). We find this contention to be without merit.

Both *Johnson* and *Wool, supra*, determined that a restriction on a prisoner's right to go through the formal ceremony of marriage does not amount to an infringement on a fundamental right because those aspects of a marriage which make it a basic civil right—"cohabitation, sexual intercourse, and the begetting and raising of children"—are already precluded by the fact of incarceration. *Johnson*, 365 F.Supp. at 380; *Wool*, 505 F.Supp. at 932. This argument ignores the elements of emotional support and public acknowledgement and commitment which are central to the marital relationship. Moreover, it is contrary to the *Zablocki* Court's interpretation of the decision to marry as being distinct from, but equally as important as, decisions relating to procreation and other family matters.

> [T]he decision to marry has been placed on the same level of importance as decisions relating to procreation, childbirth, child rearing, and family relationships. * * * [I]t would make little sense to recognize a right of privacy with respect to other matters of family life and not with respect to the decision to enter the relationship that is the foundation of the family in our society.

Zablocki, 434 U.S. at 386, 98 S.Ct. at 681. In *Polmaskitch, supra*, the court first determined that it had no jurisdiction of the case, and then went on to decide that a prisoner has no fundamental right to marry while incarcerated. We need not give precedential value to a decision made without jurisdiction. Thus, we hold that an inmate's decision to marry is a fundamental right protected by the Constitution. *See Bradbury v. Wainwright*, 718 F.2d 1538, 1540 (11th Cir.1983).

Appellants' main argument is the same as that advanced in connection with the mail rule—that is, the district court applied the wrong legal test. They rely on *Jones v. North Carolina Prisoners' Labor Union*, 433 U.S. 119, 97 S.Ct. 2532, 53 L.Ed.2d 629 (1977), and *Bell v. Wolfish*, 441 U.S. 520, 99 S.Ct. 1861, 60 L.Ed.2d 447 (1979), as well as our own decision in *Otey v. Best*, 680 F.2d 1231 (8th Cir.1982). We discussed these cases *supra* and we adhere to our earlier analysis.

All three decisions involved regulations of the time, place or manner in which a particular right could be exercised, and all three regulations left open other means of exercising that right. Thus, the union materials in *Jones* could have been mailed individually to prison inmates rather than by bulk mail. 433 U.S. at 130 n. 8, 97 S.Ct. at 2540 n. 8. The pretrial detainees in *Wolfish* were permitted to receive all soft-covered reading materials, could receive hardback books directly from publishers, book clubs and bookstores, and had access to hardback books in the prison library. 441 U.S. at 552, 99 S.Ct. at 1881. And the Muslim death row inmate in *Otey*, while prohibited from attending worship services with the general prison population, was allowed religious visits and services in his cell, adherence to Islamic dietary requirements, and access to Muslim literature and broadcasts. 680 F.2d at 1232.

Here, in contrast, both the old marriage rule as it was applied by Superintendent Turner and the 1983 rule on its face absolutely prevent those inmates denied permission from getting married. There are no alternative means of exercising that right. When a government-imposed regulation "significantly interferes with the exercise of a fundamental right, it cannot be upheld unless it is supported by sufficiently important state interests and is closely tailored to effectuate only those interests." *Zablocki*, 434 U.S. at 388, 98 S.Ct. at 682 (citations omitted); *see also Abdul Wali v. Coughlin*, 754 F.2d 1015, 1033 (2d Cir.1985) (where official action works to deprive rather than merely limit the means of exercising a protected right, judgment of prison officials must be scrutinized under the *Martinez* standard). We therefore affirm the district court's application of strict scrutiny in evaluating the marriage rules.

THE DISTRICT COURT'S
FINDINGS OF FACT

Finally, appellants contend that certain of the district court's findings of fact are clearly erroneous. Fed.R.Civ.P. 52(a). We may not overturn findings of fact unless, after a review of the entire record, we are left with the definite and firm conviction that a mistake has been committed. *Pullman-Standard v. Swint*, 456 U.S. 273, 284 n. 14, 102 S.Ct. 1781, 1788, n. 14, 72 L.Ed.2d 66 (1982); *Aetna Casualty & Surety Co. v. General Electric Co.*, 758 F.2d 319, 323 (8th Cir.1985). As to each challenged finding, appellants concede there is supporting testimony but argue that the district court gave improper weight or significance to the finding. Having thoroughly examined the record and found substantial evidence to support each finding of fact, we hold the district court's findings are not clearly erroneous.

The thrust of appellants' argument seems to be that, even assuming the findings of fact are correct and the proper legal standard was applied, the facts of this case do not warrant the conclusion that the mail and marriage rules are unconstitutional. Since the district court based its decision on the failure of the rules to meet the least restrictive alternative requirement, we take this to be an argument that the court erred in holding that the mail and marriage rules were not the least restrictive means of serving the prison officials' objectives of security and rehabilitation.

The mail rule permitted correspondence between unrelated inmates "if the classification/treatment team of each inmate deems it in the best interest of the parties involved." While there was testimony that the question whether correspondence between two particular inmates was in their best interests was submitted to the classification/treatment team, there was other testimony indicating that in fact the team was rarely consulted. The mail room supervisor, Engelbrecht, typically rendered a decision either at the time an inmate requested permission from him or when an inmate simply went ahead and wrote a letter which was then intercepted in the mail room and diverted to Engelbrecht. The orientation booklet given to inmates on arrival at Renz stated that no correspondence between non-family inmates was permitted, apparently in the hope that inmates would be discouraged from attempting to write.

The testimony also revealed that the principal reason for refusal of inmate-to-inmate mail was the prison officials' belief that female inmates should avoid any personal relationships, friendly or romantic, with male inmates. Such relationships are detrimental to the women's rehabilitation, according to Superintendent Turner, because they may find themselves the victims of abuse which, presumably, may in turn lead them back to criminal activities. Additionally, mail was refused on the ground of security on the theory that it may contain plans for escape, violent uprisings or other illegal activities. Marriages were denied on the basis of the same protective concerns, as well as the belief that possible "love triangles" would generate violent confrontations between inmates. No specific incident of the realization of any of these concerns, involving these or any other inmates, was alleged or shown.

We agree with the district court that stopping mail and preventing marriages are not the least restrictive means of achieving these objectives. With respect to rehabilitation, efforts such as counseling, teaching of job skills to promote independence, or development of outside interests to increase the inmate's self-image and self-respect would certainly be permissible ways to help an inmate avoid detrimental relationships without impinging on the right to exchange letters with another or the right to marry. In our view, without strong evidence that the relationship in question is or will be abusive, the connection between permitting the desired correspondence or marriage and the subsequent commission of a crime caused thereby is simply too tenuous to justify denial of those constitutionally protected rights. As to the security concerns, we think the prison officials' authority to open and read all prisoner mail is sufficient to meet the problem of illegal conspiracies. As we discussed earlier, appropriate time, place or manner regulations are also permissible. And the development of violent "love triangles" is as likely to occur without a formal marriage ceremony as with one. Refusing to permit a wedding would not necessarily prevent such confrontations.

CONCLUSION

In sum, we affirm the district court's use of strict scrutiny in evaluating the constitutionality of the inmate correspondence and marriage regulations, we hold the court's findings were not clearly erroneous, and we uphold the court's conclusion that the regulations in question are unconstitutional.

VOLUME III

CHAPTER 7   RIGHT TO SELF AND PROPERTY

It has been often stated that an inmate loses a great deal of privacy when he is incarcerated and that his right to personal property must be weighed against the prison's security.

Gaunt v. Sunn, 792 F.2d 874 (9th Cir. 1986), reversed a dismissal of an action for the alleged beating of a prisoner by guards and for the denial of the prisoner's access to the courts because of threats made by the guards. A memorable statement from the opinion described the dilemma: "Prisons being the kinds of places that they are, prison guards being the kinds of people that they are, and prisoners being subject to control under often severe circumstances, we have no doubt that when threats of bodily harm are made against prisoners to discourage them from pursuing legal redress, those threats are likely to be successful." The case is included.

Burton v. Livingston, 791 F.2d 97 (8th Cir. 1986), was a civil rights action brought against prison guards for threats that allegedly violated the inmate's right to petition the court. The case is included here.

Another area of concern with regard to a prisoner's personal rights involves searches of the inmate's person. In *United States v. Smith,* 774 F.2d 1005 (10th Cir. 1985), a case not included, the court held that the prison warden's authorization of a rectal search of an inmate was not supported by a reasonable belief that contraband was concealed. *Spence v. Farrier,* 807 F.2d 753 (8th Cir. 1986), involved random urinalysis testing for drugs. The case is included.

Wright v. Newsome, 795 F.2d 964 (11th Cir. 1986), was a civil rights action in which certain personal property of the inmate was confiscated and destroyed. The case involved a procedural question and is not included here.

Introductions in previous volumes:

III: 317; VI: 449; VII: 451; VIII: 439

Kenneth GAUT, Plaintiff-Appellant,

v.

Franklin SUNN, Director of Social Services and Housing, et al., Defendants-Appellees.

No. 83-2320.

United States Court of Appeals, Ninth Circuit.

Argued Aug. 6, 1984.

Submitted April 8, 1986.

Decided June 20, 1986.

Appeal from the United States District Court for the District of Hawaii.

Before BROWNING, Chief Judge, and DUNIWAY and SNEED, Circuit Judges

PER CURIAM:

Gaut, a Hawaii state prisoner, appeals from the dismissal of his second amended complaint for failure to state a claim upon which relief can be granted. We reverse.

Gaut brought an action against state prison guards under 42 U.S.C. § 1983 (1982) for deprivation of liberty without due process of law through beatings allegedly inflicted upon him by the guards, and for denial of access to the courts through threats allegedly made by the guards. Gaut also alleged cruel and unusual punishment, a denial of medical care subsequent to the beatings, and vicarious liability on the part of prison administrators. Gaut has failed to argue that the dismissal of these causes of action was error and we do not address them.

Prison beatings which "shock the conscience" are actionable under section 1983. *Meredith v. Arizona*, 523 F.2d 481, 483 (9th Cir.1975). In *Meredith* we quoted and adopted the following standard from *Johnson v. Glick*, 481 F.2d 1028, 1033 (2d Cir.1973):

In determining whether the constitutional line has been crossed, a court must look to such factors as the need for the application of force, the relationship between the need and the amount of force that was used, the extent of injury inflicted, and whether force was applied in a good faith effort to maintain or restore discipline or maliciously and sadistically for the very purpose of causing harm.

We take the allegations of Gaut's second amended complaint as true. *North Star International v. Arizona Corporation Commission*, 720 F.2d 578, 580 (9th Cir.1983). Gaut alleges he was severely beaten, kicked, choked, and thrown against a wall by several guards when he shuffled his feet during a prison "shakedown," and was beaten again while handcuffed after he was taken to a holding unit. The complaint alleges the type of intentional, unjustified, unprovoked, and brutal conduct we have found to constitute a section 1983 claim in previous cases. *See Rutherford v. City of Berkeley*, 780 F.2d 1444, 1446-47 (9th Cir.1986); *Meredith*, 523 F.2d at 484; *Gregory v. Thompson*, 500 F.2d 59, 61-62 (9th Cir.1974); *Allison v. Wilson*, 434 F.2d 646, 647 (9th Cir.1970) (per curiam); *Allison v. California Adult Authority*, 419 F.2d 822, 823 (9th Cir.1969); *Wiltsie v. California Department of Corrections*, 406 F.2d 515, 516-17 (9th Cir.1968).

Gaut also alleged he was "threatened with bodily harm" by the defendants "to convince him to refrain from pursuing legal redress" for the beatings. This allegation made out a cause of action under section 1983 for denial of Gaut's right of access to the courts; failure to allege the threats were carried out or that Gaut was deterred from suing did not justify dismissal for failure to state a claim. *Lamar v. Steele*, 693 F.2d 559, 562 (5th Cir.1982); *Hudspeth v. Figgins*, 584 F.2d 1345, 1347-48 (4th Cir.1978) (per curiam); *Campbell v. Beto*, 460 F.2d 765, 768 (5th Cir.1972).

Prisons being the kinds of places that they are, prison guards being the kinds of people that they often are, and prisoners being subject to control under often severe circumstances, we have no doubt that when threats of bodily harm are made against prisoners to discourage them from pursuing legal redress, those threats are likely to be successful. Thus they are an improper interference with the undoubted constitutional right of the prisoner to access to the courts. As to that right, see *Bounds v.*

Smith, 430 U.S. 817, 97 S.Ct. 1491, 52 L.Ed.2d 72 (1977); *Johnson v. Avery,* 393 U.S. 483, 89 S.Ct. 747, 21 L.Ed.2d 718 (1969).

Cases cited by defendants are distinguishable. The holding of *McFadden v. Lucas,* 713 F.2d 143, 145–47 (5th Cir.1983) (*see also Johnson v. Glick,* 481 F.2d at 1033, n. 7), that threats alone are not actionable under section 1983 as assaults sufficient to shock the conscience, does not justify dismissal of a section 1983 action alleging use of threats to deny access to the courts. *Collins v. Cundy,* 603 F.2d 825, 827 (10th Cir.1979) (per curiam), is distinguishable because the threat alleged was regarded as mere verbal harassment.

Neither of Gaut's claims is precluded by *Parratt v. Taylor,* 451 U.S. 527, 101 S.Ct. 1908, 68 L.Ed.2d 420 (1981). *Parratt* does not apply to substantive due process claims, including *Meredith* claims. As we said in *Rutherford,* 780 F.2d at 1447:

Where the denial is of substantive, not merely procedural, due process, the governmental conduct involved would remain unjustified even if there existed the most stringent of procedural safeguards. Because the substantive due process is violated at the moment the harm occurs, the existence of a postdeprivation state remedy should not have any bearing on whether a cause of action exists under § 1983.

Cf. Davidson v. Cannon, — U.S. —, 106 S.Ct. 668, 670–71, 88 L.Ed.2d 677 (1986).

REVERSED and REMANDED.

SNEED, Circuit Judge, concurring in part and dissenting in part:

I concur in that part of the court's opinion holding that the complaint's allegations of being beaten, kicked, choked, and thrown against the wall state a cause of action under 42 U.S.C. § 1983 (1983). The existence of a remedy under state law that conforms to procedural due process has been made irrelevant under the law of this circuit. *Haygood v. Younger,* 769 F.2d 1350 (9th Cir.1985) (en banc). More recently this court has bypassed *Parratt v. Taylor,* 451 U.S. 527, 101 S.Ct. 1908, 68 L.Ed.2d 420 (1981), by drawing a distinction between claims resting on *substantive* due process and those resting on *procedural* due process. This distinction is employed here. *See supra* p. 875. The net effect is that in this circuit *Parratt v. Taylor* has little, if any, operative force.

I have decried this development previously. *See Mann v. City of Tucson,* 782 F.2d 790, 794–800 (9th Cir.1986) (Sneed, J., concurring). I do so again here and incorporate by reference the substance of my observations in *Mann v. City of Tucson.* Sooner or later the Supreme Court will introduce more reason into this area than presently exists. For federal courts to complain about overwork, while busily creating a comprehensive tort system applicable to all forms of misconduct by those acting under the color of state law, is to ask for scornful rejection of their complaint. Either they do not have too much to do or they want to do something other than what they are presently doing. Either way I cannot blame the public for its indifference.

Nowhere is this expansionist thrust more evident than in the court's holding here that "verbal intimidation" under the facts as alleged constitutes an actionable section 1983 claim. "Verbal intimidation" alone probably does not state a claim in tort under the law of the State of Hawaii. Hawaii Rev.Stat. § 707–715 commentary (1976). Clearly it is doubtful that it amounts to the misdemeanor "terroristic threatening," the likely source of a civil tort, that is proscribed in Hawaii Rev.Stat. § 707–715 (Supp.1986). *See In re Doe,* 3 Hawaii App. 325, 331, 650 P.2d 603, 608 (1982) (requiring psychological trauma to recover for the intentional infliction of such injury) (quoting Hawaii Rev.Stat. § 707–715 commentary (1976)) (amended 1979).[1]

1. The torts of assault and assault and battery are not defined by statute in California. This affords a court the opportunity to extend the concept of the tort beyond the limits placed by

To treat conduct of this type as meeting the constitutional standard of *Rochin v. California*, 342 U.S. 165, 72 S.Ct. 205, 96 L.Ed. 183 (1952), is to trivialize the Eighth Amendment.

The majority finds more than mere "verbal intimidation" in this case. Count five of Gaut's complaint alleges;

Plaintiff has been and continues to be verbally intimidated and threatened with bodily harm by state officials to include named defendants herein to convince him to refrain from pursuing legal redress for the events occurring on and subsequent to October 29, 1982.

No action, however, other than threats is alleged. The majority position rests on the fact that the alleged threat had as its purpose the prevention of Gaut's pursuit of legal redress. This, the court presumably reasons, contravenes a prisoner's right of access to the courts recognized in *Bounds v. Smith*, 430 U.S. 817, 97 S.Ct. 1491, 52 L.Ed.2d 72 (1977), and earlier cases.

Bounds, it will be recalled, held that the right of access requires "prison authorities to assist inmates in the preparation and filing of meaningful legal papers by providing prisoners with adequate law libraries or adequate assistance from persons trained in the law." 430 U.S. at 828, 97 S.Ct. at 1498. Obviously *Bounds* did not address the question presented by Gaut's count five allegations. Nonetheless, it is a fact that threats such as Gaut alleges do not enhance a prisoner's access to the courts. The court holds, in effect, that this verbal

discouragement, without more, transgresses the Constitution.

No case that I have been able to find precisely so holds. *Hudspeth v. Figgins*, 584 F.2d 1345 (4th Cir.1978) (per curiam), *cert. denied*, 441 U.S. 913, 99 S.Ct. 2013, 60 L.Ed.2d 386 (1979), contains language that supports the court; but in fact the prison authorities took steps to implement the threat by transferring the prisoner to a road gang as they had threatened to do. *Campbell v. Beto*, 460 F.2d 765 (5th Cir. 1972), is a similar case. The threat to punish if the prisoner filed more writs was made in the context of a course of severe mistreatment by prison officials. Moreover, the court stated that the threats, "if proved, would certainly be an appropriate justification for injunctive relief" because a prisoner's access to the court cannot be curtailed or restricted. 460 F.2d at 768. That injunctive relief, if relief is to be given, is more appropriate than damages is obvious. Here injunctive relief is unnecessary because the necessary writs were filed. Despite the threats access was obtained.

The absence of any significant restriction in fact and any overt act intended to reinforce the seriousness of the threat distinguishes this case from *Hudspeth* and *Campbell*. This case involves "verbal intimidation" only. Confronted with this form of intimidation, the Fifth Circuit had no difficulty in holding no section 1983 claim was stated. *See McFadden v. Lucas*, 713 F.2d 143, 146 (5th Cir.), *cert. denied*,

---

its corresponding statutory criminal definition. 6 Cal.Jur.3d *Assault and Other Wilful Torts* § 21 (1973). However, in civil actions for assault, the courts often apply the penal definitions and rely on criminal cases in rendering their decisions. See *Fraguglia v. Sala*, 17 Cal.App.2d 738, 742, 62 P.2d 783, 785 (1936); 4 B. Witkin, Summary of California Law § 194, at 2482 (8th ed. 1974); 6 Cal.Jur.3d *Assault and Other Wilful Torts* § 21, at 208 (1973). *McChristian v. Popkin*, 75 Cal.App.2d 249, 260, 171 P.2d 85, 92 (1946), held that the trial court correctly instructed the jury as to what constitutes an assault or battery by giving the Penal Code defini·tions thereof.

Apart from reliance on criminal definitions, a civil action for assault will lie based upon inva-

sion of the right of a person to live without being put in fear of personal harm. *Lowry v. Standard Oil Co.*, 63 Cal.App.2d 1, 7, 146 P.2d 57, 60 (1944). This case was never cited again for this proposition but the case does appear under the heading "Personal Rights" in the discussion notes to California Civil Code § 43 (Deering 1971).

Although the tort of assault is never defined by the California Civil Code, 4 B. Witkin, Summary of California Law § 194, at 2483 (8th ed. 1974) states: "Mere words, however threatening, will not amount to an assault." No civil cases have been found allowing recovery without physical injury.

464 U.S. 998, 104 S.Ct. 499, 78 L.Ed.2d 691 (1983). The court relied on Judge Friendly's opinion in *Johnson v. Glick*, 481 F.2d 1028, 1033 & n. 7 (2d Cir.), *cert. denied*, 414 U.S. 1033, 94 S.Ct. 462, 38 L.Ed.2d 324 (1973), in which he pointed out that under the common law mere words, however violent, did not amount to an assault. A similar position was reached in *Collins v. Cundy*, 603 F.2d 825 (10th Cir.1979) (per curiam), where allegations of threatening language and a refusal to mail certain legal correspondence was held not to state a section 1983 claim.

In essence the majority holds that, even though no threats were carried out and no access to the courts blocked, it is constitutional to say to a prisoner "You do as I say [anything other than not filing law suits] or I will beat you," but unconstitutional to say, "You stop filing law suits or I will beat you."

That is too fine a point for me. I respectfully dissent.

Richard W. SPENCE, et al., Appellants,

v.

Hal FARRIER, et al., Appellees.

No. 85-1902.

United States Court of Appeals,
Eighth Circuit.

Submitted June 9, 1986.

Decided Dec. 24, 1986.

Before LAY, Chief Judge, ARNOLD, Circuit Judge, and STROM,* District Judge.

STROM, District Judge.

The appellants, prisoners at the Iowa State Penitentiary, appeal from the order of the United States District Court for the Southern District of Iowa granting summary judgment against them. They allege they were deprived of constitutional rights arising under the Fourth and Fourteenth Amendments by virtue of drug testing policies and procedures at the Penitentiary.

I. BACKGROUND

Appellants filed this action pursuant to 42 U.S.C. § 1983. They sought declaratory and injunctive relief for deprivation, under color of state law, of their Fourth Amendment right to be free from an unreasonable search and seizure and their Fourteenth Amendment right to due process of law. They contend their rights were violated as a result of urinalysis testing for drugs at the Penitentiary.

Iowa State Penitentiary conducts urinalysis testing of inmates to detect and deter the use of contraband drugs. In addition to testing those suspected of using drugs, the Penitentiary tests approximately ten per cent (10%) of the prison population on a monthly basis. Inmates tested are chosen by unit managers who randomly pull cards from an index card file. There are no allegations that the selection of appellants herein was not random.

The Penitentiary uses the EMIT (Enzyme Multiple Immunoassay Test) for urinalysis testing. Any positive results are retested on the EMIT. Disciplinary reports are written on inmates who have positive EMIT results. Inmates are allowed to present defenses at a disciplinary board hearing, although they are not allowed to call expert witnesses or to have a confirmatory test by alternate methodology. Those found guilty of ingesting drugs can be subjected to sanctions, including loss of good time, transfer to a maximum security unit (ad-

---

* The Honorable Lyle E. Strom, United States District Judge for the District of Nebraska, sit- ting by designation.

ministrative segregation), and disciplinary detention (solitary confinement).

Appellants, who had been disciplined as a result of EMIT tests, challenged the constitutionality of the procedures. The district court granted defendants' motion for summary judgment, holding: (1) plaintiff's Fourth Amendment expectation of privacy in body fluids was not offended by the random selection process and that the method of generating random samples was not so susceptible to abuse as to be inherently unreasonable; (2) defendants' use of the results of EMIT without independent confirmatory tests did not violate due process as long as the positive test results provide some evidence to support the disciplinary board's decision; and (3) defendants were not required to run corroborative tests or to allow plaintiffs to call testing personnel or expert witnesses to challenge EMIT results and that failure to do so did not create an irrebuttable presumption in violation of due process. The district court did not address plaintiffs' contentions of insufficient notice for the reason that the issue was not raised in the pleadings. This appeal followed.

II. DISCUSSION

A. Fourth Amendment

Appellants first assert that the district court erred in finding that the random testing procedures at issue are reasonable within the meaning of the Fourth Amendment. A urinalysis constitutes a search or seizure for purposes of the Fourth Amendment. *See, McDonell v. Hunter,* 746 F.2d 785 (8th Cir.1984), *on remand,* 612 F.Supp. 1122, 1127 (S.D.Iowa 1986). *See also, Schmerber v. California,* 384 U.S. 757, 767–68, 86 S.Ct. 1826, 1834, 16 L.Ed.2d 908 (1966); *United States v. Williams,* 787 F.2d 1182, 1185 n. 5 (7th Cir.1986); and *Storms v. Coughlin,* 600 F.Supp. 1214, 1217–18 (S.D.N.Y.1984). Therefore, the searches must be conducted in a reasonable manner. *Schmerber v. California,* 384 U.S. at 771–72, 86 S.Ct. at 1836. However, prison administrators are accorded "wide-ranging deference in the

adoption and execution of policies and practices that in their judgment are needed to preserve internal order and discipline and to maintain institutional security." *Bell v. Wolfish,* 441 U.S. 520, 547, 99 S.Ct. 1861, 1878, 60 L.Ed.2d 447 (1979). A reasonableness analysis involves "[b]alancing the significant and legitimate security interests of the institution against the privacy interests of the inmates...." *Id.* at 560, 99 S.Ct. at 1885.

With that balancing test in mind, we hold that the procedure at issue is reasonable. The unauthorized use of narcotics is a problem that plagues virtually every penal and detention center in the country. *Block v. Rutherford,* 468 U.S. 576, 588–89, 104 S.Ct. 3227, 3234, 82 L.Ed.2d 438 (1984). Because of the prison's security needs, the prisoner's expectation of privacy in his or her body is diminished. *Storms v. Coughlin,* 600 F.Supp. at 1224. The prisoners' limited expectation of privacy does not forbid random urine collection and analysis. *Id.* at 1223. However, it is important to insure that when the state chooses to employ such intrusive random searches as these, the procedures for selecting the inmates to be tested are truly random. *Id.* There is no evidence herein that unit managers are aware of the names of the prisoners chosen, nor are there any allegations that appellants were not selected purely at random. Under the circumstances, we are unable to say that the procedure used unnecessarily exposes prisoners to the risk of harassment or that the practice lends itself to abuse. *But cf., Storms* at 1223 (procedure whereby watch commander is aware of the name of the prisoner he selects to be tested lends itself to abuse).

B. Due Process

Appellants next assert that the district court erred in finding that the testing procedures satisfied the requirements of due process. In that regard, appellants argue (1) that refusal to allow inmates to have confirmatory tests performed violates due process in that it creates an irrebuttable presumption of guilt and (2) unconfirmed

EMIT tests are inadmissible absent a showing that the test has been accepted in the scientific community.

The requirements of due process are flexible and depend on a balancing of interests affected by the relevant government action. *Superintendent, Massachusetts Correctional Institution v. Hill*, 53 U.S.L.W. 4778, 4781 (1985). This interest must be accommodated in the distinctive setting of a prison, where disciplinary proceedings "take place in a closed, tightly controlled environment peopled by those who have chosen to violate the criminal law and have been lawfully incarcerated for doing so." *Id. (quoting Wolff v. McDonnell*, 418 U.S. 539, 561, 94 S.Ct. 2963, 2977, 41 L.Ed.2d 935 (1974)). "Prison disciplinary proceedings take place in a highly charged atmosphere, and prison administrators must often act swiftly on the basis of evidence that might be insufficient in less exigent circumstances." *Id.* The requirements of due process are satisfied if some evidence supports the decision by the prison disciplinary board. *Id.; Rushing v. State*, 382 N.W.2d 141, 145 (Iowa 1986).

The EMIT test results obviously provide some evidence of drug use. EMIT tests have been found sufficiently reliable to meet the requirements of the due process clause. *See, e.g., Harmon v. Auger*, 768 F.2d 270, (8th Cir.1985) (EMIT test results are ninety-five per cent (95%) accurate and form a sufficient basis for disciplinary action); *Wycoff v. Resig*, 613 F.Supp. 1504 (N.D.Ind.1985) (a positive EMIT test confirmed by a second EMIT test or its equivalent satisfies due process); *Jensen v. Lick*, 589 F.Supp. 35 (D.N.D.1984) (prison officials could impose sanctions on prisoners based upon an unconfirmed EMIT test); *Peranzo v. Coughlin*, 608 F.Supp. 1504 (S.D.N.Y.1984) (double EMIT testing held sufficient to satisfy due process); *Hoeppner v. State*, 379 N.W.2d 23, 25 (Iowa App.1985) ("the limited rights set forth in *Wolff [v. McDonnell]* do not entitle a prisoner to an independent sample of evidence used in a disciplinary proceeding"); and *Smith v. State*, 250 Ga. 438, 298 S.E.2d 482

(1983) (the EMIT test is sufficiently reliable to stand as the only evidence in a parole revocation hearing). *But see, Higgs v. Wilson*, 616 F.Supp. 226 (W.D.Ky.1985); and *Kane v. Fair*, 33 Cr.L. 2492 (Mass.Super 1983). We hold that the EMIT test, as used at Iowa State Penitentiary with a confirmatory second test, contains sufficient indicia of reliability to provide some evidence of drug use.

Appellants also argue that use of the EMIT test as evidence at a disciplinary board hearing creates an irrebuttable presumption of guilt. Such is not the case because prisoners are allowed to present defenses. Inmates are provided an opportunity to rebut proof of the urinalysis. They can challenge the accuracy of the test and raise the defense of passive inhalation. *Harmon v. Auger*, 768 F.2d at 276–77. An inmate's rights to call witnesses and to present documentary evidence are limited to situations when "permitting him to do so will not be unduly hazardous to institutional safety and correctional goals." *Wolff v. McDonnell*, 418 U.S. at 566, 94 S.Ct. at 2979. Prison officials must have the necessary discretion to keep the hearing within reasonable limits. *Id.* "We should not be too ready to exercise oversight and put aside the judgment of prison administrators." *Id.* To allow prisoners to present expert testimony in regard to EMIT reliability would seriously interfere with the institutional goal of drug deterrence and prompt resolution of drug related infractions. The evidence herein shows that inmate's defenses are given due consideration and that charges are sometimes dismissed on grounds of irregularities in testing.

Although it is conceivable that an inmate could be unjustly disciplined as a result of EMIT tests, the margin of error is insignificant in light of institutional goals. States need not implement all possible procedural safeguards against erroneous deprivation of liberty when utilizing results of scientific testing devices in accusatory proceedings. *See, Wycoff v. Resig*, 613 F.Supp. at 1311.

Appellants' assertion that the results of the EMIT test are inadmissible because of lack of scientific support is without merit. As noted, the EMIT test has been shown to be widely accepted. *See discussion, supra.* Additionally, a prison disciplinary hearing is intended to be informal and expeditious. *See, Wolff,* 418 U.S. at 569–70, 94 S.Ct. at 2981. Evidentiary standards are therefore relaxed; inmates have no right to confrontation and cross-examination or to counsel. *Id.* It follows that the admission of positive EMIT results is not violative of due process.

C. Notice

With regard to appellants' assertion that notice is insufficient, that issue was not raised in the pleadings and will not be addressed. The matter is now moot for the reason that Iowa State Penitentiary presently follows the notice requirements mandated in *Harmon v. Auger* at 277.

In view of the foregoing, the court finds the order of the district court should be and is affirmed.

LAY, Chief Judge, dissenting.

I respectfully dissent.

I fully recognize that the Supreme Court has held that prisoners have no legitimate expectation of privacy in their prison cells, *Hudson v. Palmer,* 468 U.S. 517, 530, 104 S.Ct. 3194, 3202, 82 L.Ed.2d 393 (1984), and that it has held that random searches of cells are an effective instrument against the proliferation of weapons, illicit drugs, and other contraband in the prison setting. *Id.* at 528, 104 S.Ct. at 3201. In *Block v. Rutherford,* 468 U.S. 576, 104 S.Ct. 3227, 82 L.Ed.2d 438 (1984), the Court took judicial notice "that the unauthorized use of narcotics is a problem that plagues virtually every penal and detention center in the country." *Id.* at 588–89, 104 S.Ct. at 3234. Moreover, in *Bell v. Wolfish,* 441 U.S. 520, 99 S.Ct. 1861, 60 L.Ed.2d 447 (1979), the Court upheld the practice of body cavity searches of pretrial detainees performed by prison employees after contact visits with persons outside the institution. However,

in *Bell* the Court took care to note that in that case inmate attempts to smuggle "money, drugs, weapons, and other contraband" into the prison facility "by concealing them in body cavities are documented in this record." *Id.* at 559, 99 S.Ct. at 1884. In upholding these searches the Court stated that in each case "[t]he test of reasonableness under the Fourth Amendment * * requires a balancing of the need for the particular search against the invasion of personal rights that the search entails." *Id.* The Court continued:

> We do not underestimate the degree to which these searches may invade the personal privacy of inmates. Nor do we doubt, as the District Court noted, that on occasion a security guard may conduct the search in an abusive fashion. * * * Such abuse cannot be condoned. The searches must be conducted in a reasonable manner.

Id. at 560, 99 S.Ct. at 1885 (citations omitted).

There should be little doubt that randomly conducted urinalysis for the purposes of detecting illicit drug use by an inmate is a search that implicates the Fourth Amendment. Although prisoners are not completely divested of their constitutional rights while incarcerated, the unique constraints of the prison environment require that the inmates' rights be curtailed in a reasonable manner. We acknowledge that in balancing the rights of the inmate against the state's institutional interests, due deference must be given to prison administrators' judgments. Unless substantial evidence exists in the record to indicate that the prison officials have exaggerated their response to considerations of institutional security, courts should ordinarily defer to the expert judgments of corrections officials in such matters. *Pell v. Procunier,* 417 U.S. 817, 827, 94 S.Ct. 2800, 2806, 41 L.Ed.2d 495 (1974). There is nothing in the present record to show that prisoners in the Iowa correctional facilities must be searched on a random basis, thus subjecting prisoners to possible harassment and abuse, rather than under a reasonable suspicion standard (which is, of course, less than probable cause). The record is devoid of any facts from which the administrators could conclude that random searches of all prisoners are necessary to maintain prison discipline. Under these circumstances, the procedures here are an exaggerated response to the circumstances by the prison administration. If the prison authorities can show that security problems can be traced to the use of the reasonable suspicion standard, then the competing Fourth Amendment interests may be reevaluated and properly balanced to remedy those demonstrated problems. Here, however, there is no evidence that the state has shown any facts at all that indicate a need to conduct at-random searches.

No one is in favor of the consequences which may flow from illegal drug abuse, whether in the prison context or elsewhere. However, the majority's analysis relies on assumptions and generalizations, rather than on demonstrated facts, in affirming the district court's determination that on balance the Iowa State Penitentiary's asserted need to protect institutional security, by conducting random searches of inmates' urine, outweighs the individual inmate's privacy interests under the Fourth Amendment. In its opinion granting summary judgment to the state penitentiary, the district court made no findings of fact that the prison officials had demonstrated actual past or present drug abuse by inmates which in fact threatened the security of the institution. Moreover, a review of the record yields little, if any, factual basis to support such findings. In its brief to this court, no facts were recited by the state penitentiary to support the institution's asserted need to detect and deter the use of contraband drugs by inmates through such intrusive, random means.

I recognize that it is likely that illicit drug use by prisoners has the potential to create serious security problems in the prison setting. However, merely alleging the probability that drug abuse exists or that security problems may potentially arise from such abuse is an insufficient foundation on which to base any judicial action, especially in a case such as this which determines the scope of Fourth Amendment rights for a significant number of people. As an appellate court, we should demand from litigants and rely ourselves on facts, not dicta, even dicta drawn from Supreme Court opinions, especially when making judicial determinations with constitutional implications.

Willie **BURTON, Jr.,** Appellant,

v.

A. LIVINGSTON, Appellee.

No. 85–1941.

United States Court of Appeals,
Eighth Circuit.

Submitted Jan. 14, 1986.

Decided May 8, 1986.

Before HEANEY, ARNOLD, and WOLLMAN, Circuit Judges.

ARNOLD, Circuit Judge.

Willie Burton, Jr., an inmate at the Tucker Maximum Security Unit of the Arkansas Department of Correction, appeals from the dismissal of his 42 U.S.C. § 1983 complaint against Sgt. A. Livingston, a guard at the Cummins Unit of the Arkansas Department of Correction.

Mr. Burton alleged in his complaint that on 12 June 1984 he was in attendance at the federal courthouse in Pine Bluff, Arkansas, for a hearing on a complaint against guards at the Cummins Unit. He was accompanied to that hearing by Mr. Livingston and at least one other guard. Mr. Burton's handwritten *pro se* complaint alleged that after his appearance in court he was taken to the "holding tank" in the courthouse. Then:

Livington had continued harassing me pointing at his revolver pistol as threats; he then pull his revolver, thumb cocked it and stated, ["] nigger run so I can blow your Goddamn brains out, I want you to run so I'll be justified ["]; then another prison guard stepped between us, and move me to the opposite side of him from defendant Livington; then just out side the Court Building, as we were approaching the transporting van, def. Livington drew his pistol 357 Magnum and stated ["] nigger run, I want you to run ["], where he tried his best to scare me into running where he could shoot me in my back and say I tried to escape; I was then placed on the van and transported back to Cummins Prison Unit ... [sic]

Complaint at 3. Mr. Burton's complaint asserted that the alleged conduct of Sgt. Livingston violated the Eighth Amendment prohibition on cruel and unusual punishment and the Fourteenth Amendment Due Process and Equal Protection Clauses. He requested damages and injunctive relief. The District Court dismissed Mr. Burton's complaint *sua sponte* for failure to state a claim for which relief may be granted. The Court stated that " '[m]ere threatening language and gestures of a custodial officer do not, even if true, amount to constitutional violations.' " *Burton v. Livingston,* No. PB–C–85–289, slip op. at 2 (E.D.Ark. July 19, 1985), *quoting Coyle v. Hughs,* 436 F.Supp. 591, 593 (W.D.Okla.1977). We reverse. On the facts alleged in Mr. Burton's complaint, he has stated a claim which is entitled to be heard.

As a general rule, the federal civil-rights remedies available to a person under 42 U.S.C. § 1983 are not so broad as those available under state law, common or statutory. While a plaintiff may seek redress and win damages under state law for any unwanted touching under the common law of battery, the federal remedies under § 1983 are directed against more egregious conduct. *Johnson v. Glick,* 481 F.2d 1028, 1033 (2d Cir.), *cert. denied,* 414 U.S. 1033, 94 S.Ct. 462, 38 L.Ed.2d 324 (1973). "Not

every push or shove, even if it may later seem unnecessary in the peace of a judge's chambers, violates a prisoner's constitutional rights." *Id.* Similarly, while the common law may provide a cause of action for assault when there is no contact at all, and even for some offensive words under the law of defamation, § 1983 does not duplicate the common law in these areas.

The District Court correctly stated the general proposition that in the usual case mere words, without more, do not invade a federally protected right. See *Coyle v. Hughs,* 436 F.Supp. 591, 593 (W.D.Okla. 1977). It is also true that in most instances of "simple assault," as the term is known to the common law, there is no federal action under § 1983, see *Bolden v. Mandel,* 385 F.Supp. 761, 764 (D.Md.1974), unless actual physical injury results from the assault and the defendant's conduct is especially blameworthy. But these propositions are true not because the Due Process Clause distinguishes hypertechnically between the various forms of common-law trespass, but rather because in most instances conduct which is called "defamation" or "simple assault" does not invade a federally protected right. The Due Process Clause was intended to secure the individual from the abuse of power by government officials. *Daniels v. Williams,* — U.S. —, 106 S.Ct. 662, 665, 88 L.Ed.2d 662 (1986). The threshold level at which an individual's due-process rights are violated is different from the threshold level at which he acquires a cause of action in tort. But the difference usually has nothing to do with the common-law label attached to the underlying conduct.

Due process of law has been said to encompass a "guarantee of respect for those personal immunities which are 'so rooted in the traditions and conscience of our people as to be ranked as fundamental,' " *Rochin v. California,* 342 U.S. 165, 169, 72 S.Ct. 205, 208, 96 L.Ed. 183 (1952) (Frankfurter, J., quoting Cardozo, J., in *Snyder v. Massachusetts,* 291 U.S. 97, 105, 54 S.Ct. 330, 332, 78 L.Ed. 674 (1934)). The guarantee of due process draws a line between the power of the government, on the one hand, and the security of the individual, on the other. This line is not a fixed one like a property boundary. Its location must be surveyed anew by the court in each case through an examination of the benchmarks disclosed by the circumstances surrounding the case. Among these landmarks are the nature of the individual right, the relationship between the individual and the government, and the justification offered by the government for its conduct. Thus, a lawfully incarcerated prisoner may be said to forfeit rights which would be taken for granted in free society, when that is necessary for the order and discipline of a penal environment. See *Price v. Johnston*, 334 U.S. 266, 285, 68 S.Ct. 1049, 1060, 92 L.Ed. 1356 (1948). However, a prisoner does not lose all of his civil rights. "[T]hose that are fundamental follow him, with appropriate limitations, through the prison gate, and the walls do not foreclose his access to the courts to protect those rights." *Courtney v. Bishop*, 409 F.2d 1185, 1187 (8th Cir.), *cert. denied*, 396 U.S. 915, 90 S.Ct. 235, 24 L.Ed.2d 192 (1969).

In determining whether the conduct of a prison guard has impermissibly infringed a protected right of the prisoner, we must consider (1) the need for the guard's action; (2) the relationship between that necessity and the amount of force actually used; (3) the degree of injury to the prisoner's retained rights; and (4) whether the conduct was a good-faith effort to maintain discipline or engaged in maliciously and sadistically for the sole purpose of causing harm. See *Johnson v. Glick*, 481 F.2d at 1033.

In applying these principles to the present case, Mr. Burton's allegations must be taken as true for the purpose of determining whether he stated a claim cognizable under § 1983. A *pro se* complaint must be liberally construed and can be dismissed only if it appears to a certainty that the complainant can prove no set of facts which would entitle him to relief. *Estelle*

v. Gamble, 429 U.S. 97, 106, 97 S.Ct. 285, 292, 50 L.Ed.2d 251 (1976).

The complaint states that Sgt. Livingston pointed a lethal weapon at the prisoner, cocked it, and threatened him with instant death. This incident occurred immediately after the prisoner had given testimony against another guard in a § 1983 action. The death threat was accompanied by racial epithets which strongly suggest that the prisoner would have been treated differently had he not been black. Apparently, another guard who was present took the threat seriously enough to step between the prisoner and Sgt. Livingston. In case the point had not been made, Sgt. Livingston repeated the performance moments later. According to the uncontroverted words of the complaint, there was no provocation for the guard's action other than the prisoner's attempting to exercise his due-process and First Amendment right of access to the federal courts. The complaint describes in plain words a wanton act of cruelty which, if it occurred, was brutal despite the fact that it resulted in no measurable physical injury to the prisoner. The day has passed when an inmate must show a court the scars of torture in order to make out a complaint under § 1983. We hold that a prisoner retains at least the right to be free from the terror of instant and unexpected death at the whim of his allegedly bigoted custodians.

So far as we can tell at this early stage of the case, the guard's conduct was not motivated by the necessity of correcting a rebellious inmate or by legitimate concerns for institutional security. See *Bolden v. Mandel*, 385 F.Supp. at 764. Neither is it an instance of rough language which resulted only in bruised feelings. See *Coyle v. Hughs*, 436 F.Supp. at 593. In such cases the actions of a guard might well be *de minimis* or in any event excusable by the realities of maintaining order amongst a large population of prisoners, who are, as we are aware, "not usually the most gentle or tractable of men and women ...", *Johnson v. Glick*, 481 F.2d at 1033. This is rather a complaint that a prison guard, without provocation, and for the apparent purpose of retaliating against the prisoner's exercise of his rights in petitioning a federal court for redress, terrorized him with threats of death. Under the circumstances of this incident, the guard's actions, if proved, were a violation of Mr. Burton's rights under the First Amendment and under the Due Process and Equal Protection[1] Clauses of the Fourteenth Amendment.[2]

Reversed and remanded.

VOLUME III

CHAPTER 8   RIGHTS TO AN EFFECTIVE ORDER, DISCHARGE

In Vol. II of this series, the limitations on conditions in prisons that may prove to be inhumane were discussed. Courts are more apt to make corrections in that area than in the areas of asserted rights examined in this volume. The case of *Tanner v. Hardy,* 764 F.2d 1024 (4th Cir. 1985), involved an inmate who was sent to an institution for evaluation. After he had completed the sentence, the question was raised as to whether the institution should have moved for a release. Certainly, prisoners have a right to be released after they have completed the time prescribed in their sentences; yet often in the name of medical treatment, prisoners are held beyond that time.

Introductions in previous volumes:

James Dale TANNER, #144047,
Appellant,

v.

J. Brown HARDY, Former Acting Di-
rector, Patuxent Institution; Arthur
Kandel, Associate Director, Patuxent
Institution; Forrest Calhoun, Jr., Asso-
ciate Director, Patuxent Institution,
Appellees.

No. 84–6192.

United States Court of Appeals,
Fourth Circuit.

Argued March 8, 1985.

Decided June 21, 1985.

Before RUSSELL, MURNAGHAN, and   ERVIN, Circuit Judges.

MURNAGHAN, Circuit Judge:

James Dale Tanner, the plaintiff, has reason to complain, but the central issue raised by his appeal from a grant of summary judgment to the defendants is whether those who have been selected as defendants can be held liable in damages.

Following arrest on June 16, 1968, Tanner was charged with rape and incarcerated pending trial. His trial before the Circuit Court for St. Mary's County, Maryland, resulted in a conviction for which he was sentenced to a prison term of eight years counting from June 16, 1968. The Circuit Court for St. Mary's County sent Tanner to the Patuxent Institution for Defective Delinquents at Jessup, Maryland for an evaluation as to whether he was a "defective delinquent."[1]

Patuxent was required by the Act to make an examination of one so referred, stating findings as to defective delinquency in a written report to the court which had sentenced him. Md.Ann.Code of 1957, Art. 31B § 7(a) (repealed 1977). Tanner, upon arrival at Patuxent and consistently thereafter, refused to be interviewed by the staff or to cooperate in any way with the evaluation process. Patuxent, consequently, did not send a psychiatric evaluation to the sentencing court, but continued to hold Tanner on the grounds that the requirement of a written report of findings as to defective delinquency was only directory. *State v. Musgrove*, 241 Md. 521, 217 A.2d 247 (1966).

Thereafter, on June 19, 1972, the Supreme Court of the United States held in *McNeil v. Director, Patuxent Institution*, 407 U.S. 245, 92 S.Ct. 2083, 32 L.Ed.2d 719

(1972) that it was a denial of due process to hold an individual at Patuxent beyond the expiration of the fixed criminal sentence where doing so was based only on the original *ex parte* order referring him to Patuxent for evaluation. Approximately two months thereafter, the Patuxent staff proceeded to evaluate Tanner solely on the basis of his file and without the benefit of the personal interview which Tanner refused to provide. The Maryland Court of Appeals, in *Director, Patuxent Institution v. Cash*, 269 Md. 331, 347, 305 A.2d 833, 842 (1973), validated the procedure adopted by Patuxent of diagnosing without the benefit of a personal interview when the unavailability of the person to be evaluated was directly attributable to the individual concerned.

A manifest purpose of such incomplete diagnoses was to deal sensibly in advance with the problem which otherwise would be sure to arise upon the running of the fixed sentence imposed. With no evaluation of any kind, a likely consequence would be invocation of a rule that someone in Tanner's position would have to be released, even though an unrehabilitated defective delinquent, since a diagnosis had not been made and, consequently, none had been reviewed by the Maryland court which had requested an evaluation.

On August 21, 1972 a diagnostic staff report on Tanner, which concluded that he was a defective delinquent, was sent to the Circuit Court for St. Mary's County with a copy to the State's Attorney for the county.[2]

Despite Patuxent's valiant effort to avoid a problem they had foreseen would arise at the conclusion of Tanner's fixed eight year sentence, the Circuit Court for St. Mary's County simply sat on the diagnostic staff

---

1. *See* Md.Ann.Code of 1957, Article 31B § 5 (repealed 1977) defining a defective delinquent as one who through persistent aggravated antisocial or criminal behavior has evidenced a propensity toward criminal activity and is also intellectually deficient or emotionally unbalanced, thereby clearly demonstrating an actual danger to society.

2. The report stated that Tanner's lengthy criminal record "indicates continuous violations of the law since 1958 and a progressive increase in the seriousness of these offenses." Tanner's behavior since arriving at Patuxent Institution was described as "very unstable and negativistic." The staff concluded that he "has presented persistent aggravated anti-social behavior and appears to represent a distinct danger to society."

report. No hearing on the defective delinquency recommendation ever took place and, indeed, Patuxent received no response from the Circuit Court for St. Mary's County.[3]

The statute requires that, in such circumstances, the court summon the individual "forthwith." Md.Ann.Code of 1957, Article 31B § 8(a) (repealed 1977). Nevertheless, only deafening silence emanated from the court. Tanner simply was not summoned to appear. From all that the record discloses, the letters of October 8, 1973 represented the only effort by the defendants, officials of Patuxent, to remedy a patent error in legal procedure which, through the court's failure to act, had come to their attention. Concededly the mistake was not, in the first instance, of their making, but, nevertheless, it was one of which their professional responsibilities necessarily made them fully aware.

Sympathy necessarily extends itself to the three defendants. They were faced with a perilous situation created not by them, but by the St. Mary's County Circuit Court.[4] The risk to the safety of society in the release of Tanner was by no means negligible. At the same time, however, the

factual surroundings of what amounted to a dilemma not just for the defendants but for the plaintiff as well have by no means been sufficiently explored to make summary judgment appropriate. We are of the opinion that the case should be remanded for further development through submission of opposing affidavits or otherwise.

Through such development, it will be possible to ascertain whether, indeed, the defendants did all that it was reasonable to expect they should do to insure that Tanner was not deprived of his rights. Unlike the situation here, the defendant sheriff in *Bryan v. Jones*, 530 F.2d 1210 (5th Cir. 1976), *cert. denied*, 429 U.S. 865, 97 S.Ct. 174, 50 L.Ed.2d 145 (1976) had been misled by a typographical error not his responsibility. Here, however, the defendants did not rely on any erroneous documents or instructions. They were fully aware of the Circuit Court's failure to do what the law unambiguously called on it to do. The law permitted no discretion on the part of a state court judge to do otherwise.

Even if the defendants did not have to take any action prior to June 16, 1976, the date of expiration of Tanner's sentence, it

---

3. On October 8, 1973, Patuxent again sent the diagnostic staff report to the presiding judge in St. Mary's County as well as to the State's Attorney and to the Commissioner of Correction. In those letters, Patuxent asserted that "[t]here is nothing to indicate that any change has occurred in this patient since the original evaluation."

4. A question which presents itself is whether the Maryland Circuit Court judge, in the first instance, had anything beyond a purely ministerial responsibility to summon Tanner to appear forthwith, once the diagnostic staff report, accompanied by a recommendation that he be found a defective delinquent, reached the court. If so, perhaps judicial immunity of an absolute kind did not apply. *See McCray v. State of Maryland*, 456 F.2d 1 (4th Cir.1972). In *McCray*, the court stated that absolute immunity is conferred upon judges in order to allow them to "*exercise discretion* vigorously and effectively" without the fear of being subjected to burdensome lawsuits. *Id.* at 3 (emphasis added). However, the court suggested that "[w]hen a judge acts in a non-judicial capacity [and merely performs a *mandatory* ministerial function such as scheduling a hearing] he *pro tanto* loses his

absolute immunity and is subject to liability as any other state official." *Id.* at 4 n. 7.

On that basis, maybe the Circuit Court judge, who may well have been more at fault than the three individual defendants, should have been sued. *Cf.* F.R.Civ.Proc. 19(b) ("If a person ... described [as an indispensable party] cannot be made a party, the court shall determine whether in equity and good conscience the action should proceed among the parties before it, or should be dismissed."). However, such a suit was not instituted by the plaintiff, nor have the defendants sought to bring him or his estate in as a third-party defendant. Judge Philip Dorsey is no longer living and, from all that the record discloses, limitations would already have set in were he or his estate or the beneficiaries thereof now to be sued. Md.Cts. & Jud. Proc.Code Ann. § 5-101 (1984); Md.Est. & Trusts Code Ann. § 8-103(a) (1974). *See also Burket v. Aldridge*, 241 Md. 423, 216 A.2d 910 (1966) (Whether suit is brought against a tortfeasor during his lifetime, or against his personal representative after his death, it must be filed both within three years from date of injury and within six months from the qualification of personal representative.)

becomes a tangled question of fact whether the defendants had any basis for continuing to confine Tanner at Patuxent until September 9, 1976, *i.e.*, for nearly three illegal months of unjustified imprisonment, when his sentence had expired on June 16, 1976. The defendants were aware of Tanner's June 16, 1976 petition for a writ of *habeas corpus*. They delayed replying until September 9, 1976, when they joined Tanner in his request for his release.

· It is a well established principle that qualified immunity, which is the most in the way of immunity to which the defendants are entitled, *see Procunier v. Navarette*, 434 U.S. 555, 561, 98 S.Ct. 855, 859, 55 L.Ed.2d 24 (1978) (State prison officials and officers were not entitled to absolute immunity in § 1983 action but were entitled to qualified immunity), is a matter on which the burden of proof is allocated to the defendants. *Harlow v. Fitzgerald*, 457 U.S. 800, 819, 102 S.Ct. 2727, 2738, 73 L.Ed.2d 396 (1982).

The defendants on remand may, indeed, bolster their contention that, faced with the terrible choices presented to them of a) keeping a man illegally imprisoned beyond the term of his sentence or b) releasing someone who, had the Circuit Court of St. Mary's County only acted as it properly should have done, might well have been determined to be a defective delinquent who should not be released from prison, they acted properly in relying on legal advice of the Maryland Attorney General's office. However, to insure an adequate factual basis for that good faith immunity defense there should be detailed information as to whether and when such advice was given and the degree of mature consideration accorded the matter by the Assistant Attorney General to whom the defendants turned and who gave the advice. After all, while the question was a tortured one, the answer seems relatively free from doubt, namely, that one's constitutional right to liberty could not be subverted in the manner here involved. *See McNeil v. Director, Patuxent Institution*, 407 U.S. at 250, 92 S.Ct. at 2087. *See also Martin*

v. Director, Patuxent Institution, 18 Md. App. 505, 512–14, 308 A.2d 212, 216–217, *cert. denied*, 269 Md. 762 (1973), *cert. denied*, 414 U.S. 1160, 94 S.Ct. 921, 39 L.Ed.2d 113 (1974) (With respect to the inmate's constitutional right to liberty, the issue of defective delinquency *may* be tried after the expiration of the sentence *provided* it is tried *within a reasonable time* after the Patuxent Institution made its findings on the inmate's condition). It may well be that the lawyer's advice, in the particular circumstances of the case, was an insufficient basis for insulating the defendants from liability. The receipt of advice from a lawyer is, after all, only one of a number of factors to be considered in determining whether a qualified immunity applies. *See McElveen v. County of Prince William*, 725 F.2d 954, 958 n. 5 (4th Cir.1984) ("Although consultation with an attorney is not proof of the [State's] good faith it is certainly *indicia* of good faith and therefore should be considered in evaluating the State's [qualified immunity] defense.") (emphasis in original) (citation omitted).

That does, of course, raise an additional question on which fleshing out of the facts on remand might prove helpful. Perhaps that Assistant Attorney General, if the statute of limitations has not expired, should be joined as a defendant.

In conclusion, the district court's award of summary judgment in favor of the defendants must be reversed and remanded in order to permit adequate exploration of the question of whether the defendants had a clear and unmistakable duty to release Tanner on June 16, 1976, or at least a duty to advocate Tanner's release without waiting approximately three months before doing so. We have, after all, charged prison officials with a duty to know and act in accordance with a Supreme Court decision rendered only twelve days before the date on which they performed in a manner contrary to the law so recently laid down. *See Arebaugh v. Dalton*, 730 F.2d 970, 972 (4th Cir.1984) (§ 1983 action remanded on qualified immunity issue in order to determine whether state officials had "good faith explanation" for failing to know or act upon relevant Supreme Court decision announced and published twelve days before alleged violation occurred.)

Following argument, it was brought to our attention that Arthur Kandel, one of the appellees, had died. The district court, upon remand, shall decide whether a substitution of parties is proper pursuant to F.R.Civ.P. 25(a)(1) (Substitution of Parties (a) Death).

REVERSED AND REMANDED.

VOLUME IV
SUPPLEMENT

PAROLE

VOLUME IV

CHAPTER 1   THE PLACE OF PAROLE IN THE PRISON SYSTEM

The parole system has come to play an important role in the scheme of prisons. Parole was a method of shortening the time in prison, and the idea behind it was to reward a prisoner who conducted himself in a constructive manner while in custody. It was thought that the parole system was reformatory and would help the inmate gain strength and resistance to temptation, bolster his self control, and readjust his attitude toward social controls and standards. *McCoy v. Harris,* 108 Utah 407, 160 P.2d 721 (1945). However, in practice, the parole system never obtained the desired end, and the system has increasingly come under attack. The parole system has been abolished in the federal system. Doubtless, it will be abolished in other systems as well.

No cases seemed to consider the general philosophy of the parole system and how it should function. Certainly, a prisoner who has behaved and obeyed the rules has come to expect to be given a parole when eligible. The parole system has also been used to relieve the overcrowding of many prisons.

Introductions in previous volumes:

IV: 1; VI: 505; VII: 475; VIII: 479

VOLUME IV

CHAPTER 2   THE LEGALITY OF PAROLE BOARDS AND THEIR ACTS

In this section, we seek to consider the functioning of parole boards and constitutional limitations on their functions. Since parole boards are established by statutes in different jurisdictions, their conduct is governed by those statutes. Certain constitutional principles, however, govern their proceedings, regardless of jurisdiction.

Lynch v. United States Parole Comm'n., 768 F.2d 491 (2d Cir. 1985), questioned whether the Parole Commission was bound to follow the recommendation of hearing examiners and whether a failure to disclose an inmate's presentence report to this counselor violated due process rights.

In *Fendler v. United States Parole Comm'n.,* 774 F.2d 975 (9th Cir. 1985), the inmate was entitled to a copy of his presentence report under the Freedom of Information Act. The case teaches the application of the Freedom of Information Act as it pertains to the Parole Commission.

In *Harper v. Jeffries,* 808 F.2d 281 (3d Cir. 1986), the court gave quasi-judicial immunity in a civil rights action to officials of the Parole Board. The case is not reproduced here.

Introductions in previous volumes:

IV: 29; VI: 517; VII: 477; VIII: 481

Vincent LYNCH, Petitioner-Appellee,

v.

**UNITED STATES PAROLE COMMIS-
SION and Michael Quinlan,
Warden, Respondents-Appellants.**

No. 960, Docket 84–2383.

United States Court of Appeals,
Second Circuit.

Argued March 11, 1985.

Decided July 22, 1985.

Before TIMBERS, CARDAMONE and PIERCE, Circuit Judges.

PIERCE, Circuit Judge:

On March 17, 1969, Vincent Lynch was convicted in the United States District Court for the Southern District of New York on one count of robbery and one count of conspiracy. On December 2, 1976, while on parole based on his 1969 conviction, he was convicted of further federal offenses and sentenced to prison. As discussed below, he eventually received a pa-role hearing before a panel of Hearing Examiners ("Examiners"), who recommended that his former parole be revoked and that he be continued to a presumptive parole date on November 9, 1986. The National Parole Commission ("Commission"), however, disagreed with the presumptive parole date recommended by the Examiners, and in a Notice of Action determined that Lynch was to be continued to a ten-year reconsideration hearing in September of 1991. Lynch objected to this extension of his time to be served, and after unsuccessfully pursuing his administrative remedies, sought the subject writ of habeas corpus pursuant to 28 U.S.C. § 2255 (1982).

After oral argument before Vincent L. Broderick, *Judge*, the petition was granted, subject to the grant of a new parole hearing. The district court found at least four distinct violations of Lynch's due process rights: (1) the Commission deviated from the recommendation of the Examiners, yet failed to state additional reasons beyond those considered by the Examiners; (2) the Commission failed to give adequate consideration to the parole status of Lynch's co-defendants; (3) the Commission delayed for almost eight months producing documents requested by Lynch under the Privacy Act and the Freedom of Information Act; and (4) although the Examiners had Lynch's pre-sentence report before them at the parole hearing, Lynch's counsel was denied access to the report. For the reasons set forth below, the judgment of the district court is affirmed in part and reversed in part.

BACKGROUND

In 1969, Lynch was sentenced to ten years imprisonment. On July 31, 1974, he was released on parole, and was to remain under parole supervision until September 4, 1978.

While on parole, Lynch committed a series of offenses involving the extortion of money from alleged narcotics dealers, which led in June 1976 to his indictment in the Southern District of Florida on charges of extortion and conspiracy. He failed to appear in that court and, pursuant to a bench warrant was arrested on November 16, 1976, by federal agents in Brooklyn, New York. He was returned to Florida and on December 2, 1976, he was convicted in the Southern District of Florida of conspiracy and racketeering charges, for which he was sentenced to twenty years imprisonment. He subsequently pleaded guilty to state charges in Florida related to the same acts for which he had received his federal sentence, and was sentenced to

three years to run concurrently with the sentences imposed on the federal convictions. He has completed serving his state sentence.

As a result of Lynch's parole violations, brought about by his Florida convictions, which occurred while he was serving his 1969 sentence, a parole violation warrant was lodged against him as a detainer while he was serving his Southern District of Florida prison sentence. Lynch was thereafter scheduled for a parole revocation hearing. This was to be combined with an initial parole hearing on his new sentence, and was originally set for November 1980. On October 16, 1980, however, Lynch was assaulted by other inmates at the Federal Correctional Institution—Lompoc, and sustained serious injuries, including the loss of an eye and permanent liver damage. On the advice of counsel, Lynch did not appear at the hearing. He was thereafter notified that his hearing would be held on the next docket after December 15, 1980, at the Springfield Medical Center for Federal Prisoners. On December 29, 1980, Lynch's parole representative, Benson Weintraub, made a request under the Freedom of Information Act ("FOIA") and the Privacy Act for all documents in Lynch's file. Weintraub also requested that the parole hearing be continued for 120 days, to allow for production and review of the documents. At that time, Lynch was scheduled for a hearing on the January 1981 docket at Springfield. Lynch's transfer to Otisville, N.Y., on January 8, 1981, however, resulted in rescheduling of the hearing to March 1981, apparently independently of Weintraub's request for a continuance, which was received by the Commission on January 15, 1981.

After its review of Weintraub's request for an adjournment, the Commission became aware that Weintraub was not an attorney.[1] Accordingly, its Regional Counsel, Henry Sadowski, notified Lynch on March 3, 1981, that Weintraub would not be permitted to make legal arguments on

---

1. Parole representatives are not required to be licensed attorneys. However, Mr. Weintraub was in the process of becoming a licensed attorney, receiving his license in the District of Columbia in August of 1981.

Lynch's behalf unless a supervisory attorney were present. The Commission produced for Lynch the information that was contained in his parole violation file. This file, however, did not include all the documents requested by Weintraub.

Lynch then retained an attorney, Lawrence M. Hermann, to represent him at the parole hearing, scheduled for March 25, 1981. On March 18, Hermann requested a delay of the hearing, partly because the requested documents had not yet been produced and partly because he had not had sufficient time to prepare for the hearing.

Hermann's request for a continuance was granted, and the parole hearing was rescheduled to May 29, 1981. On that date, Lynch requested another postponement, stating that he wished to retain a different attorney. In early July 1981, Thomas Sear, Lynch's present counsel, was appointed to represent Lynch. On July 14, Sear asked for a postponement on the ground that the documents requested had still not been produced, stating that he considered it "absolutely essential" that he have an opportunity to review the documents before the hearing.

Finally, on September 2, 1981, approximately eight months after Lynch made his FOIA and Privacy Act requests, copies of all disclosable documents, with the exception of the pre-sentence report, were sent to Sear. The Commission explained this delay by stating that it had received a large influx of similar requests, which were processed in order of their receipt. During the period of the delay, however, on August 31, 1981, new parole guidelines became effective, which had the effect of increasing the minimum recommended time to be served by an offender with Lynch's characteristics from 78 or more months to 100 or more months.

Lynch ultimately received a hearing before a panel of Hearing Examiners on September 22, 1981, which combined two procedures: a parole revocation hearing concerning the offenses committed while he was on parole from the Southern District of New York sentence imposed on the 1969

robbery and conspiracy convictions, and an initial parole hearing on his new, Southern District of Florida, federal sentence for racketeering and conspiracy. At this hearing, Lynch's counsel, Sear, requested disclosure of the Southern District of Florida pre-sentence report, which the Examiners had before them. The Examiners refused to disclose the report, stating that the pre-sentence report was a "court document" which they had no authority to release to him without the sentencing court's permission. The Examiners, however, offered to grant Lynch another continuance, so that his counsel might obtain court permission. Lynch chose not to request a continuance, his counsel noting the already-extensive delays in holding the hearing and stating that "we are anxious for you to review the substance of this case." At one point in the ensuing proceedings, the Examiners quoted to Lynch and his counsel a portion of the presentence report which contained a statement by a witness made at Lynch's trial, and which tended to support a finding that Lynch, in the course of his offenses committed while on parole, had beaten his victims. Lynch contested this charge, claiming that although he had been involved in a fight with the witness, it had nothing to do with the charges of which he was convicted. The Examiners apparently did not find Lynch's explanation credible, since they noted in their recommendation that Lynch had in fact beaten his victims.

After the hearing, the Examiners sent a recommendation in Lynch's case to the Commission. The Examiners reviewed the history of Lynch's criminal offenses, and his history of misconduct while in prison. The latter included five infractions, one of which related to Lynch's attempt to introduce marijuana into a federal penal institution by threatening to kill a prison staff member and his family. Lynch's salient factor score, a measure designed to predict as far as possible the likelihood of his committing another offense were he to be released on parole, was computed as 3. Commission regulations also provide for a rating of offense severity; these ratings are designed to group comparable offenses together in terms of their gravity. Lynch's offense severity rating was calculated as Greatest II—the most serious group of offenses.[2] The Examiners noted that Commission guidelines for Greatest II offenses provided no suggested maximum term of incarceration before release on parole, and that the guideline range for a Greatest II offense coupled with a salient factor score of 3 was 100 or more months in prison. If Lynch were required to serve out the remainder of his 1969 ten-year sentence on robbery and conspiracy in addition to the twenty-year sentence imposed for his offenses committed while on parole in full, he would have to serve 199 months beyond the time he already served.

Nevertheless, the Examiners recommended that Lynch be paroled after serving ten years (120 months) on all the federal offenses. Accordingly, the panel recommended that parole on the 1969 convictions be revoked and that Lynch be continued to a presumptive parole on November 9, 1986, after serving 120 months.

The recommendation of the Examiners was reviewed by the Commission's Regional Office. The Regional Commissioner disagreed with the Examiners' recommendation that Lynch be continued to a presumptive parole date after serving 120 months and, pursuant to 28 C.F.R. § 2.24(a), referred the case to the National Commissioners for additional votes. The Commissioners reviewed the case, and issued a Notice of Action dated November 10, 1981, in which it was determined that Lynch was to be continued to a ten-year reconsideration hearing in September, 1991. This decision was based in part upon a comparison of the relative severity of Lynch's offenses with those specified in the next-lowest category, Greatest I, and upon his history of misconduct while in prison.

Pursuant to 28 C.F.R. § 2.25, Lynch appealed the decision of the National Commissioners to the Regional Commissioner, who

denied the appeal. Lynch then appealed, pursuant to *id.* § 2.26, to the National Appeals Board, which affirmed the decision of the Commissioners in a Notice of Action on Appeal dated July 8, 1982. The Notice of Action noted that there was no recommended maximum time to be served before parole in a Greatest II offense case, that Lynch had a record of poor institutional adjustment, and that he had failed to report for arrest in the Southern District of Florida. The only mitigating factor, the Board found, was the injury sustained by Lynch as a result of his being attacked while in prison, and this did not suffice to reduce the recommended time to be served prior to parole.

Lynch thereafter requested a reconsideration before the Regional Commissioner, alleging that Lynch had new information regarding the parole treatment of his co-defendants. The request for reconsideration was denied on November 19, 1982. The reasons for denial were stated in a letter to Lynch's counsel, to wit, that Lynch had the lowest salient factor score of any of the racketeering co-defendants; that he was the only co-defendant who was on federal parole at the time the offenses were committed; and that he had made a "very poor institutional adjustment and received numerous misconduct reports." Joint Appendix at 290.

Having thus exhausted his administrative remedies, Lynch filed the instant petition for a writ of habeas corpus in the Southern District of New York. Judge Broderick granted the writ subject to an order that the Commission conduct a new parole hearing in Lynch's case, directing specifically that the Commission apply the parole guidelines that were in effect prior to September, 1981, and that the Commission render a decision no more severe than that recommended by the Examiners unless additional factors not considered by the Examiners were stated.

---

2. The offense severity ratings now in effect use a terminology different from those under which Lynch's case was evaluated; the intent of the

rating d̲e̲v̲i̲c̲e, however, remains the same. *See* 28 C.F.R. § 2.20 (1984).

The Commission filed a timely notice of appeal, and argues that its original determination, continuing Lynch to a reconsideration hearing in 1991, should be reinstated. According to the Commission, it adequately considered the status of Lynch's co-defendants; did not deprive Lynch of due process by relying upon, yet failing to disclose to counsel Lynch's pre-sentence report; did not deprive Lynch of due process by delaying his parole hearing; and with or without new or additional evidence was not required to abide by the recommendation of the Examiners. In response, Lynch challenges each of these arguments and additionally claims that because a new hearing has been held, in compliance with the district court's order, this appeal is now moot. We turn now to these contentions.

DISCUSSION

We reject Lynch's claim that this appeal is moot. The Commission diligently, but unsuccessfully, applied for stays pending appeal both in the district court and in this Court. The applications failing, it held the hearing ordered by the district court, but on the present appeal asserts that its original determination of Lynch's case was proper in all respects, and that the district court erred in requiring a new hearing to be held. The Commission also challenges the terms under which the hearing was to be held, namely, that the parole guidelines in effect before September 1981 were to be applied, and that reasons not already considered by the Examiners must be proffered to support any deviation from the original recommendation of the Examiners. In the event the Commission is successful on this appeal, it asserts that it will reinstate the original determination of Lynch's case continuing him to a reconsideration hearing in 1991. Accordingly, we conclude that the issues in this case remain "live," see Murphy v. Hunt, 455 U.S. 478, 481, 102 S.Ct. 1181, 1183, 71 L.Ed.2d 353 (1982) (per curiam). Although Lynch has had a new hearing pursuant to the district court's order, on appeal the Commission continues to assert the validity of its original determination and seeks to reinstate it. The parties

clearly have a "legally cognizable interest in the outcome," id. We conclude that the appeal is not moot. United States v. Ferri, 686 F.2d 147, 157 n. 14 (3d Cir.1982), cert. denied, 459 U.S. 1211, 103 S.Ct. 1205, 75 L.Ed.2d 446 (1983); see Allen v. Hadden, 738 F.2d 1102, 1106–07 (10th Cir.1984).

Turning, then, to the merits, we consider first the Commission's argument that it was not required to adopt the recommendation of the Examiners and in any event stated sufficient reasons for not doing so. We agree.

It is the Commission, and not the Examiners, which is vested with the responsibility to make the parole decision. The hearing examiners are merely empowered to make recommendations to the Commission. 18 U.S.C. § 4203(c)(2) (1982); 28 C.F.R. § 2.23, 2.24 (1984). The Commission in its Notice of Action stated that Lynch was to be continued to another hearing in 1991 because his earlier release "would depreciate the seriousness of [his] offense," and would not adequately account for his history of misconduct while incarcerated. This determination by the Commissioners may be disturbed only upon a showing of abuse of discretion, or arbitrary and capricious action. Iuteri v. Nardoza, 732 F.2d 32, 37 (2d Cir.1984); Lieberman v. Gunnell, 726 F.2d 75, 77 (2d Cir.1984); Bialkin v. Baer, 719 F.2d 590, 593 (2d Cir.1983). This is not a case in which the Commission determined to continue a prisoner for a period beyond the maximum recommended by the guidelines; in such cases, it has been held that the Commission may not confine a prisoner beyond the applicable guideline range based upon the severity of the offense, because that factor was used to select the guideline range in the first place. See Alessi v. Quinlan, 711 F.2d 497, 500 (2d Cir.1983) (citing cases). Rather, an offense of Greatest II severity involves no maximum recommended time to be served prior to parole. The Commissioners' decision therefore did not exceed the guidelines. Although the Commission is required to state "with particularity" its reasons for denying parole, 18 U.S.C. § 4206(b) (1982), when the determination does not exceed a maximum term set forth in the guidelines, it is a sufficient statement of reasons to deny parole for the Commission to note the severity of a prisoner's offense and his poor institutional record. *Reynolds v. McCall*, 701 F.2d 810, 814 (9th Cir.1983); *Shahid v. Crawford*, 599 F.2d 666, 671–72 (5th Cir.1979); *Garcia v. United States Board of Parole*, 557 F.2d 100, 105 (7th Cir.1977); *see* 18 U.S.C. § 4206(a)(1) (1982).

Lynch quotes from the Commission's Procedures Manual the proposition that a Notice of Action modifying the recommendation of a panel of examiners "should reflect ... a brief statement of the reasons for the change." This language, however, does not require the Commission to set forth *detailed* reasons for declining to follow the recommendation of the Examiners. The reasons given by the Commission for making its determination were sufficient. *Reynolds v. McCall*, 701 F.2d at 814; *Shahid v. Crawford*, 599 F.2d at 671–72; *Garcia v. Board of Parole*, 557 F.2d at 105. Moreover, it is clear that the internal procedures manual of an executive agency does not create due process rights in the public. *E.g., Schweiker v. Hansen*, 450 U.S. 785, 789, 101 S.Ct. 1468, 1471, 67 L.Ed.2d 685 (1981) (Social Security Administration claims manual is for internal use; it has no legal force and does not bind the Administration); *Morton v. Ruiz*, 415 U.S. 199, 233–35, 94 S.Ct. 1055, 1073–1074, 39 L.Ed.2d 270 (1974) (Bureau of Indian Affairs manual is for internal use only); *United States v. New York Telephone Co.*, 644 F.2d 953, 959 n. 10 (2d Cir.1981) (Internal Revenue Service manual does not have the effect of law); *United States v. Fifty-Three Eclectus Parrots*, 685 F.2d 1131, 1136 (9th Cir.1982) (Customs Service manual is an internal agency guide, not intended for use of general public). In our view, the same principles apply to prisoners and the parole commission manual. For these reasons, we conclude that the Commission was not bound to follow the recommendation of the Examiners, and was not re-

quired to set forth factors not considered by the Examiners in deviating from their recommendation.

Next, we address the Commission's argument that it was not bound to consider the parole status of Lynch's co-defendants, and that in any event it did so. The district court held that due process required the Commission to consider the parole status of Lynch's co-defendants at the time of his initial parole determination, and that no subsequent consideration could remedy the failure to do so. We disagree. Nothing in the Commission's regulations mandates that such information be considered. The district court referred to the Commission's Procedures Manual, which provides that information regarding the parole status of co-defendants "will be obtained where possible." This language does not require that such information be considered, rather, it merely recommends that such information be considered "where possible." Moreover, as discussed above, the Procedures Manual simply does not create due process rights in inmates.

Lynch relies upon *Melvin v. Petrovsky*, 720 F.2d 9 (8th Cir.1983), for the proposition that consideration of the parole status of co-defendants is mandatory. In *Petrovsky*, however, a co-defendant was for no apparent reason given an offense severity rating different from that given the petitioning defendant, and the Commission had at no time taken this into account. Here, by contrast, the Commission did consider the parole status of Lynch's co-defendants, albeit not until Lynch requested reconsideration of his parole determination. The Commission's reasons for denying reconsideration on this basis were: (1) Lynch had the lowest salient factor score of any of his racketeering co-defendants; (2) Lynch was the only defendant on federal parole at the time the offenses were committed; and (3) Lynch had made a poor institutional adjustment and had received numerous misconduct reports. Unlike *Petrovsky*, then, Lynch did receive consideration of the parole treatment of his co-defendants; that it took place after the initial hearing before the Examiners did not, under *Petrovsky*, violate Lynch's due process rights. Finally, we disagree with *Petrovsky* to the extent that it suggests that the Commission's Procedures Manual *requires* consideration of the parole status of co-defendants. The Manual merely states that such information will be obtained and considered "where possible." Given that the Manual does not create due process rights in inmates, and that its own language does not mandate consideration of co-defendants' parole treatment, we hold that on the facts of this case, Lynch's due process rights clearly were not violated.

We turn next to the adequacy of the consideration given Lynch's injuries sustained while in prison, as a mitigating factor to be applied in fixing a parole date. The Commission has not raised this as an issue on appeal, apparently construing the district court's decision as rejecting Lynch's argument that this factor was inadequately considered. Lynch, on the other hand, claims that the Commission's failure to address his physical disabilities "constituted a basis for the [district c]ourt's granting the petition." Whatever the correct interpretation of the district court's decision on this point, the Commission expressly does not challenge that part of the district court's order requiring it to "address all relevant circumstances, including Mr. Lynch's physical condition." Reply Brief for Respondents-Appellants at 6 & n. *. In view of our ultimate disposition of this case, we will not address this question further, but note only that 18 U.S.C. § 4207(5) (1982) requires the Commission to "consider . . . reports of physical . . . examination[s] of the offender."

We turn to the Commission's argument that its use of Lynch's pre-sentence report without disclosing it to his counsel was proper and did not violate his due process rights. There exists, in this connection, an issue with respect to whether Lynch himself had access to the report; the district court declined to make a finding of fact on this question. Whether or not

Lynch had such access, however, we hold that the district court correctly ruled that the failure to disclose the report to Lynch's counsel violated Lynch's due process rights.

The Commission argues that it was sufficient that at Lynch's initial hearing, the Examiners read aloud an excerpt from the report that related to Lynch's beating his victims. This is claimed to satisfy due process because, according to the Commission, "[i]t is clear that the Commission relied upon only [this] small excerpt." Brief for Respondents-Appellants at 39 n. *. We do not, however, view it as being "clear" that this was the only significant information in the report. The report contained numerous other allegations as to Lynch's past behavior, any or all of which might have formed part of the reason for the Commission's decision to continue Lynch to another hearing in 1991. The failure to disclose the complete report is not now mitigated by self-serving declarations that only the portion read aloud was actually considered.

The cases relied upon by the Commission, *Nunez-Guardado v. Hadden*, 722 F.2d 618 (10th Cir.1983), and *Bowles v. Tennant*, 613 F.2d 776 (9th Cir.1980), provide it little support. *Nunez-Guardado* involved effective disclosure of all material information contained in the pre-sentence report, without disclosure of the actual document. *Bowles* did not involve a pre-sentence report at all. We take no position on the correctness of *Nunez-Guardado* or *Bowles*, and, in any event, we do not consider the disclosure herein of two sentences, read aloud to the inmate's counsel at the hearing, to constitute a sufficient disclosure under those decisions.

Section 4208(b) of title 18, U.S.Code, provides that a prisoner must be given "reasonable access" to all documents used by the Commission in making its determination. While the section is silent as to the right of the prisoner's counsel to see the report, in our view "reasonable access," at a minimum, requires that the prisoner be afforded the opportunity to review the report with his counsel.[2] This interpretation is buttressed by the text of Fed.R.Crim.P. 32(c)(3), which, although it does not speak to the question of access to the report after sentencing, does deal with access of defendant's counsel to the report. As it stood in 1981, at the time of Lynch's parole hearing, the Rule provided that the report was disclosable to the defendant *or* his counsel. The Commission reads this to mean that once disclosure has been made to either defendant or counsel, the Rule is complied with and no further disclosure may properly be made. The better interpretation of the language as it read in 1981, it seems to us, is that disclosure to one does not bar disclosure to the other. The Rule contains no prohibition of disclosure to counsel merely because disclosure was made to defendant. *See United States v. Charmer Industries*, 711 F.2d 1164, 1167 (2d Cir.1983) (court considers questions as to "whether and under what circumstances a presentence report ... may be disclosed to persons other than the defendant, his attorney, or the prosecuting attorney"). Finally, we note that Rule 32(c)(3) was amended in 1983 to permit disclosure to defendant *and* his attorney. This amendment, however, contemplated no change in prior practice except in the situation where disclosure was made *only* to counsel, and not to the defendant. The amendment was designed to require counsel to review the report with the defendant, because "much of the content of the presentence report will ordinarily be outside the knowledge of counsel." Fed.R.Crim.P. 32(c)(3)(A), (B), (C) Advisory Committee Note to 1983 Amendment.

The foregoing confirms our conclusion that "reasonable access" to the report, in light of the standards for disclosure contained in Rule 32(c)(3), requires that access

be afforded to both defendant *and* his counsel. The "or" contained in the pre-1983 version of the Rule is better read as an inclusive word, rather than an exclusive one. It would be irrational to hold that "reasonable access" has been afforded to the report where defendant is permitted to see it, but counsel, who represents defendant and must make decisions that will later bind defendant, has no such right. Consequently, we reject the Commission's strained interpretation of the disclosure requirement.

The Commission argues that Lynch's counsel waived his right to object to the Commission's failure to disclose the report to him, by not requesting the continuance offered by the Examiners to seek court permission to view the document. We do not agree. As discussed above, there was no valid justification for refusing to disclose the report; there likewise was no justification for imposing further delays upon Lynch with respect to the parole hearing to which he was entitled. Although Lynch's counsel did not protest the non-disclosure in subsequent proceedings before the Commission, we do not believe he thereby waived Lynch's due process right to disclosure to counsel. The Commission cites no authority that would require such a result, and we are aware of none. Whether any subsequent objection to the Commission would have been availing is doubtful, in view of the Commission's adamant position herein that disclosure of the report to Lynch was sufficient and that no further disclosure was required or proper. We therefore hold that, under these circumstances, counsel did not waive his client's rights. We consider it necessary, however, to caution that in the future, given our clear holding herein that counsel may obtain disclosure of defendant's pre-

---

2. The exceptions to this rule are codified in 18 U.S.C. § 4208(c), and provide that if reasonable access to the report would seriously disrupt the prisoner's institutional program; reveal confidential sources of information; or result in harm to any person, then the agency having

custody of the material must summarize "the basic contents of the material withheld" and "furnish such summary to the inmate," a phrase we construe to have the same meaning as to provide "reasonable access" to the summary.

sentence report in connection with parole proceedings (subject to the limits set forth in 18 U.S.C. § 4208(c) (1982)), failure to timely raise this issue before the Commission may lead to a finding that the right to object to non-disclosure has been waived.

Next, we address the Commission's contention that the delay in holding Lynch's hearing did not violate his due process rights because Lynch himself was responsible for the delay, and because the delay did not prejudice Lynch. While some of the delay was caused by Lynch, the Commission must also share in the responsibility, and it is apparent that, as the district court found, several factors caused the delay in Lynch's hearing, including his transfer, his change in representatives, and the Commission's delay in producing the requested documents. Nevertheless, it appears that if the Commission had not delayed the production of the requested documents, the hearing would have been held no later than July 1981.

Commission regulations require that documents requested by the prisoner under the Privacy Act (and under the FOIA, which are treated as Privacy Act requests) be produced within forty working days of receipt of the request. 28 C.F.R. § 2.56 (1984). Lynch's request was received by the Commission on January 15, 1981, yet the documents were not produced until September 2 of that year. Clearly, the Commission failed to comply with its own regulations. It seeks to excuse this failure, first, by pointing to a "large influx of similar requests," and second, by citing cases which hold that the FOIA was not intended as a discovery device in pending or prospective proceedings. We do not find these justifications persuasive.

That the Commission received many requests for information does not justify its failure to adhere to its regulations, and certainly does not justify such an extensive delay, of approximately eight months, in producing documents which the agency's regulations require must be produced within forty working days. The Commission's reliance on cases interpreting the breadth of individual rights under FOIA is misplaced; the Commission itself has conceded that Lynch's request was not made solely under FOIA, but also under the Privacy Act. Brief for Respondents-Appellants at 4. We therefore reject the Commission's argument that Lynch's counsel improperly delayed the parole hearing for two additional months by "misusing the Freedom of Information Act." The delay occasioned by the failure to produce the documents was attributable in substantial part to the Commission, due to its failure to timely produce the requested documents and to comply with its own regulations.

Finally, the Commission argues that Lynch was not prejudiced by the delay in the hearings. We disagree. The Commission concedes that had the hearing been held before September 1981, the guidelines applicable to Lynch would have provided for a recommended incarceration of 78 or more months before parole. At the time the hearing was held, the guidelines had recently been changed to provide for a recommended incarceration of 100 or more months. This change is apparently attributable to an adverse lowering of Lynch's salient factor score from 4 to 3 under the new guidelines, and the increased minimum recommended term of incarceration sufficiently demonstrates prejudice to Lynch resulting from the delay in the hearing.

The Commission correctly points out that neither the pre- nor post-September 1981 guidelines applicable to this case provide a *maximum* recommended term of incarceration, and that deviation from the guidelines may be justified where, as in Lynch's case, the prisoner has a poor institutional record. This, however, overlooks the fact that the Commission in this case *did* п fact rely on the guidelines, noting that in Lynch's case they provided a recommended *minimum* term of 100 or more months incarceration. We need not spec-

ulate as to the possible result had the recommended minimum term been only 78 or
more months. Because the application of
the new guidelines was the direct result of
the Commission's failure to follow its regulations and timely disclose the documents
requested by Lynch, we hold that the district judge ruled correctly in requiring the
Commission to hold a new hearing and to
apply the pre-September 1981 guidelines to
Lynch. However, consistent with the earlier discussed analysis, a Commission decision which imposed a greater term of incarceration than that originally recommended
by the Hearing Examiners, but which is
within the applicable guideline range, need
not advert to factors beyond those considered by the Examiners.

CONCLUSION

For the foregoing reasons, the judgment
of the district court which granted the writ
of habeas corpus and ordered a new parole
hearing is affirmed insofar as it was based
upon the Commission's delay in disclosing
requested documents and the refusal of the
Examiners to disclose Lynch's pre-sentence
report. Accordingly, the Commission's redetermination of Lynch's case, in compliance with the district court's order, is to
remain in effect. The judgment is reversed
to the extent that it was based upon the
Commission's alleged failure to consider
the parole status of Lynch's co-defendants,
and the Commission's deviation from the
Examiners' recommendation.

Affirmed in part; reversed in part.

Robert H. FENDLER,
Plaintiff-Appellant,

v.

UNITED STATES PAROLE
COMMISSION, et al.,
Defendants-Appellees.

Nos. 84–2239, 84–2497.

United States Court of Appeals,
Ninth Circuit.

Submitted Aug. 23, 1985.*

Decided Oct. 22, 1985.

---

* The panel unanimously finds this case suitable for decision without oral argument. Fed.R. App.P. 34(a); Ninth Circuit Rule 3(f).

On Appeal From the United States District Court for the Northern District of California.

Before SNEED and BEEZER, Circuit Judges, and TAKASUGI,** District Judge.

BEEZER, Circuit Judge:

Robert H. Fendler brought this action against the United States Parole Commission and the nine individual members of the Commission. Under a variety of legal theories, Fendler sought to obtain various documents from the Commission and to correct alleged inaccuracies in the Commission's files. The district court rejected Fendler's claims. We affirm in part and reverse in part.

I

Background

Robert Fendler is presently serving a ten-year prison term that was imposed following his convictions on charges of mail fraud, transportation of stolen goods, and racketeering. Fendler's convictions arose out of his activities relating to two financial institutions in Arizona. Litigation regarding Fendler's activities has come before us on two previous occasions. *Fendler v. Goldsmith*, 728 F.2d 1181 (9th Cir.1983) (petition for a writ of habeas corpus following state court convictions); *Davis v. Fendler*, 650 F.2d 1154 (9th Cir.1981) (appeal from default judgment in favor of investors). Fendler is now seeking parole. The Commission set a presumptive parole date for July 26, 1986. Fendler claims that the Commission's decision was influenced by false information in the Commission's files.

Initially, Fendler sought a copy of his presentence report under the Freedom of Information Act. Although the report was prepared for use in the district court that sentenced Fendler, the Commission's files contained a copy. On September 23, 1983, the district court ruled in favor of Fendler and ordered the Commission to deliver a copy of the report to Fendler. After reconsideration, the district court modified that order on November 10, 1983. Under the modified order, Fendler could review the report, but could not retain a copy. The district court stated that this modification was based on a review of "the Local Criminal Rules of Court for the Central District of California, the venue where plaintiff was sentenced." On January 30, 1984, the district court authorized Fendler to take verbatim notes from the report. Concluding that Fendler had obtained all the relief to which he was entitled, the district court granted summary judgment for the Commission on July 6, 1984.

In a separate action, Fendler sought to correct the allegedly inaccurate information in his file under nine different theories. The district court dismissed eight of Fendler's claims on September 18, 1984, and granted summary judgment for the Commission on the ninth on October 24, 1984. Fendler appeals from the dismissal of seven of the nine claims.

II

The Presentence Report

Under the Freedom of Information Act, federal agencies are required to make their records available on request. 5 U.S.C. § 552(a)(3). In *Berry v. Department of Justice*, 733 F.2d 1343, 1346–54 (9th Cir.1984), we held that presentence reports are "agency records" when they are in the possession of government agencies. Accordingly, the district court correctly concluded that the presentence report was subject to FOIA.

** The Honorable Robert M. Takasugi, District Judge, United States District Court for the Central District of California, sitting by designation.

The district court concluded, however, that Fendler was entitled only to view the report and to take verbatim notes. Fendler argues that he is entitled to a copy. We agree. As we observed in *Berry*, "FOIA speaks in terms of disclosure and nondisclosure. It does not recognize degrees of disclosure, such as permitting viewing, but not copying, of documents." 733 F.2d at 1355 n. 19. The district court based its ruling on a local rule that limits a criminal defendant's right to a copy of the presentence report. A similar limitation is contained in Fed.R.Crim.P. 32(c)(3)(E). Those rules are irrelevant in a FOIA action. As we noted in *Berry*, "the Federal Rules of Criminal Procedure speak to the courts, [while] FOIA speaks to the agencies. Rule 21 limits disclosure by the Courts; FOIA may require disclosure by the agencies." 733 F.2d at 1355 n. 19 (citations omitted).

The Commission argues, however, that FOIA exemption (3) bars disclosure of the presentence report. 5 U.S.C. § 552(b)(3). In *Berry*, we recognized that exemption (3) applied to presentence reports. 733 F.2d at 1354 & n. 17. The district court did not make express findings regarding exemption (3). We remand for consideration of the Commission's arguments regarding exemption (3) in light of our decision in *Berry*.

The Commission also argues that we should remand to allow consideration of FOIA exemption (5), 5 U.S.C. § 552(b)(5). We disagree. The Commission did not raise exemption (5) before the district court. As a general rule, the government may not raise new FOIA exemptions on appeal. *See Ryan v. Department of Justice*, 617 F.2d 781, 792 (D.C.Cir.1980). The decision to allow the consideration of new FOIA exemptions on remand is discretionary. *See Schanen ex rel. Tillet v. United States Department of Justice*, 762 F.2d 805, 807–08 (9th Cir.1985); *Carson v. United States Department of Justice*, 631 F.2d 1008, 1015 n. 29 (D.C.Cir.1980). The District of Columbia Circuit offered the following analysis:

From a practical standpoint, there are at least three situations in which an agency might be led to invoke an exemption on appeal for the first time. First, an agency might invoke an exemption for the first time on appeal in order to gain a tactical advantage over the requestor. Clearly, it is not consistent with the broad remedial purpose of the FOIA to permit such agency maneuvering. Second, an agency might be forced to invoke an exemption for the first time on appeal because of a substantial change in the factual context of the case or because of an interim development in applicable legal doctrine. Third, the agency might have an "afterthought" following district court proceedings. Normally, if an agency gives thorough and proper consideration to the disclosability of documents when it should, that is, when it receives the request in the first instance, then it should be able to cite all possibly relevant exemptions well before the appellate stage. However, we recognize that there could be circumstances where, through pure mistake, the Government attorneys had not invoked the correct exemption in the district court. If the value of the material which otherwise would be subject to disclosure were obviously high, *e.g.*, confidential information compromising the nation's foreign relations or national security, and it appeared highly likely was intended to be protected by one of the nine enumerated exemptions, then under 28 U.S.C. § 2016, the appellate court would have discretion to "remand the cause and ... require such further proceedings to be had as may be just under the circumstances." Such discretion might likewise be exercised in the second example above-cited.

Jordan v. United States Department of Justice, 591 F.2d 753, 780 (D.C.Cir.1978) (en banc). The present case presents the third situation described in *Jordan*. Under the facts of this case, we conclude that it would be inappropriate to allow the Commission to raise exemption (5) on remand.

The Commission argues, however, that we should follow the Fifth Circuit's decision in *Cotner v. United States Parole Commission*, 747 F.2d 1016 (5th Cir.1984).

In *Cotner*, the Fifth Circuit allowed the Commission to raise additional FOIA exemptions on remand in light of the Solicitor General's decision to abandon the government's position that presentence reports are exempt from FOIA as "court records." *Id.* at 1018–19. *But see Crooker v. United States Parole Commission*, 760 F.2d 1, 2 (1st Cir.1985). *Cotner* is distinguishable from the present case because the district court in *Cotner* had held that FOIA did not apply to presentence reports. Under those circumstances, the Commission had no reason to raise the exemptions and the plaintiff was not significantly prejudiced by the delay in raising the exemptions. *See Berry*, 733 F.2d at 1352 n. 13; *Carson*, 631 F.2d at 1015 n. 29. In the present case, on the other hand, the Commission lost before the district court. In addition to the "court records" argument, the Commission raised exemption (3) and several other defenses. Under these circumstances, we can see no justification for the Commission's failure to raise exemption (5). Accordingly, we decline to allow the Commission to raise that exemption on remand.

III

Correction of Inaccuracies

A. *The Privacy Act*

Under the Privacy Act, an individual may "request amendment of an agency record pertaining to him." 5 U.S.C. § 552a(d)(2). If the agency refuses to amend the record, the individual may bring a civil action against the agency. *Id.* § 552a(g)(1). The Privacy Act exempts "reports identifiable to an individual compiled at any stage of the process of enforcement of the criminal laws from arrest or indictment through release from supervision." *Id.* § 552a(j)(2)(C). The Commission has promulgated rules implementing that exemption. 28 C.F.R. § 16.85(b)(3), (9) (1984). Accordingly, the district court properly dismissed Fendler's Privacy Act claims.

B. *Expungement*

Fendler also seeks to have the allegedly false statements in the Commission's file expunged. Federal courts have the equitable power "to order the expungement of Government records where *necessary* to vindicate rights secured by the Constitution or by statute." *Chastain v. Kelley*, 510 F.2d 1232, 1235 (D.C.Cir.1975) (emphasis added); *see Reuber v. United States*, 750 F.2d 1039, 1068 (D.C.Cir.1984) (Bork, J., concurring) ("The district court must ... find that there is a real and immediate threat of irreparable harm before it can allow expungement...."). In this case, expungement is not necessary to vindicate Fendler's rights. Initially, it is apparent that Fendler can challenge the allegedly inaccurate statements through Commission procedures. *See United States v. Stevenson*, 573 F.2d 1105, 1108 (9th Cir.1978) (refusing to expunge portions of a presentence report because the defendant would have an opportunity to challenge those portions in his parole proceeding). In addition, Fendler can challenge the parole determination by petitioning for a writ of habeas corpus. Accordingly, Fendler is not entitled to expungement.

C. *Equitable Relief*

Fendler also seeks to enjoin the Commission from considering the allegedly false statements in his file. In essence, Fendler is attempting to shorten the duration of his confinement by preventing consideration of those statements. As a result, Fendler's exclusive remedy is a petition for a writ of habeas corpus. *See Preiser v. Rodriguez*, 411 U.S. 475, 488–90, 93 S.Ct. 1827, 1835–36, 36 L.Ed.2d 439 (1973); *Tedder v. United States Board of Parole*, 527 F.2d 593, 594 n. 1 (9th Cir. 1975). Because Fendler failed to exhaust his administrative remedies before bringing the present action, the district court properly dismissed this claim. *See Ruviwat v. Smith*, 701 F.2d 844, 845 (9th Cir.1983).

IV

Bivens *Claims*

Fendler claims that the individual Commission members violated his constitutional rights by withholding various documents from him. *See Bivens v. Six Un-*

known Named Agents of Federal Bureau of Narcotics, 403 U.S. 388, 91 S.Ct. 1999, 29 L.Ed.2d 619 (1971). We have held, however, that parole board members are entitled to absolute quasijudicial immunity from suit for actions taken when processing parole applications. *See Anderson v. Boyd*, 714 F.2d 906, 908–09 (9th Cir.1983) (suit under section 1983). But even if we concluded that the individual Commission members are not entitled to absolute immunity, it is apparent that the members are entitled to qualified immunity because Fendler has not alleged a violation of a clearly established constitutional right. *See Mitchell v. Forsyth*, ⸺ U.S. ⸺, 105 S.Ct. 2806, 2817–20, 86 L.Ed.2d 411 (1985); *Davis v. Scherer*, ⸺ U.S. ⸺, 104 S.Ct. 3012, 3018–19, 82 L.Ed.2d 139 (1984). Accordingly, the district court properly dismissed Fendler's *Bivens* claims.

V

Conclusion

In No. 84–2239, we reverse the district court's order denying Fendler a copy of his presentence report and remand for further proceedings in accordance with this opinion. In No. 84–2497, we affirm the dismissal of Fendler's claim.

AFFIRMED IN PART, REVERSED IN PART, AND REMANDED.

VOLUME IV

CHAPTER 3   PAROLE GRANTING

With considerable interest in his parole hearing, an inmate understandably would be greatly disappointed should parole be denied. It is not surprising, then, to find challenges to the reasons given by parole commissions for denial of parole. In *Huggins v. Isenbarger,* 798 F.2d 203 (7th Cir. 1986), the inmate challenged the denial of parole because of the "seriousness of offense" reason given by the board in a civil rights action. The court stated that release on parole is neither the liberty nor the property of an individual for the purposes of due process. However, the board must act responsibly and follow statutory guidelines in parole matters. The case is set out here.

Introductions in previous volumes:

IV: 61; VI: 521; VII: 483; VIII: 491

Robert T. HUGGINS,
Plaintiff-Appellant,

v.

John ISENBARGER, Chairman,
Indiana Parole Board,
Defendant-Appellee.

No. 85–3036.

United States Court of Appeals,
Seventh Circuit.

Submitted June 24, 1986.

Decided Aug. 8, 1986.

Before CUMMINGS, Chief Judge, and
CUDAHY and EASTERBROOK, Circuit
Judges.

PER CURIAM.

Sentenced in 1964 to life in prison for
first degree murder, Robert Huggins has
tried to secure release by clemency or parole. Five times the Governor of Indiana
declined to commute Huggins' sentence.
In 1984, after serving 20 years, he became
eligible for parole. So far the state's parole board has declined at least thrice to
release Huggins. Each time the board sent
Huggins a form preprinted "it was the
decision of the Indiana Parole Board not to
grant parole at this time for the following
reasons" followed by a handlettered notation. The notation for February 1984 is:
"SeRIOUSness of offense." The notation
for February 1985 is: "A—Seriousness of
the offense". There is no "B".

Insisting that the state had paroled
or granted clemency to other murderers,
Huggins filed this suit under 42 U.S.C.
§ 1983, arguing that the due process clause
of the fourteenth amendment entitles him
to a better reason. As he puts it, "seriousness of the offense" is "too broad and

general to comply with due process." In
this circuit, at least, such a contention may
be raised in § 1983 litigation as well as
habeas corpus. *Walker v. Prisoner Review Board*, 694 F.2d 499, 501 (7th Cir.
1982). See also *In re United States Parole Commission*, 793 F.2d 338 (D.C.Cir.
1986). But cf. *Billiteri v. United States
Board of Parole*, 541 F.2d 938, 946–47 (2d
Cir.1976); *Bijeol v. Benson*, 513 F.2d 965,
967 (7th Cir.1975).

The district court concluded that
Indiana's parole statutes and regulations
do not establish a "liberty" or "property"
interest within the meaning of the due process clause, and it therefore dismissed the
complaint for failure to state a claim on
which relief may be granted. The court
observed that *Averhart v. Tutsie*, 618 F.2d
479, 480–82 (7th Cir.1980), had come to this
conclusion about Indiana's system. Although there had been amendments to
Indiana's statute and rules since *Averhart*,
the court relied on *Higgason v. Duckworth*, 573 F.Supp. 669, 670–71 (N.D.Ind.
1983), which concluded that the amended
system still does not establish a "liberty"
or "property" interest. The principal question for decision is whether *Higgason* is
correct.

The statute in force until October 1980,
Ind.Code § 11-1-1-9, entitled the prisoner
to appear before the parole board (§ 11-1-
1-9(c)) and required the board to "consider
all pertinent information regarding each
prisoner ... including the circumstances of
his offense, his previous social history and
criminal record, his conduct, employment,
and attitude in prison, and the reports of
such physical and mental examinations as
have been made." Ind.Code § 11-1-1-9(b).
The only rules guiding the board's exercise
of discretion stated: "A parole shall be

ordered only for the best interest of society, not as an award of clemency; it shall not be considered to be a reduction of sentence or pardon. A prisoner shall be placed on parole only when arrangements have been made for his proper employment, or for his maintenance and care, and only when the Indiana parole board believes that he is able and willing to fulfill the obligations of a law-abiding citizen." Ind.Code § 11-1-1-9(c). The Supreme Court of Indiana, interpreting this statute, held that "our Legislature has invested the Parole Board with almost total discretion in such matters." *Murphy v. Indiana Parole Board*, 272 Ind. 200, 397 N.E.2d 259, 263 (1979).

The decision of the Supreme Court of Indiana made for an easy analysis under *Greenholtz v. Inmates of the Nebraska Penal and Correctional Center*, 442 U.S. 1, 99 S.Ct. 2100, 60 L.Ed.2d 668 (1979). *Greenholtz* established that a prisoner's desire to be released on parole is neither liberty nor property within the meaning of the due process clause unless the state establishes an entitlement that depends on the application of rules to facts. If parole is discretion and nothing but, then there is no liberty or property interest. If rules of law require the parole officials to act in specified ways, then there is a protected interest, a "legitimate claim of entitlement". *Board of Regents v. Roth*, 408 U.S. 564, 577, 92 S.Ct. 2701, 2709, 33 L.Ed.2d 548 (1972). The essential ingredient is "an entitlement that stands or falls on the application of rules to facts. To the extent a request appeals to discretion rather than to rules, there is no property." *Scott v. Village of Kewaskum*, 786 F.2d 338, 339–40 (7th Cir.1986). See also *Achacoso-Sanchez v. INS*, 779 F.2d 1260, 1264 (7th Cir.1985). Because the judgment of conviction removes, for the duration of the sentence, the prisoner's "natural" liberty, the right to freedom that antedates governments, the definition of a liberty interest in parole or other early release is the same as the definition of a property interest. See *Greenholtz*, 442 U.S. at 11–12, 99 S.Ct. at 2105–06. Indiana's former parole statute,

as the Supreme Court of Indiana understood it, did not call for the application of rules to facts but left parole officials with unbounded discretion.

The new statute, like the old, requires the parole board to meet with the prisoner and to consider his background. Ind.Code § 11-13-3-3(b), (i). Two new provisions restrict the board's discretion. Section 11-13-3-3(h) provides that the board "shall adopt rules, under IC 4-22-2, and make available to offenders the criteria considered in making parole release determinations. The criteria must include the: (1) nature and circumstances of the crime for which the offender is committed; (2) offender's prior criminal record; (3) offender's conduct and attitude during commitment; and (4) offender's parole plan." With these criteria in mind, the board must decide whether to release an applicant. The statute does not say what combination of criteria requires release. It does say (§ 11-13-3-3(j)):

> If parole is denied, the parole board shall give the person written notice of the denial and the reasons for the denial. The parole board may not parole a person if it determines that there is a substantial reason to believe that he:
>
> (1) will engage in further specified criminal activity; or
>
> (2) will not conform to appropriate specified conditions of parole.

Huggins argues that this statute means that the board shall release an eligible prisoner *unless* he will "engage in further specified criminal activity" or "will not conform to appropriate specified conditions of parole." If so, the new statute establishes a liberty or property interest under the analysis of *Greenholtz*.

United States ex rel. Scott v. Illinois Parole and Pardon Board, 669 F.2d 1185 (7th Cir.), *cert. denied*, 459 U.S. 1048, 103 S.Ct. 468, 74 L.Ed.2d 617 (1982), held that a statute with a structure similar to the new Indiana law does restrict the parole officials' discretion and establish a liberty or property interest. This case shows, however, that a similar structure is not enough to require an identical outcome. The district court, whose interpretation of Indiana law deserves some deference, concluded that it does not. We read the Illinois statute in *Scott* as confining the parole officials' discretion, granting that the same language could be read differently. 669 F.2d at 1189. Indiana's language must be read differently.

Section 11-13-3-3(j) is phrased in the negative; it sometimes forbids release but never requires release. The regulations issued under § 11-13-3-3(h) could restrain the board's discretion, which would establish a liberty or property interest, see *Hewitt v. Helms*, 459 U.S. 460, 471-72, 103 S.Ct. 864, 871-72, 74 L.Ed.2d 675 (1983), but they do not. The regulations, codified at 220 I.A.C. § 1.1-2-3, enlarge the list of considerations beyond those enumerated in § 11-13-3-3(h), but they do not attach weights to any factor or fetter the board's discretion in the least. The substantive regulation, 220 I.A.C. § 1.1-2-3(j), tracks the statutory language by sometimes forbidding parole but never requiring parole. Neither the statute nor any regulation requires the board to give a particular reason for denying parole. It may, for example, give a reason that is not among the two criteria that compel it (under § 11-13-3-3(j)) to deny parole. This is enough to establish that the statute leaves the parole officials with discretion.

It is not important that the statute and regulation require the parole board to hold meetings with applicants for parole. Liberty or property is defined by the substantive criteria that guide the decision, not by the procedural trappings. *Hewitt*, 459 U.S. at 471, 103 S.Ct. at 875; *Olim v. Wakinekona*, 461 U.S. 238, 248-51, 103 S.Ct. 1741, 1747-48, 75 L.Ed.2d 813 (1983). Cf. *Cleveland Board of Education v. Loudermill*, 470 U.S. 532, 105 S.Ct. 1487, 1491-93, 84 L.Ed.2d 494 (1985). It is also unimportant that the board releases many murderers. The essential liberty or property interest comes from rules, not from empirical regularities under discretionary regimes. Connecticut pardoned or granted clemency to a

very large portion of its prisoners, yet this did not establish a liberty or property interest when the executive officials retained full discretion in each case. *Connecticut Board of Pardons v. Dumschat*, 452 U.S. 458, 101 S.Ct. 2460, 69 L.Ed.2d 158 (1981).

We recognize that some decisions seem to look the other way, holding that just about any time a law or regulation gives parole officials a list of things to consider it has established a liberty or property interest. E.g., *Parker v. Corrothers*, 750 F.2d 653 (8th Cir.1984). But still other courts have come to the conclusion we did in *Averhart*, that only when the state's system significantly restricts the parole officials' discretion and grants a legitimate claim of entitlement to parole has the state created a liberty or property interest. E.g., *Berard v. Vermont Parole Board*, 730 F.2d 71 (2d Cir.1984). *Berard*, *Averhart*, and like cases capture the meaning of *Greenholtz*, *Dumschat*, *Hewitt*, and the Supreme Court's other recent decisions. We therefore adhere to *Averhart*. Under the analysis of that case, the new Indiana regime (as the Executive Branch of Indiana interprets and administers that regime) is no different from the old, and a prisoner has neither a liberty nor a property interest in his application for parole.

Only one issue remains. Huggins apparently maintains that the state's system violates the equal protection clause of the fourteenth amendment, both because some prisoners are released while others are not, and because some prisoners (those sentenced for crimes committed after 1977) are released automatically. Huggins does not say that the state treats one class of prisoners differently from any other, so the point that some are let out and some are kept in is a truism rather than a legal objection. The change in 1977 is attributable to Indiana's decision to adopt a system of determinate sentences, as the federal courts soon will under legislation enacted in 1984. Determinate sentences abolish discretionary parole; parole officials then simply monitor people released on good time credits. The observation that people sentenced under a system of determinate sentences are released "automatically" at some time does not show that people sentenced under a different system are entitled to be let go. Indeed the ex post facto clause of the Constitution may prevent the application to Huggins of today's system. Cf. *Weaver v. Graham*, 450 U.S. 24, 101 S.Ct. 960, 67 L.Ed.2d 17 (1981). It does not violate the equal protection clause to require people sentenced before 1977 to serve out their sentences under the system that was in place when they committed their crimes. *Raimondo v. Belletire*, 789 F.2d 492, 497 (7th Cir.1986).

AFFIRMED

EASTERBROOK, Circuit Judge, concurring.

Ind.Code § 11-13-3-3 is a state law, and as in so many diversity cases our job is to figure out the meaning of a state's law while the state courts remain silent. That we must interpret the law is a consequence of litigation under § 1983. The exhaustion of state remedies required prior to a petition for habeas corpus would have given Indiana's courts an opportunity to construe the new statute. I doubt that cases of this sort should be brought under § 1983. Huggins wants out, sooner or later; just as a criminal defendant seeking a new trial must use habeas corpus, so a prisoner seeking a new parole hearing should. See *Preiser v. Rodriguez*, 411 U.S. 475, 93 S.Ct. 1827, 36 L.Ed.2d 439 (1973); *Hanson v. Heckel*, 791 F.2d 93 (7th Cir.1986); *United States ex rel. Johnson v. McGinnis*, 734 F.2d 1193 (7th Cir.1984). But while *Walker* governs, § 1983 is an available avenue, and we are driven to construe state law without the guidance of the state's courts.

What should we make of the new statute? No court of Indiana has decided whether the new statute restricts the parole officials' discretion. Indiana could interpret its law as Huggins does. We held in *Scott* that a similar statute creates a liberty or property interest. The legislative history in Indiana might show that the

parole officials are to grant release whenever release is not forbidden. There is no inevitable reading of a complex statute. Context and history tell the story, which is why statutory construction is an art rather than a science.

Our task is affected by the fact that although diversity litigation usually is between private parties, with the state as neutral lawgiver, this suit is against the state. We do not have an interpretation of § 11-13-3-3 from the Judicial Branch of Indiana, but we have an interpretation from the state's Executive Branch. The parole officials interpret § 11-13-3-3 to give them discretion to deny parole based on the seriousness of the offense, a criterion not listed in § 11-13-3-3(j), which demonstrates that they do not read that statute as directing release whenever release is not forbidden. The Attorney General of Indiana interprets the new statute as granting parole officials the same unbridled discretion as the old one did. The Attorney General's brief in this court states that neither the new statute nor any of its implementing regulations constrains the board to grant parole under any set of facts.

If the Supreme Court of Indiana had come to this conclusion, our case would be as easy as *Averhart* was. To what extent does the Attorney General's interpretation of § 11-13-3-3 fill the gap? We cannot proceed as if the matter were open to utterly independent consideration. No rule of federal law requires states to confide certain powers to the judicial branch alone. However Indiana wishes to distribute its powers internally, this is no concern of the federal government unless the distribution denies the state a republican form of government. See *Whalen v. United States*, 445 U.S. 684, 689 n. 4, 100 S.Ct. 1432, 1436 n. 4, 63 L.Ed.2d 715 (1980); *Mayor of Philadelphia v. Educational Equal Opportunity League*, 415 U.S. 605, 615 n. 13, 94 S.Ct. 1323, 1330 n. 13, 39 L.Ed.2d 630 (1974); *Prentis v. Atlantic Coast Line Co.*, 211 U.S. 210, 225, 29 S.Ct. 67, 69, 53 L.Ed. 150 (1908); *Dreyer v. Illi-*

nois, 187 U.S. 71, 84, 23 S.Ct. 28, 32, 47 L.Ed. 79 (1902); *United Beverage Co. of South Bend v. Indiana Alcoholic Beverage Commission*, 760 F.2d 155 (7th Cir. 1985). Cf. *Bates v. State Bar of Arizona*, 433 U.S. 350, 359–62, 97 S.Ct. 2691, 2696–98, 53 L.Ed.2d 810 (1977) (recognizing that state courts may exercise legislative powers); *University of Tennessee v. Elliott*, — U.S. —, 106 S.Ct. 3220, 92 L.Ed.2d 635 (1986) (findings of fact made by states' executive agencies have preclusive effect in federal civil rights litigation). The allocation is for the state to decide under domestic law, and it may give the Executive Branch powers that overlap those of the Judicial Branch. See *Felder v. Estelle*, 693 F.2d 549, 554–55 (5th Cir.1982) (Higginbotham, J., concurring); cf. *Barrera v. Young*, 794 F.2d 1264, 1268–70 (7th Cir. 1986).

The Executive Branch of any government has the authority to interpret the law, if only to the extent necessary to decide how to execute that law. The authority of judges to interpret and sometimes decline to enforce a statute is implied from the need to decide cases that are properly before them and from the hierarchy of rules that applies. See *Marbury v. Madison*, 1 Cranch (5 U.S.) 137, 170–80, 2 L.Ed. 60 (1803). The announcement of legal rules is a byproduct of the process of adjudication. The interpretation of the law is a principal function of judges, but it is also an important function of other branches of government. Each branch of the government interprets the law, with equal authority, when necessary for resolution of the problem at hand—adjudication in the case of judges, implementation in the case of executive officials. See Learned Hand, *The Bill of Rights* 3–18, 27–30 (1958). We have held that in interpreting the law executive officials share the attributes of judges and are entitled to absolute immunity. *Carson v. Block*, 790 F.2d 562, 565 (7th Cir.1986); *Henderson v. Lopez*, 790 F.2d 44, 46–47 (7th Cir.1986); *Mother Goose Nursery Schools, Inc. v. Sendak*, 770 F.2d 668 (7th Cir.1985), *cert. denied*, — U.S. —, 106 S.Ct. 884, 88 L.Ed.2d 919 (1986). Ours is not a case of immunity, but the underlying question is the same: When do executive officials have the authority to interpret the law on behalf of their jurisdiction?

That the Attorney General comes before us as an advocate does not diminish his role. The nature of the judicial system forces the Attorney General to advocate as well as to interpret, but a federal court is not authorized on that account to give the Attorney General's views lesser weight than they would receive if they appeared in a bound volume of legal opinions. The statements of law in his brief are the views of the highest responsible official of the Executive Branch of Indiana. Some views expressed in briefs may be poorly considered, but some views expressed in judicial opinions also are poorly considered. Cases get reversed, and briefs may have a more complete exposition of the law than do judicial opinions. Indiana could adopt a principle of domestic law under which briefs are treated solely as advocacy; this is the rule the federal courts use when a lawyer (as opposed to an administrative agency in opinions or regulations) tries to explain the basis of a decision. *SEC v. Chenery Corp.*, 318 U.S. 80, 92–95, 63 S.Ct. 454, 461–63, 87 L.Ed. 626 (1943). But the Supreme Court often gives special consideration to the statutory analysis in the Opinions of the Attorney General or the brief of the Solicitor General representing agencies of the Executive Branch. E.g., *Japan Whaling Ass'n v. American Cetacean Society*, — U.S. —, — - —, 106 S.Ct. 2860, 2867–68, 92 L.Ed.2d 166 (1986); *Haig v. Agee*, 453 U.S. 280, 291, 101 S.Ct. 2766, 2774, 69 L.Ed.2d 640 (1981). That the first complete elaboration of the legal position is presented in a brief does not authorize a court to sneeze at the position. Officials often formulate legal positions in the course of litigation, as the bearing of a particular statute becomes evident. A state should be entitled to decide for itself the status of legal interpretations contained in briefs. At all events, the Attorney General's views were not formulated only for use in this litigation. The

Attorney General appears on behalf of the Indiana Parole Board, which adopted in its regulations the legal view that it has unfettered discretion under § 11–13–3–3. This existing view is authoritative under state law, at least for the moment.

In Indiana, as in the federal system and the other states, judicial interpretations of the law by the highest court supersede the executive interpretations. Cf. *United States v. Mendoza*, 464 U.S. 154, 104 S.Ct. 568, 78 L.Ed.2d 379 (1984) (interpretations of law by lower federal courts bind the Executive Branch only with respect to the litigants involved). If the Supreme Court of Indiana had spoken on the meaning of § 11–13–3–3, we would follow its decisions. It has not, however, and until it does the prevailing construction is the one of the Executive Branch of Indiana's government. Any position that disregarded the executive's views would raise profound questions in a federal system, one in which states rather than the national government establish the meaning of state law. See *Pennhurst State School & Hospital v. Halderman*, 465 U.S. 89, 104 S.Ct. 900, 79 L.Ed.2d 67 (1984) (*Pennhurst II*), which concluded that principles of sovereign immunity implicit in the federal structure of our nation prevent a federal court from granting injunctive relief against state officials based on an interpretation of state law that differs from the interpretation placed on that law by the state's Executive Branch (the defendant in *Pennhurst II*). *Pennhurst II* was a strong case for interpretation of state law by a federal court. The Supreme Court of Pennsylvania had construed the state's law differently from the construction defended by the Executive Branch of the state; moreover, a decision based on the state court's construction of state law would have enabled the federal court to avoid a question of federal constitutional law. Still, the Court concluded, the federal court must not grant a remedy against the state based on its own construction of state law. In our case, by contrast, no state court has spoken, and accepting the Executive Branch's construction of state law will enable us to avoid a constitutional question.

Because in Indiana the views of the Supreme Court trump the views of the Attorney General, the Executive Branch does not always speak for the state. This suggests the same sort of caution a federal court exercises when determining whether the Supreme Court of a state would adopt a legal position articulated by a lower court. See *King v. Order of Travelers*, 333 U.S. 153, 68 S.Ct. 488, 92 L.Ed. 608 (1948) (in diversity cases federal courts are not absolutely bound by the construction of an intermediate state court); *Williams, McCarthy, Kinley, Rudy & Picha v. Northwestern National Insurance Group*, 750 F.2d 619, 624–25 (7th Cir.1984). So, too, when a state's construction of its domestic law (by any branch of its government) affects the enforcement of federal rights, there is a second inquiry: whether the state's construction is reasoned, consistent, and sufficient to justify the effect on the federal interest. See *Henry v. Mississippi*, 379 U.S. 443, 85 S.Ct. 564, 13 L.Ed.2d 408 (1965); *Hathorn v. Lovorn*, 457 U.S. 255, 262–63, 102 S.Ct. 2421, 72 L.Ed.2d 824 (1982); *James v. Kentucky*, 466 U.S. 341, 104 S.Ct. 1830, 80 L.Ed.2d 346 (1984). But the interpretation of § 11–13–3–3 does not undercut a federal interest. If the statute means what the Attorney General says it does, there is no federal interest at all.

The Attorney General's understanding of Indiana law is not so far out of line that the Supreme Court of Indiana is certain to go the other way. The court discusses the statute and its implementing regulations. These do not compel a conclusion that the parole board has unfettered discretion, but they permit such a conclusion. Similar indicia would lead a court to accept the interpretation given to a law by a federal agency. E.g., *Chevron U.S.A., Inc. v. Natural Resources Defense Council, Inc.*, 467 U.S. 837, 842–45, 104 S.Ct. 2778, 2781–83, 81 L.Ed.2d 694 (1984); *Watkins v. Blinzinger*, 789 F.2d 474, 478 (7th Cir.1986). A federal court owes still greater respect for a state agency's construction of state law. So to the extent a federal court is authorized to venture an independent opinion, I think it likely that the Supreme Court of Indiana will support the Attorney General's view that the new statute and regulations leave the parole board with discretion. Parole in Indiana does not depend on the application of rules to facts; a prisoner's appeal is to discretion rather than to legitimate claims of entitlement; the statute and regulation therefore do not establish a liberty or property interest.

The court is able to resolve today's case without deciding the appropriate treatment of the considered views of the Executive Branch of a state's government. Similarly, I have outlined some views without suggesting a firm answer to the question how federal courts should deal with the Executive Branch's views. I hope, however, that avoidance in this case does not mean inattention in the future. Neither the district court nor the parties discussed the question. *Pennhurst II* has put federal courts out of the business of issuing relief against state officials based on state law, but this case shows that questions of state law are inescapable, because the entitlements established by state law become the basis of claims under the Constitution. I should think it regrettable if a federal court were to order a state to change its practices on the ground that its Executive Branch does not understand state law—even though the formal basis for the order is the due process clause of the fourteenth amendment. Both the parties and the courts should take care in tomorrow's cases to consider the role a state's construction of its own law plays in constitutional litigation.

James WRIGHT, Plaintiff-Appellant,

v.

Lanson NEWSOME, Warden,
Defendant-Appellee.

No. 85–8897

Non-Argument Calendar.

United States Court of Appeals,
Eleventh Circuit.

Aug. 6, 1986.

Appeal from the United States District Court for the Southern District of Georgia.

Before FAY, JOHNSON and CLARK, Circuit Judges.

PER CURIAM:

James Wright appeals from the district court's dismissal of his pro se 42 U.S.C. § 1983 action for failure to state a claim upon which relief could be granted. We reverse and remand for further proceedings.

I. FACTS

Wright is an inmate at Georgia State Prison ("GSP"). Taking the facts alleged in the complaint as true, Sergeant Fred Brown ordered fellow GSP correctional officers Pedro Diaz and Eddie Mincey to search Wright's cell on March 28, 1984. In the course of the search, Diaz and Mincey destroyed seven of Wright's photographs and some legal papers. They also seized legal pleadings concerning Wright's challenge to his conviction and a law book belonging to Wright. The pleadings and law book have not been returned.

Wright informed other correctional officers on duty that day about the search and seizure. Unit Manager Sikes declined to photograph the damage in the cell or file a damage report but told Wright to file a grievance. Wright sent a letter to Warden Lanson Newsome informing him of the search and requesting the return of his papers and book, apparently to no avail. He also presented a claim against the Department of Corrections to the Claims Advisory Board pursuant to O.C.G.A. § 28–5–

85. The Board rejected the claim on July 16, 1985, after giving Wright an opportunity to present evidence in support of his allegations at one of its meetings, finding insufficient evidence of Department of Corrections negligence.

On August 27, 1985, Wright filed the current civil rights lawsuit pro se, naming Newsome, Diaz, Mincey and unknown "John Does and Richard Does" (correctional officers or other agents of Newsome) as defendants. He alleged First and Fourteenth Amendment violations of his right to access to the courts and to procedural due process of law. He also invoked the court's pendent jurisdiction over his claims under Georgia law for destruction of his property and conversion. He requested declaratory and injunctive relief and damages. He simultaneously asked the court to allow him to proceed in forma pauperis under 28 U.S.C. § 1915.

In an order dated September 6, 1985, prior to service of the complaint on the defendants, the district court dismissed Wright's procedural due process claim on the ground that Wright has access to adequate state remedies for the alleged unauthorized deprivation of his property and so cannot state a claim under the due process clause. *Hudson v. Palmer*, 468 U.S. 517, 104 S.Ct. 3194, 82 L.Ed.2d 393 (1984); *Parratt v. Taylor*, 451 U.S. 527, 101 S.Ct. 1908, 68 L.Ed.2d 420 (1981). It also dismissed his state law claims. With respect to Wright's access to the courts claim, the court ordered Wright to submit a statement of the facts supporting his claim and a description of the relief requested within twenty days. The court ordered service of the order and the complaint on the defendants and invited them to respond to the access to courts claim.

Wright responded to the order by filing a "Motion to Amend" in which he restated the facts contained in his initial complaint and added allegations that the defendants' misconduct was in retaliation for prior lawsuits and administrative grievances he had filed, that black inmates had filed other grievances notifying Newsome of the "outrageous" treatment of blacks by Diaz and Mincey, and that the seizure and destruction of property were committed pursuant to established state procedure. Apparently in support of the latter assertion, Wright stated that officials at GSP have been subject to court orders issued in connection with two law suits concerning GSP "shakedown" procedures and the destruction and confiscation of inmates' legal materials. Finally, Wright included a discussion of the cases supporting his claims.

The district court's order notwithstanding, the defendants have never been served and have not appeared before this court on appeal. Needless to say, they did not respond to the court's order.

The district court denied the motion to amend and dismissed the access to courts claim, thereby disposing of Wright's complaint in its entirety. The court stated that "[p]laintiff's new allegation of 'retaliation' is put forth not out of sincerity, but out of convenience to get around the 'adequate post-deprivation state remedy' requirement of *Hudson*" and found that "plaintiff seeks to file in a federal district court solely because he believes that his claim could be unsuccessful in a state forum." The court also pointed out that Wright had not alleged specific facts but had merely stated conclusions of law. Hence the court dismissed the complaint for failure to state a claim upon which relief can be granted. Wright appeals without the aid of counsel.

II. ISSUES

On appeal, Wright argues that he properly alleged that the deprivation of his property was effected pursuant to established state procedure and so stated a claim under the due process clause as interpreted in *Parratt* and *Hudson*. He further argues that he alleged facts sufficient to state a claim of retaliation for the exercise of constitutional rights and of interference with his right to access to the courts. We agree that the district court abused its discretion in denying Wright's motion to amend his complaint and erred as a matter of law in concluding that he failed to state any claim for which relief can be granted.

III. ANALYSIS

When reviewing the dismissal of a complaint under Fed.R.Civ.P. 12(b)(6), we may not affirm unless it appears beyond doubt that the plaintiff can prove no set of facts in support of the claims in the complaint that would entitle him or her to relief. *Haines v. Kerner*, 404 U.S. 519, 520–21, 92 S.Ct. 594, 596, 30 L.Ed.2d 652 (1972). We must keep in mind that allegations in a pro se complaint are to be held to less stringent standards than are pleadings drafted by an attorney, *id.*, and that all pleadings are to be construed to do substantial justice. Fed.R.Civ.P. 8(f). Finally, we note that the complaint of an in forma pauperis plaintiff may be dismissed prior to service on the defendant only if the action is frivolous or malicious. 28 U.S.C. § 1915(d).

We acknowledge that certain of the facts and issues discussed *infra* are not technically part of the complaint because they were contained in the motion to amend, which was denied. For the sake of orderliness, we point out that Fed.R.Civ.P. 15(a) allows a plaintiff to amend the complaint "as a matter of course at any time before a responsive pleading is served." As the defendants had not been served when Wright attempted to amend his complaint, the district court abused its discretion in denying the amendment. Our discussion therefore refers to the complaint as if the motion to amend had been granted.

A. *Procedural Due Process*

In *Parratt v. Taylor*, 451 U.S. 527, 101 S.Ct. 1908, 68 L.Ed.2d 420 (1981), the Supreme Court held that the allegation of an unauthorized deprivation of property does not state a procedural due process claim where an adequate state remedy exists to redress the deprivation. In *Logan v. Zimmerman Brush Co.*, 455 U.S. 422, 102 S.Ct. 1148, 71 L.Ed.2d 265 (1982), the Court explained that post-deprivation remedies do not satisfy the due process requirement where the deprivation of property is effected pursuant to established state procedure, rather than through random, unauthorized action. In *Hudson v. Palmer*, 468 U.S. 517, 104 S.Ct. 3194, 82 L.Ed.2d 393 (1984), the Court further clarified its holding in *Parratt* by explaining that post-deprivation remedies may provide due process where the deprivation was intentional, rather than negligent, so long as it was random or unauthorized. In this case, if Wright sufficiently alleged facts demonstrating that the deprivation was the result of established state procedure, the district court erred in holding that he must resort to state post-deprivation remedies.

Contrary to the district court's finding, Wright has not merely stated conclusions of law but has alleged facts that, if true, would support the finding that the deprivation in this case was the result of established state procedure. Diaz and Mincey were ordered to search the cell by a superior. *See Neary v. Dugger*, 766 F.2d 456, 457 (11th Cir.1985) (allegation of confiscation during search conducted pursuant to established state procedure states claim of deprivation without due process). According to Wright's allegations, confiscations of legal materials at GSP have taken place in the past and continue despite court orders to the contrary and notice to the warden and other responsible officials. Thus it could be inferred that searches and consequent confiscations unaccompanied by procedural safeguards are the sanctioned standard operating procedure at GSP. Moreover, this case does not involve a situation in which predeprivation process would not have been feasible. *See Rittenhouse v. DeKalb County*, 764 F.2d 1451, 1454–55 (11th Cir.1985), *cert. denied,* —— U.S. ——, 106 S.Ct. 1193, 89 L.Ed.2d 308 (1986) (explaining that established state procedure requirement focuses on feasibility of predeprivation process). As the allegations sufficiently charged that the taking was the result of established state procedure, the court improperly relied upon *Parratt* and its progeny.

The district court also dismissed Wright's pendent state law claims at the same time it dismissed the due process claim on the basis of *Parratt*. The court did not explain this decision and, given that the access to courts federal claim remained in the case, there was no apparent reason to dismiss the pendent claims. Certainly, *Parratt* does not require a federal court to decline to exercise pendent jurisdiction over a claim simply because it rests on a state cause of action that provides the adequate post-deprivation remedy necessitating dismissal of the federal due process claim so long as the court has jurisdiction upon other grounds. In this case, of course, we have determined that the district court's dismissal of Wright's due process claim was in error. Any other reason that the court may have had for dismissing the state claims with the due process claim no longer exists, and we reverse the dismissal of the pendent state claims.

B. *Access to the Courts*

The district court discounted Wright's retaliation claim, finding that Wright was only trying to salvage an otherwise defective pleading. As noted above, however, Wright's allegations must be accepted as true.[1]

The allegation that prison officials seized Wright's pleadings and law book and destroyed other legal papers clearly states a claim of denial of access to the courts. Prison officials may not deny or obstruct an inmate's access to the courts. *Johnson v. Avery*, 393 U.S. 483, 89 S.Ct. 747, 21 L.Ed.2d 718 (1969). The facts stated in Wright's initial complaint state a constitutional claim standing alone and are not dependent on being framed in terms of retaliation to convert an otherwise insufficient claim into a federally cognizable one. It is the fact that Wright was denied his *legal* papers and *law* books, and not the deprivation, that brings this claim within the scope of constitutional protection. The district court incorrectly stated the law when it suggested that Wright needed to allege retaliation to salvage his complaint.

Wright also sufficiently alleged facts bringing actions that might not otherwise be offensive to the Constitution, such as the search itself or the confiscation and destruction of nonlegal materials (if not in violation of the due process clause), within the scope of the Constitution by alleging that the actions were taken in retaliation for filing lawsuits and administrative grievances. This type of retaliation violates both the inmate's right of access to the courts, *Hooks v. Kelley*, 463 F.2d 1210 (5th Cir.1972), and the inmate's First Amendment rights. *See Bridges v. Russell*, 757 F.2d 1155 (11th Cir.1985). The district court erred in dismissing the retaliation claim for failure to state a claim for which relief can be granted.

The district court's denial of Wright's motion to amend and dismissal of his complaint are reversed and this case is remanded to the district court for further proceedings.

REVERSED and REMANDED.

---

1. We do not mean to suggest that the district court does not have the power under 28 U.S.C. § 1915(d) to dismiss the complaint of a plaintiff seeking to proceed in forma pauperis if the action is maliciously brought. In such a case, however, the district court must have reason to believe the suit is not brought in a good faith. In this case, the district court did not explain its suspicions, and the record does not support its findings with respect to Wright's lack of good faith.

VOLUME IV

CHAPTER 4   PAROLE CONDITIONS

In many cases, parole is not granted without attached conditions. In *Alonzo v. Rozanski*, 808 F.2d 637 (7th Cir. 1986), the condition of the parole was that the individual remain in Illinois. The parolee wanted to move to Florida to be with his girlfriend, but the court held he had neither liberty nor property interest in his place of residence. The case is included.

In *People v. Allegri*, 487 N.E.2d 606 (Ill. 1985), the defendant had been paroled on the condition that she refrain from violating any state law and report regularly for psychological counseling. By restraining a thirteen year old boy, she had violated the criminal code, but she raised insanity as her defense. The court held insanity was not a defense in a revocation hearing.

In *United States v. Garcia*, 771 F.2d 1369 (9th Cir. 1985), the question arose whether a parolee's guilty plea made without adequate warning of his rights was sufficient to revoke a parole granted on the condition that parolee obey all state and federal laws. The case is reproduced here.

Normally, when a parolee is released on parole, a state returns him to the county of his commitment. The case of *Prison Law Office v. Koenig*, 233 Cal.Rept. 590 (Cal.App. 1st Dist. 1986), challenged this practice. In most cases, as in *Koenig*, the concept of returning the prisoner to the original county where he was committed is upheld.

Introductions in previous volumes:

IV: 201; VI: 557; VII: 493; VIII: 499

Philip J. ALONZO, Petitioner-Appellant,

v.

John J. ROZANSKI, III, United States
Probation Officer, et al.,
Respondents-Appellees.

No. 86–1586.

United States Court of Appeals,
Seventh Circuit.

Argued Dec. 16, 1986.
Decided Dec. 29, 1986.

Before BAUER, Chief Judge, and
CUMMINGS and EASTERBROOK,
Circuit Judges.

EASTERBROOK, Circuit Judge.

Until he entered prison in 1983 for several narcotics offenses, Philip Alonzo lived in Lombard, Illinois. He was paroled in June 1985, with 2½ years remaining on his term, to be followed by three years' special parole. As 28 C.F.R. § 2.33(b) provides, he was paroled to the place of his legal residence and required to obtain the permission of the probation service before leaving the

Northern District of Illinois. See also 18 U.S.C. § 4209, which authorizes the Parole Commission to impose conditions on its charges.

Alonzo wants to move to Florida to live with his girlfriend in a house he recently bought. The probation officer in Florida opposed the move, citing the "immense problems" his office had supervising the drug offenders who already lived there. Alonzo then filed a petition for a writ of habeas corpus under 28 U.S.C. § 2241, contending that this decision is arbitrary and capricious, thereby (he says) denying him due process of law. The defendants moved for summary judgment, which the district court granted on the ground that Alonzo, as a parolee, has neither a liberty nor a property interest in his place of residence. 635 F.Supp 496. Unless "life, liberty, or property" is at stake, the due process clause of the fifth amendment does not apply, and officials may act for such reasons (and with such procedures) as they choose. (They may not act for reasons, such as race, forbidden by other portions of the Constitution, but Alonzo does not contend that they acted for substantively prohibited reasons.)

The district court gave the right reason for the right conclusion. Alonzo committed crimes, and the punishment for these crimes includes stripping him of control over where he shall live. While in prison Alonzo had no say at all about where he could go. A prisoner has neither a liberty nor a property interest in the place of his confinement. *Meachum v. Fano*, 427 U.S. 215, 96 S.Ct. 2532, 49 L.Ed.2d 451 (1976); *Olim v. Wakinekona*, 461 U.S. 238, 103 S.Ct. 1741, 75 L.Ed.2d 813 (1983); *Miller v. Henman*, 804 F.2d 421 (7th Cir.1986). Alonzo's control of abode was extinguished, for the entire term of his sentence, by the judgment of conviction. Some choice was

restored to Alonzo when he was paroled, but Alonzo received no more than statutes and binding regulations gave him. How much freedom Alonzo received is a question of positive rather than natural law. Positive law allows a parolee to move without restraint in the district of his release, unless the conditions attached to his parole enlarge or restrict that liberty. Alonzo does not claim that any statute, regulation, or term of his release gives him an interest in living outside Illinois. Sections 2.33(b) and 2.38(b) give him an opportunity to ask the Commission to designate a new place of residence,* but the regulations do not contain criteria that require the Commission to act in any particular way in response to particular facts. Alonzo has no more than a hope, a unilateral expectation, a right to appeal to the Commission's discretion. Such expectations do not create liberty or property interests. See *Connecticut Board of Pardons v. Dumschat*, 452 U.S. 458, 101 S.Ct. 2460, 69 L.Ed.2d 158 (1981); *Huggins v. Isenbarger*, 798 F.2d 203 (7th Cir.1986). Alonzo needs more than a unilateral expectation. He needs, and does not have, a "legitimate claim of entitlement", *Board of Regents v. Roth*, 408 U.S. 564, 577, 92 S.Ct. 2701, 2709, 33 L.Ed.2d 548 (1972).

We therefore join the Ninth Circuit in holding that the decision where a parolee shall be allowed to live is not subject to the due process clause of the fifth amendment. *Bagley v. Harvey*, 718 F.2d 921, 924 (9th Cir.1983). See also *Greenholtz v. Nebraska Inmates*, 442 U.S. 1, 9–11, 99 S.Ct. 2100, 2104–06, 60 L.Ed.2d 668 (1979) (an application for release on parole implicates liberty or property only to the extent statutes and regulations create a legitimate claim of entitlement). Alonzo relies on *Arciniega v. Freeman*, 404 U.S. 4, 92 S.Ct. 22, 30 L.Ed.2d 126 (1971), for the

---

* 28 C.F.R. § 2.33(b) provides that a parolee shall be released to the place of his legal residence "unless the Commission is satisfied that another place of residence will serve the public interest more effectively or will improve the probability of the applicant's readjustment." 28 C.F.R. § 2.38(b) states that a "parolee may be transfer-

red to a new district of supervision with the permission of the probation officers of both the transferring and receiving district, provided such transfer is not contrary to instructions from the Commission." The statute, 18 U.S.C. § 4209, gives the Commission equal discretion.

contrary proposition. *Arciniega* dealt with the application of a condition of parole, but only because a violation of the condition led to the revocation of parole. Being out of jail is a form of liberty interest, which revocation of parole extinguishes. Compare *Morrissey v. Brewer*, 408 U.S. 471, 480–82, 92 S.Ct. 2593, 2599–601, 33 L.Ed.2d 484 (1972), with *Jago v. Van Curen*, 454 U.S. 14, 102 S.Ct. 31, 70 L.Ed.2d 13 (1981). The deprivation of "liberty" in *Arciniega* was covered by the due process clause. The unfavorable reaction to Alonzo's request is not, which makes all the difference.

AFFIRMED.

109 Ill.2d 309
93 Ill.Dec. 781
The PEOPLE of the State of
Illinois, Appellee,

v.

Anita ALLEGRI, Appellant.

No. 61000.

Supreme Court of Illinois.

Dec. 20, 1985.

SIMON, Justice:

The defendant, Anita Allegri, entered a negotiated plea of guilty in the circuit court of Champaign County to the offense of unlawful restraint (Ill.Rev.Stat.1981, ch. 38, par. 10–3(a)). She was charged with unlawfully attempting to take a two-year-old child from his father. The sentence was 30 months' probation conditioned upon her periodic incarceration in the county correctional facility as a work-release prisoner. In addition, her probation required her to refrain from violating any State laws and to report on a regular basis for psychological counseling.

Six months later the State charged her with a probation violation and sought to revoke her probation. The evidence demonstrated that the defendant had unlawfully restrained a 13-year-old boy in violation of the criminal code (Ill.Rev.Stat.1981, ch.

38, par. 10–3(a)) and, as a result of that infraction, a condition of her probation had been violated.

Her defense was that she was insane (Ill.Rev.Stat.1981, ch. 38, par. 6–2(a)) and could not be adjudged to have violated her probation because she was unable to control herself. Psychiatric testimony established that the defendant suffered from paranoid schizophrenia. The trial court made a specific finding that the State had failed to rebut this evidence, and that if the defense of insanity was available in a probation-revocation proceeding, the defendant would prevail.

The trial court ruled, however, that in a probation-revocation proceeding the defense of insanity was not available to the probationer. The defendant appealed, and the appellate court affirmed the trial court's ruling with one judge dissenting (127 Ill.App.3d 1041, 83 Ill.Dec. 192, 469 N.E.2d 1126). We allowed the defendant's petition for leave to appeal (94 Ill.2d R. 315 (a)). Thus, the question we are called upon to answer is whether insanity is an available defense in a probation-revocation proceeding, a question which this court has never considered.

The defendant argues that the insanity defense is appropriate here because the underlying basis for the probation revocation is a violation of the criminal code. She suggests that the criminal code is silent as to whether the defense is available in a revocation proceeding, and that the defense should therefore be applied because the legislature did not specifically exclude it.

Not only is defendant's statutory argument unsound, but her position would require that we ignore the legislative purpose behind probation.

The issue presented requires us to construe section 6–2(a) of the Criminal Code of 1961. It provides:

> "Insanity. (a) A person is not criminally responsible for conduct if at the time of such conduct, as a result of mental disease or mental defect, he lacks substantial capacity either to appreciate the criminality of his conduct or to conform his conduct to the requirements of law." (Ill.Rev.Stat.1981, ch. 38, par. 6–2(a).)

To determine legislative intent, we first look to the plain meaning of the statute as found in the words of section 6–2(a). (See, e.g., People v. Boykin (1983), 94 Ill.2d 138, 141, 68 Ill.Dec. 321, 445 N.E.2d 1174; 2A Sutherland, Statutory Construction sec. 48 (4th ed. 1984).) Examination of this statute reveals that the legislature did not directly address whether the insanity defense applied to probation-revocation proceedings. The use of the words "criminally responsible" and "criminality of his conduct," though, indicates that the legislature was concerned with the possibility of conviction of an offense in the absence of criminal intent. While this language is not conclusive, it does suggest that the General Assembly's intent was that the insanity de-

fense should apply only to proceedings in which guilt or innocence is to be determined. A probation-revocation hearing is not, however, such a proceeding. (Gagnon v. Scarpelli (1973), 411 U.S. 778, 93 S.Ct. 1756, 36 L.Ed.2d 656.) It takes place only after the defendant has already been convicted, sentenced to probation, and then has violated the conditions of the probation.

Similarly, section 5–2–4 of the Unified Code of Corrections (Ill.Rev.Stat.1981, ch. 38, par. 1005–2–4), which sets forth the procedure for treating defendants who are found not guilty by reason of insanity, also supports the conclusion that the insanity defense is not available in revocation proceedings. It requires a hearing to determine whether a defendant *acquitted* by reason of insanity should be involuntarily committed to a mental health facility. But, because the defendant in a probation-revocation proceeding has already been found guilty rather than acquitted, commitment of a defendant to a mental health facility by reason of his acquittal has no relevance to such a proceeding. This is especially true because a probation-revocation proceeding is not one which leads to the acquittal or conviction of a defendant.

While the legislature did not explicitly exclude a defense based on insanity in a probation-revocation proceeding, this defense is inconsistent with the purpose of probation revocation. Probation is a form of judgment after the defendant has been found guilty. (People ex rel. Barrett v. Bardens (1946), 394 Ill. 511, 517, 68 N.E.2d 710.) The appellate court properly characterized probation as a privilege. It is employed when the defendant's continued presence in society would not be threatening and the defendant's rehabilitation would be enhanced. (See, e.g. People v. Molz (1953), 415 Ill. 183, 188, 113 N.E.2d 314; Knight v. Estelle (5th Cir.1974), 501 F.2d 963, 964.) A violation of probation demonstrates to the court that the defendant is a threat to society and that his continued presence outside of jail is unwarranted.

The insanity defense had no bearing on the real issue at defendant's revocation hearing, which was whether the defendant's continued presence in society presents a danger. When the defendant unlawfully restrained a child, she demonstrated the threat which her continued freedom poses for society. That threat is no less real because defendant's insanity would excuse her from criminal responsibility.

Personal culpability is not required for a court to revoke a sentence of probation. (*People v. Davis* (1984), 123 Ill. App.3d 349, 353, 78 Ill.Dec. 705, 462 N.E.2d 824 (defendant's failure to be accepted in drug- and alcohol-treatment program justified revocation).) This point is illustrated by section 5–6–2(c) of the Unified Code of Corrections, which provides that the "court may at any time terminate probation or conditional discharge if warranted by the conduct of the offender and the ends of justice." (Ill.Rev.Stat.1981, ch. 38, par. 1005–6–2(c).) The legislature's choice of the word "conduct" strongly suggests that the key question in a revocation proceeding is whether the objective acts of the defendant require revocation, not whether he is legally responsible for such acts. Indeed, the statute has no requirement that such conduct even be of a criminal nature, let alone criminally culpable. As the appellate court properly noted, if "insanity applied as a defense, the trial court would have no statutory authority to modify or revoke probation even though the defendant's actions clearly establish a violation of probation and a frustration of its purposes." 127 Ill.App.3d 1041, 1044, 83 Ill.Dec. 192, 469 N.E.2d 1126.

Defendant also contends that this court has, by implication, approved of the use of the affirmative defense of self-defense in probation-revocation proceedings. (*People v. Cooper* (1977), 66 Ill.2d 509, 6 Ill.Dec. 870, 363 N.E.2d 817.) In *Cooper*, this court reversed an appellate court's evidentiary ruling but did not specifically consider the appellate court's approval of the use of self-defense at a probation-revocation proceeding. Regardless of the correctness of the appellate court decision on that issue, it does not provide a meaningful analogy to the defendant's situation.

Self-defense provides a justification, so that action which society otherwise seeks to prevent becomes permissible under the circumstances. Insanity, on the other hand, is an excuse for the individual's behavior. It does not turn unacceptable behavior into permissible conduct, but only excuses the individual from criminal punishment for having violated a penal statute. Because conduct excused on the basis of insanity is no more desirable, nor less criminal, than inexcusable conduct, section 5–2–4 requires involuntary admission into a mental health facility for those defendants who are declared insane, while acquittal by reason of self-defense allows the accused immediate freedom. Therefore, whether or not self-defense is applicable in a probation-revocation proceeding, an issue we do not decide here, it has no bearing on the applicability of the insanity defense in that type of proceeding.

Other States and the Federal courts have considered this problem in the context of probation or parole revocations, and our research reveals that the conclusion we reach is in accord with their decisions. (See, *e.g.*, *Steinberg v. Police Court* (6th Cir.1979), 610 F.2d 449; *Knight v. Estelle* (5th Cir.1974), 501 F.2d 963; *Pierce v. State Department of Social & Health Services* (1982), 97 Wash.2d 552, 646 P.2d 1382; *State ex rel. Lyons v. Department of Health & Social Services* (1981), 105 Wis.2d 146, 312 N.W.2d 868; *People v. Breaux* (1980), 101 Cal.App.3d 468, 161 Cal. Rptr. 653; *State v. O'Meal* (1977), 116 Ariz. 307, 569 P.2d 249; *Trumbly v. State* (Alaska 1973), 515 P.2d 707.) In *Knight v. Estelle* (5th Cir.1974), 501 F.2d 963, for example, the Federal appellate court for the fifth circuit examined Texas law in a case involving parole revocation (which does not significantly differ from probation revocation for our purposes. (See *Gagnon v. Scarpelli* (1973), 411 U.S. 778, 93 S.Ct. 1756, 36 L.Ed.2d 656).) The court noted:

"[I]f the parolee has committed the physical act, the attempt to reintegrate him into society has obviously failed * * *. Whether the act which made the failure apparent was culpable or punishable is no concern of the revocation authority, which does not sit to punish. Its concern is whether the law has been obeyed, not whether it has been culpably broken." (501 F.2d 963, 964.)

We believe our General Assembly enacted the probation provision for the same reasons and intended that the same procedure apply.

Additionally, we note the dilemma which would confront a sentencing judge were we to reverse the appellate court. In cases where probation seems appropriate but there exists some risk that the defendant will commit an excusable offense during the probationary period, the judge would have to choose between sentencing the defendant to an unnecessary period of incarceration or granting probation at the risk of having made an uncorrectable error. We can find no just reason to saddle trial judges with such a Hobson's choice.

Finally, the State contends that the defendant's right to due process does not require that the insanity defense be made applicable to a probation-revocation hearing. We need not directly address this argument, as the defendant has failed to argue this particular issue in this court and has instead chosen to rely solely on the statutory language.

It is critical to note that in refusing to recognize the insanity defense in a revocation proceeding, the court is not imposing criminal punishment on the defendant for her present excusable conduct. The criminal punishment results from the past conduct which was not excused by insanity and for which defendant has been duly convicted. We therefore hold that the circuit and appellate courts properly found that the insanity defense does not apply in probation revocation proceedings.

Judgment affirmed.

MILLER, J., took no part in the consideration or decision of this case.

WARD, Justice, dissenting:

I cannot accept the majority's holding that insane persons cannot plead their disability at a probation-revocation hearing and are subject to punishment, though they were not mentally responsible for the conduct that the State says violated their probation. It is not questioned that such persons could have pleaded insanity and could not have been found guilty if the insanity existed when the criminal charges were brought. In the event of later developing disability and conduct violating terms of probation the majority's view is that the probationer's "continued presence outside of jail is unwarranted." (109 Ill.2d at 314, 93 Ill.Dec. at 782, 487 N.E.2d at 607.) The majority's conclusion is founded on what I consider to be the strange construction that the General Assembly, in section 6–2(a) of the Criminal Code of 1961, intended that the defense of insanity would apply only to trial proceedings at which the guilt of the accused was to be determined. It appears obvious to me that the General Assembly, in enacting the statute making insanity a defense, intended to insure fairness toward persons with the specified mental disease or mental defect. It is inconceivable that the General Assembly intended that this fairness to handicapped persons would not be extended to all proceedings and especially to those in which punishment was sought by the State.

The majority says, too, that the real issue at the probation-revocation hearing was whether the defendant's continued presence in society presented a danger. I consider that the important question here is whether this court should approve the denial of a hearing to a woman who, it is claimed, because of mental deficiency could not adequately understand or control conduct for which the State seeks her punishment.

To support its position the majority cites a decision which held that whether the conduct that violated the terms of probation was culpable is of no concern and that the only concern is whether the terms of probation have been observed. That is a view I cannot share.

The majority concludes by stating that it need not, on the ground of waiver, address the question whether the right to due process requires recognition of the insanity defense in a probation-revocation hearing. I believe that the question of due process and also the question of constitutional protection against cruel and unusual punishments are involved and that here both protections were ignored. *Ford v. Wainwright* (11th Cir.1985), 752 F.2d 526, *cert. granted* (1985), —— U.S. ——, 106 S.Ct. 566, 88 L.Ed.2d 552.

GOLDENHERSH, J., joins in this dissent.

UNITED STATES of America,
Plaintiff-Appellee,

v.

Reynaldo GARCIA, Jr.,
Defendant-Appellant.

No. 84–1275.

United States Court of Appeals,
Ninth Circuit.

Argued and Submitted May 13, 1985.

Decided Sept. 23, 1985.

On Appeal from the United States District Court for the Eastern District of California.

Before MERRILL, TANG, and FLETCHER, Circuit Judges.

MERRILL, Circuit Judge:

Pursuant to 28 U.S.C. § 1291 (1982), Reynaldo Garcia appeals the revocation of his probation, arguing that the district court relied upon invalid evidence.

I

On April 4, 1983, Garcia was sentenced by the United States District Court for the Eastern District of California to fifteen years in prison for violating the Racketeer Influenced and Corrupt Organizations Act (RICO), 18 U.S.C. § 1962(d) (1982). The execution of this sentence was suspended, and the appellant was placed on probation for a period of five years. As a condition of probation, Garcia agreed to comply with all federal, state and local laws. He acknowledges that he was advised of this condition and that he fully understood it.

Garcia resettled in Missouri. On February 13, 1984, a petition for revocation of probation was filed in the Eastern District of California alleging that Garcia had violated the condition of his probation that he obey all federal, state and local laws.

The petition charged Garcia with four violations of Kansas City and Missouri ordinances, including disorderly conduct, breach of the peace, assault and willful damaging of the property of another. Garcia pleaded guilty to three of these charges. As to the fourth violation charged, the district court was not furnished with a court document indicating what disposition was made.[1] Garcia has never sought to overturn any of his Missouri convictions.

Because the Municipal Court of Kansas City is not a court of record, the district court found that no evidence existed that Garcia had been apprised of his constitutional rights and had waived them prior to pleading guilty. The district court nevertheless held that the evidence showed that Garcia had violated laws in contravention of a condition of his probation. Accordingly, appellant's probation was revoked and he was ordered committed to prison for a period of five years.

---

1. It is "not a ground for revocation that a probationer has merely been *charged* with a crime." *United States v. Webster,* 492 F.2d 1048, 1051 (D.C.Cir.1974) (emphasis in original).

II

This court recently held that "[t]he standard of proof required [for probation revocation] is that evidence and facts be such as reasonably to satisfy the judge that the probationer's conduct has not been as required by [his] conditions of probation. The judge may revoke probation when reasonably satisfied that a [local,] state or federal law has been violated, and conviction is not essential." *United States v. Guadarrama*, 742 F.2d 487, 489 (9th Cir. 1984) (citations omitted); *accord United States v. Carrion*, 457 F.2d 808, 809 (9th Cir.1972).[2]

certified copy of a probationer's conviction in itself constitutes sufficient proof that a probationer has committed a crime in violation of the terms of his probation. *United States v. Lustig*, 555 F.2d 751, 753 (9th Cir.1977) (per curiam), *cert. denied*, 434 U.S. 1045, 98 S.Ct. 889, 54 L.Ed.2d 796 (1978). Here, certified copies of several Missouri convictions were introduced at the hearing to revoke appellant's probation.

Garcia contends that the Missouri convictions were invalid and may not, therefore, form the basis for revocation of probation, relying on *Boykin v. Alabama*, 395 U.S. 238, 89 S.Ct. 1709, 23 L.Ed.2d 274 (1969). He argues that the requirement in *Boykin* that the record affirmatively show that a guilty plea was intelligent and voluntary was not satisfied.

The question, however, is not whether the convictions or the guilty pleas on which they were based were valid. Garcia is not being punished for commission of those offenses; he has already been punished. The question is whether he should now receive the punishment to which he was sentenced for the RICO violation.

In *United States v. Lustig*, this court held that a probationer may not collaterally attack a prior conviction in a probation revocation hearing. 555 F.2d at 753. *See also United States v. Carrion*, 457 F.2d 808, 809 (9th Cir.1972) (per curiam). Lustig's prior convictions were said to pose "issues that are ... not properly before [the court] and may not here be asserted as grounds for reversing the district court's order...." 555 F.2d at 753. The reason for this rule is that the validity of the conviction furnishing a basis to revoke probation is not itself a prerequisite to revocation. "Probation may be revoked where the judge is reasonably satisfied that a state or federal law has been violated." *Id.*

The court in *Lustig* said nothing about the situation where the invalidity of prior convictions was alleged to be facially apparent. Even assuming, however, that the guilty pleas in this case were facially invalid, the admission of the resulting convictions at a subsequent probation revocation hearing as evidence that federal or state laws had been violated was not necessarily

2. In this case, a letter from Garcia's probation officer was submitted in addition to the Missouri convictions. The letter reported the convictions and provided additional information concerning the underlying offenses.

The record indicates, however, that the district court relied only upon the convictions in revoking probation. No mention is made of the probation officer's letter in the court's memorandum decision. In *Gagnon v. Scarpelli*, 411 U.S. 778, 93 S.Ct. 1756, 36 L.Ed.2d 279 (1973), the Supreme Court held that among the minimum elements of due process required in revoking probation was "'a written statement by the factfinders as to the evidence relied on and reasons for revoking [probation or] parole,'" *id.* at 786, 93 S.Ct. at 1761, *quoting Morrissey v. Brewer*, 408 U.S. 471, 489, 92 S.Ct. 2593, 2604, 33 L.Ed.2d 484 (1972). We must assume, there-

fore, that the letter was not among the evidence relied upon in revoking probation.

In probation revocation hearings, where the ultimate decision is "predictive and subjective in nature," *Black v. Romano*, — U.S —, 105 S.Ct. 2254, 2259, 85 L.Ed.2d 636 (1985), and the sentencing court is granted broad discretion, *United States v. Dane*, 570 F.2d 840, 843 (9th Cir.1977), *cert. denied*, 436 U.S. 959, 98 S.Ct. 3075, 57 L.Ed.2d 1124 (1978), the first inquiry of an appellate court should be into the admissibility and sufficiency of the evidence actually relied upon by the trier of fact. Only if that evidence is deficient should the court ascertain whether other evidence might have supported revocation and whether a remand is necessary in order for the district court to exercise its discretion upon the basis of that additional evidence.

foreclosed. As an initial matter, we note that the Federal Rules of Evidence concerned with the exclusion of hearsay and certain types of documents do not apply in probation revocation hearings. *See* Fed.R. Evid. 1101(d)(3).

We have also not been referred to any reason to believe that exclusion of the convictions as evidence in the federal courts would serve to deter the use of allegedly improper procedures by the Missouri judicial system. *Cf. United States v. Rea,* 678 F.2d 382, 388–90 (2d Cir.1982) (deterrence of future unlawful conduct held sufficient to exclude from a probation revocation hearing evidence seized by a probation officer in violation of the Fourth Amendment); *United States v. Vandemark,* 522 F.2d 1019, 1020–21 (9th Cir.1975); *United States v. Winsett,* 518 F.2d 51, 52–55 (9th Cir. 1975) (evidence obtained in violation of the Fourth Amendment is admissible in probation revocation proceedings if, at the time of the search, the law enforcement officers did not know or have reason to believe that the subject was on probation).

The crucial issue in this case is, therefore, whether the admission of the Missouri convictions is inconsistent with due process. Though probation revocation is not a stage of a criminal prosecution, it does result in a loss of liberty, *Gagnon v. Scarpelli,* 411 U.S. 778, 782, 93 S.Ct. 1756, 1759, 36 L.Ed.2d 656 (1973), and the probationer consequently cannot be denied due process. *Morrissey v. Brewer,* 408 U.S. 471, 482, 92 S.Ct. 2593, 2600, 33 L.Ed.2d 484 (1972). *See Gagnon,* 411 U.S. at 781–82, 93 S.Ct. at 1759; *United States v. Dane,* 570 F.2d 840, 843 (9th Cir.1977, *cert. denied,* 436 U.S. 959, 98 S.Ct. 3075, 57 L.Ed.2d 1124 (1978). In defining the scope of the due process protection in revocation proceedings, the Supreme Court has insisted upon procedural guarantees sufficient

to assure that the finding of a violation will be "based on verified facts and that the exercise of discretion will be informed by an accurate knowledge of the parolee's behavior." *Morrissey,* 408 U.S. at 484, 92 S.Ct. at 2601. *See Gagnon,* 411 U.S. at 785, 93 S.Ct. at 1761.

The evidence constituting the basis for the revocation of probation must, therefore, be reliable.[3] The absence of evidence of the voluntary and intelligent nature of a guilty plea raises doubts that the guilty plea was intelligent and voluntary. An innocent person may be coerced into pleading guilty or be led to believe that, by pleading guilty, he will obtain more sympathetic treatment.

It is noteworthy, however, that upon the introduction of the challenged evidence of probation violations, Garcia did not seek to rebut the assertion that he had committed the acts covered by the state convictions. He does not dispute that he had a full opportunity to show that he did not violate the conditions of probation. *See Black v. Romano,* — U.S. —, 105 S.Ct. 2254, 2258, 85 L.Ed.2d 636 (1985).

Instead, Garcia told the district court: When I walked out of prison ... I had dreams. I thought that things were going to turn out the way that others told me they were. The reality of it was no, they didn't. Mistakes were made along the way.... I realize that I made these mistakes. I'll pay the price if I have to.

Later, Garcia engaged in the following colloquy with the court:
The Court: [L]ife is stressful.... I get mad ... but I don't throw tires cut of windows. I don't spit on people. Do you see what I'm saying?
The Defendant: Yes, I do.

Further, the appellant pleaded guilty to varied offenses on a number of separate

---

3. This emphasis upon reliability is consistent with the approach taken by the Supreme Court in disallowing the use of *uncounseled* convictions in subsequent proceedings. The crucial factor in those cases was the belief that uncounseled convictions are not reliable as evidence in subsequent proceedings. *See Lewis v. United*

States, 445 U.S. 55, 67, 100 S.Ct. 915, 921, 63 L.Ed.2d 198 (1980); *Loper v. Beto,* 405 U.S. 473, 483–84, 92 S.Ct. 1014, 1019, 31 L.Ed.2d 374 (1972); *see also Linkletter v. Walker,* 381 U.S. 618, 639 and n. 20, 85 S.Ct. 1731, 1743 and n. 20, 14 L.Ed.2d 601 (1965).

dates before several different judges. He was arrested by a different police officer on each occasion. The likelihood that all of the guilty pleas were unreliable is, therefore, quite low.

The circumstances of this case indicate that the Missouri convictions were reliable evidence of law violations, and, consequently, their introduction into evidence did not violate due process. The district court could reasonably have concluded that state law had been violated and did not, therefore, abuse its discretion in revoking probation. *See United States v. Guadarrama*, 742 F.2d at 489.

Judgment affirmed.

PRISON LAW OFFICE, Plaintiff
and Appellant,

v.

Ronald KOENIG, as Chairman of the
California Board of Prison Terms et
al., Defendants and Respondents.

A026985.

Court of Appeal, First District,
Division 4.

Sept. 11, 1986.

Review Denied Dec. 31, 1986.

CHANNELL, Associate Justice.

In this case of first impression, appellant Prison Law Office challenges the constitutionality of Penal Code section 3003,[1] providing for return of a parolee to the county of his or her commitment when released on parole. The Prison Law Office contends that the trial court improperly granted summary judgment to respondent Ronald Koenig, Chairman of the Board of Prison Terms.[2] We find the provision constitutional on its face and thus affirm the judgment.

I. FACTS

After the Board of Prison Terms formulated a policy of releasing parolees to the county of commitment, appellant Prison Law Office brought an action to enjoin implementation of the policy on procedural grounds and to declare it unconstitutional as a matter of substantive law. Subsequently, the Legislature codified this policy in section 3003. (See Stats.1982, ch. 1407,

§ 1, pp. 5363–5364.) The new statute, rather than the policy, then became the focus of the litigation.[3]

After surviving a demurrer, the Prison Law Office requested that the Board produce documents and answer interrogatories, seeking certain factual information. The Board objected that the answers and documents sought were irrelevant to the sole issue in the case—the purely legal question of the constitutionality of section 3003. The trial court granted a motion to compel discovery. Before complying with the discovery order, the Board filed a motion for summary judgment; the Prison Law Office countered with a similar motion. After a hearing, the trial court granted the Board's motion, denied that made by the Prison Law Office, and dissolved the earlier order compelling discovery. The trial court later entered judgment on its summary judgment order. The Prison Law Office filed a timely appeal from that judgment.[4] The sole issue on

---

1. All statutory references are to the Penal Code, unless otherwise indicated.

2. Koenig, present Chairman of the California Board of Prison Terms, has been substituted for Raymond C. Brown and Albert Leddy, former Chairmen of the Board.

3. At this point, the procedural challenge to the Board policy became moot. The parties agree

that the sole issue on appeal is the substantive one—the constitutionality of section 3003.

4. Initially, the Prison Law Office appealed from an order denying its motion for summary judgment and granting the Board's motion for summary judgment. However, as an order granting summary judgment is not an appealable order (*Islander Yachts, Inc. v. One Freeport 36–Foot Vessel* (1985) 173 Cal.App.3d 1081, 1086, fn. 6, 219 Cal.Rptr. 654; see 9 Witkin, Cal. Procedure

appeal is whether section 3003,[5] providing for the return of a parolee to the county of commitment, is constitutional. The Prison Law Office contends both that its motion for summary judgment should have been granted and that the Board's motion should have been denied.[6]

II. TYPE OF CONSTITUTIONAL ATTACK

It is unclear from the record on appeal whether the Prison Law Office challenges section 3003 on its face or as applied. The Prison Law Office has consistently phrased its challenge in terms of a constitutional test concerning whether the requirement of a release to the county of commitment (1) bears any relationship to the crime for which the parolee was incarcerated, (2) relates to non-criminal conduct, and (3) requires or forbids conduct not reasonably related to future criminality. (See *People v. Dominguez* (1967) 256 Cal. App.2d 623, 627–628, 64 Cal.Rptr. 290; see also *People v. Knox* (1979) 95 Cal.App.3d 420, 427, 157 Cal.Rptr. 238 [*Dominguez* test held applicable to parole condition].) This standard may be appropriate to test a challenge to the application of section 3003 to a particular parolee under a particular

set of circumstances, but that is not the situation presented by this appeal. The Prison Law Office brought this action without alleging that the law had, in fact, been improperly applied to any particular parolee, nor does the complaint list any parolee as plaintiff. The complaint lists only two plaintiffs—a taxpayer who is not a party to this appeal and the Prison Law Office. The Prison Law Office amended its pleadings twice, but did not alter the thrust of its constitutional attack or attempt to add other plaintiffs. Therefore, we construe the Prison Law Office challenge as an attack only on the statute's facial constitutionality. On the Prison Law Office's petition for rehearing, we gave this question further consideration, but have come to the same conclusion.

The fact that the Prison Law Office does not have standing to raise a challenge to the application of section 3003 reinforces our conclusion. At trial, the Board demurred to the Prison Law Office's complaint on the ground that it had no standing to sue. The trial court overruled the demurrer and ruled for the Board on the merits. We still assume that the Prison Law Office had standing to make such a facial constitutional challenge. However,

---

(3d ed. 1985) Appeal, § 76, p. 100) and because no appealable final judgment had issued (see Cal. Rules of Court, rule 2(c)), we dismissed the appeal. Since that time, a judgment was issued. Under rule 2(c) of the California Rules of Court, we treat the notice of appeal, filed before judgment was rendered, as filed immediately after entry of judgment. (*Classen v. Weller* (1983) 145 Cal.App.3d 27, 34, fn. 1, 192 Cal.Rptr. 914.) On the parties' joint petition, we vacated our dismissal. We now proceed to determine the merits of this appeal.

5. Until July 1, 1986, section 3003 provided: "(a) An inmate who is released on parole shall be returned to the county from which he or she was committed. [¶] (b) Notwithstanding subdivision (a), an inmate may be returned to another county in a case where that would be in the best interests of the public and of the parolee. If the authority setting the conditions of parole decides on a return to another county, it shall place its reasons in writing in the parolee's permanent record. In making its decision, the authority may consider, among others, the following factors: [¶] (1) The need to protect the

life or safety of a victim, the parolee, a witness or any other person. [¶] (2) Public concern that would reduce the chance that the inmate's parole would be successfully completed. [¶] (3) The verified existence of a work offer, or an educational or vocational training program. [¶] (4) The last legal residence of the inmate having been in another county. [¶] (5) The existence of family in another county with whom the inmate has maintained strong ties and whose support would increase the chance that the inmate's parole would be successfully completed. [¶] (c) An inmate may be paroled to another state pursuant to any other provision of law." (See Stats.1982, ch. 1407, § 1, pp. 5363–5364.)

On July 1, 1986, an amended version of section 3003 took effect. (See Stats.1985, ch. 1419, §§ 2, 3.)

6. The fact that both parties moved for summary judgment, does not conclusively establish the absence of a triable issue of fact; the trial court must independently determine the motions. (*Trailer Train Co. v. State Bd. of Equalization* (1986) 180 Cal.App.3d 565, 580, fn. 10, 225 Cal. Rptr. 717.)

the Prison Law Office's request for rehearing—on the ground that it did, in fact, raise a challenge to the application of the statute—raises doubts about its standing to raise this type of challenge. The answers submitted to our request for letter briefs on the standing issue convince us that the Prison Law Office does not have standing to challenge the application of this provision. (See *In re Cregler* (1961) 56 Cal.2d 308, 313, 14 Cal.Rptr. 289, 363 P.2d 305; *City of Vallejo v. Adult Books* (1985) 167 Cal.App.3d 1169, 1175, 213 Cal.Rptr. 143, *cert. den.*, —U.S. ——, 106 S.Ct. 1374, 89 L.Ed.2d 601.)

III. CONSTITUTIONALITY

The pleadings and briefs, drafted in terms of the inapplicable *Dominguez* test, do not state explicitly the basis of the constitutional challenge (e.g., federal or state constitution, "equal protection" or "substantive due process," 14th Amend., etc.). Thus, we will interpret the constitutional challenge broadly. If the challenge is based on substantive due process (U.S. Const., 14th Amend.; Cal. Const., art. I, § 7), the statute must meet the rational basis test—it must not be unreasonable, arbitrary, or capricious, but must have a real and substantial relation to the object sought to be obtained. (*Goggin v. State Personnel Bd.* (1984) 156 Cal.App.3d 96, 107, 202 Cal.Rptr. 587; *Nebbia v. New York* (1934) 291 U.S. 502, 525, 54 S.Ct. 505, 510-11, 78 L.Ed. 940; see *West Coast Hotel Co. v. Parrish* (1937) 300 U.S. 379, 391, 57 S.Ct. 578, 581, 81 L.Ed. 703 [liberty may properly be restrained, consistent with due process, if restriction protects health, safety, morals, or welfare].) If we construe this as an equal protection challenge (U.S. Const., 14th Amend.; Cal. Const., art. I, § 7), the rational basis test requires that distinctions drawn by a challenged statute must bear some rational relationship to a conceivable state purpose. (*Goggin v. State Personnel Bd., supra*, 156 Cal.App.3d at p. 107, 202 Cal.Rptr. 587.) The goal of equal distribution of parolees throughout the state is a legitimate, reasonable state goal. The conclusion that the Legislature ap-

pears to have drawn—that to release parolees to the county of commitment will spread the parolee population throughout the state—is also reasonable. Under either substantive due process or equal protection analysis, section 3003 is constitutional. (*Ibid.*)

Section 3003 does not mandate return of a parolee to the commitment county in every case. The Legislature recognizes that the best interests of the public and the parolee may mandate release to another county—even to another state. (See § 3003, subds. (b), (c).) A non-inclusive list of factors—including the parolee's last legal residence, the county where the parolee has a verifiable work offer, and the county where the parolee's family resides—may be considered when the Board decides where the parolee should be released. (§ 3003, subd. (b)(3)-(5).) The Board's opportunity to consider these factors also supports the conclusion that section 3003 is a reasonable means to achieve the legitimate governmental ends of effective parole supervision and successful reintegration of parolees into society. Section 3003 is constitutional on its face.

Next, the Prison Law Office contends that we must subject section 3003 to "special scrutiny" because the statute burdens a parolee's fundamental rights, such as the right to intrastate travel, free speech, and free association. The cited California cases all refer to the rights of probationers, not the rights of parolees. Probation and parole are quite different concepts. "Probation involves *judicial* action taken before the prison door is closed, whereas parole involves *executive* action taken after the door has been closed on a convict." (*People v. Borja* (1980) 110 Cal. App.3d 378, 381, 167 Cal.Rptr. 813, emphasis in original.) Parole is the conditional release of a prisoner who has already served part of his or her state prison sentence. Once released from confinement, a prisoner on parole is not free from legal restraint, but is constructively a prisoner in the legal custody of state prison authorities until officially discharged from parole. (*Id.*, at p. 382, 167 Cal.Rptr. 813; see § 3056.) Clearly, the liberty of a parolee is "partial and restricted," (*People v. Denne* (1956) 141 Cal.App.2d 499, 508, 297 P.2d 451; see *People v. Anglin* (1971) 18 Cal.App.3d 92, 95, 95 Cal.Rptr. 588), not the equivalent of that of an average citizen (see *Morrissey v. Brewer* (1972) 408 U.S. 471, 482, 92 S.Ct. 2593, 2600–01, 33 L.Ed.2d 484), as the Prison Law Office seems to contend. Although a parolee is entitled to basic rights entitling him or her to constitutional protection against arbitrary or oppressive official action, a parolee's rights are not necessarily tested by the same rules that apply to citizens who are possessed of full civil rights. (*People v. Howard* (1978) 79 Cal. App.3d 46, 49, 143 Cal.Rptr. 342.) Insofar as is necessary for the maintenance of parole guardianship, the status of a parolee is no different than that of a prisoner. (*Ibid.; People v. Anglin, supra,* 18 Cal.App.3d at p. 95, 95 Cal.Rptr. 588.)

By allowing a parolee to serve the remainder of his or her sentence outside prison walls, the state does not relinquish its right to regulate the parolee's basic conduct during the remainder of the term of parole. By definition, a prisoner is one who must live within prison walls—one whose rights are severely restricted. (See § 2601.) Courts have traditionally recognized a state's right to require a parolee to live in a particular place. (See *Morrissey v. Brewer, supra,* 408 U.S. at p. 477, 92 S.Ct. at p. 2598; *In re Schoengarth* (1967) 66 Cal.2d 295, 300, 57 Cal.Rptr. 600, 425 P.2d 200; *In re Faucette* (1967) 253 Cal.App.2d 338, 341, 61 Cal.Rptr. 97 [parolee has no right to choose residence].) If the state may constitutionally restrict a prisoner's liberty by incarcerating him, and may require a parolee to live in a particular place during the parole period, then a statute specifying in which county a parolee will probably spend his or her term of parole also passes constitutional muster.

The Prison Law Office also suggests that the statute is overbroad. It poses a hypothetical situation in which the statute can be applied in violation of a parolee's constitutional rights, arguing that the statute must therefore be invalid. However, when a statute is attacked as unconstitutional on its face, the attacker cannot prevail by suggesting that, in some future hypothetical situation, constitutional problems may arise as to a particular application of the statute. Instead, the challenger must demonstrate that the act's provisions inevitably pose a present total and fatal conflict with applicable prohibitions. (*Pacific Legal Foundation v. Brown* (1981) 29 Cal.3d 168, 180–181, 172 Cal.Rptr. 487, 624 P.2d 1215; *People v. Harris* (1985) 165 Cal.App.3d 1246, 1255, 212 Cal.Rptr. 216.) The Prison Law Office has not done so.

As a procedural matter, a motion for summary judgment must be granted if there is no triable issue of material fact and the moving party is entitled to judgment as a matter of law. (Code Civ.Proc., § 437c, subd. (c); see *Coast-United Advertising, Inc. v. City of Long Beach* (1975) 51 Cal.App.3d 766, 769, 124 Cal.Rptr. 487; see also *Grant v. Avis Rent a Car System, Inc.* (1984) 158 Cal.App.3d 813, 816, 204 Cal.Rptr. 869.) Section 3003 is constitutional on its face; therefore, the trial court properly denied the Prison Law Office's motion for summary judgment.

[12] Finally, the Prison Law Office contends that, in order to determine the constitutionality of section 3003, certain factual questions must first be answered. it argues the trial court therefore erred when granting the Board's motion for summary judgment. However, this argument rests on its earlier assertion that the three-pronged, fact-specific *Dominguez* test applies. Having rejected this contention, we further reject the contention that the Prison Law Office must be allowed to complete discovery before the trial court could properly rule on the Board's motion for summary judgment, which presented only a question of law.

The judgment is affirmed.

ANDERSON, P.J., concurs.

POCHÉ, Associate Justice, concurring.

I concur in the result. I agree with the basic premise of my colleagues: the instant facial attack is not the proper method to raise constitutional challenges to Penal Code section 3003.[1] For all we know, 99.9 percent of prison inmates in this state are tried, convicted and committed from the county of their residence and hence under section 3003 are paroled back home, and the .1 percent of the inmates who commit crimes outside of their county residence are deemed by the Department of Corrections to fall outside of the presumption of section 3003 and are also paroled to their home county. Since such home town delivery would not support any constitutional objection to section 3003 that I am aware of, the statute must prevail over the general objection of the Prison Law Office. (Cf. *People v. Harris* (1985) 165 Cal.App.3d 1246, 1255–1256, 212 Cal.Rptr. 216 [and cases cited therein].)

I express no other opinion as to the constitutionality of the statute.

VOLUME IV

CHAPTER 5 SUPERVISION AND REVOCATION

Introductions in previous volumes:

John Larry RAY, Petitioner-Appellant,

v.

R.D. BREWER, Respondent-Appellee.

Darrell HILL, Petitioner-Appellant,

v.

Dutch BREWER, Warden, Federal Correctional Institution at Oxford, Wisconsin, Respondent-Appellee.

Nos. 85–1964, 86–1312.

United States Court of Appeals, Seventh Circuit.

Submitted Nov. 24, 1986.*

Decided Dec. 22, 1986.

Before CUMMINGS, CUDAHY, and MANION, Circuit Judges.

PER CURIAM.

At issue in these consolidated appeals is whether the habeas corpus petitioners were deprived without due process of the statutory good time awarded to them before their release on parole. In *Hill v. Brewer*, No. 86–1312, the district court vacated its earlier order granting the plaintiff's writ of habeas corpus and dismissed the petition. In *Ray v. Brewer*, No. 85–1964, the district court dismissed the habeas petition and denied petitioner's motion to vacate the dismissal. We affirm both orders for the following reasons.

I. FACTS

A. *Hill v. Brewer*

Petitioner Darrell Hill, an inmate at the Federal Correctional Institution at Oxford, Wisconsin, filed a petition for a writ of habeas corpus on August 6, 1984. He alleged that the forfeiture of his good time credits accompanying his parole revocation violated his right to due process. Hill claimed first that he did not receive notice that the forfeiture of the good time he had earned prior to parole release was one of the consequences of parole revocation. Second, he alleged that he did not have any opportunity to be heard in connection with the good time forfeiture. The respondents contended that the federal parole authorities treated previously-earned good time as "used up" once a prisoner was paroled or released. On April 21, 1985, the district court held that Hill had a right to notice and that a writ of habeas corpus would issue unless the respondents demonstrated that Hill had received such notice. The court granted the writ on May 3, 1985, but stayed the writ's execution for 90 days to give the respondents an opportunity to provide Hill with a forfeiture hearing, which was later given on August 1, 1985. The Parole Commission (Commission) again forfeited Hill's good-time credits.

On November 7, 1985, the court held that the pre-decisional component of the hearing was valid, but the court gave the respondents thirty days to show that the Commission properly exercised its discretion. On December 6, 1985, the respondents filed a photocopy of a declaration by Carol Pavilack Getty, the Regional Commissioner for the Northern Central Region of the U.S. Parole Commission. The court examined this declaration, and it subsequently held that because the Commission stated its reasons in acting, it thus properly exercised its discretion. Because this forfeiture hearing comported with due process, the district court vacated its earlier grant of Hill's petition.

---

* After preliminary examination of the briefs, the court notified the parties that it had tentatively concluded that oral argument would not be helpful to the court in this case. The notice provided that any party might file a "Statement as to Need of Oral Argument." *See* Rule 34(a), Fed.R.App.P.; Circuit Rule 14(f). No such statement having been filed, the appeal has been submitted on the briefs and record.

This same court recently examined an identical argument in *Conley v. Brewer*, 652 F.Supp. 106 (W.D.Wis.1986). Here, in denying the petition for habeas corpus, the court expressly overruled its opinion in *Hill* and accepted the Commission's justification for not notifying parolees that their good time will be unavailable to them if they are returned to prison to serve a parole violator term. *Conley*, at 110.

B. *Ray v. Brewer*

Ray also is currently confined at the same penitentiary as Hill. He is serving three sentences: (1) a parole violator term for an eighteen-year sentence imposed on April 23, 1971; (2) a three-year sentence imposed on July 28, 1981, to run consecutively to any previous sentence; and (3) a two-year sentence imposed on January 28, 1983, to run concurrently with any other sentence. Ray was paroled on September 18, 1978, and after he violated his parole, he was given a mandatory revocation hearing. While Ray was credited with all time served on parole, he was not credited for the good time earned prior to his release.

On February 25, 1985, Ray filed his petition for writ of habeas corpus claiming that he was deprived of his good time without a due process hearing. The district court dismissed his petition on April 22, 1985. It held that because good time is earned solely for purposes of an eventual release under 18 U.S.C. § 4163 or § 4164, since Ray chose *parole* release rather than release pursuant to § 4163 or § 4164, his statutory good time no longer existed.

When Ray moved to vacate this judgment on the ground that this decision conflicted with *Hill v. Brewer*, the court denied the motion and held that petitioner's parole revocation was sufficient as it was

procedurally more rigorous than that required for forfeiture of good-time credits under *Wolff v. McDonnell*, 418 U.S. 539, 94 S.Ct. 2963, 41 L.Ed.2d 935 (1974).

II. DISCUSSION

We believe that the district court's reasoning in *Conley v. Brewer*, 652 F.Supp. 106 (W.D.Wis.1986) is persuasive. The court in *Conley* pursued an administrative law analysis to give due deference to the Commission's interpretation of its authorizing statute. *See United States v. Clark*, 454 U.S. 555, 565, 102 S.Ct. 805, 811, 70 L.Ed.2d 768 (1982); *Brock v. Dow Chemical USA*, 801 F.2d 926 (7th Cir.1986). We must defer to an agency's construction of its regulation except where compelling indications show that this interpretation is wrong. *United Fire Ins. Co. v. CIR*, 768 F.2d 164 (7th Cir.1985). We find no such indications here.

On November 7, 1985, the Commission issued an interpretive regulation to explain the interaction between the prison good-time statutes, 18 U.S.C. § 4161 *et seq.*, and the parole statutes, 18 U.S.C. § 4201 *et seq.* This regulation [1] demonstrates the Commission's view that all pre-parole good time expires upon a prisoner's release. Noting that there was a controversy over whether pre-parole good-time credits were "used up" by the release of a prisoner on parole or were "forfeited" in connection with a parole revocation decision, the Commission announced its interpretation that the former parole statutes did not give the parole board authority to restore any pre-release good time credits of parole violators. This interpretation of the Commission is not so unreasonable as to mandate our rejection of its view. *See FEC v. Democratic Sena-*

---

1. The regulation provides:

It is the Commission's interpretation of the statutory scheme for parole and good time that the only function of good time credits is to determine the point in a prisoner's sentence when, in the absence of parole, the prisoner is to be conditionally released on supervision.... Once an offender is conditionally released from imprisonment either by

parole or mandatory release, the good time earned during that period of imprisonment is of no further effect either to shorten the period of supervision or to shorten the period of imprisonment which the offender may be required to serve for violation of parole or mandatory release.

28 C.F.R. § 2.35(b), as amended, 50 Fed.Reg. 46, 282 (November 7, 1985).

torial Campaign Committee, 454 U.S. 27, 39, 102 S.Ct. 38, 46, 70 L.Ed.2d 23 (1981). Because the Commission's position is based on a "permissible construction" of the statute, *Chevron, U.S.A., Inc. v. Natural Resources Defense Council,* 464 U.S. 927, 104 S.Ct. 329, 78 L.Ed.2d 300 (1983), we must conclude that the interpretation of good time as "used up" upon parole release is reasonable.

Under this construction, the Commission therefore had no duty to notify parolees that their good time will be unavailable to them if they are returned to prison to serve a parole violation term. Moreover, the Commission did not abuse its discretion. *Solomon v. Elsea,* 676 F.2d 282 (7th Cir.1982). Accordingly, since both Hill's and Ray's due process arguments must fail, we affirm the dismissals of their petitions for writs of habeas corpus.

AFFIRMED.

VOLUME IV

CHAPTER 6   PAROLE TERM, GOOD TIME, CONDITIONAL RELEASE

Introductions in previous volumes:

VOLUME IV

CHAPTER 7   PAROLE AND DETAINERS, PAROLE AND FINES

It is not uncommon for a prisoner to have pending against him a detainer for a parole violation or a charge for a crime committed in another state. The Interstate Agreement on Detainers is a compact approved by Congress that sets out the usual procedure for filing a detainer. In *Carchman v. Nash,* 105 S.Ct. 3401 (1985), the requirement of this agreement — that upon demand the defendant be tried within 180 days — was held not to apply in the parole revocation proceedings. The case is included.

Introductions in previous volumes:

IV: 401; VI: 587; VII: 535; VIII: 547

Philip S. CARCHMAN, Mercer County
Prosecutor, Petitioner,

v.

Richard NASH.

NEW JERSEY DEPARTMENT OF
CORRECTIONS, Petitioner,

v.

Richard NASH.

Nos. 84–776, 84–835.

Argued April 22, 1985.

Decided July 2, 1985.

*Syllabus**

Article III of the Interstate Agreement
on Detainers (Agreement), a congressionally sanctioned interstate compact, establishes a procedure by which a prisoner incarcerated in one State (the sending State)
may demand the speedy disposition of "any
untried indictment, information or complaint" that is the basis of a detainer
lodged against him by another State (the
receiving State). If the prisoner makes
such a demand, Art. III requires the authorities in the receiving State to bring him
to trial within 180 days or the court must
dismiss the indictment, information, or
complaint, and the detainer will cease to be
of any force or effect. Respondent was
convicted on criminal charges in New Jersey Superior Court, which imposed prison
sentences and a 2-year term of probation to
follow imprisonment. Thereafter, while on
probation, respondent was charged with
criminal offenses in Pennsylvania and was
convicted and sentenced to prison there.
While he was awaiting trial in Pennsylva-

nia, the New Jersey authorities notified the New Jersey Superior Court that he had violated his probation by committing offenses in Pennsylvania, and that court issued an arrest warrant, which was lodged as a detainer with the corrections officials in Pennsylvania. Although respondent requested New Jersey officials to make a final disposition of the probation-violation charge, that State failed to bring him to trial within 180 days. Respondent then brought a habeas corpus petition in Federal District Court seeking dismissal of the probation-violation charge on the basis of New Jersey's noncompliance with Art. III. The District Court stayed respondent's federal action pending exhaustion of state court remedies. After the New Jersey courts denied respondent relief under the Agreement, revoked his probation, and resentenced him to a term of imprisonment, the District Court granted respondent's petition for a writ of habeas corpus. The Court of Appeals affirmed, holding that an outstanding probation-violation charge is an "untried indictment, information or complaint" within the meaning of Art. III.

Held: Article III does not apply to detainers based on probation-violation charges. Pp. 3405–3411.

(a) The language of the Agreement indicates that Art. III applies solely to detainers based on outstanding criminal charges. Article III by its terms applies to detainers based on an "indictment," "information," or "complaint." The most natural interpretation of these terms is that they refer to documents charging an individual with having committed a criminal offense. This interpretation is reinforced by the adjective "untried," by the requirement that the prisoner promptly be "brought to trial," and by the limitation that the receiving State obtains custody "only for the purpose of permitting prosecution" on the charges. A probation-violation charge does not accuse an individual with having committed a criminal offense in the sense of initiating a prosecution. Although such a charge might be based on the commission of a criminal offense, it does not result in the probationer's being "prosecuted" or "brought to trial" for that offense. Nor does it result in the probationer's being "prosecuted" or "brought to trial" on the offense for which he initially was sentenced to probation, since he already will have been tried and convicted of that offense. Accordingly, a detainer based on a probation-revocation charge does not come within the plain language of the Agreement. Pp. 3405–3407.

(b) The legislative history created by the Council of State Governments, the drafter of the Agreement, does not directly address the issue in this case and does not support the inference that the Council intended Art. III to apply to detainers based on probation-violation charges. And the congressional history indicates that Congress, which adopted the Agreement, considered it to apply only to detainers based on untried criminal charges. Pp. 3407–3408.

(c) The purposes of the Agreement, including the purpose of enabling prisoners to obtain prompt disposition of charges underlying detainers in order to protect them from the adverse consequences that detainers have on their treatment and rehabilitation, do not compel the conclusion that, contrary to the Agreement's plain language, Art. III was intended to apply to probation-violation detainers. Such purposes are significantly less directly advanced by application of Art. III to probation-violation detainers than by its application to criminal-charge detainers. Pp. 3408–3411.

739 F.2d 878 (CA3 1984), reversed.

———————

Philip S. Carchman, Princeton, N.J., for petitioners in both cases.

John Burke, III, Alexandria, Va., for respondent in both cases, pro hac vice, by special leave of Court.

Justice BLACKMUN delivered the opinion of the Court.

Article III of the Interstate Agreement on Detainers gives a prisoner incarcerated in one State the right to demand the speedy disposition of "any untried indictment, information or complaint" that is the basis of a detainer lodged against him by another State. These cases present the issue whether Art. III applies to detainers based on probation-violation charges.

I

The Interstate Agreement on Detainers (Agreement) is a compact among 48 States, the District of Columbia, Puerto Rico, the Virgin Islands, and the United States. The Agreement was drafted in 1956 by the Council of State Governments and was adopted in 1958 by the State of New Jersey, where it is now codified as N.J.Stat.Ann. §§ 2A:159A–1 et seq. (West 1971). The Agreement is a congressionally sanctioned interstate compact within the Compact Clause, U.S.Const., Art. I, § 10, cl. 3, and thus is a federal law subject to federal construction. Cuyler v. Adams, 449 U.S. 433, 438–442, 101 S.Ct. 703, 706–708, 66 L.Ed.2d 641 (1981).

A detainer is a request filed by a criminal justice agency with the institution in which a prisoner is incarcerated, asking the institution either to hold the prisoner for the agency or to notify the agency when release of the prisoner is imminent. See id., at 436, n. 3, 101 S.Ct., at 706, n. 3 (citing and quoting H.R.Rep. No. 91–1018, p. 2 (1970), and S.Rep. No. 91–1356, p. 2 (1970)), U.S.Code Cong. & Admin.News 1970, p. 4864; United States v. Mauro, 436 U.S. 340, 359, 98 S.Ct. 1834, 1846, 56 L.Ed.2d 329 (1978); Moody v. Daggett, 429 U.S. 78, 80–81, n. 2, 97 S.Ct. 274, 275, n. 2, 50 L.Ed.2d 236 (1976); Council of State Governments, Suggested State Legislation, Program for 1957, p. 74 (1956). Detainers generally are based on outstanding criminal charges, outstanding parole or probation violation charges, or additional sentences already imposed against the prisoner. See Dauber, Reforming the Detainer System: A Case Study, 7 Crim.L.Bull. 669, 676 (1971). See generally L. Abramson, Criminal Detainers (1979).

The Agreement is based on a legislative finding that "charges outstanding against a prisoner, detainers based on untried indictments, informations or complaints, and difficulties in securing speedy trial of persons already incarcerated in other jurisdictions, produce uncertainties which obstruct programs of prisoner treatment and rehabilitation." Art. I. As has been explained:

"The inmate who has a detainer against him is filled with anxiety and apprehension and frequently does not respond to a training program. He often must be kept in close custody, which bars him from treatment such as trustyships, moderations of custody and opportunity for transfer to farms and work camps. In many jurisdictions he is not eligible for parole; there is little hope for his release after an optimum period of training and treatment, when he is ready for return to society with an excellent possibility that he will not offend again. Instead, he often becomes embittered with continued institutionalization and the objective of the correctional system is defeated." Council of State Governments, Suggested State Legislation, Program for 1957, p. 74 (1956).

See also Cuyler v. Adams, 449 U.S., at 449, 101 S.Ct., at 712; United States v. Mauro, 436 U.S., at 353, 356, 359–360, 98 S.Ct., at 1843, 1845, 1846–1847. Accordingly, the purpose of the Agreement is "to encourage the expeditious and orderly disposition of [outstanding] charges and determination of the proper status of any and all detainers based on untried indictments, informations or complaints." Art. I.

To achieve this purpose, Art. III of the Agreement establishes a procedure by which a prisoner incarcerated in one party State (the sending State) may demand the speedy disposition of "any untried indictment, information or complaint on the basis of which a detainer has been lodged against the prisoner"[1] by another party State (the receiving State). Specifically, Art. III requires the warden to inform the prisoner that a detainer has been lodged against him and that he may request final disposition of the indictment, information, or complaint upon which the detainer is based. If the prisoner makes such a request, the warden must forward it, together with a certificate providing certain information about the prisoner's terms of confinement, to the appropriate prosecuting official and court of the receiving State. The authorities in the receiving State then must bring the prisoner to trial within 180 days, absent good cause shown, or the court must dismiss the indictment, information, or complaint with prejudice, and the detainer will cease to be of any force or effect.

II

On June 21, 1976, respondent Richard Nash, in the Superior Court of New Jersey, Law Division, Mercer County, pleaded guilty to charges of breaking and entering with intent to rape, and of assault with intent to rape. On October 29, the Superior Court sentenced respondent to 18 months in prison on each count, with the sentences to run consecutively. The court suspended two years of the sentences and imposed a 2-year term of probation to follow respondent's imprisonment. On June 13, 1978, while on probation, respondent was arrested in Montgomery County, Pa., and charged with burglary, involuntary deviate sexual intercourse, and loitering. Respondent was tried and convicted on the Pennsylvania charges on March 14, 1979, and was sentenced on July 13 of that year.

While respondent was awaiting trial in Pennsylvania, the Mercer County Probation Department, on June 21, 1978, notified the Superior Court that respondent had violated his probation by committing offenses in Pennsylvania. At the Department's request, the Superior Court issued a bench warrant for respondent's arrest. The warrant was lodged as a detainer with the appropriate corrections officials in Pennsylvania.

Beginning on April 13, 1979, respondent sent a series of letters to New Jersey officials requesting final disposition of the probation-violation charge. The State of New Jersey failed to bring respondent "to trial" on the probation-violation charge within 180 days after Art. III was invoked.

On March 6, 1980, respondent filed a petition for a writ of habeas corpus in the United States District Court for the Middle District of Pennsylvania seeking dismissal of the probation-violation charge on the basis of the State's noncompliance with Art. III. The case was transferred, pursuant to 28 U.S.C. § 1406(a), to the United States District Court for the District of New Jersey. App. to Pet. for Cert. in No. 84-776, p. 101. That court stayed respondent's federal action pending exhaustion of state court remedies. *Id.*, at 81.

Respondent then petitioned for a writ of habeas corpus in New Jersey Superior Court. The Superior Court denied respondent's motion to dismiss the probation-violation charge, ruled that respondent's Pennsylvania convictions constituted a probation violation, and ordered respondent to serve the two consecutive 18-month sentences on his New Jersey convictions, with credit for 249 days respondent had served

---

1. Article III(a) provides in pertinent part:

   "Whenever a person has entered upon a term of imprisonment in a penal or correctional institution of a party State, and whenever during the continuance of the term of imprisonment there is pending in any other party State any untried indictment, information or complaint on the basis of which a detainer has been lodged against the prisoner, he shall be brought to trial within 180 days after he shall have

caused to be delivered to the prosecuting officer and the appropriate court of the prosecuting officer's jurisdiction written notice of the place of his imprisonment and his request for final disposition to be made of the indictment, information or complaint: provided that for good cause shown in open court, the prisoner or his counsel being present, the court having jurisdiction of the matter may grant any necessary or reasonable continuance."

in 1976 and 1977. The Appellate Division affirmed the trial court's judgment, *id.*, at 44, and the New Jersey Supreme Court denied certification. *Id.*, at 43.

Respondent then returned to the United States District Court for the District of New Jersey. On March 21, 1983, the District Court granted the petition for a writ of habeas corpus, vacated respondent's probation revocation, and ordered his release from state custody.[2] 558 F.Supp. 641 (1983). Petitioner Philip S. Carchman, the Mercer County prosecutor, took an appeal to the United States Court of Appeals for the Third Circuit. Petitioner State of New Jersey, Department of Corrections, at this point sought to intervene because the District Court's decision invalidated its policy that parole- and probation-violation detainers do not fall within Art. III of the Agreement. Its motion to intervene was granted by the Court of Appeals. App. to Pet. for Cert. in — U.S. —, p. —, 105 S.Ct. 2014, p. —, 85 L.Ed.2d 296.

The Court of Appeals affirmed, holding that an outstanding probation-violation charge is an "untried indictment, information or complaint" within the meaning of Art. III of the Agreement.[3] *Nash v. Jeffes,* 739 F.2d 878 (1984). In reaching its decision, the Court of Appeals "decline[d] to adopt a technical interpretation of the relevant language of Art. III," *id.*, at 883, and instead relied on "the broader purposes of the legislation." *Id.*, at 882. The court reasoned that a principal purpose of Art. III is to enable prisoners to obtain prompt disposition of the charges underlying detainers in order to protect them from the

adverse consequences that detainers have on their treatment and rehabilitation, and that this purpose would be furthered by applying Art. III to detainers based on probation-violation charges. The Court of Appeals completed its "policy analysis," *id.*, at 883, n. 9, by concluding that the benefit to prisoners of applying Art. III to probation-violation detainers would outweigh the administrative burdens, including additional paperwork and the cost of transporting prisoners in order to provide them with probation-revocation hearings.

In view of the conflict, see n. 3, *supra,* we granted certiorari. 469 U.S. —, 105 S.Ct. 902, 83 L.Ed.2d 917 (1985).

III

A

We begin by considering the language of the Agreement. Article III by its terms applies to detainers based on "any untried indictment, information or complaint." The most natural interpretation of the words "indictment," "information," and "complaint" is that they refer to documents charging an individual with having committed a criminal offense. See Fed.Rules Crim.Proc. 3 (complaint) and 7 (indictment and information). This interpretation is reinforced by the adjective "untried," which would seem to refer to matters that can be brought to full trial, and by Article III's requirement that a prisoner who requests final disposition of the indictment, information, or complaint "shall be *brought to trial* within 180 days." (Emphasis added.)

---

2. The District Court ruled that respondent's letters requesting disposition of the detainer were sufficient to invoke Art. III, even though they did not strictly comply with Art. III's request procedures. The Court of Appeals affirmed that ruling. We assume, without deciding, that this ruling on the issue whether respondent complied with the procedures of Art. III is correct.

3. This holding conflicts with rulings of the United States Court of Appeals for the Ninth Circuit and of four state courts of last resort. See *United States v. Roach,* 745 F.2d 1252 (CA9 1984);. *Padilla v. Arkansas,* 279 Ark. 100, 648

S.W.2d 797 (1983); *Suggs v. Hopper,* 234 Ga. 242, 215 S.E.2d 246 (1975); *Clipper v. Maryland,* 295 Md. 303, 455 A.2d 973 (1983); *State v. Knowles,* 275 S.C. 312, 270 S.E.2d 133 (1980). It also conflicts with rulings of several intermediate state appellate courts. See, *e.g., People v. Jackson,* 626 P.2d 723 (Colo.App.1981); *People ex rel. Capalongo v. Howard,* 87 App.Div.2d 242, 453 N.Y.S.2d 45 (1982); *Blackwell v. State,* 546 S.W.2d 828 (Tenn.Crim.App.1976). See *Nash v. Jeffes,* 739 F.2d 878, 881, n. 4 (CA3 1984) (citing cases involving parole-and probation-violation detainers).

The language of Art. V also indicates that Art. III should be interpreted to apply solely to criminal charges. Article V(a) provides: "In response to a request made under Article III or Article IV hereof, the appropriate authority in a sending State shall offer to deliver temporary custody of such prisoner to the appropriate authority in the State where such indictment, information or complaint is pending against such person in order that speedy and efficient *prosecution* may be had." (Emphasis added.) Article V(c) provides that "in the event that an action on the indictment, information or complaint on the basis of which the detainer has been lodged is not *brought to trial* within the period provided in Article III or Article IV hereof, the appropriate court of the jurisdiction where the indictment, information or complaint has been pending shall enter an order dismissing the same with prejudice, and any detainer based thereon shall cease to be of any force or effect." (Emphasis added.) Finally, Art. V(d) provides: "The temporary custody referred to in this agreement shall be only for the purpose of permitting *prosecution* on the charge or charges contained in 1 or more untried indictments, informations or complaints which form the basis of the detainer or detainers or for *prosecution* of any other charge or charges arising out of the same transaction." (Emphasis added.)

The language of the Agreement therefore makes clear that the phrase "untried indictment, information or complaint" in Art. III refers to criminal charges pending against a prisoner. A probation-violation charge, which does not accuse an individual with having committed a criminal offense in the sense of initiating a prosecution, thus does not come within the terms of Art. III. Although the probation-violation charge might be based on the commission of a criminal offense, it does not result in the probationer's being "prosecuted" or "brought to trial" for that offense. In-

deed, in the context of the Agreement, the probation-violation charge generally will be based on the criminal offense for which the probationer already was tried and convicted and is serving his sentence in the sending State.

Nor, of course, will the probationer be "prosecuted" or "brought to trial" on the criminal offense for which he initially was sentenced to probation, since he already will have been tried and convicted for that offense. Instead, the probation-violation charge results in a probation-revocation hearing, a proceeding to determine whether the conditions of probation should be modified or the probationer should be resentenced, at which the probationer is entitled to less than the full panoply of due process rights accorded a defendant at a criminal trial. See *Gagnon v. Scarpelli*, 411 U.S. 778, 93 S.Ct. 1756, 36 L.Ed.2d 656 (1973). Cf. *Morrissey v. Brewer*, 408 U.S. 471, 92 S.Ct. 2593, 33 L.Ed.2d 484 (1972) (parole-revocation hearing).

Respondent contends that Art. III applies to more than just criminal charges, relying principally on the language of Art. I, which provides: "The party States find that *charges outstanding against a prisoner*, detainers based on untried indictments, informations or complaints, and difficulties in securing speedy trial of persons already incarcerated in other jurisdictions, produce uncertainties which obstruct programs of prisoner treatment and rehabilitation." (Emphasis added.) According to respondent, this language indicates that the drafters intended the Agreement to apply, literally, to all "charges outstanding against a prisoner," including a probation-violation charge. However, when this language which appears in the legislative declaration of purpose, is read in the context of the operative language of Arts. III and V discussed above, it is clear that the drafters meant the term "charges" to refer to criminal charges.[4]

4. Even if the term "charges" in Art. I were interpreted to refer to all charges, under normal

rules of statutory construction the specific lan-

We therefore conclude from the language of the Agreement that a detainer based on a probation-violation charge is not a detainer based on "any untried indictment, information or complaint," within the meaning of Art. III.

B

The legislative history of the Agreement does not persuade us to depart from what appears to be the plain language of the Agreement. Respondent relies principally on the following passage from comments made by the Council of State Governments, which drafted the Agreement:

"A detainer may be defined as a warrant filed against a person already in custody with the purpose of insuring that he will be available to the authority which has placed the detainer. Wardens of institutions holding men who have detainers on them invariably recognize these warrants and notify the authorities placing them of the impending release of the prisoner. Such detainers may be placed by various authorities under varying conditions, for example, when an escaped prisoner or *a parolee commits a new crime and is imprisoned in another state;* or where a man not previously imprisoned commits a series of crimes in different jurisdictions." Council of State Governments, Suggested State Legislation, Program for 1957, p. 74 (1956) (emphasis added).

This passage is the introductory paragraph of the Council's discussion of the suggested legislation. It was intended to provide a general definition of detainers and a brief description of how they might arise. The italicized passage suggests that some detainers arise from parole-violation charges, a fact not in dispute here. By its terms, however, Art. III does not apply to all detainers, but only to those based on "any untried indictment, information or complaint." [5] The above passage does not illuminate, or purport to illuminate, the scope of this phrase.

Indeed, if the above passage were interpreted to define the scope of Art. III, it would lead to the conclusion that Art. III applies to *parole*-violation detainers. This conclusion is difficult to reconcile with the procedures established by the Agreement. In particular, the prisoner invokes Art. III by "caus[ing] to be delivered *to the prosecuting officer and the appropriate court of the prosecuting officer's jurisdiction* written notice of the place of his imprisonment and his request for a final disposition to be made of the indictment, information or complaint." (Emphasis added.) This notification mechanism is efficacious in the case of criminal-charge detainers, but not in the case of parole-violation detainers, because prosecutors and judges generally are not involved in parole-revocation proceedings. If the drafters of the Agreement had intended Art. III to apply to parole-violation detainers, they likely would have devised a more appropriate notification mechanism. Furthermore, Art. III(d) provides that if the prisoner is returned to the original place of imprisonment without being tried on any indictment, information, or complaint, "the *court* shall enter an order dismissing the [indictment, information, or complaint] with prejudice." Similarly, Art. V(c) provides that if the prisoner is not brought to trial within the period provided in Art. III, "*the appropriate court of the jurisdiction* where the indictment, information or complaint has been pending shall enter an order dismissing the same with prejudice." (Emphasis added.) It is difficult to understand how these provisions would apply in the context of parole-violation charges, which generally are issued and adjudicated by a parole board or similar administrative agency, and are not "pending" in any court.

---

guage of Art. III would control over the general language of Art. I.

5. For example, Art. III clearly does not apply to a detainer based on an additional sentence already imposed against the prisoner.

We therefore conclude that the reference to parolees in the comments of the Council of State Governments does not support the inference that in drafting the Agreement the Council intended the scope of Art. III to include detainers based on parole- or probation-violation charges.

In contrast to the legislative history created by the Council of State Governments, which does not directly address the precise issue in this case, the congressional legislative history indicates that Congress, which adopted the Agreement in 1970, see Pub.L. 91–538, 84 Stat. 1397, considered the Agreement to apply only to detainers based on untried criminal charges. The Court noted in *United States v. Mauro*, 436 U.S., at 359, 98 S.Ct., at 1846, and in *Cuyler v. Adams*, 449 U.S., at 436, n. 3, 101 S.Ct., at 706, n. 3, that the House and Senate Reports on the Agreement explain: "A detainer is a notification filed with the institution in which a prisoner is serving a sentence, advising that he is wanted to face pending *criminal charges* in another jurisdiction." H.R.Rep. No. 91–1018, p. 2 (1970); S.Rep. No. 91–1356, p. 2 (1970) (emphasis added), U.S.Code Cong. & Admin.News 1970, p. 4865. The Congressional Reports also contain references to the prisoner's being "convicted on the new charges." H.R.Rep. No. 91–1018, at 2; S.Rep. No. 91–1356, at 2,

U.S.Code Cong. & Admin.News 1970, p. 4865. In addition, Senator Hruska stated in the congressional debates on the Agreement: "At the heart of this measure is the proposition that a person should be entitled to have *criminal charges* pending against him determined in an expeditious fashion." 116 Cong.Rec. 38840 (1970) (emphasis added).

C

As noted, the Court of Appeals said its decision was based not on "a technical interpretation of the relevant language of Art. III," 739 F.2d, at 883, nor on any statements in the legislative history addressing the specific issue in this case, but rather on "the broader purposes of the legislation," *id.*, at 882. We do not find that these purposes compel the conclusion that, contrary to the plain language of the Agreement, Art. III was intended to apply to probation-violation detainers.

Adoption of the Agreement was motivated in part by a practice of filing detainers based on untried criminal charges that had little basis.[*] These detainers often would be withdrawn shortly before the prisoner was released.[7] Even though unsubstantiated, the detainers would have a detrimental effect on the prisoner's treatment.[8] Ar-

---

6. One commentator has noted:
"Since the legal basis for a detainer is rarely examined, a prisoner can suffer loss of privileges and parole because of a charge for which there is not sufficient proof to obtain an indictment. Undoubtedly, detainers are sometimes used by prosecutors to exact punishment without having to try a charge which they feel would not result in a conviction." Note, Detainers and the Correctional Process, 4 Wash.U.L.Q. 417, 423 (1966) (footnote omitted).
See also *United States v. Mauro*, 436 U.S. 340, 358, and n. 25, 98 S.Ct. 1834, 1846, and n. 25, 56 L.Ed.2d 329 (1978) (noting that, because of the informality of the detainer system, detainers may be filed groundlessly or even in bad faith). The Congressional Reports note that the Agreement provides the prisoner "with a procedure for bringing about a prompt test of the substantiality of detainers placed against him by other jurisdictions." H.R.Rep. No. 91–1018, p. 2 (1970); S.Rep. No. 91–1356, p. 2 (1970), U.S. Code Cong. & Admin.News 1970, p. 4865.

7. According to the Congressional Reports, "a majority of detainers filed by States are withdrawn near the conclusion of the Federal sentence." H.R.Rep. No. 91–1018, at 3; S.Rep. No. 91–1356, at 3, U.S.Code Cong. & Admin.News 1970, p. 4866.

8. The United States Court of Appeals for the Eighth Circuit has described these effects as follows:
"[T]he inmate is (1) deprived of an opportunity to obtain a sentence to run concurrently with the sentence being served at the time the detainer is filed; (2) classified as a maximum or close custody risk; (3) ineligible for initial assignments to less than maximum security prisons (i.e., honor farms or forestry camp work); (4) ineligible for trustee [*sic*] status; (5) not allowed to live in preferred living quarters such as dormitories; (6) ineligible for study-release programs or work-release programs; (7) ineligible to be transferred to preferred medium or minimum custody institutions within the cor-

ticle III enables a prisoner to require the State lodging the detainer either to drop the charge and resulting detainer or to bring the prisoner to trial. In this way, the prisoner can clear his record of detainers based on unsubstantiated charges.

A probation-violation detainer, however, generally, as in the present case, will be based on the prisoner's commission of the crimes that resulted in his conviction and incarceration in the sending State.[9] Because the convictions conclusively establish the probation violation, see *Morrissey v. Brewer*, 408 U.S., at 490, 92 S.Ct., at 2604 (parole revocation hearing), the probation-violation charge will not be unsubstantiated. Thus, the abuses that in part motivated adoption of the Agreement generally do not occur in the context of probation-violation detainers.

The Agreement generally seeks "to encourage the expeditious and orderly disposition of [outstanding] charges,"[10] as well as the prompt "determination of the proper status of any and all detainers based on untried indictments, informations and complaints," in order to eliminate "uncertainties which obstruct programs of prisoner treatment and rehabilitation." Art. I. The uncertainties associated with probation-violation detainers, however, are less severe than the uncertainties associated with criminal-charge detainers. See Dauber, Reforming the Detainer System: A Case Study, 7 Crim.L.Bull. 669, 680 (1971) (parole- and probation-violation detainers involve less uncertainty than criminal-charge detainers). As noted above, in general the factual issue of guilt of the probation violation is conclusively established by the convictions leading to incarceration in the sending State. Disposition of the probation-violation charge underlying a detainer therefore often will result in probation being revoked and in the probationer's being resentenced to imprisonment in the receiv-

rectional system, which includes the removal of any possibility of transfer to an institution more appropriate for youthful offenders; (8) not entitled to preferred prison jobs which carry higher wages and entitle [him] to additional good time credits against [his] sentence; (9) inhibited by the denial of possibility of parole or any commutation of his sentence; (10) caused anxiety and thus hindered in the overall rehabilitation process since he cannot take maximum advantage of his institutional opportunities." *Cooper v. Lockhart*, 489 F.2d 308, 314, n. 10 (8th Cir. 1973).

9. See Brief for University of Virginia School of Law Post-Conviction Assistance Project as *Amicus Curiae* 30–31 ("[I]n most cases the conviction for which the prisoner is serving a sentence will be conclusive proof of the violation"). Although a probation-violation detainer initially might be based on an arrest, the probationer cannot invoke Art. III until he "has entered upon a term of imprisonment in a penal or correctional institution of a party State"—that is, until he has been convicted of the offense in the sending State and commenced to serve his sentence there.

10. The Court of Appeals suggested that the Agreement serves "to vindicate a prisoner's constitutional right to a speedy trial," 739 F.2d, at 883, but noted that this purpose is "not usually relevant when probation violations are involved." *Id.*, at 882. Some 13 years after the

Agreement was drafted, this Court ruled that the Sixth Amendment right to a speedy trial entitles a prisoner in a federal penitentiary who is subject to pending state criminal charges to have the State, upon demand, make a diligent, good-faith effort to bring him to trial within a reasonable time. *Smith v. Hooey*, 393 U.S. 374, 89 S.Ct. 575, 21 L.Ed.2d 607 (1969). The Congressional Reports discuss *Smith v. Hooey* and explain that enactment of the Agreement by Congress "would afford defendants in criminal cases the right to a speedy trial and diminish the possibility of convictions being vacated or reversed because of a denial of this right." S.Rep. No. 91–1356, p. 2, U.S.Code Cong. & Admin. News 1970, p. 4864. See also H.R.Rep. No. 91–1018, pp. 1–2; 116 Cong.Rec. 14,000 (1970) (remarks of Rep. Poff); *id.*, at 38,840 (remarks of Sen. Hruska). Thus, Congress, at least, enacted the Agreement in part to vindicate a prisoner's constitutional right to a speedy trial. This Court has never held, however, that a prisoner subject to a probation-violation detainer has a constitutional right to a speedy probation-revocation hearing. Cf. *Moody v. Daggett*, 429 U.S. 78, 97 S.Ct. 274, 50 L.Ed.2d 236 (1976) (a prisoner in a federal penitentiary who is subject to a federal parole-violation detainer is not constitutionally entitled to a prompt parole-revocation hearing). Thus, as the Court of Appeals suggested, it is not clear that the purpose of vindicating a prisoner's constitutional right to a speedy trial is applicable at all in the context of probation-violation detainers.

ing State. See *Moody v. Daggett*, 429 U.S. 78, 89, 97 S.Ct. 274, 279, 50 L.Ed.2d 236 (1976) (parole violation); L. Abramson, Criminal Detainers 64–65, 81 (1979). The ultimate consequence is that the detainer based on the probation-violation charge merely will be replaced by a detainer based on the reimposed sentence, with similar adverse effects on the prisoner's treatment and rehabilitation. See Dauber, *supra*, at 678–679. Since the probation revocation is based on commission of a crime serious enough to warrant incarceration in the sending State, the probationer no doubt often, as in the present case, will be sentenced to serve the full term of his suspended sentence. Thus, the uncertainties in the underlying charge, in the likelihood of the prisoner's receiving an additional sentence, and in the length of incarceration generally are less in the case of probation-violation detainers than in the case of criminal-charge detainers. Moreover, because the prisoner may not relitigate the factual issue of guilt of the probation-violation charge when it is established by a conviction in the sending State, see *Morrissey v. Brewer*, 408 U.S., at 490, 92 S.Ct., at 2604, the "most serious," see *Barker v. Wingo*, 407 U.S. 514, 532, 92 S.Ct. 2182, 2193, 33 L.Ed.2d 101 (1972), of the interests of the accused in obtaining a speedy disposition of outstanding criminal charges—the interest in " 'limit[ing] the possibilities that long delay will impair [his] ability ... to defend himself,' " *Smith v. Hooey*, 393 U.S., at 378, 89 S.Ct., at 577, quoting *United States v. Ewell*, 383 U.S. 116, 120, 86 S.Ct. 773, 776, 15 L.Ed.2d 627 (1966)—is unlikely to be strongly implicated in the probation-violation detainer context.

Indeed, it often may be desirable to delay rather than to expedite disposition of the probation-violation charge. As the Court explained in *Moody v. Daggett*, 429 U.S. 78, 97 S.Ct. 274, 50 L.Ed.2d 236 (1976), in the context of parole violations:

"[I]n cases such as this, in which the parolee admits or has been convicted of an offense plainly constituting a parole violation, the only remaining inquiry is whether continued release is justified notwithstanding the violation. This is uniquely a 'prediction as to the ability of the individual to live in society without committing antisocial acts.' *Morrissey, supra* [408 U.S.], at 480 [92 S.Ct., at 2599]. In making this prophecy, a parolee's institutional record can be perhaps one of the most significant factors. Forcing decision immediately after imprisonment would not only deprive the parole authority of this vital information, but since the other most salient factor would be the parolee's recent convictions, ... a decision to revoke parole would often be foreordained. Given the predictive nature of the hearing, it is appropriate that such hearing be held at the time at which prediction is both most relevant and most accurate—at the expiration of the parolee's intervening sentence." *Id.*, at 89., 97 S.Ct., at 279–280.

Of course, the decision whether to request expeditious disposition lies with the prisoner, and there are circumstances under which the prisoner may have a legitimate interest in obtaining prompt disposition of a probation-violation charge underlying a detainer. For example, the prisoner may believe that he can present mitigating evidence that will lead to a decision not to revoke probation. Alternatively, he may hope for the imposition of a concurrent sentence. Finally, he simply may prefer the certainty of a known sentence to the relative uncertainty of a pending probation-violation charge.

Nevertheless, as discussed above, the purposes of the Agreement are significantly less advanced by application of Art. III to probation-violation detainers than by application of Art. III to criminal-charge detainers. Whether those purposes would be advanced sufficiently by application of Art. III to probation-violation detainers to outweigh the administrative costs, and, more generally, whether the procedures of Art. III are the most appropriate means of disposing of probation-violation detainers,[11] are questions of legislative judgment that we must leave to the parties to the Agreement. Given the plain language of the Agreement and the relevant legislative history, we cannot conclude on the basis of the stated purposes of the Agreement alone that the parties to the Agreement intended Art. III to apply to probation-violation detainers. Accordingly, the judgment of the Court of Appeals is reversed.

It is so ordered.

Justice BRENNAN, with whom Justice MARSHALL and Justice STEVENS join, dissenting.

Must detainers based on outstanding charges of probation violation be disposed of within the terms of the Interstate Agreement on Detainers when such disposition is requested? Article III of the Agreement permits an inmate to invoke his rights to speedy detainer disposition by making a "request for final disposition of all untried indictments, informations or complaints on the basis of which detainers have been lodged." N.J.Stat.Ann. § 2A:159A–3 (West 1971) (hereinafter cited by Article only). No interpretive rule that I am aware of requires that "complaints" cannot subsume charges of probation violation, and no available legislative history indicates an intention to exclude detainers based on such charges from the Agree-

11. We note that some commentators have recommended, in light of the differences between probation-violation charges and criminal charges, that procedures different from those of Art. III be adopted for resolving probation-violation charges underlying detainers. See, *e.g.,* L. Abramson, Criminal Detainers 81–83 (1979); Dauber, Reforming the Detainer System: A Case Study, 7 Crim.L.Bull. 669, 704–705 (1971).

1. "Since the [Agreement] is remedial in character, it should be construed liberally in favor of the prisoner." Council of State Governments, Handbook on Interstate Crime Control 134 (1978 ed.). See also *Cuyler v. Adams,* 449 U.S. 433, 449, 101 S.Ct. 703, 712, 66 L.Ed.2d 641 (1981) ("The remedial purpose of the Agreement supports an interpretation that gives prisoners [a hearing] right").

ment. Instead, the drafters plainly intended a comprehensive solution for the problem of detainers, and the Court itself acknowledges that underlying purposes of the Agreement would be "advanced" if probation-violation detainers were subject to its strictures. *Ante,* at 3410. Article IX of the Agreement directs that "[t]his Agreement shall be liberally construed so as to effectuate its purposes," and the Council of State Governments, original author of the Agreement some 30 years ago, still agrees.[1] Nevertheless, without mention of Article IX, the Court holds that the Agreement does not apply to probation-violation detainers. I respectfully suggest that, in so holding, the Court constructs an artificial "plain language" argument that assumes its conclusion, vitiates the Agreement in significant measure, and reverses the rationale of our other major precedent construing the Agreement, *United States v. Mauro,* 436 U.S. 340, 98 S.Ct. 1834, 56 L.Ed.2d 329 (1978). Accordingly, I dissent.

I

Prior to expiration of his 2-year New Jersey probationary term, respondent Richard Nash was arrested in Pennsylvania. Upon learning of this, his probation department in New Jersey notified the New Jersey Superior Court of Nash's probable probation violation,[2] and the Superior Court

2. This notification took the form of a 1-page untitled memorandum from a probation officer to a Mercer County Superior Court judge, reciting that Nash had been arrested in Pennsylvania and that his "offenses [obviously as yet unproven] constitute a Violation of Probation." Supp. Record 6. The New Jersey Superior Court explicitly characterized this document as a "probation violation *complaint.*" App. to Pet. for Cert. in — U.S. —, p. —, 105 S.Ct. 2014, p. —, 85 L.Ed.2d 296 (emphasis added). The Court ignores this characterization, as well as the question of what the result would be under its "plain language" analysis if any signatory States routinely so labeled charges of probation violation. I do not believe the argument should turn on such labels. See n. 16, *infra.*

Probationers in New Jersey are charged with knowledge that commission of further crimes while on probation is an automatic violation

ordered that "a Bench Warrant be issued as a DETAINER." Supp. Record 3. This document was then lodged with corrections officials having custody of Nash in Pennsylvania.

The Pennsylvania officials, the New Jersey officials and courts, and Nash all treated the detainer as subject to the provisions of the Agreement. Upon its receipt, Pennsylvania notified Nash of his rights to dispose of the detainer under the Agreement. Nash then contacted New Jersey officials and requested disposition of the detainer under the Agreement, and the New Jersey officials attempted to comply with the Agreement's requirements. The New Jersey state courts reviewed Nash's case as one involving a "complaint" under Article III of the Agreement, see n. 2, *supra*, and the New Jersey District Court ruled that New Jersey's failure to comply with the time limits of the Agreement required dismissal of the New Jersey probation violation charges. 558 F.Supp. 641, 651 (1983).

II

In *Mauro, supra,* we stated that when "the purposes of the Agreement and the reasons for its adoption" are implicated, there is simply "no reason to give an unduly restrictive meaning" to the Agreement's terms. 436 U.S., at 361–362, 98 S.Ct., at 1848; accord, *Cuyler v. Adams,* 449 U.S. 443, 448–450, 101 S.Ct. 703, 711–

712, 66 L.Ed.2d 641 (1981) (looking to purposes of the Agreement in light of Article IX's "liberal construction" rule). It is therefore necessary to review the purposes underlying the Interstate Agreement on Detainers and how they relate to detainers based on charges of probation violation.

Three distinct goals generated the drafting and enactment of the Agreement: (1) definitive resolution of potential terms of incarceration so that prisoners and prison administrators can know with certainty when a prisoner is likely to be released, (2) speedy disposition of detainers to ensure that those filed for frivolous reasons do not linger, and (3) reciprocal ease for signatory States to obtain persons incarcerated in other jurisdictions for disposition of charges of wrongdoing, thereby superceding more cumbersome extradition procedures. See generally *Cuyler, supra,* at 446–450, 101 S.Ct., at 710–712; *Mauro, supra,* 436 U.S., at 359–364, 98 S.Ct., at 1846–1849; Council of State Governments, Suggested State Legislation Program for 1957, pp. 74–79 (1956) (hereinafter CSG Report). Noting that the Agreement was motivated "in part" by the second purpose—speedy disposition of detainers based on possibly unsubstantiated criminal charges—the Court then addresses that purpose alone for the remainder of its opinion. *Ante,* at 3408–3410.[3] Ignoring the other purposes,

---

under New Jersey law. *State v. Zachowski,* 53 N.J.Super. 431, 437, 147 A.2d 584, 588 (1959); cf. N.J.Stat.Ann., § 2C:45–3(a)(2) (West 1982) (warrant may be issued on probable cause that probationer "has committed another offense"). Whether or not the probation violation complaint and consequent detainer had an adequate basis when issued in this case is not before us.

3. Although the Court's conclusion apparently extends to detainers based on any type of probation-violation charge, its discussion refers only to probation violations founded on a new criminal conviction. Of course, probation-violation detainers may easily be based on arrests alone, as was the detainer in this case, or on charges of "technical" violations, the validity of which cannot be so easily presumed. See, *e.g.,* N.J.Stat. Ann., § 2C:45–1(b) (West 1982) (conditions of probation may include "meet[ing] ... family

responsibilities," maintaining employment, continuing medical or psychiatric treatment, "pursu[ing] a prescribed ... course of study," "refrain[ing] from frequenting unlawful or disreputable places or consorting with disreputable persons," etc.). Nevertheless, I am willing to concede, *arguendo,* that many probation violation detainers are based upon criminal convictions in another jurisdiction. I will also assume that "uncertainties" concerning "the factual issue of guilt" are therefore "less severe" with regard to probation-violation than outstanding-criminal-charge detainers, *ante,* at 3409, although the high rate of conviction for most criminal prosecutions suggests the differences are less real than the Court imagines. Both these assumptions are necessary for the Court to dismiss the second purpose of the Agreement as being "less advanced" in the probation-violation context. *Ante,* at 3410.

however, ignores *Mauro*. Moreover, because the one purpose discussed is obviously the least relevant to detainers based on charges stemming from conviction for new criminal conduct, the Court's silence regarding the other purposes leaves a gaping hole in its analysis.

It is unarguable that a major motivating force behind the Agreement was the first listed above: disposition of unresolved detainers so as to produce sentences of determinate length, so that in-prison programming and rehabilitation could freely occur.[4] Because in-prison educational, vocational, rehabilitation, and other treatment programs are generally (1) overcrowded and (2) designed for inmates who will shortly be released to the public world, prisoners that

The Court also employs its "factual issue of guilt" argument to dismiss the interest in obtaining speedy disposition of detainers so as not to impair a prisoner's possible defense, which it finds not as "strongly" implicated in the probation violation context. *Ante*, at 3410. Of course, this dismissal also depends on the dual assumptions that all probation violation charges will be based on criminal convictions, and that they therefore carry greater inherent substantiation. Even if all these assumptions were true, however, the Court's conclusion still leaves unexamined the other goals of the Agreement.

4. A detainer is defined by the drafters of the Agreement as any "warrant filed against a person already in custody with the purpose of insuring that he will be available to the authority which has placed the detainer" after his current custody is terminated. CSG Report 74. Because detainers often go unresolved for years, "[t]he prison administrator is thwarted in his efforts toward rehabilitation. The inmate who has a detainer against him is filled with anxiety and apprehension and frequently does not respond to a training program. He often must be kept in close custody, which bars him from treatment such as trustyships, moderations of custody and opportunity for transfer to farms and work camps. In many jurisdictions he is not eligible for parole; there is little hope for his release after an optimum period of training and treatment.... Instead, he often becomes embittered ... and the objective of the correctional system is defeated." *Id.*, at 74. See Note, The Right to a Speedy Trial and the New Detainer Statutes, 18 Rut.L.Rev. 828, 832 (1964) ("The thrust of [the Agreement] is not to protect the convict's right to a speedy trial per se, but rather to protect him from the particular disabilities engendered by an untried detainer pending against him").

may be released only to another State's prisons are put at the end of the line for such programs. In addition, because prisoners facing longer sentences are believed to be greater escape risks, they are often held in stricter custody levels and denied various in-prison benefits (such as recreational and work-release programs and trusty status). In some States prisoners with detainers may even be denied parole that they would otherwise receive, on the theory that a prisoner cannot be "paroled into" another prison.[5] Thus *any* "charges outstanding" against prisoners that might result in additional incarceration create "uncertainties" that "obstruct programs of prisoner treatment and rehabilitation." Art. I.[6] This statement in Article I repre-

5. The deleterious effects of detainers are well-recognized and recitation of authority is superfluous. A helpful summary may be found in Wexler & Hershey, Criminal Detainers in a Nutshell, 7 Crim.L.Bull. 753 (1971): "As has been carefully documented elsewhere, a prison inmate with a detainer filed against him ... may suffer several disabilities, ranging from mandatory maximum-security classification to exclusion from vocational rehabilitation programs and even to possible ineligibility for parole." See also N. Cohen & J. Gobert, The Law of Probation and Parole, § 12.01, pp. 562–563 (1983); L. Abramson, Criminal Detainers 29–34, 85–87 (1979); Bennett, "The Last Full Ounce," 23 Fed.Prob. 20 (June 1959); 9 Fed.Prob. 1 (July 1945) (entire issue devoted to "the detainer and its evils").

6. The Court seriously misunderstands what "uncertainties" the Agreement is designed to resolve. It is an uncertain *length of incarceration,* not an uncertain basis for charges, that is "produced" by a detainer and "obstructs" rehabilitation. Cf. *ante*, at 3409–3410 (discussing only uncertainties related to the "factual issue of guilt"). Prison officials generally do not inquire whether the basis for a detainer is certain or flimsy—if it suggests a possibility of additional incarceration, whether for violation of parole or for conviction of a new crime, it is considered as an additional factor in determining the inmate's security level and programming options. See, *e.g.*, Dept. of Justice, Federal Prison System, Program Statement No. 5100.2, §§ 9(B)(1), 11(A)(1) (1982). The Agreement obviously does not eliminate detainers, but merely provides the means for definitive resolution and imposition of a certain, final sentence. "The result is to permit the prisoner to secure a greater degree of

sents the legislative findings of 48 States and Congress. It is, therefore, those legislative bodies, and not merely the prisoner, who "prefer the certainty of a known sentence to the relative uncertainty of a pending probation-violation charge." *Ante*, at 3410.

Even if a detainer is withdrawn near the end of a prisoner's term, he will have been denied the benefits of less strict custody and will be released to the streets without the education, job-training, or treatment he might otherwise have received. It is therefore undisputed that prisoners with unresolved detainers are embittered not only because those detainers may have little basis in fact, but also because they have a palpably punitive effect on the prisoner's life while in prison and on his rehabilitative future following release.[7]

Prosecutors know full well that a detainer can operate to deny prisoners substantial in-prison benefits and programs, as well as delay their eventual release. Thus, as the Court acknowledges, detainers are often filed with "little basis" in order to "exert punishment" impermissibly, and are often "withdrawn shortly before" release of the prisoner after the damage has been done. *Ante*, at 3408, and n. 6.[8] The evident lawlessness of such practices as well

as their disruptive effect rehabilitation motivated adoption of the Agreement, *ibid*, in order, in large part, to end uncertainty regarding release dates. See Council of State Governments, Handbook on Interstate Crime Control 116 (1978 ed.) (the Agreement is designed "to permit the prisoner to secure a greater degree of knowledge of his own future and to make it possible for the prison authorities to provide better plans and programs for his treatment").

Obviously, a detainer based on a charge of probation violation implicates these rehabilitative concerns of the Agreement to the same extent as do detainers based on outstanding criminal charges. Accord, N. Cohen & J. Gobert, The Law of Probation and Parole, § 12.02, p. 566 (1983) ("the policies underlying [the Agreement] apply equally well to prisoners subject to a detainer based on a probation or parole violator warrant"). Both types of detainers may result in terms of additional incarceration, yet both types can also result in no additional time. Just as judges normally are permitted to impose an original sentence of brief or ~no incarceration, they also have broad discretion when resentencing for probation violations as to any subsequent term of imprisonment.[9] Thus certainty regard-

---

certainty as to his future and to enable the prison authorities to plan more effectively for his rehabilitation and return to society." S.Rep. No. 91-1356, p. 2 (1970), U.S.Code Cong. & Admin.News 1970, p. 4865.

7. "It is in their effect upon the prisoner and our attempts to rehabilitate him that detainers are most corrosive". *Smith v. Hooey*, 393 U.S. 374, 379, 89 S.Ct. 575, 578, 21 L.Ed.2d 607 (1969) (citation and stylistic punctuation omitted).

8. As Congress noted when it joined the Agreement, "withdrawal at this late stage is of dubious benefit. The damage to the rehabilitative process has been done because by then the period of treatment and training has ended. Further, this situation precludes the institutional staff from developing a well-planned program upon release." S.Rep. No. 91-1356, *supra*, at 5, U.S.Code Cong. & Admin.News 1970, p. 4866. See also Bennett, The Correctional Administrator Views Detainers, 9 Fed.Prob. 8, 9 (June 1945) ("It is ... pointless to spend funds for the training of an inmate if he is merely to be

graduated to another institution"); Heyns, The Detainer in a State Correctional System, 9 Fed. Prob. 13, 13 (June 1945) ("no State correctional agency can plan a sound program of rehabilitation for an inmate so long as he must keep answering detainers").

9. New Jersey's laws are typical. Upon finding a probation violation, the court "may impose on the defendant any sentence that might have been imposed originally for the offense for which he was convicted." N.J.Stat.Ann., § 2C:45-3(b) (West 1982). Any sentence imposed may be ordered to run concurrently with or consecutively to any sentence the inmate is serving. *Id.*, § 44-5 N.J.Stat.Ann., § 2C: (West 1982 and Supp. 1984-1985). Even revocation is not automatic despite a proven violation. § 2C:45-3(a)(4) (court "may" revoke probation upon finding a violation). Similar guidelines apply to parole violation resentencing. See N.J. Stat.Ann. §§ 30:4-123.60 through 123.65 (West 1982). See also The National Advisory Commission on Criminal Justice Standards and Goals,

ing the "factual issue of guilt" of the charge, *ante*, at 3410, is irrelevant to the uncertainty of the incarceration term. For this reason, the first listed purpose of the Agreement, certainty regarding length of incarceration, is "fully implicated," *Mauro*, 436 U.S., at 362, 98 S.Ct., at 1848, by detainers based on charges of probation violation, and "the very problems with which the Agreement is concerned," *ibid*, are present.

The result of such analysis in *Mauro* is instructive. In that case we concluded that the phrase "written request for temporary custody" in Article IV was sufficiently broad to accommodate a writ of habeas corpus *ad prosequandum* from the Federal Government to a State, even though such a writ is (as the dissent noted) in effect a command which state officials have no discretion to ignore. *Id.*, at 361–364, 98 S.Ct., at 1847–1849; see *id.*, at 366, 98 S.Ct., at 1850 (REHNQUIST, J., dissenting). We rejected just the sort of semantic formalism practiced by the Court today, which virtually echoes the *Mauro* dissent.[10] A "narrow reading" of the term "request" was inappropriate because nothing in the Agreement's history required it and "[a]ny

other reading of this section would allow the Government to gain the advantages of lodging a detainer against a prisoner without assuming the responsibilities that the Agreement intended to arise from such an action." 436 U.S., at 364, 98 S.Ct., at 1849 (footnotes omitted).

Mauro's rationale does not require that the terms of the Agreement be thrown to the winds whenever an inmate comes up with a plausible policy argument for the Agreement's application—obviously the Agreement cannot be judicially rewritten if its present language cannot accommodate probation-violation detainers. But, as we also noted in *Cuyler*, 449 U.S., at 449–450, 101 S.Ct., at 712, consideration of the "purpose, ... structure, ... language, and its legislative history" is necessary before reaching a final interpretation of the Agreement's terms. *Mauro* plainly counsels against miserly interpretation of the words when the purposes of the Agreement are implicated, as they undeniably are here.[11] These precedents and the Agreement's purposes must be kept in mind as one turns to the Court's argument that the Agreement's "plain language" cannot ac-

---

Corrections, Standard 5.4(5) (upon revocation of parole for new criminal conviction, resentencing decisions should be governed by the same "criteria and procedures [that] gover[n] initial sentencing decisions"); see generally Cohen and Gobert, The Law of Probation and Parole, § 15; *id.*, p. 646 ([m]ost jurisdictions" provide judges with "a vast array of possible sanctions to impose after a revocation").

In light of such broad grants of discretion, the Court's assertion, offered with no citation of supportive authority, that "probationer[s] no doubt often ... will be resentenced to serve the full term of [their] suspended sentence[s]," *ante*, at 3410, is surprising as well as speculative.

10. In *Mauro*, Justice REHNQUIST criticized the Court for basing its decision on the purposes of the Agreement, and suggested instead that the Court should have *"first* turn[ed] to the language of the [Agreement] before resorting to such extra-statutory interpretive aids." 436 U.S., at 366, 98 S.Ct., at 1850 (REHNQUIST, J., dissenting) (emphasis in original). Compare *ante*, at 3410–3411 (although purposes of the Agreement would be "advanced" by application to probation-violation detainers, in light of the "plain

language" of the Agreement "we cannot conclude on the basis of the stated purposes ... alone" that such a result is required).

11. "When 'interpreting a statute, the court will not look merely to a particular clause in which general words may be used, but will take in connection with it the whole statute (or statutes on the same subject) and the objects and policy of the law, as indicated by its various provisions, and give to it such construction as will carry into execution the will of the Legislature....' *Brown v. Duchesne*, 19 How. 183, 194 [15 L.Ed. 595] (1857)." *Kokoszka v. Belford*, 417 U.S. 642, 650, 94 S.Ct. 2431, 2436, 41 L.Ed.2d 374 (1974). See also 2A C. Sands, Sutherland on Statutory Construction § 46.07 (4th ed. 1984) ("The literal interpretation of the words of an act should not prevail if it creates a result contrary to the intention of the legislature"). Even if this were not already a "well-established canon of statutory construction," *Bob Jones University v. United States*, 461 U.S. 574, 586, 103 S.Ct. 2017, 2025, 76 L.Ed.2d 157 (1983), in this case the law itself directs us to apply its terms "liberally ... so as to effectuate its purposes." Art. IX.

commodate detainers based on charges of probation violation.

II

Literally applied, the "plain language" of the Agreement, *ante*, at 3411, 3415, would place far more restrictions on the Agreement's operation than the Court admits. For example, Article III states that a prisoner who makes a final disposition request "shall be brought to trial within 180 days," and provides that "[i]f trial is not had ... prior to the return of the prisoner ... the court shall enter an order dismissing" the underlying charges. Obviously, however, neither the Court nor common sense would require that a prisoner returned on a detainer and convicted on a plea of guilty or diverted into a pretrial probation plan could obtain an Article III dismissal because he had had no "trial." [12] The term "trial" is plainly used in the Agreement to represent the broader concept of "final disposition"—indeed, Article III uses the terms interchangeably. See also *ante*, at 3410 (noting interest in obtaining "speedy *disposition* of outstanding criminal charges") (emphasis added).

Similarly, the terms "indictment, information or complaint," strictly construed, would not encompass the varied types of documents used by some signatory States to initiate the criminal process. Virginia, for example, has a practice whereby criminal charges may be lodged with the court by a grand jury without involvement of a prosecutor. Va.Code § 19.2-216 (1983). The resulting document is called a "presentment" and, as petitioners admitted at oral argument, a "presentment" would not fall within their "plain language" interpretation of the Agreement. Tr. of Oral Arg. 10; see Brief for University of Virginia School of Law Post-Conviction Assistance Project as *Amicus Curiae* 13–14. Yet detainers based on presentments are, for purposes of the Agreement, no different from those based on indictments or

informations. The Court therefore properly rejects *this* plain language argument, "interpret[ing]," the phrase "indictment, information or complaint" to encompass all "documents charging an individual with having committed a criminal offense." *Ante*, at 3405.

Once the Court recognizes, albeit silently, the propriety of such interpretive efforts, its continued reliance on a strict "plain language" argument cannot persuade. Nash's argument is that the Agreement was designed to deal comprehensively with the problems caused by detainers of all kinds, and that "complaint" is a general term used to encompass any type of "charges outstanding against a prisoner," Art. I, that might form the basis for a detainer. No rule of language precludes such a conclusion. In general usage, "complaint" is defined as, *inter alia*, any "utterance expressing a grievance." Webster's New International Unabridged Dictionary 546 (2d ed. 1957). Even if restricted to its legal usage, "complaint" has been, since at least 1949 when the Federal Rules were amended, a sweeping generic term, applicable in both civil and criminal proceedings and encompassing "every action" that possibly can be filed in federal court, thereby superceding all "technical forms of pleading." Fed.Rules Civ.Proc. 1, 3, and 8(e)(1); Fed.Rule Crim.Proc. 3. Nothing in the Agreement or its legislative history indicates that "complaint" was used to *exclude* any particular type of detainer, or that its meaning was intended to be determined by its usage in only one context. Yet the Court looks only to the Federal Rules of Criminal Procedure for its definition of "complaint." *Ante*, at 3405. Neither does any rule of statutory construction require the conclusion that "complaint" as used in Article III must be a more specific term than "charges" as used in Article I; indeed, one would think that construing the Agreement as a whole would require that these terms be read as coextensive rather

---

12. Thus, just as a probation violation charge "does not result in the probationer's being ...

'brought to trial,'" *ante*, at 3406, neither necessarily does an outstanding criminal charge.

than conflicting. But cf. *ante*, at 3406, n. 4. Ultimately, no more than the fiat of a majority determines that "complaint" cannot include a probation violation charge.

IV

While I believe that the Court loses the semantic battle in this case, I am much more seriously troubled by the Court's blind eye to relevant legislative history and the purposes of the Agreement, and the consequent vitiation of the Agreement itself. Detainers based on outstanding charges of criminal acts likely constitute only between one-half and two-thirds of all detainers filed in our Nation's prisons.[13] The drafters of a uniform interstate statute would surely be surprised and disappointed to learn that their efforts had succeeded in dealing with perhaps only one-half of the problem they addressed.[14]

In fact, all the available evidence suggests that the Agreement was designed to

13. The only reported statistical studies report that 46% and 44% of the detainers, respectively, in their concededly small samples were based on outstanding criminal charges. Dauber, Reforming the Detainer System: A Case Study, 7 Crim.L.Bull. 669, 676 (1971); Heyns, The Detainer in a State Correctional System, 9 Fed. Prob. 13, 15, n. 1 (July 1945). Detainers based on charges of probation or parole violation, on the other hand, made up, respectively, 19% and 44% of the samples. *Ibid.* See also Yackle, Taking Stock of Detainer Statutes, 8 Loyola (LA) L.Rev. 88, 89 (1975) (citing unpublished survey claiming that 69% of all detainers filed nationwide were based on outstanding criminal charges). The absence of comprehensive, recent data permits only rough generalizations, but it is certainly safe to say that restriction of the Agreement to only those detainers based on outstanding criminal charges leaves a substantial number of detainers beyond the protection of the Agreement. See Brief for Attorney General of Pennsylvania, et al., as *Amicus Curiae* 6, n. 4 (surmising that probation-violation detainers make up a "significant number" of all detainers).

14. They might also be dismayed to discover that their third purpose—easing the administrative burdens of interstate prisoner transfer for signatory States—also stands partially frustrated by the Court's decision today. Once authorities have filed a detainer against a prisoner, Article IV of the Agreement enables them to obtain custody of that prisoner from another jurisdic-

"deal comprehensively" with the problem of detainers of all kinds[15]; significantly, the Court can point to absolutely no affirmative indication that the drafters of the Agreement intended to exclude probation violation detainers from its terms. As the Court acknowledges, Article I of the Agreement contains a "legislative declaration of purpose," *ante*, at 3407, to reach "charges outstanding against a person," that is, "any and all detainers." Art. I. The Court concedes the comprehensive scope of Article I, but sidesteps it by declaring that Article III "*does not apply to all detainers*, but only those based on 'any untried indictment, information, or complaint.'" *Ante*, at 3407 (emphasis added). The italicized phrase, however, merely assumes the conclusion. If the drafters of the Agreement did in fact intend to reach all detainers, as the evidence suggests, nothing in the general language of Article III requires a more restrictive reading.[16]

tion simply by filing a "written request for temporary custody." Article IV, however, also uses the phrase "indictment, information or complaint" to trigger its provisions. Thus any State that now desires to resolve probation-violation detainers in a timely manner will no longer have the option of using the Agreement, and will have to resort to the same unsatisfactory extradition procedures that originally motivated the States to draft and join the Agreement.

15. Yackle, 8 Loyola (LA) L.Rev., at 94; see also L. Abramson, Criminal Detainers 94 (1979) ("article I ... declares that the IAD applies to all situations in which an inmate faces pending charges in another jurisdiction"). The title of the Agreement itself belies the Court's attribution of a less-than-comprehensive legislative intent—we are not construing an Interstate Agreement on "Some" Detainers.

16. The Court attempts to buttress its position by relying on two examples not presented in this case. First, the Court recognizes that a comprehensive reading might require application of the Agreement to *parole*-violation detainers as well. Because Article III refers to "prosecuting officers" and "courts," and "because prosecutors and judges are generally not involved in parole revocation proceedings," language other than that currently found in Article III would have been, in the Court's view, "more appropriate" for this application. *Ante*, at 3407. Of course,

Although the terms of the Agreement were finally drafted in 1956 by the Council of State Governments, they were founded on a "statement of aims or guiding principles" drawn up in 1948. See CSG Report 74-75.[17] Those principles discuss "detainers" generally, without reference to their underlying basis, and the CSG Report declared in 1956 that those principles still "should govern the actions of prosecuting authorities, sentencing judges, prison officials *and parole authorities* to the end that detainers will not hamper the administration of correction programs and the effective rehabilitation of criminals." *Id.*, at 75 (emphasis added). Not even a suspicion that a third or more of all detainers might survive unaffected to "hamper" the correctional system is present here. Indeed, Principle III explicitly directs attention to detainers filed by nonprosecuting officials and thus not based on new criminal charges: "Prison and Parole authorities should take prompt action to settle detainers which have been filed *by them.*" *Ibid* (emphasis added).

After reprinting these "govern[ing]" principles, the CSG Report went on to introduce three legislative proposals to "dea[l] with disposition of detainers," *id.*, at 76, including its Agreement on Detainers

for application in the "interstate field." *Id.*, at 78. The CSG offered a statement of purpose for this particular proposal, "by which a prisoner may initiate proceedings to clear a detainer placed against him from another jurisdiction," again without qualification: "The Agreement on Detainers makes the clearing of detainers possible." *Ibid.*

To my mind, it requires an impossible effort to imagine that the authors of these broad principles and unqualified statements of purpose, repeatedly referring to "parole" and relying on parole experts, somehow intended a less-than-comprehensive answer to the "problems in the detainer field." *Ibid.* Rather than attempt that effort, the Court simply ignores all this historical evidence of broad purpose. Presenting a single reference to parole-violation detainers as though it were the only such reference and then dismissing it as merely a "general definition," *ante*, at 3407, the Court quickly retreats to its conclusion-assuming "plain language" argument. *Ante*, at 3407. At no point does the Court attempt to explain what rational intent might have motivated the Agreement's authors to draft only a partial solution without ever affirmatively so stating.[18]

---

courts and prosecuting officers from probation departments *are* involved in probation revocation proceedings, the only type of proceeding at issue here, so that these terms of Article III are perfectly well fulfilled in this case. More importantly, however, there is simply no reason that the terms of Article III could not accommodate disposition of parole-violation detainers, if they were applied a little less woodenly than the Court reads them. Just as "trial" in Article III must be interpreted as coextensive with the concept of "final disposition," so the other terms of Article III must be read "liberally," Art. IX, to accommodate the analogous roles that parole boards and probation officers play in the correctional system. Indeed, the New Jersey probation office, prosecutors and courts in this case made no objection to complying with the terms of Article III to dispose of Nash's probation-violation detainer.

The Court's second makeweight argument is that Article III "clearly does not apply to a detainer based on an additional sentence already imposed against the prisoner." *Ante*, at 3407, n. 5. Of course it does not, but that is

because such a detainer is *certain* and in no sense undisposed of or "untried."

17. Significantly, the 1948 drafters included representatives from the Parole and Probation Compact Administrators Association. CSG Report 74.

18. Because the Agreement is an interstate compact, its terms cannot be amended unilaterally by one or even several signatory jurisdictions. Thus the Court's reliance on Congress' 1970 description of "detainer" to support its conclusion about what the Agreement's 1957 terms may have meant, *ante*, at 3408, is therefore illegitimate; "post-passage remarks of legislators, however, explicit, cannot serve to change . . . legislative intent." *Regional Rail Reorganization Act Cases*, 419 U.S. 102, 132, 95 S.Ct. 335, 353, 42 L.Ed.2d 320 (1974). It is entirely possible that late-joining jurisdictions might have different reasons for signing the Agreement, see, *e.g., ante*, at 3409, n. 9 (Congress joined the Agreement in part to vindicate speedy trial

V

We have recently noted that remedial statutes do not "take on straitjackets upon enactment." *Dowling v. United States,* — U.S. —, —, 105 S.Ct. —, —, 85 L.Ed.2d — (1985). This should especially be true in the case of interstate compacts entered into by some 50 different legislative acts and therefore much less amenable to subsequent amendment.[19] Much has changed since 1957 in the law of corrections; a probationer is now entitled to an in-person hearing before a term of incarceration is reimposed, *Gagnon v. Scarpelli,* 411 U.S. 778, 93 S.Ct. 1756, 36 L.Ed.2d 656 (1973); see *Black v. Romano,* — U.S. —, —, 105 S.Ct. 2254, —, 85 L.Ed.2d — (1985), and the rehabilitative ethic that motivated the Agreement has, for better or worse, been largely abandoned.[20] Thus timely disposition of probation-violation detainers now requires the expense of transportation for the prisoner to and from the charging jurisdiction,[21] while the rehabilitative benefits previously thought to accrue

from such disposition are now discounted. Yet no one argues that an important remedial purpose of the Agreement as written—disposition of any detainer that could result in additional incarceration in order to produce certainty for in-prison programming—is not fully invoked by probation violation detainers. In light of this fact, policy arguments that evidence only dissatisfaction with the Agreement's underlying purposes or chosen means are illegitimate, nonjudicial bases for decision.

Ultimately, the Court's decision rests on its conclusion that although the purposes of the Agreement are "advanced" when linked to probation violation detainers, this is "significantly less" so than when the detainer is based on an outstanding criminal charge. *Ante,* at 3410. Ignoring the bulk of the legislative history as well as the purpose of the Agreement to produce certainty described above, the Court defers instead to claims of "administrative costs" and paternalistic arguments regarding the

---

rights), and even varying interpretations of the Agreement's terms. But such differences can in no way alter the original understanding that generated the particular terms as written. Indeed, New Jersey as well as 24 other States had already joined the Agreement by the time Congress considered the law. Subsequent narrowing of the terms by the remarks of federal legislators is thus particularly inappropriate in this case.

It should also be noted that Congress' discussion of detainers came in reaction to the decisions in *Smith v. Hooey,* 393 U.S. 374, 89 S.Ct. 575, 21 L.Ed.2d 607 (1969), and *Dickey v. Florida,* 398 U.S. 30, 90 S.Ct. 1564, 26 L.Ed.2d 26 (1970), cases which involved detainers based on criminal charges. See S.Rep. No. 91-1356, at 1 (1970). The Council of State Governments provided a much more comprehensive definition when it proposed the Agreement. See n. 4, *supra.* The Court does not explain why this broad statement is dismissed as merely a "general definition," *ante,* at 3407, while Congress' later and contextually-specific discussion is relied upon to demonstrate intent, *ante,* at 3408.

19. Kentucky has in fact attempted to amend the Agreement to apply explicitly to probation and parole violation detainers. Ky.Rev.Stat. § 440.-455(2) (1985). Kentucky's amendment expressly notes, however, that it can be "binding only ... between those party states which specifical-

ly execute the same" amendment. § 440.455(1). Since no other State has enacted such an amendment, Kentucky's law has no effect and, after today's decision, the will of its legislature stands frustrated.

20. See, *e.g.,* S.Rep. No. 98-225, p. 38 (1983) ("today, criminal sentencing is based largely on an outmoded rehabilitation model.... Yet almost everyone involved in the criminal justice system now doubts that rehabilitation can be induced reliably in a prison setting"); A. von Hirsch, Doing Justice: The Choice of Punishments xxxvii, 11-18 (1976); Bainbridge, The Return of Retribution, 71 ABA Journal 60 (May 1985). By comparison, in 1959 one of the framers of the Agreement, Director of the Federal Bureau of Prisons James V. Bennett, termed detainers "a vestigial remnant of the age-old concept of retributive justice. No purpose is served except the destructive expression of a primitive urge for vengeance." Bennett, "The Last Full Ounce," 23 Fed.Prob. 20 (June 1959).

21. See, *e.g., Padilla v. State,* 279 Ark. 100, 104, 648 S.W.2d 797, 799 (1983) (Smith, J., concurring) (since probation violation hearing would be "useless," reading Agreement to require transportation of prisoner from California and back for disposition of probation-violation detainer would be "holding the taxpayers of Arkansas for ransom").

"desirab[ility] of delay" [22] for prisoners. *Ante*, at 3410.[23] Thus Article IX is read out of the Agreement, and the rationale of *Mauro* is turned on its head. Rather than determining whether the purposes of the Agreement can be achieved within a fair reading of its terms, the Court decides that if the "plain language" of the Agreement is amenable to a narrow reading, advancement of the Agreement's purposes is insufficient reason to apply its directives. By this backwards reasoning the scope of the Act is now restricted to only two-thirds or less of all detainers. Consequently, as would have been the case in *Mauro* had this Court not properly exercised its authority to construe federal law, prosecutors will once again be able to file certain detainers for little or no reason and "gain the advantages of lodging a detainer against a prisoner without assuming the responsibilities that the Agreement intended." 436 U.S., at 364, 98 S.Ct., at 1849 (footnotes omitted).

I respectfully dissent.

---

22. As the Court acknowledges, a prisoner may well have "a legitimate interest in obtaining prompt disposition of a probation-violation charge." *Ante*, at 3410. Although delaying disposition of a detainer may in some circumstances be desirable, the Agreement currently leaves the decision of whether to invoke its terms up to the prisoner. *Ibid;* see Article III (disposition required only after prisoner "cause[s] to be delivered" a request for final disposition). It is a cruel irony for the Court to note legitimate interests in prompt disposition at the same time it takes the choice away, for under the Court's result a prisoner will now be unable to dispose of a probation violation detainer no matter how long it lingers or how frivolous its basis may be, unless the charging jurisdiction wants to do so. See Dauber, 7 Crim.L.Bull., at 680 (statistics indicate that "[p]arole and probation detainers: ... usually remain unresolved the longest"). As Justice STEVENS noted in his dissent in *Moody v. Daggett*, 429 U.S. 78, 94, n. 8, 97 S.Ct. 274, 282, n. 8, 50 L.Ed.2d 236 (1976), "if a prisoner would rather face the uncertainty and restrictions which might occur because of an outstanding detainer in hopes that the [federal Parole] Commission would prove more lenient at a later revocation hearing, he could certainly waive his right" to prompt disposition.

23. Reference to such arguments, as well as to alternative language the Court would find "more appropriate" for the Agreement, *ante*, at 3407, renders the Court's veiled criticism of the Court of Appeals' "policy analysis," *ante*, at 3407, completely ineffective. Indeed, *Mauro* and *Cuyler* indicate that such analysis *with regard to the policies of the Agreement* is entirely appropriate.

VOLUME V
SUPPLEMENT

CIVIL RIGHTS

VOLUME V

CONSTITUTIONALITY OF RESTRICTIONS

Upon commitment, the individual loses his liberty, but after serving his sentence, his civil rights are diminished. In this volume, limits on the state power to impose restrictions were examined. In previous introductions, especially in Vol. V, p.1, the old common law restrictions were examined, with references to common law punishment such as outlawry and the doctrine of "corruption of blood," which prevented a felon from transmitting his property to his heirs. Obviously, these kind of punishments do not apply, but a number of other restrictions do. For example, a felon cannot have a license for a firearm. *Dickerson v. New Banner Institute, Inc.,* 460 U.S. 103, 103 S.Ct. 986 (1983).

Many other restrictions, including the individual's ability to hold certain types of employment, have been placed on those convicted of crimes. Other restrictions include those related to issuing licenses of various types and property rights (not so much real property as pension rights and other benefits). Although such restrictions have come under increasing attack, there were no significant cases discussing these issues during this time period.

INDEX OF CASES

INDEX OF CASES
Volume IX

INDEX OF CASES
Volume I-IX

Cases cited in the chapter texts are indexed. Cases set forth in their complete texts are indexed, their location being indicated by italics, but cases cited in them are not indexed.

Solem v. Helm, VIII 138
Solesbee v. Balkcom, I 580
Solomon v. Benson, VI 108
Sostre v. McGinnis, II 3, 180, *228,* 338,
  441, III 175, 321, VI 217
Sostre v. Preisder, VI 108, 450, *461*
Souder v. McGuire, VI 259
Spain v. Procunier, VI 217, *219,* VII 136,
  180
Spates v. Manson, VII 400
Spence v. Farrier, IX 481, *486*
Spicer v. Hilton, VII 425
Spotted Bear v. McCall, VII 503
Sprouse v. Federal Prison Industries,
  Incorporated, II 358
St. Clair v. Cuyler, VII 417
Stachulak v. Coughlin, I 512, VI 79
Standlee v. Rhay, VI 560
Stapleton v. Frohmiller, V 427
State v. Ammons, IX 129, *130*
State v. Baker, VII 193
State v. Braithwaite, VI 615
State v. Chambers, I 312
State v. Costello, I 5
State v. Davis, V 249
State v. Dixon, I 430
State v. Dupard, VII 503
State v. Feilen, V 430
State v. Gibbons, VI 432
State v. Grady, I *133,* V 429
State v. Green, III 25, 277, 279, *282, 288*
State v. Guisinger, I 176
State v. Harris, V 3
State v. Hendrick, I 3, 387
State v. Hodgdon, VI 51
State v. Kelly, III 26
State v. Kimbrough, I 429
State v. Krol, VI 79
State v. Lane, VII 400
State v. McCoy, I 141, *166*
State v. Meyer, I 350, IV 29
State v. Mitchell, I *226*
State v. Normand, I 141
State v. Pohlabel, I 26, *57*
State v. Ramsey, IV 30
State v. Rogel, VI 6
State v. Sheldon, V 427
State v. Sittig, VI 45
State v. Slopper, V 342
State v. Snyder, V 584
State v. Spaulding, VII 193
State v. Streeter, I 295, *305*
State v. Tackett, I 241

State v. Wilson, VI 45
State v. Yates, IV 351, *366*
State Board of Registration for the Heal-
  ing Arts v. De Vore, V 178
State Board of Registration for the Heal-
  ing Arts v. Finch, V 178, *199*
State Compensation Fund Workmen's
  Compensation Appeals Board, II 357
State ex rel. Attorney General v. Irby, V
  585
State ex rel. Attorney General v. Peters,
  I 29
State ex rel. Beckman v. Bowman, V
  292, *325*
State ex rel. Collins v. Lewis, V 583
State ex rel. Djonne v. Schoen, IV 431,
  439
State ex rel. Good v. Marsh, V 427
State ex rel. Johnson v. Crane, V 427
State ex rel. Muirhead v. State Board of
  Election Commissioners, V 428, *486*
State ex rel. Pingley v. Coiner, II 10, 13,
  41, III 387
State ex rel. Smith v. Dowd, IV 401
State ex rel. Webb v. Parks, V 583
State ex rel. Wilberly v. Barham, V 427
State of Florida v. Daniel, VII 193, *242*
State of New Jersey v. Ulesky, V 535
Steffen v. Housewright, VII 451
Steinberg v. Police Court of Albany,
  New York, VII 493, *494*
Sterling v. Cupp, VI 450, VII 452
Stevenson v. Reed, VI 317
Stewert v. Rhodes, VII 193
Stickney v. List, VIII 251
Stidham v. Wyrick, VI 559
Stokes v. Bruce, II 2, 409, *415*
Stokes v. Fair, IX 259
Stone v. City of Paducah, II 360
Stone v. Egeler, II 409, 410, III 387, *437*
Storseth v. Spellman, VII 399
Strader v. Garrison, VII 15
Strickland v. Wysowatky, V 293
Sullivan v. Ford, VII 451
Svizzero v. Bensinger, II 410
Synder v. Blankenship, VII 283

T

Talley v. Stephens, II 359
Tanner v. Hardy, IX 495, *496*
Tarlton v. Clark, III 280
Tate v. Short, I 241, 257, II 358, VII 37
Tatum v. United States, V 586
Taylor v. Clement, VI 217, 466